★ 1996 ★

PEOPLE
ENTERTAINMENT
ALMANAC

★ 1996 ★
PEOPLE
ENTERTAINMENT
ALMANAC

Created and Produced by

Cader Books

LITTLE, BROWN AND COMPANY
BOSTON • NEW YORK • TORONTO • LONDON

First Edition

ISBN: 0-316-69888-1

10 9 8 7 6 5 4 3 2 1

Published simultaneously in Canada by Little, Brown & Company (Canada) Limited

Printed in the United States of America

CONTENTS

STAFF

Editor-in-Chief
Michael Cader

Executive Editor
Genevieve Field

Senior Editors
Jenny Bent, Julie Maner

Designer
Charles Kreloff

Research
Louise Anderson, Steve Baumgartner, Camille N.
Cline, Meryl Davids, Robin Dellabough, Lisa
DiMona, Rattan D'Souza, Nicole Goldstein, Amy
Joyner, Jor T. Law, Cynthia Liu, Carol Markowitz,
Megan O'Connor, Greg Oliver, Anne Shepherd,
Karen Watts, Dara Weiss, Erica Werner, Amy Winger

Photo Research
Meg Handler

Consulting Editor
Seth Godin

PEOPLE Contributors
Richard Burgheim (Supervising Editor), Betsy
Castillo, Suzanne Cheruk, Steven Dougherty, Cutler
Durkee, Nancy Eils, Jeremy Helligar, David Hilt-
brand, Anne Kilpatrick, Joanne Kroeger, Louise
Lague, Charles Leerhsen, Eric Levin, Denise Lynch,
Mary Carroll Marden, Ralph Novak, James Oberman,
John Shecut Jr., Hal Wingo

Landon Y. Jones Jr., Managing Editor; Ann S. Moore,
President; Robert D. Jurgrau, Business Manager

ACKNOWLEDGMENTS

Many people and organizations have generously lent their time, resources, and expertise to help make this project possible. Special thanks go to: Sheri Abramson, Harcourt Brace; Academy of Recording Arts and Sciences; Frank Alkyer, *Downbeat* magazine; Jennifer Allen, PMK; American Film Institute; Susan Arnold, Waldenbooks; Bridget Aschenberg, ICM; Alan Axelrod; Arnold Becker, CBS; Allison Beers, People for the American Way; Michelle Bega, Rogers & Cowan, Inc.; Phil Berk, Los Angeles Film Critics Association; Richard Betz, MTV; *Billboard* magazine; Marion Billings, M/S Billings Publicity, Ltd.; Bob Blake, National Academy of Television Arts and Sciences; Helen Blake, National Infomercial Marketing Association; Judy Boals, Berman, Boals & Flynn; Paul Boggards, Knopf; Elaine Bosman, HarperCollins; Sandy Bresler, Bresler, Kelly, and Associates; Johanne Brown, Forty Acres and a Mule Film Productions; Peter Brown, Brown and Argus; Brad Cafarelli, Bragman, Nyman, Cafarelli; Carnegie Mellon School of Drama; Alexa Cassanos, Random House; Fr. John Catoir, Christophers; Center for the Book, Library of Congress; Center for Media and Public Affairs; Robert C. Christopher, The Pulitzer Prizes; Columbia University Graduate School of Journalism; Steve Clar; Sam Cohn, ICM; Ace Collins; Barbara Contardi, Association of Comedy Artists; Sarah Cooper, O.W. Toad Ltd.; Don Corathers, *Dramatics* magazine; Angela Corio, Recording Industry Association of America; Catherine Craig, American Zoetrope; Lisa Croke, Nielsen Media Research; Crown; Leslie Dart, PMK; Gary N. DaSilva; Doreen Dean, British Academy of Film and Television; Dramatists Guild; Jennifer Dienst, Knopf; Marilyn Ducksworth, Putnam Berkley; Steve Dworman, *Infomercial Marketing Report*; Tom Evered, Blue Note Records; Kenneth Ewing; Charmaine Ferenczi, The Tantleff Office; Harry Forbes, PBS; Susan Geller, Susan Geller & Associates; Heather Gifford, National Academy of Recording Artists; Debbie Gilwood; Deborah Hanauer, Entertainment Data, Inc.; Cynthia Harris, Little, Brown; Ted Hearne, John D. and Catherine T. MacArthur Foundation; Shanan Hein, Country Music Association; Pauline Hess, *Pulse!*; Leonard Hirschan, William Morris; Patricia Hodges, Time Warner; Kay Hoffman, Berlin International Film Festival; Sally Hoffman, Random House; Hollywood Chamber of Commerce; Hollywood Foreign Press Association; Fred Horton, WYNY; Dawn Hudson, Independent Feature Project West; Susan Imber, Rubenstein Associates; Gary Ink, *Publishers Weekly*; M. Jackson, AUDELCO; Dotty Jeffries, Amblin Entertainment; Jennifer Jones, Academy of Motion Picture Arts and Sciences; Steve Jukes, Judy Daish 'Associates; Pat Kingsley; John Krier, Exhibitor Relations; Judy Krug, American Library Association; Michael Kurchwara, New York Drama Critics Circle; Douglas Langworthy, *American Theater:* New York University, Tisch School of the Arts; Steve Leggett, National Film Registry, Library of Congress; Stacey Levitt, Rachel McCallister & Associates; Ed Limato, ICM; Elizabeth Maas, The League of American Theatres and Producers; Dottie McCarthy, John F. Kennedy Center for the Performing Arts; Robin MacDonald, World Film Festival of Toronto; Ken Mandlebaum, *Theater Week*; Howard Marcantel, National Academy of Cable Programming; Valerie Marcus, Tommy Boy Records; Lisa Meredith, National Cable Forum; Jessica Morell; Jamie Morris, *Soap Opera Digest*; Art Murphy; The National Book Foundation; Gary Necessary, George Schlatter Productions; Karen Kriendler Nelson, Richard Tucker Foundation; Northwestern University School of Speech; Catherine Olim, PMK; Bob Palmer; Paramount Communications; Charlotte Parker, Parker Public Relations; Gilbert Parker, William Morris; Jeffrey Pasternack, Wylie, Aitken, & Stone; Chris Petrikin, *Variety*; Lou Pitt, ICM; Pollstar; Ronnie Pugh, Country Music Hall of Fame; Quigley Publishing Company; Joe Regal, Russell & Volkening; Tom Reidy, Tuneful Productions; Andrew Rhodes, American Society of Magazine Editors; Sandy Rice, PMK; Rock and Roll Hall of Fame; Richard Rodzinski, Van Cliburn Competition; Susan Roman, American Library Association; Ami Roosevelt; Howard Rosenstone, Rosenstone/Wender; Heidi Schaeffer, ICM; Marly Rusoff, Doubleday; Bill Schelble; Rachel Schnoll, Viking; Nancy Seltzer, Nancy Seltzer & Associates, Inc.; John Sheehan, Center for Media and Public Affairs; Paul Shefrin, The Shefrin Company; Barry Sherman, University of Georgia; Gina Smith, Country Music Association; Smithsonian Institution, Division of Community Life; Mary Stapleton, Barnes and Noble; Robert Stein, United Talent Agency; Carol Stone, PMK; Gundar Strads, Before Columbus Foundation; Jack Tantleff, The Tantleff Office; Noah Tepperman, William Morris; Nancy Trypuc, Rosenstone/Wender; Prof. Mark Tucker, Columbia University; Chris Upton, Knopf; Chris Vaccari, Harcourt Brace; Sylvester Vanetti, *Variety*; Venice International Film Festival; Sherri Weiss, HarperCollins; Liz Weiss, National Society of Film Critics; Murray Weissman, Weissman Angellotti; Moira Whalon; *Whitaker's Almanac*; Patricia Willis, Beinecke Library, Yale University; Marcia Winter, Yale School of Drama; Barbara Wise, *Variety*; Maria Zimmann, Nielsen Media Research; Marc Zubatkin, *Billboard* magazine; Kathy Zuckerman, Knopf.

PHOTO CREDITS

COVERS
Front cover (clockwise from center left): Kimberly Butler, Laurent Sola/Gamma Liaison, Brian Aris/Outline, Eika Aoshima/Onyx. Back cover (clockwise from upper left): Reno/Sygma, Archive Photos, Rob Brown/Onyx. Spine: Bonnie Schiffman/Onyx

YEAR IN REVIEW
p. 1 Los Angeles Police Department; p. 2 AP/Wide World; p. 3 United Paramount Network; TWEC; p. 4 Canapress; p. 5 Gary Boas/Retna Ltd.; Warner Bros., Regency Enterprises V.O.F., and Le Studio Canal; p. 7 AP/Wide World; p. 8 AP/Wide World; S.G./Retna Ltd.; p. 10 Courtesy of Fashion Cafe; p. 11 Stewart Fere-bee; Sony Music; p. 13 AP/Wide World; p. 14 Los Angeles Police Department(2); p. 16 Jay Blakesberg/Retna Ltd.; p. 17 Jay Blakesberg/Retna Ltd.

TIMELINE
pp. 43, 44, 45(2), 46, 47, 48(2), 49(2), 50, 51, 54, 55(2), 56, 58(2), 59, 61, 61, 63, 66 Hulton Deutsch Col-lection; p. 65 AP/Wide World; p. 67 AP/Wide World; p. 68 AP/Wide World; p. 69 Sarasota County sheriff's department/Meg Handler collection

ROYALTY
p. 73 Gareth Davies/All Action/Retna Ltd.; p. 75 Michael Melia/Retna Ltd.; p. 77 Camera Press/Retna Ltd.; p. 80 Steve Granitz/Retna Ltd.; p. 81 Gareth Davies/All Action/Retna Ltd.; p. 82 Press Association; p. 83 Camera Press London/Retna Ltd.; p. 84 Bill Davila/Retna Ltd.

SCREEN
p. 99 Michael Ferguson/Globe Photos Inc.

TUBE
p. 159 Edie Baskin/Onyx; p. 161 Capital Cities/ABC Inc.; NBC photo by: Reisig & Taylor; p. 162 NBC photo by: Chris Haston; Paramount Productions Photo: Amy Rachlin; p. 187 Capital Cities/ABC, Inc. (3)

SONG
p. 215 Jon Ragel/Onyx; p. 217 Concord Jazz; EMI; p. 218 Geffen; Atlantic; p. 219 Capitol; Arista; p. 220 Music for Little People; p. 221 A&M; Sony; BMG; EMI; p. 222 Columbia; p. 223 EMI; LaFace; p. 224 Poly-gram; MCG curb; p. 243 I.R.S. Inc.; Epic; Motown; p. 244 EMI; p. 247 MCA

PAGES
p. 289 Brian Smale/Onyx; p. 290 Harper Collins; Random House; p. 291 Random House; Viking; p. 292 Harper Collins; Doubleday; p. 293 Doubleday; Random House; p. 294 Random House; p. 295 Knopf; p. 296 Simon & Schuster; p. 297 Bantam; p. 298 Little, Brown & Co.; Harper Collins

STAGE
p. 333 Canapress; p. 341 Ivan Kyncl

THE PEOPLE REGISTER
p. 385 Camera Press/Retna Ltd.; p. 387 Aaron Rapoport/Onyx; p. 390 George Lange/Onyx; p. 394 Michael Ferguson/Globe Photos Inc.; p. 395 Bonnie Schiffmann/Onyx; p. 397 Edie Baskin/Onyx; p. 399 Steve Branitz/Retna Ltd.; Karjean MG/Retna Inc.; p. 401 Michael Ferguson/Globe Photos Inc.; p. 402 Bill Davila/Retna Ltd.; p. 409 Brian Smale/Onyx; p. 416 Ruedi Hoffman/Onyx; p. 417 NBC/Globe Photos; p. 426 Camera Press/Retna; p. 428 Alan Davidson/All Action/Retna Ltd.; p. 430 Rob Brown/Onyx; p. 431 George Holz/Onyx; p. 435 Jon Ragel/Onyx; p. 436 Armando Gallo/Retna Ltd.; p. 437 Paul Hurschmann/All Action/Retna Ltd.

★ 1996 ★

PEOPLE
ENTERTAINMENT
ALMANAC

THE YEAR
IN REVIEW

JANUARY

The Newt age begins, as the Republican Party takes control of both the House and the Senate for the first time in 40 years. New House Speaker **Newt Gingrich** presides over a 14-hour opening day, but the real media storm is over Gingrich's mother Kathleen having whispered on camera to **Connie Chung** that Newt told her **Hillary Clinton** was a "bitch."

Included in the freshman crop of representatives taking the oath of office is Congressman **Sonny Bono**. He comments, "It's great to have a No. 1 record. It's great to be a star. But to have this happen—it's awesome. The beat does go on."

One of the world's most mysterious one-name characters makes known his full appellation. For the first time since the hit show *Seinfeld* debuted in 1990, the character played by Michael

Richards, **Kramer**, reveals his first name—it's Cosmo.

The Late Late Show with Tom Snyder debuts, with guests Candice Bergen, and Kathleen and Robert Gingrich. Produced by **David Letterman**'s company Worldwide Pants, the show marks Snyder's triumphant return to network television after many years away. It was Snyder who gave way for Letterman's *Late Night* on NBC. Letterman says his company will smooth the difficulty of producing shows on both coasts by "getting a condominium in Kansas City." Meanwhile, **Charles Grodin** takes over Snyder's CNBC talk-show slot.

The latest twist in one of England's longest-running melodramas—the tangled tale of **Charles and Camilla**—surprises no one: Andrew and Camilla Parker Bowles abandon the entire charade, conceding in a joint statement that they have been "leading separate lives" since 1993. With the requisite two-year separation period behind them, Andrew, 55, and Camilla, 47, end their 21-year marriage in a London courtroom.

Viewers may still not know it, but this is the month when the number of television networks grew by 50%. The **WB Television Network** bows with a weekly Wednesday night lineup of *The Wayans Bros., The Parent 'Hood, Unhappily Ever After,* and *Muscle.* Its first night out the "network" reg-

Incoming House Speaker Newt Gingrich in front of the Capitol.

isters a rating of only 1.9, well below the 3 rating that had been projected for advertisers. Meanwhile, the competing **United Paramount Network** also launches, with regular programming on Monday and Tuesday evenings and movies on Saturday afternoons. Its slate features *Star Trek: Voyager, Platypus Man, Pig Sty, Marker,* and *The Watcher.* On the strength of the *Star Trek* franchise, UPN registers a much more significant rating of 14.7.

Hollywood's dream team finally gets a name. The new Spielberg, Katzenberg, and Geffen venture is dubbed **DreamWorks SKG.**

After a seven-month FBI investigation, the FBI charges **Qubilah Shabazz,** Malcolm X's second of six daughters, with negotiating with a hit man to murder Malcolm's longtime rival in the Nation of Islam, **Louis Farrakhan,** now 61 and the powerful leader of the NOI. Shabazz, 34, had been a witness at the gunning down of her father when she was 6. Police claim she made a down payment to a would-be killer—a former schoolmate working as an FBI informant—and say they have some 20 audio and videotapes as evidence of the plot. But the informer admits that the U.S. government promised him $45,000 to record his telephone calls with Shabazz and to testify at her trial.

TELEVISION NETWORK

The logos for the new UPN and WB television networks.

In May, Shabazz avoids a trial and a possible prison sentence by agreeing to "accept responsibility" for her involvement in the sketchy plot to kill the fiery leader, though she maintains her original plea of not guilty and her lawyers and supporters continue to say she was manipulated by the hitman/informer.

Her voice trembling, her eyes welling with tears, her heart "beating fast" she would later say, **Oprah Winfrey** reveals her "great shame" before a studio audience in Chicago. 20 years earlier, encouraged, she said, by a man "I was so in love with I would have done anything for him," she had smoked cocaine. "This is probably one of the hardest things I've ever said, here it is, here it is," Winfrey said of discussing, "my life's great big secret."

The promise of a 400-channel world becomes clearer as **The Golf Channel** tees off, the world's first 24-hour network devoted exclusively to live events from around the globe.

Violence erupts in and around U.S. movie theaters screening **John Singleton**'s controversial film *Higher Learning* over the Martin Luther King holiday weekend. Two die by gunshot outside of separate theaters in the suburbs of Washington D.C., and moviehouse owners around the U.S. report numerous arrests after a rash of brawls between black and white teens. There is even a stampede in a Canton, Ohio mall.

The R-rated film depicts racial tension and violence on a fictional college campus and shows the devastation caused by hate crimes and violence. Columbia Studios' controversial poster for the film portrays racial epithets that made some exhibitors nervous even before the film arrived in theaters.

Actress **Faye Dunaway,** 54, and composer-producer **Andrew Lloyd Webber,** 46, reach a confidential out-of-court settlement of her $6 million suit against him for breach of contract, defamation, and fraud. She had gone to court last August after Lloyd Webber abruptly closed the Los Angeles version of his musical *Sunset Boulevard* less than two weeks before Dunaway's debut, maintaining that her voice wasn't strong enough to carry the starring role of faded film star Norma Desmond.

Courtney Love, 30, widow of grunge rock star Kurt Cobain and lead singer of the group Hole, pleads guilty in a Melbourne court to committing offensive behavior on an aircraft. Love had been arrested for swearing at a flight attendant who told her not to prop her feet up on the bulkhead during a Qantas flight from Brisbane to Melbourne.

Love has more scrapes with the law in August at rock extravaganza Lollapalooza. Mid-tour, she is charged with assaulting Kathleen Hanna, a singer and bass player for the rock band Bikini Kill; later, in a closing night performance, Love is dragged off stage by a security guard for twice jumping into the audience to attack fans.

Bachelor billionaire **David Koch**, 54, executive vice president of Koch Industries, his family's oil and gas company, purchases the late **Jacqueline Kennedy Onassis**'s palatial apartment on Fifth Avenue in Manhattan for a reported $9.5 million. Onassis, who bought the 15-room duplex in 1964 for $200,000, lived there until her death in 1994.

For a moment it almost seems that Camelot has been reborn, as the Kennedys gather to say a final good-bye to **Rose Fitzgerald Kennedy**, the 104-year-old matriarch of the clan, who lies dying of complications of pneumonia. Ted Kennedy announces that evening, "Mother passed away peacefully today. She had a long and extraordinary life, and we loved her deeply. She was the most beautiful rose of all."

Keanu Reeves plays Hamlet for a 24-day SRO run in Winnipeg, Canada. Reeves, who gets $7 million per picture, agreed to take the role for $2,000 a week. Later in the year, Reeves takes on another unusual role, touring the U.S. and Japan with his rock band, Dogstar.

My So Called Life, starring **Claire Danes**, suffers the fate of only so-so ratings, broadcasting its last original episode. Loyal fans of the critically acclaimed drama campaign ardently for its reinstatement, but to no avail, though rebroadcasts will draw a healthy audience for MTV.

Mario Cuomo and **Ann Richards** join ranks with **Dan Quayle**—in the club of former-officeholders turned snack food endorsers. Cuomo and Richards liven up another lopsided Super Bowl with the debut of their commercial for Doritos. The San Francisco 49ers clobber the San Diego Chargers, 38–15.

Keanu Reeves as Hamlet.

FEBRUARY

Branford Marsalis officially takes a leave of absence from *The Tonight Show* with Jay Leno show to tour with his own hip-hop-pop-reggae band, **Buckshot LeFonque. Kevin Eubanks** steps easily into Marsalis's role.

Freedom finally looms for **Keiko**, the whale who starred in *Free Willy*. Plans are announced to free him from the cramped tank in Mexico City that he has called home since 1985. The 15-year-old whale, who weighs 3.5 tons, is to be moved to a temporary home at the Oregon Coast Aquarium, where he will be given a mate and prepared for reentry into the ocean off of the coast of Iceland. The liberation will take four years and cost $9 million, $2 million of which has been contributed by the movie's producers, Warner Bros., and New Regency Productions.

Rapper **Tupac Shakur** is sentenced to a term of 18 months to 4½ years in prison for sexually assaulting a young woman in a New York City hotel room in November 1993. Shakur's business manager, Charles Fuller, is sentenced to four months in jail and five years probation for his part in the crime. The judge denies a lawyer's request for bail pending an appeal for Shakur and Fuller.

Olympic diver **Greg Louganis** discloses to Barbara Walters and readers of his memoirs that "I do have AIDS." Louganis, who won the gold in both the 1984 and 1988 Games, apparently knew before going to Seoul in 1988 that he was H.I.V. positive and was taking the drug AZT. Louganis's announcement is accompanied by controversy over whether he should have informed the doctor who stitched the wound he incurred after hitting his head on the springboard while attempting a

Greg Louganis, holding his best-selling book.

reverse two-and-a-half. But experts agree that the doctor, as well as the diver's teammates, were most likely not at risk.

After the controversy dies down, Louganis goes on to star in the off-Broadway one-man show *The Only Thing Worse You Could Have Told Me . . . .*

The **Joffrey Ballet** is moving from its New York home to Chicago, where it will operate as the Joffrey Ballet

Aquatic star whale Keiko, who soon will be truly free.

of Chicago. The move is prompted by ongoing financial problems. Reportedly, the company explored alternate homes in Los Angeles, Washington, D.C. and Iowa City, Iowa before deciding on Chicago.

Baseball's **Darryl Strawberry**, 32, pleads guilty to tax evasion, admitting that he failed to report more than $350,000 in income he had earned from signing autographs and making personal appearances at memorabilia shows from 1986 to 1990.

Madonna hits No. 1 for the first time in three years with her "Take a Bow." Her 11th trip to the top of the charts puts her ahead of all other female vocalists in that category.

MARCH

Jamie Lee Curtis and **Jon Lovitz** create a stir on the American Comedy Awards telecast when Lovitz makes a grab for Curtis's breast and she returns the insult by reaching for his crotch. The audience is shocked by Lovitz's not-so-smooth move, but Curtis later defends the actor, saying the bizarre scene was rehearsed.

Titillation turns to tragedy as a ***Jenny Jones*** taping leads to murder. Jon Schmitz, 24, agrees to appear on the syndicated talk show under the premise that he will meet his secret admirer there. But his admirer turns out to be another male, Scott Amedure, 32. Three days later, Amedure is found dead in his Orion Township trailer, killed by two shotgun blasts to the chest. Schmitz confesses to the crime, telling police that he felt "humiliated" by his television experience. Jones later tells PEOPLE, "Getting the news was so shocking—I was devastated." But, she says, the tragedy "had nothing to do with the show. We have no responsibility whatsoever because [Schmitz] was not misled." The episode was never aired.

Eazy-E, (a.k.a. Eric Wright), 31, the founder of rap group N.W.A. and president of Ruthless Records, dies of AIDS. Before his passing he comments, "Maybe success was too good to me . . . . Like the others before me, I would like to turn my own problem into something good that will reach out to all my homeboys and their kin because I want to save their a— before it's too late . . . . I've learned in the last week that this thing is real and it doesn't discriminate. It affects everyone." Before his death at Cedars-Sinai Hospital, Eazy-E received literally thousands of phone calls—"more than for any other celebrity ever," according to hospital spokeswoman Paula Correia.

The air is filled with celebration as **Michael Jordan** resumes his basketball career. Jordan claims he has been dismayed by the baseball strike, which he perceives an obstacle to his progress. Donning a new jersey, #45, Jordan needs only a few days to regain the magic; he scores 19 points but hits only 7 of 28 shots, and the Bulls still lose to the Pacers in overtime. NBC registers what is thought to be the highest regular-season NBA ratings in over 20 years as viewers are drawn to Jordan's return. Days later, he racks up 55 points against the New York Knicks.

And in June, after Chicago is eliminated from the NBA playoffs in the second round by the Orlando Magic, Jordan announces he is ready to conquer a new medium—the big screen. The Chicago Bulls superstar will team up with cartoon king **Bugs Bunny** for *Space Jam*, a live action/animation adventure for Warner Bros. The story revolves around a group of Looney Tunes cartoon characters who are in

Michael Jordan takes to the air again in his first game back with the Chicago Bulls, facing the Indiana Pacers.

danger of being kidnapped by some outer-space villains—until Bugs is able to convince his old pal Jordan to give them a hand and wipe out the bad guys. The film won't be released until the end of next year.

Mike Tyson strides out of the Indiana Youth Center in Plainfield, Ohio, a free man for the first time in three years, and the world is watching. Many of those who have visited Tyson, now 28, claim they are initially surprised by the man prisoner No. 922235 has become. Tyson attended classes while in jail, reportedly even studying Chinese. He lined his 8-by-11-foot cell with more than 300 books and read two or three volumes, ranging from Malcolm X to Machiavelli, each week. Tyson also studied the Koran intensely, and has embraced its teachings. "Being a Muslim is probably not going to make me an angel in heaven," he said. "But it's going to make me a better person." Soon after his release, Tyson purchases multiple BMWs and announces the resumption of his boxing career, under the direction of promoter Don King.

Tyson's comeback bout with Peter McNeeley in August is stopped after one minute 29 seconds when McNeeley's manager, Vinny Vechione, abruptly bursts into the ring. Tyson collects $25 million for the outing.

America's favorite girl next door, **Julia Roberts**, 27, and her husband, singer, songwriter, **Lyle Lovett**, 37, (recovering from a broken collarbone he suffered in a recent motorcycle accident,) announce their separation in a joint statement. There is no explanation, just a one-line claim of mutual goodwill. Said the couple: "We remain close and in great support of each other."

The announcement puts a sudden end to the fragile belief, painstakingly nurtured by fans, friends, and both families during the couple's 21 months of marriage, that this improbable coupling would last. The day after the wedding, Roberts flew back to Washington to finish filming *The Pelican*

7

Brief, and Lovett resumed his concert tour—a pattern that would define the sporadic crossing of paths that was their marriage. The couple rarely spent more than a week at a time together and, in fact, kept separate residences: hers a co-op in New York City, his a clapboard farmhouse in Klein, Texas (pop 12,000).

Ironically the sad news for Lyle may be good news for some fans. "It's harder to write songs when you're happy than it is when you're miserable," Lovett said last year. "Who wants to hear how happy you are?" For the foreseeable future, that won't be his problem.

With the *Forrest Gump* sweep, **Tom Hanks** becomes the first man to win the Best Actor Oscar two years in a row since Spencer Tracy in 1937 and 1938, for *Captains Courageous* and *Boys Town*. The only others to have won acting awards two years in a row are actresses Luise Rainer (1936 and 1937) and Katharine Hepburn (1967 and 1968) and Jason Robards, for supporting actor, in 1976 and 1977.

When is feeling blue happy news? After tabulating over 10 million votes, Mars Inc. announces that the blue is the overwhelming choice of color for the newest **M&M**. Capturing over 50 percent of the vote, blue easily outpaced runner-up purple, and the distant third-place pink. The new color takes the place of tan in the candy line-up.

Touted as Latin music's Madonna, the Texas-born singer known as **Selena** was on the brink of crossover stardom—until a friend's bullet cuts short her life.

Selena, 23, had gone to confront the former president of her fan club, Yolanda Saldvar, 34. Saldvar, suspected by Selena and her family of embezzling funds, was on the verge of being fired, and she knew it. Soon after Selena arrived, say police, Saldvar shot her once in the back with a .38-caliber revolver.

The 23-year-old reigning queen of Tex-Mex music had enchanted fans with her danceable tunes. Now her tragic and bizarre murder fills them with an almost inexpressible grief, as up to 50,000 mourners, some from as far away as Canada and Guatemala, converge on Corpus Christi, Texas to pay their final respects.

For Latin music enthusiasts, the most apt comparison is with the death of John Lennon. Selena was vastly talented, deeply adored. "This was not some sexy babe groomed by a record company," says author Enrique Fernandez, one of the nation's most respected critics of Latin music. "We'll never be sure of how far she could have gone."

In August, the crossover appeal that was budding in Selena's music before she died is confirmed. ***Dreaming of You***, her bilingual, posthumous set, debuts at No. 1 on The Billboard 200 chart.

Tom Hanks (left) adopts a pose last struck by Spencer Tracy: that of the man winning the Best Actor Oscar in two consecutive years.

APRIL

Hollywood's famed celebrity oasis **Chasen's** will close its doors, taking with it more than half a century of glamour. "**Jimmy Stewart** always favored liver and onions," says Ronald Clint, the manager for 40 years. And lore has it that when a certain irresistibly dimpled child star of the '30s cried that she wanted a cocktail like her parents', a Chasen's bartender tossed together a concoction of ginger ale, grenadine, and fruit that became the Shirley Temple. The trouble is that too few of the major stars have been in lately. Bastion of an older, more conservative Hollywood, Chasen's has been eclipsed by power hot spots such as Spago and Morton's. "At some of the newer places, people are allowed to come in wearing warm-up suits, even T-shirts," says Clint. "We still require a jacket."

Noting that **MCA** is one of "six major seats at the production table" in Hollywood, the Canadian liquor conglomerate **Seagram** agrees to buy 80% of the entertainment colossus from Matsushita Electric for $5.7 billion. Led by CEO **Edgar Bronfman Jr.**, 39, Seagram had hotly pursued an increased presence in the entertainment business.

Now those who want to live like royalty have a new opportunity to do so. **Queen Elizabeth** announces that 60 apartments in various royal palaces (though outside of official security cordons) will be put up for rental. The properties became available after a reduction in royal staff employees, and the rental income will help reduce the public's cost of maintaining the royal household. Offerings include a former barracks in London's Kensington area and a cottage in the royal paddocks at Hampton Court Palace renting for $55,850 a year.

It is announced that **Arnold Schwarzenegger**, 47, was slapped with a paternity suit last December. The plaintiff is Debra Wrenn, 41, a gym employee who claims that the actor fathered her now 12-year-old daughter when the two had a one-nighter in 1982 while Wrenn was an exotic dancer in Indianapolis. (Schwarzenegger began seeing **Maria Shriver** in 1978 and the two wed in

'86.) Wrenn says she filed suit because her daughter has been diagnosed with bone cysts and needs surgery. The actor's lawyer calls Wrenn's allegations "totally false."

The final ratings for the **1994–95 television season** are in and the Fox network registers a major victory by passing CBS in what is considered a critical demographic category, adults 18 to 49. According to ratings from Nielsen Media Research, Fox garnered a rating of 5.4 among this group, versus CBS's score of 5.3. Each ratings point equals slightly fewer than one million homes. ABC leads all of the networks, as CBS plunges, due in part to recent realignment of affiliations. Altogether, the three established networks lose 7.5% of their collective audience, one of the biggest such drops since 1954. But the two aspiring networks, UPN and the WB, are barely a factor, drawing negligible ratings.

Controversy surrounds the release of ***Priest***, a Miramax film about a homosexual priest who tries to come to terms with his faith and himself. Anonymous bomb threats force a New Jersey theater owner to pull the film from two screens over Easter weekend, and **Cardinal John J. O'Connor** compares the film to scrawlings on a bathroom wall.

9

Before a crowd of 25,000 colleagues and well-wishers, **Joe Montana**, 38, announces his retirement. Appearing at a celebration of "Joe Montana Day" on a plaza near San Francisco's Bay Bridge, Montana notes, "My career was like living a dream. Like all dreams, I woke up. It's time to move on." Considered one of the greatest quarterbacks of all time, Montana led the San Francisco 49ers to four Super Bowl victories in the 1980s before finishing his career with the Kansas City Chiefs.

Supermodels **Claudia Schiffer**, **Naomi Campbell**, and **Elle Macpherson** dish up a feast for photographers and autograph hunters at the opening of Fashion Cafe, their new venture in New York City. "We're here to say hi to people," said Naomi. "We are very approachable." In July, fellow supermodel (and vegetarian) **Christy Turlington** joins the group.

Add **Luciano Pavarotti** to the list of celebs who lend their names to the marketing of a fragrance. The Italian tenor appears at London's renowned Harrods department store to launch his scent, to shouts of "Bravo" from the crowd. The less-than-svelte singer claims his cologne will "go very well with romantic music." But will men think of his hirsute image and impressive body, or the powerful allure of his voice? Harrods claims the Pavarotti introduction outpaces a similar event with **Cindy Crawford**.

MAY

The way **Martha Stewart** is living is causing grief for her neighbors in the Greens Farm section of Westport, Conn. For the last two years the lifestyle doyenne has been filming portions of her television show on her four-acre property. But residents claim that the production crews block traffic on the bucolic two-lane road, delaying commuters and school buses and endangering passers-by. "It's an accident waiting to happen," one neighbor charges. "It's a production studio in a residential zone." But town officials refuse to block Stewart's permit, granting her a three-month extension. In classic style, Martha holds a tour of her gardens and tea party to make peace with her neighbors.

While the movie world is abuzz over the mammoth costs of **Kevin Costner**'s $175 million-plus *Waterworld*, the Broadway produc-

Supermodels Elle Macpherson, Naomi Campbell, and Claudia Schiffer strike a pose in front of their new eatery.

Style-setter Martha Stewart.

ers of *On the Waterfront* are facing their own bath. Closing after 16 previews and eight regular performances, the show makes a wash out of investors' $3 million, ranking it as one of the most expensive flops in the history of the Great White Way.

Who says love is better the second, third, or fourth time around? Certainly not **Don Johnson** and **Melanie Griffith**, who married in 1976, remarried with great fanfare six years ago, split last spring, reconciled over the summer, and now appear to have gone their separate ways once more. Meanwhile, Griffith makes the scene with another actor, **Antonio Banderas**, with whom she's making a film.

A **Pablo Picasso** blue period portrait of Angel Ferandez de Soto is auctioned off by Sotheby's for $29.1 million, the highest price paid at auction in five years. The deep-pocketed buyer is later revealed to be composer **Andrew Lloyd Webber**, who bought the picture for his art foundation. The sale marks a resurgence in the previously slumping art market.

The fabled white sign that demarks **Hollywood** is unwrapped after its third facelift. The operation consumed 300 gallons of paint and primer and took 700 work-hours to complete.

Michael Jackson's latest single, "Scream," a duet with sister **Janet**, hits the airwaves. The song answers charges of child abuse made against the reclusive King of Pop. The flip side of the single offers "Childhood," another very personal song: "They view it as such strange eccentricities/'Cause I keep kidding around . . . It's been my fate to compensate/For the childhood I've never known."

Cheyenne Brando, 25, the troubled daughter of **Marlon Brando**, takes her life on Easter Sunday, in Tahiti. Cheyenne's problems have been no secret since the day, nearly five years ago, when her half brother **Christian** shot and killed her fiancé, Dag Drollet, the handsome 26-year-old son of a prominent Tahitian. Cheyenne was one of Brando's known 11 children, aged 1 to 36 years.

The reclusive Marlon receives the news of his daughter's death like a paralyzing physical blow, and a curtain of silence falls over Brando's sprawling mansion in Los Angeles. Talk show host **Larry King**, Brando's new best friend since their interview last December, notes, "When I talked to him a month ago, Marlon said that he didn't want to touch his strongest emotions anymore. He didn't want to reach that kind of pain again."

Connie Chung is fired as co-anchor of the *CBS Evening News with Dan Rather*. While Chung recovers from the shock, media critics debate whether she was victim or villain— one camp claims that CBS had unfairly blamed her for the *Evening News*'s poor ratings; the other side contends that Chung was a bantamweight who never belonged behind the anchor desk and who embarrassed CBS with gambits like her January

Michael Jackson, shown here with sister Janet, made a lot of people want to "Scream."

11

interview with Kathleen Gingrich.

President Clinton finally gives in to the urging of security experts and orders Pennsylvania Avenue closed to traffic between 15th and 17th Streets.

At the Commonwealth Park equestrian facility in Culpeper County, Va., **Christopher Reeve** suffers a tragic accident on the cross-country jumping course. When his 7-year-old chestnut Thoroughbred Eastern Express refuses a fence, Reeve is sent pitching headfirst. Though he is wearing a protective vest and helmet, the fall causes multiple fractures of the first and second cervical vertebrae in his spinal column, leaving the actor paralyzed.

With leagues of well-wishers keeping vigil outside the hospital where Reeve receives treatment, the actor undergoes surgery and regains some movement in his neck. By August, he will learn to drive his wheelchair by "sipping" and "puffing" into a plastic tube.

JUNE

Licking a stamp gets a little bit more interesting as the U.S. Postal Service unveils its latest celebrity stamp, this one honoring **Marilyn Monroe**. It's the first in a new series commemorating "The Legends of Hollywood."

The Mouse takes Manhattan, as **Disney** premieres its 33rd animated feature film, ***Pocahontas***, with a free viewing in Central Park for 100,000 lucky winners, as well as a healthy core of celebrities and friends of City Hall. Dubbed "Waltstock" by some, the screening carries a $1 million price tag.

The King of Pop and his princess go live with **Diane Sawyer** and draw over 60 million viewers (about 30 million less than when Jackson was interviewed by Oprah Winfrey, but still one of the most-watched TV events of the year). The combination interview/publicity opportu-

nity includes an answer to fans' most frequently asked question: Do **Lisa-Marie** and **Michael** have sex? "Yes, yes, yes," answers Mrs. Presley-Jackson.

Other events surrounding the release of Jackson's ***HIStory: Past, Present and Future Book 1*** double CD include rumors that the couple are pregnant and accusations of anti-semitism in one of Jackson's new releases, "They Don't Care About Us." Jackson quickly gives in to enormous public pressure and re-records the offensive portions of the song. But after all the hype, sales of the CD are disappointing by Jackson standards.

At the same time, four ex-guards of the superstar claim in court that they were fired because they knew of Jackson's alleged trysts with boys. "These men were fired because they were percipient witnesses to Michael Jackson coming and going in the middle of the night along with young boys over a period of years," argued lawyer Charles Mathews. The four men are asking for unspecified damages in the non-jury trial. Jackson's lawyers counter that the suit is an extortion attempt and deny a cover-up.

Pearl Jam cancels the last leg of its problematic United States tour, citing the ongoing difficulty of trying to perform in venues not affiliated with Ticketmaster, the mega-

The world premiere of Pocahontas *in Central Park.*

ticket-seller with which the band has sustained a long-running feud. One of the most popular rock bands in the world, Pearl Jam seemed fated not to perform for U.S. fans. The band was forced to postpone several concerts because of bad weather and security concerns, and at their last concert, lead singer **Eddie Vedder** was so overcome by stomach flu that he asked guest **Neil Young** to finish the set.

Later in the summer, the indecisive Vedder will reschedule several of the band's seven cancelled shows, using a new ticket agency, ETM.

The auctioneer calls it "a record for polyester." The white suit **John Travolta** wore in the movie *Saturday Night Fever* sells for $145,500 at an auction in New York. Seller **Gene Siskel** bought the three-piece suit with attached black shirt for just $2,000 at

a charity auction in 1979. Among the other items of movie memorabilia auctioned off are fiberglass copies of the Ten Commandments from the movie of the same name, which sell for $81,000, and the 1940 Buick Phaeton from *Casablanca* that goes for $211,000 to a man bidding by telephone from a cruise ship.

Holy opening! *Batman Forever* pulls in just shy of $53 million, which puts it more than a couple of million ahead of *Jurassic Park* for the largest three-day opening ever.

Fort Worth police arrest country music's rising star, **Ty Herndon**, 33, for allegedly exposing himself to a male undercover cop in a park notorious for public lewdness and male prostitution. They also charge Herndon with possession of a controlled substance—the 2.49

grams of methamphetamine they say they found in his wallet. This is hardly the kind of exposure the handsome country crooner was looking for. After years of struggling to make his way to the top, Herndon seemed on the verge of a breakthrough. His heart-tugging single "What Mattered Most" spent a week at No. 1 on *Billboard's* country chart, and his album of the same name hit No. 14.

Two months later, the singer credits the Tuscon rehabilitation center a Fort Worth judge ordered him to enter with saving his life. "Technically, I have to say that I'm an addict," he tells the Nashville Network Country News. "I was using drugs weekly and hiding it. But I had only seriously been involved in it about 10 months, so if 10 months is long enough to be addicted then I guess I was." The indecent exposure charge is dropped and instead of jail time, Herndon will be on probation once he finishes rehab.

An excerpt from a previously unpublished, original draft of **Mark Twain**'s *The Adventures of Huckleberry Finn* runs in *The New Yorker*'s annual fiction issue. The first half of the handwritten masterpiece was discovered in an attic in 1990, after having been presumed lost. Twain donated both parts of the early draft to the Buffalo Public Library in 1885, at the request of a young lawyer who was assembling a collection of manuscripts and letters of important authors. The lawyer, James Fraser Gluck, died a year later and the manuscript, which had no library markings, was turned over to his widow, who moved to California, where it was eventually discovered by her daughter.

Child star **Macaulay Culkin**'s mom, Patricia Brentrup, 41, is ordered by a Manhattan judge to share custody of her 14-year-old son and five of his siblings with their father, Christopher "Kit" Culkin, 51. Bruntrup was previously awarded temporary sole custody after charging that Kit had threatened to hinder the kids' acting careers. The judge changed his position after hearing Culkin's side of the story. A subsequent hearing will decide who gets long-term custody.

Hugh Grant, who had become known as the thinking woman's sex symbol, is arrested near L.A.'s Sunset Boulevard for engaging in a "lewd act" with a prostitute. The act is later identified as oral sex. The news of Grant's indiscretion shocks his fans, who knew the actor as a clever and charming 34-year-old who loved his mum and dad; adored his longtime girlfriend (29-year-old Estée Lauder model Elizabeth Hurley); and was bold enough to be naughty ("I've always had

a crush on cheerleaders. Catholic cheerleaders—my double favorite,") but not downright *nasty*. A judge sentences Grant, who pleads no contest, to two years of unsupervised probation and a fine of $1,180, and he is ordered to complete an AIDS education program. Grant's appearance on *The Tonight Show*, the debut of his Apology Tour, draws that show's third-highest ratings ever.

Meanwhile, prostitute Divine Brown's fortunes take a *Pretty Woman*-style turn for the better. After selling her story for a reported $150,000, she makes commercials for a lingerie company and a Los Angeles radio station (which pulls the promo spot shortly after its debut in the face of listener complaints).

JULY

Joey Buttafuoco, 39, pleads no contest to soliciting an undercover policewoman for sex shortly after the Independence Day weekend. Buttafuoco's illicit affair with a New York teenager led to the girl shooting his wife. The automobile repairman, whose notoriety has made a mini-celebrity of him, is still on probation after serving four months of a six-month prison sentence in New York state for statutory rape.

An Englishman travels to Los Angeles, engages prostitute Divine Brown, and becomes a mug shot heard about around the world.

14

Sharon Stone, 37, and jeweler Harry Winston settle a $12 million lawsuit she filed last year after Winston forced her to return a $400,000 diamond necklace she had worn while promoting the movie *Sliver*. The company said the necklace was a loan; she said it was a gift. As part of the settlement, Winston will donate an unspecified sum to the American Foundation for AIDS Research.

George Michael, 32, settles a two-year dispute with Sony Music, during which he had demanded his release from a 15-year, $12 million contract. On the same day, it is announced that he has signed a new North American contract with DreamWorks SKG.

Rapper **Queen Latifah**, 25, is carjacked and her companion shot in the chest near New York's Apollo Theater in Harlem. The Queen and two friends are sitting in Latifah's parked 1995 green BMW, when two gunmen order them out of the car. All three comply, but 22-year old Sean Moon is shot anyway. Latifah—famous for speaking out against violence, sexism, and racism—declares "I hope this is a lesson that we have to wake up and try to do something about the violence in our community."

The rights to the music of legendary rock guitarist **Jimi Hendrix**, valued at up to $90 million, are awarded to the singer's father and his family. Since 1993, the rights to the music, name, and likeness of the 1960s acid rock star have been held up in litigation. The lawsuit, filed in Hendrix's hometown of Seattle, had effectively blocked sale of the rights to MCA Records for a reported $50 million to $75 million. Last year's *Jimi Hendrix: Woodstock* was ranked among *Billboard* magazine's top 40 albums.

The makers of **SPAM** file suit against Jim Henson Productions over a particularly piggy pig named SPA'AM who will appear in the upcoming Muppets movie *Muppet Treasure Island*. Calling the up-and-coming puppet a "grotesque and noxious appearing wild boar" and the epitome of "evil in porcine form," Hormel Foods has turned up its snout at an apology from the Muppets, who say they didn't mean to hurt anyone's feelings.

Waterworld finally washes ashore on a tide of red ink, opening nationwide to a robust but not spectacular weekend gross of over $21 million. Pilloried in the media for its spectacular record-setting production cost of $175 million long before premiering, the film sank Kevin Costner's friendship with director Kevin Reynolds, who abandoned the project during editing. It will have to earn over $100 million in the U.S. alone to even stand a chance of recouping its investment.

Seagram, the canny new owner of Universal, the studio that produced the picture, has less exposure than is commonly assumed. When Seagram purchased the MCA empire, all but $12 million of *Waterworld's* mammoth production cost was charged to the previous owners at Matsushita, so Seagram will likely see profits even on a mediocre performance. And that is how Hollywood accountants can make as much magic as their colleagues behind the cameras.

The **Walt Disney Company** surprises the entertainment world when it announces on the 31st that it's buying **Capital Cities/ABC**. The deal is valued at $19 billion. Chairman Michael Eisner ups the ante further when mere weeks later he hires superagent Mike Ovitz to serve as his "partner" and company president.

The day after Disney's acquisition, Westinghouse Electric announces its agreement to purchase of **CBS** for $5.4 billion.

AUGUST

The much talked-about marriage of former Playboy playmate of the year and Guess jeans model **Anna Nicole Smith**, 27, to Texas oilman J. Howard Marshall, ends with the multi-millionaire's death at the age of 90. The two were married in June of 1994, and Smith has spent much of her time since then battling in probate court with Marshall's son, E. Pierce Marshall, over the elder Marshall's estate, estimated to be worth $500 million. The money is in a trust pending a court ruling on the case. Smith and the younger Marshall extend their dispute to the disposal of Marshall's remains. The family prevails in their desire for cremation (Smith favored a mausoleum), but they agree to split the ashes.

Grateful Dead guru **Jerry Garcia**, 53, dies of an apparent heart attack at the Serenity Knolls rehabilitation center in Marin County, California. The singer, lead guitarist, and figurehead behind the legendary Grateful Dead had checked into the Betty Ford clinic for treatment of heroin addiction following the wrap-up of a tour. But he left the Ford center suddenly two weeks into his treatment, and was subsequently persuaded by friends to enter the San Francisco-area facility. The Dead's devoted following of Deadheads plunge into mourning at the loss of Jerry; to many who have idolized the band from its formation in 1966, it is a sad ending to the "feelgood" era that the Dead carried well into the '90s with their record-grossing tours.

Heidi Fleiss is convicted on eight counts of conspiracy, tax evasion, and money laundering, with the federal jury undecided on two other counts of filing false loan applications. The Hollywood Madam was previously convicted on state pandering charges last December and sentenced to three years in prison. She faces up to five more years in prison on the new federal convictions. After two years of rumors about the entries in Fleiss's notorious "little black book," the only star called to the stand is **Charlie Sheen**, 29. In videotaped testimony, Sheen admits to paying women who worked for Fleiss more than $53,000 for "heterosexual services."

One week after winning the right to enter the all-male Citadel, **Shannon Faulkner**, 20, quits the corps of cadets she had fought so long to enter. Faulkner says that she realized she had to quit The Citadel to preserve her emotional and physical health: "The past 2½ years came crashing down on me in an instant."

Faulkner collapsed from heat exhaustion shortly after beginning the school's traditional "Hell Week" for incoming cadets—seven days of rigorous physical training—in temperatures that often topped 100 degrees; she spent the rest of the week in the school infirmary. Faulkner summed up later, "I don't think there's any dishonor in leaving. I think there's dis-justice in my staying and killing myself just for the political point."

Jerry Garcia.

New York Yankee greats gather in Dallas to lay to rest **Mickey Mantle**, dead of cancer, in a funeral filled with warm feelings and good humor. As such household names as Yogi Berra, Whitey Ford, Johnny Blanchard, Reggie Jackson, and Bobby Murcer look on, Bobby Richardson, another former teammate who is now a lay minister, recalls some ribald moments from The Mick's past — but then touchingly remembers the day when a depressed Mantle came to him for help in finding God. He also speaks of the irony of how Mantle cleaned up his life—only to have it end so quickly. In an interview last year with NBC sportscaster Bob Costas, Mantle talked publicly for the first time about his alcoholism.

Calvin Klein bows to pressure from both child welfare advocates and the general public and suspends his new jeans campaign. Critics liken the ads to soft-core child pornography. The designer maintains that they convey the "spirit, independence, and inner worth of today's young people." The ads, which were shot in a deliberately amateurish style by fashion photographer Steven Meisel, depict denim-clad pubescent boys and girls in what some call provocative poses.

SEPTEMBER

After ten years in the planning, the $92 million I. M. Pei-designed **Rock and Roll Hall of Fame and Museum** opens in Cleveland, paying tribute to 40 years of rock and to the jazz, blues, and gospel artists who laid down the roots of the genre. Among the stars performing at the opening are Chuck Berry, Bruce Springsteen, Little Richard, Bob Dylan, and the Pretenders. The museum acquired such precious artifacts as the Sun Studios control room where Elvis Presley recorded his first songs and Janis Joplin's psychedelic '65 Porsche. Handwritten lyrics, instruments, films, videos, and archives line the halls. The museum also boasts the first rock and roll automatic teller machine, a multi-functional unit modeled after a classic '60s-style jukebox that plays rock favorites while processing transactions.

Miss America's bathing suit competition is in the swim— so decide an overwhelming 79% of the more than 898,000 callers who vote on the fate of the pageant's longstanding tradition on the 75th anniversary of the event. This year's winner, the 24-year-old Miss Oklahoma, agrees with the majority, saying "the suit is modest enough that I don't feel like it compromises any of my beliefs."

After five weeks of negotiations **Time Warner** and **Turner Broadcasting System** agree to merge, creating the world's largest communications company, outpacing the earlier merger of rival

Aretha Franklin performs at the opening of the Rock and Roll Hall of Fame and Museum.

Walt Disney and Capital Cities/ABC. The iconoclastic entrepreneur Ted Turner will serve as Vice Chairman of the new entity. Turner comments, "I'm tired of being little for my whole life. This is a chance to see the world from a different perspective.

Following two years away from professional competition due to her stabbing in Germany, **Monica Seles** returns to the U.S. Open finals, narrowly losing to Steffi Graf, but gaining even greater respect from her fans.

The first issue of *George* arrives on newsstands, right on the heels of editor-in-chief **John F. Kennedy Jr.**'s cameo appearance on *Murphy Brown*. The fledgling magazine's famous boss describes *George* as "a lifestyle magazine with politics at its core." Although met with mixed reviews, the magazine has the support of a $20 million commitment from Hachette Filipacchi Magazines. According to Pierre Salinger, a lifelong friend and press secretary to Kennedy's father, the highly-publicized launch comes at a crucial moment for Kennedy. Says Salinger: "John has reached the stage in life where he wants to be known for something other than chasing girls."

THE O.J.-OMETER

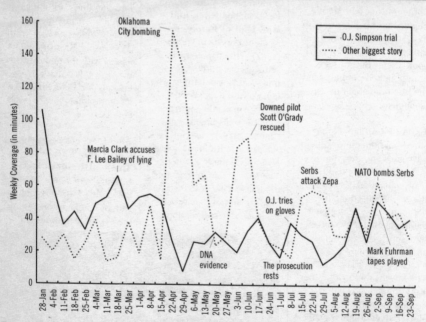

From the beginning of testimony in late January through closing arguments in late September, O.J. Simpson's murder trial ranked as the top network TV news story almost every week. The above graph documents this national obsession, comparing the Simpson-trial coverage with the other leading news story of the week. The graph points indicate the number of minutes of network news attention in a given week—Simpson versus the other leading news story. Call-outs help to put the peaks and valleys in perspective. (Source: Tyndall Reports)

18

REMEMBRANCES

GEORGE FRANCIS ABBOTT

It is only fitting that this legendary playwright, director, actor, and producer had his first hit with a show entitled *Broadway*, which he cowrote and directed in 1926. In the course of George Abbott's lengthy and illustrious career, Broadway became his home and, sometimes, a substitute family. By the time he died at the age of 107, he had racked up an impressive list of honors: a shared Pulitzer with Jerome Weidman for the book of 1959's *Fiorello!* and Tonys for 1954's *Pajama Game*, 1955's *Damn Yankees*, and 1962's *A Funny Thing Happened on the Way to the Forum*. His career was capped by a special Distinguished Career Achievement Tony in 1976 and a Kennedy Center award in 1982. Abbott died in his sleep of a stroke in January in Miami Beach.

CHEYENNE BRANDO

In a tragic end to a turbulent life, Cheyenne Brando, Marlon's 25-year-old daughter, hanged herself in her mother's house in Tahiti on Easter Sunday. Cheyenne's struggles with drugs and depression had come to a head five years earlier, when her half-brother Christian shot and killed her fiancé, Dag Drollet, the 26-year-old son of a prominent Tahitian politician

turned bank president, in the den of the Brando home in Los Angeles. As one friend said, Cheyenne was "sometimes very sad." She is survived by 4-year-old Tuki, her son by Drollet.

When a member of his entourage called Marlon with the sad news on Easter Sunday evening, he moaned, "Oh, God, no," and slumped to the floor. The doctor who was summoned advised against the 7½-hour flight to Tahiti.

In his deepest moment of grief, Brando and his one-time blood enemy, Jacques-Denis Drollet, the father of the slain Dag, agreed to bury Cheyenne next to her lover. Still, in many ways it's hard to imagine Brando playing the role of an involved parent. His neglect was extravagant, his love largely unexpressed. The actor has at least 11 children, ages 1 year to 36 years: five by his three wives (Anna Kashfi, Movita Castenada and Tarita Teriipia, all ex-actors), three by his Guatemalan housekeeper Christina Ruiz and an additional three from other affairs. "The family kept changing shape," Christian Brando (the son of Kashfi) once said. "I'd sit down at the breakfast table and say, 'Who are *you?*'"

Alcoholism runs in the family, as Brando made painfully clear in his 1994 autobiography. His mother,

Dorothy, "cared more about drinking than caring for us," he wrote. And father Marlon Sr.'s blood "consisted of compounds of alcohol, testosterone, adrenaline and anger."

More than anything, that could explain the long list of drug rehabs and mental hospitals that Cheyenne visited in Paris, San Francisco, Stockbridge, Mass., and Tahiti. As Peter Manso, who spent three weeks with Cheyenne while researching his 1994 biography *Brando*, observed, "Cheyenne was like a wounded bird."

PETER COOK

"One of the ways to avoid being beaten by the system," Peter Cook once said, "is to laugh at it." That's just what the deadpan, demonic British performer did for nearly 40 years, making what his longtime sidekick, Dudley Moore, called a "massive contribution to comedy" until his death, at 57, in London in January.

The son of a Colonial Service officer, Cook grew up in the English seaside town of Torquay. At Cambridge University he joined the Footlights, the resident satirical troupe, and proved to be, as Monty Python's John Cleese once conceded, "the funniest and most original of us all."

In 1959 Cook teamed up with fellow Cantabrigian

Jonathan Miller, who became a director, and two Oxford grads, Alan Bennett and Moore, to create the wickedly witty revue *Beyond the Fringe*. The show won accolades at the Edinburgh Festival and on the London stage, then crossed the Atlantic to gain a special Tony Award on Broadway in 1962. It also brought Cook and Moore together as the Mutt and Jeff (Cook stood 6'4" to Moore's 5'2") of sophisticated satire. In 1967 they costarred with Raquel Welch in the cult film *Bedazzled*, which Cook wrote, and their revue *Good Evening* was the surprise hit of Broadway's 1973-74 season.

Cook once called their relationship "ideal," adding, when Moore went off to Hollywood to star in *10* and *Arthur*, "I doubt I will ever do anything better."

Alas, he didn't. Cook made a string of mediocre movies in the '70s and '80s. And he so despised doing *The Two of Us*, a 1981 sitcom on CBS, that he walked off the show.

A lifelong drinker and smoker, Cook saw his health decline in recent years, and was admitted to London's Royal Free Hospital in January. Shortly before his death, he mused, "I suppose I might have some regrets, but I can't remember what they are."

HOWARD COSELL

A former lawyer who worked at ABC television and radio from 1953 to 1992, Cosell was in his 50s when he became celebrated for his role on ABC's groundbreaking *Monday Night Football* in 1970. The show was the first to bring sports to prime-time television and helped make football a national institution. His strident "tell it like it is" broadcasting style earned him the distinction of being named both "most loved sportscaster" and "most hated sportscaster" in a *TV Guide* poll taken in the mid-'70s. "Howard Cosell was one of the most original people ever to appear on American television," said ABC News president Roone Arledge, who was head of ABC Sports at the time.

Cosell—who died in April at 77 of a heart embolism—was known as a champion of the underdog and for sticking to his guns when it came to voicing his often controversial opinions. In the '60s, he was the first sportscaster to call Muhammad Ali by his Muslim name, as the heavyweight champ desired, in place of his given name Cassius Clay. In 1967, when the New York boxing commission stripped Ali of his title for his refusal to fight in the Vietnam War, Cosell called the decision "imbecilic," and was deluged with hate mail. Cosell defended his position, saying, "Nobody gives a damn about the professional football players who dodge the draft. But Muhammad was different, he was black and boastful."

Soon after Cosell's death, Ali said of him, "Howard Cosell was a good man and he lived a good life. I have been interviewed by many people, but I enjoyed interviews with Howard the best. We always put on a good show. I hope to meet him one day in the hereafter. I can hear Howard saying, 'Muhammad, you're not the man you used to be.'"

EAZY-E

In the end, it wasn't the gun-toting gangstas he rapped about that brought him down. It was a quiet killer—a killer without attitude, known as AIDS. That's why there was such an outpouring of shock and confusion when rap pioneer Eazy-E died in March at Cedars-Sinai Medical Center in Los Angeles, about 3½ weeks after learning he had AIDS. During his final days, fans swamped hospital phone lines with up to 2,500 calls a day. "Eazy-E, he's like the brother next door," said rapper Method Man, "and when you see it happening to him, it's time to wake up and smell the coffee."

At 31, the rapper (born Eric Wright) had parlayed his gritty vision of urban life into a multimillion-dollar recording empire. The son of Richard Wright, a retired postal worker and his wife, Kathie, a school administrator, Eazy-E took $25,000 he had earned dealing drugs in the crime-ridden Compton section of L.A. and launched Ruthless Records in 1986. His 1988 solo album, *Eazy-Duz-It*, went double platinum, but it was the formation of N.W.A (Niggas with Attitude), with Dr. Dre and Ice Cube, that made gangsta rap a force to be reckoned with. The group's 1988 debut album, *Straight Outta Compton*, sold 3 million copies and angered the FBI, which complained it incited violence against police. "Records don't make anybody do nothing," Wright said. "You make yourself do that."

Wright often boasted of his sexual prowess, having fathered (and supported) eight children—ranging from Eric, 10, to Dominick, 1—by seven different women. How Wright contracted AIDS is a mystery, but he was most likely a victim of denial and misinformation. In 1991 he said, "I use condoms. I don't want to f—k around with AIDS or herpes. But in case I need it I got a big-a— bottle of tetracycline and another gang of pills." On his deathbed, Wright wrote a cautionary message to his fans, "to save [them] before it's too late."

J. WILLIAM FULBRIGHT

During his 30 years in the Senate, J. William Fulbright (D–Arkansas) posted many eloquent dissents. The Senator, who died of a stroke in February in Washington at the age of 89, once observed that dissent, "is an act of faith. Like medicine, the test

of its value is not its taste but its effect." Joe McCarthy called him "Senator Halfbright," and he was LBJ's most scathing Vietnam critic. To become a senator, Congressman Fulbright (in '44) defeated the governor who had dumped him as University of Arkansas president. A Rhodes scholar who believed in the power of education to reshape the world, he was the legislative father of the prestigious international fellowship program that still bears his name. The father of two daughters, he was married for 53 years to Elizabeth Williams, a onetime Philadelphia socialite. In 1990, a widower, he married Harriet Mayor, then 61 and director of the Fulbright Association.

JERRY GARCIA

The charismatic and visionary musician Jerry Garcia, whose band, the Grateful Dead, has become emblematic of an era and a state of mind, died in August at a drug treatment center in Marin County, Calif. Garcia, who died in his sleep of a heart attack, had just celebrated his 53rd birthday. Garcia had a long history of drug abuse and excessive personal habits that had led to health problems in the past, and was reportedly being treated for heroin addiction at the time of his death.

Garcia had been a fixture on the rock scene for over three decades, and his death

stunned the musical community. "There's no way to measure his greatness or magnitude as a person or as a player," Bob Dylan wrote in a statement. "He was that great, much more than a superb musician with an uncanny ear and dexterity . . . His playing was moody, awesome, sophisticated, hypnotic and subtle." Jann Wenner, publisher of *Rolling Stone*, said in a statement, "Jerry Garcia was an American original."

The Grateful Dead were one of rock's longest-lived and most beloved institutions. Formed in 1965, when a Bay Area jug band switched to electric instruments, the Dead created an all-American fusion of bluegrass, blues, country, rhythm-and-blues, folk, and rock, all augmented with improvisation. They never played a song in the same way twice.

Unlike almost every other band, the Dead built their reputation on live performances, conducting lengthy, free-form shows without a set list. The Dead's fans savored the group's unpredictability, seeing as many concerts as possible and sometimes following the band for a full-length tour. Barefoot and wearing tie-dyes, dancing and smoking marijuana, the Dead's audiences hung on to the aesthetic, and many of the attitudes, of the '60s.

The Dead played their last date on July 9 at Soldier Field in Chicago. Garcia is survived by his third wife, Deborah Koons, who first met him at a concert in the early '70s and who he'd married on Valentine's Day 1994. He is also survived by four daughters from his first two marriages: Heather, 32, Annabelle, 25, Teresa, 21, and Keelin, 6.

ALEXANDER GODUNOV

Brilliantly talented yet filled with fatal self-doubt, Alexander Godunov was that quintessential Cold War creature, a star in his own country who could achieve brighter fame only by leaving it. The strapping, 6'3" dancer stunned Soviet audiences in 1971, when at age 21 he made his debut in *Swan Lake* at the Bolshoi Ballet in Moscow. "He was a phenomenal success," says Konstantin Kosterev, the Bolshoi Opera's accompanist and one of Godunov's closest friends.

Godunov would remain larger-than-life for nearly two decades. His defection to the U.S. in 1979 almost caused an international crisis, and throughout the '80s he and actress Jacqueline Bisset were a romantic duo of astounding leonine beauty. When Godunov made his film debut as an Amish farmer in 1985's *Witness*, critics predicted he would become a screen idol.

But in a pitiful ending to an extraordinary life, Godunov was found dead in his West Hollywood apartment in May. He died, says his spokeswoman, Evelyn Shriver, of the cumulative effects of acute alcoholism. He had probably been dead for at least a couple of days before his body was discovered.

Godunov had seemed on the brink of recapturing the promise of his early film roles. He spent March on location in Budapest, playing a terrorist in the thriller *The Zone*, his first significant movie part in years. "He never drank in excess in my presence," says producer Oliver Hess. "This has shocked the hell out of me." Yet even as a young Bolshoi dancer, Godunov drank heavily. Still, says Shriver, "you couldn't tell from looking at him that drinking was taking its toll. He continued to do hours at the ballet barre and was in great shape."

BURL IVES

Poet Carl Sandburg once called Burl Ives "the mightiest ballad singer of this or any other century." On-screen, too, Ives carved an imposing presence, portraying cranky cattle barons (1958's *The Big Country*, for which he won a Best Supporting Actor Oscar) and crafty patriarchs—most memorably, Big Daddy in the 1958 film version of *Cat on a Hot Tin Roof*. But the actor himself, it seems, was a gentle giant. "He possessed this wonderful, teddy-bear warmth," Elizabeth Taylor recalled after Ives, 85, died of mouth cancer in April at his home in Anacortes, Wash. "I loved him, and I will miss him." So will generations of kids who grew up singing Ives's signature songs "Big Rock Candy Mountain" and "Blue Tail Fly."

In all, Ives appeared in at least a dozen plays and 26 movies. In 1955, he became Big Daddy when director Elia Kazan, then casting the Broadway production of *Cat on a Hot Tin Roof*, saw him punching out a nightclub heckler. On TV he narrated the Christmas cartoon perennial *Rudolph the Red-Nosed Reindeer*, and played a lawyer on NBC's *The Bold Ones* (1969-72) and a southern senator in 1977's *Roots*.

ROSE KENNEDY

To many, she was the queen mother of American politics. Rose Kennedy—who died in Cape Cod in January, at 104, of complications from pneumonia—founded a dynasty that knew both giddy triumph and crushing tragedy for the better part of the 20th century.

Rose's father, John "Honey Fitz" Fitzgerald was the first Irish-American congressman from Boston—and later mayor of the city—and Rose, the oldest of his six children, learned early to savor both the bright lights and bare-knuckle infighting of politics. Although she was accepted at Wellesley College, Honey Fitz, wedded to convention, sent her to convent schools. At age 20, in 1914, she married Joe Kennedy, a saloon keeper's son of whom her father disapproved. By the time of their marriage, Joe, 26, was already the country's youngest bank president, and together he and his new bride set out to start a family and fashion a dynasty. Joe, who is rumored to have dabbled in bootlegging in the 1920s, eventually amassed a fortune (his wealth was estimated at more than $250 million in 1957) in banking, real estate, and stock holdings. The Kennedys had nine children—Joseph Jr., John, Rosemary, Kathleen, Eunice, Patricia, Robert, Jean and Edward—homes in Massachusetts, New York and Palm Beach—and more family troubles than were generally known. Joe was a notorious philanderer, but in its way the marriage worked, in large part because Rose enjoyed the perks she derived from Joe's money and connections. The couple's most insurmountable conflict came over their eldest daughter Rosemary, who was mentally retarded. In 1941, without seeking Rose's approval, Joe agreed to have the 23-year-old lobotomized, believing the operation would help control her behavior. Twenty years passed before Rose learned the truth, and according to intimates it was the one act for which she never forgave her husband. Rosemary never spoke intelligibly

again and, at 76, remains institutionalized.

In 1961 Rose's crowning success came as she stood by her son and his wife, Jacqueline Bouvier Kennedy, as Jack was sworn in as the first Catholic President of the United States. But later that year Joe Sr. was felled by a stroke from which he never fully recovered. Then came Jack's assassination, followed, five years later, by Bobby's. The Chappaquiddick scandal was next. When Mary Jo Kopechne drowned in Ted Kennedy's car on July 18, 1969, Ted's—and Rose's—presidential ambitions were dashed. Rose remained active in the family until she suffered a stroke in 1984. After that she returned to the Hyannis Port compound and her faith, saying her rosary daily.

MICKEY MANTLE

The mood was surprisingly buoyant at Mickey Mantle's August funeral—fitting perhaps for an irrepressible man's man who used to slip snakes into his teammates' pants. The 2,000 mourners at Lovers Lane United Methodist Church in Dallas alternated between laughter and tears. Eulogizing Mantle, NBC broadcaster Bob Costas recalled how millions of boys who grew up in the '50s and '60s slavishly imitated everything Mickey did. "Always so hard on himself, he finally came to accept and appreciate that distinc-

tion between a role model and a hero," Costas said of Mantle, who died of liver cancer at 63.

Despite his success, Mantle was shot through with human frailty. Driven to alcoholism, he could be surly, crude, and downright obscene to his adoring public. But after years of abusing himself and shortchanging those who loved him, in 1994 he entered the Betty Ford Center. Sober, Mantle revealed himself to be the warm, self-effacing character who had so often inspired loyalty and love in friends and teammates.

"For all those years I lived the life of somebody I didn't know. A cartoon character," Mantle said in April 1994. "I still can't remember much of the last 10 years . . . but I'm looking forward to the memories I'll have in the next 10." As it turned out, he had 16 months left.

The raw crew-cut kid emerged from poverty in Commerce, Okla., where his father, Elvin "Mutt" Mantle, worked eight hours a day in a zinc mine. A semipro pitcher, Mutt named his eldest son after Hall of Fame catcher Gordon "Mickey" Cochrane, the sparkplug of the Depression-era Philadelphia Athletics and Detroit Tigers. The elder Mantle drilled his son hours a day, teaching him to hit both right- and left-handed. Signed by the New York Yankees in 1949, just after he had graduated from high school, Mantle was called up to the majors in 1951. The shortstop turned outfielder had an astonishing blend of power and speed. In his 18-year career he hit 536 home runs, though constantly hobbled by injuries and chronic bone disease in his left leg, and led the Yanks to seven world championships.

The extent of his illness wasn't known on May 28, when Mantle was rushed to Baylor University Medical Center in Dallas with severe abdominal pain. Diagnosed with liver cancer, he underwent a transplant on June 8. At first the operation seemed a success. Then came word that the cancer had spread and was swiftly overwhelming his lungs, heart cavity, and other vital organs.

As one of Mantle's last wishes, he wanted to establish a donor awareness program, called Mickey's Team, at Baylor. To date, Mantle's medical travails have inspired a twofold increase in the number of people requesting donor cards.

Yet Mantle's gracious endgame was not untouched by controversy. His liver transplant, a mere 48 hours after his name went on a waiting list, fueled a contentious debate about medical ethics. Skeptics wondered whether Mantle was given preferential treatment, effectively jumping ahead of more than 250 Texans awaiting new livers. His doctors insisted that Mantle received this new liver so quickly

because he was the sickest patient on the waiting list. Though his epitaph has yet to be written, Mantle may have already provided the wry last word himself. He liked to tell a story about his death and his arrival at the Pearly Gates, where St. Peter shook his head and sent him away. Resigned, Mantle turned to go, only to be summoned back. "Before you go," St. Peter remarked, "God wants to know if you'd sign these six dozen balls."

ELIZABETH MONTGOMERY

Elizabeth Montgomery's final request was to die as she had lived, quietly and privately. After weeks spent battling a vicious cancer, Montgomery, 62, slipped away in May. She was at home in Beverly Hills, surrounded by the people she loved most: her fourth husband, actor Robert Foxworth, 53, and her three children from her third marriage, to *Bewitched* producer William Asher.

Montgomery's quiet death was in keeping with the dignified life of the woman who found fame as Samantha Stephens, a blithe, blonde witch determined to be the perfect wife to a sputteringly flustered adman named Darrin. The daughter of movie star Robert Montgomery and stage actress Elizabeth Allen, Montgomery had firm notions about how Hollywood royalty should behave. That meant keeping her personal life far from the lime-

light. Although she never stopped acting, she hadn't given an interview in 20 years.

Bewitched, which began airing in 1964, was Montgomery's first TV series, and was a good fit for a mother and actress. The births of Elizabeth's children were blended into the production schedule—when Samantha was pregnant with her TV son Adam in 1969, Montgomery was pregnant with Rebecca.

Montgomery owned 20 percent of *Bewitched* and made millions in its first run and residuals. The show, now enjoying renewed popularity on Nick at Nite, went off the air in 1972. A few years later Montgomery embarked on the second phase of her career, as the doyenne of TV movies. She wanted to move away from *Bewitched*, and though one wall of a hallway of her home was lined with photos of her TV movie roles, there were no pictures from the show that made her famous.

Although Montgomery mostly kept to herself, she was happy to use her celebrity clout to back favorite liberal causes. Critical of Reagan-Bush policies in Central America, Montgomery narrated the 1988 documentary *Coverup: Behind the Iran-Contra Affair* and *The Panama Deception*, which won an Oscar in 1993. She worked with AIDS Project Los Angeles and AmFAR, the American Foundation for AIDS Research.

According to author Edna Buchanan, Montgomery was a star without a star attitude. "Elizabeth just acted like a terrific, friendly, wonderful, buoyant person," Buchanan said. The magic didn't end with Samantha.

GINGER ROGERS

Almost 70 years ago, when a teenage Ginger Rogers had just graduated from dancing the Charleston in Texas to performing in vaudeville in New York City, she was pleased to discover how effortlessly she was able to establish rapport with an audience. "I realized that there was a trick," she said later, "and that was being warm with them." A simple enough credo, but it carried Rogers through 73 movies, including the 10 unforgettable musicals in which, paired with Fred Astaire, she whirled across elegant Art Deco sets trailing feathers and chiffon, setting an unmatchable standard for dancing on film. There were also her straight-shooting performances in 1937's *Stage Door,* 1940's *Kitty Foyle,* and 1942's *The Major and the Minor.* Robust yet glamorous, with a purposeful stride and a beauty mark on the left side of her chin, Rogers was, as *Time* pronounced in 1941, "the flesh-and-blood symbol of the United States working girl."

Rogers died in April at the age of 83. Strongly reli-

gious, she always credited her indomitability to a life-long faith in Christian Science. Rogers relied on that faith when she died serenely at her three-bedroom home in Ranch Mirage, Calif.

Rogers was born Virginia Katherine McMath on July 16, 1911. At age 14, Ginger won a state-wide Charleston contest that ultimately led her to Broadway. In 1930's *Girl Crazy,* the 19-year-old Rogers, who had a pleasantly girlish voice, introduced Gershwin's *Embraceable You* and *But Not for Me.* That same year, she made her movie debut in *Young Man in Manhattan,* in which she uttered a line that would become a catch phrase: "Cigarette me, big boy." Her first screen hits came three years later, in *42nd Street* and *Gold Diggers of 1933.*

SELENA

Listening to the four albums that vaulted onto the pop charts in the wake of her death, it's clear that 23-year-old superstar Selena was more than just a bustier-clad "Tex-Mex Madonna." With its trembling, tear-in-the-throat sob, her husky voice was rooted in both early-period Madonna and conjunto balladeering, and her songs were steeped in the same tales of unrequited passion that play such a large part in Latin music. Beneath the glitz and chirpy synthesizers was a living, breathing folk tradition.

But that beautiful music

was brought to an abrupt end with a single bullet, fired, according to police, from the gun of Yolanda Saldvar, 34, the former president of Selena's fan club. Selena had gone to confront Saldvar over a suspected embezzlement of funds. For Selena's family, who knew Saldvar well, the rush of events had a surreal quality. "The ultimate sorrow a human can feel is when someone dies," her father, Abraham Quintanilla Jr., told PEOPLE. "I felt like this was all a dream." Selena sang Tejano—the contemporary offshoot of conjunto, a century-old blend of German dance music (played on accordions) and Mexican folk melodies. Spanish for "Texan," Tejano is enormously popular in the Southwest. Still, Tejano artists had never crossed into the world of MTV. Selena was on the verge of changing that when she was murdered—she was in the process of recording her first English-language album, which was finished posthumously. *Dreaming of You,* a collection of old and new Selena songs, made its debut in *Billboard's* No. 1 spot.

MARGARET CHASE SMITH

It was a rainy Washington morning in June 1950 when Margaret Chase Smith, a first-term Republican senator from Maine, bumped into fellow legislator Joseph McCarthy of Wisconsin.

McCarthy, the country's ranking political bully, had recently embarked on an innuendo-filled crusade against alleged Communists in government. "Margaret," she recalled him saying, "you look awfully glum this morning." Smith responded in a determined Yankee twang, "I'm making a speech today. And you're not going to like it."

She was right. Smith, who died in May at age 97 at her home in Skowhegan, Maine, would deliver the seminal address of her remarkable 32-year congressional career that afternoon. Reading what she called a Declaration of Conscience, which she had written at her kitchen table a few days earlier, she became the first politician to denounce McCarthy's fear-mongering on the Senate floor: "I don't want to see the Republican party ride to political victory on the four horsemen of calumny—fear, ignorance, bigotry, and smear."

In time, Smith's congressional career would span the terms of six Presidents as she became the first woman to win election to both houses of Congress. But she disliked such distinctions. "Isn't a woman a human being?" she once asked. "Why can't she just be a person?"

Smith's career in Washington started late. She was born in the little Maine mill town of Skowhegan, where her mother was a waitress and her father was a town barber. The oldest of six children, she started work at age 12 and, a few years after graduating from high school, joined the local *Independent Reporter* as circulation manager. In 1930 she married its co-owner, Clyde H. Smith, then 21 years her senior.

It was her husband, with his involvement in local Republican politics, who introduced Smith to her life's work. In 1936 he was elected to the U.S. House from Maine's second congressional district. She worked as his full-time secretary in Washington, and when he died of a heart attack in 1940, she was elected to fill his unexpired term. From then on she seemed unstoppable, crossing party lines to endorse government-financed medical care and federal aid to education. Smith's political career ended in 1972 when Democrat William D. Hathaway defeated her in her bid for a fifth Senate term. "I think a lot of people thought she was taking it [her place in Congress] for granted," says Hathaway, now 71. But Smith—who had never accepted contributions from individuals or interest groups—said she simply lost pace with modern campaign strategies. "She proved integrity could always be good politics," says Maine Gov. Angus King. "She had an absolute rock-bottom sense of self."

KRISTEN TAYLOR

On July 7, five days after she collapsed and died at her parents' home in Pembroke Pines, Fla., 200 friends and family members gathered to say farewell to 17-year-old model Kristen Taylor, whose life had seemed so full of promise. Like her parents, Barbara and Ken, Taylor's supermodel sister Niki was too distraught to speak. Sister Joelle, 24, gave a eulogy, followed by more than a dozen of Taylor's teenage friends, and then the mourners gathered in a circle, clutching candles.

Following Taylor's mysterious death, rumors had spread quickly. In New York, fashion insiders postulated privately that, in the hours before she died, Taylor might have been using Primatene Mist, a non-prescription asthma remedy, to get an over-the-counter high. They wondered whether she had coped with stress by abusing booze or drugs, and whether Barbara, 48, and Ken, 54, had pressured her into a life before the cameras. And they whispered that Taylor, like many models, must have starved herself until her body was vulnerable to any minor shock. However, a few weeks later the results of an autopsy indicated that the cause of death was previously undetected bronchial asthma. It was unclear if her use of Primatene Mist contributed to her death.

Those who knew the 5' 11", 127-lb. Taylor refused

to believe that she had any sinister secrets. "If you had something negative to say about Kristen, you didn't know her," said her best friend Melissa Bucci. Says Barbara: "Her physical beauty captured everyone's eye, but her inner beauty is what we will remember."

LANA TURNER

The "Sweater Girl" whose buxom good looks graced many a GI's pinup, Lana Turner was a consummate '40s Hollywood star. A sex symbol whose acting was generally mediocre, Turner, who died of natural causes at 75 in Los Angeles in June, recalled in 1969, "It was all beauty and it was all power. Once you had it made, they protected you; they gave you stardom. The ones who kept forging ahead became higher and higher and brighter and brighter and they were stars. And they were treated like stars. We had the best."

The actress's best performance was as a dissatisfied wife who seduces a drifter into killing her husband in *The Postman Always Rings Twice* (1946). She was a star at MGM for 17 years, and also appeared memorably as a rebellious student in *These Glamour Girls* (1939), a shallow performer in *Ziegfeld Girl* (1941), and an alcoholic actress in *The Bad and the Beautiful* (1952).

Turner was discovered in 1937 by a reporter as she sipped a soda in a Holly-wood ice cream parlor while cutting secretarial class at her high school. The encounter led to her first film, *They Won't Forget*. Wearing a skintight sweater and skirt, she sauntered along a street, spoke not one line, was murdered in the first reel, and began a quick climb to stardom.

Her stormy personal life, peppered by many marriages and publicized romances, was as lurid as many of her films, but her identity as a sex symbol served to insulate her career from scandal's consequences. The most sensational incident occurred in 1958 when her lover, Johnny Stompanato, threatened to disfigure her and was stabbed to death with a carving knife by her 14-year-old daughter, Cheryl Crane. A jury exonerated her daughter with a finding of justifiable homicide.

Her 1982 memoir, *Lana: The Lady, the Legend, the Truth*, focused on her eight marriages and many romances. The memoir also recalled a suicide attempt, two abortions, three stillbirths, alcoholism, and her religious awakening in 1980.

★

Original "Hollywood Madam" **Elizabeth Adams**, 60, after heart surgery, in Los Angeles. A mentor (then competitor) of Heidi Fleiss, she furnished women to the rich and powerful for up to $2,000 a day. "Madam Alex" kept authorities at bay for 25 years by informing for the police, but was convicted of pandering in 1988.

The decomposed body of B-movie director **Al Adamson** (1970's *Horror of the Blood Monsters*, 1971's *Dracula vs. Frankenstein*), 66, was found wrapped in linens and buried beneath the newly tiled floor of his Indio, Calif., home in August, five weeks after he was last seen alive. Police arrested and brought homicide charges against Fred Fulford, 46, an independent contractor who had recently been renovating and living in Adamson's home.

Brazilian guitarist **Laurindo Almeida**, 77, who contributed to the score of *The Godfather* and won five Grammys for his classical guitar compositions, of cancer, in Los Angeles.

Danny Arnold, 70, an Emmy-winning TV writer-producer who created *Barney Miller*, of heart failure, in Los Angeles.

Raspy-voiced actor and comedian **Rick Aviles**, 41, whose movie credits include playing the lowlife who killed Patrick Swayze in *Ghost*, of heart failure, in Los Angeles.

Wall Street whiz **Jeffrey P. Beck**, 48, a mergers-and-acquisitions specialist who was nicknamed Mad Dog because he would howl after completing a particularly profitable megadeal, and who served as an adviser on the film *Wall Street*, of a heart attack, in Manhattan.

Ruth Disney Beecher, 91, the only sister of studio founder Walt Disney, in Portland, Ore.

Former Columbia Pictures president **David Begelman**, 74, an apparent suicide by gunshot, at his Los Angeles home. Begelman was accused in 1977 of cashing studio checks he had made payable to other people. He pleaded no contest to felony grand theft. David McClintick chronicled his activities in the 1982 book *Indecent Exposure*.

British screenwriter **Charles Bennett**, 95, who collaborated with Alfred Hitchcock on the screenplays for such 1930s film noir classics as *The Thirty-Nine Steps* and *The Man Who Knew Too Much*, of natural causes, in Los Angeles.

Publicity guru **Edward Bernays**, 103, who helped to bolster the role of public relations and corporate communications in business, and advised every President from Calvin Coolidge through Dwight Eisenhower, in Cambridge, Mass.

Entertainment chronicler **Earl Blackwell**, 85, of Parkinson's disease, in New York City. Blackwell founded Celebrity Service, a trade bulletin, in 1939.

Newscaster **Frank Blair**, 79, a mainstay on NBC's *Today Show* for 23 years, of an undisclosed cause at his home in Hilton Head, SC, on March 14, exactly 20 years

to the day after he last delivered a *Today* newscast.

Helen J. Boiardi, 90, who, with her husband, Hector, created Chef Boy-ar-dee, one of America's first packaged-convenience-food companies, of natural causes in Shaker Heights, Ohio. The familiar chef's face appearing on their labels had belonged to Hector, who died in 1985.

British playwright and screenwriter **Robert Bolt**, 70, who wrote such classic films as *Lawrence of Arabia* (1962), *Doctor Zhivago* (1965), and *A Man for All Seasons* (1966), of undisclosed causes, in Hampshire, England.

Canadian director **Philip Borsos**, 41, whose films included *The Grey Fox* (1983), of leukemia, in Vancouver.

Screenwriter **Robert Paul Breslo**, 37, of complications due to AIDS, in New York City. Breslo adapted the Carson McCullers story *A Domestic Dilemma* for a 1991 HBO TV movie produced by Jonathan Demme. "I was in awe of his gift," says Demme, who cast Breslo in a small role in *Philadelphia*.

Actor **Paul Brinegar**, 77, who dished out the grub as Wishbone, the surly chuckwagon cook on *Rawhide* (1959-66), in Los Angeles, of emphysema.

Actor **Don Brockett**, 65, who had been rolling out

dough and whipping up entrees as Chef Brockett on TV's *Mister Rogers' Neighborhood* since 1967, of a heart attack, in Pittsburgh.

Former Supreme Court Chief Justice **Warren E. Burger**, 87, the longest-reigning Chief Justice of this century—17 years—of congestive heart failure, in Washington.

Glenn Burke, 42, a former outfielder with the Los Angeles Dodgers and Oakland Athletics who, in 1982, two years after leaving the game, became the first major leaguer to publicly acknowledge his homosexuality, of complications from AIDS, in San Leandro, Calif. Burke once said that homophobia—some of his teammates knew he was gay—had driven him out of baseball.

Philip Burton, 90, a Welsh stage director and drama teacher who was both father figure and mentor to actor Richard Burton (who adopted his name), of a stroke, in Davenport, Fla.

Bob Caron, 75, the tail gunner on the "Enola Gay" when it dropped the atomic bomb on Hiroshima in 1945, of pneumonia, in Denver. In an interview published last year, Caron said of the bombing, which left as many as 100,000 dead instantly, "No remorse, no bad dreams, we accomplished our mission."

Fabio Casartelli, 24, Olympic medalist and star Tour de France cyclist, of

28

severe head injuries received when he fell from his bicycle after failing to make a sharp curve during a high-speed descent along the Portet d'Aspet mountain pass in the Pyrenees, France. The death renewed calls for competitors to wear helmets.

Nobel laureate and University of Chicago astrophysicist **Subrahmanyan Chandrasekhar**, 84, whose research into the evolution of stars helped lead to the discovery of black holes, of a heart attack, in Chicago.

Edda Ciano, 84, the oldest of Benito Mussolini's five children and his favorite, of cardiac arrest related to lung and kidney failure, in Rome. She renounced her famous surname in 1944 when her dictator father ordered the execution of her husband, Count Galeazzo Ciano, Italy's foreign minister, after he voted for Il Duce's removal following the Allied invasion of Italy.

British director **Jack Clayton**, 73, whose films included *Room at the Top* (1959) and *The Great Gatsby* (1974), of heart and liver problems, in Slough, England.

Record producer **David Cole**, 32, who was half of the creative team behind the neodisco group C+C Music Factory and scored a monster hit with the dance anthem "Gonna Make You Sweat (Everybody Dance

Now)" in 1991, of complications of spinal meningitis in Manhattan.

Jazz balladeer **Earl Coleman**, 69, of cardiac arrest, in New York City. Coleman recorded with Charlie Parker, among others.

Actor **Elisha Cook Jr.**, 88, of stroke-related complications, in Big Pine, Calif. Cook appeared in more than 100 movies, including *Shane*, *Rosemary's Baby*, and, most memorably, as Sydney Greenstreet's bug-eyed bodyguard in *The Maltese Falcon.*

Comic actor **Severn Darden**, 65, who helped found Chicago's famous Second City improvisational troupe in 1959, of heart failure, in Santa Fe.

Girvies Davis, 37, the convicted murderer who campaigned for clemency on the Internet, was executed by lethal injection at Stateville Correctional Center in Joliet, Ill. He was sentenced to death in 1980 for murdering an elderly man during a robbery.

Winston Dean, 88, the father of screen legend James Dean, of pneumonia.

Cheese manufacturer **Victor Dorman**, 80, who in the mid-'50s invented sliced cheese, of complications from muscular dystrophy, in Delray Beach, Fla.

Photojournalist **Alfred Eisenstaedt**, 96, who snapped the famous V-J Day

photo of a sailor and a girl kissing, of cardiac arrest, while vacationing.

1950s bandleader **Les Elgart**, 76, who cowrote the 1954 instrumental "Bandstand Boogie," which became the theme song for Dick Clark's long-running *American Bandstand*, of a heart attack, in Dallas.

Author **Stanley Elkin**, 65, whose 17 darkly comic novels and collections include the highly praised *A Bad Man* (1967) and *Van Gogh's Room at Arles* (1992), of a heart attack, in St. Louis.

Juan Manuel Fangio, 84, five-time Formula One world auto-racing champion during the 1950s (a record that still stands); known for his technical artistry on the track and his gentlemanly behavior off it; in Buenos Aires, Argentina.

St. Elsewhere star and three-time Emmy winner **Ed Flanders**, who played St. Eligius Hospital's quietly anguished Dr. Westphall on the classic NBC series from 1982 to 1987, shot himself at age 60 in his N. Calif. ranch home.

Game show host **Art Fleming**, 70, who gave the answers so that contestants could ask the questions on TV's *Jeopardy!* from the show's start in 1964 to '75, and then again from '78 to '79, of pancreatic cancer, in Crystal River, Fla.

Melvin Franklin, 52, one of the best known voices in the legendary soul group the

Temptations, of complications from brain seizures, in Los Angeles.

Animator **Isadore "Friz" Freleng**, 89, who helped create such cartoon characters as Sylvester the Cat and Tweety Bird and who, as head animator at Warner Bros., regularly drew Bugs Bunny and Daffy Duck, of natural causes, in Los Angeles. Freleng won five Oscars for his work.

Ernie Furtado, 72, of cancer, in Amagansett, N.Y. Furtado was a jazz bassist and composer known for his intense and passionate music, a fixture on the New York music and club scene in the early '50s.

Eva Gabor, 74, called "the good Gabor" and best known as socialite-turned-farm wife Lisa Douglas on TV's *Green Acres*, of respiratory distress, in Los Angeles.

Rory Gallagher, 46, one of the pioneers of blues and rock guitar and a champion of the Irish rock scene, from complications from a liver transplant, in London.

Playwright and actor **Michael V. Gazzo**, 71, who played Mafia lieutenant Frank Pentangeli in *The Godfather, Part II* (1974), following a stroke in Los Angeles.

Actor **Kevin John Gee**, 40, who played the valet Ito on *Another World*, of pneumonia, in New York City.

Tennis star **Pancho Gonzalez**, 67, of stomach cancer in Las Vegas. The best player never to win a Wimbledon singles title, Gonzalez was known for his strong serve and fiery on-court personality. He won the U.S. singles title in 1948 and '49, and in 1969 won the longest match in Wimbledon history: a 112-game marathon that spanned five hours and 12 minutes over two days.

L.C. Graves, 76, the homicide detective who wrestled the gun away from Jack Ruby after Ruby shot Lee Harvey Oswald in the basement of the Dallas police station on Nov. 24, 1963, of heart failure, in Kaufman, Tex.

Screenwriter **Eleanor Griffin**, 91, who shared an Oscar for cowriting the original story of 1938's *Boys' Town*, of natural causes, in Woodland Hills, Calif.

Veteran actor **Harry Guardino**, 69, who appeared in numerous films (including several with friend Clint Eastwood), stage productions, and television shows, of lung cancer at Desert Hospital in Palm Springs. He was seen most recently in the comedy *Breaking Legs*, which he took on tour with Danny Aiello.

Pulitzer Prize-winning writer **Albert Hackett**, 95, of pneumonia, in New York City. Hackett won a 1956 Pulitzer for *The Diary of Anne Frank*, which he cowrote with his first wife and collaborator, Frances Goodrich.

Actor **Antony Hamilton**, 42, who played secret agent Jack Striker in the TV series *Cover Up* (1984-85), of pneumonia, in Los Angeles. Hamilton, originally a leading dancer with the Australian Ballet, joined *Cover Up* to replace actor Jon-Erik Hexum, who had accidentally shot himself fatally in the head with a blank from a gun used as a prop.

Dorothy Handford, 71, a program assistant at Minnesota Public Radio whose home-baked cinnamon rolls inspired Garrison Keillor to enshrine her on his *Prairie Home Companion* radio show as the proprietor of Dorothy's Chatterbox Cafe, of cancer, in St. Paul, Minn.

Counterculture clothing designer **Holly Harp**, 55, who dressed rock icons Janis Joplin and Grace Slick in tie-dye and fringe, of cancer, in Los Angeles.

Former radio personality **Phil Harris**, 89, the voice of Baloo the Bear in Disney's 1967 animated classic *The Jungle Book*, of heart failure, at his home in Rancho Mirage, Calif. Harris led his own swing bands before playing Jack Benny's wisecracking, bourbon-swilling sidekick on the comic's radio show, which ran from 1936 to 1952 and garnered Harris his own program, which ran for eight years.

Dr. Thomas A. Harris, 85, a psychiatrist and the

author of the best-selling self-help book *I'm O.K.—You're O.K.* (1969), of a heart attack, in Sacramento, Calif.

Blues singer and guitarist **Ted Hawkins**, 58, whose plaintive but gutsy style earned him critical acclaim for works such as the 1982 album *Watch Your Step*, of a stroke, in Los Angeles.

Julius Hemphill, 57, legendary jazz saxophonist and cofounder of the World Saxophone Quartet, of complications from diabetes, in New York City.

James Alfred Wight, 78, who under the pen name **James Herriot** became a best-selling author with 1972's *All Creatures Great and Small*, of prostate cancer, in Yorkshire, England. His books, 18 in all, sold 60 million copies worldwide and inspired two movies and a TV series.

Novelist **Patricia Highsmith**, 74, whose psychologically rich thrillers have been a staple on mystery shelves for 45 years, of leukemia, in Locarno, Switzerland.

Actor **John Howard**, 82, known best for his roles in *Lost Horizon* and *The Philadelphia Story*, of heart failure, in Santa Rosa, Calif.

Trumpet player **Percy Humphrey**, 90, of natural causes, in New Orleans. Humphrey, who at the peak of his career led the Eureka Brass Band, was known as the oldest active jazz musician in New Orleans.

Comedy writer **Edward James**, 87, who created the radio version of *Father Knows Best* in 1949, and, in 1954, helped move it to TV, of complications of emphysema, in Escondido, Calif.

Chords member **Jimmy Keyes**, in his 60s, cause of death unstated, in the Bronx, N.Y. Keyes was a co-writer of the hit song "Sh-Boom."

Playwright **Sidney Kingsley**, 88, whose best-known work was *Dead End* (1935), a drama of life in the slums, of a stroke, in Oakland, N.J.

Screenwriter **Howard Koch**, 93, of pneumonia, in Kingston, N.Y. Koch wrote the radio script for Orson Welles's *War of the Worlds* before moving to films; he won an Academy Award for *Casablanca*.

Jailed British gangster **Ronnie Kray**, 61, after a heart attack, in Slough, England. Before they were imprisoned for murder in 1969, the thuggish Ronnie and his twin brother, Reggie, ran swindles and extorted payoffs from nightclubs and pubs, causing them to be crowned Kings of Crime by the British press. A movie depicting their brutal rise, *The Krays*, was released in 1990. Reggie is serving a life sentence.

Political and social activist **Maggie Kuhn**, 89, who led the fight against age discrimination by helping to found the Gray Panthers in 1970, of cardiopulmonary arrest, in Philadelphia.

Singer and movie star **Priscilla Lane**, 77, blondest, youngest, and longest-lived of the three performing Lane Sisters (the others were Rosemary and Lola), of natural causes, at a nursing home in Andover, Mass.

Comedian **Jerry Lester**, 85, host of the first successful late-night TV talk and variety show, *Broadway Open House*, in 1950-51, of complications from Alzheimer's disease, in Miami.

Evelyn Lincoln, 85, John F. Kennedy's devoted secretary from 1953, his first year in the U.S. Senate, until his assassination 10 years later, of complications after cancer surgery, in Washington. Although Lincoln published two best-selling memoirs, the loyal secretary once said that much of what she had written in her diary about JFK would remain secret.

Onnie Lee Logan, 85, midwife and memoirist; in Mobile, Ala. For half a century, Logan delivered the babies of impoverished black families. In 1989 she published her reminiscences, *Motherwit: An Alabama Midwife's Story*, which became a best-selling feminist classic.

Director **Arthur Lubin**, 96, who, between his *Francis the Talking Mule* movies and his *Mr. Ed* TV series, pretty much had a lock on the gabby equine franchise, of complications from a stroke, in Glendale, Calif.

Adored baseball umpire **Ron Luciano**, 57, committed suicide by carbon monoxide poisoning as he sat in his 1987 Cadillac in the garage of his wood-frame house in his upstate hometown of Endicott, N.Y. The 6'4", 300-lb. ump labored to cast off the traditional dour air of the man in blue, and produced four memoirs, including the best-seller *The Umpire Strikes Back*. Obviously, there was a side to Luciano that the public didn't see.

British-born actress and film noir pinup girl **Ida Lupino**, 77, who played Humphrey Bogart's girlfriend in *High Sierra* and became a pioneering woman director, of colon cancer, in Burbank, Calif.

Children's author **Roger MacBride**, 65, guardian of Laura Ingalls Wilder's series of *Little House on the Prairie* books, of heart failure, in Miami Beach. MacBride assumed control of the Wilder estate in 1968 upon the death of Wilder's daughter, Rose Wilder Lane. He wrote three children's books of his own, and ran for President in 1976 as the candidate of the Libertarian Party.

Oil mogul **J. Howard Marshall II**, 90, husband of **Anna Nicole Smith**, 27, in Houston. The fate of Marshall's fortune, estimated at $550 million, is still being contested.

Fashion designer **Vera Maxwell**, 93, who helped pioneer sportswear for American women and dressed Grace Kelly, Pat Nixon and Rosalynn Carter, among others, of a stroke, in Puerto Rico.

Actor **Doug McClure**, 59, who defined cowhand bonding and branding for a generation of viewers in the popular series *The Virginian* (1962-1971), of lung cancer, in Sherman Oaks, Calif.

Former Ziegfeld Follies dancer **Dorothy McHugh**, 87, best known for her medical-alert commercials, in which she cried, "I've fallen, and I can't get up," after suffering several strokes, in Philadelphia.

Scriptwriter **Herb Meadow**, 83, who cocreated the western TV series *Have Gun Will Travel* (1957-63), of a heart attack, in Los Angeles.

Poet **James Merrill**, 68, who published 15 volumes of poetry and was awarded every major prize given for verse, of a heart attack, in Tucson. Merrill won the Pulitzer for *Divine Comedies*, and had finished correcting proofs on his latest work, *A Scattering of Salts*, just before his death.

Pianist **Arturo Benedetti Michelangeli**, 75, of undisclosed causes, in Lugano, Switzerland. A WWII pilot and sometime auto racer, the famously reclusive classical keyboard wizard was known for his remarkable technical facility as well as his idiosyncratic personality, which at times led him to cancel performances abruptly.

Silent-film actress **Patsy Ruth Miller**, 91, in Palm Desert, Calif. At the age of 18, Miller earned her niche in film history as Esmeralda, the gypsy girl literally swept off her feet by Lon Chaney's Hunchback of Notre Dame. After the talkies drove Miller from the screen in 1931, she became an award-winning writer of short stories and radio scripts.

Colorado housewife **Virginia Tighe Morrow**, 72, who 41 years ago sparked a national debate on reincarnation after she claimed under hypnosis to have lived before, of breast cancer, near Denver. In 1952 businessman and amateur hypnotist Morey Bernstein offered to hypnotize Morrow to relieve her allergies. When he did, she spoke in a heavy brogue of a past as a 19th-century Irishwoman known as Bridey Murphy. Morrow shunned fame and profit after Bernstein wrote the 1956 bestseller *The Search for Bridey Murphy*.

Director **Gilbert Moses**, 52, a cofounder in 1963 of the Free Southern Theater, an influential black touring troupe based in Jackson, Miss., of multiple myeloma, in Manhattan. He directed such socially conscious off-Broadway works as *Slave Ship* (1969) and *The Taking of Miss Janie* (1975). For TV, he directed two segments of the 1977 miniseries *Roots* and, more recently, *Law & Order*.

Esther Muir, 92, a former Broadway actress who found fame—and a faceful of wallpaper paste—in the Marx Brothers' film *A Day at the Races* (1937), of natural causes, in Mount Kisco, N.Y.

Fashion designer **Jean Muir**, 66, known for her superbly tailored, elegantly simple outfits, of cancer, in London.

Veteran NBC sportscaster **Lindsey Nelson**, 76, known for his easygoing on-air manner and the eyesore sports jackets he sought out for their loudness, of complications of Parkinson's disease and pneumonia, in Atlanta. He is recognized in the National Baseball Hall of Fame.

Carroll O'Connor's 32-year-old son **Hugh O'Connor**, a part-time actor, committed suicide in the Pacific Palisades section of Los Angeles. Hugh, who played Sgt. Lonnie Jamison to his father's starring role as Chief Bill Gillespie on CBS's *In the Heat of the Night*, had been fighting a drug habit for half his life and was reportedly deeply depressed.

British music hall performer **Tessie O'Shea**, 82, who won a Tony award as a fish-and-chips peddler in Noël Coward's *The Girl Who Came to Supper* (1963), of congestive heart failure, in Leesburg, Fla.

Golf pro **Harvey Penick**, 90, for 48 years the head pro at the Austin Country Club and the best-selling author of *Harvey Penick's Little Red Book* (1992), of pneumonia, in Austin, Texas.

British tennis champ **Fred Perry**, 85, who in 1936 became the last Englishman to win a Wimbledon singles title, of heart failure, in Melbourne.

Donald Pleasence, 75, the bald, beady-eyed British character actor who specialized in playing screen villains, of complications from heart valve surgery, at his home in the South of France.

British stage actor **Eric Porter**, 67, who played Soames Forsyte in *The Forsyte Saga*, the BBC series that became a U.S. hit via public TV in 1969, of cancer, in London.

Cartoonist **George Price**, 93, whose drawings depicting his skewed view of domestic life were a staple of *The New Yorker* for more than 60 years, after a brief illness, in Englewood, N.J.

Actress **Katherine DeMille Quinn**, 83, the first wife of movie star Anthony Quinn and the adopted daughter of biblical-epic director Cecil B. DeMille, of Alzheimer's disease, in Tucson, Ariz. She appeared in such movies as *Call of the Wild* (1935) and *Unconquered* (1947).

Grammy-winning country singer **Charlie Rich**, 62, of natural causes, in Hammond, La. Rich, known as the Silver Fox because of his mane, is best remembered for his '70s hits "Behind Closed Doors" and "The Most Beautiful Girl in the World."

Republican **George Romney**, 88, three-term governor of Michigan during the '60s and for four years Richard Nixon's Secretary of Housing and Urban Development, of a heart attack, in Bloomfield Hills, Mich. Romney's presidential hopes were dashed after he stated that U.S. generals had "brainwashed" him during his 1965 tour of Vietnam.

Bob Ross, 52, the bushy-haired host of the popular *Joy of Painting* public television program who parlayed the success of *Joy of Painting* into an industry of art books and supplies, of cancer, in Orlando.

Composer **Miklos Rozsa**, 88, who won Oscars for scoring *Spellbound*, *A Double Life*, and *Ben Hur*, three weeks after suffering a stroke, in Los Angeles.

Producer **Matthew Rushton**, 43, of AIDS, in Los Angeles. Most recently, Rushton served as executive producer on *Mrs. Doubtfire*.

Poet **May Sarton**, 83, of breast cancer, in York, Maine. Although she wrote more than 20 novels, Sarton, a lesbian and self-imposed recluse, was best known for her poetry about solitude, love, and feminist consciousness.

Hope Montgomery Scott, 90, the accomplished horse-woman and Main Line Philadelphia socialite whose life was the model for Katherine Hepburn in 1940's *The Philadelphia Story*, from injuries after falls at her estate. Scott combined two mighty names in Philadelphia society. Her father was the financier, Col. Robert Montgomery, and she married Edgar Scott, heir to the Pennsylvania Railroad fortune.

Bluesman **Sunnyland Slim** (born Albert Luandrew), 87, whose booming voice and rollicking piano helped shape the hearty electrified Chicago sound of the '50s, of renal failure, in Chicago.

Cowboy star **John Smith**, 63, who played deputy sheriff Lane Temple on TV's *Cimarron City* (1958-59) and rancher Slim Sherman on *Laramie* (1959-63), of cirrhosis and heart problems, in Los Angeles.

British poet **Sir Stephen Spender**, 86, of natural causes, in London. Spender, who was knighted in 1983, ushered in an era of socially conscious poetry.

Industrial designer **Brooks Stevens**, 83, who overhauled the Harley-Davidson motorcycle's look in 1949 and put the sizzle in Oscar Mayer's promotional "Wienermobile" in 1958, of heart failure, in Milwaukee.

Former anchorman **John Cameron Swayze**, 89, for 20 years the voice of Timex watches ("It takes a licking and keeps on ticking"), of natural causes, at his home in Sarasota, Fla. Swayze began his broadcasting career on the radio in his native Kansas before joining NBC television in 1949 to host *The Camel News Caravan*, a 15-minute news program whose nearly eight-year run made famous Swayze's authoritative yet folksy delivery and his trademark signoff, "That's the story, glad we could get together."

Ringo's ex **Maureen Tigrett**, 47, of complications from a bone-marrow transplant. Tigrett, who was married to Ringo Starr from 1965-75 and had three children by him, is the first of the Beatle wives to die.

Radio newscaster **Dallas Townsend**, 76, who wrote and anchored CBS radio's *World News Roundup* for 25 years, of injuries suffered in a fall, in Montclair, N.J.

Group Capt. **Peter Townsend**, 80, in Paris. The dashing WWII fighter ace will always be remembered for his intense but thwarted romance with Britain's Princess Margaret in the '50s. Margaret, then third in line to the throne, and Townsend, a divorced war hero 16 years her senior, fell madly and publicly in love when Margaret was in her early 20s. They were expected to announce their engagement upon Margaret's 25th birthday, but the Palace had let it be known that Townsend's divorce made him an unsuitable mate. Rather than turn her back on the royal family—which had been rocked in 1936 by King Edward VIII's abdication to marry a divorcée—Margaret reluctantly announced the couple's parting in 1955.

Retired salesman **Salvatore Travolta**, 82, father of John Travolta, of a heart ailment, in Santa Barbara, Calif.

British writer **Kathleen Tynan**, 57, best known for *The Life of Kenneth Tynan*, her compelling 1987 biography of her husband, the influential drama critic, of cancer, in London.

Ex-Minnesota Twins shortstop **Zoilo Versalles**, 55, who in 1965 became the first Latin American to be named the American League's most valuable player, in Bloomington, Minn. No cause of death was released. After leaving baseball in 1971 due to a back injury, the Cuban-born Versalles worked odd jobs and had to sell his trophies to make ends meet.

Super retailer **James L. "Bud" Walton**, 73, who cofounded the Wal-Mart Stores empire in 1962 with his late brother Sam, of an aneurysm following surgery, in Miami. His personal fortune was estimated at $1 billion.

Actor **Willard Waterman**, 80, who from 1950 to 56 played the title character,

34

water commissioner Throckmorton P. Gildersleeve, on the radio and in the TV comedy *The Great Gildersleeve*, of bone-marrow disease, in Burlingame, Calif.

David Wayne, 81, who won Broadway's first Tony Award for supporting actor in a musical as the leprechaun in the 1947 fantasy *Finian's Rainbow*, of lung cancer, in Santa Monica.

Celebrity barber **Clyde Vernon Waynick**, 68, who was known to snip Elvis Presley's hair when the King visited Nashville, of cancer, in the country music capital.

Sylvia Weinberger, 89, the Colonel Sanders of chopped liver, in Fort Lauderdale.

Actress **Patricia Welsh**, 80, who provided the distinctive, gravelly voice of E.T., of pneumonia, in Green Valley, Ariz.

Casino worker **William R. Wilcoxson**, 54, who on April 23 received the heart of nurse Rebecca Anderson, 37, after she was killed by falling debris while trying to help victims at the Oklahoma City bombing site, from a lung infection related to the transplant, in Oklahoma City.

Novelist **Isabel Wilder**, 95, sister of playwright Thornton Wilder, after a long illness, in Hamden, Conn.

Novelist and screenwriter **Calder Willingham**, 72, whose first book *End As a Man*, a Gothic tale of students at a military academy, made him a literary star in 1947, of lung cancer, in Laconia, N.H. In 1967 he and cowriter Buck Henry received an Oscar nomination for their screenplay of *The Graduate*.

Legendary radio personality **Wolfman Jack**, 57, of a heart attack at his home in Belvedere, N.C. With his distinctive raspy voice and trademark howl, Wolfman Jack was known to a genera-tion of radio listeners all over the country. Wolfman played himself in the 1973 hit George Lucas film *American Graffiti*, and his numerous television credits included an eight-year stint as host of NBC-TV's *Midnight Special*.

Author and former British intelligence official **Peter Wright**, 78, whose best-selling 1987 exposé *Spycatcher* claimed KGB moles had occupied high British intelligence posts, of pneumonia, in Australia.

Society fixture **Jerome Zipkin**, 80, often referred to in *Women's Wear Daily* simply as the "social moth," of lung cancer, in New York City. Zipkin, a real estate heir known for his quick wit and biting insults, served as the confidant and fiercely devoted friend of such rich and famous ladies who lunch as Betsy Bloomingdale, Pat Buckley, and Nancy Reagan.

MARRIAGES

Roseanne's ex **Tom Arnold**, 36, and college student Julie Champnella, 22, in Dearborn, Mich. "Any sorrow I previously experienced is all washed away by the joy I feel right now," Arnold said at the nuptials. The 550 guests were treated to a make-your-own-sundae bar and a hot dog stand wheeled in at midnight. It was the bride's first marriage, Arnold's second.

West Virginia businessman and Wampanoag tribesman **Black Beaver** (Robert MacDiarmid) and tribal chairwoman **Soaring Feather** (Beverly Wright), in Martha's Vineyard.

Nicolas Cage, 31, and **Patricia Arquette**, 27, in a private ceremony at an undisclosed location. Arquette has a son, Enzo, 6, from a relationship with rocker Paul Rossi, and Cage has a son, Weston, 4, by actress Kristina Fulton . . . . Wild at heart or true romance?

Ex-teen dream **Shaun Cassidy**, 36, and actress Susan Diol, 30, in Westwood, Calif. It is the second marriage for both.

Professional golfer **John Daly**, 28, known for his prodigious driver and intemperate behavior, and former model Paulette Dean, 23, at the Little Church of the West in Las Vegas. At the time of their marriage the couple were expecting a baby. Daly has a daughter, Shynah, 2, from his second marriage. This latest union is his third, Dean's first.

Model-cum-photographer **Janice Dickinson**, 40, who was kissed off by Sylvester Stallone after a DNA test showed that her daughter Savannah Rodin wasn't his, and real estate developer Albert Gersten, 43, at his West Hollywood nightclub, the Gate.

Former Nixon aide and convicted Watergate conspirator **John Ehrlichman**, 69, and Atlanta restaurateur Karen Hilliard (age unavailable) in Glen Ellen, Calif. It was wedding number three for both. He has six children from previous marriages; she has two.

Princess Elena of Spain, 31, and dashing banker **Jaime de Marichalar**, 31, in the Cathedral of Seville in front of 1300 guests, including members of 38 royal families. It was Spain's first royal wedding since 1906; 600 million people worldwide tuned in to watch.

NYPD Blue's **Dennis Franz**, 50, and businesswoman Joanie Zeck, 47, in Carmel, Calif., after a 13-year relationship.

Actress **Melissa Gilbert**, 30, and actor **Bruce Boxleitner**, 44, on New Year's Day. The actress played Laura Ingalls on *Little House on the Prairie* from 1974 to 1983; her sister Sara is a regular on *Roseanne*.

Boxleitner is best known for starring in *The Scarecrow and Mrs. King*. It's the second marriage for both. Gilbert has a son, Dakota, 5; Boxleitner has two sons, Sam, 14, and Lee, 9.

Eagle **Don Henley**, 47, and model Sharon Summerall, 32, in Malibu. The invitations were printed on recycled paper, and disposable items used at the nuptials were recycled.

Oscar-winning actress **Holly Hunter**, 37 (*The Piano*), and Oscar-winning cinematographer **Janusz Kaminski**, 35 (*Schindler's List*), in Los Angeles. It was the first marriage for both.

Massachusetts **Sen. John Kerry**, 51, and **Teresa Heinz**, 56—widow of Sen. H. John Heinz of Pennsylvania, who died in a plane crash in 1991—on the porch of her summer house in Nantucket, Mass. Heinz, who is vice chairwoman of the Environmental Defense Fund and chairwoman of Heinz Philanthropies, was led down the aisle by her three grown sons from her first marriage. Kerry's two grown daughters from his first marriage, which ended in divorce, also took part in the ceremony.

Lisa Kudrow, 31, who stars on NBC's *Friends* and has a recurring role as the dim waitress on *Mad About You*, tied the knot with French adman Michel Stern, 37, in Malibu before 225 guests. It is her first marriage.

Two months after ex-wife Heather Locklear took a new mate, rocker **Tommy Lee**, 32, wed another blond TV pinup, *Baywatch*'s **Pamela Anderson**, 27, in Mexico. The bride wore a white bikini; the groom wore only shorts. Judge Pedro Solis Rodriguez, called in to perform the ceremony, commented, "My impression was that it was [done] at a moment's notice."

Martin Lawrence, 29, of *Martin* fame, and Patricia Southall, 24, a former Miss Virginia who was first runner-up in 1994's Miss USA Pageant, in Norfolk, Va.

Impressionist **Rich Little**, 54, and stage partner Jeannette Markey, 28, at the MGM Grand Hotel in Las Vegas.

Former *Petticoat Junction* star **Meredith MacRae**, 48, and office-supply company president Philip Neal, 54, at Los Angeles's Hotel Bel Air.

Denise Matthews, 36, the Prince protégé formerly known as Vanity, and Los Angeles Raiders defensive end **Anthony Smith**, 27, in California, after knowing each other for one month.

Queen Elizabeth, Prince Charles and King Hussein were among the royals gathered in London's Greek Orthodox Cathedral of Saint Sophia for the July 1 nuptials of exiled **Crown Prince Pavlos of Greece**, 28, and American heiress **Marie-Chantal Miller**, 26,

daughter of Robert W. Miller, 62, co-founder of Duty Free Shoppers Ltd., the world's largest duty-free shopping chain. Pavlos is the oldest son of the former King Constantine and Queen Anne-Marie, who have lived in London since Greece adopted a constitutional government in 1974. Pavlos and his wife will move to Manhattan, where she is a director of an art collection. Pavlos, who has a master's degree in international relations from Georgetown University, will work for a firm that brokers oil tankers.

The children of Rev. and Mrs. **Sun Myung Moon**, the Unification Church heads who in 1992 married 30,000 couples at once, were married into arranged unions in a joint ceremony in New York. Son Kwon-Jin Moon, 20, wed Hwa-Yun Chun, and daughter Sun-Jin Moon, 19, wed In-Sup Park.

NYPD Blue actor **Gail O'Grady**, 32, and her manager Steven Fenton, 28, surprised the 100 guests at their August Beverly Hills engagement party by having a minister turn up and conduct wedding vows. It is O'Grady's third marriage, Fenton's first.

Revlon tycoon **Ron Perelman**, 52, and Democratic political activist **Patricia Duff**, in a civil ceremony several weeks after the Dec. 13 birth of their daughter Caleigh Sophia.

Hangin' with Mr. Cooper's **Holly Robinson**, 30, and Philadelphia Eagle quarterback **Rodney Peete**, 29, in West Los Angeles. Reverend Jesse Jackson officiated at the wedding.

Former *General Hospital* hunk **Tristan Rogers**, 48, (he played Robert Scorpio) and his live-in love Teresa Parkerson, 31, on a ranch in Agoura, Calif. Their daughter Sara, 2, was the flower girl.

Today Show weatherman **Al Roker**, 40, and *Dateline NBC* correspondent **Deborah Roberts**, 34. He proposed on New Year's Day at the Grand Canyon. It's Roker's third marriage; he has a daughter Courtney, 7.

Roseanne, 43, two months pregnant, and her former bodyguard Ben Thomas, 28, on Valentine's Day. Guests included *Roseanne*'s Laurie Metcalf, Garry Shandling, Rosie's first husband, Bill Pentland, and her four children.

Rapper-actor **Tupac Shakur**, 23, and girlfriend Keisha Morris, age unavailable, at the Clinton Correctional Facility in Dannemora, N.Y. Shakur was found guilty in December of sexually abusing a fan in 1993, and was sentenced to 4½ years in jail.

Model **Stephanie Seymour**, 26, and millionaire *Interview* magazine owner **Peter Brant**, 48, in Paris. Their son Peter Jr., 16 months, served as ring-bearer and model Naomi Campbell was maid of honor. Seymour also has son Dylan, 6, from a first marriage. Brant has five children from his previous marriage to Sandra Brant.

Monaco's **Princess Stephanie**, 30, and her ex-bodyguard Daniel Ducruet, 31, the father of her two children, in a simple civil ceremony in Monaco. Prince Rainier, Princess Caroline and Prince Albert were on hand.

Ukelele-strumming singer and celebrity oddball **Tiny Tim**, 72, and Susan Gardener, 39, in Minnetonka, Minn. It is his third marriage, her first.

Musician **Ike Turner**, 63, divorced from Tina Turner for 19 years, wed dancer-singer Jeanette Bazzell, 32, on July 4, in Las Vegas. It is her first marriage.

Neo-folkie **Suzanne Vega**, 35, and music producer and keyboardist Mitchell Froom, 31, at City Hall in New York City. The two already had a 10-month-old daughter, Ruby. It is her first marriage, his second. Froom has a daughter from his first marriage.

Wings' **Steven Weber**, 34, and MTV's Los Angeles bureau chief, **Juliette Hohnen**, 30, at Highclere Castle outside her native London. It was Weber's second marriage, Hohnen's first.

Beach Boys founding genius **Brian Wilson**, 52, and California girl Melinda Ledbetter, 47, at—where else?—a surf-side chapel in Palos Verdes Peninsula, Calif. It was Wilson's second marriage; present at the wedding were his first wife, Marilyn, and his formerly estranged daughters Carnie, 26, and Wendy, 25 (two-thirds of the singing group Wilson Phillips), plus the groom's cousin Beach Boy Mike Love, who two months previously had won a $5 million judgment against Wilson in a lawsuit over song rights. Wilson met Ledbetter, a former model turned car saleswoman, when she sold him a new gold Cadillac Seville in 1986.

PARTINGS

Christie Brinkley, 42, and real estate developer **Ricky Taubman**, 46, separated after seven months of marriage. Brinkley was reportedly distressed over how Taubman handles money. Their son, Jack, is living with Brinkley.

Extreme's **James Brolin**, 54, and his wife, *WKRP in Cincinnati's* **Jan Smithers**, 45, after a decade of marriage. They have a daughter, Molly Elizabeth, 7.

James Brown, 62, and his third wife, Adrienne, after a decade of marriage.

Tough guy actor **James Caan**, 55, and his wife

Ingrid, 34, after four years. The couple have one son, Alexander, 4. Caan has been married twice previously and has two other children.

British MP **Winston Churchill**, 54, grandson of Sir Winston and son of U.S. Ambassador to France Pamela Harriman and the late journalist Randolph Churchill, and his wife Minnie, 54, after 30 years. Minnie had stood by him when Fleet Street trumpeted news of his alleged affairs—in the late '70s with Soraya Khashoggi, ex-wife of Saudi Arabian arms dealer Adnan Khashoggi, and in '92 with American socialite Jan Cushing. The Churchills have four grown children.

Best-selling spy novelist **Tom Clancy**, 48, was sued for divorce by Wanda, 46, his wife of 25 years and the mother of his four children, on the grounds of desertion and adultery. In papers filed on April 10 in Baltimore circuit court, Wanda claimed that he deserted her on March 6 and "committed adultery" with attorney Katherine Huang, 26.

Singer **Phil Collins**, 44, instigated divorce proceedings against second wife Jill, 38, after a decade of marriage. The couple have a daughter, Lily, 5. They have been separated since last May after Collins sent Jill a fax saying, "I am so sick and tired of your attitude I will not be coming back." Collins has taken up housekeeping in Hermance, Switzerland, with his new Swiss girlfriend, translator Orianne Cevey, 22.

The 23-year on-again, off-again romance between **Melanie Griffith**, 37, and **Don Johnson**, 45, is officially off again. The couple went ahead with the divorce Griffith initiated more than a year before to end their second marriage, which lasted six years. The two were previously wed in 1976 for six months. Together, they have a daughter, Dakota, 5, and, separately, two other kids.

Former Olympic figure skater **Dorothy Hamill**, 39, and her husband, sports physician Kenneth Forsythe, 51, announced that they are separating after eight years of marriage. They have one child, Alexandra, 6.

Actress **Mariette Hartley**, 54, and husband producer-director Patrick Boyriven, 57, after 16 years of marriage and three kids.

British actor **John Hurt**, 55, and his third wife, film assistant Jo Dalton, 36, after five years of marriage and two sons. Hurt departed their mansion in Ireland late last year, and the British press later reported that Dalton was having an affair with the landscape gardener.

Actor **Joanne Whalley-Kilmer**, 30, and Batman **Val Kilmer**, 35, co-stars of the films *Willow* and *Kill Me Again*, after seven-and-a-half years of marriage, citing "irreconcilable differences."

Ex-James Bond star **Roger Moore**, 67, and his third wife Luisa, 56, after 27 years of marriage and three children. Moore, who played 007 in seven films, has been keeping company with Danish socialite Christina "Kiki" Tholstrup, 53, a former pal of Luisa's.

Former Led Zeppelin guitarist **Jimmy Page**, 51, and Patricia Ecker (age unavailable) an American ex-waitress and model, after nine years.

Camilla Parker Bowles, 47, and her husband Andrew, 55, after 21 years. The couple released a joint statement conceding that they've been "leading separate lives" since 1993. The Parker Bowleses have two children, Tom, 20, and Laura, 16.

Iolanda Quinn (age unavailable) filed for a separation from husband of 29 years **Anthony Quinn**, 59. She declared she was tired of being "publicly humiliated;" Anthony has admitted to fathering a daughter, Patricia, with his former secretary Kathy Benvin, 32, in Sept. 1993. The Quinns have three grown children.

Actress **Barbara Rush**, 65, and her husband public relations czar Warren Cowan, 74, after five years of marriage.

Fresh Prince of Bel-Air star **Will Smith** and his wife Sheree, both 26, after three years. They have a son, Willard III, known as Trey, 2.

Princess Diana's brother **Charles, Earl Spencer**, 30, and his wife of six years, Victoria, 30. Victoria, a former model, had been undergoing treatment for alcoholism and anorexia in a Surrey clinic. The couple has four children, ages 1 to 4.

Actress **Elizabeth Taylor**, 63, and seventh husband, construction worker Larry Fortensky, announced Thursday that they had split up in a "trial separation." The marriage, which Las Vegas odds-makers had predicted would last only a year, in fact endured for nearly four. A joint and tersely-worded statement released through Taylor's publicist in New York, Chen Sam, said: "We both need our own space for a while, so we have agreed to a trial separation. We both hope this is only temporary."

Sylvester Stallone, 48, and his fiancée, model **Angie Everhart**, 25, after less than three months of engagement. Not one to sit home moping, Stallone is rumored to be planning to marry an ex-flame, model-actress Jennifer Flavin.

Picket Fences' venerable Judge Bone, **Ray Walston**, 80, was sued for divorce in Los Angeles superior court by his wife of 51 years, Ruth, 79, on grounds of irreconcilable differences. They have an adult daughter.

BIRTHS

Yasir Arafat, 65, and his wife **Suha**, 32; their first child together, Zahwa Arafat. Arafat has, over the years, adopted more than 50 orphans from refugee camps.

Onetime Olympic figure skater **Tai Babilonia**, 35, and her husband, TV sitcom music engineer-producer Cary Butler, 29; their first child, Scout Gabriel.

Country singer **Suzy Bogguss**, 38, and her husband, songwriter Doug Crider, 35; their first child together, Benton Charles.

Jon Bon Jovi, 34, and his wife Dorothea (age unavailable); their second child together, Jesse James Louis.

Christie Brinkley, 41, and her husband, real estate developer **Rick Taubman**, 46; their first child, Jack Paris. Brinkley has a daughter, Alexa, 9, with ex-husband Billy Joel, and Taubman has a son, Wyatt, 8, from an earlier marriage.

Stanley Burrell, 32, better known as rapper **M.C. Hammer**, and his wife Stephanie, 28; their third child, Stanley Kirk Jr. They also have Akiba, 7, and Sarah, 2.

Actor **Darren E. Burrows**, 29, who plays Ed Chigliak on *Northern Exposure*, and his wife, chef Melinda Delgado, 30; their first child, William Franklin.

Connie Chung, 48, and **Maury Povich**, 56, adopted a baby boy, Matthew Jay Povich, after a lengthy and well-documented effort to become parents.

Tom Cruise, 34, and **Nicole Kidman**, 31; their second adopted baby, Connor Antony Kidman Cruise.

Kerry Kennedy Cuomo, 35, daughter of Robert F. Kennedy, and **Andrew Cuomo**, 37, son of ex-New York Gov. Mario Cuomo; their first children, twins Cara Ethel and Mariah Matilda Kennedy Cuomo.

Daniel Day-Lewis, 38, and sometime lover **Isabelle Adjani**, 39; their first child together, a son whose name was not disclosed. Adjani has a teenage son by director Bruno Nuytten.

Actor **Pat Finn**, 29, and his wife, Donna, 31; their first child, Cassidy Marie.

Michael J. Fox, 33, and his wife, actress **Tracy Pollan**, 34; their second and third children together, twin girls Aquinnah Kathleen and Schuyler Frances.

Marvin Gaye III, 29, the musician son of the Motown great, and wife Jenny-Joi Fennimore, 20; their first child, Marvin IV, on April 1—the 11th anniversary of Marvin Gaye's death.

Actor **Tony Goldwyn**, 34, and his wife, production designer Jane Musky, 40; their second child together, Tess Frances.

Deirdre Hall, 47, who plays the shrink Marlena Evans on *Days of Our Lives*, and TV producer Steve Sohmer, 53, had their second son, Tully, by a surrogate mother, the same woman who'd given birth to their first son.

Earvin "Magic" Johnson, 35, and his wife Cookie, 35, adopted a newborn daughter, Elisa, Magic's third child, and their second together.

French actress **Sophie Marceau**, 28, *Braveheart*'s Isabelle, Princess of Wales, and her boyfriend of 10 years, Polish director **Andrzej Zulawski**, 52; their first child, Vincent.

Mary Matalin, 41, and **James Carville**, 50; their first child, Matalin Mary Carville.

John Cougar Mellencamp, 43, and his wife, model Elaine Irwin, 25; their second child and Mellencamp's fifth, Speck Wildhorse.

Actor **Dudley Moore**, 60, and his wife, Nicole Rothschild, 31; their first child, Nicholas Anthony. Moore also has Patrick, 18, from his previous marriage to actress Tuesday Weld, and Rothschild has Lauren, 8, and Christopher, 6, from her first marriage.

Liam Neeson, 43, and his wife **Natasha Richardson**, 32; their first child, Micheál Richard Antonio.

TV diva **Roseanne**, 42, and her husband of six months,

former bodyguard Ben Thomas, 28; their first child together, **Buck**, the product of in-vitro fertilization. It's Thomas's first child. Roseanne has Jessica, 20, Jennifer, 19, Jake, 17, and Brandi, 24, whom she gave up for adoption at birth (the two reunited in 1989).

Rosie O'Donnell, 33, became a single mother, adopting a baby boy, Parker Jaren.

Actress **Linda Purl** (*Robin's Hoods*), 39, and her husband, screenwriter Alexander Cary, 31; their first child, son Lucius Jackson Arthur Plantagenet Cary.

Mary Lou Retton, 27, and her husband, former University of Texas quarterback Shannon Kelley, 29; their first child, Shayla Rae Kelley.

Pat Sajak, 48, and his wife Lesly, 29; their second child together, Maggie Marie.

Bob Seger, 49, and his wife, Nita, 31; their second child, Samantha Char Seger.

Paul Simon, 53, and **Edie Brickell**, 29; their second child together, Lulu.

Gene Siskel, 49, and his wife, former TV producer **Marlene Iglitzen**, 42; their third child together, Will Nathaniel.

Mötley Crüe bassist **Nikki Sixx**, 36, and his wife, Brandi, 26, an ex-model; their third child together, Decker Nilsson.

Actress-singer **Jill Whelan**, 28, best known as perky Vicki Stubing on *The Love Boat*, and her husband Brad St. John, 33; their first child, Harrison Robert.

Montel Williams, 38, and his wife Grace, 30; Montel's fourth child and their second together, Wynter-Grace Dolores.

THE PEOPLE TIMELINE

A POP CULTURE TIMELINE OF THE 20TH CENTURY

Here is a selective chronicle of the events and inventions, milestones and hallmarks, people and productions that have entertained us and changed life in our century.

1900

THE BROWNIE BOX CAMERA, the first consumer-oriented camera, is introduced by Eastman Kodak. It sells for $1.

PHILOSOPHER Friedrich Nietzsche dies after 11 years of madness.

THE HOT DANCE around the nation is the cake walk, invented by African Americans in the late 18th century.

STAGE ACTRESS SARAH BERNHARDT, 56, makes her film debut in *Hamlet's Duel.* She plays Hamlet.

BOOKER T. WASHINGTON publishes his autobiography, *Up from Slavery.*

FERDINAND VON ZEPPELIN'S famous airship makes its first flight on July 20.

1901

VICTORIA, Queen of England and Ireland, and Empress of India, dies on January 22 at age 82, marking the end of the Victorian Era.

THE VICTOR TALKING MACHINE COMPANY is formed by Emile Berliner and Eldridge Johnson. "His Master's Voice" is the registered trademark for their gramophones, called Victrolas.

1902

BEATRIX POTTER creates the first of her legendary Peter Rabbit children's stories.

1903

THE GREAT TRAIN ROBBERY, starring Max Anderson, is released, marking the debut of the first male movie star.

THE WORLD SERIES is launched, pitting the winners of the National and the American Leagues against each other: this year, the Boston Red Stockings triumph over the Pittsburgh Pirates.

ORVILLE AND WILBUR WRIGHT fly the first powered, heavier-than-air airplane at Kitty Hawk, N.C., on December 17.

1904

HELEN KELLER graduates with honors from Radcliffe, thanks to years of devoted assistance from Anne Sullivan, who will go down in history as the Miracle Worker.

FREUD introduces the idea of neuroses in *The Psychopathology of Everyday Life,* his first major work on psychoanalysis.

THE TEDDY BEAR makes its debut. Created by the German Richard Sterb, it is inspired by President Theodore Roosevelt, who refused to kill a bear cub on a hunting trip.

1905

THE WORLD'S FIRST all–motion picture theater opens in Pittsburgh. The cost is 10¢ for a showing of *Poor But Honest.*

ALBERT EINSTEIN publishes his theory of the photoelectric effect, which is later essential in the development of the TV camera.

Sarah Bernhardt.

1906

Jelly Roll Morton at the piano.

FERDINAND "JELLY ROLL" MORTON, jazz's first great composer, writes "The King Porter Stomp."

THE SAN FRANCISCO EARTHQUAKE kills hundreds on April 18 and causes hundreds of millions of dollars in damage throughout the Bay Area as the city crashes and burns.

UPTON SINCLAIR publishes *The Jungle,* his exposé of the meat-packing industry, which prompts Congress to pass labor reform laws in addition to the Pure Food and Drug Act and the Meat Packing Act of 1906.

1907

FLORENZ ZIEGFELD offers his first version of the *Ziegfeld Follies,* an extravaganza that will continue for 24 years.

HENRY ADAMS'S masterful autobiography, *The Education of Henry Adams,* is published privately; the Nobel Prize for Biography will be awarded to Adams posthumously in 1919.

COLOR PHOTOGRAPHY becomes practical for the first time due to the development of a new method by the brothers Auguste and Louis Lumière.

THE FIRST MOTION PICTURE with both sound and color is shown in Cleveland.

THE RINGLING BROTHERS buy out their archrivals, Barnum and Bailey, although the two circuses will be operated separately until 1919.

1908

A L'ECU D'OR becomes the earliest dated pornographic film.

THE FIRST MODEL T, known as the Tin Lizzy, is produced on October 1 at Ford's Detroit plant.

THE FIRST COMMERCIAL color film, G. A. Smith's *A Visit to the Seaside* (Britain), is released.

1909

ROLLER COASTERS become increasingly popular in amusement parks all over the country.

VITAGRAPH'S *Les Misérables* becomes the first feature film produced in the United States.

THE FIRST ANIMATED CARTOON, *Gertie the Dinosaur,* is released.

ROBERT EDWIN PEARY becomes the first person ever to reach the North Pole.

1910

AUTHOR MARK TWAIN (Samuel Longhorne Clemens) dies at 74.

Mark Twain.

THOMAS EDISON demonstrates his "kinetophone," which successfully displays talking motion pictures.

THE BOY SCOUTS of America is founded by William D. Boyce, who takes his inspiration from the English program started by Sir Robert Baden-Powell.

T. S. ELIOT writes *The Love Song of J. Alfred Prufrock* while a Harvard undergraduate; it becomes one of the seminal works of the Modernist movement when it is published in 1915.

1911

JEAN, Larry Trimble's pet collie, becomes the first canine star on the big screen. Hired by Vitagraph, she earns $10 more per week than Trimble earns as an actor-writer.

IRVING BERLIN writes "Alexander's Ragtime Band," melding the rhythms of black ragtime into American popular music.

1912

SEIZING ON A CRAZE that has millions of Americans doing the tango, the turkey trot, the hesitation waltz, and the one-step, Victor releases a series of recordings intended for dancing.

THE *TITANIC* sinks after hitting an iceberg on April 14, drowning 1,595 people.

ZANE GREY publishes his most famous Western, *Riders of the Purple Sage*.

THE FIRST BLUES SONG is published by W. C. Handy. Originally called "Memphis Blues," it becomes a hit as "Mr. Crump."

PERHAPS THE BEST all-around athlete in history, Native American track-and-field star Jim Thorpe dominates the Olympics, winning gold medals for both the pentathlon and the decathlon. But his medals are taken away from him when it is discovered that he played semipro baseball two years before.

STUNT FLYING becomes a staple across the country, taking a terrible toll of pioneering aviators.

1913

DUKE ELLINGTON writes his first song, "Soda Fountain Rag," at the age of 14.

BILLBOARD magazine publishes its first song-popularity chart by listing leading songs in vaudeville as well as bestselling sheet music.

THE FIRST CROSSWORD puzzle is published in the *New York World*.

1914

CHARLIE CHAPLIN creates the legendary Little Tramp in his second film, *Kid's Auto Races*.

BERT WILLIAMS, a popular vaudevillian, stars in *Darktown Jubilee*, one of the first movies to use an African-American actor rather than white actors in blackface. The movie causes a riot in Brooklyn, N.Y.

THE TARZAN SAGA begins with the publication of *Tarzan of the Apes* by Edgar Rice Burroughs.

ASCAP—the American Society of Composers, Authors, and Publishers—is formed to empower artists to collect fees for the performance and use of their work.

THE PANAMA CANAL opens on May 18.

WORLD WAR I breaks out on July 28. One of the many consequences is that movie production outside of the United States will be suspended, allowing American filmmakers to dominate the industry.

1915

ALBERT EINSTEIN proposes the General Theory of Relativity.

AUDREY MUNSON reveals all as she becomes the first leading lady to appear on the screen nude in *Inspiration*.

MARGARET SANGER is jailed for writing about birth control in her book *Family Limitation*.

THE MOST FAMOUS MOVIE of the silent era, D. W. Griffith's *The Birth of a Nation*, opens in New York City to great success, but is bitterly criticized for its racism.

THE DIVINE Sarah Bernhardt finally faces the end of her stage career when her leg is amputated at the age of 71; the next year, however, she stages what proves at last to be her final one-for-the-road, this time playing Portia in *The Merchant of Venice* with an artificial leg.

THE PROVINCETOWN PLAYERS are organized in Massa-chusetts and become the first to present the works of playwright Eugene O'Neill. The next year the group moves its already highly influential theater to New York where it begins the off-Broadway theater movement.

USING VACUUM tubes, AT&T introduces long-distance service between New York and San Francisco.

THE MOVIE BUSINESS takes root in Hollywood, California, land of good weather and cheap labor. By 1915, half of all American films are made there.

1916

NOTORIOUS SIBERIAN MONK Grigory Rasputin is murdered. Rasputin had

Grigory Rasputin.

been a confidant and advisor to the Czarina after using his hypnotic powers to "cure" the Empress's heir, Alexis, of hemophilia.

TWO VERY DIFFERENT major American writers die—action-adventure writer Jack London, author of *Call of the Wild,* and expatriate novelist Henry James, author of *Portrait of a Lady.*

THE DADA MOVEMENT is founded in Zurich as an anti-art, anti-literature protest against the atrocities of the Great War.

1917

"THE DIXIE JAZZ BAND ONE-STEP" by Nick LaRocca's Original Dixieland Jazz Band, a group of white musicians, is the first jazz record to be released in the United States.

MATA HARI, a Dutch dancer, is executed by the French as a spy for Germany.

THE FIRST PULITZER PRIZES are awarded, in the categories of biography, history, and journalism. The award for drama is added the following year.

1918

PRESIDENT WOODROW WILSON proclaims his Fourteen Points for world peace; World War I comes to an end on November 11.

DAYLIGHT SAVING TIME is introduced in America.

1919

JACK DEMPSEY, known as the Manassa Mauler, wins the world heavyweight boxing championship.

Jack Dempsey in fighting stance.

1920

PROHIBITION begins with the enactment of the Eighteenth Amendment, which makes it illegal to produce, sell, or drink alcoholic beverages.

HERCULE POIROT is introduced in Agatha Christie's first novel, *The Mysterious Affair at Styles.*

MAMIE SMITH becomes the first African-American singer to record a vocal blues performance with "Crazy Blues."

THE NATION'S FIRST RADIO stations— KDKA, Pittsburgh and WWJ, Detroit— hit the airwaves.

1921

THE FIRST MISS AMERICA pageant is held on September 9, won by Margaret Gorman, Miss Washington, D.C.

READER'S DIGEST begins publication.

1922

THE FIRST 3-D feature film is released when Nat Deverich creates *Power of Love.*

NANOOK OF THE NORTH by Robert J. Flaherty is released and comes to be regarded as one of the greatest documentaries ever filmed.

THE TECHNICOLOR film process makes its initial successful run.

JAMES JOYCE'S *Ulysses* is published in Paris by the expatriate American Sylvia Beach; though one of the greatest novels of the century, it remains banned in the United States until December 6, 1933, when a judge rules that the book does not contain "the leer of a sensualist."

1923

LEE DEFOREST devises a method of recording sound directly on film. Producers utilize the technology to create vaudeville shorts.

THE COVERED WAGON, the first of the great Western epics, is released to huge success.

TIME magazine begins publication, providing the news in a flavorful, succinct format.

1924

STAGE LEGENDS Alfred Lunt and Lynn Fontanne first appear together as a team in a play called *The Guardsman.*

THE FIRST MILLION-SELLERS in America are instrumentals: Paul Whiteman's *Whispering* and Ben Selvin's *Dardanella.*

NATHAN LEOPOLD and Richard Loeb are tried for the "thrill killing" of 14-year-old Robert Franks; Clarence Darrow's pioneering insanity plea saves them from execution.

THE *LITTLE ORPHAN ANNIE* comic strip is created by Harold Gray.

1925

THE FIRST national spelling bee is held.

THE AGE OF THE CHARLESTON bounces into dancehalls across America.

THE NEW YORKER is founded on February 21, edited by Harold Ross. The first issue bears the image of Eustace Tilley, who will come to serve as the magazine's unofficial symbol and patriarch.

THE WSM BARN DANCE—renamed the *Grand Ole Opry* in 1928—premieres in November.

THE CLASSIC NOVEL of the Jazz Age, *The Great Gatsby* by F. Scott Fitzgerald, is published.

1926

TELEVISION is invented in Scotland by John Logie Baird, but the Depression and World War II stifle development of the industry until the '50s.

DEFORD BAILEY is the first African American musician to appear on Nashville's *Grand Ole Opry* show. He becomes nationally known as "The Harmonica Wizard," and

remains a regular until 1941.

RUDOLPH VALENTINO, the most popular of all male silent film stars and a worldwide sex symbol, dies at age 31 of a ruptured appendix and a gastric ulcer.

Rudolph Valentino.

NBC RADIO is founded.

NEW YORK TALKS to London in the first successful transatlantic radiotelephone conversation.

MAE WEST writes and stars in a play called *Sex,* the performance that launches her

Mae West.

career as the greatest sex symbol of the era and that also inspires the police to close the show and sentence West to 10 days in a workhouse.

THE BOOK-OF-THE-MONTH-CLUB is founded, the first of the mail-order book programs. The first offering is Sylvia Townsend Warner's novel, *Lolly Willowes.*

MINIATURE GOLF is introduced in Lookout Mountain, Tennessee, and from there it expands to over 40,000 courses within three years.

THE SUN ALSO RISES, the classic novel of disillusionment in the postwar years, is written by Ernest Hemingway.

1927

THE AGE OF THE TALKIES arrives with the Warner Bros. release of the wildly successful film *The Jazz Singer,* starring Al Jolson.

THE FIRST CAR RADIOS are introduced.

CHARLES LINDBERGH makes the first non-stop solo flight across the Atlantic, from New York to Paris.

Charles Lindbergh and his famous plane.

1928

TELEVISION comes to a home in Schenectady, N.Y., and begins receiving regularly scheduled broadcasts, three afternoons a week, on its one and one-half-inch-square screen.

WOMEN COMPETE in the Olympics (in Amsterdam) for the first time.

AMELIA EARHART becomes the first woman to fly across the Atlantic Ocean when she lands in London.

MICKEY MOUSE debuts in Walt Disney's first cartoon, *Plane Crazy*. The public however, first meets him in *Steamboat Willie*, which is released before its progenitor.

1929

THE FIRST ACADEMY AWARDS are presented at the Hollywood Roosevelt Hotel in Los Angeles, May 16. Douglas Fairbanks Sr. presents all of the awards in five minutes. The first winner for Best Picture is the now-forgotten Clara Bow vehicle, *Wings*.

VIRGINIA WOOLF publishes her feminist classic, *A Room of One's Own*.

CBS (Columbia Broadcasting System) is founded by William S. Paley, age 27.

THE MUSEUM OF MODERN ART (MOMA) opens in New York with an exhibition of works by Cezanne, Gaugin, Seurat, and Van Gogh.

ON BLACK THURSDAY, October 24, the stock market crashes, abruptly beginning the transition from the Roaring Twenties to the Great Depression.

KODAK introduces 16mm color movie film.

1930

SINCLAIR LEWIS becomes the first American to win the Nobel Prize for Literature.

THE FIRST SUPERMARKET opens in Queens, N.Y., offering low prices, and a huge selection; it achieves tremendous success overnight.

THE HAYS OFFICE creates a production code to enforce self-censorship in the film business.

GRANT WOOD paints *American Gothic*.

GARBO TALKS, in Eugene O'Neill's *Anna Christie*, her first speaking role.

Garbo poses.

1931

THE WORLD'S TALLEST building, the Empire State Building, is opened to the public. RCA and NBC install a TV transmitter atop the building.

AL "SCARFACE" CAPONE, all-time great American gangster, goes to jail for tax evasion.

THE WHITNEY MUSEUM, founded by sculptor and railroad heiress Gertrude Vanderbilt Whitney, opens in New York City.

SCRABBLE is invented by New York architect Alfred Butts, but the game is turned down by every manufacturer; not until 1948 is Scrabble widely distributed, and not until 1952 does word of mouth turn it into a bonanza.

1932

THE LINDBERGH BABY is kidnapped on May 1, only to be discovered dead 12 days later, after the parents pay a $50,000 ransom.

OF THEE I SING, a musical comedy written by George and Ira Gershwin with book by George S.

Kaufman and Morrie Ryskind, becomes the first musical to win a Pulitzer Prize.

BIG-TIME VAUDEVILLE begins its final fade-out as the last two-a-day show opens at the Palace on Broadway.

1933

ECSTASY, in which Hedy Lamarr appears nude, becomes the first film in which a sexual experience is depicted.

FRANCES PERKINS becomes the first woman to hold a Cabinet post when she is appointed secretary of labor by Franklin Delano Roosevelt.

THE FIRST DRIVE-IN cinema is built in Camden, N.J., accommodating 400 cars, and opens with *Wife Beware*.

PRESIDENT ROOSEVELT holds the first Fireside Chat on March 12, a radio address to the entire nation.

PROHIBITION is repealed with the ratification of the 21st Amendment on December 5. The watering holes that soon cover the country—bars, saloons, cocktail lounges—have a new feature, the jukebox.

THE FIRST NATIONAL FOOTBALL LEAGUE championship play-off pits the Chicago Bears against the New York Giants on December 17. The Bears win, 23–21.

1934

THE APOLLO THEATRE stages its first live show in Harlem.

BENNY GOODMAN begins his radio show *Let's Dance*, establishing himself as the "King of Swing."

JOHN DILLINGER, Public Enemy No. 1, is gunned down in Chicago by FBI agents.

1935

THE FEDERAL THEATRE Project is instituted by Congress as part of the Works Progress Administration. An attempt to assist an ailing theater community hit badly by the Depression, it is disbanded in 1939.

BECKY SHARP, the first full-length color feature film, opens.

THE FIRST NIGHT BASEBALL game in the major leagues is played between the Cincinnati Reds and the Philadelphia Phillies. Cincinnati wins, 2–1.

GEORGE AND DOROTHY GERSHWIN'S opera *Porgy and Bess* opens.

1936

JESSE OWENS wins four gold medals in track events at the Berlin Olympics, infuriating German chancellor Adolf Hitler, who preaches the mental and physical supremacy of Aryan whites over all other races.

MARGARET MITCHELL'S *Gone with the Wind* is published, selling a million copies in six months and winning the Pulitzer Prize in 1937. It will be her only book.

FRANKLIN DELANO ROOSEVELT is reelected president in the greatest Democratic landslide ever, carrying 48 states.

EUGENE O'NEILL, the great American dramatist, is awarded the Nobel Prize for Literature.

1937

VENTRILOQUIST EDGAR BERGEN and Charlie McCarthy premiere on NBC. They will remain hugely popular with audiences when the show makes the move from radio to TV.

Jesse Owens in gold-medal form.

JOHN STEINBECK'S *Of Mice and Men* is published.

THE FIRST worldwide radio broadcast to be received in the United States brings us the coronation of King George VI of England on May 12.

1938

WALT DISNEY'S *Snow White and the Seven Dwarfs* tops the movie charts, making Disney internationally famous, and goes on to become an all-time classic.

OUR TOWN, by Thornton Wilder, is produced (and not in a high school theater). It wins a Pulitzer.

HEAVYWEIGHT BOXING champion Joe Louis defends his title with a first-round knockout of German boxer Max Schmeling, a Nazi hero who symbolizes the notion of Aryan superiority. His victory is viewed

Joe Louis.

as a triumph both for African Americans and for democracy.

THE DIRIGIBLE *Hindenburg* bursts into flames as it lands in New Jersey on May 6, marking the virtual end of lighter-than-air transportation. Simultaneously, the first coast-to-coast radio broadcast is conducted by Herbert Morrison, who reports on the disaster.

THE RADIO PLAY *War of the Worlds* (based on the novel by H.G. Wells) is broadcast on October 30 by Orson Welles, causing widespread panic among listeners who believe its story of an invasion from Mars.

1939

THE FIRST GOLDFISH is swallowed by a Harvard undergrad, beginning a fad that quickly sweeps across the nation and sets off such variations on the theme as eating light bulbs and biting snakes' heads off.

MARIAN ANDERSON, world-famous African-American contralto, is denied permission to sing in Washington D.C.'s Constitution Hall by the Daughters of the American Revolu-

tion. Undaunted, she is sponsored by Eleanor Roosevelt in a triumphant performance on the steps of the Lincoln Memorial in front of 75,000 fans.

ROBERT KANE creates the cartoon character Batman.

THE GOLDEN GATE Exposition is held in San Francisco.

LOU NOVA squares off against Max Baer in the first televised prizefight, direct from Yankee Stadium. Nova wins in 11 rounds.

RHETT BUTLER'S infamous observation in the film version of *Gone with the Wind*, "Frankly, my dear, I don't give a damn," breaks the taboo against cursing in the movies.

AT THE NEW YORK WORLD'S FAIR thousands ogle RCA TV sets featuring a 12-inch screen reflected in a cabinet-lid mirror.

1940

RICHARD WRIGHT'S masterpiece, *Native Son*, is published to wide acclaim; it is later adapted for a successful Broadway run.

A WORKABLE COLOR TV is announced by Peter Goldmark, chief television engineer at CBS.

THE COTTON CLUB, Harlem's famous jazz nightclub, closes down.

CONGRESS passes the Selective Service Act, the first U.S. peacetime draft law ever.

1941

THE FIRST TV AD comes on the air, marking the advent of commercial television; the spot, for Bulova watches, lasts 10 seconds and costs the company $9.

PEARL HARBOR is bombed by Japan on December 7, a day of infamy that ushers the U.S. into World War II.

1942

RODGERS AND HAMMERSTEIN transform the musical comedy with their production of *Oklahoma!*

PHYSICISTS John Atanasoff and Clifton Berry develop the first fully electronic computer.

CAPITOL RECORDS is launched by Glenn

Wallichs, who invents the art of record promotion by sending copies of new record releases to prominent disc jockeys.

BING CROSBY releases "White Christmas," from the film *Holiday Inn*, and it becomes the biggest-selling song from a movie in history.

1943

FRANK LLOYD WRIGHT begins work on the Solomon R. Guggenheim Museum in New York. Founded in 1939 as the Museum of Non-Objective Painting, the building opens its doors in 1959.

GEORGE WASHINGTON CARVER, 81, dies in Tuskegee, Ala. Born into slavery, he developed inventive uses for peanuts, soybeans, and other traditional Southern crops, which proved to be a boon to agriculture in the region.

1944

BILLBOARD introduces the first country music charts, first called "Most-Played Juke Box Hillbilly Records" and then changed to

"Folk Records" before being relabeled "Country & Western" in 1949.

PAPER SHORTAGES during World War II force the publishing business to experiment with softcover bindings for its books, with stunning success.

1945

SMELL-O-VISION is created by Swiss inventor Hans E. Laube, who develops a "smell pack" that is stimulated by TV waves to produce an odor to accompany what is being shown on the screen.

WORLD WAR II comes to an end. Germany surrenders on May 8 (V-E Day). The only atomic bombs ever to be used in war are dropped by the U.S. on Hiroshima on August 6 and Nagasaki three days later, leading to the surrender of Japan on August 15 (V-J Day).

1946

DR. BENJAMIN SPOCK revolutionizes the way Americans raise their families with his *Common Sense Book of Baby and Child Care*.

WINSTON CHURCHILL coins the term "iron curtain" in a speech at Westminster College in Missouri.

THE U.S. detonates a nuclear bomb on Bikini Atoll on July 5 in the South Pacific. Five days later, designer Louis Reard commemorates the blast at a fashion show in Paris, where a certain itsy-bitsy, teeny-weeny two-piece bathing suit makes its first appearance.

THE CANNES FILM FESTIVAL premieres in September.

THE FIRST TV SOAP OPERA, *Faraway Hill*, debuts on the DuMont network.

CONSUMERS RUSH to buy the new 10-inch RCA TV set for $375. This "Model T of television" ushers in the TV age.

1947

THE POLAROID Land camera is patented by Dr. Edwin Land, providing prints that develop inside the camera within a minute. It enters the market the following year, selling for $90.

JACKIE ROBINSON becomes the first African American to sign with a major-league baseball

team. His first game with the Brooklyn Dodgers is an exhibition game against the New York Yankees.

NBC'S *KRAFT TELEVISION* Theatre introduces serious drama. Overnight, cheese sales soar and Madison Avenue melts.

FLYING SAUCER! The first sighting is reported on June 25, according to one source.

THE WORLD SERIES is broadcast on TV for the first time, and four million baseball fans watch the New York Yankees and the Brooklyn Dodgers battle it out. The Yanks go on to win the series.

THE FIRST ANTOINETTE PERRY (TONY) AWARDS for excellence in the theater are handed out. No best play award is included, but José Ferrer wins as best actor, and best actress awards go to Ingrid Bergman and Helen Hayes.

THE TRANSISTOR is invented by Bell Telephone Laboratories; it becomes one of the most significant advances in the history of consumer electronics, paving the way for the miniaturization of TV sets, radios, and gear like CD players that haven't yet been invented.

1948

TED MACK'S ORIGINAL AMATEUR HOUR premieres in January. By year's end, the first "ratings sweep" declares it the most popular show on TV.

THE PHONOGRAPH RECORDING market is fraught with competition as companies come up with improvements on the old 78 rpm disks. Columbia introduces the first long-playing commercial record, the 33⅓ rpm disk, and RCA releases the 45.

LEE STRASBERG takes over the Actor's Studio, introducing the Method acting techniques that will profoundly influence such students as Marlon Brando, Paul Newman, James Dean, and Marilyn Monroe.

THE MOTORCYCLE CLAN Hell's Angels is formed.

THE ED SULLIVAN SHOW premieres to an initially poor viewer response. The influential variety program will stay on the air until 1971.

THE TERM "COLD WAR" is popularized by a speech before the Senate War Investigation Committee.

TV SET SALES skyrocket, with an estimated 250,000 sets installed every month.

NORMAN MAILER'S first novel, *The Naked and the Dead*, comes out. It remains one of the most important fictional works about World War II.

1949

CHIC YOUNG'S *Blondie* is the most popular comic strip in the world.

THE FIRST CABLE television systems go into homes.

ARTHUR MILLER'S play *Death of a Salesman*, the first dramatic tragedy to feature a common man as a protagonist, wins a Pulitzer Prize.

UNERRING *CRUSADER RABBIT* debuts as the first made-for-TV animated cartoon.

1950

GWENDOLYN BROOKS is the first African American to win a Pulitzer Prize, for her work *Annie Allen*.

MCCARTHYISM begins in February when the obscure U.S. senator Joseph McCarthy alleges that the federal government is infested with Communists.

GOOD OL' CHARLIE BROWN enters American culture as Charles Schulz creates the legendary comic strip *Peanuts*.

TELEVISION takes its first late-night variety plunge with *Broadway Open House*, and "dumb blonde" Dagmar (Jennie Lewis) becomes the first boob-tube sex symbol.

THE FIRST AMERICAN TROOPS land in Korea on July 1 after soldiers from North Korea invade South Korea. Although the move is described as a United Nations action, American soldiers comprise the vast majority of foreign troops. With news footage being aired on American TVs, it is also the first living-room war.

HOLLYWOOD buys its first million-dollar property: Columbia acquires the rights to the successful Broadway play *Born Yesterday* from the writer Garson Kanin.

A. C. NIELSEN begins gathering ratings data for TV, employing electronic viewing records along with written logs to determine the popularity of shows.

BELL LABORATORIES and Western Electric create the first telephone answering machine.

THE SITCOM laugh track is introduced on *The Hank McCune Show*, a program that has the added distinction of being canceled mid-season.

THE FIRST CREDIT CARD is introduced through the Diners Club.

THE CISCO KID, starring Duncan Renaldo and Leo Carillo, is the first TV series filmed in color. At the time, there are fewer than 100 experimental color sets in the U.S.

THE 1949 NOBEL PRIZE for Literature is retroactively awarded to William Faulkner. No prize had been awarded the previous year because none of the candidates had won a majority of the votes.

1951

PAY-PER-VIEW dies a premature death after Zenith begins testing its "Phonevision" in Chicago. Viewers can dial a phone number and watch a recent feature film for $1. But skittish movie studios decide not to make first-run films available, fearing the consequences.

SENATE HEARINGS on organized crime rivet the nation. Mobster Frank Costello allows only his hands to be shown.

UNIVAC I, the first commercially built computer, goes into operation at the Census Bureau in Philadelphia.

CBS broadcasts the first commercial color telecast on June 25 with a one-hour special from New York to four other cities.

NBC begins the first network coast-to-coast programming.

AMOS 'N' ANDY bows with TV's first all-black cast. Though canceled in 1953, reruns air until 1966, when protests about racial stereotyping force withdrawal of the show from syndication.

I LOVE LUCY debuts to tremendous success, creating the mold for TV sitcoms.

CLEVELAND DJ Alan Freed, the first to introduce black R&B to a white audience on station WJW, coins the term "rock and roll."

CBS debuts its "unblinking eye," which evolves into

TV's most famous logo.

GIAN CARLO MENOTTI'S *Amahl and the Night Visitors* becomes the first made-for-TV opera on Christmas Eve. It becomes a perennial seasonal favorite.

1952

THE REVISED STANDARD edition of the Old Testament, only the third authorized Protestant revision in 341 years, becomes a No. 1 bestseller and sets records by selling 1.6 million copies in eight weeks; the old record was held by *Gone with the Wind*, which sold 1 million books in six months.

THE MOUSETRAP, originally a play created by Agatha Christie for the 80th birthday of Britain's Queen Mary, premieres in London. It will become the single longest-running theatrical work of all time.

MAD **MAGAZINE** and the *National Enquirer* make their debuts.

UNIDENTIFIED FLYING OBJECTS capture the imagination of Americans. No longer looked on as simply science fiction, the

national fascination with UFOs even prompts the U.S. Air Force to publish possible photographs of the phenomena.

THE FIRST HYDROGEN BOMB is detonated on November 1, and Americans' fear of complete annihilation intensifies.

BWANA DEVIL leads a resurgence of popularity for 3-D movies, Hollywood's attempt to combat the appeal of "free" TV.

PANTY RAIDS occur in epic proportions at college sororities across the nation.

TWO OF TELEVISION'S biggest all-time hits—the *Today* show, hosted by Dave Garroway, and *Guiding Light*—begin broadcasting on NBC and CBS, respectively; both programs are still going strong today.

THE MARILYN MONROE image crystallizes with four film

Marilyn Monroe.

releases, helping movie theaters draw Americans away from their TV sets.

ART LINKLETTER tosses a *House Party* on September 1, and the bash lasts longer (17 years) than any daytime variety show. People *are* funny.

VEEP HOPEFUL Richard Nixon makes a politician's first direct TV appeal on September 23, citing his dog, Checkers, in his successful quest to beat fundmisuse charges and save his career.

CHRISTINE JORGENSON returns from Denmark where she had undergone the first publicized sexchange operation.

1953

I LOVE LUCY features the birth of Little Ricky on January 19 as the real Lucille Ball gives birth to Desi Arnaz Jr. The landmark show draws a 92 percent share of TV sets in use, or 44 million viewers—a record to date. Turns out the "dual birth" was no happy accident, since Desi Junior was born by a scheduled caesarean section. The event received more media attention than Dwight Eisenhower's inauguration, which took place the following day. Eisenhower and Nixon

Hugh Hefner.

form the first Republican administration in 24 years.

DESI JR. scores again when the first issue of *TV Guide* is published, featuring him on the cover.

AT AGE 27, Queen Elizabeth II is crowned as England's monarch.

JULIUS AND ETHEL ROSENBERG are executed, the only American civilians ever to receive such a penalty for espionage.

THE DISC JOCKEY Top 40 radio format is established on KOWH, an Omaha station. It features a limited number of records played over and over, hourly news breaks, and sporadic chatter from the announcer.

CINEMASCOPE premieres with *The Robe,* and its wide-screen format becomes a huge hit with filmgoers.

***PLAYBOY* MAGAZINE** is founded by 27-year-old Hugh Hefner with a first issue featuring the nude Marilyn Monroe on its cover.

THE FIRST ROCK AND ROLL song hits the Billboard charts: Bill Haley and His Comets' "Crazy, Man, Crazy."

THE RCA compatible color television is approved by the FCC and becomes the industry standard.

HOUSTON'S KUHT debuts as the country's first noncommercial educational TV station; within 10 years there will be 75 other such stations.

1954

MARILYN MONROE marries former New York Yankees star Joe DiMaggio, a second marriage for both. Alas, the match is not meant to be—Marilyn files for divorce nine months later.

TELEVISION JOURNALIST Edward R. Murrow launches the first major attack on Joseph McCarthy's witch-hunt tactics on CBS's *See It Now,* inspiring a groundswell of support for the senator's critics and ultimately precipitating his downfall.

SEGREGATION in schools is declared unconstitutional on May 14 in the landmark case, *Brown vs. Board of Education.*

ELVIS PRESLEY cuts his first record, the double-sided 45 "That's All Right

Elvis Presley.

(Mama)"/"Blue Moon of Kentucky."

THE FIRST COLOR TV sets and the first transistor radios are marketed.

TONIGHT!, later known as *The Tonight Show,* premieres with Steve Allen as host.

SWANSON brings out the very first TV dinners—ominously, turkey—for 69¢.

1955

CONTRALTO MARIAN ANDERSON becomes the first African American to sing a major role at the Metropolitan Opera, appearing as Ulrica in Verdi's *Masked Ball.*

A NEW ERA in domestic politics is launched with the first filmed presidential press conference. Both TV and motion picture newsreel photographers cover the event.

WALT DISNEY'S TV show, *Disneyland,* first appears on ABC and quickly becomes one of the most successful programs on the tube. One segment, "Davy Crockett, Indian Fighter," instigates a full-blooded Davy Crockett mania, which sweeps the country. Over 3,000 Crockett-related items sell in crazy numbers, from coonskin caps to Bill Hayes's song "Ballad of Davy Crockett," which rises to the top of the charts.

ANN LANDERS launches her advice column in the *Chicago Sun-Times*.

BILL HALEY and His Comets' "Rock Around the Clock" goes to No. 1 on *Billboard*'s charts on June 6, marking the undisputable ascent of rock and roll.

DISNEYLAND, the first theme amusement park, opens south of Los Angeles in Anaheim.

JAMES DEAN stars in *Rebel Without a Cause*, his second and penultimate starring role before crashing his Porsche later in the year and dying at age 26. His death gives rise to his enduring status as a cult hero, embodying the spirit of rebelliousness so sought after by America's younger generation.

BOB KEESHAN debuts as the Captain on *Captain Kangaroo*, which goes on to become the longest-running kids' show. *The Mickey Mouse Club* begins as well.

IN ONE OF THE greatest record deals of all time, RCA buys Elvis's contract—for an unprecedented $40,000—from Sam Phillips's Sun Records.

COMIC BOOK popularity reaches unprecedented heights, with sales soaring beyond a billion copies. Concern over their violent content increases in due measure, prompting New York State to ban the sale of certain graphic comics to minors.

1956

ACTOR GRACE KELLY retires from Hollywood and marries Prince Rainier III of Monaco, a member of the thousand-year-old Grimaldi dynasty, in one of the most publicized marriages of the century.

BEAT POET ALAN GINSBERG'S *"Howl" and Other Poems* is released and its publisher is promptly brought up on obscenity charges that are later successfully defended in court.

MARILYN MONROE weds husband No. 3, Pulitzer- and Tony Award-winning playwright Arthur Miller (it's his second mar-

riage). The two are divorced in 1961.

DEAN MARTIN and Jerry Lewis are a team no more. They split on July 25, exactly 10 years after they first appeared together in Atlantic City.

NBC'S Huntley and Brinkley are TV's first co-anchors: "Goodnight, Chet." "Goodnight, David."

IN HIS FIRST YEAR of stardom, Elvis releases "Don't Be Cruel"/"Hound Dog," a double-sided 45 that still stands as the biggest hit of all time on *Billboard*'s charts. His appearance on Ed Sullivan's *Toast of the Town* on September 9, shot discreetly above the pelvis, earns the highest rating for any regularly scheduled program, drawing an estimated audience of 50 million people. He also appears in his first movie, *Love Me Tender*.

1957

LEONARD BERNSTEIN is named the first American musical director of the New York Philharmonic.

JERRY LEE LEWIS scandalizes the nation when he mar-. ries his 13-year-old

Slick Jerry Lee Lewis.

cousin, Myra Gale Brown—also committing bigamy by failing to divorce his first wife, Jane Mitcham.

BOBBY FISCHER, 14, wins the U.S. chess championship.

THE HULA HOOP is introduced and takes America by storm, selling over 45 million by 1958.

DICK CLARK'S *American Bandstand* moves from a local Philadelphia station to its national debut on ABC. It becomes the longest-running variety show in TV history.

THE SOVIET UNION launches *Sputnik*, setting off the space race.

LEAVE IT TO BEAVER debuts on CBS, presenting the audience with the most typically American family to date.

THE NAT "KING" COLE SHOW, the first major series with an African-American host, is canceled after a year, for lack of a national sponsor.

1958

ALVIN AILEY founds the American Dance Theatre.

BILLBOARD begins its Hot 100 chart; the first No. 1 record is "Poor Little Fool" by Ricky Nelson.

VLADIMIR NABOKOV'S sensational novel *Lolita* is published by Putnam after being rejected as too obscene by four other American publishers.

DEEJAYS AT ST. LOUIS'S KWK radio station complete their "Record Breaking Week" when, at the insistence of the management, "undesirable" records are given a final play on the airwaves and then ceremoniously destroyed. Most of the sacrificed recordings are of rock and roll music.

SCIENTISTS at the ESSO Gas Research Center—now EXXON—announce on July 28 that they have found that drivers waste gas when they listen to rock and roll because they tend to jiggle the pedals in time with the beat.

VAN CLIBURN becomes the first American to win a gold medal at the Tchaikovsky International Piano Festival. His subsequent recording of the composer's *Piano Concerto No. 1* is the first classical record to go gold.

THE BROOKLYN DODGERS and the New York Giants move to California, bringing major-league baseball to the West Coast.

THE GRAMMY AWARDS are launched. Ignoring the rising predominance of rock and roll, the organizers present best album of the year to Henry Mancini and name "Volare" by Domenico Modugno as best song.

QUIZ SHOW scandals erupt with an initial investigation of answer-feeding on a program called *Dotto* prompted by a complaint by contestant Eddie Hilgemeier. By the end of the year most quiz shows are pulled off the air.

1959

BUDDY HOLLY, Ritchie Valens, and The Big Bopper are tragically killed in February when their single-engine light aircraft crashes in a snow-

storm about 10 minutes after takeoff.

BARBIE is introduced to the toy world, created by Ruth and Elliot Handler, who founded Mattel in 1945. The doll's proportions, if copied on a human scale, would be 33-18-28. Barbie was named for the Handlers' daughter, Barbara, just as their son, Ken, was later honored when his parents created a male companion doll.

ISLAND IN THE SUN, starring James Mason, Dorothy Dandridge, Harry Belafonte, and Joan Fontaine, becomes the first film to portray interracial romance.

THE U.S. POSTMASTER GENERAL bans *Lady Chatterly's Lover* by D. H. Lawrence, but sales skyrocket after courts hold that the book is not obscene.

AMERICANS SEE THE WORLD from a new perspective as *Explorer VI* sends down the first photograph of Earth taken from outer space.

THE TELEPHONE-BOOTH JAMMING fad hits this year and fades almost as quickly. The fad first catches hold on the West Coast and moves quickly across the country, the record being set

with 32 squashed students at Modesto Junior College in California.

MOTOWN RECORDS is founded in Detroit by songwriter Berry Gordy Jr.

IS TELEVISION KING? In December, for the first time, TV rings up more in commercial sales ($1.24 billion) than Hollywood cashes in box-office receipts ($1.235 billion).

1960

ELVIS PRESLEY'S army career, which began in March of 1958, comes to a close.

A CONGRESSIONAL investigation into payola determines that radio deejays have been receiving payments from record companies to play their disks. Dick Clark and Alan Freed are the particular focus of allegations, and Freed eventually loses his job.

SMELL-O-VISION hits theaters as Michael Todd Jr.'s film *Scent of Mystery* is released to general indifference.

PSYCHO, directed by Alfred Hitchcock, sets new movie attendance records

Master director Alfred Hitchcock.

and earns a mint as one of the most frightening films ever made.

THE TWIST is introduced by 19-year-old Chubby Checker.

BEN-HUR collects a record 11 Oscars out of 12 nominations.

THE FANTASTICKS debuts May 3. It will become the longest-running off-Broadway show ever, hitting its 14,000th performance on March 2, 1994—and still going strong at the Sullivan Street Playhouse in Greenwich Village. Since its beginning, notable performers have included Kevin Kline, Richard Chamberlain, and Jerry Orbach.

THE FLINTSTONES debuts as prime time's first animated sitcom.

BIRTH CONTROL PILLS become available for widespread use as the FDA approves

the public sale of Enovid at $10 to $11 for a month's supply.

1961

THE FIRST FRENCH KISS on the Hollywood big screen takes place between Natalie Wood and Warren Beatty in *Splendor in the Grass.*

SOPRANO LEONTYNE PRICE, 34, debuts at New York's Metropolitan Opera House in *Il Trovatore* and receives a 45-minute ovation.

BOB DYLAN gives his first solo performance, opening for blues musician John Lee Hooker in New York City's Gerde's Folk City.

ABC'S WIDE WORLD OF SPORTS with Jim McKay is introduced and runs on Saturday afternoons, showing us "the thrill of victory and the agony of defeat."

ALAN B. SHEPARD JR. becomes the first American astronaut to go into space on May 5.

SATURDAY NIGHT AT THE MOVIES debuts as the first regular TV showcase for major motion pictures.

Jacqueline Kennedy lights up the White House.

1962

JACQUELINE KENNEDY takes the country on a televised tour of the White House.

THE FIRST USE OF NUDITY in advertising appears in *Harper's Bazaar* in a barebreasted photo by Richard Avedon.

THE FIRST JAMES BOND movie, *Dr. No*, is released starring Sean Connery, 32.

DIRECT-DIAL long-distance telephone service begins in the United States.

MARILYN MONROE dies of a barbituate overdose at age 36 on August 5.

THE VIRGINIAN makes its debut as the first

90-minute TV series. In a nine-year run, its cast includes Lee Majors, David Hartman, and Lee J. Cobb as a frontier judge.

JOHNNY CARSON takes over *The Tonight Show*, where he will reign as King of Television until he retires in 1992.

1963

WEIGHT WATCHERS enters the market, turning dieting into big business.

POP ART is given its first major show at the Guggenheim Museum in New York. Artists on display include Andy

Warhol, Jasper Johns, and Roy Lichtenstein.

BETTY FRIEDAN publishes her landmark feminist tract, *The Feminine Mystique*.

JULIA CHILD bubbles up on *The French Chef* and becomes public TV's first star; she'll keep TV cooking for the next 10 years.

WHISKEY A-GO-GO opens in Los Angeles, beginning its tenure as Hollywood's longest-lived club devoted to cutting-edge rock music.

THE BEATLES release their first single in the U.S., "Please Please Me," in February along with their LP *Introducing The Beatles*.

CLEOPATRA, with Elizabeth Taylor and

Elizabeth Taylor as Cleopatra.

Richard Burton, scores as both the top money-maker of the year and one of the biggest flops in movie history as its vast costs far overrun its huge budget; Taylor alone receives $1.75 million for her participation.

PEBBLES FLINTSTONE is born to parents Wilma and Fred on February 22 at the Bedrock Rockapedia Hospital.

TROLLS are introduced. Billed as good-luck charms, their ugliness is a charm indeed, producing sales in the millions.

THE FUGITIVE debuts September 17; David Janssen runs. He'll catch the one-armed man—and a then record prime-time audience—in the '67 finale. That episode still ranks as the third-most-watched episode of a television series ever.

PRESIDENT JOHN F. KENNEDY, 46, is assassinated in Dallas on November 22. The immediacy of television's coverage of the surrounding events transforms TV into a witness to history and binds together a nation in mourning.

1964

5,000 SCREAMING FANS greet The Beatles at Kennedy Airport in New York on February 7, when the band arrives for its first American tour. Two days later the Fab Four appear on *The Ed Sullivan Show*. They draw an estimated 75 percent of all TV viewers, making it the most-watched hour of television to date. Songs include "All My Loving," "She Loves You," and "I Want To Hold Your Hand."

THE MOOG, the first commercial music synthesizer, is developed.

ELIZABETH TAYLOR finally meets her match, again, as she marries husband No. 5, Richard Burton, just 10 days after getting a divorce from Eddie Fisher. The two had met on the set of *Cleopatra*.

THE HOME VIDEO recorder is invented in Japan by the Sony Corporation.

MARSHALL MCLUHAN declares that the "medium is the message" in his book *Understanding Media*. Nobody gets it, but everybody talks about it.

LYNDON B. JOHNSON'S "daisy" campaign

spot airs once on September 7, suggesting that Republican opponent Barry Goldwater is nuke-happy. Fallout: LBJ wins in a landslide.

PEYTON PLACE airs September 15 as the first prime-time soap and becomes a smash hit.

G.I. JOE is introduced by Hasbro and sells for $4.

MARTIN LUTHER KING JR. receives the Nobel Peace Prize. Jean-Paul Sartre is awarded the Nobel Prize for Literature and becomes the first person to reject the honor.

1965

SOUPY SALES asks his loyal young viewers to send him "those little green pieces of paper" from dad's wallet, "and I'll send *you* a postcard from Puerto Rico." The January 1 stunt draws a big enough response to get Sales suspended by the station, but viewers protest and he is reinstated.

BELL-BOTTOMS grace the nation's hips, and lava lamps make a splash, selling 2.5 million units this year alone.

THE FIRST AMERICAN COMBAT TROOPS not deployed in an advisory capacity land in South Vietnam, turning a local conflict into an undeclared large-scale international war.

THE NATIONAL ENDOWMENT for the Arts and Humanities is established by Congress.

"(I CAN'T GET NO) SATISFACTION," the classic Rolling Stones tune, becomes a No. 1 hit in the United States, sealing the British invasion as one of the dominant musical developments of the decade.

THE BEATLES play before 55,000 fans at New York's Shea Stadium August 15 to open their third U.S. tour.

THE SOUND OF MUSIC is released, eventually overtaking *Gone with the Wind* to rank for a time as the top box-office earner ever.

GO-GO DANCING and its accompanying little white boots quickly wax and then wane in popularity among discotheque goers.

CINEMA'S 34-year rule against nudity is broken when a scene in *The Pawnbroker* is approved by the ratings board as essential to the plot.

CBS AND NBC adopt virtually all-color formats starting with the fall season.

BILL COSBY becomes the first African-American TV star, in *I Spy.*

SONY introduces the first commercial home video tape recorder. The size of an overnight bag, it costs $995.

1966

"YESTERDAY," the most recorded song in the history of popular music, is released by Paul McCartney in the first solo by a Beatle. The record label, however, still reads "Beatles."

CINEMA'S BLUE LANGUAGE ban finally falls with *Who's Afraid of Virginia Woolf?*

THE SUPREMES become the first female group to top the U.S. album chart with *Supremes a Go Go.*

JOHN LENNON makes his most infamous remark on August 5 by saying that he and his Beatles bandmates are "more popular than Jesus." Subsequently radio stations across the country take Beatles songs off the air.

LSD is pulled off the market by its manufacturer, Sandoz Pharmaceuticals, after being banned by the government in response to controversy over the hallucinogen's recreational uses.

STAR TREK is launched September 8 and remains on the air until 1969. It will become one of the few series to be more popular in syndication than in its network run.

"PAUL IS DEAD." For those who believe, November 9 marks the date of the Beatle's supposed decapitation.

STEREO CASSETTE TAPE RECORDERS are introduced, a breakthrough for tape cartridges.

1967

THE FIRST SUPER BOWL is held on January 15, broadcast in color on both CBS and NBC; setting a model for future contests, the Green Bay Packers defeat the Kansas City Chiefs in a lopsided game, 35–10.

THE BLACK PANTHER PARTY is founded in Oakland by Huey Newton and Bobby Seale.

OTIS REDDING, 26, dies in a plane crash in December. One month later, his biggest hit, the chart-topping "Sittin' on the Dock of the Bay," is released.

ELVIS PRESLEY weds Priscilla Beaulieu on May 1 at the Aladdin Hotel in Las Vegas.

THE MONTEREY INTERNATIONAL POP FESTIVAL in California features such performers as Janis Joplin, Jimi Hendrix, The Mamas and the Papas, and the Grateful Dead.

RIOTING breaks out in Detroit as racial tension builds; over 17,000 people are arrested in what proves to be the worst U.S. riot of the century.

FOLKSINGER PETE SEEGER is finally allowed to appear on TV (on *The Smothers Brothers Comedy Hour*) after having been blacklisted for 17 years for his leftist politics.

HAIR has its off-Broadway premiere at the Public Theatre in New York.

ROLLING STONE magazine begins publication under the direction of 21-year-old Jann Wenner.

PRESIDENT LYNDON B. JOHNSON signs a law insuring federal support for public TV, and the Corporation for Public Broadcasting is created.

THE FIRST SO-CALLED SPAGHETTI WESTERN, Sergio Leone's *A Fistful of Dollars*, is released in the United States. Filmed in 1964, it stars Clint Eastwood.

INTERRACIAL ROMANCE unfolds on TV as Mia and Paul fall for each other on *Love Is a Many-Splendored Thing*.

BOXER MUHAMMAD ALI is stripped of his heavyweight title after refusing to serve in the army during the Vietnam War.

THE FIRST HUMAN HEART transplant is performed by Dr. Christiaan Barnard in South Africa on Louis Washkansky, who lives for 18 days.

MAO TSE-TUNG'S QUOTATIONS, better known as the Red Book, is the biggest-selling read in the world this year.

Martin Luther King Jr. giving his famous "I have a dream" speech in Washington, D.C.

MOVIE RATINGS are introduced by the Motion Picture Association of America. The original classifications are G, M (mature audience), R, and X. M is changed to GP two years later, and then PG (parental guidance) a year after that. PG-13 is invented in 1984 as the result of a dispute over the violence in *Indiana Jones and the Temple of Doom,* and in 1990 the nefarious X is replaced by NC-17.

ARTHUR CLARKE and Stanley Kubrick's *2001: A Space Odyssey* is released, introducing the evil computer Hal, an antihero who becomes a cultural icon.

THE EARLIEST-KNOWN HEIDI scandal: With 50 seconds left and the New York Jets leading the Oakland Raiders, NBC cuts from the game to the movie *Heidi.* The Raiders go on to win by scoring two touchdowns in nine seconds.

CIVIL RIGHTS LEADER Martin Luther King Jr. is assassinated April 4 at age 39 on the balcony outside of his motel room in Memphis, Tenn. Days later, many American cities erupt in riots.

ROBERT F. KENNEDY, 42, is assassinated June 5 by Sirhan Sirhan in a Los Angeles hotel after winning the California Democratic presidential primary. As a response, David Crosby writes "A Long Time Coming."

AT THE SUMMER OLYMPIC GAMES in Mexico City, American runners Tommy Smith and John Car-

los give the black power salute as they receive their gold and bronze medals, resulting in their suspension from competition.

PRESIDENTIAL CANDIDATE Richard Nixon appears on *Laugh-In* and says, "Sock it to me!"

JULIA, premiering September 17, is the first TV series to star a black woman in a non-menial role as Diahann Carroll plays a nurse who is also a single parent.

MIKE WALLACE and Harry Reasoner start grilling as *60 Minutes* starts ticking September 24; the news program will eventually top the ratings.

1969

THE BEATLES stage their last public performance January 30 from a rooftop in London.

JIM MORRISON, lead singer for The Doors, is arrested for lewd and lascivious behavior after exposing himself at a concert in Miami.

DIANA ROSS invites 350 special guests to the trendy Daisy Club in Beverly Hills to see the new Motown act, The Jackson Five.

1968

CARDIGAN-CARRYING MISTER ROGERS opens his Neighborhood February 19, beginning a 27-year run that will establish a PBS record.

JOHN LENNON and Yoko Ono tie the knot on Gibraltar March 20.

THE FIRST FULL-FRONTAL male nudity appears in film with Alan Bates and Oliver Reed in Ken Russell's *Women in Love.*

THE ALTAMONT FESTIVAL—starring such acts as The Rolling Stones, Santana, Jefferson Airplane, and Crosby, Stills, Nash & Young—is struck by tragedy when the Hell's Angels security force beats to death an 18-year-old boy.

CAST MEMBERS of the play *Oh! Calcutta!* are arrested for indecent exposure in Los Angeles.

THE SUPREME COURT rules that laws prohibiting the private possession of obscene material by adults are unconstitutional.

PRINCE CHARLES is officially titled Prince of Wales.

UPON WALKING ON THE MOON on July 20, Neil Armstrong proclaims, "That's one small step for a man, one giant leap for mankind."

ACTRESS SHARON TATE, wife of director Roman Polanski, is found murdered along with four oth-ers—the victims of Charles Manson's cult, known as The Family. Although not present at the house that night, would-be rock musician and psychopath Manson is convicted of the grisly killings and imprisoned.

THE WOODSTOCK Music and Art Festival is held August 15–17 in upstate New York. Playing before an audience of around 400,000, featured performers include The Who, Grateful Dead, Janis Joplin, Joe Cocker, Santana, Jimi Hendrix, Jefferson Airplane, and Crosby, Stills & Nash.

SESAME STREET debuts, starring Big Bird, Oscar, Bert, Ernie, Cookie Monster, Grover, and Kermit; it marks a radical breakthrough for children's TV programming.

TINY TIM marries Miss Vickie before 45 million witnesses on *The Tonight Show.*

1970

RECORDING TOGETHER for the last time, the Beatles cut "I Me Mine" January 3. The historic breakup happens on April 10, when Paul McCartney announces that he will not record with John Lennon again. By the end of the year, John, Paul, George, and Ringo have all released albums of their own.

EVERYTHING You Always Wanted to Know About Sex, but Were Afraid To Ask by Dr. David Reuben becomes a No. 1 bestseller.

JIMI HENDRIX and Janis Joplin both die drug-related deaths this year at age 27.

Jimi Hendrix.

THE FILM VERSION of *M*A*S*H,* with Elliott Gould and Donald Sutherland, is officially banned from military installations for "reducing the conventions and paraphernalia of war to total idiocy."

MIDNIGHT COWBOY is the first and only X-rated film to win Best Picture at the Academy Awards.

MASTERPIECE THE-ATRE is introduced on National Educational Television, hosted by Alistair Cooke and featuring BBC dramas.

TV'S PARTRIDGE FAM-ILY records "I Think I Love You," which becomes a smash hit first in the show's story line and then in real life, and makes David Cassidy a teen idol.

WATERBEDS hit the market, and although technical problems often produce flooding, sales skyrocket.

MONDAY NIGHT FOOT-BALL takes its bow September 21 (with the New York Jets vs. the Cleveland Browns) and strains U.S. marriages, but Don Meredith, Howard Cosell, and Frank Gifford will boost ABC's ratings.

1971

CIGARETTE ADS are banned January 2 and TV networks lose $200 million in annual advertising.

CBS'S controversial *All in the Family* is introduced, featuring the bigoted Archie Bunker, whose offensive diatribes and hilarious family members drive the show's great popularity.

EXCERPTS FROM THE PENTAGON PAPERS, leaked by Daniel Ellsberg, are published in the *New York Times*, showing that presidential administrations had indeed recognized the futility of the Vietnam War but escalated involvement anyway and then lied about it. The Nixon administration attempts to block publication but the Supreme Court rules in favor of the newspaper on First Amendment grounds.

BILL GRAHAM closes down Fillmore East and Fillmore West in New York City and San Francisco, unable to pay the increasing prices charged by the musicians he has showcased for so long.

MUHAMMAD ALI'S conviction for draft evasion is overturned by the Supreme Court, which rules that the boxer's pacifist religious convictions were sincere.

JIM MORRISON, 27, dies in a bathtub in Paris on July 3.

HOSTED BY GEORGE HARRISON, the Concert for Bangladesh initiates the rise of the celebrity fundraiser. The concert features Ringo Starr, Eric Clapton, and Bob Dylan, but while its success is great, only a small fraction of its proceeds ever reach the starving people of Bangladesh.

LEGENDARY ALLMAN BROTHERS Band member Duane Allman is killed October 29 in a motorcycle accident near Macon, Ga.

1972

MS., edited by Gloria Steinem, publishes its premiere issue in January.

RECLUSIVE MULTIMILLIONAIRE Howard Hughes exposes as a hoax an upcoming "autobiography" supposedly written with, but actually forged by, author Clifford Irving.

PONG, the first commercial computer game, is created by Atari.

BURT REYNOLDS poses nude for the centerfold of *Cosmopolitan*.

AT THE SUMMER OLYMPICS in Munich, 11 Israeli Olympians are killed by Arab terrorists, and the games are suspended for the first time in history.

JONATHAN LIVINGSTON SEAGULL establishes itself as the bestselling book since *Gone with the Wind*.

DEEP THROAT becomes one of the most successful porn films ever made; produced on a budget of $40,000, it goes on to gross around $40 million.

THE HOME BOX OFFICE cable channel goes on the air in Wilkes-Barre, Pa., with 365 subscribers. The first offering is a Paul Newman movie, *Sometimes a Great Notion*.

1973

ROE V. WADE is upheld by the Supreme Court, legalizing unrestricted abortion in the first trimester of pregnancy.

A CEASE-FIRE agreement is signed on January 27 that essentially ends the Vietnam War.

SACHEEN LITTLEFEATHER refuses Marlon Brando's Oscar for Best Actor on his behalf to protest the treatment of Native Americans. (Brando had been nominated for *The Godfather*.)

Marlon Brando as the Godfather.

PBS'S *STEAMBATH* takes on a taboo as Valerie Perrine becomes the first woman to bare her breasts in a dramatic TV program.

AT THE AGE OF 38, Seiji Ozawa becomes the youngest permanant conductor of the Boston Symphony.

A BREAK-IN at Democratic party headquarters at the Watergate Hotel is discovered, eventually leading to the only resignation of a sitting president in American history when Richard Nixon is forced to leave office on August 9 of the following year.

PUNK/NEW WAVE club CBGB and OMFUG (which stands for Country, Bluegrass, Blues, and Other Music for Uplifting Gourmandizers) opens its doors on Manhattan's divey Bowery, becoming home to such performers as Blondie, Talking Heads, Patti Smith, The Ramones, The Police, Joan Jett, and Sid Vicious. As Joey Ramone put it 20 years later, "It's a birthplace. It's like a big womb there. It's very primitive, very primal."

BILLIE JEAN KING trounces male chauvinist Bobby Riggs in tennis's ballyhooed "Battle of the Sexes."

THE AMERICAN PSYCHIATRIC ASSOCIATION reverses its traditional position and declares that homosexuality is not a mental illness.

1974

THE AUTOBIOGRAPHY OF MISS JANE PITTMAN, starring Cicely Tyson, becomes one of TV's most highly praised and successful special programs, going on to win nine Emmys.

HEIRESS PATRICIA HEARST is kidnapped by the Symbionese Liberation Army, which she later joins and with which she commits a robbery. 19 months after her kidnapping, Hearst is captured and convicted.

AFTER 10 YEARS OF MARRIAGE, Cher files for divorce from her husband and performing partner Sonny Bono. She marries Gregg Allman of the Allman Brothers Band only four days after the divorce is finalized.

PEOPLE magazine, featuring Mia Farrow on the cover, is launched by Time, Inc., in February.

EVEL KNIEVEL fails his attempt to jump the Snake River Canyon on his motorcycle, but survives.

1,000 FANS at a David Cassidy concert in London are injured during a frenzy following the teen idol's appearance. One concertgoer dies.

FLORIDA TV commentator Chris Chubbuck announces her own suicide at the end of the news broadcast, and proceeds to shoot herself in the head on the air.

ALEKSANDR SOLZHENITSYN is expelled from Russia for his dissident writings; this year *The Gulag Archipelago* is also published in the West.

STREAKING becomes a momentary fad, primarily on college campuses, although the madness eventually extends to telecasts of the Academy Awards and *The Tonight Show.*

RUSSIAN DANCER EXTRAORDINAIRE Mikhail Barishnikov defects to the West, electrifying the American dance scene.

KAREN SILKWOOD is killed in a suspicious car crash on November 13. A laboratory worker at the Kerr-McGee plutonium plant, she dies on her way to meet with a reporter to discuss safety hazards at her workplace.

1975

THE VIETNAM WAR officially comes to an end.

JOHN LENNON wins a four-year-long battle against American immigration authorities when they drop his case for humanitarian reasons due to the pregnancy of Yoko Ono.

SATURDAY NIGHT LIVE hits the airwaves

from New York City, with guest host George Carlin.

RICHARD BURTON and Elizabeth Taylor marry for the second time, only a year after their divorce.

THE VIDEOCASSETTE recorder/player is introduced by Sony.

MOOD RINGS are introduced and reach their peak in only a few months, selling more than 20 million before passing from popular fancy. Meanwhile, maintenance-free pet rocks also hit the short-term big time.

1976

THE MINISERIES comes to commercial TV, as *Rich Man, Poor Man* airs, starring Peter Strauss, Susan Blakely, and Nick Nolte.

BRITAIN'S PRINCESS MARGARET scandalizes the world with an illicit liaison on the island of Mustique with brewery heir Roddy Llewellyn. She and her husband, Lord Snowden, separate later this year.

GONE WITH THE WIND is telecast over two evenings on NBC, earning the highest ratings to date.

1977

ALEX HALEY'S novel *Roots*, a story of his quest for his ancestors in Africa and America, is made into the most successful miniseries in history. It wins a record nine Emmys, and mesmerizes the country for over a week, drawing approximately 130 million people to watch at least one of its eight episodes.

STUDIO 54 opens its doors in New York, becoming the quintessential glamorous nightclub until owners Steve Rubell and Ian Shrager are arrested for tax evasion in 1980.

GEORGE LUCAS releases *Star Wars*, which goes on to become the fourth-highest-grossing movie of all time.

THE KING IS DEAD: Elvis Presley, 42, passes on at Graceland, his palatial estate in Memphis, Tenn., on August 16.

SOAP introduces prime time's first gay character—Billy Crystal as Jodie Dallas.

RONALD ZAMORA, 15, confesses to murder and claims TV made him do it; he will be convicted in the first televised trial.

SATURDAY NIGHT FEVER premieres in New York on December 14, launching the disco era.

1978

FORMER FIRST LADY Betty Ford helps break the stigma of addiction by entering a rehabilitation clinic.

THE WORLD'S FIRST test-tube baby, Louise Brown, is born July 25 in England.

AT 25 HOURS and $25 million, the dramatization of James Michener's *Centennial* is the most outsized program yet produced for TV.

JIM JONES leads his followers to a mass death in Jonestown, Guyana, on November 18. 1,914 of his cult commit suicide or kill each other.

SONY invents the revolutionary Walkman, the first portable cassette player.

1979

RAP MUSIC is ushered into the commercial age when the Sugarhill Gang releases "Rapper's Delight."

Earlier in the year a Brooklyn group called The Fatback Band had produced "King Tim III (Personality Jock)," a disk widely regarded as the first rap record.

WHILE THE WOMEN on TV's *Charlie's Angels* changed outfits on average eight times per show, a guest appearance this year by Farrah Fawcett (who left the show in 1977) easily breaks the record: in one hour-long program she changes clothes 12 times.

1980

THE U.S. HOCKEY TEAM beats the Soviet Union during the Winter Olympics at Lake Placid, on their way to winning their first gold medal since 1960—and only their second gold since the Olympics began.

POST-IT NOTES enter the market, revolutionizing the office and the refrigerator.

TED KOPPEL'S *Nightline*, begun as an ABC series following the status of U.S. hostages in Iran, brings hard news in the wee hours.

COMEDIAN RICHARD PRYOR is badly burned when a flammable drug mixture used to make "freebase," a cocaine derivative, explodes in his face.

WITH SUCH BLOCKBUSTER musicals as *A Chorus Line*, *Oh! Calcutta!*, and *Evita* on the boards, Broadway box offices collect almost $200 million, a dramatic increase over a five-year period. Road shows during this period experience an even greater success.

TV'S FIRST ALL-NEWS SERVICE begins with Ted Turner's Cable News Network on

The triumphant U.S. Hockey Team.

June 1. Broadcasting 24 hours a day, the network loses $16 million in a year, but grabs seven million viewers.

HALF THE NATION'S VIEWERS tune in on November 21 to find out "Who Shot J.R.?," more viewers than for any other single TV show in history.

MARK DAVID CHAPMAN shoots and kills John Lennon on December 8 outside the singer's apartment in New York City.

1981

HOMOSEXUAL MEN across the country are struck down by a wave of cancer and pneumonia that is traced to a mysterious breakdown in the body's disease-fighting system. It will be referred to later as Acquired Immune Deficiency Syndrome, or AIDS.

HILL STREET BLUES premieres.

TICKETS TO BROADWAY'S *The Life and Adventures of Nicholas Nickleby* go on sale at the Plymouth Theatre for a record-setting $100 each.

PRESIDENT RONALD REAGAN is shot in an assassination

attempt on March 30 that leaves his press secretary, James Brady, paralyzed for life. John Hinckley apparently undertakes the assassination in an attempt to impress Jodie Foster.

President Ronald Reagan.

THE VIDEO GAME PAC-MAN devours the market as young people everywhere are seized with acute Pac-mania.

CHARLES, PRINCE OF WALES, and Lady Diana Spencer are married July 29 at Saint Paul's Cathedral in London.

MTV unveils music for your eyes on August 1. The channel's opener: "Video Killed the Radio Star," by The Buggles.

SANDRA DAY O'CONNOR becomes the first woman Supreme Court justice in U.S. history.

PRIVATE SATELLITE DISHES sprout after the FCC gives them

the okay. By the end of the '80s, there will be two million nationwide.

1982

OZZY OSBOURNE bites the head off a live bat thrown at him during a performance on January 20, a moment that is immortalized in heavy metal chronicles.

THE REVEREND SUN MYUNG MOON performs a mass ceremony at Madison Square Garden, marrying some 4,150 of his followers, the "Moonies."

MICHAEL JACKSON'S *Thriller* is released. Selling over 20 million copies in 1983 and 1984 alone, it becomes the biggest-selling album in history.

JOHN BELUSHI dies March 5 of an overdose of cocaine and heroin in a Hollywood hotel room.

CHARLES AND DI produce their first offspring, Prince William, on June 21, the latest heir to the British throne.

PRINCESS GRACE dies on September 14 after an automobile accident.

THE WATCHMAN, Sony's portable

microtelevision, is invented.

THE FIRST ARTIFICIAL HEART is transplanted into Barney C. Clark, age 61, in Utah. He lives for 112 days.

1983

CABLE TV subscribers reach the 30 million mark.

SINGER KAREN CARPENTER dies of anorexia nervosa on February 4.

*M*A*S*H* ends its 11-year, 14-Emmy run with the largest audience ever to watch a single TV show.

ASTRONAUT SALLY RIDE becomes the first American woman in space as she blasts off June 18 with four colleagues aboard the space shuttle *Challenger*.

VANESSA WILLIAMS becomes the first African American to win the Miss America pageant. She relinquishes her title two months before her term ends in 1984, when it is discovered that revealing nude photos of the singer are going to be published in *Penthouse*.

THE CHILLING TV DRAMA *The Day*

After, with Jason Robards, explores the aftermath of nuclear war, hardening both pro- and anti-freeze positions.

CABBAGE PATCH DOLLS, introduced by Coleco Industries, become the holy grail of the holiday season.

1984

HOME TAPING OF TV programming is held not to be in violation of copyright law by the Supreme Court, which throws out a suit brought against Sony by MCA and Walt Disney.

SURROGATE CONCEPTION is successful for the first time in California.

GERALDINE FERRARO becomes the first woman to run for vice president as presidential candidate Walter Mondale names the Queens congresswoman as his running mate; the pair lose the election to President Reagan and Vice President George Bush in a landslide.

GYMNAST MARY LOU RETTON wins two gold, two silver, and two bronze Olympic medals for the U.S.

SIDNEY BIDDLE BARROWS is arrested. Known as the Mayflower Madam, she included numerous famous and powerful people among her clients.

THE COSBY SHOW premieres, becoming the most popular series of the decade before going off the air in 1993.

THE FIRST ALL-RAP RADIO format is introduced by KDAY in Los Angeles.

RUN-DMC becomes the first rap group to have an album—*Run-DMC*—certified gold.

BOB GELDOF and Band Aid's "Do They Know It's Christmas" raises money to help feed the starving people of Africa.

1985

"WE ARE THE WORLD" is recorded by 45 pop music superstars under the auspices of USA for Africa.

CRACK COCAINE hits the streets, further devastating already blighted urban areas.

PIANO MAN BILLY JOEL and supermodel Christie Brinkley tie the knot.

MADONNA begins her road debut, The Virgin Tour, on April 10.

THE MUSIC INDUSTRY'S benefit for African famine relief, Live Aid, is staged in London and Philadelphia and beamed all over the world.

ROCK HUDSON becomes the first major public figure to die of AIDS, at 59, on October 2.

1986

THE SPACE SHUTTLE *CHALLENGER* explodes January 28 shortly after launching, killing everyone on board, including schoolteacher Christa McAuliffe, the first private citizen to go into space.

FILIPINO FIRST LADY Imelda Marcos is revealed to possess 2,700 pairs of shoes.

ARNOLD SCHWARZENEGGER and Maria Shriver are married.

JOHNNY CARSON stops talking to Joan Rivers when she accepts an offer to host a late-night show on the Fox network.

CAROLINE KENNEDY marries artist-designer Edwin Schlossberg.

PRINCE ANDREW marries Sarah Ferguson in London on July 23.

THE OPRAH WINFREY SHOW, originally a local program called *A.M. Chicago,* goes national on September 8. Its host quickly establishes herself as one of the most successful personalities in show business.

TURNER BROADCASTING colorizes black-and-white classics and directors, stars and movie buffs see red. First to run: Jimmy Cagney's *Yankee Doodle Dandy.*

Vice-presidential candidate Geraldine Ferraro.

1987

JESSICA HAHN is implicated in a scandal with TV evangelist Jim Bakker.

VAN GOGH'S *Irises* is auctioned at $53.9 million, the highest price ever paid for a painting at the time.

PRINCE CHARLES and Diana begin leading separate lives in March as their marriage starts to deteriorate.

PRESIDENTIAL CANDIDATE Gary Hart's connection with model Donna Rice destroys his political aspirations, and he is forced to withdraw from the race.

GARRISON KEILLOR broadcasts his last radio show, *A Prairie Home Companion*, from Lake Wobegon on June 13 and moves to New York City.

PORN QUEEN CICCIOLINA wins a seat in Italian parliament on June 16.

BRUCE WILLIS and Demi Moore are married November 21 in Las Vegas.

1988

TV PREACHER JIMMY SWAGGART admits his involvement with pornography and prostitutes. His February 21 statement, "I have sinned," deals a serious setback to electronic evangelism.

COMPACT DISCS outsell vinyl albums for the first time: the Recording Industry Association of America reports unit sales of 149.7 million CDs to 72.4 million records.

SONNY BONO is elected mayor of Palm Springs, California.

THE VERY LAST Playboy Club in America closes July 30 in Lansing, Mich.

ACTRESS ROBIN GIVENS files for divorce on October 7 from world heavyweight champion Mike Tyson, claiming that the fighter is violent.

TALK SHOW HOST PHIL DONAHUE wears a dress on November 18 to boost his ratings.

BENAZIR BHUTTO of Pakistan becomes the first woman to lead an Islamic nation.

PAN AM FLIGHT 103 explodes over Lockerbie, Scotland, killing all 259 passengers.

THE ERA of the personal video arrives when Sony introduces the Video Walkman, an ultracompact VCR with a three-inch color screen.

1989

LATE-NIGHT TV gets its first regular African-American host on January 3 with comedian Arsenio Hall.

Talk-show host Arsenio Hall.

VIRTUAL REALITY, the term as well as the equipment to achieve it, is invented by Jaron Lanier.

NOVELIST SALMAN RUSHDIE is forced into hiding after a death threat is issued by Islamic militants angry over what they see as sacrilege in his book *The Satanic Verses*.

KIM BASINGER steps in to rescue near-bankrupt Braselton, Ga., by buying the town for a reported $20 million.

LUCILLE BALL, perhaps the most beloved television star in history, dies on April 26.

ACTOR ROB LOWE is identified by Fulton County, Ga. officials in a soft-porn video with an underaged girl.

PLAYBOY FOUNDER Hugh Hefner marries former *Playboy* Playmate Kimberley Conrad.

JOSE MENENDEZ and his wife, Kitty, are found murdered August 20 in their $4 million Beverly Hills mansion. Their sons, Lyle and Erik, will later be accused of murdering their parents for money, though at their trials the brothers claim that years of sexual and psychological abuse by their parents drove them to kill in self-defense.

PETE ROSE, Cincinnati Reds manager and one of the greatest baseball players in history, is banned from the game for life for gambling.

TV GUIDE boasts a picture on the cover of the newly slim Oprah Winfrey, but the image turns out to be a composite of Oprah's head and Ann-Margret's body.

PRINCESS ANNE issues a palace statement on August

31 that she is officially separating from her husband, Mark Phillips.

THE BERLIN WALL falls on November 9.

SAN FRANCISCO GIANTS pitcher Dave Dravecky retires after an aborted comeback attempt from cancer in his pitching arm.

1990

THE SIMPSONS spins off from *The Tracey Ullman Show* and makes the fledgling Fox network a real contender as a fourth network.

NELSON MANDELA is released from prison after 27 years of incarceration for leading a campaign against the South African government.

"ICE ICE BABY" by Vanilla Ice becomes the first rap record to top the U.S. singles chart.

SONY creates the first portable compact disc player, the Discman.

M. C. HAMMER releases *Please Hammer Don't Hurt 'Em*, which becomes the biggest-selling rap record in history.

DONALD AND IVANA TRUMP divorce.

MILLI VANILLI is accused of fraud for using voices other than its own on its Grammy-winning album, *Girl You Know It's True*. The group is forced to surrender the award.

IN THE FIRST such ruling against a music group in the U. S., a Florida judge declares 2 Live Crew's album *As Nasty As They Wanna Be* obscene and bans all sales of the rap recording to minors. The move ignites a campaign against censorship in the music business.

TWIN PEAKS debuts on ABC as a two-hour movie with limited commercial interruption.

SEINFELD, a show about "nothing," quietly debuts on May 31.

AMERICA RELIVES the war between the states with Ken Burns's indelible PBS documentary *The Civil War*.

IN AN EFFORT to raise money for AIDS research, the *Red Hot & Blue* album is released on October 30, featuring such stars as U2, David Byrne, and The Neville Brothers performing Cole Porter songs.

1991

OPERATION DESERT SHIELD turns into Desert Storm on January 16 as the Allied forces attack Iraq to liberate Kuwait. CNN's Bernard Shaw, Peter Arnett, and John Holliman cover the events for the world, broadcasting from downtown Baghdad.

THE GODFATHER OF SOUL, James Brown, is released from a Georgia prison after serving two years of a six-year sentence for aggravated assault, not stopping for police, and carrying a gun.

RODNEY KING'S beating by Los Angeles police is recorded by an observer with a home video camera on March 3.

DR. JACK KEVORKIAN'S attempts to help people commit suicide first come to light.

WILLIAM KENNEDY SMITH, nephew of Teddy Kennedy, is accused of rape by a Florida woman; after a harrowing trial, he is exonerated.

PAUL REUBENS, creator of the much-admired *Pee-Wee's Playhouse* and the character Pee-Wee Herman, is busted in Florida for indecent exposure.

Paul Reubens, a.k.a. Pee-Wee Herman, after his infamous arrest.

LIZ TAYLOR marries husband number seven, 39-year-old Larry Fortensky, a carpenter she met at the Betty Ford Center where they were both being treated for alcohol and drug dependency. The wedding, held on Michael Jackson's estate, draws such guests as Nancy Reagan.

THE ANITA HILL/ CLARENCE THOMAS hearings galvanize the nation with charges of sexual harassment against the Supreme Court nominee; Thomas is narrowly approved for the post.

MAGIC JOHNSON announces his retirement from professional basketball because he has tested positive for the HIV virus.

MEDIA MOGUL TED TURNER and actress-cum-fitness-guru Jane Fonda are married.

1992

ARTHUR ASHE, tennis star and beloved public figure, dies of AIDS.

MIKE TYSON is convicted of raping beauty contestant Desiree Washington.

TAMMY FAYE BAKKER files for divorce from husband Jim, who's still in prison on a fraud conviction and not eligible for parole for another three years.

FERGIE AND ANDY separate after six years of marriage.

A *MURPHY BROWN* segment in which the unmarried Murphy gives birth spurs the wrath of Vice President Dan Quayle and instigates a nationwide debate over family values.

LONG ISLAND TEENAGER Amy Fisher shoots Mary Jo Buttafuoco.

JOHNNY CARSON ends his reign over late-night talk shows on May 22 with his last appearance on *The Tonight Show.*

CANDIDATE BILL CLINTON appears on *The Arsenio Hall Show,* complete with dark shades and saxophone, to perform "Heartbreak Hotel"

with the show's "posse."

WOODY ALLEN and Mia Farrow begin a bitter custody battle over their son Satchel, 4, and two children they adopted together, Moses, 14, and daughter Dylan, 7. The dispute is fueled by Allen's affair with Farrow's adopted daughter Soon-Yi Previn.

THE TORONTO BLUE JAYS become the first non-American team to win that most American of sports championships, the World Series, with a 4–2 series win over Ted Turner's Atlanta Braves.

PRINCE CHARLES and Princess Diana formally separate.

1993

THE U.S. POSTAL SERVICE releases its commemorative Elvis stamp, featuring the youthful Elvis, the overwhelming selection of the voting public.

BILL WYMAN leaves The Rolling Stones in January. He is 56.

DR. DRE'S album *The Chronic* (named after a very potent form of marijuana) reaches No. 1 on the *Billboard* charts and

becomes the most successful hard-core rap album to date.

MICHAEL JACKSON tells interviewer Oprah Winfrey that his lightened skin color is due to a rare skin disease, and says that he is in love with Brooke Shields. Later in the year Jackson is accused of having fondled a 13-year-old Los Angeles boy.

THE ROCK AND ROLL HALL OF FAME, designed by I. M. Pei, finally breaks ground. Pete Townshend notes: "Let's hope it doesn't become a monolith to a bunch of dinosaurs." The Hall opens its doors in Cleveland in 1995.

PRINCE, born Prince Rogers Nelson, turns 35 and, in a most confusing commemoration, changes his name to a symbol that no one knows how to pronounce.

JULIA ROBERTS, 25, and Lyle Lovett, 35, wed.

ACTOR RIVER PHOENIX, 23, dies on October 31. The young actor had a reputation for clean living, but coroners find high levels of cocaine and morphine as well as Valium and marijuana in Phoenix's system.

1994

NANCY KERRIGAN is attacked in January by a club-wielding assailant, but battles back from the resulting knee injury to win a silver medal in the Winter Olympics. American rival Tonya Harding finishes a disappointing eighth, and is later banned from the U.S. Figure Skating Association for life after a grand jury concludes that she helped to plan the attack on Kerrigan with ex-husband Jeff Gillooly.

LORENA BOBBITT is acquitted of all charges of malicious wounding when the jury concludes that the 24-year-old manicurist was temporarily insane when she cut her husband's penis off with a kitchen knife in June 1993.

A MAJOR EARTHQUAKE hits Los Angeles on January 18, and 61 people die as it rolls to 6.6 on the Richter scale. Many celebrities experience severe damage to their homes, including Denzel Washington, Jeff Bridges, Arsenio Hall, Warren Beatty, Jack Nicholson, and David Caruso. Tom Arnold sums it up: "We had too much stuff, and God let us know real quick."

MICHAEL JORDAN
quits basketball and signs a contract with the Chicago White Sox, fulfilling his childhood dream of becoming a baseball player. He is assigned to the Birmingham Barons, a Class AA team, and finishes the season with a batting average of .202.

STEVEN SPIELBERG
finally claims Oscars for Best Picture and Best Director with *Schindler's List*, which receives a total of seven awards. His *Jurassic Park* wins another three.

KURT COBAIN takes his own life with a shotgun on April 8 in his Seattle-area lakeside home. He joins a long and sad list of fellow rock stars: Janis Joplin, Jimi Hendrix, Jim Morrison—all dead at 27.

BARBARA STREISAND,
52, conquers stage fright to make a stunning return with her first paid concerts in 22 years. The 13-city tour

draws packed audiences at every step of the way, and her New York show at Madison Square Garden officially smashes the record for the highest total concert gross at one venue.

'60S SUPERGROUPS
take the country by storm. The Eagles reassemble for a worldwide tour, and Jimmy Page and Robert Plant reinflate Led Zeppelin for MTV and a new album. The aging Rolling Stones take to the road with "Voodoo Lounge," humbling critics of their so-called Geritol Tour with the highest U.S. concert grosses of all time.

JACQUELINE BOUVIER KENNEDY ONASSIS dies at age 64 on May 19. She had been diagnosed just four months before with non-Hodgkin's lymphoma, a cancer of the lymphatic system.

NICOLE BROWN SIMPSON, 35, and Ronald Goldman, 25, are brutally murdered in front of Simpson's Brentwood condominium. After an

eerie low-speed chase watched live on television by 95 million people, Nicole's ex-husband O.J. Simpson surrenders to police and is charged with the murders.

THE POPE proves his popularity as his book, *Crossing the Threshold of Hope*, sells over 1.6 million copies to become one of the year's top sellers.

NEVERLAND meets Graceland as Michael Jackson and Lisa Marie Presley get hitched in a secret ceremony in the Dominican Republic.

WOODSTOCK '94, held on the 25th anniversary of the original, devolves into a free-for-all of mud, mosh pits, and acts old (the Allman Brothers Band, Bob Dylan) and new (Green Day, Nine Inch Nails).

HEATHER WHITESTONE is the first disabled person to win the Miss America pageant in September. Almost completely deaf, Heather must be told by

another contestant that she has won.

DREAMWORKS SKG,
the first new major studio in 55 years, is formed in Hollywood by record mogul David Geffen, director Steven Spielberg, and former Disney executive Jeffrey Katzenberg, the man who brought us *The Lion King*.

THE WORLD SERIES is canceled for the first time ever after major league baseball players and team owners fail to come to an agreement in their labor dispute. Meanwhile, the National Hockey League shuts down over collective bargaining issues.

GEORGE FOREMAN,
45, recaptures the heavyweight title he lost to Muhammad Ali 20 years ago. He defeats Michael Moore in Las Vegas with a 10th-round knockout.

FORMER PRESIDENT
Ronald Reagan bravely shares the news that he has been diagnosed with Alzheimer's disease, an incurable brain disorder.

ROYALTY

THE MERRY MEN AND WOMEN OF WINDSOR

"I want to be as famous as the queen of England," the ambitious young Andy Warhol proclaimed back in the 1950s. He might as well have said that he wanted to be as famous as the Atlantic Ocean. The current British royal family has something that vast and immemorial about it. In the three centuries of its reign, other crowned families of Europe have been executed or packed off. But the Windsors still occupy the throne, as implacable and seemingly enduring as the planet Jupiter.

It hasn't been easy. The Windsors are expected to behave like the Cleavers even when they're feeling like the Simpsons. Being famous is more than their fate; in a sense it's their job. As the real decision-making power of the monarchy has dwindled, the public symbolism has become more important. On more than one occasion in the past, however, Britons have seemed ready to rid themselves of a dynasty that could look costly, shiftless, and Teutonic. The lessons of the past are not lost on the Windsors, who take their family history not just as a source of pride but also as a series of warnings to the present. Like her father, George VI, Elizabeth II has been a model of dignity and decorum. But a stroll among her ancestors in

the National Portrait Gallery is enough to remind her of any number of hot-blooded blue bloods in her line.

Where does the Windsor saga begin? Actually, with the German Hanoverian kings. The royals like to consider Queen Victoria their matriarch because, while she was from the House of Hanover herself, her marriage to Prince Albert of Saxe-Coburg-Gotha established the present branch of the family tree. So emphasizing Albert's line allows the Windsors to distance themselves from Victoria's Hanoverian predecessors. Starting with **George I**, who was imported to England from Germany in 1714, the five increasingly preposterous rulers had made the British people rue almost the very idea of royalty.

After monarchs who alternated between extravagant skirt-chasing and outright incompetence, **Victoria** acceded to the crown in 1837, the niece of the last Hanoverian king, William IV. Immediately she made it her business to undo their legacy. She brought the monarchy a bit of wholesome romance through a devoted marriage to her German husband, **Prince Albert**. Indeed the transformation of the royal reputation may be Albert's achievement even more than Victoria's. With the middle classes taking

power from the spoiled and lazy aristocrats, Albert gave them a royal family that the common man could both look up to and identify with: wreathed in pomp and ceremony but frugal, sober, dutiful, and monogamous.

Though Victoria's name has come to stand for prudishness, it was as much Albert who brought the moralizing strain to their marriage. As a young woman, the Queen didn't blush to size him up bluntly in her diary. ("Such a pretty mouth," she noted. "A beautiful figure, broad in the shoulders, and a fine waist.") But Albert worried that their children would take after his wayward parents, who had divorced in a tangle of adulteries. Above all he vowed that Edward, heir to the throne, would be raised in an atmosphere of hard schooling and abstinence. Naturally, Edward grew up to be dim, jolly, and goatish.

Upon Albert's death in 1861, Victoria, just 42 years old, plunged down a black hole of widowhood. Albert's bedroom was kept as it was on the day of his death, even to the extent of having fresh bedclothes laid out every night. She eventually roused herself sufficiently to regain the public's affection, and lived long enough to see her nine children and forty grandchildren married into most of the royal families of

Europe. On her deathbed she was supported by her grandson Kaiser Wilhelm of Germany, who 13 years later would lead his nation into war against hers.

When Victoria died in 1901, after the longest reign in her nation's history, her reputation for rectitude had become so stultifying that her womanizing heir, son **Edward VII**, found himself lionized for the same habits that had caused so much trouble for so many Hanoverian kings. Throughout his life the insatiable Edward conducted a series of lengthy affairs with some of the most celebrated beauties of the day, including the actresses Lillie Langtry and Sarah Bernhardt. With prosperity at home and vast empire abroad, the public was willing to overlook the moral lapses of a robust and even randy monarch. After nine popular years on the throne he was followed by **George V**, prim, exacting, and a stickler for impeccable dress. George led the country through World War I when he changed the family name from the Germanic Saxe-Coburg-Gotha to Windsor. He also encouraged closer ties between the royals and the people by allowing the Windsors to marry British nobles and commoners. Indeed among the first to benefit from this new trend was the present Queen Mother, a noblewoman who married George's son Albert, the future George VI.

George VI became the monarch, however, only after his elder brother abdicated. Crowned **Edward VIII** in 1936, the young man was already intent upon marriage to Wallis Warfield Simpson, a divorced American married to a British businessman. But the government would hear nothing of it and presented Edward with a choice—the lady or the land—hoping that he would choose the former and in the process remove a king who showed signs of Nazi sympathies. After a reign of almost a year, he resigned and, bearing the newly invented title of Duke of Windsor, he left England for the Conti-

nent and Wallis Simpson. They would return home only for rare visits—and, decades later, to be buried.

England was shaken—indeed on the night of Edward's abdication the sentries around Buckingham Palace were issued live ammunition for the first time in modern history. The public's reaction may have been overestimated, but when Edward's younger brother, Albert, now **George VI**, came to the throne in December 1936, all of Britain was poised for the worst.

For that matter, so was Albert. He had never expected to be king (formal

The Queen Mother.

FOLLOW THE ROYAL LINE

The Windsors are but the latest of many families to rule the kingdom. Here is the complete lineage for Britain's crown according to *Whitaker's Almanac*, listed by year of accession.

Saxons and Danes

Egbert	827
Ethelwulf	839
Ethelbald	858
Ethelbert	858
Ethelred	866
Alfred the Great	871
Edward the Elder	899
Athelstan	925
Edmund	940
Edred	946
Edwy	955
Edgar	959
Edward the Martyr	975
Ethelred II	978
Edmund Ironside	1016
Canute the Dane	1017
Harold I	1035
Hardicanute	1040
Edward the Confessor	1042
Harold II	1066

The House of Normandy

William I	1066
William II	1087
Henry I	1100
Stephen	1135

The House of Plantagenet

Henry II	1154
Richard I	1189
John	1199
Henry III	1216
Edward I	1272
Edward II	1307
Edward III	1327
Richard II	1377

The House of Lancaster

Henry IV	1399
Henry V	1413
Henry VI	1422

The House of York

Edward IV	1461
Edward V	1483
Richard II	1483

The House of Tudor

Henry VII	1485
Henry VIII	1509
Edward VI	1547
Jane	1553
Mary I	1553
Elizabeth I	1558

The House of Stuart

James I (VI of Scotland)	1603
Charles I	1625

[Commonwealth declared, 1649]

The House of Stuart (restored)

Charles II	1660
James II (VII of Scotland)	1685
William II and Mary II	1689
Anne	1702

The House of Hanover

George I	1714
George II	1727
George III	1760
George IV	1820
William IV	1830
Victoria	1837

The House of Saxe-Coburg

Edward VII	1901

The House of Windsor

George V	1910
Edward VIII	1936
George VI	1936
Elizabeth II	1952

speaking engagements left him shaken and depressed), and when he learned he was suddenly to take the throne, he went to his mother, Queen Mary, and wept for an hour. No wonder it was rumored that George VI was too frail to survive the coronation ceremony.

But his very narrowness and humility turned out to be qualities that were once again in favor among the British people. George VI and his wife, the current **Queen Mother**, Elizabeth, provided Britain with a center of gravity during the grim days of World War II, remaining in Buckingham Palace even when London was being fractured by German bombs and refusing to send Princesses Elizabeth and Margaret out of the country. No wonder Adolf Hitler called her "the most dangerous woman in Europe." King George's family represented what the English wanted during these terrible years: a conscientious and principled king, a winning queen, and two likable young princesses, Elizabeth and Margaret.

Still thriving at 95, the Queen Mother has become a beloved national institution. Adored for her approachability and cheerful mien, the QM was described by photographer Cecil Beaton as "the great mother figure and nanny of us all." A red-hot number in the '20s, she still likes "drinky-poos" (gin and tonic) before dinner, but she has never forgiven President Jimmy Carter for his shameful breach of etiquette: he kissed her on the lips.

London merchants quake when they see her coming. It's not her taste in tulle, it's that she reportedly rarely pays her accounts. And she's still keen as a tack. Says one old friend of her wicked wit: "She doesn't take prisoners."

Born Lady Elizabeth Bowes-Lyon, the serenely beautiful young woman was the Di of her day. But fearing life in the royal fishbowl, she twice rejected marriage proposals from the painfully shy, stammering Prince Albert, who called her "the most wonderful person in the world."

It is amazing that this five-foot-tall aristocrat, the last Empress of India and the honorary colonel of 18 regiments, who has probably never cooked a meal or made a bed, is considered "everybody's mum." But the festivities surrounding her 90th birthday in 1990 confirmed the devotion she has long inspired.

When King George, a heavy smoker, died of lung cancer in 1952 at the age of 57, his daughter **Elizabeth II** took up the scepter knowing that her main job would be to preserve the gains her parents had made. Admittedly, Elizabeth is a figurehead, a constitutional monarch who reigns but does not rule. Yet no one trifles with the 68-year-old woman known at Buckingham

Queen Elizabeth II.

Palace as The Boss. Part of her power is ex officio: It is bad form to contradict Her Most Excellent Majesty, Elizabeth the Second, by the Grace of God, of the United Kingdom of Great Britain and Northern Ireland and of Her other Realms and Territories, Queen, Head of the Commonwealth, Defender of the Faith. It is also hard to disagree with someone whom *Fortune* reckons as the world's richest woman.

But much of Elizabeth's authority arises from the immovable force of her character. This is the monarch who at 27 overrode the objections of advisers and

ordered her coronation to be televised because, she said, "I have to be seen to be believed." And who continued to appear in public and ride in open cars after her husband's favorite uncle, Lord Mountbatten, was assassinated by an IRA bomb in 1979. And who in 1982 coolly kept a disturbed intruder talking on the edge of her bed until she could summon help.

She grew up during the London blitz and matured in the ensuing period of austerity. The world's wealthiest woman still wanders around Buckingham Palace turning off lights. The heat is kept low and there are no objections; there never are. And when one of her favorite dogs killed a hare, the Queen carefully picked it up and presented it to the kitchen staff. "We can eat this," she announced.

When Elizabeth II rings, a staff of 300 jumps. When the queen is in London, the PM calls on her every Tuesday to brief her on government business. Though not a quick study, Elizabeth is assiduous, has a phenomenal memory, and frequently embarrasses ministers by knowing more about the issues than they do.

Elizabeth's hold on her subjects begins with her family. When as a 13-year-old she met a dashing cadet, she instantly decided that he was Midshipman Right. Five years later she had not changed her mind, and so in 1947 she married **Prince Philip** of Greece, a great-

THE VULGAR SUBJECT OF MONEY

Loaded as they are, money is something the Windsors prefer not to tarnish themselves with. They never carry cash, not a penny. And it's not because they carry American Express instead. Elizabeth's famous pocketbook is a stage prop. It sometimes contains only mints for her horses. Otherwise, the Windsors come in contact with currency the way other people encounter God—mostly on Sundays. Before church, Charles is reportedly provided with a £5 note for the collection plate; he likes to have it sprayed and ironed by his valet, then neatly creased and left for him beneath his clove box. You know, the box that holds your before-dinner clove. You probably have one around somewhere.

The Windsor wealth is complicated. A considerable portion is their own, acquired by them or their ancestors with personal funds. That would include Sandringham and Balmoral, two of the royal country estates, which they own the way the Cartwrights owned the Ponderosa. Both were purchased during Queen Victoria's reign. But the greater part of the wealth that surrounds them is held in trust for the nation. That means the Windsors can wear it, sit on it, eat off it and go lightheartedly skipping down its glinting corridors. They just can't sew any name tags on it or cart it off to Christie's for auction.

If Britain should ever decide to get rid of the royal family, though, it would be a messy divorce. There's some confusion about which of their property belongs to the state and which is their own. In particular, who rightly possesses the lavish gifts from foreign potentates? Like the 2,000-year-old necklace from Egypt's former King Farouk?

And some of the royal's riches actually do benefit the public. It seems that Windsor Castle, their weekend residence, where construction began in the 11th century, may be perched atop oil deposits worth an estimated $1 billion. Queen Elizabeth II has given a white-gloved thumbs-up for exploratory drilling on a site somewhere between the royal household golf course and the royal household cricket ground. Any revenue generated will go directly to the Treasury.

By anyone's count, though, the total number is a whopper. *Fortune* has calculated that the Queen is one of the richest people in the world and two years ago they estimated her net worth at $7.8 billion. But a recent London *Sunday Times* report placed her total at a paltry $680 million, though most surveys still put the Windsor wealth well into the billions. Charles, meanwhile, was believed to be worth about $400 million as of 1991, which would still place him among Britain's 40 wealthiest people. To paraphrase Mel Brooks: It is good to be Queen.

great-grandchild of Queen Victoria. Britain's sceptered marriage has survived for almost fifty years.

Although Elizabeth has inevitably dominated her husband in the public realm, in the world of the Windsor family the duke of Edinburgh has had authority over educating the children: first Prince Charles and Princess Anne, later Princes Andrew and Edward. But Elizabeth's will is what holds the family and the royal public image together.

Her own image is not universally admired, at least from a fashion point of view. Dressing in a style that can be characterized as pseudo-frumpy, the queen stays out of the tabloids and gets her work done. While her hair is done every Monday at four p.m. by Charles Martyn, her hairdresser for the last two decades, she reads state papers and seldom glances in the mirror. Not everyone is happy about her diffidence. "I sometimes wish she had been a bit more of a clothes person," wistfully admits her couturier of four decades, Sir Hard Amies. "She doesn't care, basically. She listens to our advice, then goes off and wears shabby shoes because they're comfortable." But in fact Elizabeth does care about her appearance. Her outfits—the boxy, brightly colored clothes, clunky handbags, unfashionable reading glasses—are chosen with great deliberation to be unthreatening to women,

unobtrusive to men, and easily seen by the crowds that line her path. If she were chic, she would be French, but this queen is British to her bones. That means a love of silver service and afternoon tea, bland food, sweetish wine, jigsaw puzzles, Dick Francis mysteries, and, most of all, tramps in the country amid her Thoroughbreds and her dogs. The queen feeds her six corgis and two dorgis (a dachshund-corgi mix) herself, cutting up their meat and mixing it with biscuits in their separate bowls set out every afternoon by a footman.

No one takes better care of business than Her Majesty, who has long since realized that her maritally unstable offspring have created a throne-threatening PR problem for the House of Windsor. At the close of 1992, in a now-famous speech she noted, "It has turned out to be an *annus horribilis*." If not the language of the common man, it was certainly a sentiment commonly understood. And things got even more horrible a few days after that speech. On the Queen's 45th wedding anniversary, a fire gutted a corner of Windsor Castle, causing damages of up to $60 million. As a debate brewed over who should bear the cost of repairs, Elizabeth, with her unerring sense for image damage control, proclaimed that she would give up a centuries-old royal perk by commencing to pay

income tax on her private fortune, as well as pony up $8.5 million toward refurbishing the Castle. And perhaps most tellingly, the Queen announced that she was removing from the Civil List the Princes Andrew and Edward and the Princesses Anne and Margaret. That meant that she was switching from the public to her personal dole the annual upkeep of this spoiled quartet, not to mention their spendthrift spouses, present or future. And in 1993 she went one step further, conceding that marketing the mystique of the monarchy was in order. On August 7, she opened 19 state rooms in Buckingham Palace to public tours (leaving 631 rooms still off-limits) while she and the family were taking their annual summer retreat to Balmoral.

Ultimately, when verbal snipers zero in on every other royal soul, Elizabeth has risen above criticism. Her popularity continues unabated despite the scandals whirling around almost all of her children, chief among them Charles, Prince of Wales, and his wife, Princess Diana.

THE HEIRS AND THE ERRORS

Pity **Charles, the Prince of Wales**. Not only must he spend his life waiting to become king of England, he isn't even left in peace in the meantime. The windsurfing-parachuting-scuba-diving Action Prince of the '70s and the oratorical Philosopher Prince of the '80s has become in the public mind the Selfish Prince of the '90s. Whatever exquisite pleasures he pursues, he stands accused of conduct unbefitting a Man with Royal Responsibilities.

Charles has tried to please. Until he was 32 years old he lived at home with his parents. Then he found a lovely bride and promptly fulfilled his duty to begat heirs. Now all he can do is try not to go bonkers with boredom waiting for his hardy mum to pass him the scepter. Elizabeth is ticking away better than Big Ben, and Charles could end up like his great-great-grandfather, King Edward VII, who held the title of Prince of

Wales for almost 60 years before his mother, Queen Victoria, passed away.

But in the meantime, Charles has been a relatively energetic prince of Wales. He has eschewed some preferred hobbies of heirs apparent—falconing, gambling, and conspicuous wenching (although lately that seems to be slipping)—and contributed eloquently and provocatively to the public discourse on the preservation of architecture, the environment, and the language. True enough, he has become a tad eccentric. He awakens to farming programs on the radio. He eats odd vegetable dishes like nettle soup and sells organic bread stoneground from whole meal grown on his own farm. He believes in homeopathic medicine, frets about disappearing peat bogs, and collects antique lavatory seats. Yet all of these activities are at worst harmless, at best valuable, for an extraordinarily wealthy, inordinately spoiled gentleman patiently biding his time. As heir apparent he gets no income from the Civil List, but he does receive ample income from several estates—plus claim, by law and ancient tradition, to any whales that wash ashore.

There had been a fatal flaw in Charles's childhood: he didn't have one. Unlike prior generations of royal children, who were educated by palace tutors, he was sent

Prince Charles in a now-typical pose: contemplative, and ever-waiting.

to boarding schools—notably Gordonstoun, in harsh northeastern Scotland, a boot camp with books. In the '60s, when the youth of the world were exploding with passion, Charles was attending Trinity College, Cambridge, playing the cello in his tweeds. His mother, the titular head of the diminished British Commonwealth, had precious little time for him. She mostly wanted him to behave, and he did. While his upbringing didn't prepare him to be a regular guy, it certainly taught him how to be a king. But that hasn't been enough to keep together his marriage with **Lady Diana Spencer**. Despite having two adored sons, **Prince William** and **Prince Harry**, in December, 1992 the Prince and Princess of Wales announced an official separation that finally ended the long charade of their once idealized, now desperately unhappy, marriage.

Shortly thereafter, the last hope of a happy ending quickly faded. A racy taped phone chat between Prince Charles and his confidante, Camilla Parker Bowles was published worldwide. Charles revealed, among other steamy things, his surprising desire to live inside her "trousers or something." He purportedly declared his love for her and gushed, "In the next life, I should like to come back as your knickers."

Then came new revelations of a sexually charged phone conversation in which Diana discussed with *her* confidant, James Gilbey, her fear of getting pregnant. So in December, when the tearful princess announced that she was greatly curtailing her public life, it appeared that the Palace had finally succeeded in reining her in. "The dream is over. The people's darling will never become queen," proclaimed columnist John Casey in the *Evening Standard*, urging Brits to dump Diana and rally round the "slightly absurd" Charles.

In 1994, the second year of their official separation, the union of the prince and princess seemed to unspool with a special savagery and at indecent length in every possible medium. Worse, Charles and the House of Windsor itself seemed to lose in the process the public sympathy they so desperately tried to engender. The fire was fueled by the principals themselves, cooperating with unseemly disclosures and partisan biographies about lovers old and new, alienation of feelings, eating disorders and suicide attempts. Caught in this murderous crossfire, Charles and Diana found themselves the villains of a klieg-lit reality that had finally, and sadly, overtaken the soft-focus fairy tale.

The Prince of Wales turned into the Prince of Wails. Struggling to overcome his image as the diffident twit who allowed his marriage to founder, Charles

She may have lost her prince, but Princess Diana still retains her glamor.

rolled up his tailor-made sleeves and wrestled with the demon of publicity. First in a TV documentary and later in the sympathetic biography *Prince of Wales*, based on his diaries and letters, Charles worked closely with TV broadcaster Jonathan Dimbleby. The journalist cast him as an emotionally deprived pawn abandoned to nannies by Queen Elizabeth and bullied into a charade marriage by Prince Philip. Charles maintained in his TV

As Prince William and Prince Harry grow up they are looking more to their futures than back to their once-rancourous home.

interview that he remained faithful to the most glamorous woman in Britain "until it became clear that the marriage had irretrievably broken down." (But another '94 tome, *Camilla: The King's Mistress*, claims that Charles spent the night before his wedding with Parker Bowles.) And then Charles's vestigial dignity was puddled around his ankles after massively unflattering revelations in early 1995 from Ken Stronach, the valet charged with washing Charles's shorts and tucking his teddy into bed with him.

Stronach confided that he had scrubbed grass stains from the knees of Charles's pajamas after the prince's open-air trysts with Camilla;

that he had watched Charles hurl a heavy bootjack at Diana after she called him a "f--king animal"; and that Stronach had rumpled guest-room sheets to obscure the fact that Camilla shared the prince's bed. The pile of dirty linen was further added to by Charles's former housekeeper Wendy Berry, now living in exile, who defied the prince in publishing her account of palace life. But *The House-keeper's Diary* covered ground that is now familiar: more tales of shouted expletives and broken china.

Finally, in January, 1995, Camilla and her husband Andrew abandoned the charade that their union was intact, ending their 21-year marriage. Palace insiders are convinced that, along with Charles's startling confessions, Camilla's split is part of an elaborate long-range plan designed to bring their 25-year relationship out of the shadows—and, perhaps, set the stage for another royal marriage.

As for Diana, her startling decision in late 1993 to abandon most of her royal duties only added to her troubles. Soon thereafter she became embroiled in a top-less-photo scandal when a paparazzo caught her sunbathing in Spain. She was then accused of adultery with ex-Army officer James Hewitt, whose story was recounted by Anna Pasternak in the shamelessly florid *Princess in Love*. Diana was also linked with dashing mil-

lionaire Oliver Hoare, a married London art dealer who had offered to act as go-between for the Waleses when their marriage was collapsing. And she, wrote *News of the World*, had rung his Chelsea manse some 300 times over a period of 18 months beginning in 1992, often reportedly staying on the line, saying nothing, while the anxious Hoare demanded, "Who's there?"

Behind the headlines, Diana was a woman adrift without the charity work that had sustained her. She filled her days with shopping, lunch dates, and workouts. By year's end, impatient with "retirement," she reentered public life via her work for the Red Cross—"returning to the things she does best," as a friend put it.

A minor fuss over Diana's flirtation with English rugby star Will Carling, 29, was more revealing for its implications than its content, renewing concerns about the princess's growing remoteness. Now 34 and in her third year of post-separation limbo, Diana seems desperate to find people she can trust. "I can't speak to a man without people assuming I'm up to no good," she reportedly told friends. One observer tends to agree. The princess, he says, is "living in a gilded cage. She can do everything, and she can do nothing."

In any case, Charles and his wife have reached a kind of détente. Despite her attempts to upstage him in public, their private relationship is slightly more civil than it once was.

While some have speculated that the Camilla scandal will inspire the Queen to pass over him and make William her heir, Charles himself has no doubt that he will be the next monarch.

If you're heartbroken that Diana might not be queen and hasn't had the romance of the century, don't dab your eyes—there are no tears in her teacup. "Most people think that of the two—Charles and Diana—Diana is the one with steel," asserts Brian Hoey, author of *The New Court*. "She's her own woman, and she knows exactly what she wants to do, in the same way the Queen Mother did and does. She's a very tough lady. She's had to be."

For Diana is first and foremost a Spencer. That means she is more English than half the royal family, according to a recent genealogical study. Way down yonder in the 21st century, when her son Prince William accedes to the throne, he will have more English blood in him than any monarch since James I, who, though mostly Scottish, was 25% English.

Indeed Di was never cowed by the royal family. She first took aim at Charles when she was sweet 16 during a pheasant shoot. And she pursued the heir as only a Sloaney English seductress

would—disguised in tartans, tweeds, twin-sets, and pearls, a cross between Mary Poppins and Mata Hari. And the world knows, she got her man.

Immediately and single-handedly she lent fresh glamour and force to a fairly dowdy dynasty. As princess of Wales she put her life and soul into the most wrenching social issues without ever flinching. "Against the advice of friends," adds author Hoey, "she was the first royal to shake hands without a glove with an AIDS patient. She knew that that photograph would help allay fears. It was a very brave thing to do."

Diana began with one overriding duty—to produce an heir, preferably male—and she was fortunate enough within two years of her marriage to produce two towheads, known as the heir

and the spare. And now the boys must ricochet among very different worlds, something to which Wills and Harry are still adjusting. By all accounts, William, who lives with the burden of being Charles's heir, has felt the pain most acutely.

Now 13, the boy who seems destined to be king is leaving childhood behind. A rambunctious toddler who grew into a reserved primary-schooler, William is learning to cope with the peculiar demands of royal life. Like younger brother Harry, he must prepare for a role that will become more public over time, and one that will expose his every misstep. William's head now reaches the shoulder of his 5' 10" mother and he has grown into a thoughtful young man with a strong sense of duty and little of the Windsor's emotional detach-

The Windsor heirs are becoming more accustomed to public appearances. Here Wills orchestrates a group shot while on vacation with brother Harry and cousins Beatrice and Eugenie.

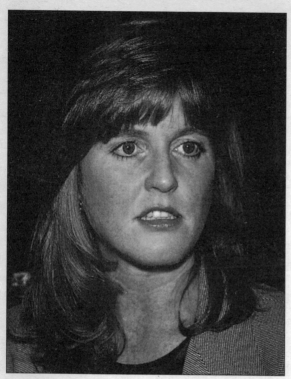

Sarah, Duchess of York.

ment. Says one Wales watcher: "He's a very gentle, nice boy."

Although William and Harry are hardly ready to abandon food fights and water guns, their recent public performances have left no doubt that the age of innocence is behind them. With Diana, they tour historic sites in Wales and visit homeless shelters in London. With Charles, they practice chatting up strangers before holiday church services near Sandringham and Balmoral.

And now William is attending Eton, one of England's most exclusive public—meaning private—schools. He is the first heir to the British throne to attend the institution, which has been educational home to British luminaries, including Gladstone, Pitt the Elder, and 18 other prime ministers, since 1440.

Of course Diana and Charles are not the only royals having trouble making peace with the idea of a loveless marriage. Hitched for 16 years, Charles's younger sister, **Princess Anne,** and Captain Mark Phillips were initially drawn together by their passion for horses (both are extraordinary equestrians). But Anne's interests were much broader—she is president of the Save the Children Fund and was even nominated for the Nobel Peace Prize a few years back. Says Anne of her work, "You have to decide at the end of the day if you can live with yourself." You also have to decide if you can live with your husband, and the affirmative answer increasingly came into doubt. Finally the couple separated in 1989, and after divorcing, Anne married long-time love Timothy Laurence, five years her junior, in December 1992. As close to her mother as any of her siblings, Anne staged her second wedding as an intimate family affair, attended by only a handful of relatives including her two children with Phillips, **Peter** and **Zara**.

Anne's second brother, rowdy **Prince Andrew, Duke of York**, has had his share—perhaps the lion's share—of marital bad luck as well. After a plucky performance in the Falklands conflict, helicopter pilot Andy seemed interested mainly in oat-sowing and club-crawling with a string of steamy ladies, culminating in former soft-porn star Koo Stark. What well-bred English girl would marry Andrew and put up with him?

And so when the prince's roving eye fell upon Sarah Ferguson in 1985, the nation breathed a collective sigh of relief. A strapping, worldly wench who loved a good time, Fergie seemed perfectly suited to her happy-go-lucky hubby. But while **Sarah, Duchess of York**, produced two lovely daughters, **Princesses Beatrice** and **Eugenie**, she also committed gaffe after gaffe. If the Yorks often struck the public as a pair of heedless hedonists, at least they originally seemed besotted with each other—a touching assumption not applicable to all Windsor marriages. But Fergie's erratic behavior quickly brought that into doubt as well. After a series of romantic trysts and crass missteps on her part, the Duchess was formally separated from the Duke in 1992. Later that year London tabs were abrim with graphic photos of Fergie on the Riviera cavorting topless with her American-born "financial advisor," John Bryan, who was shown smooching the bare instep of her foot while her two young daughters looked on.

She later confessed that the publication of those photos had been her "most humiliating experience." Fergie admitted that, "During the first years of my marriage I probably had an excessive ego. The St. Tropez photos forced me to change and care more about others than myself."

Earlier this year Andrew and Fergie vacationed together with their children and were seen looking affectionate together in public, but aides of the couple refused to speculate on the chances of a reconciliation.

The youngest of Elizabeth's four children, **Prince Edward** seems like a dinghy in the wake of bigger boats, bobbing and bailing as his three older siblings surge ahead with their lives, however troubled. More underestimated than underdeveloped, however, Edward has blazed a difficult path that has brought him both criticism and success. Brits, and his queenly mother, are ambivalent about him for quitting the Royal Marines in 1987, a move that earned him the label "Wimp of Windsor" and that fueled speculation about his sexual preference.

But Edward's independence of mind may make him the most interesting member of the royal family yet. He has become, for instance, the first child of a reigning monarch to—gulp—take a real job, initially as a gofer with Andrew Lloyd Webber's Really Useful Theatre Company. After becoming overseas manager of *Cats* and *Starlight Express*, Edward left Webber's company and now is joint managing director of a television production company, Ardent Productions. His business cards read simply, "Edward Windsor." Loyal to his dreams as well as the British ideal of monarchy, the queen's youngest child is, ran one editorial, "on the way to becoming the first really modern royal."

A ROYAL CALENDAR

A listing of birthdays and other special royal milestones. (Source: *Whitaker's Almanac*)

Prince Andrew	February 19, 1960
Prince Edward	March 10, 1964
Princess Eugenie	March 23, 1990
Queen Elizabeth	April 21, 1926
The Queen's coronation	June 2, 1953
Prince Philip	June 10, 1921
Prince William	June 21, 1982
Princess Diana	July 1, 1961
Queen Mother	August 4, 1900
Princess Beatrice	August 8, 1988
Princess Anne	August 15, 1950
Princess Margaret	August 21, 1930
Prince Henry	September, 15, 1984
Duchess of York (Sarah)	October 15, 1959
Prince Charles	November 14, 1948
The Queen's wedding	November 20, 1947

He also may be on his way to becoming the next married royal. Dating 31-year-old London public relations rep Sophie Rhys-Jones—a Di look-alike who is distantly related to the princess—for over two years now, Edward has been trying to take things slowly. Given the spectacular failure of his three older siblings' marriages, it's hard to blame him for being a bit commitment-shy, but even his Mum may be getting a tad impatient. "The Queen is happy with Sophie," says one Palace insider. "But she wants them to make up their minds. It's beginning to be make or break time." Whether or not a royal alignment lies around the corner, the lovers are finding life together sweet. "Basically," said Rhys-Jones in June, "we are simply two people who are happy enjoying each other's company."

Edward's fascination with the theater is hardly unusual among the Windsors. Indeed if the family reigned in Beverly Hills instead of Westminster, the queen's younger sister, **Princess Margaret**, would be the family's Elizabeth Taylor. She has been onstage since age six, when she had a walk-on part in her father's coronation. With her theatrical props—a tortoise-shell cigarette holder, a tumbler of Famous Grouse whisky, and a circle of intimates in the arts—the Princess has played varied roles: tragic lover, wife, mother, divorcée, and regal grand dame. She emanates star quality, complete with romantic intrigues, erratic public behavior, mysterious health problems, and Sunset Boulevard brass. "I can't imagine anything more wonderful," she once said, "than being who I am."

Precocious and irrepressible as a child, the violet-eyed and theatrical Margaret wrapped George VI around her finger. Other men proved harder to keep. As a teenager she fell hard for a dashing fighter pilot named Peter Townsend, 16 years her senior, but finally passed him up at 22 when her union with the divorced Townsend was declared acceptable only if she gave up her claim to the throne and her royal income and if she would live abroad for five years.

Several years later Margaret walked the aisle with photographer Antony Armstrong-Jones (who became **Lord Snowdon** after the wedding). She produced two children with the artistic commoner: David (**Viscount Linley**) and **Lady Sarah Armstrong-Jones**. But their 18-year marriage was not a picture-book affair. Initially rejecting separation as too scandalous, both partners discreetly sizzled with old and new flames until the tabs ran pictures of Margaret and her lover Roddy Llewellyn, a gardener and wanna-be pop singer 17 years her junior. An uncontested divorce was granted in 1978.

But Margaret's son, David, did his part to show the happy side of royal life—his marriage in 1993 to Serena Stanhope, a blue blood with cover-girl looks, was a windfall for the monarchy, and their lavish nuptials at St. Margaret's Church were billed as the Wedding of the Year, drawing 650 guests.

As dazzling as the lives of the Windsors seem, ultimately being royal carries with it an incalculable personal price tag. Family members live with the nozzles of public fascination open full against them. And it's an irony of their station that even though they live their whole lives in public, they can barely speak their minds there. But the true value of the royal family lies in the realm of moist eyes and lumps in the throat. They have, at least until now, given Britain a symbol of nationhood, something as sumptuous and venerable as a work of art—a source of incalculable pride and pleasure.

SUCCESSION: THE BUCK HOUSE BULLPEN

Under rules codified in the eighteenth century, rightful candidates to the British crown move up inexorably except for two disqualifiers: they cannot be Catholic (or marry into that faith) or be born out of wedlock. Unlike some European monarchies, which abide by the centuries-old Salic law—the exclusion of women from succession—the Court of St. James owes its vitality in great part to females. Victoria and the current queen, for instance, are two of history's longest-reigning sovereigns. This is not to say that Britain's accession rules are not sexist; a monarch is succeeded by his or her eldest son, then by that son's sons in descending order of age, and only then by that son's daughters. The line starts again with the monarch's next youngest son, and so on, ending with the sovereign's daughters and their children. After the offspring are accounted for, the sovereign's brothers come next, followed finally by sisters. From there the line marches through uncles, aunts, and full courts of cousins, including, currently at No. 32, James Lascelles, 41, a onetime deejay in Albuquerque, N.M.

Herewith, the top 25 in the royal bullpen:

1. HRH The Prince of Wales
   (Prince Charles), 46
2. HRH Prince William of Wales, 13
   (son of Prince Charles)
3. HRH Prince Henry of Wales, 11
   (second son of Prince Charles)
4. HRH The Duke of York (Prince Andrew), 35
   (second son of Queen Elizabeth)
5. HRH Princess Beatrice of York, 7
   (daughter of Prince Andrew)
6. HRH Princess Eugenie of York, 5
   (second daughter of Prince Andrew)
7. HRH Prince Edward, 31
   (third son of Queen Elizabeth)
8. HRH The Princess Royal (Princess Anne), 45
   (daughter of Queen Elizabeth—
   for now, the highest ranking divorced royal)
9. Peter Phillips, 19
   (the highest ranking commoner, son of Princess Anne)
10. Zara Phillips, 14
    (daughter of Princess Anne)
11. HRH Princess Margaret, 65
    (sister of Queen Elizabeth)
12. Viscount Linley (David), 33
    (son of Princess Margaret)
13. Lady Sarah Armstrong-Jones, 31
    (daughter of Princess Margaret)
14. HRH The Duke of Gloucester, 51
    (grandson of King George V, Queen Elizabeth's cousin)
15. The Earl of Ulster (Alexander), 21
    (son of the duke of Gloucester)
16. Lady Davina Windsor, 18
    (daughter of the duke of Gloucester)
17. Lady Rose Windsor, 15
    (second daughter of the duke of Gloucester)
18. HRH The Duke of Kent (Edward), 60
    (cousin to both Queen Elizabeth and Prince Philip
    and son of George, duke of Kent, younger brother of
    Kings Edward VII and George VI)
19. Lord Downpatrick, 7
    (son of the duke of Kent's eldest son, the earl of St.
    Andrews, who was dropped from the line when he
    married a Catholic)
20. Lord Nicholas Windsor, 25
    (second son of the duke of Kent)
21. Lady Helen "Melons" Windsor, 31
    (daughter of the duke of Kent)
22. Lord Frederick Windsor, 16
    (son of Prince Michael of Kent, who was dropped
    from the line for marrying a Catholic; Queen Eliza-
    beth's cousin Prince Michael is the younger brother
    of the duke of Kent)
23. Lady Gabriella Windsor, 14
    (daughter of Prince Michael)
24. HRH Princess Alexandra, 59
    (Queen Elizabeth's cousin, granddaughter of King
    George V)
25. James Ogilvy, 31
    (son of Princess Alexandra)

ROYAL HOUSES AROUND THE WORLD

Most of them have little or no actual political power, but hereditary monarchies are clinging to their traditional thrones in several countries. Herewith an international round-up of places where the crown still glitters.

BELGIUM

Current monarch: King Albert II (crowned 1993)

King Albert II, prince of Liège, was born on June 6, 1934. He is the son of King Leopold III and Queen Astrid, princess of Sweden, and the brother of the late King Baudouin of Belgium.

The Royal Family:

King Albert II was married to Paola Ruffo di Calabria, the daughter of a princely Italian family, in 1959. The king and queen have three children: Prince Philippe (b. 1960), Princess Astrid (b. 1962), who is now married to the Archduke Lorenz of East Austria, and Prince Laurent (b. 1963). The royal palace is in Brussels.

DENMARK

Current monarch: Queen Margrethe II (crowned 1972)

Margrethe Alexandrine Thorhildur Ingrid, the eldest daughter of King Frederik IX and Queen Ingrid of Denmark, was born on April 16, 1940.

The Royal Family:

Margarethe married French diplomat Henri-Marie-Jean-André, count de Laborde de Monpezat, in 1967 (he changed his name to Prince Henrik upon marriage). The queen and consort have two sons, Prince Frederik (b. 1968) and Prince Joachim (b. 1969). Crown Prince Frederik, as the official heir to the Danish throne, will eventually become King Frederik X. Besides the official residence in

Copenhagen, the family also has a small mansion in southern France at Cahors, the home district of Prince Henrik.

JAPAN

Current monarch: Emperor Akihito (crowned 1989)

Born on December 23, 1933, Emperor Akihito is the eldest son of the late Emperor Hirohito (posthumously known as Emperor Showa) and Empress Nagako.

The Royal Family:

Emperor Akihito married Michiko Shoda in 1959. She is the eldest daughter of the Shoda family, a prominent name in Japanese industrial and academic circles. The emperor and empress live in the imperial palace in Tokyo, and they have three children: Crown Prince Naruhito (b. 1960; married in 1993 to Crown Princess Masako amid much public attention), Prince Akishino (b. 1965; married in 1990 to Princess Akishino), and Princess Sayako (b. 1969).

LIECHTENSTEIN

Current monarch: Prince Hans Adam II (crowned 1989)

His Serene Highness Prince Hans Adam II is the eldest son of the late Prince Franz Josef II of Liechtenstein and Countess Gina von Wilczek. He was born on February 14, 1945.

The Princial Family:

Hans Adam II married Countess Marie Kinsky von Wchinitz and Tettau of Prague in 1967. The

couple has four children: Crown Prince Alois (b. 1968; married to Duchess Sophie of Bavaria in 1993), Prince Maximilian (b. 1969), Prince Constantin (b. 1972), and Princess Tatjana (b. 1973). The royal family resides in the Vaduz Castle.

LUXEMBOURG

Current monarch: Grand Duke Jean (crowned 1964)

Grand Duke Jean was born on January 5, 1921. He is the eldest son of the late Grand Duchess Charlotte and Prince Felix of Luxembourg, prince of Bourbon Parma. He is the direct descendant of French kings Henri IV, Louis XIII, and Louis XIV.

The Royal Family:

Grand Duke Jean was married to Princess Joséphine-Charlotte of Belgium in 1953. She is the daughter of Prince Leopold of Belgium and Princess Astrid of Sweden, and the sister of the late King Baudouin of Belgium. The royal couple resides in the Castle of Colmar-Berg in Luxembourg, and they have five children: Princess Marie-Astrid (b. 1954), Prince Henri (b. 1955; the hereditary grand duke of Luxembourg), Prince Jean and his twin sister Princess Margaretha (b. 1957), and Prince Guillaume (b. 1963).

MONACO

Current monarch: Prince Rainier III (crowned 1949)

The Sovereign Prince of Monaco and head of the House of Grimaldi, Prince Rainier III, was born on May 31, 1923. He is the grandson of the late Prince Louis II of Monaco and the son of Princess Charlotte and Prince Pierre, count of Polignac.

The Royal Family:

Prince Rainier III married American actress Grace Kelly (1928–1982) in 1956. She was the daughter of John B. and Margaret Kelly of Philadelphia. The couple had three children: Princess Caroline (b. 1957), Crown Prince Albert (b. 1958), and Princess Stephanie (b. 1965; married in 1995 to her French-born former bodyguard Daniel Ducruet, 31). The royal palace is in Monte Carlo, and the family owns a private residence in Paris.

THE NETHERLANDS

Current monarch: Queen Beatrix (crowned 1980)

Beatrix Wilhemina Armgard was born on January 31, 1938, the first child of Queen Juliana and Prince Bernhard of the Netherlands.

The Royal Family:

Queen Beatrix was married to a German diplomat, Claus von Amsberg, in 1966, and the royal couple now resides in the Huis ten Bosch Palace in the Hague. The queen and prince have three sons: Prince Willem-Alexander Claus Georg Ferdinand (b. 1967), Prince Johan Friso Bernhard Christiaan David (b. 1968), and Prince Constantijn Christof Frederik Aschwin (b. 1969).

NORWAY

Current monarch: King Harald (crowned 1991)

Born on February 21, 1937, King Harald is the firstborn son of the late King Olav V and Princess Märtha.

The Royal Family

The announcement that King Harald was to marry commoner Sonja Haraldsen in 1968 triggered much debate about the future of the Norwegian monarchy. Since their marriage, however, Queen Sonja has been accepted by the public. The king and queen, who reside in the royal palace in Oslo, have a daughter, Princess Märtha Louise (b. 1971), and a son, Crown Prince Haakon (b. 1973).

SPAIN

Current monarch: King Juan Carlos (crowned 1975)

Juan Carlos Víctor María de Borbón y Borbón was born on January 5, 1938. He is the first son of Don Juan de Borbón y Battenberg and Doña María de las Mercedes de Borbón y Orléans, and the grandson of King Alfonso XIII and Queen Victoria Eugenia, who was herself the granddaughter of Queen Victoria of England.

The Royal Family:

King Juan Carlos married Princess Sofía, the daughter of King Paul I and Queen Fredericka of Greece, in 1961. The king and queen have three children: Princess Elena (b. 1963), Princess Cristina (b. 1965), and Crown Prince Felipe (b. 1968). Princess Elena, next in line for the throne, married banker Jaime de Marichalar, 31, in March 1995. It was Spain's first royal wedding since 1906. The Palacio de La Zarzuela, their official residence, is situated five kilometers outside of Madrid. The royal family's summer residence, the Palace of Marivent, is in the city of Palma de Mallorca on the island of Mallorca.

SWEDEN

Current monarch: Carl XVI Gustaf (crowned 1973)

Carl XVI Gustaf was born on April 30, 1946, the youngest child and only son of Prince Gustaf Adolf of Sweden and Princess Sibylla of Sachsen-Coburg-Gotha.

The Royal Family

Carl XVI Gustaf married commoner Silvia Renate Sommerlath, daughter of Walther and Alice Sommerlath of the Federal Republic of Germany, in 1976. The king and queen have three children: Princess Victoria (b. 1977), Prince Carl Philip (b. 1979), and Princess Madeleine (b. 1982). In 1980 the Swedish act of succession was changed to allow females the same rights of succession as males; the crown passes to the eldest child regardless of sex. Thus, eldest daughter Victoria has been named the crown princess and successor to Carl XVI Gustaf. The family lived in the royal palace in Stockholm until 1981, when they moved to Drottningholm Palace on the outskirts of the city.

SCREEN

PICKS & PANS 1995

Here's what we at PEOPLE think of the year in film. From classic comebacks like the sultry, French *Belle de Jour* to Disney's colorful *Pocahontas*, we found much to recommend. (Where there's an asterisk, there's a movie we loved.) On the other hand, there were some losers by our lights, like *Billy Madison* and *S.F.W.*, and PEOPLE critics don't mince words.

AMATEUR
Isabelle Huppert, Martin Donovan, Elina Lowensohn, Damian Young
While handsomely filmed and amusing in a deadpan way, *Amateur* never draws you in. (R)

*APOLLO 13
Tom Hanks, Kevin Bacon, Ed Harris, Bill Paxton, Gary Sinise, Kathleen Quinlan
Tense and kinetic, this space adventure is as thrilling as movies get. (PG)

BABE
James Cromwell, Magda Szubanski
This children's fantasy, about a pig raised by border collies on a picturesque farm, is certainly cute, but also kinda weird. (G)

THE BABY-SITTERS CLUB
Schuyler Fisk, Rachel Leigh Cook
America's preadolescent girls deserve better than this drivel based on Ann M. Martin's bestsellers. (PG)

BAD BOYS
Martin Lawrence, Will Smith, Téa Leoni, Theresa Randle
If this buddy action comedy began with 100 points of entertainment value, and we subtracted 10 points for each "Oh, *expletive!*" and 25 points for each car chase or gratuitous explosion, that would leave *Bad Boys* with about minus 250. (R)

BAD COMPANY
Laurence Fishburne, Ellen Barkin, Frank Langella, David Ogden Stiers, Michael Murphy, Gia Carides
This brutal, cynical, often watchable thriller is an exercise in maligning the CIA. (R)

THE BASKETBALL DIARIES
Leonardo DiCaprio, Mark Wahlberg
This adaptation of poet-rocker Jim Carroll's teenage autobiography could use an infusion of authentic adolescent poetry. (R)

*BATMAN FOREVER
Val Kilmer, Tommy Lee Jones, Jim Carrey, Nicole Kidman, Chris O'Donnell
Despite some shortcomings, this second sequel is playful, original, and lots of fun.

BEFORE SUNRISE
Ethan Hawke, Julie Delpy
A tiny comedy about an American traveler and a French graduate student who share one night in Vienna. The endless talking goes nowhere, like the film. (R)

*BEFORE THE RAIN
Katrin Cartlidge, Rade Serbedzija, Gregoire Colin, Labina Mitevska
How Macedonia's persistent conflict between Orthodox Slavs and Muslims affects the lives of its people is the focus in a series of three interconnected and violence-filled stories. (R)

*BELLE DE JOUR
Catherine Deneuve
Time proves to have been very good to this heartless 1967 tale of a well-off, sexually repressed Parisian housewife who passes afternoons working in a brothel. Deneuve's Belle ranks with the great movie performances. (R)

BILLY MADISON
Adam Sandler
This vehicle for *Saturday Night Live*'s Opera Man and Canteen Boy is just too wee and cute, as if Sandler had honed his skills performing for elves. (PG-13)

BOYS ON THE SIDE
Whoopi Goldberg, Mary-Louise Parker, Drew Barrymore
Following the growing friendship between three women, this film is a draggy, mawkish affair. Its big goober of wisdom? Love is someone who'll stand by you when times are tough. (R)

*THE BRADY BUNCH MOVIE
Shelley Long, Gary Cole
The unexpected success of this film version of the '70s family sitcom can be credited to the clever spin it puts on the original's Plasticine awfulness. All the performances send up the smiling opacity that passed for acting in the old series. (PG-13)

BRAVEHEART
Mel Gibson, Patrick McGoohan
An old-fashioned historic romance that aspires to epic breadth but comes across as basically wide in the hips. (R)

*THE BRIDGES OF MADISON COUNTY
Clint Eastwood, Meryl Streep
The movie, thank goodness, is better than the book. What's more surprising is that it's an accomplished piece of filmmaking. (PG-13)

THE BROTHERS MCMULLEN
Edward Burns, Mike McGlone, Jack Mulcahy, Maxine Bahns
As talky and crisis-laden as a soap opera, but appealingly offbeat. (R)

*BURNT BY THE SUN
Nikita Mikhalkov, Nadia Mikhalkov
A comically elegiac look at life under Stalin that is filled with a sense of underlying menace. (R)

BUSHWHACKED
Daniel Stern, Anthony Heald, Ann Dowd, Jon Polito
Nobody should be offended by this ensemble juvenile comedy. Nobody should become indignant at the waste of talent. Nobody should be too entertained either. (PG)

BYE BYE, LOVE
Matthew Modine, Randy Quaid, Paul Reiser
A tedious, almost laugh-free comedy of two days in the lives of three divorced dads. (PG-13)

CAMILLA
Jessica Tandy, Hume Cronyn, Bridget Fonda
Jessica Tandy adds grace and wit to an uninspiring movie about a young musician who embarks on a journey of self-realization when she befriends a former concert violinist. (PG-13)

CASPER
Christina Ricci, Bill Pullman, Eric Idle, Cathy Moriarity, Amy Brenneman
The lame script and less-than-exciting conclusion succeed in restoring Casper to his rightful place—that of a fourth-rate cartoon character right in there with Foghorn Leghorn, Pepe Le Pew, and Gladstone Gander. (PG)

*CIRCLE OF FRIENDS
Chris O'Donnell, Minnie Driver, Geraldine O'Rawe, Saffron Burrows
Charm is given a very good name in this adaptation of Maeve Binchy's winsome coming-of-age novel set in 1950s Ireland. (PG)

*CLUELESS
Alicia Silverstone, Stacey Dash
Though it wants in plot, there's a heaping helping of attitude, up-to-the-second slang, and underlying sweetness. (PG-13)

*CONGO
Ernie Hudson, Laura Linney, Dylan Walsh, Tim Curry
Dynamic, funny, and much less bogged down in technology than most Michael Crichton-derived movies. An unusually disarming action film. (PG-13)

CRIMSON TIDE
Gene Hackman, Denzel Washington, George Dzundza
A visually stunning but aurally dim film that seems to have been blended from parts of *The Hunt for Red October*, *The Caine Mutiny Court-Martial*, *In the Heat of the Night*, and *Run Silent, Run Deep*. (R)

*CRUMB
Documentary
This affectionate, unsettling documentary makes clear that

TOP MOVIES OF 1995

Week by week, here are the movies that have ranked No. 1 at the box office so far in 1995. (Source: *Variety*)

Film	Week (end of)
Dumb and Dumber	January 5
Dumb and Dumber	January 12
Legends of the Fall	January 19
Legends of the Fall	February 2
Legends of the Fall	February 9
The Quick and the Dead	February 16
The Brady Bunch Movie	February 23
The Brady Bunch Movie	March 2
Man of the House	March 9
Outbreak	March 16
Outbreak	March 23
Outbreak	March 30
Tommy Boy	April 6
Bad Boys	April 13
Bad Boys	April 20
While You Were Sleeping	April 27
While You Were Sleeping	May 3
French Kiss	May 11
Crimson Tide	May 18
Die Hard With a Vengeance	May 26
Casper	June 1
Casper	June 8
Congo	June 15
Batman Forever	June 22
Pocahontas	June 29
Apollo 13	July 6
Apollo 13	July 13
Apollo 13	July 20
Apollo 13	July 27
Waterworld	August 3
Waterworld	August 10
Dangerous Minds	August 17
Mortal Kombat	August 24

Robert Crumb, the creator of Fritz the Cat, is driven by dark and eccentric muses.

*THE CURE
Joseph Mazzello, Brad Renfro, Annabella Sciorra, Diana Scarwid
While this is about an 11-year-old boy with AIDS, it is moving, surprisingly unsentimental, and admirably unhysterical. (PG-13)

DANGEROUS MINDS
Michelle Pfeiffer
Liver may be good for you, but that never made it taste any better. The same is true here. (R)

DEATH AND THE MAIDEN
Sigourney Weaver, Ben Kingsley, Stuart Wilson
An airless adaptation of the acclaimed play by Ariel Dorfman about a woman confronted with a man she believes was her torturer 15 years in the past. Less a movie than a polemic. (R)

DEMON KNIGHT
Billy Zane, Jada Pinkett, William Sadler, C.C.H. Pounder, Brenda Bakke
Spun off from the TV series *Tales of the Crypt*, this feature is gorier, more obscene (though less sexy), and more pretentious than the TV show. (R)

DESPERADO
Antonio Banderas
The follow-up to director Robert Rodriguez's low-budget 1993 hit *El Mariachi*, this movie is extremely violent in the by now familiar cartoon manner, with little variation from one action sequence to the next. And please, no more Quentin Tarantino cameos! (R)

DIE HARD WITH A VENGEANCE
Bruce Willis, Samuel L. Jackson
While not as dopey as the first two films in the series, this *Die Hard* is just as violent, obscene, and implausible. (R)

DOLORES CLAIBORNE
Kathy Bates, Jennifer Jason Leigh, Christopher Plummer, David Strathairn
If this movie works at all, it's strictly due to the tough-talking Bates character—she is beaten down but never beaten. (R)

*DON JUAN DEMARCO
Marlon Brando, Johnny Depp, Faye Dunaway
Once you get over the initial shock of just how jumbo Brando's belly has become, you will discover plenty of other diversions worthy of attention in this winningly offbeat comedy. (R)

THE ENGLISHMAN WHO WENT UP A HILL BUT CAME DOWN A MOUNTAIN
Hugh Grant, Tara Fitzgerald, Colm Meaney
There's little substance in this whimsically comic tale of how, in 1917, an entire Welsh village goes to work piling a local hill with enough dirt to call it a mountain. (PG)

EXOTICA
Bruce Greenwood, Mia Kirshner, Elias Koteas
Atom Egoyan's sixth film, set in an upscale strip club, is exasperatingly chilled-out, until a twist near the end floods it with regretful sadness. (R)

*FAR FROM HOME: THE ADVENTURES OF YELLOW DOG
Mimi Rogers, Bruce Davison, Jesse Bradford
A refreshingly straightforward family movie about the courage a 14-year-old boy shows after he and his Yellow Labrador are knocked overboard during a storm and washed ashore on the Canadian Pacific Coast. (PG)

FIRST KNIGHT
Sean Connery, Richard Gere, Julia Ormond, Ben Cross, Sir John Gielgud
This ageless story lends itself to romanticization much more than it does to the literal-minded,

serious treatment it is accorded here. (PG-13)

FLUKE
Matthew Modine, Eric Stoltz, Nancy Travis, Max Pomeranc, Comet the dog
PETA—People for the Ethical Treatment of Actors, that is—ought to come down hard on this convoluted dog movie which condemns Modine, Stoltz, and Travis to silly supporting roles behind Comet the dog. (PG)

FORGET PARIS
Billy Crystal, Debra Winger
Although it includes some snappy lines, this romantic comedy is draggy, repetitious, and unconvincing. (PG-13)

FREE WILLY 2: THE ADVENTURE HOME
Jason James Richter, Francis Capra, Elizabeth Peña, Mary Kate Schellhardt
Prepare for another hour and a half's worth of warm fuzzies—and not much else. (PG)

*FRENCH KISS
Meg Ryan, Kevin Kline
This romantic comedy is like the perfect croissant: light, buttery, and a touch sweet. (PG-13)

FRIDAY
Ice Cube, Anna Maria Horsford, Regina King, Chris Tucker, Nia Long
This is not one of those Fridays to thank God for. The trudging, 'hood comedy has no momentum. It lurches from one punch-up curse-out to another. (R)

FUNNY BONES
Oliver Platt, Jerry Lewis, Lee Evans
Attempting to sketch the connection between British vaudeville and American comedy, this picture wobbles desperately between humor and psychosis. (R)

THE GLASS SHIELD
Michael Boatman, Lori Petty
A character study as police thriller, it lacks originality but gains power as it goes along. (PG-13)

A GOOFY MOVIE
Animated
After 63 years, Goofy gets a full-length feature. Sadly, one cannot say that a star is born. (G)

*A GREAT DAY IN HARLEM
Documentary
Jazz fans are the obvious audience for this engaging little film, but it's so lively, good-natured, and full of unforced affection that others, too, will find it thoroughly enjoyable. (Not rated)

HEAVYWEIGHTS
Tom McGowan, Aaron Schwartz, Ben Stiller, Jerry Stiller
Think of this as *Meatballs* with extra cheese. It's a summer-camp epic in which the chubby kids, instead of being comic relief, are the whole story. (PG)

HIDEAWAY
Jeff Goldblum, Christine Lahti
A man's near-death experience gives him a psychic connection to a mad killer. Even in the most bizarre tales, there must be a seedbed of logic. No such thing here. (R)

HIGHLANDER: THE FINAL DIMENSION
Christopher Lambert
How come Lambert, the film's Scottish hero, speaks with a French accent? Other than this petit problem, there's naught else to dwell on while watching this murky mess. (PG-13)

THE HUNTED
Christopher Lambert, John Lone, Joan Chen, Yoshio Harada
Tired of action movies where everyone gets shot to smithereens? Try this one, where they get sliced and diced with massive Japanese swords. (R)

IMMORTAL BELOVED
Gary Oldman, Isabella Rossellini, Valeria Golino, Johanna Ter Steege
This movie is more enjoyable than it has any right to be. If

nothing else—and its opulent 19th-century costumes and sets aside there isn't much else—you will come out of this bio-cum-mystery about Ludwig van Beethoven humming. (R)

THE INCREDIBLY TRUE ADVENTURE OF 2 GIRLS IN LOVE
Laurel Holloman, Nicole Parker
A fairly predictable but nonchalant comedy. It's a good midsummer movie, light when the air outside is heavy. (R)

IN THE MOUTH OF MADNESS
Sam Neill
Another horrific concoction from director John Carpenter. It gets under the skin, but Neill's understated performance undercuts the scariness. (R)

THE INDIAN IN THE CUPBOARD
Hal Scardino, Litefoot, Rishi Bhat, Lindsay Crouse, Richard Jenkins
This kids' flick plays like a fairly clever, thought-provoking *Twilight Zone* episode stretched beyond its outer limits. (PG)

JEFFERSON IN PARIS
Nick Nolte, Greta Scacchi, Thandie Newton, Simon Callow
Like all Merchant-Ivory films, this stately biographical epic is glacially paced. Yet even after 200 years, Thomas Jefferson maintains his preternatural versatility; he makes a great movie subject. (PG-13)

THE JERKY BOYS—THE MOVIE
Johnny Brennan, Kamal, Alan Arkin
This stupifyingly pea-brained comedy is custom-tailored to the talents (a generous word choice) of its beefy stars, Brennan and Kamal, two New Yorkers who acquired modest fame by making prank phone calls. (R)

JOHNNY MNEMONIC
Keanu Reeves
Directed by multimedia artist Robert Longo, this action-adventure flick is a violent jumble. (R)

JUDGE DREDD
Sylvester Stallone, Armand Assante, Diane Lane, Rob Schneider, Joan Chen
This simpleminded movie has a certain wham!-bam! charm for the first third, but loses all hope from there on out. (R)

JURY DUTY
Pauly Shore, Tia Carrere, Stanley Tucci, Abe Vigoda
The bright side of this insipid courtroom comedy is that it is only 86 minutes long. (PG-13)

*JUST CAUSE
Sean Connery, Laurence Fishburne, Blair Underwood, Kate Capshaw, Ruby Dee, Ed Harris, Christopher Murray, Daniel J. Travanti, Ned Beatty
As eerily perverse and tension-ridden as *Silence of the Lambs*, only better paced and spiced with more twists. (R)

1995'S TOP GROSSERS
This list is by no means final—it was compiled while most of these hits were still playing widely, and more blockbusters are likely to arrive with the year-end holidays—but as of August 17, these were the year's most popular films. (Source: *Variety*)

1. *Batman Forever*
2. *Apollo 13*
3. *Pocahontas*
4. *Die Hard With a Vengeance*
5. *Casper*
6. *Crimson Tide*
7. *While You Were Sleeping*
8. *Congo*
9. *Waterworld*
10. *The Bridges of Madison County*

A KID IN KING ARTHUR'S COURT
Thomas Ian Nicholas, Art Malik
This lame effort owes a nod to Mark Twain. In no way does it improve upon the original. (PG)

KIDS
Leo Fitzpatrick, Chloe Sevigny
How can you be doomed and boring at the same time? This controversial exercise in teen nihilism feels like the work of a grownup having problems with his inner child. (Not rated)

KISS OF DEATH
Nicolas Cage, David Caruso, Helen Hunt, Samuel L. Jackson
Although based on the classic 1947 crime thriller of the same title, this grim and unfocused but absorbing bloody-nose fest shares only the title and its basic premise with the original. (R)

LADYBIRD, LADYBIRD
Crissy Rock, Vladimir Vega
This emotionally crushing movie is based on the true case of a woman who nearly loses custody of her children after she takes up with a physically abusive boyfriend. (Not rated)

THE LAST GOOD TIME
Armin Mueller-Stahl, Olivia d'Abo
The best that can be said about this film is that the acting is good. Other than that, the movie feels tiny tiny tiny, underlit, and emotionally remote. (Not rated)

LITTLE ODESSA
Tim Roth, Edward Furlong, Vanessa Redgrave, Maximilian Schell
This tale of small-time mobsters and hoods in Brooklyn's Brighton Beach is fine to look at, but that's not the same as setting up a story so there's an emotional payoff. (R)

A LITTLE PRINCESS
Liesel Matthews, Liam Cunningham
The movie takes pointless liberties with Frances Hodgson Burnett's story in period, setting, characters, dialogue, plot twists, and theme, in the process obliterating the novel's charm. (G)

*LITTLE WOMEN
Winona Ryder, Susan Sarandon, Trini Alvarado, Samanth Mathis, Kirsten Dunst, Claire Danes, Christian Bale
This fondly faithful adaptation of Louisa May Alcott's classic novel captures the original's inspiring mix of feminism and family values. (PG)

LIVING IN OBLIVION
Steve Buscemi, Catherine Keener, Dermot Mulroney, James Le Gros
A shrewdly funny, if narrowly focused, film about the world of low-budget, independent filmmaking. (R)

LOSING ISAIAH
Jessica Lange, Halle Berry, David Straithairn
This laborious chronicle of a child-custody battle between a black birth mother and a white adoptive mother insists on having things both ways, never managing to find itself in spite of some hefty acting. (R)

LOVE AND HUMAN REMAINS
Thomas Gibson, Ruth Marshall
Often amusing and mildly disturbing, this dark comedy has a hip charm but is bleak at heart. (R)

MAD LOVE
Chris O'Donnell, Drew Barrymore
Buried deep in here is a story about what happens when a young guy realizes that the girl he's in love with is nuts. But what we get is a mess. (PG-13)

THE MADNESS OF KING GEORGE
Nigel Hawthorne, Helen Mirren, Rupert Everett
This tart little drama focuses on the repercussions of one of the king's bouts with chronic mental illness. Despite the warmth and spark of performances, *King George* is both unmoving and uninvolving. (Not rated)

MAJOR PAYNE
Damon Wayans, Karyn Parsons, William Kickey, Michael Ironside, Steven Martini
As heavy-handed and annoying as its title, this military school comedy attempts a kind of backhanded tribute to *The Donna Reed Show*. But why?!? (PG-13)

A MAN OF NO IMPORTANCE
Albert Finney, Brenda Fricker, Tara Fitzgerald, Michael Gambon
Albert Finney gives an utterly breathtaking performance as a bus conductor who recites from the work of his favorite playwright-poet, Oscar Wilde. The movie, however, is not quite up to the charms of the playwright-poet who inspires it. (R)

MAN OF THE HOUSE
Chevy Chase, Farrah Fawcett, Jonathan Taylor Thomas
Once you get past the fact that a bunch of white guys are dressing as Native Americans and giving themselves names like Squatting Dog, this comedy is an inoffensive bit of fluff chronicling the growing bond between a kid and his prospective stepfather. (PG)

THE MANGLER
Robert Englund
There's naught that stands out in *Mangler* other than its gory shots of arms, heads, and bodies being crushed and a dying man hocking bloody sputum directly onto the camera lens. (R)

MARTHA AND ETHEL
Documentary
This sometimes moving if rather stiff and attenuated documentary chronicles the lives and times of two nannies and the post–World War II families who employed them. (G)

MIAMI RHAPSODY
Sarah Jessica Parker, Mia Farrow, Antonio Banderas, Paul Mazursky
This relationship pic desperately wants to say something warm and

witty and wise about the current state of marriage, but manages only to say something about the size of its debt to sources as diverse as *Annie Hall* and *Love, American Style*. (PG-13)

MIGHTY MORPHIN POWER RANGERS: THE MOVIE
Karan Ashley, Johnny Yong Bosch, Steve Cardenas, Jason David Frank, Amy Jo Johnson, David Yost, Paul Freeman
For anyone over age 8, this is an interminable film, with no other purpose but to indoctrinate toddlers in the bash-'em-and-trash-'em basics so that they can one day become connoisseurs of films like *Judge Dredd*. (PG)

MORTAL KOMBAT
Christopher Lambert, Linden Ashby, Talisa Soto, Cary-Hiroyuki Tagawa, Bridgette Wilson
This isn't the worst video game-inspired movie ever. But the main theme seems to be martial artlessness, and most of the sequences appear to have been filmed in cellars. (PG-13)

MURDER IN THE FIRST
Kevin Bacon, Christian Slater, Gary Oldman
Bacon plays a miserable prisoner who kills another inmate after three years in solitary confinement. But his badges of suffering feel like accessories not connected to the inner man. (R)

MURIEL'S WEDDING
Toni Collette, Rachel Griffiths
This story about an ugly duckling praying to become a swan tries to be uplifting. It tries even harder to be charming. It succeeds at being trying. (R)

MY FAMILY/MI FAMILIA
Jimmy Smits, Esai Morales, Edward James Olmos
An ambitious, sprawling, uneven but well-intentioned multigenerational saga about a Mexican-American family. (R)

THE NET
Sandra Bullock, Dennis Miller
This paranoid "technothriller" never generates enough tension to make computers seem any more menacing than a temperamental toaster. (PG-13)

NINE MONTHS
Hugh Grant, Julianne Moore, Robin Williams
A romantic comedy that will appeal to those who like their laughs obvious. (PG-13)

*NOBODY'S FOOL
Paul Newman, Jessica Tandy, Bruce Willis, Melanie Griffith
A sharply observant movie about a depressed and otherwise uninviting hamlet and the roguish shenanigans of its most notorious ne'er-do-well (Newman). Sentimental without being saccharine, moving without being maudlin, and generous toward its small-town characters. (R)

1994'S OVERSEAS MONEYMAKERS

Foreign shores provide a welcome second wind for Hollywood's hits—and misses. For example, while *Schindler's List* and *Four Weddings and a Funeral* were successes in the U.S., these adult-appeal hits were many times more profitable abroad. At the same time, homegrown disappointments like *Beverly Hills Cop III* and *The Specialist* compensated overseas, proving star-powered action travels well, too. (Source: *Variety*)

Rank	Title	Gross (in millions)
1.	*The Lion King*	$358
2.	*Schindler's List*	221
3.	*True Lies*	218
4.	*The Flintstones*	210
5.	*Mrs. Doubtfire*	204
6.	*Four Weddings and a Funeral*	190
7.	*Forrest Gump*	187
8.	*Speed*	162
9.	*Philadelphia*	124
10.	*A Perfect World*	104
11.	*Demolition Man*	101
12.	*The Mask*	98
13.	*The Pelican Brief*	94
14.	*The Specialist*	86
15.	*Cool Runnings*	85
16.	*Maverick*	81
17.	*Naked Gun 33⅓*	80
18.	*Free Willy*	76
19.	*Clear and Present Danger*	73
20.	*Beverly Hills Cop III*	70

*OUTBREAK
Dustin Hoffman, Morgan Freeman, Rene Russo, Donald Sutherland, Cuba Gooding Jr., Kevin Spacey
Though it often strains for effect, *Outbreak*'s strength is its ability to make the audience willingly—and breathlessly—suspend disbelief until the credits crawl. (R)

PANTHER
Kadeem Hardison, Marcus Chong
Historical or not, the chronicle of the Black Panthers is hard to cram into two hours. Ultimately the narrative stress is too great, and *Panther* breaks down. (R)

PARTY GIRL
Parker Posey
The movie is a vehicle for the sullen, self-absorbed Posey, who looks like a very young Katharine Hepburn, but with a backbone as soft as linguine. (R)

THE PEREZ FAMILY
Marisa Tomei, Anjelica Huston
Tomei is an actress who's best when a role provides some edge, some venom, some boldness. This one doesn't. (R)

*POCAHONTAS
Animated
Pocahontas never has a bad hair day. And as good as her hair is, the movie is even better. (G)

*THE POSTMAN (IL POSTINO)
Massimo Triosi, Philippe Noiret
This Italian comedy, set on an island off Naples, features a touching friendship between Chilean poet Pablo Neruda (Noiret) and a postman (Triosi). (PG)

*PRIEST
Linus Roache, Tom Wilkinson
Though this story of a tormented gay priest has sparked controversy, it's a touching tale. (R)

THE QUICK AND THE DEAD
Sharon Stone, Gene Hackman, Lance Henriksen, Russell Crowe, Gary Sinise, Leonardo DiCaprio
It's a tribute to the charisma of Hackman and Stone that this convoluted, pretentious feminist western grabs and holds attention as well as it does. (R)

READY TO WEAR
Julia Roberts, Tim Robbins, Anouk Aimée, Lauren Bacall, Kim Basinger, Sophia Loren, Marcello Mastroianni
This rag-tag send-up of the fashion world lacks pungency and sharp commentary and has none of *The Player*'s satiric bite. (R)

ROB ROY
Liam Neeson, Jessica Lange, Tim Roth, John Hurt, Eric Stoltz, Brian Cox
While this is about an 18th-century Scottish outlaw, the best way to enjoy it is to ignore the silly feudal feuding and royal politics. Think of it as a western. (R)

ROOMMATES
Peter Falk, D. B. Sweeney, Julianne Moore, Ellen Burstyn
By the end of this putative comedy about a geriatric baker's relationship with his orphaned grandson, so many body organs have come into play that the movie no longer has room on its sleeve to wear its heart. (PG)

*SAFE
Julianne Moore
This satire, about a woman with "20th-century disease," is numbingly fascinating. (R)

SAFE PASSAGE
Susan Sarandon, Sam Shepard
In the role of a woman estranged from her husband and fearful for the life of one of her seven sons, Susan Sarandon acts with a conviction that is the only bearable aspect of this aggressively bittersweet picture. (PG-13)

*THE SECRET OF ROAN INISH
Jenny Courtney, Eileen Colgan, Mich Lally, Richard Sheridan, Susan Lynch
This magical film, set on the west coast of Ireland, focuses on a 10-year-old girl who becomes convinced that her younger brother, who as a baby drifted out to sea when the tide carried off his cradle, is still alive. (PG)

S.F.W.
Stephen Dorff
This movie is cruddy, in-your-face ugly, generally substandard—and proud of it. (R)

*SHALLOW GRAVE
Kerry Fox, Christopher Eccleston, Ewan McGregor
This mordant black comedy is too stylish and too clever by half. Even so, it has some devilishly funny moments. (R)

SMOKE
Harvey Keitel, William Hurt, Stockard Channing, Forest Whitaker
The characters link up and interact like a Manhattan Project for lost souls, but the movie just drifts and drifts and drifts. (R)

SOMETHING TO TALK ABOUT
Julia Roberts, Dennis Quaid, Robert Duvall, Gena Rowlands, Kyra Sedgwick
Callie Khouri, writer of *Thelma & Louise*, disappoints with this grimly humorless, philosophically jejune movie. (R)

SPECIES
Natasha Henstridge, Ben Kingsley
As a chase film this unsophisticated sci-fi fails miserably, but horror afficianados will get their money's worth. (R)

STRAWBERRY AND CHOCOLATE
Jorge Perrugoria, Vladimir Cruz, Mirta Ibarra
Set in Cuba, this film works best when it forsakes its political agenda for storytelling. (R)

STUART SAVES HIS FAMILY
Al Franken
Imagine Richard Simmons in a revival of *Days of Wine and Roses*. (PG-13)

THE SUM OF US
Jack Thompson, Russell Crowe
This adaptation of the off-Broadway play about a father's relationship with his gay son is meant to be comic but often comes off as arch. (Not rated)

TALES FROM THE HOOD
Corbin Bernson, Rosalind Cash
This movie relies too heavily on garish effects and the performance of Clarence Williams III. (R)

TALL TALE: THE UNBELIEVABLE ADVENTURES OF PECOS BILL
Scott Glenn, Oliver Platt, Nick Stahl, Stephen Lang, Roger Aaron Brown, Catherine O'Hara, Patrick Swayze
Dang it if Disney's western for kids doesn't seem like *The Wizard of Oz* in chaps, sharing that classic's structure but minus its imagination and charm. (PG)

*TANK GIRL
Lori Petty, Malcolm McDowell, Naomi Watts, Jeff Kober, Ice-T
You would have to go back to the Batman TV series to find a comic-book-to-screen transposition that is this much no-pretense, flat-out fun. (R)

TOM & VIV
Willem Dafoe, Miranda Richardson
There is an essential flaw to this film about T. S. Eliot's wretched marriage to Vivienne Haigh-Wood: Tom is the more interesting character, but Viv gets most of the screen time. (PG-13)

TOMMY BOY
Chris Farley, David Spade, Bo Derek, Brian Dennehy, Julie Warner, Rob Lowe
Spade and Farley fare no better—and no worse, which isn't saying much—than most of their *Saturday Night Live*-to-celluloid predecessors. (PG-13)

TOP DOG
Chuck Norris, Reno the dog
This is an innocuously entertaining Norris action film, with a standard ration of punch-ups and a relatively tasteful, if uninspired, script. (PG-13)

*THE UNDERNEATH
Peter Gallagher, Alison Elliott
Disorienting camera angles and a silvery, aquarium-blue hue push this film toward self-indulgence, but make it a joy to watch. (R)

A WALK IN THE CLOUDS
Keanu Reeves, Aitana Sanchez-Gijon, Anthony Quinn, Giancarlo Giannini
This far-fetched romantic story by the Mexican director of *Like Water for Chocolate* never achieves the lightfootedness its title promises. (PG-13)

THE WALKING DEAD
Allen Payne, Eddie Griffin, Joe Morton, Roger Floyd
Billed as defining the "black experience in Vietnam," this film is so convoluted it makes the real war seem a model of clarity and common sense. (R)

WATERWORLD
Kevin Costner, Jeanne Tripplehorn, Dennis Hopper
The simple fact is that widescreen H_2O is terribly monotonous to look at. (PG-13)

*WHILE YOU WERE SLEEPING
Sandra Bullock, Bill Pullman, Peter Gallagher
A pleasant but wispy romantic comedy featuring a lonely heroine who is mistaken for the fiancée of a man in a coma by his family. (PG)

WIGSTOCK: THE MOVIE
Documentary
A little of this goes a long way and, even at just 86 minutes, *Wigstock* seems, pardon the expression, padded. (Not rated)

THE WILD BUNCH
William Holden, Robert Ryan
Now fully restored, Sam Peckinpah's rugged, profoundly pessimistic epic about the final days of a band of robbers remains both the apotheosis and annihilator of the western. (R)

THE TOP 100 FILMS OF ALL TIME

The following lists the largest money-making movies of all time based on domestic (U.S. and Canada) box-office grosses. Figures are accurate through August 24, 1995; summer blockbusters (such as *Batman Forever* and *Apollo 13*) are still earning. (Source: *Variety*)

Rank	Film (year of release)	B.O. Gross	Rank	Film (year of release)	B.O. Gross
1.	E.T., the Extra-Terrestrial (1982)	$399,804,539	51.	101 Dalmatians (1961)	143,992,148
2.	Jurassic Park (1993)	357,100,000	52.	The Jungle Book (1967)	142,000,000
3.	Forrest Gump (1994)	329,650,110	53.	National Lampoon's Animal House (1978)	141,600,000
4.	Star Wars (1977)	322,000,000	54.	A Few Good Men (1992)	141,340,178
5.	The Lion King (1994)	312,775,367	55.	Look Who's Talking (1989)	140,088,813
6.	Home Alone (1990)	285,761,243	56.	Sister Act (1992)	139,605,150
7.	Return of the Jedi (1983)	263,700,000	57.	Platoon (1986)	137,963,328
8.	Jaws (1975)	260,000,000	58.	Teenage Mutant Ninja Turtles (1990)	135,265,915
9.	Batman (1989)	251,188,924	59.	Pocahontas (1995)	135,096,948
10.	Raiders of the Lost Ark (1981)	242,374,454	60.	Superman (1978)	134,218,018
11.	Ghostbusters (1984)	238,600,000	61.	The Rocky Horror Picture Show (1975)	134,200,000
12.	Beverly Hills Cop (1984)	234,760,478	62.	The Godfather (1972)	133,698,921
13.	The Empire Strikes Back (1980)	222,700,000	63.	The Silence of the Lambs (1991)	130,726,716
14.	Mrs. Doubtfire (1993)	219,131,586	64.	Honey, I Shrunk the Kids (1989)	130,724,172
15.	Ghost (1990)	217,631,306	65.	The Flintstones (1994)	130,522,921
16.	Aladdin (1992)	217,350,219	66.	An Officer and a Gentleman (1982)	129,795,549
17.	Back to the Future (1985)	208,242,016	67.	Close Encounters of the Third Kind (1977)	128,290,347
18.	Terminator 2: Judgment Day (1991)	204,843,345	68.	Coming to America (1988)	128,152,301
19.	Indiana Jones and the Last Crusade (1989)	197,171,806	69.	Rocky IV (1985)	127,873,414
20.	Gone with the Wind (1939)	191,749,436	70.	Dumb and Dumber (1994)	127,158,115
21.	Dances with Wolves (1990)	184,208,848	71.	Smokey and the Bandit (1977)	126,737,428
22.	The Fugitive (1993)	183,875,760	72.	Sleepless in Seattle (1993)	126,700,000
23.	Indiana Jones and the Temple of Doom (1984)	179,870,271	73.	City Slickers (1991)	124,000,000
24.	Pretty Woman (1990)	178,406,268	74.	Good Morning Vietnam (1987)	123,922,370
25.	Batman Forever (1995)	178,386,979	75.	Rocky III (1982)	122,823,192
26.	Tootsie (1982)	177,200,000	76.	Clear and Present Danger (1994)	121,957,859
27.	Top Gun (1986)	176,781,728	77.	The Bodyguard (1992)	121,823,192
28.	Snow White and the Seven Dwarfs (1937)	175,263,233	78.	Wayne's World (1992)	121,697,323
29.	"Crocodile" Dundee (1986)	174,634,806	79.	Speed (1994)	121,248,145
30.	Rain Man (1988)	172,825,435	80.	The Hunt for Red October (1990)	120,709,868
31.	Home Alone 2: Lost in New York (1992)	172,704,311	81.	The Mask (1994)	119,913,630
32.	Three Men and a Baby (1987)	167,780,960	82.	Hook (1991)	119,654,823
33.	Robin Hood: Prince of Thieves (1991)	165,493,908	83.	Blazing Saddles (1974)	119,500,000
34.	The Exorcist (1973)	165,000,000	84.	Total Recall (1990)	119,394,839
35.	Batman Returns (1992)	162,831,698	85.	On Golden Pond (1981)	118,710,777
36.	The Sound of Music (1965)	160,476,331	86.	Back to the Future Part II (1989)	118,450,002
37.	The Firm (1993)	158,340,292	87.	Basic Instinct (1992)	117,727,224
38.	Fatal Attraction (1987)	156,645,693	88.	Die Hard 2 (1990)	117,500,000
39.	The Sting (1973)	156,000,000	89.	Rocky (1976)	117,235,247
40.	Apollo 13 (1995)	155,311,315	90.	The Towering Inferno (1974)	116,000,000
41.	Who Framed Roger Rabbit (1988)	154,112,492	91.	The Karate Kid Part II (1986)	115,103,979
42.	Beverly Hills Cop II (1987)	153,665,036	92.	American Graffiti (1973)	115,000,000
43.	Grease (1978)	153,112,492	93.	Big (1988)	114,968,774
44.	Rambo: First Blood Part II (1985)	150,415,432	94.	The Addams Family (1991)	113,502,246
45.	Gremlins (1984)	148,168,459	95.	Ghostbusters II (1984)	112,494,738
46.	Lethal Weapon 2 (1989)	147,253,986	96.	One Flew over the Cuckoo's Nest (1975)	112,000,000
47.	True Lies (1994)	146,260,993	97.	Twins (1988)	111,936,388
48.	Beauty and the Beast (1991)	145,863,363	98.	Doctor Zhivago (1965)	111,721,913
49.	The Santa Clause (1994)	144,800,000	99.	Star Trek IV: The Voyage Home (1986)	109,713,132
50.	Lethal Weapon 3 (1992)	144,731,527	100.	"Crocodile" Dundee II (1988)	109,306,210

THE TOP 100 FILMS OF 1994

These are the movies that captured our hearts—and wallets—last year. Films are ranked according to their North American box-office grosses. (Starred films were released in 1993 but earned much of their income in 1994; grosses include 1994 only.) (Source: *Variety*)

Rank	Film	B.O. Gross	Rank	Film	B.O. Gross
1.	The Lion King	$298,879,911	51.	Shadowlands*	25,768,608
2.	Forrest Gump	298,096,620	52.	My Father, the Hero	25,479,558
3.	True Lies	146,260,993	53.	Wyatt Earp	25,052,500
4.	The Santa Clause	134,560,221	54.	In the Name of the Father*	25,010,410
5.	The Flintstones	130,522,921	55.	The Piano*	24,676,885
6.	Clear and Present Danger	121,715,132	56.	Renaissance Man	24,332,324
7.	Speed	121,248,145	57.	Blue Chips	22,354,402
8.	The Mask	118,644,781	58.	Mary Shelley's Frankenstein	22,024,639
9.	Mrs. Doubtfire*	107,430,221	59.	Quiz Show	21,840,003
10.	Maverick	101,631,272	60.	Sister Act 2*	21,680,052
11.	Interview with the Vampire*	100,006,085	61.	Drop Zone	21,274,027
12.	The Client	92,115,211	62.	The Air Up There	21,011,318
13.	Schindler's List*	91,077,929	63.	Iron Will	21,006,361
14.	Philadelphia	76,878,958	64.	Reality Bites	20,982,557
15.	Ace Ventura: Pet Detective	72,217,396	65.	Intersection	20,928,892
16.	Star Trek Generations	70,432,156	66.	Jason's Lyric	20,452,161
17.	Stargate	68,228,515	67.	The Cowboy Way	20,279,854
18.	Wolf	65,011,757	68.	Corrina, Corrina	20,164,171
19.	Pulp Fiction	62,391,023	69.	With Honors	20,043,254
20.	Dumb and Dumber	59,072,700	70.	Only You	20,042,048
21.	Grumpy Old Men*	57,962,756	71.	Color of Night	19,721,814
22.	The Specialist	55,834,548	72.	8 Seconds	19,623,396
23.	Four Weddings and a Funeral	52,700,832	73.	Little Giants	19,288,821
24.	The Little Rascals	51,932,954	74.	House Party 3	19,281,235
25.	Naked Gun 33⅓	51,109,400	75.	Richie Rich	19,175,387
26.	The Crow	50,693,162	76.	Getting Even With Dad	18,438,164
27.	Angels in the Outfield	50,236,831	77.	Sugar Hill	18,272,447
28.	Natural Born Killers	50,177,396	78.	Love Affair	18,250,211
29.	When a Man Loves a Woman	50,021,959	79.	The Professional	18,007,189
30.	The Pelican Brief*	48,782,677	80.	Jurassic Park*	17,854,274
31.	Disclosure	46,250,464	81.	Milk Money	17,837,658
32.	D2: The Mighty Ducks	45,640,410	82.	Street Fighter	17,662,440
33.	The River Wild	45,167,745	83.	Wes Craven's New Nightmare	17,412,282
34.	Timecop	44,454,024	84.	My Girl 2	17,359,799
35.	City Slickers II: The Legend of Curly's Gold	43,622,150	85.	The Jungle Book	17,345,474
36.	Beverly Hills Cop III	42,610,021	86.	Miracle on 34th Street	16,867,213
37.	Tombstone*	39,648,712	87.	Baby's Day Out	16,827,402
38.	The Paper	38,824,341	88.	Lightning Jack	16,821,273
39.	On Deadly Ground	38,590,458	89.	Andre	16,819,465
40.	It Could Happen to You	37,939,757	90.	Blink	16,696,219
41.	The Shadow	32,060,771	91.	The War	16,551,365
42.	I Love Trouble	30,806,194	92.	Terminal Velocity	16,478,879
43.	Major League II	30,626,182	93.	Monkey Trouble	16,453,258
44.	Blank Check	30,577,969	94.	The Shawshank Redemption	16,424,889
45.	Blown Away	30,155,037	95.	Above the Rim	16,192,320
46.	Junior	30,204,485	96.	The Getaway	16,096,272
47.	In the Army Now	28,864,707	97.	Little Women	15,999,996
48.	Guarding Tess	27,058,304	98.	No Escape	15,339,030
49.	A Low Down Dirty Shame	26,524,388	99.	Bad Girls	15,240,435
50.	Beethoven's 2nd*	26,338,216	100.	Threesome	14,815,317

THE TOP 50 FOREIGN-LANGUAGE FILMS

Last year produced only one foreign hit, Ang Lee's *Eat Drink Man Woman*, which proved even more popular than his *The Wedding Banquet*, set in America. Similarly, 1995 has contributed only *Il Postino (The Postman)* to the hit list. (Source: *Variety*)

Rank	Film (year of U.S. release, director, country of origin)	Rank	Film (year of U.S. release, director, country of origin)
1.	*Like Water for Chocolate* (1993, Arau, Mexico)	26.	*Swept Away* (1975, Wertmüller, Italy)
2.	*I Am Curious (Yellow)* (1969, Sjoman, Sweden)	27.	*La Cage aux folles II* (1981, Molinaro, France)
3.	*La Dolce Vita* (1960, Fellini, Italy)	28.	*Belle Epoque* (1993, Trueba, Spain)
4.	*La Cage aux folles* (1979, Molinaro, France/Italy)	29.	*Il Postino (The Postman)* (1995, Radford, Italy)
5.	*Z* (1969, Costa-Gavras, France)	30.	*Cyrano de Bergerac* (1990, Rappeneau, France)
6.	*A Man and a Woman* (1966, Lelouch, France)	31.	*Indochine* (1992, Wargnier, France)
7.	*Cinema Paradiso* (1990, Tornatore, Italy/France)	32.	*Europa, Europa* (1991, Holland, France/Germany)
8.	*Emmanuelle* (1975, Jaeckin, France)	33.	*Jean de Florette* (1987, Berri, France)
9.	*Das Boot* (1982, Peterson, Germany)	34.	*King of Hearts* (1967, de Broca, France/England)
10.	*Story of O* (1975, Jaeckin, France)	35.	*Au revoir, les enfants* (1988, Malle, France)
11.	*8½* (1963, Fellini, Italy)	36.	*Madame Rosa* (1978, Mizrahi, France)
12.	*Yesterday, Today and Tomorrow* (1964, de Sica, Italy)	37.	*Babette's Feast* (1988, Axel, Denmark)
13.	*Marriage Italian Style* (1964, de Sica, Italy)	38.	*Farewell My Concubine* (1993, Chen, Hong Kong)
14.	*Elvira Madigan* (1967, Widerberg, Sweden)	39.	*The Garden of the Finzi-Continis* (1971, de Sica, Italy)
15.	*Dear John* (1964, Lindgren, Sweden)	40.	*Manon of the Spring* (1987, Berri, France)
16.	*Cousin, Cousine* (1976, Tacchella, France)	41.	*La Femme Nikita* (1990, Besson, France/Italy)
17.	*My Life as a Dog* (1987, Hallström, Sweden)	42.	*Seven Beauties* (1976, Wertmüller, Italy)
18.	*Fanny and Alexander* (1983, Bergman, Sweden)	43.	*Bread and Chocolate* (1978, Brusati, Italy)
19.	*Women on the Verge of a Nervous Breakdown* (1988, Almodóvar, Spain)	44.	*Amarcord* (1974, Fellini, Italy)
20.	*Eat Drink Man Woman* (1994, Lee, Taiwan)	45.	*Mediterraneo* (1991, Salvatores, Italy)
21.	*Ran* (1985, Kurosawa, Japan)	46.	*The Emigrants* (1972, Troell, Sweden)
22.	*Two Women* (1961, de Sica, Italy)	47.	*Get Out Your Handkerchiefs* (1979, Blier, France)
23.	*Without a Stitch* (1970, Meineche, Denmark)	48.	*Entre nous* (1983, Kurys, France)
24.	*The Wedding Banquet* (1993, Lee, Taiwan)	49.	*Tie Me Up, Tie Me Down* (1990, Almodóvar, Spain)
25.	*Diva* (1982, Beineix, France)	50.	*The Return of Martin Guerre* (1982, Vigne, France)

ALL-TIME INTERNATIONAL BOX-OFFICE CHAMPS

At home *E.T.* is still the king of the hits, but once you factor in international revenues, *Jurassic Park* rules. These are the biggest films worldwide, and the results are surprisingly different from the list of North American favorites. (Source: *Variety*)

Rank	Film, Year of Release	B.O. Gross (millions)	Rank	Film, Year of Release	B.O. Gross (millions)
1.	*Jurassic Park*, 1993	$913.1	11.	*Jaws*, 1975	458.0
2.	*The Lion King*, 1994	772.3	12.	*Pretty Woman*, 1990	454.4
3.	*E.T., the Extra-Terrestrial*, 1982	701.1	13.	*Mrs. Doubtfire*, 1993	423.1
4.	*Forrest Gump*, 1994	673.7	14.	*Batman*, 1989	411.2
5.	*Ghost*, 1990	517.6	15.	*The Bodyguard*, 1992	407.6
6.	*Star Wars*, 1977	513.0	16.	*Rain Man*, 1988	405.8
7.	*Indiana Jones and the Last Crusade*, 1989	494.8	17.	*The Empire Strikes Back*, 1980	405.0
8.	*Aladdin*, 1992	497.0	18.	*Dances With Wolves*, 1990	394.2
9.	*Terminator 2: Judgment Day*, 1991	490.0	19.	*Robin Hood: Prince of Thieves*, 1991	390.5
10.	*Home Alone*, 1990	474.7	20.	*The Jungle Book*, 1967	384.0

THE TOP INDEPENDENT FILMS

Made outside the realm of the largest movie companies, independent films tradition-
ally feature trimmer budgets, untapped talent, or an idiosyncratic vision. Yet these
upstarts sometimes find their audiences. From art-house hits to drive-in classics,
here are the "little" films that scored big. (Source: *Variety*)

Rank	Film (year of release)	B.O. Gross	Rank	Film (year of release)	B.O. Gross
1.	Teenage Mutant Ninja Turtles (1990)	$135,265,915	51.	Caligula (1980)	23,438,119
2.	Dumb and Dumber (1994)*	127,158,115	52.	Circle of Friends (1995)	23,389,975
3.	The Mask (1994)*	119,913,630	53.	The Care Bears Movie (1985)	22,934,622
4.	Pulp Fiction (1994)*	107,864,762	54.	Crimes of the Heart (1986)	22,905,522
5.	The Graduate (1968)	104,397,102	55.	Missing in Action (1984)	22,812,411
6.	The Amityville Horror (1979)	86,432,519	56.	My Tutor (1983)	22,587,834
7.	Teenage Mutant Ninja Turtles II (1991)	78,656,813	57.	Much Ado About Nothing (1993)	22,550,957
8.	The Muppet Movie (1979)	76,341,718	58.	In Search of Historic Jesus (1980)	22,438,771
9.	Dirty Dancing (1987)	63,446,382	59.	A Nightmare on Elm Street 5 (1989)	22,168,359
10.	The Crying Game (1992)	62,548,947	60.	The Bermuda Triangle (1978)	22,167,397
11.	In Search of Noah's Ark (1977)	55,734,818	61.	Don Juan DeMarco (1995)*	22,032,635
12.	Papillon (1973)	53,267,431	62.	The Player (1992)	21,706,101
13.	Four Weddings and a Funeral (1994)	52,700,832	63.	Like Water for Chocolate (1993)	21,665,468
14.	The Crow (1993)*	50,693,162	64.	The Fog (1980)	21,378,361
15.	A Nightmare on Elm Street 4 (1988)	49,369,899	65.	Weekend Pass (1984)	21,058,033
16.	Halloween (1978)	47,000,000	66.	A Room with a View (1986)	20,966,644
17.	Grizzly Adams (1975)	46,394,177	67.	The Groove Tube (1974)	20,447,386
18.	A Nightmare on Elm Street 3 (1987)	44,793,222	68.	Action Jackson (1988)	20,256,955
19.	Love at First Bite (1979)	43,884,929	69.	I Am Curious (Yellow) (1969)	20,238,100
20.	Cabaret (1972)	42,764,873	70.	A Force of One (1979)	20,166,378
21.	Time Bandits (1981)	42,365,581	71.	Corrina, Corrina (1994)*	20,160,280
22.	Teenage Mutant Ninja Turtles III (1993)	42,273,609	72.	8 Seconds (1994)*	19,603,103
23.	The Piano (1993)*	40,157,856	73.	La Dolce Vita (1960)	19,516,348
24.	Benji (1974)	39,522,601	74.	House (1986)	19,444,631
25.	The Sword and the Sorcerer (1982)	39,103,425	75.	House Party 2 (1991)	19,438,638
26.	Freddy's Dead: The Final Nightmare (1991)	34,972,033	76.	The Lion in Winter (1968)	19,328,972
27.	Teen Wolf (1985)	33,086,611	77.	House Party 3 (1994)	19,281,235
28.	Mortal Kombat (1995)*	32,753,183	78.	Willard (1971)	19,216,447
29.	The Lawnmower Man (1992)	32,100,816	79.	Joe (1970)	19,184,332
30.	Dressed to Kill (1980)	31,898,776	80.	The Octagon (1980)	18,971,384
31.	Adventures of the Wilderness Family (1976)	31,223,187	81.	Across the Great Divide (1977)	18,806,332
32.	The Texas Chainsaw Massacre (1974)	30,859,623	82.	Macon County Line (1974)	18,765,338
33.	A Nightmare on Elm Street, Part 2 (1985)	29,999,213	83.	Windwalker (1980)	18,636,482
34.	Carnal Knowledge (1971)	28,623,684	84.	Good Guys Wear Black (1978)	18,327,664
35.	National Lampoon's Loaded Weapon (1993)	27,979,399	85.	Posse (1993)	18,289,763
36.	Menace II Society (1993)	27,899,866	86.	The Sure Thing (1985)	18,135,531
37.	Soul Man (1986)	27,820,000	87.	Wes Craven's New Nightmare (1994)*	18,078,206
38.	Friday (1995)*	27,184,130	88.	The Private Eyes (1980)	18,014,386
39.	The Jazz Singer (1980)	27,118,436	89.	The Howling (1981)	17,985,893
40.	El Cid (1961)	26,620,818	90.	The Pom Pom Girls (1976)	17,883,410
41.	House Party (1990)	26,385,627	91.	Halloween 4 (1988)	17,768,757
42.	Private Lessons (1981)	26,278,365	92.	For the Love of Benji (1977)	17,731,884
43.	Howards End (1992)*	25,966,555	93.	The Betsy (1978)	17,685,173
44.	Chariots of the Gods (1973)	25,948,371	94.	Take This Job and Shove It (1981)	17,569,029
45.	Shadowlands (1993)	25,842,377			
46.	A Nightmare on Elm Street (1984)	25,504,513			
47.	Escape from New York (1981)	25,244,626			
48.	sex, lies and videotape (1989)	24,741,667			
49.	The Emerald Forest (1985)	24,468,550			
50.	Beyond and Back (1978)	23,784,396			

Note: As the specialty-film scene has expanded, some indie
production mainstays have linked up with major Hollywood
houses. Movies from these "studio-affiliated indies" are
noted by an asterisk.

Figures as of August 24, 1995.

THE TOP DOCUMENTARY FILMS

The media furor over documentary Oscars may make you think the format's popularity is growing. Not exactly. *Hoop Dreams* was the most-seen "straight" documentary in years, but its gross doesn't approach that of several recent concert films. And most of those can't top the Cinerama spectacles and tabloid-like exposés from days gone by. IMAX films—more commonly found at museums or amusement parks than in cinemas—are also (in all senses) big winners. (Source: *Variety*)

Rank	Film (year of release)	B.O. Gross	Rank	Film (year of release)	B.O. Gross
1.	To Fly (1976)	$82,500,000	15.	Blue Planet (1990)	22,800,000
2.	In Search of Noah's Ark (1977)	55,700,000	16.	In Search of Historic Jesus (1980)	22,400,000
3.	The Dream Is Alive (1985)	55,200,000	17.	The Bermuda Triangle (1978)	22,200,000
4.	Grand Canyon: The Hidden Secrets (1984)	52,800,000	18.	The Late Great Planet Earth (1977)	19,500,000
5.	Raw (1987)	50,500,000	19.	The Vanishing Wilderness (1973)	17,000,000
6.	This Is Cinerama (1952)	41,600,000	20.	Richard Pryor Here and Now (1983)	16,200,000
7.	Richard Pryor Live on the Sunset Strip (1982)	36,300,000	21.	Richard Pryor Live In Concert (1979)	15,800,000
8.	Woodstock (1970)	34,800,000	22.	Truth or Dare (1991)	15,000,000
9.	Seven Wonders of the World (1956)	32,100,000	23.	You So Crazy (1994)	10,200,000
10.	Cinerama Holiday (1955)	29,600,000	24.	Endless Summer (1966)	9,400,000
11.	Beavers (1988)	26,400,000	25.	Dirt (1979)	9,200,000
12.	Chariots of the Gods (1973)	25,900,000	26.	U2: Rattle and Hum (1988)	8,600,000
13.	Beyond and Back (1978)	23,800,000	27.	Hoop Dreams (1994)	6,800,000
14.	To the Limit (1989)	23,500,000	28.	Roger & Me (1989)	6,700,000

OLD MONEY WALLOPS THE NOUVEAU RICHE

The top-grossing domestic movies of all time are nearly all recently released films, thanks to ever-increasing ticket prices. But what if the playing field is leveled? Exhibitor Relations has compiled the following inflation-adjusted list of the highest-grossing films of all time. Figures are as of July, 1995.

Rank	Title	Opening Date	Adjusted Gross
1.	Gone with the Wind	1939	$827,745,000
2.	Star Wars	1977	602,125,561
3.	The Ten Commandments	1958	546,270,000
4.	The Sound of Music	1965	535,349,040
5.	Jaws	1975	534,088,670
6.	E.T., the Extra-Terrestrial	1982	529,265,056
7.	Doctor Zhivago	1965	517,644,850
8.	The Jungle Book	1967	463,059,892
9.	Snow White	1937	454,530,000
10.	101 Dalmations	1961	414,101,557
11.	Ben-Hur	1959	408,660,000
12.	The Exorcist	1973	393,171,429
13.	The Sting	1973	371,725,714
14.	Jurassic Park	1993	359,655,396
15.	The Graduate	1967	356,832,711
16.	Return of the Jedi	1983	349,134,431
17.	Fantasia	1940	346,291,304
18.	The Empire Strikes Back	1980	345,691,450
19.	Forrest Gump	1994	332,080,039
20.	The Godfather	1972	327,955,589

THE BIGGEST HITS, YEAR-BY-YEAR

The following are the top five movies of the year based on data from *Variety*, beginning with 1939, when a Hollywood legend, *Gone with the Wind*, hit the theaters. Dollar figures listed are rentals (the amount of money collected by the studio), rather than box-office grosses, a relatively new method of measuring a film's box-office strength. (Figures for 1941 films, with the exception of *Sergeant York*, are rough estimates.)

1939

1. *Gone with the Wind*	$77,641,106
2. *The Wizard of Oz*	4,544,851
3. *The Hunchback of Notre Dame* (tie)	1,500,000
3. *Jesse James* (tie)	1,500,000
3. *Mr. Smith Goes to Washington* (tie)	1,500,000

1940

1. *Fantasia*	$41,660,000
2. *Pinocchio*	40,442,000
3. *Boom Town*	4,586,415
4. *Rebecca* (tie)	1,500,000
4. *Santa Fe Trail* (tie)	1,500,000

1941

1. *Sergeant York*	$6,135,707
2. *Dive Bomber* (tie)	1,500,000
2. *Honky Tonk* (tie)	1,500,000
2. *The Philadelphia Story* (tie)	1,500,000
2. *A Yank in the R.A.F.* (tie)	1,500,000

1942

1. *Bambi*	$47,265,000
2. *Mrs. Miniver*	5,390,009
3. *Yankee Doodle Dandy*	4,719,681
4. *Random Harvest*	4,665,501
5. *Casablanca*	4,145,178

1943

1. *This Is the Army*	$8,301,000
2. *For Whom the Bell Tolls*	7,100,000
3. *The Outlaw*	5,075,000
4. *The Song of Bernadette*	5,000,000
5. *Stage Door Canteen*	4,339,532

1944

1. *Going My Way*	$6,500.000
2. *Meet Me in St. Louis*	5,132,202
3. *Since You Went Away*	4,924,756
4. *30 Seconds over Tokyo*	4,471,080
5. *White Cliffs of Dover*	4,045,250

1945

1. *The Bells of St. Mary's*	$8,000,000
2. *Leave Her to Heaven*	5,500,000
3. *Spellbound*	4,970,583
4. *Anchors Aweigh*	4,778,679
5. *The Valley of Decision*	4,566,374

1946

1. *Song of the South*	$29,228,717
2. *The Best Years of Our Lives* (tie)	11,300,000
2. *Duel in the Sun* (tie)	11,300,000
4. *The Jolson Story*	7,600,000
5. *Blue Skies*	5,700,000

1947

1. *Welcome Stranger*	$6,100,000
2. *The Egg and I*	5,500,000
3. *Unconquered*	5,250,000
4. *Life with Father*	5,057,000
5. *Forever Amber*	5,000,000

1948

1. *The Red Shoes*	$5,000,000
2. *Red River*	4,506,825
3. *The Paleface*	4,500,000
4. *The Three Musketeers*	4,306,876
5. *Johnny Belinda*	4,266,000

1949

1. *Samson and Delilah*	$11,500,000
2. *Battleground*	5,051,143
3. *Jolson Sings Again* (tie)	5,000,000
3. *The Sands of Iwo Jima* (tie)	5,000,000
5. *I Was a Male War Bride*	4,100,000

1950

1. *Cinderella*	$41,087,000
2. *King Solomon's Mines*	5,586,000
3. *Annie Get Your Gun*	4,919,394
4. *Cheaper by the Dozen*	4,425,000
5. *Father of the Bride*	4,054,405

1951

1. *Quo Vadis?*	$11,901,662
2. *Alice in Wonderland*	7,196,000
3. *Show Boat*	5,533,000
4. *David and Bathsheba*	4,720,000
5. *The Great Caruso*	4,531,000

1952

1. *This Is Cinerama*	$15,400,000
2. *The Greatest Show on Earth*	14,000,000
3. *The Snows of Kilimanjaro*	6,500,000
4. *Ivanhoe*	6,258,000
5. *Hans Christian Andersen*	6,000,000

1953

1. Peter Pan	$37,584,000
2. The Robe	17,500,000
3. From Here to Eternity	12,200,000
4. Shane	9,000,000
5. How To Marry a Millionaire	7,300,000

1954

1. White Christmas	$12,000,000
2. 20,000 Leagues Under the Sea	11,267,000
3. Rear Window	9,812,271
4. The Caine Mutiny	8,700,000
5. The Glenn Miller Story	7,590,994

1955

1. Lady and the Tramp	$40,249,000
2. Cinerama Holiday	12,000,000
3. Mister Roberts	8,500,000
4. Battle Cry	8,100,000
5. Oklahoma!	7,100,000

1956

1. The Ten Commandments	$43,000,000
2. Around the World in 80 Days	23,120,000
3. Giant	14,000,000
4. Seven Wonders of the World	12,500,000
5. The King and I	8,500,000

1957

1. The Bridge on the River Kwai	$17,195,000
2. Peyton Place	11,500,000
3. Sayonara	10,500,000
4. Old Yeller	10,050,000
5. Raintree County	5,962,839

1958

1. South Pacific	$17,500,000
2. Auntie Mame	9,300,000
3. Cat on a Hot Tin Roof	8,785,162
4. No Time for Sergeants	7,500,000
5. Gigi	7,321.423

1959

1. Ben-Hur	$36,992,088
2. Sleeping Beauty	21,998,000
3. The Shaggy Dog	12,317,000
4. Operation Petticoat	9,321,555
5. Darby O'Gill and the Little People	8,336,000

1960

1. Swiss Family Robinson	$20,178,000
2. Psycho	11,200,000
3. Spartacus	10,300,454
4. Exodus	8,331,582
5. The Alamo	7,918,776

1961

1. 101 Dalmatians	$68,648,000
2. West Side Story	19,645,570
3. The Guns of Navarone	13,000,000
4. El Cid	12,000,000
5. The Absent-Minded Professor	11,426,000

1962

1. How the West Was Won	$20,932,883
2. Lawrence of Arabia	20,310,000
3. The Longest Day	17,600,000
4. In Search of the Castaways	9,975,000
5. The Music Man	8,100,000

1963

1. Cleopatra	$26,000,000
2. It's a Mad Mad Mad Mad World	20,849,786
3. Tom Jones	16,925,988
4. Irma La Douce	11,921,784
5. The Sword in the Stone	10,475,000

1964

1. Mary Poppins	$45,000,000
2. Goldfinger	22,997,706
3. The Carpetbaggers	15,500,000
4. My Fair Lady	12,000,000
5. From Russia with Love	9,924,279

1965

1. The Sound of Music	$79,748,000
2. Doctor Zhivago	47,116,811
3. Thunderball	28,621,434
4. Those Magnificent Men in Their Flying Machines	14,000,000
5. That Darn Cat	12,628,000

1966

1. Hawaii	$15,553,018
2. The Bible	15,000,000
3. Who's Afraid of Virginia Woolf?	14,500,000
4. A Man for All Seasons	12,750,000
5. Lt. Robin Crusoe, USN	10,164,000

1967

1. The Jungle Book	$60,964,000
2. The Graduate	44,090,729
3. Guess Who's Coming to Dinner	25,500,000
4. Bonnie and Clyde	22,800,000
5. The Dirty Dozen	20,403,826

1968

1. Funny Girl	$26,325,000
2. 2001: A Space Odyssey	25,521,917
3. The Odd Couple	20,000,000
4. Bullitt	19,000,000
5. Romeo and Juliet	17,473,000

1969

1. *Butch Cassidy and the Sundance Kid*	$46,039,000
2. *The Love Bug*	23,150,000
3. *Midnight Cowboy*	20,499,282
4. *Easy Rider*	19,100,000
5. *Hello, Dolly!*	15,200,000

1970

1. *Love Story*	$50,000,000
2. *Airport*	45,220,118
3. *M*A*S*H*	36,720,000
4. *Patton*	28,100,000
5. *The Aristocats*	26,462,000

1971

1. *Fiddler on the Roof*	$38,251,196
2. *Billy Jack*	32,500,000
3. *The French Connection*	26,315,000
4. *Summer of '42*	20,500,000
5. *Diamonds Are Forever*	19,726,829

1972

1. *The Godfather*	$86,275,000
2. *The Poseidon Adventure*	42,000,000
3. *What's Up Doc?*	28,000,000
4. *Deliverance*	22,600,000
5. *Jeremiah Johnson*	21,900,000

1973

1. *The Exorcist*	$89,000,000
2. *The Sting*	78,212,000
3. *American Graffiti*	55,128,175
4. *Papillon*	22,500,000
5. *The Way We Were*	22,457,000

1974

1. *The Towering Inferno*	$52,000,000
2. *Blazing Saddles*	47,800,000
3. *Young Frankenstein*	38,823,000
4. *Earthquake*	35,849,994
5. *The Trial of Billy Jack*	31,100,000

1975

1. *Jaws*	$129,549,325
2. *One Flew over the Cuckoo's Nest*	59,939,701
3. *The Rocky Horror Picture Show*	40,020,000
4. *Shampoo*	23,822,000
5. *Dog Day Afternoon*	22,500,000

1976

1. *Rocky*	$56,524,972
2. *A Star Is Born*	37,100,000
3. *King Kong*	36,915,000
4. *Silver Streak*	30,018,000
5. *All the President's Men*	30,000,000

1977

1. *Star Wars*	*$193,500,000*
2. *Close Encounters of the Third Kind*	*82,750,000*
3. *Saturday Night Fever*	*74,100,000*
4. *Smokey and the Bandit*	*58,949,939*
5. *The Goodbye Girl*	*41,839,170*

1978

1. *Grease*	$96,300,000
2. *Superman*	82,800,000
3. *National Lampoon's Animal House*	70,826,000
4. *Every Which Way but Loose*	51,900,000
5. *Jaws 2*	50,431,964

1979

1. *Kramer vs. Kramer*	$59,986,335
2. *Star Trek: The Motion Picture*	56,000,000
3. *The Jerk*	42,989,656
4. *Rocky II*	42,169,387
5. *Alien*	40,300,000

1980

1. *The Empire Strikes Back*	$141,600,000
2. *9 to 5*	59,100,000
3. *Stir Crazy*	58,364,420
4. *Airplane!*	40,610,000
5. *Any Which Way You Can*	40,500,000

1981

1. *Raiders of the Lost Ark*	$115,598,000
2. *Superman II*	65,100,000
3. *On Golden Pond*	61,174,744
4. *Arthur*	42,000,000
5. *Stripes*	40,886,589

1982

1. *E.T., the Extra-Terrestrial*	$228,618,939
2. *Tootsie*	96,292,736
3. *Rocky III*	66,262,796
4. *An Officer and a Gentleman*	55,223,000
5. *Porky's*	54,000,000

1983

1. *Return of the Jedi*	$168,002,414
2. *Terms of Endearment*	50,250,000
3. *Trading Places*	40,600,000
4. *WarGames*	38,519,833
5. *Superman III*	37,200,000

1984

1. *Ghostbusters*	$130,211,324
2. *Indiana Jones and the Temple of Doom*	109,000,000
3. *Beverly Hills Cop*	108,000,000
4. *Gremlins*	79,500,000
5. *The Karate Kid*	43,432,881

1985

1. *Back to the Future*	$104,408,738
2. *Rambo: First Blood Part II*	78,919,250
3. *Rocky IV*	76,023,246
4. *The Color Purple*	47,900,000
5. *Out of Africa*	43,103,469

1986

1. *Top Gun*	$79,400,000
2. *"Crocodile" Dundee*	70,227,000
3. *Platoon*	69,742,143
4. *The Karate Kid, Part II*	58,362,026
5. *Star Trek IV: The Voyage Home*	56,820,071

1987

1. *Three Men and a Baby*	$81,313,000
2. *Beverly Hills Cop II*	80,857,776
3. *Fatal Attraction*	70,000,000
4. *Good Morning, Vietnam*	58,103,000
5. *The Untouchables*	36,866,530

1988

1. *Rain Man*	$86,813,000
2. *Who Framed Roger Rabbit*	81,244,000
3. *Coming to America*	65,000,000
4. *"Crocodile" Dundee II*	57,300,000
5. *Twins*	57,715,127

1989

1. *Batman*	$150,500,000
2. *Indiana Jones and the Last Crusade*	115,500,000
3. *Lethal Weapon 2*	79,500,000
4. *Back to the Future Part II*	72,319,630
5. *Honey, I Shrunk the Kids*	72,007,000

1990

1. *Home Alone*	$140,099,000
2. *Ghost*	98,200,000
3. *Pretty Woman*	81,905,530
4. *Dances with Wolves*	81,537,971
5. *Teenage Mutant Ninja Turtles*	67,650,000

1991

1. *Terminator 2: Judgment Day*	$112,500,000
2. *Robin Hood: Prince of Thieves*	86,000,000
3. *Beauty and the Beast*	69,415,000
4. *Hook*	65,000,000
5. *City Slickers*	60,750,000

1992

1. *Home Alone 2: Lost in New York*	$103,377,614
2. *Batman Returns*	100,100,000
3. *Aladdin*	82,539,083
4. *Lethal Weapon 3*	80,000,000
5. *A Few Good Men*	71,000,000

1993

1. *Jurassic Park*	$208,000,000
2. *Mrs. Doubtfire*	109,761,240
3. *The Fugitive*	92,600,000
4. *The Firm*	77,047,044
5. *Sleepless in Seattle*	64,930,137

1994

1. *Forrest Gump*	$129,597,800
2. *The Lion King*	124,459,970
3. *True Lies*	64,221,360
4. *The Flintstones*	60,035,940
5. *Speed*	55,764,220

SEX FIRSTS ON THE SILVER SCREEN

- The first kiss appeared in *The Widow Jones* (1896).
- The first French kiss took place between Natalie Wood and Warren Beatty in *Splendor in the Grass* (1961).
- The first leading lady to kiss another was Marlene Dietrich in Josef von Sternberg's *Morocco* (1930).
- The first kiss in a Japanese film was finally allowed in *Twenty-Year-Old Youth* (1946).
- The longest single kiss on record took place between Regis Toomey and Jane Wyman in *You're in the Army Now* (1940); the smooch lasted three minutes and five seconds. (Naomi Levine spent 50 minutes being kissed in Andy Warhol's 50-minute film *Kiss*, but she had three partners.)
- The first leading lady to appear nude was Audrey Munson in *Inspiration* (1915).
- The first full male nudity featured Alan Bates and Oliver Reed in Ken Russell's *Women in Love* (1969).
- The first time sex was depicted was in *Ecstasy* with Hedy Lamarr (Czechoslovakia, 1932).
- The earliest known pornographic film was *A l'ecu d'or* (France, 1908).
- The first hard-core pornographic feature shown in American cinemas was *Deep Throat* (1972).
- The first film about homosexuality was Richard Oswald's *Anders als die Andern* (Germany, 1919).
- The first American film about homosexuality was Joseph Mankiewicz's *Suddenly Last Summer* (1959).

THE 100 BEST MOVIES OF ALL TIME

They are the celluloid touchstones of our inner life, the enduring echoes of various generations and the most bittersweet of social commentaries played out 10 yards high. PEOPLE's movie critic Ralph Novak selects 100 of the greatest.

ADAM'S RIB (1949)
The funniest of the five Hepburn-Tracy battle-of-the-sexes comedies.

THE ADVENTURES OF ROBIN HOOD (1938)
Errol Flynn's charisma and zest as Robin of Sherwood are all but impossible to equal.

THE AFRICAN QUEEN (1951)
Humphrey Bogart is a dipsomaniacal boatman and Katharine Hepburn is his unlikely traveling companion, a spinster, in John Huston's ingratiatingly ribald saga of an East Africa river trip during World War I.

AIRPLANE! (1980)
The Zucker brothers and Jim Abrahams created this telling but zany satire of air crisis movies, especially the *Airport* series.

ALL ABOUT EVE (1950)
The *Wizard of Oz* of cynicism, this Joseph Mankiewicz-written and directed film features Bette Davis as a stage star who takes in and is taken in by a manipulative young rival, Anne Baxter.

ALL THAT JAZZ (1979) ✓
Director-choreographer Bob Fosse hung his own pretension and vast talent out to dry in this lively autobiographical musical about a critically ill showbiz junkie (Roy Scheider) trying to direct a movie and play at the same time, as Fosse himself often did.

AMARCORD (1974)
Fellini's later films were light on plot but heavy on vivid images. This nostalgic trip to the director's home village is a stunning mix of history, nostalgia, and impressionism.

APOLLO 13 (1995)
This film is based on a real incident, so the ending is a foregone conclusion. Yet director Ron Howard and his splendid cast maintain an extraordinary level of tension.

BAMBI (1942)
In a sumptuously animated feature, the dear little cartoon deer and his ingratiating playmates more than compensate for the traumatic death of Bambi's mom in a forest fire.

THE BAND WAGON (1953)
Fred Astaire's last musical proves that even in his fifties, the old master could pick them up and lay them down with elegance and grace.

BEAU GESTE (1939)
This captivating, old-fashioned desert action film, directed by William Wellman, has Gary Cooper, Ray Milland, and Robert Preston as English brothers trying to hide a family scandal by joining the Foreign Legion.

BEAUTY AND THE BEAST (1946)
This live-action French version of the great romantic fable, directed by Jean Cocteau, is more elegant and sophisticated than the Disney version. However, the animated feature, with Broadway-style music by Howard Ashman and Alan Menken, is more playful and more fun.

BENNY & JOON (1993)
Johnny Depp, as a misfit who worships Buster Keaton, charms the mildly retarded Mary Stuart Masterson, to the chagrin of her solicitous brother, Aidan Quinn.

THE BEST YEARS OF OUR LIVES (1946)
Celebrating the end of World War II with a cinematic catharsis, this multi-character drama sketches the problems faced by returning servicemen and their families.

THE BIRDS (1963)
"The Birds is Coming!" said the hype of the day. "And Grammar has went!" said *Mad* magazine. Hitchcock's loony tale of ordinary domestic birds gone ferocious made audiences around the country see seagulls in a different light.

THE BIG SLEEP (1946)
While its plot is often confounding and always implausible, this grim private-eye caper includes Humphrey Bogart as Philip Marlowe and Lauren Bacall as a confused (and confusing) client.

BILL (1981)
The highlight of Mickey Rooney's second career was his portrayal of a retarded man facing life outside an institution in this exceptional TV movie costarring Dennis Quaid.

BIRTH OF THE BLUES (1941)
In an affable musical that's a very loose interpretation of the history of jazz, Bing Crosby, Mary Martin, the great trombonist/singer Jack Teagarden, and, of all people, Brian Donlevy (as a hot cornet), invent Dixieland.

BLACK AND WHITE IN COLOR (1977)
The movies' best take on European colonialism in Africa, this French-African production looks at the supreme arrogance of Frenchmen and Germans squabbling over colonial territory as an extension of World War I.

BLADE RUNNER (1982)
From Ridley Scott, the director of *Thelma and Louise*, an eerie, futuristic cops-and-crooks film.

BLAZING SADDLES (1973)
Mel Brooks parodies the traditional Western (especially *High Noon*) in this funny spoof featuring Gene Wilder, Cleavon Little, Harvey Korman, and Madeline Kahn.

BLOW-UP (1966)
A lot of people invested this British-Italian thriller with a heavier load of philosophical import than it can bear, but it is an engrossing mystery about a photographer who inadvertently photographs a murder.

THE BLUE ANGEL (1930)
Most Marlene Dietrich films seem campy now. So does this one, but her seduction of a conservative professor, Emil Jannings, seems totally reasonable given the feline sensuousness of her Lola-Lola

BODY HEAT (1981)
An updated, sexier version of *Double Indemnity*, director Lawrence Kasdan's atmospheric first film stars Kathleen Turner as the dissatisfied wife who schemes to become a rich widow.

BOYZ N THE HOOD (1991)
A rare movie about black youth that doesn't glamorize the violence, obscenity, and illiteracy it decries.

BREAKFAST AT TIFFANY'S (1961)
Audrey Hepburn is an irresistibly winsome country girl who charms New York City in Truman Capote's precious story, which includes an unfortunately racist bit by Mickey Rooney as a Chinese neighbor.

BREATHLESS (1959)
Jean-Paul Belmondo does his famous Bogart imitation as a capricious Parisian crook who picks up American papergirl Jean Seberg to go on a minor crime spree.

THE BRIDGE ON THE RIVER KWAI (1957)
The heart of this World War II epic directed by David Lean is the psychological battle between Alec Guinness, ranking officer among Allied prisoners in a Japanese POW camp in Burma, and Sessue Hayakawa, the camp commandant.

THE BROTHERS KARAMAZOV (1958)
Dostoevsky's novels require a lot of transposing to turn into movies, but his examination of families and morality wades through the philosophizing in crisp fashion.

BULLITT (1968)
The plot is routine: noble cop battles corrupt system, but the cop is moody Steve McQueen, his girlfriend is moody Jacqueline Bisset, and director Peter Yates stages a rollicking chase up and down the hilly streets of San Francisco.

BUS STOP (1956)
Marilyn Monroe finally got to act, in this version of the William Inge play about a naive cowboy, Don Murray, who goes bonkers over Marilyn as an irresistibly flouncy saloon singer.

BUTCH CASSIDY AND THE SUNDANCE KID (1969)
Paul Newman and Robert Redford turn the charm all the way up as two outlaws with an uncommonly light-hearted attitude toward their criminal pursuits.

CABARET (1972)
Liza Minnelli got to sing the title song and otherwise found the role of her career as Sally Bowles, an American marooned in between-wars Germany.

THE CAINE MUTINY (1954)
Humphrey Bogart has the central part of ball-bearing-jiggling Capt. Queeg, but Fred MacMurray nicely handles a tough role as a coward who foments a mutiny, but then wilts under courtroom pressure.

THE CANTERVILLE GHOST (1944)
Impossibly cute little Margaret O'Brien and Robert Young help Charles Laughton do good deeds to end his career as a ghost.

CANYON PASSAGE (1946)
An unusual Western with no big stars compensates with vivid performances by usually supporting actors. Dana Andrews, Ward Bond, Brian Donlevy, and Lloyd Bridges step out front and center.

CAPTAIN BLOOD (1935)
Errol Flynn swashbuckles to beat the band as a doctor turned pirate.

CARNAL KNOWLEDGE (1971)
Mike Nichols directs Jules Pfeiffer's script about sexually dysfunctional Americans of various ilk. Jack Nicholson, Art Garfunkel, Candice Bergen, Ann-Margret, and Rita Moreno are among them.

CASABLANCA (1942)
Cliché-filled (though it invented most of them) and florid, this is still an unfailingly entertaining film.

CHINATOWN (1974)
Most famous for private eye Jack Nicholson's bandaged nose, Roman Polanski's perverse thriller keeps you guessing until the end.

CITIZEN KANE (1941)
Orson Welles's prodigiously innovative debut is best appreciated by those who know about publisher William Randolph Hearst, on whom Welles loosely based Kane. But it is an absorbing saga in any case.

THE CONVERSATION (1974)
Modest but engrossing, Francis Coppola's meditation on the permutations of paranoia centers on surveillance expert Gene Hackman.

COOL HAND LUKE (1967)
Paul Newman, in a classic '60s rebel turn, is a small time crook who refuses to obey the rules at a Southern chain-gang prison.

CRASH DIVE (1943)
While this is a World War II submarine movie, it is less memorable for its action sequences than for a mouth-watering eating scene when submariners Dana Andrews and Tyrone Power, returning from a long mission without fresh food, gorge themselves at an officers' club.

CRIMES AND MISDEMEANORS (1989)
Woody Allen finally merges his biting wit with his dramatic sensibilities in a tale of adultery, murder, and deceit.

A DAY AT THE RACES (1937)
Harpo does his "Dr. Hackenbush" charade, Chico and Groucho unreel their racetrack tipsheet routine, and Groucho tries to seduce the ultimate straight woman, Margaret Dumont.

DR. STRANGELOVE (1964)
Stanley Kubrick manages to satirize everyone's fear of nuclear war, directing Peter Sellers, George C. Scott, Sterling Hayden, and Keenan Wynn through Terry Southern's cataclysmic comedy.

DOUBLE INDEMNITY (1944)
Like three Thoroughbreds streaking around a muddy oval, Fred MacMurray, Barbara Stanwyck, and Edward G. Robinson, navigate Billy Wilder's holey plot about an insurance adjustor who helps a woman murder her husband.

E.T., THE EXTRA-TERRESTRIAL (1982)
Steven Spielberg's schmaltzy tale of an extraterrestrial stranded on Earth is all fiction, no science, but winning in any case.

THE EMPIRE STRIKES BACK (1980)
The second installment in the *Star Wars* saga introduces Yoda the Muppet/guru and brings Billy Dee Williams into the interplanetary cliffhanger plot.

FORT APACHE (1948)
John Wayne is an honorable cavalry officer who is overruled by racist commander Henry Fonda while fighting Apaches. The young adult Shirley Temple strikes up a romance with real-life husband John Agar.

FULL METAL JACKET (1987)
Stanley Kubrick examines Vietnam in particular and human bloodlust in general, with Matthew Modine and Vincent D'Onofrio as Marines.

THE GAY DIVORCEE (1934)
The Astaire-Rogers musicals are all wonderful, but this one has the sexy dance to "Night and Day," a young Betty Grable, and a great character name, "Hortense Ditherwell," played by Alice Brady.

GOLDFINGER (1964)
The third and still best James Bond movie revolves around villain Gert Frobe's crafty plot to rob Fort Knox.

GONE WITH THE WIND (1939)
Many of its little mysteries are now moot: Atlanta survived; Rhett and Scarlett are forever linked; tomorrow was another day. There still isn't any more ambitious, grander epic movie romance.

THE GODFATHER (1972)
You have to ignore the amorality of Francis Coppola romanticizing the ugly, cowardly business of organized crime, but if you can stomach it, there's a sprawling, eventful story acted by an all-star cast.

GRAND ILLUSION (1937)
World War I French POWs confront their articulate, sympathetic captor (Erich von Stroheim) in Jean Renoir's subtle anti-war drama.

THE GRAPES OF WRATH (1940)
Directed by John Ford within vivid living memory of the Great Depression, this adaptation of John Steinbeck's novel follows the migration of a family from the Dust Bowl to the migrant worker camps of California.

HAMLET (1948)
Mel Gibson's eyes were bluer and Richard Burton was more palpably sexual, but Shakespeare's poetry never fell more trippingly from a cinematic tongue than it did from Laurence Olivier's in this profound interpretation, directed by Olivier and shot in Denmark.

HIS GIRL FRIDAY (1940)
Rosalind Russell is the ace reporter, Cary Grant the ruthless newspaper editor in this witty, bantering variation on Ben Hecht's *The Front Page*.

THE HOUND OF THE BASKERVILLES (1939)
The movies' best Sherlock Holmes, Basil Rathbone, joins Nigel Bruce as Watson in solving the mystery of the devil dog of the moors.

THE HUSTLER (1961)
Paul Newman, at his intense, ironic best, is a pool hustler who challenges "Minnesota Fats," Jackie Gleason, in a bitter match.

IT HAPPENED ONE NIGHT (1934)
In the very definition of romantic comedy, Frank Capra directs Clark Gable and Claudette Col-

bert through a sparring courtship.

JAILHOUSE ROCK (1957)
"Love Me Tender" was Elvis Presley's best movie song and *Viva Las Vegas!* had Ann-Margret, but this film's production number of the title song typified the cockeyed tone and zeal of the logic-poor Elvis films.

JAWS (1975)
In spite of Richard Dreyfuss's unconvincing performance as a hotshot ichthyologist, Steven Spielberg's judicious use of his mechanical great white shark, Roy Scheider's steadiness as the embattled sheriff, and Robert Shaw's old salt turn make this the biggest fish in the monster movie pond.

KING SOLOMON'S MINES (1950)
Dazzling wildlife photography and a slow-kindling romance between Deborah Kerr and Stewart Granger elevate this version of the H. Rider Haggard story, lamely redone in 1985 with Sharon Stone and Richard Chamberlain.

LA DOLCE VITA (1960)
Fellini skewered the early, Italian version of yuppies in this uncompromising satire.

LA STRADA (1954)
A touring carnival becomes an allegory for life in Fellini's moving fable, with Anthony Quinn as a strong man, Richard Basehart as a gentle clown, and the future Mrs. Fellini, Giulietta Masina.

THE LITTLE COLONEL (1935)
The matchless child star Shirley Temple, then 6, tap dances with Bill "Bojangles" Robinson and holds her own with inveterate scene stealer Lionel Barrymore.

LONG DAY'S JOURNEY INTO NIGHT (1962)
Director Sidney Lumet didn't try to gild the lily of Eugene

O'Neill's powerful, anxiety-ridden play about a drug-addicted woman, her frustrated actor husband, and their two troubled sons.

LONGTIME COMPANION (1990)
The most ambitious and affecting drama about the gay community's response to AIDS.

LOST IN A HAREM (1944)
Abbott and Costello build on their "Slowly I turned" routine in a Middle East romp.

THE MALTESE FALCON (1941)
Humphrey Bogart, as Sam Spade, defined the detective genre in searching for "the stuff dreams are made of." John Huston directed an expert cast that included his father Walter in a brief role.

MEAN STREETS (1973)
Martin Scorsese nailed the tone of street crime in this tale of Little Italy with Harvey Keitel and Robert DeNiro. His other Mob movies seemed pale copies.

MUTINY ON THE BOUNTY (1935)
Charles Laughton is the haughty Captain Bligh, Clark Gable the stalwart first mate who becomes a reluctant mutineer in the sea adventure based on a real event.

PINOCCHIO (1940)
Disney's lovable if pedantic tale about a puppet turning into a boy includes the best Disney song, "When You Wish Upon A Star."

THE PINK PANTHER (1964)
The first Inspector Clouseau comedy profited from David Niven, Robert Wagner, Claudia Cardinale, and Fran Jeffries, as well as star Peter Sellers.

PLATOON (1986)
Vietnam vet Oliver Stone directs a war story as morality play, with Tom Berenger, Willem Dafoe, and Charlie Sheen.

THE POSTMAN ALWAYS RINGS TWICE (1946)
Lana Turner and John Garfield generate real heat as an adulterous couple plotting to murder the woman's husband. The 1981 remake was more explicit, yet less sexy.

PSYCHO (1960)
Often successfully parodied but rarely equalled, Alfred Hitchcock's creepy tale of murder at the Bates Hotel shocks after many viewings.

RAIDERS OF THE LOST ARK (1981)
Steven Spielberg's ingenuity at recreating old-fashioned adventure films and Harrison Ford's sturdy but witty portrayal of Indiana Jones make this a fun-filled diversion.

RED RIVER (1948)
John Wayne should have received his Oscar for this thoughtful Western, in which he is a tough rancher who becomes a mentor to young gunman Montgomery Clift.

THE ROAD TO UTOPIA (1945)
Crosby and Hope clown wittily; Crosby and Lamour sing. And Hillary Brooke, usually Abbott and Costello's foil, joins veteran villain Douglas Dumbrille for evil relief.

SCENES FROM A MARRIAGE (1973)
In what was originally a TV series in Sweden, Ingmar Bergman painfully traces the disintegration of a middle-class marriage, with Liv Ullmann and Erland Josephson.

SCHINDLER'S LIST (1993)
Steven Spielberg unearthed this long but wrenching story of a Polish businessman who sheltered Jews during World War II, with Liam Neeson subtly moving as Schindler.

THE SEARCHERS (1956)
John Ford and John Wayne teamed up on this elegantly paced Western epic in which Wayne and his "nephew," Jeffrey Hunter, search for Wayne's niece, who by the end has grown into Natalie Wood.

THE SEVEN SAMURAI (1954)
Kurosawa's bloody, colorful Japanese Western about seven mercenaries was turned into the 1960 American Western *The Magnificent Seven.*

THE SEVENTH SEAL (1957)
Bergman's imposing meditation on religion and free will features Max Von Sydow as a disillusioned knight playing a high stakes chess game with Death.

SOME LIKE IT HOT (1959)
Jack Lemmon and Tony Curtis are musicians who go into drag to hide from gangsters they've seen commit the St. Valentine's Day Massacre. Marilyn Monroe is the star of the all-woman band they end up with.

THE SPY WHO LOVED ME (1977)
The opening is the most exciting in the James Bond series, and there are Richard Kiel as the steel-toothed Jaws and beautiful Barbara Bach, too.

THE THIRD MAN (1949)
This often confusing but gripping thriller set in postwar Vienna relies on Joseph Cotten as a writer, Orson Welles as a mysterious fugitive, and Anton Karas's intriguing zither rendition of the film's theme.

THE STING (1973)
Paul Newman and Robert Redford turn their Butch and Sundance rapport to '20s gangland Chicago and try to dupe dandyhoodlum Robert Shaw in a tricky, ingratiating plot.

STAR WARS (1977)
George Lucas blended revolutionary special effects with a grand sense of fun to start his saga of young hero Luke Skywalker and dark villain Darth Vader.

A STREETCAR NAMED DESIRE (1951)
Marlon Brando's revolutionary naturalistic acting style as anguished chauvinist pig Stanley Kowalski still echoes in the performances of every serious young American actor.

THE TREASURE OF THE SIERRA MADRE (1948)
Most famous for its "We don't need no stinking badges" line, John Huston's morality play/action-adventure is absorbing from start to finish, with Humphrey Bogart, Walter Huston, and Tim Holt as greed-stricken gold prospectors in Mexico.

THE WOLF MAN (1941)
What might have been a routine werewolf movie is elevated by the unexpectedly touching acting of Lon Chaney Jr. as the tortured man who turns into a vicious wolf when there's a full moon.

A WALK IN THE SUN (1945)
A modest action film captures the deceptive banality of war, with Dana Andrews, Lloyd Bridges, John Ireland, and Richard Conte on a patrol in Italy.

WITNESS FOR THE PROSECUTION (1957)
The cleverest courtroom drama features Tyrone Power, Marlene Dietrich, and Charles Laughton acting Agatha Christie's story and Billy Wilder directing. Beware of surprises.

THE WIZARD OF OZ (1939)
The most fun for adults of any kids' movie, this extravaganza seems exceptionally good-natured, despite jockeying for position among Judy Garland, Ray Bolger, Jack Haley, and Bert Lahr.

YANKEE DOODLE DANDY (1942)
James Cagney's gangly dancing and lippy attitude make him an impressive George M. Cohan.

YOUNG FRANKENSTEIN (1974)
Mel Brooks's parody of the Frankenstein movies never lets up, with Peter Boyle as the monster, Gene Wilder as Dr. Frankenstein, and Marty Feldman as the faithful Igor.

HOLLYWOOD'S FOOTPRINTS OF FAME

The first footprints at Grauman's Chinese Theater, as it was originally called, were made by Norma Talmadge in 1927 when, legend holds, she accidentally stepped in wet concrete outside the building. Since then over 180 stars have been immortalized, along with their hands, feet—and sometimes noses (Jimmy Durante), fists (John Wayne), and legs (Betty Grable). Following the most recent induction of Whoopi Goldberg (braids and all) in 1995, the Forecourt of the Stars at Mann's includes:

Abbott & Costello
Don Ameche
Julie Andrews
Edward Arnold
Fred Astaire
Gene Autry
John Barrymore
Freddie Bartholomew
Anne Baxter
Wallace Beery
Jack Benny
Edgar Bergen
Joan Blondell
Humphrey Bogart
Charles Boyer
Joe E. Brown
Yul Brynner
George Burns
Cantinflas
Eddie Cantor
Maurice Chevalier
Gary Cooper
Jackie Cooper
Jeanne Crain
Joan Crawford
Bing Crosby
Tom Cruise
Bebe Daniels
Linda Darnell
Marion Davies
Bette Davis
Doris Day
Olivia DeHavilland
Cecil B. DeMille
Kirk Douglas
Marie Dressler
Donald Duck
Irene Dunne
Jimmie Durante
Deanna Durbin
Clint Eastwood
Nelson Eddy
Douglas Fairbanks
Alice Faye
Rhonda Fleming
Henry Fonda

Joan Fontaine
Harrison Ford
Clark Gable
Ava Gardner
Judy Garland
Greer Garson
Janet Gaynor
Mel Gibson
Whoopi Goldberg
Betty Grable
Cary Grant
Rosa Grauman (founder Sid
    Grauman's mother)
Sid Grauman
Ann Harding
Jean Harlow
Rex Harrison
William S. Hart
Susan Hayward
Rita Hayworth
Van Heflin
Sonja Henie
Jean Hersholt
Charlton Heston
Bob Hope
Rock Hudson
George Jessel
Van Johnson
Al Jolson
Danny Kaye
Michael Keaton
Gene Kelly
Deborah Kerr
Alan Ladd
Dorothy Lamour
Charles Laughton
Jack Lemmon
Mervyn LeRoy
Harold Lloyd
Sophia Loren
Myrna Loy
George Lucas
William Lundigan
Jeanette MacDonald
Ali MacGraw
Shirley MacLaine

Victor McLaglen
Steve McQueen
Fredric March
Dean Martin
Tony Martin
The Marx Brothers
James Mason
Marcello Mastroianni
Lauritz Melchior
Ray Milland
Hayley Mills
Carmen Miranda
Tom Mix
Marilyn Monroe
Colleen Moore
Eddie Murphy
George Murphy
Hildegarde Neff
Pola Negri
Paul Newman
Jack Nicholson
Jack Oakie
Margaret O'Brien
Donald O'Connor
Louella Parsons
Gregory Peck
Mary Pickford
Ezio Pinza
Sidney Poitier
Dick Powell
Eleanor Powell
William Powell
Tyrone Power
Anthony Quinn
George Raft
Burt Reynolds
Debbie Reynolds
The Ritz Brothers
Edward G. Robinson
May Robson
Ginger Rogers
Roy Rogers
Mickey Rooney
Jane Russell
Rosalind Russell
Peter Sellers

Norma Shearer
Jean Simmons
Frank Sinatra
Red Skelton
Steven Spielberg
Sylvester Stallone
Barbara Stanwyck
Star Trek crew (William
    Shatner, Leonard Nimoy,
    DeForest Kelley, James
    Doohan, Nichelle Nichols,
    George Takei, Walter
    Koenig)
Star Wars characters
George Stevens
Jimmy Stewart
Gloria Swanson
Constance Talmadge
Norma Talmadge
Elizabeth Taylor
Robert Taylor
Shirley Temple
Danny Thomas
Gene Tierney
John Travolta
Lana Turner
Rudy Vallee
Dick Van Dyke
W. S. Van Dyke
Raoul Walsh
John Wayne
Clifton Webb
Oskar Werner
Richard Widmark
Esther Williams
Jane Withers
Natalie Wood
Joanne Woodward
Monty Woolley
Jane Wyman
Diana Wynyard
Loretta Young
Adolph Zukor

THE BRIGHTEST STARS, BY YEAR

In today's high-pressure movie business, the most valuable commodity is a star who shines so bright that he or she can "open" a movie—filling seats on the basis of pure popularity regardless of the allure of the film. Every year since 1933, Quigley Publishing has polled more than 500 moviehouse owners nationwide to determine which stars they regarded as the surest-fire box-office draw.

1933

1. Marie Dressler
2. Will Rogers
3. Janet Gaynor
4. Eddie Cantor
5. Wallace Beery
6. Jean Harlow
7. Clark Gable
8. Mae West
9. Norma Shearer
10. Joan Crawford

1934

1. Will Rogers
2. Clark Gable
3. Janet Gaynor
4. Wallace Beery
5. Mae West
6. Joan Crawford
7. Bing Crosby
8. Shirley Temple
9. Marie Dressler
10. Norma Shearer

1935

1. Shirley Temple
2. Will Rogers
3. Clark Gable
4. Fred Astaire & Ginger Rogers
5. Joan Crawford
6. Claudette Colbert
7. Dick Powell
8. Wallace Beery
9. Joe E. Brown
10. James Cagney

1936

1. Shirley Temple
2. Clark Gable
3. Fred Astaire and Ginger Rogers
4. Robert Taylor
5. Joe E. Brown
6. Dick Powell
7. Joan Crawford
8. Claudette Colbert

9. Jeanette MacDonald
10. Gary Cooper

1937

1. Shirley Temple
2. Clark Gable
3. Robert Taylor
4. Bing Crosby
5. William Powell
6. Jane Withers
7. Fred Astaire & Ginger Rogers
8. Sonja Henie
9. Gary Cooper
10. Myrna Loy

1938

1. Shirley Temple
2. Clark Gable
3. Sonja Henie
4. Mickey Rooney
5. Spencer Tracy
6. Robert Taylor
7. Myrna Loy
8. Jane Withers
9. Alice Faye
10. Tyrone Power

1939

1. Mickey Rooney
2. Tyrone Power
3. Spencer Tracy
4. Clark Gable
5. Shirley Temple
6. Bette Davis
7. Alice Faye
8. Errol Flynn
9. James Cagney
10. Sonja Henie

1940

1. Mickey Rooney
2. Spencer Tracy
3. Clark Gable
4. Gene Autry
5. Tyrone Power
6. James Cagney

7. Bing Crosby
8. Wallace Beery
9. Bette Davis
10. Judy Garland

1941

1. Mickey Rooney
2. Clark Gable
3. Abbott & Costello
4. Bob Hope
5. Spencer Tracy
6. Gene Autry
7. Gary Cooper
8. Bette Davis
9. James Cagney
10. Spencer Tracy

1942

1. Abbott & Costello
2. Clark Gable
3. Gary Cooper
4. Mickey Rooney
5. Bob Hope
6. James Cagney
7. Gene Autry
8. Betty Grable
9. Greer Garson
10. Spencer Tracy

1943

1. Betty Grable
2. Bob Hope
3. Abbott & Costello
4. Bing Crosby
5. Gary Cooper
6. Greer Garson
7. Humphrey Bogart
8. James Cagney
9. Mickey Rooney
10. Clark Gable

1944

1. Bing Crosby
2. Gary Cooper
3. Bob Hope
4. Betty Grable
5. Spencer Tracy
6. Greer Garson

7. Humphrey Bogart
8. Abbott & Costello
9. Cary Grant
10. Bette Davis

1945

1. Bing Crosby
2. Van Johnson
3. Greer Garson
4. Betty Grable
5. Spencer Tracy
6. Humphrey Bogart (tie)
6. Gary Cooper (tie)
8. Bob Hope
9. Judy Garland
10. Margaret O'Brien

1946

1. Bing Crosby
2. Ingrid Bergman
3. Van Johnson
4. Gary Cooper
5. Bob Hope
6. Humphrey Bogart
7. Greer Garson
8. Margaret O'Brien
9. Betty Grable
10. Roy Rogers

1947

1. Bing Crosby
2. Betty Grable
3. Ingrid Bergman
4. Gary Cooper
5. Humphrey Bogart
6. Bob Hope
7. Clark Gable
8. Gregory Peck
9. Claudette Colbert
10. Alan Ladd

1948

1. Bing Crosby
2. Betty Grable
3. Abbott & Costello
4. Gary Cooper
5. Bob Hope

6. Humphrey Bogart
7. Clark Gable
8. Cary Grant
9. Spencer Tracy
10. Ingrid Bergman

1949

1. Bob Hope
2. Bing Crosby
3. Abbott & Costello
4. John Wayne
5. Gary Cooper
6. Cary Grant
7. Betty Grable
8. Esther Williams
9. Humphrey Bogart
10. Clark Gable

1950

1. John Wayne
2. Bob Hope
3. Bing Crosby
4. Betty Grable
5. James Stewart
6. Abbott & Costello
7. Clifton Webb
8. Esther Williams
9. Spencer Tracy
10. Randolph Scott

1951

1. John Wayne
2. Dean Martin & Jerry Lewis
3. Betty Grable
4. Abbott & Costello
5. Bing Crosby
6. Bob Hope
7. Randolph Scott
8. Gary Cooper
9. Doris Day
10. Spencer Tracy

1952

1. Dean Martin & Jerry Lewis
2. Gary Cooper
3. John Wayne
4. Bing Crosby
5. Bob Hope
6. James Stewart
7. Doris Day
8. Gregory Peck
9. Susan Hayward
10. Randolph Scott

1953

1. Gary Cooper
2. Dean Martin & Jerry Lewis
3. John Wayne
4. Alan Ladd
5. Bing Crosby
6. Marilyn Monroe
7. James Stewart
8. Bob Hope
9. Susan Hayward
10. Randolph Scott

1954

1. John Wayne
2. Dean Martin & Jerry Lewis
3. Gary Cooper
4. James Stewart
5. Marilyn Monroe
6. Alan Ladd
7. William Holden
8. Bing Crosby
9. Jane Wyman
10. Marlon Brando

1955

1. James Stewart
2. Grace Kelly
3. John Wayne
4. William Holden
5. Gary Cooper
6. Marlon Brando
7. Dean Martin & Jerry Lewis
8. Humphrey Bogart
9. June Allyson
10. Clark Gable

1956

1. William Holden
2. John Wayne
3. James Stewart
4. Burt Lancaster
5. Glenn Ford
6. Dean Martin & Jerry Lewis
7. Gary Cooper
8. Marilyn Monroe
9. Kim Novak
10. Frank Sinatra

1957

1. Rock Hudson
2. John Wayne
3. Pat Boone
4. Elvis Presley

5. Frank Sinatra
6. Gary Cooper
7. William Holden
8. James Stewart
9. Jerry Lewis
10. Yul Brynner

1958

1. Glenn Ford
2. Elizabeth Taylor
3. Jerry Lewis
4. Marlon Brando
5. Rock Hudson
6. William Holden
7. Brigitte Bardot
8. Yul Brynner
9. James Stewart
10. Frank Sinatra

1959

1. Rock Hudson
2. Cary Grant
3. James Stewart
4. Doris Day
5. Debbie Reynolds
6. Glenn Ford
7. Frank Sinatra
8. John Wayne
9. Jerry Lewis
10. Susan Hayward

1960

1. Doris Day
2. Rock Hudson
3. Cary Grant
4. Elizabeth Taylor
5. Debbie Reynolds
6. Tony Curtis
7. Sandra Dee
8. Frank Sinatra
9. Jack Lemmon
10. John Wayne

1961

1. Elizabeth Taylor
2. Rock Hudson
3. Doris Day
4. John Wayne
5. Cary Grant
6. Sandra Dee
7. Jerry Lewis
8. William Holden
9. Tony Curtis
10. Elvis Presley

1962

1. Doris Day
2. Rock Hudson

3. Cary Grant
4. John Wayne
5. Elvis Presley
6. Elizabeth Taylor
7. Jerry Lewis
8. Frank Sinatra
9. Sandra Dee
10. Burt Lancaster

1963

1. Doris Day
2. John Wayne
3. Rock Hudson
4. Jack Lemmon
5. Cary Grant
6. Elizabeth Taylor
7. Elvis Presley
8. Sandra Dee
9. Paul Newman
10. Jerry Lewis

1964

1. Doris Day
2. Jack Lemmon
3. Rock Hudson
4. John Wayne
5. Cary Grant
6. Elvis Presley
7. Shirley MacLaine
8. Ann-Margret
9. Paul Newman
10. Jerry Lewis

1965

1. Sean Connery
2. John Wayne
3. Doris Day
4. Julie Andrews
5. Jack Lemmon
6. Elvis Presley
7. Cary Grant
8. James Stewart
9. Elizabeth Taylor
10. Richard Burton

1966

1. Julie Andrews
2. Sean Connery
3. Elizabeth Taylor
4. Jack Lemmon
5. Richard Burton
6. Cary Grant
7. John Wayne
8. Doris Day
9. Paul Newman
10. Elvis Presley

1967

1. Julie Andrews
2. Lee Marvin
3. Paul Newman
4. Dean Martin
5. Sean Connery
6. Elizabeth Taylor
7. Sidney Poitier
8. John Wayne
9. Richard Burton
10. Steve McQueen

1968

1. Sidney Poitier
2. Paul Newman
3. Julie Andrews
4. John Wayne
5. Clint Eastwood
6. Dean Martin
7. Steve McQueen
8. Jack Lemmon
9. Lee Marvin
10. Elizabeth Taylor

1969

1. Paul Newman
2. John Wayne
3. Steve McQueen
4. Dustin Hoffman
5. Clint Eastwood
6. Sidney Poitier
7. Lee Marvin
8. Jack Lemmon
9. Katharine Hepburn
10. Barbra Streisand

1970

1. Paul Newman
2. Clint Eastwood
3. Steve McQueen
4. John Wayne
5. Elliott Gould
6. Dustin Hoffman
7. Lee Marvin
8. Jack Lemmon
9. Barbra Streisand
10. Walter Matthau

1971

1. John Wayne
2. Clint Eastwood
3. Paul Newman
4. Steve McQueen
5. George C. Scott
6. Dustin Hoffman
7. Walter Matthau
8. Ali MacGraw

9. Sean Connery
10. Lee Marvin

1972

1. Clint Eastwood
2. George C. Scott
3. Gene Hackman
4. John Wayne
5. Barbra Streisand
6. Marlon Brando
7. Paul Newman
8. Steve McQueen
9. Dustin Hoffman
10. Goldie Hawn

1973

1. Clint Eastwood
2. Ryan O'Neal
3. Steve McQueen
4. Burt Reynolds
5. Robert Redford
6. Barbra Streisand
7. Paul Newman
8. Charles Bronson
9. John Wayne
10. Marlon Brando

1974

1. Robert Redford
2. Clint Eastwood
3. Paul Newman
4. Barbra Streisand
5. Steve McQueen
6. Burt Reynolds
7. Charles Bronson
8. Jack Nicholson
9. Al Pacino
10. John Wayne

1975

1. Robert Redford
2. Barbra Streisand
3. Al Pacino
4. Charles Bronson
5. Paul Newman
6. Clint Eastwood
7. Burt Reynolds
8. Woody Allen
9. Steve McQueen
10. Gene Hackman

1976

1. Robert Redford
2. Jack Nicholson
3. Dustin Hoffman
4. Clint Eastwood
5. Mel Brooks
6. Burt Reynolds

7. Al Pacino
8. Tatum O'Neal
9. Woody Allen
10. Charles Bronson

1977

1. Sylvester Stallone
2. Barbra Streisand
3. Clint Eastwood
4. Burt Reynolds
5. Robert Redford
6. Woody Allen
7. Mel Brooks
8. Al Pacino
9. Diane Keaton
10. Robert De Niro

1978

1. Burt Reynolds
2. John Travolta
3. Richard Dreyfuss
4. Warren Beatty
5. Clint Eastwood
6. Woody Allen
7. Diane Keaton
8. Jane Fonda
9. Peter Sellers
10. Barbra Streisand

1979

1. Burt Reynolds
2. Clint Eastwood
3. Jane Fonda
4. Woody Allen
5. Barbra Streisand
6. Sylvester Stallone
7. John Travolta
8. Jill Clayburgh
9. Roger Moore
10. Mel Brooks

1980

1. Burt Reynolds
2. Robert Redford
3. Clint Eastwood
4. Jane Fonda
5. Dustin Hoffman
6. John Travolta
7. Sally Field
8. Sissy Spacek
9. Barbra Streisand
10. Steve Martin

1981

1. Burt Reynolds
2. Clint Eastwood
3. Dudley Moore
4. Dolly Parton

5. Jane Fonda
6. Harrison Ford
7. Alan Alda
8. Bo Derek
9. Goldie Hawn
10. Bill Murray

1982

1. Burt Reynolds
2. Clint Eastwood
3. Sylvester Stallone
4. Dudley Moore
5. Richard Pryor
6. Dolly Parton
7. Jane Fonda
8. Richard Gere
9. Paul Newman
10. Harrison Ford

1983

1. Clint Eastwood
2. Eddie Murphy
3. Sylvester Stallone
4. Burt Reynolds
5. John Travolta
6. Dustin Hoffman
7. Harrison Ford
8. Richard Gere
9. Chevy Chase
10. Tom Cruise

1984

1. Clint Eastwood
2. Bill Murray
3. Harrison Ford
4. Eddie Murphy
5. Sally Field
6. Burt Reynolds
7. Robert Redford
8. Prince
9. Dan Aykroyd
10. Meryl Streep

1985

1. Sylvester Stallone
2. Eddie Murphy
3. Clint Eastwood
4. Michael J. Fox
5. Chevy Chase
6. Arnold Schwarzenegger
7. Chuck Norris
8. Harrison Ford
9. Michael Douglas
10. Meryl Streep

1986

1. Tom Cruise
2. Eddie Murphy
3. Paul Hogan
4. Rodney Dangerfield
5. Bette Midler
6. Sylvester Stallone
7. Clint Eastwood
8. Whoopi Goldberg
9. Kathleen Turner
10. Paul Newman

1987

1. Eddie Murphy
2. Michael Douglas
3. Michael J. Fox
4. Arnold Schwarzenegger
5. Paul Hogan
6. Tom Cruise
7. Glenn Close
8. Sylvester Stallone
9. Cher
10. Mel Gibson

1988

1. Tom Cruise
2. Eddie Murphy
3. Tom Hanks
4. Arnold Schwarzenegger
5. Paul Hogan
6. Danny DeVito
7. Bette Midler
8. Robin Williams
9. Tom Selleck
10. Dustin Hoffman

1989

1. Jack Nicholson
2. Tom Cruise
3. Robin Williams
4. Michael Douglas
5. Tom Hanks
6. Michael J. Fox
7. Eddie Murphy
8. Mel Gibson
9. Sean Connery
10. Kathleen Turner

1990

1. Arnold Schwarzenegger
2. Julia Roberts
3. Bruce Willis
4. Tom Cruise
5. Mel Gibson
6. Kevin Costner
7. Patrick Swayze
8. Sean Connery
9. Harrison Ford
10. Richard Gere

1991

1. Kevin Costner
2. Arnold Schwarzenegger
3. Robin Williams
4. Julia Roberts
5. Macaulay Culkin
6. Jodie Foster
7. Billy Crystal
8. Dustin Hoffman
9. Robert De Niro
10. Mel Gibson

1992

1. Tom Cruise
2. Mel Gibson
3. Kevin Costner
4. Jack Nicholson
5. Macaulay Culkin
6. Whoopi Goldberg
7. Michael Douglas
8. Clint Eastwood
9. Steven Seagal
10. Robin Williams

1993

1. Clint Eastwood
2. Tom Cruise
3. Robin Williams
4. Kevin Costner
5. Harrison Ford
6. Julia Roberts
7. Tom Hanks
8. Mel Gibson
9. Whoopi Goldberg
10. Sylvester Stallone

1994

1. Tom Hanks
2. Jim Carrey
3. Arnold Schwarzenegger
4. Tom Cruise
5. Harrison Ford
6. Tim Allen
7. Mel Gibson
8. Jodie Foster
9. Michael Douglas
10. Tommy Lee Jones

STAR LIGHT, STAR BRIGHT

PEOPLE analyzed Quigley Publishing's list of the top 10 stars of every year since 1933 to come up with an all-time list of the most popular actors ever. Here they are, along with their total scores. (We awarded points on a descending scale of 10, based on the year-by-year Quigley rankings.)

Rank	Actor	Score	Rank	Actor	Score	Rank	Actor	Score
1.	John Wayne	172	19.	Shirley Temple	49	36.	Elvis Presley (tie)	29
2.	Clint Eastwood	165	20.	Spencer Tracy (tie)	48	36.	Jack Nicholson (tie)	29
3.	Bing Crosby	111	20.	Barbra Streisand (tie)	48	38.	Jane Fonda (tie)	28
4.	Gary Cooper	102	22.	Steve McQueen	47	38.	Tom Hanks (tie)	28
5.	Clark Gable	91	23.	Dean Martin		38.	Will Rogers (tie)	28
6.	Burt Reynolds	90		& Jerry Lewis (tie)	46	38.	Robin Williams (tie)	28
7.	Bob Hope	84	23.	Mickey Rooney (tie)	46	42.	Mel Gibson	27
8.	Paul Newman	76	23.	Arnold		43.	Garson Greer (tie)	24
9.	Doris Day	72		Schwarzenegger (tie)	46	43.	John Travolta (tie)	24
10.	Rock Hudson	69	26.	Elizabeth Taylor	44	45.	Woody Allen (tie)	22
11.	Betty Grable	66	27.	Dustin Hoffman	42	45.	Michael Douglas (tie)	22
12.	Cary Grant	62	28.	Jack Lemmon	40	45.	Jerry Lewis (tie)	22
13.	Eddie Murphy (tie)	57	29.	Julie Andrews (tie)	35	48.	Glenn Ford (tie)	21
13.	Abbott & Costello (tie)	57	29.	Harrison Ford (tie)	35	48.	Julia Roberts (tie)	21
15.	James Stewart	56	31.	Humphrey Bogart (tie)	34	50.	Michael J. Fox (tie)	20
16.	Robert Redford	55	31.	Gary Cooper (tie)	34	50.	Paul Hogan (tie)	20
17.	Tom Cruise	52	33.	William Holden	33	50.	Lee Marvin (tie)	20
18.	Sylvester Stallone	50	34.	Sean Connery	32	50.	Robert Taylor (tie)	20
			35.	Kevin Costner	30			

THE HOLLYWOOD BLACKLIST

The House Committee on Un-American Activities investigated the entertainment business for subversive activities—i.e., communist connections—starting in 1947. By the end of the hearings in 1958, roughly 100 film, television, radio, theater, and music industry figures had been questioned. Approximately one-third of them provided the committee with the names of others who were alleged sympathizers. The remainder, insisting that their political beliefs were a private matter, took either the First or the Fifth Amendment and refused to name names; some of these men and women were jailed, almost all were blacklisted, and many had their careers ruined.

The following were some of the most well known of the informers who identified over 300 supposed communist sympathizers:

Lee J. Cobb, actor (*On the Waterfront*, *Twelve Angry Men*, *Death of a Salesman*, *Exodus*, "The Virginian")

Sterling Hayden, actor (*The Asphalt Jungle*, *Johnny Guitar*, *Dr. Strangelove*)

Roy Huggins, writer/director/producer ("Cheyenne," "Maverick," "The Rockford Files")

Elia Kazan, director (*Gentleman's Agreement*, *On the Waterfront*, *A Streetcar Named Desire*)

Isobel Lennart, screenwriter (*East Side, West Side*, *Anchors Aweigh*, *Meet Me in Las Vegas*)

Clifford Odets, playwright (*Waiting for Lefty*, *Golden Boy*)

Jerome Robbins, dancer/choreographer/assoc. director, New York City Ballet (*Fancy Free*, *Interplay*,

Dances at a Gathering)

Robert Rossen, director (*Body and Soul*, *All the King's Men*)

Budd Schulberg, screenwriter/novelist (*On the Waterfront*)

Leo Townsend, screenwriter (*Night and Day*, *Beach Blanket Bingo*, *Bikini Beach*)

The following, six of them Oscar winners at some point in their careers, refused to incriminate themselves or to inform on others, and as a result were either jailed, blacklisted, or forced to leave the country.

Herschel Bernardi, actor (*The Front*)

Howard Da Silva, actor (*Mommy Dearest*)

Carl Foreman, director/screenwriter (screenwriter, *High Noon*)

Dashiell Hammett, novelist (*The Thin Man*, *The Maltese Falcon*)

Lillian Hellman, playwright/screenwriter (*The Little Foxes*, *The Watch on the Rhine*)

Howard Koch, radio writer/screenwriter/playwright ("War of the Worlds," *Casablanca*)

Ring Lardner Jr., screenwriter (*Woman of the Year*, *Laura*, *M*A*S*H*)

Philip Loeb, actor ("The Goldbergs")

Joseph Losey, director (*The Concrete Jungle*, *The Damned*, *The Servant*, *Modesty Blaise*, *Boom!*, *The Go-Between*)

Albert Maltz, screenwriter/playwright (*This Gun for Hire*, *Destination Tokyo*, *The House I Live In*, *Pride of the Marines*, *The Robe*)

Arthur Miller, playwright/screenwriter (*The Crucible*, *Death of a Salesman*, *The Misfits*)

Zero Mostel, actor/comedian (*A Funny Thing Happened on the Way to the Forum*, *The Producers*, *Fiddler on the Roof*)

Dorothy Parker, short-story writer/screenwriter ("Laments for the Living," *A Star is Born*)

John Randolph, actor (*Come Back, Little*

Sheba, *Serpico*)

Paul Robeson, actor/singer (*Show Boat*, *The Emperor Jones*)

Waldo Salt, screenwriter (*Midnight Cowboy*, *Serpico*, *Coming Home*)

Robert Adrian Scott, screenwriter/producer (producer, *Murder, My Sweet*, *Crossfire*)

Pete Seeger, musician (coauthor, "If I Had a Hammer")

Gale Sondergaard, actress (*Anthony Adverse*, *A Night to Remember*, *The Spider Woman*)

Dalton Trumbo, screenwriter (*Kitty Foyle*, *Thirty Seconds over Tokyo*, *The Brave One* [under the name of Robert Rich], *Exodus*, *Hawaii*, *Spartacus*)

Sam Wanamaker, actor (*The Spy Who Came in from the Cold*, *Private Benjamin*)

Nedrick Young, screenwriter (*The Defiant Ones*, *Inherit the Wind*)

SUPERSTAR FILMOGRAPHIES

Here are filmographies for some of the most important, most popular, and most intriguing people in Hollywood today. The filmographies list only full-length feature films to which these actors and directors contributed significantly. Films are listed by their year of release, including some early works by now-famous figures that have been released directly onto video years after completion.

WOODY ALLEN
Director/screenwriter/actor

What's New, Pussycat? (screenwriter/actor, 1965)

What's Up, Tiger Lily? (director/screenwriter/actor, 1966)

Casino Royale (co-screenwriter/actor, 1967)

Take the Money and Run (director/co-screenwriter/actor, 1969)

Bananas (director/screenwriter/actor, 1971)

Play It Again, Sam (screenwriter/actor, 1972)

Everything You Always Wanted To Know About Sex* (*but were afraid to ask) (director/co-screenwriter/actor, 1972)

Sleeper (director/screenwriter/actor, 1973)

Love and Death (director/screenwriter/actor, 1975)

The Front (actor, 1976)

Annie Hall (director/co-screenwriter/actor, 1977; Academy Awards for best picture, best director, best original screenplay)

Interiors (director/screenwriter/actor, 1978)

Manhattan (director/co-screenwriter/actor, 1979)

Stardust Memories (director/screenwriter/actor, 1980)

A Midsummer Night's Sex Comedy (director/screenwriter/actor, 1982)

Zelig (director/screenwriter/actor, 1983)

Broadway Danny Rose (director/screenwriter/actor, 1984)

The Purple Rose of Cairo (director/screenwriter, 1985)

Hannah and Her Sisters (director/screenwriter/actor, 1986; Academy Award for best original screenplay)

Radio Days (director/screenwriter/actor, 1987)

King Lear (actor, 1987)

September (director/screenwriter, 1987)

Another Woman (director/screenwriter, 1988)

"Oedipus Wrecks," in New York Stories (director/co-screenwriter/actor, 1989)

Crimes and Misdemeanors (director/screenwriter/actor, 1989)

Alice (director/screenwriter, 1990)

Scenes from a Mall (actor, 1991)

Shadows and Fog (director/screenwriter/actor, 1992)

Husbands and Wives (director/screenwriter/actor, 1992)

Manhattan Murder Mystery (director/screenwriter/actor, 1993)

Bullets over Broadway (director/co-screenwriter, 1994)

Mighty Aphrodite (director/screenwriter/actor, 1995)

SANDRA BULLOCK
Actor

Who Shot Patakango? (1990)

Religion, Inc. (1990—videotape)

When the Party's Over (1992)

Who Do I Gotta Kill? (1992)

Love Potion No. 9 (1992)

The Vanishing (1993)

Fire on the Amazon (1992—videotape)

Demolition Man (1992)

The Thing Called Love (1993)

Wrestling Ernest Hemingway (1993)

Speed (1994)

While You Were Sleeping (1995)

The Net (1995)

GLENN CLOSE
Actor

The World According to Garp (1982)

The Big Chill (1983)

The Stone Boy (1984)

Greystoke: The Legend of Tarzan, Lord of the Apes (Voice, 1984)

The Natural (1984)

Jagged Edge (1985)

Maxie (1985)

Fatal Attraction (1987)

Dangerous Liaisons (1988)

Light Years (cartoon voice, 1988)

Immediate Family (1989)

Hamlet (1990)

Reversal of Fortune (1990)

Meeting Venus (1991)

The Paper (1994)

The House of the Spirits (1994)

Mary Reilly (1995)

SEAN CONNERY
Actor

No Road Back (1956)

Action of the Tiger (1957)

Another Time, Another Place (1958)

Hell Drivers (1957)

Time Lock (1957)

A Night to Remember (1958)

Tarzan's Greatest Adventure (1959)

Darby O'Gill and the Little People (1959)

On the Fiddle (1961)

The Frightened City (1961)

The Longest Day (1962)

Dr. No (1962)

From Russia with Love (1963)

Goldfinger (1964)

Woman of Straw (1964)

Marnie (1964)

Thunderball (1965)

The Hill (1965)

A Fine Madness (1966)

You Only Live Twice (1967)

Shalako (1968)

Bowler and Bonnet (1969, director)

The Molly Maguires (1970)

The Red Tent (1971)

The Anderson Tapes (1971)

Diamonds Are Forever (1971)

The Offence (or Something like the Truth, 1973)

Zardoz (1974)

Murder on the Orient Express (1974)

Ransom (1974)

The Wind and the Lion (1975)

The Man Who Would Be King (1975)

The Terrorists (1975)

Robin and Marian (1976)

The Next Man (1976)

A Bridge Too Far (1977)

The Great Train Robbery (1979)

Meteor (1979)

Cuba (1979)

Outland (1981)

Time Bandits (1981)

Wrong Is Right (1981)

G'ole (1982)

Five Days One Summer (1982)

Never Say Never Again (1983)

Sword of the Valiant (1984)

Highlander (1985)

The Name of the Rose (1986)

The Untouchables (1987; Academy Award for best supporting actor)

The Presidio (1988)

Memories of Me (1988)

Indiana Jones and the Last Crusade (1989)

Family Business (1989)

The Hunt for Red October (1990)

The Russia House (1990)

Highlander II: The Quickening (1991)

Robin Hood: Prince of Thieves (1991)

Medicine Man (1992)

Rising Sun (1993)

A Good Man in Africa (1994)

Just Cause (1995)

First Knight (1995)

FRANCIS FORD COPPOLA
Director/producer/screenwriter

Dementia 13 (director/screenwriter, 1963)

Is Paris Burning? (screenwriter, 1966)

This Property Is Condemned (screenwriter, 1966)

You're a Big Boy Now (director/screenwriter, 1966)

Finian's Rainbow (director, 1968)

The Rain People (director/screenwriter, 1969)

Patton (co-screenwriter, 1970; Academy Award for best screenplay)

The Godfather (director/co-screenwriter, 1972; Academy Award for best screenplay)

The Conversation (director/co-producer/screenwriter, 1974)

The Godfather, Part II (director/co-producer/coscreenwriter, 1974; Academy Awards for best director, best picture, best screenplay)

The Great Gatsby (screenwriter, 1974)

Apocalypse Now (director/producer/co-screenwriter/musical co-composer, 1979)

One from the Heart (director/co-screenwriter, 1982)

The Outsiders (director/producer, 1983)

Rumble Fish (director/co-screenwriter, 1983)

The Cotton Club (director/co-screenwriter, 1984)

Rip Van Winkle (for cable television) (director, 1985)

Captain EO (director, 1986)

Peggy Sue Got Married (director, 1986)

Gardens of Stone (director/co-producer, 1987)

Tucker: The Man and His Dream (director, 1988)

"Life Without Zoe," in *New York Stories* (director/co-screenwriter, 1989)

The Godfather, Part III (director/producer/co-screenwriter, 1990)

Bram Stoker's Dracula (director/producer, 1992)

Mary Shelley's Frankenstein (producer, 1994)

Don Juan DeMarco (co-producer, 1995)

KEVIN COSTNER
Actor/director/producer

Shadows Run Black (actor, 1981)

Night Shift (actor, 1982)

Stacy's Knights (actor, 1982)

The Big Chill (played corpse, all other scenes edited out, 1983)

The Gunrunner (actor, 1983)

Table for Five (actor, 1983)

Testament (actor, 1983)

American Flyers (actor, 1985)

Fandango (actor, 1985)

Silverado (actor, 1985)

Sizzle Beach, U.S.A. (actor, 1986)

No Way Out (actor, 1987)

The Untouchables (actor, 1987)

Bull Durham (actor, 1988)

Chasing Dreams (actor, 1989)

Field of Dreams (actor, 1989)

Dances with Wolves (actor/director/producer, 1990; Academy Awards for best picture, best director)

Revenge (actor, 1990)

Robin Hood: Prince of Thieves (actor, 1991)

JFK (actor, 1991)

The Bodyguard (actor/producer, 1992)

A Perfect World (actor, 1993)

Wyatt Earp (actor/producer, 1994)

Rapa Nui (co-producer, 1994)

The War (actor, 1994)

Waterworld (actor/producer, 1995)

TOM CRUISE
Actor

Endless Love (1981)

Taps (1981)

Losin' It (1983)

The Outsiders (1983)

Risky Business (1983)

All the Right Moves (1983)

Legend (1986)

Top Gun (1986)

The Color of Money (1986)

Cocktail (1988)

Rain Man (1988)

Born on the Fourth of July (1989)

Days of Thunder (1990)

Far and Away (1992)

A Few Good Men (1992)

The Firm (1993)

Interview with the Vampire (1994)

CLINT EASTWOOD
Actor/director/producer

Francis in the Navy (actor, 1955)

Lady Godiva (actor, 1955)

Never Say Goodbye (actor, 1955)

Revenge of the Creature (actor, 1955)

Tarantula (actor, 1955)

The Traveling Saleslady (actor, 1956)

Star in the Dust (actor, 1956)

Escapade in Japan (actor, 1957)

Ambush at Cimarron Pass (actor, 1958)

Lafayette Escadrille (actor, 1958)

A Fistful of Dollars (actor, 1964)

For a Few Dollars More (actor, 1965)

The Good, the Bad, and the Ugly (actor, 1966)

Coogan's Bluff (actor, 1968)

Hang 'Em High (actor, 1968)

The Witches (actor, 1968)

Where Eagles Dare (actor, 1968)

Paint Your Wagon (actor, 1969)

Kelly's Heroes (actor, 1970)

Two Mules for Sister Sara (actor, 1970)

The Beguiled (actor, 1971)

Dirty Harry (actor, 1971)

Play Misty For Me (actor/director, 1971)

Joe Kidd (actor, 1972)

Breezy (actor, 1973)

High Plains Drifter (actor/director, 1973)

Magnum Force (actor, 1973)

Thunderbolt and Lightfoot (actor, 1974)

The Eiger Sanction (actor/director, 1974)

The Outlaw Josey Wales (actor/director, 1975)

The Enforcer (actor, 1976)

The Gauntlet (actor/director, 1977)

Every Which Way but Loose (actor, 1978)

Escape from Alcatraz (actor, 1979)

Any Which Way You Can (actor, 1980)

Bronco Billy (actor/director, 1980)

Firefox (actor/director/producer, 1982)

Honkytonk Man (actor/director/producer, 1982)

Sudden Impact (actor/director/producer, 1983)

City Heat (actor, 1984)

Tightrope (actor/producer, 1984)

Pale Rider (actor/director/producer, 1985)

Heartbreak Ridge (actor/director/producer, 1986)

Bird (director/producer, 1988)

The Dead Pool (actor/producer, 1988)

Pink Cadillac (actor, 1989)

The Rookie (actor/director, 1990)

White Hunter, Black Heart (actor/director/producer, 1990)

Unforgiven (actor/director/producer, 1992; Academy Awards for best director and best film)

In the Line of Fire (actor/producer, 1993)

A Perfect World (actor/director, 1993)

The Bridges of Madison County (actor/director, 1995)

JODIE FOSTER
Actor/director

Napoleon and Samantha (1972)

Kansas City Bomber (1972)

Tom Sawyer (1973)

One Little Indian (1973)

Alice Doesn't Live Here Anymore (1974)

Echoes of a Summer (1976)

Bugsy Malone (1976)

Taxi Driver (1976)

The Little Girl Who Lives Down the Lane (1976)

Freaky Friday (1977)

Candleshoe (1977)

Moi, fleur bleue (1977)

Il Casotto (1977)

Carny (1980)

Foxes (1980)

O'Hara's Wife (1982)

Les Sang des autres (The Blood of Others) (1984)

The Hotel New Hampshire (1984)

Mesmerized (actor/co-producer, 1986)

Siesta (1987)

Five Corners (1988)

The Accused (1988; Academy Award for best actress)

Stealing Home (1988)

Backtrack (1989)

The Silence of the Lambs (1991; Academy Award for best actress)

Little Man Tate (actor/director, 1991)

Shadows and Fog (1992)

Sommersby (1993)

Maverick (1994)

Nell (1994)

Home for the Holidays (director, 1995)

MEL GIBSON
Actor/director

Summer City (1977)

Tim (1979)

Mad Max (1979)

Attack Force Z (1981)

Gallipoli (1981)

The Road Warrior (1981)

The Year of Living Dangerously (1982)

The Bounty (1984)

Mrs. Soffel (1984)

The River (1984)

Mad Max Beyond Thunderdome (1985)

Lethal Weapon (1987)

Tequila Sunrise (1988)

Lethal Weapon 2 (1989)

Air America (1990)

Bird on a Wire (1990)

Hamlet (1990)

Forever Young (1992)

Lethal Weapon 3 (1992)

The Man Without a Face (actor/director, 1993)

Maverick (1994)

Braveheart (actor/director/producer, 1995)

Pocahontas (cartoon voice, 1995)

WHOOPI GOLDBERG
Actor

The Color Purple (1985)

Jumpin' Jack Flash (1986)

Burglar (1987)

Fatal Beauty (1987)

Clara's Heart (1988)

The Telephone (1988)

Beverly Hills Brats (1989)

Homer and Eddie (1989)

Ghost (1990; Academy Award for best supporting actress)

The Long Walk Home (1990)

Soapdish (1991)

The Player (1992)

Sarafina! (1992)

Sister Act (1992)

Made in America (1993)

Sister Act 2: Back in the Habit (1993)

Corrina, Corrina (1994)

The Lion King (cartoon voice, 1994)

The Pagemaster (cartoon voice, 1994)

The Little Rascals (1994)

Star Trek: Generations (1994)

Boys on the Side (1995)

Moonlight & Valentino (1995)

TOM HANKS
Actor

He Knows You're Alone (1980)

Splash (1984)

Bachelor Party (1984)

The Man with One Red Shoe (1985)

Volunteers (1985)

The Money Pit (1986)

Nothing in Common (1986)

Everytime We Say Goodbye (1986)

Dragnet (1987)

Big (1988)

Punchline (1988)

The Burbs (1989)

Turner and Hooch (1989)

Joe Versus the Volcano (1990)

The Bonfire of the Vanities (1990)

Radio Flyer (1992)

A League of Their Own (1992)

Sleepless in Seattle (1993)

Philadelphia (1993; Academy Award for best actor)

Forrest Gump (1994; Academy Award for best actor)

Apollo 13 (1995)

Toy Story (cartoon voice, 1995)

ANTHONY HOPKINS
Actor

The Lion in Winter (1968)

Hamlet (1969)

The Looking Glass War (1970)

When Eight Bells Toll (1971)

Young Winston (1972)

A Doll's House (1973)

The Girl From Petrovka (1974)

Juggernaut (1974)

All Creatures Great and Small (1975)

Audrey Rose (1977)

A Bridge Too Far (1977)

International Velvet (1978)

Magic (1978)

A Change of Seasons (1980)

The Elephant Man (1980)

The Bounty (1984)

Blunt (1986)

The Good Father (1986)

84 Charing Cross Road (1987)

The Dawning (1988)

A Chorus of Disapproval (1987)

Desperate Hours (1990)

The Silence of the Lambs (1991; Academy Award for best actor)

The Remains of the Day (1993)

Shadowlands (1993)

The Trial (1993)

The Road to Wellville (1994)

Legends of the Fall (1994)

SPIKE LEE
Director/producer/screenwriter/actor

She's Gotta Have It (director/producer/screenwriter/actor, 1986)

School Daze (director/producer/screenwriter/actor, 1988)

Do the Right Thing (director/producer/screenwriter/actor, 1989)

Mo' Better Blues (director/producer/screenwriter/actor, 1990)

Lonely in America, (actor, 1990)

Jungle Fever (director/producer/screenwriter/actor, 1991)

Malcolm X (director/producer/co-screenwriter/actor, 1992)

Crooklyn (director/producer/co-screenwriter/actor, 1994)

Clockers (director/co-producer/co-screenwriter, 1995)

DEMI MOORE
Actor

Choices (1981)

Parasite (1982)

Young Doctors in Love (1982)

Blame It on Rio (1984)

No Small Affair (1984)

St. Elmo's Fire (1985)

About Last Night (1986)

One Crazy Summer (1986)

Wisdom (1986)

The Seventh Sign (1988)

We're No Angels (1989)

Ghost (1990)

Mortal Thoughts (actor/co-producer, 1991)

Nothing but Trouble (1991)

The Butcher's Wife (1991)

A Few Good Men (1992)

Indecent Proposal (1993)

Disclosure (1994)

The Scarlet Letter (1995)

JACK NICHOLSON
Actor/producer/screenwriter/director

Cry Baby Killer (1958)

Studs Lonigan (1960)

Too Soon To Love (1960)

The Wild Ride (1960)

Little Shop of Horrors (1961)

The Broken Land (1962)

The Raven (1963)

The Terror (1963)

Thunder Island (screenwriter, 1963)

Ensign Pulver (1964)

Back Door to Hell (1964)

The Fortune (1965)

Flight to Fury (actor/screenwriter, 1966)

Ride in the Whirlwind (actor/producer/screenwriter, 1966)

Hell's Angels on Wheels (1966)

The Shooting (actor/producer, 1967)

The Trip (screenwriter, 1967)

St. Valentine's Day Massacre (1967)

Head (actor/producer/screenwriter, 1968)

Psych-Out (1968)

Easy Rider (1969)

Five Easy Pieces (1970)

On a Clear Day You Can See Forever (1970)

Rebel Rousers (1970)

Carnal Knowledge (1971)

Drive, He Said (director/producer/screenwriter, 1971)

A Safe Place (1971)

The King of Marvin Gardens (1972)

The Last Detail (1973)

Chinatown (1974)

The Fortune (1975)

One Flew over the Cuckoo's Nest (1975; Academy Award for best actor)

The Passenger (1975)

Tommy (1975)

The Last Tycoon (1976)

The Missouri Breaks (1976)

Goin' South (actor/director, 1978)

The Shining (1980)

The Border (1981)

The Postman Always Rings Twice (1981)

Reds (1981)

Terms of Endearment (1983; Academy Award for best supporting actor)

Prizzi's Honor (1985)

Heartburn (1986)

Broadcast News (1987)

Ironweed (1987)

The Witches of Eastwick (1987)

Batman (1989)

The Two Jakes (actor/director, 1990)

Man Trouble (1992)

A Few Good Men (1992)

Hoffa (1992)

Wolf (1994)

The Crossing Guard (1995)

MICHELLE PFEIFFER
Actor

The Hollywood Knights (1980)

Falling in Love Again (1980)

Charlie Chan and the Curse of the Dragon Queen (1981)

Grease 2 (1982)

Scarface (1983)

Into the Night (1985)

Ladyhawke (1985)

Sweet Liberty (1986)

Amazon Women on the Moon (1987)

The Witches of Eastwick (1987)

Dangerous Liaisons (1988)

Married to the Mob (1988)

Tequila Sunrise (1988)

The Fabulous Baker Boys (1989)

The Russia House (1990)

Frankie and Johnny (1991)

Batman Returns (1992)

Love Field (1992)

The Age of Innocence (1993)

Wolf (1994)

Dangerous Minds (1995)

JULIA ROBERTS
Actor

Satisfaction (1988)

Mystic Pizza (1988)

Blood Red (1989)

Steel Magnolias (1989)

Pretty Woman (1990)

Flatliners (1990)

Sleeping with the Enemy (1991)

Dying Young (1991)

Hook (1991)

The Player (1992)

The Pelican Brief (1993)

I Love Trouble (1994)

Ready to Wear (1994)

Something To Talk About (1995)

Mary Reilly (1995)

MEG RYAN
Actor

Rich and Famous (1981)

Amityville 3-D (1983)

Armed and Dangerous (1986)

Top Gun (1986)

Innerspace (1987)

Promised Land (1987)

D.O.A. (1988)

The Presidio (1988)

When Harry Met Sally . . . (1989)

Joe Versus the Volcano (1990)

The Doors (1991)

Prelude to a Kiss (1992)

Sleepless in Seattle (1993)

Flesh and Bone (1993)

When a Man Loves a Woman (1994)

I.Q. (1994)

French Kiss (actor/coproducer, 1995)

ARNOLD SCHWARZENEGGER
Actor

Hercules in New York (1974)

Stay Hungry (1976)

Pumping Iron (1977)

The Villain (1979)

Conan the Barbarian (1982)

Conan the Destroyer (1984)

The Terminator (1984)

Commando (1985)

Red Sonja (1985)

Raw Deal (1986)

Predator (1987)

The Running Man (1987)

Red Heat (1988)

Twins (1988)

Total Recall (1989)

Kindergarten Cop (1990)

Terminator 2: Judgment Day (1991)

Last Action Hero (1993)

True Lies (1994)

Junior (1994)

MARTIN SCORSESE
Director/producer/screenwriter

Who's That Knocking at My Door? (director/screenwriter/actor, 1969)

Street Scenes 1970

(director/actor, 1970)

Boxcar Bertha (director, 1972)

Mean Streets (director/screenwriter, 1973)

Alice Doesn't Live Here Anymore (director, 1974)

Taxi Driver (director, 1976)

New York, New York (director, 1977)

American Boy: A Profile of Steven Prince (director, 1978)

The Last Waltz (director/actor, 1978)

Raging Bull (director/actor, 1980)

The King of Comedy (director/actor, 1983)

After Hours (director, 1985)

The Color of Money (director, 1986)

The Last Temptation of Christ (director, 1988)

"Life Lessons," in *New York Stories* (director, 1989)

GoodFellas (director/co-screenwriter, 1990)

Made in Milan (director, 1990)

The Grifters (producer, 1990)

Cape Fear (director, 1991)

The Age of Innocence (director/co-screenwriter, 1993)

Clockers (co-producer, 1995)

Casino (director/co-screenwriter, 1995)

STEVEN SPIELBERG
Director/producer/screenwriter

Duel (director, 1971)

The Sugarland Express (director/co-screenwriter,1974)

Jaws (director, 1975)

Close Encounters of the Third Kind (director/screenwriter, 1977)

1941 (director, 1979)

Raiders of the Lost Ark (director, 1981)

E.T., the Extra-Terrestrial (director/co-producer, 1982)

Poltergeist (co-producer/co-screenwriter, 1982)

"Kick the Can" in *Twilight Zone—The Movie* (director/co-producer, 1983)

Indiana Jones and the Temple of Doom (director, 1984)

The Color Purple (director/co-producer, 1985)

Special Academy Award presented in 1986, the Irving G. Thalberg Award, for consistently high quality of filmmaking

Empire of the Sun (director/co-producer, 1987)

Always (director/co-producer, 1989)

Indiana Jones and the Last Crusade (director, 1989)

Hook (director, 1991)

An American Tail II: Fievel Goes West (co-producer, 1991)

Jurassic Park (director, 1993)

Schindler's List (director/producer, 1993; Academy Awards for best director, best picture)

SYLVESTER STALLONE
Actor/director/screenwriter

A Party at Kitty and Stud's (reissued as *The Italian Stallion*) (actor, 1970)

Bananas (actor, 1971)

The Lords of Flatbush (actor/co-screenwriter, 1974)

Capone (actor, 1975)

Death Race 2000 (actor, 1975)

Farewell, My Lovely (actor, 1975)

No Place to Hide (actor, 1975)

The Prisoner of Second Avenue (actor, 1975)

Cannonball (actor, 1976)

Rocky (actor/screenwriter/fight choreographer, 1976)

F.I.S.T. (actor/co-screenwriter, 1978)

Paradise Alley (actor/director/screenwriter, 1978)

Rocky II (actor/director/screenwriter/fight choreographer, 1979)

Victory (actor, 1981)

Nighthawks (actor, 1981)

First Blood (actor/co-screenwriter, 1982)

Rocky III (actor/director/screenwriter/fight choreographer, 1982)

Staying Alive (director/co-producer/co-screenwriter, 1983)

Rhinestone (actor/co-screenwriter, 1984)

Rambo: First Blood, Part II (actor/co-screenwriter, 1985)

Rocky IV (actor/director/screenwriter, 1985)

Cobra (actor/screenwriter, 1986)

Over the Top (actor/co-screenwriter, 1987)

Rambo III (actor/co-screenwriter, 1988)

Lock Up (actor, 1989)

Tango and Cash (actor, 1989)

Rocky V (actor/screenwriter, 1990)

Oscar (actor, 1991)

Stop! or My Mom Will Shoot (actor, 1992)

Cliffhanger (actor/co-screenwriter, 1993)

Demolition Man (actor, 1993)

The Specialist (actor, 1994)

Judge Dredd (actor, 1995)

Assassins (actor, 1995)

SHARON STONE
Actor

Stardust Memories (1980)

Deadly Blessing (1981)

Bolero (France) (1981)

Irreconcilable Differences (1984)

King Solomon's Mines (1985)

Allan Quartermain and the Lost City of Gold (1987)

Action Jackson (1988)

Above the Law (1988)

Personal Choice (Beyond the Stars) (1989)

Blood and Sand (1989)

Total Recall (1990)

He Said, She Said (1991)

Scissors (1991)

Year of the Gun (1991)

Basic Instinct (1992)

Where Sleeping Dogs Lie (1992)

Diary of a Hitman (1992)

Sliver (1993)

Intersection (1994)

The Specialist (1994)

The Quick and the Dead (1995)

Casino (1995)

MERYL STREEP
Actor

Julia (1977)

The Deer Hunter (1978)

Manhattan (1979)

The Seduction of Joe Tynan (1979)

Kramer vs. Kramer (1979; Academy Award for best supporting actress)

The French Lieutenant's Woman (1981)

Sophie's Choice (1982; Academy Award for best actress)

Still of the Night (1982)

Silkwood (1983)

Falling in Love (1984)

Plenty (1985)

Out of Africa (1985)

Heartburn (1986)

Ironweed (1987)

A Cry in The Dark (1988)

She-Devil (1989)

Postcards from the Edge (1990)

Defending Your Life (1991)

Death Becomes Her (1992)

The House of the Spirits (1994)

The River Wild (1994)

The Bridges of Madison County (1995)

EMMA THOMPSON
Actor/screenwriter

Henry V (1989)

The Tall Guy (1989)

Impromptu (1990)

Dead Again (1991)

Howard's End (1992)

Peter's Friends (1992)

Much Ado About Nothing (1993)

The Remains of the Day (1993)

In the Name of the Father (1993)

Junior (1994)

Carrington (1995)

Sense and Sensibility (actor/screenwriter, 1995)

DENZEL WASHINGTON
Actor

Carbon Copy (1981)

A Soldier's Story (1984)

Power (1986)

Cry Freedom (1987)

Glory (1989; Academy Award for best supporting actor)

For Queen and Country (1989)

Reunion (1989)

The Mighty Quinn (1989)

Mo' Better Blues (1990)

Heart Condition (1990)

Ricochet (1991)

Mississippi Masala (1991)

Malcolm X (1992)

Much Ado About Nothing (1993)

The Pelican Brief (1993)

Philadelphia (1993)

Crimson Tide (1995)

Virtuosity (1995)

Devil in a Blue Dress (1995)

TOP FILM SOUNDTRACKS

We love to go to the movies, but a good soundtrack means we can take them home with us, too. And fans do, as this list indicates.

Soundtrack	Sales (in millions)
The Bodyguard	15
Dirty Dancing	11
Purple Rain	11
Saturday Night Fever	11
Grease	8
Footloose	8
The Lion King	8
Top Gun	7

THE TOP VIDEOS, YEAR-BY-YEAR

Billboard magazine has been tracking bestselling videos since 1980 and started ranking video rentals in 1982. Sales lists are now dominated by children's videos and exercise tapes with a growing smattering of soft porn, while rentals are led by a combination of certified hits and sleepers that viewers passed up at the box office.

1980

Sales
1. The Godfather
2. Saturday Night Fever
3. Superman
4. M*A*S*H
5. The Godfather, Part II
6. Blazing Saddles
7. 10
8. Grease
9. The Sound of Music
10. Halloween

1981

Sales
1. Airplane
2. Caddyshack
3. 9 to 5
4. Superman
5. Alien
6. Star Trek
7. Fame
8. Ordinary People
9. Elephant Man
10. Popeye

1982

Sales
1. Clash of the Titans
2. An American Werewolf in London
3. Atlantic City
4. Stir Crazy
5. The Jazz Singer
6. Blue Lagoon
7. Kramer vs. Kramer
8. Casablanca
9. Raging Bull
10. Jane Fonda's Workout

Rentals
1. Clash of the Titans
2. An American Werewolf in London
3. Arthur
4. Star Wars
5. Fort Apache, the Bronx
6. For Your Eyes Only
7. On Golden Pond
8. Stripes
9. The Cannonball Run
10. Superman II

1983

Sales
1. Jane Fonda's Workout
2. Star Trek II: The Wrath of Khan
3. An Officer and a Gentleman
4. The Compleat Beatles
5. Rocky III
6. Playboy Vol. I
7. Poltergeist
8. Star Wars
9. Blade Runner
10. Road Warrior

Rentals
1. An Officer and a Gentleman
2. Star Trek II: The Wrath of Khan
3. The Road Warrior
4. Rocky III
5. Poltergeist
6. First Blood
7. Das Boot
8. Night Shift
9. Blade Runner
10. Sophie's Choice

1984

Sales
1. Jane Fonda's Workout
2. Raiders of the Lost Ark
3. Making Michael Jackson's "Thriller"
4. Flashdance
5. Duran Duran
6. Risky Business
7. 48 Hrs.
8. Do It Debbie's Way
9. Trading Places
10. The Jane Fonda Workout Challenge

Rentals
1. Raiders of the Lost Ark
2. Risky Business
3. Flashdance
4. 48 Hrs.
5. Tootsie
6. Mr. Mom
7. Sudden Impact
8. Trading Places
9. Blue Thunder
10. Making Michael Jackson's "Thriller"

1985

Sales
1. Jane Fonda's Workout
2. Prime Time
3. Making Michael Jackson's "Thriller"
4. Purple Rain
5. Gone with the Wind
6. The Jane Fonda Workout Challenge
7. Raiders of the Lost Ark
8. Raquel, Total Beauty and Fitness
9. We Are the World—The Video Event
10. Wham! The Video

Rentals
1. The Karate Kid
2. The Terminator
3. Police Academy
4. Romancing the Stone
5. Revenge of the Nerds
6. The Natural
7. Starman
8. The Empire Strikes Back
9. Bachelor Party
10. Splash

1986

Sales
1. Jane Fonda's New Workout
2. Jane Fonda's Workout
3. Pinocchio
4. Beverly Hills Cop
5. The Sound of Music
6. Jane Fonda's Prime Time Workout
7. Casablanca
8. Gone with the Wind
9. The Wizard of Oz
10. The Best of John Belushi

Rentals
1. Back to the Future
2. Beverly Hills Cop
3. Prizzi's Honor
4. Witness
5. Ghostbusters
6. Rambo: First Blood, Part II
7. Return of the Jedi
8. Cocoon
9. Mask
10. Gremlins

1987

Sales
1. Jane Fonda's Low Impact Aerobic Workout
2. Jane Fonda's New Workout
3. Sleeping Beauty
4. Top Gun
5. Callanetics
6. The Sound of Music
7. Kathy Smith's Body Basics
8. Indiana Jones and the Temple of Doom
9. Star Trek III: The Search for Spock
10. Star Trek II: The Wrath of Khan

Rentals
1. Short Circuit
2. Top Gun
3. Back to School
4. Indiana Jones and the Temple of Doom
5. Down and Out in Beverly Hills
6. The Color of Money
7. Ferris Bueller's Day Off
8. Stand By Me
9. Ruthless People
10. Aliens

1988

Sales
1. Lady and the Tramp
2. Callanetics
3. Jane Fonda's Low Impact Aerobic Workout
4. Star Trek IV: The Voyage Home
5. Start Up with Jane Fonda
6. An American Tale
7. Jane Fonda's New Workout
8. Pink Floyd: The Wall
9. Dirty Dancing
10. Sleeping Beauty

Rentals
1. Dirty Dancing
2. Lethal Weapon
3. Fatal Attraction
4. The Untouchables
5. The Witches of Eastwick
6. No Way Out
7. Outrageous Fortune

8. Robocop
9. Stakeout
10. Tin Men

1989

Sales

1. Cinderella
2. E.T., the Extra-Terrestrial
3. Jane Fonda's Complete Workout
4. Moonwalker
5. Callanetics
6. Dirty Dancing
7. The Wizard of Oz: The Fiftieth Anniversary Edition
8. Lethal Weapon
9. U2 Rattle and Hum
10. Pink Floyd: The Delicate Sound of Thunder

Rentals

1. Big
2. Die Hard
3. A Fish Called Wanda
4. Three Men and a Baby
5. Beetlejuice
6. Coming to America
7. Cocktail
8. Twins
9. Bull Durham
10. "Crocodile" Dundee II

1990

Sales

1. Bambi
2. New Kids on the Block: Hangin' Tough Live
3. The Little Mermaid
4. Lethal Weapon 2
5. The Wizard of Oz: The Fiftieth Anniversary Edition
6. Batman
7. Honey, I Shrunk the Kids
8. The Land Before Time
9. Who Framed Roger Rabbit
10. Teenage Mutant Ninja Turtles: Cowabunga, Shredhead

Rentals

1. Look Who's Talking
2. When Harry Met Sally

3. Parenthood
4. K-9
5. Dead Poets Society
6. Steel Magnolias
7. Sea of Love
8. Robocop
9. Stakeout
10. Tin Men

1991

Sales

1. Pretty Woman
2. The Little Mermaid
3. Peter Pan
4. The Jungle Book
5. Three Tenors in Concert
6. Richard Simmons: Sweatin' to the Oldies
7. Teenage Mutant Ninja Turtles: The Movie
8. The Terminator
9. Ducktales: The Movie
10. Total Recall

Rentals

1. Ghost
2. Pretty Woman
3. GoodFellas
4. Bird on a Wire
5. Flatliners
6. The Hunt for Red October
7. Kindergarten Cop
8. Total Recall
9. Sleeping with the Enemy
10. Another 48 Hrs.

1992

Sales

1. Fantasia
2. 101 Dalmations
3. The Jungle Book
4. Robin Hood: Prince of Thieves
5. Cherfitness: A New Attitude
6. Fievel Goes West
7. 1992 Playboy Video Playmate Calendar
8. Home Alone
9. The Rescuers Down Under
10. Playboy: Sexy Lingerie IV

Rentals

1. Thelma and Louise

2. The Silence of the Lambs
3. The Fisher King
4. City Slickers
5. Backdraft
6. Cape Fear
7. The Hand That Rocks the Cradle
8. Father of the Bride
9. Deceived
10. What About Bob?

1993

Sales

1. Beauty and the Beast
2. Pinocchio
3. 101 Dalmations
4. Playboy Celebrity Centerfold: Jessica Hahn
5. Sister Act
6. Playboy Playmate of the Year 1993: Anna Nicole Smith
7. Cindy Crawford/Shape Your Body Workout
8. Home Alone 2: Lost in New York
9. Disney's Sing Along Songs: Friend Like Me
10. Beethoven

Rentals

1. Sister Act
2. Patriot Games
3. Under Siege
4. A League of Their Own
5. A Few Good Men
6. Scent of a Woman
7. Unforgiven
8. Sneakers
9. Passenger 57
10. The Bodyguard

1994

Sales

1. Aladdin
2. Playboy Celebrity Centerfold: Dian Parkinson
3. Yanni: Live at the Acropolis
4. Free Willy
5. Mrs. Doubtfire
6. The Fugitive
7. The Return of Jafar
8. The Fox and the Hound
9. Ace Ventura: Pet Detective

10. Beauty and the Beast
11. Playboy: 1994 Playmate of the Year
12. The Bodyguard
13. Playboy 1994 Video Playmate Calendar
14. Beethoven's 2nd
15. Homeward Bound: The Incredible Journey
16. Dennis the Menace
17. The Secret Garden
18. Pinocchio
19. Penthouse: 25th Anniversary Swimsuit Video
20. The Three Tenors in Concert 1994
21. Thumbelina
22. We're Back!: A Dinosaur Story
23. Batman: Mask of the Phantasm
24. Playboy: College Girls
25. D2: The Mighty Ducks

Rentals

1. Sleepless in Seattle
2. Philadelphia
3. In the Line of Fire
4. The Pelican Brief
5. The Fugitive
6. The Firm
7. Carlito's Way
8. Sliver
9. Ace Ventura: Pet Detective
10. Mrs. Doubtfire
11. Grumpy Old Men
12. Rising Sun
13. Cliffhanger
14. Tombstone
15. A Perfect World
16. Malice
17. Cool Runnings
18. The Joy Luck Club
19. Indecent Proposal
20. Dave
21. Four Weddings and a Funeral
22. Demolition Man
23. Schindler's List
24. On Deadly Ground
25. The Ref

EXTRA! EXTRA! HOW TO GET IN THE BIG PICTURE

Did you envy those glamorous hordes of Scotsmen in *Braveheart*? Do you dream of being on-screen with Brad Pitt? Well, don't sit around waiting to be discovered. Here's how to get your face on the silver screen (or at least in a car commercial). (For more detailed information, check *Back to One*, by Cullen Chambers.)

CASTING AGENCIES

The easiest way to land a bit part in the movies, on TV, or on the radio is to register with a casting agency. There are hundreds of these in the L.A. area. Most charge a modest registration fee of $20 or under, or no fee at all. The following are some of the best known and reputed. The proper registration procedure is noted at the end of each entry.

Academy Kids Management
(casts children only)
Vineland Studios
4942 Vineland Ave. #103
N. Hollywood, Calif. 91601
(818) 769-8091
By appointment

Anna Miller Casting
P.O. Box 66
Sunland, Calif. 91041
(213) 957-4696
By appointment

Bill Dance Casting
3518 W. Cahuenga Blvd. #210
Los Angeles, Calif. 90068
(213) 878-1131
Walk-ins Monday through
Thursday from noon to 1 p.m.

Cast of Thousands
4011 W. Magnolia
Burbank, Calif. 91050
(818) 955-9995
Walk-ins Tuesday from
2 to 5 p.m.

Central/Cenex Casting
The largest casting agency in
the entertainment industry.
Central Casting handles
union actors; Cenex handles

non-union actors.
1700 Burbank Blvd.
Burbank, Calif. 91506
Central: (818) 562-2700
Cenex: (818) 562-2800
Central: walk-ins Tuesday
(last name A through L) and
Thursday (last name M
through Z) 2 to 3:30 p.m.
Cenex: walk-ins Monday,
Wednesday, and Friday from
10 to 11:30 a.m.

Lane Model and Talent Agency
14071 Windsor Place
Santa Ana, Calif. 92705
(714) 731-1420
Send photo and resumé

Messenger Associates Casting
P.O. Box 2380
Toluca Lake, Calif. 91601
(818) 508-5486

HOW THE MIGHTY HAVE RISEN

They're big stars now—but they weren't born that way. These Hollywood idols began their movie careers as lowly extras.

Lucille Ball	Janet Gaynor	Mary Tyler Moore
Gary Cooper	Whoopi Goldberg	Ronald Reagan
Bill Cosby	Mark Harmon	Burt Reynolds
Kevin Costner	Dustin Hoffman	Tom Selleck
Robert De Niro	Bob Hope	Suzanne Somers
Robert Duvall	Casey Kasem	Sylvester Stallone
Clark Gable	Michael Landon	Donald Sutherland
Teri Garr	Sophia Loren	John Wayne
	Marilyn Monroe	

Send photo and resumé, then call for appointment

Rainbow Casting
12501 Chandler Blvd. #206
N. Hollywood, Calif. 91607
(818) 752-2278
Walk-ins Monday through Thursday from 11 a.m. to 2 p.m.

Screen Children Agency
(casts children only)
12444 Ventura Blvd. #103
Studio City, Calif. 91604
(818) 846-4300
Send photo and resumé

PAYMENT

Extra work may be a rich experience, but it's not a very lucrative one. A typical salary for eight hours is $40; children can claim somewhat higher wages. The money's a little better if you're in Actors Equity, Screen Actors Guild, or the American Federation of Television and Radio Artists—yet you needn't join a union to get in on the action, and you'll still get salary "bumps" for almost anything you do beyond standing around in a crowd scene. Time-and-a-half is paid for shifts between eight and 10 hours; double time is paid for anything over 10 hours.

TRADE SOURCES

These magazines list casting calls and give up-to-the-minute facts on curent films and theater productions.

Backstage
1515 Broadway
New York, N.Y., 10036-8986
(212) 764-7300
published: weekly
cost per issue: $2.25

Backstage West
5055 Wilshire Blvd.
Los Angeles, Calif. 90036
(213) 525-2356
published: weekly
cost per issue: $1.85

Dramalogue
146 Gordon Ave.
Hollywood, Calif.
(213) 464-5079
published: weekly
cost per issue: $1.85

Hollywood Reporter
5055 Wilshire Blvd.
Los Angeles, Calif. 90036
(213) 525-2000
published: weekdays
cost per issue: $1.00

Daily Variety
5700 Wilshire Blvd.
Los Angeles, Calif.,
(213) 857-6600
published: weekdays
cost per issue: $.95

TALKING THE TALK

On the set, what separates the men from the boys (or the women from the girls) is whether they know how to separate the "gaffer" from the "flipper."

craft services
on-set catering

flipper
cosmetic false teeth for children

gaffer
lighting and electrical equipment crew member

golden time
overtime after the 16th hour for theatrical talent

honey wagon
truck or towed vehicle containing dressing rooms, production offices, and/or mobile restrooms

hot set
a set that is ready for use and is not to be disturbed

P&G
performers with a clean-cut, all-American look like that favored by Proctor & Gamble for its ads

sight-and-sound
parents' right under union contract to be within sight and sound of their child performer at all times

wild track
soundtrack with no apparent relationship to the picture it accompanies

OSCAR—DECADE-BY-DECADE

67, an age for savoring life's achievements—even though one's joints might creak. "He rattles," says Olivia de Havilland, holding her 1949 Oscar to the phone receiver and shaking him to illustrate. Ernest Borgnine, a 1955 winner, complains that his Oscar "flakes." Jack Lemmon, who took his *Mr. Roberts* Oscar home in 1956, says the statue rusted: "I had to send him back to the Academy to be redipped." But, ah, how nice to have the old guy around.

Sure, like any sexagenarian, Oscar has taken his lumps. He's been called "a cruel joke" (Marion Davies), "a heartbreaker" (Orson Welles), and "something to be feared" (George C. Scott). But don't count him out. Oscar's imprimatur can add $25 million or more to a winning film's gross, double an actor's salary, and at least triple the size of his ego.

What a shock, then, to learn that Oscar started life as a patsy. In 1927, MGM kingpin Louis B. Mayer and 35 cronies decided to form an Academy of Motion Picture Arts and Sciences. Forget the high-toned blather of the first charter seeking "the improvement and advancement of the . . . profession." What Mayer really wanted was to stop the advance of film unions. An Academy would keep labor disputes in the hands of the studios. As a carrot to actors, writers,

directors, and technicians, Mayer formed a committee to find "some little way" of rewarding merit in film.

While Mayer finagled, MGM art director Cedric Gibbons doodled a sketch of a naked man with a sword, standing on a reel of film. Today Oscar is a thirteen-and-a-half inch, eight-and-a-half pound trophy cast in a metal alloy, then plated in turn with copper, nickel, silver, and finally gold. At Oscar's debut in 1929, some laughed. Screenwriter Frances (*The Champ*) Marion believed Hollywood had found its ideal symbol, "an athletic body . . . with half his head, that part which held his brains, completely sliced off."

But, hey, Oscar didn't need brains. The studio bosses controlled the nominations and virtually hand-picked the winners. It took years for Oscar to clean house—the Academy did not even start using sealed envelopes until 1941. Since then the Academy, which has grown from a scant 36 members in 1927 to the 4,523 voting members of today, has tried to discourage machinations, especially ad campaigns, to influence voting. It hasn't succeeded, of course. But Oscar, by dint of sheer perseverance, has become, in the words of 1957 winner Alec (*The Bridge on the River Kwai*) Guinness, "the most highly

prized [award] of all." At this point, the grandstanding and costuming have become as much a reason for tuning in the Oscars as finding out the winners. "Well, hell—let's face it," says Katharine Hepburn, recipient of a record four Oscars for acting, "It's our track meet. It's painful but it's thrilling."

THE FIRST DECADE

1927-1936

Oscar threw his first party in 1929. The press stayed away. A black-tie crowd clapped politely as all 12 awards were distributed in under five minutes. The three Best Actor nominees didn't bother to show up. Janet Gaynor, first Best Actress winner, gamely tried to act thrilled. "Had I known what it would come to mean in the next few years," she said later, "I'm sure I'd have been overwhelmed." It was the first and last Oscar bust. The Depression and the sound era soon made movies into the ideal escapism, and Oscar's touch came to mean box-office gold. Some aspired to win. Others conspired. As ever in Hollywood, greed, jealousy, and raw ambition added up to a helluva show.

The first Best Actor winner, Emil Jannings, had scooted home to Germany before collecting his Oscar scroll. His later Nazi propaganda films—done, he said, under duress—

made him a favorite with Hitler. Marlene Dietrich disputed the Fuhrer on the talents of her *Blue Angel* costar: "He was a terrible ham."

★

First ceremony: Hollywood's elite jammed the Roosevelt Hotel to hear Al Jolson put down the Oscar as a "paperweight." Jolie's film, *The Jazz Singer*—an early talkie—had been disqualified; only silent films were eligible. The Academy was suspicious of new trends. Some things never change.

★

The WWI air extravaganza *Wings*, starring Buddy Rogers, Clara Bow, and Richard Arlen, was the first Best Picture winner. With tinted color in the battle scenes and noise machines in the theaters to simulate plane crashes, here was a primitive *Top Gun* that showed the Academy's early fondness for spectacle.

★

In 1930, Norma Shearer, winner for *The Divorcée*, posed for a photograph with Oscar two days *before* the ceremony. "She sleeps with the boss," sniped Joan Crawford. Rumor had it that MGM's Irving Thalberg pressured employees to vote for his wife.

★

Oscar's first tie: Fredric March (*Dr. Jekyll and Mr. Hyde*) and Wallace Beery (*The Champ*) shared the 1931 gold. Both had recently adopted children. "Odd,"

said March, "that Wally and I were given awards for best male performance."

★

Clark Gable and Claudette Colbert both took Oscars for Frank Capra's 1934 comedy, *It Happened One Night*, as did Capra and the film—the only clean sweep in Academy history until *One Flew over the Cuckoo's Nest* duplicated the feat in 1975. No one expected it. Everybody still thinks Gable won for *Gone with the Wind*.

★

The Academy invented a new category, Best Song, prompted by Fred Astaire & Ginger Rogers's dancing and singing of "The Continental" in 1934's *The Gay Divorcee*.

★

Bette Davis collected an award for 1935's *Dangerous*, and gave the statue its name. Reflecting that the trophy "resembled the backside" of her first husband, bandleader Harmon Oscar Nelson Jr., she dubbed her prize Oscar. The moniker stuck.

THE SECOND DECADE

1937–1946

The Oscar ceremony was establishment now, broadcast on radio. In 1939 Gone with the Wind *became the most popular and profitable film ever. But this was also a time of war, as reflected in movies from* Mrs. Miniver *to* The Best Years of Our Lives. *Winston Churchill hailed* Miniver *as "propaganda*

worth a hundred battleships." As a wartime cost-cutting measure, the Academy ended its elaborate banquets and took the show inside a theater, where food and drink could no longer distract from the ego battles.

Walt Disney is given a special honorary award for 1938's *Snow White and the Seven Dwarfs*, featuring one large Oscar and seven tiny ones.

★

Gone with the Wind, then the costliest movie in history ($3,957,000) wins eight Oscars, a record not broken until 1958's *Gigi*. Leigh was the triumphant victor, Gable the disgruntled loser. "This was my last chance," he groaned. He was right.

Hattie McDaniel, Miss Scarlett's maid, was the first black actor to win an Oscar. Hattie sobbed on accepting her plaque (supporting players didn't receive full statues until 1943).

★

Playing George M. Cohan in 1942, James Cagney—America's favorite tough guy—became the first actor to win an Oscar for a musical. "Don't forget," said Jimmy in his acceptance speech, "it was a pretty good part."

★

Bogie told Ingrid Bergman in *Casablanca* that their wartime love story "didn't amount to a hill of beans in this crazy world." Except for winning the Best Picture

Oscar of 1943 and the hearts of all romantics.

★

Barry Fitzgerald's role as a twinkly old priest in 1944's *Going My Way* made him a popular winner. But at home a few days later, he forgot that wartime Oscars were made of plaster instead of bronze and decapitated his prize with a golf club.

★

The Lost Weekend, the Best Picture of 1945, offered an unsparing portrait of an alcoholic, by Ray Milland. "I gave it everything I had," said the actor. He must have. Accepting the Oscar, a speechless Milland simply bowed and departed.

THE THIRD DECADE

1947–1956

No sooner had the war ended over there than the Academy embarked on its own war at home. The enemy? Television. The little black box was emptying movie theaters at an alarming rate. The studios retaliated at first with sex, violence, and Cinema-scope, then gave in. So did Oscar. The Academy Awards were telecast for the first time in 1953. Variety's headline heralded a new era: "1ST MAJOR PIX-TV WEDDING BIG CLICK."

Many years prior, actor Walter Huston said he asked his son, John, "If you ever become a writer or director, please find a good part for your old man." John complied with *Treasure of the*

Sierra Madre and won 1948 Oscars for them both.

★

Joseph Mankiewicz's crackerjack 1950 comedy *All About Eve* still holds the record—14 nominations. Though *Eve* won six Oscars, including Best Picture, co-stars Bette Davis and Anne Baxter both lost to *Born Yesterday*'s Judy Holliday.

★

Vivien Leigh copped her second Best Actress Oscar in 1951 for *A Streetcar Named Desire*. When the award was announced in Hollywood, Leigh was in New York starring in *Antony and Cleopatra* with then-husband Laurence Olivier.

★

In Hollywood, Donald O'Connor watched Shirley Booth's reaction in New York on being named 1952's Best Actress for *Come Back, Little Sheba*. Meanwhile, the largest single audience (about 80 million) in TV's five-year history saw the first Oscarcast.

★

Having fought to play Maggio in 1953's *From Here to Eternity*, Frank Sinatra triumphed. Said the Best Supporting Actor, "I ducked the party and took a walk. Just me and Oscar." The salty version of James Jones's Army-barracks novel won a whopping eight Oscars, including Best Picture. And Deborah Kerr's sexy roll on the sand with Burt Lancaster cracked her saintly image.

★

A year before her royal wedding in 1956, *The Country Girl*'s Grace Kelly scored an upset victory over Judy Garland in *A Star is Born*. Kelly confided: "I wanted to win so badly, I was afraid that I would stand up no matter which name was read out."

★

First-time film producer Michael Todd nabbed the 1956 Best Picture Oscar with his star-studded *Around the World in 80 Days*. "Imagine this—and being married to Liz, too," he enthused.

THE FOURTH DECADE

1957–1966

The times they were a-changing. Drugs, hippies, the youth movement, civil rights demonstrations, the Kennedy assassination: Many films dealt with these social and political upheavals. But you couldn't tell by Oscar. Relevant was out; big was in. The Academy awarded either historical epics (Ben-Hur, The Bridge on the River Kwai, Lawrence of Arabia, A Man for All Seasons) or blockbuster musicals (Gigi, West Side Story, My Fair Lady, The Sound of Music). The most controversial move on the Academy's part was to issue a formal slap to those who tried to "buy" Oscar nominations by purchasing self-congratulatory ads in the trade papers. Few paid heed.

Joanne Woodward, the new Mrs. Paul Newman, collected her 1957 Oscar for *The Three*

Faces of Eve in a $100 dress she made herself. Joan Crawford claimed Hollywood glamour "had been set back twenty years." When Paul finally won his Oscar, twenty-nine years later, clothes weren't a problem. He didn't show up at all.

★

In 1959, Best Picture *Ben-Hur* took a record eleven Oscars, including Best Actor for Charlton Heston, who got the part after Burt Lancaster dropped out. "It was hard work," said Chuck, who drove a mean chariot. But some questioned his talents. "That Heston," said actor Aldo Ray, "what a hamola."

★

Denounced in Congress in 1950 for her adulterous affair with Roberto Rossellini, Ingrid Bergman ended her decade-long Hollywood exile by presenting a 1959 Best Picture Oscar to *Gigi* producer Arthur Freed. She said her recipe for happiness was "good health and a poor memory."

★

Sporting a tracheotomy scar from a near-fatal bout of pneumonia, Liz Taylor scored a sympathy Oscar for 1960's *Butterfield 8*. In 1966 Liz won Oscar No. 2 for *Who's Afraid of Virginia Woolf?*, but railed at the Academy when fifth husband Richard Burton failed to win too.

★

"I'd like to think it will help," said Sidney Poitier after Anne Bancroft opened

the envelope and, for 1963's *Lilies of the Field*, he became the first black Best Actor winner. "But I don't believe my Oscar will be a magic wand that will wipe away the restrictions on job opportunities for Negro actors."

★

Sisters and Best Actress nominees Lynn and Vanessa Redgrave, cited respectively for 1966's *Georgy Girl* and *Morgan!*, were only the second sister nominees in Oscar history. And they came from a notable British acting family to boot. Maybe so. But Liz Taylor still whupped them both.

THE FIFTH DECADE

1967–1976

Oscar neared its half-century mark in a reactionary mood. Breakthrough films such as Bonnie and Clyde, The Graduate, *and* Easy Rider *ended up losers. In 1968, the year of* 2001: A Space Odyssey, Oliver! *won the Best Picture prize. Yikes. No wonder a streaker felt the need to defame one of the decade's Academy telecasts. Then, a rebel cry was heard in filmland. Newcomers Dustin Hoffman and Jon Voight dared to duke it out with the Duke, John Wayne, for the statue. They failed, but their X-rated* Midnight Cowboy *took the Best Picture prize in 1969. Jane Fonda raised hackles with her Vietnam views and won anyway. The warring*

factions of the Academy were creating sparks.

For the second time in Oscar history, a tie was declared. *Funny Girl's* Barbra Streisand and *The Lion in Winter's* Katharine Hepburn received the same number of votes from the 1968 Academy's 3,030 members. Designer Edith Head was "shocked," not by the tie but by Streisand's tacky peekaboo pantsuit.

★

John Wayne had to let it all hang out in 1969 as bloated, one-eyed Rooster Cogburn to finally collect his first Oscar at 62 after 250 movies. "Wow," drawled the Duke, "if I had known, I would have put that eye patch on 35 years earlier."

★

Deriding the Oscars as a "meat parade," George C. Scott declined his nomination as 1970's Best Actor. "My God!" exclaimed Goldie Hawn as she opened the envelope and read the winner's name, "It's George C. Scott."

★

When Marlon Brando was voted 1972's Best Actor, he sent Apache Sacheen Littlefeather to reject the Oscar for all the Native Americans Hollywood had demeaned. "Childish," scowled Charlton Heston. "Wonderful," gushed Jane Fonda.

★

Would-be comic Robert Opel snuck backstage at the 1974 Oscars ceremony, flustering emcee David Niven as the cameras cut away to spare home viewers the streaker's shortcomings. The hit of a dull show, Opel was found murdered five years later in his San Francisco sex shop.

★

Struggling actor Sylvester Stallone took half a week to write a script for himself about an underdog fighter. He lost the Best Actor Oscar, but the sleeper film won the title as Best Picture of 1976. "*Rocky* will be remembered," said Sly with typical modesty. As time would tell, the real issue is if Rocky will ever go away.

THE SIXTH DECADE

1977–1986

Oscar had a goal now. Ignoring the films of George Lucas and Steven Spielberg became a full-time job. The Hardy Boys of the zap-happy set combined their youthful fantasies with dazzling special effects to create eight of the top 10 box office hits of all time (E.T., Star Wars, Return of the Jedi, The Empire Strikes Back, Jaws, Raiders of the Lost Ark, Indiana Jones, and Back to the Future). Not a Best Picture winner in the bunch. The Academy, doing penance for scorning Vietnam in the previous decade, annointed politically themed films from The Deer Hunter to Platoon. A vote for Gandhi, the movie, was a vote for Gandhi, the man. Oscar, typically late,

began sporting a social conscience.

Accepting her Best Supporting Actress Oscar for 1976's *Julia*, Vanessa Redgrave dismissed as "Zionist hoodlums" those who showed up to protest her politics. The audience booed, Vanessa had to dine later with her two bodyguards, and a confused Jack Nicholson cracked, "What are these Zionists? I've been skiing."

★

"It's simply terrific. This is something," sputtered Diane Keaton after accepting the 1977 Best Actress prize for *Annie Hall* from first winner Janet Gaynor. Her co-star and former boyfriend Woody Allen stayed home and shrugged off the Academy as meaningless: "I just don't think they know what they're doing."

★

Robert Redford and Warren Beatty have never won Oscars for their acting. That might make sense. Instead, each (Redford for 1980's *Ordinary People* and Beatty for 1981's *Reds*) took the prize as Best Director—a pinnacle Hitchcock, Bergman, Fellini, and Orson Welles never reached. Go figure.

Jane Fonda rushed from the 1982 Academy Awards show to present her ailing father and *On Golden Pond* costar, Henry, with the long-overdue first Oscar of his 47-year career. "Hell, if I hadn't won, I wouldn't be able to walk with my head up anymore,"

Fonda said to his wife, Shirlee. He died five months later.

★

Gidget gets respect: For 1984's *Places in the Heart*, Sally Field won a second Oscar and spoke the words that will haunt her forever: "You like me! You like me!"

★

Perennial also-ran Paul Newman won for reprising his 1961 *Hustler* role in 1986's *The Color of Money*. "After losing six times, I felt it cruel and unusual punishment to attend," said the no-show.

★

Writer-director Oliver Stone took the 1986 Best Picture Oscar for *Platoon*, based on his wartime experiences in Vietnam—a film almost no studio wanted to make.

★

In 1987 Marlee Matlin of *Children of a Lesser God* became the first hearing-impaired Best Actress winner. "After I'm alone I'm going to scream," she said.

THE SEVENTH DECADE

1987 and counting

Oscar continues his old traditions by heaping awards on elder statesmen — from Clint Eastwood, Paul Newman, and Sean Connery to Jack Palance, Jessica Tandy, and Martin Landau—who should have been recognized long before. Best Director continues to be a fickle category— many films, such as The Prince of Tides, are honored with numerous nominations for everyone but the director. But the drought finally ends for traditional punching bag Steven Spielberg. Of course it took the culturally significant Schindler's List *to get the Oscar monkey off of Spielberg's back (after three previous Best Director nominations), rather than his second-highest grossing movie of all time,* Jurassic Park— *making it clear that he was chosen as best director, not most successful. In 1995,* Forrest Gump *bucks the conventional wisdom that box-office favorites don't play well in Academy-land, becoming the highest-grossing picture ever to claim the Best Picture Award.*

In 1988, a barely dressed, slightly tattooed Cher wins Best Actress and announces, "I don't think that this means I am somebody, but I guess I'm on my way."

★

The telecast hits new lows in production values in 1989, with the dreadful Snow White musical opening giving Oscar a black eye.

★

Whoopi Goldberg becomes only the second African-American woman to claim an acting award, as Best Supporting Actress for her role in 1990's *Ghost*.

★

Jack Palance shows he's no old-timer by performing one-handed push-ups by way of accepting his Best Supporting Actor statuette for *City Slickers*. And he provides Oscar host Billy Crystal with a year's worth of material.

★

Anna Paquin, 11, is the youngest winner since 1973, taking Best Supporting Actress for her role in 1993's *The Piano*.

★

Lizzy Gardiner, the winner for best costume design on *Priscilla, Queen of the Desert*, makes a memorable imprint on the 1995 ceremonies in her dress fashioned from American Express gold cards.

★

After five previous nominations and one award (for 1982's *Tootsie*) and several years of relative obscurity, Jessica Lange, 45, takes the Best Actress Oscar in 1995 for her portrayal of the rebellious wife of an Army officer in *Blue Sky*. Maybe the performance sweetened with age: Orion Pictures' financial woes kept the film—and Lange's comeback performance—on a bank vault floor for three years before its release.

IN THE NAME OF PRODUCTION

More and more celebrity actors are starting their own production companies. But how did they get such funny names? Here's a list of some luminary-owned companies and the inspiration behind their appellations.

Actor	Production Company	Where the Name Came From
Kevin Costner	TIG Productions	The nickname of his grandmother
Robert Duvall	Butcher's Run Films	The name of a farm he once owned in Virginia
Clint Eastwood	Malpaso Productions	A creek in Carmel, Calif., and a Spanish expression meaning "dangerous step," which critics mistakenly assumed he made in forming the company
Jodie Foster	Egg Pictures	The egg as a symbol of protection
Michael J. Fox	Snowback Productions	Canadian slang for someone who crosses the border to the United States
Tom Hanks	Clavius Base	The otherworldly planet in Stanley Kubrick's *2001: A Space Odyssey*
Dustin Hoffman	Punch Productions	After the Punchinello character in *Punch and Judy* shows
Meg Ryan	Prufrock Pictures	Alluding to one of her favorite poems, T. S. Eliot's "Love Song of J. Alfred Prufrock"
Wesley Snipes	Amen Ra Films	The Egyptian sun god
Patrick Swayze	Troph Productions	His nickname in high school because he won so many sports trophies
Denzel Washington	Mundy Lane Entertainment	The street he grew up on in Mount Vernon, N.Y.

THE ACADEMY AWARDS

	1927–28	1928–29	1929–30
Picture	*Wings*	*Broadway Melody*	*All Quiet on the Western Front*
Actor	Emil Jannings, *The Last Command; The Way of All Flesh*	Warner Baxter, *In Old Arizona*	George Arliss, *Disraeli*
Actress	Janet Gaynor, *Seventh Heaven; Street Angel; Sunrise*	Mary Pickford, *Coquette*	Norma Shearer, *The Divorcée*
Director	Frank Borzage, *Seventh Heaven;* Lewis Milestone, *Two Arabian Knights*	Frank Lloyd, *The Divine Lady; Weary River; Drag*	Lewis Milestone, *All Quiet on the Western Front*
Adapted Screenplay	Benjamin Glazer, *Seventh Heaven*	—	—
Original Story	Ben Hecht, *Underworld*	Hans Kraly, *The Patriot*	Frances Marion, *The Big House*
Cinematography	*Sunrise*	*White Shadows in the South Seas*	*With Byrd at the South Pole*
Interior Decoration	*The Dove* and *The Tempest*	*The Bridge of San Luis Rey*	*King of Jazz*
Sound	—	—	*The Big House*

OSCAR RECORDS

Most awards in any category: Walt Disney, 26 regular and six special

Most awards to a single film: *Ben-Hur* in 1959, with 11

Most nominated films: *All About Eve*, with 14, and *From Here to Eternity, Judgment at Nuremberg,* and *Mary Poppins* with 13 each

Most nominated films to receive no awards: *The Turning Point* and *The Color Purple,* with 11 each

Most Best Actor awards: Spencer Tracy, Fredric March, Gary Cooper, Marlon Brando, Dustin Hoffman, and Tom Hanks, with two each

Most Best Director awards: John Ford with four, for *The Informer, The Grapes of Wrath, How Green Was My Valley,* and *The Quiet Man*

Most Best Actress awards: Katharine Hepburn with four, for *Morning Glory, Guess Who's Coming to Dinner, The Lion in Winter,* and *On Golden Pond*

Best Actress awards for debut performances: Shirley Booth for *Come Back, Little Sheba,* Barbra Streisand for *Funny Girl,* and Marlee Matlin for *Children of a Lesser God*

Youngest Best Supporting Actress winners: Tatum O'Neal for *Paper Moon* and Anna Paquin for *The Piano,* both at age 11

First African-American Oscar winner: Hattie McDaniel, Best Supporting Actress, in *Gone with the Wind*

	1930–31	1931–32	1932–33
Picture	Cimarron	Grand Hotel	Cavalcade
Actor	Lionel Barrymore, A Free Soul	Wallace Beery, The Champ; Fredric March, Dr. Jekyll and Mr. Hyde	Charles Laughton, The Private Life of Henry VIII
Actress	Marie Dressler, Min and Bill	Helen Hayes, The Sin of Madelon Claudet	Katharine Hepburn, Morning Glory
Supporting Actor	—	—	—
Supporting Actress	—	—	—
Director	Norman Taurog, Skippy	Frank Borzage, Bad Girl	Frank Lloyd, Cavalcade
Adapted Screenplay/ Screenplay	Howard Estabrook, Cimarron	Edwin Burke, Bad Girl	Victor Heerman and Sarah Y. Mason, Little Women
Original Story	John Monk Saunders, The Dawn Patrol	Francis Marion, The Champ	Robert Lord, One Way Passage
Song	—	—	—
Score	—	—	—
Cinematography	Tabu	Shanghai Express	A Farewell to Arms
Interior Decoration	Cimarron	Transatlantic	Cavalcade
Film Editing	—	—	—
Sound	Paramount Studio Sound Department	Paramount Studio Sound Department	A Farewell to Arms
Short Films	—	Flower and Trees (Cartoons); The Music Box (Comedy); Wrestling Swordfish (Novelty)	The Three Little Pigs (Cartoons); So This Is Harris (Comedy); Krakatoa (Novelty)

POPULAR AND PRAISED

Few films claim the hearts of both the movie-going public and the majority of the Academy of Motion Picture Arts and Sciences. In fact, only 12 of the top 100 money-makers of all time have won best-picture Oscars. Those films are listed below, ranked in order of amount grossed. (Source: *Variety*)

1.	Forrest Gump	1994
2.	Gone with the Wind	1939
3.	Dances with Wolves	1990
4.	Rain Man	1988
5.	The Sound of Music	1965
6.	The Sting	1973
7.	Platoon	1986
8.	The Godfather	1972
9.	The Silence of the Lambs	1991
10.	Rocky	1976
11.	One Flew over the Cuckoo's Nest	1975
12.	Terms of Endearment	1938

1934	**1935**	**1936**	**1937**
It Happened One Night	Mutiny on the Bounty	The Great Ziegfeld	The Life of Emile Zola
Clark Gable, It Happened One Night	Victor McLaglen, The Informer	Paul Muni, The Story of Louis Pasteur	Spencer Tracy, Captains Courageous
Claudette Colbert, It Happened One Night	Bette Davis, Dangerous	Luise Rainer, The Great Ziegfeld	Luise Rainer, The Good Earth
—	—	Walter Brennan, Come and Get It	Joseph Schildkraut, The Life of Emile Zola
—	—	Gale Sondergaard, Anthony Adverse	Alice Brady, In Old Chicago
Frank Capra, It Happened One Night	John Ford, The Informer	Frank Capra, Mr. Deeds Goes to Town	Leo McCarey, The Awful Truth
Robert Riskin, It Happened One Night	Dudley Nichols, The Informer	Pierre Collings and Sheridan Gibney, The Story of Louis Pasteur (Screenplay)	Heinz Herald, Geza Herczeg, and Norman Reilly Raine, The Life of Emile Zola (Screenplay)
Arthur Caesar, Manhattan Melodrama	Ben Hecht and Charles MacArthur, The Scoundrel	Pierre Collings and Sheridan Gibney, The Story of Louis Pasteur (Story)	William A. Wellman and Robert Carson, A Star is Born (Story)
"The Continental" (The Gay Divorcée)	"Lullaby of Broadway" (Gold Diggers of 1935)	"The Way You Look Tonight" (Swing Time)	"Sweet Leilani" (Waikiki Wedding)
One Night of Love	The Informer	Anthony Adverse	100 Men and a Girl
Cleopatra	A Midsummer Night's Dream	Anthony Adverse	The Good Earth
The Merry Widow	The Dark Angel	Dodsworth	Lost Horizon
Eskimo	A Midsummer Night's Dream	Anthony Adverse	Lost Horizon
One Night of Love	Naughty Marietta	San Francisco	The Hurricane
The Tortoise and the Hare (Cartoons); La Cucaracha (Comedy); City of Wax (Novelty)	Three Orphan Kittens (Cartoons); How To Sleep (Comedy); Wings over Mt. Everest (Novelty)	Country Cousin (Cartoons); Bored of Education (One-Reel); The Public Pays (Two-Reel); Give Me Liberty (Color)	The Old Mill (Cartoons); Private Life of the Gannetts (One-Reel); Torture Money (Two-Reel); Penny Wisdom (Color)

DISNEY'S WINNING TUNES

Disney has dominated the Oscar Best Song category in recent years, winning five out of six times since 1989. In total, the studio has won eight times in this category, tying it with MGM; the two still trail Paramount, with 15 wins; and Fox with 10. Disney winners:

Song	Film	Year
"When You Wish Upon a Star"	Pinocchio	1940
"Zip-a-Dee-Doo-Dah"	Song of the South	1947
"Chim Chim Cher-ee"	Mary Poppins	1964
"Under the Sea"	The Little Mermaid	1989
"Sooner or Later"	Dick Tracy	1990
"Beauty and the Beast"	Beauty and the Beast	1991
"A Whole New World"	Aladdin	1992
"Can You Feel the Love Tonight"	The Lion King	1994

	1938	**1939**	**1940**
Picture	*You Can't Take It with You*	*Gone with the Wind*	*Rebecca*
Actor	Spencer Tracy, *Boys Town*	Robert Donat, *Goodbye, Mr. Chips*	James Stewart, *The Philadelphia Story*
Actress	Bette Davis, *Jezebel*	Vivien Leigh, *Gone with the Wind*	Ginger Rogers, *Kitty Foyle*
Supporting Actor	Walter Brennan, *Kentucky*	Thomas Mitchell, *Stagecoach*	Walter Brennan, *The Westerner*
Supporting Actress	Fay Bainter, *Jezebel*	Hattie McDaniel, *Gone with the Wind*	Jane Darwell, *The Grapes of Wrath*
Director	Frank Capra, *You Can't Take It with You*	Victor Fleming, *Gone with the Wind*	John Ford, *The Grapes of Wrath*
Screenplay	Ian Dalrymple, Cecil Lewis, and W. P. Lipscomb, *Pygmalion*	Sidney Howard, *Gone with the Wind*	Donald Ogden Stewart, *The Philadelphia Story*
Original Screenplay/ Original Story	Eleanore Griffin and Dore Schary, *Boys Town*	Lewis R. Foster, *Mr. Smith Goes to Washington*	Preston Sturges, *The Great McGinty*; Benjamin Glazer and John S. Toldy, *Arise, My Love*
Song	"Thanks for the Memory" *(Big Broadcast of 1938)*	"Over the Rainbow" *(The Wizard of Oz)*	"When You Wish upon a Star" *(Pinocchio)*
Score/Original Score	*Alexander's Ragtime Band*; *Adventures of Robin Hood*	*Stagecoach*; *The Wizard of Oz*	*Tin Pan Alley*; *Pinocchio*
Cinematography	*The Great Waltz*	*Wuthering Heights* (B&W); *Gone with the Wind* (Color)	*Rebecca* (B&W); *The Thief of Bagdad* (Color)
Interior Decoration	*Adventures of Robin Hood*	*Gone with the Wind*	*Pride and Prejudice* (B&W); *The Thief of Bagdad* (Color)
Film Editing	*Adventures of Robin Hood*	*Gone with the Wind*	*North West Mounted Police*
Sound	*The Cowboy and the Lady*	*When Tomorrow Comes*	*Strike Up the Band*
Special Effects	—	*The Rains Came*	*The Thief of Bagdad*
Short Films	*Ferdinand the Bull* (Cartoons); *That Mothers Might Live* (One-Reel); *Declaration of Independence* (Two-Reel)	*The Ugly Duckling* (Cartoons); *Busy Little Bears* (One-Reel); *Sons of Liberty* (Two-Reel)	*Milky Way* (Cartoons); *Quicker 'N a Wink* (One-Reel); *Teddy, the Rough Rider* (Two-Reel)
Documentaries	—	—	—

66 I hope that at the end of another 50 years of service in the theater, your children and your children's children will have enough courage to vote for me again. 99

—Charles Coburn, Best Supporting Actor for *The More the Merrier*, 1943

1941	1942	1943	1944
How Green Was My Valley	*Mrs. Miniver*	*Casablanca*	*Going My Way*
Gary Cooper, *Sergeant York*	James Cagney, *Yankee Doodle Dandy*	Paul Lukas, *Watch on the Rhine*	Bing Crosby, *Going My Way*
Joan Fontaine, *Suspicion*	Greer Garson, *Mrs. Miniver*	Jennifer Jones, *The Song of Bernadette*	Ingrid Bergman, *Gaslight*
Donald Crisp, *How Green Was My Valley*	Van Heflin, *Johnny Eager*	Charles Coburn, *The More the Merrier*	Barry Fitzgerald, *Going My Way*
Mary Astor, *The Great Lie*	Teresa Wright, *Mrs. Miniver*	Katina Paxinou, *For Whom the Bell Tolls*	Ethel Barrymore, *None but the Lonely Heart*
John Ford, *How Green Was My Valley*	William Wyler, *Mrs. Miniver*	Michael Curtiz, *Casablanca*	Leo McCarey, *Going My Way*
Sidney Buchman and Seton I. Miller, *Here Comes Mr. Jordan*	George Froeschel, James Hilton, Claudine West, and Arthur Wimperis, *Mrs. Miniver*	Julius J. Epstein, Philip G. Epstein, and Howard Koch, *Casablanca*	Frank Butler and Frank Cavett, *Going My Way*
Harry Segall, *Here Comes Mr. Jordan*; Herman J. Mankiewicz and Orson Welles, *Citizen Kane*	Michael Kanin and Ring Lardner Jr., *Woman of the Year*; Emeric Pressburger, *The Invaders*	Norman Krasna, *Princess O'Rourke*; William Saroyan, *The Human Comedy*	Lamar Trotti, *Wilson*; Leo McCarey, *Going My Way*
"The Last Time I Saw Paris" (*Lady Be Good*)	"White Christmas" (*Holiday Inn*)	"You'll Never Know" (*Hello, Frisco, Hello*)	"Swinging on a Star" (*Going My Way*)
All That Money Can Buy (Dramatic); *Dumbo* (Musical)	*Now, Voyager* (Dramatic or Comedy); *Yankee Doodle Dandy* (Musical)	*The Song of Bernadette* (Dramatic or Comedy); *This Is the Army* (Musical)	*Since You Went Away* (Dramatic or Comedy); *Cover Girl* (Musical)
How Green Was My Valley (B&W); *Blood and Sand* (Color)	*Mrs. Miniver* (B&W); *The Black Swan* (Color)	*The Song of Bernadette* (B&W); *The Phantom of the Opera* (Color)	*Laura* (B&W); *Wilson* (Color)
How Green Was My Valley (B&W); *Blossoms in the Dust* (Color)	*This Above All* (B&W); *My Gal Sal* (Color)	*The Song of Bernadette* (B&W); *The Phantom of the Opera* (Color)	*Gaslight* (B&W); *Wilson* (Color)
Sergeant York	*The Pride of the Yankees*	*Air Force*	*Wilson*
That Hamilton Woman	*Yankee Doodle Dandy*	*This Land Is Mine*	*Wilson*
I Wanted Wings	*Reap the Wild Wind*	*Crash Dive*	*Thirty Seconds over Tokyo*
Lend a Paw (Cartoons); *Of Pups and Puzzles* (One-Reel); *Main Street on the March* (Two-Reel)	*Der Fuehrer's Face* (Cartoons); *Speaking of Animals and Their Families* (One-Reel); *Beyond the Line of Duty* (Two-Reel)	*Yankee Doodle Mouse* (Cartoons); *Amphibious Fighters* (One-Reel); *Heavenly Music* (Two-Reel)	*Mouse Trouble* (Cartoons); *Who's Who in Animal Land* (One-Reel); *I Won't Play* (Two-Reel)
Churchill's Island	*Battle of Midway*; *Kokoda Front Line*; *Moscow Strikes Back*; *Prelude to War*	*December 7th* (Shorts); *Desert Victory* (Features)	*With the Marines at Tarawa* (Shorts); *The Fighting Lady* (Features)

139

	1945	**1946**	**1947**
Picture	*The Lost Weekend*	*The Best Years of Our Lives*	*Gentleman's Agreement*
Actor	Ray Milland, *The Lost Weekend*	Fredric March, *The Best Years of Our Lives*	Ronald Colman, *A Double Life*
Actress	Joan Crawford, *Mildred Pierce*	Olivia de Havilland, *To Each His Own*	Loretta Young, *The Farmer's Daughter*
Supporting Actor	James Dunn, *A Tree Grows in Brooklyn*	Harold Russell, *The Best Years of Our Lives*	Edmund Gwenn, *Miracle on 34th Street*
Supporting Actress	Anne Revere, *National Velvet*	Anne Baxter, *The Razor's Edge*	Celeste Holm, *Gentleman's Agreement*
Director	Billy Wilder, *The Lost Weekend*	William Wyler, *The Best Years of Our Lives*	Elia Kazan, *Gentleman's Agreement*
Screenplay	Charles Brackett and Billy Wilder, *The Lost Weekend*	Robert E. Sherwood, *The Best Years of Our Lives*	George Seaton, *Miracle on 34th Street*
Original Screenplay/ Original Story	Richard Schweizer, *Marie-Louise*; Charles G. Booth, *The House on 92nd Street*	Muriel and Sydney Box, *The Seventh Veil*; Clemence Dane, *Vacation from Marriage*	Sidney Sheldon, *The Bachelor and the Bobby-Soxer*; Valentine Davies, *Miracle on 34th Street*
Song	"It Might As Well Be Spring" *(State Fair)*	"On the Atchison, Topeka and Santa Fe" *(The Harvey Girls)*	"Zip-A-Dee-Doo-Dah" *(Song of the South)*
Score—Dramatic or Comedy/ Musical	*Spellbound*; *Anchors Aweigh*	*The Best Years of Our Lives*; *The Jolson Story*	*A Double Life*; *Mother Wore Tights*
Cinematography	*The Picture of Dorian Gray* (B&W); *Leave Her to Heaven* (Color)	*Anna and the King of Siam* (B&W); *The Yearling* (Color)	*Great Expectations* (B&W); *Black Narcissus* (Color)
Costume Design	—	—	—
Interior Decoration, through 1946; Art Direction—Set Decoration, from 1947	*Blood on the Sun* (B&W); *Frenchman's Creek* (Color)	*Anna and the King of Siam* (B&W); *The Yearling* (Color)	*Great Expectations* (B&W); *Black Narcissus* (Color)
Film Editing	*National Velvet*	*The Best Years of Our Lives*	*Body and Soul*
Sound	*The Bells of St. Mary's*	*The Jolson Story*	*The Bishop's Wife*
Special Effects	*Wonder Man*	*Blithe Spirit*	*Green Dolphin Street*
Short Films	*Quiet Please* (Cartoons); *Stairway to Light* (One-Reel); *Star in the Night* (Two-Reel)	*The Cat Concerto* (Cartoons); *Facing Your Danger* (One-Reel); *A Boy and His Dog* (Two-Reel)	*Tweetie Pie* (Cartoons); *Goodbye Miss Turlock* (One-Reel); *Climbing the Matterhorn* (Two-Reel)
Documentaries	*Hitler Lives?* (Shorts); *The True Glory* (Features)	*Seeds of Destiny* (Shorts)	*First Steps* (Shorts); *Design for Death* (Features)

> 66 What can I tell ya? I'd like to thank the makers of Maalox for making all this possible. 99
>
> —Marvin Hamlisch, Best Dramatic Score for *The Way We Were*, 1973

1948	1949	1950	1951
Hamlet	*All the King's Men*	*All About Eve*	*An American in Paris*
Laurence Olivier, *Hamlet*	Broderick Crawford, *All the King's Men*	José Ferrer, *Cyrano de Bergerac*	Humphrey Bogart, *The African Queen*
Jane Wyman, *Johnny Belinda*	Olivia de Havilland, *The Heiress*	Judy Holliday, *Born Yesterday*	Vivien Leigh, *A Streetcar Named Desire*
Walter Huston, *Treasure of Sierra Madre*	Dean Jagger, *Twelve O'Clock High*	George Sanders, *All About Eve*	Karl Malden, *A Streetcar Named Desire*
Claire Trevor, *Key Largo*	Mercedes McCambridge, *All the King's Men*	Josephine Hull, *Harvey*	Kim Hunter, *A Streetcar Named Desire*
John Huston, *Treasure of Sierra Madre*	Joseph L. Mankiewicz, *A Letter to Three Wives*	Joseph L. Mankiewicz, *All About Eve*	George Stevens, *A Place in the Sun*
John Huston, *Treasure of Sierra Madre*	Joseph L. Mankiewicz, *A Letter to Three Wives*	Joseph L. Mankiewicz, *All About Eve*	Michael Wilson and Harry Brown, *A Place in the Sun*
Richard Schweizer and David Wechsler, *The Search*	Douglas Morrow, *The Stratton Story*; Robert Pirosh, *Battleground* (Story and Screenplay)	Edna and Edward Anhalt, *Panic in the Streets*; Charles Brackett, Billy Wilder, and D.M. Marshman Jr., *Sunset Boulevard* (Story and Screenplay)	Paul Dehn and James Bernard, *Seven Days to Noon*; Alan Jay Lerner, *An American in Paris* (Story and Screenplay)
"Buttons and Bows" (*The Paleface*)	"Baby, It's Cold Outside" (*Neptune's Daughter*)	"Mona Lisa" (*Captain Carey, USA*)	"In the Cool, Cool, Cool of the Evening" (*Here Comes the Groom*)
The Red Shoes; *Easter Parade*	*The Heiress*; *On the Town*	*Sunset Boulevard*; *Annie Get Your Gun*	*A Place in the Sun*; *An American in Paris*
The Naked City (B&W); *Joan of Arc* (Color)	*Battleground* (B&W); *She Wore a Yellow Ribbon* (Color)	*The Third Man* (B&W); *King Solomon's Mines* (Color)	*A Place in the Sun* (B&W); *An American in Paris* (Color)
Hamlet (B&W); *Joan of Arc* (Color)	*The Heiress* (B&W); *Adventures of Don Juan* (Color)	*All About Eve* (B&W); *Samson and Delilah* (Color)	*A Place in the Sun* (B&W); *An American in Paris* (Color)
Hamlet (B&W); *The Red Shoes* (Color)	*The Heiress* (B&W); *Little Women* (Color)	*Sunset Boulevard* (B&W); *Samson and Delilah* (Color)	*A Streetcar Named Desire* (B&W); *An American in Paris* (Color)
The Naked City	*Champion*	*King Solomon's Mines*	*A Place in the Sun*
The Snake Pit	*Twelve O'Clock High*	*All About Eve*	*The Great Caruso*
Portrait of Jennie	*Mighty Joe Young*	*Destination Moon*	*When Worlds Collide*
The Little Orphan (Cartoons); *Symphony of a City* (One-Reel); *Seal Island* (Two-Reel)	*For Scent-imental Reasons* (Cartoons); *Aquatic House Party* (One-Reel); *Van Gogh* (Two-Reel)	*Gerald McBoing-Boing* (Cartoons); *Grandad of Races* (One-Reel); *In Beaver Valley* (Two-Reel)	*Two Mouseketeers* (Cartoons); *World of Kids* (One-Reel); *Nature's Half Acre* (Two-Reel)
Toward Independence (Shorts); *The Secret Land* (Features)	*A Chance To Live* and *So Much for So Little* (Shorts); *Daybreak in Udi* (Features)	*Why Korea?* (Shorts); *The Titan: Story of Michelangelo* (Features)	*Benjy* (Shorts); *Kon-Tiki* (Features)

66 I guess this proves there are as many nuts in the Academy as anywhere else. 99

—Jack Nicholson, Best Actor for
One Flew Over the Cuckoo's Nest, 1975

	1952	1953	1954
Picture	*The Greatest Show on Earth*	*From Here to Eternity*	*On the Waterfront*
Actor	Gary Cooper, *High Noon*	William Holden, *Stalag 17*	Marlon Brando, *On the Waterfront*
Actress	Shirley Booth, *Come Back, Little Sheba*	Audrey Hepburn, *Roman Holiday*	Grace Kelly, *The Country Girl*
Supporting Actor	Anthony Quinn, *Viva Zapata!*	Frank Sinatra, *From Here to Eternity*	Edmond O'Brien, *The Barefoot Contessa*
Supporting Actress	Gloria Grahame, *The Bad and the Beautiful*	Donna Reed, *From Here to Eternity*	Eva Marie Saint, *On the Waterfront*
Director	John Ford, *The Quiet Man*	Fred Zinnemann, *From Here to Eternity*	Elia Kazan, *On the Waterfront*
Screenplay	Charles Schnee, *The Bad and the Beautiful*	Daniel Taradash, *From Here to Eternity*	George Seaton, *The Country Girl*
Story/Story and Screenplay	Frederic M. Frank, Theodore St. John, and Frank Cavett, *The Greatest Show on Earth*; T.E.B. Clarke, *The Lavender Hill Mob*	Ian McLellan Hunter, *Roman Holiday*; Charles Brackett, Walter Reisch, and Richard Breen, *Titanic*	Philip Yordan, *Broken Lance*; Budd Schulberg, *On the Waterfront*
Song	"High Noon (Do Not Forsake Me, Oh My Darlin')" *(High Noon)*	"Secret Love" *(Calamity Jane)*	"Three Coins in the Fountain" *(Three Coins in the Fountain)*
Score—Dramatic or Comedy/Musical	*High Noon; With a Song in My Heart*	*Lili; Call Me Madam*	*The High and the Mighty; Seven Brides for Seven Brothers*
Cinematography	*The Bad and the Beautiful* (B&W); *The Quiet Man* (Color)	*From Here to Eternity* (B&W); *Shane* (Color)	*On the Waterfront* (B&W); *Three Coins in the Fountain* (Color)
Costume Design	*The Bad and the Beautiful* (B&W); *Moulin Rouge* (Color)	*Roman Holiday* (B&W); *The Robe* (Color)	*Sabrina* (B&W); *Gate of Hell* (Color)
Art Direction—Set Decoration	*The Bad and the Beautiful* (B&W); *Moulin Rouge* (Color)	*Julius Caesar* (B&W); *The Robe* (Color)	*On the Waterfront* (B&W); *20,000 Leagues Under the Sea* (Color)
Film Editing	*High Noon*	*From Here to Eternity*	*On the Waterfront*
Foreign Language Film	—	—	—
Sound	*Breaking the Sound Barrier*	*From Here to Eternity*	*The Glenn Miller Story*
Special Effects	*Plymouth Adventure*	*The War of the Worlds*	*20,000 Leagues Under the Sea*
Short Films	*Johann Mouse* (Cartoons); *Light in the Window* (One-Reel); *Water Birds* (Two-Reel)	*Toot, Whistle, Plunk and Boom* (Cartoons); *The Merry Wives of Windsor Overture* (One-Reel); *Bear Country* (Two-Reel)	*When Magoo Flew* (Cartoons); *This Mechanical Age* (One-Reel); *A Time Out of War* (Two-Reel)
Documentaries	*Neighbours* (Shorts); *The Sea Around Us* (Features)	*The Alaskan Eskimo* (Shorts); *The Living Desert* (Features)	*Thursday's Children* (Shorts); *The Vanishing Prairie* (Features)

1955	1956	1957	1958
Marty	Around the World in 80 Days	The Bridge on the River Kwai	Gigi
Ernest Borgnine, Marty	Yul Brynner, The King and I	Alec Guinness, The Bridge on the River Kwai	David Niven, Separate Tables
Anna Magnani, The Rose Tattoo	Ingrid Bergman, Anastasia	Joanne Woodward, The Three Faces of Eve	Susan Hayward, I Want to Live!
Jack Lemmon, Mister Roberts	Anthony Quinn, Lust for Life	Red Buttons, Sayonara	Burl Ives, The Big Country
Jo Van Fleet, East of Eden	Dorothy Malone, Written on the Wind	Miyoshi Umeki, Sayonara	Wendy Hiller, Separate Tables
Delbert Mann, Marty	George Stevens, Giant	David Lean, The Bridge on the River Kwai	Vincente Minnelli, Gigi
Paddy Chayefsky, Marty	James Poe, John Farrow, and S.J. Perelman, Around the World in 80 Days (Adapted)	Pierre Boulle, The Bridge on the River Kwai (Adapted)	Alan Jay Lerner, Gigi (Adapted)
Daniel Fuchs, Love Me or Leave Me; William Ludwig and Sonya Levien, Interrupted Melody	Dalton Trumbo (aka Robert Rich), The Brave One; Albert Lamorisse, The Red Balloon	George Wells, Designing Woman	Nathan E. Douglas and Harold Jacob Smith, The Defiant Ones
"Love is a Many-Splendored Thing" (Love Is a Many-Splendored Thing)	"Whatever Will Be, Will Be (Que Será, Será)" (The Man Who Knew Too Much)	"All the Way" (The Joker Is Wild)	"Gigi" (Gigi)
Love is a Many-Splendored Thing; Oklahoma!	Around the World in 80 Days; The King and I	The Bridge on the River Kwai	The Old Man and the Sea; Gigi
The Rose Tattoo (B&W); To Catch a Thief (Color)	Somebody up There Likes Me (B&W); Around the World in 80 Days (Color)	The Bridge on the River Kwai	The Defiant Ones (B&W); Gigi (Color)
I'll Cry Tomorrow (B&W); Love Is a Many-Splendored Thing (Color)	The Solid Gold Cadillac (B&W); The King and I (Color)	Les Girls	Gigi
The Rose Tattoo (B&W); Picnic (Color)	Somebody up There Likes Me (B&W); The King and I (Color)	Sayonara	Gigi
Picnic	Around the World in 80 Days	The Bridge on the River Kwai	Gigi
—	La Strada (Italy)	The Nights of Cabiria (Italy)	My Uncle (France)
Oklahoma!	The King and I	Sayonara	South Pacific
The Bridges at Toko-Ri	The Ten Commandments	The Enemy Below	tom thumb
Speedy Gonzales (Cartoon); Survival City (One-Reel); The Face of Lincoln (Two-Reel)	Mister Magoo's Puddle Jumper (Cartoons); Crashing the Water Barrier (One-Reel); The Bespoke Overcoat (Two-Reel)	Birds Anonymous (Cartoons); The Wetback Hound (Live Action)	Knighty Knight Bugs (Cartoons); Grand Canyon (Live Action)
Men Against the Arctic (Shorts); Helen Keller in Her Story (Features)	The True Story of the Civil War (Shorts); The Silent World (Features)	Albert Schweitzer (Features)	AMA Girls (Shorts); White Wilderness (Features)

	1959	**1960**	**1961**
Picture	*Ben-Hur*	*The Apartment*	*West Side Story*
Actor	Charlton Heston, *Ben-Hur*	Burt Lancaster, *Elmer Gantry*	Maximilian Schell, *Judgment at Nuremburg*
Actress	Simone Signoret, *Room at the Top*	Elizabeth Taylor, *Butterfield 8*	Sophia Loren, *Two Women*
Supporting Actor	Hugh Griffith, *Ben-Hur*	Peter Ustinov, *Spartacus*	George Chakiris, *West Side Story*
Supporting Actress	Shelley Winters, *The Diary of Anne Frank*	Shirley Jones, *Elmer Gantry*	Rita Moreno, *West Side Story*
Director	William Wyler, *Ben-Hur*	Billy Wilder, *The Apartment*	Robert Wise and Jerome Robbins, *West Side Story*
Adapted Screenplay	Neil Paterson, *Room at the Top*	Richard Brooks, *Elmer Gantry*	Abby Mann, *Judgment at Nuremberg*
Story and Screenplay	Russell Rouse and Clarence Greene, story; Stanley Shapiro and Maurice Richlin, screenplay, *Pillow Talk*	Billy Wilder and I.A.L. Diamond, *The Apartment*	William Inge, *Splendor in the Grass*
Song	"High Hopes" *(A Hole in the Head)*	"Never on Sunday" *(Never on Sunday)*	"Moon River" *(Breakfast at Tiffany's)*
Score	*Ben-Hur* (Dramatic or Comedy); *Porgy and Bess* (Musical)	*Exodus* (Dramatic or Comedy); *Song Without End (The Story of Franz Liszt)* (Musical)	*Breakfast at Tiffany's* (Dramatic or Comedy); *West Side Story* (Musical)
Cinematography	*The Diary of Anne Frank* (B&W); *Ben-Hur* (Color)	*Sons and Lovers* (B&W); *Spartacus* (Color)	*The Hustler* (B&W); *West Side Story* (Color)
Costume Design	*Some Like It Hot* (B&W); *Ben-Hur* (Color)	*The Facts of Life* (B&W); *Spartacus* (Color)	*La Dolce Vita* (B&W); *West Side Story* (Color)
Art Direction—Set Decoration	*The Diary of Anne Frank* (B&W); *Ben-Hur* (Color)	*The Apartment* (B&W); *Spartacus* (Color)	*The Hustler* (B&W); *West Side Story* (Color)
Film Editing	*Ben-Hur*	*The Apartment*	*West Side Story*
Foreign Language Film	*Black Orpheus* (France)	*The Virgin Spring* (Sweden)	*Through a Glass Darkly* (Sweden)
Sound	*Ben-Hur*	*The Alamo*	*West Side Story*
Sound Effects (Editing)	—	—	—
Visual Effects	—		
Special Effects	*Ben-Hur*	*The Time Machine*	*The Guns of Navarone*
Short Films	*Moonbird* (Cartoons); *The Golden Fish* (Live Action)	*Munro* (Cartoons); *Day of the Painter* (Live Action)	*Ersatz (The Substitute)* (Cartoons); *Seawards the Great Ships* (Live Action)
Documentaries	*Glass* (Shorts); *Serengeti Shall Not Die* (Features)	*Giuseppina* (Shorts); *The Horse with the Flying Tail* (Features)	*Project Hope* (Shorts); *Le Ciel et la boue (Sky Above and Mud Beneath)* (Features)

1962	1963	1964	1965
Lawrence of Arabia	*Tom Jones*	*My Fair Lady*	*The Sound of Music*
Gregory Peck, *To Kill a Mockingbird*	Sidney Poitier, *Lilies of the Field*	Rex Harrison, *My Fair Lady*	Lee Marvin, *Cat Ballou*
Anne Bancroft, *The Miracle Worker*	Patricia Neal, *Hud*	Julie Andrews, *Mary Poppins*	Julie Christie, *Darling*
Ed Begley, *Sweet Bird of Youth*	Melvyn Douglas, *Hud*	Peter Ustinov, *Topkapi*	Martin Balsam, *A Thousand Clowns*
Patty Duke, *The Miracle Worker*	Margaret Rutherford, *The V.I.P.s*	Lila Kedrova, *Zorba the Greek*	Shelley Winters, *A Patch of Blue*
David Lean, *Lawrence of Arabia*	Tony Richardson, *Tom Jones*	George Cukor, *My Fair Lady*	Robert Wise, *The Sound of Music*
Horton Foote, *To Kill a Mockingbird*	John Osborne, *Tom Jones*	Edward Anhalt, *Beckett*	Robert Bolt, *Doctor Zhivago*
Ennio de Concini, Alfredo Giannetti, and Pietro Germi, *Divorce—Italian Style*	James R. Webb, *How the West Was Won*	S. H. Barnett, story; Peter Stone and Frank Tarloff, screenplay, *Father Goose*	Frederic Raphael, *Darling*
"Days of Wine and Roses" (*Days of Wine and Roses*)	"Call Me Irresponsible" (*Papa's Delicate Condition*)	"Chim Chim Cher-ee" (*Mary Poppins*)	"The Shadow of Your Smile" (*The Sandpiper*)
Lawrence of Arabia (Original); *The Music Man* (Adaptation)	*Tom Jones* (Original); *Irma La Douce* (Adaptation)	*Mary Poppins* (Original); *My Fair Lady* (Adaptation)	*Doctor Zhivago* (Original); *The Sound of Music* (Adaptation)
The Longest Day (B&W); *Lawrence of Arabia* (Color)	*Hud* (B&W); *Cleopatra* (Color)	*Zorba the Greek* (B&W); *My Fair Lady* (Color)	*Ship of Fools* (B&W); *Doctor Zhivago* (Color)
Whatever Happened to Baby Jane? (B&W); *The Wonderful World of the Brothers Grimm* (Color)	*8½* (B&W); *Cleopatra* (Color)	*The Night of the Iguana* (B&W); *My Fair Lady* (Color)	*Darling* (B&W); *Doctor Zhivago* (Color)
To Kill a Mockingbird (B&W); *Lawrence of Arabia* (Color)	*America America* (B&W); *Cleopatra* (Color)	*Zorba the Greek* (B&W); *My Fair Lady* (Color)	*Ship of Fools* (B&W); *Doctor Zhivago* (Color)
Lawrence of Arabia	*How the West Was Won*	*Mary Poppins*	*The Sound of Music*
Sundays and Cybèle (France)	*8½* (Italy)	*Yesterday, Today and Tomorrow* (Italy)	*The Shop on Main Street* (Czechoslovakia)
Lawrence of Arabia	*How the West Was Won*	*My Fair Lady*	*The Sound of Music*
—	*It's a Mad, Mad, Mad, Mad World*	*Goldfinger*	*The Great Race*
—	*Cleopatra*	*Mary Poppins*	*Thunderball*
The Longest Day	—	—	—
The Hole (Cartoons); *Heureux Anniversaire* (Live Action)	*The Critic* (Cartoons); *An Occurrence at Owl Creek Bridge* (Live Action)	*The Pink Phink* (Cartoons); *Casals Conducts: 1964* (Live Action)	*The Dot and the Line* (Cartoons); *The Chicken* (*Le Poulet*) (Live Action)
Dylan Thomas (Shorts); *Black Fox* (Features)	*Chagall* (Shorts); *Robert Frost: A Lover's Quarrel with the World* (Features)	*Nine from Little Rock* (Shorts); *Jacques-Yves Cousteau's World Without Sun* (Features)	*To Be Alive!* (Shorts); *The Eleanor Roosevelt Story* (Features)

	1966	1967	1968
Picture	A Man for All Seasons	In the Heat of the Night	Oliver!
Actor	Paul Scofield, A Man for All Seasons	Rod Steiger, In the Heat of the Night	Cliff Robertson, Charly
Actress	Elizabeth Taylor, Who's Afraid of Virginia Woolf?	Katharine Hepburn, Guess Who's Coming to Dinner	Katharine Hepburn, The Lion in Winter; Barbra Streisand, Funny Girl
Supporting Actor	Walter Matthau, The Fortune Cookie	George Kennedy, Cool Hand Luke	Jack Albertson, The Subject Was Roses
Supporting Actress	Sandy Dennis, Who's Afraid of Virginia Woolf?	Estelle Parsons, Bonnie and Clyde	Ruth Gordon, Rosemary's Baby
Director	Fred Zinnemann, A Man for All Seasons	Mike Nichols, The Graduate	Carol Reed, Oliver!
Adapted Screenplay	Robert Bolt, A Man for All Seasons	Stirling Silliphant, In the Heat of the Night	James Goldman, The Lion in Winter
Story and Screenplay	Claude Lelouch, story; Pierre Uytterhoeven and Claude Lelouch, screenplay, A Man and a Woman	William Rose, Guess Who's Coming to Dinner?	Mel Brooks, The Producers
Song	"Born Free" (Born Free)	"Talk to the Animals" (Doctor Dolittle)	"The Windmills of Your Mind" (The Thomas Crown Affair)
Score	Born Free (Original); A Funny Thing Happened on the Way to the Forum (Adaptation)	Thoroughly Modern Millie (Original); Camelot (Adaptation)	The Lion in Winter (Nonmusical); Oliver! (Musical)
Cinematography	Who's Afraid of Virginia Woolf? (B&W); A Man for All Seasons	Bonnie and Clyde	Romeo and Juliet
Costume Design	Who's Afraid of Virginia Woolf? (B&W); A Man for All Seasons (Color)	Camelot	Romeo and Juliet
Art Direction—Set Decoration	Who's Afraid of Virginia Woolf? (B&W); Fantastic Voyage (Color)	Camelot	Oliver!
Film Editing	Grand Prix	In the Heat of the Night	Bullitt
Foreign Language Film	A Man and a Woman (France)	Closely Watched Trains (Czechoslovakia)	War and Peace (U.S.S.R.)
Sound	Grand Prix	In the Heat of the Night	Oliver!
Sound Effects (Editing)	Grand Prix	The Dirty Dozen	—
Visual Effects	Fantastic Voyage	Doctor Dolittle	2001: A Space Odyssey
Short Films	Herb Alpert and the Tijuana Brass Double Feature (Cartoons); Wild Wings (Live Action)	The Box (Cartoons); A Place to Stand (Live Action)	Winnie the Pooh and the Blustery Day (Cartoons); Robert Kennedy Remembered (Live Action)
Documentaries	A Year Toward Tomorrow (Shorts); The War Game (Features)	The Redwoods (Shorts); The Anderson Platoon (Features)	Why Man Creates (Shorts); Journey into Self (Features)

1969	1970	1971	1972
Midnight Cowboy	*Patton*	*The French Connection*	*The Godfather*
John Wayne, *True Grit*	George C. Scott, *Patton*	Gene Hackman, *The French Connection*	Marlon Brando, *The Godfather*
Maggie Smith, *The Prime of Miss Jean Brodie*	Glenda Jackson, *Women in Love*	Jane Fonda, *Klute*	Liza Minnelli, *Cabaret*
Gig Young, *They Shoot Horses, Don't They?*	John Mills, *Ryan's Daughter*	Ben Johnson, *The Last Picture Show*	Joel Grey, *Cabaret*
Goldie Hawn, *Cactus Flower*	Helen Hayes, *Airport*	Cloris Leachman, *The Last Picture Show*	Eileen Heckart, *Butterflies Are Free*
John Schlesinger, *Midnight Cowboy*	Franklin J. Schaffner, *Patton*	William Friedkin, *The French Connection*	Bob Fosse, *Cabaret*
Waldo Salt, *Midnight Cowboy*	Ring Lardner Jr., *M*A*S*H*	Ernest Tidyman, *The French Connection*	Mario Puzo and Francis Ford Coppola, *The Godfather*
William Goldman, *Butch Cassidy and the Sundance Kid*	Francis Ford Coppola and Edmund H. North, *Patton*	Paddy Chayefsky, *The Hospital*	Jeremy Larner, *The Candidate*
"Raindrops Keep Fallin' on My Head" *(Butch Cassidy and the Sundance Kid)*	"For All We Know" *(Lovers and Other Strangers)*	"Theme from *Shaft*" *(Shaft)*	"The Morning After" *(The Poseidon Adventure)*
Butch Cassidy and the Sundance Kid (Nonmusical); *Hello Dolly!* (Musical)	*Love Story* (Original Score); *Let It Be* (Original Song Score)	*Summer of '42* (Dramatic); *Fiddler on the Roof* (Adapted)	*Limelight* (Dramatic); *Cabaret* (Adapted)
Butch Cassidy and the Sundance Kid	*Ryan's Daughter*	*Fiddler on the Roof*	*Cabaret*
Anne of the Thousand Days	*Cromwell*	*Nicholas and Alexandra*	*Travels with My Aunt*
Hello Dolly!	*Patton*	*Nicholas and Alexandra*	*Cabaret*
Z	*Patton*	*The French Connection*	*Cabaret*
Z (Algeria)	*Investigation of a Citizen Above Suspicion* (Italy)	*The Garden of the Finzi-Continis* (Italy)	*The Discreet Charm of the Bourgeoisie* (France)
Hello Dolly!	*Patton*	*Fiddler on the Roof*	*Cabaret*
—	—	—	—
Marooned	*Tora! Tora! Tora!*	*Bedknobs and Broomsticks*	—
It's Tough to Be a Bird (Cartoons); *The Magic Machines* (Live Action)	*Is It Always Right To Be Right?* (Cartoons); *The Resurrection of Broncho Billy* (Live Action)	*The Crunch Bird* (Animated); *Sentinels of Silence* (Live Action)	*A Christmas Carol* (Animated); *Norman Rockwell's World . . . An American Dream* (Live Action)
Czechoslovakia 1968 (Shorts); *Arthur Rubinstein—The Love of Life* (Features)	*Interviews with My Lai Veterans* (Shorts); *Woodstock* (Features)	*Sentinels of Silence* (Shorts); *The Hellstrom Chronicle* (Features)	*This Tiny World* (Shorts); *Marjoe* (Features)

	1973	**1974**	**1975**
Picture	*The Sting*	*The Godfather Part II*	*One Flew over the Cuckoo's Nest*
Actor	Jack Lemmon, *Save the Tiger*	Art Carney, *Harry and Tonto*	Jack Nicholson, *One Flew over the Cuckoo's Nest*
Actress	Glenda Jackson, *A Touch of Class*	Ellen Burstyn, *Alice Doesn't Live Here Anymore*	Louise Fletcher, *One Flew over the Cuckoo's Nest*
Supporting Actor	John Houseman, *The Paper Chase*	Robert De Niro, *The Godfather Part II*	George Burns, *The Sunshine Boys*
Supporting Actress	Tatum O'Neal, *Paper Moon*	Ingrid Bergman, *Murder on the Orient Express*	Lee Grant, *Shampoo*
Director	George Roy Hill, *The Sting*	Francis Ford Coppola, *The Godfather Part II*	Milos Forman, *One Flew over the Cuckoo's Nest*
Adapted Screenplay	William Peter Blatty, *The Exorcist*	Francis Ford Coppola and Mario Puzo, *The Godfather Part II*	Lawrence Hauben and Bo Goldman, *One Flew over the Cuckoo's Nest*
Original Screenplay	David S. Ward, *The Sting*	Robert Towne, *Chinatown*	Frank Pierson, *Dog Day Afternoon*
Song	"The Way We Were" *(The Way We Were)*	"We May Never Love Like This Again" *(The Towering Inferno)*	"I'm Easy" *(Nashville)*
Score	*The Way We Were* (Original); *The Sting* (Adaptation)	*The Godfather Part II* (Original); *The Great Gatsby* (Adaptation)	*Jaws* (Original); *Barry Lyndon* (Adaptation)
Cinematography	*Cries and Whispers*	*The Towering Inferno*	*Barry Lyndon*
Costume Design	*The Sting*	*The Great Gatsby*	*Barry Lyndon*
Art Direction—Set Decoration	*The Sting*	*The Godfather Part II*	*Barry Lyndon*
Film Editing	*The Sting*	*The Towering Inferno*	*Jaws*
Foreign Language Film	*Day for Night* (France)	*Amarcord* (Italy)	*Dersu Uzala* (U.S.S.R.)
Sound	*The Exorcist*	*Earthquake*	*Jaws*
Visual Effects	—	—	—
Short Films	*Frank Film* (Animated); *The Bolero* (Live Action)	*Closed Mondays* (Animated); *One-Eyed Men Are Kings* (Live Action)	*Great* (Animated); *Angel and Big Joe* (Live Action)
Documentaries	*Princeton: A Search for Answers* (Shorts); *The Great American Cowboy* (Features)	*Don't* (Shorts); *Hearts and Minds* (Features)	*The End of the Game* (Shorts); *The Man Who Skied down Everest* (Features)

> **66** This is all so exciting. I've decided to keep making one movie every 36 years. **99**
>
> —George Burns, Best Supporting Actor for *The Sunshine Boys*, 1975

1976	1977	1978	1979
Rocky	Annie Hall	The Deer Hunter	Kramer vs. Kramer
Peter Finch, Network	Richard Dreyfuss, The Goodbye Girl	Jon Voight, Coming Home	Dustin Hoffman, Kramer vs. Kramer
Faye Dunaway, Network	Diane Keaton, Annie Hall	Jane Fonda, Coming Home	Sally Field, Norma Rae
Jason Robards, All the President's Men	Jason Robards, Julia	Christopher Walken, The Deer Hunter	Melvyn Douglas, Being There
Beatrice Straight, Network	Vanessa Redgrave, Julia	Maggie Smith, California Suite	Meryl Streep, Kramer vs. Kramer
John G. Avildsen, Rocky	Woody Allen, Annie Hall	Michael Cimino, The Deer Hunter	Robert Benton, Kramer vs. Kramer
William Goldman, All the President's Men	Alvin Sargent, Julia	Oliver Stone, Midnight Express	Robert Benton, Kramer vs. Kramer
Paddy Chayefsky, Network	Woody Allen and Marshall Brickman, Annie Hall	Nancy Dowd, story; Waldo Salt and Robert C. Jones, screenplay, Coming Home	Steve Tesich, Breaking Away
"Evergreen" (A Star Is Born)	"You Light Up My Life" (You Light Up My Life)	"Last Dance" (Thank God It's Friday)	"It Goes Like It Goes" (Norma Rae)
The Omen (Original); Bound for Glory (Adaptation)	Star Wars (Original); A Little Night Music (Adaptation)	Midnight Express (Original); The Buddy Holly Story (Adaptation)	A Little Romance (Original); All That Jazz (Adaptation)
Bound for Glory	Close Encounters of the Third Kind	Days of Heaven	Apocalypse Now
Fellini's Casanova	Star Wars	Death on the Nile	All That Jazz
All the President's Men	Star Wars	Heaven Can Wait	All That Jazz
Rocky	Star Wars	The Deer Hunter	All That Jazz
Black and White in Color (Ivory Coast)	Madame Rosa (France)	Get Out Your Handkerchiefs (France)	The Tin Drum (Federal Republic of Germany)
All the President's Men	Star Wars	The Deer Hunter	Apocalypse Now
—	Star Wars	—	Alien
Leisure (Animated); In the Region of Ice (Live Action)	Sand Castle (Animated); I'll Find a Way (Live Action)	Special Delivery (Animated); Teenage Father (Live Action)	Every Child (Animated); Board and Care (Live Action)
Number Our Days (Shorts); Harlan County, U.S.A. (Features)	Gravity Is My Enemy (Shorts); Who Are the DeBolts? And Where Did They Get Nineteen Kids? (Features)	The Flight of the Gossamer Condor (Shorts); Scared Straight! (Features)	Paul Robeson: Tribute to an Artist (Shorts); Best Boy (Features)

> 66 I haven't had an orthodox career and I wanted more than anything to have your respect. The first time I didn't feel it, but this time I feel it and I can't deny the fact you like me—right now, you *like* me! 99
>
> —Sally Field, Best Actress for *Places in the Heart*, 1984 (she had also won in 1979 for *Norma Rae*)

	1980	1981	1982
Picture	*Ordinary People*	*Chariots of Fire*	*Gandhi*
Actor	Robert De Niro, *Raging Bull*	Henry Fonda, *On Golden Pond*	Ben Kingsley, *Gandhi*
Actress	Sissy Spacek, *Coal Miner's Daughter*	Katharine Hepburn, *On Golden Pond*	Meryl Streep, *Sophie's Choice*
Supporting Actor	Timothy Hutton, *Ordinary People*	John Gielgud, *Arthur*	Louis Gossett Jr., *An Officer and a Gentleman*
Supporting Actress	Mary Steenburgen, *Melvin and Howard*	Maureen Stapleton, *Reds*	Jessica Lange, *Tootsie*
Director	Robert Redford, *Ordinary People*	Warren Beatty, *Reds*	Richard Attenborough, *Gandhi*
Adapted Screenplay	Alvin Sargent, *Ordinary People*	Ernest Thompson, *On Golden Pond*	Costa-Gavras and Donald Stewart, *Missing*
Original Screenplay	Bo Goldman, *Melvin and Howard*	Colin Welland, *Chariots of Fire*	John Briley, *Gandhi*
Song	"Fame" *(Fame)*	"Arthur's Theme (Best That You Can Do)" *(Arthur)*	"Up Where We Belong" *(An Officer and a Gentleman)*
Original Score	*Fame*	*Chariots of Fire*	*E.T., the Extra-Terrestrial; Victor/Victoria* (Song Score/Adaptation)
Cinematography	*Tess*	*Reds*	*Gandhi*
Costume Design	*Tess*	*Chariots of Fire*	*Gandhi*
Art Direction—Set Decoration	*Tess*	*Raiders of the Lost Ark*	*Gandhi*
Film Editing	*Raging Bull*	*Raiders of the Lost Ark*	*Gandhi*
Foreign Language Film	*Moscow Does Not Believe in Tears* (U.S.S.R.)	*Mephisto* (Hungary)	*Volver A Empezar (To Begin Again)* (Spain)
Sound	*The Empire Strikes Back*	*Raiders of the Lost Ark*	*Gandhi*
Sound Effects (Editing)	—	—	*E.T., the Extra-Terrestrial*
Makeup	—	*An American Werewolf in London*	*Quest for Fire*
Visual Effects	—	*Raiders of the Lost Ark*	*E.T., the Extra-Terrestrial*
Short Films	*The Fly* (Animated); *The Dollar Bottom* (Live Action)	*Crac* (Animated); *Violet* (Live Action)	*Tango* (Animated); *A Shocking Accident* (Live Action)
Documentaries	*Karl Hess: Toward Liberty* (Shorts); *From Mao to Mozart: Isaac Stern in China* (Features)	*Genocide* (Shorts); *Close Harmony* (Features)	*If You Love This Planet* (Shorts); *Just Another Missing Kid* (Features)

1983	1984	1985	1986
Terms of Endearment	Amadeus	Out of Africa	Platoon
Robert Duvall, Tender Mercies	F. Murray Abraham, Amadeus	William Hurt, Kiss of the Spider Woman	Paul Newman, The Color of Money
Shirley MacLaine, Terms of Endearment	Sally Field, Places in the Heart	Geraldine Page, The Trip to Bountiful	Marlee Matlin, Children of a Lesser God
Jack Nicholson, Terms of Endearment	Haing S. Ngor, The Killing Fields	Don Ameche, Cocoon	Michael Caine, Hannah and Her Sisters
Linda Hunt, The Year of Living Dangerously	Peggy Ashcroft, A Passage to India	Anjelica Huston, Prizzi's Honor	Dianne Wiest, Hannah and Her Sisters
James L. Brooks, Terms of Endearment	Milos Forman, Amadeus	Sydney Pollack, Out of Africa	Oliver Stone, Platoon
James L. Brooks, Terms of Endearment	Peter Shaffer, Amadeus	Kurt Luedtke, Out of Africa	Ruth Prawer Jhabvala, A Room with a View
Horton Foote, Tender Mercies	Robert Benton, Places in the Heart	William Kelley, Pamela Wallace, and Earl W. Wallace, Witness	Woody Allen, Hannah and Her Sisters
"Flashdance . . . What a Feeling" (Flashdance)	"I Just Called To Say I Love You" (The Woman in Red)	"Say You, Say Me" (White Nights)	"Take My Breath Away" (Top Gun)
The Right Stuff; Yentl (Song Score/Adaptation)	A Passage to India; Purple Rain (Song Score)	Out of Africa	'Round Midnight
Fanny & Alexander	The Killing Fields	Out of Africa	The Mission
Fanny & Alexander	Amadeus	Ran	A Room with a View
Fanny & Alexander	Amadeus	Out of Africa	A Room with a View
The Right Stuff	The Killing Fields	Witness	Platoon
Fanny & Alexander (Sweden)	Dangerous Moves (Switzerland)	The Official Story (Argentina)	The Assault (The Netherlands)
The Right Stuff	Amadeus	Out of Africa	Platoon
The Right Stuff	—	Back to the Future	Aliens
—	Amadeus	Mask	The Fly
Return of the Jedi	Indiana Jones and the Temple of Doom	Cocoon	Aliens
Sundae in New York (Animated); Boys and Girls (Live Action)	Charade (Animated); Up (Live Action)	Anna & Bella (Animated); Molly's Pilgrim (Live Action)	A Greek Tragedy (Animated); Precious Images (Live Action)
Flamenco at 5:15 (Shorts); He Makes Me Feel Like Dancin' (Features)	The Stone Carvers (Shorts); The Times of Harvey Milk (Features)	Witness to War: Dr. Charlie Clements (Shorts); Broken Rainbow (Features)	Women—For America, for the World (Shorts); Artie Shaw: Time Is All You've Got and Down and out in America (Features)

	1987	**1988**	**1989**
Picture	*The Last Emperor*	*Rain Man*	*Driving Miss Daisy*
Actor	Michael Douglas, *Wall Street*	Dustin Hoffman, *Rain Man*	Daniel Day-Lewis, *My Left Foot*
Actress	Cher, *Moonstruck*	Jodie Foster, *The Accused*	Jessica Tandy, *Driving Miss Daisy*
Supporting Actor	Sean Connery, *The Untouchables*	Kevin Kline, *A Fish Called Wanda*	Denzel Washington, *Glory*
Supporting Actress	Olympia Dukakis, *Moonstruck*	Geena Davis, *The Accidental Tourist*	Brenda Fricker, *My Left Foot*
Director	Bernardo Bertolucci, *The Last Emperor*	Barry Levinson, *Rain Man*	Oliver Stone, *Born on the Fourth of July*
Adapted Screenplay	Mark Peploe and Bernardo Bertolucci, *The Last Emperor*	Christopher Hampton, *Dangerous Liaisons*	Tom Schulman, *Dead Poets Society*
Original Screenplay	John Patrick Shanley, *Moonstruck*	Ronald Bass and Barry Morrow, *Rain Man*	Alfred Uhry, *Driving Miss Daisy*
Song	"(I've Had) The Time of My Life" *(Dirty Dancing)*	"Let the River Run" *(Working Girl)*	"Under the Sea" *(The Little Mermaid)*
Original Score	*The Last Emperor*	*The Milagro Beanfield War*	*The Little Mermaid*
Cinematography	*The Last Emperor*	*Mississippi Burning*	*Glory*
Costume Design	*The Last Emperor*	*Dangerous Liaisons*	*Henry V*
Art Direction—Set Decoration	*The Last Emperor*	*Dangerous Liaisons*	*Batman*
Film Editing	*The Last Emperor*	*Who Framed Roger Rabbit*	*Born on the Fourth of July*
Foreign Language Film	*Babette's Feast* (Denmark)	*Pelle the Conqueror* (Denmark)	*Cinema Paradiso* (Italy)
Sound	*The Last Emperor*	*Bird*	*Glory*
Sound Effects (Editing)	—	*Who Framed Roger Rabbit*	*Indiana Jones and the Last Crusade*
Makeup	*Harry and the Hendersons*	*Beetlejuice*	*Driving Miss Daisy*
Visual Effects	*Innerspace*	*Who Framed Roger Rabbit*	*The Abyss*
Short Films	*The Man Who Planted Trees* (Animated); *Ray's Male Heterosexual Dance Hall* (Live Action)	*Tin Toy* (Animated); *The Appointments of Dennis Jennings* (Live Action)	*Balance* (Animated); *Work Experience* (Live Action)
Documentaries	*Young at Heart* (Shorts); *The Ten-Year Lunch: The Wit and the Legend of the Algonquin Round Table* (Features)	*You Don't Have To Die* (Shorts); *Hotel Terminus: The Life and Times of Klaus Barbie* (Features)	*The Johnstown Flood* (Shorts); *Common Threads: Stories from the Quilt* (Features)

> 66 Gee, this isn't what I imagined it would be like in the bathtub. 99
>
> —Dianne Wiest, Best Supporting Actress for *Hannah and Her Sisters*, 1986

1990	1991	1992	1993
Dances with Wolves	The Silence of the Lambs	Unforgiven	Schindler's List
Jeremy Irons, Reversal of Fortune	Anthony Hopkins, The Silence of the Lambs	Al Pacino, Scent of a Woman	Tom Hanks, Philadelphia
Kathy Bates, Misery	Jodie Foster, The Silence of the Lambs	Emma Thompson, Howards End	Holly Hunter, The Piano
Joe Pesci, GoodFellas	Jack Palance, City Slickers	Gene Hackman, Unforgiven	Tommy Lee Jones, The Fugitive
Whoopi Goldberg, Ghost	Mercedes Ruehl, The Fisher King	Marisa Tomei, My Cousin Vinny	Anna Paquin, The Piano
Kevin Costner, Dances with Wolves	Jonathan Demme, The Silence of the Lambs	Clint Eastwood, Unforgiven	Steven Spielberg, Schindler's List
Michael Blake, Dances with Wolves	Ted Tally, The Silence of the Lambs	Ruth Prawer Jhabvala, Howards End	Steven Zaillian, Schindler's List
Bruce Joel Rubin, Ghost	Callie Khouri, Thelma & Louise	Neil Jordan, The Crying Game	Jane Campion, The Piano
"Sooner or Later (I Always Get My Man)" (Dick Tracy)	"Beauty and the Beast" (Beauty and the Beast)	"A Whole New World" (Aladdin)	"Streets of Philadelphia" (Philadelphia)
Dances with Wolves	Beauty and the Beast	Aladdin	Schindler's List
Dances with Wolves	JFK	A River Runs Through It	Schindler's List
Cyrano de Bergerac	Bugsy	Bram Stoker's Dracula	The Age of Innocence
Dick Tracy	Bugsy	Howards End	Schindler's List
Dances with Wolves	JFK	Unforgiven	Schindler's List
Journey of Hope (Switzerland)	Mediterraneo (Italy)	Indochine (France)	Belle Epoque (Spain)
Dances with Wolves	Terminator 2: Judgment Day	The Last of the Mohicans	Jurassic Park
The Hunt for Red October	Terminator 2: Judgment Day	Bram Stoker's Dracula	Jurassic Park
Dick Tracy	Terminator 2: Judgment Day	Bram Stoker's Dracula	Mrs. Doubtfire
Total Recall	Terminator 2: Judgment Day	Death Becomes Her	Jurassic Park
Creature Comforts (Animated); The Lunch Date (Live Action)	Manipulation (Animated); Session Man (Live Action)	Mona Lisa Descending a Staircase (Animated); Omnibus (Live Action)	The Wrong Trousers (Animated); Black Rider (Live Action)
Days of Waiting (Shorts); American Dream (Features)	Deadly Deception: General Electric, Nuclear Weapons and Our Environment (Shorts); In the Shadow of the Stars (Features)	Educating Peter (Shorts); The Panama Deception (Features)	Defending Our Lives (Shorts); Am a Promise: The Children of Stanton Elementary School (Features)

> 66 When I was little, my mother said, 'I want you to be something.' I don't think that this means that I am somebody, but I guess I'm on my way. 99
> —Cher, Best Actress for Moonstruck, 1987

1994

Picture	*Forrest Gump*
Actor	Tom Hanks, *Forrest Gump*
Actress	Jessica Lange, *Blue Sky*
Supporting Actor	Martin Landau, *Ed Wood*
Supporting Actress	Dianne Wiest, *Bullets over Broadway*
Director	Robert Zemeckis, *Forrest Gump*
Adapted Screenplay	Eric Roth, *Forrest Gump*
Original Screenplay	Roger Avary and Quentin Tarantino, *Pulp Fiction*
Best Song	"Can You Feel the Love Tonight" (*The Lion King*)
Original Score	*The Lion King*
Cinematography	*Legends of the Fall*
Costume Design	*The Adventures of Priscilla, Queen of the Desert*
Art Direction—Set Decoration	*The Madness of King George*
Film Editing	*Forrest Gump*
Foreign Language Film	*Burnt by the Sun*
Sound	*Speed*
Sound Effects (Editing)	*Speed*
Makeup	*Ed Wood*
Visual Effects	*Forrest Gump*
Short Films	*Bob's Birthday* (Animated); *Franz Kafka's It's a Wonderful Life* and *Trevor* (Live Action)
Documentaries	*A Time for Justice* (Shorts); *Maya Lin: A Strong Clear Vision* (Features)

MORE OSCAR RECORDS

Oldest Best Actor winner:
Henry Fonda, 76, for *On Golden Pond*

Oldest Best Actress winner:
Jessica Tandy, 80, for *Driving Miss Daisy*

Most nominations before winning an Oscar:
Geraldine Page, with eight

Women directors whose films were nominated for Best Picture:
Randa Haines for *Children of a Lesser God*, Penny Marshall for *Awakenings*, Barbara Streisand for *The Prince of Tides*, and Jane Campion for *The Piano*

Two-time Best Supporting Actresses:
Shelley Winters for *The Diary of Anne Frank* and *A Patch of Blue*, and Dianne Wiest for *Hannah and Her Sisters* and *Bullets over Broadway*

Most popular Oscar-winning film genre: drama (44% of all winners)

Least popular Oscar-winning film genre: suspense-thriller (two winning films: *Rebecca* in 1940, and *The Silence of the Lambs* in 1991)

Films that won all top five Oscars:
It Happened One Night in 1934, *One Flew over the Cuckoo's Nest* in 1975, and *The Silence of the Lambs* in 1991

Shortest Best Picture Winner:
Annie Hall (94 minutes)

Westerns that won Best Picture:
Cimarron in 1930/1, *Dances With Wolves* in 1990, and *Unforgiven* in 1992

FILM AWARDS

NATIONAL SOCIETY OF FILM CRITICS
Annual Awards for Best Film
1966 Blow-Up
1967 Persona
1968 Shame
1969 Z
1970 M*A*S*H
1971 Claire's Knee
1972 The Discreet Charm of the Bourgeoisie
1973 Day for Night
1974 Scenes from a Marriage
1975 Nashville
1976 All The President's Men
1977 Annie Hall
1978 Get Out Your Handkerchiefs
1979 Breaking Away
1980 Melvin and Howard
1981 Atlantic City
1982 Tootsie
1983 Night of the Shooting Stars
1984 Stranger Than Paradise
1985 Ran
1986 Blue Velvet
1987 The Dead
1988 The Unbearable Lightness of Being
1989 Drugstore Cowboy
1990 GoodFellas
1991 Life Is Sweet
1992 Unforgiven
1993 Schindler's List
1994 Pulp Fiction

SUNDANCE FILM FESTIVAL
GRAND JURY PRIZE
1978 Girlfriends
1979 Spirit in the Wind
1981 Heartland
     Gal Young Un
Dramatic
1982 Street Music
1983 Purple Haze
1984 Old Enough
1985 Blood Simple
1986 Smooth Talk
1987 Waiting for the Moon
     Trouble with Dick
1988 Heat and Sunlight
1989 True Love
1990 Chameleon Street
1991 Poison
1992 In the Soup
1993 Ruby in Paradise
     Public Access

1994 What Happened Was . . .
1995 The Brothers McMullen

FILMMAKERS TROPHY
Dramatic
1989 Powwow Highway
1990 House Party
1991 Privilege
1992 Zebrahead
1993 Fly By Night
1994 Clerks
1995 Angela

AUDIENCE AWARD
Dramatic
1989 sex, lies and videotape
1990 Longtime Companion
1991 One Cup of Coffee
1992 The Waterdance
1993 El Mariachi
1994 Spanking the Monkey
1995 Picture Bride

CANNES FILM FESTIVAL
Palme d'Or for Best Film
1946 La Bataille du rail (France)
1947 Antoine et Antoinette (France)
1948 No festival
1949 The Third Man (G.B.)
1950 No festival
1951 Miracle in Milan (Italy)
     Miss Julie (Sweden)
1952 Othello (Morocco)
     Two Cents Worth of Hope (Italy)
1953 Wages of Fear (France)
1954 Gate of Hell (Japan)
1955 Marty (U.S.)
1956 World of Silence (France)
1957 Friendly Persuasion (U.S.)
1958 The Cranes are Flying (U.S.S.R.)
1959 Black Orpheus (France)
1960 La Dolce Vita (Italy)
1961 Viridiana (Spain)
     Une Aussi longue absence (France)
1962 The Given Word (Brazil)
1963 The Leopard (Italy)
1964 The Umbrellas of Cherbourg (France)
1965 The Knack (G.B.)
1966 A Man and a Woman (France)
     Signore e Signori (Italy)
1967 Blow-Up (G.B.)
1968 Festival disrupted; no awards given
1969 If . . . (G.B.)
1970 M*A*S*H (U.S.)

1971 The Go-Between (G.B.)
1972 The Working Class Goes to Paradise (Italy)
     The Mattei Affair (Italy)
1973 Scarecrow (U.S.)
     The Hireling (G.B.)
1974 The Conversation (U.S.)
1975 Chronicle of the Burning Years (Algeria)
1976 Taxi Driver (U.S.)
1977 Padre Padrone (Italy)
1978 L'Albero Degli Zoccoli (Italy)
1979 The Tin Drum (Germany)
     Apocalypse Now (U.S.)
1980 All That Jazz (U.S.)
     Kagemusha (Japan)
1981 Man of Iron (Poland)
1982 Missing (U.S.)
     Yol (Turkey)
1983 The Ballad of Narayama (Japan)
1984 Paris, Texas (Germany)
1985 When Father Was Away On Business (Yugoslavia)
1986 The Mission (G.B.)
1987 Under the Sun of Satan (France)
1988 Pelle the Conqueror (Denmark)
1989 sex, lies and videotape (U.S.)
1990 Wild at Heart (U.S.)
1991 Barton Fink (U.S.)
1992 The Best Intentions (Denmark)
1993 The Piano (New Zealand)
     Farewell My Concubine (Hong Kong)
1994 Pulp Fiction (U.S.)
1995 Underground (Bosnia)

VENICE FILM FESTIVAL
Golden Lion [for Best Film or Best Foreign Film]
1932 No official award
1933 No festival
1934 Man of Aran (G.B.)
1935 Anna Karenina (U.S.)
1936 Der Kaiser von Kalifornien (Germany)
1937 Un Carnet debal (France)
1938 Olympia (Germany)
1939 No award given
1940 Der Postmeister (Germany)
1941 Ohm Kruger (Germany)
1942 Der grosse König (Germany)
1943 No festival
1944 No festival
1945 No festival
1946 The Southerner (U.S.)
1947 Sirena (Czechoslovakia)
1948 Hamlet (G.B.)

1949   Manon (France)
1950   Justice is Done (France)
1951   Rashomon (Japan)
1952   Forbidden Games (France)
1953   No award given
1954   Romeo and Juliet (Italy/G.B.)
1955   Ordet (Denmark)
1956   No award given
1957   Aparajito (India)
1958   Muhomatsu no Issho (Japan)
1959   Il Generale della Rovere (Italy)
1960   Le Passage du Rhin (France)
1961   Last Year at Marienbad (France)
1962   Childhood of Ivan (U.S.S.R.)
1963   Le Mani sulla città (Italy)
1964   Red Desert (Italy)
1965   Of a Thousand Delights (Italy)
1966   Battle of Algiers (Italy)
1967   Belle de Jour (France)
1968   Die Aristen in der Zirkuskuppel
        (Germany)

*Jury and award system discontinued
1969–79*
1980   Gloria (U.S.)
        Atlantic City (France/Canada)
1981   Die Bleierne Zeit (Germany)
1982   The State of Things (Germany)
1983   Prénom Carmen (France/
        Switzerland)
1984   Year of the Quiet Sun (Poland)
1985   Sans toit ni loi (Vagabonde)
        (France)
1986   Le Rayon vert (France)
1987   Au revoir, les enfants (France)
1988   The Legend of the Holy Drinker
        (Italy)
1989   A City of Sadness (Taiwan)
1990   Rosencrantz and Guildenstern
        Are Dead (G.B.)
1991   Urga (U.S.S.R./France)
1992   The Story of Qiu Ju (China)
1993   Blue (France)
        Short Cuts (U.S.)
1994   Before the Rain (Macedonia)
        Vive L'Amour (Taiwan)

BERLIN FILM FESTIVAL AWARD

Golden Bear Award for Best Film
1953   The Wages of Fear (France)
1954   Hobson's Choice (G.B.)
1955   The Rats (Germany)
1956   Invitation to the Dance (G.B.)
1957   Twelve Angry Men (U.S.)
1958   The End of the Day (Sweden)
1959   The Cousins (France)
1960   Lazarillo de Tormes (Spain)
1961   La Notte (Italy)
1962   A Kind of Loving (G.B.)
1963   Oath of Obedience (Germany)
        The Devil (Italy)
1964   Dry Summer (Turkey)

1965   Alphaville (France)
1966   Cul-de-Sac (G.B.)
1967   Le Depart (Belgium)
1968   Ole Dole Duff (Sweden)
1969   Early Years (Yugoslavia)
1970   No award
1971   The Garden of the Finzi-Continis
        (Italy)
1972   The Canterbury Tales (Italy)
1973   Distant Thunder (India)
1974   The Apprenticeship of Duddy
        Kravitz (Canada)
1975   Orkobefogadas (Hungary)
1976   Buffalo Bill and the Indians
        (U.S.) [award declined]
1977   The Ascent (U.S.S.R.)
1978   The Trouts (Spain)
        The Words of Max (Spain)
1979   David (Germany)
1980   Heartland (U.S.)
        Palermo Oder Wolfsburg
        (Germany)
1981   Di Presa Di Presa (Spain)
1982   Die Sehnsucht der Veronica Voss
        (Germany)
1983   Ascendancy (G.B.)
        The Beehive (Spain)
1984   Love Streams (U.S.)
1985   Wetherby (G.B.)
        Die Frau und der Fremde
        (Germany)
1986   Stammhein (Germany)
1987   The Theme (U.S.S.R.)
1988   Red Sorghum (China)
1989   Rain Man (U.S.)
1990   Music Box (U.S.)
        Larks on a String
        (Czechoslovakia)
1991   House of Smiles (Italy)
1992   Grand Canyon (U.S.)
1993   The Woman from the Lake of
        Scented Souls (China)
        The Wedding Banquet
        (Taiwan/U.S.)
1994   In the Name of the Father
        (UK/Ireland)
1995   Live Bait (France)

INDEPENDENT SPIRIT AWARDS

These prizes are considered the Oscars of
the independent film world.

Best Feature
1986   After Hours
1987   Platoon
1988   River's Edge
1989   Stand and Deliver
1990   sex, lies and videotape
1991   The Grifters
1992   Rambling Rose
1993   The Player

1994   Short Cuts
1995   Pulp Fiction

Best First Feature
1987   Spike Lee, director
        She's Gotta Have It
1988   Emile Ardolino, director
        Dirty Dancing
1989   Donald Petrie, director
        Mystic Pizza
1990   Michael Lehmann, director
        Heathers
1991   Whit Stillman, producer/director
        Metropolitan
1992   Matty Rich, director
        Straight Out of Brooklyn
1993   Neal Jimenez and Michael
        Steinberg, directors
        The Waterdance
1994   Robert Rodriguez, director
        El Mariachi
1995   David O. Russell, director
        Spanking the Monkey

Best Director
1986   Martin Scorsese
        After Hours
1987   Oliver Stone
        Platoon
1988   John Huston
        The Dead
1989   Ramon Menendez
        Stand and Deliver
1990   Steven Soderbergh
        sex, lies and videotape
1991   Charles Burnett
        To Sleep with Anger
1992   Martha Coolidge
        Rambling Rose
1993   Carl Franklin
        One False Move
1994   Robert Altman
        Short Cuts
1995   Quentin Tarantino
        Pulp Fiction

Best Screenplay
1986   Horton Foote
        The Trip to Bountiful
1987   Oliver Stone
        Platoon
1988   Neal Jimenez
        River's Edge
1989   Ramon Menendez and Tom
        Musca
        Stand and Deliver
1990   Gus Van Sant Jr. and Daniel Yost
        Drugstore Cowboy
1991   Charles Burnett
        To Sleep with Anger
1992   Gus Van Sant Jr.
        My Own Private Idaho

1993	Neal Jimenez
	The Waterdance
1994	Robert Altman and Frank Barhydt
	Short Cuts
1995	David O. Russell
	Spanking the Monkey

Best Cinematographer

1986	Toyomichi Kurita
	Trouble In Mind
1987	Bob Richardson
	Platoon
1988	Haskell Wexler
	Matewan
1989	Sven Nykvist
	The Unbearable Lightness of Being
1990	Robert Yeoman
	Drugstore Cowboy
1991	Fred Elmes
	Wild at Heart
1992	Walt Lloyd
	Kafka
1993	Frederick Elmes
	Night on Earth
1994	Lisa Rinzler
	Menace II Society
1995	John Thomas
	Barcelona

Best Actor

1986	M. Emmet Walsh
	Blood Simple
1987	James Woods
	Salvador
1988	Dennis Quaid
	The Big Easy
1989	Edward James Olmos
	Stand and Deliver
1990	Matt Dillon
	Drugstore Cowboy
1991	Danny Glover
	To Sleep with Anger
1992	River Phoenix
	My Own Private Idaho
1993	Harvey Keitel
	Bad Lieutenant
1994	Jeff Bridges
	American Heart
1995	Samuel L. Jackson
	Pulp Fiction

Best Actress

1986	Geraldine Page
	The Trip to Bountiful
1987	Isabella Rossellini
	Blue Velvet
1988	Sally Kirkland
	Anna
1989	Jodie Foster
	Five Corners

1990	Andie MacDowell
	sex, lies and videotape
1991	Anjelica Huston
	The Grifters
1992	Judy Davis
	Impromptu
1993	Fairuza Balk
	Gas, Food, Lodging
1994	Ashley Judd
	Ruby in Paradise
1995	Linda Fiorentino
	The Last Seduction

Best Supporting Actor

1988	Morgan Freeman
	Street Smart
1989	Lou Diamond Phillips
	Stand and Deliver
1990	Max Perlich
	Drugstore Cowboy
1991	Bruce Davison
	Longtime Companion
1992	David Strathairn
	City of Hope
1993	Steve Buscemi
	Reservoir Dogs
1994	Christopher Lloyd
	Twenty Bucks
1995	Chazz Palmintieri
	Bullets over Broadway

Best Supporting Actress

1988	Anjelica Huston
	The Dead
1989	Rosanna De Soto
	Stand and Deliver
1990	Laura San Giacomo
	sex, lies and videotape
1991	Sheryl Lee Ralph
	To Sleep with Anger
1992	Diane Ladd
	Rambling Rose
1993	Alfre Woodard
	Passion Fish
1994	Lili Taylor
	Household Saints
1995	Dianne Wiest
	Bullets over Broadway

Best Foreign Film

1986	Kiss of the Spider Woman
1987	A Room with a View
1988	My Life as a Dog
1989	Wings of Desire
1990	My Left Foot
1991	Sweetie
1992	An Angel at My Table
1993	The Crying Game
1994	The Piano
1995	Red

MTV MOVIE AWARDS

Best Movie

1992	Terminator 2: Judgment Day
1993	A Few Good Men
1994	Menace II Society
1995	Pulp Fiction

Best Male Performance

1992	Arnold Schwarzenegger
	Terminator 2: Judgment Day
1993	Denzel Washington
	Malcolm X
1994	Tom Hanks
	Philadelphia
1995	Brad Pitt
	Interview with the Vampire

Best Female Performance

1992	Linda Hamilton
	Terminator 2: Judgment Day
1993	Sharon Stone
	Basic Instinct
1994	Janet Jackson
	Poetic Justice
1995	Sandra Bullock
	Speed

Breakthrough Performance

1992	Edward Furlong
	Terminator 2: Judgment Day
1993	Marisa Tomei
	My Cousin Vinny
1994	Alicia Silverstone
	The Crush
1995	Kirsten Dunst
	Interview with the Vampire

Most Desirable Male

1992	Keanu Reeves
	Point Break
1993	Chistian Slater
	Untamed Heart
1994	William Baldwin
	Sliver
1995	Brad Pitt
	Legends of the Fall

Most Desirable Female

1992	Linda Hamilton
	Terminator 2: Judgment Day
1993	Sharon Stone
	Basic Instinct
1994	Janet Jackson
	Poetic Justice
1995	Sandra Bullock
	Speed

Best On-Screen Duo

| 1992 | Mike Myers and Dana Carvey |
| | *Wayne's World* |

1993	Mel Gibson and Danny Glover
	Lethal Weapon 3
1994	Harrison Ford and Tommy Lee Jones
	The Fugitive
1995	Keanu Reeves and Sandra Bullock
	Speed

Best Villain
1992	Rebecca DeMornay
	The Hand That Rocks the Cradle
1993	Jennifer Jason Leigh
	Single White Female
1994	Alicia Silverstone
	The Crush
1995	Dennis Hopper
	Speed

Best Comedic Performance
1992	Billy Crystal
	City Slickers
1993	Robin Williams
	Aladdin
1994	Robin Williams
	Mrs. Doubtfire
1995	Jim Carrey
	Dumb and Dumber

Best Song
1992	Bryan Adams
	"(Everything I Do) I Do It For You" (*Robin Hood: Prince of Thieves*)
1993	Whitney Houston
	"I Will Always Love You" (*The Bodyguard*)
1994	Michael Jackson
	"Will You Be There" (*Free Willy*)
1995	Stone Temple Pilots
	"Big Empty" (*The Crow*)

Best Kiss
1992	Macaulay Culkin and Anna Chlumsky
	My Girl
1993	Marisa Tomei and Christian Slater
	Untamed Heart
1994	Woody Harrelson and Demi Moore
	Indecent Proposal
1995	Jim Carrey and Lauren Holly
	Dumb and Dumber

Best Action Sequence
1992	Terminator 2: Judgment Day
1993	Lethal Weapon 3
1994	The Fugitive
1995	Speed

Best New Filmmaker Award
1992	John Singleton
	Boyz N the Hood
1993	Carl Franklin
	One False Move
1994	Steven Zaillian
	Searching for Bobby Fischer
1995	Steve James
	Hoop Dreams

Lifetime Achievement Award
1992	Jason Voorhees
	Friday the 13th
1993	The Three Stooges
1994	Richard Roundtree
	Shaft film series
1995	Jackie Chan

DIRECTOR'S GUILD AWARDS

Year	Film	Director
1948–49	A Letter To Three Wives	Joseph Mankiewicz
1949–50	All The King's Men	Robert Rossen
1950–51	All About Eve	Joseph Mankiewicz
1951	A Place in the Sun	George Stevens
1952	The Quiet Man	John Ford
1953	From Here to Eternity	Fred Zinnemann
1954	On the Waterfront	Elia Kazan
1955	Marty	Delbert Mann
1956	Giant	George Stevens
1957	Bridge on the River Kwai	David Lean
1958	Gigi	Vincente Minnelli
1959	Ben-Hur	William Wyler
1960	The Apartment	Billy Wilder
1961	West Side Story	Robert Wise and Jerome Robbins
1962	Lawrence of Arabia	David Lean
1963	Tom Jones	Tony Richardson
1964	My Fair Lady	George Cukor
1965	The Sound of Music	Robert Wise
1966	A Man for All Seasons	Fred Zinnemann
1967	The Graduate	Mike Nichols
1968	The Lion In Winter	Anthony Harvey
1969	Midnight Cowboy	John Schlesinger
1970	Patton	Franklin J. Schaffner
1971	The French Connection	William Friedkin
1972	The Godfather	Francis Ford Coppola
1973	The Sting	George Roy Hill
1974	The Godfather, Part II	Francis Ford Coppola
1975	One Flew over the Cuckoo's Nest	Milos Forman
1976	Rocky	John G. Avildsen
1977	Annie Hall	Woody Allen
1978	The Deer Hunter	Michael Cimino
1979	Kramer vs. Kramer	Robert Benton
1980	Ordinary People	Robert Redford
1981	Reds	Warren Beatty
1982	Gandhi	Richard Attenborough
1983	Terms of Endearment	James L. Brooks
1984	Amadeus	Milos Forman
1985	The Color Purple	Steven Spielberg
1986	Platoon	Oliver Stone
1987	The Last Emperor	Bernardo Bertolucci
1988	Rain Man	Barry Levinson
1989	Born on the Fourth of July	Oliver Stone
1990	Dances with Wolves	Kevin Costner
1991	The Silence of the Lambs	Jonathan Demme
1992	Unforgiven	Clint Eastwood
1993	Schindler's List	Steven Spielberg
1994	Forrest Gump	Robert Zemeckis

TUBE

PICKS & PANS 1994–95

The new shows of the 1994-95 season go to school—here are their report cards with some very surprising grades. The shows at the top of the ratings charts don't always wind up at the top of this class, but don't worry: no one fails (the lowest grade is a D+) and there are even a few A's for the teacher's pets.

Homicide: Life on the Street	NBC	A	Both amusing and educational, one of the few series worth setting aside time to watch.
The Jon Stewart Show	SYN	A	Fresh and consistently amusing, Stewart seems like Letterman's younger, hipper brother.
Chicago Hope	CBS	A-	Intelligent, fleet, emotionally complex, and lightly dusted with producer David Kelley's sense of the absurd, the best hospital show since *St. Elsewhere.*
My So-Called Life	ABC	A-	A lyrical coming-of-age story that is not just extraordinary TV but also the best piece of filmmaking of the year.
Newsradio	NBC	A-	A nervier, more sophisticated version of *WKRP in Cincinnati*, with a marvelous ensemble cast and a lunatic sense of humor.
Politically Incorrect with Bill Maher	COM	A-	Imagine *The McLaughlin Group* after the panelists have had a few beers.
Star Trek: Voyager	UPN	A-	More action-oriented and less morally ponderous than the recent *Star Trek* series.
Cybill	CBS	B+	This amusing sitcom radiates a zippy tartness.
Due South	CBS	B+	Squeezes fresh life out of an old buddy formula.
Earth 2	NBC	B+	Needs a more energetic atmosphere, but has a superior cast and a cohesive if not always convincing futuristic zeitgeist.
Extreme	ABC	B+	High-altitude derring-do, rugged, breathtaking scenery, a happening soundtrack, and an appealing, fresh-faced cast.
Something Wilder	NBC	B+	There's nothing wild about it, but there is a lot to like about this sweet, innocuous sitcom.
Thunderbirds	Fox	B+	The adventures of these futuristic flyboys are still wonderfully hokey-looking and absolutely distinctive.
The Tick	Fox	B+	With the sardonic wit of *The Simpsons*, this is hysterical cartoon entertainment for grownups.
The Cosby Mysteries	NBC	B	Cosby's imperishable charm makes a flimsy vehicle seem like a cushy ride.
The Five Mrs. Buchanans	CBS	B	The humor is obvious, but the pacing is snappy and the characters are sharply delineated.
Friends	NBC	B	A barrage of banter with an arch coyness that suggests a Gen X Neil Simon play.
Hope and Gloria	NBC	B	Smartly conceived and lively, the show exhibits a healthy sense of the absurd.
House of Buggin'	Fox	B	Leguizamo possesses energy and comic flair, but he needs a stronger supporting cast and consistent, inventive writing.
Legend	UPN	B	It's nice to see a Western that doesn't take the genre too seriously.
The Marshall	ABC	B	A crisp and slick adventure hour which is losing definition because of a string of unfocused scripts.

Me and the Boys	ABC	B	Bland but likable, driven by comic Steve Harvey, whose style recalls the mellower Richard Pryor.
New York Undercover	Fox	B	Flawed but bold—like *21 Jump Street* set to a slammin' hip-hop soundtrack.
Pride and Joy	NBC	B	Often clever humor delivered in stagy declamations—imagine a tennis match with no volleys, just serves.
Under One Roof	CBS	B	A wholesome, heartwarming homily on family values that rings true but unfortunately not too deep.
VR.5	Fox	B	Jumbled but jazzy, trading on a paranoid, conspiratorial tone that recalls *The Prisoner* and MTV's *Dead at 21*.
Women of the House	CBS	B	Implausible and forced, but the writing is usually articulate.
Blue Skies	ABC	B-	Has an easy jocularity, but the key cast members need a good deal more comedic seasoning.
ER	NBC	B-	Pure adrenaline rush during the emergency sequences, but hackneyed in its lull periods.
In the House	NBC	B-	A revamped *Who's the Boss* which scores low on the yucks-meter.
Marker	UPN	B-	Escapist adventure whose quality will fluctuate from week to week depending on the sturdiness of the scripts.
McKenna	ABC	B-	Will rise or fall depending on whether star Eric Close can achieve heartthrob status.
Muscle	WB	B-	Makes a crass bid to create the tone of *Soap,* not realizing that there's a difference between funny and offensive.
Sliders	Fox	B-	Sci-fi lite, rendered with gee-whiz energy and a sense of levity.
Under Suspicion	CBS	B-	Sort of a one-note show, but that note, while thin, is piercing.
The Wright Verdicts	CBS	B-	Conventional and formulaic, the parlor-game plotting is more than passable, but the writing is undistinguished.
Amazing Grace	NBC	C+	Striking when it sticks to the spiritual, but unfortunately spends too much time trying to imitate *Picket Fences*.
Double Rush	CBS	C+	Aspires to be a pedal-pushing version of *Taxi,* but the cast and writing are grievously uneven.
The Great Defender	Fox	C+	A light, almost flimsy drama which tries to provide an irreverent look at the seamier side of jurisprudence.

The cast of last season's biggest hit, Friends.

Cast members of My So-Called Life, *a favorite of ours, if not of viewers everywhere.*

M.A.N.T.I.S.	Fox	C+	Mantis's costume is cool, but the plots and action scenes are luke-warm at best.
Medicine Ball	Fox	C+	A tepid hodgepodge of borrowings from *ER, Chicago Hope,* and *University Hospital.*
My Wildest Dreams	Fox	C+	Series star Lisa Ann Walter has a saucy presence, but the show-goes to outrageous lengths for a punch line.
On Our Own	ABC	C+	Energetic but utterly silly.
The Parent 'Hood	WB	C+	Tries to be a '90s *Cosby Show,* but the structure, timing, and humor are all strictly standard, even a little clichéd.
Party of Five	Fox	C+	Incredibly dull melodrama with a high-gloss cast of characters showing hopeful signs of growing more selfish, randy, and funky.
Pig Sty	UPN	C+	Genial but simpy—the post-collegiate version of *Animal House.*
University Hospital	SYN	C+	Flimsy material lent a surprising vitality by the show's young leads.
Wild Oats	Fox	C+	A brittle and often crude sitcom that succeeds in being the wrong kind of hysterical.
All-American Girl	ABC	C	In its own warped fashion, similar to *The Many Loves of Dobie Gillis*—only with rickshaw jokes.
The Boys Are Back	CBS	C	A vacuous eyesore of a vehicle for returning sitcom favorites Hal Linden and Suzanne Pleshette.
Fortune Hunter	Fox	C	This 007 knockoff is so callow and cartoonish, it won't make any-one forget Roger Moore—or even George Lazenby.
The George Wendt Show	CBS	C	Running-on-empty humor with a woeful supporting cast.
Get Smart	Fox	C	A dumbed-up version of the original TV classic.
High Sierra Search and Rescue	NBC	C	Mawkish, formulaic melodrama.
The Office	CBS	C	This false farce wastes a good cast on dull, overdone material.
Platypus Man	UPN	C	A likable star with curdled ingredients: hit-or-miss humor, an anemic supporting cast, gag-me gags, and feeble plotting.
Hardball	Fox	C-	As obnoxiously boisterous and flip as a beer-soaked bleacher bum.
Sweet Justice	NBC	C-	Stilted plots, contrived courtroom scenes, wild overacting, and more bad Southern accents than a Canadian high-school produc-tion of *Cat on a Hot Tin Roof.*
A Whole New Ballgame	ABC	C-	The jokes hit about .213—a little light for the majors.
Madman of the People	NBC	D+	Tart curmudgeon Dabney Coleman in one of the season's worst.

Homicide drew one of our top marks, and is slowly building in the ratings as well.

Even some of the smartest, hippest talk couldn't keep Jon Stewart on the air.

THE CABLE DIRECTORY

The following is a complete list of all national cable television networks, as of our press date, according to the 1995 National Cable Television Association Guide.

Action Pay Per View
independent action, sci-fi, thriller movies

Adam & Eve
adult movies

All News Channel
continuous newscasts

American Movie Classics (AMC)
Hollywood's greatest films

America's Talking
all talk

ANA Network
programming in Arabic and English for Arab-Americans

Arts & Entertainment Television Network
original biographies, mysteries, and specials

Asian American Satellite TV
Chinese-language news, drama, movies, sports, education, and entertainment

Black Entertainment Television (BET)
music videos, sports, drama, sit-coms, concerts, specials, talk shows, gospel, news

The Box
viewer-programmed music videos of all types

Bravo Cable Network
cultural offerings including films, arts specials, interviews

Cable Health Club
aerobics, fitness, health

Cable News Network (CNN)
news, weather, sports

Cable Video Store
movies and special events

Canal de Noticias NBC
Spanish-language news

Canal Sur
Latin American newscasts, entertainment and sports

The Cartoon Network
cartoons

Catalog 1
electronic catalog shopping mall

Channel America Television Network
sports, music, talk shows, movies, religious programming

CineLatino
Spanish-language movies

Cinemax
contemporary and classic films

Classic Arts Showcase
nonprofit arts programming

Country Music Television (CMT)
country music videos

CNBC
business, money, and talk programming

CNN International (CNNI)
global news, business, weather, and sports

Comedy Central
all-comedy programming

The Computer Network (c/net)
computers, on-line services, interactive media, and video games

Consumer Resource Network (CRN)
marketer-supported information

Courtroom Television Network (Court TV)
live and taped trial coverage and legal features

The Crime Channel
crime-related programming, including series, movies, and news

C-SPAN (Cable Satellite Public Affairs Network)
straight news from Washington and around the nation

C-SPAN 2
live coverage of the U.S. Senate and public affairs programming

Deep Dish TV
educational programming

The Discovery Channel
nature, history, technology, and adventure

The Disney Channel
family entertainment

E! Entertainment Television
celebrity interviews, news, features

Encore
films of the '60s–'80s

Encore Thematic Multiplex
movies, with "mood on demand" viewing options

ESPN
broad appeal and narrow interest sports programming

ESPN2
live and original sports programming

EWTN: The Catholic Cable Network
religious programming in English and Spanish

Faith & Values Channel
interfaith religious programming

The Family Channel
varied programming for children and families

The Filipino Channel
news, drama, sitcoms, and cultural programs from the Philippines

Flix
movies from the '60s–'90s

FoxNet
regular Fox network programs

fX
entertainment and lifestyle programming for ages 18–49

fXM: Movies from Fox
movies scheduled by genre

Galavisión
Spanish-language movies, sports, news

Game Show Network
new and classic game shows

GEMS International Television
Spanish-language women's programming

The Golf Channel
golf tournaments and instruction

Home Box Office (HBO)
films, specials, sports

Headline News
half-hour newscasts, from CNN

The History Channel
Historical documentaries, movies, and miniseries

Home & Garden Television
lifestyle programming

Home Shopping Network I
discount shopping at home

Home Shopping Network II
more shopping at home

The Idea Channel
leading scholars in discussions on a variety of topics

The Independent Film Channel
independent films

The Inspirational Network (ISNP)
cross-denominational family programming

International Channel
multinational programming in 22 different languages

Jewish Television Network
news, public affairs, arts and entertainment

Jones Computer Network (JCN)
computer instruction, news, commentary, courses

Kaleidoscope: America's Disability Channel
programming by and for people with disabilities

KTLA/UV
Los Angeles station with movies, specials, local news and sports

Ladbroke Racing Channel
live thoroughbred and harness racing

The Learning Channel
educational programming for all ages

Lifetime Television
entertainment and information programming aimed at women

Mind Extension University (ME/U): The Educational Network
educational for-credit programming

MOR Music TV
music video hits from the '50s–'90s

The Movie Channel (TMC)
current and classic movies

MTV: Music Television
music videos and pop culture programming

MTV Latino
Spanish-language pop culture programming, including American and Latin music videos

MuchMusic USA
rock, rap, country, and alternative videos

NASA Television
space program coverage and other educational material

The Nashville Network (TNN)
country music entertainment

NET—Political NewsTalk Network
original programming focusing on Washington D.C.'s intrigue and issues

Network One
adult entertainment including movies, action and adventure, and music

NewSport
sports news and scores

NewsTalk Television
news-based interactive talk channel

Newsworld International
news from the United States and around the world

Nickelodeon/Nick at Nite
kids' programming during the day; TV classics after hours

The '90s Channel
social and political documentaries

Nostalgia Television
entertainment, lifestyle, and information for adults

Outdoors Motorsports Channel (OMC)
programming for the outdoorsman or -woman

Planet Central
environmentally themed programming

Playboy TV
adult entertainment

Prime SportsChannel Networks
national sports

Product Information Network (PIN)
infomercials

Q2
electronic retailing

QVC
home-shopping service

Request Television
pay-per-view movies and events

Sci-Fi Channel
fantasy, horror, and sci-fi series, movies, originals

Scola
international TV news, broadcast to schools

Shop at Home
electronic retailing

Showtime
movies, series, specials, boxing, other entertainment

SingleVision
lifestyle and infotainment programming for singles

Spice
adult movies

STARZ!
first-run movie releases from Universal, Miramax, Columbia, and other leading distributors

TBS
movies, sports, comedies, kids' shows

Telemundo
Spanish-language programming with movies, game shows, news, music, soap operas, and sports

Television Food Network (TVFN)
food, fitness, health, nutrition

The Travel Channel
travel news, documentaries, live events

Trinity Broadcasting Network
religious programming

Trio
family entertainment

Turner Classic Movies
nearly 400 movies per month

Turner Network Television (TNT)
vintage and original films, sports, kids' shows, specials

TV Asia
programming from the Asian continent, mostly in English

TV-JAPAN
news, sports, drama, education, and kids' shows from Japan

U Network
student-produced programming in all genres

Univision
Spanish-speaking programs, with movies, sports, national newscasts

USA Network
all-entertainment network

ValueVision
home shopping

Via TV Network
television shopping network

Video Catalog Channel
home shopping for antiques and collectibles

Video Hits One (VH1)
music videos targeted to the 25-to-35-year-old audience

Viewer's Choice
films, sports, musical events

Viewer's Choice: Continuous Hits 1, 2, 3
three channels offering recent movies

Viewer's Choice: Hot Choice
action-adventure and adult-appeal movies and specials

Viva Television Network
Spanish-language entertainment, culture, educational programs

The Weather Channel
local, national, and international weather information

WGN/UV
Chicago station featuring specials, news, movies, local sports

The Worship Network
Christian worship and music set to scenic videos

WPIX/UV
New York station with specials, news, movies, local sports

WSBK
Boston station offering movies, specials, and local sports

WWOR/EMI Service
New York station with programs from the '60s, '70s plus the Mets

Z Music
Christian videos, specials, news, and entertainment

CABLE'S TOP 20 NETWORKS

Ranked by the number of subscribers, these are cable's leading networks. (Source: Nielsen Media Research)

1. Cable News Network (CNN)
2. ESPN
3. TBS
4. The Nashville Network (TNN)
5. USA Network
5. The Discovery Channel
5. Turner Network Televison (TNT)
8. C-SPAN
9. The Family Channel
10. A&E Television Network
11. MTV
12. Lifetime Television
12. Nickelodeon/Nick at Nite
14. Headline News
15. The Weather Channel
16. American Movie Classics (AMC)
17. CNBC
18. QVC
19. Video Hits One (VH1)
20. Black Entertainment Television (BET)

THE MOST POPULAR SHOWS ON TV

The following chart shows America's TV favorites every year beginning in 1949.
(Sources: *Variety* [1949–50, month of October] and Nielsen Media Research)

1949–50

1.	The Texaco Star Theater	NBC
2.	Toast of the Town	
	(Ed Sullivan)	CBS
3.	Arthur Godfrey's	
	Talent Scouts	CBS
4.	Fireball Fun for All	NBC
5.	Philco Television	
	Playhouse	NBC
6.	Fireside Theatre	NBC
7.	The Goldbergs	CBS
8.	Suspense	CBS
9.	The Ford Television	
	Theater	CBS
10.	Cavalcade of Stars	DUMONT

1950–51

1.	The Texaco Star Theater	NBC
2.	Fireside Theatre	NBC
3.	Your Show of Shows	NBC
4.	Philco Television Playhouse	NBC
5.	The Colgate Comedy Hour	NBC
6.	Gillette Cavalcade of Sports	NBC
7.	Arthur Godfrey's	
	Talent Scouts	CBS
8.	Mama	CBS
9.	Robert Montgomery Presents	NBC
10.	Martin Kane, Private Eye	NBC
11.	Man Against Crime	CBS
12.	Somerset Maugham	
	Theatre	NBC
13.	Kraft Television Theatre	NBC
14.	Toast of the Town	
	(Ed Sullivan)	CBS
15.	The Aldrich Family	NBC
16.	You Bet Your Life	NBC
17.	Armstrong Circle Theater (tie)	NBC
17.	Big Town (tie)	CBS
17.	Lights Out (tie)	NBC
20.	The Alan Young Show	CBS

1951–52

1.	Arthur Godfrey's	
	Talent Scouts	CBS
2.	The Texaco Star Theater	NBC
3.	I Love Lucy	CBS
4.	The Red Skelton Show	NBC
5.	The Colgate Comedy Hour	NBC
6.	Fireside Theatre	NBC
7.	The Jack Benny Program	CBS
8.	Your Show of Shows	NBC
9.	You Bet Your Life	NBC
10.	Arthur Godfrey and	
	His Friends	CBS
11.	Mama	CBS
12.	Philco Television	
	Playhouse	NBC
13.	Amos 'n' Andy	CBS
14.	Big Town	CBS
15.	Pabst Blue Ribbon Bouts	CBS
16.	Gillette Cavalcade of Sports	NBC
17.	The Alan Young Show	CBS
18.	All-Star Revue (tie)	NBC
18.	Dragnet (tie)	NBC
20.	Kraft Television Theatre	NBC

1952–53

1.	I Love Lucy	CBS
2.	Arthur Godfrey's	
	Talent Scouts	CBS
3.	Arthur Godfrey and	
	His Friends	CBS
4.	Dragnet	NBC
5.	The Texaco Star Theater	NBC
6.	The Buick Circus Hour	NBC
7.	The Colgate Comedy Hour	NBC
8.	Gangbusters	NBC
9.	You Bet Your Life	NBC
10.	Fireside Theatre	NBC
11.	The Red Buttons Show	CBS
12.	The Jack Benny Program	CBS
13.	Life with Luigi	CBS
14.	Pabst Blue Ribbon Bouts	CBS
15.	Goodyear Television	
	Playhouse	NBC
16.	The Life of Riley	NBC
17.	Mama	CBS
18.	Your Show of Shows	NBC
19.	What's My Line?	CBS
20.	Strike It Rich	CBS

1953–54

1.	I Love Lucy	CBS
2.	Dragnet	NBC
3.	Arthur Godfrey's	
	Talent Scouts (tie)	CBS
3.	You Bet Your Life (tie)	NBC
5.	The Bob Hope Show	NBC
6.	The Buick-Berle Show	NBC
7.	Arthur Godfrey and	
	His Friends	CBS
8.	The Ford Television Theater	NBC
9.	The Jackie Gleason Show	CBS
10.	Fireside Theatre	NBC
11.	The Colgate Comedy	
	Hour (tie)	NBC
11.	This Is Your Life (tie)	NBC
13.	The Red Buttons Show	CBS
14.	The Life of Riley	NBC
15.	Our Miss Brooks	CBS
16.	Treasury Men in Action	NBC
17.	All-Star Revue	
	(Martha Raye)	NBC
18.	The Jack Benny Program	CBS
19.	Gillette Cavalcade of Sports	NBC
20.	Philco Television Playhouse	NBC

1954–55

1.	I Love Lucy	CBS
2.	The Jackie Gleason Show	CBS
3.	Dragnet	NBC
4.	You Bet Your Life	NBC
5.	Toast of the Town	
	(Ed Sullivan)	CBS
6.	Disneyland	ABC
7.	The Bob Hope Show	NBC
8.	The Jack Benny Program	CBS
9.	The Martha Raye Show	NBC
10.	The George Gobel Show	NBC
11.	The Ford Television Theater	NBC
12.	December Bride	CBS
13.	The Buick-Berle Show	NBC
14.	This Is Your Life	NBC
15.	I've Got a Secret	CBS
16.	Two for the Money	CBS
17.	Your Hit Parade	NBC
18.	The Millionaire	CBS
19.	General Electric Theater	CBS
20.	Arthur Godfrey's	
	Talent Scouts	CBS

1955–56

1.	The $64,000 Question	CBS
2.	I Love Lucy	CBS
3.	The Ed Sullivan Show	CBS
4.	Disneyland	ABC
5.	The Jack Benny Program	CBS
6.	December Bride	CBS
7.	You Bet Your Life	NBC
8.	Dragnet	NBC
9.	I've Got a Secret	CBS
10.	General Electric Theater	CBS
11.	Private Secretary (tie)	CBS
11.	The Ford Television Theater (tie)	NBC
13.	The Red Skelton Show	CBS
14.	The George Gobel Show	NBC
15.	The $64,000 Challenge	CBS
16.	Arthur Godfrey's Talent Scouts	CBS
17.	The Lineup	CBS
18.	Shower of Stars	CBS
19.	The Perry Como Show	NBC
20.	The Honeymooners	CBS

1956–57

1.	I Love Lucy	CBS
2.	The Ed Sullivan Show	CBS
3.	General Electric Theater	CBS
4.	The $64,000 Question	CBS
5.	December Bride	CBS
6.	Alfred Hitchcock Presents	CBS
7.	I've Got a Secret (tie)	CBS
7.	Gunsmoke (tie)	CBS
9.	The Perry Como Show	NBC
10.	The Jack Benny Program	CBS
11.	Dragnet	NBC
12.	Arthur Godfrey's Talent Scouts	CBS
13.	The Millionaire (tie)	CBS
13.	Disneyland (tie)	ABC
15.	Shower of Stars	CBS
16.	The Lineup	CBS
17.	The Red Skelton Show	CBS
18.	You Bet Your Life	NBC
19.	The Life and Legend of Wyatt Earp	ABC
20.	Private Secretary	CBS

1957–58

1.	Gunsmoke	CBS
2.	The Danny Thomas Show	CBS
3.	Tales of Wells Fargo	NBC
4.	Have Gun, Will Travel	CBS
5.	I've Got a Secret	CBS
6.	The Life and Legend of Wyatt Earp	ABC
7.	General Electric Theater	CBS
8.	The Restless Gun	NBC
9.	December Bride	CBS
10.	You Bet Your Life	NBC
11.	Alfred Hitchcock Presents (tie)	CBS
11.	Cheyenne (tie)	ABC
13.	The Tennessee Ernie Ford Show	NBC
14.	The Red Skelton Show	CBS
15.	Wagon Train (tie)	NBC
15.	Sugarfoot (tie)	ABC
15.	Father Knows Best (tie)	CBS
18.	Twenty-One	NBC
19.	The Ed Sullivan Show	CBS
20.	The Jack Benny Program	CBS

1958–59

1.	Gunsmoke	CBS
2.	Wagon Train	NBC
3.	Have Gun, Will Travel	CBS
4.	The Rifleman	ABC
5.	The Danny Thomas Show	CBS
6.	Maverick	ABC
7.	Tales of Wells Fargo	NBC
8.	The Real McCoys	ABC
9.	I've Got a Secret	CBS
10.	Wyatt Earp	ABC
11.	The Price Is Right	NBC
12.	The Red Skelton Show	CBS
13.	Zane Grey Theater (tie)	CBS
13.	Father Knows Best (tie)	CBS
15.	The Texan	CBS
16.	Wanted: Dead or Alive (tie)	CBS
16.	Peter Gunn (tie)	NBC
18.	Cheyenne	ABC
19.	Perry Mason	CBS
20.	The Tennessee Ernie Ford Show	NBC

1959–60

1.	Gunsmoke	CBS
2.	Wagon Train	NBC
3.	Have Gun, Will Travel	CBS
4.	The Danny Thomas Show	CBS
5.	The Red Skelton Show	CBS
6.	Father Knows Best (tie)	CBS
6.	Sunset Strip (tie)	ABC
8.	The Price Is Right	NBC
9.	Wanted: Dead or Alive	CBS
10.	Perry Mason	CBS
11.	The Real McCoys	ABC
12.	The Ed Sullivan Show	CBS
13.	The Bing Crosby Show	ABC
14.	The Rifleman	ABC
15.	The Tennessee Ernie Ford Show	NBC
16.	The Lawman	ABC
17.	Dennis the Menace	CBS
18.	Cheyenne	ABC
19.	Rawhide	CBS
20.	Maverick	ABC

1960–61

1.	Gunsmoke	CBS
2.	Wagon Train	NBC
3.	Have Gun, Will Travel	CBS
4.	The Andy Griffith Show	CBS
5.	The Real McCoys	ABC
6.	Rawhide	CBS
7.	Candid Camera	CBS
8.	The Untouchables (tie)	ABC
8.	The Price Is Right (tie)	NBC
10.	The Jack Benny Program	CBS
11.	Dennis the Menace	CBS
12.	The Danny Thomas Show	CBS
13.	My Three Sons (tie)	ABC
13.	77 Sunset Strip (tie)	ABC
15.	The Ed Sullivan Show	CBS
16.	Perry Mason	CBS
17.	Bonanza	NBC
18.	The Flintstones	ABC
19.	The Red Skelton Show	CBS
20.	Alfred Hitchcock Presents	CBS

1961–62

1.	Wagon Train	NBC
2.	Bonanza	NBC
3.	Gunsmoke	CBS
4.	Hazel	NBC
5.	Perry Mason	CBS
6.	The Red Skelton Show	CBS
7.	The Andy Griffith Show	CBS
8.	The Danny Thomas Show	CBS
9.	Dr. Kildare	NBC
10.	Candid Camera	CBS
11.	My Three Sons	ABC
12.	The Garry Moore Show	CBS
13.	Rawhide	CBS
14.	The Real McCoys	ABC
15.	Lassie	CBS
16.	Sing Along with Mitch	NBC
17.	Dennis the Menace (tie)	CBS
17.	Marshal Dillon (tie) (Gunsmoke reruns)	CBS
19.	Ben Casey	ABC
20.	The Ed Sullivan Show	CBS

1962–63

1.	The Beverly Hillbillies	CBS
2.	Candid Camera (tie)	CBS
2.	The Red Skelton Show (tie)	CBS
4.	Bonanza (tie)	NBC
4.	The Lucy Show (tie)	CBS
6.	The Andy Griffith Show	CBS
7.	Ben Casey (tie)	ABC
7.	The Danny Thomas Show (tie)	CBS
9.	The Dick Van Dyke Show	CBS
10.	Gunsmoke	CBS
11.	Dr. Kildare (tie)	NBC
11.	The Jack Benny Program (tie)	CBS
13.	What's My Line?	CBS
14.	The Ed Sullivan Show	CBS
15.	Hazel	NBC
16.	I've Got a Secret	CBS
17.	The Jackie Gleason Show	CBS
18.	The Defenders	CBS
19.	The Garry Moore Show (tie)	CBS
19.	To Tell the Truth (tie)	CBS

1963–64

1.	The Beverly Hillbillies	CBS
2.	Bonanza	NBC
3.	The Dick Van Dyke Show	CBS
4.	Petticoat Junction	CBS
5.	The Andy Griffith Show	CBS
6.	The Lucy Show	CBS
7.	Candid Camera	CBS
8.	The Ed Sullivan Show	CBS
9.	The Danny Thomas Show	CBS
10.	My Favorite Martian	CBS
11.	The Red Skelton Show	CBS
12.	I've Got a Secret (tie)	CBS
12.	Lassie (tie)	CBS
12.	The Jack Benny Program (tie)	CBS
15.	The Jackie Gleason Show	CBS
16.	The Donna Reed Show	ABC
17.	The Virginian	NBC
18.	The Patty Duke Show	ABC
19.	Dr. Kildare	NBC
20.	Gunsmoke	CBS

1964–65

1.	Bonanza	NBC
2.	Bewitched	ABC
3.	Gomer Pyle, U.S.M.C.	CBS
4.	The Andy Griffith Show	CBS
5.	The Fugitive	ABC
6.	The Red Skelton Hour	CBS
7.	The Dick Van Dyke Show	CBS
8.	The Lucy Show	CBS
9.	Peyton Place (II)	ABC
10.	Combat	ABC
11.	Walt Disney's Wonderful World of Color	NBC
12.	The Beverly Hillbillies	CBS
13.	My Three Sons	ABC
14.	Branded	NBC
15.	Petticoat Junction (tie)	CBS
15.	The Ed Sullivan Show (tie)	CBS
17.	Lassie	CBS
18.	The Munsters (tie)	CBS
18.	Gilligan's Island (tie)	CBS
20.	Peyton Place (V)	ABC

1965–66

1.	Bonanza	NBC
2.	Gomer Pyle, U.S.M.C.	CBS
3.	The Lucy Show	CBS
4.	The Red Skelton Hour	CBS
5.	Batman (II)	ABC
6.	The Andy Griffith Show	CBS
7.	Bewitched (tie)	ABC
7.	The Beverly Hillbillies (tie)	CBS
9.	Hogan's Heroes	CBS
10.	Batman (I)	ABC
11.	Green Acres	CBS
12.	Get Smart	NBC
13.	The Man from U.N.C.L.E.	NBC
14.	Daktari	CBS
15.	My Three Sons	CBS
16.	The Dick Van Dyke Show	CBS
17.	Walt Disney's Wonderful World of Color (tie)	NBC
17.	The Ed Sullivan Show (tie)	CBS
19.	The Lawrence Welk Show (tie)	ABC
19.	I've Got a Secret (tie)	CBS

1966–67

1.	Bonanza	NBC
2.	The Red Skelton Hour	CBS
3.	The Andy Griffith Show	CBS
4.	The Lucy Show	CBS
5.	The Jackie Gleason Show	CBS
6.	Green Acres	CBS
7.	Daktari (tie)	CBS
7.	Bewitched (tie)	ABC
7.	The Beverly Hillbillies (tie)	CBS
10.	Gomer Pyle, U.S.M.C. (tie)	CBS
10.	The Virginian (tie)	NBC
10.	The Lawrence Welk Show (tie)	ABC
10.	The Ed Sullivan Show (tie)	CBS
14.	The Dean Martin Show (tie)	CBS
14.	Family Affair (tie)	CBS
16.	Smothers Brothers Comedy Hour	CBS
17.	The CBS Friday Night Movie (tie)	CBS
17.	Hogan's Heroes (tie)	CBS
19.	Walt Disney's Wonderful World of Color	NBC
20.	Saturday Night at the Movies	NBC

1967–68

1. The Andy Griffith Show — CBS
2. The Lucy Show — CBS
3. Gomer Pyle, U.S.M.C. — CBS
4. Gunsmoke (tie) — CBS
4. Family Affair (tie) — CBS
4. Bonanza (tie) — NBC
7. The Red Skelton Hour — CBS
8. The Dean Martin Show — NBC
9. The Jackie Gleason Show — CBS
10. Saturday Night at the Movies — NBC
11. Bewitched — ABC
12. The Beverly Hillbillies — CBS
13. The Ed Sullivan Show — CBS
14. The Virginian — NBC
15. The CBS Friday Night Movie (tie) — CBS
15. Green Acres (tie) — CBS
17. The Lawrence Welk Show — ABC
18. Smothers Brothers Comedy Hour — CBS
19. Gentle Ben — CBS
20. Tuesday Night at the Movies — NBC

1968–69

1. Rowan and Martin's Laugh-In — NBC
2. Gomer Pyle, U.S.M.C. — CBS
3. Bonanza — NBC
4. Mayberry R.F.D. — CBS
5. Family Affair — CBS
6. Gunsmoke — CBS
7. Julia — NBC
8. The Dean Martin Show — NBC
9. Here's Lucy — CBS
10. The Beverly Hillbillies — CBS
11. Mission: Impossible (tie) — CBS
11. Bewitched (tie) — ABC
11. The Red Skelton Hour (tie) — CBS
14. My Three Sons — CBS
15. The Glen Campbell Goodtime Hour — CBS
16. Ironside — NBC
17. The Virginian — NBC
18. The F.B.I. — ABC
19. Green Acres — CBS
20. Dragnet — NBC

1969–70

1. Rowan and Martin's Laugh-In — NBC
2. Gunsmoke — CBS
3. Bonanza — NBC
4. Mayberry R.F.D. — CBS
5. Family Affair — CBS
6. Here's Lucy — CBS
7. The Red Skelton Hour — CBS
8. Marcus Welby, M.D. — ABC
9. The Wonderful World of Disney — NBC
10. The Doris Day Show — CBS
11. The Bill Cosby Show — NBC
12. The Jim Nabors Hour — CBS
13. The Carol Burnett Show — CBS
14. The Dean Martin Show — NBC
15. My Three Sons (tie) — CBS
15. Ironside (tie) — NBC
15. The Johnny Cash Show (tie) — ABC
18. The Beverly Hillbillies — CBS
19. Hawaii Five-O — CBS
20. Glen Campbell Goodtime Hour — CBS

1970–71

1. Marcus Welby, M.D. — ABC
2. The Flip Wilson Show — NBC
3. Here's Lucy — CBS
4. Ironside — NBC
5. Gunsmoke — CBS
6. The ABC Movie of the Week — ABC
7. Hawaii Five-O — CBS
8. Medical Center — CBS
9. Bonanza — NBC
10. The F.B.I. — ABC
11. The Mod Squad — ABC
12. Adam-12 — NBC
13. Rowan and Martin's Laugh-In (tie) — NBC
13. The Wonderful World of Disney (tie) — NBC
15. Mayberry R.F.D. — CBS
16. Hee Haw — CBS
17. Mannix — CBS
18. The Men from Shiloh — NBC
19. My Three Sons — CBS
20. The Doris Day Show — CBS

1971–72

1. All in the Family — CBS
2. The Flip Wilson Show — NBC
3. Marcus Welby, M.D. — ABC
4. Gunsmoke — CBS
5. The ABC Movie of the Week — ABC
6. Sanford and Son — NBC
7. Mannix — CBS
8. Funny Face (tie) — CBS
8. Adam-12 (tie) — NBC
10. The Mary Tyler Moore Show — CBS
11. Here's Lucy — CBS
12. Hawaii Five-O — CBS
13. Medical Center — CBS
14. The NBC Mystery Movie — NBC
15. Ironside — NBC
16. The Partridge Family — ABC
17. The F.B.I. — ABC
18. The New Dick Van Dyke Show — CBS
19. The Wonderful World of Disney — NBC
20. Bonanza — NBC

1972–73

1. All in the Family — CBS
2. Sanford and Son — NBC
3. Hawaii Five-O — CBS
4. Maude — CBS
5. Bridget Loves Bernie (tie) — CBS
5. The NBC Sunday Mystery Movie (tie) — NBC
7. The Mary Tyler Moore Show (tie) — CBS
7. Gunsmoke (tie) — CBS
9. The Wonderful World of Disney — NBC
10. Ironside — NBC
11. Adam-12 — NBC
12. The Flip Wilson Show — NBC
13. Marcus Welby, M.D. — ABC
14. Cannon — CBS
15. Here's Lucy — CBS
16. The Bob Newhart Show — CBS
17. ABC Tuesday Movie of the Week — ABC
18. NFL Monday Night Football — ABC
19. The Partridge Family (tie) — ABC
19. The Waltons (tie) — CBS

1973–74

1.	All in the Family	CBS
2.	The Waltons	CBS
3.	Sanford and Son	NBC
4.	M*A*S*H	CBS
5.	Hawaii Five-O	CBS
6.	Maude	CBS
7.	Kojak (tie)	CBS
7.	The Sonny and Cher Comedy Hour (tie)	CBS
9.	The Mary Tyler Moore Show (tie)	CBS
9.	Cannon (tie)	CBS
11.	The Six Million Dollar Man	ABC
12.	The Bob Newhart Show (tie)	CBS
12.	The Wonderful World of Disney (tie)	NBC
14.	The NBC Sunday Mystery Movie	NBC
15.	Gunsmoke	CBS
16.	Happy Days	ABC
17.	Good Times (tie)	CBS
17.	Barnaby Jones (tie)	CBS
19.	NFL Monday Night Football (tie)	ABC
19.	The CBS Friday Night Movie (tie)	CBS

1974–75

1.	All in the Family	CBS
2.	Sanford and Son	NBC
3.	Chico and the Man	NBC
4.	The Jeffersons	CBS
5.	M*A*S*H	CBS
6.	Rhoda	CBS
7.	Good Times	CBS
8.	The Waltons	CBS
9.	Maude	CBS
10.	Hawaii Five-O	CBS
11.	The Mary Tyler Moore Show	CBS
12.	The Rockford Files	NBC
13.	Little House on the Prairie	NBC
14.	Kojak	CBS
15.	Police Woman	NBC
16.	S.W.A.T.	ABC
17.	The Bob Newhart Show	CBS
18.	The Wonderful World of Disney (tie)	NBC
18.	The Rookies (tie)	ABC
20.	Mannix	CBS

1975–76

1.	All in the Family	CBS
2.	Rich Man, Poor Man	ABC
3.	Laverne and Shirley	ABC
4.	Maude	CBS
5.	The Bionic Woman	ABC
6.	Phyllis	CBS
7.	Sanford and Son (tie)	NBC
7.	Rhoda (tie)	CBS
9.	The Six Million Dollar Man	ABC
10.	The ABC Monday Night Movie	ABC
11.	Happy Days	ABC
12.	One Day at a Time	CBS
13.	The ABC Sunday Night Movie	ABC
14.	The Waltons (tie)	CBS
14.	M*A*S*H (tie)	CBS
16.	Starsky and Hutch (tie)	ABC
16.	Good Heavens (tie)	ABC
18.	Welcome Back, Kotter	ABC
19.	The Mary Tyler Moore Show	CBS
20.	Kojak	CBS

1976–77

1.	Happy Days	ABC
2.	Laverne and Shirley	ABC
3.	The ABC Monday Night Movie	ABC
4.	M*A*S*H	CBS
5.	Charlie's Angels	ABC
6.	The Big Event	NBC
7.	The Six Million Dollar Man	ABC
8.	The ABC Sunday Night Movie (tie)	ABC
8.	Baretta (tie)	ABC
8.	One Day at a Time (tie)	CBS
11.	Three's Company	ABC
12.	All in the Family	CBS
13.	Welcome Back, Kotter	ABC
14.	The Bionic Woman	ABC
15.	The Waltons (tie)	CBS
15.	Little House on the Prairie (tie)	NBC
17.	Barney Miller	ABC
18.	60 Minutes (tie)	CBS
18.	Hawaii Five-O (tie)	CBS
20.	NBC Monday Night at the Movies	NBC

1977–78

1.	Laverne and Shirley	ABC
2.	Happy Days	ABC
3.	Three's Company	ABC
4.	Charlie's Angels (tie)	ABC
4.	All in the Family (tie)	CBS
4.	60 Minutes (tie)	CBS
7.	Little House on the Prairie	NBC
8.	M*A*S*H (tie)	CBS
8.	Alice (tie)	CBS
10.	One Day at a Time	CBS
11.	How the West Was Won	ABC
12.	Eight Is Enough	ABC
13.	Soap	ABC
14.	The Love Boat	ABC
15.	NBC Monday Night Movie	NBC
16.	NFL Monday Night Football	ABC
17.	Barney Miller (tie)	ABC
17.	Fantasy Island (tie)	ABC
19.	The Amazing Spider-Man (tie)	CBS
19.	Project U.F.O. (tie)	NBC

1978–79

1.	Laverne and Shirley	ABC
2.	Three's Company	ABC
3.	Mork & Mindy	ABC
4.	Happy Days (tie)	ABC
4.	The Ropers (tie)	ABC
6.	What's Happening!! (tie)	ABC
6.	Alice (8:30) (tie)	CBS
8.	M*A*S*H	CBS
9.	One Day at a Time (Monday)	CBS
10.	Taxi	ABC
11.	60 Minutes (tie)	CBS
11.	Charlie's Angels (tie)	ABC
13.	Angie	ABC
14.	Alice (9:30)	CBS
15.	All in the Family	CBS
16.	WKRP in Cincinnati (tie)	CBS
16.	Soap (tie)	ABC
18.	Eight Is Enough	ABC
19.	All in the Family	CBS
20.	Barney Miller (tie)	ABC
20.	CBS Sunday Night Movie (tie)	CBS

1979–80

1.	60 Minutes	CBS
2.	Three's Company	ABC
3.	That's Incredible	ABC
4.	M*A*S*H	CBS
5.	Alice	CBS
6.	Dallas	CBS
7.	Flo	CBS
8.	The Jeffersons	CBS
9.	The Dukes of Hazzard	CBS
10.	One Day at a Time	CBS
11.	WKRP in Cincinnati	CBS
12.	Goodtime Girls	ABC
13.	Archie Bunker's Place	CBS
14.	Taxi	ABC
15.	Eight Is Enough	ABC
16.	Little House on the Prairie	NBC
17.	House Calls	CBS
18.	Real People	NBC
19.	CHiPs	NBC
20.	Happy Days	ABC

1980–81

1.	Dallas	CBS
2.	60 Minutes	CBS
3.	The Dukes of Hazzard	CBS
4.	Private Benjamin	CBS
5.	M*A*S*H	CBS
6.	The Love Boat	ABC
7.	The NBC Tuesday Night Movie	NBC
8.	House Calls	CBS
9.	The Jeffersons (tie)	CBS
9.	Little House on the Prairie (tie)	NBC
11.	The Two of Us	CBS
12.	Alice	CBS
13.	Real People (tie)	NBC
13.	Three's Company (tie)	ABC
15.	The NBC Movie of the Week (tie)	NBC
15.	One Day at a Time (tie)	CBS
17.	Too Close for Comfort (tie)	ABC
17.	Magnum, P.I. (tie)	CBS
19.	Diff'rent Strokes (tie)	NBC
19.	NFL Monday Night Football (tie)	ABC

1981–82

1.	Dallas (9:00)	CBS
2.	Dallas (10:00)	CBS
3.	60 Minutes	CBS
4.	Three's Company (tie)	ABC
4.	CBS NFL Football Post 2 (tie)	CBS
6.	The Jeffersons	CBS
7.	Joanie Loves Chachi	ABC
8.	The Dukes of Hazzard (9:00)	CBS
9.	Alice (tie)	CBS
9.	The Dukes of Hazzard (8:00) (tie)	CBS
11.	The ABC Monday Night Movie (tie)	ABC
11.	Too Close for Comfort (tie)	ABC
13.	M*A*S*H	CBS
14.	One Day at a Time	CBS
15.	NFL Monday Night Football	ABC
16.	Falcon Crest	CBS
17.	Archie Bunker's Place (tie)	CBS
17.	The Love Boat (tie)	ABC
19.	Hart to Hart	ABC
20.	Trapper John, M.D.	CBS

1982–83

1.	60 Minutes	CBS
2.	Dallas	CBS
3.	M*A*S*H (tie)	CBS
3.	Magnum, P.I. (tie)	CBS
5.	Dynasty	ABC
6.	Three's Company	ABC
7.	Simon & Simon	CBS
8.	Falcon Crest	CBS
9.	NFL Monday Night Football	ABC
10.	The Love Boat	ABC
11.	One Day at a Time (Sunday)	CBS
12.	Newhart (Monday)	CBS
13.	The Jeffersons (tie)	CBS
13.	The A Team (tie)	NBC
15.	The Fall Guy (9:00)	ABC
16.	Newhart (Sunday, 9:30)	CBS
17.	The Mississippi	CBS
18.	9 to 5	ABC
19.	The Fall Guy	ABC
20.	The ABC Monday Night Movie	ABC

1983–84

1.	Dallas	CBS
2.	Dynasty	ABC
3.	The A Team	NBC
4.	60 Minutes	CBS
5.	Simon & Simon	CBS
6.	Magnum, P.I.	CBS
7.	Falcon Crest	CBS
8.	Kate & Allie	CBS
9.	Hotel	ABC
10.	Cagney & Lacey	CBS
11.	Knots Landing	CBS
12.	The ABC Sunday Night Movie (tie)	ABC
12.	The ABC Monday Night Movie (tie)	ABC
14.	TV's Bloopers & Practical Jokes	NBC
15.	AfterMASH	CBS
16.	The Fall Guy	ABC
17.	The Four Seasons	CBS
18.	The Love Boat	ABC
19.	Riptide	NBC
20.	The Jeffersons	CBS

1984–85

1.	Dynasty	ABC
2.	Dallas	CBS
3.	The Cosby Show	NBC
4.	60 Minutes	CBS
5.	Family Ties	NBC
6.	The A Team (tie)	NBC
6.	Simon & Simon (tie)	CBS
8.	Knots Landing	CBS
9.	Murder, She Wrote	CBS
10.	Falcon Crest (tie)	CBS
10.	Crazy Like a Fox (tie)	CBS
12.	Hotel	ABC
13.	Cheers	NBC
14.	Riptide (tie)	NBC
14.	Who's the Boss? (tie)	ABC
16.	Magnum, P.I.	CBS
17.	Hail to the Chief	ABC
18.	Newhart	CBS
19.	Kate & Allie	CBS
20.	The NBC Monday Night Movie	NBC

1985–86

1.	The Cosby Show	NBC
2.	Family Ties	NBC
3.	Murder, She Wrote	CBS
4.	60 Minutes	CBS
5.	Cheers	NBC
6.	Dallas (tie)	CBS
6.	Dynasty (tie)	ABC
6.	The Golden Girls (tie)	NBC
9.	Miami Vice	NBC
10.	Who's the Boss?	ABC
11.	Perfect Strangers	ABC
12.	Night Court	NBC
13.	The CBS Sunday Night Movie	CBS
14.	Highway to Heaven (tie)	NBC
14.	Kate & Allie (tie)	CBS
16.	NFL Monday Night Football	ABC
17.	Newhart	CBS
18.	Knots Landing (tie)	CBS
18.	Growing Pains (tie)	ABC
20.	227	NBC

1986–87

1.	The Cosby Show	NBC
2.	Family Ties	NBC
3.	Cheers	NBC
4.	Murder, She Wrote	CBS
5.	Night Court	NBC
6.	The Golden Girls	NBC
7.	60 Minutes	CBS
8.	Growing Pains	ABC
9.	Moonlighting	ABC
10.	Who's the Boss?	ABC
11.	Dallas	CBS
12.	Nothing in Common	NBC
13.	Newhart	CBS
14.	Amen	NBC
15.	227	NBC
16.	Matlock (tie)	NBC
16.	CBS Sunday Night Movie (tie)	CBS
16.	NBC Monday Night Movie (tie)	NBC
19.	NFL Monday Night Football (tie)	ABC
19.	Kate & Allie (tie)	CBS

1987–88

1.	The Cosby Show	NBC
2.	A Different World	NBC
3.	Cheers	NBC
4.	Growing Pains (Tuesday)	ABC
5.	Night Court	NBC
6.	The Golden Girls	NBC
7.	Who's the Boss?	ABC
8.	60 Minutes	CBS
9.	Murder, She Wrote	CBS
10.	The Wonder Years	ABC
11.	Alf	NBC
12.	Moonlighting (tie)	ABC
12.	L.A. Law (tie)	NBC
14.	NFL Monday Night Football	ABC
15.	Matlock (tie)	NBC
15.	Growing Pains (Wednesday) (tie)	ABC
17.	Amen	NBC
18.	Family Ties	NBC
19.	Hunter	NBC
20.	The CBS Sunday Night Movie	CBS

1988–89

1.	Roseanne (9:00) (tie)	ABC
1.	The Cosby Show (tie)	NBC
3.	Roseanne (8:30) (tie)	ABC
3.	A Different World (tie)	NBC
5.	Cheers	NBC
6.	60 Minutes	CBS
7.	The Golden Girls	NBC
8.	Who's the Boss?	ABC
9.	The Wonder Years	ABC
10.	Murder, She Wrote	CBS
11.	Empty Nest	NBC
12.	Anything but Love	ABC
13.	Dear John	NBC
14.	Growing Pains	ABC
15.	Alf (tie)	NBC
15.	L.A. Law (tie)	NBC
17.	Matlock	NBC
18.	Unsolved Mysteries (tie)	NBC
18.	Hunter (tie)	NBC
20.	In the Heat of the Night	NBC

1989–90

1.	Roseanne	ABC
2.	The Cosby Show	NBC
3.	Cheers	NBC
4.	A Different World	NBC
5.	America's Funniest Home Videos	ABC
6.	The Golden Girls	NBC
7.	60 Minutes	CBS
8.	The Wonder Years	ABC
9.	Empty Nest	NBC
10.	Chicken Soup	ABC
11.	NFL Monday Night Football	ABC
12.	Unsolved Mysteries	NBC
13.	Who's the Boss?	ABC
14.	L.A. Law (tie)	NBC
14.	Murder, She Wrote (tie)	CBS
16.	Grand	NBC
17.	In the Heat of the Night	NBC
18.	Dear John	NBC
19.	Coach	ABC
20.	Matlock	NBC

1990–91

1.	Cheers	NBC
2.	60 Minutes	CBS
3.	Roseanne	ABC
4.	A Different World	NBC
5.	The Cosby Show	NBC
6.	NFL Monday Night Football	ABC
7.	America's Funniest Home Videos	ABC
8.	Murphy Brown	CBS
9.	America's Funniest People (tie)	ABC
9.	Designing Women (tie)	CBS
9.	Empty Nest (tie)	NBC
12.	Golden Girls	NBC
13.	Murder, She Wrote	CBS
14.	Unsolved Mysteries	NBC
15.	Full House	ABC
16.	Family Matters	ABC
17.	Coach (tie)	ABC
17.	Matlock (tie)	NBC
19.	In the Heat of the Night	NBC
20.	Major Dad	CBS

1991–92

1.	60 Minutes	CBS
2.	Roseanne	ABC
3.	Murphy Brown	CBS
4.	Cheers	NBC
5.	Home Improvement	ABC
6.	Designing Women	CBS
7.	Coach	ABC
8.	Full House	ABC
9.	Murder, She Wrote (tie)	CBS
9.	Unsolved Mysteries (tie)	NBC
11.	Major Dad (tie)	CBS
11.	NFL Monday Night Football (tie)	ABC
13.	Room For Two	ABC
14.	The CBS Sunday Night Movie	CBS
15.	Evening Shade	CBS
16.	Northern Exposure	CBS
17.	A Different World	NBC
18.	The Cosby Show	NBC
19.	Wings	NBC
20.	America's Funniest Home Videos (tie)	ABC
20.	Fresh Prince of Bel Air (tie)	NBC

1992–93

1.	60 Minutes	CBS
2.	Roseanne	ABC
3.	Home Improvement	ABC
4.	Murphy Brown	CBS
5.	Murder, She Wrote	CBS
6.	Coach	ABC
7.	NFL Monday Night Football	ABC
8.	The CBS Sunday Night Movie (tie)	CBS
8.	Cheers (tie)	NBC
10.	Full House	ABC
11.	Northern Exposure	CBS
12.	Rescue: 911	CBS
13.	20/20	ABC
14.	The CBS Tuesday Night Movie (tie)	CBS
14.	Love & War (tie)	CBS
16.	Fresh Prince of Bel Air (tie)	NBC
20.	Fresh Prince of Bel Air (tie) NBC	
16.	Hangin' with Mr. Cooper (tie)	ABC
16.	The Jackie Thomas Show (tie)	ABC
19.	Evening Shade	CBS
20.	Hearts Afire (tie)	CBS
20.	Unsolved Mysteries (tie)	NBC

1993–94

1.	Home Improvement	ABC
2.	60 Minutes	CBS
3.	Seinfeld	NBC
4.	Roseanne	ABC
5.	Grace Under Fire	ABC
6.	These Friends of Mine	ABC
7.	Frasier	NBC
8.	Coach (tie)	ABC
8.	NFL Monday Night Football (tie)	ABC
10.	Murder, She Wrote	CBS
11.	Murphy Brown	CBS
12.	Thunder Alley	ABC
13.	The CBS Sunday Night Movie	CBS
14.	20/20	ABC
15.	Love & War	CBS
16.	Primetime Live (tie)	ABC
16.	Wings (tie)	NBC
18.	NYPD Blue	ABC
19.	Homicide	NBC
20.	Northern Exposure	CBS

1994–95

1.	Seinfeld	NBC
2.	ER	NBC
3.	Home Improvement	ABC
4.	Grace Under Fire	ABC
5.	NFL Monday Night Football	ABC
6.	60 Minutes	CBS
7.	NYPD Blue	ABC
8.	Friends	NBC
9.	Roseanne (tie)	ABC
9.	Murder, She Wrote (tie)	CBS
11.	Mad About You	NBC
12.	Madman of the People	NBC
13.	Ellen	ABC
14.	Hope & Gloria	NBC
15.	Frasier	NBC
16.	Murphy Brown	CBS
17.	20/20	ABC
18.	CBS Sunday Movie	CBS
19.	NBC Monday Night Movies	NBC
20.	Dave's World	CBS

HOSTS WITH THE MOST FUTURE

Monty Hall, Bob Barker, and Pat Sajak are well-known game-show masters, but an unexpected host of TV legends have apprenticed as quiz masters. Here are just a few, along with the dates of their hosting duties:

Johnny Carson	*Earn Your Vacation*	1954
	Who Do You Trust?	1957-62
Walter Cronkite	*It's News to Me*	1954
Buddy Hackett	*You Bet Your Life*	1980
Moss Hart	*Answer Yes or No*	1950
Ernie Kovacs	*Time Will Tell*	1954
	Take a Good Look	1959-61
Oscar Levant	*G.E. Guest House*	1951
Jack Paar	*Bank on the Stars*	1953
Carl Reiner	*The Celebrity Game*	1964-65
Rod Serling	*Liar's Club*	1969
Dick Van Dyke	*Mother's Day*	1958-59
	Laugh Line	1959
Mike Wallace	*Guess Again*	1951
	Who's the Boss?	1954
	The Big Surprise	1956-57
	Who Pays	1959

1994–95 SPECIAL RATINGS

The following are Nielsen ratings for a variety of special categories for the most recent season. (Source: Nielsen Media Research, 1995)

QUIZ AND GAME SHOWS

1.	Wheel of Fortune	Kingsworld/ Camelot
2.	Jeopardy	Kingsworld/ Camelot
3.	Wheel of Fortune (Weekend)	Kingsworld/ Camelot
4.	The Price Is Right 2	CBS
5.	The Price Is Right 1	CBS
6.	The Price Is Right	Paramount/ Premier
7.	Star Search	Rysher Entertainment
8.	Love Connection	Warner
9.	Family Feud	All American TV
10.	Soul Train	Tribune Entertainment

SATURDAY MORNING CHILDREN'S PROGRAMS

1.	X-Men	Fox
2.	Spider Man–Saturday	Fox
3.	The Tick	Fox
4.	Batman & Robin	Fox
5.	Red Planet	Fox
6.	Animaniacs–Saturday (tie)	Fox
6.	Eek!Stravaganza (tie)	Fox
6.	Power Rangers–Saturday (tie)	Fox
9.	Bugs Bunny/Tweety Show II	ABC
10.	Disney's Aladdin	CBS

SOAPS

1.	The Young and the Restless	CBS
2.	All My Children	ABC
3.	General Hospital	ABC
4.	The Bold and the Beautiful	CBS
5.	Days of Our Lives	NBC
6.	One Life To Live	ABC
7.	As the World Turns	CBS
8.	Guiding Light	CBS
9.	Another World	NBC
10.	Loving	ABC

SYNDICATED TALK SHOWS

1.	The Oprah Winfrey Show	Kingwood/ Camelot
2.	Ricki Lake	Columbia Tristar TV
3.	The Jenny Jones Show	Warner Brothers TV
4.	Sally Jessy Raphael	Multimedia
5.	Live–Regis & Kathy Lee	Buena Vista TV
6.	The Maury Povich Show	Paramount/ Premier
7.	The Montel Williams Show	Paramount/ Premier
8.	Donahue	Multimedia
9.	Geraldo (tie)	Tribune Entertainment
9.	Rush Limbaugh (tie)	Multimedia

THE TOP INFOMERCIALS

This unique form of advertising in the guise of programming was first seen on American television in 1984 when advertising was deregulated, and the affliction has metastasized since. The following list presents the top-grossing infomercials, based on the total dollars taken in during each ad's most profitable year. (Source: *Steve Dworman's Infomercial Marketing Report*)

1. Jane Fonda: Fitness Trends for the Nineties (treadmill)
2. Psychic Friends Network (1-900 psychic line)
3. Bruce Jenner: PowerWalk Plus (treadmill)
4. Connie Selleca and John Tesh: Growing in Love and Hidden Keys
5. Jake Steinfeld: Body by Jake (hip and thigh exercise machine)
6. Barbara De Angelis: Making Love Work
7. Health Rider (fitness machine)
8. Popeil Pasta Maker
9. Anthony Robbins: Personal Power #4 (self-improvement)
10. Victoria Principal's Principal Secret (skin care products)
10. Your Psychic Experience
10. Fantom Vacuum (household appliance)
10. Mega-Memory (self-improvement)
10. Super Slicer (kitchen aid)

PBS'S MOST POPULAR PROGRAMS

Viewers often associate PBS with cultural programming and British imports, but for the most part it's wild animals that draw the viewers.

1. *National Geographic Special:* "The Incredible Machine" (1975)
2. *National Geographic Special:* "The Sharks" (1982)
3. *National Geographic Special:* "Land of the Tigers" (1985)
4. *National Geographic Special:* "The Grizzlies" (1987)
5. *National Geographic Special:* "Polar Bear Alert" (1982)
6. *National Geographic Special:* "Rain Forest" (1983)
7. *National Geographic Special:* "In the Shadow of Vesuvius" (1987)
8. *National Geographic Special:* "In the Realm of the Alligator" (1986)
8. *National Geographic Special:* "Save the Panda" (1983)
10. *National Geographic Special:* "Lions of the African Night" (1987)
11. *National Geographic Special:* "Among Wild Chimpanzees" (1984)
12. *The Civil War:* "Most Hallowed Ground" (1990)
13. *National Geographic Special:* "Living Sands of Namib" (1978)
13. *National Geographic Special:* "Etosha" (1981)
13. *Death of a Princess* (1980)

WHAT'S IN A NAME?

Is a favorite show any less sweet by a different name? The creators often thought so. And so many of the most popular shows of all time began with names other than those that became familiar to millions. A sampling follows (when a show had multiple names, they are listed in sequence).

Original Name	Final Name	Original Name	Final Name
The Alley Cats	Charlie's Angels	Mr. Solo/Solo	The Man From U.N.C.L.E.
The Brady Brood	The Brady Bunch		
45 Minutes from Harlem	Diff'rent Strokes	Occupation Unknown	What's My Line?
Country Cousins/		Oil	Dynasty
The Eddie Albert Show	Green Acres	Ozark Widow/Dern Tootin'/	
Cyborg	The Six Million Dollar Man	Whistle Stop	Petticoat Junction
		The Rise and Shine Revue	Today
Danny Doyle	I Spy		
Eye-Opener	CBS Morning Show	Spencer's Mountain	The Waltons
Family Business	The Partridge Family	Sunset 77	77 Sunset Strip
The Flagstones	The Flintstones	Those Were the Days	All in the Family
McHale's Men	McHale's Navy	Wally and the Beaver	Leave It to Beaver

THE TOP 50 TELEVISION SHOWS

These single broadcasts drew the largest audiences in TV history. (Source: Nielsen Media Research)

Rank	Program	Date
1.	M*A*S*H	February 28, 1983
2.	Dallas (Who Shot J.R.?)	November 21, 1980
3.	Roots, Part 8 (conclusion)	January 30, 1977
4.	Super Bowl XVI	January 24, 1982
5.	Super Bowl XVII	January 30, 1983
6.	Winter Olympics	February 23, 1994
7.	Super Bowl XX	January 26, 1986
8.	Gone with the Wind, Part 1	November 7, 1976
9.	Gone with the Wind, Part 2	November 8, 1976
10.	Super Bowl XII	January 15, 1978
11.	Super Bowl XIII	January 21, 1979
12.	Bob Hope Christmas Show	January 15, 1970
13.	Super Bowl XVIII (tie)	January 22, 1984
13.	Super Bowl XIX (tie)	January 20, 1985
15.	Super Bowl XIV	January 20, 1980
16.	The Day After	November 20, 1983
17.	Roots, Part 6 (tie)	January 28, 1977
17.	The Fugitive (tie)	August 29, 1967
19.	Super Bowl XXI	January 25, 1987
20.	Roots, Part 5	January 27, 1977
21.	Super Bowl XXVIII (tie)	January 29, 1994
21.	Cheers (tie)	May 20, 1993
23.	The Ed Sullivan Show (TV debut of The Beatles)	February 9, 1964
24.	Super Bowl XXVII	January 31, 1993
25.	Bob Hope Christmas Show	January 14, 1971
26.	Roots, Part 3	January 25, 1977
27.	Super Bowl XI (tie)	January 9, 1977
27.	Super Bowl XV (tie)	January 25, 1981
29.	Super Bowl VI	January 16, 1972
30.	Roots, Part 2	January 24, 1977
31.	The Beverly Hillbillies	January 8, 1964
32.	Roots, Part 4 (tie)	January 26, 1977
32.	The Ed Sullivan Show (with The Beatles) (tie)	February 16, 1964
34.	Super Bowl XXIII	January 22, 1989
35.	The 43rd Academy Awards	April 7, 1970
36.	The Thorn Birds, Part 3	March 29, 1983
37.	The Thorn Birds, Part 4	March 30, 1983
38.	NFC championship game	January 10, 1982
39.	The Beverly Hillbillies	January 15, 1964
40.	Super Bowl VII	January 14, 1973
41.	Thorn Birds, Part 2	March 28, 1983
42.	Super Bowl IX (tie)	January 12, 1975
42.	The Beverly Hillbillies (tie)	February 26, 1964
44.	Super Bowl X (tie)	January 18, 1976
44.	Airport (tie)	November 11, 1973
44.	Love Story (tie)	October 1, 1972
44.	Cinderella (tie)	February 22, 1965
44.	Roots, Part 7 (tie)	January 29, 1977
49.	The Beverly Hillbillies	March 25, 1964
50.	The Beverly Hillbillies	February 6, 1964

MOST WATCHED MOVIES ON TELEVISION

This list includes network prime-time feature films, both those made specifically for TV (*) and those made for theatrical release. Although *The Wizard of Oz* only appears twice in this list, it has earned high ratings for five different broadcasts, making it overall the most popular movie ever shown on TV. (Source: Nielsen Media Research)

Rank	Movie	Air Date
1.	Gone with the Wind, Part 1	November 7, 1976
2.	Gone with the Wind, Part 2	November 8, 1976
3.	The Day After*	November 20, 1983
4.	The Thorn Birds, Part 3*	March 29, 1983
5.	The Thorn Birds, Part 4*	March 30, 1983
6.	The Thorn Birds, Part 2*	March 28, 1983
7.	Love Story (tie)	October 1, 1972
7.	Airport (tie)	November 11, 1973
9.	The Thorn Birds, Part 1*	March 27, 1983
10.	The Godfather, Part 2	November 18, 1974
11.	Jaws	November 4, 1979
12.	The Poseidon Adventure	October 27, 1974
13.	The Birds (tie)	January 16, 1968
13.	True Grit (tie)	November 12, 1972
15.	Patton	November 19, 1972
16.	The Bridge on the River Kwai	September 25, 1966
17.	Jeremiah Johnson (tie)	January 18, 1976
17.	Helter Skelter, Part 2 (tie)*	April 2, 1976
19.	Rocky (tie)	February 4, 1979
19.	Ben-Hur (tie)	February 14, 1971
21.	The Godfather, Part 1	November 16, 1974
22.	Little Ladies of the Night (tie)*	January 16, 1977
22.	Shogun, Part 3 (tie)*	September 17, 1980
24.	The Wizard of Oz	December 13, 1959
25.	The Burning Bed*	October 8, 1984
26.	The Wizard of Oz	January 26, 1964
27.	Shogun, Part 4*	September 18, 1980
28.	Planet of the Apes (tie)	September 14, 1973
28.	Helter Skelter, Part 1 (tie)*	April 1, 1976
30.	Holocaust, Part 4*	April 19, 1978

PEOPLE'S FAVORITE 50 TV STARS

Designating TV immortals is like wearing a Boston Red Sox cap in the Yankee Stadium bleachers: you're just asking for an argument. After long debate with colleagues, PEOPLE TV reviewer David Hiltbrand enshrined these diverse talents into our cathode-ray Cooperstown.

JAMES ARNESS
As the flinty Marshall of Dodge City, Arness, the rec room John Wayne left a pair of boots impossible to fill.

LUCILLE BALL
The immortal diva of ditsiness.

RONA BARRETT
The Pandora of TV celebrity gossip.

MILTON BERLE
TV's first great comic. In the early days of the medium, Berle's notoriety sold more television sets than Montgomery Ward.

CAROL BURNETT
From the silly to the sentimental, this lovable, elastic performer could play it all. Her variety show was simply splendid.

RAYMOND BURR
In dramas from *Perry Mason* to *Ironside*, his imposing basso profundo presence always stood in sharp relief to prime time's usual pip-squeak chorus.

JOHNNY CARSON
Somehow the silky master of late-night festivities always managed to make a demanding gig look so damn easy.

RICHARD CHAMBERLAIN
In the era of mammoth miniseries, this classy, inscrutable actor reigned supreme.

DICK CLARK
We honor him for *American Bandstand*. A pop culture icon whose influence was so refreshing and far-reaching that we are willing to overlook everything Clark has done since, even *Bloopers, Bleepers and Practical Jokes*.

HOWARD COSELL
Yes, he was smug and pedantic, but his autonomous thinking and rigorous candor made him a lightning rod among sportscasters.

WALTER CRONKITE
He was called without hyperbole "the most trusted man in America," a signal honor for a network news anchor.

BOB DENVER
Both as a beatnik and a castaway, his goofy, droopy, sad sack persona fit the tube perfectly.

PHIL DONAHUE
With boundless energy and enthusiasm, he single-handedly invented the liberating area of the daytime talk show. (Look what they did to his song, Ma.)

PATTY DUKE
She is literally a child of the medium and we have watched her progress through all the stages of her often painful life. But in front of the camera, she has never been anything less than fearless, uncompromising, and passionate.

PETER FALK
Okay, his repertoire was limited, but that hardly matters given that he plays the befuddled-like-a-fox Lt. Columbo with such remarkable virtuosity.

FRED FLINTSTONE
This cartoon caveman can join our bowling team any time with or without shoes. Yabba dabba doo!

ANNETTE FUNICELLO
Why? Because we love her.

JAMES GARNER
The most cherished, effortlessly charismatic actor ever to work on the small screen.

JACKIE GLEASON
The title still applies: The Great One.

CURT GOWDY
America's supernal sportsman.

KELSEY GRAMMER
Whether drowning his sorrows with chardonnay in Boston or jolting them with double lattes in Seattle, his consummate creation, the fastidious and fustian Dr. Frasier Crane, stands with the sitcom immortals.

BRYANT GUMBEL
His assets: self-possession, preparation and quick wits serve him as well on Election Night as they do at the Olympics.

LARRY HAGMAN
His acting range is hard to discern, only because he submerges himself so completely in every role he takes, from Col. Nelson to J.R. Ewing Jr.

MONTY HALL
We wouldn't trade this most engaging of game show hosts for anything, not even what's behind the curtain Carol is standing in front of.

KERMIT THE FROG
The unassuming amphibian has made learning a joy for generations of enthralled young viewers.

CHARLES KURALT
The wizard of backroads wanderlust.

JACK LALANNE
This fitness advocate was totally

aerobicized way, way before working out was cool.

MICHAEL LANDON

Both as an actor and as a story-teller, he was simple, direct and earnest. Maybe that's why he was able to touch us so deeply.

DAVID LETTERMAN

He's the post-modern late night host: cynical, absurdist, brainy and decidedly ambivalent about the pop culture maelstrom in which he swirls.

SUSAN LUCCI

The most acclaimed character in the annals of daytime drama is her captivating, conniving, ruthless (and appallingly Emmyless) Erica Kane Cudahy Chandler etc., etc..

JOHN MADDEN

The irrepressible observer of football's boom-crash opera.

ELIZABETH MONTGOMERY

Hocus schmocus! The real magic of *Bewitched* was her sparkling surplus of charm.

MARY TYLER MOORE

The princess of prime time.

EDWARD R. MURROW

Towering TV news pioneer.

RICKY NELSON

Not only was the proverbial boy next door devilishly cute, the kid could really sing.

BOB NEWHART

He lavished his dry, deft, delicious comic touch over a sterling succession of sitcoms, always playing a flustered Everyman surrounded by eccentrics.

CARROLL O'CONNOR

Only an extraordinary actor could make a mean bigot like Archie Bunker so irresistibly sympathetic.

THE ORIGINAL NOT-READY-FOR-PRIME-TIME PLAYERS

Saturday Night Live became an instant sensation in 1975 thanks to a crackerjack assault team of unknown comics that included John Belushi, Chevy Chase, Gilda Radner, Dan Aykroyd and (soon thereafter) Bill Murray.

DONNA REED

The radiant domestic goddess of the Eisenhower era.

FRED ROGERS

The host of PBS's longest running kids' show is gentle, devout, soft-spoken and didactic. Sheesh, how in the world did this guy ever get on the air?

PHIL SILVERS

His hilarious, unrestrained portrayal of the avaricious Sgt. Bilko still outranks almost everything else on TV. Ten hut! You are in the presence of comic genius.

ED SULLIVAN

His posture was ungainly, his diction stilted and his appearance cadaverous. But it didn't matter because his show—the most prestigious, eclectic and enduring variety hour in the history of television—had all the magnetism the man lacked.

ROSEANNE

Bold, brassy, and bullet-proof, she introduced a bracing note of realism to the sitcom, radically rejiggering TV's oldest formula.

ARTHUR TREACHER

Seated at the right hand of Merv Griffin, this unflappable Englishman was the quintessential second banana.

MIKE WALLACE

The indefatigable pit bull of TV journalism.

BARBARA WALTERS

It's no accident this indomitable lady was the one to bust up the boys' club of network anchors. A gutsy, hard-working dame with a knack for snagging scoops and a flair for presentation, she's singularly dexterous at straddling the worlds of news and entertainment.

LAWRENCE WELK

The Slavic-accented band leader put the fizz in champagne music for uh-one, uh-two, uh-three decades.

BETTY WHITE

A true TV trouper, equally adept on game shows, talk shows and sitcoms.

OPRAH WINFREY

The sweet voice of enlightenment soars above the demented din of her bottom-sucking competitors.

JONATHAN WINTERS

The most inspired improvisational comic the tube has ever seen.

PEOPLE'S 50 FORMATIVE SHOWS

The mark of all great television shows is their profound, or at least pervasive, impact on the pop culture. No sooner are they on the air than it's impossible to remember how we got along without them. Herewith, PEOPLE's shows of shows.

THE ADVENTURES OF SUPERMAN
More than 40 years later, this show starring George Reeves as the Man of Steel is still the only good superhero series TV has ever produced.

ALL IN THE FAMILY
At the heart of this epochal sitcom were the corrosive working-class prejudices of Archie Bunker, a Northern redneck. His political arguments with his liberal live-in son-in-law make *Crossfire* seem tame.

ALL MY CHILDREN
The soap trend-setter has tackled big social and medical issues without ever losing a grip on its primary imperative: addictive story-telling.

THE ANDY GRIFFITH SHOW
The precursor of the so-called rusticoms of the '60s, this quiet masterpiece had heart, humor, wisdom and (often overlooked), an outstanding cast. The launching pad for *Gomer Pyle, U.S.M.C* and *Mayberry R.F.D.*

THE BEVERLY HILLBILLIES
Yee ha! The most outrageous yokel yuk-fest this side of *Li'l Abner.* Bonus points for TV's most recognizable theme song.

BONANZA
It was that larger-than-life clan, the Cartwrights, that made the Ponderosa worth visiting every week.

THE BULLWINKLE SHOW
Jay Ward's kaleidoscopic, pun-crammed cartoon about a dense moose and a plucky flying squirrel delighted kids of all ages.

BURNS AND ALLEN
This iconoclastic '50s show gleefully disregarded TV tradition, including the observance of "the fourth wall." The comic chemistry between this old vaudeville team has never been duplicated.

CANDID CAMERA
"When you least expect it/You're elected/You're the star today." Alan Funt milked hilarious results from simply filming people in situations when they thought no one was watching.

CHARLIE'S ANGELS
A brilliant TV concept: staff a standard detective show with a gorgeous trio (Farrah Fawcett, Kate Jackson, and Jaclyn Smith) in sausage-skin clothing. This was producer Aaron Spelling's first megahit and his finest hour.

CHEERS
The pluperfect pinnacle of the sitcom genre.

THE COSBY SHOW
Witty, warm, and winning, the domestic experiences of the Huxtables touted family values without sermonizing.

THE DICK VAN DYKE SHOW
The first TV comedy to thoroughly exploit dual settings. For the first half of the '60s, the only place on the planet funnier than the Petrie household was Rob's office at the apocryphal *Alan Brady Show.*

DRAGNET
The show's deliberately laconic style ("Just the facts, ma'am") only underscored the gritty power of its tales of cops and miscreants.

DYNASTY
The squabbles of the Carringtons proved that the rich really are different than you and me: they dress swankily while hatching Byzantine plots of revenge against one another.

FAWLTY TOWERS
John Cleese starred as an apoplectic innkeeper in this import, a remarkably seamless slapstick farce.

GUNSMOKE
TV's archetypal and longest running Western.

HILL STREET BLUES
Creator Steven Bochco spiced up his precinct house gumbo with a rich slate of characters, multi-tiered narratives, wry humor and a dash of fatalism.

THE HONEYMOONERS
The antics of a bus driver and a sewer worker in a Brooklyn tenement yielded a priceless vein of American humor. Jackie Gleason and Art Carney were sublime.

JEOPARDY
The thinking person's game show.

L.A. LAW
A powerhouse legal drama complex, unpredictable, imaginative and always rewarding.

THE LARRY SANDERS SHOW
This sardonic backstage tour of a talk show is TV's funniest satire, perhaps because we love to see the medium mock itself.

LEAVE IT TO BEAVER
Took the familiar family sitcom formula of the '50s and gave it a devious adolescent twist. Show stealer: Eddie Haskell ("Good morning, Mrs. Cleaver. You're looking particularly lovely today.")

MARY HARTMAN, MARY HARTMAN
And now for something com-

pletely different. This soap opera spoof presented everyday life in Fernwood, Ohio as a pastiche of country song, floor wax commercial, and Kurt Vonnegut novel.

THE MARY TYLER MOORE SHOW
A magical confluence of concept, cast, and material made this the high watermark of '70s television.

M*A*S*H
Hands-down, the most successful series ever spun off from a feature film. The comedy lasted eight years longer than the Korean War had.

MIAMI VICE
Against a gaudy SoFlo backdrop of neon and pastels, cute cops chase after well-armed cocaine cowboys in flashy sport scars and cigarette boats. The only reason TV has ever furnished to stay home on Friday nights.

MISSION: IMPOSSIBLE
Your mission, should you decide to accept it, is to name a better adventure series than this taut, gripping espionage exercise.

THE MONKEES
Rock music reared its unruly head in primetime with this madcap, faux-psychedelic '60s comedy about a perky pop quartet. Groundbreaking for its time, even if the show soon settled into lame Stooges schtick.

NIGHTLINE
A provident opportunity to hash out the day's big news event.

N.Y.P.D. BLUE
The most electrifying cop show since *Naked City* (1958-63). Acute and suspenseful, *Blue* roars by like a runaway train.

THE ODD COUPLE
Opposites amuse, but never so much as in this impeccably cast, tone-perfect comedy about a pair of mismatched, middle-aged, Manhattan neo-bachelors.

THE ROCKFORD FILES
The couch potato's choice: a sly, undemanding, endlessly entertaining delight.

ROSEANNE
An adventurous, abrasive, authentic and always amusing examination of the struggles of a working-class family.

ROWAN AND MARTIN'S LAUGH-IN
With zany banter, double entendres and go-go dancers (including Goldie Hawn), this late-'60s comedy cavalcade nudged TV into the age of hipsters.

ST. ELSEWHERE
Piquant and volatile, this Jack-in-the-box drama about a lesser Boston hospital ran from intense tragedy to bawdy comedy.

SEINFELD
An hermetic, exquisitely maintained comedy of contemporary urban manners and mores.

SESAME STREET
This jauntily educational PBS series for pre-schoolers is culturally diverse, inventive and altogether admirable.

77 SUNSET STRIP
The most influential of the Sputnik-era private eye series was this ultra-cool conceit which starred Efrem Zimbalist Jr. and Roger Smith as a pair of suave, college-educated judo experts.

THE SIMPSONS
You'd need a shelf full of books like this Almanac and a crack research staff to run down all the pop culture references in a single episode of this puckish cartoon about the post-nuclear family.

60 MINUTES
The ultimate news magazine.

STAR TREK
This notorious cult favorite was little-honored during its original '60s run but became a rerun staple and has launched a thriving industry of spin-offs.

THIRTYSOMETHING
Though dismissed by cynics as yuppie whining, this was in fact a drama of rare pathos, complexity and insight.

TODAY
The oldest, and in our book, the best of the matinal infotainment bandwagons.

THE TONIGHT SHOW
It's a tradition as comfortable as flannel pajamas: awaiting the Sandman while watching Johnny's (and now Jay's) guests play musical chairs.

THE TWILIGHT ZONE
This spine-tingling supernatural anthology was penetrating, often profound, but above all, singularly spooky.

WALT DISNEY PRESENTS
Over four decades, under a variety of banners and working alternately for each of the three major networks, the Disney studio consistently turned out the tube's finest, most indelible family fare.

THE X-FILES
"The truth is out there." Really out there. But week after week, this suspenseful series transforms paranormal and outright bizarre concepts into gripping, credible drama.

YOU BET YOUR LIFE
This '50s series was ostensibly a quiz show, but in fact that was merely a pretext for host Groucho Marx to sharpen his legendary wit on a succession of contestants.

YOUR SHOW OF SHOWS
The apex of the variety show, this '50s favorite thrived on the astoundingly versatile comedic talents of Sid Caesar and Imogene Coco and a stable of writers that included Mel Brooks, Larry Gelbart, Neil Simon, and Woody Allen.

NICK AT NITE'S CLASSIC TV COUNTDOWN

Nick at Nite celebrated its tenth anniversary in 1995, and also held its seventh annual New Year's countdown of the year's best reruns, hosted by Casey Kasem. Nick at Nite selects these shows based on viewer requests, ratings, and critical commentary, as well as the guest-star quotient (celebrities before they hit it big), historical importance (first episodes, marriages, and births), and quintessential moments or bizarre plot twists.

1994 SELECTIONS

1 *I Love Lucy,* "Lucy Makes a TV Commercial"

Lucy is seen in dozens of countries, and has run continuously ever since she and Desi and Fred and Ethel hit the airwaves. Among the many classics within this classic sitcom, the pitching of Vitameatavegamin stands out as her single finest performance.

2 *Taxi,* "Reverend Jim: A Space Odyssey"

The very very Reverend Jim (Christopher Lloyd) had made an earlier appearance in the garage, to marry Latka to a lady of the evening so that he could avoid deportation. But in this episode he becomes a permanent member of the gang, taking his legendary driver's exam and answering the question "What does a yellow light mean?"

3 *Bewitched,* "Divided, He Falls"

Darrin is split into two Darrins—the fun side and the serious side—by Endora, of course. The "fun" Dick York is unreal: "Sam, why don't you 'whap' us up some champagne. The gang'll be crazy about it! They'll love it love it love it!"

4 *The Dick Van Dyke Show,* "Coast to Coast Big Mouth"

Laura Petrie is chosen from the audience to be in a game show. During the on-air interview, she is tricked into revealing that

Alan Brady is bald. Carl Reiner, as Alan Brady, rants hilariously in the classic scene where he tells his toupees they're out of work.

5 *The Mary Tyler Moore Show,* "Love is All Around"

The episode that started it all, as Mary flees from a broken engagement to a fresh start in Minneapolis, where in quick order she "steals" Rhoda's apartment, and interviews with Lou Grant at WJM. In that classic interview she orders a Brandy Alexander and, most importantly, displays her famous "spunk."

6 *Alfred Hitchcock Presents,* "Man from the South"

Steve McQueen takes up Peter Lorre on a simple wager. Lorre's character says it best: "Is that so strange? He wins, he takes the car, I win, I take his finger. Is that so strange?" The episode is sterling Hitchcock, with true suspense, great performances, and a final twist that leaves you reeling.

7 *Dragnet,* "The LSD Story"

This episode is more popularly known as "Blue Boy" after its antagonist, a teenage boy who has painted his face blue and yellow and buried his head in the ground on an acid trip. Blue Boy's lunatic ravings and Joe Friday's moralizing have made this episode one of Nick at Nite's all-time most requested. It was also the very first episode in Jack

Webb's "comeback" tour with the show. *Dragnet* had been off the air since 1959, but motivated in part by America's growing drug problem, producer-writer-director-star Webb decided in 1967 to revive the show.

8 *I Dream of Jeannie,* "Jeannie the Guru"

After all the obvious storylines had been done, the creators of *I Dream of Jeannie* really hit their stride by taking the plots further and further "out of sight." This was the ninety-ninth episode, and it's a hippie-filled, counter-cultural, only-in-the-'60s doozie.

9 *I Love Lucy,* "Job Switching"

Lucy and Ethel in the chocolate factory. Nick at Nite researchers believe that aside from moments that were included in show openers—Rob's trip over the ottoman, Mary's hat toss, the ski-jumper wiping out on *Wide World of Sports*—this is the single most recognized scene in television history.

10 *The Mary Tyler Moore Show,* "Chuckles Bites the Dust"

Chuckles the Clown is the host of a kiddie show on WJM. In a terrible accident, while dressed as a peanut, Chuckles is shucked—and killed—by a rogue elephant. Mary can't believe how quickly people begin making sick jokes about the tragedy . . . until the classic funeral scene.

The following are the highest-ranking episodes of other classic TV series shown on Nick at Nite.

Get Smart, "The Groovy Guru"

Larry Storch guest-stars as the evil hippie high-priest who is hypnotizing our nation's youth with the psychedelic sounds of his rock group minions The Sacred Cows. Max and 99 infiltrate his headquarters only to be trapped in a chamber of rock-and-roll horrors where high-volume music may be the last thing they ever hear.

Mork and Mindy, "Mork Goes Erk"

Morgan Fairchild, as Susan Taylor, invites Mork, Mindy, and Mr. Bickley to join her EST-like encounter group. Ellsworth, the cynical, mean-spirited, invective-hurling leader of the ERK (Ellsworth Revitalization Conditioning) group is played by none other than David Letterman. Letterman has seldom been seen out of the friendly confines of his own show since.

Mr. Ed, "Clint Eastwood Meets Mr. Ed"

Guest-starring, naturally, Clint Eastwood, who was then better known as Rowdy Yates of *Rawhide* than as a movie star. The story is Mr. Ed's romancing of a filly who happens to be Eastwood's. Naturally, Wilbur is the one who gets in trouble, and Clint plays the heavy.

F-Troop, "Bye Bye Balloon"

Harvey Korman guest stars in the role of Colonel Heinrich Von Zeppel, a Prussian balloonist who arrives at Fort Courage to whip the men into shape. The episode also features the classic moment when the hot-air balloon floats over the Hekawi camp and Chief Wild Eagle calls out memorably: "It . . . is . . . balloon!"

The Partridge Family, "Soul Club"

Thanks to a crazy booking mix-up, Shirley drives the bus into downtown Detroit to play a club owned by guest stars Richard Pryor and Lou Gossett Jr. If they can't attract an audience, the club will go under. The gang goes to work, Reuben hustles, Keith writes a song that's "kind of an afro thing," and Danny recruits a group of militant African-American martial arts students to join the cause. Very seventies, and very cool.

The Patty Duke Show, "The Cousins"

It wasn't until this, the thirty-sixth episode of the show, that the makers of *The Patty Duke Show* went back and told the origin of the story, returning to the fateful day that the worldly and intellectual Cathy Lane arrived in Brooklyn Heights. But have no fear, psychopathologists have now firmly established that you cannot "lose your mind when cousins are two of a kind."

The Donna Reed Show, "The Foundling"

A true classic starring the "Perfect American Mom." Donna finds a baby on the doorstep, and while she searches for the mother the whole Stone family, the maid, and the milkman all fall in love with the little guy. In the end, it's a real tearjerker, and Donna tries to explain away her tears by saying, "I guess I just like cheese."

Green Acres, "Don't Trust Little Old Ladies"

Green Acres was a strange and wonderful show like none other. It combined surrealism and nonsense that Salvador Dali and Lewis Carroll would have admired, and never more so than in this episode, where a little old lady's weather predictions lead

Oliver to dream that he and Lisa are mechanical characters in a Bavarian clock. The final scene is Oliver and Lisa at night out in the field among tomato plants that are being warmed by flaming pancakes.

My Three Sons, "Coincidence"

In its early years this long-running show often tried unusual stories and plot devices. "Coincidence" could well have been an episode of the *Twilight Zone:* Steve is fed up with the chaos of his house, but then, shortly after an encounter with a leprechaun-like gentleman (played by Billy Barty), he arrives at a parallel female version of his own household, meeting a woman and her three daughters: Mike, Bobby, and Kip.

Car 54, Where Are You?, "How Smart Can You Be?"

This is the classic episode in which Gunther Toody poses the questions: "Could Leonard Bernstein subsist on termites? Is he nocturnal? Does he have strong blunt claws?" The episode also includes Toody's classic monologue on nonchalance and its impact on major league ballplayers, and whether Yogi Berra or Mickey Mantle is more nonchalant, or even too nonchalant.

The Bob Newhart Show, "Death Be My Destiny"

Bob steps into the open elevator shaft, and his close call with "Mr. Death" creates a phobia that he can't beat. It's a case of "psychologist, analyze thyself," and a memorable episode.

HOW TO GET TICKETS TO TELEVISION SHOWS

Say what you want about television, but at least it's free (more or less). Not only that, but you can also obtain free tickets to see shows, game shows, and situation comedies, most of which tape in New York, Chicago, or Los Angeles. Here's how.

CHARLES PEREZ

Send a letter or postcard with the number of tickets desired, the approximate date you would like to attend, and your phone number so a ticket representative can contact you, to *The Charles Perez Show*, 3rd Floor, 514 West 57th Street, New York, NY 10019. Allow two to three weeks to receive your tickets. You must be at least 17 to attend.

DONAHUE

Send a postcard indicating the number of tickets desired to *Donahue*, 30 Rockefeller Plaza, New York, NY 10112. Tickets are available to those 16 or over; please allow two to four weeks for delivery. For an updated New York taping schedule call (212) 664-3056.

GERALDO

Call (212) 265-1283 for recorded information about tickets and the New York taping schedule, or send a self-addressed stamped envelope with ticket requests to Geraldo Tickets, CBS Television, 524 W. 57th Street, New York, NY 10019.

THE GORDON ELLIOT SHOW

Call (212) 975-8540 to speak with a ticket representative or leave a message with the number of tickets required and the date you would like to attend. Scheduling for this New York show is done about one month in advance, and you must be at least 18 to attend.

THE JENNY JONES SHOW

Call (312) 836-9400 to make reservations at least six to eight weeks in advance. For standby information call (312)-836-9485 with the specific date you would like to attend this Chicago show. The minimum age is 18.

JERRY SPRINGER SHOW

To receive tickets by mail, call (312) 321-5350 or write P.O. Box 4113, Chicago, IL 60654 with your name, address, phone number, number of tickets, and date desired. Requests should be sent one month in advance. Tickets are generally mailed out two to three weeks before the taping, and there is a minimum age of 16 required to attend.

LATE NIGHT WITH CONAN O'BRIEN

Mail one postcard per show (no letters) with name, address, and number of tickets desired to *Late Night* Tickets, c/o NBC, 30 Rockefeller Plaza, New York, NY 10112. The wait list is about one month, and the ticket office will do their best to accommodate specific requests. Tickets are only available to those 16 or over. A limited number of day-of-taping general admission and standby tickets are available Monday through Friday at 9:00 a.m. at the page desk in the downstairs main NBC lobby (same address as above). Standbys are given out on a first-come–first-serve basis, and only one per person. Standbys do not guarantee admission. For more information call (212) 664-3055, or (212) 664-3056 for an updated schedule of shows.

LATE SHOW WITH DAVID LETTERMAN

Send a postcard with name and address to Tickets, Ed Sullivan Theater, 1697 Broadway, New York, NY 10019. Available to those 16 and older, the tickets are usually mailed within six months; if no response is received, another card should be sent. Only two tickets are issued per request, and specific dates cannot generally be accommodated. There are, however, a number of standby tickets available every day at the theater; numbers are issued each day at noon (though a waiting line forms much earlier) and distributed at 5:00. It is recommended that the studio audience dress warmly since the studio is kept cold during taping.

LEEZA

Free tickets are available on a first-come–first-serve basis from the Paramount Studios Visitor Center on 860 North Gower Street in Hollywood up to five days prior to taping. For recorded ticket and taping information call the Paramount Studio guest relations line at (213) 956-5575. Production schedules vary from week to week, so the most precise information is available by speaking with a representative from the Paramount business office at (213) 956-1777 from 9:00 to 5:00, Monday through Friday.

LIVE WITH REGIS AND KATHIE LEE

For ticket and New York taping information call (212) 456-3537.

To request tickets by mail, send a postcard with your name, address, phone number, and the number of tickets desired (limit of four per request) to Live Tickets, Ansonia Station, P.O. Box 777, New York, NY 10023-0777. There is an eight to ten month wait for tickets, and audience members must be 18 or over to attend the taping. On the morning of each show, a limited number of standby tickets are issued at the ticket office on W. 67th Street and Columbus Avenue at 8:00 a.m., but these tickets do not guarantee admission to the taping.

MAURY POVICH

For ticket information and New York taping schedules call the ticket hotline, (212) 989-3622, and leave a message indicating your name, address, phone number, and the number of tickets (the maximum is two) and dates desired. Booking is generally done one month in advance, and a representative will mail the tickets and information to you. Standby tickets are available starting at 9:15 a.m. on the day of the taping at the studio on 221 West 26th Street. You must be at least 16 to attend.

THE MONTEL WILLIAMS SHOW

Call the ticket line at (212) 560-3003 for tickets and the New York taping schedule. To request tickets by mail, send a postcard with your name, address, phone number, and the number of tickets desired to Montel Williams Tickets, 356 West 57th Street, New York, NY 10019. There is a minimum age of 18.

OPRAH

Tickets are not available by mail, but show information can be obtained and reservations to appear in the studio audience in Chicago can be made by calling (312) 591-9222. These lines are often busy, so try calling early in the day.

THE RICKI LAKE SHOW

To request tickets by mail, send a postcard with your address and number of tickets desired to The Ricki Lake Show, Ticket Office, 401 Fifth Avenue, 7th Floor, New York, NY 10016. There is a limit of four tickets per request, and you must be at least 18 to attend the New York taping. For further information and schedules of topics, speak with a representative at (212) 889-6767.

RUSH LIMBAUGH: THE TELEVISION SHOW

For free tickets call (212) 397-7367, Monday through Thursday, 10 a.m.–12:30 p.m. For further New York taping schedules and information call (212) 397-4675.

SALLY JESSY RAPHAEL

Call (212) 582-1722 for ticket and New York taping information between 8:30 a.m. and 5:00 p.m. Monday through Friday, or send a postcard with your address and the number of tickets desired to Sally Jessy Raphael Tickets, P.O. Box 1400, Radio City Station, New York, NY 10101.

SATURDAY NIGHT LIVE

To obtain tickets for next season, send *one* postcard (no letters) with your name and complete address to *Saturday Night Live* Tickets, c/o NBC, 30 Rockefeller Plaza, New York, NY 10112. NBC accepts postcards during the month of August only, and these requests will be entered into a lottery drawing for tickets during the upcoming season. If you are are selected, you will be notified by mail two weeks in advance that you have received two tickets to either the dress rehearsal or the live taping. It is not possible to request specific dates, but standby tickets are available (fifty for the dress rehearsal and fifty for the live taping). These are distributed on Saturday mornings, the Saturdays of original shows only, at 9:15 a.m. at the side entrance of the GE Building on W. 49th Street, opposite the Rockefeller Center Garage. Standbys are given on a first-come–first-serve basis, and only one per person. Standby tickets do not guarantee admission, though last season's critical pans led to the best availability in years. You must be 16 or over to attend. For more information call (212) 664-3055, or to speak with a ticket representative call (212) 664-3056.

THE TONIGHT SHOW WITH JAY LENO

Send a self-addressed, stamped envelope with the date of the show you would like to see and the number of tickets desired to NBC Tickets, 3000 W. Alameda Ave., Burbank, CA 91523. Tickets are also available at the Burbank ticket counter on the day of the taping. The counter is located just off the California Street side of the studio facility, and hours are 8:00 a.m.–5:00 p.m., Monday through Friday. The minimum age to attend is 16. For recorded ticket distribution information, taping schedules, group bookings, and directions to the Burbank, California studios, call NBC Studios at (818) 840-3537.

SITCOMS

SEINFELD

Tickets are available by mail only. Send a self-addressed, stamped envelope with the date of the show that you would like to see and the number of tickets needed to *Seinfeld* Tickets, 3662 Katella Avenue, Los Alamitos, CA 90720. Your request should be received at least one month before the taping you wish to attend. Tickets are distributed in order of the requests received, and are mailed one week in advance of the taping. One must be 18 or over to attend. For more information call (310) 795-5254.

ELLEN, FRASIER, MARTIN, AND WINGS

No tickets are distributed by mail. A limited number of reservations are available by phone, and tickets can also be picked up at the Paramount ticket box starting five working days in advance of a show on a first-come–first-serve basis. The ticket box is located at 860 North Gower Street in Hollywood, between Santa Monica Boulevard and Melrose Avenue. It is open Monday through Friday from 8:30 a.m. to 4:00 p.m. To reserve tickets and for information about studio tours, shooting schedules, and ticket availability, call Paramount Studio guest relations at (213) 956-5575, or the Paramount business office at (213) 956-1777.

OTHER SERIES

Audiences Unlimited distributes limited numbers of tickets for most of the situation comedies shot before live audiences in the Los Angeles area. They have tickets for the favorites—such as *Roseanne, Friends,* and *Home Improvement*—as well as for newer sitcoms and even award shows. For a recorded message giving a weekly list of tickets available, the times and locations of taping, call (818) 506-0067. A one-month advance show taping-filming schedule is available by sending a self-addressed, stamped envelope to Audiences Unlimited, 100 Universal City Plaza, Building 153, Universal City, CA 91608. Tickets are available by mail from the same address. They are mailed 10 days to two weeks prior to show date and are limited for all shows, so include alternate choices.

A limited number of free tickets are also available from Audiences Unlimited's four box offices.

1. Fox Television Center, 5746 Sunset Boulevard, Hollywood; the office is open 8:30 a.m.–6:00 p.m. Monday through Friday; tickets are distributed starting on Wednesdays for shows scheduled for the following week.
2. Glendale Galleria, Central and Broadway, Glendale; tickets are distributed daily at the information desk, starting on Wednesdays for shows scheduled for the following week.
3. The Oaks, 222 W. Hillcrest, Thousand Oaks; tickets are distributed daily at the information desk, starting on Fridays for shows scheduled for the following week.
4. Fox Hills Mall, Sepulveda and Slausen, Culver City; tickets are distributed daily at the information desk, starting on Fridays for shows scheduled for the following week.

All tickets are available on a first-come-first-serve basis and occasionally on the day of the show, but earlier arrival is suggested for the best selection. Some of the more popular shows such as *Home Improvement* and *Roseanne* tend to go first or have tickets available only by mail, so it is best to call or write ahead for tickets.

HOW TO GET ON AUDIENCE-PARTICIPATION SHOWS

We all play along with the game shows when we watch at home, but only a few of us make it onto the air to play the games for real. Here are the wheres and hows on becoming a contestant on the leading shows.

AMERICAN GLADIATORS

The show holds open tryouts for its competitors once a year (usually in April or May). Details on the locations, times, and requirements for the tryouts are not readily available until early spring. For further information, call the *American Gladiators* hotline in Calif. at (310) 284-9181.

JEOPARDY!

To be a contestant on *Jeopardy!* you must pass a fifty-question test. Los Angeles test dates are available from the *Jeopardy!* contestant line, (310) 280-5367, Monday through Friday from 10:00 to 4:30. The test dates are scheduled intermittently throughout the year, so call two to three weeks prior to being in the Los Angeles area to schedule an appointment. For information about out-of-town contestant searches watch your local *Jeopardy!* station for announcements. Successful test-takers are then invited to play a mock version of the game, and if that goes well they may be called to be scheduled as a contestant, up to one month to one year after the tryout. To inquire about general taping information and schedules, and to request tickets for the Los Angeles studio audience, call (310) 280-8856.

MTV

MTV airs several shows with audience participants and dancers, among them *The Grind* and the annual spring break and summertime specials. Many of these shows require auditions and/or advance reservations. Call MTV's Viewer Services Twenty-Four-Hour Hotline at (212) 258-8700 for the latest schedules of shows requiring live audiences and information on their procedures to follow to become a participant. MTV representatives are available to answer questions from 9:30 to 5:30, Monday through Friday.

NICKELODEON

Nickelodeon produces several kids' shows that require audience participation, such as *Guts* and *Legends of the Hidden Temple*. These shows are filmed on erratic schedules at Universal Studios Theme Park in Orlando, Fla. Call Nickelodeon's Viewer Services in New York (212) 258-7579 or in Fla. (407) 363-8500 at least two weeks in advance of being in Orlando to find out taping schedules. Free tickets are distributed at the theme park on a first-come-first-serve basis on the day of the taping. To gain access to the theme park, you have to purchase the regular-price admission pass. (Call (407) 363-8000 for general theme park information.) Tickets do not guarantee admission to the tapings, and there are different age limits for kids who wish to participate as contestants.

THE PRICE IS RIGHT

Since all of the contestants on *The Price Is Right* are randomly selected from the audience, call CBS Tickets in Los Angeles at (213) 852-2458 for the most up-to-date taping schedule and ticket information. *The Price Is Right* is usually taped twice daily on Mondays, Tuesdays, and Wednesdays at 1:15 and 4:45. Tickets can be obtained by mail (allow four to six weeks for delivery) from the CBS ticket window, Television City, 7800 Beverly Boulevard, Los Angeles, CA 90036. Tickets are also available from the ticket window up to one week in advance of the taping. Ticketholders then must wait at this location for the 1:15 show starting at 8 a.m., and for the 4:45 show starting at 11:00 a.m. to receive name tags and gain admission. (However, the lines begin forming at least two hours prior to distribution times.)

WHEEL OF FORTUNE

Contestant auditions are held sporadically throughout the year, both in Los Angeles and during contestant searches around the U.S. The most up-to-date information on audition schedules is available by calling (213) 520-5555 Monday through Friday, from 10:00 a.m. to 6:00 p.m. Pacific Standard Time.

STARS WITH SOAPY ROOTS

Many of the most familiar faces in the entertainment world first appeared on the small screen of daytime TV. Test your soap-opera memory against our list.

Actor	Character	Soap
Dame Judith Anderson	Minx Lockridge	Santa Barbara
Richard Dean Anderson	Dr. Jeff Webber	General Hospital
Kevin Bacon	Tim Werner	Guiding Light
Alec Baldwin	Billy Allison Aldrich	The Doctors
Bonnie Bedelia	Sandy Porter	Love of Life
Robby Benson	Bruce Carson	Search for Tomorrow
Tom Berenger	Timmy Siegel	One Life To Live
Corbin Bernsen	Kenny Graham	Ryan's Hope
Ellen Burstyn	Dr. Kate Bartok	The Doctors
Tia Carrere	Jade Soong	General Hospital
Dixie Carter	Olivia Brandeis "Brandy" Henderson	The Edge of Night
Nell Carter	Ethel Green	Ryan's Hope
Shaun Cassidy	Dusty Walker	General Hospital
Jill Clayburgh	Grace Bolton	Search for Tomorrow
Dabney Coleman	Dr. Tracy Brown	Bright Promise
Ted Danson	Tim Conway	Somerset
Ruby Dee	Martha Frazier	Guiding Light
Julia Duffy	Penny Davis	The Doctors
Olympia Dukakis	Barbara Moreno	Search for Tomorrow
Morgan Fairchild	Jennifer Phillips	Search for Tomorrow
Mike Farrell	Scott Banning	Days of Our Lives
Laurence Fishburne	Joshua West	One Life To Live
Morgan Freeman	Roy Bingham	Another World
Kelsey Grammer	Dr. Canard	Another World
Richard Grieco	Rick Gardner	One Life To Live
Charles Grodin	Matt Crane	The Young Marrieds

Luke Perry on Loving.

Demi Moore on General Hospital.

Tommy Lee Jones on One Life to Live.

Actor	Character	Soap
Larry Hagman	Ed Gibson	The Edge of Night
Mark Hamill	Kent Murray	General Hospital
David Hasselhoff	Bill "Snapper" Foster	The Young and the Restless
Hal Holbrook	Grayling Dennis	The Brighter Day
Lauren Holly	Julie Chandler	All My Children
Kate Jackson	Daphne Harridge	Dark Shadows
James Earl Jones	Dr. Jim Frazier	Guiding Light
Tommy Lee Jones	Dr. Mark Toland	One Life To Live
Raul Julia	Miguel Garcia	Love of Life
Kevin Kline	Woody Reed	Search for Tomorrow
Don Knotts	Wilbur Peabody	Search for Tomorrow
Diane Ladd	Kitty Styles	The Secret Storm
Judith Light	Karen Martin	One Life To Live
Hal Linden	Larry Carter	Search for Tomorrow
Ray Liotta	Joey Perini	Another World
Cleavon Little	Captain Hancock	Another World
Marsha Mason	Judith Cole	Love of Life
Demi Moore	Jackie Templeton	General Hospital
Luke Perry	Ned Bates	Loving
Regis Philbin	Malachy Malone	Ryan's Hope
Phylicia Rashad	Courtney Wright	One Life To Live
Christopher Reeve	Benno ("Beanie" or "Ben") Harper	Love of Life
Eric Roberts	Ted Bancroft	Another World
Meg Ryan	Betsy Stewart	As the World Turns
Susan Sarandon	Sarah	Search for Tomorrow
Kyra Sedgwick	Julia Shearer	Another World
Tom Selleck	Jed Andrews	The Young and the Restless
Grant Show	Rick Hyde	Ryan's Hope
Christian Slater	D. J. LaSalle	Ryan's Hope
Rick Springfield	Dr. Noah Drake	General Hospital
John Stamos	Blackie Parrish	General Hospital
Marisa Tomei	Marcy Thompson	As the World Turns
Janine Turner	Laura Templeton	General Hospital
Kathleen Turner	Nola Dancy Aldrich	The Doctors
Cicely Tyson	Martha Frazier	Guiding Light
Blair Underwood	Bobby Blue	One Life To Live
Joan Van Ark	Janene Whitney	Days of Our Lives
Christopher Walken	Michael Bauer	Guiding Light
Sigourney Weaver	Avis Ryan	Somerset
Billy Dee Williams	Dr. Jim Frazier	Guiding Light
JoBeth Williams	Brandy Sheloo	Guiding Light
Robin Wright	Kelly Capwell	Santa Barbara

PRIME TIME'S TOP 40

There's something infectious about television theme songs. Here are the ones that hit highest on the *Billboard* charts. (The list excludes songs that were hits prior to their adoption as television anthems.)

Song	Show	Performer	Chart Position/Year
I'll Be There for You*	Friends	The Rembrandts	1/1995
S.W.A.T.	S.W.A.T.	Rhythm Heritage	1/1975
Welcome Back	Welcome Back, Kotter	John Sebastian	1/1976
Miami Vice	Miami Vice	Jan Hammer	1/1985
Believe It or Not	The Greatest American Hero	Joey Scarbury	2/1981
Dragnet	Dragnet	Ray Anthony Orchestra	3/1953
Secret Agent Man	Secret Agent Man	Johnny Rivers	3/1966
Hawaii Five-O	Hawaii Five-O	The Ventures	4/1969
Happy Days	Happy Days	Pratt and McClain	5/1976
Makin' It	Makin' It	David Naughton	5/1979
Peter Gunn	Peter Gunn	Ray Anthony Orchestra	8/1959
Three Stars Will Shine Tonight	Dr. Kildare	Richard Chamberlain	10/1962
The Rockford Files	The Rockford Files	Mike Post	10/1975
Hill Street Blues	Hill Street Blues	Mike Post and Larry Carlton	10/1981
Zorro	Zorro	The Chordettes	17/1958
Batman	Batman	The Marketts	17/1966
Different Worlds	Angie	Maureen McGovern	18/1979
Bonanza	Bonanza	Al Caiola	19/1961
Keep Your Eye on the Sparrow	Baretta	Rhythm Heritage	20/1976
Mr. Lucky	Mr. Lucky	Henry Mancini Orchestra	21/1960
The Dukes of Hazzard	The Dukes of Hazzard	Waylon Jennings	21/1980
Moonlighting	Moonlighting	Al Jarreau	23/1987
Making Our Dreams Come True	Laverne & Shirley	Cyndi Grecco	25/1976
Magnum, P.I.	Magnum, P.I.	Mike Post	25/1982
Ben Casey	Ben Casey	Valjean	28/1962
Blue Star	Medic	Felicia Sanders	29/1955
Route 66	Route 66	Nelson Riddle Orchestra	30/1962
Ballad of Paladin	Have Gun Will Travel	Duane Eddy	33/1962
Seattle	Here Come the Brides	Perry Como	38/1969
The Men	The Men	Isaac Hayes	38/1972
Mission: Impossible	Mission: Impossible	Lalo Schifrin	41/1968
Those Were the Days	All in the Family	Carroll O'Connor and Jean Stapleton	43/1971
The Ballad of Jed Clampett	Beverly Hillbillies	Lester Flatt and Earl Scruggs	44/1962
Charlie's Angels	Charlie's Angels	Henry Mancini	45/1977
Dynasty	Dynasty	Bill Conti	52/1982
My Three Sons	My Three Sons	Lawrence Welk Orchestra	55/1961

*Was not released as an A-side single, but reached No. 1 on *Billboard*'s Hot 100 Airplay Chart.

THE GREATEST COMMERCIALS OF ALL TIME

The editors of *Advertising Age* recently selected the 50 best TV spots of the past 50 years. Judged on the basis of their creativity, durability, and longevity, these are the commercials that made us laugh, cry, and most importantly—buy.

1940s

Gillette
A well-recognized radio jingle—"Look sharp, feel sharp . . ." is put to animation in one of the first regularly run TV commercials.

Lucky Strike
Dancing cigarettes twirl and swing and wind up in the Luckies pack for the concluding L.S.M.F.T. slogan—Lucky Strike Means Fine Tobacco.

Texaco
The be-all and end-all of the early days of commercial TV, with the singing "men from Texaco . . . who work from Maine to Mexico" getting every product plug imaginable into their weekly song.

1950s

Alka-Seltzer
Speedy Alka-Seltzer, the walking, talking tablet from early '50s-style "stop motion" became a certified classic before giving way to the creative revolution of the '60s.

Anacin
This early spot positioned Anacin as a "tension headache" remedy by fancifully diagramming a tension headache—and probably causing them all over America.

Chevrolet
When Dinah Shore sang "See the USA in your Chevrolet" on her popular TV show, America made the car the No. 1 nameplate on the new interstate highway system and in suburbia.

Timex
The famous "takes a licking and keeps on ticking" watch torture test began its 20-year-plus run.

1960s

Maxwell House
With the catchy "Good to the Last Drop" slogan and a catchier audiovisual mnemonic (the bubbling coffee sound), Maxwell House evoked the smell and flavor of brewed coffee, and sales percolated from the very start.

Lyndon Johnson
This seminal political commercial—a young girl picking petals from a daisy along with the countdown to a nuclear explosion—ran only once before it was withdrawn by the candidate.

Marlboro
Rugged cowboys and theme music from the movie *The Magnificent Seven* drove the campaign that revived sagging Marlboro, previously a brand targeted to women.

Noxzema
One of the earliest examples of overtly sexy TV advertising has former Miss Sweden Gunilla Knutson eyeing the camera and cooing the double-entendre "Take it off, take it all off" for Noxzema shave cream while the music from "The Stripper" plays.

Cracker Jack
Character actor Jack Gilford walks through a sleeping rail-car when a hand pops out from an upper-berth curtain with a box of Cracker Jack, intended for someone on the other side of the aisle. But deadpan Gilford intercepts it, helps himself and passes it back and forth to the unknowing passengers in a hilarious routine.

Hertz
People glide through the air and into a moving open convertible as "Hertz puts you in the driver's seat." Its endurance was enhanced by later parodies.

Benson & Hedges
To tout the cigarette brand's 100-millimeter size, the "disadvantages" of length are humorously demonstrated—popping a balloon, getting caught in an elevator door, etc.

Alka-Seltzer
"Mamma Mia, atsa some spicy meatball!" From the first frame to the last, the heartburn joke is propelled ever forward.

1970s

Budweiser
This classic annual TV Christmas card lives on as the beer-wagon team of Clydesdales trots through a picturesque snow-covered small town.

Volkswagen
"Funeral" has a deceased tycoon reading his will as limos enter the cemetery. He berates his spendthrift wife, partner, and sons—whom we see in limos—and leaves them almost nothing. To his nephew, who's driving a VW Beetle, he gives "my entire fortune of $100 billion dollars."

Coca-Cola

Bill Backer and Billy Davis's "I'd Like To Buy the World a Coke," sung by young people from numerous nations on a hilltop in Italy in 1971, became the pop song, "I'd Like To Teach the World To Sing."

Lite Beer from Miller

Who more natural to turn a "female-oriented" low-calorie beer called Lite into a manly brew? Ex-jocks. And with this long-running "Everything you ever wanted in a beer—and less" campaign, Miller Lite beer shot to the top of the market.

Xerox

Could Brother Dominick produce 500 more sets of his hand-lettered manuscript? Yes, with the "miracle" coming from the Xerox 9200 copier.

Life Cereal

Two brothers get their younger sibling Mikey to try Life and, surprise, he likes it. "Hey, Mikey" entered the lexicon.

American Express

With competition from bank charge cards increasing, American Express began its "Do you know me?" campaign to suggest empowerment through the Green Card.

American Express

For its Travelers Cheques, Karl Malden brought his *Streets of San Francisco* detective persona to these AmEx commercials. But the spots ran far longer than the TV series, and "Don't leave home without 'em" became embedded in the collective American consciousness.

McDonald's

With an energetic crew cleaning and singing "You deserve a break today," McDonald's established two themes: (1) its outlets were not "greasy spoons" and (2)

mothers weren't short-changing their families by patronizing the quick-service restaurant leader.

Dannon

"In [what was then Soviet] Georgia, where they eat a lot of yogurt, a lot of people live past 100," says one spot from a series for Dannon yogurt, which fondly filmed a village of centenarians enjoying free samples. One ends: "eighty-nine-year-old Renan Topagua . . . ate two cups. That pleased his mother very much."

Southern Airways

Possibly the funniest spot ever filmed, this one for a now-defunct airline portrays coach-class travel as akin to transatlantic steerage, in contrast to the Roman orgy going on in first class.

7UP

Geoffrey Holder's deep voice and a tropical setting were just the right touches to introduce the "uncola nut," 7UP's answer to Coke and Pepsi's key ingredient. A palpably refreshing point of differentiation.

Sunsweet

Opens with an arrogant man saying, "I warn you in advance, I'm not going to like your prunes." He says prunes are both pitted and wrinkled. A hand holds out a box of Sunsweet prunes and the man discovers they don't have pits. He finds them sweet and moist, but still complains about the wrinkles. Closing stentorian VO: "Today the pits, tomorrow the wrinkles."

Polaroid

When Mariette Hartley joined James Garner for these repartee-filled spots, Polaroid and its One-Step and SX-70 moved from novelty to mainstream in the camera business.

Chanel

This 1979 work from director Ridley Scott was one of the first in a "new wave" of highly visual "graphics" approaches that swept in from the U.K. A woman lolls by a swimming pool; a man dives, emerges at her feet; an airplane's shadow passes—for the simple message: "Chanel . . . share the fantasy."

1980s

Bartles & Jaymes

Classic "plain folks" approach features homespun codgers Frank Bartles and Ed Jaymes on a porch as Frank (Ed never speaks) introduces the product in staccato monotone and ends with the campaign tagline "Thank you for your support."

Chrysler

One of the most effective executive ad spokesmen ever, Chrysler's Lee Iacocca helped bring his company back from the brink of bankruptcy with blunt-talking commercials challenging consumers: "If you can find a better car, buy it."

Wendy's

"Where's the beef?!" Clara Peller barked and a pop culture phenomenon was born.

Eastman Kodak

In "Daddy's Little Girl," snapshots record a child's life up to her wedding, whereupon no father of daughters can keep from choking up. Sentimental yet restrained, this masterpiece reminds parents to capture Kodak memories while they can.

Eveready Energizer

One of TV's cleverest campaigns made its debut in '89 with the first Energizer Bunny parodies. The pink drum-thumper, itself a parody of one used by rival Duracell, romps through three

15 second "commercials"—dead-on sendups of coffee, wine, and decongestant spots.

Federal Express
Fast-talker John Moschitta humorously sets FedEx's role in a fast-paced world.

Ronald Reagan
This "feel-good" spot for his 1984 reelection campaign shows patriotic vignettes while musing on the theme "It's Morning Again in America."

Coca-Cola
The fearsome brute, Pittsburgh Steelers' defender Mean Joe Greene, took a long swig of Coca-Cola and suddenly was humanized enough to toss his jersey to a young fan. Maudlin or no, the 1980 vignette is perhaps the most beloved of all commercials.

AT&T
One of the best in the AT&T series stressing the human side of long-distance calling, the husband asks his crying wife what's wrong. "Joey called. Is everything alright? Yes. Then why are you crying? 'Cause Joey said, 'I called just to say I love you, Mom.' "

Isuzu
Nobody had ever heard of Isuzu before "lying" car salesman (correct information was simultaneously shown) David Leisure became one of the most popular characters in America.

Nike
Bo Diddley strums his guitar and then athlete Bo Jackson does the same with far less success, causing the legendary musician to intone, "Bo, you don't know diddley." A takeoff on earlier "Bo knows" spots in which Jackson is shown to excel in a variety of athletics.

Cheer
In a departure from staid Procter & Gamble's messages, this spot features a silent deadpan presenter smudging a handkerchief and putting it in a cocktail shaker with water, ice, and a dash of Cheer. As an opera aria plays, he removes the hanky, shows it's now spotless, hangs it on a line to dry, and marches off-camera.

Apple Macintosh
Ridley Scott also directed this Orwellian nightmare of tyranny and enslavement, broadly suggesting that Big Brother and IBM were one and the same. "1984" is the greatest commercial ever.

Pepsi-Cola
After being the "Pepsi generation" for one generation, at least, Pepsi-Cola signed the pop music icon of the '80s, Michael Jackson, to position the soft drink as "the choice of a new generation," in one of the largest celebrity endorsement agreements in advertising history.

Calvin Klein
Teen-age supermodel Brooke Shields took Calvin Klein (and the jeans market in general) to new heights of sophistication in this campaign, done by noted photographer Richard Avedon, as she purred, "Know what comes between me and my Calvins? Nothing!"

California Raisins
Hip Claymation raisins, some wearing sunglasses, shuffle to Marvin Gaye's '60s hit, "I Heard It Through the Grapevine."

1990s

Bud Light
The spot that made "Yes . . . I AM!" the first big advertising catch phrase of the '90s, this has a cheeky young man talking his way into a limousine reserved for a Dr. Galazkiewicz by claiming to be "Dr. Gally-wick-its," first making certain the driver had stocked the limo with Bud Light.

Hallmark
Long a user of emotion-evoking advertising, Hallmark Cards pulled out all the stops in this two-minute spot centered on a "surprise" one hundreth birthday party (she knows). Noteworthy, too, is the mainstreaming of the African-American family; the appeal here is universal.

Levi's for Women
Breathtaking painted-glass animation expressed a distinctly female perspective, and by the time women viewers filtered the message through their own psyches, Levi's for Women was given credit for truly understanding them.

Coca-Cola
It was advertising done by a Hollywood talent agency, Creative Artists Agency. It was computer-animated imagery such as never seen before. It was a heartstopper for Madison Avenue and a heart-warmer for American viewers. The Coca-Cola "Polar Bears" spot was a carbonated watershed, part of an "Always"-themed, logo-centered effort featuring one of the best jingles ever.

THE EMMY AWARDS

As the television industry has grown, so has the business of television awards. So much so that the Emmys are now presented in two separate ceremonies to accommodate the wealth of categories. The following presents a wide selection of winners in major areas through the years.

	1949	1950
Actor	—	Alan Young
Actress	—	Gertrude Berg
Drama	—	*Pulitzer Prize Playhouse*, ABC
Variety Program	—	*The Alan Young Show*, CBS
Game Show	—	*Truth or Consequences*, CBS
Children's Show	*Time for Beany*, KTLA	*Time for Beany*, KTLA

	1951	1952	1953
Actor	Sid Caesar	Thomas Mitchell	Donald O'Connor, *Colgate Comedy Hour*, NBC
Actress	Imogene Coca	Helen Hayes	Eve Arden, *Our Miss Brooks*, CBS
Drama	*Studio One*, CBS	*Robert Montgomery Presents*, NBC	*U.S. Steel Hour*, ABC
Mystery, Action, or Adventure	—	*Dragnet*, NBC	*Dragnet*, NBC
Comedy	*Red Skelton Show*, NBC	*I Love Lucy*, CBS	*I Love Lucy*, CBS
Comedian	Red Skelton, NBC	Lucille Ball, CBS; Jimmy Durante, NBC	—
Variety Program	*Your Show of Shows*, NBC	*Your Show of Shows*, NBC	*Omnibus*, CBS
Game Show	—	*What's My Line?*, CBS	*This is Your Life*, NBC; *What's My Line?*, CBS
Children's Program	—	*Time for Beany*, KTLA	*Kukla, Fran & Ollie*, NBC

	1954	1955	1956
Actor	Danny Thomas, *Make Room for Daddy*, ABC	Phil Silvers, *The Phil Silvers Show*, CBS	Robert Moss, *Father Knows Best*, NBC
Actress	Loretta Young, *The Loretta Young Show*, NBC	Lucille Ball, *I Love Lucy*, CBS	Loretta Young, *The Loretta Young Show*, NBC
Drama	*U.S. Steel Hour*, ABC	*Producers' Showcase*, NBC	*Playhouse 90*, CBS
Mystery, Action, or Adventure	*Dragnet*, NBC	*Disneyland*, ABC	—
Comedy	*Make Room for Daddy*, ABC	*The Phil Silvers Show*, CBS	—
Comedian	—	Phil Silvers, CBS; Nanette Fabray, NBC	Sid Caesar, *Caesar's Hour*, NBC; Nanette Fabray, *Caesar's Hour*, NBC
Variety Series	*Disneyland*, ABC	*The Ed Sullivan Show*, CBS	—
Game Show	*This Is Your Life*, NBC	*The $64,000 Question*, CBS	—
Children's Program	*Lassie*, CBS	*Lassie*, CBS	—

	1957	1958–59	1959–60
Drama	*Gunsmoke*, CBS	*The Alcoa Hour/Goodyear Playhouse*, NBC; *Playhouse 90*, CBS	*Playhouse 90*, CBS
Actor—Series	—	Raymond Burr, *Perry Mason*, CBS (Drama)	Robert Stack, *The Untouchables*, ABC
Actress—Series	—	Loretta Young, *The Loretta Young Show*, NBC (Drama)	Jane Wyatt, *Father Knows Best*, CBS
Supporting Actor—Series	—	Dennis Weaver, *Gunsmoke*, CBS	—
Supporting Actress—Drama Series	—	Barbara Hale, *Perry Mason*, CBS	—
Director—Drama	—	George Schaefer, *Little Moon of Aloban*, NBC; Jack Smight, *Eddie*, NBC	Robert Mulligan, *The Moon and Sixpence*, NBC
Writer—Drama	—	James Costigan, *Little Moon of Alban*, NBC; Alfred Brenner, and Ken Hughes, *Eddie*, NBC	Rod Serling, *The Twilight Zone*, CBS
Comedy	*The Phil Silvers Show*, CBS	*The Jack Benny Show*, CBS	*Art Carney Special*, NBC
Actor—Comedy Series	Robert Young, *Father Knows Best*, NBC	Jack Benny, *The Jack Benny Show*, CBS	Dick Van Dyke, *The Dick Van Dyke Show*, CBS
Actress—Comedy Series	Jane Wyatt, *Father Knows Best*, NBC	Jane Wyatt, *Father Knows Best*, CBS & NBC	Jane Wyatt, *Father Knows Best*, CBS
Supporting Actor—Comedy Series	Carl Reiner, *Caesar's Hour*, NBC	Tom Poston, *The Steve Allen Show*, NBC	—
Supporting Actress—Comedy Series	Ann B. Davis, *The Bob Cummings Show*, CBS and NBC	Ann B. Davis, *The Bob Cummings Show*, NBC	—
Director—Comedy/Comedy Series	—	Peter Tewksbury, *Father Knows Best*, CBS	Ralph Levy and Bud Yorkin, *The Jack Benny Hour Specials*, CBS
Writer—Comedy/Comedy Series	Nat Hiken, Billy Friedberg, Phil Sharp, Terry Ryan, Coleman Jacoby, Arnold Rosen, Sidney Zelinko, A.J. Russell, and Tony Webster, *The Phil Silvers Show*, CBS	Sam Perrin, George Balzer, Hal Goldman, and Al Gordon, *The Jack Benny Show*, CBS	Sam Perrin, George Balzer, Hal Goldman, and Al Gordon, *The Jack Benny Show*, CBS
Variety Program	*The Dinah Shore Chevy Show*, NBC	*The Dinah Shore Chevy Show*, NBC	*The Fabulous Fifties*, CBS
Game Show	—	*What's My Line?* CBS	—
Children's Program	—	—	*Huckleberry Hound*, SYN

	1960–61	1961–62	1962–63
Actor	Raymond Burr, *Perry Mason*, CBS	E.G. Marshall, *The Defenders*, CBS	E.G. Marshall, *The Defenders*, CBS
Actress	Barbara Stanwyck, *The Barbara Stanwyck Show*, NBC	Shirley Booth, *Hazel*, NBC	Shirley Booth, *Hazel*, NBC
Drama	*Macbeth*, NBC	*The Defenders*, CBS	*The Defenders*, CBS
Director—Drama	George Schaefer, *Macbeth*, NBC	Franklin Schaffner, *The Defenders*, CBS	Stuart Rosenberg, *The Defenders*, CBS
Writer—Drama	Rod Serling, *The Twilight Zone*, CBS	Reginald Rose, *The Defenders*, CBS	Robert Thorn, Reginald Rose, *The Defenders*, CBS
Comedy	*The Jack Benny Show*, CBS	*The Bob Newhart Show*, NBC	*The Dick Van Dyke Show*, CBS
Director—Comedy	Sheldon Leonard, *The Danny Thomas Show*, CBS	Nat Hiken, *Car 54, Where Are You?*, NBC	John Rich, *The Dick Van Dyke Show*, CBS
Writer—Comedy	Sherwood Schwartz, Dave O'Brien, Al Schwartz, Martin Ragaway, and Red Skelton, *The Red Skelton Show*, CBS	Carl Reiner, *The Dick Van Dyke Show*, CBS	Carl Reiner, *The Dick Van Dyke Show*, CBS
Variety Program	*Astaire Time*, NBC	*The Garry Moore Show*, CBS	*The Andy Williams Show*, NBC
Individual Performance—Variety or Music Program/Series	Fred Astaire, *Astaire Time*, NBC	Carol Burnett, *The Garry Moore Show*, CBS	Carol Burnett, *Julie and Carol at Carnegie Hall*, CBS; *Carol and Company*, CBS
Panel, Quiz or Audience Participation	—	—	*College Bowl*, CBS
Children's Program	*Young People's Concert: Aaron Copland's Birthday Party*, CBS	*New York Philharmonic Young People's Concerts with Leonard Bernstein*, CBS	*Walt Disney's Wonderful World of Color*, NBC

THE RATINGS CONNECTION

Having the No. 1 rated show for a season doesn't necessarily guarantee Emmy success . . . or does it? Here is a list of the No. 1 shows that have also won the top honors—along with those that have achieved the dubious distinction of winning the ratings race but losing the Emmy battle.

EMMY WINNERS	EMMY LOSERS
Texaco Star Theatre	Arthur Godfrey's Talent Scouts
I Love Lucy	Wagon Train
The $64,000 Question	The Beverly Hillbillies
Gunsmoke	Bonanza
Rowan and Martin's Laugh-In	The Andy Griffith Show
All in the Family	Marcus Welby, M.D.
60 Minutes	Happy Days
The Cosby Show	Laverne & Shirley
Cheers	Three's Company
Seinfeld	Dallas
	Dynasty
	Roseanne
	Home Improvement

	1963–64	1964–65	1965–66
Drama	The Defenders, CBS	In 1964–65 the entire award system was changed for one year, and there were no awards given in individual categories that in any way match the categories from other years.	The Fugitive, ABC
Actor—Drama Series	Jack Klugman, The Defenders, CBS		Bill Cosby, I Spy, NBC
Actress—Drama Series	Shelley Winters, Two Is The Number, NBC		Barbara Stanwyck, The Big Valley, ABC
Supporting Actor—Drama Series	Albert Parker, One Day In The Life of Ivan Denisovich, NBC	—	James Daly, Eagle in a Cage, NBC
Supporting Actress—Drama Series	Ruth White, Little Moon of Alban, NBC	—	Lee Grant, Peyton Place, ABC
Writer—Drama	Ernest Kinay, The Defenders, CBS	—	Sidney Pollack, The Game, NBC
Director—Drama	Tom Gries, East Side/West Side, CBS	—	Millard Lampell, Eagle in a Cage, NBC
Comedy	The Dick Van Dyke Show, CBS	—	The Dick Van Dyke Show, CBS
Actor—Comedy Series	Dick Van Dyke, The Dick Van Dyke Show, CBS	—	Dick Van Dyke, The Dick Van Dyke Show, CBS
Actress—Comedy Series	Mary Tyler Moore, The Dick Van Dyke Show, CBS	—	Mary Tyler Moore, The Dick Van Dyke Show, CBS
Supporting Actor—Comedy Series	—	—	Don Knotts, The Andy Griffith Show, CBS
Supp. Actress—Comedy Series	—	—	Alice Pearce, Bewitched, ABC
Director—Comedy	Jerry Paris, The Dick Van Dyke Show, CBS	—	William Asher, Bewitched, ABC
Writer—Comedy	Carl Reiner, Sam Denoff, and Bill Penky, The Dick Van Dyke Show, CBS	—	Bill Persky, Sam Denoff, The Dick Van Dyke Show, CBS
Variety Program	The Danny Kaye Show, CBS	—	The Andy Williams Show, NBC
Director—Variety or Music	Robert Scheerer, The Danny Kaye Show, CBS	—	Alan Handley, The Julie Andrews Show, NBC
Writer—Variety	—	—	Al Gordon, Hal Goldman, and Sheldon Keller, An Evening with Carol Channing, CBS
Children's Program	Discovery '63-'64, ABC	—	A Charlie Brown Christmas, CBS

WINNING TEAMS

These married power couples all sport matching Emmys, and one duo (William Daniels and Bonnie Bartlett of *St. Elsewhere*) even won theirs for playing a husband and wife on TV.

Hume Cronyn & Jessica Tandy
William Daniels & Bonnie Bartlett
Danny DeVito & Rhea Perlman
Phil Donahue & Marlo Thomas
Alfred Lunt & Lynn Fontanne
George C. Scott & Colleen Dewhurst

	1966–67	**1967–68**	**1968–69**
Drama Series	*Mission: Impossible*, CBS	*Mission: Impossible*, CBS	*NET Playhouse*, NET
Actor—Drama Series	Bill Cosby, *I Spy*, NBC	Bill Cosby, *I Spy*, NBC	Carl Betz, *Judd, for the Defense*, ABC
Actress—Drama Series	Barbara Bain, *Mission: Impossible*, CBS	Barbara Bain, *Mission: Impossible*, CBS	Barbara Bain, *Mission: Impossible*, CBS
Supporting Actor— Drama	Eli Wallach, *The Poppy Is Also a Flower*, ABC	Milburn Stone, *Gunsmoke*, CBS	—
Supporting Actress— Drama	Agnes Moorehead, *The Wild, Wild West*, CBS	Barbara Anderson, *Ironside*, NBC	Susan Saint James, *The Name of the Game*, NBC
Director—Drama	Alex Segal, *Death of a Salesman*, CBS	Paul Bogart, *Dear Friends*, CBS	David Green, *The People Next Door*, CBS
Writer—Drama	Bruce Geller, *Mission: Impossible*, CBS	Loring Mandel, *Do Not Go Gentle into That Good Night*, CBS	J.P. Miller, *The People Next Door*, CBS
Comedy	*The Monkees*, NBC	*Get Smart*, NBC	*Get Smart*, NBC
Actor—Comedy Series	Don Adams, *Get Smart*, NBC	Don Adams, *Get Smart*, NBC	Don Adams, *Get Smart*, NBC
Actress—Comedy Series	Lucille Ball, *The Lucy Show*, CBS	Lucille Ball, *The Lucy Show*, CBS	Hope Lange, *The Ghost and Mrs. Muir*, NBC
Supporting Actor— Comedy Series	Don Knotts, *The Andy Griffith Show*, CBS	Werner Klemperer, *Hogan's Heroes*, CBS	Werner Klemperer, *Hogan's Heroes*, CBS
Supporting Actress— Comedy Series	Frances Bavier, *The Andy Griffith Show*, CBS	Marion Lorne, *Bewitched*, ABC	—
Director—Comedy/ Comedy Series	James Frawley, *The Monkees*, NBC	Bruce Bilson, *Get Smart*, NBC	—
Writer—Comedy/ Comedy Series	Buck Henry and Leonard Stern, *Get Smart*, NBC	Allan Burns and Chris Hayward, *He and She*, CBS	Alan Blye, Bob Einstein, Murray Roman, Carl Gottlieb, Jerry Music, Steve Martin, Cecil Tuck, Paul Wayne, Cy Howard, and Mason Williams, *The Smothers Brothers Comedy Hour*, CBS
Variety Program	*The Andy Williams Show*, NBC	*Rowan and Martin's Laugh-In*, NBC	*Rowan and Martin's Laugh-In*, NBC
Director—Variety or Music	Fielder Cook, *Brigadoon*, ABC	Jack Haley, Jr., *Movin' with Nancy*, NBC	—
Writer—Variety or Music	Mel Brooks, Sam Denoff, Bill Persky, Carl Reiner, and Mel Tolkin, *The Sid Caesar, Imogene Coca, Carl Reiner, Howard Morris Special*, CBS	Chris Beard, Phil Hahn, Jack Hanrahan, Coslough Johnson, Paul Keyes, Marc London, Allan Manings, David Panich, Hugh Wedlock, and Digby Wolfe, *Rowan and Martin's Laugh-In*, NBC	—
Children's Program	*Jack and the Beanstalk*, NBC	—	—

	1969–70	1970–71	1971–72
Drama	*Marcus Welby, M.D.,* ABC	*The Bold Ones: The Senator,* NBC	*Elizabeth R,* PBS
Actor—Drama Series	Robert Young, *Marcus Welby, M.D.,* ABC	Hal Holbrook, *The Bold Ones: The Senator,* NBC	Peter Falk, *Columbo,* NBC
Actress—Drama Series	Susan Hampshire, *The Forsyte Saga,* NET	Susan Hampshire, *The First Churchills,* PBS	Glenda Jackson, *Elizabeth R.,* PBS
Supporting Actor—Drama Series	James Brolin, *Marcus Welby, M.D.,* ABC	David Burns, *The Price,* NBC	Jack Warden, *Brian's Song,* ABC
Supporting Actress—Drama Series	Gail Fisher, *Mannix,* CBS	Margaret Leighton, *Hamlet,* NBC	Jenny Agutter, *The Snow Goose,* NBC
Director—Drama Series	—	Daryl Duke, *The Bold Ones: The Senator,* NBC	Alexander Singer, *The Bold Ones: The Lawyers,* NBC
Writer—Drama	Richard Levinson and William Link, *My Sweet Charlie,* NBC	Joel Oliansky, *The Bold Ones: The Senator,* NBC	Richard L. Levinson and William Link, *Columbo,* NBC
Comedy	*My World and Welcome to It,* NBC	*All in the Family,* CBS	*All in the Family,* CBS
Actor—Comedy Series	William Windom, *My World and Welcome to It,* NBC	Jack Klugman, *The Odd Couple,* ABC	Carroll O'Connor, *All in the Family,* CBS
Actress—Comedy Series	Hope Lange, *The Ghost and Mrs. Muir,* ABC	Jean Stapleton, *All in the Family,* CBS	Jean Stapleton, *All in the Family,* CBS
Supporting Actor—Comedy Series	Michael Constantine, *Room 222,* ABC	Edward Asner, *The Mary Tyler Moore Show,* CBS	Edward Asner, *The Mary Tyler Moore Show,* CBS
Supporting Actress—Comedy Series	Karen Valentine, *Room 222,* ABC	Valerie Harper, *The Mary Tyler Moore Show,* CBS	Valerie Harper, *The Mary Tyler Moore Show,* CBS; Sally Struthers, *All in the Family, CBS*
Director—Comedy Series	—	Jay Sandrich, *The Mary Tyler Moore Show,* CBS	John Rich, *All in the Family,* CBS
Writer—Comedy Series	—	James L. Brooks and Allan Burns, *The Mary Tyler Moore Show,* CBS	Burt Styler, *All in the Family,* CBS
Drama/Comedy Special	—	—	*Brian's Song,* ABC
Variety or Music Series	*The David Frost Show,* SYN	*The David Frost Show, SYN* (Talk); *The Flip Wilson Show,* NBC (Music)	*The Dick Cavett Show,* ABC (Talk), *The Carol Burnett Show,* CBS (Music)
Director—Variety or Music	—	Mark Warren, *Rowan and Martin's Laugh-In,* NBC	Art Fisher, *The Sonny & Cher Comedy Hour,* CBS
Writer—Variety or Music	—	Herbert Baker, Hal Goodman, Larry Klein, Bob Weiskopf, Bob Schiller, Norman Steinberg, and Flip Wilson, *The Flip Wilson Show,* NBC	Don Hinkley, Stan Hart, Larry Siegel, Woody Kling, Roger Beatty, Art Baer, Ben Joelson, Stan Burns, Mike Marmer, and Arnie Rosen, *The Carol Burnett Show,* CBS
Daytime Drama Series	—	—	*The Doctors,* NBC
Children's Program	*Sesame Street,* NET	*Sesame Street,* PBS	*Sesame Street,* PBS

	1972–73	**1973–74**	**1974–75**
Drama	*The Waltons*, CBS	*Upstairs, Downstairs*, PBS	*Upstairs, Downstairs*, PBS
Actor—Drama Series	Richard Thomas, *The Waltons*, CBS	Telly Savalas, *Kojak*, CBS	Robert Blake, *Baretta*, ABC
Actress—Drama Series	Michael Learned, *The Waltons*, CBS	Michael Learned, *The Waltons*, CBS	Jean Marsh, *Upstairs, Downstairs*, PBS
Supporting Actor— Drama/Drama Series	Scott Jacoby, *That Certain Summer*, ABC	Michael Moriarty, *The Glass Menagerie*, ABC	Will Geer, *The Waltons*, CBS
Supporting Actress— Drama/Drama Series	Ellen Corby, *The Waltons*, CBS	Joanna Miles, *The Glass Menagerie*, ABC	Ellen Corby, *The Waltons*, CBS
Director—Drama	Joseph Sargent, *The Marcus Nelson Murders*, CBS	John Korty, *The Autobiography of Miss Jane Pittman*, CBS	George Cukor, *Love Among the Ruins*, ABC
Director—Drama Series	Jerry Thorpe, *Kung Fu*, ABC	Robert Butler, *The Blue Knight*, NBC	Bill Bain, *Upstairs, Downstairs*, PBS
Writer—Drama Series	John McGreevey, *The Waltons*, CBS	Joanna Lee, *The Waltons*, CBS	Howard Fast, *Benjamin Franklin*, CBS
Comedy	*All in the Family*, CBS	*M*A*S*H*, CBS	*The Mary Tyler Moore Show*, CBS
Actor—Comedy Series	Jack Klugman, *The Odd Couple*, ABC	Alan Alda, *M*A*S*H*, CBS	Tony Randall, *The Odd Couple*, ABC
Actress—Comedy Series	Mary Tyler Moore, *The Mary Tyler Moore Show*, CBS	Mary Tyler Moore, *The Mary Tyler Moore Show*, CBS	Valerie Harper, *Rhoda*, CBS
Supporting Actor— Comedy Series	Ted Knight, *The Mary Tyler Moore Show*, CBS	Rob Reiner, *All in the Family*, CBS	Ed Asner, *The Mary Tyler Moore Show*, CBS
Supporting Actress— Comedy Series	Valerie Harper, *The Mary Tyler Moore Show*, CBS	Cloris Leachman, *The Mary Tyler Moore Show*, CBS	Betty White, *The Mary Tyler Moore Show*, CBS
Director—Comedy Series	Jay Sandrich, *The Mary Tyler Moore Show*, CBS	Jackie Cooper, *M*A*S*H*, CBS	Gene Reynolds, *M*A*S*H*, CBS
Writer—Comedy Series	Michael Ross, Bernie West, and Lee Kalcheim, *All in the Family*, CBS	Treva Silverman, *The Mary Tyler Moore Show*, CBS	Ed. Weinberger and Stan Daniels, *The Mary Tyler Moore Show*, CBS
Drama/Comedy Special	*A War of Children*, CBS	*The Autobiography of Miss Jane Pittman*, CBS	*The Law*, NBC
Variety Series	*The Julie Andrews Hour*, ABC	*The Carol Burnett Show*, CBS	*The Carol Burnett Show*, CBS
Director—Variety or Music	Bill Davis, *The Julie Andrews Hour*, ABC	Dave Powers, *The Carol Burnett Show*, CBS	Dave Powers, *The Carol Burnett Show*, CBS

	1972–73	**1973–74**	**1974–75**
Writer—Variety or Music Series	Stan Hart, Larry Siegel, Gail Parent, Woody Kling, Roger Beatty, Tom Patchett, Jay Tarses, Robert Hilliard, Arnie Kogen, Bill Angelos, and Buz Kohan, *The Carol Burnett Show*, CBS	Ed Simmons, Gary Belkin, Roger Beatty, Arnie Kogen, Bill Richmond, Gene Perret, Rudy De Luca, Barry Levinson, Dick Clair, Jenna McMahon, and Barry Harman, *The Carol Burnett Show*, CBS	Ed Simmons, Gary Belkin, Roger Beatty, Arnie Kogen, Bill Richmond, Gene Perret, Rudy De Luca, Barry Levinson, Dick Clair, and Jenna McMahon, *The Carol Burnett Show*, CBS
Variety, Music, or Comedy Special	*Singer Presents Liza with a "Z"*, CBS	*Lilly Tomlin*, CBS	*An Evening with John Denver*, ABC
Miniseries/Limited Series	*Tom Brown's Schooldays*, PBS	*Columbo*, NBC	*Benjamin Franklin*, CBS
Actor—Miniseries/Limited Series	Anthony Murphy, *Tom Brown's Schooldays*, PBS	William Holden, *The Blue Knight*, NBC	Peter Falk, *Columbo*, NBC
Actress—Miniseries/Limited Series	Susan Hampshire, *Vanity Fair*, PBS	Mildred Natwick, *The Snoop Sisters*, NBC	Jessica Walter, *Amy Prentiss*, NBC
Daytime Drama Series	*The Edge of Night*, CBS	*The Doctors*, NBC	*The Young and the Restless*, CBS
Actor—Daytime Drama Series	—	Macdonald Carey, *Days of Our Lives*, NBC	Macdonald Carey, *Days of Our Lives*, NBC
Actress—Daytime Drama Series	—	Elizabeth Hubbard, *The Doctors*, NBC	Susan Flannery, *Days of Our Lives*, NBC
Host—Game Show	—	Peter Marshall, *The Hollywood Squares*, NBC	Peter Marshall, *The Hollywood Squares*, NBC
Host—Talk or Service	—	Dinah Shore, *Dinah's Place*, NBC	Barbara Walters, *Today*, NBC
Game Show	—	*Password*, ABC	*Hollywood Squares*, NBC
Talk, Service or Variety Series	—	*The Merv Griffin Show*, SYN	*Dinah!* SYN
Children's Special	—	*Marlo Thomas and Friends in Free To Be . . . You and Me*, ABC	*Yes, Virginia, There Is a Santa Claus*, ABC
Children's Entertainment Series	—	*Zoom*, PBS	Star Trek, NBC

	1975–76	**1976–77**	**1977–78**
Drama	*Police Story*, NBC	*Upstairs, Downstairs*, PBS	*The Rockford Files*, NBC
Actor—Drama Series	Peter Falk, *Columbo*, NBC	James Garner, *The Rockford Files*, NBC	Edward Asner, *Lou Grant*, CBS
Actress—Drama Series	Michael Learned, *The Waltons*, CBS	Lindsay Wagner, *The Bionic Woman*, ABC	Sada Thompson, *Family*, ABC
Supporting Actor—Drama Series	Anthony Zerbe, *Harry-O*, ABC	Gary Frank, *Family*, ABC	Robert Vaughn, *Washington: Behind Closed Doors*, ABC
Supp. Actress—Drama Series	Ellen Corby, *The Waltons*, CBS	Kristy McNichol, *Family*, ABC	Nancy Marchand, *Lou Grant*, CBS
Director—Drama Series	David Greene, *Rich Man, Poor Man*, ABC	David Greene, *Roots*, ABC	Marvin J. Chomsky, *Holocaust*, NBC
Writer—Drama Series	Sherman Yellen, *The Adams Chronicles*, PBS	Ernest Kinoy, and William Blinn, *Roots*, ABC	Gerald Green, *Holocaust*, NBC
Comedy	*The Mary Tyler Moore Show*, CBS	*The Mary Tyler Moore Show*, CBS	*All in the Family*, CBS
Actor—Comedy Series	Jack Albertson, *Chico and the Man*, NBC	Carroll O'Connor, *All in the Family*, CBS	Carroll O'Connor, *All in the Family*, CBS
Actress—Comedy Series	Mary Tyler Moore, *The Mary Tyler Moore Show*, CBS	Beatrice Arthur, *Maude*, CBS	Jean Stapleton, *All in the Family*, CBS

	1975–76	1976–77	1977–78
Supporting Actor— Comedy Series	Ted Knight, *The Mary Tyler Moore Show*, CBS	Gary Burghoff, *M*A*S*H*, CBS	Rob Reiner, *All in the Family*, CBS
Supporting Actress—Comedy Series	Betty White, *The Mary Tyler Moore Show*, CBS	Mary Kay Place, *Mary Hartman, Mary Hartman*, SYN	Julie Kavner, *Rhoda*, CBS
Director—Comedy/ Comedy Series	Gene Reynolds, *M*A*S*H*, CBS	Alan Alda, *M*A*S*H*, CBS	Paul Bogart, *All in the Family*, CBS
Writer— Comedy Series	David Lloyd, *The Mary Tyler Moore Show*, CBS	Allan Burns, James L. Brooks, Ed. Weinberger, Stan Daniels, David Lloyd, and Bob Ellison, *The Mary Tyler Moore Show*, CBS	Bob Weiskopf and Bob Schiller (Teleplay); Barry Harman, and Harve Brosten (Story), *All in the Family*, CBS
Drama/Comedy Special	*Eleanor and Franklin*, ABC	*Eleanor and Franklin: The White House Years*, ABC	*The Gathering*, ABC
Variety Series	*NBC's Saturday Night*, NBC	*Van Dyke and Company*, NBC	*The Muppet Show*, SYN
Limited Series	*Upstairs, Downstairs*, PBS	*Roots*, ABC	*Holocaust*, NBC
Actor— Limited Series	Hal Holbrook, *Sandburg's Lincoln*, NBC	Christopher Plummer, *The Moneychangers*, NBC	Michael Moriarty, *Holocaust*, NBC
Actress— Limited Series	Rosemary Harris, *Notorious Women*, PBS	Patty Duke Astin, *Captains and the Kings*, NBC	Meryl Streep, *Holocaust*, NBC
Daytime Drama Series	*Another World*, NBC	*Ryan's Hope*, ABC	*Days of Our Lives*, NBC
Actor—Daytime Drama Series	Larry Haines, *Search for Tomorrow*, CBS	Val Dufour, *Search for Tomorrow*, CBS	James Pritchett, *The Doctors*, NBC
Actress—Daytime Drama Series	Helen Gallagher, *Ryan's Hope*, ABC	Helen Gallagher, *Ryan's Hope*, ABC	Laurie Heineman, *Another World*, NBC
Host—Game Show	Allen Ludden, *Password*, ABC	Bert Convy, *Tattletales*, CBS	Richard Dawson, *Family Feud*, ABC
Host—Talk or Service Series	Dinah Shore, *Dinah!*, SYN	Phil Donahue, *Donahue*, SYN	Phil Donahue, *Donahue*, SYN
Game Show	*The $20,000 Pyramid*, ABC	*Family Feud*, ABC	*The Hollywood Squares*, NBC
Talk, Service or Variety Series	*Dinah!*, SYN	*The Merv Griffin Show*, SYN	*Donahue*, SYN
Children's Entertainment Series	*Big Blue Marble*, SYN	*Zoom!*, PBS	*Captain Kangaroo*, CBS

	1978–79	1979–80	1980–81
Drama	*Lou Grant*, CBS	*Lou Grant*, CBS	*Hill Street Blues*, NBC
Actor—Drama Series	Ron Leibman, *Kaz*, CBS	Ed Asner, *Lou Grant*, CBS	Daniel J. Travanti, *Hill Street Blues*, NBC
Actress—Drama Series	Mariette Hartley, *The Incredible Hulk*, CBS	Barbara Bel Geddes, *Dallas*, CBS	Barbara Babcock, *Hill Street Blues*, NBC
Supporting Actor—Drama Series	Stuart Margolin, *The Rockford Files*, NBC	Stuart Margolin, *The Rockford Files*, NBC	Michael Conrad, *Hill Street Blues*, NBC
Supporting Actress—Drama Series	Kristy McNichol, *Family*, ABC	Nancy Marchand, *Lou Grant*, CBS	Nancy Marchand, *Lou Grant*, CBS
Director—Drama Series	Jackie Cooper, *The White Shadow*, CBS	Roger Young, *Lou Grant*, CBS	Robert Butler, *Hill Street Blues*, NBC
Writer—Drama Series	Michele Gallery, *Lou Grant*, CBS	Seth Freeman, *Lou Grant*, CBS	Michael Kozoll and Steven Bochco, *Hill Street Blues*, NBC
Comedy	*Taxi*, ABC	*Taxi*, ABC	*Taxi*, ABC
Actor—Comedy Series	Carroll O'Connor, *All in the Family*, CBS	Richard Mulligan, *Soap*, ABC	Judd Hirsch, *Taxi*, ABC
Actress—Comedy Series	Ruth Gordon, *Taxi*, ABC	Cathryn Damon, *Soap*, ABC	Isabel Sanford, *The Jeffersons*, CBS
Supporting Actor—Comedy Series	Robert Guillaume, *Soap*, ABC	Harry Morgan, M*A*S*H, CBS	Danny De Vito, *Taxi*, ABC
Supporting Actress—Comedy Series	Sally Struthers, *All in the Family*, CBS	Loretta Swit, *M*A*S*H*, CBS	Eileen Brennan, *Private Benjamin*, CBS
Director—Comedy Series	Noam Pitlik, *Barney Miller*, ABC	James Burrows, *Taxi*, ABC	James Burrows, *Taxi*, ABC
Writer—Comedy Series	Alan Alda, *M*A*S*H*, CBS	Bob Colleary, *Barney Miller*, ABC	Michael Leeson, *Taxi*, ABC
Drama/Comedy Special	*Friendly Fire*, ABC	*The Miracle Worker*, NBC	*Playing for Time*, CBS
Variety Program	*Steve & Eydie Celebrate Irving Berlin*, NBC	*Baryshnikov on Broadway*, ABC	*Lily: Sold Out*, CBS
Director—Variety or Music	—	Dwight Hemion, *Baryshnikov on Broadway*, ABC	Don Mischer, *The Kennedy Center Honors: A National Celebration of the Performing Arts*, CBS

	1978–79	1979–80	1980–81
Writer—Variety or Music	—	Buz Kohan, *Shirley MacLaine. . . Every Little Movement*, CBS	Jerry Juhl, David Odell, Chris Langham, *The Muppet Show*, SYN
Limited Series	*Roots: The Next Generations*, ABC	*Edward & Mrs. Simpson*, SYN	*Shogun*, NBC
Actor—Limited Series	Peter Strauss, *The Jericho Mile*, ABC	Powers Boothe, *Guyana Tragedy: The Story of Jim Jones*, CBS	Anthony Hopkins, *The Bunker*, CBS
Actress—Limited Series	Bette Davis, *Strangers: The Story of a Mother and Daughter*, CBS	Patty Duke Astin, *The Miracle Worker*, NBC	Vanessa Redgrave, *Playing for Time*, CBS
Supporting Actor— Limited Series or Special	Marlon Brando, *Roots: The Next Generations*, ABC	George Grizzard, *The Oldest Living Graduate*, NBC	David Warner, *Masada*, ABC
Supporting Actress— Limited Series or Special	Esther Rolle, *Summer of My German Soldier*, NBC	Mare Winningham, *Amber Waves*, ABC	Jane Alexander, *Playing for Time*, CBS
Director—Limited Series or Special	David Greene, *Friendly Fire*, ABC	Marvin J. Chomsky, *Attica*, ABC	James Goldstone, *Kent State*, NBC
Writer—Limited Series or Special	Patrick Nolan and Michael Mann, *The Jericho Mile*, ABC	David Chase, *Off the Minnesota Strip*, ABC	Arthur Miller, *Playing for Time*, CBS
Daytime Drama Series	*Ryan's Hope*, ABC	*Guiding Light*, CBS	*General Hospital*, ABC
Actor—Daytime Drama Series	Al Freeman, Jr., *One Life to Live*, ABC	Douglass Watson, *Another World*, NBC	Douglass Watson, *Another World*, NBC
Actress—Daytime Drama Series	Irene Dailey, *Another World*, NBC	Judith Light, *One Life to Live*, ABC	Judith Light, *One Life to Live*, ABC
Supporting Actor— Daytime Drama Series	Peter Hansen, *General Hospital*, ABC	Warren Burton, *All My Children*, ABC	Larry Haines, *Search for Tomorrow*, CBS
Supporting Actress— Daytime Drama Series	Suzanne Rogers, *Days of Our Lives*, NBC	Francesca James, *All My Children*, ABC	Jane Elliot, *General Hospital*, ABC
Host—Game Show	Dick Clark, *The $20,000 Pyramid*, ABC	Peter Marshall, *The Hollywood Squares*, NBC	Peter Marshall, *The Hollywood Squares*, NBC
Host—Talk or Service	Phil Donahue, *Donahue*, SYN	Phil Donahue, *Donahue*, SYN	Hugh Downs, *Over Easy*, PBS
Game Show	*The Hollywood Squares*, NBC	*The Hollywood Squares*, NBC; *The $20,000 Pyramid*, ABC	*The $20,000 Pyramid*, ABC
Talk, Service or Variety Series	*Donahue*, SYN	*Donahue*, SYN	*Donahue*, SYN
Children's Program	*Christmas Eve on Sesame Street*, PBS	—	*Donahue and Kids*, NBC
Children's Entertainment Series	*Kids Are People Too*, ABC	*Hot Hero Sandwich*, NBC	*Captain Kangaroo*, CBS

	1981–82	**1982–83**	**1983–84**
Drama	*Hill Street Blues*, NBC	*Hill Street Blues*, NBC	*Hill Street Blues*, NBC
Actor—Drama Series	Daniel J. Travanti, *Hill Street Blues*, NBC	Ed Flanders, *St. Elsewhere*, NBC	Tom Selleck, *Magnum, P.I.*, CBS
Actress—Drama Series	Michael Learned, *Nurse*, CBS	Tyne Daly, *Cagney & Lacey*, CBS	Tyne Daly, *Cagney & Lacey*, CBS
Supporting Actor—Drama Series	Michael Conrad, *Hill Street Blues*, NBC	James Coco, *St. Elsewhere*, NBC	Bruce Weitz, *Hill Street Blues*, NBC
Supporting Actress—Drama Series	Nancy Marchand, *Lou Grant*, CBS	Doris Roberts, *St. Elsewhere*, NBC	Alfre Woodard, *Hill Street Blues*, NBC
Director—Drama Series	Harry Harris, *Fame*, NBC	Jeff Bleckner, *Hill Street Blues*, NBC	Corey Allen, *Hill Street Blues*, NBC
Writer—Drama Series	Steven Bochco, Anthony Yerkovich, Jeffrey Lewis, and Michael Wagner (Teleplay); Michael Kozoll and Steven Bochco (Story), *Hill Street Blues*, NBC	David Milch, *Hill Street Blues*, NBC	John Ford Noonan (Teleplay); John Masius, and Tom Fontana (Story), *St. Elsewhere*, NBC
Comedy	*Barney Miller*, ABC	*Cheers*, NBC	*Cheers*, NBC
Actor—Comedy Series	*Alan Alda*, M*A*S*H, CBS	Judd Hirsch, *Taxi*, NBC	John Ritter, *Three's Company*, ABC
Actress—Comedy Series	Carol Kane, *Taxi*, ABC	Shelley Long, *Cheers*, NBC	Jane Curtin, *Kate & Allie*, CBS
Supporting Actor—Comedy Series	Christopher Lloyd, *Taxi*, ABC	Christopher Lloyd, *Taxi*, NBC	Pat Harrington, Jr., *One Day at a Time*, CBS
Supp. Actress—Comedy Series	Loretta Swit, *M*A*S*H*, CBS	Carol Kane, *Taxi*, NBC	Rhea Perlman, *Cheers*, NBC
Director—Comedy Series	Alan Rafkin, *One Day at a Time*, CBS	James Burrows, *Cheers*, NBC	Bill Persky, *Kate & Allie*, CBS
Writer—Comedy Series	Ken Estin, *Taxi*, ABC	Glen Charles, Les Charles, *Cheers*, NBC	David Angel, *Cheers*, NBC
Drama/Comedy Special	*A Woman Called Golda*, SYN	*Special Bulletin*, NBC	*Something About Amelia*, ABC
Variety, Music, or Comedy Program	*Night of 100 Stars*, ABC	*Motown 25: Yesterday, Today, Forever*, NBC	*The 6th Annual Kennedy Center Honors: A Celebration of the Performing Arts*, CBS
Individual Performance—Variety or Music Program	—	Leontyne Price, *Live From Lincoln Center: Leontyne Price, Zubin Mehta, and the New York Philharmonic*, PBS	Cloris Leachman, *Screen Actors Guild 50th Anniversary Celebration*, CBS
Director—Variety or Music	Dwight Hemion, *Goldie and Kids Listen to Us*, ABC	Dwight Hemion, *Sheena Easton Act I*, NBC	Dwight Hemion, *Here's Television Entertainment*, NBC
Writer—Variety or Music	John Candy, Joe Flaherty, Eugene Levy, Andrea Martin, Rick Moranis, Catherine O'Hara, Dave Thomas, Dick Blasucci, Paul Flaherty, Bob Dolman, John McAndrew, Doug Steckler, M. Bert Rich, Jeffrey Barron, Michael Short, Chris Cluess, Stuart Kreisman, and Brian McConnachie, *SCTV Comedy Network*, NBC	John Candy, Joe Flaherty, Eugene Levy, Andrea Martin, Martin Short, Dick Blasucci, Paul Flaherty, John McAndrew, Doug Steckler, Bob Dolman, Michael Short, and Mary Charlotte Wilcox, *SCTV Network*, NBC	Steve O'Donnell, Gerard Mulligan, Sanford Frank, Joseph E. Toplyn, Christopher Elliott, Matt Wickline, Jeff Martin, Ted Greenberg, David Yazbek, Merrill Markoe, and David Letterman, *Late Night with David Letterman*, NBC

	1981–82	**1982–83**	**1983–84**
Limited Series	*Marco Polo*, NBC	*Nicholas Nickleby*, SYN	*Concealed Enemies*, PBS
Actor—Limited Series or Special	Mickey Rooney, *Bill*, CBS	Tommy Lee Jones, *The Executioner's Song*, NBC	Laurence Olivier, *King Lear*, SYN
Actress—Limited Series or Special	Ingrid Bergman, *A Woman Called Golda*, SYN	Barbara Stanwyck, *The Thorn Birds*, ABC	Jane Fonda, *The Dollmaker*, ABC
Supporting Actor—Limited Series or Special	Laurence Olivier, *Brideshead Revisited*, PBS	Richard Kiley, *The Thorn Birds*, ABC	Art Carney, *Terrible Joe Moran*, CBS
Supporting Actress—Limited Series or Special	Penny Fuller, *Elephant Man*, ABC	Jean Simmons, *The Thorn Birds*, ABC	Roxana Zal, *Something About Amelia*, ABC
Director—Limited Series or Special	Marvin J. Chomsky, *Inside the Third Reich*, ABC	John Erman, *Who Will Love My Children?* ABC	Jeff Bleckner, *Concealed Enemies*, PBS
Writer—Limited Series or Special	Corey Blechman (Teleplay); Barry Morrow (Story), *Bill*, CBS	Marshall Herskovitz (Teleplay); Edward Zwick, Marshall Herskovitz (Story), *Special Bulletin*, NBC	William Hanley, *Something About Amelia*, ABC
Daytime Drama Series	*The Guiding Light*, CBS	*The Young & The Restless*, CBS	*General Hospital*, ABC
Actor—Daytime Drama Series	Anthony Geary, *General Hospital*, ABC	Robert Woods, *One Life to Live*, ABC	Larry Bryggman, *As the World Turns*, CBS
Actress—Daytime Drama Series	Robin Strasser, *One Life To Live*, ABC	Dorothy Lyman, *All My Children*, ABC	Erika Slezak, *One Life To Live*, ABC
Supporting Actor—Daytime Drama Series	David Lewis, *General Hospital*, ABC	Darnell Williams, *All My Children*, ABC	Justin Deas, *As the World Turns*, CBS
Supporting Actress—Daytime Drama Series	Dorothy Lyman, *All My Children*, ABC	Louise Shaffer, *Ryan's Hope*, ABC	Judi Evans, *The Guiding Light*, CBS
Host—Game Show	Bob Barker, *The Price Is Right*, CBS	Betty White, *Just Men!*, NBC	Bob Barker, *The Price Is Right*, CBS
Host—Talk or Service	Phil Donahue, *Donahue*, SYN	Phil Donahue, *Donahue*, SYN	Gary Collins, *Hour Magazine*, SYN
Game Show	*Password Plus*, NBC	*The New $25,000 Pyramid*, CBS	*The $25,000 Pyramid*, CBS
Talk or Service Series	*The Richard Simmons Show*, SYN	*This Old House*, PBS	*Woman to Woman*, SYN
Children's Program	*The Wave*, ABC	*Big Bird in China*, NBC	*He Makes Me Feel Like Dancin'*, NBC
Children's Series	*Captain Kangaroo*, CBS	*Smurfs*, NBC	*Captain Kangaroo*, CBS

	1984–85	1985–86	1986–87
Drama	*Cagney and Lacey*, CBS	*Cagney & Lacey*, CBS	*L. A. Law*, NBC
Actor—Drama Series	William Daniels, *St. Elsewhere*, NBC	William Daniels, *St. Elsewhere*, NBC	Bruce Willis, *Moonlighting*, ABC
Actress—Drama Series	Tyne Daly, *Cagney & Lacey*, CBS	Sharon Gless, *Cagney & Lacey*, CBS	Sharon Gless, *Cagney & Lacey*, CBS
Supporting Actor—Drama Series	Edward James Olmos, *Miami Vice*, NBC	John Karlen, *Cagney & Lacey*, CBS	John Hillerman, *Magnum, P.I.*, CBS
Supporting Actress—Drama Series	Betty Thomas, *Hill Street Blues*, NBC	Bonnie Bartlett, *St. Elsewhere*, NBC	Bonnie Bartlett, *St. Elsewhere*, NBC
Director—Drama Series	Karen Arthur, *Cagney & Lacey*, CBS	Georg Stanford Brown, *Cagney & Lacey*, CBS	Gregory Hoblit, *L.A. Law*, NBC
Writer—Drama Series	Patricia M. Green, *Cagney & Lacey*, CBS	Tom Fontana, John Tinker, and John Masius, *St. Elsewhere*, NBC	Steven Bochco, Terry Louise Fisher, *L.A. Law*, NBC
Comedy	*The Cosby Show*, NBC	*The Golden Girls*, NBC	*The Golden Girls*, NBC
Actor—Comedy Series	Robert Guillaume, *Benson*, ABC	Michael J. Fox, *Family Ties*, NBC	Michael J. Fox, *Family Ties*, NBC
Actress—Comedy Series	Jane Curtin, *Kate & Allie*, CBS	Betty White, *The Golden Girls*, NBC	Rue McClanahan, *The Golden Girls*, NBC
Supporting Actor—Comedy Series	John Larroquette, *Night Court*, NBC	John Larroquette, *Night Court*, NBC	John Larroquette, *Night Court*, NBC
Supporting Actress—Comedy Series	Rhea Perlman, *Cheers*, NBC	Rhea Perlman, *Cheers*, NBC	Jackée Harry, *227*, NBC
Director—Comedy Series	Jay Sandrich, *The Cosby Show*, NBC	Jay Sandrich, *The Cosby Show*, NBC	Terry Hughes, *The Golden Girls*, NBC
Writer—Comedy Series	Ed. Weinberger, Michael Leeson, *The Cosby Show*, NBC	Barry Fanaro and Mort Nathan, *The Golden Girls*, NBC	Gary David Goldberg, Alan Uger, *Family Ties*, NBC
Drama/Comedy Special	*Do You Remember Love*, CBS	*Love Is Never Silent*, NBC	*Promise*, CBS
Variety, Music, or Comedy Program	*Motown Returns to the Apollo*, NBC	*The Kennedy Center Honors: A Celebration of the Performing Arts*, CBS	*The 1987 Tony Awards*, CBS
Individual Performance—Variety or Music Program	George Hearn, *Sweeney Todd*, PBS	Whitney Houston, *The 28th Annual Grammy Awards*, CBS	Robin Williams, *A Carol Burnett Special: Carol, Carl, Whoopi & Robin*, ABC
Director—Variety or Music	Terry Hughes, *Sweeney Todd*, PBS	Waris Hussein, *Copacabana*, CBS	Don Mischer, *The Kennedy Center Honors: A Celebration of the Performing Arts*, CBS
Writer—Variety or Music	Gerard Mulligan, Sandy Frank, Joe Toplyn, Chris Elliott, Matt Wickline, Jeff Martin, Eddie Gorodetsky, Randy Cohen, Larry Jacobson, Kevin Curran, Fred Graver, Merrill Markoe, and David Letterman, *Late Night with David Letterman*, NBC	David Letterman, Steve O'Donnell, Sandy Frank, Joe Toplyn, Chris Elliott, Matt Wickline, Jeff Martin, Gerard Mulligan, Randy Cohen, Larry Jacobson, Kevin Curran, Fred Graver, and Merrill Markoe, *Late Night with David Letterman*, NBC	Steve O'Donnell, Sandy Frank, Joe Toplyn, Chris Elliott, Matt Wickline, Jeff Martin, Gerard Mulligan, Randy Cohen, Larry Jacobson, Kevin Curran, Fred Graver, Adam Resnick, and David Letterman, *Late Night with David Letterman*, NBC

	1984–85	**1985–86**	**1986–87**
Miniseries	*The Jewel in the Crown*, PBS	*Peter the Great*, NBC	*A Year in the Life*, NBC
Actor—Miniseries	Richard Crenna, *The Rape of Richard Beck*, ABC	Dustin Hoffman, *Death of a Salesman*, CBS	James Woods, *Promise*, CBS
Actress—Miniseries	Joanne Woodward, *Do You Remember Love*, CBS	Marlo Thomas, *Nobody's Child*, CBS	Gena Rowlands, *The Betty Ford Story*, ABC
Supporting Actor—Miniseries or Special	Karl Malden, *Fatal Vision*, NBC	John Malkovich, *Death of a Salesman*, CBS	Dabney Coleman, *Sworn to Silence*, ABC
Supporting Actress—Miniseries/ Limited Series or Special	Kim Stanley, *Cat on a Hot Tin Roof*, PBS	Colleen Dewhurst, *Between Two Women*, CBS	Piper Laurie, *Promise*, CBS
Director—Miniseries or Special	Lamont Johnson, *Wallenberg: A Hero's Story*, NBC	Joseph Sargent, *Love Is Never Silent*, NBC	Glenn Jordan, *Promise*, CBS
Writer—Miniseries or Special	Vickie Patik, *Do You Remember Love*, CBS	Ron Cowen and Daniel Lipman (Teleplay); Sherman Yellen (Story), *An Early Frost*, NBC	Richard Friedenberg (Teleplay); Kenneth Blackwell, Tennyson Flowers, and Richard Friedenberg (Story), *Promise*, CBS
Daytime Drama Series	*The Young and the Restless*, CBS	*The Young and the Restless*, CBS	*As the World Turns*, CBS
Actor—Daytime Drama Series	Darnell Williams, *All My Children*, ABC	David Canary, *All My Children*, ABC	Larry Bryggman, *As the World Turns*, CBS
Actress—Daytime Drama Series	Kim Zimmer, *Guiding Light*, CBS	Erika Slezak, *One Life To Live*, ABC	Kim Zimmer, *Guiding Light*, CBS
Supporting Actor—Daytime Drama Series	Larry Gates, *Guiding Light*, CBS	John Wesley Shipp, *As the World Turns*, CBS	Gregg Marx, *As the World Turns*, CBS
Supporting Actress—Daytime Drama Series	Beth Maitland, *The Young and the Restless*, CBS	Leann Hunley, *Days of Our Lives*, NBC	Kathleen Noone, *All My Children*, ABC
Ingenue— Daytime Drama Series	Tracey E. Bregman, *The Young and the Restless*, CBS	Ellen Wheeler, *Another World*, NBC	Martha Byrne, *As the World Turns*, CBS
Younger Leading Man— Daytime Drama Series	Brian Bloom, *As the World Turns*, CBS	Michael E. Knight, *All My Children*, ABC	Michael E. Knight, *All My Children*, ABC
Host—Game Show	Dick Clark, *The $25,000 Pyramid*, CBS	Dick Clark, *The $25,000 Pyramid*, CBS	Bob Barker, *The Price Is Right*, CBS
Host—Talk or Service	Phil Donahue, *Donahue*, SYN	Phil Donahue, *Donahue*, SYN	Oprah Winfrey, *The Oprah Winfrey Show*, SYN
Game Show	*The $25,000 Pyramid*, CBS	*The $25,000 Pyramid*, CBS	*The $25,000 Pyramid*, CBS
Talk, Service or Variety Series	*Donahue*, SYN	*Donahue*, SYN	*The Oprah Winfrey Show*, SYN
Children's Program	*Displaced Person*, PBS	*Anne of Green Gables*, PBS	*Jim Henson's The Storyteller: Hans My Hedgehog*, NBC
Children's Series	*Sesame Street*, PBS	*Sesame Street*, PBS	*Sesame Street*, PBS

	1987–88	1988–89	1989–90
Drama	*thirtysomething*, ABC	*L.A. Law*, NBC	*L.A. Law*, NBC
Actor—Drama Series	Richard Kiley, *A Year in the Life*, NBC	Carroll O'Connor, *In the Heat of the Night*, NBC	Peter Falk, *Columbo*, ABC
Actress—Drama Series	Tyne Daly, *Cagney & Lacey*, CBS	Dana Delany, *China Beach*, ABC	Patricia Wettig, *thirtysomething*, ABC
Supporting Actor—Drama Series	Larry Drake, *L.A. Law*, NBC	Larry Drake, *L.A. Law*, NBC	Jimmy Smits, *L.A. Law*, NBC
Supporting Actress—Drama Series	Patricia Wettig, *thirtysomething*, ABC	Melanie Mayron, *thirtysomething*, ABC	Marg Helgenberger, *China Beach*, ABC
Director—Drama Series	Mark Tinker, *St. Elsewhere*, NBC	Robert Altman, *Tanner '88*, HBO	Thomas Carter, *Equal Justice*, ABC; Scott Winant, *thirtysomething*, ABC
Writer—Drama Series	Paul Haggis, Marshall Herskovitz, *thirtysomething*, ABC	Joseph Dougherty, *thirtysomething*, ABC	David E. Kelley, *L.A. Law*, NBC
Comedy	*The Wonder Years*, ABC	*Cheers*, NBC	*Murphy Brown*, CBS
Actor—Comedy Series	Michael J. Fox, *Family Ties*, NBC	Richard Mulligan, *Empty Nest*, NBC	Ted Danson, *Cheers*, NBC
Actress—Comedy Series	Beatrice Arthur, *The Golden Girls*, NBC	Candice Bergen, *Murphy Brown*, CBS	Candice Bergen, *Murphy Brown*, CBS
Supporting Actor—Comedy Series	John Larroquette, *Night Court*, NBC	Woody Harrelson, *Cheers*, NBC	Alex Rocco, *The Famous Teddy Z*, CBS
Supporting Actress—Comedy Series	Estelle Getty, *The Golden Girls*, NBC	Rhea Perlman, *Cheers*, NBC	Bebe Neuwirth, *Cheers*, NBC
Director—Comedy Series	Gregory Hoblit, *Hooperman*, ABC	Peter Baldwin, *The Wonder Years*, ABC	Michael Dinner, *The Wonder Years*, ABC
Writer—Comedy Series	Hugh Wilson, *Frank's Place*, CBS	Diane English, *Murphy Brown*, CBS	Bob Brush, *The Wonder Years*, ABC
Drama/Comedy Special	*Inherit the Wind*, NBC	*Day One*, CBS	*Caroline?* CBS; *The Incident*, CBS
Variety, Music, or Comedy Program	*Irving Berlin's 100th Birthday Celebration*, CBS	*The Tracey Ullman Show*, FOX	*In Living Color*, FOX
Individual Performance—Variety or Music Program	Robin Williams, *ABC Presents a Royal Gala*, ABC	Linda Ronstadt, *Canciones de Mi Padre*, PBS	Tracey Ullman, *The Best of the Tracey Ullman Show*, FOX
Director—Variety or Music	Patricia Birch and Humphrey Burton, *Celebrating Gershwin*, PBS	Jim Henson, *The Jim Henson Hour*, NBC	Dwight Hemion, *The Kennedy Center Honors: A Celebration of the Performing Arts*, CBS

1987–88 1988–89 1989–90

	1987–88	1988–89	1989–90
Writer—Variety or Music	Jackie Mason, *Jackie Mason on Broadway*, HBO	James Downey, head writer; John Bowman, A. Whitney Brown, Gregory Daniels, Tom Davis, Al Franken, Shannon Gaughan, Jack Handey, Phil Hartman, Lorne Michaels, Mike Myers, Conan O'Brien, Bob Odenkirk, Herb Sargent, Tom Schiller, Robert Smigel, Bonnie Turner, Terry Turner, and Christine Zander, writers; George Meyer, additional sketches, *Saturday Night Live*, NBC	Billy Crystal, *Billy Crystal: Midnight Train to Moscow*, HBO; James L. Brooks, Heide Perlman, Sam Simon, Jerry Belson, Marc Flanagan, Dinah Kirgo, Jay Kogen, Wallace Wolodarsky, Ian Praiser, Marilyn Suzanne Miller, Tracey Ullman, *The Tracey Ullman Show*, FOX
Miniseries	*The Murder of Mary Phagan*, NBC	*War and Remembrance*, ABC	*Drug Wars: The Camarena Story*, NBC
Actor—Miniseries or Special	Jason Robards, *Inherit the Wind*, NBC	James Woods, *My Name is Bill W.*, ABC	Hume Cronyn, *Age-Old Friends*, HBO
Actress—Miniseries or Special	Jessica Tandy, *Foxfire*, CBS	Holly Hunter, *Roe vs. Wade*, NBC	Barbara Hershey, *A Killing in a Small Town*, CBS
Supporting Actor—Miniseries or Special	John Shea, *Baby M*, ABC	Derek Jacobi, *The Tenth Man*, CBS	Vincent Gardenia, *Age-Old Friends*, HBO
Supporting Actress—Miniseries or Special	Jane Seymour, *Onassis: The Richest Man in the World*, ABC	Colleen Dewhurst, *Those She Left Behind*, NBC	Eva Marie Saint, *People Like Us*, NBC
Director—Miniseries or Special	Lamont Johnson, *Gore Vidal's Lincoln*, NBC	Simon Wincer, *Lonesome Dove*, CBS	Joseph Sargent, *Caroline?* CBS
Writer—Miniseries or Special	William Hanley, *The Attic: The Hiding of Anne Frank*, CBS	Abby Mann, Robin Vote, and Ron Hutchison, *Murderers Among Us: The Simon Wiesenthal Story*, HBO	Terrence McNally, *Andre's Mother*, PBS
Daytime Drama Series	*Santa Barbara*, NBC	*Santa Barbara*, NBC	*Santa Barbara*, NBC
Actor—Daytime Drama Series	David Canary, *All My Children*, ABC	David Canary, *All My Children*, ABC	A. Martinez, *Santa Barbara*, NBC
Actress—Daytime Drama Series	Helen Gallagher, *Ryan's Hope*, ABC	Marcy Walker, *Santa Barbara*, NBC	Kim Zimmer, *Guiding Light*, CBS
Supp. Actor—Daytime Drama	Justin Deas, *Santa Barbara*, NBC	Justin Deas, *Santa Barbara*, NBC	Henry Darrow, *Santa Barbara*, NBC
Supporting Actress—Daytime Drama Series	Ellen Wheeler, *All My Children*, ABC	Debbi Morgan, *All My Children*, ABC; Nancy Lee Grahn, *Santa Barbara*, NBC	Julia Barr, *All My Children*, ABC
Ingenue—Daytime Drama Series	Julianne Moore, *As the World Turns*, CBS	Kimberly McCullough, *General Hospital*, ABC	Cady McClain, *All My Children*, ABC
Younger Leading Man—Daytime Drama Series	Billy Warlock, *Days of Our Lives*, NBC	Justin Gocke, *Santa Barbara*, NBC	Andrew Kavovit, *As the World Turns*, CBS
Host—Game Show	Bob Barker, *The Price Is Right*, CBS	Alex Trebek, *Jeopardy!*, SYN	Alex Trebek, *Jeopardy!*, SYN; Bob Barker, *The Price Is Right*, CBS
Host—Talk or Service Show	Phil Donahue, *Donahue*, SYN	Sally Jessy Raphael, *Sally Jessy Raphael*, SYN	Joan Rivers, *The Joan Rivers Show*, SYN
Game Show	*The Price Is Right*, CBS	*The $25,000 Pyramid*, CBS	*Jeopardy!*, SYN
Talk, Service, or Variety Series	*The Oprah Winfrey Show*, SYN	*The Oprah Winfrey Show*, SYN	*Sally Jessy Raphael*, SYN
Children's Program	*The Secret Garden*, CBS	*Free To Be . . . A Family*, ABC	*A Mother's Courage: The Mary Thomas Story*, NBC
Children's Series	*Sesame Street*, PBS	*Newton's Apple*, PBS	*Reading Rainbow*, PBS

	1990–91	**1991–92**	**1992–93**
Drama	*L.A. Law*, NBC	*Northern Exposure*, CBS	*Picket Fences*, CBS
Actor—Drama Series	James Earl Jones, *Gabriel's Fire*, ABC	Christopher Lloyd, *Avonlea*, DIS	Tom Skerritt, *Picket Fences*, CBS
Actress—Drama Series	Patricia Wettig, *thirtysomething*, ABC	Dana Delany, *China Beach*, ABC	Kathy Baker, *Picket Fences*, CBS
Supporting Actor— Drama Series	Timothy Busfield, *thirtysomething*, ABC	Richard Dysart, *L.A. Law*, NBC	Chad Lowe, *Life Goes On*, ABC
Supporting Actress— Drama Series	Madge Sinclair, *Gabriel's Fire*, ABC	Valerie Mahaffey, *Northern Exposure*, CBS	Mary Alice, *I'll Fly Away*, NBC
Director—Drama Series	Thomas Carter, *Equal Justice*, ABC	Eric Laneuville, *I'll Fly Away*, NBC	Barry Levinson, *Homicide—Life on the Street*, NBC
Writer—Drama Series	David E. Kelley, *L.A. Law*, NBC	Andrew Schneider and Diane Frolov, *Northern Exposure*, CBS	Tom Fontana, *Homicide—Life on the Street*, NBC
Comedy	*Cheers*, NBC	*Murphy Brown*, CBS	*Seinfeld*, NBC
Actor—Comedy Series	Burt Reynolds, *Evening Shade*, CBS	Craig T. Nelson, *Coach*, ABC	Ted Danson, *Cheers*, NBC
Actress—Comedy Series	Kirstie Alley, *Cheers*, NBC	Candice Bergen, *Murphy Brown*, CBS	Roseanne Arnold, *Roseanne*, ABC
Supporting Actor— Comedy Series	Jonathan Winters, *Davis Rules*, ABC	Michael Jeter, *Evening Shade*, CBS	Michael Richards, *Seinfeld*, NBC
Supp. Actress—Comedy Series	Bebe Neuwirth, *Cheers*, NBC	Laurie Metcalf, *Roseanne*, ABC	Laurie Metcalf, *Roseanne*, ABC
Director—Comedy Series	James Burrows, *Cheers*, NBC	Barnet Kellman, *Murphy Brown*, CBS	Betty Thomas, *Dream On*, HBO
Writer—Comedy Series	Gary Dontzig and Steven Peterman, *Murphy Brown*, CBS	Elaine Pope and Larry Charles, *Seinfeld*, NBC	Larry David, *Seinfeld*, NBC
Variety, Music, or Comedy Program	*The 63rd Annual Academy Awards*, ABC	*The Tonight Show Starring Johnny Carson*, NBC	*Saturday Night Live*, NBC
Individual Performance— Variety or Music Program	Billy Crystal, *The 63rd Annual Academy Awards*, ABC	Bette Midler, *The Tonight Show Starring Johnny Carson*, NBC	Dana Carvey, *Saturday Night Live*, NBC
Director—Variety or Music	Hal Gurnee, *Late Night with David Letterman*, NBC	Patricia Birch, *Unforgettable with Love: Natalie Cole Sings the Songs of Nat King Cole*, PBS	Walter C. Miller, *The 1992 Tony Awards*, CBS
Writer—Variety or Music	Hal Kanter and Buz Kohan, writers; Billy Crystal, David Steinberg, Bruce Vilanch, and Robert Wuhl (Special Material), *The 63rd Annual Academy Awards*, ABC	Hal Kanter and Buz Kohan, writers); Billy Crystal, Marc Shaiman, David Steinberg, Robert Wuhl, and Bruce Vilanch, special material, *The 64th Annual Academy Awards*, ABC	Judd Apatow, Robert Cohen, David Cross, Brent Forrester, Jeff Kahn, Bruce Kirschbaum, Bob Odenkirk, Sultan Pepper, Dino Stamatopoulos, Ben Stiller, *The Ben Stiller Show*, FOX
Made for Television Movie	—	*Miss Rose White* Hallmark Hall of Fame, NBC	*Barbarians at the Gate*, HBO; *Stalin*, HBO
Miniseries	*Separate but Equal*, ABC	*A Woman Named Jackie*, NBC	*Prime Suspect 2*, PBS

	1990–91	1991–92	1992–93
Actor—Miniseries or Special	John Gielgud, *Summer's Lease*, PBS	Beau Bridges, *Without Warning: The James Brady Story*, HBO	Robert Morse, *Tru*, PBS
Actress—Miniseries or Special	Lynn Whitfield, *The Josephine Baker Story*, HBO	Gena Rowlands, *Face of a Stranger*, CBS	Holly Hunter, *The Positively True Adventures of the Alleged Texas Cheerleader-Murdering Mom*, HBO
Supporting Actor—Miniseries or Special	James Earl Jones, *Heat Wave*, TNT	Hume Cronyn, *Neil Simon's Broadway Bound*, ABC	Beau Bridges, *The Positively True Adventures of the Alleged Texas Cheerleader-Murdering Mom*, HBO
Supporting Actress—Miniseries or Special	Ruby Dee, *Decoration Day*, NBC	Amanda Plummer, *Miss Rose White*, NBC	Mary Tyler Moore, *Stolen Babies*, LIF
Director—Miniseries or Special	Brian Gibson, *The Josephine Baker Story*, HBO	Daniel Petrie, *Mark Twain and Me*, DIS	James Sadwith, *Sinatra*, CBS
Writer—Miniseries or Special	Andrew Davies, *House of Cards*, PBS	John Falsey and Joshua Brand, *I'll Fly Away*, NBC	Jane Anderson, *The Positively True Adventures of the Alleged Texas Cheerleader-Murdering Mom*, HBO
Daytime Drama Series	*As the World Turns*, CBS	*All My Children*, ABC	*All My Children*, ABC
Actor—Daytime Drama Series	Peter Bergman, *The Young and the Restless*, CBS	Peter Bergman, *The Young and the Restless*, CBS	Michael Zaslow, *Guiding Light*, CBS
Actress—Daytime Drama Series	Finola Hughes, *General Hospital*, ABC	Erika Slezak, *One Life to Live*, ABC	Hillary B. Smith, *One Life to Live*, ABC
Supporting Actor—Daytime Drama Series	Bernie Barrow, *Loving*, ABC	Thom Christopher, *One Life to Live*, ABC	Justin Deas, *Guiding Light*, CBS
Supporting Actress—Daytime Drama Series	Jess Walton, *The Young and the Restless*, CBS	Maeve Kinkead, *Guiding Light*, CBS	Susan Haskell, *One Life to Live*, ABC
Younger Actress—Daytime Drama Series	Anne Heche, *Another World*, NBC	Tricia Cast, *The Young and the Restless*, CBS	Melissa Hayden, *Guiding Light*, CBS
Younger Leading Man—Daytime Drama Series	Rick Hearst, *Guiding Light*, CBS	Kristoff St. John, *The Young and the Restless*, CBS	Roger Howarth, *One Life to Live*, ABC
Host—Game Show	Bob Barker, *The Price Is Right*, CBS	Bob Barker, *The Price Is Right*, CBS	—
Host—Talk or Service Show	Oprah Winfrey, *The Oprah Winfrey Show*, SYN	Oprah Winfrey, *The Oprah Winfrey Show*, SYN	Oprah Winfrey, *The Oprah Winfrey Show*, SYN
Game Show	*Jeopardy!*, SYN	*Jeopardy!*, SYN	
Talk, Service, or Variety Series	*The Oprah Winfrey Show*, SYN	The Oprah Winfrey Show, SYN	*The Oprah Winfrey Show*, SYN
Children's Program	*You Can't Grow Home Again: A 3-2-1 Contact Extra*, PBS	*Mark Twain and Me*, DIS	
Children's Series	*Sesame Street*, PBS	*Sesame Street*, PBS	*Sesame Street*, PBS

	1993-94	**1994-95**
Drama	*Picket Fences*, CBS	*NYPD Blue*, ABC
Actor—Drama Series	Dennis Franz, *NYPD Blue*, ABC	Mandy Patinkin, *Chicago Hope*, CBS
Actress—Drama Series	Sela Ward, *Sisters*, NBC	Kathy Baker, *Picket Fences*, CBS
Supporting Actor—Drama Series	Fyvush Finkel, *Picket Fences*, CBS	Ray Walston, *Picket Fences*, CBS
Supporting Actress—Drama Series	Leigh Taylor-Young, *Picket Fences*, CBS	Julianna Margulies, *ER*, NBC
Director—Drama Series	Daniel Sackheim, *NYPD Blue*, ABC	Mimi Leder, *ER*, NBC
Writer—Drama Series	*NYPD Blue*, ABC	*ER*, NBC
Comedy	*Frasier*, NBC	*Frasier*, NBC
Actor—Comedy Series	Kelsey Grammer, *Frasier*, NBC	Kelsey Grammer, *Frasier*, NBC
Actress—Comedy Series	Candice Bergen, *Murphy Brown*, CBS	Candice Bergen, *Murphy Brown*, CBS
Supporting Actor—Comedy Series	Michael Richards, *Seinfeld*, NBC	David Hyde Pierce, *Frasier*, NBC
Supp. Actress—Comedy Series	Laurie Metcalf, *Roseanne*, ABC	Christine Baranski, *Cybill*, CBS
Director—Comedy Series	James Burrows, *Frasier*, NBC	David Lee, *Frasier*, NBC
Writer—Comedy Series	*Frasier*, NBC	*Frasier*, NBC
Variety, Music, or Comedy Program	*Late Show With David Letterman*, CBS	*The Tonight Show With Jay Leno*, NBC
Individual Performance—Variety or Music Program	Tracey Ullman, *Tracey Ullman Takes On New York*, HBO	Barbra Streisand, *Barbra Streisand: The Concert*, HBO
Director—Variety or Music	Walter C. Miller, *The Tony Awards*, CBS	Jeff Margolis, *The 67th Annual Academy Awards*, ABC
Writer—Variety or Music	*Dennis Miller Live*, HBO	*Dennis Miller Live*, HBO
Made for Television Movie	*And the Band Played On*, HBO	*Indictment: The McMartin Trial*, HBO
Miniseries	*Mystery: Prime Suspect 3*, PBS	*Joseph*, TNT

	1993-94	**1994-95**
Actor—Miniseries or Special	Hume Cronyn, *Hallmark Hall of Fame: To Dance With the White Dog*, CBS	Raul Julia, *The Burning Season*, HBO
Actress—Miniseries or Special	Kirstie Alley, *David's Mother*, CBS	Glenn Close, *Serving in Silence: The Margarethe Cammermeyer Story*, NBC
Supporting Actor—Miniseries or Special	Michael Goorjian, *David's Mother*, CBS	Donald Sutherland, *Citizen X*, HBO
Supporting Actress—Miniseries or Special	Cicely Tyson, *Oldest Living Confederate Widow Tells All*, CBS	Judy Davis, *Serving in Silence: The Margarethe Cammermeyer Story*, NBC
Director—Miniseries or Special	John Frankenheimer, *Against the Wall*, HBO	John Frankenheimer, *The Burning Season*, HBO
Writer—Miniseries or Special	*David's Mother*, CBS	*Serving in Silence: The Margarethe Cammermeyer Story*, NBC
Daytime Drama Series	*General Hospital*, ABC	
Actor—Daytime Drama Series	Justin Deas, *Guiding Light*, CBS	
Actress—Daytime Drama Series	Erika Slezak, *One Life to Live*, ABC	
Supporting Actor—Daytime Drama Series	Jerry Ver Dorn, *Guiding Light*, CBS	
Supporting Actress—Daytime Drama Series	Rena Sofer, *General Hospital*, ABC	
Younger Actress—Daytime Drama Series	Sarah Michelle Gellar, *All My Children*, ABC	
Younger Leading Man—Daytime Drama Series	Jonathan Jackson, *General Hospital*, ABC	
Host—Game Show	—	
Host—Talk or Service Show	Oprah Winfrey, *The Oprah Winfrey Show*, SYN	
Game Show	*Jeopardy!*, SYN	
Talk, Service, or Variety Series	*The Oprah Winfrey Show*, SYN	
Children's Program	*A Child Betrayed: The Calvin Mire Story*, HBO	
Children's Series	*Nick News*, NIK	

EMMY LOSERS

Despite their numerous contributions to the world of TV, the following performers have never taken home that elusive Emmy. *All My Children*'s Susan Lucci has been snubbed the most with 15 nominations but no wins.

Gracie Allen
Desi Arnaz
Edgar Bergen
Charles Durning
Judy Garland
Jackie Gleason
Andy Griffith
Angela Lansbury
Susan Lucci
Ed Sullivan*

*the recipient of a Trustees Award in 1971, but never won in a competitive category.

SONG

PICKS & PANS 1995

Here are PEOPLE's candid assessments of the year's albums, listed alphabetically by artist. Our favorites are marked with an asterisk. If you're looking for a good listen, you don't have to stick with popular music; some of our favorites are Gregorian chants—see the Benedictine Monks's *The Soul of Chant*—and Cecilia Bartoli's ethereal arias in *Mozart Portraits*. But don't get us wrong: we regard the Beatles' *Live at the BBC* as pure-pop bliss.

HEAD OVER HEELS
Paula Abdul

While Abdul remains a somewhat anemic balladeer, she settles comfortably into her narrow range on this album. Sounding husky and positively sexy, she finds a pop persona that really works.

*THANK YOU FOR THE MUSIC
Abba

Thrilling pure-pop abandon that proves that Abba was more than shrill harmonies, banal lyrics, and tacky stage wear.

REFLECTIONS
After 7

True to its title, After 7's *Reflections* is mostly about looking back musically. The gently swinging songs are packed with soaring harmonies, silky arrangements, and sweet words of love.

AND THE MUSIC SPEAKS
All-4-One

The group's idealized version of love can be wonderfully soothing, but the one-dimensional romanticism rings callow and shallow.

*JULIE ANDREWS—BROADWAY: THE MUSIC OF RICHARD RODGERS
Julie Andrews

Julie Andrews discharges her debt to Rodgers and Hammerstein with a voice almost as pure as when it first echoed through the Alps some 30 years ago.

WONDERFUL
Adam Ant

With his first album in five years, Ant reminds us that he is a modestly talented fellow whose real genius was for selling a fad.

*MOZART PORTRAITS
Cecilia Bartoli

Every syllable of these Mozart arias is infused with life.

*NO WAYS TIRED
Fontella Bass

This collection of traditional sounding gospel numbers *rocks*.

*LIVE AT THE BBC
The Beatles

A 56-song compilation of live performances on the English radio network between 1963 and 1965; every number is rendered with flawless harmony and deft musicianship.

THE ANDREW LLOYD WEBBER ALBUM
Laurie Beechman

Beechman tackles the songs of the mega-successful composer and comes up a winner.

REACHIN' BACK
Regina Belle

Belle's newest collection of covers doesn't offer any surprises, but that doesn't matter. Her lovely voice is clearly the main attraction here.

KING
Belly

With a few exceptions, their new songs offer a bunch of great riffs without any real center.

*THE SOUL OF CHANT
The Benedictine Monks of Santo Domingo de Silos

Better than last year's *Chant*, the monks' voices, gently colored by an organ accompaniment, admirably reflect the music's calm, ethereal beauty.

POST
Björk

With her piercing wail and unpeggable pop tunes, Björk remains an acquired taste.

HOME
Blessid Union of Souls

Essentially bereft of soul with overproduced string arrangements and emetic lyrics.

SOUP
Blind Melon

A crock pot filled with disparate ingredients, from early Led Zepish riffs to Dead-inspired fills.

THESE DAYS
Bon Jovi

On its sixth studio release, Bon Jovi strike a skillful balance between the obligatory raucous pile drivers that fill stadiums and the emotional ballads that give an album legs.

*BOXING GANDHIS
Boxing Gandhis

A smart, sophisticated update of '70s R&B and rock, this gritty, passionate CD gives the funk genre a rootsy kick in the booty.

CHEAPNESS & BEAUTY
Boy George

Cheapness & Beauty is at its best on the fresh breeze of the title tune and the fragile "If I Could Fly"—when George dumps the cheap, hard-rock sounds and puts melodic beauty first.

MISTY EYED ADVENTURES
Máire Brennan

Adventures like these may not be as in-your-face as a gun-toting gangsta-rap tirade, but they pack a similar wallop.

*SIXTEEN STONE
Bush
Crammed with exceedingly catchy, soulful, and witty songs.

HURT CITY
Stacy Dean Campbell
This 28-year-old son of the Southwest has enough sob in his voice to make the old-fashioned country-music weepers he's partial to sound great.

LITTLE ACTS OF TREASON
Carlene Carter
The granddaughter of country singing legend Maybelle Carter, daughter of June Carter and 1950s hitmaker Carl Smith, and stepdaughter of Johnny Cash, gives us more of her joyous vocal abandon.

*HAPPY DAYS
Catherine Wheel
Catherine Wheel makes angst gorgeous as well as purifying.

*WHIRLIGIG
The Caulfields
A winning combination of witty wordplay and memorable melodies toughed up with blasts of rock-guitar crunch.

*THE DARK BEFORE THE DAWN
Cyrus Chestnut
Chestnut shows an orchestral command of the keyboard and a sophisticated sense of swing.

*THE LONG BLACK VEIL
The Chieftains
A hearty mixture of irreverence and respect for tradition—the listening just gets better and better.

DUBLIN BLUES
Guy Clark
A fine and sturdy album from a fabled songwriter.

*DEMI-CENTENNIAL
Rosemary Clooney
It's all here: taste, musicianship, simplicity, and directness, the

voice that's equal parts sun and seductiveness.

*KOJAK VARIETY
Elvis Costello
Catchy yet obscure songs only an old record fanatic would know—Costello seems to be having more fun on this record than he has had in years.

WINDOW
Christopher Cross
Vintage Cross with maddeningly melodic tunes that make it seem like it's 1981 again.

*THE HONEYMOON IS OVER
The Cruel Sea
A stellar marriage of instrumentals and vocal workouts. This Australian group might be in for a long honeymoon with U.S. fans.

TERENCE TRENT D'ARBY'S VIBRATOR
Terence Trent D'Arby
D'Arby continues to push his considerable talent and his tunes over the top.

*THE COMPLETE LIVE AT THE PLUGGED NICKEL 1965
Miles Davis
This boxed set is your chance to experience the mercurial magic of the late trumpeter near the beginning of his long, successful association with saxophonist Wayne Shorter, pianist Herbie Hancock, bassist Ron Carter, and drummer Tony Williams.

*BOHEME
Deep Forest
Wherever Deep Forest puts

down its roots, it manages to conjure up a haunting musical hybrid. On this enthralling album the inspiration is Balkan rather than African.

*TWISTED
Del Amitri
Their low-key approach casts a lovely, elegiac spell.

LEARNING ENGLISH, LESSON ONE
Die Toten Hosen
For aging punk rock fans, listening to this album is as nostalgic as thumbing through your high school yearbook.

THE FRENCH ALBUM
Céline Dion
A Europop collection that sounds stilted to American ears and showcases Dion's emotionality rather than her elegance.

*LIVE . . . AGAIN
Don Pullen & the African Brazilian Connection
A lively, joyous session at the 1993 Montreux Jazz Festival.

THANK YOU
Duran Duran
A gaudy and haphazard collection of borrowed songs that makes for interesting listening, even when the results are ludicrous.

*MTV UNPLUGGED
Bob Dylan
A powerhouse set of mostly classic originals that Dylan approaches with dignity.

HELL FREEZES OVER
Eagles
Those old bittersweet love songs and gorgeous melodies are enough to remind us why the Eagles once soared so high.

MY CHERIE
Sheena Easton
Easton shows off her technical ability, but a chilliness seeps into otherwise well-crafted ballads.

AND SO MUCH MORE
Linda Eder
A powerful pop-inflected voice dabbed with tinges of Streisand and Maureen McGovern.

*ELASTICA
Elastica
Reminiscent of Debbie Harry and Gary Numan—when the songs work, they're vastly enjoyable.

*HEARTACHES & HARMONIES
The Everly Brothers
Four discs containing 103 songs is a lot of Everlys—but with a harmonic blend as sweet as theirs, it's time well spent.

WAITING FOR THE PUNCHLINE
Extreme
Songs that are virtual clones of the Pearl Jam style, without the sincerity or originality.

*KING FOR A DAY, FOOL FOR A LIFETIME
Faith No More
A comedown from 1992's superb *Angel Dust*, it still takes enough sharp left turns to leave its listeners alternately smiling and confused.

A SECRET LIFE
Marianne Faithfull
Faithfull's voice bears the tread marks of her indulgent past, and her songs have the poignant ring of a ravaged survivor.

SUCH SWEET SORROW
Michael Feinstein
Not a particularly felicitous match of material and talent.

*FOO FIGHTERS
Foo Fighters
On such monster stompers as "Good Grief" and "Watershed," former Nirvana drummer Dave Grohl's knockout punch seems to be aimed squarely at anyone who (wrongly) assumed that Nirvana was just another one-talent wonder.

MR. MOONLIGHT
Foreigner
Mick Jones hasn't lost his knack for crafting terse, canny, hook-bristling rock tunes.

LABOR OF LOVE
Radney Foster
Simple, buoyant melodies and a good old shuffle beat.

*JUDY GARLAND
The Complete Decca Masters (Plus)
Garland when she was glorious: a voice combining youthful exuberance and exhilaration and unforced torchiness.

*THAT'S MY KICK & GEMINI
Erroll Garner
These two albums on one CD present Garner at his best—a geyser of melodic ideas, ebullient chords, extravagant introductions, and tidally irresistible rhythm.

OLYMPIAN
Gene
Gene is England's latest Next Big Thing to feature wham-glam guitars and a fey front man with a warbly twang.

THINK WITH YOUR HEART
Debbie Gibson
A voice this unremarkable needs

inspired production and strong songs, but gets neither here.

I NEED A BREAK
Noah Gordon
Gordon's toasty twang manages to make even the most average numbers memorable.

CLINTON GREGORY
Clinton Gregory
This impressive major-label debut should bring Gregory the recognition he deserves.

FAMILY
Roy Hargrove
The 25-year-old trumpeter is again in solid form, but he seems too eager to prove his maturity to the jazz establishment.

KEEP THE FIRE BURNIN'
Dan Hartman
A posthumous compilation of vintage recordings which presents Hartman as a bland tenor with a knack for churning out picture-perfect hooks.

*TO BRING YOU MY LOVE
P J Harvey
Harvey's raw, dense music rivals that of Bob Dylan himself for sheer gut-wrenching melodrama.

ONLY EVERYTHING
Juliana Hatfield
Hatfield goes electric—a startling, and for the most part unbecoming, transformation.

*BRANDED
Isaac Hayes
Hayes retains his gift of musical gab with long, hypnotic songs

that continuously develop their musical themes.

COVER TO COVER
The Jeff Healey Band

The blind Canadian guitarist, who has attracted a following with his fiery six-string prowess, doffs an obliging hat to a few of his blues idols and other artists on this 12-song cover collection.

*BAND OF GYPSYS
Jimi Hendrix

An essential recording of Hendrix's 1969 New Year's Eve concert at the Fillmore East which delivers his brilliance with marvelous clarity.

VOODOO SOUP
Jimi Hendrix

This collection of songs that would have made up Hendrix's fourth studio album ends up sounding more like a rehearsal than a studio session.

*LAUGHING AT LIFE
Milt Hinton

The grand old jazzman takes us on an ebullient ride through scads of plucky standards.

*CHILL OUT
John Lee Hooker

The growlin' grandpa of the blues is back in fine form, with his stark guitar strumming bumping against a voice no one can beat for its world-weary authenticity.

*I LOVE YOU, PARIS
Shirley Horn

Lacks cohesiveness, but still manages to be haunting, heartbreaking, and self-revealing without being self-indulgent.

*AN EVENING WITH LENA HORNE
Lena Horne

Horne's range and sheer vocal power have diminished, but she can still imbue a lyric with such emotion that listeners may well feel they're eavesdropping.

OCTOPUS
The Human League

The synthesizer trio still tinkle about as soullessly as they did in 1982.

*FOREVER BLUE
Chris Isaak

An emotional collection, which poignantly captures the sound of a heart breaking in two.

HISTORY: PAST, PRESENT AND FUTURE—BOOK 1
Michael Jackson

It was a marketing masterstroke bundling Jackson's 15 new songs with 15 of his greatest hits. The oldies disc ensures strong sales, even if the new material won't make history. And it won't.

*TOMORROW THE GREEN GRASS
The Jayhawks

A very consistent and charismatic disc with a comfortable folksy feeling.

*FLACO JIMENEZ
Flaco Jimenez

The merry squeal of the 55-year-old Texan's accordian merges

with his electrified band to rollick, frolic, and swing.

THE SHOW, THE AFTER PARTY, THE HOTEL
Jodeci

On their first two efforts, which both went platinum, the foursome came across as the unbuttoned alternative to Boyz II Men's straitlaced romantics. With *The Show* they go all the way—and a bit too far in the rude-boy direction.

MADE IN ENGLAND
Elton John

John's chops and love affair with his craft show little sign of fatigue, but Bernie Taupin's song writing is too often banal.

*ONE
George Jones & Tammy Wynette

They're reunited and it feels so good.

THIS IS HOW WE DO IT
Montell Jordan

With a few exceptions, this album doesn't demonstrate any new moves.

LYRICAL GANGSTA
Ini Kamoze

With his sharp, staccato arrangements and reedy, singsong delivery, Kamoze often comes across like a hip-hop singer toying with Rasta patois.

YELLING AT MARY
Mary Karlzen

A polished work of folk-tinged rock.

*WANTED MAN
Paul Kelly

Gracefully woven blues, jazz, and power-pop in a lush tapestry of songs.

*WELCOME TO THE REAL WORLD
Frankie Knuckles

The second album by New York City club DJ and producer Frankie Knuckles maximizes the euphoric drama of house music and its anticipatory rush.

*NOW THAT I'VE FOUND YOU
Alison Krauss
The best under-30 female vocalist in Nashville, Krauss ushers bluegrass into the '90s.

*SOUTH OF I-10
Sonny Landreth
A blues-tinged, Cajun-spiced rock gumbo that's as strong as the Louisiana heat.

*LEADBELLY'S LAST SESSIONS
Leadbelly
This mother lode of music from an American original includes the bulk of his repertoire recorded a year before his death in 1949.

*MEDUSA
Annie Lennox
Her grand alto makes this cover album into a gorgeous patchwork quilt.

*PAPA'S DREAM
Los Lobos with Lalo Guerrero
Delicious kids' music from both sides of the border.

*THE IMPOSSIBLE BIRD
Nick Lowe
Beautifully crafted ballads and a smart sense of fun.

*BIZARRE FRUIT
M People
Dance music that stuffs in all the best elements of timeless R&B: soaring melodies, gospel backdrops, joy in repetition, and big, distinctive vocals.

THE SNAKE
Shane MacGowan
Shane MacGowan is the kind of

singer who could turn "Ave Maria" into a bawdy drinking tune. Sure it's sloppy-sounding, but it's lots of fun.

ABOVE
Mad Season
Another Seattle grunge lineup, with Pearl Jam's Mike McCready, Alice in Chain's Layne Staley, and Screaming Trees's Barrett Martin—the results are intriguing if erratic.

IF MY HEART HAD WINGS
Melissa Manchester
Manchester's fans won't be disappointed—as long as they remember they're not living in a perfect world.

PROTECTION
Massive Attack
This follow-up is sluggish, often sounding uninspired and drunk on its own languor.

*GETTIN' TO IT
Christian McBride
Jazz bassist McBride proves he can move with the groove while possessing a musical wisdom well beyond his years.

WHEN YOU GET A LITTLE LONELY
Maureen McCormick
The Brady Bunch's Marcia, McCormick possesses a sweet voice, but doesn't bring much conviction to the material.

*YOU GOTTA LOVE THAT!
Neal McCoy
A highly listenable and satifisfying follow-up album.

I REMEMBER YOU
Brian McKnight
Instead of resorting to the gratuitous flourishes and poses that dominate current twentysomething soul, McKnight woos listeners with hip classic soul.

PARIS
Malcolm McLaren
This is essentially souvenir-stand kitsch, but superior and impeccably produced pop nevertheless.

*FOR LADY DAY, VOLUME 1
Carmen McRae
A lush, smoky, and intimate homage to Billie Holiday.

TIGERLILY
Natalie Merchant
Merchant's uneven debut away from 10,000 Maniacs is most striking when she loosens up and takes her gospel-tinged lilt to dynamic musical ground.

WE LIVE HERE
Pat Metheny Group
Metheny sets his usually sonorous, rounded guitar melodies to some vaguely hiphoppish beats, and there's nothing alienating about his more streetwise approach.

*BETTE OF ROSES
Bette Midler
Midler's new effort reminds us that she is a lovely vocalist who can handle pop ballads with a delicate but sure grasp.

DRAGONFLY
Mae Moore
The simple, folkie melodies combine with Moore's reedy voice to give the record a moony, subdued mood.

*JAGGED LITTLE PILL
Alanis Morissette
Canadian singer-songwriter Morissette, 20, is quickly making a name for herself with this phenomenal U.S. debut. A constantly surprising and satisfying, collection of rock tunes.

*YES
Morphine
Overflows with both the raw, rock edge of the great Eddie Cochran and the smoky, hard-boiled mystery of Raymond Chandler.

DAYS LIKE THIS
Van Morrison
His 24th studio album finds the Irish minstrel in a looser, more festive mood—but one can't help

wishing that he had spent a little more time suffering in the studio.

*MEDITATIONS
Bheki Mseleku
An eclectic journey through musical idioms that never loses its resonance.

*MY BROTHER THE COW
Mudhoney
Punk rage and fury combined with memorable choruses and tight grooves.

UNTAMED
Heather Myles
A blend of different musical styles which offer Myles's full-throated vocals and honest, no-nonsense delivery.

*POVERTY'S PARADISE
Naughty By Nature
Vividly captures the joy and frustration of inner-city life in all its rundown glory.

BECAUSE THEY CAN
Nelson
The identical-twin, blond himbo sons of the late singer Rick Nelson really don't need a "Kick Me" album title to suggest the question: Why in the world would they make another record?

JUST ONE LOVE WILLIE NELSON: A CLASSIC & UNRELEASED COLLECTION
Willie Nelson
The Willie of *Just One Love* is the Icon in Repose, an ultra-laid-back elder statesman making classy, if unsurprising, music.

*THE TATTOOED HEART
Aaron Neville
Leaves an indelible impression of a veteran vocalist reveling in his considerable gifts.

*PERSONAL BEST: THE HARRY NILSSON ANTHOLOGY
Harry Nilsson
This two-disc box set makes it clear that Nilsson's versatile tenor could handle big-band crooning, irreverent clowning, or furious rocking.

WOWEE ZOWEE
Pavement
Feels less like Pavement than like a lazily blazed trail.

*VITALOGY
Pearl Jam
Every tune seems more open and inviting than anything the band has done before.

*LEAD ME ON
Kelly Joe Phelps
Released last summer on a small label in Portland, Ore., this album is beginning to gain well-deserved attention. Phelps's unadorned brand of country blues is hypnotic.

*THE POLICE LIVE!
The Police
11 years after officially disbanding, the trio finally offers live recordings, from a 1979 Boston show and a 1983 Atlanta show. While the first disc in the boxed set is the meatier offering, for real Police fans the whole package is worth the price of admission.

*DUMMY
Portishead
Obscure and challenging; fascinating and deeply felt.

*THE COMPLETE BUD POWELL ON VERVE
*BUD POWELL: THE COMPLETE BLUE NOTE AND ROOST RECORDINGS
Bud Powell
Both collections are a must for serious jazz lovers.

*HEART AND SOUL
Elvis Presley
A collection of the King's love songs—delicious work from one of America's greatest singers.

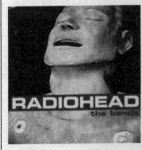

THE BENDS
Radiohead
Wide-ranging tunes chronicling excruciating experience—still, these *Bends* won't hurt at all.

ANOTHER NIGHT
Real McCoy
A database of overused sound effects—just listening is exhausting.

*OYSTER
Heather Nova
This Bermuda-born, London-based singer reveals a beautiful, delicate—and powerful—voice in this excellent collection of dreamy pop-rock tunes.

*THE SWING AND I
Eric Reed
Jazz pianist Reed mines each crisp chord and economical line for maximum rhythmic thrust and meaning.

*L.P.
The Rembrandts
Those who cut to the *Friends* theme song will miss the highlights of an album that can stand quite nicely on its own.

*FEELS LIKE HOME
Linda Ronstadt
Deliciously downbeat, *Home* may be where the hurt is, but it's worth repeat visits.

DREAMING OF YOU
Selena
Compounding the tragedy of Selena's murder in March is the fact that the 23-year-old Tejano singer was bidding to cross over from regional success in the Latino market to mainstream pop appeal. In view of the evidence here, it appears that Selena was destined to make a significant impact on the Top 40.

*BOOMBASTIC
Shaggy
Shaggy's second album is the real reggae thing, but the dreads-less dance hall deejay also has some crossover tricks up his sleeve.

SLOW HOT WIND
Janis Siegel and Fred Hersch
Siegel, of the jazz group Manhattan Transfer, has a flexible voice with a strong sense of phrasing, and no small pleasure here is pianist-arranger Fred Hersch.

GOOD NEWS FROM THE NEXT WORLD
Simple Minds
A simple-minded formula of fuzz-box guitar licks and yelping, pseudo-sincere vocals.

THE RAPTURE
Siouxsie and the Banshees
Never fails to be engrossing, with oblique, offbeat thrills.

*GOOD NEWS IN HARD TIMES
The Sisters of Glory
While other modern gospel ensembles like the Sounds of Blackness and the Boys Choir of Harlem turn youngsters on to God by adding contemporary pop and R&B elements to their music, these Sisters smartly stick to traditional Sunday-morning basics.

WASPS' NESTS
The 6ths
Smart, sad wistful songs about love—bubblegum music for passive-aggressive people.

*SUBHUMAN RACE
Skid Row
Their most raucous, intense, and impressive effort yet.

IT'S FIVE O'CLOCK SOMEWHERE
Slash's Snakepit
Songs that pack plenty of fury but little else.

*SMART
Sleeper
Singer-songwriter Louise Wener has Liz Phair's raunch and Chrissie Hynde's vocal chops.

*MURDER LOVE
Snow
Once again Snow drops nasal, tongue-twisting vocals over polished arrangements, sounding sexy without slipping into forced bravado.

*JILL SOBULE
Jill Sobule
Airy but inventive acoustic folk—Sobule's natural tonality is lucid and lissome.

DARE TO LOVE
Jimmy Somerville
This Scottish pop singer became known as a gay activist in the '80s, after "Smalltown Boy," his ode to coming out, became a dance club staple. Now he's back with an uneven album that is full of angry reflections on AIDS, prejudice, and forbidden love.

*LET YOUR DIM LIGHT SHINE
Soul Asylum
If Soul Asylum is out to make soulful brooding their specialty, they've just about perfected the art—this dim light gets pretty dazzling.

*CANDY RAIN
Soul for Real
The four brothers revel in loose, jazzy R&B, offering more human-sounding performances than Boyz II Men and All-4-One.

*PURE PHASE
Spiritualized
Ambient, and heavy on psychedelic caresses—the musical equivalent of a spectacular light show.

A VERY FINE LOVE
Dusty Springfield
Springfield's experienced contralto makes these tunes so contagious they seem to be daring you not to sing along.

*GREATEST HITS
Bruce Springsteen
This collection of Springsteen's sing-along standards is marked

by passion. The Boss continues to imbue his songs with an exalted significance.

GREETINGS FROM THE GUTTER
Dave Stewart
Stewart has a tough time finding his own voice, but thanks to his stellar guitar picking and crack songwriting he rules the *Gutter*.

A SPANNER IN THE WORKS
Rod Stewart
Stewart, 50, is finally acting his age. This mature return to his blue-eyed soulful roots seems to cry, "Pardon my excessive, overindulgent, 'Do Ya Think I'm Sexy?' period."

*SECOND COMING
The Stone Roses
A potpourri of classic mop-top rock, hippy psychedelia, and insistent funk.

I SHOULD COCO
Supergrass
Supergrass mow through some songs with punky exuberance while gently drifting through others with catchy melodies reeking of '60s pop.

*100% FUN
Matthew Sweet
Strong, accessible, and consistent in quality and tone.

*CRAZYSEXYCOOL
TLC
With its sharp funk and libidinous R&B, the album really lives up to its title.

RAOUL AND THE KINGS OF SPAIN
Tears for Fears
Tears for Fears' Roland Orzabal has downsized his trademark pomp and pretension. He and his studio musicians play it straight and, at times, surprisingly rough.

JACKY TERRASSON
Jacky Terrasson
Jazz pianist Terrasson is a brooding modernist with a classicist's touch.

*HANKY PANKY
The The
A whole album of Hank Williams Sr. covers backed up with the band's usual eclectic mix of dark, thumping, rock and haunting melodies.

*CARRY THE DAY
Henry Threadgill
An impressive album by an innovative, important musician who takes chances but never loses his integrity—or his wit.

UNIVERSITY
Throwing Muses
The band takes a newly supercharged stance that starts to wear thin about halfway through.

A HUNDRED LOVERS
Timbuk3
The team that brought us "The Future's So Bright, I Gotta Wear Shades" continues to churn out more wry, if inconsistent, sketches on modern life.

LEARNING HOW TO FLY
Tuck & Patti
Eschewing big production and backing tracks, this is an unadorned and hummable collection of cabaret-pop.

BALANCE
Van Halen
Serviceable but lumpy melodies overshadowed and engulfed by incendiary guitar—Eddie's technical virtuosity and sheer propulsion has rarely sounded better.

*NO DEEPER BLUE
Townes Van Zandt
Something to prize, these melancholy, rough-hewn songs exist beyond fashion.

BATMAN FOREVER SOUNDTRACK
various artists
Most of these tunes would hold up *sans* Batman: Brandy, Mazzy Star, and Massive Attack with Tracey Thorn all offer good tracks, though the album starts to dip near the end because of filler by also-rans.

*SAM COOKE'S SAR RECORDS STORY
various artists
A two-CD collection of soul music which proves Cooke's belief that even pop music could be a sanctified art form.

ENCOMIUM: A TRIBUTE TO LED ZEPPELIN
various artists
A harmless nostalgia trip that will have you remembering how many great songs Led Zeppelin left us.

THE ENVELOPE PLEASE . . . ACADEMY AWARD-WINNING SONGS (1934-1993)
various artists
At three hours plus, this five-CD collection of Best Original Songs is about as long as the Academy Awards telecast itself, but for pure fun, it deserves an Oscar.

FRIDAY ORIGINAL MOTION PICTURE SOUNDTRACK
various artists
At its best, the album is an arresting amalgam of disparate genres.

LOST IN BOSTON III
various artists
This third installment of musical tunes that never made it to Broadway includes numbers scrapped from *The Music Man, Gypsy, Guys and Dolls,* and *Where's Charley?,* among others.

POCAHONTAS SOUNDTRACK
various artists
With its wide open feel, the score at its best is reminiscent of Aaron Copland. But the folks at Disney try too hard to make Vanessa Williams's end-title rendering of "Colors of the Wind" into a "Big Breakout Ballad/Academy Award Contender."

*READY TO WEAR (PRET-A-PORTER) SOUNDTRACK
various artists
Deep, delicious, and diverse.

TUBE TUNES—VOLS. I–III
various artists
These three volumes of TV music from the '70s and '80s are like a photo gallery of kitsch.

UP & DOWN CLUB SESSIONS VOL. I & II
various artists
These two volumes of live recordings from performers at San Francisco's Up & Down Club—in which supermodel Christy Turlington is a business partner—back up their boast that the club "spawned San Francisco's acid/new jazz movement."

LIVE ON
Wailing Souls
With this follow-up to their 1992 Grammy-nominated *All Over the World,* Lloyd "Bread" McDonald and Winston "Pipe" Matthews keep the momentum going with more percolating reggae.

AFFECTION
Jody Watley
After scoring six Top 10 singles and a pair of platinum albums in the late '80s, the 1987 Best New

Artist Grammy winner watched her rising star burn out in the early '90s. But on this album she is an assured artist who acknowledges current musical trendsetters without aping them.

JAZZ WAGON
Jon Weber
Musical sophistication and dexterity don't prevent this first album from having a dulling song-to-song sameness.

*STANLEY ROAD
Paul Weller
With this remarkable, personal work, the former singer-songwriter of the Jam returns from a few years in the creative wilderness to embrace the role of rock elder statesman.

THIRTY YEARS OF MAXIMUM R&B
The Who
An expansive if somewhat repetitive collection of Who classics.

*THE SWEETEST DAYS
Vanessa Williams
Imbued with timeless maturity and sophistication.

HOG WILD
Hank Williams Jr.
Should keep Bocephus's rowdy reputation intact and unshaded.

*THE FINER THINGS
Steve Winwood
An overstuffed but valuable retrospective which resonates with Winwood's yearning, funky-choir-boy vocals, felicitous writing, and expressive arrangements.

CONVERSATION PEACE
Stevie Wonder
Wonder's gift for transcendent melody takes an ill-timed leave of absence on this studio album of pedestrian songs lacking his usual celebratory bounce.

*THINKIN' ABOUT YOU
Trisha Yearwood
Yearwood just gets better and better, and she has never sounded more emotionally connected with the lyrics she's warbling than on these 10 cuts.

*ELECTR-O-PURPLE
Yo La Tengo
One of their best albums, typically pensive and tautly constructed.

*DREAMLAND
Yellowjackets
With their 12th album, the Yellowjackets have once again put luster in their melodies and bite in their backbeat.

*MIRROR BALL
Neil Young
Call it the Dream Team of Grunge. Young has written all the songs here, but Pearl Jam, Seattle's reigning royalty-in-ripped-jeans, provides him enough explosive garage-band fuel to blow the doors off most rockers half his age.

*MUTINEER
Warren Zevon
Another solid piece of work from one of rock's most dependable and underrated songwriters.

ROCK AND ROLL HALL OF FAME

Cleveland's Rock and Roll Hall of Fame opened in September, 1995. The new home of Buddy Holly's high school diploma, John Lennon's Sgt. Pepper jacket, and Wilson Pickett's guitar, the Hall will also continue to select the greatest rock and roll musicians for induction every January. In order to be eligible, a nominee must have released a record at least 25 years prior to induction; the Early Influences list honors the formative figures of rock music.

1986

Chuck Berry
James Brown
Ray Charles
Sam Cooke
Fats Domino
The Everly Brothers
Buddy Holly
Jerry Lee Lewis
Elvis Presley
Little Richard

Early Influences
Robert Johnson
Jimmie Rodgers
Jimmy Yancey

Nonperformers
Alan Freed
Sam Phillips

Lifetime Achievement
John Hammond

1987

The Coasters
Eddie Cochran
Bo Diddley
Aretha Franklin
Marvin Gaye
Bill Haley
B. B. King
Clyde McPhatter
Ricky Nelson
Roy Orbison
Carl Perkins
Smokey Robinson
Big Joe Turner
Muddy Waters
Jackie Wilson

Early Influences
Louis Jordan
T-Bone Walker
Hank Williams

Nonperformers
Leonard Chess
Ahmet Ertegun
Jerry Leiber and Mike Stoller
Jerry Wexler

1988

The Beach Boys
The Beatles
The Drifters
Bob Dylan
The Supremes

Early Influences
Woody Guthrie
Leadbelly
Les Paul

Nonperformer
Berry Gordy Jr.

1989

Dion
Otis Redding
The Rolling Stones
The Temptations
Stevie Wonder

Early Influences
The Ink Spots
Bessie Smith
The Soul Stirrers

Nonperformer
Phil Spector

1990

Hank Ballard
Bobby Darin
The Four Seasons
The Four Tops
The Kinks
The Platters
Simon & Garfunkel
The Who

Early Influences
Louis Armstrong
Charlie Christian
Ma Rainey

Nonperformers
Lamont Dozier
Gerry Goffin and Carole King
Brian Holland and Eddie Holland

1991

LaVern Baker
The Byrds
John Lee Hooker
The Impressions
Wilson Pickett
Jimmy Reed
Ike and Tina Turner

Early Influences
Howlin' Wolf

Nonperformer
Dave Bartholomew
Ralph Bass

Lifetime Achievement
Nesuhi Ertegun

1992

Bobby "Blue" Bland
Booker T & The MG's
Johnny Cash
Jimi Hendrix Experience
The Isley Brothers
Sam and Dave
The Yardbirds

Early Influences
Elmore James
Professor Longhair

Nonperformers
Leo Fender
Doc Pomus
Bill Graham

1993

Ruth Brown
Cream
Creedence Clearwater Revival
The Doors
Etta James
Frankie Lymon & The Teenagers
Van Morrison
Sly & The Family Stone

Early Influence
Dinah Washington

Nonperformers
Dick Clark
Milt Gabler

1994

The Animals
The Band
Duane Eddy
Grateful Dead
Elton John
John Lennon
Bob Marley
Rod Stewart

Early Influence
Willie Dixon

Nonperformer
Johnny Otis

1995

The Allman Brothers Band
Al Green
Janis Joplin
Led Zeppelin
Martha & The Vandellas
Neil Young
Frank Zappa

Early Influence
The Orioles

Nonperformers
Paul Ackerman

JAZZ HALL OF FAME

Downbeat magazine, the country's leading jazz publication, conducts an annual poll of both readers and critics to determine the greatest luminaries of the jazz world. The honorees:

	Readers' poll	Critics' poll		Readers' poll	Critics' poll
1952	Louis Armstrong	—	1974	Buddy Rich	Ben Webster
1953	Glenn Miller	—	1975	Cannonball Adderley	Cecil Taylor
1954	Stan Kenton	—	1976	Woody Herman	King Oliver
1955	Charlie Parker	—	1977	Paul Desmond	Benny Carter
1956	Duke Ellington	—	1978	Joe Venuti	Rahsaan Roland Kirk
1957	Benny Goodman	—	1979	Ella Fitzgerald	Lennie Tristano
1958	Count Basie	—	1980	Dexter Gordon	Max Roach
1959	Lester Young	—	1981	Art Blakey	Bill Evans
1960	Dizzy Gillespie	—	1982	Art Pepper	Fats Navarro
1961	Billie Holiday	Coleman Hawkins	1983	Stephane Grappelli	Albert Ayler
1962	Miles Davis	Bix Beiderbecke	1984	Oscar Peterson	Sun Ra
1963	Thelonious Monk	Jelly Roll Morton	1985	Sarah Vaughan	Zoot Sims
1964	Eric Dolphy	Art Tatum	1986	Stan Getz	Gil Evans
1965	John Coltrane	Earl Hines	1987	Lionel Hampton	Johnny Dodds,
1966	Bud Powell	Charlie Christian			Thad Jones,
1967	Billy Strayhorn	Bessie Smith			Teddy Wilson
1968	Wes Montgomery	Sidney Bechet,	1988	Jaco Pastorius	Kenny Clarke
		Fats Waller	1989	Woody Shaw	Chet Baker
1969	Ornette Coleman	Pee Wee Russell,	1990	Red Rodney	Mary Lou Williams
		Jack Teagarden	1991	Lee Morgan	John Carter
1970	Jimi Hendrix	Johnny Hodges	1992	Maynard Ferguson	James P. Johnson
1971	Charles Mingus	Roy Eldridge,	1993	Gerry Mulligan	Edward Blackwell
		Django Reinhardt	1994	Dave Brubeck	Frank Zappa
1972	Gene Krupa	Clifford Brown	1995	(to be named	Julius Hemphill
1973	Sonny Rollins	Fletcher Henderson		December 1995)	

COUNTRY MUSIC HALL OF FAME

Located in Nashville along with everything else in country music, the Country Music Hall of Fame inducts its honorees each autumn. The enshrined elite:

1962	Roy Acuff	1972	Jimmie Davis	1985	Lester Flatt and Earl Scruggs
1963	(elections held but no one candidate received enough votes)	1973	Patsy Cline, Chet Atkins	1986	Wesley Rose, The Duke of Paducah
1964	Tex Ritter	1974	Owen Bradley, Frank "Pee Wee" King	1987	Rod Brasfield
1965	Ernest Tubb	1975	Minnie Pearl	1988	Roy Rogers, Loretta Lynn
1966	James R. Denny, George D. Hay, Uncle Dave Macon, Eddy Arnold	1976	Paul Cohen, Kitty Wells	1989	Jack Stapp, Hank Thompson, Cliffie Stone
		1977	Merle Travis		
		1978	Grandpa Jones	1990	Tennessee Ernie Ford
1967	Red Foley, J. L. Frank, Jim Reeves, Stephen H. Sholes	1979	Hubert Long, Hank Snow	1991	Boudleaux and Felice Bryant
		1980	Connie B. Gay, Original Sons of the Pioneers, Johnny Cash	1992	George Jones, Frances Preston
1968	Bob Wills				
1969	Gene Autry	1981	Vernon Dalhart, Grant Turner	1993	Willie Nelson
1970	Original Carter Family (A. P. Carter, Maybelle Carter, Sara Carter), Bill Monroe	1982	Lefty Frizzell, Marty Robbins, Roy Horton	1994	Merle Haggard
		1983	Little Jimmy Dickens		
1971	Arthur Edward Satherley	1984	Ralph Peer, Floyd Tillman		

TOP CONCERT APPEARANCES

The following survey lists the most successful North American individual concert appearances, based on box-office grosses, for 1994 and for all time. A concert appearance is defined here as all performances in a visit to a single town. (Source: Pollstar)

1994

1. Barbra Streisand — New York City
2. Elton John/Billy Joel — East Rutherford, New Jersey
3. Barbra Streisand — Las Vegas
4. Barbra Streisand — Anaheim, California
5. The Rolling Stones — East Rutherford, New Jersey
6. The Rolling Stones/Seal — Oakland, California
7. Barbra Streisand — Auburn Hills, Michigan
8. Elton John/Billy Joel — Philadelphia
9. The Rolling Stones/ Buddy Guy/ Red Hot Chili Peppers — Pasadena, California
10. Luis Miguel — Mexico City
11. Pink Floyd — Montreal, Quebec
12. Pink Floyd — Oakland, California
13. Pink Floyd — Mexico City
14. The Eagles — Mansfield, Massachusetts
15. The Eagles/Sheryl Crow — East Rutherford, New Jersey
16. Pink Floyd — Philadelphia
17. The Eagles — Irvine, California
18. Pink Floyd — Foxboro, Massachusetts
19. The Eagles — Mountain View, California
20. Pink Floyd — Pasadena, California

ALL TIME

1. Barbra Streisand — New York City, 1994
2. Elton John/Billy Joel — East Rutherford, New Jersey, 1994
3. Barbra Streisand — Las Vegas, 1993
4. Barbra Streisand — Anaheim, California, 1994
5. The Rolling Stones/ Living Colour/ Mar & Magette/ Dou Dov n' Diaye Rose — New York City, 1989
6. Bette Midler — New York City, 1993
7. The Rolling Stones — East Rutherford, New Jersey, 1994
8. The Rolling Stones/ Seal — Oakland, California, 1994
9. The Rolling Stones/ Guns N' Roses/ Living Colour — Los Angeles, 1989
10. Madonna — Mexico City, 1993
11. Paul Simon/Simon & Garfunkel — New York City, 1993
12. Barbra Streisand — Auburn Hills, Michigan, 1994
13. Elton John/Billy Joel — Philadelphia, 1994
14. Bruce Springsteen & The E Street Band — East Rutherford, New Jersey, 1985
15. Paul McCartney — Mexico City, 1993
16. Bruce Springsteen — East Rutherford, New Jersey, 1992
17. The Rolling Stones/ Buddy Guy/ Red Hot Chili Peppers — Pasadena, California, 1994
18. Bruce Springsteen & The E Street Band — Los Angeles, 1985
19. Luis Miguel — Mexico City, 1994
20. The Rolling Stones — Atlantic City, New Jersey, 1989

TOP CONCERT TOURS

These are the most successful North American tours of all time, along with year-by-year leaders since 1985, when Pollstar first began tracking the concert industry. The rankings are based on grosses rather than attendance. (Source: Pollstar)

ALL TIME

Rank	Artist	Year of tour
1.	The Rolling Stones	1994
2.	Pink Floyd	1994
3.	The Rolling Stones	1989
4.	The Eagles	1994
5.	New Kids on the Block	1990
6.	U2	1992
7.	Barbra Streisand	1994
8.	Grateful Dead	1994
9.	Elton John/Billy Joel	1994
10.	Grateful Dead	1993
11.	Billy Joel	1990
12.	The Who	1989
13.	Bruce Springsteen & The E Street Band	1985
14.	Paul McCartney	1990
15.	Bon Jovi	1989
16.	U2	1987
17.	Grateful Dead	1991
18.	Grateful Dead	1992
19.	Guns N' Roses/Metallica	1992
20.	Rod Stewart	1993

1985

Rank	Artist	Cities played
1.	Bruce Springsteen & The E Street Band	21
2.	Tina Turner	90
3.	Bryan Adams	129
4.	Kenny Rogers	80
5.	Prince & The Revolution	22
6.	Foreigner	105
7.	Willie Nelson and Family	97
8.	Ratt	139
9.	Grateful Dead	40
10.	REO Speedwagon	94
11.	Mötley Crüe	91
12.	Iron Maiden	81
13.	Daryl Hall and John Oates	51
14.	Phil Collins	28

15.	Dio, featuring Ronnie James Dio	92
16.	AC/DC	57
17.	Chicago	48
18.	U2	30
19.	Triumph	74
20.	Dire Straits	41

1986

Rank	Artist	Cities/Shows
1.	ZZ Top	91/132
2.	Van Halen	77/109
3.	Neil Diamond	22/64
4.	Alabama	127/127
5.	Kenny Rogers	116/143
6.	Journey	52/69
7.	The Monkees	174/211
8.	Bob Dylan and Tom Petty	31/41
9.	Lionel Richie	40/60
10.	Bill Cosby	23/46
11.	Bob Seger & The Silver Bullet Band	40/60
12.	Billy Joel	32/42
13.	David Lee Roth	74/78
14.	Aerosmith	80/81
15.	Stevie Wonder	49/53
16.	Loverboy	118/118
17.	Run–D.M.C.	82/82
18.	Grateful Dead	16/39
19.	Julio Iglesias	51/71
20.	Beach Boys	90/97

1987

Rank	Artist	Cities/Shows
1.	U2	50/79
2.	Bon Jovi	104/130
3.	Pink Floyd	28/60
4.	Grateful Dead	37/84
5.	David Bowie	31/45
6.	Mötley Crüe	92/100
7.	Whitney Houston	77/89

8.	Huey Lewis & The News	89/101
9.	Boston	37/69
10.	Alabama	117/127
11.	Genesis	18/30
12.	Heart	82/88
13.	Madonna	19/22
14.	Billy Joel	42/57
15.	Kenny Rogers	78/99
16.	Luther Vandross	51/65
17.	Tina Turner	71/78
18.	Bryan Adams	81/84
19.	Def Leppard	58/59
20.	Fleetwood Mac	45/48

1988

Rank	Artist	Cities/Shows
1.	Pink Floyd	23/35
2.	Van Halen's "Monsters of Rock"	23/26
3.	Def Leppard	94/112
4.	Grateful Dead	33/80
5.	Aerosmith	96/105
6.	Michael Jackson	19/54
7.	AC/DC	105/110
8.	Rod Stewart	82/88
9.	"Rat Pack/Ultimate Event"	23/41
10.	George Michael	32/46
11.	Whitesnake	83/84
12.	Bruce Springsteen & The E Street Band	21/43
13.	Robert Plant	88/92
14.	Luther Vandross/Anita Baker	26/42
15.	INXS	75/81
16.	John Cougar Mellencamp	45/54
17.	Kenny Rogers	88/167
18.	New Edition	67/70
19.	Randy Travis	98/119
20.	Sting	75/79

1989

Rank	Artist	Cities/Shows
1.	The Rolling Stones	33/60
2.	The Who	27/39
3.	Bon Jovi	129/143
4.	Grateful Dead	33/73
5.	New Kids on the Block	112/143
6.	Neil Diamond	29/69
7.	Metallica	134/140
8.	Elton John	32/47
9.	Rod Stewart	61/71
10.	Beach Boys/Chicago	57/59
11.	Poison	82/83
12.	R.E.M.	84/87
13.	Cinderella	135/136
14.	Barry Manilow	44/123
15.	George Strait	90/104
16.	New Edition	48/49
17.	Kenny Rogers	85/115
18.	Alabama	77/79
19.	Reba McEntire	111/126
20.	Randy Travis	88/105

1990

Rank	Artist	Cities/Shows
1.	New Kids on the Block	122/152
2.	Billy Joel	53/95
3.	Paul McCartney	21/32
4.	Grateful Dead	27/63
5.	Janet Jackson	62/89
6.	Aerosmith	92/101
7.	M. C. Hammer	132/138
8.	Mötley Crüe	103/108
9.	Phil Collins	27/56
10.	Eric Clapton	48/57
11.	David Bowie	41/51
12.	Madonna	12/32
13.	KISS	121/121
14.	Rush	56/63
15.	Depeche Mode	32/33
16.	Randy Travis	98/125
17.	Whitesnake	99/101
18.	Fleetwood Mac	54/62
19.	Kenny Rogers	66/105
20.	Alabama	102/103

1991

Rank	Artist	Cities/Shows
1.	Grateful Dead	27/76
2.	ZZ Top	85/106
3.	The Judds	116/126
4.	Rod Stewart	47/59
5.	Paul Simon	72/76
6.	Guns N' Roses	30/43
7.	Bell Biv Devoe/Johnny Gill/Keith Sweat	66/72
8.	Michael Bolton	70/103
9.	Garth Brooks	94/111
10.	Clint Black	92/100
11.	AC/DC	57/60
12.	Sting	64/81
13.	Luther Vandross	50/60
14.	Scorpions	90/93
15.	Van Halen	42/46
16.	Frank Sinatra	30/53
17.	Randy Travis	93/107
18.	Jimmy Buffett	37/51
19.	Jane's Addiction (includes "Lollapalooza")	56/66
20.	Yes	55/57

1992

Rank	Artist	Cities/Shows
1.	U2	61/73
2.	Grateful Dead	23/55
3.	Guns N' Roses/Metallica	25/25
4.	Neil Diamond	26/69
5.	Bruce Springsteen	36/59
6.	Genesis	24/28
7.	Elton John	32/49
8.	Metallica	87/102
9.	Eric Clapton	30/37
10.	Hammer	123/130
11.	Bryan Adams	92/94
12.	Jimmy Buffett	43/64
13.	"Lollapalooza II"	29/35
14.	Garth Brooks	78/79
15.	Reba McEntire	102/111
16.	Ozzy Osbourne	80/88
17.	John Mellencamp	44/55
18.	Harry Connick Jr.	43/87
19.	Def Leppard	72/77
20.	Rush	52/55

1993

Rank	Artist	Cities/Shows
1.	Grateful Dead	29/81
2.	Rod Stewart	54/68
3.	Neil Diamond	43/75
4.	Paul McCartney	23/23
5.	Bette Midler	29/71
6.	Billy Joel	22/39
7.	Garth Brooks	29/54
8.	Jimmy Buffett	32/52
9.	Reba McEntire	97/105
10.	Kenny G	82/97
11.	"Lollapalooza III"	29/34
12.	Aerosmith	61/66
13.	Clint Black/Wynonna	70/73
14.	Van Halen	32/40
15.	Alan Jackson	98/105
16.	Luther Vandross	42/49
17.	Peter Gabriel	31/38
18.	Def Leppard	90/91
19.	Depeche Mode	40/49
20.	Elton John	27/34

1994

Rank	Artist	Cities/Shows
1.	The Rolling Stones	43/60
2.	Pink Floyd	39/59
3.	The Eagles	32/54
4.	Barbra Streisand	6/22
5.	Grateful Dead	29/84
6.	Elton John/Billy Joel	14/21
7.	Aerosmith	71/76
8.	"Lollapalooza IV"	33/43
9.	Phil Collins	41/59
10.	Reba McEntire	96/102
11.	Bette Midler	44/54
12.	Billy Joel	40/49
13.	Michael Bolton	84/93
14.	Metallica	49/50
15.	ZZ Top	93/96
16.	Janet Jackson	63/72
17.	Brooks & Dunn	95/99
18.	Alan Jackson	93/99
19.	Jimmy Buffett	25/43
20.	Rod Stewart	33/34

BILLBOARD'S TOP 10 SINGLES

Chart-toppers of the past half-century are a nostalgia trip. The '52 list featured both George Clooney's mother and Carrie Fisher's father. Tony Bennett cracked the Top 10 the year before.

1946

1. "Prisoner of Love," Perry Como
2. "To Each His Own," Eddy Howard
3. "The Gypsy," Ink Spots
4. "Five Minutes More," Frank Sinatra
5. "Rumors Are Flying," Frankie Carle
6. "Oh! What It Seemed To Be," Frankie Carle
7. "Personality," Johnny Mercer & The Pied Pipers
8. "South America, Take It Away," Bing Crosby & The Andrews Sisters
9. "The Gypsy," Dinah Shore
10. "Oh! What It Seemed To Be," Frank Sinatra

1947

1. "Near You," Francis Craig
2. "Peg O' My Heart," Harmonicats
3. "Heartaches," Ted Weems
4. "Linda," Ray Noble Orchestra & Buddy Clark (tie)
5. "Smoke, Smoke, Smoke (That Cigarette)," Tex Williams (tie)
6. "I Wish I Didn't Love You So," Vaughn Monroe
7. "Peg O' My Heart," Three Suns
8. "Anniversary Song," Al Jolson
9. "Near You," Larry Green Orchestra
10. "That's My Desire," Sammy Kaye

1948

1. "Twelfth Street Rag," Pee Wee Hunt
2. "Manana," Peggy Lee
3. "Now Is the Hour," Bing Crosby
4. "A Tree in the Meadow," Margaret Whiting
5. "My Happiness," Jon & Sandra Steele
6. "You Can't Be True, Dear," Ken Griffin & Jerry Wayne
7. "Little White Lies," Dick Haymes
8. "You Call Everybody Darlin'," Al Trace
9. "My Happiness," Pied Pipers
10. "I'm Looking Over a Four Leaf Clover," Art Mooney

1949

1. "Riders in the Sky," Vaughn Monroe Orchestra
2. "That Lucky Old Sun," Frankie Laine
3. "You're Breaking My Heart," Vic Damone
4. "Some Enchanted Evening," Perry Como
5. "Slipping Around," Jimmy Wakely & Margaret Whiting
6. "I Can Dream, Can't I?" Andrews Sisters & Gordon Jenkins
7. "Cruising Down the River," Russ Morgan Orchestra
8. "A Little Bird Told Me," Evelyn Knight & The Stardusters
9. "Mule Train," Frankie Laine
10. "Jealous Heart," Al Morgan

1950

1. "Goodnight Irene," Gordon Jenkins & The Weavers
2. "Mona Lisa," Nat King Cole
3. "Third Man Theme," Anton Karas
4. "Sam's Song," Gary & Bing Crosby
5. "Simple Melody," Gary & Bing Crosby
6. "Music, Music, Music," Teresa Brewer
7. "Third Man Theme," Guy Lombardo
8. "Chattanoogie Shoe Shine Boy," Red Foley
9. "Harbor Lights," Sammy Kaye
10. "It Isn't Fair," Sammy Kaye & Don Cornell

1951

1. "Too Young," Nat King Cole
2. "Because of You," Tony Bennett
3. "How High the Moon," Les Paul & Mary Ford
4. "Come On-A My House," Rosemary Clooney
5. "Be My Love," Mario Lanza
6. "On Top of Old Smoky," Weavers
7. "Cold, Cold Heart," Tony Bennett
8. "If," Perry Como
9. "Loveliest Night of the Year," Mario Lanza
10. "Tennessee Waltz," Patti Page

1952

1. "Blue Tango," Leroy Anderson
2. "Wheel of Fortune," Kay Starr
3. "Cry," Johnnie Ray
4. "You Belong to Me," Jo Stafford
5. "Auf Wiederseh'n, Sweetheart," Vera Lynn
6. "I Went to Your Wedding," Patti Page
7. "Half as Much," Rosemary Clooney
8. "Wish You Were Here," Eddie Fisher & Hugo Winterhalter
9. "Here in My Heart," Al Martino
10. "Delicado," Percy Faith

1953

1. "Song From Moulin Rouge," Percy Faith
2. "Vaya con Dios," Les Paul & Mary Ford
3. "Doggie in the Window," Patti Page
4. "I'm Walking Behind You," Eddie Fisher
5. "You, You, You," Ames Brothers
6. "Till I Waltz Again with You," Teresa Brewer
7. "April in Portugal," Les Baxter
8. "No Other Love," Perry Como
9. "Don't Let the Stars Get in Your Eyes," Perry Como
10. "I Believe," Frankie Laine

1954

1. "Little Things Mean a Lot," Kitty Kallen
2. "Wanted," Perry Como
3. "Hey, There," Rosemary Clooney
4. "Sh-Boom," Crew Cuts
5. "Make Love to Me," Jo Stafford
6. "Oh! My Pa-Pa," Eddie Fisher
7. "I Get So Lonely," Four Knights
8. "Three Coins in the Fountain," Four Aces
9. "Secret Love," Doris Day
10. "Hernando's Highway," Archie Bleyer

1955

1. "Cherry Pink and Apple Blossom White," Perez Prado
2. "Rock Around the Clock," Bill Haley & His Comets

3. "The Yellow Rose of Texas," Mitch Miller
4. "Autumn Leaves," Roger Williams
5. "Unchained Melody," Les Baxter
6. "The Ballad of Davy Crockett," Bill Hayes
7. "Love Is a Many-Splendored Thing," Four Aces
8. "Sincerely," McGuire Sisters
9. "Ain't That a Shame," Pat Boone
10. "Dance with Me Henry," Georgia Gibbs

1956

1. "Heartbreak Hotel," Elvis Presley
2. "Don't Be Cruel," Elvis Presley
3. "Lisbon Antigua," Nelson Riddle
4. "My Prayer," Platters
5. "The Wayward Wind," Gogi Grant
6. "Hound Dog," Elvis Presley
7. "The Poor People of Paris," Les Baxter
8. "Whatever Will Be Will Be (Que Sera Sera)," Doris Day
9. "Memories Are Made of This," Dean Martin
10. "Rock and Roll Waltz," Kay Starr

1957

1. "All Shook Up," Elvis Presley
2. "Love Letters in the Sand," Pat Boone
3. "Little Darlin'," Diamonds
4. "Young Love," Tab Hunter
5. "So Rare," Jimmy Dorsey
6. "Don't Forbid Me," Pat Boone
7. "Singing the Blues," Guy Mitchell
8. "Young Love," Sonny James
9. "Too Much," Elvis Presley
10. "Round and Round," Perry Como

1958

1. "Volare (Nel Blu Dipinto Di Blu)," Domenico Modugno
2. "All I Have To Do Is Dream/ Claudette," Everly Brothers
3. "Don't/I Beg of You," Elvis Presley
4. "Witch Doctor," David Seville
5. "Patricia," Perez Prado
6. "Sail Along Silvery Moon/Raunchy," Billy Vaughn
7. "Catch a Falling Star/Magic Moments," Perry Como
8. "Tequila," Champs
9. "It's All in the Game," Tommy Edwards
10. "Return to Me," Dean Martin

1959

1. "The Battle of New Orleans," Johnny Horton
2. "Mack the Knife," Bobby Darin
3. "Personality," Lloyd Price
4. "Venus," Frankie Avalon
5. "Lonely Boy," Paul Anka
6. "Dream Lover," Bobby Darin
7. "The Three Bells," Browns
8. "Come Softly to Me," Fleetwoods
9. "Kansas City," Wilbert Harrison
10. "Mr. Blue," Fleetwoods

1960

1. "Theme from *A Summer Place*," Percy Faith
2. "He'll Have To Go," Jim Reeves
3. "Cathy's Clown," Everly Brothers
4. "Running Bear," Johnny Preston
5. "Teen Angel," Mark Dinning
6. "It's Now or Never," Elvis Presley
7. "Handy Man," Jimmy Jones
8. "I'm Sorry," Brenda Lee
9. "Stuck on You," Elvis Presley
10. "The Twist," Chubby Checker

1961

1. "Tossin' and Turnin'," Bobby Lewis
2. "I Fall to Pieces," Patsy Cline
3. "Michael," Highwaymen
4. "Cryin'," Roy Orbison
5. "Runaway," Del Shannon
6. "My True Story," Jive Five
7. "Pony Time," Chubby Checker
8. "Wheels," String-a-Longs
9. "Raindrops," Dee Clark
10. "Wooden Heart (Muss I Denn)," Joe Dowell

1962

1. "Stranger on the Shore," Mr. Acker Bilk
2. "I Can't Stop Loving You," Ray Charles
3. "Mashed Potato Time," Dee Dee Sharp
4. "Roses Are Red," Bobby Vinton
5. "The Stripper," David Rose
6. "Johnny Angel," Shelley Fabares
7. "Loco-motion," Little Eva
8. "Let Me In," Sensations
9. "The Twist," Chubby Checker
10. "Soldier Boy," Shirelles

1963

1. "Sugar Shack," Jimmy Gilmer & The Fireballs
2. "Surfin' USA," Beach Boys

3. "The End of the World," Skeeter Davis
4. "Rhythm of the Rain," Cascades
5. "He's So Fine," Chiffons
6. "Blue Velvet," Bobby Vinton
7. "Hey Paula," Paul & Paula
8. "Fingertips II," Little Stevie Wonder
9. "Washington Square," Village Stompers
10. "It's All Right," Impressions

1964

1. "I Want To Hold Your Hand," Beatles
2. "She Loves You," Beatles
3. "Hello, Dolly!" Louis Armstrong
4. "Oh, Pretty Woman," Roy Orbison
5. "I Get Around," Beach Boys
6. "Everybody Loves Somebody," Dean Martin
7. "My Guy," Mary Wells
8. "We'll Sing in the Sunshine," Gale Garnett
9. "Last Kiss," J. Frank Wilson & The Cavaliers
10. "Where Did Our Love Go," Supremes

1965

1. "Wooly Bully," Sam the Sham & The Pharaohs
2. "I Can't Help Myself," Four Tops
3. "(I Can't Get No) Satisfaction," Rolling Stones
4. "You Were on My Mind," We Five
5. "You've Lost That Lovin' Feelin'," Righteous Brothers
6. "Downtown," Petula Clark
7. "Help!," Beatles
8. "Can't You Hear My Heartbeat," Herman's Hermits
9. "Crying in the Chapel," Elvis Presley
10. "My Girl," Temptations

1966

1. "The Ballad of the Green Berets," S/Sgt. Barry Sadler
2. "Cherish," Association
3. "(You're My) Soul and Inspiration," Righteous Brothers
4. "Reach Out I'll Be There," Four Tops
5. "96 Tears," ? & the Mysterians
6. "Last Train to Clarksville," Monkees
7. "Monday, Monday," Mamas & the Papas
8. "You Can't Hurry Love," Supremes
9. "Poor Side of Town," Johnny Rivers
10. "California Dreamin'," Mamas & the Papas

1967

1. "To Sir with Love," Lulu
2. "The Letter," Box Tops
3. "Ode to Billie Joe," Bobby Gentry
4. "Windy," Association
5. "I'm a Believer," Monkees
6. "Light My Fire," Doors
7. "Somethin' Stupid," Nancy Sinatra & Frank Sinatra
8. "Happy Together," Turtles
9. "Groovin'," Young Rascals
10. "Can't Take My Eyes Off You," Frankie Valli

1968

1. "Hey Jude," Beatles
2. "Love Is Blue (L'Amour Est Blue)," Paul Mauriat
3. "Honey," Bobby Goldsboro
4. "(Sittin' on) The Dock of the Bay," Otis Redding
5. "People Got To Be Free," Rascals
6. "Sunshine of Your Love," Cream
7. "This Guy's in Love with You," Herb Alpert
8. "The Good, the Bad and the Ugly," Hugo Montenegro
9. "Mrs. Robinson," Simon & Garfunkel
10. "Tighten Up," Archie Bell & The Drells

1969

1. "Sugar, Sugar," Archies
2. "Aquarius/Let the Sunshine In," Fifth Dimension
3. "I Can't Get Next to You," Temptations
4. "Honky Tonk Women," Rolling Stones
5. "Everyday People," Sly & The Family Stone
6. "Dizzy," Tommy Roe
7. "Hot Fun in the Summertime," Sly & The Family Stone
8. "I'll Never Fall in Love Again," Tom Jones
9. "Build Me Up Buttercup," Foundations
10. "Crimson and Clover," Tommy James & The Shondells

1970

1. "Bridge over Troubled Water," Simon & Garfunkel
2. "(They Long To Be) Close to You," Carpenters
3. "American Woman/No Sugar Tonight," Guess Who

4. "Raindrops Keep Fallin' on My Head," B. J. Thomas
5. "War," Edwin Starr
6. "Ain't No Mountain High Enough," Diana Ross
7. "I'll Be There," Jackson 5
8. "Get Ready," Rare Earth
9. "Let It Be," Beatles
10. "Band of Gold," Freda Payne

1971

1. "Joy to the World," Three Dog Night
2. "Maggie May/Reason To Believe," Rod Stewart
3. "It's Too Late/I Feel the Earth Move," Carole King
4. "One Bad Apple," Osmonds
5. "How Can You Mend a Broken Heart," Bee Gees
6. "Indian Reservation," Raiders
7. "Go Away Little Girl," Donny Osmond
8. "Take Me Home, Country Roads," John Denver with Fat City
9. "Just My Imagination (Running Away with Me)," Temptations
10. "Knock Three Times," Dawn

1972

1. "The First Time Ever I Saw Your Face," Roberta Flack
2. "Alone Again (Naturally)," Gilbert O'Sullivan
3. "American Pie," Don McLean
4. "Without You," Nilsson
5. "Candy Man," Sammy Davis Jr.
6. "I Gotcha," Joe Tex
7. "Lean on Me," Bill Withers
8. "Baby Don't Get Hooked on Me," Mac Davis
9. "Brand New Key," Melanie
10. "Daddy Don't You Walk So Fast," Wayne Newton

1973

1. "Tie a Yellow Ribbon 'Round the Ole Oak Tree," Tony Orlando & Dawn
2. "Bad, Bad Leroy Brown," Jim Croce
3. "Killing Me Softly with His Song," Roberta Flack
4. "Let's Get It On," Marvin Gaye
5. "My Love," Paul McCartney & Wings
6. "Why Me," Kris Kristofferson
7. "Crocodile Rock," Elton John
8. "Will It Go Round in Circles," Billy Preston
9. "You're So Vain," Carly Simon
10. "Touch Me in the Morning," Diana Ross

1974

1. "The Way We Were," Barbra Streisand
2. "Seasons in the Sun," Terry Jacks
3. "Love's Theme," Love Unlimited Orchestra
4. "Come and Get Your Love," Redbone
5. "Dancing Machine," Jackson 5
6. "The Loco-motion," Grand Funk Railroad
7. "TSOP," MFSB
8. "The Streak," Ray Stevens
9. "Bennie and the Jets," Elton John
10. "One Hell of a Woman," Mac Davis

1975

1. "Love Will Keep Us Together," Captain & Tennille
2. "Rhinestone Cowboy," Glen Campbell
3. "Philadelphia Freedom," Elton John
4. "Before the Next Teardrop Falls," Freddy Fender
5. "My Eyes Adored You," Frankie Valli
6. "Shining Star," Earth, Wind & Fire
7. "Fame," David Bowie
8. "Laughter in the Rain," Neil Sedaka
9. "One of These Nights," Eagles
10. "Thank God I'm a Country Boy," John Denver

1976

1. "Silly Love Songs," Wings
2. "Don't Go Breaking My Heart," Elton John & Kiki Dee
3. "Disco Lady," Johnnie Taylor
4. "December, 1963 (Oh, What a Night)," Four Seasons
5. "Play That Funky Music," Wild Cherry
6. "Kiss and Say Goodbye," Manhattans
7. "Love Machine, Pt. 1," Miracles
8. "50 Ways To Leave Your Lover," Paul Simon
9. "Love Is Alive," Gary Wright
10. "A Fifth of Beethoven," Walter Murphy & The Big Apple Band

1977

1. "Tonight's the Night (Gonna Be Alright)," Rod Stewart
2. "I Just Want To Be Your Everything," Andy Gibb
3. "Best of My Love," Emotions
4. "Love Theme from *A Star Is Born* (Evergreen)," Barbra Streisand
5. "Angel in Your Arms," Hot
6. "I Like Dreamin'," Kenny Nolan
7. "Don't Leave Me This Way," Thelma Houston

8. "(Your Love Has Lifted Me) Higher and Higher," Rita Coolidge
9. "Night Fever," Alan O'Day
10. "Torn Between Two Lovers," Mary MacGregor

1978

1. "Shadow Dancing," Andy Gibb
2. "Night Fever," Bee Gees
3. "You Light Up My Life," Debby Boone
4. "Stayin' Alive," Bee Gees
5. "Kiss You All Over," Exile
6. "How Deep Is Your Love," Bee Gees
7. "Baby Come Back," Player
8. "Love Is Thicker Than Water," Andy Gibb
9. "Boogie Oogie Oogie," A Taste of Honey
10. "Three Times a Lady," Commodores

1979

1. "My Sharona," Knack
2. "Bad Girls," Donna Summer
3. "Le Freak," Chic
4. "Da Ya Think I'm Sexy," Rod Stewart
5. "Reunited," Peaches & Herb
6. "I Will Survive," Gloria Gaynor
7. "Hot Stuff," Donna Summer
8. "Y.M.C.A.," Village People
9. "Ring My Bell," Anita Ward
10. "Sad Eyes," Robert John

1980

1. "Call Me," Blondie
2. "Another Brick in the Wall," Pink Floyd
3. "Magic," Olivia Newton-John
4. "Rock with You," Michael Jackson
5. "Do That to Me One More Time," Captain & Tennille
6. "Crazy Little Thing Called Love," Queen
7. "Coming Up," Paul McCartney
8. "Funkytown," Lipps, Inc.
9. "It's Still Rock and Roll to Me," Billy Joel
10. "The Rose," Bette Midler

1981

1. "Bette Davis Eyes," Kim Carnes
2. "Endless Love," Diana Ross & Lionel Richie
3. "Lady," Kenny Rogers
4. "(Just Like) Starting Over," John Lennon
5. "Jessie's Girl," Rick Springfield
6. "Celebration," Kool & The Gang
7. "Kiss on My List," Daryl Hall & John Oates

8. "I Love a Rainy Night," Eddie Rabbitt
9. "9 to 5," Dolly Parton
10. "Keep On Loving You," REO Speedwagon

1982

1. "Physical," Olivia Newton-John
2. "Eye of the Tiger," Survivor
3. "I Love Rock 'n' Roll," Joan Jett & The Blackhearts
4. "Ebony and Ivory," Paul McCartney & Stevie Wonder
5. "Centerfold," The J. Geils Band
6. "Don't You Want Me," Human League
7. "Jack and Diane," John Cougar
8. "Hurts So Good," John Cougar
9. "Abracadabra," Steve Miller Band
10. "Hard To Say I'm Sorry," Chicago

1983

1. "Every Breath You Take," The Police
2. "Billie Jean," Michael Jackson
3. "Flashdance . . . What a Feeling," Irene Cara
4. "Down Under," Men at Work
5. "Beat It," Michael Jackson
6. "Total Eclipse of the Heart," Bonnie Tyler
7. "Maneater," Daryl Hall & John Oates
8. "Baby Come to Me," Patti Austin with James Ingram
9. "Maniac," Michael Sembello
10. "Sweet Dreams (Are Made of This)," Eurythmics

1984

1. "When Doves Cry," Prince
2. "What's Love Got To Do with It," Tina Turner
3. "Say Say Say," Paul McCartney & Michael Jackson
4. "Footloose," Kenny Loggins
5. "Against All Odds (Take a Look at Me Now)," Phil Collins
6. "Jump," Van Halen
7. "Hello," Lionel Richie
8. "Owner of a Lonely Heart," Yes
9. "Ghostbusters," Ray Parker Jr.
10. "Karma Chameleon," Culture Club

1985

1. "Careless Whisper," Wham! featuring George Michael
2. "Like a Virgin," Madonna
3. "Wake Me Up Before You Go-Go," Wham!
4. "I Want To Know What Love Is," Foreigner
5. "I Feel for You," Chaka Khan

6. "Out of Touch," Daryl Hall & John Oates
7. "Everybody Wants To Rule the World," Tears for Fears
8. "Money for Nothing," Dire Straits
9. "Crazy for You," Madonna
10. "Take on Me," a-ha

1986

1. "That's What Friends Are For," Dionne & Friends
2. "Say You, Say Me," Lionel Richie
3. "I Miss You," Klymaxx
4. "On My Own," Patti LaBelle & Michael McDonald
5. "Broken Wings," Mr. Mister
6. "How Will I Know," Whitney Houston
7. "Party All the Time," Eddie Murphy
8. "Burning Heart," Survivor
9. "Kyrie," Mr. Mister
10. "Addicted to Love," Robert Palmer

1987

1. "Walk Like an Egyptian," Bangles
2. "Alone," Heart
3. "Shake You Down," Gregory Abbott
4. "I Wanna Dance with Somebody (Who Loves Me)," Whitney Houston
5. "Nothing's Gonna Stop Us Now," Starship
6. "C'est La Vie," Robbie Nevil
7. "Here I Go Again," Whitesnake
8. "The Way It Is," Bruce Hornsby & The Range
9. "Shakedown," Bob Seger
10. "Livin' On a Prayer," Bon Jovi

1988

1. "Faith," George Michael
2. "Need You Tonight," INXS
3. "Got My Mind Set on You," George Harrison
4. "Never Gonna Give You Up," Rick Astley
5. "Sweet Child o' Mine," Guns N' Roses
6. "So Emotional," Whitney Houston
7. "Heaven Is a Place on Earth," Belinda Carlisle
8. "Could've Been," Tiffany
9 "Hands to Heaven," Breathe
10. "Roll with It," Steve Winwood

1989

1. "Look Away," Chicago
2. "My Prerogative," Bobby Brown
3. "Every Rose Has Its Thorn," Poison
4. "Straight Up," Paula Abdul
5. "Miss You Much," Janet Jackson

6. "Cold Hearted," Paula Abdul
7. "Wind Beneath My Wings," Bette Midler
8. "Girl You Know It's True," Milli Vanilli
9. "Baby, I Love Your Way/Freebird Medley," Will to Power
10. "Giving You the Best That I Got," Anita Baker

1990

1. "Hold On," Wilson Phillips
2. "It Must Have Been Love," Roxette
3. "Nothing Compares 2 U," Sinéad O'Connor
4. "Poison," Bell Biv Devoe
5. "Vogue," Madonna
6. "Vision of Love," Mariah Carey
7. "Another Day in Paradise," Phil Collins
8. "Hold On," En Vogue
9. "Cradle of Love," Billy Idol
10. "Blaze of Glory," Jon Bon Jovi

1991

1. "(Everything I Do) I Do It for You," Bryan Adams
2. "I Wanna Sex You Up," Color Me Badd

3. "Gonna Make You Sweat," C+C Music Factory
4. "Rush Rush," Paula Abdul
5. "One More Try," Timmy T.
6. "Unbelievable," EMF
7. "More Than Words," Extreme
8. "I Like the Way (The Kissing Game)," Hi-Five
9. "The First Time," Surface
10. "Baby Baby," Amy Grant

1992

1. "End of the Road," Boyz II Men
2. "Baby Got Back," Sir Mix-A-Lot
3. "Jump," Kris Kross
4. "Save the Best for Last," Vanessa Williams
5. "Baby-Baby-Baby," TLC
6. "Tears in Heaven," Eric Clapton
7. "My Lovin' (You're Never Gonna Get It)," En Vogue
8. "Under the Bridge," Red Hot Chili Peppers
9. "All 4 Love," Color Me Badd
10. "Just Another Day," Jon Secada

1993

1. "I Will Always Love You," Whitney Houston
2. "Whoomp! (There It Is)," Tag Team
3. "Can't Help Falling in Love," UB40
4. "That's the Way Love Goes," Janet Jackson
5. "Freak Me," Silk
6. "Weak," SWV
7. "If I Ever Fall in Love," Shai
8. "Dreamlover," Mariah Carey
9. "Rump Shaker," Wreckx-N-Effect
10. "Informer," Snow

1994

1. "The Sign," Ace of Base
2. "I Swear," All-4-One
3. "I'll Make Love to You," Boyz II Men
4. "The Power of Love," Céline Dion
5. "Hero," Mariah Carey
6. "Stay (I Missed You)," Lisa Loeb & Nine Stories
7. "Breathe Again," Toni Braxton
8. "All for Love," Bryan Adams/Rod Stewart/Sting
9. "All That She Wants," Ace of Base
10. "Don't Turn Around," Ace of Base

RAP WRAPPED UP

More than a decade after its initial breakthrough, rap has become a permanent part of the pop music landscape. Here, selected by PEOPLE music critic Jeremy Helligar, are some of the best albums the genre has to offer.

1. Arrested Development, *3 Years, 5 Months and 2 Days in the Life of . . .* (1992)
2. A Tribe Called Quest, *Midnight Marauders* (1993)
3. Beastie Boys, *Licensed to Ill* (1986)
4. Beastie Boys, *Paul's Boutique* (1989)
5. Da Brat, *Funkdafied* (1994)
6. De La Soul, *3 Feet High & Rising* (1989)
7. Digable Planets, *Blowout Comb* (1994)
8. Dr. Dre, *The Chronic* (1993)
9. Grandmaster Flash & The Furious Five, *Greatest Hits* (1987)
10. L.L. Cool J, *Mama Said Knock You Out* (1990)
11. Naughty By Nature, *Poverty's Paradise* (1995)
12. N.W.A., *Straight Outta Compton* (1989)
13. Public Enemy, *It Takes a Nation of Millions to Hold Us Back* (1988)
14. Run-D.M.C., *Run-D.M.C.* (1984)
15. Run-D.M.C., *King of Rock* (1985)
16. Run-D.M.C., *Raising Hell* (1986)
17. Salt-N-Pepa, *Black's Magic* (1990)
18. various artists, *Above the Rim* soundtrack (1994)
19. Whodini, *Escape* (1984)
20. Yo-Yo, *You Better Ask Somebody* (1993)

BILLBOARD'S TOP 10 ALBUMS

The times certainly have been a-changin' to judge from *Billboard*'s list of top-selling albums since tabulation began almost 40 years ago.

1956

1. *Calypso*, Harry Belafonte
2. *My Fair Lady*, original cast
3. *The King and I*, soundtrack
4. *The Eddy Duchin Story*, soundtrack
5. *Elvis Presley*, Elvis Presley
6. *High Society*, soundtrack
7. *Songs for Swingin' Lovers*, Frank Sinatra
8. *Belafonte*, Harry Belafonte
9. *The Platters*, Platters
10. *Oklahoma!*, soundtrack

1957

1. *My Fair Lady*, original cast
2. *Hymns*, Tennessee Ernie Ford
3. *Oklahoma!*, soundtrack
4. *Around the World in 80 Days*, soundtrack
5. *The King and I*, soundtrack
6. *Calypso*, Harry Belafonte
7. *Love Is the Thing*, Nat King Cole
8. *The Eddy Duchin Story*, soundtrack
9. *Songs of the Fabulous Fifties*, Roger Williams
10. *Film Encores*, Mantovani

1958

1. *My Fair Lady*, original cast
2. *The Music Man*, original cast
3. *Johnny's Greatest Hits*, Johnny Mathis
4. *South Pacific*, soundtrack
5. *Come Fly with Me*, Frank Sinatra
6. *Around the World in 80 Days*, soundtrack
7. *Warm*, Johnny Mathis
8. *South Pacific*, original cast
9. *Ricky*, Ricky Nelson
10. *The King and I*, soundtrack

1959

1. *Music from "Peter Gunn,"* Henry Mancini
2. *Gigi*, soundtrack
3. *South Pacific*, soundtrack
4. *From the Hungry i*, Kingston Trio
5. *The Kingston Trio at Large*, Kingston Trio
6. *Sing Along with Mitch*, Mitch Miller
7. *Inside Shelley Berman*, Shelley Berman
8. *Exotica, Vol. 1*, Martin Denny
9. *My Fair Lady*, original cast
10. *Flower Drum Song*, original cast

1960

1. *The Sound of Music*, original cast
2. *Inside Shelley Berman*, Shelley Berman
3. *The Button-Down Mind of Bob Newhart*, Bob Newhart
4. *Sixty Years of Music America Loves Best, Vol. I*, various artists
5. *Here We Go Again*, Kingston Trio
6. *Sold Out*, Kingston Trio
7. *Heavenly*, Johnny Mathis
8. *South Pacific*, soundtrack
9. *Faithfully*, Johnny Mathis
10. *Outside Shelley Berman*, Shelley Berman

1961

1. *Camelot*, original cast
2. *Great Motion Picture Themes*, various artists
3. *Never on Sunday*, soundtrack
4. *The Sound of Music*, original cast
5. *Exodus*, soundtrack
6. *Knockers Up*, Rusty Warren
7. *G.I. Blues*, Elvis Presley/soundtrack
8. *Sing Along with Mitch*, Mitch Miller
9. *Calcutta*, Lawrence Welk
10. *Tonight in Person*, Limeliters

1962

1. *West Side Story*, soundtrack
2. *Breakfast at Tiffany's*, Henry Mancini
3. *Blue Hawaii*, Elvis Presley/soundtrack
4. *West Side Story*, original cast
5. *The Sound of Music*, original cast
6. *Time Out*, Dave Brubeck
7. *Camelot*, original cast
8. *Your Twist Party*, Chubby Checker
9. *Knockers Up*, Rusty Warren
10. *Judy at Carnegie Hall*, Judy Garland

1963

1. *West Side Story*, soundtrack
2. *Peter, Paul and Mary*, Peter, Paul and Mary
3. *Moving*, Peter, Paul and Mary
4. *Joan Baez in Concert*, Joan Baez
5. *I Left My Heart in San Francisco*, Tony Bennett
6. *Moon River and Other Great Movie Themes*, Andy Williams
7. *Lawrence of Arabia*, soundtrack
8. *Days of Wine and Roses*, Andy Williams

9. *Oliver*, original cast
10. *Modern Sounds in Country and Western Music, Vol. 2*, Ray Charles

1964

1. *Hello, Dolly!*, original cast
2. *In the Wind*, Peter, Paul and Mary
3. *Honey in the Horn*, Al Hirt
4. *The Barbra Streisand Album*, Barbra Streisand
5. *West Side Story*, soundtrack
6. *Peter, Paul and Mary*, Peter, Paul & Mary
7. *The Second Barbra Streisand Album*, Barbra Streisand
8. *Meet the Beatles*, Beatles
9. *The Third Barbra Streisand Album*, Barbra Streisand
10. *Moon River and Other Great Movie Themes*, Andy Williams

1965

1. *Mary Poppins*, soundtrack
2. *Beatles '65*, Beatles
3. *The Sound of Music*, soundtrack
4. *My Fair Lady*, soundtrack
5. *Fiddler on the Roof*, original cast
6. *Goldfinger*, soundtrack
7. *Hello, Dolly!*, original cast
8. *Dear Heart*, Andy Williams
9. *Introducing Herman's Hermits*, Herman's Hermits
10. *Beatles VI*, Beatles

1966

1. *Whipped Cream and Other Delights*, Herb Alpert & The Tijuana Brass
2. *The Sound of Music*, soundtrack
3. *Going Places*, Herb Alpert & The Tijuana Brass
4. *Rubber Soul*, Beatles
5. *What Now My Love*, Herb Alpert & The Tijuana Brass
6. *If You Can Believe Your Eyes and Ears*, Mamas & the Papas
7. *Dr. Zhivago*, soundtrack
8. *Revolver*, Beatles
9. *Color Me Barbra*, Barbra Streisand
10. *Ballad of the Green Berets*, S/Sgt. Barry Sadler

1967

1. *More of the Monkees*, Monkees
2. *The Monkees*, Monkees

3. *Dr. Zhivago*, soundtrack
4. *The Sound of Music*, soundtrack
5. *The Temptations' Greatest Hits*, Temptations
6. *A Man and a Woman*, soundtrack
7. *S.R.O.*, Herb Alpert & The Tijuana Brass
8. *Whipped Cream and Other Delights*, Herb Alpert & The Tijuana Brass
9. *Going Places*, Herb Alpert & The Tijuana Brass
10. *Sgt. Pepper's Lonely Hearts Club Band*, Beatles

1968

1. *Are You Experienced?*, Jimi Hendrix Experience
2. *The Graduate*, Simon & Garfunkel/soundtrack
3. *Disraeli Gears*, Cream
4. *Magical Mystery Tour*, Beatles/soundtrack
5. *Diana Ross and the Supremes' Greatest Hits*, Diana Ross & The Supremes
6. *Sgt. Pepper's Lonely Hearts Club Band*, Beatles
7. *The Doors*, The Doors
8. *Parsley, Sage, Rosemary and Thyme*, Simon & Garfunkel
9. *Vanilla Fudge*, Vanilla Fudge
10. *Blooming Hits*, Paul Mauriat & His Orchestra

1969

1. *In-a-Gadda-Da-Vida*, Iron Butterfly
2. *Hair*, original cast
3. *Blood, Sweat and Tears*, Blood, Sweat and Tears
4. *Bayou Country*, Creedence Clearwater Revival
5. *Led Zeppelin*, Led Zeppelin
6. *Johnny Cash at Folsom Prison*, Johnny Cash
7. *Funny Girl*, soundtrack
8. *The Beatles (The White Album)*, Beatles
9. *Donovan's Greatest Hits*, Donovan
10. *The Association's Greatest Hits*, Association

1970

1. *Bridge over Troubled Water*, Simon & Garfunkel
2. *Led Zeppelin II*, Led Zeppelin
3. *Chicago*, Chicago
4. *Abbey Road*, Beatles
5. *Santana*, Santana
6. *Get Ready*, Rare Earth

7. *Easy Rider*, soundtrack
8. *Butch Cassidy and the Sundance Kid*, soundtrack
9. *Joe Cocker!*, Joe Cocker
10. *Three Dog Night Was Captured Live at the Forum*, Three Dog Night

1971

1. *Jesus Christ Superstar*, various artists
2. *Tapestry*, Carole King
3. *Close to You*, Carpenters
4. *Pearl*, Janis Joplin
5. *Abraxas*, Santana
6. *The Partridge Family Album*, Partridge Family
7. *Sweet Baby James*, James Taylor
8. *Tea for the Tillerman*, Cat Stevens
9. *Greatest Hits*, Sly & The Family Stone
10. *Chicago III*, Chicago

1972

1. *Harvest*, Neil Young
2. *Tapestry*, Carole King
3. *American Pie*, Don McLean
4. *Teaser and the Firecat*, Cat Stevens
5. *Hot Rocks, 1964–71*, Rolling Stones
6. *Killer*, Alice Cooper
7. *First Take*, Roberta Flack
8. *America*, America
9. *Music*, Carole King
10. *Madman Across the Water*, Elton John

1973

1. *The World Is a Ghetto*, War
2. *Summer Breeze*, Seals & Crofts
3. *Talking Book*, Stevie Wonder
4. *No Secrets*, Carly Simon
5. *Lady Sings the Blues*, Diana Ross
6. *They Only Come Out at Night*, Edgar Winter Group
7. *I Am Woman*, Helen Reddy
8. *Don't Shoot Me, I'm Only the Piano Player*, Elton John
9. *I'm Still in Love with You*, Al Green
10. *Seventh Sojourn*, Moody Blues

1974

1. *Goodbye Yellow Brick Road*, Elton John
2. *John Denver's Greatest Hits*, John Denver
3. *Band on the Run*, Paul McCartney & Wings
4. *Innervisions*, Stevie Wonder
5. *You Don't Mess Around with Jim*, Jim Croce
6. *American Graffiti*, soundtrack
7. *Imagination*, Gladys Knight & The Pips
8. *Behind Closed Doors*, Charlie Rich

9. *The Sting*, soundtrack
10. *Tres Hombres*, ZZ Top

1975

1. *Elton John—Greatest Hits*, Elton John
2. *John Denver's Greatest Hits*, John Denver
3. *That's the Way of the World*, Earth, Wind & Fire
4. *Back Home Again*, John Denver
5. *Phoebe Snow*, Phoebe Snow
6. *Heart Like a Wheel*, Linda Ronstadt
7. *Captain Fantastic and the Brown Dirt Cowboy*, Elton John
8. *An Evening with John Denver*, John Denver
9. *AWB*, Average White Band
10. *On the Border*, Eagles

1976

1. *Frampton Comes Alive*, Peter Frampton
2. *Fleetwood Mac*, Fleetwood Mac
3. *Wings at the Speed of Sound*, Wings
4. *Greatest Hits, 1971–1975*, Eagles
5. *Chicago IX—Chicago's Greatest Hits*, Chicago
6. *The Dream Weaver*, Gary Wright
7. *Desire*, Bob Dylan
8. *A Night at the Opera*, Queen
9. *History—America's Greatest Hits*, America
10. *Gratitude*, Earth, Wind & Fire

1977

1. *Rumours*, Fleetwood Mac
2. *Songs in the Key of Life*, Stevie Wonder
3. *A Star Is Born*, Barbra Streisand/Kris Kristofferson/soundtrack
4. *Hotel California*, Eagles
5. *Boston*, Boston
6. *A New World Record*, Electric Light Orchestra
7. *Part 3*, K.C. & The Sunshine Band
8. *Silk Degrees*, Boz Scaggs
9. *Night Moves*, Bob Seger & The Silver Bullet Band
10. *Fleetwood Mac*, Fleetwood Mac

1978

1. *Saturday Night Fever*, Bee Gees/various artists/soundtrack
2. *Grease*, John Travolta/Olivia Newton-John/soundtrack
3. *Rumours*, Fleetwood Mac
4. *The Stranger*, Billy Joel
5. *Aja*, Steely Dan
6. *Feels So Good*, Chuck Mangione

7. *The Grand Illusion*, Styx
8. *Simple Dreams*, Linda Ronstadt
9. *Point of Know Return*, Kansas
10. *Slowhand*, Eric Clapton

1979

1. *52nd Street*, Billy Joel
2. *Spirits Having Flown*, Bee Gees
3. *Minute by Minute*, Doobie Brothers
4. *The Cars*, The Cars
5. *Breakfast in America*, Supertramp
6. *Live and More*, Donna Summer
7. *Pieces of Eight*, Styx
8. *Bad Girls*, Donna Summer
9. *Parallel Lines*, Blondie
10. *Blondes Have More Fun*, Rod Stewart

1980

1. *The Wall*, Pink Floyd
2. *The Long Run*, Eagles
3. *Off the Wall*, Michael Jackson
4. *Glass Houses*, Billy Joel
5. *Damn the Torpedoes*, Tom Petty & The Heartbreakers
6. *Against the Wind*, Bob Seger & The Silver Bullet Band
7. *In the Heat of the Night*, Pat Benatar
8. *Eat to the Beat*, Blondie
9. *In Through the Out Door*, Led Zeppelin
10. *Kenny*, Kenny Rogers

1981

1. *Hi Infidelity*, REO Speedwagon
2. *Double Fantasy*, John Lennon & Yoko Ono
3. *Greatest Hits*, Kenny Rogers
4. *Christopher Cross*, Christopher Cross
5. *Crimes of Passion*, Pat Benatar
6. *Paradise Theatre*, Styx
7. *Back in Black*, AC/DC
8. *Voices*, Daryl Hall & John Oates
9. *Zenyatta Mondatta*, The Police
10. *The River*, Bruce Springsteen

1982

1. *Asia*, Asia
2. *Beauty and the Beat*, The Go-Go's
3. *4*, Foreigner
4. *American Fool*, John Cougar
5. *Freeze-Frame*, The J. Geils Band
6. *Escape*, Journey
7. *Get Lucky*, Loverboy
8. *Bella Donna*, Stevie Nicks
9. *Chariots of Fire*, Vangelis/soundtrack
10. *Ghost in the Machine*, The Police

1983

1. *Thriller*, Michael Jackson
2. *Business as Usual*, Men at Work

3. *Synchronicity*, The Police
4. *H2O*, Daryl Hall & John Oates
5. *1999*, Prince
6. *Lionel Richie*, Lionel Richie
7. *Jane Fonda's Workout Record*, Jane Fonda
8. *Pyromania*, Def Leppard
9. *Kissing To Be Clever*, Culture Club
10. *Olivia's Greatest Hits, Vol. 2*, Olivia Newton-John

1984

1. *Thriller*, Michael Jackson
2. *Sports*, Huey Lewis & The News
3. *Can't Slow Down*, Lionel Richie
4. *An Innocent Man*, Billy Joel
5. *Colour by Numbers*, Culture Club
6. *1984*, Van Halen
7. *Eliminator*, ZZ Top
8. *Sychronicity*, Police
9. *Footloose*, soundtrack
10. *Seven and the Ragged Tiger*, Duran Duran

1985

1. *Born in the U.S.A.*, Bruce Springsteen
2. *Reckless*, Bryan Adams
3. *Like a Virgin*, Madonna
4. *Make It Big*, Wham!
5. *Private Dancer*, Tina Turner
6. *No Jacket Required*, Phil Collins
7. *Beverly Hills Cop*, various artists/soundtrack
8. *Suddenly*, Billy Ocean
9. *Purple Rain*, Prince & The Revolution
10. *Songs from the Big Chair*, Tears for Fears

1986

1. *Whitney Houston*, Whitney Houston
2. *Heart*, Heart
3. *Scarecrow*, John Cougar Mellencamp
4. *Afterburner*, ZZ Top
5. *Brothers in Arms*, Dire Straits
6. *Control*, Janet Jackson
7. *Welcome to the Real World*, Mr. Mister
8. *Promise*, Sade
9. *No Jacket Required*, Phil Collins
10. *Primitive Love*, Miami Sound Machine

1987

1. *Slippery When Wet*, Bon Jovi
2. *Graceland*, Paul Simon
3. *Licensed To Ill*, Beastie Boys
4. *The Way It Is*, Bruce Hornsby & The Range
5. *Control*, Janet Jackson
6. *The Joshua Tree*, U2
7. *Fore!*, Huey Lewis & The News

8. *Night Songs*, Cinderella
9. *Rapture*, Anita Baker
10. *Invisible Touch*, Genesis

1988

1. *Faith*, George Michael
2. *Dirty Dancing*, soundtrack
3. *Hysteria*, Def Leppard
4. *Kick*, INXS
5. *Bad*, Michael Jackson
6. *Appetite for Destruction*, Guns N' Roses
7. *Out of the Blue*, Debbie Gibson
8. *Richard Marx*, Richard Marx
9. *Tiffany*, Tiffany
10. *Permanent Vacation*, Aerosmith

1989

1. *Don't Be Cruel*, Bobby Brown
2. *Hangin' Tough*, New Kids on the Block
3. *Forever Your Girl*, Paula Abdul
4. *New Jersey*, Bon Jovi
5. *Appetite for Destruction*, Guns N' Roses
6. *The Raw & the Cooked*, Fine Young Cannibals
7. *GNR Lies*, Guns N' Roses
8. *Traveling Wilburys*, Traveling Wilburys
9. *Hysteria*, Def Leppard
10. *Girl You Know It's True*, Milli Vanilli

1990

1. *Janet Jackson's Rhythm Nation 1814*, Janet Jackson
2. *. . . But Seriously*, Phil Collins
3. *Soul Provider*, Michael Bolton
4. *Pump*, Aerosmith
5. *Please Hammer Don't Hurt 'Em*, M.C. Hammer
6. *Forever Your Girl*, Paula Abdul
7. *Dr. Feelgood*, Mötley Crüe
8. *The End of Innocence*, Don Henley
9. *Cosmic Thing*, The B-52's
10. *Storm Front*, Billy Joel

1991

1. *Mariah Carey*, Mariah Carey
2. *No Fences*, Garth Brooks
3. *Shake Your Money Maker*, The Black Crowes
4. *Gonna Make You Sweat*, C+C Music Factory
5. *Wilson Phillips*, Wilson Phillips
6. *To the Extreme*, Vanilla Ice
7. *Please Hammer Don't Hurt 'Em*, M.C. Hammer
8. *The Immaculate Collection*, Madonna
9. *Empire*, Queensryche
10. *I'm Your Baby Tonight*, Whitney Houston

1992

1. *Ropin' the Wind,* Garth Brooks
2. *Dangerous,* Michael Jackson
3. *Nevermind,* Nirvana
4. *Some Gave All,* Billy Ray Cyrus
5. *Achtung Baby,* U2
6. *No Fences,* Garth Brooks
7. *Metallica,* Metallica
8. *Time, Love, & Tenderness,* Michael Bolton
9. *Too Legit To Quit,* Hammer
10. *Totally Krossed Out,* Kris Kross

1993

1. *The Bodyguard,* soundtrack
2. *Breathless,* Kenny G
3. *Unplugged,* Eric Clapton
4. *Janet,* Janet Jackson
5. *Some Gave All,* Billy Ray Cyrus
6. *The Chronic,* Dr. Dre
7. *Pocket Full of Kryptonite,* Spin Doctors
8. *Ten,* Pearl Jam
9. *The Chase,* Garth Brooks
10. *Core,* Stone Temple Pilots

1994

1. *The Sign,* Ace of Base
2. *Music Box,* Mariah Carey
3. *Doggy Style,* Snoop Doggy Dogg
4. *The Lion King* soundtrack
5. *August & Everything After,* Counting Crows
6. *VS.,* Pearl Jam
7. *Toni Braxton,* Toni Braxton
8. *Janet,* Janet Jackson
9. *Bat Out of Hell II: Back into Hell,* Meatloaf
10. *The One Thing,* Michael Bolton

BILLBOARD NUMBER ONES FOR 1995

Week-by-week, here are the most popular albums and songs so far in 1995. (Source: *Billboard.*)

The Hits, Garth Brooks January 7 "On Bended Knee," Boyz II Men	*Me Against the World,* 2PAC April 15 "This is How We Do It," Montell Jordan	*Pulse,* Pink Floyd June 24 "Have You Ever Really Loved a Woman?" Bryan Adams
The Hits, Garth Brooks January 14 "On Bended Knee," Boyz II Men	*Me Against the World,* 2PAC April 22 "This is How We Do It," Montell Jordan	*Cracked Rear View,* July 1 Hootie & The Blowfish "Have You Ever Really Loved a Woman?" Bryan Adams
The Hits, Garth Brooks January 21 "On Bended Knee," Boyz II Men	*The Lion King* soundtrack April 29 "This is How We Do It," Montell Jordan	*HIStory,* Michael Jackson July 8 "Waterfalls," TLC
The Hits, Garth Brooks January 28 "Creep," TLC	*Throwing Copper,* Live May 6 "This is How We Do It," Montell Jordan	*HIStory,* Michael Jackson July 15 "Waterfalls," TLC
The Hits, Garth Brooks February 4 "Creep," TLC	*Friday* soundtrack May 13 "This is How We Do It," Montell Jordan	*Pocahontas* soundtrack July 22 "Waterfalls," TLC
Balance, Van Halen February 11 "Creep," TLC	*Friday* soundtrack May 20 "This is How We Do It," Montell Jordan	*Cracked Rear View,* July 29 Hootie & The Blowfish "Waterfalls," TLC
The Hits, Garth Brooks February 18 "Creep," TLC	*Cracked Rear View,* May 27 Hootie & The Blowfish "This is How We Do It," Montell Jordan	*Dreaming of You,* Selena August 5 "Waterfalls," TLC
The Hits, Garth Brooks February 25 "Take a Bow," Madonna	*Cracked Rear View,* June 3 Hootie & The Blowfish "Have You Ever Really Loved a Woman?" Bryan Adams	*E. 1999 Eternal,* August 12 Bone Thugs N Harmony "Waterfalls," TLC
The Hits, Garth Brooks March 4 "Take a Bow," Madonna	*Cracked Rear View,* June 10 Hootie & The Blowfish "Have You Ever Really Loved a Woman?" Bryan Adams	*E. 1999 Eternal,* August 19 Bone Thugs N Harmony "Waterfalls," TLC
II, Boyz II Men March 11 "Take a Bow," Madonna	*Cracked Rear View,* June 17 Hootie & The Blowfish "Have You Ever Really Loved a Woman?" Bryan Adams	*Cracked Rear View* August 26 Hootie & The Blowfish "Kiss from a Rose," Seal
Greatest Hits, March 18 Bruce Springsteen "Take a Bow" Madonna		*Dangerous Minds* September 2 soundtrack "You Are Not Alone," Michael Jackson
Greatest Hits, March 25 Bruce Springsteen "Take a Bow," Madonna		
Me Against the World, 2PAC April 1 "Take a Bow," Madonna		
Me Against the World, 2PAC April 8 "Take a Bow," Madonna		

THE BESTSELLING ALBUMS OF ALL TIME

The Recording Industry Association of America tracks monthly album sales and awards gold and platinum certification based on the sale of 500,000 units for gold, one million units for platinum, and two million units or more for multiplatinum. Here are the albums which top the lists, organized by category, as of September 1995.

ROCK/POP

24 million
Michael Jackson, *Thriller*, 1982

22 million
Eagles, *Their Greatest Hits, 1971–1975*, 1977

17 million
Fleetwood Mac, *Rumours*, 1977

15 million
Boston, *Boston*, 1976
Whitney Houston/various artists, *The Bodyguard* soundtrack, 1992
Bruce Springsteen, *Born in the U.S.A.*, 1984

14 million
Eagles, *Hotel California*, 1976

13 million
Guns N' Roses, *Appetite for Destruction*, 1987
Pink Floyd, *The Dark Side of the Moon*, 1973

12 million
Whitney Houston, *Whitney Houston*, 1985
Meat Loaf, *Bat Out of Hell*, 1977
Bruce Springsteen, *Bruce Springsteen & The E Street Band Live, 1975–1985*, 1986

11 million
Bee Gees/various artists, *Saturday Night Fever* soundtrack, 1977
Bon Jovi, *Slippery When Wet*, 1986
Def Leppard, *Hysteria*, 1987
Elton John, *Greatest Hits*, 1974
Prince, *Purple Rain*, 1984
various artists, *Dirty Dancing* soundtrack, 1987
Led Zeppelin, *Led Zeppelin IV*, 1971

10 million
AC/DC, *Back in Black*, 1980
M.C. Hammer, *Please Hammer Don't Hurt 'Em*, 1990
Carole King, *Tapestry*, 1971
Pink Floyd, *The Wall*, 1979
Lionel Richie, *Can't Slow Down*, 1984

9 million
The Beatles, *Abbey Road*, 1969
Billy Joel, *The Stranger*, 1977
Def Leppard, *Pyromania*, 1983
Journey, *Escape*, 1981
Madonna, *Like a Virgin*, 1984
George Michael, *Faith*, 1987
R.E.O. Speedwagon, *Hi-Infidelity*, 1982

8 million
Ace of Base, *The Sign*, 1993
Aerosmith, *Greatest Hits*, 1980
The Beatles, *Sgt. Pepper's Lonely Hearts Club Band*, 1967
Michael Bolton, *Time, Love and Tenderness*, 1991
Mariah Carey, *Mariah Carey*, 1991
Mariah Carey, *Music Box*, 1993
Green Day, *Dookie*, 1994
Whitney Houston, *Whitney*, 1987
Michael Jackson, *Bad*, 1987
Billy Joel, *Greatest Hits Volume I & II*, 1985
Journey, *Journey's Greatest Hits*, 1988
Madonna, *The Immaculate Collection*, 1991
Metallica, *Metallica*, 1991
New Kids on the Block, *Hangin' Tough*, 1988
Pearl Jam, *Ten*, 1991
Van Halen, *Van Halen*, 1978
Whitesnake, *Whitesnake*, 1987

COUNTRY

13 million
Garth Brooks, *No Fences*, 1990

11 million
Garth Brooks, *Ropin' the Wind*, 1991

8 million
Billy Ray Cyrus, *Some Gave All*, 1992

6 million
Garth Brooks, *The Chase*, 1991
Garth Brooks, *Garth Brooks*, 1989
Patsy Cline, *Greatest Hits*, 1967

5 million
Garth Brooks, *The Hits*, 1994
Garth Brooks, *In Pieces*, 1993
Brooks & Dunn, *Brand New Man*, 1991
Alan Jackson, *A Lot About Livin' (And a Little About Love)*, 1992

4 million
Alabama, *Feels So Right*, 1981
Alabama, *Mountain Music*, 1982
Brooks & Dunn, *Hard Workin' Man*, 1993
Alan Jackson, *Don't Rock the Jukebox*, 1991
Waylon Jennings, *Greatest Hits*, 1979
Wynonna, *Wynonna*, 1992
Tim McGraw, *Not a Moment Too Soon*, 1994
Anne Murray, *Greatest Hits*, 1980
Willie Nelson, *Always on My Mind*, 1982
Willie Nelson, *Stardust*, 1990
Randy Travis, *Always and Forever*, 1990

3 million
Alabama, *Alabama's Greatest Hits*, 1986
Alabama, *The Closer You Get*, 1983
Alabama, *Roll On*, 1984
Clint Black, *Killin' Time*, 1989

Garth Brooks, *The Garth Brooks Collection,* 1994
Vince Gill, *I Still Believe in You,* 1992
Alan Jackson, *Who I Am,* 1994
Reba McEntire, *It's Your Call,* 1992
Reba McEntire, *Greatest Hits, Vol. II,* 1993
John Michael Montgomery, *Kickin' It Up,* 1994
The Statler Brothers, *Best of The Statler Brothers,* 1975
George Strait, *Pure Country,* 1992
Randy Travis, *Storms of Life,* 1992

JAZZ

8 million
Kenny G, *Breathless,* 1992

4 million
Kenny G, *Silhouette,* 1988

3 million
Kenny G, *Kenny G Live,* 1989
Kenny G, *Duotones,* 1986
Kenny G, *Miracles,* 1994
George Benson, *Breezin',* 1984

Platinum
George Benson, *Weekend in L.A.,* 1978
George Benson, *Give Me the Night,* 1980
George Benson, *In Flight,* 1977
Herbie Hancock, *Future Shock,* 1983
Bob James/David Sanborn, *Double Vision,* 1991
Al Jarreau, *Breakin' Away,* 1982
Chuck Mangione, *Feels So Good,* 1977
Spyro Gyra, *Morning Dance,* 1979

RAP

10 million
M.C. Hammer, *Please Hammer Don't Hurt 'Em,* 1990

7 million
Vanilla Ice, *To the Extreme,* 1990

5 million
The Beastie Boys, *Licensed To III,* 1986

4 million
Arrested Development, *3 Years, 5 Months and 2 Days in the Life of . . .,* 1992
Kris Kross, *Totally Krossed Out,* 1992
Snoop Doggy Dogg, *Doggystyle,* 1993

3 million
D.J. Jazzy Jeff and The Fresh Prince, *He's the D.J., I'm the Rapper,* 1988
Dr. Dre, *The Chronic,* 1992
Hammer, *Too Legit To Quit,* 1992
Salt-N-Pepa, *Very Necessary,* 1993

2 million
various artists, *Above the Rim* soundtrack, 1994
Cypress Hill, *Black Sunday,* 1993
Eazy-E, *Eazy-Duz-It,* 1988
L.L. Cool J, *Bigger and Deffer,* 1987
L.L. Cool J, *Mama Said Knock You Out,* 1990
M.C. Hammer, *Let's Get It Started,* 1988
various artists, *Murder Was the Case* soundtrack, 1994
N.W.A., *Straight Outta Compton,* 1989
Tone-Loc, *Loc'd After Dark,* 1989
Warren G., *Regulate . . . G Funk Era,* 1994

CLASSICAL

2 million
Benedictine Monks of Santo Domingo de Silos, *Chant,* 1994
Carreras, Domingo, Pavarotti, *The Three Tenors in Concert,* 1990

Platinum
Wendy Carlos, *Switched on Bach,* 1986
Carreras, Domingo, Pavarotti with Mehta, *The Three Tenors in Concert 1994,* 1994
London Symphony Orchestra for Victoria's Secret, *Classics by Request, Volume I,* 1988*
London Symphony Orchestra for Victoria's Secret, *Classics by Request, Volume II,* 1989*
London Symphony Orchestra for Victoria's Secret, *Classics by Request, Volume III,* 1990*
London Symphony Orchestra for Victoria's Secret, *Classics by Request, Volume IV,* 1991*
London Symphony Orchestra for Victoria's Secret, *Classics by Request, Volume V,* 1992*
Luciano Pavarotti, *O Holy Night,* London, 1985
Royal Philharmonic Orchestra, *Hooked on Classics,* 1982
Piotr Tchaikovsky performed by Van Cliburn with the RCA Symphony Orchestra/Kirill Kondrashin, *Piano Concerto No. 1 in B-flat Minor, Op. 23,* 1982

*albums sold exclusively through the Victoria's Secret stores and catalog and thus not eligible for certification by RIAA.

DESERT ISLAND DISCS

Since 1983, *Pulse!* (the magazine published by Tower Records/Video) has been asking major recording artists, "If you were stranded on a desert island, what 10 records would you want with you?" The following is a sampling from its archives.

BILLY JOEL

Take Five	Dave Brubeck
Rubber Soul	The Beatles
Hot Rocks, 1964–69	The Rolling Stones
Adagio for Strings	Samuel Barber, performed by Leonard Bernstein and the New York Philharmonic
Led Zeppelin	Led Zeppelin
Axis: Bold As Love	Jimi Hendrix Experience
The Complete Tatum Solo Masterpieces, Volumes 1–9	Art Tatum
John Barleycorn Must Die	Traffic
Otis Redding's Greatest Hits	Otis Redding
The Genius of Ray Charles	Ray Charles

ANTHONY KIEDIS (RED HOT CHILI PEPPERS)

I Against I	Bad Brains
Talking Book	Stevie Wonder
Anything by	Bob Marley and the Wailers
Hardcore Jollies	Funkadelic
Greatest Hits	James Brown
Greatest Hits	Marvin Gaye
Greatest Hits	Billie Holiday
Are You Experienced?	Jimi Hendrix Experience

SUZANNE VEGA

Eli and the 13th Confession	Laura Nyro
Songs of Leonard Cohen	Leonard Cohen
The Velvet Underground and Nico	The Velvet Underground
Sounds of Silence	Simon and Garfunkel
Synchronicity (side 2)	The Police
Hatful of Hollow	The Smiths
Somebody's Got To Do It	Frank Christian
Working on Wings to Fly	Cindy Kallet
2	Cindy Kallet

MICHAEL STIPE (R.E.M.)

Pink Flag	Wire
Marquee Moon	Television
Horses	Patti Smith
Rhapsody in Blue	George Gershwin
Experiment in Terror	Henry Mancini
Fellini Satyricon	soundtrack
The Velvet Underground	The Velvet Underground
154	Wire
Exotica 2	Martin Denny
Sound of the Sand	David Thomas & the Pedestrians

ICE-T

On Fire	Stetsasonic
Yo! Bum Rush the Show	Public Enemy
Salt-N-Pepa	Salt-N-Pepa
Licensed to Ill	Beastie Boys
Motor-Booty Affair	Parliament
The Best of the Delfonics	The Delfonics
Down by Law	MC Shan
All LPs	AC/DC
All LPs	Judas Priest

TOM PETTY

Good Vibrations: Thirty Years of The Beach Boys	The Beach Boys
The Byrds	The Byrds
Greatest Hits	The Searchers
Rainin' in My Heart	Slim Harpo
The Chess Box	Howlin' Wolf
Elvis—The King of Rock & Roll:The Complete '50s Masters	Elvis Presley
Grevious Angel	Gram Parsons
Greatest Hits	Wilson Pickett
$1,000,000 Worth of Twang	Duane Eddy
A Date With the Everly Brothers	The Everly Brothers

CARLY SIMON

Tea for the Tillerman	Cat Stevens
Caverna Magica	Andreas Vollenweider
Midnight Love	Marvin Gaye
Alchemy—Live	Dire Straits
Winter	George Winston
Water Music	George Frideric Handel
Porgy and Bess	any version
Puccini Arias	Kiri Te Kanawa
Paradise and Lunch	Ry Cooder
Greatest Hits	The Temptations
I Musici, Concerto in A Minor, Concerto in D Minor, Brandenburg Concertos	Johann Sebastian Bach

K.D. LANG

The Patsy Cline Story	Patsy Cline
Hard Hitting Songs for Hard Hit People	Hazel Dickens
Season of Glass	Yoko Ono
Country Hits, Vol. 7 (K-Tel)	various artists
Mingus	Joni Mitchell
Latin à la Lee	Peggy Lee
Any album by	Kate Bush

Wild, Wild Young Women	various artists
Ella and Oscar	Ella Fitzgerald and Oscar Peterson
Rickie Lee Jones	Rickie Lee Jones

DWIGHT YOAKAM

The Best of Buck Owens, Vols. I, II, III	Buck Owens
Buckaroo	Buck Owens
The Songs That Made Him Famous	Johnny Cash
The Columbia Sessions	Stanley Brothers
The Best of Merle Haggard	Merle Haggard
The Georgia Satellites	The Georgia Satellites
Can't Stand the Weather	Stevie Ray Vaughan
. . . And a Time To Dance	Los Lobos
Rockin' George Jones	George Jones
Get Yer Ya-Ya's Out	The Rolling Stones
Green River	Creedence Clearwater Revival
Riptide	Robert Palmer

ROSANNE CASH

Atlantic Rhythm and Blues 1947–1974	various artists
Paradise and Lunch	Ry Cooder
A Hard Day's Night	The Beatles
Graceland	Paul Simon
Gorilla	James Taylor
Blonde on Blonde	Bob Dylan
Desire	Bob Dylan
Infidels	Bob Dylan
King of America	Elvis Costello
My Aim Is True	Elvis Costello
Born To Run	Bruce Springsteen
Hard Promises	Tom Petty

LENNY KRAVITZ

Kaya	Bob Marley and the Wailers
Catch a Fire	Bob Marley and the Wailers
Electric Ladyland	Jimi Hendrix Experience
Smash Hits	Jimi Hendrix Experience
Plastic Ono Band	John Lennon
Innervisions	Stevie Wonder
Houses of the Holy	Led Zeppelin
Zoso (Led Zeppelin IV)	Led Zeppelin
Past Masters	The Beatles
What's Going On	Marvin Gaye

DAVE PIRNER (SOUL ASYLUM)

Bitches Brew	Miles Davis
The Complete Recordings	Robert Johnson
Out of Step	Minor Threat
Exile on Main Street	The Rolling Stones
Loaded	The Velvet Underground
Horses	Patti Smith
The Stooges	The Stooges
Poor Boy	Woodie Guthrie
Pearl	Janis Joplin
Up on the Sun	Meat Puppets

JOAN BAEZ

The Brandenburg Concertos	Johann Sebastian Bach
The Beethoven String Quartets	various artists
The Final Cut	Pink Floyd
Brahms Alto Rhapsody, Op. 53	Kathleen Ferrier
Jussi Bjoerling Arias Vols. I & II	
Tristan und Isolde	Wagner, sung by Birgit Nilsson
Chopin Etudes	Maurizio Pollini
Blonde on Blonde	Bob Dylan
Scottish Fantasy	Max Bruch, performed by Jascha Heifetz
Compilation "Dance" tape	Steve Winwood, Stevie Wonder, Ruben Blades, U2, Peter Gabriel, Talk Talk, Tears for Fears, Foreigner, Eurythmics

THE ROCK OF AGES: PEOPLE'S FAVORITE 50

Steve Dougherty has been PEOPLE's chief music writer since 1985. Herewith, his completely subjective list of the 50 albums he'd stock in his personal jukebox.

THE BAND (1969)
The Band
Robbie Robertson's songs are like mini-novels with a back beat, and the heartland vocals by Richard Manuel, Levon Helm, and Rick Danko may qualify this as the greatest American rock album of all time.

A HARD DAY'S NIGHT (1964), **RUBBER SOUL** (1965), **THE BEATLES** (1969)
The Beatles
John Lennon, at the height of his vocal and writing powers, dominates all three discs; and for a change, the Cute One rocks as well.

CHUCK BERRY'S GOLDEN HITS (1967)
Chuck Berry
The brown-eyed handsome man told Tchaikovsky the news: There is indeed such a thing as a three-minute masterpiece.

THE RISE AND FALL OF ZIGGY STARDUST AND THE SPIDERS FROM MARS (1972)
David Bowie
Music had never glittered quite like this before and glam rock never sounded so good again.

20 ALL-TIME GREATEST HITS (1991)
James Brown
You'll feel good! But then, you knew that you would.

BUFFALO SPRINGFIELD 1958–77 (1976)
Buffalo Springfield
This is evidence of why many a hippie tear spilled at the break-up of the supergroup that spawned Neil Young, Stephen Stills, and Jim Messina.

20 ESSENTIAL TRACKS FROM THE BOXED SET: 1965–1990 (1992)
The Byrds
America's Beatles invented country rock and inspired Dylan to electrify folk.

LONDON CALLING (1979)
The Clash
They pronounced rock dead, then celebrated its resurrection on this, a double album without a lame cut in the lot.

MY AIM IS TRUE (1977)
Elvis Costello
He looked punk, acted mean, sounded nasty, and hit right on target in his album debut.

LAYLA AND OTHER ASSORTED LOVE SONGS (1970)
Derek and the Dominoes
Eric Clapton and Duane Allman. 'Nuff said.

THE CHRONIC (1992)
Dr. Dre (with Snoop Doggy Dogg)
Hip hop's auteur and his pet rapper share their bemused family values.

BRINGING IT ALL BACK HOME (1965), **HIGHWAY 61 REVISITED** (1965), **JOHN WESLEY HARDING** (1968)
Bob Dylan
For all who question the lasting fuss over the rheumy rock laureate, three masterworks.

I NEVER LOVED A MAN (THE WAY I LOVE YOU) (1967)
Aretha Franklin
They invented soul so she could be queen.

WHAT'S GOIN' ON (1971)
Marvin Gaye
Motown's sex star made hearts and minds quicken with this ambitious song cycle.

ARE YOU EXPERIENCED? (1967)
Jimi Hendrix Experience
That voice. Those songs. That guitar. We're still asking, "Where did this guy come from?"

R.E.M., *Murmur*

The Clash, *London Calling*

Marvin Gaye, *What's Goin' On*

ARTHUR (DECLINE AND FALL OF THE BRITISH EMPIRE) (1969), MUSWELL HILLBILLIES (1971)
The Kinks
Tommy without the pretensions: these are two of plaintive mod genius Ray Davies's brilliantly realized theme albums.

ORIGINAL GOLDEN HITS, VOLS. 1 AND 2 (1969)
Jerry Lee Lewis
Killer tracks from The Killer: all is forgiven.

GROOVIEST 17 ORIGINAL HITS (1959)
Little Richard
"Good Golly Miss Molly," "Tutti Fruiti," "Lucille," "Long Tall Sally," "Rip It Up." Macon, Georgia's absolutely fabulous former dishwasher screamed 'em all to life at New Orleans's Specialty Records studio.

COURT AND SPARK (1974)
Joni Mitchell
The ultimate chick singer whips one on the boys.

MOBY GRAPE (1967)
Moby Grape
San Francisco's one-masterpiece wonder squeezed all their juice into this ignored collection.

THE BEST OF VAN MORRISON (1990)
Van Morrison
Romance for the soul.

NEVERMIND (1991)
Nirvana
Full of as much old-fashioned tube amplifier feedback as neo-punk martyr Kurt Cobain's fabled rage, this is a call to get with it for all classic rock-fixated geezers who insist that the music ain't what it used to be.

TEAR THE ROOF OFF (1993)
Parliament Funkadelic
So they did and something memorable was born.

THE 10 MOST OVERRATED ALBUMS

For those contrarians who would rather smash discs than play them, here is a flip-side list of legendary non-legends in the annals of rock.

SERGEANT PEPPER'S LONELY HEARTS CLUB BAND (1967)
The Beatles
"A Day in the Life" does not a great album make. Ballyhooed as not only the Beatles', but rock's best ever, it paved the way for a generation of self-indulgent studio dweebs.

PET SOUNDS (1966)
The Beach Boys
The "masterpiece" that inspired *Pepper* and committed similar crimes.

4 WAY STREET (1971)
Crosby, Stills, Nash and Young
They could have used a stop sign.

DARK SIDE OF THE MOON (1973)
Pink Floyd
In which the band defined ponderous.

ELVIS (TV SPECIAL) (1968)
Elvis Presley
The gig that was trumpeted as his return to '50s form. Leatherclad in Vegas a year after the summer of love, The King was already out of touch with current culture and his music.

EXILE ON MAIN STREET (1972)
The Rolling Stones
For revisionists, the Stones don't get any better. But they did, and would again, without so much filler.

THE JOSHUA TREE (1987)
U2
Bono and the boys provide two great songs—"Bullet the Blue Sky," "Where the Street Have No Name"—and a lot of cuts that seem interesting at first but end up all sounding the same.

THE DREAM OF THE BLUE TURTLES (1985)
Sting
The Police man lured listeners with his pop status, then stung them with stingy jazz.

TOMMY (1969)
The Who
Maybe if Pete had left it to critics to call his own composition "A Rock Opera," it wouldn't make us want to gag.

And, finally: **THE COMPACT DISC ITSELF**
It's not the pop, scratch and hum we miss—it's what's lost in the digital mix. Sound waves, like rock, should roll, rather than get chopped up into chewy bytes.

THE SUN SESSIONS (1987), **ELVIS' GOLDEN RECORDS, VOL. 1** (1958)
Elvis Presley
Rock and roll at its best.

1999 (1982)
Prince
From when he had a name and all the critics loved him in New York, and everywhere else.

MURMUR (1983)
R.E.M.
The debut album that brought "Radio Free Europe" to the promised land. What's it about? Who knows? Who cares?

HISTORY OF OTIS REDDING (1968)
Otis Redding
The greatest soul ever told.

TIM (1985)
The Replacements
Put "Swingin' Party" on replay, never let it stop.

BEGGAR'S BANQUET (1968), **STICKY FINGERS** (1971), **THE SINGLES COLLECTION** (1989)
The Rolling Stones
The first two are mid-career classics. In the last, an obscure collection of mostly mono, many never released in the U.S. singles, finds the Stones paying tribute to their black American heroes.

NEVER MIND THE BOLLOCKS HERE'S THE SEX PISTOLS (1977)
Sex Pistols
Unlistenable then, unbeatable now, it mocks, it taunts, it screams, and you can dance to it!

ANTHOLOGY (1981)
Sly & the Family Stone
Rock's original rainbow coalition invented the party jam.

BETWEEN HEAVEN AND HELL (1992)
Social Distortion
Tatooed front man Mike Ness looks like he stepped from the gates of San Quentin; he sings Patsy Cline's "Making Believe (You Still Love Me)" like a prison yard angel.

BACK TO MONO (1991)
Phil Spector
Actually four CDs, offering unforgettable visits by (mostly) girl groups to the little man's Great Wall of Sound.

BORN TO RUN (1975)
Bruce Springsteen
The Boss as rock-and-roll tradesman, re-defining the exuberant yearning to get out on the highway with a guitar strapped 'cross his back.

STORYTELLER (Boxed Set, 1992)
Rod Stewart
Remember that before he turned out the lights and cuddled up to the Manilow inside him, Rod the mod was an underrated lyricist who rivaled Van Morrison in the U.K. soul crooner department.

HITSVILLE USA: THE MOTOWN SINGLES COLLECTION (1992)
The Supremes, The Four Tops, Smokey Robinson & The Miracles, The Jackson Five, The Temptations, et.al.
The soundtrack of the '60s, courtesy of Detroit's big wheel, Berry Gordy. (And it's got Mary Wells and Marvin Gaye too.)

GIRLFRIEND (1991)
Matthew Sweet
With former Television star Richard Lloyd, Sweet made the album of the year only to be ignored by radio and its customers, who didn't buy it.

TALKING HEADS 77 (1977)
Talking Heads
Leading the punk revolt from these shores, art school misfit David Byrne makes his bow as one of rock's strangest, and most talented, characters.

ACHTUNG, BABY (1991)
U2
The Dubliners finally drop the earnest facade, as well as the endlessly repeated rhythm guitar riff, that launched them and deliver a sonic treat recorded in the cold war capital of Berlin.

WHAT UP, DOG? (1988)
Was (Not Was)
The now feuding brothers Was married Don's '70s funk with David's post-modern poetry and created a true pop original.

MEATY BEATY BIG AND BOUNCY (1971)
The Who
Known for their big productions, including the overrated *Tommy* and underrated *Quadrophenia*, the London mods rocked Top 40 radio with these high explosives.

AFTER THE GOLD RUSH (1970)
Neil Young
One nugget from four brilliant decades of work by the once and current rocker.

TELY FREE (1967)
Frank Zappa
Innovative, mocking, shocking, and funny as hell.

THE NAME OF THIS BAND IS . . .

From Abba to ZZ Top, here's the scoop on how our favorite bands came up with their famous names.

ABBA: an acronym made up of the first initials of the band members' names—Agnetha Fältskog, Benny Andersson, Björn Ulvaeus, and Anni-Frid Lyngstad.

The B-52's: the Southern term for the bouffant hairdos favored by band members Kate Pierson and Cindy Wilson.

Chicago: originally named the Chicago Transit Authority, and shortened to Chicago after they were threatened with a lawsuit by the city.

Devo: the band felt it essential to name themselves after the theory of "de-evolution"—the idea that mankind is moving backwards instead of forwards.

Duran Duran: took the name from the villain in the 1967 science fiction film *Barbarella*.

Fine Young Cannibals: from the 1960 film *All the Fine Young Cannibals*, starring Natalie Wood and Robert Wagner.

Guns N' Roses: a combination of two bands that members had previously played in—L.A. Guns and Hollywood Rose.

Hole: band leader Courtney Love chose the name after a line in the Greek tragedy *Medea*: "There's a hole burning deep inside of me." She says she picked it because "I knew it would confuse people."

Hüsker Dü: it means "Do You Remember?" in Swedish, and was the title of a board game popular in the '50s.

Jane's Addiction: allegedly, Jane is a Hollywood hooker through whom the band members met in Los Angeles.

L7: a slang term from the '50s meaning "square" which guitarist Suzy Gardner learned from watching *The Flinstones*.

Pearl Jam: named after Eddie Vedder's grandmother Pearl, who was married to a Native American and made hallucinogenic preserves from peyote.

Pink Floyd: a combination of the names of two Georgia bluesmen, Pink Anderson and Floyd Council.

The Police: an ironic reference to drummer Stewart Copeland's father, former chief of the CIA's Political Action Staff.

Soundgarden: named after a beach sculpture by Lake Washington in Seattle which hums in the wind.

10,000 Maniacs: the misremembered title of a cult horror film, *2,000 Maniacs*.

UB40: since the band members were all unemployed, they chose the name of the British unemployment benefit card.

Velvet Underground: from the title of an obscure book about sadomasochism.

ZZ Top: after Texas bluesman Z. Z. Hill

CHANGE OF TUNE

Like the best-laid plans, the best-named bands often went astray before deciding on a final moniker. Here are some enduring groups with their long lost early names.

Final Name	Original Name	Final Name	Original Name
The Bangles	Supersonic Bangs; Bangs	Journey	Golden Gate Rhythm Section
The Beach Boys	Carl and the Passions	Led Zeppelin	New Yardbirds
The Beatles	Johnny and the Moondogs	Lynyrd Skynyrd	My Backyard
The Bee Gees	Rattlesnakes	The Mamas and the Papas	New Journeymen
Black Sabbath	Earth	The Righteous Brothers	Paramours
Buffalo Springfield	The Herd	Salt-N-Pepa	Supernature
The Byrds	Beefeaters	Simon and Garfunkel	Tom and Jerry
Creedence Clearwater Revival	The Golliwogs	Styx	Trade Winds; TW4
Culture Club	Praise of Lemmings	Sonny and Cher	Caesar and Cleo
The Cure	Obelisk; Goat Band	Steppenwolf	Sparrow
Depeche Mode	Composition of Sound	The Supremes	Primettes
Dire Straits	Cafe Racers	Talking Heads	Artistics
Earth, Wind & Fire	Salty Peppers	The Temptations	The Elgins
Grateful Dead	Warlocks	U2	Feedback; the Hype

THE 50 BEST COUNTRY ALBUMS

Seeking a collection of country albums to get the essence of Nashville? PEOPLE's Ralph Novak ardently (if arbitrarily) touts this starter set—or any of them—for a great listen.

THE BEST OF EDDY ARNOLD (1967)
Eddy Arnold
The Tennessee Plowboy was the very definition of smooth.

RUDOLPH THE RED-NOSED REINDEER (1949)
Gene Autry
Autry may not have had the best voice of the movies' singing cowboys or the best horse, but he got the best tunes to sing.

THINKIN' PROBLEM (1994)
David Ball
No problem—it's brilliant.

HOT TAMALE BABY (1986)
Marcia Ball
The Louisiana Texas country circuit knows no spicier number than this lanky belter.

ONE OF A KIND (1990)
Susi Beatty
Cancer hit this bright, witty singer just as she was getting started. More's the pity.

THE BELLAMYS' GREATEST HITS (1982)
The Bellamy Brothers
"If I Said You Had a Beautiful Body, Would You Hold It Against Me?" is country's cleverest tune.

LYING TO THE MOON (1990)
Matraca Berg
A lyrical voice and poignant music make Berg the most promising female singer-songwriter in country.

SOMEWHERE BETWEEN (1988)
Suzy Bogguss
A rhythmic, soft-rock style and a shrewd ear for material earned Bogguss her strong following.

WALK ON (1982)
Karen Brooks
Her career didn't last much past this striking debut album, but the lively, sweet-voiced horsewoman made it fun while it lasted.

HOMETOWN GIRL (1987)
Mary Chapin Carpenter
Carpenter indelibly introduced herself and her evocative story songs with this rollicking album.

JOHNNY CASH IN FOLSOM PRISON (1968)
Johnny Cash
Cash's rumbly voice and style helped bring country & western into the mainstream.

SEVEN-YEAR ACHE (1981)
Rosanne Cash
Lots of fun, this playful album backed by Albert Lee's guitar arrived before Cash descended into her often morose pit of contemplation.

PATSY CLINE (1957)
Patsy Cline
Country's best torch singer built a noble body of work before her premature death in a plane crash.

AIN'T LIVING LONG LIKE THIS (1981)
Rodney Crowell
Nobody writes better country songs than old Rodney and nobody sings 'em better, either.

FIGHTING FIRE WITH FIRE (1991)
Davis Daniel
He may be too subtle for stardom, but his smooth style makes for splendid listening.

EB '84 (1984)
The Everly Brothers
The Everly Brothers' comeback was short-lived, no fault of this collection, which is as rich as any of their historic '50s material.

WHEN I CALL YOUR NAME (1989)
Vince Gill
He might have to envy some of the younger generation of male singers their hats. They have to envy him that ethereal tenor.

SONGS I'LL ALWAYS SING (1976)
Merle Haggard
The best younger singers sound like the old Okie; none really equals him.

LUXURY LINER (1977)
Emmylou Harris
Country's best backup singer has cut many glorious solo albums, not least this one and *Elite Hotel*.

HIGHWAYMEN (1985)
The Highwaymen
Listening to Willie Nelson, Waylon Jennings and Kris Kristofferson sing is like hearing Mt. Rushmore burst into song.

DON'T ROCK THE JUKEBOX (1991)
Alan Jackson
Showing an edifying respect for his elders, the sweetly twangy Jackson updates honky tonk.

GREATEST HITS (1979)
Waylon Jennings
Jennings always had the grittiest voice and the best band of all country's Lone Star outlaws.

WINE-COLORED ROSES (1986)
George Jones
Not only the title song but "You Never Looked this Good When You were Mine," a playful duet

with Patti Page, grace this latter-day effort by country's answer to Frank Sinatra.

TELL SOMEBODY (1990)
Sass Jordan
Canadian country performers can tend to the softer side but Jordan rocks with the livliest of them.

THE COWBOY ALBUM (1992)
Frankie Laine
Laine wasn't exactly a country singer. But once he recorded the unforgettable theme from *High Noon*, you had to consider him at least an honorary cowpoke.

SPEECHLESS (1986)
Albert Lee
Nashville's most prolific, melodious electric guitarist is at his best improvising behind vocal stars, but he can hold center stage, too.

ANTHOLOGY—VOLS. I & II (1991)
Brenda Lee
Her visibility, but not her singing ability, declined after "I'm Sorry."

PONTIAC (1988)
Lyle Lovett
Nobody beats Lyle in the big hair department, and few can match his eclectic approach to country music, either.

THE VERY BEST OF LORETTA LYNN AND CONWAY TWITTY (1979)
Loretta Lynn and Conway Twitty
Simply put, Country's best duet.

GREATEST HITS, VOL. II (1985)
Ronnie Milsap
Milsap's affinity for Motown tunes explains his uncommonly rhythmic approach to Nashville music.

SOMETHING IN RED (1991)
Lorrie Morgan
Country's Sheena Easton struts her considerable stuff.

GREATEST HITS (1980)
Ann Murray
She sings a bit earnestly, but there is no one warmer or more ingratiating.

WILLIE NELSON SINGS KRIS KRISTOFFERSON (1979)
Willie Nelson
Modern country's best songs sung by its best singer. What else do you want?

WILL THE CIRCLE BE UNBROKEN II (1990)
Nitty Gritty Dirt Band
A multi-guest collaboration brings the neo-folk Dirtsters in touch with their Nashville roots.

'80S LADIES (1987)
K. T. Oslin
Blooming very late but very full, Oslin wrote and sang these songs with passion and wit.

COAT OF MANY COLORS (1971)
Dolly Parton
Forget everything else. It was this voice and this songwriting skill that made Parton a star.

TRIO (1987)
Dolly Parton, Linda Ronstadt, & Emmylou Harris,
The closest thing on earth to a heavenly choir made this one-time collaboration memorable.

ELVIS IN NASHVILLE (1988)
Elvis Presley
Another town in Tennessee claimed him, but what better country song is there than "Are You Lonesome Tonight?"

COWBOYS IN LOVE (1994)
Riders in the Sky
Ranger Doug, Too Slim and Side Meat masterfully spoof the cowboy myth and its music.

DON'T CHEAT IN OUR HOMETOWN (1983)
Ricky Skaggs
A versatile, glib instrumentalist, Skaggs also proved he is a happily twangy, expressive singer.

COUNTRY JAMBOREE (1972)
Sesame Street Troupe (Plus Crystal Gayle, et al)
A typical Sesame Street blend of fun and learning teaches kids the joys of country music.

COME ON JOE (1987)
Jo-el Sonnier
Blending Cajun country and Randy Newman, the Louisiana performer made a late but impressive splash.

GREATEST HITS (1983)
Ray Stevens
Stevens's spoofs are always unique; his countrified, banjo-heavy version of "Misty" is a masterwork of non-verbal parody.

HEROES AND FRIENDS (1990)
Randy Travis
Even Roy Rogers shows up on this collaboration between Travis and many of his idols and contemporaries.

ERNEST TUBB FAVORITES (1968)
Ernest Tubb
If he had never recorded anything but "Waltz Across Texas," the Texas Troubadour would have made his contribution.

WHAT DO I DO WITH ME? (1991)
Tanya Tucker
The onetime teen-aged temptress aged very well.

COUNTRY MUSIC HALL OF FAME SERIES (1991)
Kitty Wells
Maybe God didn't make honky tonk angels, but He must have had a hand in this poignant voice.

40 GREATEST HITS (1978)
Hank Williams
If country music ever had a Gershwin, it was Hank the Elder.

GREATEST HITS (1947)
Tex Williams
Williams sang wittily and his band swung almost as much as Wills's.

A BOB WILLS ANTHOLOGY (1973)
Bob Wills
The flagship band of Western Swing made "San Antonio Rose" everybody's gal.

GREAT TITLES TO COUNTRY SONGS

A case could be made that the aptest aphorists of pop culture are country songwriters. Herewith, some of C & W's quirkier titles.

"Divorce Me C.O.D.," Merle Travis

"Don't You Think This Outlaw Bit's Done Got Out of Hand," Waylon Jennings

"Heaven's Just a Sin Away," The Kendells

"I Cheated Me Right Out of You," Moe Bandy

"She Was Bitten on the Udder by an Adder," Jethro Burns

"I Forgot More Than You'll Ever Know," Davis Sisters

"I'll Never Get Out of This World Alive," Hank Williams Sr.

"I'm Gonna Hire a Wino to Decorate Our Home," David Frizzell

"I'm the Only Hell (Mama Ever Raised)," Johnny Paycheck

"It's Not Love (But It's Not Bad)," Merle Haggard

"I've Enjoyed About as Much of This as I Can Stand," Porter Wagoner

"The Lord Knows I'm Drinkin'," Cal Smith

"Mama's in the Graveyard, Papa's in the Pen (Papa Loved Mama and Mama Loved Men)," Garth Brooks

"Marriage Has Ruined More Good Love Affairs," Jan Howard

"Maximum Security to Minimum Wage," Don King

"Now I Lay Me Down To Cheat," David Allan Coe

"She's Actin' Single (I'm Drinkin' Doubles)," Gary Stewart

"She Got the Goldmine (I Got the Shaft)," Jerry Reed

"Sleeping Single (in a Double Bed)," Barbara Mandrell

"Take an Old Cold Tater and Wait," Little Jimmy Dickens

"Take This Job and Shove It," Johnny Paycheck

"Yonder Comes a Sucker," Jim Reeves

"You Just Hurt My Last Feeling," Sammi Smith

"You're Gonna Ruin My Bad Reputation," Ronnie McDowell

"You're Out Doing What I'm Here Doing Without," Gene Watson

"You're the Reason Our Kids Are Ugly," Loretta Lynn

"Waitin' in Your Welfare Line," Buck Owens

"What's Made Milwaukee Famous (Has Made a Loser Out of Me)," Jerry Lee Lewis

"When It's Springtime in Alaska (It's Forty Below)," Johnny Horton

PEOPLE'S 20 TRAILBLAZERS OF C & W MUSIC

Many of these legendary divas and dudes of the Grand Ole Opry are now dead, but their music and influence live forever—from Nashville to Austin to Bakersfield, wherever country artists are at work.

Roy Acuff	Lefty Frizzell	Ernest Tubb
Eddy Arnold	Bill Monroe	Kitty Wells
Gene Autry	Minnie Pearl	Hank Williams Sr.
Boudleaux Bryant	Tex Ritter	Bob Wills
The Carter Family	Marty Robbins	
Patsy Cline	Jimmie Rodgers	
Spade Cooley	Roy Rogers	
Tennessee Ernie Ford	Hank Snow	

JAZZ: ESSENTIAL LISTENING

Not encyclopedic or definitive, this is simply a list of 50 marvelous jazz albums. The recordings here date from the '20s to the '90s, and they cover a range of styles. Any jazz purist, or for that matter, impurist, will find sins of omission and commission on this list. All we, the jazz jury at PEOPLE, can say is that these albums have enriched our lives immeasurably and given us an almost embarrassing amount of pleasure. To us, these recordings are the easiest sort of listening, full of wit, passion, invention, and beauty.

Louis Armstrong	*Hot Fives and Sevens,* Vol. II or III (1926–27)
Chet Baker	*My Funny Valentine* (1954)
Count Basie	*The Original American Decca Recordings* (1937–39)
Bix and Tram Beiderbecke	*The Bix Beiderbecke Story,* Vol. II (1927–28)
Art Blakey & The Jazz Messengers	*Buhaina's Delight* (1961)
Clifford Brown and Max Roach	*Clifford Brown and Max Roach* (1954–55)
Betty Carter	*Betty Carter* (1966)
Ornette Coleman	*The Shape of Jazz To Come* (1959–60)
Ornette Coleman	*Free Jazz* (1960)
John Coltrane	*Coltrane* (1957)
John Coltrane	*Meditations* (1965)
Miles Davis	*Kind of Blue* (1959)
Miles Davis and Gil Evans	*Porgy and Bess* (1958)
Paul Desmond and Gerry Mulligan	*Two of a Mind* (1962)
Eric Dolphy	*Out to Lunch* (1964)
Duke Ellington	*The Blanton-Webster Band* (1940-42)
Duke Ellington & The Jungle Band	*Rockin' in Rhythm,* Vol. III (1929–31)
Bill Evans	*The Village Vanguard Sessions* (1961)
Art Farmer	*Something To Live For* (1987)
Ella Fitzgerald	*The Gershwin Songbook* (1959)
Ella Fitzgerald	*The Intimate Ella* (1960)
Stan Getz	*The Roost Quartets 1950-51* (1950–51)
Benny Goodman	*Carnegie Hall Concert* (1938)
Charlie Haden & Quartet	*Haunted Heart* (1990)
Lionel Hampton	*The Complete Lionel Hampton* (1937–41)
Herbie Hancock	*Maiden Voyage* (1965)
Coleman Hawkins	*Body and Soul: The Complete Coleman Hawkins,* Vol. I (1929–40)
Coleman Hawkins	*The Complete Coleman Hawkins* (1944)
Fletcher Henderson and Don Redman	*Developing an American Orchestra, 1923–1937* (1923–37)
Billie Holiday	*The Quintessential Billie Holiday,* Vol. III, IV, or V (1937–39)
James P. Johnson	*Snowy Morning Blues* (1930, 1944)
Abbey Lincoln	*The World Is Falling Down* (1990)
Charles Mingus	*New Tijuana Moods* (1957)
Thelonious Monk	*The Unique Thelonious Monk* (1956)
Thelonious Monk	*Alone in San Francisco* (1959)
Thelonious Monk	*Monk's Dream* (1962)
Gerry Mulligan	*What Is There To Say?* (1958–59)

Oliver Nelson	*Blues and the Abstract Truth* (1961)	Sonny Rollins	*A Night at the Village Vanguard*, Vols. I and II (1957)
King Oliver	*King Oliver's Jazz Band 1923* (1923)	John Scofield	*Time on My Hands* (1989)
Charlie Parker	*The Charlie Parker Story* (1945)	Art Tatum	*The Tatum Solo Masterpieces*, Vol. III (1953–55)
Charlie Parker (with Dizzy Gillespie, Max Roach, Bud Powell, and Charles Mingus)	*The Greatest Jazz Concert Ever* (1953)	Cecil Taylor	*Unit Structures* (1966)
		Sarah Vaughan and Clifford Brown	*Sarah Vaughan With Clifford Brown* (1954)
		Fats Waller	*The Joint Is Jumpin'* (1929–43)
Bud Powell	*The Amazing Bud Powell*, Vol. I (1949–51)	Lester Young	*The Complete Lester Young* (1943–44)
Bud Powell	*The Genius of Bud Powell* (1951)		

JAZZ TODAY

A new generation of stars is emerging in jazz. Steeped in tradition, technically prodigious, often daring, and always fired by the energy and passion of youth, they are a formidable lot, as varied in style as they are united in their allegiance to the verities of swing, the blues, and improvisation. But the roots of jazz are not necessarily ruled by the spring chickens. Our favorite jazz masters paved the way for today's prodigies. Here are some standout albums by the old and new schools.

THE NEW GENERATION

James Carter, *The Real Quietstorm* (1995)
(saxophone/flute/clarinet)

Javon Jackson, *For One Who Knows* (1995)
(saxophone)

Leroy Jones , *Mo' Cream From The Crop* (1994)
(trumpet)

Keb' Mo', *Keb' Mo'* (1994)
(guitar)

Marcus Printup, *Song for the Beautiful Woman* (1995)
(trumpet)

Eric Reed, *The Swing And I* (1995)
(piano)

Jacky Terrasson, *Jacky Terrasson* (1995)
(piano)

THE ROOTS OF JAZZ

Geri Allen, *Twenty One* (1994)
(piano)

Marty Ehrlich, *Can You Hear A Motion?* (1994)
(various instruments)

Kenny Garrett, *Triology* (1995)
(alto sax)

Hank Jones and Charlie Haden, *Steal Away: Spirituals, Hymns, and Folk Songs* (1995)
(piano; bass)

Abbey Lincoln, *A Turtle's Dream* (1994)
(vocals)

Steve Turre, *Rhythm Within* (1995)
(trombone)

Cassandra Wilson, *Blue Skies* (1988)
(vocals)

50 GREAT CLASSICAL RECORDINGS

We can't really presume to pick a classical library for all tastes, but PEOPLE's editors will hazard this tendentious consensus of outstanding recordings:

Johann Sebastian Bach	*Brandenburg Concertos*, Munich Bach Orchestra/Karl Richter
Johann Sebastian Bach	*The Well-Tempered Clavier, BWV 846-893*, Davitt Moroney
Samuel Barber	*Adagio for Strings*, Saint Louis Symphony Orchestra/Leonard Slatkin
Béla Bartók	*String Quartets Nos. 1–6*, Emerson Quartet
Ludwig van Beethoven	*Symphonies Nos. 1–9, Complete Cycles*, Berlin Philharmonic/Herbert von Karajan
Ludwig van Beethoven	*Piano Sonata in C Minor, Op. 13, "Pathétique,"* Wilhelm Kempff
Ludwig van Beethoven	*Piano Sonata in C-sharp Minor, Op. 27, No. 2, "Moonlight,"* Wilhelm Kempff
Hector Berlioz	*Symphonie fantastique*, French National Radio Orchestra/Sir Thomas Beecham
Leonard Bernstein	*Chichester Psalms*, John Paul Bogart; Camerata Singers, New York Philharmonic/Leonard Bernstein
Georges Bizet	*Carmen*, Agnes Baltsa, José Carreras; Chorus of the Paris Opéra, Berlin Philharmonic/Herbert von Karajan
Johannes Brahms	*Violin Concerto in D, Op. 77,* Itzhak Perlman; Chicago Symphony Orchestra/Carlo Maria Giulini
Benjamin Britten	*War Requiem, Op. 66*, Lorna Haywood, Anthony Rolfe Johnson, Benjamin Luxon; Atlanta Boy Choir, Atlanta Symphony Orchestra & Chorus/Robert Shaw
Frédéric Chopin	*26 Preludes*, Dmitri Alexeev
Aaron Copland	*Appalachian Spring*, New York Philharmonic/Leonard Bernstein
Claude Debussy	*Images*, Claudio Arrau
Antonín Dvořák	*Symphony No. 9 in E Minor, Op. 95, "From the New World,"* London Symphony Orchestra/István Kertész
César Franck	*Symphony in D Minor*, Berlin Radio Symphony Orchestra/Vladimir Ashkenazy
George Gershwin	*Rhapsody in Blue*, Columbia Symphony Orchestra, New York Philharmonic/Leonard Bernstein
George Gershwin	*Porgy and Bess*, Willard White, Leona Mitchell; Cleveland Orchestra & Chorus/Lorin Maazel
George Frideric Handel	*Messiah*, Heather Harper, Helen Watts, John Wakefield, John Shirley-Quirk; London Symphony Orchestra & Choir/Sir Colin Davis
Joseph Haydn	*Symphonies Nos. 93-104, "London,"* Royal Concertgebouw Orchestra/Sir Colin Davis
Joseph Haydn	*String Quartets, Op. 76, "Erdödy,"* Takács Quartet
Charles Ives	*Three Places in New England*, Boston Symphony Orchestra/Michael Tilson Thomas
Franz Liszt	*Les Préludes*, Philadelphia Orchestra/Riccardo Muti
Gustav Mahler	*Symphony No. 9 in D*, Vienna Philharmonic/Bruno Walter
Felix Mendelssohn	*Violin Concerto in E Minor, Op. 64,* Kyung Wha Chung; Montreal Symphony Orchestra/ Charles Dutoit

Wolfgang Amadeus Mozart	*Symphony No. 41 in C, K. 551, "Jupiter,"* Columbia Symphony Orchestra/Bruno Walter
Wolfgang Amadeus Mozart	*A Little Night Music, K. 525*, Prague Chamber Orchestra/Sir Charles Mackerras
Wolfgang Amadeus Mozart	*The Marriage of Figaro*, Samuel Ramey, Lucia Popp; London Opera Chorus, London Philharmonic Orchestra/Sir George Solti
Wolfgang Amadeus Mozart	*Don Giovanni*, Eberhard Wächter, Joan Sutherland, Elisabeth Schwarzkopf; Philharmonia Orchestra & Chorus/Carlo Maria Giulini
Modest Mussorgsky	*Pictures at an Exhibition*, Montreal Symphony Orchestra/Charles Dutoit
Giacomo Puccini	*La Bohème*, Mirella Freni, Luciano Pavarotti; Chorus of the Deutsche Oper Berlin, Berlin Philharmonic/Herbert von Karajan
Sergei Prokofiev	*Symphony No. 1 in D, Op. 25, "Classical,"* Berlin Philharmonic/Herbert von Karajan
Sergei Rachmaninoff	*Piano Concerto No. 2 in C Minor, Op. 18*, Vladimir Ashkenazy; London Symphony Orchestra/André Previn
Nikolai Rimsky-Korsakov	*Scheherazade, Op. 35*, Royal Concertgebouw Orchestra/Kirill Kondrashin
Gioacchino Rossini	*The Barber of Seville*, Leo Nucci, William Matteuzzi, Cecilia Bartoli; Chorus & Orchestra of the Teatro Comunale di Bologna/Giuseppe Patanè
Camille Saint-Saëns	*The Carnival of the Animals*, Montreal Symphony Orchestra, London Sinfonietta/Charles Dutoit
Domenico Scarlatti	*Keyboard Sonatas*, Vladimir Horowitz
Arnold Schoenberg	*Verklärte Nacht (Transfigured Night), Op. 4*, Jiri Najnar, Vaclav Bernasek; Talich Quartet
Franz Schubert	*Die Schöne Müllerin, D. 795; Winterreise, D. 911*, Dietrich Fischer-Dieskau, Gerald Moore
Robert Schumann	*Op. 19, "Carnaval: Pretty Scenes on Four Notes,"* Artur Rubinstein
Dmitri Shostakovich	*Symphony No. 5 in D Minor, Op. 47*, Royal Concertgebouw Orchestra/Bernard Haitink
Jean Sibelius	*Symphony No. 5 in E-flat, Op. 82*, Boston Symphony Orchestra/Sir Colin Davis
Igor Stravinsky	*The Rite of Spring*, New York Philharmonic, Cleveland Orchestra/Pierre Boulez
Piotr Ilyich Tchaikovsky	*Symphony No. 6 in B Minor, Op. 74, "Pathétique,"* Leningrad Philharmonic/Evgeny Mravinsky
Piotr Ilyich Tchaikovsky	*Piano Concerto No. 1 in B-flat Minor, Op. 23*, Van Cliburn; RCA Symphony Orchestra/Kirill Kondrashin
Giuseppe Verdi	*Requiem*, Elisabeth Schwárzkopf, Christa Ludwig, Nicolai Gedda, Nicolai Ghiaurov; Philharmonia Orchestra & Chorus/Carlo Maria Giulini
Giuseppe Verdi	*La Traviata*, Joan Sutherland, Luciano Pavarotti; London Opera Chorus, National Philharmonic Orchestra/Richard Bonynge
Antonio Vivaldi	*Concertos for Violin, Strings, and Continuo, Op. 8, Nos. 1–4, "The Four Seasons,"* Alan Loveday; Academy of St. Martin-in-the-Fields/Sir Neville Marriner
Richard Wagner	*The Ring of the Nibelung*, Birgit Nilsson, Wolfgang Windgassen; Chorus & Orchestra of the Bayreuth Festival/Karl Böhm

THE 50 GREATEST CLASSICAL COMPOSERS

They're all dead white men, but they sure could write a tune. Here are the classics of the classical composers as selected by PEOPLE:

Johann Sebastian Bach (German, 1685–1750)

Samuel Barber (American, 1910–81)

Béla Bartók (Hungarian, 1881–1945)

Ludwig van Beethoven (German, 1770–1827)

Hector Berlioz (French, 1803–69)

Leonard Bernstein (American, 1918–90)

Georges Bizet (French, 1838–75)

Johannes Brahms (German, 1833–97)

Benjamin Britten (British, 1913–76)

John Cage (American, 1912–92)

Elliott Carter (American, b. 1908)

Frédéric Chopin (Polish, 1810–49)

Aaron Copland (American, 1900–90)

François Couperin (French, 1668–1733)

Claude Debussy (French, 1862–1918)

Antonín Dvorák (Czech, 1841–1904)

Gabriel Fauré (French, 1845–1924)

César Franck (Belgian/French, 1822–90)

George Gershwin (American, 1898–1937)

George Frideric Handel (German/British, 1685–1759)

Franz Joseph Haydn (Austrian, 1732–1809)

Paul Hindemith (German, 1895–1963)

Charles Ives (American, 1874–1954)

Leos Janácek (Czech, 1854–1928)

Franz Liszt (Hungarian, 1811–86)

Gustav Mahler (Bohemian/Austrian, 1860–1911)

Felix Mendelssohn (German, 1809–47)

Claudio Monteverdi (Italian, 1567–1643)

Wolfgang Amadeus Mozart (Austrian, 1756–91)

Giovanni da Palestrina (Italian, c. 1525–94)

Sergei Prokofiev (Russian, 1891–1953)

Giacomo Puccini (Italian, 1858–1924)

Sergei Rachmaninoff (Russian, 1873–1943)

Jean-Philippe Rameau (French, 1683–1764)

Maurice Ravel (French, 1875–1937)

Camille Saint-Saëns (French, 1835–1921)

Domenico Scarlatti (Italian, 1685–1757)

Arnold Schoenberg (Austrian, 1874–1951)

Franz Schubert (Austrian, 1797–1828)

Dmitri Shostakovich (Russian, 1906–75)

Jean Sibelius (Finnish, 1865–1957)

Johann Strauss (Austrian, 1825–99)

Richard Strauss (German, 1864–1949)

Igor Stravinsky (Russian, 1882–1971)

Piotr Ilyitch Tchaikovsky (Russian, 1840–93)

Georg Philipp Telemann (German, 1681–1767)

Ralph Vaughan Williams (British, 1872–1958)

Giuseppe Verdi (Italian, 1813–1901)

Antonio Vivaldi (Italian, 1678–1741)

Richard Wagner (German, 1813–83)

MAJOR AMERICAN SYMPHONY ORCHESTRAS

From Miami to Seattle, American cities are supporting some of the finest symphonies in the world. The following orchestras, 25 of the most important in the U.S., are listed with their conductors or music directors.

Orchestra	Conductor	Location
Atlanta Symphony Orchestra	Yoel Levi	Atlanta, GA
Baltimore Symphony Orchestra	David Zinman	Baltimore, MD
Boston Symphony Orchestra	Seiji Ozawa	Boston, MA
Buffalo Philharmonic Orchestra	Maximiano Valdes	Buffalo, NY
Chicago Symphony Orchestra	Daniel Barenboim	Chicago, IL
Cincinnati Symphony Orchestra	Jesús Lopez-Cobos	Cincinnati, OH
Cleveland Orchestra	Christoph von Dohnányi	Cleveland, OH
Detroit Symphony Orchestra	Neeme Järvi	Detroit, MI
Houston Symphony	Christoph Eschenbach	Houston, TX
Los Angeles Chamber Orchestra	Christof Perick	Los Angeles, CA
Los Angeles Philharmonic	Esa-Pekka Salonen	Los Angeles, CA
Louisville Orchestra	Wayne S. Brown	Louisville, KY
Minnesota Orchestra	Edo de Waart	Minneapolis, MN
National Symphony Orchestra	Leonard Slatkin	Washington, DC
New Jersey Symphony Orchestra	Zdenek Macal	Newark, NJ
New World Symphony	Michael Tilson Thomas	Miami Beach, FL
New York Philharmonic	Kurt Masur	New York, NY
Philadelphia Orchestra	Wolfgang Sawallisch	Philadelphia, PA
Pittsburgh Symphony Orchestra	Lorin Maazel	Pittsburgh, PA
Rochester Philharmonic Orchestra	Peter Bay	Rochester, NY
St. Louis Symphony Orchestra	Leonard Slatkin	St. Louis, MO
St. Paul Chamber Orchestra	Hugh Wolff	St. Paul, MN
San Francisco Symphony	Herbert Blomstedt	San Francisco, CA
Seattle Symphony	Gerard Schwarz	Seattle, WA
Utah Symphony Orchestra	Joseph Silverstein	Salt Lake City, UT

MUSICAL PERIODS

As it turns out, classical music isn't all classical. To help you sort out baroque quartets and romantic symphonies from classical sonatas and modern operas, here's the chronological breakdown of musical periods:

PERIOD	DATES
Renaissance	1450–1600
Baroque	1600–1750
Classical	1750–1825
Romantic	1825–1910
Modern	1910–present

CLIFF'S CLUES TO OPERA PLOTS

Opera is drama expressed musically, verbally, and visually—the ultimate experience for ears, eyes, and emotions. If you're intimidated by the prospect of sitting through three or more hours of heightened drama in a foreign language, but are intrigued by the passionate, mysterious world of divas and Don Juans, start here, with our summaries of 10 classics. (Dates given indicate the first staged production.)

THE BARBER OF SEVILLE (1782)

Composed by Gioacchino Rossini, text by Sterbini. Based on the novel by Beaumarchais. Set in Seville, Spain, in the 17th century.

Count Almaviva, a Grandee of Spain, loves Rosina, the young ward and bride-to-be of Dr. Bartolo. With the help of Figaro, the town barber and busybody, the Count enters his rival's home disguised as a drunken soldier, then as a music teacher. Having gained access to Rosina, he easily persuades her to take his hand. Almaviva then convinces a notary, procured by Bartolo for his own marriage to Rosina, to marry him to Rosina in Bartolo's absence.

LA BOHÈME (1896)

Composed by Giacomo Puccini, text by Luigi Illica and Giuseppe Giacosa. Based on the novel Scènes de la vie de Bohème by Henri Murger. Set in Paris, France, in the 17th century.

Rodolfo, a poet, lives in the Latin Quarter of Paris with his dear friends—a painter, a philosopher, and a musician—who defy their hunger with cheerfulness and pranks. The quartet of friends is so poor that they resort to burning Rodolfo's poetry to keep warm. But

Rodolfo's heart is soon warmed by the frail and consumptive Mimi, who knocks on his door one night, her candle extinguished by a winter draft. The two fall in love, but Mimi grows weaker and weaker. Eventually, her sickness and Rodolfo's overprotectiveness drive the two apart. Mimi's last request is to return to Rodolfo's attic room, where they first met, and where she will die in his arms.

DON CARLOS (1867)

Composed by Giuseppe Verdi, text by G. Méry and C. du Locle. Based on the play by Friedrich von Schiller. Set in France and Spain, during the Spanish Inquisition.

Don Carlos, infante of Spain, is torn between a futile love for Queen Elizabeth, his stepmother, to whom he was once engaged, and a fierce desire to bring freedom to Flanders, a Protestant country under Spanish (Catholic) domain. The queen's attendant, who is deeply in love with Carlos, tells the king, untruthfully, that Carlos and Elizabeth have been unfaithful to him. Carlos is sent to death, ostensibly for demanding to be let go to Flanders. Elizabeth remains at her husband's side, and

Carlos escapes his death in the last moments of the opera, saved by the King's father, who takes Carlos into the cloister.

DON GIOVANNI (1787)

Composed by Wolfgang Amadeus Mozart, text by Lorenzo da Ponte. Based on the text Il Convitato by Giovanni Bertati. Set in Seville at the end of the 18th century.

The insatiable lover, Don Juan, jaunts from lass to lass, breaking hearts and wreaking havoc before he is finally dragged into Hell by the statue of the Commendatore who he killed in a duel after attempting to seduce his daughter, Doña Anna.

ELEKTRA (1909)

Composed by Richard Strauss, text by Hugo von Hofmannsthal. Adapted from the play by Sophocles. Set in ancient Mycenae.

Her soul withered by grief, Elektra is bent on avenging the seven-year-old murder of her father, Agamemnon, at the hands of her mother, Klytämnestra, and her mother's lover, Aegisth. Elektra persuades her brother Orest to murder Klytämnestra and Aegisth. The murders send Elektra into a dance of joy that becomes a frenzied dance of death, ending in the explosion of her heart.

LUCIA DI LAMMERMOOR (1835)
Composed by Gaetano Donizetti, text by Salvatore Cammarano. Based on the novel The Bride of Lammermoor *by Sir Walter Scott. Set in Scotland in 1700.*

Her mother's death is slowly but inexorably driving the tragic Lucia to madness. She loves Edgardo, but their promised union is sabotaged by her brother, who forces her to marry Arturo, a wealthy man she does not love. Tormented by visions of ghosts and spirits and devastated over the loss of Edgardo, Lucia murders her groom on their wedding night, then experiences a series of hallucinations before collapsing and dying of a broken heart.

RIGOLETTO (1851)
Composed by Giuseppe Verdi, text by Francesco Maria Piave. Based on Victor Hugo's Le Roi s'amuse. *Set Mantua, Italy, in the 16th century.*

Rigoletto, a court jester, intends to have the Duke of Mantua murdered for seducing his daughter, Gilda, but brings about the murder of the girl, instead.

The first of a "romantic trilogy," *Rigoletto* is followed by *Il Trovotore* and *La Traviata*.

TOSCA (1900)
Composed by Giacomo Puccini, text by Giuseppe Giacosa and Luigi Illica. Based on the play La Tosca *by Victorien Sardou. Set in Rome, in 1800.*

Floria Tosca, a prima donna, is passionately pursued by the evil Scarpia, chief of the Roman police. Yet Tosca loves Cavaradossi, a painter and a liberal patriot. She attempts to save her lover from execution when he is accused of aiding a fugitive, by pretending to yield to Scarpia's wishes, then killing him. But her actions unwittingly help to destroy her true love, Cavaradossi.

LA TRAVIATA (1853)
Composed by Giuseppe Verdi, text by Francesco Maria Piave. Based on Alexandre Dumas's play La Tame aux Camélias. *Set in Paris and vicinity in 1850.*

Violetta, a courtesan, renounces her life of pleasure in order to be with her gentlemanly lover, Alfredo.

But Alfredo's father persuades Violetta that she is a blight on his family and that she must leave Alfredo for the good of his career. She returns to her former protector, with whom Alfredo fights a duel. Alfredo is subsequently forced to flee the country, and will return only to find Violetta dying of consumption.

TRISTAN AND ISOLDE (1865)
Composed and written by Richard Wagner. Set in a ship at sea, in England, and in Ireland, in a legendary time.

Tristan is dispatched to Ireland by his uncle, King Marke, to win him Isolde's hand. Yet Tristan and Isolde have long loved one another, each believing their love to be unrequited. On board the vessel that brings them to Cornwall, they drink what they believe to be a death potion, but is in fact a love potion. King Marke later discovers them in a midnight embrace. Tristan, wounded by one of the king's knights, flees to France. Isolde follows, finds him dying, and she too dies by his side.

THE WORLD'S LARGEST OPERA HOUSES

These houses showcase the world's best singers and stand as monuments to the grandeur of opera.

Opera House	Location	Total Capacity
The Metropolitan Opera	New York, NY	4,065
Cincinnati Opera	Cincinnati, OH	3,630
Lyric Opera of Chicago	Chicago, IL	3,563
San Francisco Opera	San Francisco, CA	3,476
The Dallas Opera	Dallas, TX	3,420

MTV VIDEO MUSIC AWARDS

BEST VIDEO OF THE YEAR

1984	The Cars	*You Might Think*
1985	Don Henley	*The Boys of Summer*
1986	Dire Straits	*Money for Nothing*
1987	Peter Gabriel	*Sledgehammer*
1988	INXS	*Need You Tonight/Mediate*
1989	Neil Young	*This Note's for You*
1990	Sinead O'Connor	*Nothing Compares 2 U*
1991	R.E.M.	*Losing My Religion*
1992	Van Halen	*Right Now*
1993	Pearl Jam	*Jeremy*
1994	Aerosmith	*Cryin'*
1995	TLC	*Waterfalls*

BEST MALE VIDEO

1984	David Bowie	*China Girl*
1985	Bruce Springsteen	*I'm on Fire*
1986	Robert Palmer	*Addicted to Love*
1987	Peter Gabriel	*Sledgehammer*
1988	Prince	*U Got the Look*
1989	Elvis Costello	*Veronica*
1990	Don Henley	*The End of the Innocence*
1991	Chris Isaak	*Wicked Game* (Concept)
1992	Eric Clapton	*Tears in Heaven* (Performance)
1993	Lenny Kravitz	*Are You Gonna Go My Way*
1994	Tom Petty and the Heartbreakers	*Mary Jane's Last Dance*
1995	Tom Petty and the Heartbreakers	*You Don't Know How It Feels*

BEST FEMALE VIDEO

1984	Cyndi Lauper	*Girls Just Want To Have Fun*
1985	Tina Turner	*What's Love Got To Do with It*
1986	Whitney Houston	*How Will I Know*
1987	Madonna	*Papa Don't Preach*
1988	Suzanne Vega	*Luka*
1989	Paula Abdul	*Straight Up*
1990	Sinead O'Connor	*Nothing Compares 2 U*
1991	Janet Jackson	*Love Will Never Do Without You*
1992	Annie Lennox	*Why*
1993	k.d. lang	*Constant Craving*
1994	Janet Jackson	*If*
1995	Madonna	*Take a Bow*

BEST CONCEPT VIDEO

1984	Herbie Hancock	*Rockit*
1985	Glenn Frey	*Smuggler's Blues*
1986	a-ha	*Take On Me*
1987	Peter Gabriel/ Stephen Johnson	*Sledgehammer*
1988	Pink Floyd	*Learning To Fly*

BEST GROUP VIDEO

1984	ZZ Top	*Legs*
1985	USA for Africa	*We Are the World*
1986	Dire Straits	*Money for Nothing*
1987	Talking Heads	*Wild Wild Life*
1988	INXS	*Need You Tonight/Mediate*
1989	Living Colour	*Cult of Personality*
1990	The B-52's	*Love Shack*
1991	R.E.M.	*Losing My Religion*

1992	U2	*Even Better Than the Real Thing*
1993	Pearl Jam	*Jeremy*
1994	Aerosmith	*Cryin'*
1995	TLC	*Waterfalls*

BEST NEW ARTIST IN A VIDEO

1984	Eurythmics	*Sweet Dreams (Are Made of This)*
1985	'Til Tuesday	*Voices Carry*
1986	a-ha	*Take On Me*
1987	Crowded House	*Don't Dream It's Over*
1988	Guns N' Roses	*Welcome to the Jungle*
1989	Living Colour	*Cult of Personality*
1990	Michael Penn	*No Myth*
1991	Jesus Jones	*Right Here, Right Now*
1992	Nirvana	*Smells Like Teen Spirit*
1993	Stone Temple Pilots	*Plush*
1994	Counting Crows	*Mr. Jones*
1995	Hootie & the Blowfish	*Hold My Hand*

BEST RAP VIDEO

1989	D.J. Jazzy Jeff & The Fresh Prince	*Parents Just Don't Understand*
1990	M.C. Hammer	*U Can't Touch This*
1991	L.L. Cool J	*Mama Said Knock You Out*
1992	Arrested Development	*Tennessee*
1993	Arrested Development	*People Everyday*
1994	Snoop Doggy Dogg	*Doggy Dogg World*
1995	Dr. Dre	*Keep Their Heads Ringin'*

BEST DANCE VIDEO

1989	Paula Abdul	*Straight Up*
1990	M.C. Hammer	*U Can't Touch This*
1991	C + C Music Factory	*Gonna Make You Sweat (Everybody Dance Now)*
1992	Prince & The New Power Generation	*Cream*
1993	En Vogue	*Free Your Mind*
1994	Salt-N-Pepa w/ En Vogue	*Whatta Man*
1995	Michael and Janet Jackson	*Scream*

BEST METAL/HARD ROCK VIDEO

1989	Guns N' Roses	*Sweet Child o' Mine*
1990	Aerosmith	*Janie's Got a Gun*
1991	Aerosmith	*The Other Side*
1992	Metallica	*Enter Sandman*
1993	Pearl Jam	*Jeremy*
1994	Soundgarden	*Black Hole Sun*
1995	White Zombie	*More Human Than Human*

BEST R&B VIDEO

1993	En Vogue	*Free Your Mind*
1994	Salt-N-Pepa w/ En Vogue	*Whatta Man*
1995	TLC	*Waterfalls*

BEST VIDEO FROM A FILM

1987	Talking Heads	*Wild Wild Life*
1988	Los Lobos	*La Bamba*
1989	U2 with B.B. King	*When Love Comes to Town*
1990	Billy Idol	*Cradle of Love [Ford Fairlaine]*
1991	Chris Isaak	*Wicked Game [Wild at Heart]*
1992	Queen	*Bohemian Rhapsody [Wayne's World]*
1993	Alice in Chains	*Would? [Singles]*
1994	Bruce Springsteen	*Streets of Philadelphia [Philadelphia]*
1995	Seal	*Kiss From a Rose [Batman Forever]*

BEST CHOREOGRAPHY IN A VIDEO

1994	Salt-N-Pepa w/ En Vogue; Frank Gatson, Randy Connors	*Whatta Man*
1995	Michael and Janet Jackson; Lavelle Smith, Travis Payne, Tina Landon, Sean Cheeseman	*Scream*

BEST ALTERNATIVE VIDEO

1991	Jane's Addiction	*Been Caught Stealing*
1992	Nirvana	*Smells Like Teen Spirit*
1993	Nirvana	*In Bloom* (Version 1—Dresses)
1994	Nirvana	*Heart-Shaped Box*
1995	Weezer	*Buddy Holly*

BEST SPECIAL EFFECTS IN A VIDEO

1984	Herbie Hancock	*Rockit*
1985	Tom Petty & The Heartbreakers; Tony Mitchell, Kathy Dougherty, Peter Cohen	*Don't Come Around Here No More*
1986	a-ha; Michael Patterson	*Take On Me*
1987	Peter Gabriel; Stephen Johnson, Peter Lord	*Sledgehammer*
1988	Squeeze; Jim Francis, Dave Barton	*Hourglass*
1989	Michael Jackson; Jim Blashfield	*Leave Me Alone*
1990	Tears For Fears; Jim Blashfield	*Sowing the Seeds of Love*
1991	Faith No More; David Faithful, Ralph Ziman	*Falling to Pieces*
1992	U2; Simon Taylor	*Even Better Than the Real Thing*
1993	Peter Gabriel; Real World Productions/ Colossal Pictures	*Steam*
1994	Peter Gabriel; Brett Leonard/ Angel Studios	*Kiss That Frog*
1995	The Rolling Stones; Fred Raimondi	*Love Is Strong*

BEST DIRECTION IN A VIDEO

1984	ZZ Top; Tim Newman	*Sharp Dressed Man*
1985	Don Henley; John Baptiste Mondino	*The Boys of Summer*
1986	a-ha; Steven Barron	*Take On Me*
1987	Peter Gabriel; Stephen Johnson	*Sledgehammer*
1988	George Michael; Andy Morahan, George Michael	*Father Figure*
1989	Madonna; David Fincher	*Express Yourself*
1990	Madonna; David Fincher	*Vogue*
1991	R.E.M.; Tarsem	*Losing My Religion*
1992	Van Halen; Mark Fenske	*Right Now*
1993	Pearl Jam; Mark Pellington	*Jeremy*
1994	R.E.M.; Jake Scott	*Everybody Hurts*
1995	Weezer; Spike Jonze	*Buddy Holly*

BREAKTHROUGH VIDEO

1988	INXS	*Need You Tonight/Mediate*
1989	Art of Noise, featuring Tom Jones	*Kiss*
1990	Tears for Fears	*Sowing the Seeds of Love*
1991	R.E.M.	*Losing My Religion*
1992	Red Hot Chili Peppers	*Give It Away*
1993	Los Lobos	*Kiko & The Lavender Moon*
1994	R.E.M.	*Everybody Hurts*
1995	Weezer	*Buddy Holly*

VIDEO VANGUARD AWARD

1984	The Beatles, David Bowie, Richard Lester
1985	David Byrne, Kevin Godley and Lol Creme, Russell Mulcahy
1986	Madonna and Zbigniew Rybeznski
1987	Julien Temple and Peter Gabriel
1988	Michael Jackson
1989	George Michael
1990	Janet Jackson
1994	Tom Petty
1995	R.E.M.

MICHAEL JACKSON VIDEO VANGUARD AWARD

1991	Bon Jovi, Wayne Isham
1992	Guns N' Roses

VIEWER'S CHOICE AWARD

1984	Michael Jackson	*Thriller*
1985	USA for Africa	*We Are the World*
1986	a-ha	*Take On Me*
1987	U2	*With or Without You*
1988	INXS	*Need You Tonight/Mediate*
1989	Madonna	*Like a Prayer*
1990	Aerosmith	*Janie's Got a Gun*
1994	Aerosmith	*Cryin'*
1995	TLC	*Waterfalls*

THE GRAMMY AWARDS

Even more so than most award-giving bodies, the National Academy of Recording Arts and Sciences has switched, added, deleted, and renamed its various award categories on a regular basis. The following chart gathers the majority of continuing categories that honor mainstream musical achievement. This means you won't find the awards for polka or jacket liner notes, but you will find years of musical greats (and electorate gaffes) in an easy-to-follow format.

	1958	1959	1960
Record of the Year	Domenico Modugno, "Nel Blu Dipinto Di Blu (Volare)"	Bobby Darin, "Mack the Knife"	Percy Faith, "Theme from A Summer Place"
Album of the Year	Henry Mancini, *The Music from Peter Gunn*	Frank Sinatra, *Come Dance with Me*	Bob Newhart, *Button Down Mind*
Song of the Year	Domenico Modugno, "Nel Blu Dipinto Di Blu (Volare)"	Jimmy Driftwood, "The Battle of New Orleans"	Ernest Gold, "Theme from *Exodus*"
Pop Vocal, Female	Ella Fitzgerald, *Ella Fitzgerald Sings the Irving Berlin Song Book*	Ella Fitzgerald, "But Not for Me"	Ella Fitzgerald, *Mack the Knife, Ella in Berlin*
Pop Vocal, Male	Perry Como, "Catch a Falling Star"	Frank Sinatra, *Come Dance with Me*	Ray Charles, *Genius of Ray Charles*
New Artist	—	Bobby Darin	Bob Newhart
Pop Vocal, Duo or Group with Vocal	Louis Prima and Keely Smith, "That Old Black Magic"	Mormon Tabernacle Choir, "Battle Hymn of the Republic"	Eydie Gormé and Steve Lawrence, "We Got Us"
Rhythm and Blues Song	Champs, "Tequila"	Dinah Washington, "What a Diff'rence a Day Makes"	Ray Charles, "Let the Good Times Roll"
Jazz, Soloist	—	Ella Fitzgerald, *Ella Swings Lightly*	—
Jazz, Group	Count Basie, *Basie*	Jonah Jones, *I Dig Chicks*	André Previn, *West Side Story*
Jazz, Big Band/ Large Ensemble Performance	—	—	Henry Mancini, *The Blues and the Beat*
Folk Recording	—	Kingston Trio, *The Kingston Trio at Large*	Harry Belafonte, *Swing Dat Hammer*
Cast Show Album	*The Music Man*	*Porgy and Bess*	*The Sound of Music*
Comedy Recording (Spoken Word/Musical)	David Seville, "The Chipmunk Song"	Shelley Berman, *Inside Shelley Berman*; Homer & Jethro, *The Battle of Kookamonga*	Bob Newhart, *Button Down Mind Strikes Back*; Paul Weston and Jo Stafford, *Jonathan and Darlene Edwards in Paris*
Classical Orchestral Performance	Felix Slatkin, Hollywood Bowl Symphony, *Gaîeté Parisienne*	Charles Munch, conductor, Boston Symphony, *Debussy: Images for Orchestra*	Fritz Reiner, conductor, Chicago Symphony, *Bartók: Music for Strings, Percussion and Celeste*
Opera Recording	Roger Wagner Chorale, *Virtuoso*	Erich Leinsdorf, conductor, Vienna Philharmonic, *Mozart: The Marriage of Figaro*	Erich Leinsdorf, conductor, Rome Opera House Chorus and Orchestra, *Puccini: Turandot* (Solos: Tebaldi, Nilsson, Bjoerling, Tozzi)
Chamber Music Performance	Hollywood String Quartet, *Beethoven: Quartet 130*	Artur Rubinstein, *Beethoven: Sonata No. 21 in C, Op. 53; "Waldstein" Sonata No. 18 in E Flat, Op. 53, No. 3*	Laurindo Almeida, *Conversations with the Guitar*

	1961	**1962**	**1963**
Record of the Year	Henry Mancini, "Moon River"	Tony Bennett, "I Left My Heart in San Francisco"	Henry Mancini, "The Days of Wine and Roses"
Album of the Year	Judy Garland, *Judy at Carnegie Hall*	Vaughn Meader, *The First Family*	Barbra Streisand, *The Barbra Streisand Album*
Song of the Year	Henry Mancini and Johnny Mercer, "Moon River"	Leslie Bricusse and Anthony Newley, "What Kind of Fool Am I"	Johnny Mercer and Henry Mancini, "The Days of Wine and Roses"
(Pop) Vocal, Female	Judy Garland, *Judy at Carnegie Hall*	Ella Fitzgerald, *Ella Swings Brightly with Nelson Riddle*	Barbra Streisand, *The Barbra Streisand Album*
(Pop) Vocal, Male	Jack Jones, "Lollipops and Roses"	Tony Bennett, "I Left My Heart in San Francisco"	Jack Jones, "Wives and Lovers"
New Artist	Peter Nero	Robert Goulet	Swingle Singers
Pop Vocal, Duo or Group with Vocal	Lambert, Hendricks & Ross, *High Flying*	Peter, Paul & Mary, "If I Had a Hammer"	Peter, Paul & Mary, "Blowin' in the Wind"
Rhythm and Blues Song	Ray Charles, "Hit the Road, Jack"	Ray Charles, "I Can't Stop Loving You"	Ray Charles, "Busted"
Jazz, Soloist/Small Group	André Previn, *André Previn Plays Harold Arlen*	Stan Getz, *Desafinado*	Bill Evans, *Conversations with Myself*
Jazz, Big Band/Large Ensemble Performance	Stan Kenton, *West Side Story*	Stan Kenton, *Adventures in Jazz*	Woody Herman Band, *Encore: Woody Herman, 1963*
Contemporary Folk	Belafonte Folk Singers, *Belafonte Folk Singers at Home and Abroad*	Peter, Paul & Mary, "If I Had a Hammer"	Peter, Paul & Mary, "Blowin' in the Wind"
Cast Show Album	*How To Succeed in Business Without Really Trying*	*No Strings*	*She Loves Me*
Comedy Recording	Mike Nichols and Elaine May, *An Evening with Mike Nichols and Elaine May*	Vaughn Meader, *The First Family*	Allen Sherman, *Hello Mudduh, Hello Faddah*
Classical Album	Igor Stravinsky, conductor, Columbia Symphony, *Stravinsky Conducts, 1960: Le Sacre du Printemps; Petruchka*	Vladimir Horowitz, *Columbia Records Presents Vladimir Horowitz*	Benjamin Britten, conductor, London Symphony Orchestra and Chorus, *Britten: War Requiem*
Classical Orchestral Performance	Charles Munch, conductor, Boston Symphony, *Ravel: Daphnis et Chloe*	Igor Stravinsky, conductor, Columbia Symphony, *Stravinsky: The Firebird Ballet*	Erich Leinsdorf, conductor, Boston Symphony, *Bartók: Concerto for Orchestra*
Opera Recording	Gabriele Santini, conductor, Rome Opera Chorus and Orchestra *Puccini: Madama Butterfly*	Georg Solti, conductor, Rome Opera House Orchestra and Chorus (Solos: Price, Vickers, Gorr, Merrill, Tozzi), *Verdi: Aïda*	Erich Leinsdorf, conductor, RCA Italiana Orchestra and Chorus (Solos: Price, Tucker, Elias), *Puccini: Madama Butterfly*
Chamber Music Performance	Jascha Heifetz, Gregor Piatigorsky, William Primrose, *Beethoven: Serenade, Op. 8; Kodaly: Duo for Violin & Cello, Op. 7*	Jascha Heifetz, Gregor Piatigorsky, William Primrose, *The Heifetz-Piatigorsky Concerts with Primrose, Pennario and Guests*	Julian Bream Consort, *An Evening of Elizabethan Music*

	1964	1965	1966
Record of the Year	Stan Getz and Astrud Gilberto, "The Girl from Ipanema"	Herb Alpert & The Tijuana Brass, "A Taste of Honey"	Frank Sinatra, "Strangers in the Night"
Album of the Year	Stan Getz and Joao Gilberto, *Getz/Gilberto*	Frank Sinatra, *September of My Years*	Frank Sinatra, *Sinatra: A Man & His Music*
Song of the Year	Jerry Herman, "Hello, Dolly!"	Paul Francis Webster and Johnny Mandel, "The Shadow of Your Smile (Love Theme from *The Sandpiper*)"	John Lennon and Paul McCartney, "Michelle"
Pop Vocal, Female	Barbra Streisand, "People"	Barbra Streisand, *My Name Is Barbra*	Eydie Gorme, "If He Walked into My Life"
Pop Vocal, Male	Louis Armstrong, "Hello, Dolly!"	Frank Sinatra, "It Was a Very Good Year"	Frank Sinatra, "Strangers in the Night"
Rock Vocal Female, Male	Petula Clark, "Downtown"	Petula Clark, "I Know a Place"; Roger Miller, "King of the Road"	Paul McCartney, "Eleanor Rigby"
New Artist	The Beatles	Tom Jones	—
Pop Vocal, Duo or Group	The Beatles, *A Hard Day's Night*	Anita Kerr Quartet, *We Dig Mancini*	Anita Kerr Quartet, "A Man and a Woman"
Rock Performance, Duo or Group with Vocal	—	Statler Brothers, "Flowers on the Wall"	The Mamas & The Papas, "Monday, Monday"
Rhythm and Blues Song	Nancy Wilson, "How Glad I Am"	James Brown, "Papa's Got a Brand New Bag"	Ray Charles, "Crying Time"
R&B Vocal	—	—	Ray Charles, "Crying Time"
R&B Duo or Group with Vocal	—	—	Ramsey Lewis, "Hold It Right There"
Country Song	Roger Miller, "Dang Me"	Roger Miller, "King of the Road"	Bill Sherrill and Glenn Sutton, "Almost Persuaded"
Country Vocal, Female	Dottie West, "Here Comes My Baby"	Jody Miller, "Queen of the House"	Jeannie Seely, "Don't Touch Me"
Country Vocal, Male	Roger Miller, "Dang Me"	Roger Miller, "King of the Road"	David Houston, "Almost Persuaded"
Jazz, Group	Stan Getz, *Getz/Gilberto*	Ramsey Lewis Trio, *The "In" Crowd*	Wes Montgomery, *Goin' Out of My Head*
Jazz, Big Band/ Large Ensemble Performance	Laurindo Almeida, *Guitar from Ipanema*	Duke Ellington Orchestra, *Ellington '66*	—
Gospel Performance, Duo, Group, Choir or Chorus	—	George Beverly Shea and Anita Ker Quartet, *Southland Favorites*	Porter Wagoner & the Blackwood Bros., *Grand Old Gospel*
Folk Recording	Gale Garnett, *We'll Sing in the Sunshine*	Harry Belafonte, Miriam Makeba, *An Evening with Belafonte/Makeba*	Cortelia Clark, *Blues in the Street*
Cast Show Album	*Funny Girl*	*On a Clear Day You Can See Forever*	*Mame*
Comedy Recording	Bill Cosby, *I Started Out as a Child*	Bill Cosby, *Why Is There Air?*	Bill Cosby, *Wonderfulness*

	1964	**1965**	**1966**
Classical Album	Leonard Bernstein, conductor, New York Philharmonic, *Bernstein: Symphony No. 3*	Vladimir Horowitz, *Horowitz at Carnegie Hall: An Historic Return*	Morton Gould conductor, Chicago Symphony, *Ives: Symphony No. 1 in D Minor*
Classical Orchestral Performance	Erich Leinsdorf, conductor, Boston Symphony, *Mahler: Symphony No. 5 in C Sharp Minor*; Berg: *Wozzeck Excerpts*	Leopold Stokowski, conductor, American Symphony, *Ives: Symphony No. 4*	Erich Leinsdorf, conductor, Boston Symphony, *Mahler: Symphony No. 6 in A Minor*
Opera Recording	Herbert von Karajan, conductor, Vienna Philharmonic and Chorus (Solos: Price, Corelli, Merrill, Freni), *Bizet: Carmen*	Karl Bohm, conductor, Orchestra of German Opera, Berlin, (Solos: Fischer-Dieskau, Lear, Wunderlich), *Berg: Wozzeck*	Georg Solti, conductor, Vienna Philharmonic (Solos: Nilsson, Crespin, Ludwig, King, Hotter), *Wagner: Die Walküre*
Chamber Music Performance	Jascha Heifetz, Gregor Piatigorsky (Jacob Lateiner, piano), *Beethoven: Trio No. 1 in E Flat, Op. 1, No. 1*	Juilliard String Quartet, *Bartók: The Six String Quartets*	Boston Symphony Chamber Players, *Boston Symphony Chamber Players*

	1967	**1968**	**1969**
Record of the Year	5th Dimension, "Up, Up and Away"	Simon & Garfunkel, "Mrs. Robinson"	5th Dimension, "Aquarius/Let the Sunshine In"
Album of the Year	The Beatles, *Sgt. Pepper's Lonely Hearts Club Band*	Glen Campbell, *By the Time I Get to Phoenix*	Blood, Sweat & Tears, *Blood, Sweat & Tears*
Song of the Year	Jim Webb, "Up, Up and Away"	Bobby Russell, "Little Green Apples"	Joe South, "Games People Play"
Pop Vocal, Female	Bobbie Gentry, "Ode to Billie Joe"	Dionne Warwick, "Do You Know the Way To San Jose"	Peggy Lee, "Is That All There Is"
Pop Vocal, Male	Glen Campbell, "By the Time I Get to Phoenix"	José Feliciano, "Light My Fire"	Harry Nilsson, "Everybody's Talkin"
New Artist	Bobbie Gentry	José Feliciano	Crosby, Stills & Nash
Pop Vocal	5th Dimension, "Up, Up and Away"	Simon & Garfunkel, "Mrs. Robinson"	5th Dimension, "Aquarius/Let the Sunshine In"
Rock Performance, Duo or Group	5th Dimension, "Up, Up and Away"	—	—
Rhythm and Blues Song	Aretha Franklin, "Respect"	Otis Redding and Steve Cropper, "(Sittin' On) the Dock of the Bay"	Richard Spencer, "Color Him Father"
R&B Vocal, Female	Aretha Franklin, "Respect"	Aretha Franklin, "Chain of Fools"	Aretha Franklin, "Share Your Love With Me"
R&B Vocal, Male	Lou Rawls, "Dead End Street"	Otis Redding, "(Sittin' On) the Dock of the Bay"	Joe Simon, "The Chokin' Kind"

	1967	1968	1969
R&B Duo or Group with Vocal	Sam & Dave, "Soul Man"	The Temptations, "Cloud Nine"	The Isley Brothers, "It's Your Thing"
Country Song	John Hartford, "Gentle on My Mind"	Bobby Russell, "Little Green Apples"	Shel Silverstein, "A Boy Named Sue"
Country Vocal, Female	Tammy Wynette, "I Don't Wanna Play House"	Jeannie C. Riley, "Harper Valley P.T.A."	Tammy Wynette, "Stand By Your Man"
Country Vocal, Male	Glen Campbell, "Gentle on My Mind"	Johnny Cash, "Folsom Prison Blues"	Johnny Cash, "A Boy Named Sue"
Country Performance, Duo or Group with Vocal	Johnny Cash and June Carter, "Jackson"	Flatt & Scruggs, "Foggy Mountain Breakdown"	Waylon Jennings & The Kimberlys, "MacArthur Park"
Jazz, Group	Cannonball Adderley Quintet, *Mercy, Mercy, Mercy*	Bill Evans Trio, *Bill Evans at the Montreux Jazz Festival*	Wes Montgomery, *Willow Weep For Me*
Jazz, Big Band/ Large Ensemble Performance	Duke Ellington, *Far East Suite*	Duke Ellington, *And His Mother Called Him Bill*	Quincy Jones, "Walking in Space"
Gospel Performance, Duo, Group, Choir or Chorus	Porter Wagoner & The Blackwood Bros. Quartet, *More Grand Old Gospel*	Happy Goodman Family, *The Happy Gospel of the Happy Goodmans*	Porter Wagoner & the Blackwood Bros., *In Gospel Country*
Folk Recording	John Hartford, "Gentle on My Mind"	Judy Collins, "Both Sides Now"	Joni Mitchell, *Clouds*
Cast Show Album	*Cabaret*	*Hair*	*Promises, Promises*
Comedy Recording	Bill Cosby, *Revenge*	Bill Cosby, *To Russell, My Brother, Whom I Slept With*	Bill Cosby, *The Best of Bill Cosby*
Classical Album	Pierre Boulez, conductor, Orchestra and Chorus of Paris National Opera (Solos: Berry, Strauss, Uhl, Doench), *Berg: Wozzeck;* Leonard Berstein, conductor, London Symphony, *Mahler: Symphony No. 8 in E Flat Major ("Symphony of a Thousand")*	—	Walter Carlos, *Switched-On Bach*
Classical Orchestral Performance	Igor Stravinsky, conductor, Columbia Symphony, *Stravinsky: Firebird & Petrouchka Suites*	Pierre Boulez, conductor, New Philharmonic Orchestra, *Boulez Conducts Debussy*	Pierre Boulez, conductor, Cleveland Orchestra, *Boulez Conducts Debussy, Vol. 2: "Images Pour Orchestre"*
Opera Recording	Pierre Boulez, conductor, Orchestra and Chorus of Paris National Opera (Solos: Berry, Strauss, Uhl, Doench), *Berg: Wozzeck*	Erich Leinsdorf, conductor, New Philharmonic Orchestra and Ambrosian Opera Chorus (Soloists: Price, Troyanos, Raskin, Milnes, Shirley, Flagello), *Mozart: Cosi fan tutte*	Herbert von Karajan, conductor, Berlin Philharmonic (Soloists: Thomas, Stewart, Stolze, Dernesch, Keleman, Dominguez, Gayer, Ridderbusch), *Wagner: Siegfried*
Chamber Music Performance	Ravi Shankar and Yehudi Menuhin, *West Meets East*	E. Power Biggs with Edward Tarr Brass Ensemble and Gabrieli Consort, Vittorio Negri, conductor, *Gabrieli: Canzoni for Brass, Winds, Strings & Organ*	The Philadelphia, Cleveland, and Chicago Brass Ensembles, *Gabrieli: Antiphonal Music of Gabrieli (Canzoni for Brass Choirs)*

264

	1970	**1971**	**1972**
Record of the Year	Simon & Garfunkel, "Bridge Over Troubled Water"	Carole King, "It's Too Late"	Roberta Flack, "The First Time Ever I Saw Your Face"
Album of the Year	Simon & Garfunkel, *Bridge Over Troubled Water*	Carole King, *Tapestry*	George Harrison and Friends (Ravi Shankar, Bob Dylan, Leon Russell, Ringo Starr, Billy Preston, Eric Clapton, Klaus Voorman, others), *The Concert for Bangla Desh*
Song of the Year	Paul Simon, "Bridge Over Troubled Water"	Carole King, "You've Got a Friend"	Ewan MacColl, "The First Time Ever I Saw Your Face"
Pop Vocal, Female	Dionne Warwick, "I'll Never Fall In Love Again"	Carole King, "Tapestry"	Helen Reddy, "I Am Woman"
Pop Vocal, Male	Ray Stevens, "Everything Is Beautiful"	James Taylor, "You've Got a Friend"	Nilsson, "Without You"
New Artist	The Carpenters	Carly Simon	America
Pop Vocal, Duo or Group with Vocal	Carpenters, "Close to You"	Carpenters, *Carpenters*	Roberta Flack and Donny Hathaway, "Where Is the Love"
Rhythm and Blues Song	Ronald Dunbar, General Johnson, "Patches"	Bill Withers, "Ain't No Sunshine"	Barrett Strong and Norman Whitfield, "Papa Was a Rolling Stone"
R&B Vocal, Female	Aretha Franklin, "Don't Play That Song"	Aretha Franklin, "Bridge Over Troubled Water"	Aretha Franklin, "Young, Gifted & Black"
R&B Vocal, Male	B.B. King, "The Thrill Is Gone"	Lou Rawls, "A Natural Man"	Billy Paul, "Me and Mrs. Jones"
R&B Duo or Group with Vocal	The Delfonics, "Didn't I (Blow Your Mind This Time)"	Ike and Tina Turner, "Proud Mary"	The Temptations, "Papa Was a Rolling Stone"
Country Song	Marty Robbins, "My Woman, My Woman, My Wife"	Kris Kristofferson, "Help Me Make It Through the Night"	Ben Peters, "Kiss an Angel Good Mornin'"
Country Vocal, Female	Lynn Anderson, "Rose Garden"	Sammi Smith, "Help Me Make It Through the Night"	Donna Fargo, "Happiest Girl in the Whole U.S.A."
Country Vocal, Male	Ray Price, "For the Good Times"	Jerry Reed, "When You're Hot, You're Hot"	Charley Pride, *Charley Pride Sings Heart Songs*
Country Performance, Duo or Group with Vocal	Johnny Cash and June Carpenter, "If I Were a Carpenter"	Conway Twitty and Loretta Lynn, "After the Fire Is Gone"	The Statler Brothers, "Class of '57"
Traditional Blues Recording	T-Bone Walker, "Good Feelin'"	Muddy Waters, *They Call Me Muddy Waters*	Muddy Waters, *The London Muddy Waters Session*
Jazz, Soloist	—	Bill Evans, *The Bill Evans Album*	Gary Burton, *Alone at Last*
Jazz, Group	Bill Evans, *Alone*	Bill Evans Trio, *The Bill Evans Album*	Freddie Hubbard, *First Light*
Jazz, Big Band/ Large Ensemble Performance	Miles Davis, *Bitches Brew*	Duke Ellington, *New Orleans Suite*	Duke Ellington, *Togo Brava Suite*
Gospel Performance, Duo, Group, Choir or Chorus	Oak Ridge Boys, "Talk About the Good Times"	Charley Pride, "Let Me Live"	Blackwood Brothers, *L-O-V-E*
Cast Show Album	*Company*	*Godspell*	*Don't Bother Me I Can't Cope*
Comedy Recording	Flip Wilson, *The Devil Made Me Buy This Dress*	Lily Tomlin, *This Is a Recording*	George Carlin, *FM & AM*

	1970	**1971**	**1972**
Classical Album	Colin Davis, conductor, Royal Opera House Orchestra and Chorus (Solos: Vickers, Veasey Lindholm), *Berlioz: Les Troyens*, Philips	Vladimir Horowitz, *Horowitz Plays Rachmaninoff*	Georg Solti, conductor, Chicago Symphony, Vienna Boys Choir, Vienna State Opera Chorus, Vienna Singverein Chorus and soloists, *Mahler: Symphony No. 8 in E Flat Major (Symphony of a Thousand)*
Classical Orchestral Performance	Pierre Boulez, conductor, Cleveland Orchestra, *Stravinsky: Le Sacre du printemps*	Carlo Maria Giulini, conductor, Chicago Symphony, *Mahler: Symphony No. 1 in D Major*	Georg Solti, conductor, Chicago Symphony, *Mahler: Symphony No. 7 in E Minor*
Opera Recording	Colin Davis, conductor, Royal Opera House Orchestra and Chorus (Solos: Vickers, Veasey, Lindholm), *Berlioz: Les Troyens*	Erich Leinsdorf, conductor, London Symphony and John Alldis Choir (Solos: Price, Domingo, Milnes, Bumbry, Raimondi), *Verdi: Aida*	Colin Davis, conductor, BBC Symphony/Chorus of Covent Garden (Solos: Gedda, Eda-Pierre, Soyer, Berbie), *Berlioz: Benvenuto Cellini*
Chamber Music Performance	Eugene Istomin, Isaac Stern, Leonard Rose, *Beethoven: The Complete Piano Trios*	Juilliard Quartet, *Debussy: Quartet in G Minor/Ravel: Quartet in F Major*	Julian Bream and John Williams, *Julian & John*

	1973	**1974**	**1975**
Record of the Year	Roberta Flack, "Killing Me Softly with His Song"	Olivia Newton-John, "I Honestly Love You"	Captain & Tennille, "Love Will Keep Us Together"
Album of the Year	Stevie Wonder, *Innervisions*	Stevie Wonder, *Fulfillingness' First Finale*	Paul Simon, *Still Crazy After All These Years*
Song of the Year	Norman Gimbel and Charles Fox, "Killing Me Softly with His Song"	Marilyn and Alan Bergman, Marvin Hamlisch, "The Way We Were"	Stephen Sondheim, "Send In the Clowns"
Pop Vocal, Female	Roberta Flack, "Killing Me Softly with His Song"	Olivia Newton-John, "I Honestly Love You"	Janis Ian, "At Seventeen"
Pop Vocal, Male	Stevie Wonder, "You Are the Sunshine of My Life"	Stevie Wonder, *Fulfillingness' First Finale*	Paul Simon, *Still Crazy After All These Years*
New Artist	Bette Midler	Marvin Hamlisch	Natalie Cole
Pop Vocal, Duo or Group with Vocal	Gladys Knight & The Pips, "Neither One of Us (Wants To Be the First To Say Goodbye)"	Paul McCartney & Wings, "Band on the Run"	Eagles, "Lyin' Eyes"
Rhythm and Blues Song	Stevie Wonder, "Superstition"	Stevie Wonder, "Living for the City"	H. W. Casey, Richard Finch, Willie Clarke, and Betty Wright, "Where Is the Love"
R&B Vocal, Female	Aretha Franklin, "Master of Eyes"	Aretha Franklin, "Ain't Nothing Like the Real Thing"	Natalie Cole, "This Will Be"
R&B Vocal, Male	Stevie Wonder, "Superstition"	Stevie Wonder, "Boogie On Reggae Woman"	Ray Charles, "Living for the City"

	1973	1974	1975
R&B Duo or Group with Vocal	Gladys Knight & The Pips, "Midnight Train to Georgia"	Rufus, "Tell Me Something Good"	Earth, Wind & Fire, "Shining Star"
Country Song	Kenny O'Dell, "Behind Closed Doors"	Norris Wilson and Bill Sherrill, "A Very Special Love Song"	Chips Moman and Larry Butler, "(Hey Won't You Play) Another Somebody Done Somebody Wrong Song"
Country Vocal, Female	Olivia Newton-John, "Let Me Be There "	Anne Murray, "Love Song"	Linda Ronstadt, "I Can't Help It (If I'm Still in Love with You)"
Country Vocal, Male	Charlie Rich, "Behind Closed Doors"	Ronnie Milsap, "Please Don't Tell Me How the Story Ends"	Willie Nelson, "Blue Eyes Crying in the Rain"
Country Performance, Duo or Group with Vocal	Kris Kristofferson and Rita Coolidge, "From the Bottle to the Bottom"	The Pointer Sisters, "Fairytale"	Kris Kristofferson and Rita Coolidge, "Lover Please"
Traditional Blues Recording	Doc Watson, *Then and Now*	Doc and Merle Watson, *Two Days in November*	Muddy Waters, *The Muddy Waters Woodstock Album*
Jazz, Soloist	Art Tatum, *God Is in the House*	Charlie Parker, *First Recordings!*	Dizzy Gillespie, *Oscar Peterson and Dizzy Gillespie*
Jazz, Group	Supersax, *Supersax Plays Bird*	Oscar Peterson, Joe Pass, and Niels Pedersen, *The Trio*	Return to Forever featuring Chick Corea, *No Mystery*
Jazz, Big Band/ Large Ensemble Performance	Woody Herman, *Giant Steps*	Woody Herman, *Thundering Herd*	Phil Woods with Michel Legrand & His Orchestra, *Images*
Cast Show Album	*A Little Night Music*	*Raisin*	*The Wiz*
Comedy Recording	Cheech & Chong, *Los Cochinos*	Richard Pryor, *That Nigger's Crazy*	Richard Pryor, *Is It Something I Said?*
Classical Album	Pierre Boulez, conductor, New York Philharmonic, *Bartók: Concerto for Orchestra*	Georg Solti, conductor, Chicago Symphony, *Berlioz: Symphonie Fantastique*	Georg Solti, conductor, Chicago Symphony, *Beethoven: Symphonies (9) Complete*
Classical Orchestral Performance	Pierre Boulez, conductor, New York Philharmonic, *Bartók: Concerto for Orchestra*	Georg Solti, conductor, Chicago Symphony, *Berlioz: Symphonie Fantastique*	Pierre Boulez, conductor, New York Philharmonic, *Ravel: Daphnis et Chloë*
Opera Recording	Leonard Bernstein, conductor, Metropolitan Opera Orchestra and Manhattan Opera Chorus (Solos: Horne, McCracken, Maliponte, Krause), *Bizet: Carmen*	Georg Solti, conductor, London Philharmonic (Soloists: Caballé, Domingo, Milnes, Blegen, Raimondi), *Puccini: La Bohème*	Colin Davis, conductor, Royal Opera House, Covent Garden (Solos: Caballé, Baker, Gedda, Ganzarolli, Van Allen, Cotrubas), *Mozart: Cosi fan tutte*
Chamber Music Performance	Gunther Schuller and New England Ragtime Ensemble, *Joplin: The Red Back Book*	Artur Rubinstein, Henryk Szeryng, and Pierre Fournier, *Brahms: Trios (complete)/Schumann: Trio No. 1 in D Minor*	Artur Rubinstein, Henryk Szeryng, and Pierre Fournier, *Shubert: Trios Nos. 1 in B Flat Major Op. 99 & 2 in E Flat Major Op. 100*

	1976	**1977**	**1978**
Record of the Year	George Benson, "This Masquerade"	Eagles, "Hotel California"	Billy Joel, "Just the Way You Are"
Album of the Year	Stevie Wonder, *Songs in the Key of Life*	Fleetwood Mac, *Rumours*	The Bee Gees and others, *Saturday Night Fever*
Song of the Year	Bruce Johnston, "I Write the Songs"	Joe Brooks, "You Light Up My Life"; Barbra Streisand, "Love Theme from *A Star Is Born* (Evergreen)"	Billy Joel, "Just the Way You Are"
(Pop) Vocal, Female	Linda Ronstadt, *Hasten Down the Wind*	Barbra Streisand, "Love Theme from *A Star Is Born* (Evergreen)"	Anne Murray, "You Needed Me"
(Pop) Vocal, Male	Stevie Wonder, *Songs in the Key of Life*	James Taylor, "Handy Man"	Barry Manilow, "Copacabana (At the Copa)"
New Artist	Starland Vocal Band	Debby Boone	A Taste of Honey
Pop Vocal, Duo or Group with Vocal	Chicago, "If You Leave Me Now"	The Bee Gees, "How Deep Is Your Love"	The Bee Gees, *Saturday Night Fever*
Rhythm and Blues Song	Boz Scaggs and David Paich, "Lowdown"	Leo Sayer and Vini Poncia, "You Make Me Feel Like Dancing"	Paul Jabara, "Last Dance"
R&B Vocal, Female	Natalie Cole, "Sophisticated Lady (She's a Different Lady)"	Thelma Houston, "Don't Leave Me This Way"	Donna Summer, "Last Dance"
R&B Vocal, Male	Stevie Wonder, "I Wish"	Lou Rawls, *Unmistakably Lou*	George Benson, "On Broadway"
R&B Duo or Group with Vocal	Marilyn McCoo and Billy Davis, Jr., "You Don't Have To Be a Star (To Be in My Show)"	Emotions, "Best of My Love"	Earth, Wind & Fire, "All 'n All"
Country Song	Larry Gatlin, "Broken Lady"	Richard Leigh, "Don't It Make My Brown Eyes Blue"	Don Schlitz, "The Gambler"
Country Vocal, Female	Emmylou Harris, *Elite Hotel*	Crystal Gayle, "Don't It Make My Brown Eyes Blue"	Dolly Parton, *Here You Come Again*
Country Vocal, Male	Ronnie Milsap, "(I'm a) Stand by My Woman Man"	Kenny Rogers, "Lucille"	Willie Nelson, "Georgia on My Mind"
Country Performance, Duo or Group with Vocal	Amazing Rhythm Aces, "The End Is Not in Sight (The Cowboy Tune)"	The Kendalls, "Heaven's Just a Sin Away"	Waylon Jennings and Willie Nelson, "Mamas Don't Let Your Babies Grow Up To Be Cowboys"
Ethnic or Traditional Recording	John Hartford, *Mark Twang*	Muddy Waters, *Hard Again*	Muddy Waters, *I'm Ready*
Jazz, Soloist	Count Basie, *Basie & Zoot*	Oscar Peterson, *The Giants*	Oscar Peterson, *Montreux '77, Oscar Peterson Jam*
Jazz, Group	Chick Corea, *The Leprechaun*	Phil Woods, *The Phil Woods Six—Live from the Showboat*	Chick Corea, *Friends*
Jazz, Big Band/ Large Ensemble Performance	Duke Ellington, *The Ellington Suites*	Count Basie & His Orchestra, *Prime Time*	Thad Jones and Mel Lewis, *Live in Munich*
Cast Show Album	*Bubbling Brown Sugar*	*Annie*	*Ain't Misbehavin'*
Comedy Recording	Richard Pryor, *Bicentennial Nigger*	Steve Martin, *Let's Get Small*	Steve Martin, *A Wild and Crazy Guy*
Classical Album	Artur Rubinstein with Daniel Barenboim, conductor, London Philharmonic, *Beethoven: The Five Piano Concertos*	Leonard Bernstein, Vladimir Horowitz, Isaac Stern, Mstislav Rostropovich, Dietrich Fischer-Dieskau, Yehudi Menuhin, Lyndon Woodside, *Concert of the Century* (recorded live at Carnegie Hall May 18, 1976)	Itzhak Perlman with Carlo Maria Giulini, conductor, Chicago Symphony, *Brahms: Concerto for Violin in D Major*

	1976	1977	1978
Classical Orchestral Performance	Georg Solti, conductor, Chicago Symphony, *Strauss: Also Sprach Zarathustra*	Carlo Maria Giulini, conductor, Chicago Symphony, *Mahler: Symphony No. 9 in D Major*	Herbert von Karajan, conductor, Berlin Philharmonic, *Beethoven: Symphonies (9) Complete*
Opera Recording	Lorin Maazel conductor, Cleveland Orchestra and Chorus (Solos: Mitchell, White), *Gershwin: Porgy & Bess*	John De Main, conductor, Houston Grand Opera Production (Solos: Albert, Dale, Smith, Shakesnider, Lane, Brice, Smalls), *Gershwin: Porgy & Bess*	Julius Rudel, conductor, New York City Opera Orchestra and Chorus (Solos: Sills, Titus), *Lehar: The Merry Widow*
Chamber Music Performance	David Munrow, conductor, The Early Music Consort of London, *The Art of Courtly Love*	Juilliard Quartet, *Schöenberg: Quartets for Strings*	Itzhak Perlman and Vladimir Ashkenazy, *Beethoven: Sonatas for Violin and Piano*

GRAMMY AWARD RECORDS

In 1957, the newly-formed National Academy of Recording Arts & Sciences first conceived of a peer award to recognize outstanding achievement in the recording field. The Grammys, named after the gramophone statuette, have since expanded from 28 categories to 81. The following artists have all set records in the annals of Grammy history:

Youngest winner: Barbra Streisand, age 22 when *The Barbra Streisand Album* was named 1963's best LP

Winningest winner: Georg Solti, the conductor of the Chicago Symphony, has won 30 awards

Winningest female: Aretha Franklin, with 15 awards (and an uninterrupted winning streak from 1967 to 1974)

Most awards in a single year: Michael Jackson in 1983, with seven for Album of the Year *Thriller* and one for *E.T., the Extra-Terrestrial* as Best Recording for Children

Most country awards: Chet Atkins with 13

Most jazz awards: Ella Fitzgerald with 13

Most comedy awards: Bill Cosby with nine

Most opera awards: Leontyne Price with 13

	1979	**1980**	**1981**
Record of the Year	The Doobie Brothers, "What a Fool Believes"	Christopher Cross, "Sailing"	Kim Carnes, "Bette Davis Eyes"
Album of the Year	Billy Joel, *52nd Street*	Christopher Cross, *Christopher Cross*	John Lennon and Yoko Ono, *Double Fantasy*
Song of the Year	Kenny Loggins and Michael McDonald, "What a Fool Believes"	Christopher Cross, "Sailing"	Donna Weiss and Jackie DeShannon, "Bette Davis Eyes"
Pop Vocal, Female	Dionne Warwick, "I'll Never Love This Way Again"	Bette Midler, "The Rose"	Lena Horne, *Lena Horne: The Lady and Her Music Live on Broadway*
Pop Vocal, Male	Billy Joel, *52nd Street*	Kenny Loggins, "This Is It"	Al Jarreau, *Breakin' Away*
Rock Vocal, Female	Donna Summer, "Hot Stuff"	Pat Benatar, *Crimes of Passion*	Pat Benatar, "Fire and Ice"
Rock Vocal, Male	Bob Dylan, "Gotta Serve Somebody"	Billy Joel, *Glass Houses*	Rick Springfield, "Jessie's Girl"
New Artist	Rickie Lee Jones	Christopher Cross	Sheena Easton
Pop Vocal, Duo or Group with Vocal	The Doobie Brothers, *Minute by Minute*	Barbra Streisand and Barry Gibb, "Guilty"	The Manhattan Transfer, "Boy from New York City"
Rock Performance, Duo or Group with Vocal	The Eagles, "Heartache Tonight"	Bob Seger & The Silver Bullet Band, *Against the Wind*	The Police, "Don't Stand So Close to Me"
Rhythm and Blues Song	David Foster, Jay Graydon, and Bill Champlin, "After the Love Has Gone"	Reggie Lucas and James Mtume, "Never Knew Love Like This Before"	Bill Withers, William Salter, and Ralph MacDonald, "Just the Two of Us"
R&B Vocal, Female	Dionne Warwick, "Déjà Vu"	Stephanie Mills, "Never Knew Love Like This Before"	Aretha Franklin, "Hold on, I'm Comin'"
R&B Vocal, Male	Michael Jackson, "Don't Stop 'Till You Get Enough"	George Benson, *Give Me the Night*	James Ingram, "One Hundred Ways"
R&B Duo or Group with Vocal	Earth, Wind & Fire, "After the Love Has Gone"	Manhattans, "Shining Star"	Quincy Jones, *The Dude*
Country Song	Bob Morrison and Debbie Hupp, "You Decorated My Life"	Willie Nelson, "On the Road Again"	Dolly Parton, "9 to 5"
Country Vocal, Female	Emmylou Harris, *Blue Kentucky Girl*	Anne Murray, "Could I Have This Dance"	Dolly Parton, "9 to 5"
Country Vocal, Male	Kenny Rogers, "The Gambler"	George Jones, "He Stopped Loving Her Today"	Ronnie Milsap, "(There's) No Gettin' Over Me"
Country Performance, Duo or Group with Vocal	Charlie Daniels Band, "The Devil Went Down to Georgia"	Roy Orbison and Emmylou Harris, "That Lovin' You Feelin' Again"	Oak Ridge Boys, "Elvira"
Ethnic or Traditional Recording	Muddy Waters, *Muddy "Mississippi" Waters Live*	Dr. Isaiah Ross, Maxwell Street Jimmy, Big Joe William, Son House, Rev. Robert Wilkins, Little Brother Montgomery, and Sunnyland Slim, *Rare Blues*	B. B. King, *There Must Be a Better World Somewhere*
Jazz Vocal, Female	Ella Fitzgerald, *Fine and Mellow*	Ella Fitzgerald, *A Perfect Match/Ella & Basie*	Ella Fitzgerald, *Digital III at Montreux*
Jazz Vocal, Male	—	George Benson, "Moody's Mood"	Al Jarreau, "Blue Rondo à la Turk"
Jazz, Soloist	Oscar Peterson, *Jousts*	Bill Evans, *I Will Say Goodbye*	John Coltrane, *Bye, Bye Blackbird*

	1979	1980	1981
Jazz, Group	Gary Burton and Chick Corea, *Duet*	Bill Evans, *We Will Meet Again*	Chick Corea and Gary Burton, *Chick Corea and Gary Burton in Concert, Zurich, October 28, 1979*
Jazz, Big Band/ Large Ensemble Performance	Duke Ellington, *At Fargo, 1940 Live*	Count Basie and Orchestra, *On the Road*	Gerry Mulligan & His Orchestra, *Walk on the Water*
Jazz Fusion Performance, Vocal or Instrumental	Weather Report, *8:30*	Manhattan Transfer, "Birdland"	Grover Washington Jr., *Winelight*
Cast Show Album	*Sweeney Todd*	*Evita*	*Lena Horne: The Lady and Her Music Live on Broadway*
Comedy Recording	Robin Williams, *Reality... What a Concept*	Rodney Dangerfield, *No Respect*	Richard Pryor, *Rev. Du Rite*
Classical Album	Georg Solti, conductor, Chicago Symphony Orchestra, *Brahms: Symphonies (4) Complete*	Pierre Boulez, conductor, Orchestre d l'Opera de Paris (Solos: Stratas, Minton, Mazura, Toni Blankenheim), *Berg: Lulu*	Georg Solti, conductor, Chicago Symphony Orchestra and Chorus (Solos: Buchanan, Zakai), *Mahler: Symphony No. 2 in C Minor*
Classical Orchestral Performance	Georg Solti, conductor, Chicago Symphony, *Brahms: Symphonies (4) Complete*	Georg Solti, conductor, Chicago Symphony, *Bruckner: Symphony No. 6 in A Major*	Georg Solti, conductor, Chicago Symphony, *Mahler: Symphony No. 2 in C Minor*
Opera Recording	Colin Davis, conductor, Orchestra and Chorus of the Royal Opera House, Covent Garden (Solos: Vickers, Harper, Summers), *Britten: Peter Grimes*	Pierre Boulez, conductor, Orchestre d l'Opera de Paris (Solos: Stratas, Minton, Mazura, Blankenheim), *Berg: Lulu*	Charles Mackerras, conductor, Vienna Philharmonic (Solos: Zahradnicek, Zitek, Zidek), *Janacek: From the House of the Dead*
Chamber Music Performance	Dennis Russel Davies, conductor, St. Paul Chamber Orchestra, *Copland: Appalachian Spring*	Itzhak Perlman and Pinchas Zukerman, *Music for Two Violins (Moszkowski: Suite for Two Violins/Shostakovich: Duets/ Prokofiev: Sonata for Two Violins)*	Itzhak Perlman, Lynn Harrell, and Vladimir Ashkenazy, *Tchaikovsky: Piano Trio in A Minor*

FAMOUS LOSERS

The following artists have never won a Grammy in a competitive category, although many have been nominated. Asterisks indicate that the performers have, however, belatedly received the NARAS Lifetime Achievement Award.

AC/DC
Beach Boys
Chuck Berry*
Jackson Browne
The Byrds
Cher
Patsy Cline*
Sam Cooke
Elvis Costello
Creedence Clearwater Revival
Cream
Bing Crosby*

Fats Domino*
The Doors
The Drifters
The Four Tops
Peter Frampton
Benny Goodman*
Grateful Dead
Jimi Hendrix*
The Jackson 5
Janis Joplin
Led Zeppelin
Little Richard

Van Morrison
Pretenders
Queen
Cat Stevens
Diana Ross
Lawrence Welk
Kitty Wells*
The Who
Hank Williams, Sr.*
Neil Young

	1982	1983	1984
Record of the Year	Toto, "Rosanna"	Michael Jackson, "Beat It"	Tina Turner, "What's Love Got To Do with It"
Album of the Year	Toto, *Toto IV*	Michael Jackson, *Thriller*	Lionel Richie, *Can't Slow Down*
Song of the Year	Johnny Christopher, Mark James, and Wayne Thompson, "Always on My Mind"	Sting, "Every Breath You Take"	Graham Lyle and Terry Britten, "What's Love Got To Do with It"
Pop Vocal, Female	Melissa Manchester, "You Should Hear How She Talks About You"	Irene Cara, "Flashdance . . . What a Feeling"	Tina Turner, "What's Love got To Do with It"
Pop Vocal, Male	Lionel Richie, "Truly"	Michael Jackson, *Thriller*	Phil Collins, "Against All Odds (Take a Look at Me Now)"
Rock Vocal, Female	Pat Benatar, "Shadows of the Night"	Pat Benatar, "Love Is a Battlefield"	Tina Turner, "Better Be Good to Me"
Rock Vocal, Male	John Cougar, "Hurts So Good"	Michael Jackson, "Beat It"	Bruce Springsteen, "Dancing in the Dark"
New Artist	Men at Work	Culture Club	Cyndi Lauper
Pop Vocal, Duo or Group with Vocal	Joe Cocker and Jennifer Warnes, "Up Where We Belong"	The Police, "Every Breath You Take"	Pointer Sisters, "Jump (For My Love)"
Rock Performance, Duo or Group with Vocal	Survivor, "Eye of the Tiger"	The Police, *Synchronicity*	Prince and the Revolution, *Purple Rain*
Rhythm and Blues Song	Jay Graydon, Steve Lukather, and Bill Champlin, "Turn Your Love Around"	Michael Jackson, "Billie Jean"	Prince, "I Feel for You"
R&B Vocal, Female	Jennifer Holliday, "And I Am Telling You I'm Not Going"	Chaka Khan, *Chaka Khan*	Chaka Khan, "I Feel for You"
R&B Vocal, Male	Marvin Gaye, "Sexual Healing"	Michael Jackson, "Billie Jean"	Billy Ocean, "Caribbean Queen (No More Love on the Run)"
R&B Duo or Group with Vocal	Dazz Band, "Let It Whip"; Earth, Wind & Fire, "Wanna Be With You"	Rufus & Chaka Khan, "Ain't Nobody"	James Ingram and Michael McDonald, "Yah Mo B There"
Country Song	Johnny Christopher, Wayne Thompson, and Mark James, "Always on My Mind"	Mike Reed, "Stranger in My House"	Steve Goodman, "City of New Orleans"
Country Vocal, Female	Juice Newton, "Break It To Me Gently"	Anne Murray, "A Little Good News"	Emmylou Harris, "In My Dreams"
Country Vocal, Male	Willie Nelson, "Always on My Mind"	Lee Greenwood, "I.O.U."	Merle Haggard, "That's the Way Love Goes"
Country Performance, Group	Alabama, *Mountain Music*	Alabama, *The Closer You Get*	The Judds, "Mama He's Crazy"
Traditional Blues Recording	Clarence "Gatemouth" Brown, *Alright Again*	B. B. King, *Blues 'n' Jazz*	John Hammond, Stevie Ray Vaughan & Double Trouble, Sugar Blue, Koko Taylor & The Blues Machine, Luther "Guitar Junior" Johnson, and J. B. Hutto & The New Hawks, *Blues Explosion*
Reggae Recording	—	—	Black Uhuru, *Anthem*
Jazz Vocal, Female	Sarah Vaughan, *Gershwin Live!*	Ella Fitzgerald, *The Best Is Yet to Come*	—
Jazz Vocal, Male	Mel Torme, *An Evening with George Shearing and Mel Torme*	Mel Torme, *Top Drawer*	Joe Williams, *Nothin' but the Blues*
Jazz, Soloist	Miles Davis, *We Want Miles*	Wynton Marsalis, *Think of One*	Wynton Marsalis, *Hot House Flowers*

	1982	1983	1984
Jazz, Group	Phil Woods Quartet, *"More" Live*	The Phil Woods Quartet, *At the Vanguard*	Art Blakey & The Jazz Messengers, *New York Scene*
Jazz, Big Band/ Large Ensemble Performance	Count Basie & His Orchestra, *Warm Breeze*	Rob McConnell and The Boss Brass, *All in Good Time*	Count Basie & His Orchestra, *88 Basie Street*
Jazz Fusion Performance	Pat Metheny Group, *Offramp*	Pat Metheny Group, *Travels*	Pat Metheny Group, *First Circle*
Gospel Performance, Female	—	Amy Grant, "Ageless Medley"	Amy Grant, "Angels"
Gospel Performance, Male	—	Russ Taff, *Walls of Glass*	Michael W. Smith, *Michael W. Smith 2*
Gospel Performance, Duo, Group, Choir or Chorus	—	Sandi Patti and Larnelle Harris, "More Than Wonderful"	Debby Boone and Phil Driscoll, "Keep the Flame Burning"
Ethnic or Traditional Folk Recording	Queen Ida, *Queen Ida and the Bon Temps Zydeco Band on Tour*	Clifton Chenier & His Red Hot Louisiana Band, *I'm Here*	Elizabeth Cotten, *Elizabeth Cotten Live!*
Cast Show Album	*Dreamgirls*	*Cats (Complete Original Broadway Cast Recording)*	*Sunday in the Park with George*
Comedy Recording	Richard Pryor, *Live on the Sunset Strip*	Eddie Murphy, *Eddie Murphy: Comedian*	"Weird Al" Yankovic, "Eat It"
Classical Album	Glenn Gould, *Bach: The Goldberg Variations*	Georg Solti, conductor, Chicago Symphony, *Mahler: Symphony No. 9 in D Major*	Neville Marriner, conductor, Academy of St. Martin-in-the-Fields/Ambrosian Opera Chorus/Choristers of Westminster Abbey, *Amadeus (Original Soundtrack)*
Classical Orchestral Performance	James Levine, conductor, Chicago Symphony, *Mahler: Symphony No. 7 in E Minor (Song of the Night)*	Georg Solti, conductor, Chicago Symphony, *Mahler: Symphony No. 9 in D Major*	Leonard Slatkin, conductor, St. Louis Symphony, *Prokofiev: Symphony No. 5 in B Flat, Op. 100*
Opera Recording	Pierre Boulez, conductor, Bayreuth Festival Orchestra (Solos: Jones, Altmeyer, Wenkel, Hofmann, Jung, Jerusalem, Zednik, McIntyre, Salminen, Becht), *Wagner: Der Ring des Nibelungen*	James Levine, conductor, The Metropolitan Opera Orchestra and Chorus (Solos: Stratas, Domingo, MacNeill), *Verdi: La Traviata*	Lorin Maazel, conductor, Orchestre National de France/Choeurs et Maitrise de Radio France (Solos: Johnson, Esham, Domingo, Raimondi), *Bizet: Carmen*
Chamber Music Performance	Richard Stoltzman and Richard Goode, *Brahms: The Sonatas for Clarinet & Piano, Op. 120*	Mstislav Rostropovich and Rudolph Serkin, *Brahms: Sonata for Cello & Piano in E Minor, Op. 38 & Sonata in F Major, Op. 99*	Juilliard String Quartet, *Beethoven: The Late String Quartets*

	1985	**1986**	**1987**
Record of the Year	USA for Africa, "We Are the World"	Steve Winwood, "Higher Love"	Paul Simon, "Graceland"
Album of the Year	Phil Collins, *No Jacket Required*	Paul Simon, *Graceland*	U2, *The Joshua Tree*
Song of the Year	Michael Jackson and Lionel Richie, "We Are the World"	Burt Bacharach and Carole Bayer Sager, "That's What Friends Are For"	James Horner, Barry Mann, and Cynthia Weil, "Somewhere Out There"
Pop Vocal, Female	Whitney Houston, "Saving All My Love for You"	Barbra Streisand, *The Broadway Album*	Whitney Houston, "I Wanna Dance with Somebody (Who Loves Me)"
Pop Vocal, Male	Phil Collins, *No Jacket Required*	Steve Winwood, "Higher Love"	Sting, *Bring on the Night*
Rock Vocal, Female	Tina Turner, "One of the Living"	Tina Turner, "Back Where You Started"	—
Rock Vocal, Male	Don Henley, "The Boys of Summer"	Robert Palmer, "Addicted to Love"	Bruce Springsteen, *Tunnel of Love*
New Artist	Sade	Bruce Hornsby and the Range	Jody Watley
Pop Vocal, Duo or Group with Vocal	USA for Africa, "We Are the World"	Dionne Warwick & Friends featuring Elton John, Gladys Knight and Stevie Wonder, "That's What Friends Are For"	Bill Medley and Jennifer Warnes, "(I've Had) The Time of My Life"
Rock Performance, Group	Dire Straits, "Money for Nothing"	Eurythmics, "Missionary Man"	U2, *The Joshua Tree*
New Age Recording	—	Andreas Vollenweider, *Down to the Moon*	Yusef Lateef, *Yusef Lateef's Little Symphony*
Rhythm and Blues Song	Narada Michael Walden and Jeffrey Cohen, "Freeway of Love"	Anita Baker, Louis A. Johnson, Gary Bias, "Sweet Love"	Bill Withers, "Lean on Me"
R&B Vocal, Female	Aretha Franklin, "Freeway of Love"	Anita Baker, *Rapture*	Aretha Franklin, *Aretha*
R&B Vocal, Male	Stevie Wonder, *In Square Circle*	James Brown, "Living in America"	Smokey Robinson, "Just To See Her"
R&B Duo or Group with Vocal	Commodores, "Nightshift"	Prince & The Revolution, "Kiss"	Aretha Franklin and George Michael, "I Knew You Were Waiting (For Me)"
Country Song	Jimmy L. Webb, "Highwayman"	Jamie O'Hara, "Grandpa (Tell Me 'Bout the Good Old Days)"	Paul Overstreet and Don Schlitz, *Forever and Ever, Amen*
Country Vocal, Female	Rosanne Cash, "I Don't Know Why You Don't Want Me"	Reba McEntire, "Whoever's in New England"	K. T. Oslin, "80's Ladies"
Country Vocal, Male	Ronnie Milsap, "Lost in the Fifties Tonight (In the Still of the Night)"	Ronnie Milsap, *Lost in the Fifties Tonight*	Randy Travis, *Always & Forever*
Country Performance, Duo or Group with Vocal	The Judds, *Why Not Me*	The Judds, "Grandpa (Tell Me 'Bout the Good Old Days)"	Dolly Parton, Linda Ronstadt, and Emmylou Harris, *Trio*
Country Vocal, Collaboration	—	—	Ronnie Milsap and Kenny Rogers, "Make No Mistake, She's Mine"
Traditional Blues Recording	B. B. King, "My Guitar Sings the Blues"	Albert Collins, Robert Cray, and Johnny Copeland, *Showdown*	Professor Longhair, *Houseparty New Orleans Style*
Contemporary Blues	—	—	Robert Cray Band, *Strong Persuader*

	1985	1986	1987
Reggae Recording	Jimmy Cliff, *Cliff Hanger*	Steel Pulse, *Babylon the Bandit*	Peter Tosh, *No Nuclear War*
Jazz Vocal, Female	Cleo Laine, *Cleo at Carnegie, the 10th Anniversary Concert*	Diane Schuur, *Timeless*	Diane Schuur, *Diane Schuur & The Count Basie Orchestra*
Jazz Vocal, Male	Jon Hendricks and Bobby McFerrin, "Another Night in Tunisia"	Bobby McFerrin, " 'Round Midnight"	Bobby McFerrin, "What Is This Thing Called Love"
Jazz, Soloist	Wynton Marsalis, *Black Codes from the Underground*	Miles Davis, *Tutu*	Dexter Gordon, *The Other Side of 'Round Midnight*
Jazz, Group	Wynton Marsalis Group, *Black Codes from the Underground*	Wynton Marsalis, *J Mood*	Wynton Marsalis, *Marsalis Standard Time, Volume I*
Jazz, Big Band/ Large Ensemble Performance	John Barry and Bob Wilber, *The Cotton Club*	The Tonight Show Band with Doc Severinsen, *The Tonight Show Band with Doc Severinsen*	The Duke Ellington Orchestra, conducted by Mercer Ellington, *Digital Duke*
Jazz Fusion Performance, Vocal or Instrumental	David Sanborn, *Straight to the Heart*	Bob James and David Sanborn, *Double Vision*	Pat Metheny Group, *Still Life (Talking)*
Gospel Performance, Female	Amy Grant, *Unguarded*	Sandi Patti, *Morning Like This*	Deniece Williams, "I Believe in You"
Gospel Performance, Male	Larnelle Harris, "How Excellent Is Thy Name"	Philip Bailey, *Triumph*	Larnelle Harris, *The Father Hath Provided*
Gospel Performance, Duo, Group, Choir or Chorus	Larnelle Harris and Sandi Patti, "I've Just Seen Jesus"	Sandi Patti & Deniece Williams, "They Say"	Mylon LeFevre & Broken Heart, *Crack the Sky*
Traditional Folk Recording	Rockin' Sidney, "My Toot Toot"	Doc Watson, *Riding the Midnight Train*	Ladysmith Black Mambazo, *Shaka Zulu*
Contemporary Folk Recording	—	Arlo Guthrie, John Hartford, Richie Havens, Bonnie Koloc, Nitty Gritty Dirt Band, John Prine and others, *Tribute to Steve Goodman*	Steve Goodman, *Unfinished Business*
Cast Show Album	*West Side Story*	*Follies in Concert*	*Les Misérables*
Comedy Recording	Whoopi Goldberg, *Whoopi Goldberg*	Bill Cosby, *Those of You With or Without Children, You'll Understand*	Robin Williams, *A Night at the Met*
Classical Album	Robert Shaw, conductor, Atlanta Symphony Orchestra and Chorus, (Solo: Aler) *Berlioz: Requiem*	Vladimir Horowitz, *Horowitz: The Studio Recordings, New York 1985*	Vladimir Horowitz, *Horowitz in Moscow*
Classical Orchestral Performance	Robert Shaw, conductor, Atlanta Symphony Orchestra, *Fauré: Pelléas et Mélisande*	Georg Solti, conductor, Chicago Symphony Orchestra, *Liszt: A Faust Symphony*	Georg Solti, conductor, Chicago Symphony Orchestra, *Beethoven: Symphony No. 9 in D Minor*
Opera Recording	Georg Solti, conductor, Chicago Symphony Orchestra and Chorus (Solos: Mazura, Langridge), *Schoenberg: Moses und Aaron*	John Mauceri, conductor, New York City Opera Chorus and Orchestra (Solos: Mills, Clement, Eisler, Lankston, Castle, Reeve, Harrold, Billings), *Bernstein: Candide*	James Levine, conductor, Vienna Philharmonic (Solos: Tomowa-Sintow, Battle, Baltsa, Lakes, Prey), *R. Strauss: Ariadne auf Naxos*
Chamber Music Performance	Emanuel Ax and Yo-Yo Ma, *Brahms: Cello and Piano Sonatas in E Major & F Major*	Yo-Yo Ma and Emanuel Ax, *Beethoven: Cello & Piano Sonata No. 4 in C and Variations*	Itzhak Perlman, Lynn Harrell, and Vladimir Ashkenazy, *Beethoven: The Complete Piano Trios*

	1988	1989	1990
Record of the Year	Bobby McFerrin, "Don't Worry, Be Happy"	Bette Midler, "Wind Beneath My Wings"	Phil Collins, "Another Day in Paradise"
Album of the Year	George Michael, *Faith*	Bonnie Raitt, *Nick of Time*	Quincy Jones, *Back on the Block*
Song of the Year	Bobby McFerrin, "Don't Worry, Be Happy"	Larry Henley and Jeff Silbar, "Wind Beneath My Wings"	Julie Gold, "From a Distance"
Pop Vocal, Female	Tracy Chapman, "Fast Car"	Bonnie Raitt, "Nick of Time"	Mariah Carey, "Vision of Love"
Pop Vocal, Male	Bobby McFerrin, "Don't Worry, Be Happy"	Michael Bolton, "How Am I Supposed to Live Without You"	Roy Orbison, "Oh Pretty Woman"
Rock Vocal, Female	Tina Turner, *Tina Live in Europe*	Bonnie Raitt, *Nick of Time*	Alannah Myles, "Black Velvet"
Rock Vocal, Male	Robert Palmer, "Simply Irresistible"	Don Henley, *The End of the Innocence*	Eric Clapton, "Bad Love"
New Artist	Tracy Chapman	No award (Milli Vanilli)	Mariah Carey
Pop Vocal, Duo or Group with Vocal	The Manhattan Transfer, *Brasil*	Linda Ronstadt and Aaron Neville, "Don't Know Much"	Linda Ronstadt with Aaron Neville, "All My Life"
Rock Performance, Duo or Group with Vocal	U2, "Desire"	Traveling Wilburys, *Traveling Wilburys, Volume I*	Aerosmith, "Janie's Got a Gun"
New Age Recording	Shadowfax, *Folksongs for a Nuclear Village*	Peter Gabriel, *Passion (Music from The Last Temptation of Christ)*	Mark Isham, *Mark Isham*
Hard Rock	Jethro Tull, *Crest of a Knave*	Living Colour, "Cult of Personality"	Living Colour, *Time's Up*
Metal	—	Metallica, "One"	Metallica, "Stone Cold Crazy"
Alternative	—	—	Sinéad O'Connor, *I Do Not Want What I Haven't Got*
Rap Performance, Solo	D.J. Jazzy Jeff & The Fresh Prince, "Parents Just Don't Understand"	Young MC, "Busta Move"	M.C. Hammer, "U Can't Touch This"
Rap Performance by a Duo or Group	—	—	Ice-T, Melle Mel, Big Daddy Kane, Kool Moe Dee, and Quincy Jones III, "Back on the Block"
Rhythm and Blues Song	Anita Baker, Skip Scarborough, and Randy Holland, "Giving You the Best That I Got"	Kenny Gamble and Leon Huff, "If You Don't Know Me By Now"	Rick James, Alonzo Mille, and M.C. Hammer, "U Can't Touch This"
R&B Vocal, Female	Anita Baker, "Giving You the Best That I Got"	Anita Baker, *Giving You the Best That I Got*	Anita Baker, *Compositions*
R&B Vocal, Male	Terence Trent D'Arby, *Introducing the Hardline According to Terence Trent D'Arby*	Bobby Brown, "Every Little Step"	Luther Vandross, "Here and Now"
R&B Duo or Group with Vocal	Gladys Knight & The Pips, "Love Overboard"	Soul II Soul featuring Caron Wheeler, "Back to Life"	Ray Charles and Chaka Khan, "I'll Be Good to You"
Country Song	K. T. Oslin, "Hold Me"	Rodney Crowell, "After All This Time"	Jon Vezner and Don Henry, "Where've You Been"

	1988	1989	1990
Country Vocal, Female	K. T. Oslin, "Hold Me"	k.d. lang, *Absolute Torch and Twang*	Kathy Mattea, "Where've You Been"
Country Vocal, Male	Randy Travis, *Old 8 x 10*	Lyle Lovett, *Lyle Lovett and His Large Band*	Vince Gill, "When I Call Your Name"
Country Performance, Duo or Group with Vocal	The Judds, "Give a Little Love"	The Nitty Gritty Dirt Band, *Will the Circle Be Unbroken, Volume 2*	The Kentucky Headhunters, *Pickin' on Nashville*
Country Vocal, Collaboration	Roy Orbison and k.d. lang, "Crying"	Hank Williams Jr. and Hank Williams Sr., "There's a Tear in My Beer"	Chet Atkins and Mark Knopfler, "Poor Boy Blues"
Traditional Blues Recording	Willie Dixon, *Hidden Charms*	John Lee Hooker and Bonnie Raitt, "I'm in the Mood"	B.B. King, *Live at San Quentin*
Contemporary Blues	The Robert Cray Band, "Don't Be Afraid of the Dark"	Stevie Ray Vaughan & Double Trouble, *In Step*	The Vaughan Brothers, *Family Style*
Reggae Recording	Ziggy Marley & The Melody Makers, *Conscious Party*	Ziggy Marley & The Melody Makers, *One Bright Day*	Bunny Wailer, *Time Will Tell—A Tribute to Bob Marley*
Jazz Vocal, Female	Betty Carter, *Look What I Got!*	Ruth Brown, *Blues on Broadway*	Ella Fitzgerald, *All That Jazz*
Jazz Vocal, Male	Bobby McFerrin, "Brothers"	Harry Connick Jr., *When Harry Met Sally . . .*	Harry Connick Jr., *We Are in Love*
Jazz, Soloist	Michael Brecker, *Don't Try This at Home*	Miles Davis, *Aura*	Oscar Peterson, *The Legendary Oscar Peterson Trio Live at the Blue Note*
Jazz, Group	McCoy Tyner, Pharaoh Sanders, David Murray, Cecil McBee, and Roy Haynes, *Blues for Coltrane: A Tribute to John Coltrane*	Chick Corea Akoustic Band, *Chick Corea Akoustic Band*	Oscar Peterson Trio, *The Legendary Oscar Peterson Trio Live at the Blue Note*
Jazz, Big Band/ Large Ensemble Performance	Gil Evans & The Monday Night Orchestra, *Bud & Bird*	Miles Davis, *Aura*	George Benson featuring the Count Basie Orchestra; Frank Foster, conductor, "Basie's Bag"
Jazz Fusion Performance, Vocal or Instrumental	Yellowjackets, *Politics*	Pat Metheny Group, *Letter from Home*	Quincy Jones, "Birdland"
Gospel Performance, Female	Amy Grant, *Lead Me On*	CeCe Winans, "Don't Cry"	—
Gospel Performance, Male	Larnelle Harris, *Christmas*	BeBe Winans, "Meantime"	—
Gospel Performance, Duo, Group, Choir or Chorus	The Winans, *The Winans Live at Carnegie Hall*	Take 6, "The Savior Is Waiting"	Rev. James Cleveland, *Having Church*
Traditional Folk Recording	Various artists, *Folkways: A Vision Shared—A Tribute to Woody Guthrie and Leadbelly*	Bulgarian State Female Vocal Choir, *Le Mystère des voix bulgares, Vol. II*	Doc Watson, *On Praying Ground*
Contemporary Folk Recording	Tracy Chapman, *Tracy Chapman*	Indigo Girls, *Indigo Girls*	Shawn Colvin, *Steady On*
Cast Show Album	*Into the Woods*	*Jerome Robbins' Broadway*	*Les Misérables, The Complete Symphonic Recording*

	1988	**1989**	**1990**
Comedy Recording	Robin Williams, *Good Morning, Vietnam*	"Professor" Peter Schickele, *P.D.Q. Bach: 1712 Overture and Other Musical Assaults*	"Professor" Peter Schickele, *P.D.Q. Bach: Oedipus Tex & Other Choral Calamities*
Classical Album	Robert Shaw, conductor, Atlanta Symphony Orchestra and Chorus, *Verdi: Requiem and Operatic Choruses*	Emerson String Quartet, *Bartók: 6 String Quartets*	Leonard Bernstein, conductor, New York Philharmonic, *Ives: Symphony No. 2 (and Three Short Works)*
Classical Orchestral Performance	Robert Shaw, conductor, Atlanta Symphony Orchestra, *Rorem: String Symphony;* Louis Lane, conductor, Atlanta Symphony Orchestra, *Sunday Morning* and *Eagles*	Leonard Bernstein, conductor, New York Philharmonic, *Mahler: Sym. No. 3 in D Min.*	Leonard Bernstein, conductor, Chicago Symphony, *Shostakovich: Symphonies No. 1, Op. 10, and No. 7, Op. 60*
Opera Recording	Georg Solti, conductor, Vienna State Opera Choir & Vienna Philharmonic (Solos: Domingo, Norman, Randova, Nimsgern, Sotin, Fischer-Dieskau), *Wagner: Lohengrin*	James Levine, conductor, Metropolitan Opera Orchestra (Solos: Lakes, Moll, Morris, Norman, Behrens, Ludwig), *Wagner: Die Walküre*	James Levine, conductor, Metropolitan Opera Orchestra (Solos: Morris, Ludwig, Jerusalem, Wlaschiha, Moll, Zednik, Rootering), *Wagner: Das Rheingold*
Chamber Music Performance	Murray Perahia and Sir Georg Solti, pianos, with David Corkhill and Evelyn Glennie, percussion, *Bartók: Sonata for Two Pianos and Percussion; Brahms: Variations on a Theme by Joseph Haydn for Two Pianos*	Emerson String Quartet, *Bartók: 6 String Quartets*	Itzhak Perlman, violin; Daniel Barenboim, piano, *Brahms: The Three Violin Sonatas*

GRAMMY CHAMPS

Who's taken home the most statuettes? Chicago Symphony conductor Sir Georg Solti must have had to build a special case just to hold all his Grammys. After Sir Georg, the following musicians have received the highest number of awards from the National Academy of Recording Arts and Sciences.

Sir Georg Solti	30	Chet Atkins	13
Quincy Jones	26	Michael Jackson	12
Vladimir Horowitz	25	Ray Charles	12
Henry Mancini	20	David Foster	12
Stevie Wonder	17	Thomas Z. Shepard	12
Leonard Bernstein	16	Sting (including The Police)	12
Pierre Boulez	16	Duke Ellington	11
Paul Simon (including Simon & Garfunkel)	16	James Mallinson	11
John T. Williams	16	Roger Miller	11
Aretha Franklin	15	Paul McCartney	
Itzhak Perlman	14	(including The Beatles and Wings)	10
Ella Fitzgerald	13	Bobby McFerrin	10
Leontyne Price	13	Artur Rubinstein	10
Robert Shaw (including Robert Shaw Chorale)	13	Robert Woods	10

	1991	1992	1993
Record of the Year	Natalie Cole (with Nat "King" Cole), "Unforgettable"	Eric Clapton, "Tears in Heaven"	Whitney Houston, "I Will Always Love You"
Album of the Year	Natalie Cole, *Unforgettable*	Eric Clapton, *Unplugged*	Whitney Houston and others, *The Bodyguard—Original Soundtrack*
Song of the Year	Irving Gordon, "Unforgettable"	Eric Clapton and Will Jennings, "Tears in Heaven"	Alan Menken and Tim Rice, "A Whole New World"
Pop Vocal, Female	Bonnie Raitt, "Something to Talk About"	k.d. lang, "Constant Craving"	Whitney Houston, "I Will Always Love You"
Pop Vocal, Male	Michael Bolton, "When a Man Loves a Woman"	Eric Clapton, "Tears in Heaven"	Sting, "If I Ever Lose My Faith In You"
Rock Vocal, Female	Bonnie Raitt, *Luck of the Draw*	Melissa Etheridge, "Ain't It Heavy"	—
Rock Vocal, Male	—	Eric Clapton, *Tears in Heaven*	—
Rock Song/ Rock Vocal Performance, Solo	Sting, "Soul Cages"	Eric Clapton and Jim Gordon, *Layla*	Meat Loaf, "I'd Do Anything for Love (But I Won't Do That)"
New Artist	Mark Cohn	Arrested Development	Toni Braxton
Pop Vocal, Duo or Group with Vocal	R.E.M., "Losing My Religion"	Celine Dion and Peabo Bryson, "Beauty and the Beast"	Peabo Bryson and Regina Belle, "A Whole New World"
Rock Performance, Duo or Group with Vocal	Bonnie Raitt and Delbert McClinton, "Good Man, Good Woman"	U2, *Achtung Baby*	Aerosmith, "Living on the Edge"
New Age Recording	Mannheim Steamroller, *Fresh Aire 7*	Enya, *Sheperd Moons*	Paul Winter Consort, *Spanish Angel*
Hard Rock	Van Halen, *For Unlawful Carnal Knowledge*	Red Hot Chili Peppers, "Give It Away"	Stone Temple Pilots, "Plush"
Metal	Metallica, *Metallica*	Nine Inch Nails, "Wish"	Ozzy Ozbourne, "I Don't Want To Change the World"
Alternative	R.E.M., *Out of Time*	Tom Waits, *Bone Machine*	U2, *Zooropa*
Rap Performance, Solo	L.L. Cool J, "Mama Said Knock You Out"	Sir Mix-A-Lot, "Baby Got Back"	Dr. Dre, "Let Me Ride"
Rap Performance by a Duo or Group	D.J. Jazzy Jeff & The Fresh Prince, "Summertime"	Arrested Development, "Tennessee"	Digable Planets, "Rebirth of Slick (Cool Like Dat)"
Rhythm and Blues Song	Luther Vandross, Marcus Miller, and Teddy Vann, "Power of Love/Love Power"	L.A. Reid, Babyface, and Daryl Simmons, "End of the Road"	Janet Jackson, James Harris III, and Terry Lewis, "That's the Way Love Goes"
R&B Vocal, Female	Patti LaBelle, *Burnin'*; Lisa Fischer; "How Can I Ease the Pain"	Chaka Khan, *The Woman I Am*	Toni Braxton, "Another Sad Love Song"
R&B Vocal, Male	Luther Vandross, *Power of Love*	Al Jarreau, *Heaven and Earth*	Ray Charles, "A Song For You"
R&B Duo or Group with Vocal	Boyz II Men, *Cooleyhigh harmony*	Boyz II Men, "End of the Road"	Sade, "No Ordinary Love"
Country Song	Naomi Judd, John Jarvis, and Paul Overstreet, "Love Can Build a Bridge"	Vince Gill and John Barlow Jarvis, "I Still Believe in You"	Lucinda Williams, "Passionate Kisses"
Country Vocal, Female	Mary-Chapin Carpenter, "Down at the Twist and Shout"	Mary-Chapin Carpenter, "I Feel Lucky"	Mary-Chapin Carpenter, "Passionate Kisses"
Country Vocal, Male	Garth Brooks, *Ropin' the Wind*	Vince Gill, *I Still Believe in You*	Dwight Yoakam, "Ain't That Lonely Yet"

	1991	1992	1993
Country Performance, Duo or Group with Vocal	The Judds, "Love Can Build a Bridge"	Emmylou Harris & The Nash Ramblers, *Emmylou Harris & The Nash Ramblers at the Ryman*	Brooks & Dunn, "Hard Workin' Man"
Country Vocal, Collaboration	Steve Wariner, Ricky Skaggs, and Vince Gill, "Restless"	Travis Tritt and Marty Stuart, "The Whiskey Ain't Workin' "	Reba McEntire and Linda Davis, "Does He Love You"
Traditional Blues Recording	B. B. King, *Live at the Apollo*	Dr. John, *Goin' Back to New Orleans*	B.B. King, *Blues Summit*
Contemporary Blues	Buddy Guy, *Damn Right, I've Got the Blues*	Stevie Ray Vaughan & Double Trouble, *The Sky Is Crying*	Buddy Guy, *Feels Like Rain*
Reggae Recording	Shabba Ranks, *As Raw as Ever*	Shabba Ranks, *X-tra Naked*	Inner Circle, *Bad Boys*
Jazz, Soloist	Stan Getz, "I Remember You"	Joe Henderson, "Lush Life"	Joe Henderson, "Miles Ahead"
Jazz, Group	Oscar Peterson Trio, *Saturday Night at the Blue Note*	Branford Marsalis, *I Heard You Twice the First Time*	Joe Henderson, *So Near, So Far (Musings for Miles)*
Jazz, Big Band/ Large Ensemble Performance	Dizzy Gillespie & The United Nation Orchestra, *Live at the Royal Festival Hall*	McCoy Tyner Big Band, *The Turning Point*	Miles Davis and Quincy Jones, *Miles and Quincy Live at Montreaux*
Jazz Fusion Performance	—	Pat Metheny, *Secret Story*	—
Gospel Performance, Duo, Group, Choir or Chorus	Sounds of Blackness, *The Evolution of Gospel*	Music & Arts Seminar Mass Choir; Edwin Hawkins, choir director, *Edwin Hawkins Music & Arts Seminar Mass Choir: Recorded Live in Los Angeles*	Brooklyn Tabernacle Choir; Carol Cymbala, choir director, *Live . . . We Come Rejoicing*
Traditional Folk Recording	Ken Burns and John Colby, *The Civil War*	The Chieftains, *Another Country*	The Chieftains, *The Celtic Harp*
Contemporary Folk Recording	John Prine, *The Missing Years*	The Chieftains, *An Irish Evening Live at the Grand Opera House, Belfast*	Nanci Griffith, *Other Voices/Other Rooms*
Cast Show Album	*The Will Rogers Follies*	*Guys and Dolls*	*The Who's Tommy*
Comedy Recording	"Professor" Peter Schickele, *P.D.Q. Bach: WTWP Classical Talkity-Talk Radio*	"Professor" Peter Schickele, *P.D.Q. Bach: Music for an Awful Lot of Winds & Percussion*	George Carlin, *Jammin' in New York*
Classical Album	Leonard Bernstein, conductor, London Symphony Orchestra (Solos: Hadley, Anderson, Ludwig, Green, Gedda, Jones), *Bernstein: Candide*	Leonard Bernstein, conductor, Berlin Philharmonic Orchestra, *Mahler: Symphony No. 9*	Pierre Boulez, conductor, Chicago Symphony Orchestra and Chorus; John Alen John Tomlinson, baritone, *Bartók: The Wooden Prince & C*
Classical Orchestral Performance	Daniel Barenboim, conductor, Chicago Symphony Orchestra, *Corigliano: Symphony No. 1*	Leonard Bernstein, conductor, Berlin Philharmonic Orchestra, *Mahler: Symphony No. 9*	Pierre Boulez, conductor, Chicago Symphony, *Bartók: The Wooden Prince*
Opera Recording	James Levine, conductor, Metropolitan Opera Orchestra and Chorus (Solos: Behrens, Studer, Schwarz, Goldberg, Weikl, Wlaschiha, Salminen), *Wagner: Götterdämmerung*	Georg Solti conductor, Vienna Philharmonic (Solos: Domingo, Varady, Van Dam, Behrens, Runkel, Jo), *R. Strauss: Die Frau Ohne Schatten*	John Nelson, conductor, English Chamber Orchestra and Ambrosian Opera Chorus (Solos: Battle, Horne, Ramey, Aler, McNair, Chance, Mackie, Doss); *Handel: Semele*
Chamber Music Performance	Isaac Stern and Jamie Laredo, violins; Yo-Yo Ma, cello; Emanuel Ax, piano, *Brahms: Piano Quartets*	Yo-Yo Ma, cello; Emanuel Ax, piano, *Brahms: Sonatas for Cello & Piano*	Anne-Sophie Mutter, violin, and James Levine, conductor, Chicago Symphony, *Berg: Violoin Concerto/Rihm: Time Chant*

1994

Record of the Year	Sheryl Crow, "All I Wanna Do"
Album of the Year	Tony Bennet, *MTV Unplugged*
Song of the Year	Bruce Springsteen, "Streets of Philadelphia"
Pop Vocal, Female	Sheryl Crow, "All I Wanna Do"
Pop Vocal, Male	Elton John, "Can You Feel the Love Tonight"
Rock Vocal, Female	Melissa Etheridge, "Come to my Window"
Rock Vocal, Male	Bruce Springsteen, "Streets of Philadelphia"
Rock Song/ Rock Vocal Performance, Solo	Bruce Springsteen, "Streets of Philadelphia"
New Artist	Sheryl Crow
Pop Vocal, Duo or Group with Vocal	All-4-One, "I Swear"
Rock Performance, Duo or Group with Vocal	Aerosmith, "Crazy"
New Age Recording	Paul Winter, "Prayer for the Wild Thing"
Hard Rock	Soundgarden, *Black Hole Sun*
Metal	Soundgarden, *Spoonman*
Alternative	Green Day, "Dookie"
Rap Performance, Solo	Queen Latifah, "U.N.I.T.Y."
Rap Performance by a Duo or Group	Salt-N-Pepa, "None of Your Business"
Rhythm and Blues Song	Babyface, "I'll Make Love to You"
R&B Vocal, Female	Toni Braxton, "Breathe Again"
R&B Vocal, Male	Babyface, "When Can I See You"
R&B Duo or Group with Vocal	Boyz II Men, "I'll Make Love to You"
Country Song	Gary Baker and Frank J. Myers, "I Swear"
Country Vocal, Female	Mary Chapin Carpenter, "Shut Up and Kiss Me"
Country Vocal, Male	Vince Gill, "When Love Finds You"

1994

Country Performance, Duo or Group with Vocal	Asleep at the Wheel with Lyle Lovett, "Blues for Dixie"
Country Vocal, Collaboration	Aaron Neville and Trisha Yearwood, "I Fall to Pieces"
Traditional Blues Recording	Eric Clapton, *From the Cradle*
Contemporary Blues	Pops Staples, *Father Father*
Reggae Recording	Bunny Wailer, *Crucial! Roots Classics*
Jazz, Soloist	Benny Carter, "Prelude to a Kiss"
Jazz, Group	Ron Carter, Herbie Hancock, Wallace Roney, Wayne Shorter & Tony Williams, *A Tribute to Miles*
Jazz, Big Band/ Large Ensemble Performance	McCoy Tyner Big Band, *Journey*
Jazz Fusion Performance	—
Gospel Performance, Duo, Group, Choir or Chorus	The Thompson Community Singers, Rev. Milton Brunson, choir director, *Through God's Eyes* and The Love Fellowship Crusade Choir, Hezekiah Walker, choir director, *Live in Atlanta at Morehouse College* (tie)
Traditional Folk Recording	Bob Dylan, *World Gone Wrong*
Contemporary Folk Recording	Johnny Cash, *American Recordings*
Cast Show Album	*Passion*
Comedy Recording	Sam Kinison, *Live From Hell*
Classical Album	Pierre Boulez, conductor, Chicago Symphony Orchestra, *Bartok: Concerto for Orch.; Four Orchestral Pieces, Op. 12*
Classical Orchestral Performance	Pierre Boulez, conductor, Chicago Symphony Orchestra, *Bartok: Concerto for Orch.; Four Orchestral Pieces, Op. 12*
Opera Recording	Kent Nagano, conductor, Orchestra and Chorus of Opera de Lyon (Solos: Cheryl Struder, Jerry Hadley, Samuel Ramey, Kenn Chester), *Floyd: Susannah*
Chamber Music Performance	Daniel Barenboim, piano; Dale Clevenger, horn; Larry Combs, clarinet (Chicago Symphony), Daniele Damiano, bassoon; Hansjorg Schellenberger, oboe (Berlin Philharmonic), *Beethoven/Mozart: Quintets*

THE COUNTRY MUSIC ASSOCIATION AWARDS

	1967	**1968**	**1969**
Entertainer	Eddy Arnold	Glen Campbell	Johnny Cash
Song	Dallas Frazier, "There Goes My Everything"	Bobby Russell, "Honey"	Bob Ferguson, "Carroll County Accident"
Female Vocalist	Loretta Lynn	Tammy Wynette	Tammy Wynette
Male Vocalist	Jack Greene	Glen Campbell	Johnny Cash
Album	Jack Greene, *There Goes My Everything*	Johnny Cash, *Johnny Cash at Folsom Prison*	Johnny Cash, *Johnny Cash at San Quentin Prison*
Single	Jack Greene, "There Goes My Everything"	Jeannie C. Riley, "Harper Valley P.T.A."	Johnny Cash, "A Boy Named Sue"
Vocal Group	The Stoneman Family	Porter Wagoner and Dolly Parton	Johnny Cash and June Carter
Musician	Chet Atkins	Chet Atkins	Chet Atkins

	1970	**1971**	**1972**
Entertainer	Merle Haggard	Charley Pride	Loretta Lynn
Song	Kris Kristofferson, "Sunday Morning Coming Down"	Freddie Hart, "Easy Loving"	Freddie Hart, "Easy Loving"
Female Vocalist	Tammy Wynette	Lynn Anderson	Loretta Lynn
Male Vocalist	Merle Haggard	Charley Pride	Charley Pride
Album	Merle Haggard, *Okie from Muskogee*	Ray Price, *I Won't Mention It Again*	Merle Haggard, *Let Me Tell You About a Song*
Single	Merle Haggard, "Okie From Muskogee"	Sammi Smith, "Help Me Make It Through the Night"	Donna Fargo, "The Happiest Girl in the Whole U.S.A."
Vocal Group	The Glaser Brother	The Osborne Brothers	The Statler Brothers
Vocal Duo	Porter Wagoner and Dolly Parton	Porter Wagoner and Dolly Parton	Conway Twitty and Loretta Lynn
Musician	Jerry Reed	Jerry Reed	Charlie McCoy

	1973	**1974**	**1975**
Entertainer	Roy Clark	Charlie Rich	John Denver
Song	Kenny O'Dell, "Behind Closed Doors"	Don Wayne, "Country Bumpkin"	John Denver, "Back Home Again"
Female Vocalist	Loretta Lynn	Olivia Newton-John	Dolly Parton
Male Vocalist	Charlie Rich	Ronnie Milsap	Waylon Jennings
Album	Charlie Rich, *Behind Closed Doors*	Charlie Rich, *A Very Special Love Song*	Ronnie Milsap, *A Legend in My Time*
Single	Charlie Rich, "Behind Closed Doors"	Cal Smith, "Country Bumpkin"	Freddy Fender, "Before the Next Teardrop Falls"
Vocal Group	The Statler Brothers	The Statler Brothers	The Statler Brothers
Vocal Duo	Conway Twitty and Loretta Lynn	Conway Twitty and Loretta Lynn	Conway Twitty and Loretta Lynn
Musician	Charlie McCoy	Don Rich	Johnny Gimble

	1976	**1977**	**1978**
Entertainer	Mel Tillis	Ronnie Milsap	Dolly Parton
Song	Larry Weiss, "Rhinestone Cowboy"	Roger Bowling & Hal Bynum, "Lucille"	Richard Leigh, "Don't It Make My Brown Eyes Blue"
Female Vocalist	Dolly Parton	Crystal Gayle	Crystal Gayle
Male Vocalist	Ronnie Milsap	Ronnie Milsap	Don Williams
Album	Waylon Jennings, Willie Nelson, Tompall Glaser, Jessi Colter, *Wanted—The Outlaws*	Ronnie Milsap, *Ronnie Milsap Live*	Ronnie Milsap, *It Was Almost Like a Song*
Single	Waylon Jennings & Willie Nelson, "Good Hearted Woman"	Kenny Rogers, "Lucille"	The Kendalls, "Heaven's Just a Sin Away"
Vocal Group	The Statler Brothers	The Statler Brothers	The Oak Ridge Boys
Vocal Duo	Waylon Jennings & Willie Nelson	Jim Ed Brown & Helen Cornelius	Kenny Rogers and Dottie West
Musician	Hargus "Pig" Robbins	Roy Clark	Roy Clark

	1979	**1980**	**1981**
Entertainer	Willie Nelson	Barbara Mandrell	Barbara Mandrell
Song	Don Schlitz, "The Gambler"	Bobby Braddock & Curly Putman, "He Stopped Loving Her Today"	Bobby Braddock & Curly Putman, "He Stopped Loving Her Today"
Female Vocalist	Barbara Mandrell	Emmylou Harris	Barbara Mandrell
Male Vocalist	Kenny Rogers	George Jones	George Jones
Album	Kenny Rogers, *The Gambler*	Original Motion Picture Soundtrack, *Coal Miner's Daughter*	Don Williams, *I Believe in You*
Single	Charlie Daniels Band, "The Devil Went Down to Georgia"	George Jones, "He Stopped Loving Her Today"	Oak Ridge Boys, "Elvira"
Vocal Group	The Statler Brothers	The Statler Brothers	Alabama
Horizon Award	—	—	Terri Gibbs
Vocal Duo	Kenny Rogers and Dottie West	Moe Bandy and Joe Stampley	David Frizzell and Shelly West
Musician	Charlie Daniels	Roy Clark	Chet Atkins

	1982	**1983**	**1984**
Entertainer	Alabama	Alabama	Alabama
Song	Johnny Christopher, Wayne Carson, Mark James, "Always On My Mind"	Johnny Christopher, Wayne Carson, Mark James, "Always On My Mind"	Larry Henley, Jeff Silbar, "Wind Beneath My Wings"
Female Vocalist	Janie Fricke	Janie Fricke	Reba McEntire
Male Vocalist	Ricky Skaggs	Lee Greenwood	Lee Greenwood
Album	Willie Nelson, *Always on My Mind*	Alabama, *The Closer You Get*	Anne Murray, *A Little Good News*
Single	Willie Nelson, "Always on My Mind"	John Anderson, "Swingin'"	Anne Murray, "A Little Good News"
Vocal Group	Alabama	Alabama	The Statler Brothers
Horizon Award	Ricky Skaggs	John Anderson	The Judds
Vocal Duo	David Frizzell and Shelly West	Merle Haggard and Willie Nelson	Willie Nelson & Julio Iglesias
Musician	Chet Atkins	Chet Atkins	Chet Atkins

	1985	**1986**	**1987**
Entertainer	Ricky Skaggs	Reba McEntire	Hank Williams Jr.
Song	Lee Greenwood, "God Bless the USA"	Paul Overstreet, Don Schlitz, "On the Other Hand"	Paul Overstreet, Don Schlitz, "Forever and Ever, Amen"
Female Vocalist	Reba McEntire	Reba McEntire	Reba McEntire
Male Vocalist	George Strait	George Strait	Randy Travis
Album	George Strait, *Does Fort Worth Ever Cross Your Mind*	Ronnie Milsap, *Lost in the Fifties Tonight*	Randy Travis, *Always and Forever*
Single	The Judds, "Why Not Me"	Dan Seals, "Bop"	Randy Travis, "Forever and Ever, Amen"
Vocal Group	The Judds	The Judds	The Judds
Horizon Award	Sawyer Brown	Randy Travis	Holly Dunn
Vocal Duo	Anne Murray and Dave Loggins	Dan Seals and Marie Osmond	Ricky Skaggs and Sharon White
Musician	Chet Atkins	Johnny Gimble	Johnny Gimble
Music Video	Hank Williams Jr., *All My Rowdy Friends Are Comin' Over Tonight*	George Jones, *Who's Gonna Fill Their Shoes*	Hank Williams Jr., *My Name Is Bocephus*

	1988	**1989**	**1990**
Entertainer	Hank Williams Jr.	George Strait	George Strait
Song	K.T. Oslin, "80's Ladies"	Max D. Barnes, Vern Gosdin, "Chiseled in Stone"	Jon Vezner, Don Henry, "Where've You Been"
Female Vocalist	K.T. Oslin	Kathy Mattea	Kathy Mattea
Male Vocalist	Randy Travis	Ricky Van Shelton	Clint Black
Album	Hank Williams Jr., *Born to Boogie*	Nitty Gritty Dirt Band, *Will the Circle Be Unbroken, Vol. II*	Kentucky HeadHunters, *Pickin' on Nashville*
Single	Kathy Mattea, "Eighteen Wheels and a Dozen Roses"	Keith Whitley, "I'm No Stranger to the Rain"	Vince Gill, "When I Call Your Name"
Vocal Group	Highway 101	Highway 101	Kentucky HeadHunters
Vocal Event	Dolly Parton, Emmylou Harris, Linda Ronstadt, *Trio*	Hank Williams Jr., Hank Williams Sr.	Lorrie Morgan, Keith Whitley
Horizon Award	Ricky Van Shelton	Clint Black	Garth Brooks
Vocal Duo	The Judds	The Judds	The Judds
Musician	Chet Atkins	Johnny Gimble	Johnny Gimble
Music Video	—	Hank Williams Jr., Hank Williams Sr., *There's a Tear in My Beer*	Garth Brooks, *The Dance*

1991   1992   1993

	1991	1992	1993
Entertainer of the Year	Garth Brooks	Garth Brooks	Vince Gill
Song of the Year	Vince Gill, Tim DuBois, "When I Call Your Name"	Vince Gill, Max D. Barnes, "Look at Us"	Vince Gill, John Barlow Jarvis, "I Still Believe in You"
Female Vocalist of the Year	Tanya Tucker	Mary-Chapin Carpenter	Mary-Chapin Carpenter
Male Vocalist of the Year	Vince Gill	Vince Gill	Vince Gill
Album of the Year	Garth Brooks, *No Fences*	Garth Brooks, *Ropin' the Wind*	Vince Gill, *I Still Believe in You*
Single of the Year	Garth Brooks, "Friends in Low Places"	Billy Ray Cyrus, "Achy Breaky Heart"	Alan Jackson, "Chattahoochee"
Vocal Group of the Year	Kentucky HeadHunters	Diamond Rio	Diamond Rio
Vocal Event of the Year	Mark O'Connor & The New Nashville Cats (featuring Vince Gill, Ricky Skaggs, and Steve Wariner)	Marty Stuart, Travis Tritt	George Jones with Vince Gill, Mark Chesnutt, Garth Brooks, Travis Tritt, Joe Diffie, Alan Jackson, Pam Tillis, T. Graham Brown, Patty Loveless, Clint Black, *I Don't Need Your Rockin' Chair*
Horizon Award	Travis Tritt	Suzy Bogguss	Mark Chesnutt
Vocal Duo of the Year	The Judds	Brooks & Dunn	Brooks & Dunn
Musician of the Year	Mark O'Connor	Mark O'Connor	Mark O'Connor
Music Video of the Year	Garth Brooks, *The Thunder Rolls*	Alan Jackson, *Midnight in Montgomery*	Alan Jackson, *Chattahoochee*

1994

	1994
Entertainer of the Year	Vince Gill
Song of the Year	Alan Jackson, Jim McBride, "Chattahoochee"
Female Vocalist of the Year	Pam Tillis
Male Vocalist of the Year	Vince Gill
Album of the Year	*Common Thread: The Songs of the Eagles*
Single of the Year	John Michael Montgomery, "I Swear"
Vocal Group of the Year	Diamond Rio
Vocal Event of the Year	Reba McEntire with Linda Davis, *"Does He Love You"*
Horizon Award	John Michael Montgomery
Vocal Duo of the Year	Brooks & Dunn
Musician of the Year	Mark O'Conner
Music Video of the Year	Martina McBride, *Independence Day*

PAGES

PICKS & PANS 1995

Here's a summary of the latest literary hits and misses—in the view of PEOPLE's discerning if idiosyncratic critics. You'll *know* when we're panning, and the picks we can recommend most enthusiastically are marked with an asterisk.

*RESERVATION BLUES
Sherman Alexie

The author uses his own experiences growing up on the Wellpinit reservation outside Spokane as a springboard for this high-flying, humor-spiked tale of culture and assimilation.

PAULA
Isabel Allende

The Chilean author follows her lineage, from the immigration of her Basque ancestors to her daughter's untimely death. But there is something unseemly about a self-centered work in the name of one's daughter; in the final sentence, Allende uses the word "I" six times even as she bids Paula farewell.

FIVE MINUTES IN HEAVEN
Lisa Alther

Alther has lost her sense of humor. Without that humor to alleviate the main character's pain, the reader just wants the character to put both herself and the rest of us out of our misery.

*IN THE TIME OF THE BUTTERFLIES
Julia Alvarez

This gorgeous and sensitive novel is an attempt to understand how three well-to-do young women came to die in the cause of revolution.

THE INFORMATION
Martin Amis

A minor novelist attempts to gain revenge on his friend for writing a successful novel. Full of quirkiness for quirkiness's sake, infuriatingly truncated passages, and self-important preciousness, *The Information* still offers compelling storytelling.

*THE COLLECTED STORIES OF LOUIS AUCHINCLOSS
Louis Auchincloss

A rich collection of gracefully crafted stories from the elder statesman of literary lawyers.

*RULE OF THE BONE
Russell Banks

Huckleberry Finn transposed to Upstate New York in the '90s, this is the tale of a white boy fleeing his depressed, small-minded hometown for Jamaica.

*DAVE BARRY'S COMPLETE GUIDE TO GUYS
Dave Barry

This laugh-out-loud original book proves Barry to be the most consistently funny, deceptively playful satirist this side of Twain and Thurber.

THE GLASS LAKE
Maeve Binchy

A soap opera set in the small Irish village of Lough Glass. *The Glass Lake* is comfort food—not great, but satisfying in its blandness and bulk.

*THE BURGLAR WHO THOUGHT HE WAS BOGART
Lawrence Block

The part-time thief with a heart of semi-precious metal and a nose for detection is back. Block is a master of the form, and *Bogart* is excellent.

BOB MARLEY: SONGS OF FREEDOM
Adrian Boot and Chris Salewicz

As overstuffed, rough-hewn, and heady as the spliffs Bob and his Wailers used to pass around, *Songs of Freedom* is a definitive volume for collectors.

DEVILS HOLE
Bill Branon

Bill Branon's new thriller focuses on hitman Arthur Arthur, a sniper with a twisted agenda and one of contemporary crime fiction's best wackos. A bull's-eye.

BOMBADIERS
Po Bronson

A kind of a *Catch-22* of the information age, where the mad rule the crazed and survival depends on turning logic inside out.

A PRIVATE VIEW
Anita Brookner

The author paints on an even tinier canvas than usual, yet—master miniaturist that she is—her sure strokes make for a picture that lingers.

*MADE IN AMERICA: AN INFORMAL HISTORY OF THE ENGLISH LANGUAGE IN THE UNITED STATES
Bill Bryson
Written with understated humor, this lively treatment of the development of American English is no lemon—it's a peach!

*THE MATISSE STORIES
A. S. Byatt
From the hands of a master, this triptych touches upon things that matter to people: thwarted dreams; loneliness and the longing to connect; the restorative power of kindness; and the pleasures of flesh, color, and creation.

THE PLAN
Stephen J. Cannell
A Mob-controlled TV network promotes their candidate for President. Flapdoodle—but say this much: Cannell knows how to craft scenes which more than compensate for the Styrofoam characters and cartoon dialogue.

*SLEEPERS
Lorenzo Carcaterra
Fact or fiction, this stunning story of what happens 10 years after four high-spirited boys are abused in a reformatory is a compelling read.

*WONDER BOYS
Michael Chabon
This ode to the perils of literary success and the travails of a sad-sack writer is an enjoyable literary romp.

THE RETURN OF MERLIN
Deepak Chopra
Author of such alternative medicine megasellers as *Ageless Body, Timeless Mind*, Chopra makes his first foray into fiction with this reworking of the Arthurian legend. Unfortunately, too much proselytizing about self-actualization diminishes his narrative flair.

LET ME CALL YOU SWEETHEART
Mary Higgins Clark
Clark's latest mystery has as many suspects as a game of Clue. Making it even tougher to solve is the fact that the murder is 10 years old.

*OFF STAGE
Betty Comden
An engaging portrait of a woman of the theater away from the stage.

*DENIAL
Bonnie Comfort
Therapist Dr. Sarah Rinsley's patient becomes obsessed with her; when she rejects his come-ons, he devises a way to destroy her professional reputation and her sanity. A page-turner with interesting characters.

FROM POTTER'S FIELD
Patricia Cornwell
In this deliciously nerve-jangling game of cat and mouse, Dr. Kay Scarpetta tracks a cunning and sadistic killer.

*MICROSERFS
Douglas Coupland
A hilarious, intimate look at the way high technology is transforming American life—for better and for worse.

GROWING UP WITH MY GRANDFATHER: MEMORIES OF HARRY TRUMAN
Clifton Truman Daniel
Daniel describes how it feels to be a low achiever in a famous American family. Perhaps fellow members of the overprivileged club can sympathize with the demons that haunted the author, but this book has a whiny tone.

NEST OF VIPERS
Linda Davies
The heroine is a foreign-currency-exchange trader who may be a bit too eager to live on the edge. First-time novelist Davies sets a promising plot in motion but doesn't seem to know quite what to do with it.

*THE CUNNING MAN
Robertson Davies
A very unconventional doctor referees the battle between science and religion, medicine and spirituality, in this latest offering from Canada's literary master.

*FOR THE GLORY
Ken Denlinger
No one who reads Denlinger's account of five years in the life of one class of Penn State football recruits will ever again think of big-time college football in terms of bonfires, rallies, and campus romance.

THE DAUGHTERS OF CAIN
Colin Dexter
Brilliant curmudgeon Inspector Morse investigates the murder of an Oxford don. Too labyrinthine for lazy beach reading, but Dexter's talent for plot-thickening makes it worth the extra effort.

*THE PAPERBOY
Pete Dexter
A lyrical and disturbing tale of filial and journalistic responsibility and the toll it takes on a father and his two sons.

HUSBANDS & WIVES
Liza Donnelly and Michael Maslin
An entertainingly irreverent husband-and-wife cartoonist team, Donnelly and Maslin's less than idyllic view of marriage informs this whole collection.

DEAD OPPOSITE: THE LIVES AND LOSS OF TWO AMERICAN BOYS
Geoffrey Douglas
The story of a Yale student shot to death and the high school dropout once accused of killing him. The murder and its aftermath are a jumping-off point for the author's troubled ruminations on race and class in America.

IN HER SISTER'S SHADOW: AN INTIMATE BIOGRAPHY OF LEE RADZIWILL
Diana Dubois
Even if you give Lee Radziwill a break—it can't have been easy being Jacqueline Kennedy Onassis's younger, plainer sister—she appears to have led a rather frivolous life, or so suggests this unauthorized biography.

*THE BOOKMAN'S WAKE
John Dunning
A cop-turned-antiquarian-book-dealer realizes that he's in a race against a serial killer. Dunning immerses the reader in an intriguing, little-known milieu without losing sight of the page-turning yarn that he's spinning.

*WHAT TO EXPECT: THE TODDLER YEARS
Arlene Eisenberg, Heidi S. Murkoff and Sandee E. Hathaway
A smart guide packed with sensible tips on tantrums, teething, toilet training, and more.

KATO KAELIN: THE WHOLE TRUTH
Marc Eliot
Based on interviews with Kato Kaelin, Marc Eliot's book suggests that on the stand Kaelin minimized the menace he sensed in Simpson's mood on the night of the killings.

*AMERICAN TABLOID
James Ellroy
Ellroy offers a cynical—and mesmerizing—take on the JFK assassination. All diabolically imagined, this is history caught between dirty sheets with a needle in its arm and marked bills on the bed.

HANGING UP
Delia Ephron
Hanging Up is a semiautobiographical novel by essayist Ephron *(Teenage Romance)*, whose own father, Henry, spent the last years of his life at a Hollywood rest home. The book effectively conveys the sadness a family feels as it prepares for the passing of a troubled patriarch.

*THE BLUE JAY'S DANCE
Louise Erdrich
Pregnancy, birth and caring for an infant inspire Erdrich's reflections on being a woman, a mother, and a writer in this affecting memoir of a daughter's first year.

DON'T CRY NOW
Joy Fielding
Becoming the prime suspect in a murder, a pretty high school teacher and classic good girl turns to sleuthing. A brisk summer read.

*FROM TIME TO TIME
Jack Finney
Finney has a dazzling way with descriptive passages and lets his talents loose in this magical sequel to the imaginative classic *Time and Again*.

HARD EVIDENCE
David Fisher
In an era of crime and more crime, this exclusive account of the FBI crime labs is basically an *Oxford Home Companion to the News*.

U2 AT THE END OF THE WORLD
Bill Flanagan
Flanagan followed one of the world's biggest rock bands on their most ambitious tour ever; trouble is, his book offers fewer insights than your average fan-club newsletter.

*INDEPENDENCE DAY
Richard Ford
Troubled Frank Bascombe's wrestling for love gives this rich and ambitious sequel to *The Sportswriter* strength and appeal.

*BY GEORGE
George Foreman and Joel Engel
Following the champ's rise from Dickensian beginnings to his late '80s comeback, *By George* spins Foreman's wonderful tale with characteristic humor.

*WILD HORSES
Dick Francis

A suspense novel marked by crisp language and a brisk pace that can be bumpy at times, but is ultimately a successful ride.

*THE DIARY OF A YOUNG GIRL
Anne Frank

This new edition includes entries that Frank's father had excised from the original. For those who haven't given the diary a second thought since writing a fifth-grade book report, it's time to refresh our memories.

THE LAST SHOT: CITY STREETS, BASKETBALL DREAMS
Darcy Frey

Amid sirens and gunfights, hoop dreams take flight in this chronicle of life and basketball on the mean streets of New York City's Coney Island.

FROM BEGINNING TO END
Robert Fulghum

Fulghum's fifth book takes a look at rituals, big and little. Sure, he's overbearing, oversimplified, and saccharine. But he's also touching, practical, and wise.

THE POLISH OFFICER
Alan Furst

Furst traces the exploits of a Polish patriot in the early days of World War II. *The Polish Officer* is saved from being a shallow documentary by the writing.

VERTICAL RUN
Joseph R. Garber

This mélange of *Die Hard 2* and *The Hot Zone* is a clever, nonstop thriller.

*OF LOVE AND OTHER DEMONS
Gabriel García Márquez

In the hands of Nobel Prize winner García Márquez, the legend of the girl bitten by a rabid dog on her 12th birthday, 200 years before, becomes a mesmerizing tale.

*ONCE UPON A MORE ENLIGHTENED TIME: MORE POLITICALLY CORRECT BEDTIME STORIES
James Finn Garner

Eight more wryly sanitized fairy tales. Garner takes an irresistable premise and delivers some sharp satire.

*A MODEL CRIME
Curtis Gathje

This careful reconstruction of a 1937 murder revisits '30s American journalism—and displays crime's longtime grip on our imaginations.

LISTEN TO MY HEART: LESSONS IN LOVE, LAUGHTER, AND LUNACY
Kathie Lee and Cody Gifford

This slim volume recounts the authors' memorable moments together. Kathie Lee brings to these vignettes the same vigor that has endeared her to millions of TV viewers.

1945
Newt Gingrich and William R. Forstchen

This juvenile, horrendously written book proceeds from the hackneyed What if Germany Had Won? premise. Folks ought to be steamed up about Gingrich's crackpot historical revision.

LOST IN HOLLYWOOD: THE FAST TIMES AND SHORT LIFE OF RIVER PHOENIX
John Glatt

The reader comes away disgusted by the story of a wasted life and angry at the people who knew Phoenix but were unable to save him.

*MARRY ME!
Wendy Goldberg and Betty Goodwin

Full of anecdotes about the courtships and proposals of famous couples, this fun book should be an inspiration to die-hard romantics.

COLOR IS THE SUFFERING OF LIGHT
Melissa Green

Green, an award-winning poet, has written a narrative of chilling fact—but it doesn't gain momentum. For all its words and its stories, *Color* fails to illuminate.

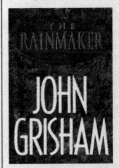

*THE RAINMAKER
John Grisham

A fully satisfying courtroom drama, most notable for its engagingly oddball characters. Grisham's most barbed book since *The Firm*, and by far his most entertaining.

SHROUDS OF GLORY FROM ATLANTA TO NASHVILLE: THE LAST GREAT CAMPAIGN OF THE CIVIL WAR
Winston Groom

There are mistakes and an attitude of slapdash "that's close enough" nonfiction in this account of the Confederacy's last offensive. But when Groom reaches the fighting at Spring Hill and Franklin, he puts his novelist's eye to searching out the telling detail and the colorful anecdote.

*MODEL: THE UGLY BUSINESS OF BEAUTIFUL WOMEN
Michael Gross

Sweeping energetically through the rise of the supermodel, Gross has obviously thought deeply about the machinations and meaning of the modeling business, and it has left him feeling very queasy.

*SNOW FALLING ON CEDARS
David Guterson
This courtroom drama skillfully shuttles between witnesses, gill-netting, the work of a coroner, internment camps, strawberry farming, and the protean nature of guilt and innocence. This is poetry masquerading as prose.

*GONE WILD
James W. Hall
Gone Wild follows an animal activist's furious effort to find her daughter's killers in Borneo. We also meet two of the more engaging psychopaths in recent crime fiction—Orlon and Rayon White. Hall's prose is exquisitely vivid.

*POISON
Kathryn Harrison
Alternating between a princess's and a pauper's stories, Harrison's powerful novel examines the psychosexual underbelly of life during the Spanish Inquisition.

EVELYN WAUGH: A BIOGRAPHY
Selina Hastings
The focus of this detailed account is not on Waugh the writer of brilliant satire, but on Waugh the wicked, witty drunk. Hastings never reconciles her subject's two sides.

TOBACCO STICKS
William Elliott Hazelgrove
Twelve-year-old Lee Hartwell narrates this spirited family saga, set amongst the social and political upheavals of 1945 Richmond, Va.

THE CLUB
Jane Heller
Knowing and naughty, this suburban mystery is engaging enough to divert—but not enough to make you forget to reapply the sunscreen.

*MEMOIR FROM ANTPROOF CASE
Mark Helprin
Convoluted, hilarious, and heart-rending, *Antproof* follows the execution of a great crime and reveals the narrator's obsession with "a filthy corruption brewed from a bean that poisons its own tree." Irresistible.

SAFE IN AMERICA
Marcie Hershman
Like Hershman's own Jewish grandparents, *America*'s Evan and Vera Eichenbaum leave Czechoslovakia before the Holocaust, but they can't escape it. In graceful prose, Hershman conveys the enormity of this family's losses, as well as the impossibility of the American promise they cling to.

*LIZ: AN INTIMATE BIOGRAPHY OF ELIZABETH TAYLOR
C. David Heymann
The juicier of the two new Taylor biographies, this salacious volume dutifully documents an abundance of choice tidbits.

*MOVING VIOLATIONS: WAR ZONES, WHEELCHAIRS, AND DECLARATIONS OF INDEPENDENCE
John Hockenberry
In this brave memoir, Hockenberry, 39, an ABC correspondent who became a paraplegic at age 19, may have reached his ultimate destination.

BORDERLINERS
Peter Hoeg
Capturing the helplessness and frustration of institutionalized children who are neither well-adjusted nor altogether retarded, *Borderliners* would be shocking even if it were not true.

*PRACTICAL MAGIC
Alice Hoffman
Written with a light hand and perfect rhythm, this tale of sister witches wraps a fantastical cocoon around its readers, conjuring up luscious images with rhapsodic prose.

THE DEATH OF COMMON SENSE
Philip K. Howard
Howard's suggestion that individual civil rights are too easily legislated will offend anyone stung by discrimination; still, the author's thoughtful arguments are impassioned and his research is convincing.

*DIRTY WHITE BOYS
Stephen Hunter
A trio of convicts tears through Texas in this full-tilt-thriller. While the violence is extreme, it is matched by tingling suspense.

FORMOSA STRAITS
Anthony Hyde
More than just a page-turner, there are history lessons—Mao Tse-Tung and his wife play key roles—and canny references to old movies, but this thriller often seems willfully convoluted.

ORIGINAL SIN
P. D. James
Overcrowded with interesting types and without a central focus, this Adam Dalgliesh mystery remains a cut above most, but occasional flashes remind the reader that she can do even better.

*FOR KEEPS
Pauline Kael
Critic Kael makes a jazzy, generous record of her mind's life span, a record sure to please her many fans as well as anyone who just plain loves movies.

*THE LIARS' CLUB
Mary Karr

Focusing on a childhood year in a godforsaken refinery town in east Texas, poet Mary Karr has written an astonishing memoir of her ferociously loving and dysfunctional family.

*MID-LIFE: NOTES FROM THE HALFWAY MARK
Elizabeth Kaye

Kaye's Didionesque prose has such shine and inventiveness, her observations are so wry, wise and poignant, that the good long cry that seems inevitable by *Mid-Life*'s end is a small price to pay.

INSIDE THE WHITE HOUSE
Ronald Kessler

Not so much political science as high-toned gossip, this bestseller sketches the behind-the-facade world of American Presidents, their families and entourages.

*ALLEY CAT BLUES
Karen Kijewski

Feisty and funny as ever, popular P. I. Kat Colorado unravels two mysteries. This one will keep you glued to your beach blanket.

ROSE MADDER
Stephen King

Though this is an engrossing story of a battered woman, its supernatural elements are neither super nor natural.

*TRUE CRIME
Andrew Klavan

When cynical, philandering reporter Steve Everett sinks his teeth into the case of a death-row inmate, he can't let go. And readers won't stop turning pages.

*THE WORKING MOM'S BOOK OF HINTS, TIPS, AND EVERYDAY WISDOM
Louise Lague

A witty compendium by a PEOPLE staffer that whacks away at outdated supermom myths.

TROPHY WIFE
Kelly Lange

Lange, an anchorwoman at KNBC-TV in L.A., has written a glitzy story of renewal and revenge that moves along briskly and painlessly and mixes well with sand and water.

HOSTILE WITNESS
William Lashner

Prosecution: If not for the existence of stereotypes, Lashner would have a hard time populating *Hostile Witness*. Defense: Lashner has fashioned a propulsive story. Verdict? A good, gritty feel and a sardonic protagonist who grows on you. No objections.

VICKI! THE TRUE-LIFE ADVENTURES OF MISS FIREBALL
Vicki Lawrence with Marc Eliot

There's a Cinderella veneer to this bittersweet memoir of the woman tapped at 18 for the then-fledgling *Carol Burnett Show*.

*SWIFTY: MY LIFE AND GOOD TIMES
Irving Lazar

Written in collaboration with Annette Tapert, this memoir of Hollywood's legendary agent and consummate host is literate, entertaining, and touching.

KATHARINE HEPBURN
Barbara Leaming

Leaming brings an outsider's valuable perspective to the life of a singular and clearly very complicated woman.

*OUR GAME
John Le Carré

In his most thoughtful work since *Smiley's People*, Le Carré explores the deconstruction of Soviet Russia and, more dramatically, the changes it has inspired among British cold warriors.

*NATIVE SPEAKER
Chang-Rae Lee

A spy is trapped in limbo between his American birth and his Korean upbringing. A family saga is the soul of this poignant first novel, featuring powerfully captured characters not soon forgotten.

RIDING THE RAP
Elmore Leonard

More dispatches from the skewed, dangerous, mundane world of people who work at crime for a living.

*TOOTH IMPRINTS ON A CORN DOG
Mark Leyner

How do you spoof a world that has become a parody of itself? Leyner's first collection of essays confirms that he's the American writer best suited for this daunting task.

*ISABEL'S BED
Elinor Lipman

The prose is spare and breezy, but there's wry wisdom beneath the chuckles in this warm, affecting tale about one smart woman letting go of her dumb choices and fumbling toward love.

THERAPY
David Lodge

Laurence "Tubby" Passmore has everything money can buy, but—surprise!—he's not happy. This cleverly written book details his wholly unpredictable course of soul-searching and redemption.

THE APOCALYPSE WATCH
Robert Ludlum

As usual, Ludlum is at his best hurtling the reader through an ever-widening conspiracy. But the overwhelming sense for a longtime Ludlum reader is "been there, done that."

MAKING MOVIES
Sidney Lumet

Maybe reticence is what makes Lumet such an enduring, versatile director, but you wish he had spent more time on the gifted actors and writers he has worked with and less on the types of lenses he prefers.

*D. H. LAWRENCE: THE STORY OF A MARRIAGE
Brenda Maddox

Maddox's sympathetic, compelling portrait shows Lawrence as a man struggling with the angels and demons of his psyche, a conflict that was both eased and exacerbated by his wife, Frieda Weekley.

OSWALD'S TALE
Norman Mailer

Mailer sifts through the magnified detritus of Lee Harvey Oswald's life. Thankfully, in the second half of this hefty tome, the Mailer who can skewer with mischievous imagery finally comes roaring out of the nonfiction closet.

LONG WALK TO FREEDOM: THE AUTOBIOGRAPHY OF NELSON MANDELA
Nelson Mandela

This is less a memoir than a political history of modern South Africa. Readers will learn much but won't find the media Mandela who has previously touched their hearts; emotion rarely breaks through.

*FIRST IN HIS CLASS: A BIOGRAPHY OF BILL CLINTON
David Maraniss

It's not a flattering portrait, yet even the President's supporters will be hard-pressed to find fault with Maraniss's meticulous research and evenhanded tone.

A BIOGRAPHY OF BILL CLINTON
FIRST IN HIS CLASS
DAVID MARANISS
WINNER OF THE PULITZER PRIZE

*AFTER DARK
Phillip Margolin

A specialist in death penalty cases defends the aloof, luscious, and maybe husband-killing prosecutor for whom he harbors an obsession. The suspicion never rests, and readers will be hard-pressed to anticipate the action.

ON THE WAY TO THE VENUS DE MILO
Pearson Marx

At its most engagingly madcap, this novel recalls the work of E. F. Benson, the popular British creator of the Lucia novels. But Marx loses her grip on the story two-thirds of the way through.

*WHEN ELEPHANTS WEEP
Jeffrey Moussaieff Masson and Susan McCarthy

Scientists like to tell you that animals have no emotions, but in this impassioned volume, the authors use examples from scientific literature to argue just the opposite.

*ALL THE DAYS AND NIGHTS
William Maxwell

An impeccable collection of stories drawing upon childhood memories, rendered with neither nostalgia nor sentiment.

A DOG'S LIFE
Peter Mayle

Parents and pet owners have a certain tendency to overestimate the appeal of their loved ones to the general public. Be advised that *A Dog's Life* is written from the point of view of the pooch. Cloyingly coy.

*FATHER'S DAY
Bill McCoy

A chronicle of the trials and tribulations of the author's debut as a daddy, *Father's Day* will have dads—and moms—smiling and muttering, "Yeah, Bill. Me too."

*THE DISTINGUISHED GUEST
Sue Miller

In Sue Miller's deft hands, mothers are always a source of beguiling fiction; her latest novel is no exception.

DR. SEUSS & MR. GEISEL
Judith and Neil Morgan

The writers of this authorized biography rhapsodize over the work and life of one of the most popular children's writers in American history. Sadly, their pedantic tone cries out for Dr. Seuss's own light touch.

MY DOG SKIP
Willie Morris

This book is a loving tribute to Morris's boyhood companion and a lyrical remembrance of vanished innocence.

MAPPLETHORPE
Patricia Morrisroe

In this readable but ultimately opaque biography, photographer Robert Mapplethorpe comes across as a green-eyed robot programmed for gay sex.

PRIVATE ALTARS
Katherine Mosby

Eccentric heroine, decaying gothic mansion, intolerant townsfolk. Mosby writes with fluid grace but fails to give fresh life to the southern gothic form.

MARTIN MULL: PAINTINGS, DRAWINGS AND WORDS
Martin Mull

Well-known as Leon Carp on *Roseanne*, Mull is a widely

exhibited painter who holds a degree in the fine arts. This book has its charms, but "Duelling Tubas" is still funnier.

SLEEPWALKING
Julie Myerson
At its best a moving, profoundly unsettling chronicle of a woman's search for self, *Sleepwalking* often overreaches. It's hard to cozy up to just about any character in this book, but its strong, self-assured prose leaves readers eager for more Myerson.

REVELATIONS FROM THE MEMPHIS MAFIA
Alanna Nash with Billy Smith, Marty Lacker, and Lamar Fike
700-plus pages of gossip about Elvis Presley's private life by three hangers-on. Only an ardent fan or devoted voyeur will enjoy this mountain of crumbs.

*VURT
Jeff Noon
Reality and technology take on a slippery, hallucinatory quality in this arresting sci-fi vision of near-future Manchester.

THE COMMODORE
Patrick O'Brian
The 17th volume of O'Brian's series following a Royal Navy captain and his doctor-naturalist-spy friend during the Napoleonic wars. The heart of the enterprise is O'Brian's nuanced depiction of human relationships as they evolve over time.

*THE MAN WHO CAST TWO SHADOWS
Carol O'Connell
A suspenseful yarn that exploits thoroughly original characters and the vivid cityscape. Even more satisfying than *Mallory's Oracle*—and that's high praise.

*THE DISNEY ENCYCLOPEDIA OF BABY AND CHILD CARE
Judith Palfrey, Irving Schulman, Samuel L. Katz, Maria I. New
Four leading pediatricians dis-

pense advice on early childhood development and health care in this first-rate, two-volume set.

THIN AIR
Robert B. Parker
Has Spenser gone sappy? One of detective fiction's best hard-boiled gumshoes should be commanding mean streets; here he's spending too much time with his psychotherapist.

THE AFTERLIFE DIET
Daniel Pinkwater
You chortle at moments, but the plot is as convoluted as a noodle kugel, and most of the characters are big bodies with no souls.

*HUNTERS AND GATHERERS
Francine Prose
Prose is sharp with dialogue and detail, her satire cutting but never cruel, in this tale of a magazine fact-checker who chooses the faintly ridiculous company of a Goddess group over men, who have the habit of breaking her heart.

*HUNTING DINOSAURS
Louis Psihoyos with John Knoebber
A colorful history of the planet's first dwellers and the equally mysterious Homo Sapiens who have devoted careers and lives to studying them.

ONE MAN TANGO
Anthony Quinn, with Daniel Paisner
Now 80 and the father of 12 children by two wives and three mistresses, the mighty Quinn reveals himself in this florid yet earthy autobiography as a world-class womanizer.

VANESSA REDGRAVE: AN AUTOBIOGRAPHY
Vanessa Redgrave
No doubt Redgrave is pleased with the book she has written—but anyone curious about her life will find it preachy, boring, and self-righteous.

MEMNOCH THE DEVIL
Anne Rice
In her fifth volume of the Vampire Chronicles, Anne Rice abandons her usual terrain and instead substitutes huge chunks of dry theology.

*FREE TO TRADE
Michael Ridpath
A satisfying course of violence, romance, and high-rolling paper chases. Hero Paul Murray gives the story legs—and Ridpath himself seems a Thoroughbred of promise.

TOM ROBBINS
Half Asleep In Frog Pajamas

*HALF ASLEEP IN FROG PAJAMAS
Tom Robbins
For all its absurdity, this disparate novel is bright with Robbins's customary verbal pyrotechnics. The author is one of the most inventive stylists writing today.

*LETTIN IT ALL HANG OUT: AN AUTOBIOGRAPHY
RuPaul
A captivating drag-to-riches story that celebrates perseverance and press-on nails.

*EAST, WEST
Salman Rushdie
These nine tales take their cue from subjects Rushdie knows well: the plight of immigrants, exiles, and the dispossessed. Rushdie's imagination is witty and delightfully multicultural.

*LITTLE GIRLS IN PRETTY BOXES
Joan Ryan

This exposé of upper-level competitive gymnastics and figure skating proves once again that perfection is always an illusion.

*AN ANTHROPOLOGIST ON MARS
Oliver Sacks

Sacks probes lives radically transformed by neurological conditions yet "no less human for being so different." After reading his compelling stories, you may well experience an awakening of your own.

*PALE BLUE DOT
Carl Sagan

This is his latest pulpit-pounder on the topic of sending humans to Mars—and despite the budgetary climate of the times, it's downright inspirational.

*MIND PREY
John Sandford

Lucas Davenport faces his most cunning adversary, a psychopathic killer who is also a skilled computer gamer. The seventh and best outing in the *Prey* series.

NOTES OF A WHITE BLACK WOMAN
Judy Scales-Trent

The daughter of two light-skinned blacks offers a series of essays, by turns poignant and pugilistic, about what it's like to straddle two worlds.

*MANDATE OF HEAVEN
Orville Schell

A strangely comic picture of China, in the midst of economic reforms, that makes the United States almost seem socialist in comparison.

*THE LOVE LETTER
Cathleen Schine

A know-it-all becomes obsessed with a love letter sent to her bookstore. Schine builds a satire that is rarely less than sublime.

*WHAT REALLY MATTERS
Tony Schwartz

Schwartz journeys to men and women whose ideas and practices convinced him that a "more meaningful life is within reach." An absorbing update on the timeless quest for enlightenment.

DREAMING: HARD LUCK AND GOOD TIMES IN AMERICA
Carolyn See

Drinking and dreaming are inextricably linked in See's family; this is her testament to the way a family can rise above its circumstances and seek its own particularly elusive redemption.

*SEARCHING FOR MERCY STREET
Linda Gray Sexton

A courageous journey into the dark terrain of remembering, forgiving, and healing through telling, from the daughter of Anne Sexton, the famous poet who committed suicide in 1974.

BLOWN SIDEWAYS THROUGH LIFE
Claudia Shear

This tour de résumé by Shear was an acclaimed, one-woman off-Broadway show in 1994—but without Shear's stage presence, these sad-funny tales from the odd-job front have no heft at all.

*IN LOVE WITH DAYLIGHT
Wilfred Sheed

A gifted, exuberant, intelligent stylist, Sheed offers a rollicking ride through the highs and lows of his battles with cancer, addiction, and depression.

*THE REPUBLIC OF LOVE
Carol Shields

Parallel lives, love-at-first-sight romance, and the nasty intrusion of reality are the stuff of this intoxicating novel.

*THE STONE DIARIES
Carol Shields

The extraordinary story of an ordinary woman whose experiences celebrate work, relationships, and family life.

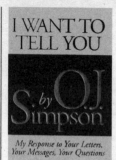

My Response to Your Letters, Your Messages, Your Questions

I WANT TO TELL YOU
O. J. Simpson

Simpson offers highly selective reflections on Nicole, press coverage of the crime, and the justice system. Most of his responses are simply self-serving previews of his defense strategy.

*MOO
Jane Smiley

Not for a minute does *Moo* lose its perfect satiric pitch or its pacing. Fast, hilarious, and, come to think of it, heartbreaking.

*RESTRAINT
Sherry Sonnett

Aside from some pacing problems and a sexual explicitness that sometimes seems more ludicrous than lubricious, it's easy to recommend this without restraint.

A PASSION FOR LIFE: THE BIOGRAPHY OF ELIZABETH TAYLOR
Donald Spoto

More flattering than the year's other Taylor bio, Spoto's cloying-

at-times portrait of the star has a certain poignance.

THE MAGIC BULLET
Harry Stein
A dose of this clunky medical thriller won't leave you feeling much more energized than before you started treatment.

COMPLETE & UTTER FAILURE: A CELEBRATION OF ALSO-RANS, RUNNERS-UP, NEVER-WERES, AND TOTAL FLOPS
Neil Steinberg
Overachievers won't relate. But for the rest of us, here's a genial exploration of defeat in its many guises. It's enough to give failure a good name.

*LOVING EDITH
Mary Tannen
Radiant young Edith unwittingly comes to work at her biological father's magazine. Tannen doesn't miss a step in this gracefully conceived gavotte.

*COME AND GO, MOLLY SNOW
Mary Ann Taylor-Hall
Shattered by her five-year-old's death, Carrie is cared for by two elderly sisters-in-law. In Taylor-Hall's hands, grief becomes a beautiful rendition of memory.

*THE RECTOR'S WIFE
Joanna Trollope
There is a bit of the soap opera in this story of a cleric's enduring wife, but it is a sin easy to forgive in light of the chance to watch a lovely, lost woman grab hold of her life.

LADDER OF YEARS
Anne Tyler
Convinced that she is no longer appreciated by her family, a 40-year-old walks out during a vacation to start life anew. Readable without quite being rewarding.

*GHOSTS OF MISSISSIPPI
Maryanne Vollers
In her riveting account of Medgar Evers's murder and the 30-year crusade to bring his killer to justice, Vollers chronicles the social change that transformed the Deep South.

ALL MY CHILDREN: THE COMPLETE FAMILY SCRAPBOOK
Gary Warner
This is a guaranteed good time for anyone plugged into the Pine Valley experience, from sporadic soapers to *AMC* addicts who've seen all 6,500 episodes.

OBJECTS IN MIRROR ARE CLOSER THAN THEY APPEAR
Katharine Weber
This first novel—about, among other things, perception versus reality—is maddeningly fuzzy around the edges.

*WANNABE: A WOULD-BE PLAYER'S MISADVENTURES IN HOLLYWOOD
Everett Weinberger
He'll never work in that town again, but he doesn't care. In this hilarious tell-all, the movie business is populated with monsters.

RAGING HEART
Sheila Weller
Tells more than any Simpson trial junkie will want to know—and leaves no reasonable doubt about who the author believes committed the crime.

*THE WEDDING
Dorothy West
A tale of class and race consciousness set on Martha's Vineyard in the 1950's. West brings a graceful style and an insider's knowledge of an elite echelon to this fascinating tale.

*EVER AFTER
William Wharton
An absorbing memorial Wharton leaves to four tragically ended lives. The author brings grace and dignity to the story of his family's life and finds the peace to continue his own.

*GREEN RIVER RISING
Tim Willocks
On its slick surface, as fine a thriller as one could ask for. Underneath, larger shadows are moving: mediations on incarceration, guilt, violence, and the nature of mankind.

*YOU SEND ME: THE LIFE AND TIMES OF SAM COOKE
Daniel Wolff, with S. R. Crain, Clifton White, and G. David Tenenbaum
Wolff and his collaborators fill a glaring void with this first and richly deserved study of one rock star.

*THE AGE OF CONSENT
Geoffrey Wolff
Wolff skillfully lays bare a world of rueful adults—and even children—whose memories are rife with ache and bitterness.

AUTOBIOGRAPHY OF A FAMILY PORTRAIT
Jacqueline Woodson
A chronicle of the coming-of-age of a black girl in an urban ghetto transcends familiar territory.

INTO THIN AIR
Thomas Zigal
Good-humored Aspen sheriff Kurt Muller, more hippie than lawman at heart, wrestles with his demons and the equally elusive bad guys amid some spectacular scenery.

FICTION AND NONFICTION BESTSELLERS

Publishers Weekly began charting the nation's top-selling hardcover fiction in 1895. The first nonfiction lists were published regularly beginning in 1917, and during World War I the trade magazine even tracked the most popular war books. (The Winston Churchill on the fiction lists, by the way, was an American novelist who died in 1947; his British statesman namesake was, of course, a bestselling and Nobel Prize-winning writer of nonfiction.) These rankings are not based on net sales figures but rather on publishers' reports of copies shipped and billed.

1900

Fiction

1. *To Have and To Hold*, Mary Johnston
2. *Red Pottage*, Mary Cholmondeley
3. *Unleavened Bread*, Robert Grant
4. *The Reign of Law*, James Lane Allen
5. *Eben Holden*, Irving Bacheller
6. *Janice Meredith*, Paul Leicester Ford
7. *The Redemption of David Corson*, Charles Frederic Goss
8. *Richard Carvel*, Winston Churchill
9. *When Knighthood Was in Flower*, Charles Major
10. *Alice of Old Vincennes*, Maurice Thompson

1901

Fiction

1. *The Crisis*, Winston Churchill
2. *Alice of Old Vincennes*, Maurice Thompson
3. *The Helmet of Navarre*, Bertha Runkle
4. *The Right of Way*, Gilbert Parker
5. *Eben Holden*, Irving Bacheller
6. *The Visits of Elizabeth*, Elinor Glyn
7. *The Puppet Crown*, Harold MacGrath
8. *Richard Yea-and-Nay*, Maurice Hewlett
9. *Graustark*, George Barr McCutcheon
10. *D'ri and I*, Irving Bacheller

1902

Fiction

1. *The Virginian*, Owen Wister
2. *Mrs. Wiggs of the Cabbage Patch*, Alice Caldwell Hegan
3. *Dorothy Vernon of Haddon Hall*, Charles Major
4. *The Mississippi Bubble*, Emerson Hough
5. *Audrey*, Mary Johnston
6. *The Right of Way*, Gilbert Parker
7. *The Hound of the Baskervilles*, A. Conan Doyle
8. *The Two Vanrevels*, Booth Tarkington

9. *The Blue Flower*, Henry van Dyke
10. *Sir Richard Calmady*, Lucas Malet

1903

Fiction

1. *Lady Rose's Daughter*, Mary Augusta Ward
2. *Gordon Keith*, Thomas Nelson Page
3. *The Pit*, Frank Norris
4. *Lovey Mary*, Alice Hegan Rice
5. *The Virginian*, Owen Wister
6. *Mrs. Wiggs of the Cabbage Patch*, Alice Hegan Rice
7. *The Mettle of the Pasture*, James Lane Allen
8. *Letters of a Self-Made Merchant to His Son*, George Horace Lorimer
9. *The One Woman*, Thomas Dixon Jr.
10. *The Little Shepherd of Kingdom Come*, John Fox Jr.

1904

Fiction

1. *The Crossing*, Winston Churchill
2. *The Deliverance*, Ellen Glasgow
3. *The Masquerader*, anonymous (Katherine Cecil Thurston)
4. *In the Bishop's Carriage*, Miriam Michelson
5. *Sir Mortimer*, Mary Johnston
6. *Beverly of Graustark*, George Barr McCutcheon
7. *The Little Shepherd of Kingdom Come*, John Fox Jr.
8. *Rebecca of Sunnybrook Farm*, Kate Douglas Wiggin
9. *My Friend Prospero*, Henry Harland
10. *The Silent Places*, Stewart Edward White

1905

Fiction

1. *The Marriage of William Ashe*, Mary Augusta Ward
2. *Sandy*, Alice Hegan Rice
3. *The Garden of Allah*, Robert Hichens

4. *The Clansman*, Thomas Dixon Jr.
5. *Nedra*, George Barr McCutcheon
6. *The Gambler*, Katherine Cecil Thurston
7. *The Masquerader*, anonymous (Katherine Cecil Thurston)
8. *The House of Mirth*, Edith Wharton
9. *The Princess Passes*, C. N. and A. M. Williamson
10. *Rose o' the River*, Kate Douglas Wiggin

1906

Fiction

1. *Coniston*, Winston Churchill
2. *Lady Baltimore*, Owen Wister
3. *The Fighting Chance*, Robert W. Chambers
4. *The House of a Thousand Candles*, Meredith Nicholson
5. *Jane Cable*, George Barr McCutcheon
6. *The Jungle*, Upton Sinclair
7. *The Awakening of Helena Ritchie*, Margaret Deland
8. *The Spoilers*, Rex Beach
9. *The House of Mirth*, Edith Wharton
10. *The Wheel of Life*, Ellen Glasgow

1907

Fiction

1. *The Lady of the Decoration*, Frances Little
2. *The Weavers*, Gilbert Parker
3. *The Port of Missing Men*, Meredith Nicholson
4. *The Shuttle*, Frances Hodgson Burnett
5. *The Brass Bowl*, Louis J. Vance
6. *Satan Sanderson*, Hallie Erminie Rives
7. *The Daughter of Anderson Crow*, George Barr McCutcheon
8. *The Younger Set*, Robert W. Chambers
9. *The Doctor*, Ralph Connor
10. *Half a Rogue*, Harold MacGrath

1908

Fiction

1. *Mr. Crewe's Career*, Winston Churchill
2. *The Barrier*, Rex Beach
3. *The Trail of the Lonesome Pine*, John Fox Jr.
4. *The Lure of the Mask*, Harold MacGrath
5. *The Shuttle*, Frances Hodgson Burnett
6. *Peter*, F. Hopkinson Smith
7. *Lewis Rand*, Mary Johnston
8. *The Black Bag*, Louis J. Vance
9. *The Man from Brodney's*, George Barr McCutcheon
10. *The Weavers*, Gilbert Parker

1909

Fiction

1. *The Inner Shrine*, anonymous (Basil King)
2. *Katrine*, Elinor Macartney Lane
3. *The Silver Horde*, Rex Beach
4. *The Man in Lower Ten*, Mary Roberts Rinehart
5. *The Trail of the Lonesome Pine*, John Fox Jr.
6. *Truxton King*, George Barr McCutcheon
7. *54-40 or Fight*, Emerson Hough
8. *The Goose Girl*, Harold MacGrath
9. *Peter*, F. Hopkinson Smith
10. *Septimus*, William J. Locke

1910

Fiction

1. *The Rosary*, Florence Barclay
2. *A Modern Chronicle*, Winston Churchill
3. *The Wild Olive*, anonymous (Basil King)
4. *Max*, Katherine Cecil Thurston
5. *The Kingdom of Slender Swords*, Hallie Erminie Rives
6. *Simon the Jester*, William J. Locke
7. *Lord Loveland Discovers America*, C. N. and A. M. Williamson
8. *The Window at the White Cat*, Mary Roberts Rinehart
9. *Molly Make-Believe*, Eleanor Abbott
10. *When a Man Marries*, Mary Roberts Rinehart

1911

Fiction

1. *The Broad Highway*, Jeffrey Farnol
2. *The Prodigal Judge*, Vaughan Kester
3. *The Winning of Barbara Worth*, Harold Bell Wright
4. *Queed*, Henry Sydnor Harrison

5. *The Harvester*, Gene Stratton Porter
6. *The Iron Woman*, Margaret Deland
7. *The Long Roll*, Mary Johnston
8. *Molly Make-Believe*, Eleanor Abbott
9. *The Rosary*, Florence Barclay
10. *The Common Law*, Robert W. Chambers

1912

Fiction

1. *The Harvester*, Gene Stratton Porter
2. *The Street Called Straight*, Basil King
3. *Their Yesterdays*, Harold Bell Wright
4. *The Melting of Molly*, Maria Thompson Daviess
5. *A Hoosier Chronicle*, Meredith Nicholson
6. *The Winning of Barbara Worth*, Harold Bell Wright
7. *The Just and the Unjust*, Vaughan Kester
8. *The Net*, Rex Beach
9. *Tante*, Anne Douglas Sedgwick
10. *Fran*, J. Breckenridge Ellis

BANNED BESTSELLERS

Books enrich our lives, but to a certain vocal part of the population they can enrage as well. While every year brings what some see as a new threat to the moral fabric of our nation, certain classics, from *The Adventures of Huckleberry Finn* to *Catcher in the Rye*, can be counted upon to rouse the ire of someone year after year. Here are the most challenged books in school libraries and curriculums, in the last year and over the last decade, according to People for the American Way:

1982–95

1. *Of Mice and Men*, John Steinbeck
2. *The Catcher in the Rye*, J. D. Salinger
3. *Scary Stories To Tell in the Dark*, Alvin Schwartz
4. *The Chocolate War*, Robert Cormier
5. *More Scary Stories To Tell in the Dark*, Alvin Schwartz
6. *The Adventures of Huckleberry Finn*, Mark Twain
7. *I Know Why the Caged Bird Sings*, Maya Angelou
8. *Go Ask Alice*, anonymous
9. *The Bridge to Terabithia*, Katherine Paterson
10. *The Witches*, Roald Dahl

1994–95

1. *More Scary Stories To Tell in the Dark*, Alvin Schwartz
2. *Scary Stories To Tell in the Dark*, Alvin Schwartz
3. *I Know Why the Caged Bird Sings*, Maya Angelou
4. *The Giver*, Lois Lowry
5. *Scary Stories 3: More Tales to Chill Your Bones*, Alvin Schwartz
6. *Halloween ABC*, Eve Merriam
7. *The Bridge to Terabithia*, Katherine Paterson
8. *The Chocolate War*, Robert Cormier
9. *Of Mice and Men*, John Steinbeck
10. *My Brother Sam Is Dead*, Christopher and James Lincoln Collier

Nonfiction

1. *The Promised Land*, Mary Antin
2. *The Montessori Method*, Maria Montessori
3. *South America*, James Bryce
4. *A New Conscience and an Ancient Evil*, Jane Addams
5. *Three Plays*, Eugène Brieux
6. *Your United States*, Arnold Bennett
7. *Creative Evolution*, Henri Bergson
8. *How to Live on Twenty-Four Hours a Day*, Arnold Bennett
9. *Woman and Labor*, Olive Schreiner
10. *Mark Twain*, Albert Bigelow Paine

1913

Fiction

1. *The Inside of the Cup*, Winston Churchill
2. *V. V.'s Eyes*, Henry Sydnor Harrison
3. *Laddie*, Gene Stratton Porter
4. *The Judgment House*, Sir Gilbert Parker
5. *Heart of the Hills*, John Fox Jr.
6. *The Amateur Gentleman*, Jeffrey Farnol
7. *The Woman Thou Gavest Me*, Hall Caine
8. *Pollyanna*, Eleanor H. Porter
9. *The Valiants of Virginia*, Hallie Erminie Rives
10. *T. Tembarom*, Frances Hodgson Burnett

Nonfiction

1. *Crowds*, Gerald Stanley Lee
2. *Germany and the Germans*, Price Collier
3. *Zone Policeman 88*, Harry A. Franck
4. *The New Freedom*, Woodrow Wilson
5. *South America*, James Bryce
6. *Your United States*, Arnold Bennett
7. *The Promised Land*, Mary Antin
8. *Auction Bridge To-Day*, Milton C. Work
9. *Three Plays*, Eugène Brieux
10. *Psychology and Industrial Efficiency*, Hugo Munsterberg

1914

Fiction

1. *The Eyes of the World*, Harold Bell Wright
2. *Pollyanna*, Eleanor H. Porter
3. *The Inside of the Cup*, Winston Churchill
4. *The Salamander*, Owen Johnson
5. *The Fortunate Youth*, William J. Locke
6. *T. Tembarom*, Frances Hodgson Burnett
7. *Penrod*, Booth Tarkington
8. *Diane of the Green Van*, Leona Dalrymple
9. *The Devil's Garden*, W. B. Maxwell

10. *The Prince of Graustark*, George Barr McCutcheon

1915

Fiction

1. *The Turmoil*, Booth Tarkington
2. *A Far Country*, Winston Churchill
3. *Michael O'Halloran*, Gene Stratton Porter
4. *Pollyanna Grows Up*, Eleanor H. Porter
5. *K*, Mary Roberts Rinehart
6. *Jaffery*, William J. Locke
7. *Felix O'Day*, F. Hopkinson Smith
8. *The Harbor*, Ernest Poole
9. *The Lone Star Ranger*, Zane Grey
10. *Angela's Business*, Henry Sydnor Harrison

1916

Fiction

1. *Seventeen*, Booth Tarkington
2. *When a Man's a Man*, Harold Bell Wright
3. *Just David*, Eleanor H. Porter
4. *Mr. Britling Sees It Through*, H. G. Wells
5. *Life and Gabriella*, Ellen Glasgow
6. *The Real Adventure*, Henry Kitchell Webster
7. *Bars of Iron*, Ethel M. Dell
8. *Nan of Music Mountain*, Frank H. Spearman
9. *Dear Enemy*, Jean Webster
10. *The Heart of Rachael*, Kathleen Norris

1917

Fiction

1. *Mr. Britling Sees It Through*, H. G. Wells
2. *The Light in the Clearing*, Irving Bacheller
3. *The Red Planet*, William J. Locke
4. *The Road to Understanding*, Eleanor H. Porter
5. *Wildfire*, Zane Grey
6. *Christine*, Alice Cholmondeley
7. *In the Wilderness*, Robert S. Hichens
8. *His Family*, Ernest Poole
9. *The Definite Object*, Jeffrey Farnol
10. *The Hundredth Chance*, Ethel M. Dell

General Nonfiction

1. *Rhymes of a Red Cross Man*, Robert W. Service
2. *The Plattsburg Manual*, O. O. Ellis and E. B. Garey
3. *Raymond*, Sir Oliver Lodge
4. *Poems of Alan Seeger*, Alan Seeger
5. *God the Invisible King*, H. G. Wells

6. *Laugh and Live*, Douglas Fairbanks
7. *Better Meals for Less Money*, Mary Green

War Books

1. *The First Hundred Thousand*, Ian Hay
2. *My Home in the Field of Honor*, Frances W. Huard
3. *A Student in Arms*, Donald Hankey
4. *Over the Top*, Arthur Guy Empey
5. *Carry On*, Coningsby Dawson
6. *Getting Together*, Ian Hay
7. *My Second Year of the War*, Frederick Palmer
8. *The Land of Deepening Shadow*, D. Thomas Curtin
9. *Italy, France and Britain at War*, H. G. Wells
10. *The Worn Doorstep*, Margaret Sherwood

1918

Fiction

1. *The U. P. Trail*, Zane Grey
2. *The Tree of Heaven*, May Sinclair
3. *The Amazing Interlude*, Mary Roberts Rinehart
4. *Dere Mable*, Edward Streeter
5. *Oh, Money! Money!*, Eleanor H. Porter
6. *Greatheart*, Ethel M. Dell
7. *The Major*, Ralph Connor
8. *The Pawns Count*, E. Phillips Oppenheim
9. *A Daughter of the Land*, Gene Stratton Porter
10. *Sonia*, Stephen McKenna

General Nonfiction

1. *Rhymes of a Red Cross Man*, Robert W. Service
2. *Treasury of War Poetry*, G. H. Clark
3. *With the Colors*, Everard J. Appleton
4. *Recollections*, Viscount Morley
5. *Laugh and Live*, Douglas Fairbanks
6. *Mark Twain's Letters*, Albert Bigelow Paine, editor
7. *Adventures and Letters of Richard Harding Davis*, Richard Harding Davis
8. *Over Here*, Edgar Guest
9. *Diplomatic Days*, Edith O'Shaughnessy
10. *Poems of Alan Seeger*, Alan Seeger

War Books

1. *My Four Years in Germany*, James W. Gerard
2. *The Glory of the Trenches*, Coningsby Dawson
3. *Over the Top*, Arthur Guy Empey

4. *A Minstrel in France*, Harry Lauder
5. *Private Peat*, Harold R. Peat
6. *Outwitting the Hun*, Lieut. Pat O'Brien
7. *Face to Face with Kaiserism*, James W. Gerard
8. *Carry On*, Coningsby Dawson
9. *Out to Win*, Coningsby Dawson
10. *Under Fire*, Henri Barbusse

1919

Fiction

1. *The Four Horsemen of the Apocalypse*, V. Blasco Ibañez
2. *The Arrow of Gold*, Joseph Conrad
3. *The Desert of Wheat*, Zane Grey
4. *Dangerous Days*, Mary Roberts Rinehart
5. *The Sky Pilot in No Man's Land*, Ralph Connor
6. *The Re-Creation of Brian Kent*, Harold Bell Wright
7. *Dawn*, Gene Stratton Porter
8. *The Tin Soldier*, Temple Bailey
9. *Christopher and Columbus*, "Elizabeth"
10. *In Secret*, Robert W. Chambers

Nonfiction

1. *The Education of Henry Adams*, Henry Adams
2. *The Years Between*, Rudyard Kipling
3. *Belgium*, Brand Whitlock
4. *The Seven Purposes*, Margaret Cameron
5. *In Flanders Fields*, John McCrae
6. *Bolshevism*, John Spargo

1920

Fiction

1. *The Man of the Forest*, Zane Grey
2. *Kindred of the Dust*, Peter B. Kyne
3. *The Re-Creation of Brian Kent*, Harold Bell Wright
4. *The River's End*, James Oliver Curwood
5. *A Man for the Ages*, Irving Bacheller
6. *Mary-Marie*, Eleanor H. Porter
7. *The Portygee*, Joseph C. Lincoln
8. *The Great Impersonation*, E. Phillips Oppenheim
9. *The Lamp in the Desert*, Ethel M. Dell
10. *Harriet and the Piper*, Kathleen Norris

Nonfiction

1. *Now It Can Be Told*, Philip Gibbs
2. *The Economic Consequences of the Peace*, John M. Keynes
3. *Roosevelt's Letters to His Children*, Joseph B. Bishop, editor
4. *Theodore Roosevelt*, William Roscoe Thayer

5. *White Shadows in the South Seas*, Frederick O'Brien
6. *An American Idyll*, Cornelia Stratton Parker

1921

Fiction

1. *Main Street*, Sinclair Lewis
2. *The Brimming Cup*, Dorothy Canfield
3. *The Mysterious Rider*, Zane Grey
4. *The Age of Innocence*, Edith Wharton
5. *The Valley of Silent Men*, James Oliver Curwood
6. *The Sheik*, Edith M. Hull
7. *A Poor Wise Man*, Mary Roberts Rinehart
8. *Her Father's Daughter*, Gene Stratton Porter
9. *The Sisters-in-Law*, Gertrude Atherton
10. *The Kingdom Round the Corner*, Coningsby Dawson

Nonfiction

1. *The Outline of History*, H. G. Wells
2. *White Shadows in the South Seas*, Frederick O'Brien
3. *The Mirrors of Downing Street*, A Gentleman with a Duster (pseudonym for Harold Begbie)
4. *The Autobiography of Margot Asquith*, Margot Asquith
6. *Peace Negotiations*, Robert Lansing

1922

Fiction

1. *If Winter Comes*, A.S.M. Hutchinson
2. *The Sheik*, Edith M. Hull
3. *Gentle Julia*, Booth Tarkington
4. *The Head of the House of Coombe*, Frances Hodgson Burnett
5. *Simon Called Peter*, Robert Keable
6. *The Breaking Point*, Mary Roberts Rinehart
7. *This Freedom*, A.S.M. Hutchinson
8. *Maria Chapdelaine*, Louis Hémon
9. *To the Last Man*, Zane Grey
10. *Babbitt*, Sinclair Lewis (tie)
10. *Helen of the Old House*, Harold Bell Wright (tie)

Nonfiction

1. *The Outline of History*, H. G. Wells
2. *The Story of Mankind*, Hendrik Willem Van Loon
3. *The Americanization of Edward Bok*, Edward Bok
4. *Diet and Health*, Lulu Hunt Peters
5. *The Mind in the Making*, James Harvey Robinson

6. *The Outline of Science*, J. Arthur Thomson
7. *Outwitting Our Nerves*, Josephine A. Jackson and Helen M. Salisbury
8. *Queen Victoria*, Lytton Strachey
9. *Mirrors of Washington*, anonymous (Clinton W. Gilbert)
10. *Painted Windows*, A Gentleman with a Duster (pseudonym for Harold Begbie)

1923

Fiction

1. *Black Oxen*, Gertrude Atherton
2. *His Children's Children*, Arthur Train
3. *The Enchanted April*, "Elizabeth"
4. *Babbitt*, Sinclair Lewis
5. *The Dim Lantern*, Temple Bailey
6. *This Freedom*, A.S.M. Hutchinson
7. *The Mine with the Iron Door*, Harold Bell Wright
8. *The Wanderer of the Wasteland*, Zane Grey
9. *The Sea-Hawk*, Rafael Sabatini
10. *The Breaking Point*, Mary Roberts Rinehart

Nonfiction

1. *Etiquette*, Emily Post
2. *The Life of Christ*, Giovanni Papini
3. *The Life and Letters of Walter H. Page*, Burton J. Hendrick, editor
4. *The Mind in the Making*, James Harvey Robinson
5. *The Outline of History*, H. G. Wells
6. *Diet and Health*, Lulu Hunt Peters
7. *Self-Mastery Through Conscious Auto-Suggestion*, Emile Coué
8. *The Americanization of Edward Bok*, Edward Bok
9. *The Story of Mankind*, Hendrik Willem Van Loon
10. *A Man from Maine*, Edward Bok

1924

Fiction

1. *So Big*, Edna Ferber
2. *The Plastic Age*, Percy Marks
3. *The Little French Girl*, Anne Douglas Sedgwick
4. *The Heirs Apparent*, Philip Gibbs
5. *A Gentleman of Courage*, James Oliver Curwood
6. *The Call of the Canyon*, Zane Grey
7. *The Midlander*, Booth Tarkington
8. *The Coast of Folly*, Coningsby Dawson
9. *Mistress Wilding*, Rafael Sabatini
10. *The Homemaker*, Dorothy Canfield Fisher

Nonfiction

1. *Diet and Health*, Lulu Hunt Peters
2. *The Life of Christ*, Giovanni Papini
3. *The Boston Cooking School Cook Book*, Fannie Farmer, editor
4. *Etiquette*, Emily Post
5. *Ariel*, André Maurois
6. *The Cross Word Puzzle Books*, Prosper Buranelli, et al.
7. *Mark Twain's Autobiography*, Mark Twain
8. *Saint Joan*, Bernard Shaw
9. *The New Decalogue of Science*, Albert E. Wiggam
10. *The Americanization of Edward Bok*, Edward Bok

1925

Fiction

1. *Soundings*, A. Hamilton Gibbs
2. *The Constant Nymph*, Margaret Kennedy
3. *The Keeper of the Bees*, Gene Stratton Porter
4. *Glorious Apollo*, E. Barrington
5. *The Green Hat*, Michael Arlen
6. *The Little French Girl*, Anne Douglas Sedgwick
7. *Arrowsmith*, Sinclair Lewis
8. *The Perennial Bachelor*, Anne Parrish
9. *The Carolinian*, Rafael Sabatini
10. *One Increasing Purpose*, A.S.M. Hutchinson

Nonfiction

1. *Diet and Health*, Lulu Hunt Peters
2. *The Boston Cooking School Cook Book*, rev. ed., Fannie Farmer, editor
3. *When We Were Very Young*, A. A. Milne
4. *The Man Nobody Knows*, Bruce Barton
5. *The Life of Christ*, Giovanni Papini
6. *Ariel*, André Maurois
7. *Twice Thirty*, Edward Bok
8. *Twenty-Five Years*, Lord Grey
9. *Anatole France Himself*, J. J. Brousson
10. *The Cross Word Puzzle Books*, Prosper Buranelli, et al.

1926

Fiction

1. *The Private Life of Helen of Troy*, John Erskine
2. *Gentlemen Prefer Blondes*, Anita Loos
3. *Sorrell and Son*, Warwick Deeping
4. *The Hounds of Spring*, Sylvia Thompson
5. *Beau Sabreur*, P. C. Wren
6. *The Silver Spoon*, John Galsworthy
7. *Beau Geste*, P. C. Wren
8. *Show Boat*, Edna Ferber
9. *After Noon*, Susan Ertz

10. *The Blue Window*, Temple Bailey

Nonfiction

1. *The Man Nobody Knows*, Bruce Barton
2. *Why We Behave Like Human Beings*, George A. Dorsey
3. *Diet and Health*, Lulu Hunt Peters
4. *Our Times*, Vol. I, Mark Sullivan
5. *The Boston Cooking School Cook Book*, rev. ed., Fannie Farmer, editor
6. *Auction Bridge Complete*, Milton C. Work
7. *The Book Nobody Knows*, Bruce Barton
8. *The Story of Philosophy*, Will Durant
9. *The Light of Faith*, Edgar A. Guest
10. *Jefferson and Hamilton*, Claude G. Bowers

1927

Fiction

1. *Elmer Gantry*, Sinclair Lewis
2. *The Plutocrat*, Booth Tarkington
3. *Doomsday*, Warwick Deeping
4. *Sorrell and Son*, Warwick Deeping
5. *Jalna*, Mazo de la Roche
6. *Lost Ecstasy*, Mary Roberts Rinehart
7. *Twilight Sleep*, Edith Wharton
8. *Tomorrow Morning*, Anne Parrish
9. *The Old Countess*, Anne Douglas Sedgwick
10. *A Good Woman*, Louis Bromfield

Nonfiction

1. *The Story of Philosophy*, Will Durant
2. *Napoleon*, Emil Ludwig
3. *Revolt in the Desert*, T. E. Lawrence
4. *Trader Horn*, Vol. I, Alfred Aloysius Horn and Ethelreda Lewis
5. *We*, Charles A. Lindbergh
6. *Ask Me Another*, Julian Spafford and Lucien Esty
7. *The Royal Road to Romance*, Richard Halliburton
8. *The Glorious Adventure*, Richard Halliburton
9. *Why We Behave Like Human Beings*, George A. Dorsey
10. *Mother India*, Katherine Mayo

1928

Fiction

1. *The Bridge of San Luis Rey*, Thornton Wilder
2. *Wintersmoon*, Hugh Walpole
3. *Swan Song*, John Galsworthy
4. *The Greene Murder Case*, S. S. Van Dine
5. *Bad Girl*, Viña Delmar
6. *Claire Ambler*, Booth Tarkington

7. *Old Pybus*, Warwick Deeping
8. *All Kneeling*, Anne Parrish
9. *Jalna*, Mazo de la Roche
10. *The Strange Case of Miss Annie Spragg*, Louis Bromfield

Nonfiction

1. *Disraeli*, André Maurois
2. *Mother India*, Katherine Mayo
3. *Trader Horn*, Vol. I, Alfred Aloysius Horn and Ethelreda Lewis
4. *Napoleon*, Emil Ludwig
5. *Strange Interlude*, Eugene O'Neill
6. *We*, Charles A. Lindbergh
7. *Count Luckner, the Sea Devil*, Lowell Thomas
8. *Goethe*, Emil Ludwig
9. *Skyward*, Richard E. Byrd
10. *The Intelligent Woman's Guide to Socialism and Capitalism*, George Bernard Shaw

1929

Fiction

1. *All Quiet on the Western Front*, Erich Maria Remarque
2. *Dodsworth*, Sinclair Lewis
3. *Dark Hester*, Anne Douglas Sedgwick
4. *The Bishop Murder Case*, S. S. Van Dine
5. *Roper's Row*, Warwick Deeping
6. *Peder Victorious*, O. E. Rölvaag
7. *Mamba's Daughters*, DuBose Heyward
8. *The Galaxy*, Susan Ertz
9. *Scarlet Sister Mary*, Julia Peterkin
10. *Joseph and His Brethren*, H. W. Freeman

Nonfiction

1. *The Art of Thinking*, Ernest Dimnet
2. *Henry the Eighth*, Francis Hackett
3. *The Cradle of the Deep*, Joan Lowell
4. *Elizabeth and Essex*, Lytton Strachey
5. *The Specialist*, Chic Sale
6. *A Preface to Morals*, Walter Lippmann
7. *Believe It or Not*, Robert L. Ripley
8. *John Brown's Body*, Stephen Vincent Benét
9. *The Tragic Era*, Claude G. Bowers
10. *The Mansions of Philosophy*, Will Durant

1930

Fiction

1. *Cimarron*, Edna Ferber
2. *Exile*, Warwick Deeping
3. *The Woman of Andros*, Thornton Wilder
4. *Years of Grace*, Margaret Ayer Barnes
5. *Angel Pavement*, J. B. Priestley
6. *The Door*, Mary Roberts Rinehart

7. *Rogue Herries*, Hugh Walpole
8. *Chances*, A. Hamilton Gibbs
9. *Young Man of Manhattan*, Katharine Brush
10. *Twenty-Four Hours*, Louis Bromfield

Nonfiction
1. *The Story of San Michele*, Axel Munthe
2. *The Strange Death of President Harding*, Gaston B. Means and May Dixon Thacker
3. *Byron*, André Maurois
4. *The Adams Family*, James Truslow Adams
5. *Lone Cowboy*, Will James
6. *Lincoln*, Emil Ludwig
7. *The Story of Philosophy*, Will Durant
8. *The Outline of History*, H. G. Wells
9. *The Art of Thinking*, Ernest Dimnet
10. *The Rise of American Civilization*, Charles and Mary Beard

1931

Fiction
1. *The Good Earth*, Pearl S. Buck
2. *Shadows on the Rock*, Willa Cather
3. *A White Bird Flying*, Bess Streeter Aldrich
4. *Grand Hotel*, Vicki Baum
5. *Years of Grace*, Margaret Ayer Barnes
6. *The Road Back*, Erich Maria Remarque
7. *The Bridge of Desire*, Warwick Deeping
8. *Back Street*, Fannie Hurst
9. *Finch's Fortune*, Mazo de la Roche
10. *Maid in Waiting*, John Galsworthy

Nonfiction
1. *Education of a Princess*, Grand Duchess Marie
2. *The Story of San Michele*, Axel Munthe
3. *Washington Merry-Go-Round*, anonymous (Drew Pearson and Robert S. Allen)
4. *Boners: Being a Collection of Schoolboy Wisdom, or Knowledge as It Is Sometimes Written*, compiled by Alexander Abingdon; illustrated by Dr. Seuss
5. *Culbertson's Summary*, Ely Culbertson
6. *Contract Bridge Blue Book*, Ely Culbertson
7. *Fatal Interview*, Edna St. Vincent Millay
8. *The Epic of America*, James Truslow Adams
9. *Mexico*, Stuart Chase
10. *New Russia's Primer*, Mikhail Ilin

1932

Fiction
1. *The Good Earth*, Pearl S. Buck
2. *The Fountain*, Charles Morgan
3. *Sons*, Pearl S. Buck
4. *Magnolia Street*, Louis Golding
5. *The Sheltered Life*, Ellen Glasgow
6. *Old Wine and New*, Warwick Deeping
7. *Mary's Neck*, Booth Tarkington
8. *Magnificent Obsession*, Lloyd C. Douglas
9. *Inheritance*, Phyllis Bentley
10. *Three Loves*, A. J. Cronin

Nonfiction
1. *The Epic of America*, James Truslow Adams
2. *Only Yesterday*, Frederick Lewis Allen
3. *A Fortune to Share*, Vash Young
4. *Culbertson's Summary*, Ely Culbertson
5. *Van Loon's Geography*, Hendrik Willem Van Loon
6. *What We Live By*, Ernest Dimnet
7. *The March of Democracy*, James Truslow Adams
8. *Washington Merry-Go-Round*, anonymous (Drew Pearson and Robert S. Allen)
9. *The Story of My Life*, Clarence Darrow
10. *More Merry-Go-Round*, anonymous (Drew Pearson and Robert S. Allen)

1933

Fiction
1. *Anthony Adverse*, Hervey Allen
2. *As the Earth Turns*, Gladys Hasty Carroll
3. *Ann Vickers*, Sinclair Lewis
4. *Magnificent Obsession*, Lloyd C. Douglas
5. *One More River*, John Galsworthy
6. *Forgive Us Our Trespasses*, Lloyd C. Douglas
7. *The Master of Jalna*, Mazo de la Roche
8. *Miss Bishop*, Bess Streeter Aldrich
9. *The Farm*, Louis Bromfield
10. *Little Man, What Now?*, Hans Fallada

Nonfiction
1. *Life Begins at Forty*, Walter B. Pitkin
2. *Marie Antoinette*, Stefan Zweig
3. *British Agent*, R. H. Bruce Lockhart
4. *100,000,000 Guinea Pigs*, Arthur Kallet and F. J. Schlink
5. *The House of Exile*, Nora Waln

6. *Van Loon's Geography*, Hendrik Willem Van Loon
7. *Looking Forward*, Franklin D. Roosevelt
8. *Contract Bridge Blue Book of 1933*, Ely Culbertson
9. *The Arches of the Years*, Halliday Sutherland
10. *The March of Democracy*, Vol. II, James Truslow Adams

1934

Fiction
1. *Anthony Adverse*, Hervey Allen
2. *Lamb in His Bosom*, Caroline Miller
3. *So Red the Rose*, Stark Young
4. *Good-Bye, Mr. Chips*, James Hilton
5. *Within This Present*, Margaret Ayer Barnes
6. *Work of Art*, Sinclair Lewis
7. *Private Worlds*, Phyllis Bottome
8. *Mary Peters*, Mary Ellen Chase
9. *Oil for the Lamps of China*, Alice Tisdale Hobart
10. *Seven Gothic Tales*, Isak Dinesen

Nonfiction
1. *While Rome Burns*, Alexander Woollcott
2. *Life Begins at Forty*, Walter B. Pitkin
3. *Nijinsky*, Romola Nijinsky
4. *100,000,000 Guinea Pigs*, Arthur Kallet and F. J. Schlink
5. *The Native's Return*, Louis Adamic
6. *Stars Fell on Alabama*, Carl Carmer
7. *Brazilian Adventure*, Peter Fleming
8. *Forty-two Years in the White House*, Ike Hoover
9. *You Must Relax*, Edmund Jacobson
10. *The Life of Our Lord*, Charles Dickens

1935

Fiction
1. *Green Light*, Lloyd C. Douglas
2. *Vein of Iron*, Ellen Glasgow
3. *Of Time and the River*, Thomas Wolfe
4. *Time Out of Mind*, Rachel Field
5. *Good-Bye, Mr. Chips*, James Hilton
6. *The Forty Days of Musa Dagh*, Franz Werfel
7. *Heaven's My Destination*, Thornton Wilder
8. *Lost Horizon*, James Hilton
9. *Come and Get It*, Edna Ferber
10. *Europa*, Robert Briffault

Nonfiction
1. *North to the Orient*, Anne Morrow Lindbergh
2. *While Rome Burns*, Alexander Woollcott

3. *Life with Father*, Clarence Day
4. *Personal History*, Vincent Sheean
5. *Seven Pillars of Wisdom*, T. E. Lawrence
6. *Francis the First*, Francis Hackett
7. *Mary Queen of Scotland and the Isles*, Stefan Zweig
8. *Rats, Lice and History*, Hans Zinsser
9. *R. E. Lee*, Douglas Southall Freeman
10. *Skin Deep*, M. C. Phillips

1936

Fiction

1. *Gone with the Wind*, Margaret Mitchell
2. *The Last Puritan*, George Santayana
3. *Sparkenbroke*, Charles Morgan
4. *Drums Along the Mohawk*, Walter D. Edmonds
5. *It Can't Happen Here*, Sinclair Lewis
6. *White Banners*, Lloyd C. Douglas
7. *The Hurricane*, Charles Nordhoff and James Norman Hall
8. *The Thinking Reed*, Rebecca West
9. *The Doctor*, Mary Roberts Rinehart
10. *Eyeless in Gaza*, Aldous Huxley

Nonfiction

1. *Man the Unknown*, Alexis Carrel
2. *Wake Up and Live!*, Dorothea Brande
3. *The Way of a Transgressor*, Negley Farson
4. *Around the World in Eleven Years*, Patience, Richard, and Johnny Abbe
5. *North to the Orient*, Anne Morrow Lindbergh
6. *An American Doctor's Odyssey*, Victor Heiser
7. *Inside Europe*, John Gunther
8. *Live Alone and Like It*, Marjorie Hillis
9. *Life with Father*, Clarence Day
10. *I Write As I Please*, Walter Duranty

1937

Fiction

1. *Gone with the Wind*, Margaret Mitchell
2. *Northwest Passage*, Kenneth Roberts
3. *The Citadel*, A. J. Cronin
4. *And So—Victoria*, Vaughan Wilkins
5. *Drums Along the Mohawk*, Walter D. Edmonds
6. *The Years*, Virginia Woolf
7. *Theatre*, W. Somerset Maugham
8. *Of Mice and Men*, John Steinbeck
9. *The Rains Came*, Louis Bromfield
10. *We Are Not Alone*, James Hilton

Nonfiction

1. *How To Win Friends and Influence People*, Dale Carnegie
2. *An American Doctor's Odyssey*, Victor Heiser
3. *The Return to Religion*, Henry C. Link
4. *The Arts*, Hendrik Willem Van Loon
5. *Orchids on Your Budget*, Marjorie Hillis
6. *Present Indicative*, Noel Coward
7. *Mathematics for the Million*, Lancelot Hogben
8. *Life with Mother*, Clarence Day
9. *The Nile*, Emil Ludwig
10. *The Flowering of New England*, Van Wyck Brooks

1938

Fiction

1. *The Yearling*, Marjorie Kinnan Rawlings
2. *The Citadel*, A. J. Cronin
3. *My Son, My Son!*, Howard Spring
4. *Rebecca*, Daphne du Maurier
5. *Northwest Passage*, Kenneth Roberts
6. *All This, and Heaven Too*, Rachel Field
7. *The Rains Came*, Louis Bromfield
8. *And Tell of Time*, Laura Krey
9. *The Mortal Storm*, Phyllis Bottome
10. *Action at Aquila*, Hervey Allen

Nonfiction

1. *The Importance of Living*, Lin Yutang
2. *With Malice Toward Some*, Margaret Halsey
3. *Madame Curie*, Eve Curie
4. *Listen! The Wind*, Anne Morrow Lindbergh
5. *The Horse and Buggy Doctor*, Arthur E. Hertzler
6. *How To Win Friends and Influence People*, Dale Carnegie
7. *Benjamin Franklin*, Carl Van Doren
8. *I'm a Stranger Here Myself*, Ogden Nash
9. *Alone*, Richard E. Byrd
10. *Fanny Kemble*, Margaret Armstrong

1939

Fiction

1. *The Grapes of Wrath*, John Steinbeck
2. *All This, and Heaven Too*, Rachel Field
3. *Rebecca*, Daphne du Maurier
4. *Wickford Point*, John P. Marquand
5. *Escape*, Ethel Vance
6. *Disputed Passage*, Lloyd C. Douglas
7. *The Yearling*, Marjorie Kinnan Rawlings
8. *The Tree of Liberty*, Elizabeth Page
9. *The Nazarene*, Sholem Asch

10. *Kitty Foyle*, Christopher Morley

Nonfiction

1. *Days of Our Years*, Pierre van Paassen
2. *Reaching for the Stars*, Nora Waln
3. *Inside Asia*, John Gunther
4. *Autobiography with Letters*, William Lyon Phelps
5. *Country Lawyer*, Bellamy Partridge
6. *Wind, Sand and Stars*, Antoine de St. Exupéry
7. *Mein Kampf*, Adolf Hitler
8. *A Peculiar Treasure*, Edna Ferber
9. *Not Peace but a Sword*, Vincent Sheean
10. *Listen! The Wind*, Anne Morrow Lindbergh

1940

Fiction

1. *How Green Was My Valley*, Richard Llewellyn
2. *Kitty Foyle*, Christopher Morley
3. *Mrs. Miniver*, Jan Struther
4. *For Whom the Bell Tolls*, Ernest Hemingway
5. *The Nazarene*, Sholem Asch
6. *Stars on the Sea*, F. van Wyck Mason
7. *Oliver Wiswell*, Kenneth Roberts
8. *The Grapes of Wrath*, John Steinbeck
9. *Night in Bombay*, Louis Bromfield
10. *The Family*, Nina Fedorova

Nonfiction

1. *I Married Adventure*, Osa Johnson
2. *How to Read a Book*, Mortimer Adler
3. *A Smattering of Ignorance*, Oscar Levant
4. *Country Squire in the White House*, John T. Flynn
5. *Land Below the Wind*, Agnes Newton Keith
6. *American White Paper*, Joseph W. Alsop Jr. and Robert Kintnor
7. *New England: Indian Summer*, Van Wyck Brooks
8. *As I Remember Him*, Hans Zinsser
9. *Days of Our Years*, Pierre van Paassen
10. *Bet It's a Boy*, Betty B. Blunt

1941

Fiction

1. *The Keys of the Kingdom*, A. J. Cronin
2. *Random Harvest*, James Hilton
3. *This Above All*, Eric Knight
4. *The Sun Is My Undoing*, Marguerite Steen
5. *For Whom the Bell Tolls*, Ernest Hemingway
6. *Oliver Wiswell*, Kenneth Roberts

7. *H. M. Pulham, Esquire*, John P. Marquand
8. *Mr. and Mrs. Cugat*, Isabel Scott Rorick
9. *Saratoga Trunk*, Edna Ferber
10. *Windswept*, Mary Ellen Chase

Nonfiction

1. *Berlin Diary*, William L. Shirer
2. *The White Cliffs*, Alice Duer Miller
3. *Out of the Night*, Jan Valtin
4. *Inside Latin America*, John Gunther
5. *Blood, Sweat and Tears*, Winston S. Churchill
6. *You Can't Do Business with Hitler*, Douglas Miller
7. *Reading I've Liked*, Clifton Fadiman, editor
8. *Reveille in Washington*, Margaret Leech
9. *Exit Laughing*, Irvin S. Cobb
10. *My Sister and I*, Dirk van der Heide

1942

Fiction

1. *The Song of Bernadette*, Franz Werfel
2. *The Moon Is Down*, John Steinbeck
3. *Dragon Seed*, Pearl S. Buck
4. *And Now Tomorrow*, Rachel Field
5. *Drivin' Woman*, Elizabeth Pickett
6. *Windswept*, Mary Ellen Chase
7. *The Robe*, Lloyd C. Douglas
8. *The Sun Is My Undoing*, Marguerite Steen
9. *Kings Row*, Henry Bellamann
10. *The Keys of the Kingdom*, A. J. Cronin

Nonfiction

1. *See Here, Private Hargrove*, Marion Hargrove
2. *Mission to Moscow*, Joseph E. Davies
3. *The Last Time I Saw Paris*, Elliot Paul
4. *Cross Creek*, Marjorie Kinnan Rawlings
5. *Victory Through Air Power*, Major Alexander P. de Seversky
6. *Past Imperfect*, Ilka Chase
7. *They Were Expendable*, W. L. White
8. *Flight to Arras*, Antoine de St. Exupéry
9. *Washington Is Like That*, W. M. Kiplinger
10. *Inside Latin America*, John Gunther

1943

Fiction

1. *The Robe*, Lloyd C. Douglas
2. *The Valley of Decision*, Marcia Davenport
3. *So Little Time*, John P. Marquand
4. *A Tree Grows in Brooklyn*, Betty Smith
5. *The Human Comedy*, William Saroyan

6. *Mrs. Parkington*, Louis Bromfield
7. *The Apostle*, Sholem Asch
8. *Hungry Hill*, Daphne du Maurier
9. *The Forest and the Fort*, Hervey Allen
10. *The Song of Bernadette*, Franz Werfel

Nonfiction

1. *Under Cover*, John Roy Carlson
2. *One World*, Wendell L. Willkie
3. *Journey Among Warriors*, Eve Curie
4. *On Being a Real Person*, Harry Emerson Fosdick
5. *Guadalcanal Diary*, Richard Tregaskis
6. *Burma Surgeon*, Lt. Col. Gordon Seagrave
7. *Our Hearts Were Young and Gay*, Cornelia Otis Skinner and Emily Kimbrough
8. *U. S. Foreign Policy*, Walter Lippmann
9. *Here Is Your War*, Ernie Pyle
10. *See Here, Private Hargrove*, Marion Hargrove

1944

Fiction

1. *Strange Fruit*, Lillian Smith
2. *The Robe*, Lloyd C. Douglas
3. *A Tree Grows in Brooklyn*, Betty Smith
4. *Forever Amber*, Kathleen Winsor
5. *The Razor's Edge*, W. Somerset Maugham
6. *The Green Years*, A. J. Cronin
7. *Leave Her to Heaven*, Ben Ames Williams
8. *Green Dolphin Street*, Elizabeth Goudge
9. *A Bell for Adano*, John Hersey
10. *The Apostle*, Sholem Asch

Nonfiction

1. *I Never Left Home*, Bob Hope
2. *Brave Men*, Ernie Pyle
3. *Good Night, Sweet Prince*, Gene Fowler
4. *Under Cover*, John Roy Carlson
5. *Yankee from Olympus*, Catherine Drinker Bowen
6. *The Time for Decision*, Sumner Welles
7. *Here Is Your War*, Ernie Pyle
8. *Anna and the King of Siam*, Margaret Landon
9. *The Curtain Rises*, Quentin Reynolds
10. *Ten Years in Japan*, Joseph C. Grew

1945

Fiction

1. *Forever Amber*, Kathleen Winsor
2. *The Robe*, Lloyd C. Douglas
3. *The Black Rose*, Thomas B. Costain
4. *The White Tower*, James Ramsey Ullman

5. *Cass Timberlane*, Sinclair Lewis
6. *A Lion Is in the Streets*, Adria Locke Langley
7. *So Well Remembered*, James Hilton
8. *Captain from Castile*, Samuel Shellabarger
9. *Earth and High Heaven*, Gwethalyn Graham
10. *Immortal Wife*, Irving Stone

Nonfiction

1. *Brave Men*, Ernie Pyle
2. *Dear Sir*, Juliet Lowell
3. *Up Front*, Bill Mauldin
4. *Black Boy*, Richard Wright
5. *Try and Stop Me*, Bennett Cerf
6. *Anything Can Happen*, George and Helen Papashvily
7. *General Marshall's Report*, U.S. War Department General Staff
8. *The Egg and I*, Betty MacDonald
9. *The Thurber Carnival*, James Thurber
10. *Pleasant Valley*, Louis Bromfield

1946

Fiction

1. *The King's General*, Daphne du Maurier
2. *This Side of Innocence*, Taylor Caldwell
3. *The River Road*, Frances Parkinson Keyes
4. *The Miracle of the Bells*, Russell Janney
5. *The Hucksters*, Frederic Wakeman
6. *The Foxes of Harrow*, Frank Yerby
7. *Arch of Triumph*, Erich Maria Remarque
8. *The Black Rose*, Thomas B. Costain
9. *B. F.'s Daughter*, John P. Marquand
10. *The Snake Pit*, Mary Jane Ward

Nonfiction

1. *The Egg and I*, Betty MacDonald
2. *Peace of Mind*, Joshua L. Liebman
3. *As He Saw It*, Elliott Roosevelt
4. *The Roosevelt I Knew*, Frances Perkins
5. *Last Chapter*, Ernie Pyle
6. *Starling of the White House*, Thomas Sugrue and Col. Edmund Starling
7. *I Chose Freedom*, Victor Kravchenko
8. *The Anatomy of Peace*, Emery Reves
9. *Top Secret*, Ralph Ingersoll
10. *A Solo in Tom-Toms*, Gene Fowler

1947

Fiction

1. *The Miracle of the Bells*, Russell Janney
2. *The Moneyman*, Thomas B. Costain
3. *Gentleman's Agreement*, Laura Z. Hobson

4. *Lydia Bailey*, Kenneth Roberts
5. *The Vixens*, Frank Yerby
6. *The Wayward Bus*, John Steinbeck
7. *House Divided*, Ben Ames Williams
8. *Kingsblood Royal*, Sinclair Lewis
9. *East Side, West Side*, Marcia Davenport
10. *Prince of Foxes*, Samuel Shellabarger

Nonfiction

1. *Peace of Mind*, Joshua L. Liebman
2. *Information Please Almanac, 1947*, John Kieran, editor
3. *Inside U.S.A.*, John Gunther
4. *A Study of History*, Arnold J. Toynbee
5. *Speaking Frankly*, James F. Byrnes
6. *Human Destiny*, Pierre Lecomte du Noüy
7. *The Egg and I*, Betty MacDonald
8. *The American Past*, Roger Butterfield
9. *The Fireside Book of Folk Songs*, Margaret B. Boni, editor
10. *Together*, Katharine T. Marshall

1948

Fiction

1. *The Big Fisherman*, Lloyd C. Douglas
2. *The Naked and the Dead*, Norman Mailer
3. *Dinner at Antoine's*, Frances Parkinson Keyes
4. *The Bishop's Mantle*, Agnes Sligh Turnbull
5. *Tomorrow Will Be Better*, Betty Smith
6. *The Golden Hawk*, Frank Yerby
7. *Raintree County*, Ross Lockridge Jr.
8. *Shannon's Way*, A. J. Cronin

THE LONGEST WORDS

Though most of us will never attempt to use them, these are the longest unhyphenated words in that linguists' Bible, the *Oxford English Dictionary*.

WORD	LETTERS
1. pneumonoultramicroscopicsilicovolcanoconiosis	45
2. supercalifragilisticexpialidocious	34
3. pseudopseudohypoparathyroidism	30
4. floccinaucinihilipilification	29
4. triethylsulphonemethylmethane	29
6. antidisestablishmentarianism	28
6. octamethylcyclotetrasiloxane	28
6. tetrachlorodibenzoparadioxin	28
9. hepaticocholangiogastronomy	27
10. radioimmunoelectrophoresis	26
10. radioimmunoelectrophoretic	26

9. *Pilgrim's Inn*, Elizabeth Goudge
10. *The Young Lions*, Irwin Shaw

Nonfiction

1. *Crusade in Europe*, Dwight D. Eisenhower
2. *How to Stop Worrying and Start Living*, Dale Carnegie
3. *Peace of Mind*, Joshua L. Liebman
4. *Sexual Behavior in the Human Male*, A. C. Kinsey, et al.
5. *Wine, Women and Words*, Billy Rose
6. *The Life and Times of the Shmoo*, Al Capp
7. *The Gathering Storm*, Winston Churchill
8. *Roosevelt and Hopkins*, Robert E. Sherwood
9. *A Guide to Confident Living*, Norman Vincent Peale
10. *The Plague and I*, Betty MacDonald

1949

Fiction

1. *The Egyptian*, Mika Waltari
2. *The Big Fisherman*, Lloyd C. Douglas
3. *Mary*, Sholem Asch
4. *A Rage to Live*, John O'Hara
5. *Point of No Return*, John P. Marquand
6. *Dinner at Antoine's*, Frances Parkinson Keyes
7. *High Towers*, Thomas B. Costain
8. *Cutlass Empire*, Van Wyck Mason
9. *Pride's Castle*, Frank Yerby
10. *Father of the Bride*, Edward Streeter

Nonfiction

1. *White Collar Zoo*, Clare Barnes Jr.
2. *How to Win at Canasta*, Oswald Jacoby
3. *The Seven Storey Mountain*, Thomas Merton
4. *Home Sweet Zoo*, Clare Barnes Jr.
5. *Cheaper by the Dozen*, Frank B. Gilbreth Jr. and Ernestine Gilbreth Carey
6. *The Greatest Story Ever Told*, Fulton Oursler
7. *Canasta, the Argentine Rummy Game*, Ottilie H. Reilly
8. *Canasta*, Josephine Artayeta de Viel and Ralph Michael
9. *Peace of Soul*, Fulton J. Sheen
10. *A Guide to Confident Living*, Norman Vincent Peale

1950

Fiction

1. *The Cardinal*, Henry Morton Robinson
2. *Joy Street*, Frances Parkinson Keyes
3. *Across the River and into the Trees*, Ernest Hemingway
4. *The Wall*, John Hersey
5. *Star Money*, Kathleen Winsor
6. *The Parasites*, Daphne du Maurier
7. *Floodtide*, Frank Yerby
8. *Jubilee Trail*, Gwen Bristow
9. *The Adventurer*, Mika Waltari
10. *The Disenchanted*, Budd Schulberg

Nonfiction

1. *Betty Crocker's Picture Cook Book*
2. *The Baby*
3. *Look Younger, Live Longer*, Gayelord Hauser
4. *How I Raised Myself from Failure to Success in Selling*, Frank Bettger
5. *Kon-Tiki*, Thor Heyerdahl
6. *Mr. Jones, Meet the Master*, Peter Marshall
7. *Your Dream Home*, Hubbard Cobb
8. *The Mature Mind*, H. A. Overstreet
9. *Campus Zoo*, Clare Barnes Jr.
10. *Belles on Their Toes*, Frank Gilbreth Jr. and Ernestine Gilbreth Carey

1951

Fiction

1. *From Here to Eternity*, James Jones
2. *The Caine Mutiny*, Herman Wouk
3. *Moses*, Sholem Asch
4. *The Cardinal*, Henry Morton Robinson
5. *A Woman Called Fancy*, Frank Yerby
6. *The Cruel Sea*, Nicholas Monsarrat
7. *Melville Goodwin, U.S.A.*, John P. Marquand

8. *Return to Paradise*, James A. Michener
9. *The Foundling*, Cardinal Spellman
10. *The Wanderer*, Mika Waltari

Nonfiction

1. *Look Younger, Live Longer*, Gayelord Hauser
2. *Betty Crocker's Picture Cook Book*
3. *Washington Confidential*, Jack Lait and Lee Mortimer
4. *Better Homes and Gardens Garden Book*
5. *Better Homes and Gardens Handyman's Book*
6. *The Sea Around Us*, Rachel L. Carson
7. *Thorndike-Barnhart Comprehensive Desk Dictionary*, Clarence L. Barnhart, editor
8. *Pogo*, Walt Kelly
9. *Kon-Tiki*, Thor Heyerdahl
10. *The New Yorker Twenty-Fifth Anniversary Album*

1952

Fiction

1. *The Silver Chalice*, Thomas B. Costain
2. *The Caine Mutiny*, Herman Wouk
3. *East of Eden*, John Steinbeck
4. *My Cousin Rachel*, Daphne du Maurier
5. *Steamboat Gothic*, Frances Parkinson Keyes
6. *Giant*, Edna Ferber
7. *The Old Man and the Sea*, Ernest Hemingway
8. *The Gown of Glory*, Agnes Sligh Turnbull
9. *The Saracen Blade*, Frank Yerby
10. *The Houses in Between*, Howard Spring

Nonfiction

1. *The Holy Bible: Revised Standard Version*
2. *A Man Called Peter*, Catherine Marshall
3. *U.S.A. Confidential*, Jack Lait and Lee Mortimer
4. *The Sea Around Us*, Rachel L. Carson
5. *Tallulah*, Tallulah Bankhead
6. *The Power of Positive Thinking*, Norman Vincent Peale
7. *This I Believe*, Edward P. Morgan, editor; Edward R. Murrow, foreword
8. *This Is Ike*, Wilson Hicks, editor
9. *Witness*, Whittaker Chambers
10. *Mr. President*, William Hillman

1953

Fiction

1. *The Robe*, Lloyd C. Douglas
2. *The Silver Chalice*, Thomas B. Costain
3. *Désirée*, Annemarie Selinko
4. *Battle Cry*, Leon M. Uris
5. *From Here to Eternity*, James Jones
6. *The High and the Mighty*, Ernest K. Gann
7. *Beyond This Place*, A. J. Cronin
8. *Time and Time Again*, James Hilton
9. *Lord Vanity*, Samuel Shellabarger
10. *The Unconquered*, Ben Ames Williams

Nonfiction

1. *The Holy Bible: Revised Standard Version*
2. *The Power of Positive Thinking*, Norman Vincent Peale
3. *Sexual Behavior in the Human Female*, Alfred C. Kinsey, et al.
4. *Angel Unaware*, Dale Evans Rogers
5. *Life Is Worth Living*, Fulton J. Sheen
6. *A Man Called Peter*, Catherine Marshall
7. *This I Believe*, Edward P. Morgan, editor; Edward R. Murrow, foreword
8. *The Greatest Faith Ever Known*, Fulton Oursler and G.A.O. Armstrong
9. *How to Play Your Best Golf*, Tommy Armour
10. *A House Is Not a Home*, Polly Adler

1954

Fiction

1. *Not as a Stranger*, Morton Thompson
2. *Mary Anne*, Daphne du Maurier
3. *Love Is Eternal*, Irving Stone
4. *The Royal Box*, Frances Parkinson Keyes
5. *The Egyptian*, Mika Waltari
6. *No Time for Sergeants*, Mac Hyman
7. *Sweet Thursday*, John Steinbeck
8. *The View from Pompey's Head*, Hamilton Basso
9. *Never Victorious, Never Defeated*, Taylor Caldwell
10. *Benton's Row*, Frank Yerby

Nonfiction

1. *The Holy Bible: Revised Standard Version*
2. *The Power of Positive Thinking*, Norman Vincent Peale
3. *Better Homes and Gardens New Cook Book*
4. *Betty Crocker's Good and Easy Cook Book*

5. *The Tumult and the Shouting*, Grantland Rice
6. *I'll Cry Tomorrow*, Lillian Roth, Gerold Frank, and Mike Connolly
7. *The Prayers of Peter Marshall*, Catherine Marshall, editor
8. *This I Believe, 2*, Raymond Swing, editor
9. *But We Were Born Free*, Elmer Davis
10. *The Saturday Evening Post Treasury*, Roger Butterfield, editor

1955

Fiction

1. *Marjorie Morningstar*, Herman Wouk
2. *Auntie Mame*, Patrick Dennis
3. *Andersonville*, MacKinlay Kantor
4. *Bonjour Tristesse*, Françoise Sagan
5. *The Man in the Gray Flannel Suit*, Sloan Wilson
6. *Something of Value*, Robert Ruark
7. *Not As a Stranger*, Morton Thompson
8. *No Time for Sergeants*, Mac Hyman
9. *The Tontine*, Thomas B. Costain
10. *Ten North Frederick*, John O'Hara

Nonfiction

1. *Gift from the Sea*, Anne Morrow Lindbergh
2. *The Power of Positive Thinking*, Norman Vincent Peale
3. *The Family of Man*, Edward Steichen
4. *A Man Called Peter*, Catherine Marshall
5. *How to Live 365 Days a Year*, John A. Schindler
6. *Better Homes and Gardens Diet Book*
7. *The Secret of Happiness*, Billy Graham
8. *Why Johnny Can't Read*, Rudolf Flesch
9. *Inside Africa*, John Gunther
10. *Year of Decisions*, Harry S Truman

1956

Fiction

1. *Don't Go Near the Water*, William Brinkley
2. *The Last Hurrah*, Edwin O'Connor
3. *Peyton Place*, Grace Metalious
4. *Auntie Mame*, Patrick Dennis
5. *Eloise*, Kay Thompson
6. *Andersonville*, MacKinlay Kantor
7. *A Certain Smile*, Françoise Sagan
8. *The Tribe That Lost Its Head*, Nicholas Monsarrat
9. *The Mandarins*, Simone de Beauvoir
10. *Boon Island*, Kenneth Roberts

Nonfiction

1. *Arthritis and Common Sense*, rev. ed., Dan Dale Alexander
2. *Webster's New World Dictionary of the American Language*, concise ed., David B. Guralnik
3. *Betty Crocker's Picture Cook Book*, 2nd. ed.
4. *Etiquette*, Frances Benton
5. *Better Homes and Gardens Barbecue Book*
6. *The Search for Bridey Murphy*, Morey Bernstein
7. *Love or Perish*, Smiley Blanton, M.D.
8. *Better Homes and Gardens Decorating Book*
9. *How To Live 365 Days a Year*, John A. Schindler
10. *The Nun's Story*, Kathryn Hulme

1957

Fiction

1. *By Love Possessed*, James Gould Cozzens
2. *Peyton Place*, Grace Metalious
3. *Compulsion*, Meyer Levin
4. *Rally Round the Flag, Boys!*, Max Shulman
5. *Blue Camellia*, Frances Parkinson Keyes
6. *Eloise in Paris*, Kay Thompson
7. *The Scapegoat*, Daphne du Maurier
8. *On the Beach*, Nevil Shute
9. *Below the Salt*, Thomas B. Costain
10. *Atlas Shrugged*, Ayn Rand

Nonfiction

1. *Kids Say the Darndest Things!*, Art Linkletter
2. *The FBI Story*, Don Whitehead
3. *Stay Alive All Your Life*, Norman Vincent Peale
4. *To Live Again*, Catherine Marshall
5. *Better Homes and Gardens Flower Arranging*
6. *Where Did You Go? Out. What Did You Do? Nothing*, Robert Paul Smith
7. *Baruch: My Own Story*, Bernard M. Baruch
8. *Please Don't Eat the Daisies*, Jean Kerr
9. *The American Heritage Book of Great Historic Places*
10. *The Day Christ Died*, Jim Bishop

1958

Fiction

1. *Doctor Zhivago*, Boris Pasternak
2. *Anatomy of a Murder*, Robert Traver

---

3. *Lolita*, Vladimir Nabokov
4. *Around the World with Auntie Mame*, Patrick Dennis
5. *From the Terrace*, John O'Hara
6. *Eloise at Christmastime*, Kay Thompson
7. *Ice Palace*, Edna Ferber
8. *The Winthrop Woman*, Anya Seton
9. *The Enemy Camp*, Jerome Weidman
10. *Victorine*, Frances Parkinson Keyes

Nonfiction

1. *Kids Say the Darndest Things!*, Art Linkletter
2. *'Twixt Twelve and Twenty*, Pat Boone
3. *Only in America*, Harry Golden
4. *Masters of Deceit*, Edgar Hoover
5. *Please Don't Eat the Daisies*, Jean Kerr
6. *Better Homes and Gardens Salad Book*
7. *The New Testament in Modern English*, J. P. Phillips, trans.
8. *Aku-Aku*, Thor Heyerdahl
9. *Dear Abby*, Abigail Van Buren
10. *Inside Russia Today*, John Gunther

1959

Fiction

1. *Exodus*, Leon Uris
2. *Doctor Zhivago*, Boris Pasternak
3. *Hawaii*, James Michener
4. *Advise and Consent*, Allen Drury
5. *Lady Chatterley's Lover*, D. H. Lawrence
6. *The Ugly American*, William J. Lederer and Eugene L. Burdick
7. *Dear and Glorious Physician*, Taylor Caldwell
8. *Lolita*, Vladimir Nabokov
9. *Mrs. 'Arris Goes to Paris*, Paul Gallico
10. *Poor No More*, Robert Ruark

Nonfiction

1. *'Twixt Twelve and Twenty*, Pat Boone
2. *Folk Medicine*, D. C. Jarvis
3. *For 2¢ Plain*, Harry Golden
4. *The Status Seekers*, Vance Packard
5. *Act One*, Moss Hart
6. *Charley Weaver's Letters from Mamma*, Cliff Arquette
7. *The Elements of Style*, William Strunk Jr. and E. B. White
8. *The General Foods Kitchens Cookbook*
9. *Only in America*, Harry Golden
10. *Mine Enemy Grows Older*, Alexander King

1960

Fiction

1. *Advise and Consent*, Allen Drury
2. *Hawaii*, James A. Michener
3. *The Leopard*, Giuseppe di Lampedusa
4. *The Chapman Report*, Irving Wallace
5. *Ourselves To Know*, John O'Hara
6. *The Constant Image*, Marcia Davenport
7. *The Lovely Ambition*, Mary Ellen Chase
8. *The Listener*, Taylor Caldwell
9. *Trustee from the Toolroom*, Nevil Shute
10. *Sermons and Soda-Water*, John O'Hara

Nonfiction

1. *Folk Medicine*, D. C. Jarvis
2. *Better Homes and Gardens First Aid for Your Family*
3. *The General Foods Kitchens Cookbook*
4. *May This House Be Safe from Tigers*, Alexander King
5. *Better Homes and Gardens Dessert Book*
6. *Better Homes and Gardens Decorating Ideas*
7. *The Rise and Fall of the Third Reich*, William L. Shirer
8. *The Conscience of a Conservative*, Barry Goldwater
9. *I Kid You Not*, Jack Paar
10. *Between You, Me and the Gatepost*, Pat Boone

1961

Fiction

1. *The Agony and the Ecstasy*, Irving Stone
2. *Franny and Zooey*, J. D. Salinger
3. *To Kill a Mockingbird*, Harper Lee
4. *Mila 18*, Leon Uris
5. *The Carpetbaggers*, Harold Robbins
6. *Tropic of Cancer*, Henry Miller
7. *Winnie Ille Pu*, Alexander Lenard, trans.
8. *Daughter of Silence*, Morris West
9. *The Edge of Sadness*, Edwin O'Connor
10. *The Winter of Our Discontent*, John Steinbeck

Nonfiction

1. *The New English Bible: The New Testament*
2. *The Rise and Fall of the Third Reich*, William Shirer
3. *Better Homes and Gardens Sewing Book*

4. *Casserole Cook Book*
5. *A Nation of Sheep*, William Lederer
6. *Better Homes and Gardens Nutrition for Your Family*
7. *The Making of the President, 1960*, Theodore H. White
8. *Calories Don't Count*, Dr. Herman Taller
9. *Betty Crocker's New Picture Cook Book: New Edition*
10. *Ring of Bright Water*, Gavin Maxwell

1962

Fiction
1. *Ship of Fools*, Katherine Anne Porter
2. *Dearly Beloved*, Anne Morrow Lindbergh
3. *A Shade of Difference*, Allen Drury
4. *Youngblood Hawke*, Herman Wouk
5. *Franny and Zooey*, J. D. Salinger
6. *Fail-Safe*, Eugene Burdick and Harvey Wheeler

7. *Seven Days in May*, Fletcher Knebel and Charles W. Bailey II
8. *The Prize*, Irving Wallace
9. *The Agony and the Ecstasy*, Irving Stone
10. *The Reivers*, William Faulkner

Nonfiction
1. *Calories Don't Count*, Dr. Herman Taller
2. *The New English Bible: The New Testament*
3. *Better Homes and Gardens Cook Book: New Edition*
4. *O Ye Jigs & Juleps!*, Virginia Cary Hudson
5. *Happiness Is a Warm Puppy*, Charles M. Schulz
6. *The Joy of Cooking: New Edition*, Irma S. Rombauer and Marion Rombauer Becker
7. *My Life in Court*, Louis Nizer
8. *The Rothschilds*, Frederic Morton

9. *Sex and the Single Girl*, Helen Gurley Brown
10. *Travels with Charley*, John Steinbeck

1963

Fiction
1. *The Shoes of the Fisherman*, Morris L. West
2. *The Group*, Mary McCarthy
3. *Raise High the Roof Beam, Carpenters, and Seymour—An Introduction*, J. D. Salinger
4. *Caravans*, James A. Michener
5. *Elizabeth Appleton*, John O'Hara
6. *Grandmother and the Priests*, Taylor Caldwell
7. *City of Night*, John Rechy
8. *The Glass-Blowers*, Daphne du Maurier
9. *The Sand Pebbles*, Richard McKenna
10. *The Battle of the Villa Fiorita*, Rumer Godden

LITERATURE GOES TO THE MOVIES

It's no secret that many movies, both good and bad, are based on books. This list presents a small sampling of unusual, delightful, and suprising books by leading writers that were turned into well-known movies. (The dates after the titles indicate the year of the film version's release.)

Awakenings (1990), Oliver Sacks
The Blue Angel (1930, 1959), Heinrich Mann
The Body Snatcher (1945), Robert Louis Stevenson
Breakfast at Tiffany's (1961), Truman Capote
The Chant of Jimmie Blacksmith (1979), Thomas Keneally
Chitty, Chitty, Bang, Bang (1968), Ian Fleming
The Death and Life of Dith Pran (released as *The Killing Fields*, 1984), Sidney Schanberg
Deliverance (1972), James Dickey
Do Androids Dream of Electric Sheep? (released as *Blade Runner*, 1982), Philip K. Dick
Don't Look Now (1971), Daphne du Maurier
The Executioners (released as *Cape Fear*, 1962, 1991), J. D. MacDonald
The Grifters (1990), Jim Thompson
The Hamlet (originally *The Long, Hot Summer*, 1957) William Faulkner
The Last Picture Show (1971), Larry McMurtry
Legends of the Fall (1994), Jim Harrison

Little Women (1994), Louisa May Alcott
Lolita (1962), Vladimir Nabokov
Lost Moon (released as *Apollo 13*, 1995), Jim Lovell and Jeffrey Kluger
The Magnificent Ambersons (1942), Booth Tarkington
The Maltese Falcon (1941; also released as *Satan Met a Lady*, 1937), Dashiell Hammett
Mildred Pierce (1945), James M. Cain
The Natural (1984), Bernard Malamud
The Postman Always Rings Twice (1946, 1981), James M. Cain
The Seven Pillars of Wisdom (released as *Lawrence of Arabia*, 1962), T. E. Lawrence
Tales from the South Pacific (produced as the musical *South Pacific* and later released as a film, 1958), James Michener
The Turn of the Screw (released as *The Innocents*, 1961), Henry James
Two Hours to Doom (released as *Dr. Strangelove*, 1964), Peter George

Nonfiction

1. *Happiness Is a Warm Puppy*, Charles M. Schulz
2. *Security Is a Thumb and a Blanket*, Charles M. Schulz
3. *J.F.K.: The Man and the Myth*, Victor Lasky
4. *Profiles in Courage: Inaugural Edition*, John F. Kennedy
5. *O Ye Jigs & Juleps!*, Virginia Cary Hudson
6. *Better Homes and Gardens Bread Cook Book*
7. *The Pillsbury Family Cookbook*
8. *I Owe Russia $1200*, Bob Hope
9. *Heloise's Housekeeping Hints*
10. *Better Homes and Gardens Baby Book*

1964

Fiction

1. *The Spy Who Came in from the Cold*, John Le Carré
2. *Candy*, Terry Southern and Mason Hoffenberg
3. *Herzog*, Saul Bellow
4. *Armageddon*, Leon Uris
5. *The Man*, Irving Wallace
6. *The Rector of Justin*, Louis Auchincloss
7. *The Martyred*, Richard E. Kim
8. *You Only Live Twice*, Ian Fleming
9. *This Rough Magic*, Mary Stewart
10. *Convention*, Fletcher Knebel and Charles W. Bailey II

Nonfiction

1. *Four Days*, American Heritage and United Press International
2. *I Need All the Friends I Can Get*, Charles M. Schulz
3. *Profiles in Courage: Memorial Edition*, John F. Kennedy
4. *In His Own Write*, John Lennon
5. *Christmas Is Together-Time*, Charles M. Schulz
6. *A Day in the Life of President Kennedy*, Jim Bishop
7. *The Kennedy Wit*, compiled by Bill Adler
8. *A Moveable Feast*, Ernest Hemingway
9. *Reminiscences*, General Douglas MacArthur
10. *The John F. Kennedys*, Mark Shaw

1965

Fiction

1. *The Source*, James A. Michener
2. *Up the Down Staircase*, Bel Kaufman
3. *Herzog*, Saul Bellow

4. *The Looking Glass War*, John Le Carré
5. *The Green Berets*, Robin Moore
6. *Those Who Love*, Irving Stone
7. *The Man with the Golden Gun*, Ian Fleming
8. *Hotel*, Arthur Hailey
9. *The Ambassador*, Morris West
10. *Don't Stop the Carnival*, Herman Wouk

Nonfiction

1. *How To Be a Jewish Mother*, Dan Greenburg
2. *A Gift of Prophecy*, Ruth Montgomery
3. *Games People Play*, Eric Berne, M.D.
4. *World Aflame*, Billy Graham
5. *Happiness Is a Dry Martini*, Johnny Carson
6. *Markings*, Dag Hammarskjöld
7. *A Thousand Days*, Arthur Schlesinger Jr.
8. *My Shadow Ran Fast*, Bill Sands
9. *Kennedy*, Theodore C. Sorensen
10. *The Making of the President, 1964*, Theodore H. White

1966

Fiction

1. *Valley of the Dolls*, Jacqueline Susann
2. *The Adventurers*, Harold Robbins
3. *The Secret of Santa Vittoria*, Robert Crichton
4. *Capable of Honor*, Allen Drury
5. *The Double Image*, Helen MacInnes
6. *The Fixer*, Bernard Malamud
7. *Tell No Man*, Adela Rogers St. Johns
8. *Tai-Pan*, James Clavell
9. *The Embezzler*, Louis Auchincloss
10. *All in the Family*, Edwin O'Connor

Nonfiction

1. *How to Avoid Probate*, Norman F. Dacey
2. *Human Sexual Response*, William Howard Masters and Virginia E. Johnston
3. *In Cold Blood*, Truman Capote
4. *Games People Play*, Eric Berne, M.D.
5. *A Thousand Days*, Arthur M. Schlesinger Jr.
6. *Everything but Money*, Sam Levenson
7. *The Random House Dictionary of the English Language*
8. *Rush to Judgment*, Mark Lane
9. *The Last Battle*, Cornelius Ryan
10. *Phyllis Diller's Housekeeping Hints*, Phyllis Diller

1967

Fiction

1. *The Arrangement*, Elia Kazan
2. *The Confessions of Nat Turner*, William Styron (tie)
2. *The Chosen*, Chaim Potok (tie)
4. *Topaz*, Leon Uris
5. *Christy*, Catherine Marshall
6. *The Eighth Day*, Thornton Wilder
7. *Rosemary's Baby*, Ira Levin
8. *The Plot*, Irving Wallace
9. *The Gabriel Hounds*, Mary Stewart
10. *The Exhibitionist*, Henry Sutton

Nonfiction

1. *Death of a President*, William Manchester
2. *Misery Is a Blind Date*, Johnny Carson
3. *Games People Play*, Eric Berne, M.D.
4. *Stanyan Street & Other Sorrows*, Rod McKuen
5. *A Modern Priest Looks at His Outdated Church*, Father James Kavanaugh
6. *Everything but Money*, Sam Levenson
7. *Our Crowd*, Stephen Birmingham
8. *Edgar Cayce—The Sleeping Prophet*, Jess Stearn (tie)
8. *Better Homes and Gardens Favorite Ways with Chicken* (tie)
8. *Phyllis Diller's Marriage Manual*, Phyllis Diller (tie)

1968

Fiction

1. *Airport*, Arthur Hailey
2. *Couples*, John Updike
3. *The Salzburg Connection*, Helen MacInnes
4. *A Small Town in Germany*, John Le Carré
5. *Testimony of Two Men*, Taylor Caldwell
6. *Preserve and Protect*, Allen Drury
7. *Myra Breckinridge*, Gore Vidal
8. *Vanished*, Fletcher Knebel
9. *Christy*, Catherine Marshall
10. *The Tower of Babel*, Morris L. West

Nonfiction

1. *Better Homes and Gardens New Cook Book*
2. *The Random House Dictionary of the English Language: College Edition*, Laurence Urdang, editor
3. *Listen to the Warm*, Rod McKuen
4. *Between Parent and Child*, Haim G. Ginott
5. *Lonesome Cities*, Rod McKuen

6. *The Doctor's Quick Weight Loss Diet*, Erwin M. Stillman and Samm Sinclair Baker
7. *The Money Game*, Adam Smith
8. *Stanyan Street & Other Sorrows*, Rod McKuen
9. *The Weight Watcher's Cook Book*, Jean Nidetch
10. *Better Homes and Gardens Eat and Stay Slim*

1969

Fiction

1. *Portnoy's Complaint*, Philip Roth
2. *The Godfather*, Mario Puzo
3. *The Love Machine*, Jacqueline Susann
4. *The Inheritors*, Harold Robbins
5. *The Andromeda Strain*, Michael Crichton
6. *The Seven Minutes*, Irving Wallace
7. *Naked Came the Stranger*, Penelope Ashe
8. *The Promise*, Chaim Potok
9. *The Pretenders*, Gwen Davis
10. *The House on the Strand*, Daphne du Maurier

Nonfiction

1. *American Heritage Dictionary of the English Language*, William Morris, editor
2. *In Someone's Shadow*, Rod McKuen
3. *The Peter Principle*, Laurence J. Peter and Raymond Hull
4. *Between Parent and Teenager*, Dr. Haim G. Ginott
5. *The Graham Kerr Cookbook*, the Galloping Gourmet
6. *The Selling of the President 1968*, Joe McGinniss
7. *Miss Craig's 21-Day Shape-Up Program for Men and Women*, Marjorie Craig
8. *My Life and Prophecies*, Jeane Dixon with René Noorbergen
9. *Linda Goodman's Sun Signs*, Linda Goodman
10. *Twelve Years of Christmas*, Rod McKuen

1970

Fiction

1. *Love Story*, Erich Segal
2. *The French Lieutenant's Woman*, John Fowles
3. *Islands in the Stream*, Ernest Hemingway
4. *The Crystal Cave*, Mary Stewart
5. *Great Lion of God*, Taylor Caldwell
6. *QB VII*, Leon Uris

7. *The Gang That Couldn't Shoot Straight*, Jimmy Breslin
8. *The Secret Woman*, Victoria Holt
9. *Travels with My Aunt*, Graham Greene
10. *Rich Man, Poor Man*, Irwin Shaw

Nonfiction

1. *Everything You Always Wanted To Know About Sex but Were Afraid to Ask*, David Reuben, M.D.
2. *The New English Bible*
3. *The Sensuous Woman*, "J"
4. *Better Homes and Gardens Fondue and Tabletop Cooking*
5. *Up the Organization*, Robert Townsend
6. *Ball Four*, Jim Bouton
7. *American Heritage Dictionary of the English Language*, William Morris
8. *Body Language*, Julius Fast
9. *In Someone's Shadow*, Rod McKuen
10. *Caught in the Quiet*, Rod McKuen

1971

Fiction

1. *Wheels*, Arthur Hailey
2. *The Exorcist*, William P. Blatty
3. *The Passions of the Mind*, Irving Stone
4. *The Day of the Jackal*, Frederick Forsyth
5. *The Betsy*, Harold Robbins
6. *Message from Malaga*, Helen MacInnes
7. *The Winds of War*, Herman Wouk
8. *The Drifters*, James A. Michener
9. *The Other*, Thomas Tryon
10. *Rabbit Redux*, John Updike

Nonfiction

1. *The Sensuous Man*, "M"
2. *Bury My Heart at Wounded Knee*, Dee Brown
3. *Better Homes and Gardens Blender Cook Book*
4. *I'm O.K., You're O.K.*, Thomas Harris
5. *Any Woman Can!*, David Reuben, M.D.
6. *Inside the Third Reich*, Albert Speer
7. *Eleanor and Franklin*, Joseph P. Lash
8. *Wunnerful, Wunnerful!*, Lawrence Welk
9. *Honor Thy Father*, Gay Talese
10. *Fields of Wonder*, Rod McKuen

1972

Fiction

1. *Jonathan Livingston Seagull*, Richard Bach
2. *August, 1914*, Alexander Solzhenitsyn
3. *The Odessa File*, Frederick Forsyth

4. *The Day of the Jackal*, Frederick Forsyth
5. *The Word*, Irving Wallace
6. *The Winds of War*, Herman Wouk
7. *Captains and the Kings*, Taylor Caldwell
8. *Two from Galilee*, Marjorie Holmes
9. *My Name Is Asher Lev*, Chaim Potok
10. *Semi-Tough*, Dan Jenkins

Nonfiction

1. *The Living Bible*, Kenneth Taylor
2. *I'm O.K., You're O.K.*, Thomas Harris
3. *Open Marriage*, Nena and George O'Neill
4. *Harry S. Truman*, Margaret Truman
5. *Dr. Atkins' Diet Revolution*, Robert C. Atkins
6. *Better Homes and Gardens Menu Cook Book*
7. *The Peter Prescription*, Laurence J. Peter
8. *A World Beyond*, Ruth Montgomery
9. *Journey to Ixtlan*, Carlos Castaneda
10. *Better Homes and Gardens Low-Calorie Desserts*

1973

Fiction

1. *Jonathan Livingston Seagull*, Richard Bach
2. *Once Is Not Enough*, Jacqueline Susann
3. *Breakfast of Champions*, Kurt Vonnegut
4. *The Odessa File*, Frederick Forsyth
5. *Burr*, Gore Vidal
6. *The Hollow Hills*, Mary Stewart
7. *Evening in Byzantium*, Irwin Shaw
8. *The Matlock Paper*, Robert Ludlum
9. *The Billion Dollar Sure Thing*, Paul E. Erdman
10. *The Honorary Consul*, Graham Greene

Nonfiction

1. *The Living Bible*, Kenneth Taylor
2. *Dr. Atkins' Diet Revolution*, Robert C. Atkins
3. *I'm O.K., You're O.K.*, Thomas Harris
4. *The Joy of Sex*, Alex Comfort
5. *Weight Watchers Program Cookbook*, Jean Nidetch
6. *How To Be Your Own Best Friend*, Mildred Newman, et al.
7. *The Art of Walt Disney*, Christopher Finch
8. *Better Homes and Gardens Home Canning Cookbook*
9. *Alistair Cooke's America*, Alistair Cooke
10. *Sybil*, Flora R. Schreiber

1974

Fiction

1. *Centennial*, James A. Michener
2. *Watership Down*, Richard Adams
3. *Jaws*, Peter Benchley
4. *Tinker, Tailor, Soldier, Spy*, John Le Carré
5. *Something Happened*, Joseph Heller
6. *The Dogs of War*, Frederick Forsyth
7. *The Pirate*, Harold J. Robbins
8. *I Heard the Owl Call My Name*, Margaret Craven
9. *The Seven-Per-Cent Solution*, John H. Watson, M.D., Nicholas Meyer, editor
10. *The Fan Club*, Irving Wallace

Nonfiction

1. *The Total Woman*, Marabel Morgan
2. *All the President's Men*, Carl Bernstein and Bob Woodward
3. *Plain Speaking: An Oral Biography of Harry S. Truman*, Merle Miller
4. *More Joy: A Lovemaking Companion to The Joy of Sex*, Alex Comfort
5. *Alistair Cooke's America*, Alistair Cooke
6. *Tales of Power*, Carlos A. Castaneda
7. *You Can Profit from a Monetary Crisis*, Harry Browne
8. *All Things Bright and Beautiful*, James Herriot
9. *The Bermuda Triangle*, Charles Berlitz with J. Manson Valentine
10. *The Memory Book*, Harry Lorayne and Jerry Lucas

AMERICA'S POETS LAUREATE

To honor America's greatest poets, the Librarian of Congress names a poet laureate. The annointed:

Robert Penn Warren	1986–87
Richard Wilbur	1987–88
Howard Nemerov	1988–90
Mark Strand	1990–91
Joseph Brodsky	1991–92
Mona Van Duyn	1992–93
Rita Dove	1993–95
Robert Hass	1995–96

1975

Fiction

1. *Ragtime*, E. L. Doctorow
2. *The Moneychangers*, Arthur Hailey
3. *Curtain*, Agatha Christie
4. *Looking for Mister Goodbar*, Judith Rossner
5. *The Choirboys*, Joseph Wambaugh
6. *The Eagle Has Landed*, Jack Higgins
7. *The Greek Treasure: A Biographical Novel of Henry and Sophia Schliemann*, Irving Stone
8. *The Great Train Robbery*, Michael Crichton
9. *Shogun*, James Clavell
10. *Humboldt's Gift*, Saul Bellow

Nonfiction

1. *Angels: God's Secret Agents*, Billy Graham
2. *Winning Through Intimidation*, Robert Ringer
3. *TM: Discovering Energy and Overcoming Stress*, Harold H. Bloomfield
4. *The Ascent of Man*, Jacob Bronowski
5. *Sylvia Porter's Money Book*, Sylvia Porter
6. *Total Fitness in 30 Minutes a Week*, Laurence E. Morehouse and Leonard Gross
7. *The Bermuda Triangle*, Charles Berlitz with J. Manson Valentine
8. *The Save-Your-Life Diet*, David Reuben
9. *Bring on the Empty Horses*, David Niven
10. *Breach of Faith: The Fall of Richard Nixon*, Theodore H. White

1976

Fiction

1. *Trinity*, Leon Uris
2. *Sleeping Murder*, Agatha Christie
3. *Dolores*, Jacqueline Susann
4. *Storm Warning*, Jack Higgins
5. *The Deep*, Peter Benchley
6. *1876*, Gore Vidal
7. *Slapstick: or, Lonesome No More!*, Kurt Vonnegut
8. *The Lonely Lady*, Harold Robbins
9. *Touch Not the Cat*, Mary Stewart
10. *A Stranger in the Mirror*, Sidney Sheldon

Nonfiction

1. *The Final Days*, Bob Woodward and Carl Bernstein
2. *Roots*, Alex Haley

3. *Your Erroneous Zones*, Dr. Wayne W. Dyer
4. *Passages: The Predictable Crises of Adult Life*, Gail Sheehy
5. *Born Again*, Charles W. Colson
6. *The Grass Is Always Greener over the Septic Tank*, Erma Bombeck
7. *Angels: God's Secret Agents*, Billy Graham
8. *Blind Ambition: The White House Years*, John Dean
9. *The Hite Report: A Nationwide Study of Female Sexuality*, Shere Hite
10. *The Right and the Power: The Prosecution of Watergate*, Leon Jaworski

1977

Fiction

1. *The Silmarillion*, J.R.R. Tolkien; Christopher Tolkien
2. *The Thorn Birds*, Colleen McCullough
3. *Illusions: The Adventures of a Reluctant Messiah*, Richard Bach
4. *The Honourable Schoolboy*, John Le Carré
5. *Oliver's Story*, Erich Segal
6. *Dreams Die First*, Harold Robbins
7. *Beggarman, Thief*, Irwin Shaw
8. *How To Save Your Own Life*, Erica Jong
9. *Delta of Venus: Erotica*, Anaïs Nin
10. *Daniel Martin*, John Fowles

Nonfiction

1. *Roots*, Alex Haley
2. *Looking Out for #1*, Robert Ringer
3. *All Things Wise and Wonderful*, James Herriot
4. *Your Erroneous Zones*, Dr. Wayne W. Dyer
5. *The Book of Lists*, David Wallechinsky, Irving Wallace, and Amy Wallace
6. *The Possible Dream: A Candid Look at Amway*, Charles Paul Conn
7. *The Dragons of Eden: Speculations on the Evolution of Human Intelligence*, Carl Sagan
8. *The Second Ring of Power*, Carlos Castaneda
9. *The Grass Is Always Greener over the Septic Tank*, Erma Bombeck
10. *The Amityville Horror*, Jay Anson

1978

Fiction

1. *Chesapeake*, James A. Michener
2. *War and Remembrance*, Herman Wouk
3. *Fools Die*, Mario Puzo

314

4. *Bloodlines*, Sidney Sheldon
5. *Scruples*, Judith Krantz
6. *Evergreen*, Belva Plain
7. *Illusions: The Adventures of a Reluctant Messiah*, Richard Bach
8. *The Holcroft Covenant*, Robert Ludlum
9. *Second Generation*, Howard Fast
10. *Eye of the Needle*, Ken Follett

Nonfiction

1. *If Life Is a Bowl of Cherries—What Am I Doing in the Pits?*, Erma Bombeck
2. *Gnomes*, Wil Huygen and Rien Poortvliet
3. *The Complete Book of Running*, James Fixx
4. *Mommie Dearest*, Christina Crawford
5. *Pulling Your Own Strings*, Dr. Wayne W. Dyer
6. *RN: The Memoirs of Richard Nixon*, Richard Nixon
7. *A Distant Mirror: The Calamitous Fourteenth Century*, Barbara Tuchman
8. *Faeries*, Brian Froud and Alan Lee
9. *In Search of History: A Personal Adventure*, Theodore H. White
10. *The Muppet Show Book*, the Muppet People

1979

Fiction

1. *The Matarese Circle*, Robert Ludlum
2. *Sophie's Choice*, William Styron
3. *Overload*, Arthur Hailey
4. *Memories of Another Day*, Harold Robbins
5. *Jailbird*, Kurt Vonnegut
6. *The Dead Zone*, Stephen King
7. *The Last Enchantment*, Mary Stewart
8. *The Establishment*, Howard Fast
9. *The Third World War: August 1985*, Gen. Sir John Hackett, et al.
10. *Smiley's People*, John Le Carré

Nonfiction

1. *Aunt Erma's Cope Book*, Erma Bombeck
2. *The Complete Scarsdale Medical Diet*, Herman Tarnower, M.D., and Samm Sinclair Baker
3. *How to Prosper During the Coming Bad Years*, Howard J. Ruff
4. *Cruel Shoes*, Steve Martin
5. *The Pritikin Program for Diet and Exercise*, Nathan Pritikin and Patrick McGrady Jr.
6. *White House Years*, Henry Kissinger

7. *Lauren Bacall By Myself*, Lauren Bacall
8. *The Brethren: Inside the Supreme Court*, Bob Woodward and Scott Armstrong
9. *Restoring the American Dream*, Robert J. Ringer
10. *The Winner's Circle*, Charles Paul Conn

1980

Fiction

1. *The Covenant*, James A. Michener
2. *The Bourne Identity*, Robert Ludlum
3. *Rage of Angels*, Sidney Sheldon
4. *Princess Daisy*, Judith Krantz
5. *Firestarter*, Stephen King
6. *The Key to Rebecca*, Ken Follett
7. *Random Winds*, Belva Plain
8. *The Devil's Alternative*, Frederick Forsyth
9. *The Fifth Horseman*, Larry Collins and Dominique Lapierre
10. *The Spike*, Arnaud de Borchgrave and Robert Moss

Nonfiction

1. *Crisis Investing: Opportunities and Profits in the Coming Great Depression*, Douglas R. Casey
2. *Cosmos*, Carl Sagan
3. *Free to Choose: A Personal Statement*, Milton and Rose Friedman
4. *Anatomy of an Illness as Perceived by the Patient*, Norman Cousins
5. *Thy Neighbor's Wife*, Gay Talese
6. *The Sky's the Limit*, Dr. Wayne W. Dyer
7. *The Third Wave*, Alvin Toffler
8. *Craig Claiborne's Gourmet Diet*, Craig Claiborne with Pierre Franey
9. *Nothing Down*, Robert Allen
10. *Shelley: Also Known as Shirley*, Shelley Winters

1981

Fiction

1. *Noble House*, James Clavell
2. *The Hotel New Hampshire*, John Irving
3. *Cujo*, Stephen King
4. *An Indecent Obsession*, Colleen McCullough
5. *Gorky Park*, Martin Cruz Smith
6. *Masquerade*, Kit Williams
7. *Goodbye, Janette*, Harold Robbins
8. *The Third Deadly Sin*, Lawrence Sanders
9. *The Glitter Dome*, Joseph Wambaugh
10. *No Time for Tears*, Cynthia Freeman

Nonfiction

1. *The Beverly Hills Diet*, Judy Mazel
2. *The Lord God Made Them All*, James Herriot
3. *Richard Simmons' Never-Say-Diet Book*, Richard Simmons
4. *A Light in the Attic*, Shel Silverstein
5. *Cosmos*, Carl Sagan
6. *Better Homes & Gardens New Cook Book*
7. *Miss Piggy's Guide to Life*, Miss Piggy as told to Henry Beard
8. *Weight Watchers 365-Day Menu Cookbook*
9. *You Can Negotiate Anything*, Herb Cohen
10. *A Few Minutes with Andy Rooney*, Andrew A. Rooney

1982

Fiction

1. *E.T., the Extra-Terrestrial Storybook*, William Kotzwinkle
2. *Space*, James A. Michener
3. *The Parsifal Mosaic*, Robert Ludlum
4. *Master of the Game*, Sidney Sheldon
5. *Mistral's Daughter*, Judith Krantz
6. *The Valley of Horses*, Jean M. Auel
7. *Different Seasons*, Stephen King
8. *North and South*, John Jakes
9. *2010: Odyssey Two*, Arthur C. Clarke
10. *The Man from St. Petersburg*, Ken Follett

Nonfiction

1. *Jane Fonda's Workout Book*, Jane Fonda
2. *Living, Loving and Learning*, Leo Buscaglia
3. *And More by Andy Rooney*, Andrew A. Rooney
4. *Better Homes & Gardens New Cookbook*
5. *Life Extension: Adding Years to Your Life And Life to Your Years—A Practical Scientific Approach*, Durk Pearson and Sandy Shaw
6. *When Bad Things Happen to Good People*, Harold S. Kushner
7. *A Few Minutes with Andy Rooney*, Andrew A. Rooney
8. *The Weight Watchers Food Plan Diet Cookbook*, Jean Nidetch
9. *Richard Simmons' Never-Say-Diet Cookbook*, Richard Simmons
10. *No Bad Dogs: The Woodhouse Way*, Barbara Woodhouse

1983

Fiction

1. *Return of the Jedi Storybook*, Joan D. Vinge, adapt.
2. *Poland*, James A. Michener
3. *Pet Sematary*, Stephen King
4. *The Little Drummer Girl*, John Le Carré
5. *Christine*, Stephen King
6. *Changes*, Danielle Steel
7. *The Name of the Rose*, Umberto Eco
8. *White Gold Wielder: Book Three of The Second Chronicles of Thomas Covenant*, Stephen R. Donaldson
9. *Hollywood Wives*, Jackie Collins
10. *The Lonesome Gods*, Louis L'Amour

Nonfiction

1. *In Search of Excellence: Lessons from America's Best-Run Companies*, Thomas J. Peters and Robert H. Waterman Jr.
2. *Megatrends: Ten New Directions Transforming Our Lives*, John Naisbitt
3. *Motherhood: The Second Oldest Profession*, Erma Bombeck
4. *The One Minute Manager*, Kenneth Blanchard and Spencer Johnson
5. *Jane Fonda's Workout Book*, Jane Fonda
6. *The Best of James Herriot*, James Herriot
7. *The Mary Kay Guide to Beauty: Discovering Your Special Look*
8. *On Wings of Eagles*, Ken Follett
9. *Creating Wealth*, Robert G. Allen
10. *The Body Principal: The Exercise Program for Life*, Victoria Principal

1984

Fiction

1. *The Talisman*, Stephen King and Peter Straub
2. *The Aquitaine Progression*, Robert Ludlum
3. *The Sicilian*, Mario Puzo
4. *Love and War*, John Jakes
5. *The Butter Battle Book*, Dr. Seuss
6. *". . . And the Ladies of the Club,"* Helen Hooven Santmyer
7. *The Fourth Protocol*, Frederick Forsyth
8. *Full Circle*, Danielle Steel
9. *The Life and Hard Times of Heidi Abromowitz*, Joan Rivers
10. *Lincoln: A Novel*, Gore Vidal

Nonfiction

1. *Iacocca: An Autobiography*, Lee Iacocca with William Novak
2. *Loving Each Other*, Leo Buscaglia

3. *Eat to Win: The Sports Nutrition Bible*, Robert Haas, M.D.
4. *Pieces of My Mind*, Andrew A. Rooney
5. *Weight Watchers Fast and Fabulous Cookbook*
6. *What They Don't Teach You at Harvard Business School: Notes from a Street-Smart Executive*, Mark H. McCormack
7. *Women Coming of Age*, Jane Fonda with Mignon McCarthy
8. *Moses the Kitten*, James Herriot
9. *The One Minute Salesperson*, Spencer Johnson, M.D., and Larry Wilson
10. *Weight Watchers Quick Start Program Cookbook*, Jean Nidetch

1985

Fiction

1. *The Mammoth Hunters*, Jean M. Auel
2. *Texas*, James A. Michener
3. *Lake Wobegon Days*, Garrison Keillor
4. *If Tomorrow Comes*, Sidney Sheldon
5. *Skeleton Crew*, Stephen King
6. *Secrets*, Danielle Steel
7. *Contact*, Carl Sagan
8. *Lucky*, Jackie Collins
9. *Family Album*, Danielle Steel
10. *Jubal Sackett*, Louis L'Amour

Nonfiction

1. *Iacocca: An Autobiography*, Lee Iacocca with William Novak
2. *Yeager: An Autobiography*, Gen. Chuck Yeager and Leo Janos
3. *Elvis and Me*, Priscilla Beaulieu Presley with Sandra Harmon
4. *Fit for Life*, Harvey and Marilyn Diamond
5. *The Be-Happy Attitudes*, Robert Schuller
6. *Dancing in the Light*, Shirley MacLaine
7. *A Passion for Excellence: The Leadership Difference*, Thomas J. Peters and Nancy K. Austin
8. *The Frugal Gourmet*, Jeff Smith
9. *I Never Played the Game*, Howard Cosell with Peter Bonventre
10. *Dr. Berger's Immune Power Diet*, Stuart M. Berger, M.D.

1986

Fiction

1. *It*, Stephen King
2. *Red Storm Rising*, Tom Clancy
3. *Whirlwind*, James Clavell
4. *The Bourne Supremacy*, Robert Ludlum
5. *Hollywood Husbands*, Jackie Collins
6. *Wanderlust*, Danielle Steel
7. *I'll Take Manhattan*, Judith Krantz

8. *Last of the Breed*, Louis L'Amour
9. *The Prince of Tides*, Pat Conroy
10. *A Perfect Spy*, John Le Carré

Nonfiction

1. *Fatherhood*, Bill Cosby
2. *Fit for Life*, Harvey and Marilyn Diamond
3. *His Way: The Unauthorized Biography of Frank Sinatra*, Kitty Kelley
4. *The Rotation Diet*, Martin Katahn
5. *You're Only Old Once*, Dr. Seuss
6. *Callanetics: Ten Years Younger in Ten Hours*, Callan Pinckney
7. *The Frugal Gourmet Cooks with Wine*, Jeff Smith
8. *Be Happy—You Are Loved!*, Robert H. Schuller
9. *Word for Word*, Andrew A. Rooney
10. *James Herriot's Dog Stories*, James Herriot

1987

Fiction

1. *The Tommyknockers*, Stephen King
2. *Patriot Games*, Tom Clancy
3. *Kaleidoscope*, Danielle Steel
4. *Misery*, Stephen King
5. *Leaving Home: A Collection of Lake Wobegon Stories*, Garrison Keillor
6. *Windmills of the Gods*, Sidney Sheldon
7. *Presumed Innocent*, Scott Turow
8. *Fine Things*, Danielle Steel
9. *Heaven and Hell*, John Jakes
10. *The Eyes of the Dragon*, Stephen King

Nonfiction

1. *Time Flies*, Bill Cosby
2. *Spycatcher: The Candid Autobiography of a Senior Intelligence Officer*, Peter Wright with Paul Greengrass
3. *Family: The Ties That Bind . . . and Gag!*, Erma Bombeck
4. *Veil: The Secret Wars of the CIA, 1981–1987*, Bob Woodward
5. *A Day in the Life of America*, Rick Smolan and David Cohen
6. *The Great Depression of 1990*, Ravi Batra
7. *It's All in the Playing*, Shirley MacLaine
8. *Man of the House: The Life and Political Memoirs of Speaker Tip O'Neill*, Thomas P. O'Neill Jr. with William Novak
9. *The Frugal Gourmet Cooks American*, Jeff Smith
10. *The Closing of the American Mind*, Allan Bloom

1988

Fiction

1. *The Cardinal of the Kremlin*, Tom Clancy
2. *The Sands of Time*, Sidney Sheldon
3. *Zoya*, Danielle Steel
4. *The Icarus Agenda*, Robert Ludlum
5. *Alaska*, James A. Michener
6. *Till We Meet Again*, Judith Krantz
7. *The Queen of the Damned*, Anne Rice
8. *To Be the Best*, Barbara Taylor Bradford
9. *One: A Novel*, Richard Bach
10. *Mitla Pass*, Leon Uris

Nonfiction

1. *The 8-Week Cholesterol Cure*, Robert E. Kowalski
2. *Talking Straight*, Lee Iacocca with Sonny Kleinfield
3. *A Brief History of Time: From the Big Bang to Black Holes*, Steven W. Hawking
4. *Trump: The Art of the Deal*, Donald J. Trump with Tony Schwartz
5. *Gracie: A Love Story*, George Burns
6. *Elizabeth Takes Off*, Elizabeth Taylor
7. *Swim with the Sharks without Being Eaten Alive*, Harvey MacKay
8. *Christmas in America*, David Cohen, editor
9. *Weight Watchers Quick Success Program Book*, Jean Nidetch
10. *Moonwalk*, Michael Jackson

1989

Fiction

1. *Clear and Present Danger*, Tom Clancy
2. *The Dark Half*, Stephen King
3. *Daddy*, Danielle Steel
4. *Star*, Danielle Steel
5. *Caribbean*, James A. Michener
6. *The Satanic Verses*, Salman Rushdie
7. *The Russia House*, John Le Carré
8. *The Pillars of the Earth*, Ken Follet
9. *California Gold*, John Jakes
10. *While My Pretty One Sleeps*, Mary Higgins Clark

Nonfiction

1. *All I Really Need To Know I Learned in Kindergarten: Uncommon Thoughts on Common Things*, Robert Fulghum
2. *Wealth Without Risk: How To Develop a Personal Fortune Without Going Out on a Limb*, Charles J. Givens
3. *A Woman Named Jackie*, C. David Heymann

4. *It Was on Fire When I Lay Down on It*, Robert Fulghum
5. *Better Homes and Gardens New Cook Book*
6. *The Way Things Work*, David Macaulay
7. *It's Always Something*, Gilda Radner
8. *Roseanne: My Life as a Woman*, Roseanne Barr
9. *The Frugal Gourmet Cooks Three Ancient Cuisines: China, Greece, and Rome*, Jeff Smith
10. *My Turn: The Memoirs of Nancy Reagan*, Nancy Reagan with William Novak

1990

Fiction

1. *The Plains of Passage*, Jean M. Auel
2. *Four Past Midnight*, Stephen King
3. *The Burden of Proof*, Scott Turow
4. *Memories of Midnight*, Sidney Sheldon
5. *Message from Nam*, Danielle Steel
6. *The Bourne Ultimatum*, Robert Ludlum
7. *The Stand: The Complete and Uncut Edition*, Stephen King
8. *Lady Boss*, Jackie Collins
9. *The Witching Hour*, Anne Rice
10. *September*, Rosamunde Pilcher

Nonfiction

1. *A Life on the Road*, Charles Kuralt
2. *The Civil War*, Geoffrey C. Ward with Ric Burns and Ken Burns
3. *The Frugal Gourmet on Our Immigrant Heritage: Recipes You Should Have Gotten from Your Grandmother*, Jeff Smith
4. *Better Homes and Gardens New Cook Book*
5. *Financial Self-Defense: How To Win the Fight for Financial Freedom*, Charles J. Givens
6. *Homecoming: Reclaiming and Championing Your Inner Child*, John Bradshaw
7. *Wealth Without Risk: How To Develop a Personal Fortune Without Going Out on a Limb*, Charles J. Givens
8. *Bo Knows Bo*, Bo Jackson and Dick Schaap
9. *An American Life: An Autobiography*, Ronald Reagan
10. *Megatrends 2000: Ten New Directions for the 1990s*, John Naisbitt and Patricia Aburdene

1991

Fiction

1. *Scarlett: The Sequel to Margaret Mitchell's "Gone with the Wind,"* Alexandra Ripley
2. *The Sum of All Fears*, Tom Clancy
3. *Needful Things*, Stephen King
4. *No Greater Love*, Danielle Steel
5. *Heartbeat*, Danielle Steel
6. *The Doomsday Conspiracy*, Sidney Sheldon
7. *The Firm*, John Grisham
8. *Night Over Water*, Ken Follet
9. *Remember*, Barbara Taylor Bradford
10. *Loves Music, Loves to Dance*, Mary Higgins Clark

Nonfiction

1. *Me: Stories of My Life*, Katharine Hepburn
2. *Nancy Reagan: The Unauthorized Biography*, Kitty Kelley
3. *Uh-Oh: Some Observations from Both Sides of the Refrigerator Door*, Robert Fulghum
4. *Under Fire: An American Story*, Oliver North with William Novak
5. *Final Exit: The Practicalities of Self-Deliverance and Assisted Suicide for the Dying*, Derek Humphry
6. *When You Look Like Your Passport Photo, It's Time to Go Home*, Erma Bombeck
7. *More Wealth Without Risk*, Charles J. Givens
8. *Den of Thieves*, James B. Stewart
9. *Childhood*, Bill Cosby
10. *Financial Self-Defense*, Charles J. Givens

1992

Fiction

1. *Dolores Claiborne*, Stephen King
2. *The Pelican Brief*, John Grisham
3. *Gerald's Game*, Stephen King
4. *Mixed Blessings*, Danielle Steel
5. *Jewels*, Danielle Steel
6. *The Stars Shine Down*, Sidney Sheldon
7. *Tale of the Body Thief*, Anne Rice
8. *Mexico*, James A. Michener
9. *Waiting to Exhale*, Terry McMillan
10. *All Around the Town*, Mary Higgins Clark

Nonfiction

1. *The Way Things Ought To Be*, Rush Limbaugh
2. *It Doesn't Take a Hero: The Autobiography*, Gen. H. Norman Schwarzkopf

3. *How to Satisfy a Woman Every Time*, Naura Hayden
4. *Every Living Thing*, James Herriot
5. *A Return to Love*, Marianne Williamson
6. *Sam Walton: Made in America*, Sam Walton
7. *Diana: Her True Story*, Andrew Morton
8. *Truman*, David McCullough
9. *Silent Passage*, Gail Sheehy
10. *Sex*, Madonna

1993

Fiction

1. *The Bridges of Madison County*, Robert James Waller
2. *The Client*, John Grisham
3. *Slow Waltz at Cedar Bend*, Robert James Waller
4. *Without Remorse*, Tom Clancy
5. *Nightmares and Dreamscapes*, Stephen King
6. *Vanished*, Danielle Steel
7. *Lasher*, Anne Rice
8. *Pleading Guilty*, Scott Turow
9. *Like Water for Chocolate*, Laura Esquivel
10. *The Scorpio Illusion*, Robert Ludlum

Nonfiction

1. *See, I Told You So*, Rush Limbaugh
2. *Private Parts*, Howard Stern
3. *Seinlanguage*, Jerry Seinfeld
4. *Embraced by the Light*, Betty J. Eadie with Curtis Taylor
5. *Ageless Body, Timeless Mind*, Deepak Chopra
6. *Stop the Insanity*, Susan Powter
7. *Women Who Run with the Wolves*, Clarissa Pinkola Estes

8. *Men Are from Mars, Women Are from Venus*, John Gray
9. *The Hidden Life of Dogs*, Elizabeth Marshall Thomas
10. *And If You Play Golf, You're My Friend*, Harvey Penick with Bud Shrake

1994

Fiction

1. *The Chamber*, John Grisham
2. *Debt of Honor*, Tom Clancy
3. *The Celestine Prophecy*, James Redfield
4. *The Gift*, Danielle Steel
5. *Insomnia*, Steven King
6. *Politically Correct Bedtime Stories*, James Finn Garner
7. *Wings*, Danielle Steel
8. *Accident*, Danielle Steel
9. *The Bridges of Madison County*, Robert James Waller
10. *Disclosure*, Michael Crichton
11. *Nothing Lasts Forever*, Sidney Sheldon
12. *Taltos*, Anne Rice
13. *Dark Rivers of the Heart*, Dean Koontz
14. *The Lottery Winner*, Mary Higgins Clark
15. *Remember Me*, Mary Higgins Clark
16. *The Body Farm*, Patricia Cornwell/
17. *"K" Is for Killer*, Sue Grafton
18. *Everything to Gain*, Barbara Taylor Bradford
19. *Spencerville*, Nelson DeMille
20. *Wild Horses*, Dick Francis
21. *Inca Gold*, Clive Cussler
22. *Mutant Message Down Under*, Marlo Morgan
23. *Lord of Chaos*, Robert Jordan
24. *Fatal Cure*, Robin Cook
25. *Family Blessings*, LaVyrle Spencer

Nonfiction

1. *In the Kitchen with Rosie*, Rosie Daley
2. *Men Are from Mars, Women Are from Venus*, John Gray
3. *Crossing the Threshold of Hope*, John Paul II.
4. *Magic Eye I*, N.E. Thing Enterprises
5. *The Book of Virtues*, William J. Bennett
6. *Magic Eye II*, N.E. Thing Enterprises
7. *Embraced by the Light*, Betty J. Eadie with Curtis Taylor
8. *Don't Stand Too Close to a Naked Man*, Tim Allen
9. *Couplehood*, Paul Reiser
10. *Magic Eye III*, N.E. Thing Enterprises
11. *Dolly*, Dolly Parton
12. *James Herriott's Cat Stories*, James Herriott
13. *Barbara Bush*, Barbara Bush
14. *Nicole Brown Simpson*, Faye Resnick
15. *The Bubba Gump Shrimp Co. Cookbook*, Oxmoor House/Leisure Arts
16. *The Agenda*, Bob Woodward
17. *What Your Mother Couldn't Tell You and Your Father Didn't Know*, John Gray
18. *Reba: My Story*, Reba McIntire
19. *Standing Firm*, Dan Quayle
20. *The Weight Watchers Complete Cookbook and Program Basics*
21. *Old Songs in a New Cafe*, Robert James Waller
22. *Baseball*, Ken Burns and Geoffrey C. Ward
23. *First Things First*, Stephen R. Covey and A. Roger Miller
24. *The Hot Zone*, Richard Preston
25. *Midnight in the Garden of Good and Evil*, John Berendt

BESTSELLING CHILDREN'S BOOKS

Publishers Weekly started breaking out a separate children's bestseller list recently; here are results from the past three decidedly Disney-dominated years.

1992

1. *Disney's Aladdin*, adapted by Karen Kreider, illustrated by Darrell Baker
2. *Aladdin*, Walt Disney Staff
3. *The Sign of the Seahorse*, Graeme Base
4. *Walt Disney's The Little Mermaid*, adapted by Betty Birney, illustrated by Kerry Martin and Fred Marvin
5. *Walt Disney's Pinocchio*, adapted by Diane Muldrow, illustrated by Fred Marvin
6. *Walt Disney's Bambi*, adapted by Denise Lewis Patrick, illustrated by Mones
7. *Walt Disney's Snow White*, adapted by Denise Lewis Patrick, illustrated by Mones
8. *Walt Disney's Dumbo*, adapted by Rita Balducci, illustrated by Phil Ortiz and Diana Wakeman
9. *Walt Disney's Cinderella*, adapted by Rita Balducci, illustrated by Mones
10. *Brown Bear, Brown Bear, What Do You See?* (25th anniversary edition), Bill Martin Jr., illustrated by Eric Carle

1993

1. *Barney's Farm Animals*, Kimberly Kearns and Marie O'Brien, illustrated by Karen Malzeke-McDonald
2. *Barney's Favorite Mother Goose Rhymes*, Stephen White, illustrated by Mary Grace Eubank
3. *Baby Bop's Toys*, Kimberly Kearns and Marie O'Brien
4. *Barney's Color Surprise*, Mary Ann Dudko and Margie Larsen
5. *Baby Bop's Counting Book*, Mary Ann Dudko and Margie Larsen
6. *Where's Waldo? In Hollywood*, Martin Handford
7. *Aladdin (Disney Classic)*
8. *Baby Bop Discovers Shapes*, Stephen White, illustrated by Larry Daste
9. *Poky Puppy's First Christmas*, Justine Korman, illustrated by Jean Chandler
10. *Beauty and the Beast: Teapot's Tale*, Justine Korman, illustrated by Peter Emslie

1994

1. *The Lion King (Classic)*, Disney/Mouse Works
2. *The Lion King (Little Golden Book)*, Justine Korman, illustrated by D. Williams
3. *The Lion King (Big Golden Book)*, Justine Korman, illustrated by H.R. Russell
4. *Simba Roars!*, Disney/Mouse Works
5. *Aladdin's Magic Carpet Ride*, T. Slater Margulies
6. *The Christmas Bunny*, Arnold Rabin, illustrated by Carolyn Ewing
7. *The Lion King Illustrated Classic*, illustrated by Michael Humphries and Marshall Toomey
8. *The Lion King (Sturdy Shape)*, Mary Packard, illustrated by Darrell Baker
9. *The Sorcerer's Apprentice*, Don Ferguson
10. *The Very Hungry Caterpillar Board Book*, Eric Carle

LITERARY LISTENING: BESTSELLING BOOKS ON TAPE, 1994

Americans have been doing a lot of reading behind the wheel, and as this list of bestselling books on tape reveals, our tastes are pretty broad. Based on 1994's most successful audio books at Waldenbooks and Barnes & Noble, this list is not an audited ranking of bestsellers, but since the two giant chains sell a significant number of the nation's audio books, it does give us a good gauge of the year's most popular listening.

1. *The Chamber*, John Grisham
2. *Seven Habits of Highly Effective People*, Stephen R. Covey
3. *Men Are from Mars, Women Are from Venus*, John Gray
4. *Debt of Honor*, Tom Clancy
5. *Disclosure*, Miichael Crichton
6. *First Things First*, Stephen R. Covey and A. Roger Miller
7. *The Celestine Prophecy*, James Redfield
8. *See, I Told You So*, Rush Limbaugh
9. *The Client*, John Grisham
10. *The Lion King Read Along*
11. *Without Remorse*, Tom Clancy
12. *Forrest Gump*, Winston Groom
13. *The Shadow* (two-pack)
14. *Growing Younger*, Deepak Chopra
15. *Interview With the Vampire*, Anne Rice

THE PEOPLE BOOKSHELF

PEOPLE hasn't been reviewing books long enough to hazard a best-of-the-century list, but here are the books we loved the most over the past 18 years.

FICTION

The Accidental Tourist, Anne Tyler

All the Pretty Horses, Cormac McCarthy

Anagrams, Lorrie Moore

Anton the Dove Fancier, Bernard Gotfryd

August, Judith Rossner

Before and After, Rosellen Brown

Beloved, Toni Morrison

Birdy, William Wharton

The Blooding, Joseph Wambaugh

Body and Soul, Frank Conroy

The Bonfire of the Vanities, Tom Wolfe

Breathing Lessons, Anne Tyler

Cat's Eye, Margaret Atwood

Clockers, Richard Price

Collaborators, Janet Kauffman

The Collected Stories, Isaac Bashevis Singer

The Color Purple, Alice Walker

A Confederacy of Dunces, John Kennedy Toole

Dinner at the Homesick Restaurant, Anne Tyler

The Dragons of Eden, Carl Sagan

Dutch Shea Jr., John Gregory Dunne

East Is East, T. Coraghessan Boyle

Ellis Island, Mark Helprin

Enchantment, Daphne Merkin

Eye of the Needle, Ken Follett

Fanny, Erica Jong

Final Payments, Mary Gordon

The Firm, John Grisham

The First Man in Rome, Colleen McCullough

For Love, Sue Miller

Foreign Affairs, Alison Lurie

Get Shorty, Elmore Leonard

The Glass House, Laura Furman

The Good Mother, Sue Miller

Gorky Park, Martin Cruz Smith

Happy To Be There, Garrison Keillor

Her First American, Lore Segal

The Honourable Schoolboy, John Le Carré

The House of the Spirits, Isabel Allende

Illumination Night, Abbie Hoffman

An Indecent Obsession, Colleen McCollough

Labrava, Elmore Leonard

Lake Wobegon Days, Garrison Keillor

Lancelot, Walker Percy

A Lesson Before Dying, Ernest J. Gaines

Libra, Don DeLillo

A Light in the Attic, Shel Silverstein

Life Its Ownself, Dan Jenkins

Love in the Time of Cholera, Gabriel García Márquez

Machine Dreams, Jayne Anne Phillips

The Mambo Kings Play Songs of Love, Oscar Hijuelos

Maus: A Survivor's Tale, II: And Here My Troubles Begin, Art Spiegelman

Me and My Baby View the Eclipse, Lee Smith

Memoirs of an Invisible Man, H. F. Saint

Monkeys, Susan Minot

Monsignor Quixote, Graham Greene

More Die of Heartbreak, Saul Bellow

Music for Chameleons, Truman Capote

The Natural Man, Ed McClanahan

Noble House, James Clavell

Owning Jolene, Shelby Hearon

Patrimony, Philip Roth

Perfume, Patrick Süskind

Poodle Springs, Raymond Chandler and Robert B. Parker

The Pope of Greenwich Village, Vincent Park

Presumed Innocent, Scott Turow

The Progress of Love, Alice Munro

Quinn's Book, William Kennedy

Rabbit at Rest, John Updike

The Robber Bride, Margaret Atwood

Roger's Version, John Updike

The Russia House, John Le Carré

Salvador, Joan Didion

The Secret History, Donna Tartt

Seventh Heaven, Alice Hoffman

She's Come Undone, Wally Lamb

The Sicilian, Mario Puzo

Smilla's Sense of Snow, Peter Hoeg

A Soldier of the Great War, Mark Helprin

Sophie's Choice, William Styron

Talking to the Dead, Sylvia Watanabe

Tracks, Louise Erdrich

The Tree of Life, Hugh Nissenson

True Confessions, John Gregory Dunne

The Twenty-Seventh City, Jonathan Franzen

Typical American, Gish Jen

Waiting to Exhale, Terry McMillan

The White Hotel, D. M. Thomas

Winter's Tale, Mark Helprin

World's Fair, E. L. Doctorow

The Yellow Wind, David Grossman

NONFICTION

American Caesar, William Manchester

American Prospects, Joel Sternfeld

Backlash, Susan Faludi

Best Intentions, Robert Sam Anson

The Best of Dear Abby, Abigail Van Buren

Blue Highways, William Least Heat Moon

The Bookmakers's Daughter, Shirley Abbott

Cameraworks, David Hockney

The Chimpanzees of Gombe, Jane Goodall

The Culture of Narcissism, Christopher Lasch

Dave Barry Slept Here, Dave Barry

Den of Thieves, James B. Stewart

The Devil's Candy, Julie Salamon

A Distant Mirror, Barbara Tuchman

The Duke of Deception, Geoffrey Wolff

Edie, Jean Stein, edited with George Plimpton

Edith Sitwell, Victoria Glendinning

The Fatal Shore, Robert Hughes

Fatal Vision, Joe McGinniss

Fatherhood, Bill Cosby

The Forbidden Experiment, Roger Shattuck

Fungus the Bogeyman, Raymond Briggs

The Girl I Left Behind, Jane O'Reilly

The Glass House, Laura Furman

Goldwyn: A Biography, A. Scott Berg

"The Good War," Studs Terkel

The Hidden Life of Dogs, Elizabeth Marshall

Home Before Dark, Susan Cheever

Hometown, Peter Davis

House, Tracy Kidder

I Dream s World, Brian Lanker

In and Out of the Garden, Sara Midda

Ingrid Bergman: My Story, Ingrid Bergman and Alan Burgess

January Sun, Richard Stengel

The Kennedys: An American Dream, Peter Collier and David Horowitz

Kissinger, Walter Isaacson

The Knife and Gun Club, Eugene Richards

The Last Lion, William Manchester

Laura Z., A Life, Laura Z. Hobson

Lauren Bacall By Myself, Lauren Bacall

Lenin's Tomb, David Remnick

A Life of Picasso, John Richardson

Little League Confidential, Bill Geist

The Lives of John Lennon, Albert Goldman

Loitering with Intent, Peter O'Toole

Maida Heatter's Book of Great Chocolate Desserts, Maida Heatter

The Man Who Mistook His Wife for a Hat, Oliver Sacks

Means of Ascent, Robert A. Caro

The Medusa and the Snail, Lewis Thomas

Midair, Frank Conroy

Miss Manners' Guide to Excruciatingly Correct Behavior, Judith Martin

Mister Rogers Talks with Parents, Fred Rogers and Barry Head

Moonshine, Alec Wilkinson

The Non-Runner's Book, Vic Ziegel and Lewis Grossberger

On Boxing, Joyce Carol Oates

On Photography, Susan Sontag

Pablo Picasso, A Retrospective, edited by William Rubin

Payback, Joe Klein

Photoportraits, Henri Cartier-Bresson

President Kennedy, Richard Reeves

The Ragman's Son, Kirk Douglas

The Rise of Theodore Roosevelt, Edmund Morris

A Rumor of War, Philip Caputo

Saul Steinberg, Harold Rosenberg

Serpentine, Thomas Thompson

Side Effects, Woody Allen

The Sketchbooks of Picasso, Pablo Picasso

The Snow Leopard, Peter Mathiessen

The Story of English, Robert McCrum, William Cran, and Robert MacNeil

Sylvia Plachy's Unguided Tour, Sylvia Plachy

The Teamsters, Steven Brill

The Years of Lyndon Johnson: The Path to Power, Robert A. Caro

Truman, David McCullough

Why Are They Weeping?, photographed by David C. Turnley and written by Alan Cowell

Workers, Sebastião Salgado

A Writer's Beginnings, Eudora Welty

THE PEOPLE TRASH HEAP

PEOPLE's reviewers read these books because they had to—it's their job. But you have a choice. The following is a selection of books Picks & Pans reviewers judged as the worst—or most over-rated—from the past 18 years.

FICTION

Alnilam, James Dickey

American Psycho, Bret Easton Ellis

Ancient Evenings, Norman Mailer

Answer as a Man, Taylor Caldwell

Any Woman's Blues, Erica Jong

Ascent Into Hell, Andrew M. Greeley

Beast, Peter Benchley

The Big Hype, Avery Corman

A Bloodsmoor Romance, Joyce Carol Oates

The Bourne Ultimatum, Robert Ludlum

Brain, Robin Cook

Children of Light, Robert Stone

The Children's Story, James Clavell

Christine, Stephen King

The Coup, John Updike

Daddy, Danielle Steel

The Devil's Alternative, Frederick Forsyth

Doctors, Erich Segal

Elvis, Albert Goldman

Empress, Sylvia Wallace

Fever, Robin Cook

Floating Dragon, Peter Straub

.44, Jimmy Breslin and Dick Schaap

Free to Love, Ivana Trump

Friends in High Places, John Weitz

The Girl of the Sea of Cortez, Peter Benchley

Godplayer, Robin Cook

Happy Endings, Sally Quinn

Heartburn, Nora Ephron

The Holcroft Covenant, Robert Ludlum

Home Front, Patti Davis with Maureen Strange Foster

The Hope, Herman Wouk

A House of Secrets, Patti Davis

I Dream a World, Brian Lanker

Illusions: The Adventures of a Reluctant Messiah, Richard Bach

In Praise of the Stepmother, Mario Vargas Llosa

Inside, Outside, Herman Wouk

The Island, Peter Benchley

Lace, Shirley Conran

Lasher, Anne Rice

The Last Days of America, Paul Erdman

Legion, William Peter Blatty

Lord of the Dance, Andrew M. Greeley

Love and War, John Jakes

Lucky, Jackie Collins

Lust, Susan Minot

The Mammoth Hunters, Jean M. Auel

Manhattan, Neal Travis

A Matter of Honor, Jeffrey Archer

Maybe, Lillian Hellman

Megan's Book of Divorce, Erica Jong

Memories of Another Day, Harold Robbins

Men in Love, Nancy Friday

The Men's Club, Leonard Michaels

Message from Nam, Danielle Steel

Mindbend, Robin Cook

The Minstrel, Bernard Benson

Monímbo, Robert Moss and Arnaud de Borchgrave

The Mosquito Coast, Paul Theroux

The Mummy, Anne Rice

Murder in the White House, Margaret Truman

Nature's End, Whitley Streiber

and James Kunetka

The Ninth Configuration, William Peter Blatty

Of Love and Shadows, Isabel Allende

The Old Neighborhood, Avery Corman

Oliver's Story, Erich Segal

The Origin, Irving Stone

Outbreak, Robin Cook

The Paper Men, William Golding

Parachutes and Kisses, Erica Jong

The Pigeon, Patrick Süskind

The Pillars of the Earth, Ken Follett

Pinball, Jerzy Kosinski

The Plagiarist, Benjamin Cheever

Postcards from the Edge, Carrie Fisher

A Prayer for Owen Meany, John Irving

Prime Time, Joan Collins

"Q" Clearance, Peter Benchley

Queen of the Damned, Anne Rice

Regrets Only, Sally Quinn

Rock Star, Jackie Collins

The Runaway Soul, Harold Brodkey

S., John Updike

Sailor Song, Ken Kesey

Savages, Shirley Conran

Scruples, Judith Krantz

See You Later, Alligator, William F. Buckley Jr.

Slaves of New York, Tama Janowitz

Slow Waltz at Cedar Bend, Robert James Waller

Smart Women, Judy Blume

Spellbinder, Harold Robbins

Sphinx, Robin Cook

Star, Danielle Steel

The Story of Henri Todd, William F. Buckley Jr.

Story of My Life, Jay McInerney

The Talisman, Stephen King and Peter Straub

The Temple of My Familiar, Alice Walker

Texas, James Michener

Tinsel, William Goldman

Vox, Nicholson Baker

The Walnut Door, John Hersey

West of Sunset, Dirk Bogarde

Whirlwind, James Clavell

The Winners, Dominick Dunne

NONFICTION

An Affair to Remember, Maureen Donaldson and William Royce

Among the Porcupines, Carol Matthau

Andrew Wyeth: The Helga Pictures, John Wilmerding

Bardot Deneuve Fonda, Roger Vadim

The Beverly Hills Diet, Judy Mazel

Beyond Reason, Margaret Trudeau

Blown Away, A. E. Hotchner

The Book of Lists, David Wallechinsky, Irving Wallace, and Amy Wallace

Brando for Breakfast, Anna Kashfi and E. P. Stein

Brother Billy, Ruth Carter Stapleton

Bus 9 to Paradise, Leo Buscaglia

Cary Grant: The Lonely Heart, Charles Higham and Roy Moseley

Character: America's Search for Leadership, Gail Sheehy

Cruel Shoes, Steve Martin

Dance with the Devil, Kirk Douglas

Dancing in the Light, Shirley MacLaine

Elizabeth Taylor: The Last Star, Kitty Kelley

Family—The Ties That Bind . . . and Gag!, Erma Bombeck

Feminine Force: Release the Power Within to Create the Life You Deserve, Georgette Mosbacher

Flight of the Avenger: George Bush at War and in Love, Joe Hyams

Garbo: Her Story, Antoni Gronowicz

Give War a Chance, P. J. O'Rourke

Glory Days: Bruce Springsteen in the 1980s, Dave Marsh

Good Guys, Bad Guys, Shere Hite and Kate Colleran

Having It All, Helen Gurley Brown

The Hite Report on Male Sexuality, Shere Hite

How to Take Charge of Your Life, Bernard Berkowitz and Mildred Newman

I Remember, Dan Rather

In the American West, Richard Avedon

It's All in the Playing, Shirley MacLaine

The Jackson Phenomenon, Elizabeth O. Colton

Just Enough Rope, Joan Braden

The Killing of the Unicorn, Peter Bogdanovich

The Last Brother, Joe McGinniss

Laurence Olivier: A Biography, Donald Spoto

Life's Little Instruction Book, H. Jackson Brown Jr.

The Linda Evans Beauty and Exercise Book, Linda Evans

The Lives of John Lennon, Albert Goldman

Metropolitan Life, Fran Lebowitz

More Memories, Ralph Emery

Not That You Asked, Andrew A. Rooney

Now You Know, Kitty Dukakis

Number One, Billy Martin and Peter Golenbock

On Your Own, Brooke Shields

The One Minute Father, Spencer Johnson, M.D.

The One Minute Mother, Spencer Johnson, M.D.

Out on a Limb, Shirley MacLaine

A Place at the Table, Bruce Bawer

The Power to Heal, edited by Rick Smolan, Phillip Moffitt, and Matthew Naythons, M.D.

Pulling Your Own Strings, Dr. Wayne Dyer

Restoring the American Dream, Robert Ringer

Revolution from Within, Gloria Steinem

RN: The Memoirs of Richard Nixon, Richard Nixon

Running and Being, Dr. George Sheehan

The Second Seduction, Frances Lear

Secrets of a Sparrow, Diana Ross

Sex, Madonna

Shelley: Also Known As Shirley, Shelley Winters

Social Studies, Fran Lebowitz

Tennessee: Cry of the Heart, Dotson Rader

Thy Neighbor's Wife, Gay Talese

Transformation, Whitley Streiber

Uh-Oh, Robert Fulghum

Wasted: The Preppie Murder, Linda Wolfe

Willie, Willie Nelson with Bud Shrake

Women and Love, Shere Hite

Women's Work, Anne Tolstoi Wallach

Woody Allen: A Biography, Eric Lax

BIBLIOGRAPHIES OF LEADING AUTHORS

These are complete listings for a broad selection of the most popular, most admired, most discussed, and most eagerly devoured authors today. For each, all full-length works, poetry, and plays are listed, followed by the year of publication.

MARGARET ATWOOD

Fiction
The Edible Woman (1969)
Surfacing (1972)
Lady Oracle (1976)
Dancing Girls (1977)
Life Before Man (1979)
Bodily Harm (1981)
Murder in the Dark (1983)
Bluebeard's Egg (1983)
The Handmaid's Tale (1985)
Cat's Eye (1988)
Wilderness Tips (1991)
Good Bones and Simple Murders (1992)
The Robber Bride (1993)

Poetry
The Circle Game (1964)
The Animals in That Country (1968)
The Journals of Susanna Moodie (1970)
Procedures for Underground (1970)
Power Politics (1971)
You Are Happy (1974)
Two-Headed Poems (1978)
True Stories (1981)
Snake Poems (1983)
Interlunar (1984)
Morning in the Burned House (1995)

Children's books
Up in the Tree (1978)
Anna's Pet (1980)
For the Birds (1990)

Nonfiction
Survival: A Thematic Guide to Canadian Literature (1972)
Days of the Rebels, 1815–1840 (1977)
Second Words (1982)

SAUL BELLOW

Fiction
Dangling Man (1944)
The Victim (1947)
The Adventures of Augie March (1953; National Book Award)
Seize the Day (1956)
Henderson the Rain King (1959)
Herzog (1964; National Book Award)
Mr. Sammler's Planet (1970; National Book Award)
Humbolt's Gift (1975; Pulitzer Prize)
The Dean's December (1982)
More Die of Heartbreak (1987)

Nonfiction
To Jerusalem and Back: A Personal Account (1976)
It All Adds Up (1994)

Play
The Last Analysis, a Play (produced 1964)

Nobel Prize for Literature, 1976

TOM CLANCY

Fiction
The Hunt for Red October (1984)
Red Storm Rising (1986)
Patriot Games (1987)
The Cardinal of the Kremlin (1988)
Clear and Present Danger (1989)
The Sum of All Fears (1991)
Without Remorse (1993)
Debt of Honor (1994)

Nonfiction
Submarine: A Guided Tour Inside a Nuclear Warship (1993)
Armored Cav: A Guided Tour of an Armored Cavalry Regiment (1994)

PAT CONROY

Fiction
The Boo (1970)
The Water Is Wide (1972)
The Great Santini (1976)
The Lords of Discipline (1980)
The Prince of Tides (1986)
Beach Music (1995)

MICHAEL CRICHTON

Fiction
The Andromeda Strain (1969)
The Terminal Man (1972)
Westworld (screenplay, 1975)
The Great Train Robbery (1975)
Eaters of the Dead (1976)
Congo (1980)
Sphere (1987)
Jurassic Park (1990)
Rising Sun (1992)
Disclosure (1994)
The Lost World (1995)

Fiction written as John Lange
Odds On (1966)
Scratch One (1967)
Easy Go (1968; re-published as The Last Tomb, 1974)
The Venom Business (1969)
Zero Cool (1970)
Drug of Choice (1970)
Grave Descend (1970)
Binary (1972)

Fiction written as Jeffrey Hudson
A Case of Need (1968)

Fiction written as Michael Douglas (with brother Douglas Crichton)
Dealing, Or the Berkeley-to-Boston Forty-Brick Lost-Bag Blues (1971)

Nonfiction
Five Patients: The Hospital Explained (1970)
Jasper Johns (1977)

Electronic Life: How To Think about Computers (1983)
Travels (autobiography, 1988)

ROBERTSON DAVIES

Fiction
The Diary of Samuel Marchbanks (1947)
The Table Talk of Samuel Marchbanks (1949)
Tempest-Tost (1951)
Leaven of Malice (1954)
A Mixture of Frailties (1958)
Samuel Marchbanks' Almanack (1967)
Fifth Business (1970)
The Manticore (1972)
World of Wonders (1975)
The Rebel Angels (1981)
High Spirits (1982)
What's Bred in the Bone (1985)
The Papers of Samuel Marchbanks (1985)
The Lyre of Orpheus (1988)
Murther and Walking Spirits (1991)
The Cunning Man (1994)

Nonfiction
Shakespeare's Boy Actors (1939)
Shakespeare for Young Players: A Junior Course (1942)
Renown at Stratford (coauthor, 1953)
Twice Have the Trumpets Sounded (coauthor, 1954)
Thrice the Brinded Cat Hath Mew'd (coauthor, 1955)
A Voice from the Attic (1960)
The Heart of a Merry Christmas (1970)
Stephen Leacock (1970)
Feast of Stephen (1970)
The Revels History of Drama in English, Vol. 6: 1750–1880 (coauthor, 1975)
One Half of Robertson Davies: Provocative Pronounce-

ments on a Wide Rage of
Topics (1977)

*The Enthusiasms of Robertson
Davies* (1979)

*Robertson Davies: The Well-Tem-
pered Critic: One Man's
View of Theatre and Letters
in Canada* (1981)

The Mirror of Nature (1983)

Reading and Writing (1993)

Plays
Fortune, My Foe (1948)

At My Heart's Core (1952)

A Masque of Aesop (1952)

A Jig for Gypsy (1954)

Love and Libel (based on *Leaven
of Malice*, 1960)

A Masque of Mr. Punch (1962)

The Voice of the People (1968)

Hunting Stuart (1972)

King Phoenix (1972)

General Confession (1972)

Brothers in the Black Art (1974)

Question Time (1975)

Pontiac and the Green Man
(1977)

E. L. DOCTOROW

Fiction
Welcome to Hard Times (1960)

Big as Life (1966)

The Book of Daniel (1971)

Ragtime (1975; National Book
Critics Circle Award)

Loon Lake (1980)

World's Fair (1985)

Billy Bathgate (1989; National
Book Critics Circle Award)

The Waterworks (1994)

Nonfiction
*Jack London, Hemingway, and
the Constitution: Selected
Writings, 1977–1992*
(1993)

LOUISE ERDRICH

Fiction
Love Medicine (1984; National
Book Critics Circle Award)

The Beet Queen (1986)

Tracks (1988)

The Crown of Columbus (coauthor, 1991)

The Bingo Palace (1994)

The Blue Jay's Dance (1995)

Poetry
Jacklight (1984)

Baptism of Desire (1989)

JOHN GRISHAM

Fiction
A Time to Kill (1989)

The Firm (1991)

The Pelican Brief (1992)

The Client (1993)

The Chamber (1994)

The Rainmaker (1995)

MARK HELPRIN

Fiction
Winter's Tale (1983)

Refiner's Fire (1990)

A Soldier of the Great War
(1991)

Memoir from Antproof Case
(1995)

Children's books
Swan Lake (1989)

STEPHEN KING

Fiction
Carrie (1975)

Salem's Lot (1976)

The Shining (1977)

The Stand (1978)

The Dead Zone (1979)

Firestarter (1980)

Cujo (1981)

The Dark Tower: The Gunslinger
(1982)

Christine (1983)

Pet Sematary (1983)

The Talisman (coauthor, 1984)

Cycle of the Werewolf (1985)

It (1986)

The Eyes of the Dragon (1987)

Misery (1987)

The Tommyknockers (1987)

The Dark Half (1989)

*The Dark Tower II: The Drawing
of Three* (1989)

*The Dark Tower III: The Waste
Lands (1991)*

Needful Things (1991)

Gerald's Game (1992)

Dolores Claiborne (1992)

Insomnia (1994)

Rose Madder (1995)

**Fiction written as Richard
Bachman**
Rage (1977)

The Long Walk (1979)

*Roadwork: A Novel of the First
Energy Crisis* (1981)

The Running Man (1982)

Thinner (1984)

Nonfiction
Danse Macabre (1981)

JOHN LE CARRÉ
(nom de plume of David
Cornwell)

Fiction
Call for the Dead (1960)

A Murder of Quality (1962)

*The Spy Who Came in from the
Cold* (1964)

The Incongruous Spy (1964)

The Looking Glass War (1965)

A Small Town in Germany (1968)

*The Naive and Sentimental
Lover* (1971)

Tinker, Tailor, Soldier, Spy (1977)

Smiley's People (1980)

The Honourable Schoolboy
(1982)

The Little Drummer Girl (1983)

A Perfect Spy (1986)

The Russia House (1989)

The Secret Pilgrim (1991)

The Night Manager (1993)

Our Game (1995)

ROBERT LUDLUM

Fiction
The Scarlatti Inheritance (1971)

The Osterman Weekend (1972)

The Matlock Paper (1973)

The Rhineman Exchange (1974)

The Gemini Contenders (1976)

The Chancellor Manuscript
(1977)

The Holcroft Covenant (1978)

The Matarese Circle (1979)

The Bourne Identity (1980)

The Parsifal Mosaic (1982)

The Aquitaine Progression
(1984)

The Bourne Supremacy (1986)

The Icarus Agenda (1988)

The Bourne Ultimatum (1990)

The Road to Omaha (1992)

The Scorpio Illusion (1993)

The Apocalypse Watch (1995)

**Fiction written as Jonathan
Ryder**
Trevayne (1973)

The Cry of the Halidon (1974)

**Fiction written as Michael
Shepherd**
The Road to Gandolfo (1975)

NORMAN MAILER

Fiction
The Naked and the Dead (1948)

Barbary Shore (1951)

The Deer Park (1955; screenplay,
Wild 90, 1967)

Advertisements for Myself
(1959)

Deaths for the Ladies (1962)

The Presidential Papers (1963)

An American Dream (1965)

Cannibals and Christians (1966)

Existential Errands (1972)

Genius and Lust (1976)

The Executioner's Song (1979;
Pulitzer Prize; screenplay
1982)

Ancient Evenings (1983)

Tough Guys Don't Dance (1984;
screenplay 1987)

*Huckleberry Finn, Alive at One
Hundred* (1984)

Harlot's Ghost (1992)

Nonfiction
Why Are We in Vietnam? (1967)

*The Armies of the Night: History
as a Novel, the Novel as
History* (1968; Pulitzer
Prize; National Book
Award)

Miami and the Siege of Chicago
(1968; National Book
Award)

Of a Fire on the Moon (1970)

*King of the Hill: On the Fight of
the Century* (1971)

St. George and the Godfather
(1971)

The Prisoner of Sex (1971)

Marilyn: A Biography (1973)

The Faith of Graffiti (1974)

The Fight (1975)

Of Women and Their Elegance (1980)

Of a Small and Modest Malignancy, Wicked and Bristling with Dots (1980)

Pieces and Pontifications (1982)

Oswald's Tale (1995)

JAMES A. MICHENER

Fiction

Tales of the South Pacific (1947; Pulitzer Prize)

The Fires of the Spring (1949)

The Bridges of Toko-Ri (1953)

Sayonara (1954)

Hawaii (1959)

Caravans (1963)

The Source (1965)

The Drifters (1971)

Centennial (1974)

Chesapeake (1978)

The Covenant (1980)

Space (1982)

Poland (1983)

Texas (1985)

Legacy (1987)

Alaska (1988)

Caribbean (1989)

Journey (1989)

The Eagle and the Raven (1990)

The Novel (1991)

Mexico (1992)

Recessional (1994)

Children's book

South Pacific (1992)

Nonfiction

The Voice of Asia (1951)

The Floating World (1954)

The Bridge at Andau (1957)

Facing East (1961)

Iberia: Spanish Travels and Reflections (1968)

America vs. America: The Revolution in Middle-Class Values (1969)

Presidential Lottery: The Reckless Gamble in Our Electoral System (1969)

A Study of the Art of Jack Levine (1970)

Kent State: What Happened and Why (1971)

Sports in America (1976)

The World Is My Home (memoirs, 1992)

Literary Reflections: Michener on Michener, Hemingway, Capote, and Others (1993)

TONI MORRISON

Fiction

The Bluest Eye (1969)

Sula (1973)

Song of Solomon (1977; National Book Critics Circle Award)

Tar Baby (1981)

Beloved (1987; Pulitzer Prize)

Jazz (1992)

Nonfiction

Playing in the Dark: Whiteness and the Literary Imagination (1992)

Play

Dreaming Emmett (1986)

Nobel Prize for Literature, 1993

THOMAS PYNCHON

Fiction

V (1963)

The Crying of Lot 49 (1965)

Gravity's Rainbow (1973)

Vineland (1990)

ANNE RICE

Fiction

Interview with the Vampire (1976)

The Feast of All Saints (1980)

Cry to Heaven (1982)

The Vampire Lestat (1985)

The Queen of the Damned (1988)

The Mummy or *Ramses the Damned* (1989)

The Witching Hour (1990)

Tale of the Body Thief (1992)

Lasher (1993)

Taltos (1994)

Memnoch the Devil (1995)

Fiction written as A. N. Roquelaure

The Claiming of Sleeping Beauty (1983)

Beauty's Punishment (1984)

Beauty's Release: The Continued

Erotic Adventures of Sleeping Beauty (1985)

Fiction written as Anne Rampling

Exit to Eden (1985)

Belinda (1986)

PHILIP ROTH

Fiction

Goodbye, Columbus (1959; National Book Award)

Letting Go (1962)

When She Was Good (1967)

Portnoy's Complaint (1969)

Our Gang (1971)

The Breast (1972)

The Great American Novel (1973)

My Life as a Man (1974)

Reading Myself and Others (1975)

The Professor of Desire (1977)

The Ghost Writer (1979)

Zuckerman Unbound (1981)

The Anatomy Lesson (1983)

Zuckerman Bound (1985)

The Counterlife (1987)

Deception (1990)

Operation Shylock (1993)

Sabbath's Theater (1995)

Nonfiction

The Facts: A Novelist's Autobiography (1988)

Patrimony: A True Story (memoirs, 1991)

SALMAN RUSHDIE

Fiction

Grimus (1975)

Midnight's Children (1981)

Shame (1983)

The Satanic Verses (1989)

Haroun and the Sea of Stories (1991; Booker Prize)

Nonfiction

The Jaguar Smile: A Nicaraguan Journey (1987)

MAURICE SENDAK

Children's books

Kenny's Window (1956)

Very Far Away (1957)

The Sign on Rosie's Door (1960)

Chicken Soup with Rice (1962)

One Was Johnny (1962)

Alligators All Around (1962)

Pierre (1962)

Where the Wild Things Are (1963; Caldecott Medal)

Hector Protector [and] As I Went Over the Water (1965)

Higglety Pigglety Pop! or, There Must Be More to Life (1967)

In the Night Kitchen (1970)

Ten Little Rabbits: A Counting Book with Mino the Magician (1970)

Maurice Sendak's Really Rosie (1975)

Some Swell Pup; or Are You Sure You Want a Dog? (1976)

Seven Little Monsters (1977)

Outside Over There (1981)

We Are All in the Dumps with Jack and Guy (1993)

Hans Christian Anderson Award, 1970

DANIELLE STEEL

Fiction

Going Home (1973)

Passion's Promise (1977)

Now and Forever (1978)

The Promise (1978)

Season of Passion (1979)

Summer's End (1979)

To Love Again (1980)

The Ring (1980)

Loving (1980)

Remembrance (1981)

Palomino (1981)

Once in a Lifetime (1982)

Crossings (1982)

A Perfect Stranger (1982)

Thurston House (1983)

Changes (1983)

Full Circle (1984)

Family Album (1985)

Secrets (1985)

Wanderlust (1986)

Fine Things (1987)

Kaleidoscope (1987)

Zoya (1988)

Star (1989)

Daddy (1989)

Message from Nam (1990)

Heartbeat (1991)

No Greater Love (1991)

Jewels (1992)

Mixed Blessings (1992)

Vanished (1993)

Accident (1994)

The Gift (1994)

Wings (1994)

Lightning (1995)

Children's books
Max and the Babysitter (1989)

Martha's Best Friend (1989)

Max's Daddy Goes to the Hospital (1989)

Martha's New Daddy (1989)

Max's New Baby (1989)

Martha's New School (1989)

Max Runs Away (1990)

Martha's New Puppy (1990)

Max and Grandma and Grandpa Winky (1991)

Martha and Hilary and the Stranger (1991)

Freddie's Trip (1992)

Freddie's First Night Away (1992)

Freddie and the Doctor (1992)

Freddie's Accident (1992)

Poetry
Love Poems by Danielle Steel (1981)

Nonfiction
Having a Baby (1984)

ANNE TYLER

Fiction
If Morning Ever Comes (1964)

The Tin Can Tree (1965)

A Slipping-Down Life (1970)

The Clock Winder (1972)

Celestial Navigation (1974)

Searching for Caleb (1976)

Earthly Possessions (1977)

Morgan's Passing (1980)

Dinner at the Homesick Restaurant (1982)

The Accidental Tourist (1985)

Breathing Lessons (1988; Pulitzer Prize)

Saint Maybe (1991)

Ladder of Years (1995)

Children's books
Tumble Tower (1993)

JOHN UPDIKE

Fiction
The Poorhouse Fair (1959)

Rabbit, Run (1960)

The Centaur (1963; National Book Award)

Of the Farm (1965)

Couples (1968)

Rabbit Redux (1971)

A Month of Sundays (1975)

Marry Me: A Romance (1976)

The Coup (1978)

Rabbit Is Rich (1981; Pulitzer Prize; American Book Award; National Book Critics Circle Award)

The Witches of Eastwick (1984)

Roger's Version (1986)

S. (1988)

Rabbit at Rest (1990)

Memoirs of the Ford Administration (1992)

Brazil (1994)

Nonfiction
Self Consciousness (memoirs, 1989)

Play
Buchanan Dying (1974)

Children's books
The Magic Flute (1962)

The Ring (1964)

A Child's Calendar (1965)

Bottom's Dream (1969)

ALICE WALKER

Fiction
The Third Life of Grange Copeland (1970)

Meridian (1976)

The Color Purple (1982; Pulitzer)

The Temple of My Familiar (1989)

Possessing the Secret of Joy (1992)

Nonfiction
Warrior Marks (1993)

Poetry
Once (1976)

Revolutionary Petunias and Other Poems (1973)

Goodnight, Willie Lee, I'll See You in the Morning (1984)

Horses Make a Landscape Look More Beautiful (1984)

TRY ANOTHER TITLE

A title can make or break a book. Had these literary masterpieces gone to press with their original tags, who knows where they, or we, would be now.

The Title That Made History	**The Rejected Title**
All Things Bright and Beautiful, James Harriot	It Shouldn't Happen to a Vet
East of Eden, John Steinbeck	The Salinas Valley
The Great Gatsby, F. Scott Fitzgerald	Trimalchio in West Egg; Gold-hatted Gatsby; The High-bouncing Lover
The Heart is a Lonely Hunter, Carson McCullers	The Mute
Jaws, Peter Benchley	Great White; The Shark; Leviathan Rising; The Jaws of Death; A Silence in the Water
The Man with the Golden Arm, Nelson Algren	The Neon Wilderness; Night without Mercy
The Mill on the Floss, George Eliot	St. Ogg's on the Floss; The House of Tullever; Sister Maggie
Moby Dick, Herman Melville	The Whale
Roots, Alex Haley	Before This Anger
The Rose Tattoo, Tennessee Williams	The Eclipse of May 29, 1919
Treasure Island, Robert Louis Stevenson	The Sea-Cook
Valley of the Dolls, Jacqueline Susann	They Don't Build Statues to Businessmen
War and Peace, Leo Tolstoy	All's Well That Ends Well
White Noise, Don DeLillo	Panasonic

FROM GREAT BEGINNINGS, GREAT NOVELS GROW

Every great book has to start somewhere—this is how selected authors began their tales.

"At a village of la Mancha, whose name I do not wish to remember, there lived a little while ago one of those gentlemen who are wont to keep a lance in the rack, an old buckler, a lean horse, and a swift greyhound."
— *The Adventures of Don Quixote de la Mancha*, Miguel de Cervantes

"Alice was beginning to get very tired of sitting by her sister on the bank and of having nothing to do: once or twice she had peeped into the book her sister was reading, but it had no pictures or conversations in it, 'and what is the use of a book,' thought Alice, 'without pictures or conversations?' "
— *Alice in Wonderland*, Lewis Carroll

"Happy families are all alike, but an unhappy family is unhappy in its own way."
— *Anna Karenina*, Leo Tolstoy

"It was a queer, sultry summer, the summer they electrocuted the Rosenbergs, and I didn't know what I was doing in New York."
— *The Bell Jar*, Sylvia Plath

"There are songs that come free from the blue-eyed grass, from the dust of a thousand country roads."
— *The Bridges of Madison County*, Robert James Waller

"Buck did not read the newspapers, or he would have known

that trouble was brewing, not alone for himself, but for every tide-water dog, strong of muscle and with warm, long hair, from Puget Sound to San Diego."
— *The Call of the Wild*, Jack London

"I have noticed that when someone asks for you on the telephone and, finding you out, leaves a message begging you to call him up the moment you come in, and it's important, the matter is more often important to him than to you."
— *Cakes and Ale* W. Somerset Maugham

"Nobody was really surprised when it happened, not really, not at the subconscious level where savage things grow."
— *Carrie*, Stephen King

"It was love at first sight."
— *Catch-22*, Joseph Heller

"If you really want to hear about it, the first thing you'll probably want to know is where I was born, and what my lousy childhood was like, and how my parents were occupied and all before they had me, and all that David Copperfield kind of crap, but I don't feel like going into it, if you want to know the truth."
— *The Catcher in the Rye*, J. D. Salinger

" 'Where's Papa going with that ax?' said Fern to her mother as they were setting the table for breakfast."
— *Charlotte's Web*, E. B. White

"What's it going to be then, eh?"
— *A Clockwork Orange*, Anthony Burgess

"AAA CON is the first name in the phone book of most large American cities."
— *Dad*, William Wharton

"You will see, my dear, that I have kept my word and that bonnets and pom-poms do not take up all my time—there will always be some left over for you."
— *Dangerous Liaisons*, Choderlos de Laclos

"Whether I shall turn out to be the hero of my own life, or whether that station will be held by anybody else, these pages must show."
— *David Copperfield*, Charles Dickens

"I hope I will be able to confide everything to you, as I have never been able to confide in anyone, and I hope you will be a great source of comfort and support."
— *The Diary of a Young Girl* Anne Frank

"The lady was extraordinarily naked."
— *Eight Black Horses*, Ed McBain

"There were 117 psychoanalysts on the Pan Am flight to Vienna and I'd been treated by at least six of them."
— *Fear of Flying*, Erica Jong

"riverrun, past Eve and Adam's, from swerve of shore to bend of bay, brings us by a commodius

vicus of recirculation back to Howth Castle and Environs."
— *Finnegan's Wake*, James Joyce

"This is the saddest story I have ever heard."
— *The Good Soldier*, Ford Maddox Ford

"To the red country and part of the gray country of Oklahoma, the last rains came gently, and they did not cut the scarred earth."
— *The Grapes of Wrath*, John Steinbeck

"In my younger and more vulnerable years my father gave me some advice that I've been turning over in my mind ever since."
— *The Great Gatsby*, F. Scott Fitzgerald

"It is three hundred forty-eight years, six months, and nineteen days ago today that the citizens of Paris were awakened by the pealing of all the bells in the triple precincts of the City, the University, and the Town."
— *The Hunchback of Notre-Dame*, Victor Hugo

"—Something is a little strange, that's what you notice, that she's not a woman like all the others."
— *Kiss of the Spider Woman*, Manuel Puig

"Whenever my mother talks to me, she begins the conversation as if we were already in the middle of an argument."
— *The Kitchen God's Wife*, Amy Tan

"I shook the rain from my hat and walked into the room."
— *I, The Jury*, Mickey Spillane

"He did not expect to see blood."
— *Kramer Versus Kramer*, Avery Corman

"Lolita, light of my life, fire of my loins."
— *Lolita*, Vladimir Nabokov

"What can you say about a twenty-five-year-old girl who died?"
— *Love Story*, Erich Segal

"When Gregor Samsa woke up one morning from unsettling dreams, he found himself changed in his bed into a monstrous vermin."
— *Metamorphosis*, Franz Kafka

"Call me Ishmael."
— *Moby Dick*, Herman Melville

"The sun shone, having no alternative, on the nothing new."
— *Murphy*, Samuel Beckett

"It was a bright cold day in April, and the clocks were striking thirteen."
— *1984*, George Orwell

"Died on me finally."
— *Oldest Living Confederate Widow Tells All*, Allan Gurganus

"To have reason to get up in the morning, it is necessary to possess a guiding principle."
— *Ordinary People* Judith Guest

"Jinn and Phyllis were spending a wonderful holiday, in space, as far away as possible from the inhabited stars."
— *Planet of the Apes*, Pierre Boulle

"She was so deeply imbedded in my consciousness that for the first year of school I seem to have believed that each of my

teachers was my mother in disguise."
— *Portnoy's Complaint*, Philip Roth

"Under certain circumstances there are few hours in life more agreeable than the hour dedicated to the ceremony known as afternoon tea."
— *The Portrait of a Lady*, Henry James

"It began as a mistake."
— *Post Office*, Charles Bukowski

"For a long time I used to go to bed early."
— *Remembrance of Things Past* (Vol. I, *Swann's Way*), Marcel Proust

"In our family, there was no clear line between religion and fly fishing."
— *A River Runs Through It*, Norman MacLean

"It was the best of times, it was the worst of times, it was the age of wisdom, it was the age of foolishness, it was the epoch of belief, it was the epoch of incredulity, it was the season of Light, it was the season of Darkness, it was the spring of hope, it was the winter of despair, we had everything before us, we had nothing before us, we were all going direct to Heaven, we were all going direct the other way—in short, the period was so far like the present period, that some of its noisiest authorities insisted on its being received, for good or for evil, in the superlative degree of comparison only."
— *A Tale of Two Cities*, Charles Dickens

FAMOUS LAST WORDS

All good books come to an end—often, a good one. Here are some of the more memorable.

"But I reckon I got to light out for the territory ahead of the rest, because Aunt Sally she's going to adopt me and sivilize me, and I can't stand it. I been there before."
— *The Adventures of Huckleberry Finn*, Mark Twain

"The creatures outside looked from pig to man, and from man to pig, and from pig to man again; but already it was impossible to say which was which."
— *Animal Farm*, George Orwell

"The eyes and the faces all turned themselves toward me, and guiding myself by them, as by a magical thread, I stepped into the room."
— *The Bell Jar*, Sylvia Plath

"'Hurrah for Karamazov!'"
— *The Brothers Karamazov*, Fyodor Dostoevsky

"With relief, with humiliation, with terror, he understood that he too was a mere appearance, dreamt by another."
— *The Circular Ruins*, Jorge Luis Borges

"Oedipa settled back to await the crying of lot 49."
— *The Crying of Lot 49*, Thomas Pynchon

"History will call us wise."
— *Dune*, Frank Herbert

"I'll think of some way to get him back. After all, tomorrow is another day."
— *Gone with the Wind*, Margaret Mitchell

"So we beat on, boats against the current, born back ceaselessly into the past."
— *The Great Gatsby*, F. Scott Fitzgerald

"The offing was barred by a black bank of clouds, and the tranquil waterway leading to the uttermost ends of the earth flowed sombre under an overcast sky—seemed to lead into the heart of an immense darkness."
— *Heart of Darkness*, Joseph Conrad

" . . . and thence we came forth to see again the stars."
— *The Inferno*, Dante

"Who knows but that, on the lower frequencies, I speak for you?"
— *Invisible Man*, Ralph Ellison

"Florentino Ariza had kept his answer ready for 53 years, seven months, and eleven days and nights. 'Forever,' he said."
— *Love in the Time of Cholera*, Gabriel García Márquez

"For man himself is a mystery, and all humanity rests upon reverence before the mystery that is man."
— *The Magic Mountain*, Thomas Mann

"*Hot dog!*"
— *The Naked and the Dead*, Norman Mailer

"So [said the doctor]. Now vee may perhaps to begin. Yes?"
— *Portnoy's Complaint*, Philip Roth

"The God-damned fools."
— *The Reprieve*, Jean-Paul Sartre

"For now he knew what Shalimar knew: If you surrendered to the air, you could *ride* it."
— *Song of Solomon*, Toni Morrison

"He walked towards the faintly murmuring, glowing town, quickly."
— *Sons and Lovers*, D. H. Lawrence

"They endured."
— *The Sound and the Fury*, William Faulkner

"For all to be accomplished, for me to feel less lonely, all that remained to hope was that on the day of my execution there should be a huge crowd of spectators and that they should greet me with howls of execration."
— *The Stranger*, Albert Camus

"'It is a far, far better thing that I do, than I have ever done. It is a far, far better rest that I go to, than I have ever known.'"
— *A Tale of Two Cities*, Charles Dickens

"A Cock and a Bull, said Yorick— And one of the best of its kind, I ever heard."
— *The Life and Opinions of Tristram Shandy*, Laurence Sterne

"Yes I said yes I will yes."
— *Ulysses*, James Joyce

BOOKS OF THE CENTURY

To commemorate the New York Public Library's 100th anniversary, the librarians of this venerable institution identified books that, from their varying perspectives, have played defining roles in the making of the 20th century. Included are books that influenced the course of events, for good and for bad; books that interpreted new worlds; and books that simply delighted millions of patrons.

LANDMARKS OF MODERN LITERATURE

The Three Sisters, Anton Chekhov (1901)

Remembrance of Things Past, Marcel Proust (1913-27)

Tender Buttons, Gertrude Stein (1914)

The Metamorphosis, Franz Kafka (1915)

Renascence and Other Poems, Edna St. Vincent Millay (1917)

The Wild Swans at Coole, William Butler Yeats (1917)

Six Characters in Search of an Author, Luigi Pirandello (1921)

The Waste Land, T. S. Eliot (1922)

Ulysses, James Joyce (1922)

The Magic Mountain, Thomas Mann (1924)

The Great Gatsby, F. Scott Fitzgerald (1925)

To the Lighthouse, Virginia Woolf (1927)

Gypsy Ballads, Frederico García Lorca (1928)

Native Son, Richard Wright (1940)

The Age of Anxiety: A Baroque Eclogue, W. H. Auden (1947)

Invisible Man, Ralph Ellison (1952)

Lolita, Vladimir Nabokov (1955)

Fictions, Jorge Luis Borges (1944; 2nd augmented edition 1956)

One Hundred Years of Solitude, Gabriel García Márquez (1967)

Song of Solomon, Toni Morrison (1977)

PROTEST AND PROGRESS

The Battle with the Slum, Jacob Ritts (1902)

The Souls of Black Folk, W.E.B. Du Bois (1903)

The Jungle, Upton Sinclair (1906)

Twenty Years at Hull-House, Jane Addams (1910)

The House on Henry Street, Lillian Wald (1915)

The Autobiography of Lincoln Steffens, Lincoln Steffens (1931)

U.S.A., John Dos Passos (1937)

The Grapes of Wrath, John Steinbeck (1939)

Let Us Now Praise Famous Men, James Agee and Walker Evans (1941)

Strange Fruit, Lillian Smith (1944)

Growing Up Absurd, Paul Goodman (1960)

The Fire Next Time, James Baldwin (1963)

The Autobiography of Malcolm X, Malcolm X (1965)

And the Band Played On, Randy Shilts (1987)

There Are No Children Here, Alex Kotlowitz (1991)

POPULAR CULTURE & MASS ENTERTAINMENT

Dracula, Bram Stoker (1897)

The Turn of the Screw, Henry James (1898)

The Hound of the Baskervilles, Arthur Conan Doyle (1902)

Tarzan of the Apes, Edgar Rice Burroughs (1912)

Riders of the Purple Sage, Zane Grey (1912)

The Mysterious Affair at Styles, Agatha Christie (1920)

How To Win Friends and Influence People, Dale Carnegie (1936)

Gone with the Wind, Margaret Mitchell (1936)

The Big Sleep, Raymond Chandler (1939)

The Day of the Locust, Nathanael West (1939)

Peyton Place, Grace Metalious (1956)

The Cat in the Hat, Dr. Seuss (1957)

Stranger in a Strange Land, Robert A. Heinlein (1961)

Catch-22, Joseph Heller (1961)

In Cold Blood: A True Account of a Multiple Murder and Its Consequences, Truman Capote (1965)

Ball Four: My Life and Times Throwing the Knuckleball in the Big Leagues, Jim Bouton (1970)

Carrie, Stephen King (1974)

The Bonfire of the Vanities, Tom Wolfe (1987)

WOMEN RISE

The Age of Innocence, Edith Wharton (1920)

Woman Suffrage and Politics: The Inner Story of the Suffrage Movement, Carrie Chapman Catt and Nettie Rogers Shuler (1923)

My Fight for Birth Control, Margaret Sanger (1931)

Dust Tracks on a Dirt Road, Zora Neale Hurston (1942)

The Second Sex, Simone de Beauvoir (1949)

The Golden Notebook, Doris Lessing (1962)

The Feminine Mystique, Betty
  Friedan (1963)
I Know Why the Caged Bird Sings,
  Maya Angelou (1969)
Sisterhood Is Powerful: An Anthology
  of Writings from the Women's
  Liberations Movement, edited by
  Robin Morgan (1970)
Against Our Will: Men, Women and
  Rape, Susan Brownmiller (1975)
The Color Purple, Alice Walker (1982)

ECONOMICS & TECHNOLOGY

The Theory of the Leisure Class: An
  Economic Study of Institutions,
  Thorstein Veblen (1899)
The Protestant Ethic and the Spirit
  of Capitalism, Max Weber
  (1904–5)
The Education of Henry Adams,
  Henry Adams (1907)
The General Theory of Employment,
  Interest and Money, John Mey-
  nard Keynes (1936)

A Theory of the Consumption Func-
  tion, Milton Friedman (1957)
The Affluent Society, John Kenneth
  Galbraith (1958)
The Death and Life of Great Ameri-
  can Cities, Jane Jacobs (1961)
Superhighway—Super Hoax, Helen
  Leavitt (1970)
Small Is Beautiful: A Study of Eco-
  nomics as if People Mattered,
  E. F. Schumacher (1973)
The Whole Internet: User's Guide and
  Catalogue, Ed Krol (1992)

MIND & SPIRIT

Suicide: A Study in Sociology, Emile
  Durkheim (1897)
The Interpretation of Dreams,
  Sigmund Freud (1900)
Studies in the Psychology of Sex,
  Havelock Ellis (1901–28)
The Varieties of Religious Experi-
  ence: A Study in Human Nature,
  Wiilliam James (1902)

The Prophet, Kahlil Gibran (1923)
Why I Am Not a Christian, Bertrand
  Russell (1927)
Coming of Age in Samoa, Margaret
  Mead (1928)
Being and Nothingness, Jean-Paul
  Sartre (1943)
The Common Sense Book of Baby
  Care, Dr. Benjamin Spock
  (1946)
The Holy Bible, Revised Standard
  Version (1952)
The Courage to Be, Paul Tillich
  (1952)
One Flew Over the Cuckoo's Nest,
  Ken Kesey (1962)
The Politics of Ecstasy, Timothy
  Leary (1968)
On Death and Dying, Elisabeth
  Kübler-Ross (1969)
The Uses of Enchantment, Bruno
  Bettelheim (1976)

MORE BOOKS THAT SHAPE LIVES

The Library of Congress established its Center for the Book in 1977 to stimulate public
interest in books, reading, and libraries. Here is its list of the 25 books that have had the
greatest impact on readers' lives.

The Adventures of Huckleberry Finn, Mark Twain
Atlas Shrugged, Ayn Rand
The Autobiography of Benjamin Franklin
The Bible
The Catcher in the Rye, J. D. Salinger
Charlotte's Web, E. B. White
The Diary of a Young Girl, Anne Frank
Don Quixote, Miguel de Cervantes
Gone with the Wind, Margaret Mitchell
Hiroshima, John Hersey
How To Win Friends and Influence People, Dale
  Carnegie
I Know Why the Caged Bird Sings, Maya Angelou

Invisible Man, Ralph Ellison
The Little Prince, Antoine de Saint Exupéry
Little Women, Louisa May Alcott
The Lord of the Rings, J.R.R. Tolkien
Roots, Alex Haley
The Secret Garden, Frances Hodgson Burnett
To Kill a Mockingbird, Harper Lee
Treasure Island, Robert Louis Stevenson
Walden, Henry David Thoreau
War and Peace, Leo Tolstoy
What Color Is Your Parachute? Richard Nelson
  Bolles

LITERARY AWARDS

NATIONAL BOOK AWARDS

Fiction

1950 Nelson Algren
The Man with the Golden Arm

1951 William Faulkner
The Collected Stories of William Faulkner

1952 James Jones
From Here to Eternity

1953 Ralph Ellison
Invisible Man

1954 Saul Bellow
The Adventures of Augie March

1955 William Faulkner
A Fable

1956 John O'Hara
Ten North Frederick

1957 Wright Morris
The Field of Vision

1958 John Cheever
The Wapshot Chronicle

1959 Bernard Malamud
The Magic Barrel

1960 Philip Roth
Goodbye, Columbus

1961 Conrad Richter
The Waters of Kronos

1962 Walker Percy
The Moviegoer

1963 J. F. Powers
Morte D'Urban

1964 John Updike
The Centaur

1965 Saul Bellow
Herzog

1966 Katherine Anne Porter
The Collected Stories of Katherine Anne Porter

1967 Bernard Malamud
The Fixer

1968 Thornton Wilder
The Eighth Day

1969 Jerzy Kosinski
Steps

1970 Joyce Carol Oates
Them

1971 Saul Bellow
Mr. Sammler's Planet

1972 Flannery O'Connor
The Complete Stories of Flannery O'Connor

1973 John Barth
Chimera
John Williams
Augustus

1974 Thomas Pynchon
Gravity's Rainbow
Isaac Bashevis Singer

A Crown of Feathers and Other Stories

1975 Robert Stone
Dog Soldiers
Thomas Williams
The Hair of Harold Roux

1976 William Gaddis
JR

1977 Wallace Stegner
The Spectator Bird

1978 Mary Lee Settle
Blood Ties

1979 Tim O'Brien
Going After Cacciato

1980 William Styron (hardcover)
Sophie's Choice
John Irving (paperback)
The World According to Garp

1981 Wright Morris (hardcover)
Plains Song
John Cheever (paperback)
The Stories of John Cheever

1982 John Updike (hardcover)
Rabbit Is Rich
William Maxwell (paperback)
So Long, See You Tomorrow

1983 Alice Walker (hardcover)
The Color Purple
Eudora Welty (paperback)
Collected Stories of Eudora Welty

1984 Ellen Gilchrist
Victory over Japan: A Book of Stories

1985 Don DeLillo
White Noise

1986 E. L. Doctorow
World's Fair

1987 Larry Heinemann
Paco's Story

1988 Pete Dexter
Paris Trout

1989 John Casey
Spartina

1990 Charles Johnson
Middle Passage

1991 Norman Rush
Mating

1992 Cormac McCarthy
All the Pretty Horses

1993 E. Annie Proulx
The Shipping News

1994 William Gaddis
A Frolic of His Own

Nonfiction

1950 Ralph L. Rusk
Ralph Waldo Emerson

1951 Newton Arvin
Herman Melville

1952 Rachel Carson
The Sea Around Us

1953 Bernard A. De Voto
The Course of an Empire

1954 Bruce Catton
A Stillness at Appomattox

1955 Joseph Wood Krutch
The Measure of Man

1956 Herbert Kubly
An American in Italy

1957 George F. Kennan
Russia Leaves the War

1958 Catherine Drinker Bowen
The Lion and the Throne

1959 J. Christopher Herold
Mistress to an Age: A Life of Madame de Stael

1960 Richard Ellmann
James Joyce

1961 William L. Shirer
The Rise and Fall of the Third Reich

1962 Lewis Mumford
The City in History: Its Origins, Its Transformations and Its Prospects

1963 Leon Edel
Henry James, Vol. II: The Conquest of London. Henry James, Vol. III: The Middle Years

1980 Tom Wolfe (hardcover)
The Right Stuff
Peter Matthiessen (paperback)
The Snow Leopard

1981 Maxine Hong Kingston (hardcover)
China Men
Jane Kramer (paperback)
The Last Cowboy

1982 Tracy Kidder (hardcover)
The Soul of a New Machine
Victor S. Navasky (paperback)
Naming Names

1983 Fox Butterfield
China: Alive in the Bitter Sea
James Fallows (paperback)
National Defense

1984 Rovert V. Remini
Andrew Jackson and the Course of American Democracy, 1833-1845

1985 J. Anthony Lukas
Common Ground: A Turbulent Decade in the Lives of Three American Families

1986 Barry Lopez
Arctic Dreams

1987 Richard Rhodes
The Making of the Atom Bomb

1988 Neil Sheehan
A Bright Shining Lie: John Paul Vann and America in Vietnam
1989 Thomas L. Friedman
From Beirut to Jerusalem
1990 Ron Chernow
The House of Morgan: An American Banking Dynasty and the Rise of Modern Finance
1991 Orlando Patterson
Freedom
1992 Paul Monette
Becoming a Man: Half a Life Story
1993 Gore Vidal
United States: Essays 1952-1992
1994 Sherwin B. Nuland
How We Die: Reflections on Life's Final Chapter

Poetry
1950 William Carlos Williams
Paterson: Book III and Selected Poems
1951 Wallace Stevens
The Auroras of Autumn
1952 Marianne Moore
Collected Poems
1953 Archibald MacLeish
Collected Poems, 1917-1952
1954 Conrad Aiken
Collected Poems
1955 Wallace Stevens
The Collected Poems of Wallace Stevens
1956 W. H. Auden
The Shield of Achilles
1957 Richard Wilbur
Things of This World
1958 Robert Penn Warren
Promises: Poems, 1954-1956
1959 Theodore Roethke
Words for the Wind
1960 Robert Lowell
Life Studies
1961 Randall Jarrell
The Woman at the Washington Zoo
1962 Alan Dugan
Poems
1963 William Strafford
Traveling Through the Dark
1964 John Crowe Ransom
Selected Poems
1965 Theodore Roethke
The Far Field
1966 James Dickey
Buckdancer's Choice: Poems
1967 James Merrill
Nights and Days
1968 Robert Bly
The Light Around the Body

1969 John Berryman
His Toy, His Dream, His Rest
1970 Elizabeth Bishop
The Complete Poems
1971 Mona Van Duyn
To See, To Take
1972 Howard Moss
Selected Poems
Frank O'Hara
The Collected Poems of Frank O'Hara
1973 A. R. Ammons
Collected Poems, 1951-1971
1974 Allen Ginsberg
The Fall of America: Poems of These States
Adrienne Rich
Diving into the Wreck: Poems 1971-1972
1975 Marilyn Hacker
Presentation Piece
1976 John Ashbery
Self-Portrait in a Convex Mirror
1977 Richard Eberhart
Collected Poems, 1930-1976
1978 Howard Nemerov
The Collected Poems of Howard Nemerov
1979 James Merrill
Mirabell: Book of Numbers
1980 Philip Levine
Ashes
1981 Lisel Mueller
The Need To Hold Still
1982 William Bronk
Life Supports: New and Collected Poems
1983 Galway Kinnell
Selected Poems
Charles Wright
Country Music: Selected Early Poems
1991 Philip Levine
What Work Is
1992 Mary Oliver
New & Selected Poems
1993 A. R. Ammons
Garbage
1994 James Tate
A Worshipful Company of Fletchers

NEWBERY MEDAL BOOKS
For children's literature
1922 Henrik van Loon
The Story of Mankind
1923 Hugh Lofting
The Voyages of Doctor Dolittle
1924 Charles Hawes
The Dark Frigate
1925 Charles Finger
Tales from Silver Lands

1926 Arthur Chrisman
Shen of the Sea
1927 Will James
Smoky, the Cowhorse
1928 Dhan Mukerji
Gay Neck, the Story of a Pigeon
1929 Eric P. Kelly
The Trumpeter of Krakow
1930 Rachel Field
Hitty, Her First Hundred Years
1931 Elizabeth Coatsworth
The Cat Who Went to Heaven
1932 Laura Armer
Waterless Mountain
1933 Elizabeth Lewis
Young Fu of the Upper Yangtze
1934 Cornelia Meigs
Invincible Louisa
1935 Monica Shannon
Dobry
1936 Carol Brink
Caddie Woodlawn
1937 Ruth Sawyer
Roller Skates
1938 Kate Seredy
The White Stag
1939 Elizabeth Enright
Thimble Summer
1940 James Daugherty
Daniel Boone
1941 Armstrong Sperry
Call It Courage
1942 Walter Edmonds
The Matchlock Gun
1943 Elizabeth Gray
Adam of the Road
1944 Esther Forbes
Johnny Tremain
1945 Robert Lawson
Rabbit Hill
1946 Lois Lenski
Strawberry Girl
1947 Carolyn Bailey
Miss Hickory
1948 William Pène du Bois
The Twenty-One Balloons
1949 Marguerite Henry
King of the Wind
1950 Marguerite de Angeli
The Door in the Wall
1951 Elizabeth Yates
Amos Fortune, Free Man
1952 Eleanor Estes
Ginger Pye
1953 Ann Nolan Clark
Secret of the Andes
1954 Joseph Krumgold
. . . And Now Miguel
1955 Meindert DeJong
The Wheel on the School
1956 Jean Lee Latham
Carry On, Mr. Bowditch

1957	Virginia Sorenson *Miracles on Maple Hill*	1987	Sid Fleischman *The Whipping Boy*	1955	Marcia Brown *Cinderella*	

1957 Virginia Sorenson
Miracles on Maple Hill
1958 Harold Keith
Rifles for Watie
1959 Elizabeth George Speare
The Witch of Blackbird Pond
1960 Joseph Krumgold
Onion_John
1961 Scott O'Dell
Island of the Blue Dolphins
1962 Elizabeth George Speare
The Bronze Bow
1963 Madeleine L'Engle
A Wrinkle in Time
1964 Emily Neville
It's Like This, Cat
1965 Maia Wojciechowska
Shadow of a Bull
1966 Elizabeth Borton de Trevino
I, Juan de Pareja
1967 Irene Hunt
Up a Road Slowly
1968 E. L. Konigsburg
From the Mixed-Up Files of Mrs. Basil E. Frankweiler
1969 Lloyd Alexander
The High King
1970 William H. Armstrong
Sounder
1971 Betsy Byars
Summer of the Swans
1972 Robert C. O'Brien
Mrs. Frisby and the Rats of NIMH
1973 Jean Craighead George
Julie of the Wolves
1974 Paula Fox
The Slave Dancer
1975 Virginia Hamilton
M. C. Higgins, the Great
1976 Susan Cooper
The Grey King
1977 Mildred D. Taylor
Roll of Thunder, Hear My Cry
1978 Katherine Paterson
Bridge to Terabithia
1979 Ellen Raskin
The Westing Game
1980 Joan W. Blos
A Gathering of Days
1981 Katherine Paterson
Jacob Have I Loved
1982 Nancy Willard
A Visit to William Blake's Inn: Poems for Innocent and Experienced Travelers
1983 Cynthia Voight
Dicey's Song
1984 Beverly Cleary
Dear Mr. Henshaw
1985 Robin McKinley
The Hero and the Crown
1986 Patricia MacLachlan
Sarah, Plain and Tall

1987 Sid Fleischman
The Whipping Boy
1988 Russell Freedman
Lincoln: A Photobiography
1989 Paul Fleischman
Joyful Noise: Poems for Two Voices
1990 Lois Lowry
Number the Stars
1991 Jerry Spinelli
Maniac Magee
1992 Phyllis Reynolds Naylor
Shiloh
1993 Cynthia Rylant
Missing May
1994 Lois Lowry
The Giver
1995 Sharon Creech
Walk Two Moons

CALDECOTT MEDAL BOOKS
For children's picture books

1938 Helen Dean Fish, ill. by Dorothy P. Lathrop
Animals of the Bible
1939 Thomas Handforth
Mei Li
1940 Ingri and Edgar Parin d'Aulaire
Abraham Lincoln
1941 Robert Lawson
They Were Strong and Good
1942 Robert McCloskey
Make Way for Ducklings
1943 Virginia Lee Burton
The Little House
1944 James Thurber, ill. by Louis Slobodkin
Many Moons
1945 Rachel Field, ill. by Elizabeth Orton Jones
Prayer for a Child
1946 Maude and Mishka Petersham
The Rooster Crows
1947 Golden MacDonald, ill. by Leonard Weisgard
The Little Island
1948 Alvin Tresselt, ill. by Roger Duvoisin
White Snow, Bright Snow
1949 Berta and Elmer Hader
The Big Snow
1950 Leo Politi
Song of the Swallows
1951 Katherine Milhous
The Egg Tree
1952 Will Lipkind, ill. by Nicolas Mordvinoff
Finders Keepers
1953 Lynd Ward
The Biggest Bear
1954 Ludwig Bemelmans
Madeline's Rescue

1955 Marcia Brown
Cinderella
1956 John Langstaff, ill. by Feodor Rojankovsky
Frog Went A-Courtin'
1957 Janice Udry, ill. by Marc Simont
A Tree Is Nice
1958 Robert McCloskey
Time of Wonder
1959 Barbara Cooney
Chanticleer and the Fox
1960 Marie Hall Ets and Aurora Labastida
Nine Days to Christmas
1961 Ruth Robbins, ill. by Nicolas Sidjakov
Baboushka and the Three Kings
1962 Marcia Brown
Once a Mouse
1963 Ezra Jack Keats
The Snowy Day
1964 Maurice Sendak
Where the Wild Things Are
1965 Beatrice Schenk de Regniers, ill. by Beni Montresor
May I Bring a Friend?
1966 Sorche Nic Leodhas, ill. by Nonny Hogrogian
Always Room for One More
1967 Evaline Ness
Sam, Bangs & Moonshine
1968 Barbara Emberley, ill. by Ed Emberley
Drummer Hoff
1969 Arthur Ransome, ill. by Uri Shulevitz
The Fool of the World and the Flying Ship
1970 William Steig
Sylvester and the Magic Pebble
1971 Gail E. Haley
A Story a Story
1972 Nonny Hogrogian
One Fine Day
1973 Lafcadio Hearn, retold by Arlene Mosel, ill. by Blair Lent
The Funny Little Woman
1974 Harve Zemach, picts. by Margot Zemach
Duffy and the Devil
1975 Gerald McDermott
Arrow to the Sun
1976 Verna Aardema, picts. by Leo and Diane Dillon
Why Mosquitoes Buzz in People's Ears
1977 Margaret Musgrove, picts. by Leo and Diane Dillon
Ashanti to Zulu
1978 Peter Spier
Noah's Ark
1979 Paul Goble
The Girl Who Loved Wild Horses

1980 Donald Hall, picts. by Barbara
Cooney
Ox-Cart Man
1981 Arnold Lobel
Fables
1982 Chris Van Allsburg
Jumanji
1983 Blaise Cendrars, trans. and ill.
by Marcia Brown
Shadow
1984 Alice and Martin Provensen
*The Glorious Flight: Across the
Channel with Louis Blériot*
1985 Margaret Hodges, ill. by Trina
Schart Hyman
Saint George and the Dragon
1986 Chris Van Allsburg
The Polar Express
1987 Arthur Yorinks, ill. by Richard
Egielski
Hey, Al
1988 Jane Yolen, ill. by John Schoenherr
Owl Moon
1989 Karen Ackerman, ill. by Stephen
Gammell
Song and Dance Man
1990 Ed Young
Lon Po Po
1991 David Macaulay
Black and White
1992 David Wiesner
Tuesday
1993 Emily Arnold McCully
Mirette on the High Wire
1994 Allen Say
Grandfather's Journey
1995 Eve Bunting, ill. by David Diaz
Smoky Night

BOLLINGEN PRIZE IN POETRY

1949 Wallace Stevens
1950 John Crowe Ransom
1951 Marianne Moore
1952 Archibald MacLeish
William Carlos Williams
1953 W. H. Auden
1954 Leonie Adams
Louise Bogan
1955 Conrad Aiken
1956 Allen Tate
1957 e. e. cummings
1958 Theodore Roethke
1959 Delmore Schwartz
1960 Yvor Winters
1961 Richard Eberhart
John Hall Wheelock
1962 Robert Frost
1965 Horace Gregory
1967 Robert Penn Warren
1969 John Berryman
Karl Shapiro
1971 Richard Wilbur

Mona Van Duyn
1973 James Merrill
1975 A. R. Ammons
1977 David Ignatow
1979 W. S. Merwin
1981 May Swenson
Howard Nemerov
1983 Anthony E. Hecht
John Hollander
1985 John Ashbery
Fred Chappell
1987 Stanley Kunitz
1989 Edgar Bowers
1991 Laura (Riding) Jackson
Donald Justice
1993 Mark Strand
1994 Kenneth Koch

PEN/FAULKNER AWARD
Best American work of fiction
1981 Walter Abish
How German Is It?
1982 David Bradley
The Chaneysville Incident
1983 Toby Olson
Seaview
1984 John Edgar Wideman
Sent for You Yesterday
1985 Tobias Wolff
The Barracks Thief
1986 Peter Taylor
The Old Forest
1987 Richard Wiley
Soldiers in Hiding
1988 T. Coraghessan Boyle
World's End
1989 James Salter
Dusk
1990 E. L. Doctorow
Billy Bathgate
1991 John Edgar Wideman
Philadelphia Fire
1992 Don DeLillo
Mao II
1993 E. Annie Proulx
Postcards
1994 Philip Roth
Operation Shylock
1995 David Guterson
Snow Falling on Cedars

BOOKER PRIZE
British award for fiction
1969 P. H. Newby
Something To Answer For
1970 Bernice Rubens
The Elected Member
1971 V. S. Naipaul
In a Free State
1972 John Berger
G

1973 J. G. Farrell
The Siege of Krishnapur
1974 Nadine Gordimer
The Conservationist
1975 Ruth Prawer Jhabvala
Heat and Dust
1976 David Storey
Saville
1977 Paul Scott
Staying On
1978 Iris Murdoch
The Sea, the Sea
1979 Penelope Fitzgerald
Offshore
1980 William Golding
Rites of Passage
1981 Salman Rushdie
Midnight's Children
1982 Thomas Keneally
Schindler's Ark
1983 J. M. Coetzee
Life & Times of Michael K
1984 Anita Brookner
Hotel du Lac
1985 Keri Hulme
The Bone People
1986 Kingsley Amis
The Old Devils
1987 Penelope Lively
Moon Tiger
1988 Peter Carey
Oscar and Lucinda
1989 Kazuo Ishiguro
The Remains of the Day
1990 A. S. Byatt
Possession
1991 Ben Okri
The Famished Road
1992 Michael Ondaatje
The English Patient
Barry Unsworth
Sacred Hunger
1993 Roddy Doyle
Paddy Clark Ha Ha Ha
1994 James Kelman
How Late It Was, How Late

NATIONAL MAGAZINE AWARD
Public Service/Public Interest
1970 Life
1971 The Nation
1972 Philadelphia
1973 [not awarded]
1974 Scientific American
1975 Consumer Reports
1976 Business Week
1977 Philadelphia
1978 Mother Jones
1979 New West
1980 Texas Monthly
1981 Reader's Digest
1982 The Atlantic Monthly

1983 Foreign Affairs
1984 The New Yorker
1985 The Washingtonian
1986 Science 85
1987 Money
1988 The Atlantic Monthly
1989 California
1990 Southern Exposure
1991 Family Circle
1992 Glamour
1993 The Family Therapy Network
1994 Philadelphia
1995 The New Republic

Specialized Journalism

1970 Philadelphia
1971 Rolling Stone
1972 Architectural Record
1973 Psychology Today
1974 Texas Monthly
1975 Medical Economics
1976 United Mine Workers Journal
1977 Architectural Record
1978 Scientific American
1979 National Journal
1980 IEEE Spectrum

Design/Visual Excellence

1970 Look
1971 Vogue
1972 Esquire
1973 Horizon
1974 Newsweek
1975 Country Journal
     National Lampoon
1976 Horticulture
1977 Rolling Stone
1978 Architectural Digest
1979 Audubon
1980 GEO
1981 Attenzione
1982 Nautical Quarterly
1983 New York
1984 House & Garden
1985 Forbes
1986 Time
1987 Elle
1988 Life
1989 Rolling Stone
1990 Esquire
1991 Condé Nast Traveler
1992 Vanity Fair
1993 Harper's Bazaar
1994 Allure
1995 Martha Stewart Living

Reporting (Excellence)/News Reporting

1970 The New Yorker
1971 The Atlantic Monthly
1972 The Atlantic Monthly
1973 New York
1974 The New Yorker

1975 The New Yorker
1976 Audubon
1977 Audubon
1978 The New Yorker
1979 Texas Monthly
1980 Mother Jones
1981 National Journal
1982 The Washingtonian
1983 Institutional Investor
1984 Vanity Fair
1985 Texas Monthly
1986 Rolling Stone
1987 Life
1988 Baltimore Magazine
     The Washingtonian
1989 The New Yorker
1990 The New Yorker
1991 The New Yorker
1992 The New Republic
1993 IEEE Spectrum
1994 The New Yorker
1995 The Atlantic Monthly

**General Excellence
(Under 100,000 circulation)**

1981 ARTnews
1982 Camera Arts
1983 Louisiana Life
1984 The American Lawyer
1985 Manhattan, inc.
1986 New England Monthly
1987 New England Monthly
1988 The Sciences
1989 The Sciences
1990 7 Days
1991 The New Republic
1992 The New Republic
1993 Lingua Franca
1994 Print
1995 I.D. Magazine

General Excellence (100,000–400,000)

1981 Audubon
1982 Rocky Mountain Magazine
1983 Harper's Magazine
1984 Outside
1985 American Heritage
1986 3-2-1 Contact
1987 Common Cause
1988 Hippocrates
1989 American Heritage
1990 Texas Monthly
1991 Interview
1992 Texas Monthly
1993 American Photo
1994 Wired
1995 Men's Journal

General Excellence (400,000–1,000,000)

1981 Business Week
1982 Science 81
1983 Science 82
1984 House & Garden

1985 American Health
1986 Discover
1987 Elle
1988 Fortune
1989 Vanity Fair
1990 Metropolitan Home
1991 Condé Nast Traveler
1992 Mirabella
1993 The Atlantic Monthly
1994 Health
1995 The New Yorker

General Excellence (over 1,000,000)

1981 Glamour
1982 Newsweek
1983 Life
1984 National Geographic
1985 Time
1986 Money
1987 People Weekly
1988 Parents
1989 Sports Illustrated
1990 Sports Illustrated
1991 Glamour
1992 National Geographic
1993 Newsweek
1994 Business Week
1995 Entertainment Weekly

Essays and Criticism

1978 Esquire
1979 Life
1980 Natural History
1981 Time
1982 The Atlantic Monthly
1983 The American Lawyer
1984 The New Republic
1985 Boston
1986 The Sciences
1987 Outside
1988 Harper's Magazine
1989 Harper's Magazine
1990 Vanity Fair
1991 The Sciences
1992 The Nation
1993 The American Lawyer
1994 Harper's Magazine
1995 Harper's Magazine

Fiction

1978 The New Yorker
1979 The Atlantic Monthly
1980 Antaeus
1981 The North American Review
1982 The New Yorker
1983 The North American Review
1984 Seventeen
1985 Playboy
1986 The Georgia Review
1987 Esquire
1988 The Atlantic
1989 The New Yorker
1990 The New Yorker

1991 Esquire
1992 Story
1993 The New Yorker
1994 Harper's Magazine
1995 Story

Single Topic Issue
1979 Progressive Architecture
1980 Scientific American
1981 Business Week
1982 Newsweek
1983 IEEE Spectrum
1984 Esquire
1985 American Heritage
1986 IEEE Spectrum
1987 Bulletin of the Atomic Scientists
1988 Life
1989 Hippocrates
1990 National Geographic
1991 The American Lawyer
1992 Business Week
1993 Newsweek
1994 Health
1995 Discover

Personal Service/Service to the Individual
1974 Sports Illustrated
1975 Esquire
1976 Modern Medicine
1977 Harper's Magazine
1978 Newsweek
1979 The American Journal of Nursing
1980 Saturday Review
1982 Philadelphia
1983 Sunset
1984 New York
1985 The Washingtonian
1986 Farm Journal
1987 Consumer Reports
1988 Money
1989 Good Housekeeping
1990 Consumer Reports
1991 New York
1992 Creative Classroom
1993 Good Housekeeping
1994 Fortune
1995 Smart Money

Special Interests
1986 Popular Mechanics
1987 Sports Afield
1988 Condé Nast Traveler
1989 Condé Nast Traveler
1990 Arts & Antiques

1991 New York
1992 Sports Afield
1993 Philadelphia
1994 Outside
1995 Gentlemen's Quarterly

Photography
1985 Life
1986 Vogue
1987 National Geographic
1988 Rolling Stone
1989 National Geographic
1990 Texas Monthly
1991 National Geographic
1992 National Geographic
1993 Harper's Bazaar
1994 Martha Stewart Living
1995 Rolling Stone

Feature Writing
1988 The Atlantic Monthly
1989 Esquire
1990 The Washingtonian
1991 U.S. News & World Report
1992 Sports Illustrated
1993 The New Yorker
1994 Harper's Magazine
1995 Gentlemen's Quarterly

STAGE

BROADWAY SHOWS OF THE 1994–95 SEASON

It's been a rebound year for theater, with attendance hitting 9,044,763, the highest since the 1981–82 season. Here are the attractions, with (M) standing for musical, (R) for revival, and (So) for solo show

NEW PRODUCTIONS
Arcadia
A Christmas Carol
Comedy Tonight
The Flying Karamazov Brothers
     Do the Impossible!
Gentlemen Prefer Blondes (M-R)
The Glass Menagerie (R)
Chronicle of a Death Foretold
     (M)
Hamlet (R)
Having Our Say
Hedda Gabler (R)
The Heiress (R)
How To Succeed in Business
     Without Really Trying (M-R)
Indiscretions
Love! Valour! Compassion!
Medea (R)
The Molière Comedies (R)
A Month in the Country (R)
My Thing of Love

On the Waterfront
Philadelphia, Here I Come! (R)
The Play's the Thing (R)
Red Buttons on Broadway (M-
     So)
Rob Becker's Defending the
     Caveman (So)
The Rose Tattoo (R)
The Shadow Box (R)
Show Boat (M-R)
Smokey Joe's Cafe (M)
Sunset Boulevard (M)
Translations
A Tuna Christmas
What's Wrong with This Picture?
Uncle Vanya

**HOLDOVERS FROM PREVIOUS
SEASONS**
Angels in America
Beauty and the Beast (M)
Blood Brothers (M)

Broken Glass
Carousel (M-R)
Cats (M)
Crazy for You (M)
Damn Yankees (M-R)
Gray's Anatomy (So)
Grease (M-R)
Guys and Dolls (M-R)
An Inspector Calls
Jackie Mason: Politically Incorrect
     (So)
Kiss of the Spider Woman (M)
Laughter on the 23rd Floor
Les Misérables (M)
Miss Saigon (M)
Passion (M)
The Phantom of the Opera (M)
Sally Marr . . . and Her Escorts
She Loves Me (M-R)
Twilight: Los Angeles 1992 (So)
The Who's "Tommy" (M)

ON THE ROAD

The Great White Way draws most of the attention in the theater world, but for over 15 years road shows have generated the most bucks. Note that revenues in general jumped dramatically beginning in the late '70s, with the rise of blockbuster British musicals. (Source: *Variety*)

Season	Broadway box office/ total shows during most profitable week	Road box office/ total shows during most profitable week
1965–66	$53.8 million/29 shows	$32.2 million/16 shows
1970–71	$55.3 million/30 shows	$52.5 million/19 shows
1975–76	$70.8 million/29 shows	$52.6 million/19 shows
1980–81	$194.5 million/34 shows	$218.9 million/30 shows
1985–86	$190.6 million/23 shows	$235.6 million/23 shows
1990–91	$267.2 million/22 shows	$450.2 million/27 shows
1991–92	$292.4 million/28 shows	$502.7 million/25 shows
1992–93	$327.7 million/21 shows	$620.6 million/34 shows
1993–94	$356.0 million/21 shows	$687.7 million/30 shows
1994–95	$406.3 million/23 shows	$694.6 million/33 shows

LONGEST-RUNNING SHOWS ON BROADWAY

The following is a list of the longest-running shows on Broadway (as of August 30, 1995) based on the number of performances.

(M) stands for musical and (R) for revival. (Source: *League of American Theatres and Producers*)

A Chorus Line (M) (1975–90)	6,137
Oh! Calcutta! (M-R) (1976–89)	5,962
Cats (M) (1982–)	5,373
42nd Street (M) (1980–89)	3,485
Les Misérables (M) (1987–)	3,461
Grease (M) (1972–80)	3,388
Fiddler on the Roof (M) (1964–72)	3,242
Life with Father (1939–47)	3,224
Tobacco Road (1933–41)	3,182
The Phantom of the Opera (M) (1988–)	3,159
Hello, Dolly! (M) (1964–70)	2,844
My Fair Lady (M) (1956–62)	2,717
Annie (M) (1977–83)	2,377
Man of La Mancha (M) (1965–71)	2,329
Abie's Irish Rose (1922–27)	2,327
Oklahoma! (M) (1943–48)	2,212
South Pacific (M) (1949–54)	1,925
The Magic Show (M) (1974–78)	1,920
Pippin (M) (1972–77)	1,908
Gemini (1977–81)	1,819
Miss Saigon (M) (1991–)	1,813
Deathtrap (1978–82)	1,793
Harvey (1944–49)	1,775
Dancin' (M) (1978–82)	1,774
La Cage aux folles (M) (1983–87)	1,761
Hair (M) (1968–72)	1,742
The Wiz (M) (1975–79)	1,672
Born Yesterday (1946–49)	1,642
Ain't Misbehavin' (M) (1978–82)	1,604
Best Little Whorehouse in Texas (M) (1978–82)	1,584
Mary, Mary (1961–64)	1,572
Evita (M) (1979–83)	1,567
Voice of the Turtle (1943–48)	1,557
Barefoot in the Park (1963–64)	1,532
Dreamgirls (M) (1981–85)	1,521
Mame (M) (1966–70)	1,503
Crazy for You (M) (1992–)	1,460
Same Time, Next Year (1976–78)	1,453
Arsenic and Old Lace (1941–44)	1,444
The Sound of Music (M) (1959–63)	1,443
How To Succeed in Business Without Really Trying (M) (1961–65)	1,417
Hellzapoppin (M) (1938–41)	1,404
The Music Man (M) (1957–61)	1,375
Funny Girl (M) (1964–67)	1,348
Mummenschanz (M) (1977–80)	1,326
Oh! Calcutta! (M) (1969–72)	1,314
Brighton Beach Memoirs (1983–86)	1,299
Angel Street (1941–44)	1,295
Lightnin' (1918–21)	1,291
Promises, Promises (M) (1968–72)	1,281
The King and I (M) (1951–54)	1,246
Cactus Flower (1965–68)	1,234
Torch Song Trilogy (1982–85)	1,222
Sleuth (1970–73)	1,222
1776 (M) (1969–72)	1,217
Equus (1974–77)	1,209
Sugar Babies (M) (1979–82)	1,208
Guys and Dolls (M) (1950–53)	1,200
Cabaret (M) (1966–69)	1,166
Amadeus (1980–83)	1,161
Mister Roberts (1948–51)	1,157
Annie Get Your Gun (M) (1946–49)	1,147
Guys and Dolls (M-R) (1992–95)	1,143
The Seven Year Itch (1952–55)	1,141
Butterflies Are Free (1969–72)	1,128
Pins and Needles (M) (1937–40)	1,108
Plaza Suite (1968–70)	1,097
They're Playing Our Song (M) (1979–81)	1,082
Kiss Me, Kate (M) (1948–51)	1,071
Don't Bother Me, I Can't Cope (M) (1972–74)	1,065
The Pajama Game (M) (1954–56)	1,063
Shenandoah (M) (1975–77)	1,050
Teahouse of the August Moon (1953–56)	1,027
Damn Yankees (M) (1955-57)	1,019
Grand Hotel (M) (1989–92)	1,018
Never Too Late (1962–65)	1,007

BROADWAY'S FAVORITES: PLACE THAT TUNE

Know the song but can't place the musical in which it originally appeared? Here is a checklist of some Great White Way melodies that linger on.

SONG	SHOW	SONG	SHOW
"Almost Like Being in Love"	Brigadoon	"Memory"	Cats
"And I Am Telling You I'm Not Going"	Dreamgirls	"The Music of the Night"	The Phantom of the Opera
"Anything You Can Do"	Annie Get Your Gun	"My Favorite Things"	The Sound of Music
"Bali Ha'i"	South Pacific	"Oh, What a Beautiful Mornin' "	Oklahoma!
"The Ballad of Mack the Knife"	The Threepenny Opera	"Ol' Man River"	Show Boat
"Bewitched, Bothered, and Bewildered"	Pal Joey	"One Night in Bangkok"	Chess
"A Bushel and a Peck"	Guys and Dolls	"On the Street Where You Live"	My Fair Lady
"Climb Ev'ry Mountain"	The Sound of Music	"The Quest (The Impossible Dream)"	Man of La Mancha
"Everything's Coming Up Roses"	Gypsy	"Seventy-Six Trombones"	The Music Man
"Getting To Know You"	The King and I	"Shall We Dance?"	The King and I
"I Am What I Am"	La Cage aux folles	"Smoke Gets in Your Eyes"	Roberta
"I Cain't Say No"	Oklahoma!	"Some Enchanted Evening"	South Pacific
"I Could Have Danced All Night"	My Fair Lady	"The Sound of Music"	The Sound of Music
"I Don't Know How To Love Him"	Jesus Christ Superstar	"Summertime"	Porgy and Bess
"I Get a Kick out of You"	Anything Goes	"Sunrise, Sunset"	Fiddler on the Roof
"I Got Plenty o' Nothin' "	Porgy and Bess	"Tea for Two"	No, No, Nanette
"I Got Rhythm"	Girl Crazy	"Thank Heaven for Little Girls"	Gigi
"I Got the Sun in the Morning"	Annie Get Your Gun	"There Is Nothin' Like a Dame"	South Pacific
"I Feel Pretty"	West Side Story	"There's No Business Like Show Business"	Annie Get Your Gun
"I Whistle a Happy Tune"	The King and I	"This Is the Army, Mr. Jones"	This Is the Army
"If Ever I Would Leave You"	Camelot	"Till There Was You"	The Music Man
"It Ain't Necessarily So"	Porgy and Bess	"Tonight"	West Side Story
"I've Grown Accustomed to Her Face"	My Fair Lady	"You'll Never Walk Alone"	Carousel
"Let the Sunshine In"	Hair	"You're the Top"	Anything Goes
"Lover, Come Back to Me"	The New Moon	"We Need a Little Christmas"	Mame
"Luck Be a Lady"	Guys and Dolls	"What I Did for Love"	A Chorus Line
"Maria"	West Side Story		

SCHOOLS FOR STARS

Acting may be an art and a gift, but a little schooling never hurt, as indicated by the alumni rolls of these five career-nurturing institutions.

CARNEGIE MELLON SCHOOL OF DRAMA
Shari Belafonte, actor
Steven Bochco, producer
Albert Brooks, actor/director
Ted Danson, actor
Iris Rainier Dart, novelist
Barbara Feldon, actor
Mark Frost, producer
Mariette Hartley, actor
Holly Hunter, actor
Jack Klugman, actor
Judith Light, actor
Burke Moses, actor
John Pasquin, director
George Peppard, actor
George Romero, director
Laura San Giacomo, actor
Ellen Travolta, actress
Michael Tucker, actor
Blair Underwood, actor
John Wells, producer

JUILLIARD SCHOOL DRAMA DIVISION
Christine Baranski, actor
Andre Braugher, actor
Kelsey Grammer, actor
William Hurt, actor
Patti LuPone, actor/singer
Val Kilmer, actor
Perry King, actor
Kevin Kline, actor/director
Linda Kozlowski, actor
Kelly McGillis, actor
Elizabeth McGovern, actor
Gregory Mosher, director
Mandy Patinkin, actor/singer
Christopher Reeve, actor
David Ogden Stiers, actor

Jeanne Tripplehorn, actor
Robin Williams, actor

NEW YORK UNIVERSITY, TISCH SCHOOL OF THE ARTS
Alec Baldwin, actor
Barry Bostwick, actor
Bruce Davison, actor
Kathleen Dennehy, actor
Kathryn Erbe, actor
Bridget Fonda, actor
Marcia Gay Harden, actor
Mary Beth Hurt, actor
Tony Kushner, playwright
Andrew McCarthy, actor
Adam Sandler, actor
Stephen Spinella, actor
D. B. Sweeney, actor
Chandra Wilson, actor
George C. Wolfe, director

NORTHWESTERN UNIVERSITY SCHOOL OF SPEECH
Ann-Margret, actor/dancer
Warren Beatty, actor
Richard Benjamin, actor
Eric Bernt, screenwriter
Karen Black, actor
Brad Hall, actor
Charlton Heston, actor
Richard Kind, actor
Sherry Lansing, producer
Shelly Long, actor
Julia Louis-Dreyfus, actor
Dermot Mulroney, actor
Patricia Neal, actor
Jerry Orbach, actor
Paula Prentiss, actor
Tony Randall, actor
Tony Roberts, actor

David Schwimmer, actor
Peter Strauss, actor

YALE SCHOOL OF DRAMA
Angela Bassett, actor
Robert Brustein, director/writer
Christopher Durang, playwright
Jill Eikenberry, actor
John Guare, playwright
A. R. Gurney, playwright
Julie Harris, actor
Ken Howard, actor
David Henry Hwang, playwright/
    screenwriter
Albert Innaurato, playwright
Tama Janowitz, writer
Elia Kazan, director
Stacy Keach, actor
Mark Linn-Baker, actor
Santo Loquasto, set designer
Paul Newman, actor
Carrie Nye, actor
Talia Shire, actor
Meryl Streep, actor
Ted Tally, playwright/screenwriter
John Turturro, actor/director
Joan Van Ark, actor
Wendy Wasserstein, playwright
Sigourney Weaver, actor
Edmund Wilson, writer
Henry Winkler, actor/director

THEATER'S LEADING LIGHTS

Selected for their contributions to today's theater, the following artists are responsible for many of the most important and popular plays currently being produced in the English language. Each list of works notes every play, screenplay, or teleplay created by the artist (aside from one-acts), as well as major awards won by the work and the year of its first production.

BETH HENLEY
playwright/screenwriter

Parade (1975)

Crimes of the Heart (1979, screenplay 1987; Pulitzer Prize)

The Moon Watch (screenplay, 1983)

The Miss Firecracker Contest (1984; screenplay 1986)

The Wake of Jamey Foster (1984)

The Debutante Ball (1985)

The Lucky Spot (1986)

True Stories (coauthor, screenplay, 1986)

Nobody's Fool (screenplay, 1987)

Abundance (1989)

Signature (1990)

Control Freaks (1992)

Revelers (1994)

TONY KUSHNER
playwright

A Bright Room Called Day (1986)

The Illusion (adaptor, 1987)

Angels in America Part I: Millennium Approaches (1990; Tony Award; Pulitzer Prize)

Angels in America Part II: Perestroika (1993, Tony Award)

Slavs! (1994)

ANDREW LLOYD WEBBER
composer

Joseph and the Amazing Technicolor Dreamcoat (1968)

Jesus Christ Superstar (1971)

Jeeves (1974)

Evita (1976; Tony Award)

Cats (1982; Tony Award; Grammy Award)

Song and Dance (1982)

Starlight Express (1984)

The Phantom of the Opera (1986)

Aspects of Love (1989)

Sunset Boulevard (1993; Tony Award)

DAVID MAMET
playwright/screenwriter

The Duck Variations (1972)

Mackinac (children's play, 1974)

Squirrels (1974)

Sexual Perversity in Chicago (1974)

American Buffalo (1975)

The Poet and the Rent (1975)

Marranos (1975)

Reunion (1976)

Dark Pony (1977)

The Woods (1977)

The Revenge of the Space Pandas, or Binky Rudich and the Two-Speed Clock (1977)

The Water Engine: An American Fable (1977)

A Life in the Theatre (1977)

Lone Canoe or The Explorer (1979)

Lakeboat (1980)

The Postman Always Rings Twice (screenplay, 1981)

The Verdict (screenplay, 1982)

Edmond (1982)

Glengarry Glen Ross (1983; Pulitzer Prize; screenplay, 1992)

Disappearance of the Jews (1983)

Red River (adaptor, 1983)

Vermont Sketches (1984)

The Frog Prince (1984)

Joseph Dintenfass (1984)

The Spanish Prisoner (1985)

The Cherry Orchard (adaptor, 1985)

The Shawl (1985)

Three Sisters (adaptor, 1985)

The Untouchables (screenplay, 1987)

House of Games (screenplay, 1987)

Things Change (coauthor screenplay, 1987)

Speed-the-Plow (1988)

We're No Angels (screenplay, 1989)

Bobby Gould in Hell (1989)

Homicide (screenplay, 1991)

Oleanna (1992)

Hoffa (screenplay, 1992)

The Village (novel, 1994)

The Cryptogram (1994)

ARTHUR MILLER
playwright/screenwriter

Honors at Dawn (1936)

No Villain (1936)

The Half-Bridge (written 1943, never produced)

The Pussycat and the Expert Plumber Who Was a Man (radio play, 1943)

William Ireland's Confession (radio play, 1942)

The Man Who Had All the Luck (1944)

That They May Win (1944)

The Story of G.I. Joe (screenplay, 1945)

Grandpa and the Statue (radio play, 1942)

The Story of Gus (radio play, 1942)

All My Sons (1947)

Death of a Salesman (1948; Pulitzer Prize)

An Enemy of the People (adaptor, 1950)

The Crucible (1953; Tony Award)

A View from the Bridge (1955)

A Memory of Two Mondays (1955)

The Witches of Salem (screenplay, 1958)

The Misfits (screenplay, 1961)

After the Fall (1964)

Incident at Vichy (1964)

The Price (1968)

Fame (1971)

The Creation of the World and Other Business (1972; musical version, Up from Paradise, 1982)

The Archbishop's Ceiling (1977)

The American Clock (adaptor, 1979)

Playing for Time (adaptor, teleplay, 1981)

Two-Way Mirror (1982)

Danger: Memory! (1987)

The Golden Years (radio play, 1987)

Everybody Wins (screenplay, 1990)

The Ride Down Mt. Morgan (1991)

The Last Yankee (1993)

Broken Glass (1994)

Gellburg (1994)

MARSHA NORMAN
playwright/screenwriter

Getting Out (1977)

The Pool Hall (1978)

It's the Willingness (teleplay, 1978)

Third and Oak: The Laundromat (1978)

Circus Valentine (1979)

In Trouble at Fifteen (teleplay, 1980)

The Holdup (1980)

'Night, Mother (1983; Pulitzer Prize; screenplay, 1984)

Traveler in the Dark (1984)

The Fortune Teller (novel, 1988)

Sarah and Abraham (1988)

The Secret Garden (book and lyrics, 1989; Tony Award)

Face of a Stranger (teleplay, 1992)

Loving Daniel Boone (1992)

The Red Shoes (book and lyrics, 1993)

Trudy Blue (1995)

HAROLD PINTER
playwright/screenwriter

The Room (1957)

The Birthday Party (1958; screenplay, 1968; teleplay, 1987)

The Dumb Waiter (1960)

The Caretaker (1960)

A Night Out (radio play, 1960)

The Collection (teleplay, 1961)

The Servant (screenplay, 1963)

The Lover (1963)

The Pumpkin Eater (screenplay, 1964)

The Tea Party (1965)

The Quiller Memorandum (screenplay, 1966)

Accident (screenplay, 1967)

The Basement (radio 1967; stage 1969)

Landscape (1968)

The Homecoming (screenplay, 1973)

Silence (1969)

The Go-Between (screenplay, 1970)

The Last Tycoon (screenplay, 1971)

Old Times (1971)

The Proust Screenplay: A la Recherche du temps perdu (screenplay, 1973)

No Man's Land (1975)

Players (radio play, 1975)

Betrayal (1978; screenplay, 1982)

Langrishe, Go Down (adaptor, screenplay, 1978)

The Hothouse (1980)

The French Lieutenant's Woman (screenplay, 1981)

Other Places (1982)

Turtle Diary (screenplay, 1985)

Reunion (screenplay, 1989)

The Comfort of Strangers (screenplay, 1990)

The Handmaid's Tale (adaptor, screenplay, 1990)

Moonlight (1993)

The Trial (screenplay, 1993)

SAM SHEPARD
playwright/screenwriter

Up to Thursday (1965)

Dog (1965)

Rocking Chair (1965)

4-H Club (1965)

La Turista (1967)

Forensic and the Navigators (1967)

Me and My Brother (coauthor, screenplay, 1967)

Operation Sidewinder (1969)

The Unseen Hand (1969)

Zabriskie Point (coauthor, screenplay, 1970)

Cowboy Mouth (coauthor, 1971)

Ringaleenio (screenplay, 1971)

The Tooth of Crime (1972)

Blue Bitch (1973)

Nightwalk (coauthor, 1973)

Little Ocean (1974)

Geography of a Horse Dreamer (1974)

The Sad Lament of Pecos Bill on the Eve of Killing His Wife (1976)

Suicide in B Flat (1976)

Angel City (1977)

Curse of the Starving Class (1977)

Inacoma (1977)

Buried Child (1978; Pulitzer Prize)

Seduced (1978)

Tongues (coauthor, 1979)

Savage/Love (coauthor, 1979)

Jackson's Dance (coauthor, 1980)

True West (1980)

Black Bart and the Sacred Hills (1981)

Fool for Love (1983; screenplay, 1985)

Superstitions (1983)

Paris, Texas (coauthor, screenplay, 1984)

A Lie of the Mind (1985)

The War in Heaven: Angel's Monologue (coauthor, teleplay, 1985)

States of Shock (1989)

Far North (screenplay, 1992)

Silent Tongue (screenplay, 1993)

Simpatico (1994)

NEIL SIMON
playwright/screenwriter

Adventures of Marco Polo: A Musical Fantasy (book, 1959)

Heidi (book, 1959)

Come Blow Your Horn (1961)

Little Me (book, 1962; revised version 1982)

Barefoot in the Park (originally Nobody Loves Me, 1963; screenplay, 1967)

The Odd Couple (1965; Tony Award; screenplay, 1968; female version, 1985)

Sweet Charity (book, 1966)

The Star-Spangled Girl (1966)

After the Fox (screenplay, 1966)

Promises, Promises (book, 1968)

Plaza Suite (1968; screenplay, 1971)

The Last of the Red-Hot Lovers (1969; screenplay, 1972)

The Gingerbread Lady (1970)

The Out-of-Towners (screenplay, 1970)

The Prisoner of Second Avenue (1971; screenplay, 1975)

The Heartbreak Kid (screenplay, 1973)

The Sunshine Boys (1972; screenplay, 1975)

The Good Doctor (1973)

God's Favorite (1974)

California Suite (1976; screenplay 1978)

Murder by Death (screenplay, 1976)

The Goodbye Girl (screenplay, 1977; book, 1993)

Chapter Two (1977; screenplay, 1979)

The Cheap Detective (screenplay, 1978)

They're Playing Our Song (book, 1979)

I Ought To Be in Pictures (1980; screenplay, 1982)

Seems Like Old Times (screenplay, 1980)

Fools (1981)

Only When I Laugh (screenplay, 1982)

Max Dugan Returns (screenplay, 1983)

Brighton Beach Memoirs (1983; Pulitzer Prize; screenplay, 1986)

The Slugger's Wife (screenplay, 1984)

Biloxi Blues (1985; screenplay, 1988)

Broadway Bound (1986)

Rumors (1988)

Lost in Yonkers (1991; screenplay, 1993)

The Marrying Man (screenplay, 1991)

Broadway Bound (screenplay, made-for-TV movie, 1992)

Jake's Women (1992)

Laughter on the 23rd Floor (1993)

London Suite (1995)

A special Tony was awarded to Mr. Simon in 1975 for overall contribution to the theater.

STEPHEN SONDHEIM
composer/lyricist

West Side Story (lyrics, 1957)

Gypsy (lyrics, 1959)

A Funny Thing Happened on the Way to the Forum (music and lyrics, 1962)

Anyone Can Whistle (music and lyrics, 1964)

Do I Hear a Waltz? (lyrics, 1965)

The Mad Show (co-lyricist, 1966)

Company (music and lyrics, 1970; Tony Award)

Follies (music and lyrics, 1971; Tony Award)

A Little Night Music (music and lyrics, 1973; Tony Award)

Candide (revival, co-lyricist, 1973)

The Frogs (music and lyrics, 1974)

Pacific Overtures (music and lyrics, 1976)

Sweeney Todd (music and lyrics, 1979; Tony Award)

Merrily We Roll Along (1981)

Sunday in the Park with George (music and lyrics, 1984; Pulitzer Prize)

Into the Woods (1987)

Assassins (1991)

Passion (music and lyrics, 1994; Tony Award)

MUSICAL THEATER HALL OF FAME

Rock and roll has one and so do most sports, so it seems fitting that musical theater—perhaps the most American of all arts—should have one, too. The Musical Theater Hall of Fame, organized by a committee of theater experts and fans from New York University, announced its first set of inductees (greats from the past) and honorees (still-active legends) in 1993.

INDUCTEES:

Jerome Kern
George and Ira Gershwin
Richard Rodgers
Oscar Hammerstein II
Alan Jay Lerner
Frederick Loewe
Ethel Merman
Irving Berlin
Cole Porter
E. Y. "Yip" Harburg
Mary Martin

HONOREES:

Carol Channing
Jule Styne
George Abbott
Gwen Verdon
Betty Comden
Adolph Green

TOM STOPPARD
playwright

A Walk on the Water (1963)

The Dissolution of Dominic Boot (radio play, 1964)

"M" is for Moon Among Other Things (radio play, 1964)

The Gamblers (1965)

If You're Glad I'll Be Frank (radio play, 1966)

Rosencrantz and Guildenstern Are Dead (1966; Tony Award; screenplay, 1991)

Tango (adaptor, 1966)

A Separate Peace (teleplay, 1966)

Lord Malquist and Mr. Moon (novel, 1966)

Albert's Bridge (radio play, 1967)

Teeth (teleplay, 1967)

Another Moon Called Earth (teleplay, 1967)

Neutral Ground (teleplay, 1968)

The Real Inspector Hound (1968)

After Magritte (1970)

Where Are They Now? (radio play, 1970)

Dogg's Our Pet (1971)

Jumpers (1972)

Artist Descending a Staircase (radio play, 1972; stage, 1988)

The House of Bernarda Alba (adaptor, 1973)

Travesties (1974; Tony Award)

Dirty Linen, and New-found-land (1976)

The Fifteen Minute Hamlet (1976)

Professional Foul (teleplay, 1977)

Every Good Boy Deserves Favour: A Play for Actors and Orchestra (1977)

Night and Day (1978)

Undiscovered Country (adaptor, 1979)

Dogg's Hamlet, Cahoot's Mac-Beth (1979)

On the Razzle (adaptor, 1981)

The Real Thing (1982; Tony Award)

The Dog It Was That Died (radio play, 1982)

The Love for Three Oranges (adaptor, 1983)

Rough Crossing (adaptor, 1984)

Squaring the Circle: Poland 1980–81 (TV docudrama, 1984)

Dalliance (adaptor, 1986)

Largo Desolato (adaptor, 1986)

Brazil (screenplay, 1987)

Hapgood (1988)

In the Native State (radio play, 1991)

Arcadia (1993)

Indian Ink (1994)

TOMMY TUNE
director/choreographer/performer

Baker Street (actor, 1965)

A Joyful Noise (actor, 1967)

How Now Dow Jones (actor, 1968)

Seesaw (actor, 1973; Tony)

The Club (director, 1976)

Sunset (director, 1977)

The Best Little Whorehouse in Texas (co-director and choreographer, 1978)

A Day in Hollywood/A Night in the Ukraine (director and choreographer, 1980; Tony Award for best choreographer)

Cloud 9 (director, 1981)

Nine (director and choreographer, 1982; Tony Award for best director)

My One and Only (co-director, co-choreographer, actor, 1983; Tony Awards for best choreographer and best actor)

Stepping Out (director, 1987)

Grand Hotel (1989; Tony Awards for best director and best choreographer)

The Will Rogers Follies (director, choreographer, 1991; Tony Awards for best director and best choreographer)

The Best Little Whorehouse Goes Public (co-director, 1994)

Buskers (actor, 1995)

WENDY WASSERSTEIN
playwright/screenwriter

Any Woman Can't (1973)

When Dinah Shore Ruled the Earth (coauthor, 1977)

Uncommon Women and Others (teleplay, 1978)

The Sorrows of Gin (adaptor, teleplay, 1981)

Hard Sell (1980)

Isn't It Romantic? (1981)

Tender Offer (1983)

The Man in a Case (adaptor, 1985)

Miami (coauthor, book, 1985)

Drive, She Said (1988)

The Heidi Chronicles (1988; Pulitzer Prize, Tony Award)

Kiss, Kiss Darling (1991)

The Sisters Rosenzweig (1993)

The Object of My Affection (1994)

AUGUST WILSON
playwright

Black Bart and the Sacred Hills (1981)

Jitney (1982)

Joe Turner's Come and Gone (1983)

Ma Rainey's Black Bottom (1984)

Fences (1985; Pulitzer, Tony)

The Piano Lesson (1987; Pulitzer)

Two Trains Running (1990)

Seven Guitars (1995)

BREAKTHROUGH BRITISH IMPORTS

Some of the most significant and successful shows on Broadway over the last 20 years have been imported from Britain. The following list credits the major figures behind them and gives the year of their American premiere.

Amadeus, Peter Shaffer, director Peter Hall (1980)

An Inspector Calls, J. B. Priestly, director Stephen Daldry (1995)

Arcadia, Tom Stoppard, director Trevor Nunn (1995)

Aspects of Love, Andrew Lloyd Webber, Don Black, and Charles Hart, director Trevor Nunn, producer Cameron Mackintosh (1989)

Betrayal, Harold Pinter, director Peter Hall (1980)

Cats, Andrew Lloyd Webber, Trevor Nunn, director Trevor Nunn, producer Cameron Mackintosh (1982)

Equus, Peter Shaffer, director John Dexter (1974)

Evita, Andrew Lloyd Webber and Tim Rice, director Harold Prince (1979)

Hamlet, Shakespeare, director Jonathan Kent, Ralph Fiennes as Hamlet (1995)

Jesus Christ Superstar, Andrew Lloyd Webber and Tim Rice, director Tim O'Horgan (1971)

Joseph and the Amazing Technicolor Dreamcoat, Andrew Lloyd Webber and Tim Rice, director Tony Tanner (1982)

Les Liaisons Dangereuses, Christopher Hampton, Royal Shakespeare Company production, director Howard Davies (1987)

Les Misérables, by Claude-Michel Schönberg, Alain Boublil, Herbert Kretzmer, directors and adaptors Trevor Nunn and John Caird (1987)

Me and My Girl, L. Arthur Rose, Douglas Furber, Noel Gay, director Mike Ockrent (1986)

Miss Saigon, Claude-Michel Schönberg, Alain Boublil, Richard Maltby, director Nicholas Hytner (1991)

Nicholas Nickleby, David Edgar, directors Trevor Nunn and John Caird, producer Cameron Mackintosh (1986)

Noises Off, Michael Frayn, director Michael Blakemore (1983)

The Norman Conquests, Alan Ayckbourn, director Eric Thompson (1975)

Oliver!, Lionel Bart, director Peter Coe, producer Cameron Mackintosh (1984)

The Phantom of the Opera, Andrew Lloyd Webber, Charles Hart, Richard Stilgoe, director Harold Prince (1988)

Plenty, David Hare, director David Hare (1983)

The Real Thing, Tom Stoppard, director Mike Nichols (1984)

The Rocky Horror Show, Richard O'Brien, director Jim Sharman (1975)

Some Americans Abroad, Richard Nelson, director Roger Mitchell, Royal Shakespeare Company production (1990)

Starlight Express, Andrew Lloyd Webber and Richard Stilgoe, director Trevor Nunn (1987)

Sunset Boulevard, Andrew Lloyd Webber, Don Black, and Christopher Hampton (1994)

Ralph Fiennes and Francesca Annis in Hamlet.

MAJOR SHOWS THAT BEGAN IN REGIONAL THEATERS

Beginning in the '70s, the creative impetus in American drama began to shift away from the increasingly expensive Broadway venues and toward regional and nonprofit theaters. While most major playwrights once wrote directly for Broadway production, regional theaters have more commonly become the place of origination for America's most important plays. The following productions may have gone on to national and even international fame, but all began in regional theaters.

American Buffalo, by David Mamet, Goodman Theater, Chicago

Angels in America, by Tony Kushner, Eureka Theatre Company, San Francisco

Annie, by Thomas Meehan, Martin Charnin, and Charles Strouse, Goodspeed Opera House, East Haddam, Connecticut

Big River, adapted by William Hauptman from

Mark Twain, La Jolla Playhouse, La Jolla, California

Buried Child, by Sam Shepard, Magic Theater, San Francisco

California Suite, by Neil Simon, Hartman Theatre, Stamford, Connecticut

Children of a Lesser God, by Mark Medoff, Mark Taper Forum, Los Angeles

The Colored Museum, by George C. Wolfe, Crossroads Theatre Company, New Brunswick, New Jersey

Conversations with my Father, by Herb Gardner, Seattle Repertory Theatre

Crimes of the Heart, by Beth Henley, Actors Theatre of Louisville

Eastern Standard, by Richard Greenberg, Seattle Repertory Theatre

GETTING THE TICKET: THE BROADWAY TAP

Though Broadway ticket prices have risen with inflation over the past two decades, theater attendance has remained fairly steady. The prices listed below represent the net collected by management after taxes and various deductions; show-goers actually paid about 10% more. (Source: *Variety*)

Year	Average Ticket Price	Attendance	Year	Average Ticket Price	Attendance
1975-76	$9.86	7,181,898	1985-86	$29.20	6,527,498
1976-77	10.60	8,815,095	1986-87	29.74	6,968,277
1977-78	12.05	8,621,262	1987-88	31.65	8,142,722
1978-79	14.02	9,115,613	1988-89	32.88	7,968,273
1979-80	15.29	9,380,648	1989-90	35.24	8,039,106
1980-81	17.97	10,822,324	1990-91	36.53	7,314,138
1981-82	22.07	10,694,373	1991-92	39.69	7,365,528
1982-83	25.07	8,102,262	1992-93	41.71	7,856,727
1983-84	28.68	7,898,765	1993-94	43.87	8,116,031
1984-85	29.06	7,156,683	1994-95	44.92	9,044,763

Fences, by August Wilson, Yale Repertory Theatre, New Haven, Connecticut

The Gin Game, by D. L. Coburn, Long Wharf Theatre, New Haven, Connecticut

Glengarry Glen Ross, by David Mamet, Goodman Theatre, Chicago

The Heidi Chronicles, by Wendy Wasserstein, Seattle Repertory Theatre

I'm Not Rappaport, by Herb Gardner, Seattle Repertory Theatre

In the Belly of the Beast, adapted by Adrian Hall from Jack Henry Abbott, Trinity Repertory Company, Providence, Rhode Island

Into the Woods, by James Lapine and Stephen Sondheim, Old Globe Theatre, San Diego

Jelly's Last Jam, by George C. Wolfe, Jelly Roll Morton, and Susan Birkenhead, Mark Taper Forum, Los Angeles

Joe Turner's Come and Gone, by August Wilson, Yale Repertory Theatre, New Haven, Connecticut

Love Letters, by A. R. Gurney, Long Wharf Theatre, New Haven, Connecticut

Ma Rainey's Black Bottom, by August Wilson, Yale Repertory Theatre, New Haven, Connecticut

Master Harold and the Boys, by Athol Fugard, Yale Repertory Theatre, New Haven, Connecticut

'Night, Mother, by Marsha Norman, American Repertory Theatre, Cambridge, Massachusetts

Prelude to a Kiss, by Craig Lucas, South Coast Repertory, Costa Mesa, California

Quilters, by Molly Newman and Barbara Damashek, Denver Center Theatre Company

Streamers, by David Rabe, Long Wharf Theatre, New Haven, Connecticut

True West, by Sam Shepard, Steppenwolf Theatre Company, Chicago

Two Trains Running, by August Wilson, Yale Repertory Theatre, New Haven, Connecticut

The Wake of Jamey Foster, by Beth Henley, Hartford Stage Company, Hartford, Connecticut

The Who's "Tommy," by Pete Townshend and Wayne Cilento, La Jolla Playhouse, La Jolla, California

How To Succeed in Business Without Really Trying, La Jolla Playhouse, La Jolla, California

Master Class, by Terrence McNally, Philadelphia Theater Company, Pennsylvania

Twilight, by Anna Deavere Smith, Mark Taper Forum, Los Angeles, California

MAJOR REGIONAL THEATERS AND THEIR DIRECTORS

Far from the bright lights of Broadway, vibrant regional theater companies can be found in rural communities, urban neighborhoods, metropolitan centers, and suburbs around the U.S. Their repertoire ranges from the classics to musicals to modern plays to experimental, multi-media, and solo performance works. Despite deeply felt cuts in government funding, these shining companies continue to cast their light from every corner of the country.

Actors Theatre of Louisville, Louisville, Kentucky, Jon Jory, producing director

Alley Theatre, Houston, Gregory Boyd, artistic director

Alliance Theatre Company, Atlanta, Kenny Leon, artistic director

American Conservatory Theater, San Francisco, Carey Perloff, artistic director

American Repertory Theatre, Cambridge, Massachusetts, Robert Brustein, artistic director

Arena Stage, Washington, D.C., Douglas Wager, artistic director

Center Stage, Baltimore, Irene Lewis, artistic director

Dallas Theater Center, Dallas, Richard Hamburger, artistic director

Goodman Theatre, Chicago, Robert Falls, artistic director

Goodspeed Opera House, East Haddam, Connecticut, Michael P. Price, executive director

Guthrie Theater, Minneapolis, Garland Wright, artistic director

Hartford Stage Company, Hartford, Connecticut, Mark Lamos, artistic director

La Jolla Playhouse, La Jolla, California, Michael Greif, artistic director

Long Wharf Theatre, New Haven, Connecticut, Arvin Brown, artistic director

Mark Taper Forum, Los Angeles, Gordon Davidson, artistic director

McCarter Theatre Center, Princeton, New Jersey, Emily Mann, artistic director

Milwaukee Repertory Theater, Milwaukee, Joseph Hanreddy, artistic director

Old Globe Theatre, San Diego, Jack O'Brien, artistic director

Oregon Shakespeare Festival, Ashland and Portland, Oregon, Henry Woronicz, artistic director

Seattle Repertory Theatre, Seattle, Daniel Sullivan, artistic director

Shakespeare Theatre, Washington, D.C., Michael Kahn, artistic director

South Coast Repertory, Costa Mesa, California, David Emmes, producing artistic director

Steppenwolf Theatre Company, Chicago, Randall Arney, artistic director

Trinity Repertory Company, Providence, Rhode Island, Oscar Eustis, artistic director

Yale Repertory Theatre, New Haven, Connecticut, Stan Wojewodski Jr., artistic director

WHAT'S HOT IN HIGH SCHOOL DRAMA

Here's a list of the most popular full-length shows for high-school performance in the United States, over the last year and over the entire post–World War II period through 1984. In the September 1985 issue of *Dramatics* magazine, one theater educator lamented the list's conservatism—its preponderance of musicals, oldies, and relatively unadventurous shows by American playwrights.

1994

1. *A Midsummer Night's Dream*, William Shakespeare
2. *Fiddler on the Roof*, Joseph Stein, Jerry Block, and Sheldon Harnick (tie)
2. *Little Shop of Horrors*, Howard Ashman and Alan Menken (tie)
4. *Anything Goes*, Howard Lindsay, Russel Crouse, Guy Bolton, P. G. Wodehouse, and Cole Porter
5. *Arsenic and Old Lace*, Joseph Kesselring
6. *Guys and Dolls*, Frank Loesser, Jo Swerling, and Abe Burrows (tie)
6. *Our Town*, Thornton Wilder (tie)
8. *Bye Bye Birdie*, Michael Stewart, Charles Strouse, and Lee Adams
9. *You Can't Take It with You*, Moss Hart and George S. Kaufman
10. *Godspell*, Stephen Schwartz and John-Michael Tebelak (tie)
10. *Oklahoma!*, Oscar Hammerstein II and Richard Rodgers (tie)
10. *Rumors*, Neil Simon (tie)
10. *The Sound of Music*, Howard Lindsay, Russel Crouse, Richard Rodgers, and Oscar Hammerstein II (tie)
14. *The Miracle Worker*, William Gibson (tie)
14. *Up the Down Staircase*, Christopher Serge, from the novel by Bel Kaufman (tie)
16. *Annie*, Thomas Meehan, Charles Strouse, and Martin Charnin (tie)
16. *Steel Magnolias*, Robert Harling (tie)
16. *Meet Me in St. Louis*, Sally Benson, Hugh Martin, and Ralph Blane (tie)
19. *Dracula,* various adaptations based on the novel by Bram Stoker (tie)
19. *Once upon a Mattress*, Jay Thompson, Marshall Barer, Dean Fuller, and Mary Rogers (tie)
19. *Rehearsal for Murder*, adapted by D. D. Brooke from the teleplay by Richard Levinson and William Link (tie)
19. *The Wizard of Oz,* various adaptations based on the novel by L. Frank Baum (tie)

1945–1984

1. *You Can't Take It with You*, Moss Hart and George S. Kaufman
2. *Our Town*, Thornton Wilder
3. *Arsenic and Old Lace*, Joseph Kesselring
4. *Harvey*, Mary Chase
5. *The Curious Savage*, John Patrick
6. *Oklahoma!*, Richard Rodgers and Oscar Hammerstein II
7. *The Miracle Worker*, William Gibson (tie)
7. *The Diary of Anne Frank*, Frances Goodrich and Albert Hackett (tie)
9. *The Music Man*, Meredith Wilson (tie)
9. *Our Hearts Were Young and Gay*, Jean Kerr (tie)
9. *The Night of January 16*, Ayn Rand (tie)
12. *Bye Bye Birdie*, Michael Stewart, Charles Strouse, and Lee Adams
13. *The Man Who Came to Dinner*, George S. Kaufman and Moss Hart
14. *Up the Down Staircase*, Christopher Serge, from the novel by Bel Kaufman (tie)
14. *You're a Good Man, Charlie Brown*, John Gordon and Clark Gesner (tie)
14. *The Sound of Music*, Richard Rodgers and Oscar Hammerstein II (tie)
17. *Guys and Dolls*, Frank Loesser, Jo Swerling, and Abe Burrows
18. *Godspell*, John Michael Tebelak and Stephen Schwartz
19. *Teahouse of the August Moon*, John Patrick
20. *The Crucible*, Arthur Miller

THE TONY AWARDS

	1947	1948	1949
Actor (Dramatic)	Fredric March, *Years Ago*; Jose Ferrer, *Cyrano de Bergerac*	Basil Rathbone, *The Heiress*; Henry Fonda, *Mister Roberts*; Paul Kelly, *Command Decision*	Rex Harrison, *Anne of the Thousand Days*
Actress (Dramatic)	Helen Hayes, *Happy Birthday*; Ingrid Bergman, *Joan of Lorraine*	Jessica Tandy, *A Streetcar Named Desire*; Judith Anderson, *Medea*; Katharine Cornell, *Antony and Cleopatra*	Martita Hunt, *The Madwoman of Chaillot*
Supporting Actor (Dramatic)	—	—	Arthur Kennedy, *Death of a Salesman*
Supporting Actress (Dramatic)	Patricia Neal, *Another Part of the Forest*	—	Shirley Booth, *Goodbye, My Fancy*
Play	—	*Mister Roberts*	*Death of a Salesman*
Actor (Musical)	—	Paul Hartman, *Angel in the Wings*	Ray Bolger, *Where's Charley?*
Actress (Musical)	—	Grace Hartman, *Angel in the Wings*	Nanette Fabray, *Love Life*
Supporting Actor (Musical)	David Wayne, *Finian's Rainbow*	—	—
Supporting Actress (Musical)	—	—	—
Musical	—	—	*Kiss Me Kate*
Director	Elia Kazan, *All My Sons*	—	Elia Kazan, *Death of a Salesman*
Score	—	—	Cole Porter, *Kiss Me Kate*
Author (Dramatic)	—	Thomas Heggen and Joshua Logan, *Mister Roberts*	Arthur Miller, *Death of a Salesman*
Author (Musical)	—		Bella and Samuel Spewack, *Kiss Me Kate*
Scenic Designer	—	Horace Armistead, *The Medium*	Jo Mielziner, *Sleepy Hollow; Summer and Smoke; Anne of the Thousand Days; Death of a Salesman; South Pacific*
Costume Designer	—	—	Lemuel Ayers, *Kiss Me Kate*
Choreographer	Agnes de Mille, *Brigadoon*; Michael Kidd, *Finian's Rainbow*	Jerome Robbins, *High Button Shoes*	Gower Champion, *Lend an Ear*
Producer (Dramatic)	—	Leland Hayward, *Mister Roberts*	Kermit Bloomgarden and Walter Fried, *Death of a Salesman*
Producer (Musical)	—	—	Saint-Subber and Lemuel Ayers, *Kiss Me Kate*
Conductor and Musical Director	—	—	Max Meth, *As the Girls Go*
Stage Technician	—	George Gebhardt; George Pierce	—

1950	1951	1952	1953
Sydney Blackmer, *Come Back, Little Sheba*	Claude Rains, *Darkness At Noon*	Jose Ferrer, *The Shrike*	Tom Ewell, *The Seven Year Itch*
Shirley Booth, *Come Back, Little Sheba*	Uta Hagen, *The Country Girl*	Julie Harris, *I Am a Camera*	Shirley Booth, *Time of the Cuckoo*
—	Eli Wallach, *The Rose Tattoo*	John Cromwell, *Point of No Return*	John Williams, *Dial M for Murder*
—	Maureen Stapleton, *The Rose Tattoo*	Marian Winters, *I Am a Camera*	Beatrice Straight, *The Crucible*
The Cocktail Party	*The Rose Tattoo*	*The Fourposter*	*The Crucible*
Ezio Pinza, *South Pacific*	Robert Alda, *Guys and Dolls*	Phil Silvers, *Top Banana*	Thomas Mitchell, *Hazel Flagg*
Mary Martin, *South Pacific*	Ethel Merman, *Call Me Madam*	Gertrude Lawrence, *The King & I*	Rosalind Russell, *Wonderful Town*
Myron McCormick, *South Pacific*	Russell Nype, *Call Me Madam*	Yul Brynner, *The King & I*	Hiram Sherman, *Two's Company*
Juanita Hall, *South Pacific*	Isabel Bigley, *Guys And Dolls*	Helen Gallagher, *Pal Joey*	Sheila Bond, *Wish You Were Here*
South Pacific	*Guys And Dolls*	*The King & I*	*Wonderful Town*
Joshua Logan, *South Pacific*	George S. Kaufman, *Guys and Dolls*	Jose Ferrer, *The Shrike; The Fourposter; Stalag 17*	Joshua Logan, *Picnic*
Richard Rodgers, *South Pacific*	Frank Loesser, *Guys and Dolls*	—	Leonard Bernstein, *Wonderful Town*
T.S. Eliot, *The Cocktail Party*	Tennessee Williams, *The Rose Tattoo*	—	Arthur Miller, *The Crucible*
Oscar Hammerstein II and Joshua Logan, *South Pacific*	Jo Swerling and Abe Burrows, *Guys and Dolls*	—	Joseph Fields and Jerome Chodorov, *Wonderful Town*
Jo Mielziner, *The Innocents*	Boris Aronson, *The Rose Tattoo; The Country Girl; Season in the Sun*	Jo Mielziner, *The King & I*	Raoul Pene du Bois, *Wonderful Town*
Aline Bernstein, *Regina*	Miles White, *Bless You All*	Irene Sharaff, *The King and I*	Miles White, *Hazel Flagg*
Helen Tamiris, *Touch and Go*	Michael Kidd, *Guys and Dolls*	Robert Alton, *Pal Joey*	Donald Saddler, *Wonderful Town*
Gilbert Miller, *The Cocktail Party*	Cheryl Crawford, *The Rose Tattoo*	—	Kermit Bloomgarden, *The Crucible*
Richard Rodgers, Oscar Hammerstein II, Leland Hayward, and Joshua Logan, *South Pacific*	Cy Feuer and Ernest H. Martin, *Guys and Dolls*	—	Robert Fryer, *Wonderful Town*
Maurice Abravanel, *Regina*	Lehman Engel, *The Consul*	Max Meth, *Pal Joey*	Lehman Engel, *Wonderful Town; Gilbert and Sullivan Season*
Joe Lynn, master propertyman, *Miss Liberty*	Richard Raven, *The Autumn Garden*	Peter Feller, master carpenter, *Call Me Madam*	Abe Kurnit, *Wish You Were Here*

	1954	1955	1956
Actor (Dramatic)	David Wayne, *The Teahouse of the August Moon*	Alfred Lunt, *Quadrille*	Paul Muni, *Inherit the Wind*
Actress (Dramatic)	Audrey Hepburn, *Ondine*	Nancy Kelly, *The Bad Seed*	Julie Harris, *The Lark*
Featured/Supporting Actor (Dramatic)	John Kerr, *Tea and Sympathy*	Francis L. Sullivan, *Witness for the Prosecution*	Ed Begley, *Inherit the Wind*
Featured/Supporting Actress (Dramatic)	Jo Van Fleet, *The Trip to Bountiful*	Patricia Jessel, *Witness for the Prosecution*	Una Merkel, *The Ponder Heart*
Play	*The Teahouse of the August Moon*	*The Desperate Hours*	*The Diary of Anne Frank*
Actor (Musical)	Alfred Drake, *Kismet*	Walter Slezak, *Fanny*	Ray Walston, *Damn Yankees*
Actress (Musical)	Dolores Gray, *Carnival In Flanders*	Mary Martin, *Peter Pan*	Gwen Verdon, *Damn Yankees*
Featured/Supporting Actor Role (Musical)	Harry Belafonte, *John Murray Anderson's Almanac*	Cyril Ritchard, *Peter Pan*	Russ Brown, *Damn Yankees*
Featured/Supporting Actress (Musical)	Gwen Verdon, *Can-Can*	Carol Haney, *The Pajama Game*	Lotte Lenya, *The Threepenny Opera*
Musical	*Kismet*	*The Pajama Game*	*Damn Yankees*
Director	Alfred Lunt, *Ondine*	Robert Montgomery, *The Desperate Hours*	Tyrone Guthrie, *The Matchmaker; Six Characters in Search of an Author; Tamburlaine the Great*
Director (Dramatic)	—	—	—
Director (Musical)	—	—	—
Score	Alexander Borodin, *Kismet*	Richard Adler and Jerry Ross, *The Pajama Game*	Richard Adler and Jerry Ross, *Damn Yankees*
Author (Dramatic)	John Patrick, *The Teahouse of the August Moon*	Joseph Hayes, *The Desperate Hours*	Frances Goodrich and Albert Hackett, *The Diary of Anne Frank*
Author (Musical)	Charles Lederer and Luther Davis, *Kismet*	George Abbott and Richard Bissell, *The Pajama Game*	George Abbott and Douglass Wallop, *Damn Yankees*
Scenic Designer	Peter Larkin, *Ondine; The Teahouse of the August Moon*	Oliver Messel, *House of Flowers*	Peter Larkin, *Inherit the Wind; No Time for Sergeants*
Costume Designer	Richard Whorf, *Ondine*	Cecil Beaton, *Quadrille*	Alvin Colt, *The Lark/Phoenix '55/ Pipe Dream*
Choreographer	Michael Kidd, *Can-Can*	Bob Fosse, *The Pajama Game*	Bob Fosse, *Damn Yankees*
Producer (Dramatic)	Maurice Evans and George Schaefer, *The Teahouse of the August Moon*	Howard Erskine and Joseph Hayes, *The Desperate Hours*	Kermit Bloomgarden, *The Diary of Anne Frank*
Producer (Musical)	Charles Lederer, *Kismet*	Frederick Brisson, Robert Griffith, and Harold S. Prince, *The Pajama Game*	Frederick Brisson, Robert Griffith, Harold S. Prince in association with Albert B. Taylor, *Damn Yankees*
Conductor and Musical Director	Louis Adrian, *Kismet*	Thomas Schippers, *The Saint of Bleecker Street*	Hal Hastings, *Damn Yankees*
Stage Technician	John Davis, *Picnic*	Richard Rodda, *Peter Pan*	Harry Green, electrician and sound man, *The Middle of the Night; Damn Yankees*

1957	1958	1959	1960
Fredric March, *Long Day's Journey into Night*	Ralph Bellamy, *Sunrise at Campobello*	Jason Robards Jr., *The Disenchanted*	Melvyn Douglas, *The Best Man*
Margaret Leighton, *Separate Tables*	Helen Hayes, *Time Remembered*	Gertrude Berg, *A Majority of One*	Anne Bancroft, *The Miracle Worker*
Frank Conroy, *The Potting Shed*	Henry Jones, *Sunrise at Campobello*	Charlie Ruggles, *The Pleasure of His Company*	Roddy McDowall, *The Fighting Cock*
Peggy Cass, *Auntie Mame*	Anne Bancroft, *Two for the Seesaw*	Julie Newmar, *The Marriage-Go-Round*	Anne Revere, *Toys In the Attic*
Long Day's Journey into Night	*Sunrise at Campobello*	*J.B.*	*The Miracle Worker*
Rex Harrison, *My Fair Lady*	Robert Preston, *The Music Man*	Richard Kiley, *Redhead*	Jackie Gleason, *Take Me Along*
Judy Holliday, *Bells Are Ringing*	Gwen Verdon, *New Girl In Town*; Thelma Ritter, *New Girl In Town*	Gwen Verdon, *Redhead*	Mary Martin, *The Sound of Music*
Sydney Chaplin, *Bells Are Ringing*	David Burns, *The Music Man*	Russell Nype, *Goldilocks*; cast of *La Plume de ma tante*	Tom Bosley, *Fiorello!*
Edith Adams, *Li'l Abner*	Barbara Cook, *The Music Man*	Pat Stanley, *Goldilocks*; cast of *La Plume de ma tante*	Patricia Neway, *The Sound of Music*
My Fair Lady	*The Music Man*	*Redhead*	*Fiorello!*
Moss Hart, *My Fair Lady*	—	Elia Kazan, *J.B.*	—
—	Vincent J. Donehue, *Sunrise at Campobello*	—	Arthur Penn, *The Miracle Worker*
—	—	—	George Abbott, *Fiorello!*
Frederick Loewe, *My Fair Lady*	Meredith Willson, *The Music Man*	Albert Hague, *Redhead*	Jerry Bock, *Fiorello!*; Richard Rodgers, *The Sound of Music*
Eugene O'Neill, *Long Day's Journey into Night*	Dore Schary, *Sunrise at Campobello*	Archibald MacLeish, *J.B.*	William Gibson, *The Miracle Worker*
Alan Jay Lerner, *My Fair Lady*	Meredith Willson and Franklin Lacey, *The Music Man*	Herbert and Dorothy Fields, Sidney Sheldon, and David Shaw, *Redhead*	Jerome Weidman and George Abbott, *Fiorello!*; Howard Lindsay and Russel Crouse, *The Sound of Music*
Oliver Smith, *A Clearing in the Woods; Candide; Auntie Mame; My Fair Lady; Eugenia; A Visit to a Small Planet*	Oliver Smith, *West Side Story*	Donald Oenslager, *A Majority of One*	Howard Bey, *Toys in the Attic* (Dramatic); Oliver Smith, *The Sound of Music* (Musical)
Cecil Beaton, *Little Glass Clock/ My Fair Lady*	Motley, *The First Gentleman*	Robert Ter-Arutunian, *Redhead*	Cecil Beaton, *Saratoga*
Michael Kidd, *Li'l Abner*	Jerome Robbins, *West Side Story*	Bob Fosse, *Redhead*	Michael Kidd, *Destry Rides Again*
Leigh Connell, Theodore Mann, and Jose Quintero, *Long Day's Journey into Night*	Lawrence Langner, Theresa Helburn, Armina Marshall, and Dore Schary, *Sunrise at Campobello*	Alfred de Liagre, Jr., *J.B.*	Fred Coe, *The Miracle Worker*
Herman Levin, *My Fair Lady*	Kermit Bloomgarden, Herbert Greene, Frank Productions, *The Music Man*	Robert Fryer and Lawrence Carr, *Redhead*	Robert Griffith and Harold Prince, *Fiorello!*; Leland Hayward and Richard Halliday, *The Sound of Music*
Franz Allers, *My Fair Lady*	Herbert Greene, *The Music Man*	Salvatore Dell'Isola, *Flower Drum Song*	Frederick Dvonch, *The Sound of Music*
Howard McDonald (posthumous), carpenter, *Major Barbara*	Harry Romar, *Time Remembered*	Sam Knapp, *The Music Man*	John Walters, chief carpenter, *The Miracle Worker*

	1961	1962	1963
Actor (Dramatic)	Zero Mostel, *Rhinoceros*	Paul Scofield, *A Man for All Seasons*	Arthur Hill, *Who's Afraid of Virginia Woolf?*
Actress (Dramatic)	Joan Plowright, *A Taste of Honey*	Margaret Leighton, *Night of the Iguana*	Uta Hagen, *Who's Afraid of Virginia Woolf?*
Featured/Supporting Actor (Dramatic)	Martin Gabel, *Big Fish, Little Fish*	Walter Matthau, *A Shot in the Dark*	Alan Arkin, *Enter Laughing*
Featured/Supporting Actress (Dramatic)	Colleen Dewhurst, *All the Way Home*	Elizabeth Ashley, *Take Her, She's Mine*	Sandy Dennis, *A Thousand Clowns*
Play	*Becket*	*A Man for All Seasons*	*Who's Afraid of Virginia Woolf?*
Actor (Musical)	Richard Burton, *Camelot*	Robert Morse, *How To Succeed in Business Without Really Trying*	Zero Mostel, *A Funny Thing Happened on the Way to the Forum*
Actress (Musical)	Elizabeth Seal, *Irma La Douce*	Anna Maria Alberghetti, *Carnival*	Vivien Leigh, *Tovarich*
Featured/Supporting Actor (Musical)	Dick Van Dyke, *Bye, Bye Birdie*	Charles Nelson Reilly, *How To Succeed in Business Without Really Trying*	David Burns, *A Funny Thing Happened on the Way to the Forum*
Featured/Supporting Actress (Musical)	Tammy Grimes, *The Unsinkable Molly Brown*	Phyllis Newman, *Subways Are for Sleeping*	Anna Quayle, *Stop the World—I Want To Get Off*
Musical	*Bye, Bye Birdie*	*How To Succeed in Business Without Really Trying*	*A Funny Thing Happened on the Way to the Forum*
Director (Dramatic)	John Gielgud, *Big Fish, Little Fish*	Noel Willman, *A Man for All Seasons*	Alan Schneider, *Who's Afraid of Virginia Woolf?*
Director (Musical)	Gower Champion, *Bye, Bye Birdie*	Abe Burrows, *How To Succeed in Business Without Really Trying*	George Abbott, *A Funny Thing Happened on the Way to the Forum*
Score	—	Richard Rodgers, *No Strings*	Lionel Bart, *Oliver!*
Author (Dramatic)	Jean Anouilh, *Becket*	Robert Bolt, *A Man for All Seasons*	—
Author (Musical)	Michael Stewart, *Bye, Bye Birdie*	Abe Burrows, Jack Weinstock, and Willie Gilbert, *How To Succeed in Business Without Really Trying*	Burt Shevelove and Larry Gelbart, *A Funny Thing Happened on the Way to the Forum*
Scenic Designer	Oliver Smith, *Becket* (Dramatic); Oliver Smith, *Camelot* (Musical)	Will Steven Armstrong, *Carnival*	Sean Kenny, *Oliver!*
Costume Designer	Motley, *Becket;* Adrian and Tony Duquette, *Camelot*	Lucinda Ballard, *The Gay Life*	Anthony Powell, *The School for Scandal*
Choreographer	Gower Champion, *Bye, Bye Birdie*	Agnes de Mille, *Kwamina;* Joe Layton, *No Strings*	Bob Fosse, *Little Me*
Producer (Dramatic)	David Merrick, *Becket*	Robert Whitehead and Roger L. Stevens, *A Man for All Seasons*	Richard Barr and Clinton Wilder, Theatre 1963, *Who's Afraid of Virginia Woolf?*
Producer (Musical)	Edward Padula, *Bye, Bye Birdie*	Cy Feuer and Ernest Martin, *How To Succeed in Business Without Really Trying*	Harold Prince, *A Funny Thing Happened on the Way to the Forum*
Conductor and Musical Director	Franz Allers, *Camelot*	Elliot Lawrence, *How To Succeed in Business Without Really Trying*	Donald Pippin, *Oliver!*
Stage Technician	Teddy Van Bemmel, *Becket*	Michael Burns, *A Man for All Seasons*	—

1964	1965	1966	1967
Alec Guinness, *Dylan*	Walter Matthau, *The Odd Couple*	Hal Holbrook, *Mark Twain Tonight!*	Paul Rogers, *The Homecoming*
Sandy Dennis, *Any Wednesday*	Irene Worth, *Tiny Alice*	Rosemary Harris, *The Lion in Winter*	Beryl Reid, *The Killing of Sister George*
Hume Cronyn, *Hamlet*	Jack Albertson, *The Subject Was Roses*	Patrick Magee, *Marat/Sade*	Ian Holm, *The Homecoming*
Barbara Loden, *After the Fall*	Alice Ghostley, *The Sign In Sidney Brustein's Window*	Zoe Caldwell, *Slapstick Tragedy*	Marian Seldes, *A Delicate Balance*
Luther	*The Subject Was Roses*	*Marat/Sade*	*The Homecoming*
Bert Lahr, *Foxy*	Zero Mostel, *Fiddler on the Roof*	Richard Kiley, *Man of La Mancha*	Robert Preston, *I Do! I Do!*
Carol Channing, *Hello, Dolly!*	Liza Minnelli, *Flora, the Red Menace*	Angela Lansbury, *Mame*	Barbara Harris, *The Apple Tree*
Jack Cassidy, *She Loves Me*	Victor Spinetti, *Oh, What a Lovely War!*	Frankie Michaels, *Mame*	Joel Grey, *Cabaret*
Tessie O'Shea, *The Girl Who Came to Supper*	Maria Karnilova, *Fiddler on the Roof*	Beatrice Arthur, *Mame*	Peg Murray, *Cabaret*
Hello, Dolly!	*Fiddler on the Roof*	*Man of La Mancha*	*Cabaret*
Mike Nichols, *Barefoot in the Park*	Mike Nichols, *Luv/The Odd Couple*	Peter Brook, *Marat/Sade*	Peter Hall, *The Homecoming*
Gower Champion, *Hello, Dolly!*	Jerome Robbins, *Fiddler on the Roof*	Albert Marre, *Man of La Mancha*	Harold Prince, *Cabaret*
Jerry Herman, *Hello, Dolly!*	Jerry Bock and Sheldon Harnick, *Fiddler on the Roof*	Mitch Leigh and Joe Darion, *Man of La Mancha*	John Kander and Fred Ebb, *Cabaret*
John Osborne, *Luther*	Neil Simon, *The Odd Couple*	—	—
Michael Stewart, *Hello, Dolly!*	Joseph Stein, *Fiddler on the Roof*	—	—
Oliver Smith, *Hello, Dolly!*	Oliver Smith, *Baker Street/Luv/The Odd Couple*	Howard Bay, *Man of La Mancha*	Boris Aronson, *Cabaret*
Freddy Wittop, *Hello, Dolly!*	Patricia Zipprodt, *Fiddler on the Roof*	Gunilla Palmstierna-Weiss, *Marat/Sade*	Patricia Zipprodt, *Cabaret*
Gower Champion, *Hello, Dolly!*	Jerome Robbins, *Fiddler on the Roof*	Bob Fosse, *Sweet Charity*	Ronald Field, *Cabaret*
Herman Shumlin, *The Deputy*	Claire Nichtern, *Luv*	—	—
David Merrick, *Hello, Dolly!*	Harold Prince, *Fiddler on the Roof*	—	—
Shepard Coleman, *Hello, Dolly!*	—	—	—
—	—	—	—

	1968	**1969**	**1970**
Actor (Dramatic)	Martin Balsam, *You Know I Can't Hear You When the Water's Running*	James Earl Jones, *The Great White Hope*	Fritz Weaver, *Child's Play*
Actress (Dramatic)	Zoe Caldwell, *The Prime of Miss Jean Brodie*	Julie Harris, *Forty Carats*	Tammy Grimes, *Private Lives*
Featured/Supporting Actor (Dramatic)	James Patterson, *The Birthday Party*	Al Pacino, *Does a Tiger Wear a Necktie?*	Ken Howard, *Child's Play*
Featured/Supporting Actress (Dramatic)	Zena Walker, *Joe Egg*	Jane Alexander, *The Great White Hope*	Blythe Danner, *Butterflies Are Free*
Play	*Rosencrantz and Guildenstern Are Dead*	*The Great White Hope*	*Borstal Boy*
Actor (Musical)	Robert Goulet, *The Happy Time*	Jerry Orbach, *Promises, Promises*	Cleavon Little, *Purlie*
Actress (Musical)	Leslie Uggams, *Hallelujah, Baby!*; Patricia Routledge, *Darling of the Day*	Angela Lansbury, *Dear World*	Lauren Bacall, *Applause*
Featured/Supporting Actor (Musical)	Hiram Sherman, *How Now, Dow Jones*	Ronald Holgate, *1776*	Rene Auberjonois, *Coco*
Featured/Supporting Actress (Musical)	Lillian Hayman, *Hallelujah, Baby!*	Marian Mercer, *Promises, Promises*	Melba Moore, *Purlie*
Musical	*Hallelujah, Baby!*	*1776*	*Applause*
Director (Dramatic)	Mike Nichols, *Plaza Suite*	Peter Dews, *Hadrian VII*	Joseph Hardy, *Child's Play*
Director (Musical)	Gower Champion, *The Happy Time*	Peter Hunt, *1776*	Ron Field, *Applause*
Book (Musical)	—	—	—
Score	Jule Styne, Betty Comden, and Adolph Green, *Hallelujah, Baby!*	—	—
Scenic Designer	Desmond Heeley, *Rosencrantz and Guildenstern Are Dead*	Boris Aronson, *Zorba*	Howard Bay, *Cry for Us All*; Jo Mielziner, *Child's Play*
Costume Designer	Desmond Heeley, *Rosencrantz and Guildenstern Are Dead*	Louden Sainthill, *Canterbury Tales*	Cecil Beaton, *Coco*
Lighting Designer	—	—	Jo Mielziner, *Child's Play*
Choreographer	Gower Champion, *The Happy Time*	Joe Layton, *George M!*	Ron Field, *Applause*
Producer (Dramatic)	The David Merrick Arts Foundation, *Rosencrantz and Guildenstern Are Dead*	—	—
Producer (Musical)	Albert Selden, Hal James, Jane C. Nusbaum, and Harry Rigby, *Hallelujah, Baby!*	—	—

1971	1972	1973	1974
Brian Bedford, *The School for Wives*	Cliff Gorman, *Lenny*	Alan Bates, *Butley*	Michael Moriarty, *Find Your Way Home*
Maureen Stapleton, *Gingerbread Lady*	Sada Thompson, *Twigs*	Julie Harris, *The Last of Mrs. Lincoln*	Colleen Dewhurst, *A Moon for the Misbegotten* (Revival)
Paul Sand, *Story Theatre*	Vincent Gardenia, *The Prisoner of Second Avenue*	John Lithgow, *The Changing Room*	Ed Flanders, *A Moon for the Misbegotten* (Revival)
Rae Allen, *And Miss Reardon Drinks a Little*	Elizabeth Wilson, *Sticks and Bones*	Leora Dana, *The Last of Mrs. Lincoln*	Frances Sternhagen, *The Good Doctor*
Sleuth	*Sticks and Bones*	*That Championship Season*	*The River Niger*
Hal Linden, *The Rothschilds*	Phil Silvers, *A Funny Thing Happened on the Way to the Forum* (Revival)	Ben Vereen, *Pippin*	Christopher Plummer, *Cyrano*
Helen Gallagher, *No, No, Nanette*	Alexis Smith, *Follies*	Glynis Johns, *A Little Night Music*	Virginia Capers, *Raisin*
Keene Curtis, *The Rothschilds*	Larry Blyden, *A Funny Thing Happened on the Way to the Forum* (Revival)	George S. Irving, *Irene*	Tommy Tune, *Seesaw*
Patsy Kelly, *No, No, Nanette*	Linda Hopkins, *Inner City*	Patricia Elliot, *A Little Night Music*	Janie Sell, *Over Here!*
Company	*Two Gentlemen of Verona*	*A Little Night Music*	*Raisin*
Peter Brook, *Midsummer Night's Dream*	Mike Nichols, *The Prisoner of Second Avenue*	A.J. Antoon, *That Championship Season*	Jose Quintero, *A Moon for the Misbegotten* (Revival)
Harold Prince, *Company*	Harold Prince and Michael Bennett, *Follies*	Bob Fosse, *Pippin*	Harold Prince, *Candide*
George Furth, *Company*	John Guare and Mel Shapiro, *Two Gentlemen of Verona*	Hugh Wheeler, *A Little Night Music*	Hugh Wheeler, *Candide*
Stephen Sondheim, *Company*	Stephen Sondheim, *Follies*	Stephen Sondheim, *A Little Night Music*	Frederick Loewe (Music); Alan Jay Lerner (Lyrics), *Gigi*
Boris Aronson, *Company*	Boris Aronson, *Follies*	Tony Walton, *Pippin*	Franne and Eugene Lee, *Candide*
Raoul Pene du Bois, *No, No, Nanette*	Florence Klotz, *Follies*	Florence Klotz, *A Little Night Music*	Franne Lee, *Candide*
H.R. Poindexter, *Story Theatre*	Tharon Musser, *Follies*	Jules Fisher, *Pippin*	Jules Fisher, *Ulysses in Nighttown*
Donald Saddler, *No, No, Nanette*	Michael Bennett, *Follies*	Bob Fosse, *Pippin*	Michael Bennett, *Seesaw*
Helen Bonfils, Morton Gottlieb, and Michael White, *Sleuth*	—	—	—
Harold Prince, *Company*	—	—	—

	1975	**1976**	**1977**
Actor (Dramatic)	John Kani and Winston Ntshona, *Sizwe Banzi Is Dead & The Island*	John Wood, *Travesties*	Al Pacino, *The Basic Training of Pavlo Hummel*
Actress (Dramatic)	Ellen Burstyn, *Same Time, Next Year*	Irene Worth, *Sweet Bird of Youth*	Julie Harris, *The Belle of Amherst*
Featured Actor (Dramatic)	Frank Langella, *Seascape*	Edward Herrmann, *Mrs. Warren's Profession*	Jonathan Pryce, *Comedians*
Featured Actress (Dramatic)	Rita Moreno, *The Ritz*	Shirley Knight, *Kennedy's Children*	Trazana Beverley, *For Colored Girls Who Have Considered Suicide/When the Rainbow Is Enuf*
Play	*Equus*	*Travesties*	*The Shadow Box*
Actor (Musical)	John Cullum, *Shenandoah*	George Rose, *My Fair Lady*	Barry Bostwick, *The Robber Bridegroom*
Actress (Musical)	Angela Lansbury, *Gypsy*	Donna McKechnie, *A Chorus Line*	Dorothy Loudon, *Annie*
Featured Actor (Musical)	Ted Ross, *The Wiz*	Sammy Williams, *A Chorus Line*	Lenny Baker, *I Love My Wife*
Featured Actress (Musical)	Dee Dee Bridgewater, *The Wiz*	Carole Bishop, *A Chorus Line*	Delores Hall, *Your Arms Too Short To Box with God*
Musical	*The Wiz*	*A Chorus Line*	*Annie*
Director (Dramatic)	John Dexter, *Equus*	Ellis Rabb, *The Royal Family*	Gordon Davidson, *The Shadow Box*
Director (Musical)	Geoffrey Holder, *The Wiz*	Michael Bennett, *A Chorus Line*	Gene Saks, *I Love My Wife*
Book (Musical)	James Lee Barrett, *Shenandoah*	James Kirkwood and Nicholas Dante, *A Chorus Line*	Thomas Meehan, *Annie*
Score	Charlie Smalls (Music & Lyrics), *The Wiz*	Marvin Hamlisch (Music); Edward Kleban (Lyrics), *A Chorus Line*	Charles Strouse (Music); Martin Charnin (Lyrics), *Annie*
Scenic Designer	Carl Toms, *Sherlock Holmes*	Boris Aronson, *Pacific Overtures*	David Mitchell, *Annie*
Costume Designer	Geoffrey Holder, *The Wiz*	Florence Klotz, *Pacific Overtures*	Theoni V. Aldredge, *Annie*; Santo Loquasto, *The Cherry Orchard*
Lighting Designer	Neil Patrick Jampolis, *Sherlock Holmes*	Tharon Musser, *A Chorus Line*	Jennifer Tipton, *The Cherry Orchard*
Choreographer	George Faison, *The Wiz*	Michael Bennett and Bob Avian, *A Chorus Line*	Peter Gennaro, *Annie*
Reproduction of a Play or Musical	—	—	*Porgy and Bess*

1978	1979	1980	1981
Barnard Hughes, *Da*	Tom Conti, *Whose Life Is It Anyway?*	John Rubinstein, *Children of a Lesser God*	Ian McKellen, *Amadeus*
Jessica Tandy, *The Gin Game*	Constance Cummings, *Wings;* Carole Shelley, *The Elephant Man*	Phyllis Frelich, *Children of a Lesser God*	Jane Lapotaire, *Piaf*
Lester Rawlins, *Da*	Michael Gough, *Bedroom Farce*	David Rounds, *Morning's at Seven*	Brian Backer, *The Floating Light Bulb*
Ann Wedgeworth, *Chapter Two*	Joan Hickson, *Bedroom Farce*	Dinah Manoff, *I Ought To Be in Pictures*	Swoosie Kurtz, *Fifth of July*
Da	*The Elephant Man*	*Children of a Lesser God*	*Amadeus*
John Cullum, *On the Twentieth Century*	Len Cariou, *Sweeney Todd*	Jim Dale, *Barnum*	Kevin Kline, *The Pirates of Penzance*
Liza Minnelli, *The Act*	Angela Lansbury, *Sweeney Todd*	Patti LuPone, *Evita*	Lauren Bacall, *Woman of the Year*
Kevin Kline, *On the Twentieth Century*	Henderson Forsythe, *The Best Little Whorehouse in Texas*	Mandy Patinkin, *Evita*	Hinton Battle, *Sophisticated Ladies*
Nell Carter, *Ain't Misbehavin'*	Carlin Glynn, *The Best Little Whorehouse in Texas*	Priscilla Lopez, *A Day in Hollywood, a Night in the Ukraine*	Marilyn Cooper, *Woman of the Year*
Ain't Misbehavin'	*Sweeney Todd*	*Evita*	*42nd Street*
Melvin Bernhardt, *Da*	Jack Hofsiss, *The Elephant Man*	Vivian Matalon, *Morning's at Seven*	Peter Hall, *Amadeus*
Richard Maltby Jr., *Ain't Misbehavin'*	Harold Prince, *Sweeney Todd*	Harold Prince, *Evita*	Wilford Leach, *The Pirates of Penzance*
Betty Comden and Adolph Green, *On the Twentieth Century*	Hugh Wheeler, *Sweeney Todd*	Tim Rice, *Evita*	Peter Stone, *Woman of the Year*
Cy Coleman (Music); Betty Comden and Adolph Green (Lyrics), *On the Twentieth Century*	Stephen Sondheim (Music & Lyrics), *Sweeney Todd*	Andrew Lloyd Webber (Music); Tim Rice (Lyrics), *Evita*	John Kander (Music); Fred Ebb (Lyrics), *Woman of the Year*
Robin Wagner, *On the Twentieth Century*	Eugene Lee, *Sweeney Todd*	John Lee Beatty, *Talley's Folly;* David Mitchell, *Barnum*	John Bury, *Amadeus*
Edward Gorey, *Dracula*	Franne Lee, *Sweeney Todd*	Theoni V. Aldredge, *Barnum*	Willa Kim, *Sophisticated Ladies*
Jules Fisher, *Dancin'*	Roger Morgan, *The Crucifer of Blood*	David Hersey, *Evita*	John Bury, *Amadeus*
Bob Fosse, *Dancin'*	Michael Bennett and Bob Avian, *Ballroom*	Tommy Tune and Thommie Walsh, *A Day in Hollywood, a Night in the Ukraine*	Gower Champion, *42nd Street*
Dracula	—	Elizabeth I. McCann, Nelle Nugent, Ray Larsen, producers, *Morning's at Seven*	Joseph Papp, producer, *The Pirates of Penzance*

	1982	1983	1984
Actor (Dramatic)	Roger Rees, *The Life and Adventures of Nicholas Nickleby*	Harvey Fierstein, *Torch Song Trilogy*	Jeremy Irons, *The Real Thing*
Actress (Dramatic)	Zoe Caldwell, *Medea*	Jessica Tandy, *Foxfire*	Glenn Close, *The Real Thing*
Featured Actor (Dramatic)	Zakes Mokae, *Master Harold . . . and the Boys*	Matthew Broderick, *Brighton Beach Memoirs*	Joe Mantegna, *Glengarry Glen Ross*
Featured Actress (Dramatic)	Amanda Plummer, *Agnes of God*	Judith Ivey, *Steaming*	Christine Baranski, *The Real Thing*
Play	*The Life and Adventures of Nicholas Nickleby*	*Torch Song Trilogy*	*The Real Thing*
Actor (Musical)	Ben Harney, *Dreamgirls*	Tommy Tune, *My One and Only*	George Hearn, *La Cage Aux Folles*
Actress (Musical)	Jennifer Holliday, *Dreamgirls*	Natalia Makarova, *On Your Toes*	Chita Rivera, *The Rink*
Featured Actor (Musical)	Cleavant Derricks, *Dreamgirls*	Charles "Honi" Coles, *My One and Only*	Hinton Battle, *The Tap Dance Kid*
Featured Actress (Musical)	Liliane Montevecchi, *"Nine"*	Betty Buckley, *Cats*	Lila Kedrova, *Zorba*
Musical	*"Nine"*	*Cats*	*La Cage aux folles*
Director (Dramatic)	Trevor Nunn and John Caird, *The Life and Adventures of Nicholas Nickleby*	Gene Saks, *Brighton Beach Memoirs*	Mike Nichols, *The Real Thing*
Director (Musical)	Tommy Tune, *"Nine"*	Trevor Nunn, *Cats*	Arthur Laurents, *La Cage aux folles*
Book (Musical)	Tom Eyen, *Dreamgirls*	T. S. Eliot, *Cats*	Harvey Fierstein, *La Cage aux folles*
Score	Maury Yeton (Music & Lyrics), *"Nine"*	Andrew Lloyd Webber (Music); T. S. Eliot (Lyrics), *Cats*	Jerry Herman (Music & Lyrics), *La Cage aux folles*
Scenic Designer	John Napier and Dermot Hayes, *The Life and Adventures of Nicholas Nickleby*	Ming Cho Lee, *K2*	Tony Straiges, *Sunday in the Park with George*
Costume Designer	William Ivey Long, *"Nine"*	John Napier, *Cats*	Theoni V. Aldredge, *La Cage aux folles*
Lighting Designer	Tharon Musser, *Dreamgirls*	David Hersey, *Cats*	Richard Nelson, *Sunday in the Park with George*
Choreographer	Michael Bennett and Michael Peters, *Dreamgirls*	Thommie Walsh and Tommy Tune, *My One and Only*	Danny Daniels, *The Tap Dance Kid*
Reproduction of a Play or Musical	Barry and Fran Weissler, CBS Video Enterprises, Don Gregory, producers, *Othello*	Alfred De Liagre Jr., Roger L. Stevens, John Mauceri, Donald R. Seawell, Andre Pastoria, producers, *On Your Toes*	Robert Whitehead, Roger L. Stevens, producers, *Death of a Salesman*

1985	1986	1987	1988
Derek Jacobi, *Much Ado About Nothing*	Judd Hirsch, *I'm Not Rappaport*	James Earl Jones, *Fences*	Ron Silver, *Speed-the-Plow*
Stockard Channing, *Joe Egg*	Lily Tomlin, *The Search for Signs of Intelligent Life in the Universe*	Linda Lavin, *Broadway Bound*	Joan Allen, *Burn This*
Barry Miller, *Biloxi Blues*	John Mahoney, *The House of Blue Leaves*	John Randolph, *Broadway Bound*	B. D. Wong, *M. Butterfly*
Judith Ivey, *Hurlyburly*	Swoosie Kurtz, *The House of Blue Leaves*	Mary Alice, *Fences*	L. Scott Caldwell, *Joe Turner's Come and Gone*
Biloxi Blues	*I'm Not Rappaport*	*Fences*	*M. Butterfly*
—	George Rose, *The Mystery of Edwin Drood*	Robert Lindsay, *Me and My Girl*	Michael Crawford, *The Phantom of the Opera*
—	Bernadette Peters, *Song & Dance*	Maryann Plunkett, *Me and My Girl*	Joanna Gleason, *Into the Woods*
Ron Richardson, *Big River*	Michael Rupert, *Sweet Charity*	Michael Maguire, *Les Misérables*	Bill McCutcheon, *Anything Goes*
Leilani Jones, *Grind*	Bebe Neuwirth, *Sweet Charity*	Frances Ruffelle, *Les Misérables*	Judy Kaye, *The Phantom of the Opera*
Big River	*The Mystery of Edwin Drood*	*Les Misérables*	*The Phantom of the Opera*
Gene Saks, *Biloxi Blues*	Jerry Zaks, *The House of Blue Leaves*	Lloyd Richards, *Fences*	John Dexter, *M. Butterfly*
Des McAnuff, *Big River*	Wilford Leach, *The Mystery of Edwin Drood*	Trevor Nunn and John Caird, *Les Misérables*	Harold Prince, *The Phantom of the Opera*
William Hauptman, *Big River*	Rupert Holmes, *The Mystery of Edwin Drood*	Alain Boublil and Claude-Michel Schönberg, *Les Misérables*	James Lapine, *Into the Woods*
Roger Miller (Music & Lyrics), *Big River*	Rupert Holmes (Music & Lyrics), *The Mystery of Edwin Drood*	Claude-Michel Schönberg (Music); Herbert Kretzmer, and Alain Boublil (Lyrics), *Les Misérables*	Stephen Sondheim (Music & Lyrics), *Into the Woods*
Heidi Landesman, *Big River*	Tony Walton, *The House of Blue Leaves*	John Napier, *Les Misérables*	Maria Bjornson, *The Phantom of the Opera*
Florence Klotz, *Grind*	Patricia Zipprodt, *Sweet Charity*	John Napier, *Starlight Express*	Maria Björnson, *The Phantom of the Opera*
Richard Riddell, *Big River*	Pat Collins, *I'm Not Rappaport*	David Hersey, *Starlight Express*	Andrew Bridge, *The Phantom of the Opera*
—	Bob Fosse, *Big Deal*	Gillian Gregory, *Me and My Girl*	Michael Smuin, *Anything Goes*
The Shubert Organization, Emanuel Azenberg, Roger Berlind, Ivan Bloch, MTM Enterprises, Inc., producers, *Joe Egg*	Jerome Minskoff, James M. Nederlander, Arthur Rubin, Joseph Harris, producers, *Sweet Charity*	Jay H. Fuchs, Steven Warnick, Charles Patsos, producers, *All My Sons*	Lincoln Center Theater, Gregory Mosher, Bernard Gersten, producers, *Anything Goes*

	1989	**1990**	**1991**
Actor (Dramatic)	Philip Bosco, *Lend Me a Tenor*	Robert Morse, *Tru*	Nigel Hawthorne, *Shadowlands*
Actress (Dramatic)	Pauline Collins, *Shirley Valentine*	Maggie Smith, *Lettice & Lovage*	Mercedes Ruehl, *Lost in Yonkers*
Featured Actor (Dramatic)	Boyd Gaines, *The Heidi Chronicles*	Charles Durning, *Cat on a Hot Tin Roof*	Kevin Spacey, *Lost in Yonkers*
Featured Actress (Dramatic)	Christine Baranski, *Rumors*	Margaret Tyzack, *Lettice & Lovage*	Irene Worth, *Lost in Yonkers*
Play	*The Heidi Chronicles*	*The Grapes of Wrath*	*Lost in Yonkers*
Actor (Musical)	Jason Alexander, *Jerome Robbins' Broadway*	James Naughton, *City of Angels*	Jonathan Pryce, *Miss Saigon*
Actress (Musical)	Ruth Brown, *Black and Blue*	Tyne Daly, *Gypsy*	Lea Salonga, *Miss Saigon*
Featured Actor (Musical)	Scott Wise, *Jerome Robbins' Broadway*	Michael Jeter, *Gypsy*	Hinton Battle, *Miss Saigon*
Featured Actress (Musical)	Debbie Shapiro, *Jerome Robbins' Broadway*	Randy Graff, *City of Angels*	Daisy Eagan, *The Secret Garden*
Musical	*Jerome Robbins' Broadway*	*City of Angels*	*The Will Rogers Follies*
Director (Dramatic)	Jerry Zaks, *Lend Me a Tenor*	Frank Galati, *The Grapes of Wrath*	Jerry Zaks, *Six Degrees of Separation*
Director (Musical)	Jerome Robbins, *Jerome Robbins' Broadway*	Tommy Tune, *Grand Hotel, the Musical*	Tommy Tune, *The Will Rogers Follies*
Book (Musical)	—	Larry Gelbart, *City of Angels*	Marsha Norman, *The Secret Garden*
Score	—	Cy Colman (Music); David Zippel (Lyrics), *City of Angels*	Cy Coleman (Music); Betty Comden and Adolph Green (Lyrics), *The Will Rogers Follies*
Scenic Designer	Santo Loquasto, *Cafe Crown*	Robin Wagner, *City of Angels*	Heidi Landesman, *The Secret Garden*
Costume Designer	Claudio Segovia, Hector Orezzoli, *Black and Blue*	Santo Loquasto, *Grand Hotel, the Musical*	Willa Kim, *The Will Rogers Follies*
Lighting Design	Jennifer Tipton, *Jerome Robbins' Broadway*	Jules Fisher, *Grand Hotel, the Musical*	Jules Fisher, *The Will Rogers Follies*
Choreographer	Cholly Atkins, Henry LeTang, Frankie Manning, Fayard Nicholas, *Black and Blue*	Tommy Tune, *Grand Hotel, the Musical*	Tommy Tune, *The Will Rogers Follies*
Reproduction of a Play or Musical	Lincoln Center Theater, Gregory Mosher, Bernard Gersten, producers, *Our Town*	Barry and Fran Weissler, Kathy Levin, Barry Brown, producers, *Gypsy*	Barry and Fran Weissler, Pace Theatrical Group, *Fiddler on the Roof*

1992	1993	1994	1995
Judd Hirsch, *Conversations with My Father*	Ron Leibman, *Angels in America: Millennium Approaches*	Stephen Spinella, *Angels in America: Perestroika*	Ralph Fiennes, *Hamlet*
Glenn Close, *Death and the Maiden*	Madeline Kahn, *The Sisters Rosensweig*	Diana Rigg, *Medea*	Cherry Jones, *The Heiress*
Larry Fishburne, *Two Trains Running*	Stephen Spinella, *Angels in America: Millennium Approaches*	Jeffrey Wright, *Angels in America: Perestroika*	John Glover, *Love! Valour! Compassion!*
Brid Brennan, *Dancing at Lughnasa*	Debra Monk, *Redwood Curtain*	Jane Adams, *An Inspector Calls*	Frances Sternhagen, *The Heiress*
Dancing at Lughnasa	*Angels in America: Millennium Approaches*	*Angels in America: Perestroika*	*Love! Valour! Compassion!*
Gregory Hines, *Jelly's Last Jam*	Brent Carver, *Kiss of the Spider Woman—The Musical*	Boyd Gaines, *She Loves Me*	Matthew Broderick, *How to Succeed in Business Without Really Trying*
Faith Prince, *Guys and Dolls*	Chita Rivera, *Kiss of the Spider Woman—The Musical*	Donna Murphy, *Passion*	Glenn Close, *Sunset Boulevard*
Scott Waara, *The Most Happy Fella*	Anthony Crivello, *Kiss of the Spider Woman—The Musical*	Jarrod Emick, *Damn Yankees*	George Hearn, *Sunset Boulevard*
Tonya Pinkins, *Jelly's Last Jam*	Andrea Martin, *My Favorite Year*	Audra Ann McDonald, *Carousel*	Gretha Boston, *Show Boat*
Crazy for You	*Kiss of the Spider Woman—The Musical*	*Passion*	*Sunset Boulevard*
Patrick Mason, *Dancing at Lughnasa*	George C. Wolfe, *Angels in America: Millennium Approaches*	Stephen Baldry, *An Inspector Calls*	Gerald Gutierrez, *The Heiress*
Jerry Zaks, *Guys and Dolls*	Des McAnuff, *The Who's Tommy*	Nicholas Hynter, *Carousel*	Harold Prince, *Show Boat*
William Finn and James Lapine, *Falsettos*	Terrence McNally, *Kiss of the Spider Woman—The Musical*	James Lapine, *Passion*	*Sunset Boulevard*
William Finn, *Falsettos*	John Kander (Music); Fred Ebb (Lyrics), *Kiss of the Spider Woman—The Musical;* Pete Townshend (Music and Lyrics), *The Who's Tommy*	Stephen Sondheim, *Passion*	*Sunset Boulevard*
Tony Walton, *Guys and Dolls*	John Arnone, *The Who's Tommy*	Bob Crowley, *Carousel*	John Napier, *Sunset Boulevard*
William Ivey Long, *Crazy for You*	Florence Klotz, *Kiss of the Spider Woman—The Musical*	Ann Hould-Ward, *Beauty and the Beast*	Florence Klotz, *Show Boat*
Jules Fisher, *Jelly's Last Jam*	Chris Parry, *The Who's Tommy*	Rick Fisher, *An Inspector Calls*	Andrew Bridge, *Sunset Boulevard*
Susan Stroman, *Crazy for You*	Wayne Cilento, *The Who's Tommy*	Kenneth McMillan, *Carousel*	Susan Stroman, *Show Boat*
Dodger Productions, Roger Berlind, Jujamcyn Theaters/TV Asahi, Kardana Productions, John F. Kennedy Center for the Performing Arts, *Guys and Dolls*	Roundabout Theatre Company and Todd Haimes, *Anna Christie*	Noel Pearson, the Shubert Organization, Capital Cities/ABC, Joseph Harris, *An Inspector Calls* (Dramatic); Lincoln Center Theater, Andre Bishop, Bernard Gersten, the Royal National Theater, Cameron Mackintosh, the Rodgers & Hammerstein Organization, *Carousel* (Musical)	-

PEOPLE
EXTRAS

THE MOST INTRIGUING PEOPLE: 1974–PRESENT

Every December, in the Christmas double issue, the PEOPLE editors single out the 25 most intriguing people of the past year. We reprint here the complete roll of honorees, with a brief description for each, to remind readers of the notable and notorious from the past 21 years.

1974

Gerald Ford—The president copes with an office he didn't seek and savage inflation

Patty Hearst—The kidnapped newspaper heiress turned terrorist might be another face in the crowd—but in disguise

Joe Hirshhorn—He heaps the land with beauty by donating 2,000 sculptures and 4,000 paintings to Smithsonian's new Hirshhorn Museum

Kay Graham—The publisher of the *Washington Post* emerges as the big winner of Watergate

Yasir Arafat—A tough soldier takes the point for Palestine and addresses the United Nations

Faye Dunaway—A panther of an actress springs back to the top in *Chinatown, The Towering Inferno,* and *Three Days of the Condor*

Alexander Solzhenitsyn—The Russian exile's Nobel honors are late but sweet

Nelson Rockefeller—The vice president–elect has his finances questioned by Congress; being rich turns out to be a problem

Leon Jaworski—The Watergate prosecutor knew Nixon was lying, but couldn't say it

Erica Jong—A hit author who is like her uninhibited heroine in *Fear of Flying*

Francis Ford Coppola—*Godfather II* confirms him as cinema's creative king

Muhammad Ali—The title isn't enough for the world heavyweight champ—he wants another son

Pat Nixon—The last First Lady deals stoically with her husband's fall from grace

John Glenn—Could the Ohio senator and former astronaut be the Ike of the '70s?

Sherlock Holmes—He emerges from Victorian England as the most omnipresent literary figure of 1974

Carter Heyward—One of 11 women ordained as Episcopal priests (the ordinations were later declared invalid) defies her church to serve her God

Stevie Wonder—A blind artist brings soul to all his music

Alexander Calder—Now it seems every U.S. city must have one of his stabiles

Charlie Finley—The owner of the Oakland A's doesn't win friends, just the World Series

Ella Grasso—The first woman in American history to capture a governorship without inheriting the office from her husband. In this year of political women, Conn.'s governor-elect is the biggest name of all

J. Kenneth Jamieson—Exxon's chief has big profits and big problems

Jimmy Connors—He catches fire; his romance catches cold

Gunnar Myrdal—Nobel Prize winner in economics is honored for his "pioneering work in the theory of money and economic fluctuations"

Valerie Harper—*Rhoda*'s a winner on her own, and so much for TV taboos

Mikhail Barishnikov—The former Kirov Ballet star defects

to Toronto, and ballet is changed forever

1975

Betty Ford—The president's secret weapon is a refreshing First Lady high on being herself

Richard Zanuck—Son of Darryl F., he makes his own name coproducing Hollywood's most toothsome grosser ever (*Jaws*)

Frank E. Fitzsimmons—The boss of 2.2 million teamsters is Nixon's buddy and shows he is "not Hoffa's puppet"

Charles Manson—He's in prison, but may have influenced Squeaky Fromme in her failed assassination attempt on President Ford

Daniel Patrick Moynihan—Fighting Irishman at the U.N. talks tough—and, many Americans feel, talks sense too

James Coleman—The University of Chicago professor blamed for busing says it backfired

Indira Gandhi—After six months of rule in India, her popularity soars

Cher Bono Allman—Move over Liz 'n' Dick, this ricochet bride is the new First Lady of splitsville

Andrei Sakharov—The Nobel Peace Prize winner is a man under siege in his own country

Teng Hsiao-Ping—After years of obscurity, a tough, blunt, outspoken man steps into the big shoes of Chinese leadership

Patty Hearst—Was she a volunteer terrorist or a victim of her captors?

Christina Onassis—The only daughter of the late shipping magnate Aristotle Onassis has the ships and the gold, and marries her father's rival

Leonard Matlovich—The ex–Air Force sergeant is discharged after admitting his homosexuality and sets up the Matlovich Foundation for Civil Rights

Dolly Parton—There's a brain under that beehive of Nashville's new queen-in-waiting

Fred Lynn—An all-American boy dazzles Boston and baseball in his miraculous rookie year

Frank Borman—An ex-astronaut takes the controls of a company in a financial tailspin and gets Eastern Airlines off the ground

Rosemary Rogers—The master of the erotic gothic takes her readers past the bedroom door

Werner Erhard—In the wake of TM and Zen, a former encyclopedia huckster is the smooth guru of est

Woody Allen—A winning klutz moves from snappy one-liners to triple creative threat—actor, director, and author with his latest, *Without Feathers*

Marabel Morgan—The Florida housewife behind *The Total Woman* cashes in on the antifeminist backlash

Jerry Brown—California loves its young governor who avoids the mansion, limos, and labels

Don King—A flashy ex-con turned promoter is the new lord of the rings

Hercule Poirot—Who kills the famed Belgian detective after 55 years? No, not the butler, but Dame Agatha Christie

Anwar Sadat—The president of Egypt opens the Suez Canal, closed since the Six Day War in 1967

Gelsey Kirkland—The prima ballerina of the American Ballet dances a triumphant *Giselle*, highlighting a great year in ballet

1976

Jimmy Carter—The president-elect wants to be the "citizen president"

Farrah Fawcett-Majors—The shape of things to come? The nation watches an "Angel" turn into a star

Andrew Wyeth—Is he America's most popular painter? The thought grieves some critics, who see him as "the rich man's Norman Rockwell"

Betty Williams—After seven bloody years, an anguished mother whose three children were killed starts her own movement and asks Ulster to give peace a chance

Andrew Young—The first black ambassador to the United Nations. When this former congressman speaks, Jimmy Carter listens

Juan Carlos I—The new Spanish king takes aim at Franco's fascist legacy and hands power to the people

Linda Ronstadt—A vagabond grows into country rock's First Lady

Reverend Sun Myung Moon—Troubles build up for the mysterious head of the Unification Church

Bert Jones—A cool, calm Colt is pro football's man with the golden arm

Julius Nyerere—Tanzania's superstar of black African diplomacy acts as a buffer between ruling white Ian Smith's government and the black nationalists of Rhodesia

Carl Sagan—The Viking I expedition on Mars provides vicarious adventure for a would-be space explorer

Fred Silverman—Since TV's superprogrammer switched channels, ABC enjoys Happy Days and Mashes CBS

Liz Ray—The woman whose affair with Representative Wayne Hays set off the steamiest Washington sex scandal in years brings out a book and gets religion

C. W. McCall—After "Convoy," the year's bestselling single, Rubberduck is king of the road

Shere Hite—That report on women's sexuality becomes a bestseller, and its author moves on to men

Donald Kendall—With the Soviets part of the Pepski Generation, Pepsico's chief is now waging war on Coke

Vivian Reed—The star of Broadway's *Bubbling Brown Sugar* proves that black is beautiful at the box office

Ron Kovic—Crippled Vietnam veteran turned antiwar activist and author of *Born on the Fourth of July* sells movie rights for

PEOPLE'S COVER CHAMPS

Their fame far exceeded the usual 15 minutes. The saga of their lives held readers rapt. Here are the titleholders for the most times on the cover of PEOPLE.

Personality	Number of Covers
Princess Diana	35
Jacqueline Kennedy Onassis	13
Elizabeth Taylor	13
Sarah Ferguson	12
Michael Jackson	11
Cher	10

$150,000—and is a new breed of Yankee Doodle Dandy

Chevy Chase—He's hot and you're not: *Saturday Night's* stumblebum says so much for tepid TV

Regine—The queen mother of the disco craze opens clubs all over the globe

Har Gobind Khorana—A shy genius gives the world its first man-made working gene

Nadia Comaneci—The Rumanian Olympic champion prepares for the 1980 games in Moscow. In Montreal she was just about perfect—now she wants even more.

Robert Redford—The actor turns producer with *All the President's Men* and shows he's not just a pretty face

Don Shomron—The Israeli general who led the Entebbe raid to save 105 hostages is a global hero and can't understand why

King Kong—Producer Dino De Laurentis sees and monkey does—$200 million, he hopes

1977

Jimmy Carter—The first year at 1600: he likes it, Rosalynn is chilly, and Amy's adjusting

Diane Keaton—Her gamble on *Looking for Mr. Goodbar* put Woody Allen's flaky foil in the Hollywood catbird seat

General Omar Torrijos—Ratify the canal treaties or bring in the marines, says Panama's strongman

Steven Ross—An impresario of all parlors (originally funeral), the founder-chairman of Warner Communications is the greatest showman on earth

Midge Costanza—Assertive and quick-tongued, she's Carter's pipeline to the people as the assistant for public liaison

Anwar Sadat and Menachem Begin—Is it a possible secret weapon of peace that the president of Egypt and the prime minister of Israel are so much alike?

Ted Turner—After the Americas Cup the sea gets a little choppy for the cable entrepreneur and baseball team owner

Margaret Trudeau—The runaway wife of Canada's prime minister, Pierre Trudeau, says of her old life, "Politics is an ugly and thankless role. What I did was never really appreciated."

Robert Byrd—A self-made fiddler calls the tunes in the world's most exclusive club

Susanne Albrecht—A brutal murder of an old friend makes her the dark queen of German terrorism.

Lily Tomlin—The actress/comedian won a Tony for her one-woman show *Appearing Nitely*. "Is this the country to whom I'm speaking?" Happily for America the answer is yes

Billy Carter—President Carter's baby brother and typical southern "sly ole boy" has an agent and a career as spokesman for products such as Billy Beer. He may be a royal pain to some, but his brother is still amused

Anita Bryant—After a *très* ungay year, she's still praising God and passing the orange juice

Shaun Cassidy—The star of *The Hardy Boys* moonlights as a pop star, and preadolescent America is swooning

Jacqueline Onassis—Quits her editor's job at Viking and gets $25 million from stepdaughter Christina Onassis

Jasper Johns—The enigmatic master of pop art—known for depictions of the stars and stripes, targets, alphabets, and lightbulbs—stays on target

Toni Morrison—"O-o-o-oooh she done fly" into the literary top rank with *Song of Solomon*

Dr. Robert Linn—His liquid protein diet has him in fat city, but some unexplained deaths worry the FDA

Tracy Austin—Out of the cradle and onto the courts comes a new tennis wunderkind, at 14 the youngest player ever to be invited to Wimbledon

Rosalyn Yalow—All this: winner of the 1977 Nobel Prize for medicine, first laureate educated only in the United States, sixth woman science winner, second woman medicine winner

Reggie Jackson—Once just a hot dog; now he's a candy bar and a millionaire Yankee hero

Stevie Nicks—A songwriting soprano with fragile vocal cords casts her sexy spell on rock

George Lucas—From the void he created the droid and a new "force" in film

Princess Caroline—Grace and Rainier's grown-up little girl will wed Junot next July

1978

Pope John Paul II—A tough Polish priest molds the papacy to his own ebullient personality

Queen Noor al-Hussein—The blue-jeaned American queen says of her king, "I'd be delighted to have his child"

G. William Miller—The chairman of the Federal Reserve says of inflation, in effect, "We have nothing to fear but fear itself"

Teng Hsiao-Ping—The tough vice-premier gives China less of Mao, and more of himself

Brooke Shields—Pretty baby at 13: One horse, three movies, beaucoup bucks, but no beau

Melvin Gottlieb—The dream this Princeton physicist pursues is limitless energy from nuclear fusion

Louise Brown—The first test-tube baby is doing just fine, thank you, but the fuss is far from over

Reverend Jim Jones—When this religious demagogue felt his encampment was threatened by Congress and newsmen, he offered a deadly communion to his followers

John Belushi—With the hit movie *Animal House*, TV's man of mugs is becoming a hard act to outgross—in every way

Jimmy Carter—At Camp David he negotiates peace between Egypt and Israel, but back in the White House he looks for antidotes to rising inflation and helps Amy practice her pitch on the violin

Jim Fixx—His *The Complete Book of Running*, a how-to book on the simplest sport in the world, is the year's runaway bestseller

Garry Marshall—TV writer and producer of the hits *Laverne and Shirley* and *Happy Days*, continues his successful career with *Mork and Mindy*

Arlene Blum—The University of California biochemist who led the first all-woman expedition up Annapurna, the tenth highest peak in the world, loses two fellow climbers

Howard Jarvis—The crusader against high property taxes may have changed the future of U.S. politics following the endorsement of his Proposition 13 by California voters in June

Miss Piggy—The famed Muppet pig states, "I want children, my career, and the frog—not necessarily in that order"

Luciano Pavarotti—It's supertenor, opera's newest sex symbol

Cheryl Tiegs—This model's photos still bring out the beast, and earn her $2,000 for a day's work, but her new goal is survival in the TV jungle

Meat Loaf—Rock's newest (and heftiest) hero takes a Texas-size bite into the music biz

Sir Freddie Laker—The founder of the Skytrain revolutionized air fares with cheap transatlantic flights and has a knighthood to prove his success

Nancy Lopez—The golfer has a fantastic year, finishing first in nine out of 25 tournaments and is named Rookie Player and Golfer of the Year

John Travolta—Stayin' Alive is the word for the solitary new superstar besieged by his fans

James Crosby—The man who brought big-time gambling to Atlantic City hopes for the city's economic rebirth

John Irving—His novel *The World According to Garp* is on the bestseller list and revenues allow the down-to-earth Vermonter to work full-time on his upcoming work, *The Hotel New Hampshire*

Donna Summer—The queen of disco is softening her act, but she'd still love to love you, baby

Burt Reynolds—Life isn't always easy for a star working on a new image: sensitivity

1979

Rosalynn Carter—The First Lady skirts the charge that she is involved in government policy formation, and instead emphasizes the Carters as a family

Aleksandr Godunov—The Russian danseur defects to the United States "to dance more often," but his volatile personality may be the reason he has yet to perform

Marvin Mitchelson—The millionaire divorce lawyer makes "palimony" a household threat

Bo Derek—Shows the world that she's a 10 as costar to Dudley Moore, and is credited with bringing sex back to films

Lee Iacocca—Struggles valiantly to get Chrysler into gear under the threat of bankruptcy

Sly Stallone—Comes off the canvas for the biggest movie purse of the year, *Rocky II*, and is already thinking ahead to *Rocky III*

Megan Marshack—After a year of seclusion, former vice

president Nelson Rockefeller's secretary and companion on the night of his death is back in New York

Mani Said al-Otaiba—Leader of OPEC, he writes poetry and tames his Arab colleagues with cordial threats

Joan Kennedy—Impressing the nation, she sobers up to be at Ted's side for the campaign

Johnny Carson—Carson announces that he plans to give up his 17-year reign and $2.5-million contract at NBC and may entertain offers from ABC

Ayatollah Khomeini—The fate of the hostages is still unknown, but Iran's fanatic ruler leads his nation toward chaos with growing social and economic problems

Tom Wolfe—After six years of writer's block, his latest, *The Right Stuff*, is his biggest seller

Joan Baez—The brave antiwarrior raises her voice for the boat people and refugees of Cambodia and is accused of changing her tune on Vietnam

Sebastian Coe—After setting three world records, this British runner takes time out to prepare for the Olympics in Moscow, complete his postgraduate studies, and take a break from all the "razzmatazz"

Gloria Vanderbilt—Living up to her genes, the poor little rich girl brings new chic to a bottom line with her top-grossing designer jeans

Bruce Babbitt—The Arizona governor and member of the presidential commission to investigate Three Mile Island believes nuclear power is a necessary evil

Meryl Streep—A big year for the most intelligent actress now at work, with *Manhattan*, *Kramer vs. Kramer*, and *The Deer Hunter*

Willie Stargell—Captain of the Pittsburgh Pirates, voted MVP this year, but didn't need an award to get the respect and love of his team

PEOPLE'S BEST AND WORST DRESSED

Who are the biggest fashion victors and victims? The following celebrities found themselves on PEOPLE's Best Dressed and Worst Dressed lists most often.

ALL-TIME WINNERS

3 Times
Princess Caroline
Princess Diana
Kevin Costner
Jackie Onassis

2 Times
Corbin Bernsen
Delta Burke
Cher
Tom Cruise
Mel Gibson
Don Johnson
Angela Lansbury
Cyndi Lauper
Donna Mills
Julia Roberts
Liz Taylor
Prince William
Bruce Willis

ALL-TIME SINNERS

5 Times
Sarah Ferguson
Madonna

4 Times
Arsenio Hall
Daryl Hannah

3 Times
Rosanna Arquette
The artist formerly known as Prince
Kim Basinger
Demi Moore
Roseanne

2 Times
Paula Abdul
Cher
Geena Davis
Princess Diana
Andrea Evans
Goldie Hawn
Elton John
Princess Stephanie
Liz Taylor
Ivana Trump
Raquel Welch

1995'S BEST AND WORST

10 Best Dressed
Marcia Clark
George Clooney
Cindy Crawford
Jodie Foster
Elizabeth Hurley
Nicole Kidman
Serena Linley
Chris O'Donnell
Denzel Washington
Oprah Winfrey

10 Worst Dressed
Drew Barrymore
Crystal Bernard
Nicolas Cage
Tony Curtis
Fran Drescher
Melissa Etheridge
Pamela Lee
Demi Moore
Lori Petty
Tori Spelling

Pope John Paul II—Good receptions all over the world indicate a fine first year for the new pope, although his message is often a bitter pill to swallow.
Paul Volcker—The chairman of the Federal Reserve leads an exemplary frugal life, which he brings to the office
Jesse Jackson—Reverend Jackson jets around the world offering support and often inflammatory statements
Dan Aykroyd—*Saturday Night Live* loses the brilliant actor/writer, who is moving on to make more movies
Margaret Thatcher—The first female prime minister of England is not a promotion for feminist ideals but advocates a nostalgic return "to economic Calvinism: hard work, self reliance, and upward mobility"
William Webster—America's top cop takes aim at a tough target: modernizing and de-Hooverizing the FBI
Deborah Harry—Gentlemen and record buyers prefer this platinum blondie: she switches disco to a new wavelength

1980

Ronald Reagan—He wins the presidency by a landslide
Goldie Hawn—*Private Benjamin* liberates a beloved ding-a-ling, promoting her to captain of her soul
Lech Walesa—An unemployed electrician becomes a working-class hero to Poland and the free world
Colonel Charlie Beckwith—The commander of the failed mission to rescue American hostages in Iran emerges as a quiet hero
Herbert Boyer—If nothing else, his forays into genetic engineering can turn this scientist into a multimillionaire

Mary Cunningham—Blond, beautiful, and no longer at Bendix, she's looking for room at the top

Fidel Castro—He grinned after solving 125,000 problems, but now he faces a new one: Reagan

Mel Weinberg—A king con artist sets up Abscam for the FBI and snares some unsuspecting politicians

Sugar Ray Leonard—Who is the greatest? A tough little man wins the boxing championship and the title

Robert Redford—First time behind the scenes, a superstar directs a fine film and says, "I'll phase out acting"

Jean Harris—Was the death of Scarsdale Diet's Dr. Tarnower an accident or murder? Only the quiet headmistress knows

Stephen King—A mild downeaster discovers terror is the ticket

Grete Waitz—A swift Norwegian teacher gives the cold shoulder to the other women runners in the world

Baron St. Helens—An English diplomat's name lives on as a killer volcano

The Reverend Jerry Falwell—A TV preacher sells America on flag, family, and freedom, of sorts

Pat Benatar—Rock finds its missing lynx: she's doing time in the top 10 for what she calls *Crimes of Passion*

Lee Rich—Like J. R. Ewing's assailant, the producer behind *Dallas* aims to please, and does

Sonia Johnson—In the battle for the Equal Rights Amendment, a Mormon feminist waits for the balloon to go up

Sam Shepard—Mr. Funk of off-Broadway may be the Redford of the '80s—if he can play his way

Richard Pryor—Having been through the fire, he's back with a new self and, he says, no bad habits

Eudora Welty—The critics bow before the small-town tales of a masterly Southern writer

Soichiro Honda—The Henry Ford of the Japanese auto industry is known as "Pop" to his workers

Beverly Sills—Bubbles from Brooklyn has stopped singing and begun bossing the company she once graced, the New York City Opera

Dan Rather—When asked if he can hold Walter Cronkite's audience, the new CBS Atlas shrugs

Brooke Shields—From *Blue Lagoon* to blue ads for blue jeans, nothing is coming between her and success

1981

Ronald Reagan—The president survives an assassination attempt, promises 25% tax cuts over the next three years, and says time will tell if he'll run again in '84

Elizabeth Taylor—Old Violet Eyes gets a Tony nominination for her first Broadway performance, in *The Little Foxes*

Lech Walesa—Poland's patriarch of Solidarity is a man of faith and bold deeds, organizing 10 million Poles to stand up to their government

Bradford Smith—Though his Voyager project took us to the planets, he may face a permanent grounding from Reagan's budget axe

Bryant Gumbel—The new *Today* show host aims to be king of the mountain on morning TV

Crown Prince Fahd—The Saudi heir-apparent works to preserve peace between Israel and radical Arab nations

Rabbit Angstrom—John Updike's fictional hero returns fat, rich, and ready for the '80s

Ted Turner—In his one-man air war, cable's Captain Courageous stares down the big guns of network TV

Princess Diana—A kindergarten teacher becomes a princess, beguiles the world, and produces an heir

Gloria Monty—Producing ABC's *General Hospital*, she's behind the biggest bubble in showbiz: soap operas

David Stockman—Reagan's budget director is nearly done in by his own hand, the one that would tighten the nation's belt

Lena Horne—A glamorous grandmother wants audiences to wonder, "how does the old broad do it?"

John McEnroe—He's number one in tennis, but superbrat's score with the public is still love-hate

Edgar Bronfman—Seagram's liquor baron enlivens a year of corporate merger mania

Barbara Mandrell—No heehaw, a new country queen takes on TV and wins

Thomas Sowell—Ronald Reagan's favorite black intellectual attracts attention and decides he doesn't like it

Wolfgang Amadeus Mozart—After two centuries, Austria's child prodigy has become the world's favorite composer

Tom Selleck—More modest than macho, he's the hot-as-a-pistol heartthrob of *Magnum P.I.*

Mick Jagger—Mr. Rolling Stone finds sweet satisfaction with rock's richest tour ever

Richard Viguerie—The New Right's buoyant fundraiser helps purge the Senate of four of its most powerful Democrats

Nicholas Nickleby—At $100 a seat it could have been a bleak house on Broadway, but Dickens proved a smash

Sandra Day O'Connor—Up at 4 a.m. to read briefs, she learns that a woman justice's work is never done

Harrison Ford—He's the new breed of action star—little ego, medium fame, big bucks

YEAR-BY-YEAR, THE BEST (AND WORST) SELLING PEOPLE ISSUES

For each of our first 20 years, here are the regular weekly issues that fared best and worst at the newsstand.

	Best Seller	Worst Seller
1974	The Johnny Carsons	J. Paul Getty
1975	Cher & Gregg Allman	Liv Ullmann
1976	Cher, Gregg & Baby	Nancy Reagan
1977	Tony Orlando	Julie Andrews
1978	Olivia Newton-John	Vice President & Mrs. Mondale
1979	A Readers' Poll	Fleetwood Mac
1980	John Lennon, A Tribute	Paul Simon
1981	Charles & Diana	Justice Sandra Day O'Connor
1982	Princess Grace, A Tribute	"Annie," the musical
1983	Karen Carpenter, A Tribute	America's First Woman in Space, Sally Ride
1984	Michael Jackson	How To Make Your Kid a Star
1985	Rock Hudson	Bisset & Godunov
1986	Andrew & Fergie	The Raid on Libya
1987	Fergie & Di	Michael Caine
1988	Burt & Loni	Our American Hostages
1989	Lucy, A Tribute	Abbie Hoffman, Death of a Radical
1990	Patrick Swayze	Campus Rape
1991	Jeffrey Dahmer	Richard & Jeramie Dreyfuss
1992	Princess Diana	Betty Rollin: "I Helped My Mother Die"
1993	Julia & Lyle, A Wedding Album	Hillary Clinton
1994	O.J. and Nicole, The Shocking Story	Kelsey Grammer

Fernando Valenzuela—Baseball almost struck out, but a Mexican rookie conjures up a magical season

Elizabeth McGovern—A talented beauty soars from high school to stardom as a dippy sex kitten in *Ragtime*

1982

Ronald Reagan—Two years into his term, the president enjoys his "confinement" in the White House

Joan Jett—Rock's latest leading lady earns her stripes with a hard look and her hit song, *I Love Rock and Roll*

Ariel Sharon—Stunned by backlash from the Beirut massacre, the defiant Israeli defense minister battles on

Princess Stephanie—Numbed by her mother's death, a sad teenager has lost her zest for life

Jessica Lange—A talented beauty gets a monkey off her back with two major films, *Tootsie* and *Frances*

Herschel Walker—Forget the Heisman—Georgia's got the trophy that counts: the best running back in football, bar none

Larry Gelbart—After 10 years, *M*A*S*H* departs, but the man who wrote the show has a wacky new hit called *Tootsie*

Margaret Thatcher—With Churchill to inspire her, a dogged prime minister triumphs in a nasty little war in the Falkland Islands

Dr. William DeVries—A surgeon touches the soul with a new machine, the artificial heart

Princess Diana—She may have those newlywed blues, but she's still Britain's darling

Yuri Andropov—Emerging from the shadows of the Soviet KGB, a master spy takes over Brezhnev's Kremlin

George Wallace—Politically recast as a friend of blacks, he seeks their votes and forgiveness—and gets both

Paolo Rossi—A handsome soccer hero leads Italy to the World Cup and wins back the hearts of his countrymen

Randall Forsberg—A Massachusetts scholar sounds a nationwide call to (freeze) arms

Norma Kamali—Wowing Seventh Avenue has been no sweat for fashion's Greta Garbo

E.T.—An alien finds his home in Hollywood

Richard Gere—*Officer* makes a star, if not quite a gentleman, out of a movie maverick

Sam Knox—An authority on the scourge of the sexes offers some consoling facts to legions of herpes victims

Andrew Lloyd Webber—From the Bible to back alleys, Broadway's hottest composer strikes all the right notes

Evelyn Waugh—A curmudgeon's elegy for England's upper crust, *Brideshead Revisited* becomes the TV event of 1982

Barbra Streisand—At 40, the Brooklyn songbird returns to the Old World to conquer a new one—directing *Yentl*

Ted Koppel—A clear-eyed newshawk surveys war and peace and revolutionizes night-owl journalism on *Nightline*

Kiri Te Kanawa—New Zealand's diva hits the top in opera and wins a royal title by acting nothing like a dame

Reverend Sun Myung Moon—The Unification Church's controversial leader is convicted of tax evasion, but he still wins converts

Paul Newman—*The Verdict* is in: a risky role may win Blue Eyes that elusive Oscar gold

Bill Agee and Mary Cunningham—The Bendix takeover didn't take, but this famous couple makes one merger that works

1983

Ronald Reagan—After harrowing events in Granada and Lebanon, the president finishes a tough year on a tougher note with the bombing of Syrian antiaircraft nests in the mountains east of Beirut

Debra Winger—A Hollywood sexpot turns serious actress and scores on her own *Terms*

Fidel Castro—The aging lion of revolution in Latin America gets savvy—and pulls in his claws

The Cabbage Patch Kids—Glassy of eye and poker of face, this chubby, alien horde masks a plot to take over the planet

Jesse Jackson—An explosive orator's campaign breeds fusion and fission for the Democrats

William Gates—Dropping out of Harvard pays off for a computer whiz kid who's making hard cash from Microsoft software

Sam Shepard—He has it all as a laureate of stage and screen but just wants anonymity

Chun Byung In—The career of an "infallible" pilot ends in the debris of Korean Air Lines flight 007, shot down over Soviet airspace in August

Mr. T—The terror of *The A-Team* is indisputably the show-business maniac of the year

Ben Lexcen—An impish Aussie designer and his magic keel haul the America's Cup Down Under after 132 years of U.S. ownership

Joan Rivers—Where's Johnny Carson? Home, watching a *Tonight Show* guest host skewer guests and boost his ratings

Robert Mastruzzi—A Bronx high school principal won't let his school be less than the best

Eddie Murphy—He makes folks mad, but he's got it made

Matthew Broderick—Oh, to be young and hot in Hollywood; yet instead of acting up, the leader of the brat pack is buttoned-down

genes
Harvey F
funny boy takes **D**
gay mad whirl with *La C   x folles*

Philip Johnson—The grand old man of architecture comes full circle, designing the downfall of his own glass box

Vanessa Williams—A thorny crown goes with the job of being the first black Miss America

Richard Chamberlain—He gets no awards from his peers, but the public hails the king of miniseries

Michael Jackson—Thanks to a *Thriller* album, the former small fry of the Jacksons becomes the biggest star in pop

Rei Kawakubo—Japan's Stravinsky of fashion rocks the West with her atonal, asymmetric sad rags

Konrad Kujau—A Nazi-obsessed amateur forger fakes the Führer's diaries and nearly fools the world

Alice Walker—*The Color Purple*, her protagonist's letters to God, bring her a bestseller and a Pulitzer

Alfred Hitchcock—Three years after his death, five buried treasures from the master of suspense prove to be the movie event of 1983

Jennifer Beals—Dazzling looks and a ripped wardrobe turn a dancing Yalie into a flashy star

1984

Geraldine Ferraro—A tough, savvy, political pioneer loses the battle for vice president but wins a historic war for women

Bruce Springsteen—*Born in the U.S.A.* reaches for 5 million sales and the Boss transcends mere legend to become a symbol of all that once was right about America

myko—For nearly half a century, this most durable diplomat has been the poker face of Soviet foreign policy

José Napoleón Duarte—On the broad shoulders of this gutsy president rest El Salvador's hopes of emerging from a nightmare civil war

Mary Lou Retton—L.A.'s golden girl Olympian marches to a new beat as Madison Avenue's million-dollar baby

Richard Gere—This elusive screen actor seems bent on preserving the silence that marks him as a Hollywood enigma

Peter Ueberroth—An organizational wizard turns the L.A. Olympic Games into a glowing personal triumph

Joe Kittinger—In the year's greatest adventure, a hard-nosed pilot transforms a POW fantasy into a dream come true with a solo flight across the Atlantic in a hot-air balloon

Farrah Fawcett—With *The Burning Bed*, her career surges, and at 37 she's a happy mother-to-be—proud papa Ryan O' Neal hopes they're altar-bound

Clint Eastwood—As *Tightrope*'s kinky cop he reveals new and darker dimensions that leave astonished critics cheering

Betty Ford—The former First Lady publicly tackles her problems with alcohol and painkillers—and helps cure a nation's ills

John Malkovich—A versatile young Chicago actor storms Broadway in *Death of a Salesman* and stakes a claim on Oscar in two of the year's best movies, *Places in the Heart* and *The Killing Fields*

John Henry—This equine geriatric marvel has traveled from coast to coast and convincingly proved that the race is not always to the youngest

Sparky Anderson—He managed the Detroit Tigers to victory in the World Series and also leads the league in rough-hewn rhetoric

Tina Turner—After eight years of deep rivers and high mountains, a self-professed "Soul Survivor" strides back into the rock and roll promised land with her new album, *Private Dancer*

William Kennedy—At 56, Albany's patient author watches the work of a lifetime pay off with a Pulitzer Prize, *The Cotton Club*, movie deals, and a $264,000 MacArthur "genius grant"

Lee Iacocca—With his autobiography riding atop the bestseller list, Chrysler's blunt shirt-sleeve philosopher offers a plan to fix the sputtering economy

Vanessa Williams—The first black Miss America's reign is distinguished by dignity, delight, and talent—until the discovery that she had posed nude forces her resignation

Kathleen Turner—The star of *Romancing the Stone* mixes sex and sensitivity to become the hottest actress since Streep

James Baker—President Ronald Reagan remains curiously ageless as his chief of staff grows older quickly—could there be a connection?

Kathleen Morris—A controversial Minnesota prosecutor vows to continue the legal fight against sexual abuse of children

John Torrington—From his ice-shrouded tomb in the Canadian Arctic, a 19th-century explorer sheds new light on the chilling fate of Britain's ill-fated Franklin expedition

Bill Murray—This ghostbuster is the comedy star of the year's biggest box-office hit ($220 million), but if you think it's gone to his head—get outta here

Baby Fae—A wondering world watches as a child with a transplanted baboon heart fights for life

Michael Jackson—PEOPLE ran five covers, 73 photos, and 33,205 words on the singer during 1984—what more is there to say?

1985

Bob Geldof—Moved by scenes of mass starvation, this scruffy Irishman raises a cry with a song and rouses the world to save the hungry

Joe Kennedy—The best-known name in American politics surfaces again as Bobby's eldest son announces for the congressional seat once held by his Uncle Jack

Corazon Aquino—As the ghost of her assassinated husband haunts the rule of Philippine president Ferdinand Marcos, a housewife rides an emotional swell to political prominence

Steven Rosenberg—By energizing the body's natural defenses, a surgeon at the National Cancer Institute may have made the biggest step in 30 years toward a cancer cure

Rambo—His deeds are the stuff of cinema legend from here to Haiphong, but to the folks of one small western town, he's just a local boy with a preposterous set of pecs

Akira Kurosawa—Japan's feisty grand old man of the movies comes back from despair to film *Ran*, a feudal version of *King Lear* that may turn out to be his greatest triumph

Nelson Mandela—Banished behind prison walls since 1964, a legendary black leader may yet save South Africa from the horror of racial war

William Perry—He can block, run, and do endorsements. The 308-pound Refrigerator is the big surprise of the football season

Uli Derickson—TWA Flight 847's flight attendant becomes the heroine of a hijacking

Bernhard Goetz—New York's subway vigilante acted out our angriest fantasies, but a year later the questions remain—is he a hero or a villain, a victim or a criminal?

William Hurt—His risky transvestite role in *Kiss of the Spider Woman* makes him an Oscar favorite as Best Actor, but he'd rather hide from the world than try to be world-famous

Hulk Hogan—The World Wrestling Federation's heavyweight champion's favorite subjects are his biceps, his California home, and milk, his breakfast of champions

Cathleen Webb—The New Hampshire housewife says she faked a rape that sent a man to prison for years, and suddenly finds herself an unlikely celebrity

Madonna—She's a big girl now—rich, famous, and married to actor Sean Penn—but once upon a time, the reigning queen of all things pop was just another wannabe

Rupert Murdoch—The empire-building publisher of the *New York Post* and freshly minted American citizen takes on television, Hollywood, and morality

Dwight Gooden—Vulnerable only to kryptonite, baseball's best pitcher is quiet but deadly, playing a game he hasn't learned how to lose

Don Johnson—Every woman wants his body, every man wants his clothes—that's why he's America's Friday night vice

Princess Diana—No matter where she is she embodies dreams and always looks just like a princess

Mel Fisher—In a season of shipwreck salvagings, Captain Audacious ends a 17-year search for buried treasure, pulling 34 tons of Spanish silver from the Key West waters

PEOPLE'S MOST BEA
IN THE WORLD

Every year PEOPLE faces the difficult task of c
of the most stunning celebrities we've seen all year. He
face of beauty in 1995, and a look at the stars who have dazzl
their way onto more than one of our Most Beautiful People lists.

ALL-TIME BEAUTIES

5 Times
John F. Kennedy Jr.

4 Times
Tom Cruise
Mel Gibson
Julia Roberts

3 Times
Halle Berry
Kevin Costner
Michelle Pfeiffer
Claudia Schiffer
Denzel Washington

2 Times
Antonio Banderas
Cindy Crawford
Whitney Houston
Daniel Day Lewis
Paul Newman
Demi Moore
Paulina Porizkova
Jason Priestly
Isabella Rossellini
Katarina Witt

1995'S MOST BEAUTIFUL PEOPLE
Babyface
Irene Bedard
Halle Berry
Carlos Betancourt
Yasmine Bleeth
Amy Brenneman
Jeff Buckley
George Clooney
Courtney Cox
Tim Daly
Julie Delpy

Kirsten Dunst
Debrah Farentino
Frederic Fekkai
Jason Frank
Jon Frankel
John Grisham
Trip Hawkins
Faith Hill
Grant Hill
Lauren Holly
Elizabeth Hurley
John F. Kennedy Jr.
Dexter Scott King
Laura Leighton
Jared Leto
Elle Macpherson
Chiara Mastroianni
Vanessa Marcil
Lonette McKee
Demi Moore
Julianne Moore
Cara Oculato
Julia Ormond
Vincent Perez
Brad Pitt
Keanu Reeves
Claudia Schiffer
Lori Singer
Gloria Steinem
Patrick Stewart
Queen Silvia
Jimmy Smits
Kent Steffes
T-Boz
Vivienne Tam
Mike Tyson
Steve Young
Scott Wolf
Russell Wong

...l J. Fox—The comedy star of the year's No. 1 movie, *Back to the Future*, and the No. 2 TV show, *Family Ties*, puts on the dog as the boy king of Hollywood

Mengele's Bones—Discovery of the moldering remains of the Nazis' infamous "Angel of Death" ends the most intense manhunt of the century

Whoopi Goldberg—She's been on welfare and on Broadway; now she's on-screen in *The Color Purple*

Rock Hudson—His name stood for Hollywood's golden age of wholesome heroics and light-hearted romance—until he becames the most famous person to die of AIDS

The Springsteens—The storybook year of Beauty and the Boss ends on a harmonious note with Bruce and Julianne Phillips at ease at last in New Jersey

Gracie Mansion—A hip gallery owner brings world fame to the brassy, flashy, sometimes trashy art that grows in Manhattan's revitalized East Village

1986

Sarah, Duchess of York—Breaking out of the royal mold, a commoner marries her prince and wins a nation's heart without losing her independent personality

Ivan Boesky—It isn't insight but inside tips that make this risk arbitrageur the demon of Wall Street

Dr. Seuss—*You're Only Old Once!* made us hoot, made us cheer / Seuss wrote it for oldsters, it came out this year

Bette Midler—No longer the wacked-out Divine Miss M, she becomes a mother and mainstream box-office draw in two hugely successful Disney films

David Letterman—The *Late Night* host's askew humor finally finds a home in the heartland

Pat Robertson—A television preacher bids to move from God's House to the White House

Daniel Ortega—The 41-year-old president of Nicaragua wears baseball caps, wields his own AK-47, and bedevils the Reagan state department

Raymond Hunthausen—Seen by the Vatican as the shepherd who strayed, Seattle's progressive archbishop believes he's keeping the faith

Bob Hoskins—A pudgy, pint-size dynamo known as the Cockney Cagney shapes up as the actor of the year with appearances in *Sweet Liberty* and *Mona Lisa*

Oliver North—After a series of bombshell disclosures, the question remains—was the President's marine a hero or a loose cannon?

Terry Waite—An envoy from the Church of England inspires international trust and obtains freedom for hostages in Beirut

Paul Hogan—An Aussie smoothy makes *Crocodile Dundee* America's favorite easy-watching movie

Howard the Duck—George Lucas's feathered friend turns out to be a turkey, as *Howard the Duck* loses $35 million

Greg LeMond—Becoming the first American to win the Tour de France is no easy feat for the 25-year-old cyclist, who has to battle a mentor's betrayal

Run–D.M.C.—Rap's Kings of (Hollis) Queens persuade skeptical rock fans to "Walk This Way"

Debi Thomas—The U.S. women's figure-skating champion finds the time to study microbiology at Stanford

Helga—A Pennsylvania housekeeper bewitches the art world, as it is revealed that she posed for hundreds of previously unknown Andrew Wyeth paintings

Vanna White—The latest in the line of Lite Celebrities, the letter-turning bombshell of *Wheel of Fortune* rakes in endorsements, writes a book, and leaves some wondering why she's famous at all

Beth Henley—A Mississippi playwright goes Hollywood with a trio of quirky comedies: *True Stories, Nobody's Fool,* and *Crimes of the Heart*

Jerome P. Horwitz—AZT, the anticancer drug he developed 22 years ago, is now our best hope in the battle against AIDS

David Byrne—Letting down his avant-garde, the Talking Head celebrates a wondrous, wacky America in his movie *True Stories*

William Rehnquist—In all matters large and small, the new chief justice of the Supreme Court goes his own way

Tom Cruise—A fave rave of the teen scene grows up to be the box-office *Top Gun* of 1986

Max Headroom—With electrons for blood, computers for brains, and an ego as big as all TV, this nonhuman talk show host is Chairman of the Tube

Whitney Houston—Singer Cissy Houston's shy daughter emerges as pop's prettiest commercial monster

1987

Ronald Reagan—Entering his eighth year in office, the president remains vigorous and completes his term with a Hollywood finish

Mikhail Gorbachev—The Russian leader who put a human face on communism takes the West by storm and ushers in an age of optimism

Baby Jessica McClure—Up and running after her fall down a Midland, Texas, well and her televised rescue, she gets on with a normal toddler's life

Gary Hart—Undaunted by negative press on his personal life, the Colorado senator re-enters the 1988 presidential race

Oliver North—An all-American marine charms his way through the Iran-Contra hearings. Will he ever pay for his involvement in the arms-for-hostages scandal?

Michael Douglas—Playing a lech in *Fatal Attraction* and a slimy corporate raider in *Wall Street,* Kirk's son steps into the spotlight

Patient Zero—Randy Shilts's book *And the Band Played On* identifies French Canadian Gaetan Dugas as a major transmitter of the AIDS virus. 40 of the 248 homosexuals diagnosed with the disease in 1982 had either had sexual relations with the flight steward or with someone else who had

Donald Trump—Emerging as an icon for the '80s, this real estate mogul is pushing his way around in the media and in the marketplace

Cher—Sonny's onetime partner, who says she "refuses to accept other people's limitations," soars as her roles in *The Witches of Eastwick* and *Moonstruck* bring her power, happiness, and a wider audience

Christian Lacroix—A new designer's whimsical approach to his trade revolutionizes the high-fashion world and caters to the most chic of the stars

Oprah Winfrey—The leading voice among talk show hosts is using television to fight apartheid as well as racism at home

Vincent Van Gogh—Despite bouts with depression so severe they drove him to suicide, Vincent Van Gogh is emerging as the most marketable Postimpressionist of the twentieth century

Magic Johnson—This talented point guard is leading the Los Angeles Lakers to the top of the NBA—and smiling all the way

Church Lady—*Saturday Night Live*'s most biting holy roller flourishes in a year of sex scandals, church scams, and other *special* sins

Princess Diana—Hints of discord follow the princess into her sixth year of marriage, as she and Charles spend more and more time apart and she begins to test the limits of acceptable royal behavior

Donna Fawn Hahn—Rice, Hall, and Jessica, the women who fell with Gary Hart, Ollie North, and Jim Bakker, are actually all the same person— the three faces of Eve

Bono—Struggling with sainthood, this rock musician spray-paints a work of art in San Francisco and tries to chip away at his heroic status

Brigitte Nielsen—Newly divorced from Sylvester Stallone, she remains notorious for her leggy sexuality and questionable motives in love

Tracey Ullman—Host of her own show on Fox, this British comedian astonishes and delights her audience, always hoping to avoid the bland

Jerry Garcia—Despite more than just a touch of grey, the middle-aged hippie priest is still getting by—and is singing to a new generation of Deadheads

Glenn Close—A 40-year-old actress battles her earth-mother image and becomes a screen siren with fatal attraction

Garrison Keillor—The creator of National Public Radio's *A Prairie Home Companion* is happy with life in the aftermath of his show

William Casey—Dying before he is able to testify in the Iran-Contra hearings, Ronald Reagan's CIA director admitted using any means necessary to defend the free world as he saw it

Dennis Quaid—His sure-footed sex appeal and engaging grin ignite the screen in *The Big Easy*

Tammy Faye Bakker—Hurt by a drug addiction and her hus-

makeu
line audienc
self a national jo

1988

George Bush—The president-elect is a gentleman of the old school and a family man who is not above a bare-knuckled brawl when it comes to politics

Jodie Foster—No longer haunted by would-be Reagan assassin John Hinckley, she makes an acclaimed comeback as a rape victim who fights back in *The Accused*

Roseanne Barr—Looking at her, it's difficult to distinguish art from life—Roseanne plays the larger-than-life housewife both on and off the small screen

Athina Roussel—Now only three, she will inherit over $1 billion when she turns 18—but money won't buy the love she lost with the death of her mother, Christina Onassis

The Cyberpunk—The nerds rise again, as "misfit" hackers wreak havoc on America's information networks

Florence Griffith Joyner—She may have won four medals as a sprinter at the Seoul Olympics, but she's still got two feet firmly on the ground

Lisa Marie Presley—The King's daughter lives down a princess image by marrying a sober fellow and settling down

Benazir Bhutto—A Radcliffe-and-Oxford-educated feminist becomes prime minister of Pakistan and discovers the challenges posed in being the first woman to lead an Islamic nation

Liz Taylor—In another roller-coaster year, Liz writes an upbeat autobiography, raises millions to fight AIDS, and descends again into a drug addiction so severe that a staffer

Ford Center calls
ale version of Elvis"

Michelle Pfeiffer—*Married to the Mob, Tequila Sunrise,* and *Dangerous Liaisons* prove that this actress is more than just a pretty face

Jesse Jackson—He may not have clinched the nomination, but Jesse Jackson's presidential campaign shows that he is a political force to be reckoned with

Phantom of the Opera— Rising from his lonely catacomb, this anguished spirit of the night beguiles us once again with a vision of the tragic depths of love

Merv Griffin—At 63, the former talk show host becomes a billionaire and takes over ownership of Trump's Resorts International, beating Donald at his own game

Anne Tyler—With her new novel *Breathing Lessons* and a film adaptation of her 1985 bestseller, *The Accidental Tourist,* a reclusive novelist is faced by an adoring public

Orel Hershiser—Squeaky clean or tough and mean? Off the diamond he may be an angel, but this World Series MVP is uncompromising when he pitches

Shi Peipu—Posing as a woman throughout his 20-year relationship with French diplomat Bernard Boursicot, a onetime singer with the Peking opera inspires David Hwang's Tony Award–winning play, *M. Butterfly*

Kevin Costner—*Bull Durham*'s down-to-earth romantic lead sends hearts aflutter and critics abuzz

Tracy Chapman—A serious black folk musician sings about a revolution and becomes one of the most successful recording artists of the year

David Hockney—25 years after making the move from England to sunny California, artist David Hockney and his bright canvases are the talk of the art scene

Jessica Rabbit—The hottest woman on celluloid isn't a woman at all, according to fans of this sultry 'toon

Stephen Hawking—Plagued by Lou Gehrig's disease, a Cambridge University mathematics professor works to unwind the mysteries of the universe—and writes a bestselling book

Tom Hanks—A familiar face hits the *Big* time with his portrayal of a 13-year-old trapped in a 35-year-old's body

Fergie—The Duchess of York's first year with the Windsors is not the fairy tale it had been cut out to be

Mike Tyson—The heavyweight champion's most formidable opponent proves to be his beautiful wife, Robin Givens

Sage Volkman—Thanks to a strong will and the miracles of modern surgery, a six-year-old burn survivor gets back her smile

1989

George and Barbara Bush—After a successful meeting with Gorbachev abroad, George turns his gaze to domestic matters while Barbara helps Millie write her book

Jack Nicholson—As *Batman*'s Joker, he romps in a role that fits him as closely as his white grease paint

Arsenio Hall—This hippest night-owl of them all hops to the top of the talk-show totem pole

Julio Berumen—The San Francisco Bay Area earthquake's pluckiest survivor takes his first steps with a new leg

Princess Anne—Once Britain's least-liked royal, she becomes an object of desire

Mikhail Gorbachev—He shrugs when the Eastern Bloc cracks and proves he's serious about perestroika

Salman Rushdie—For publishing the controversial *The*

Satanic Verses he now lives with the threat he'll perish

John Goodman—The TV Barr-tender and newly minted movie star is an extra-large hit in any medium

Gaia—The Greek earth goddess lends her name to James Lovelock's daring theory that the planet itself is alive

Manuel Noriega—The Panamanian dictator gives American leaders fits, but he may be nearing his last hurrah

Michael Milken—A junk bond entrepreneur makes $1.1 billion financing corporate takeovers—but his indictment brings an era to an end

Paula Abdul—No longer just Janet Jackson's footwork coach, she steps out as a song-and-dance sensation

Deborah Gore Dean—As the HUD scandal unravels, it's clear that she saw government as a game show and helped her friends win valuable prizes

Robert Fulghum—His unlikely bestseller, *All I Really Need To Know I Learned in Kindergarten,* goes to the head of the class

Madonna—In another typical year, she irks some Christians, splits from Sean, dallies with Warren, and gets canned by Pepsi

Spike Lee—The director raises a ruckus—and important questions—with his film *Do The Right Thing*

Ellen Barkin—She's tough, vulnerable, smart, very sexy, and doesn't quite add up; which may be why she's so riveting on-screen

Billy Crystal—Learning that an orgasm can be faked, he becomes a genuine sex symbol in *When Harry Met Sally . . .*

Pete Rose—Charlie Hustle battles bad press, baseball commissioner A. Bartlett Giamatti, and his own demons

Pablo Escobar—A Colombian drug lord markets death by the kilo while evading an outraged citizenry

Michelle Pfeiffer—In *The Fabulous Baker Boys* she adds a dash of hot pepper to a delicious dish

Elizabeth Morgan—Jailed for shielding her daughter from alleged sexual abuse, she is freed at last

Robert Mapplethorpe—The photographer rattles the art world and Jesse Helms with a shocking retrospective

Captain Al Haynes—In crash-landing a crippled DC-10 in Sioux City, Iowa, he saves lives with grit and cool

Donna Karan—Her DKNY collection secures the designer's position as high fashion's newest mogul

1990

George Bush—His place in history insecure, he faces a sea of troubles—and his most daunting crisis lies before him in the treacherous Middle East

Sinead O'Connor—Her haunting rebel voice is heard in an age of flashing legs and lip sync

Julia Roberts—After becoming the first hit female star of the '90s in *Pretty Woman*, she's sitting pretty

Ken Burns—The producer of the 11-hour epic *The Civil War* makes a big bang in an unlikely place—public television

Patrick Swayze—More mesomorphic than ectoplasmic in *Ghost*, he's every woman's dream of a heavenly body

Neil Bush—His questionable involvement with a Denver S&L puts a First Family face on the $500-billion S&L scandal

Delta Burke—She has unkind words for her *Designing Women* producers; the next thing she loses may not be pounds

Saddam Hussein—His invasion of Kuwait—bloody politics as usual for him—brings the world to the brink of war

Michael Ovitz—The man everyone in Hollywood would like to know spins gold out of tinsel

Nancy Cruzan—Finally off life support after eight years in a coma, she dramatizes the need for living wills

Colin Powell—America's top man in uniform raises the world's shield in the desert against Saddam Hussein

Fidel Castro—Cuba's leader stands alone and defiant after watching the lights go out all over the Communist world

Effi Barry—She's a model of wifely decorum as husband Marion, Washington's mayor, goes up in a puff of smoke

Dr. Anthony Fauci—He's used to taking the heat: he's America's point man in the fight against AIDS

M.C. Hammer—He brings showbiz flash and footwork to rap—and cashes in with the year's hottest LP

Bart Simpson—TV's intemperate urchin suits his audience to a T(shirt)—while authority figures have a cow

Nancy Ziegenmeyer—A housewife and rape victim goes public to fight a once-unmentionable crime

Nelson Mandela—He steps from the dim recesses of a South African jail into the harsh reality of freedom

Francis Ford Coppola—The acclaimed director stages the movies' most ambitious mob scene with his sequel *The Godfather, Part III*

Keenan Ivory Wayans—His *In Living Color* brings howls of laughter and out-Foxes the network establishment

Claudia Schiffer—No guesswork about this supermodel's

gen[...] many, vi[...]

William Sty[...] *Visible*, an accoun[...] depression, helps fello[...] ers see the light

Laura Palmer—Wasn't washed up when she was washed up—she's the Girl Most Likely To Pique on *Twin Peaks*

THE SEXIEST MAN ALIVE

PEOPLE has honored someone with this title beginning in 1985. Here is a look at the magazine's hunks of the year. Discerning readers will recall the drought of 1994, when no one made the honor roll.

1985
Mel Gibson

1986
Mark Harmon

1987
Harry Hamlin

1988
John F. Kennedy Jr.

1989
Sean Connery

1990
Tom Cruise

1991
Patrick Swayze

1992
Nick Nolte

1993
Richard Gere and Cindy Crawford (The Sexiest Couple Alive)

1994
No winner

1995
Brad Pitt

Bo Jackson—He can hit, run, rattle, and roll—and score on Madison Avenue

Princess Caroline—Eight years after her mother's death Monaco's First Lady is coping once more with tragedy in the year of her husband's violent death

1991

George and Barbara Bush—The First Couple's first concerns are war, peace, and their kids

Jodie Foster—As an actor she's known as BLT (bossy little thing) because she isn't silent as a lamb, but the first-time director commands respect on the set with *Little Man Tate*

Magic Johnson—He copes with testing HIV-positive by mounting a full-court press against AIDS

Julia Roberts—With a busted engagement and a box-office bust that's no sleeper, she ends the year flying off to Never-Never Land

Luke Perry—This hunk steals not only the *Beverly Hills 90210* spotlight but also the hearts of girls in all zip codes

Anita Hill—Her testimony doesn't stop Clarence Thomas, but it starts a national debate on sexual harassment

Garth Brooks—His country album *Ropin' the Wind* crosses over to lasso the attention of all America

Princess Diana—Surviving digs at her marriage and her AIDS activism, she turns a very regal 30

William Kennedy Smith—He beats a charge of rape, but his famous family may never be the same again

Terry Anderson—Unbowed after nearly seven years as a Beirut hostage, he emerges eager to catch up

Boris Yeltsin—By elbowing aside both Gorby and the Krem-lin hard-liners, he becomes Russia's new voice

Kenneth Branagh—Taking a break from the Bard, he goes Hollywood with the hit noir thriller *Dead Again*

Anjelica Huston—Recovered from the loss of a father and a lover, she emerges as Morticia, the *Addams*'s coolest ghoul

Jeffrey Dahmer—His confession could not explain why his grisly serial killings went so long undetected

Elizabeth Taylor—She must be the world's most incurable romantic; will altar trip No. 8 be her last?

Robert Bly—He says there's a bit of "hairy primate" in us all, and *Iron John*'s (mostly male) readers go ape

John Singleton—His *Boyz 'n the Hood* opens middle-class eyes to inner-city life—not bad for a 23-year-old

Naomi Campbell—With her drop-dead looks and her diva's temperament, she reigns over high-fashion runways

Axl Rose—Lowering the sonic boom onstage and off befits the rock monster who is Guns N' Roses' lead pistol

The 4,600-Year-Old Man—Freed from an Alpine deep freeze, he becomes the modern world's unlikeliest souvenir

Mariah Carey—She becomes pop's queen by sharing her musical *Emotions*, not by truth-or-baring her life

Derek Humphry—His best-selling suicide manual, *Final Exit*, ignites a passionate public debate about the right to die

Pee-Wee Herman—Loses his image at an X-rated theater—but not his public, nor the support of Hollywood

Norman Schwarzkopf—A hero after the Gulf, he now faces the challenges of a post-army career

Jimmy Connors—Written off as a tennis has-been, he defi-antly returns to the present tense at the U.S. Open

1992

Bill Clinton—The president-elect and his family recoup from a rough campaign and prepare to leave Little Rock behind for Washington

Hillary Clinton—Barbara's successor is a savvy lawyer who loves her country and her husband and is determined to make a difference

Cindy Crawford—She shows the brains behind the beauty, becoming a video celebrity

Ross Perot—Trying to crash the two major parties, he goes from can-do to quitter and back

Denzel Washington—As a mesmerizing *Malcolm X* he catapults to superstardom

Princess Diana—She dumps her hubby but gets to keep the kids, the perks, and the palace

Woody Allen—His breakup with Mia Farrow is like *Annie Hall Goes Ballistic*

Larry King—*Larry King Live* is the whistle-stop that White House contenders have to visit this year

Barney—The purple dino fossilizes the Ninja Turtles and gives kid-vid a Jurassic spark

Billy Ray Cyrus—All pecs and no talent, said critics, but he's raising Nashville's pulse

Terry McMillan—She can breathe easy now that her novel *Waiting To Exhale* is a surprise smash

Gregory K.—He changes his name and sets legal precedents by divorcing his mother

Desiree Washington—She scores a knockout in court over heavyweight champ Mike Tyson

Diane English—The producer makes *Murphy Brown* a single mom and herself a lightning rod

Madonna—She bares her bod, blankets the media, and leaves

fans asking, "What next?"
George Smoot—He finds the missing ripples that confirm the universe began with a Big Bang
Katie Couric—With political know-how and a chipper personality, she boosts the *Today* show
Fabio—Once a fantasy figure on romance-novel covers, he actually moves and speaks
Arthur Ashe—He brings eloquence, guts, and grace to his instructive fight against AIDS
Dana Carvey—Whether he's doing Bush, Perot, or *Wayne*'s Garth, he's always hilariously on target
Bernadine Healy—The first woman to head the National Institute of Health is brash and brainy, and gives women's health research a shot in the arm
Carol Moseley Braun—The first black woman to be a U.S. senator defies naysayers to win a place in the history books
Henri Matisse—Sybarite and family man, this glorious painter has crowds standing in line to see his work
Whoopi Goldberg—The actor is suddenly a Hollywood force more prolific than some studios
Sharon Stone—She shows a *Basic Instinct* for sensuality and stardom—and doesn't sit like a lady

1993

Bill Clinton—The president faces tough issues and a skeptical nation
Hilary Rodham Clinton—She reflects on family life and the value of prayer while heading the committee on health care reform
Princess Diana—She may be out of power in the palace, but she still has a place in Britons' hearts
Michael Jackson—The pop star can moonwalk but he can't hide from career-threatening allegations of child abuse

Yasir Arafat—With a handshake seen around the world, the PLO leader makes peace with his sworn enemy
Oprah Winfrey—This talk show host becomes the world's highest-paid entertainer, sheds 60 pounds, and stays single
Andrew Wiles—A shy Princeton prof you've never heard of awes the great minds of math
David Letterman—Once an after-hour prankster, now he's the leader of the late-night pack
Janet Reno—She wows Washington with her guts and candor, though you can't please everyone
Susan Powter—Her hot *Stop The Insanity!* suggests anger might be the best weight-loss prescription
Howard Stern—Radio's raffish raconteur exposes his *Private Parts,* and everybody wants a peek
Baby Jessica—She focuses our eyes and hearts on the tangled arguments over parental rights
Lyle Lovett—Country's wry specialist in heartache and rue wins the hand of winsome Julia Roberts
Ol' Man River—The Mississippi inspires words of awe and rage, from days gone byto last summer's rampaging floods
Jerry Seinfeld—He's got TV's most buzzed-about sitcom, a hot book—and an 18-year-old girlfriend
Katherine Ann Power—In facing her bloody past she prompts a rethinking of '60s ideals
Eddie Vedder—His hellbound vocals make Pearl Jam jell. Now he's got just one problem—he's a star
Vincent Foster—His suicide brings sadness and self-examination to Clinton's inner circle
Sheik Omar Abdel Rahman—A blind cleric is accused of inciting his U.S. followers to bomb and kill

Michael Jordan—His surprise retirement shows that even the highest fliers need to be well grounded
Rush Limbaugh—He bashes liberals for fun, profit, and the devotion of a fanatic following on air and in print
Shannen Doherty—Unlike *Beverly Hills 90210*'s Brenda, the feisty actress runs amok in several zip codes
Tommy Lee Jones—He's not the man you want on your tail, but you sure want to see him on the big screen
Lorena Bobbitt—She provokes the national imagination with an act few could view with detachment
Tom Hanks—Seen this year in three diverse and challenging roles, this star doesn't get caught up in the glitz of Hollywood

1994

Bill Clinton—Foiled by failed politics and gloating Republicans, the president strives to restore voter confidence
Tim Allen—Good things come in threes for the still-climbing star; with a hit film, book, and sitcom, he has the last ho-ho-ho
O.J. Simpson—Once an All-American, he finds his greatest fame as the murder suspect of the decade
The Pope—Despite failing health he delivers his message to millions in a book that lands at No. 1
Princess Diana—She tries to resume private life amid allegations of adultery and instability
Gerry Adams—The Sinn Fein leader calls for his Irish countrymen to lay down their arms
Shannon Faulkner—The 19-year-old "Lady Bulldog" fights tenaciously to become the Citadel's first female cadet

Michael Fay—In Singapore, the American teen is charged with vandalism and sentenced to a caning that sets off a worldwide debate: Is it spanking or torture?

Whitney Houston—Pop's top songstress takes her show on the road but walks a rocky path at home

Ricki Lake—Less than 3.6 rating points from Oprah, she trounces her competition, walks down the aisle, and lands in jail for an antifur protest

Vinton Cerf—The hearing-impaired Father of the Internet is working toward a universal network—his brainchild has doubled every year for the past six

Michael Jordan—Basketball's king tries the summer game, gracing baseball during the labor strife that threatened to steal the season

Heather Locklear—When not luring living rooms to join sizzling *Melrose Place*, she's planning her real life marriage to Bon Jovi's Richie Sambora

Jim Carrey—He may look *Dumb and Dumber*, but that comic *Mask* shows off rare slapstick style

Tonya Harding—The feisty figure skating champion slides into scandal and ices her dream

Jeffrey Katzenberg—The Disney exec ditches Mickey and Pluto for Spielberg and Geffen

Nadja Auermann—Forget the waif: This year's supermodel is a German import who gives fashion a shot of '30s glamour

Aldrich Ames—For nine years before his arrest, this rogue CIA agent brazenly betrayed his country

Christine Todd Whitman—New Jersey's new governor becomes a darling of G.O.P. moderates and moves up in line for the 1996 ticket

James Redfield—His philosophical thriller, *The Celestine Prophecy*, breathes new life into New Age

Andre Agassi—With Brooke in his court and a win at the U.S. Open, tennis's reformed bad boy serves notice he's back to stay

Liz Phair—Alternative rock's hottest star looks perky and sings dirty, communicating that wholesome girls have prurient thoughts

Power Rangers—Six multicultural teenage superheroes battle evil (and the once invincible Barney), but adults worry they are models of violence

John Travolta—From disco prancing to ponytailed *Pulp Fiction*, he proves to be Hollywood's most durable comeback kid

Newt Gingrich—The new Speaker of the House uses tough talk to tame Democrats

THE
PEOPLE
REGISTER

THE PEOPLE 400

In last year's Almanac we created an imaginary guest list of the 400 most compelling, fastest-rising, and indisputably established stars and starmakers, for a party to put Mrs. Astor's original 400 or Truman Capote's Black and White Ball to shame. With this year's edition we welcome 50 newcomers to our dance, which meant an equal number had to sit this one out. Below we present a preview of the comings and goings among our elite. Celebs who are gone from this listing are not forgotten; you can find them (among others) in the Register of Thousands, beginning on page 442.

A HEARTY WELCOME

Billie Joe Armstrong
Nadja Auermann
Tyra Banks
Tom Brokaw
Sandra Bullock
Naomi Campbell
Mary Chapin Carpenter
George Clooney
Chris Cornell
Courteney Cox
Sheryl Crow
Clare Danes
Kenneth "Babyface" Edmonds
Anthony Edwards
Melissa Etheridge

Linda Fiorentino
Laurence Fishburne
David Geffen
Vince Gill
Bridget Hall
Lauren Holly
Elizabeth Hurley
Samuel L. Jackson
Jeffrey Katzenberg
Val Kilmer
Jessica Lange
Pamela Lee
Joan Lunden
Toni Morrison
Paul Newman
Chris O'Donnell
Julia Ormond

Chazz Palminteri
Jane Pauley
Tom Petty
Liz Phair
Dan Rather
Trent Reznor
Adam Sandler
Brooke Shields
Alicia Silverstone
Jon Stewart
Martha Stewart
Michael Stipe
Quentin Tarantino
John Tesh
Uma Thurman
John Travolta
Mike Tyson
Elijah Wood
Robert Zemeckis

AND A FOND FAREWELL

Bryan Adams
Kathy Baker
Scott Bakula
Clive Barker
Beck
Shari Belafonte
Mayim Bialik
Beau Bridges
Jane Campion
Keith Carradine
David Cassidy
Stockard Channing
Billy Corgan
Lolita Davidovich
Calvert Deforest
Linda Evangelista

Donald Fagen
Louis Farrakhan
Sherilynn Fenn
Zlata Filipovic
Peter Gabriel
Cynthia Geary
Balthazar Getty
Tonya Harding
Mickey Hart
Barbara Hershey
Chrissie Hynde
Kathy Ireland
John Irving
Bo Jackson
Jesse Jackson
Beverly Johnson
Nancy Kerrigan
Ralph Lauren
Nelson Mandela
Kate Moss
Martina Navratilova
Lena Olin
Anna Paquin
Ross Perot
Paula Poundstone
Pat Riley
Rita Rudner
Tom Skerritt
Janine Turner
Scott Turow
Richard Tyler
Vendela
Vera Wang
Cassandra Wilson

THE NUMBERS BEHIND THE LUMINARIES

Are the PEOPLE 400 really different from you and me? We analyzed the stats on registrants, and here's what we found:

Average year of birth	1954
Average number of children	1.34
400 members without children	159
Average number of marriages	1.34
Members currently married	196
Members currently engaged	11
Members currently separated/divorced	92
Members never married	102

ANDRÉ AGASSI

Birthplace: Las Vegas, NV
Birthdate: 4/29/70
Occupation: Tennis player
Education: Nick Bollettieri Tennis Academy
Facts: His father was so determined that André would grow up to be a tennis star that he hung a ball and racquet over the infant's crib and, as soon as his son could sit up, gave him a Ping-Pong paddle and a balloon.

Celebrated his fourth birthday by hitting balls for 15 minutes with tennis great Jimmy Connors.

At the end of 1993 he was injured, overweight, and No. 24 in the tennis world. A year later, he bounced back to No. 2.
Infamy: Admitted to using marijuana as a young teen player.
Relationship: Brooke Shields
Famous Relative: Mike Agassi, former Iranian Olympic boxer, father
Major Titles: Semi-finalist, French Open, 1988; Semi-finalist, U.S. Open, 1988; Wimbledon, 1992; U.S. Open, 1994; Australian Open, 1995
Address: ATP Tour North America, 200 ATP Tour Blvd., Ponte Vedra Beach, FL 32082

TROY AIKMAN

Birthplace: Cerritos, CA
Birthdate: 11/21/66
Occupation: Football player
Education: Attended University of Oklahoma, UCLA
Signature: Quarterback for the Dallas Cowboys
Facts: Number one pick in the NFL's 1989 draft.

By age 27, he had won two Super Bowls, the youngest of only five quarterbacks in history to do so.

The Cowboys gave him the largest rookie contract in NFL history: six years for $11,037,000.

In the 1990 season, he was hit so often that he was dubbed "Troy Ache-man."
Infamy: In 1993 Aikman became the first player in football history to leave the NFL Pro Bowl early (he had a charity meeting early the next day). Paul Tagliabue fined him $10,000 for leaving after the third quarter.
Original Job: Baseball player
Relationship: Janine Turner
Major Award: Named MVP of the 1993 Super Bowl
Address: Dallas Cowboys Foot-

ball Club, One Cowboy Parkway, Irving, TX 75063

JASON ALEXANDER

Real Name: Jay Scott Greenspan
Birthplace: Newark, NJ
Birthdate: 9/23/59
Occupation: Actor
Education: Boston University
Debut: (Film) *The Burning*, 1981; (TV) *Senior Trip!*, 1981
Signature: *Seinfeld*
Facts: *Seinfeld* creator Larry David modeled the George character after himself.

Is an accomplished dancer and operatic tenor.
Marriage: Daena E. Title
Child: Gabriel
Major Awards: Tony, Best Actor, *Jerome Robbins' Broadway*, 1989; Grammy, Best Cast Show Album, *Jerome Robbins' Broadway* (with others), 1989
Quote: "I started losing my hair when I was a wee kid of 16."
Address: NBC Television, 3000 West Alameda Ave., Burbank, CA 91523

TIM ALLEN

Real Name: Tim Allen Dick
Birthplace: Denver, CO
Birthdate: 6/13/53
Occupation: Comedian, actor
Education: Western Michigan University
Debut: (TV) *Showtime Comedy Club All-Stars II*
Signature: *Home Improvement*
Facts: Has nine brothers and sisters.

His personal staff did not submit his name to the Academy of Television Arts and Sciences by the 1994 deadline, so he could not be considered for an Emmy (actors are responsible for submitting their own names).

Appeared in Mr. Goodwrench commercials.
Infamy: He served 28 months in

jail in 1978 for attempting to sell cocaine.
Original Job: Creative director for an advertising agency
Marriage: Laura Deibel
Child: Kady
Major Award: Golden Globe, Best Actor in a Comedy Series, *Home Improvement*, 1995
Address: *Home Improvement*, Walt Disney Studios, 500 S. Buena Vista St., Burbank, CA 91521

WOODY ALLEN

Real Name: Allen Stewart Konigsberg; legal name Heywood Allen
Birthplace: Brooklyn, NY
Birthdate: 12/1/35
Occupation: Actor, director, writer
Education: Attended NYU, CCNY
Debut: (Film) *What's New Pussycat?*, 1965
Signature: *Annie Hall*
Facts: Plays clarinet every Monday night at Michael's Pub in Manhattan. Missed the Academy Awards ceremony for *Annie Hall* because it was on a Monday night.

Among his many neuroses: takes his temperature every two hours during the day, won't take showers if the drain is in the middle.

Was suspended from New York University for inattention to his work.
Infamy: After details became known of his affair with Soon-Yi, Mia Farrow's oldest adopted daughter, Farrow accused him of sexual abuse of her younger children. In 1993, he was denied custody but retained visitation rights of their adopted children, Dylan (since renamed Eliza) and Moses, and biological son Satchel (since renamed Seamus).
Original Job: During high school, he supplied comic snippets to newspaper columnists Walter Winchell and Earl Wilson; he later became a hired gag-writer on a retainer of $25 a week.
Marriages: Harlene Rosen (divorced), Louise Lasser (divorced)
Children: Eliza (formerly Dylan, adopted), Moses (adopted), Seamus (formerly Satchel)
Major Awards: Oscar, Best Director, *Annie Hall*, 1977; Oscar, Best Original Screenplay, *Annie Hall*, 1977; Oscar, Best Original Screenplay, *Hannah and Her Sisters*, 1986; Golden

Globe, Best Screenplay, *The Purple Rose of Cairo*, 1986
Address: Rollins & Joffe, 130 W. 57th St., New York, NY 10019

TORI AMOS

Real Name: Myra Ellen Amos
Birthdate: 8/22/64
Occupation: Singer, songwriter
Education: High school
Debut: (Album) *Y Kant Tori Read?*, 1988
Signature: "Crucify"
Facts: She started playing the piano at age three. At age five she won a scholarship to study piano in a conservatory in Baltimore but was kicked out by age 11 for refusing to practice.

Father was an evangelical preacher, a fact that figures heavily into her sex-laden lyrics in songs like "Leather" and "God."
Original Job: Piano player in Los Angeles lounges
Relationship: Eric Rosse
Quote: "I have vivid memories of being a prostitute in another life."
Address: Atlantic Records, 75 Rockefeller Plaza, New York, NY 10019

MAYA ANGELOU

Real Name: Margueritte Annie Johnson
Birthplace: St. Louis, MO
Birthdate: 4/4/28
Occupation: Writer, actor, singer, dancer
Education: California Labor School
Debut: (Film) *Calypso Heatwave*, 1957
Signature: *I Know Why the Caged Bird Sings*
Facts: Nicknamed "Maya" by her brother, who called her "My" or "Mine."

At age seven, she was raped by her mother's boyfriend. Several days after her testimony at the trial, her assailant was found dead—killed by her uncles. She blamed herself for the death and did not speak for the next five years.

Tried to join the army in the late 1940s, but was turned down after a security check revealed that the California Labor School was listed as subversive.

Has received over 30 honorary degrees.
Infamy: In the late 1950s, she worked as a madam, managing two prostitutes in San Diego. Her guilty conscience caused her to quit after only a short stint.
Original Job: The first black—

and the first female—streetcar conductor in San Francisco at age 16

Marriages: Tosh Angelos (divorced), Paul Du Feu (divorced)
Child: Guy Johnson
Major Award: Grammy, Best Spoken Word Recording, *On the Pulse of Morning,* 1993
Address: Wake Forest University, Department of Humanities, P.O. Box 7314, Reynolds Station, Winston-Salem, NC 27106

GIORGIO ARMANI

Birthplace: Piacenza, Italy
Birthdate: 7/11/34
Occupation: Fashion designer
Facts: Entered medical school but after two years decided to join the military.

Designed uniforms for the Italian Air Force (1980).
Original Job: Medical Assistant for Italian military, window dresser in a Milan department store
Major Awards: Neiman-Marcus Award, Distinguished Service in the Field of Fashion, 1979; Cutty Sark Award, Outstanding International Designer, 1981
Address: 650 Fifth Ave., New York, NY 10019

BILLIE JOE ARMSTRONG

Birthplace: Rodeo, CA
Birthdate: 2/17/72
Occupation: Singer, songwriter, guitarist
Debut: (Album) *Kerplunk!,* 1991
Signature: Green Day
Facts: Like fellow bandmate Mike Dirnt; grew up poor in a broken home in a depressed small town.

When Tre Cool joined Green Day in 1990, his father bought a used bookmobile, built bunks and equipment racks, and drove the group around during its early tours.
Infamy: In 1994 performed a New York City gig in the nude.

At a 1994 Boston show, moshing turned to chaos and mayhem, and three young women were injured. When the set came to a jolting halt, a few thousand fans remained to protest vehemently, hurling bottles toward the stage and confronting police.
Marriage: Adrienne
Major Award: Grammy, Best Alternative Music Performance, *Dookie,* 1994

Address: Warner Brothers Recording, 3300 Warner Blvd., Burbank, CA 91505

TOM ARNOLD

Birthplace: Ottumwa, IA
Birthdate: 3/6/59
Occupation: Actor
Education: Attended Indian Hills Community College in Ottumwa, Iowa
Debut: (TV) *Roseanne*
Signature: *True Lies*
Facts: The 26,000 square foot, 30-room house that the Arnolds shared is the largest residence in Iowa.

Converted to Judaism when he married Roseanne.

After the breakup with Roseanne, started a new production company, Clean Break Productions.
Infamy: He was once arrested for urinating in public at a McDonald's restaurant.

He was a cocaine addict when Roseanne recruited him to work on her show.

Roseanne claimed that he physically abused her during their marriage, a charge he denies.
Original Job: Ham packer at a Hormel plant, box stacker, bartender, bouncer
Marriage: Roseanne Barr (separated); Julie Champnella
Address: William Morris Agency, 151 El Camino Dr., Beverly Hills, CA 90212

THE ARTIST FORMERLY KNOWN AS PRINCE

Real Name: Prince Rogers Nelson
Birthplace: Minneapolis, MN
Birthdate: 6/7/58
Occupation: Singer, songwriter, actor
Education: High school dropout
Debut: (Album) *For You,* 1978
Signature: *Purple Rain*
Facts: Named after the Prince Roger Trio, a jazz group led by his father.

Can play over two dozen instruments.

Now known as a symbol, or referred to as "the artist formerly known as Prince."
Major Awards: Grammy, Best Rock Performance—Duo or Group, *Purple Rain* (with The Revolution), 1984; Grammy, Best Rhythm and Blues Song, "I Feel for You," 1984; Grammy, Best Soundtrack Album, *Purple Rain* (with The Revolution, John

L. Nelson, Lisa & Wendy), 1984; Grammy, Best R&B Duo or Group, "Kiss" (with The Revolution), 1986; Oscar, Best Original Song, "Purple Rain," 1984
Address: Creative Artists Agency, 9830 Wilshire Blvd., Beverly Hills, CA 90212

NADJA AUERMANN

Birthplace: Berlin, Germany
Birthdate: 1971
Occupation: Supermodel
Facts: Tired of her lack of success with the waif look, she had Julien d'Ys chop her hair and bleach it platinum-blonde. Magazine covers and a reported five-figure catwalk fee quickly followed.

Called "the stork" by classmates in West Berlin, because of her disproportionately long legs.
Relationship: Alexandre Bougault
Address: Elite Modeling Agency, 111 East 22nd St., New York, NY 10010

DAN AYKROYD

Birthplace: Ottawa, Canada
Birthdate: 7/1/52
Occupation: Actor, writer
Education: Attended Carleton University
Debut: (TV) *Saturday Night Live,* 1975; (Film) *1941,* 1979
Signature: *Ghostbusters*
Facts: His grandfather was a Mountie.

Was expelled for delinquency from St. Pius X Preparatory Seminary.

Had a cameo role in *Indiana Jones and the Temple of Doom,* 1984.

A police buff, he rides an Ontario Provincial Police motorcycle, collects police badges, sometimes rides shotgun with detectives in squad cars, and owns, in partnership with several Toronto police officers, a Toronto bar called Crooks.

He is very interested in the supernatural and has an extensive collection of books on the subject. He admits, "I've never seen a full apparition, but I once saw what could be termed ectoplasmic light, and that scared the hell out of me."
Original Job: Stand-up comedian
Marriage: Maureen Lewis (divorced), Donna Dixon
Children: Oscar, Mark, Lloyd
Major Award: Emmy, Best Writing in a Comedy, Variety, or

Music Series, *Saturday Night Live,* 1977
Address: Creative Artists Agency, 9830 Wilshire Blvd., Beverly Hills, CA 90212

ALEC BALDWIN

Real Name: Alexander Rae Baldwin III
Birthplace: Massapequa, NY
Birthdate: 4/3/58
Occupation: Actor
Education: NYU, attended Lee Strasberg Theatre Institute
Debut: (TV) *The Doctors*
Signature: *The Hunt for Red October*
Facts: He is not naturally tall, dark, and handsome—he dyes his fair hair black.

Originally wanted to be a lawyer.

Was engaged to Janine Turner (*Northern Exposure*); she had the wedding dress ready and the invitations were sent out when they broke up.
Original Job: Waiter and doorman at Studio 54
Marriage: Kim Basinger
Famous Relatives: William Baldwin, actor, brother; Stephen Baldwin, actor, brother; Daniel Baldwin, actor, brother
Address: Creative Artists Agency, 9830 Wilshire Blvd., Beverly Hills, CA 90212

STEPHEN BALDWIN

Birthplace: Massapequa, NY
Birthdate: 1966
Occupation: Actor
Debut: (TV) *The Prodigious Hickey,* 1987; (Film) *Homeboy,* 1988
Signature: *Threesome*
Facts: Worked as a Calvin Klein model before he started acting.

He played the teenage "Buffalo Bill" Cody on the TV series *The Young Riders,* 1989–92.

Older sister Elizabeth is the head of his fan club.
Original Job: Worked in a Manhattan pizza parlor when he was discovered by an agent
Marriage: Kennya
Child: Alaia
Famous Relatives: Alec Baldwin, actor, brother; William Baldwin, actor, brother; Daniel Baldwin, actor, brother
Address: Box 447, Camillus, NY 13031

WILLIAM BALDWIN

Birthplace: Massapequa, NY
Birthdate: 1963

Occupation: Actor
Education: State University of New York at Binghamton
Debut: (Film) *Born on the Fourth of July*, 1989
Signature: *Backdraft*
Facts: Original ambition was to play professional baseball with the New York Yankees.

In one day he went from an acting agent to a modeling agent and then to a photographer and did a modeling shoot for Calvin Klein jeans. Claims he lived for a year on the money he made on that one shoot.
Original Job: Worked for a year on Capitol Hill as an aide to Rep. Thomas Downey (D, NY)
Marriage: Chynna Phillips
Famous Relatives: Alec Baldwin, actor, brother; Stephen Baldwin, actor, brother; Daniel Baldwin, actor, brother
Quote: "I can honestly say that if Alec had never gone into the business, I wouldn't be an actor."
Address: Creative Artists Agency, 9830 Wilshire Blvd., Beverly Hills, CA 90212

ANTONIO BANDERAS

Birthplace: Málaga, Spain
Birthdate: 1960
Occupation: Actor
Education: School of Dramatic Art, Málaga, Spain
Debut: (Stage) *Los Tarantos*, 1981; (Film) *Labyrinth of Passion*, 1982
Signature: *Philadelphia*
Facts: Modeled for Ralph Lauren and Gucci.

Would love to play the Hunchback of Notre Dame, but thinks he won't be able to because of his good looks.
Original Job: Model, waiter
Marriage: Ana Leza (separated), Melanie Griffith (relationship)
Quote: "I thought to myself, 'Oh my God. How disgusting.' Then I went to the first rehearsal and it was . . . so easy. I didn't lose my fingers, my ear didn't fall down. Nothing happens if you're sure of who you are." (On his first kiss in a role as a homosexual, in the 1988 Almodóvar movie *Law of Desire*.)
Address: Creative Artists Agency, 9830 Wilshire Blvd., Beverly Hills, CA 90212

TYRA BANKS

Birthplace: Inglewood, CA
Birthdate: 12/73
Occupation: Model, actor

Education: High school
Debut: (TV) *Fresh Prince of Bel Air*, 1994; (Film) *Higher Learning*, 1995
Facts: The August before she was to enroll in college, she was asked by a French modeling agent to work at the couture shows in Paris. Within a week of that first stroll, "Miss Tyra" (as the fashion cognoscenti call her) had accumulated 25 more bookings.

Became the second-ever black model (Lana Ogilvie was the first) under contract with Cover Girl Cosmetics.

Singleton saw her on the cover of *Essence* and felt she'd be perfect for a part in his *Higher Learning*. He arranged for an audition, and during the drawn-out casting process they fell in love.
Relationship: John Singleton
Address: Creative Artists Agency, 9830 Wilshire Blvd., Beverly Hills, CA 90212

ELLEN BARKIN

Birthplace: Bronx, NY
Birthdate: 4/16/54
Occupation: Actor
Education: High School of the Performing Arts, Hunter College
Debut: (Film) *Diner*, 1982
Signature: *Sea of Love*
Facts: At New York's High School of the Performing Arts, she was often passed over for roles because she wasn't considered pretty enough.
Original Job: Waitress
Marriage: Gabriel Byrne (separated), David Arquette (relationship)
Children: Romy Marion, Jack
Address: 3100 N. Damon Way, Burbank, CA 91505

CHARLES BARKLEY

Birthplace: Leeds, AL
Birthdate: 2/20/63
Occupation: Basketball player
Education: Attended Auburn University
Facts: He is the shortest player (6' 6") ever to lead the NBA in rebounding.

At birth, he was anemic and weighed only six pounds, 12 ounces. Doctors administered blood transfusions to keep him alive.

During his college years, he battled a weight problem, at one point exceeding 300 pounds. Schoolmates nicknamed him "Boy Gorge," "The Round Mound

of Rebound," and "The Leaning Tower of Pizza."

Turned down offers of over $500,000 from trade shows because he believes that fans should not have to pay for autographs.
Infamy: During the 1989–90 season, he racked up nearly $36,000 in fines, setting an NBA record. His misconduct included spitting on a referee, making a bet with another player, and fighting.

In March 1991 Barkley spit at a fan yelling racial epithets at him, but missed and hit an eight-year-old girl instead.
Marriage: Maureen
Child: Christiana
Address: Phoenix Suns, 2910 N. Central Ave., Phoenix, AZ 85012

DREW BARRYMORE

Birthplace: Los Angeles, CA
Birthdate: 2/22/75
Occupation: Actor
Education: High school dropout
Debut: (Film) *Altered States*, 1980
Signature: *E.T., the Extra-Terrestrial*
Facts: Starred in a TV commercial for Gainsburgers when she was 11 months old.

After drug rehabilitation, she starred in *Fifteen and Getting Straight* (1989), a TV movie about drug abuse, and wrote her own autobiography, *Little Lost Girl*, at age 14 to clear the air. Credits musician David Crosby for helping her get over drugs.
Infamy: Began drinking at age nine and started taking drugs at 10.

In 1992, posed nude for *Interview* magazine.

In 1995, posed nude for *Playboy*.

While on the *Late Show with David Letterman* in 1995, pulled down her trousers to display tattoos on her behind, then pulled up her shirt and flashed her breasts at Letterman.
Marriage: Jeremy Thomas (divorced), Eric Erlander (relationship)
Famous Relatives: John Barrymore Jr., actor and director, father; Ethel Barrymore, actor, great-aunt; Lionel Barrymore, actor, great-uncle; John Barrymore Sr., actor, grandfather
Major Award: Golden Globe, Best Actress in a Miniseries or Telefilm, *Guncrazy*, 1993
Address: United Talent Agency, 9560 Wilshire Blvd., Suite 500, Beverly Hills, CA 90212

KIM BASINGER

Birthplace: Athens, GA
Birthdate: 12/8/53
Occupation: Actor
Education: Attended University of Georgia
Debut: (Film) *Hard Country*, 1981
Signature: *9 1/2 Weeks*
Facts: Filed for bankruptcy in May 1993 after an $8.1 million verdict was rendered against her in favor of Main Line Pictures, after she dropped out of the movie *Boxing Helena*. Had to limit her monthly living expenses to $10,000 under bankruptcy plan. An appeals court later reversed the verdict, setting the stage for another trial.

Developed agoraphobia while a model. Threw her modeling portfolio off the Brooklyn Bridge.

Was involved with the artist formerly known as Prince before marrying Alec Baldwin.
Infamy: In 1983, she appeared in an eight-page *Playboy* spread.

Bought Braselton, a town in Georgia, for $20 million in 1989, with plans to develop it into a tourist attraction. Dumped her interest in the town after she declared bankruptcy, leaving residents angry and fearful for their futures.
Original Job: Breck shampoo model, then a Ford model; pursued a singing career under the nom-de-chant Chelsea.
Marriages: Ron Britton (divorced), Alec Baldwin
Address: Creative Artists Agency, 9830 Wilshire Blvd., Beverly Hills, CA 90212

ANGELA BASSETT

Birthplace: New York, NY
Birthdate: 8/16/58
Occupation: Actor
Education: Yale University
Debut: (Film) *FX*, 1986
Signature: *What's Love Got To Do With It*
Facts: Helped integrate her high school, where she was on the honor roll and the cheerleading squad. Went to college on a scholarship.
Original Job: Hair stylist, photo researcher at *U.S. News and World Report*
Major Award: Golden Globe, Best Actress in a Comedy or Musical, *What's Love Got to Do With It*, 1994
Address: Ambrosio/Mortimer & Associates, 9150 Wilshire Blvd., Suite 175, Beverly Hills, CA 90212

KATHY BATES

Real Name: Kathleen Doyle Bates
Birthplace: Memphis, TN
Birthdate: 6/28/48
Occupation: Actor
Education: Southern Methodist University
Debut: (Film) *Taking Off*, 1971; (Stage) *Casserole*, 1975; (TV) *The Love Boat*, 1977
Signature: *Misery*
Facts: She lost the screen roles of characters she originated on the stage (Frankie in *Frankie and Johnny in the Claire de Lune* and Lenny McGrath in *Crimes of the Heart*) to Michelle Pfeiffer and Diane Keaton.

Terrence McNally created the character Frankie (in *Frankie and Johnny in the Claire de Lune*) with her in mind.
Original Job: Singing waitress in the Catskills, cashier in the gift shop of Museum of Modern Art in New York
Marriage: Tony Campisi
Major Award: Oscar, Best Actress, *Misery*, 1990; Golden Globe, Best Actress in a Drama, *Misery*, 1990
Address: c/o S. Smith, 121 N. San Vicente Blvd., Beverly Hills, CA 90211

WARREN BEATTY

Real Name: Henry Warren Beaty
Birthplace: Richmond, VA
Birthdate: 3/30/37
Occupation: Actor, producer, director, screenwriter
Education: Attended Northwestern University
Debut: (Film) *Splendor in the Grass*, 1961
Signature: *Shampoo*
Facts: Rejected football scholarships to go to drama school.

Is famed for his reluctance to do interviews and his tendency to pause for a minute or more before giving a yes or no answer.

The longtime womanizer broke the hearts of many famous actresses, including Natalie Wood, Leslie Caron, and Joan Collins. (Collins even had a wedding dress hanging in a wardrobe for almost a year.)
Original Job: Bricklayer, dishwasher, construction worker, piano player
Marriage: Annette Bening
Children: Kathlyn, Benjamin
Famous Relative: Shirley MacLaine, actor, sister
Major Awards: Golden Globe, Most Promising Newcomer—

Male, 1962; Golden Globe, Best Actor in a Comedy, *Heaven Can Wait*, 1979; Oscar, Best Director, *Reds*, 1981; Golden Globe, Best Director, *Reds*, 1982
Quote: "For me, the highest level of sexual excitement is in a monogamous relationship."
Address: Creative Artists Agency, 9830 Wilshire Blvd., Beverly Hills, CA 90212

ANNETTE BENING

Birthplace: Topeka, KS
Birthdate: 5/5/58
Occupation: Actor
Education: Mesa College, San Francisco State University, American Conservatory Theater, San Francisco
Debut: (Stage) *Coastal Disturbances*, 1986; (Film) *The Great Outdoors*, 1988
Signature: *The Grifters*
Fact: Originally cast as Catwoman in *Batman Returns*, she got pregnant and lost the role to Michelle Pfeiffer.
Original Job: Cook on a charter boat for a year, to pay for college
Marriages: Steve White (divorced), Warren Beatty
Children: Kathlyn, Benjamin
Address: Creative Artists Agency, 9830 Wilshire Blvd., Beverly Hills, CA 90212

TONY BENNETT

Real Name: Anthony Dominick Benedetto
Birthplace: Astoria, NY
Birthdate: 8/3/26
Occupation: Singer
Education: Attended Manhattan's School of Industrial Art
Debut: (Album) *The Boulevard of Broken Dreams*, 1950
Signature: "I Left My Heart in San Francisco"
Facts: Marched with Martin Luther King Jr. in Selma in 1965 at the urging of Harry Belafonte.

Used the name Joe Bari until Bob Hope introduced him as Tony Bennett in 1950.

Served two years as an infantryman in Europe during World War II.

An avid painter, his works have been exhibited in galleries around the country.
Original Job: Singing waiter
Marriages: Patricia Beech (divorced), Sandra Grant (divorced)
Children: Danny, Daegal, Joanna, Antonia
Major Awards: Grammy, Best Pop Vocal—Male, "I Left My Heart in

San Francisco," 1962; Grammy, Record of the Year, "I Left My Heart in San Francisco," 1962; Grammy, Album of the Year, *MTV Unplugged*, 1994; Grammy, Best Traditional Pop Vocal Performance, *MTV Unplugged*, 1994
Address: William Morris Agency, 151 El Camino Dr., Beverly Hills, CA 90212

CANDICE BERGEN

Birthplace: Beverly Hills, CA
Birthdate: 5/9/46
Occupation: Actor, photojournalist
Education: Attended University of Pennsylvania
Debut: (Film) *The Group*, 1966
Signature: *Murphy Brown*
Facts: Her father's puppet, Charlie McCarthy, had a bigger bedroom and more clothes than she did as a child.

As a photojournalist, was published in *Life* and *Playboy*.

Wrote a play, *The Freezer*, which is included in *Best Short Plays of 1968*.
Original Job: Model
Marriage: Louis Malle
Child: Chloe
Famous Relative: Edgar Bergen, ventriloquist, father
Major Awards: Emmy, Best Actress in a Comedy Series, *Murphy Brown*, 1989, 1990, 1992, 1993; Golden Globe, Best Actress in a Comedy Series, *Murphy Brown*, 1989, 1992, 1993
Address: William Morris Agency, 151 El Camino Dr., Beverly Hills, CA 90212

HALLE BERRY

Birthplace: Cleveland, OH
Birthdate: 8/14/68
Occupation: Actor
Education: Attended Cuyahoga Community College
Debut: (TV) *Living Dolls*, 1989
Signature: *Boomerang*

Facts: Elected prom queen her senior year in high school, she was accused of stuffing the ballot box. Was forced to share the title with a "white, blond, blue-eyed, all-American girl."

Raised by her white mother after her black father left when she was four years old.

Lost 80 percent of the hearing in her left ear from an injury sustained from a physically abusive lover. (She rarely wears her hearing aid.)

Her husband's name is tattooed on her rear end.

Learned she was a diabetic when she collapsed in a coma while filming the TV series *Living Dolls*.

She was first runner-up in the 1986 Miss USA pageant.

Played a crackhead in Spike Lee's *Jungle Fever* (1991) and did not bathe for days to prepare for the role.
Infamy: Sued by a Chicago dentist (and former boyfriend) who claims she never repaid the $80,000 she borrowed from him. Refused to settle and spending $50,000 defending herself, won in court.
Original Job: Model
Marriage: David Justice
Address: William Morris Agency, 151 El Camino Dr., Beverly Hills, CA 90212

JOSIE BISSETT

Birthplace: Seattle, WA
Birthdate: 10/5/69
Occupation: Actor
Debut: (Film) *Desire*, 1989
Signature: *Melrose Place*
Facts: Appeared in the TV miniseries based on Danielle Steel's book *Secrets*.

Played recurring role of Cara on *The Hogan Family*, 1990–91.
Infamy: As an unknown, starred in *Desire*, an Italian exploitation film about an American pianist who seeks enrollment in a prestigious music school in Venice. Bissett appears in the nude and in simulated sex scenes.
Original Job: Model
Marriage: Rob Estes
Address: International Creative Management, 8942 Wilshire Blvd., Beverly Hills, CA 90211

CLINT BLACK

Birthplace: Long Branch, NJ
Birthdate: 2/4/62
Occupation: Singer, songwriter
Education: High school
Debut: (Album) *Killin' Time*, 1989

Signature: "Killin' Time"
Facts: He was the first country artist since Freddy Fender to reach No. 1 with his first charted single.

Recorded a R&B record with The Pointer Sisters, who were surprised at his ability to sing in this genre.

Appeared in the 1994 movie *Maverick*.

Infamy: In 1992 Black fired his manager of five years, Bill Ham, and hired his wife's mother as his personal assistant. Ham filed a breach of contract suit in Los Angeles Superior Court, and Black filed a $2 million countersuit. The case was settled out of court.

Original Job: Construction worker
Marriage: Lisa Hartman
Address: RCA Records, 6363 Sunset Blvd., Suite 429, Hollywood, CA 90028

STEVEN BOCHCO

Birthplace: New York, NY
Birthdate: 12/16/43
Occupation: Producer, screenwriter
Education: Carnegie Institute of Technology
Debut: (TV) *A Fade to Black*, 1967
Signature: *NYPD Blue*
Facts: *Hill Street Blues* won 26 Emmys.

His father, Rudolph Bochco, was a child prodigy violinist who later played with orchestras in Broadway shows and with leading artists at Carnegie Hall.

Wrote material for *Ironside* and was the story editor for *Columbo*.

Turned down the presidency of CBS Entertainment in 1987.
Original Job: Assistant to the head of the story department at Universal Studios
Marriage: Barbara Bosson
Children: Jesse, Melissa
Famous Relative: Alan Rachins, actor, brother-in-law
Major Awards: Emmy, Outstanding Drama Series, *Hill Street Blues*, 1981, 1982, 1983, 1984; Emmy, Outstanding Drama Series, *L.A. Law*, 1987, 1989, 1990, 1991; George Foster Peabody Award; Edgar Allan Poe Award
Address: Fox Studios, 10201 W. Pico Blvd., Los Angeles, CA 90064

MICHAEL BOLTON

Real Name: Michael Bolotin
Birthplace: New Haven, CT

Birthdate: 2/26/53
Occupation: Singer, songwriter
Education: High school dropout
Debut: (EP) *Blackjack* (with Blackjack), 1979; (Album) *Michael Bolton* (solo), 1983
Facts: Wrote ballads and love songs for other artists, including Laura Branigan, Cher, The Pointer Sisters, and Barbra Streisand.

After the breakup of his band, Blackjack, he began recording solo in 1983.

In the mid '80s, he was a regular opening act for metal acts such as Ozzy Osbourne and Krokus.

A research library in the New York Medical College was dedicated to him in 1993 for his work as honorary chairman of This Close for Cancer Research.
Infamy: After a two-week trial in 1994, a jury ruled that Bolton's "Love Is a Wonderful Thing" is remarkably similar to the Isley Brothers song "Love Is a Wonderful Thing."
Marriages: Maureen McGuire (divorced), Nicollette Sheridan (relationship)
Children: Isa, Holly, Taryn
Major Awards: Grammy, Best Pop Vocal—Male, "How Am I Supposed to Live Without You," 1989; Grammy, Best Pop Vocal—Male, "When a Man Loves a Woman," 1991; American Music Awards, Favorite Male Vocalist, 1992; American Music Awards, Favorite Pop/Rock Album, 1992
Address: Columbia Records, 1801 Century Park W., Los Angeles, CA 90067

JON BON JOVI

Real Name: John Bongiovi
Birthplace: Sayreville, NJ
Birthdate: 5/2/62
Occupation: Singer, songwriter
Education: High school
Debut: (Album) *Bon Jovi*, 1984
Signature: Bon Jovi
Facts: Polygram executives gave the band a contract with the following conditions: John Bongiovi would become Jon Bon Jovi and only he would be given a contract. The other four members of the band would become Jon Bon Jovi's employees.

His first solo album, *Blaze of Glory* (1990), was "written for and inspired by" the film *Young Guns II*, in which he had a cameo role.

Title of Bon Jovi's album, *7800° Fahrenheit*, refers to the temperature of an exploding volcano.

Infamy: Had a legal dispute with cousin Tony Bongiovi, who owned the Record Plant, a New York City recording studio, over the extent to which Tony had aided his cousin's career. In 1984, Tony brought a lawsuit against Bon Jovi, the outcome of which gave him a producer's credit, a fee, royalties from Bon Jovi's first album, a cash award, and a one percent royalty from the group's next two albums.
Original Job: Floor sweeper at the Record Plant
Marriage: Dorothea Hurley
Children: Stephanie Rose, Jesse James Louis
Major Awards: Golden Globe, Best Song, "Blaze of Glory," 1991; American Music Awards, Best Pop/Rock Single, "Blaze of Glory," 1991
Address: Mercury, 825 8th Ave., New York, NY 10019

BONO

Real Name: Paul Hewson
Birthplace: Dublin, Ireland
Birthdate: 5/10/60
Occupation: Singer, songwriter
Education: High school
Debut: (EP) *U2:3* (with U2), 1979
Signature: U2
Facts: Got his nickname from a billboard advertising Bono Vox, a hearing aid retailer.

In November 1987, U2 opened for themselves at the L.A. Coliseum as the country-rock group The Dalton Brothers.
Infamy: Was the first winner in Grammy history to say "f—"during its live telecast (1994).
Marriage: Alisa
Children: Eve, Jordan
Major Awards: Grammy, Album of the Year, *The Joshua Tree*, 1987; Grammy, Best Rock Performance—Duo or Group, *The Joshua Tree*, 1987; Grammy, Best Video—Long Form, *Where the Streets Have No Name*, 1988; Grammy, Best Rock Performance—Duo or Group, "Desire," 1988; Grammy, Best Rock Performance—Duo or Group, *Achtung Baby*, 1992; Grammy, Best Alternative Performance, *Zooropa*, 1993
Address: Island Records, 14 East 4th St., New York, NY 10003

KENNETH BRANAGH

Birthplace: Belfast, Northern Ireland
Birthdate: 12/10/60

Occupation: Actor, director
Education: Attended the Royal Academy of Dramatic Arts
Debut: (Stage) *Another Country*, 1982
Signature: *Henry V*
Facts: The first installment of Branagh's autobiography, *Beginning*, is already in paperback.

Grew up in poverty in the shadow of a tobacco factory in Belfast.

Co-founded England's Renaissance Theater Company.
Marriage: Emma Thompson
Address: William Morris Agency, 151 El Camino Dr., Beverly Hills, CA 90212

MARLON BRANDO

Birthplace: Omaha, NE
Birthdate: 4/3/24
Occupation: Actor
Education: Expelled from Shattuck Military Academy, attended New School for Social Research
Debut: (Stage) *I Remember Mama*, 1944; (Film) *The Men*, 1950
Signature: *The Godfather*
Fact: Exiled himself on his private island, Tetiaroa, near Tahiti, which he bought after filming *Mutiny on the Bounty* there in 1960.

Wrote an autobiography, *Brando: Songs My Mother Taught Me* (1994) to raise money for son Christian's legal fees, but the book was panned for omitting his many wives and lovers, the latter including Shelley Winters and Rita Moreno.
Infamy: Son Christian killed daughter Cheyenne's boyfriend and is serving time for manslaughter (1990). Distraught, Cheyenne took her own life in 1995.
Original Job: Tile fitter, elevator operator
Marriages: Anna Kashfi (divorced), Movita Castenada (annulled), Tarita Teripia (divorced)
Children: Christian Devi, Miko, Rebecca, Simon Tehotu, Cheyenne (deceased), Ninna Priscilla
Major Awards: Oscar, Best Actor, *On the Waterfront*, 1955; Golden Globe, Best Actor, *On the Waterfront*, 1955; Oscar, Best Actor, *The Godfather*, 1972; Golden Globe, Best Actor, *The Godfather*, 1973; Emmy, Best Supporting Actor in a Limited Series, *Roots*, 1979; Golden Globe, World Film Favorite—Male, 1956, 1973, 1974

Address: International Creative Management, 8942 Wilshire Blvd., Beverly Hills, CA 90211

TONI BRAXTON

Birthplace: Severn, MD
Birthdate: 1968
Occupation: Singer
Education: Attended Bowie State University
Signature: "Breathe Again"
Fact: Learned to sing in a church choir. Her three sisters sing backup vocals on her albums. She and her sisters were only allowed to listen to gospel music, but she would "sneak into empty rooms to watch *Soul Train*."
Major Awards: Grammy, Best New Artist, 1993; Grammy, Best R&B Vocal—Female, "Another Sad Love Song," 1993; Grammy, Best R&B Vocal—Female, "Breathe Again," 1994
Address: LaFace Records, 3350 Peachtree Rd., #1500, Atlanta, GA 30326

JEFF BRIDGES

Birthplace: Los Angeles, CA
Birthdate: 12/4/49
Occupation: Actor
Education: High school, Herbert Berghof Studio
Debut: (Film) *The Company She Keeps*, 1950; (TV) *Sea Hunt*, 1957
Signature: *The Fabulous Baker Boys*
Facts: Joined the Coast Guard Reserves in 1968 to avoid the draft.

At age 16, he wrote a song included on the soundtrack of the 1969 film *John and Mary*, which starred Dustin Hoffman and Mia Farrow, and sold two compositions to Quincy Jones. To date, he has written over 200 songs.

Has exhibited his paintings and photographs in art galleries.
Infamy: In high school, developed a dependency on marijuana. He joined DAWN (Developing Adolescents Without Narcotics) and kicked the habit.
Marriage: Susan Gaston
Children: Isabelle, Jessica, Hayley
Famous Relatives: Lloyd Bridges, actor, father; Beau Bridges, actor, brother
Address: Creative Artists Agency, 9830 Wilshire Blvd., Beverly Hills, CA 90212

CHRISTIE BRINKLEY

Birthplace: Malibu, CA
Birthdate: 2/2/54
Occupation: Supermodel
Education: Attended UCLA
Debut: (Film) *National Lampoon's Vacation*, 1983
Signature: Cover Girl Cosmetics model
Facts: An avid Francophile, Brinkley transferred from her local high school to the Lycée Français in Los Angeles. She later dropped out of college and worked at odd jobs selling ice cream, clothes, and plants to earn money for a ticket to Paris.

Designed the cover for Billy Joel's *River of Dreams* album.

Married husband Taubman atop a ski mountain, a symbolic acknowledgment of the helicopter crash they both survived while heli-skiing in 1994.
Original Job: Painter
Marriages: Jean Francois Allaux (divorced), Billy Joel (divorced), Rick Taubman (separated)
Children: Alexa Ray, Jack Paris
Famous Relative: Don Brinkley, scriptwriter, producer, father
Address: William Morris Agency, 151 El Camino Dr., Beverly Hills, CA 90212

MATTHEW BRODERICK

Birthplace: New York, NY
Birthdate: 3/21/62
Occupation: Actor
Debut: (Stage) *Torch Song Trilogy*, 1982; (Film) *Max Dugan Returns*, 1983
Signature: *Ferris Bueller's Day Off*
Fact: Was heavily influenced by father James Broderick, who played the father in the TV series *Family* and died of cancer in 1982.
Infamy: While on vacation in Northern Ireland in 1987 with his then-girlfriend, actress Jennifer Grey, Broderick suffered a broken leg when the car he was driving collided with another automobile, killing its two occupants. Broderick was acquitted of one count of manslaughter and reckless driving.
Relationship: Sarah Jessica Parker
Famous Relative: James Broderick, character actor, father
Major Awards: Tony, Best Supporting Actor, *Brighton Beach Memoirs*, 1983; Tony, Best Actor (Musical), *How To Succeed in Business Without Really Trying*, 1995
Address: Creative Artists Agency, 9830 Wilshire Blvd., Beverly Hills, CA 90212

TOM BROKAW

Birthplace: Yankton, SD
Birthdate: 2/6/40
Occupation: Anchor, correspondent, managing editor
Education: University of South Dakota
Debut: (TV) KTIV, Sioux City, IA, 1960
Signature: *NBC Nightly News*
Facts: Served as president of high school student body. Also met future wife who became Miss South Dakota in high school.

Began with NBC as their White House correspondent in 1973.

Was the only network anchor present at the collapse of the Berlin Wall in 1989.
Marriage: Meredith
Children: Jennifer, Andrea, Sarah
Address: NBC, 30 Rockefeller Plaza, NY, NY 10112

GARTH BROOKS

Real Name: Troyal Garth Brooks
Birthplace: Tulsa, OK
Birthdate: 2/7/62
Occupation: Singer, songwriter
Education: Oklahoma State University
Debut: (Album) *Garth Brooks*, 1989
Signature: *Ropin' the Wind*
Facts: In 1990 at age 28, Garth became the youngest member of Nashville's Grand Ole Opry.

Brooks met his future wife while working as a bouncer. (He threw her out for fighting.)

In 1991, *Ropin' the Wind* became the first country album ever to reach No. 1 on the *Billboard* pop chart.

The video for "The Thunder Rolls," about a cheating husband shot by his battered wife after coming home drunk, was banned by Country Music Television and The Nashville Network. Thousands of shelters for battered women in America used the video in group counseling sessions.

Brooks' half sister is his bassist, his brother handles the books, and a college roommate is one of his guitarists.
Original Job: Bouncer in a nightclub
Marriage: Sandy Mahl
Children: Taylor Mayne Pearl, August Anna
Famous Relative: Colleen Carroll, singer, mother
Major Award: Grammy, Best Country Vocal—Male, *Ropin' the Wind*, 1991

Address: 1109 17th Ave. S., Nashville, TN 37212

JAMES L. BROOKS

Birthplace: North Bergen, NJ
Birthdate: 5/9/40
Occupation: Producer, director, actor, screenwriter
Education: Attended New York University
Debut: (TV) *Room 222*, 1969; (Film) *Starting Over*, 1979
Signature: Creator of *The Mary Tyler Moore Show* and others
Facts: Founded Gracie Films, which produces *The Simpsons*, in 1984.

With fellow writer Allan Burns, created *The Mary Tyler Moore Show* in 1970.
Original Job: Copyboy for CBS News
Marriages: Marianne Catherine Morrissey (divorced), Holly Beth Holmberg
Children: Amy Lorraine, Chloe, Cooper
Major Awards: Emmy, Best Writing in a Comedy Series, *The Mary Tyler Moore Show*, 1971, 1977; Emmy, Best Comedy Series, *The Mary Tyler Moore Show*, 1975, 1976, 1977; Emmy, Best Comedy Series, *Taxi*, 1979, 1980, 1981; Emmy, Outstanding Variety, Music, or Comedy Program, *The Tracey Ullman Show*, 1989; Emmy, Outstanding Animated Program, *The Simpsons*, 1990, 1991; Oscar, Best Director, *Terms of Endearment*, 1983; Oscar, Best Adapted Screenplay, *Terms of Endearment*, 1984; Golden Globe, Best Adapted Screenplay, *Terms of Endearment*, 1984
Address: International Creative Management, 8942 Wilshire Blvd., Beverly Hills, CA 90211

MEL BROOKS

Real Name: Melvin Kaminsky
Birthplace: Brooklyn, NY
Birthdate: 6/28/26
Occupation: Actor, writer, director, producer
Education: Attended Boston College
Debut: (Stage) *Broadway Revue*, 1949; (TV) *Your Show of Shows*, 1950
Signature: *Blazing Saddles*
Facts: Fought in Battle of the Bulge during World War II.

Co-creator of the TV series *Get Smart*.
Original Job: Drummer
Marriages: Florence Baum (divorced), Anne Bancroft

Children: Stephanie, Nicholas, Edward, Maximillian
Major Awards: Emmy, Writing in a Variety or Music Program, *Howard Morris Special*, 1967; Oscar, Best Original Screenplay, *The Producers*, 1968
Address: Creative Artists Agency, 9830 Wilshire Blvd., Beverly Hills, CA 90212

PIERCE BROSNAN

Birthplace: Navan, County Meath, Ireland
Birthdate: 5/16/52
Occupation: Actor
Debut: (Stage) *Wait Until Dark*, 1976; (Film) *The Mirror Crack'd*, 1980; (TV) *Remington Steele*, 1982
Signature: *Remington Steele*
Facts: Wife, Cassandra (best known for playing Countess Lisl in *For Your Eyes Only*, 1981), introduced Brosnan to Albert Broccoli, producer of the 007 series. Brosnan almost replaced Roger Moore as James Bond, but couldn't get out of his contract with NBC's *Remington Steele*.
In 1994, he finally played Bond in a movie.
Ran away with the circus as a fire eater in his teens.
Original Job: Commercial artist
Marriage: Cassandra Harris (deceased), Keely Shaye-Smith (relationship)
Children: stepdaughter Charlotte, stepson Christoper, Sean
Address: Creative Artists Agency, 9830 Wilshire Blvd., Beverly Hills, CA 90212

BOBBY BROWN

Birthplace: Boston, MA
Birthdate: 2/5/69
Occupation: Singer, dancer
Debut: (Album) *King of Stage* (solo), 1987; (Film) *Ghostbusters II*, 1989
Signature: "My Prerogative"
Facts: In 1989, became the first teenager since Stevie Wonder to have an album (*Don't Be Cruel*) at the top of the *Billboard* charts.
Turned away from life on the street in 1980, after he witnessed the fatal stabbing of his best friend by another youth.
Made his unofficial debut at age three, when his mother put him up on stage during a James Brown concert.
His wedding reception cost $1 million and was attended by 800 guests.
Infamy: Fined $580 for lewd-

ness on stage at a concert in Augusta, GA, 1993.
Brown was arrested at a Columbus, GA concert in 1989 for dancing suggestively with a woman he pulled from the audience, which violated a local ordinance "prohibiting the simulation of sexual intercourse" onstage.
Filed a multimillion-dollar lawsuit against his former business managers in 1994, alleging that they mismanaged his $27 million in earnings and took him to the verge of financial ruin.
Arrested in 1995 for aggravated assault for beating a man in Orlando, FL.
Marriage: Whitney Houston
Children: Bobbi Kristina Brown and three children from previous relationships
Major Award: Grammy, Best R&B Vocal—Male, "Every Little Step," 1989
Address: MCA Music Entertainment Group, 70 Universal City Plaza, Universal City, CA 91608

JACKSON BROWNE

Birthplace: Heidelberg, Germany
Birthdate: 10/9/48
Occupation: Singer, songwriter
Education: High school
Debut: (Album) *Jackson Browne*, 1972
Signature: "Tender is the Night"
Facts: Wanted to play the piano as a child, but his father was a Dixieland jazz fan and insisted that Jackson learn to play the trumpet.
Recorded with Tim Buckley and Nico in 1967 in New York City and was a member of Andy Warhol's entourage.
Co-wrote "Take It Easy" with Glenn Frey of the Eagles, which was their first hit single. Produced Warren Zevon's first album.
Albums reflect difficult phases in his life: his fourth record, *The Pretender* (1976), is associated with his first wife's suicide. The title song of *I'm Alive* seems to allude to his breakup with actress Daryl Hannah in 1992, after a rocky ten-year relationship.
Infamy: Accused of beating former longtime girlfriend Daryl Hannah.
Marriages: Phyllis Major (deceased), Lynne Sweeney (divorced), Dianna Cohen (relationship)
Children: Ryan Daniel, Ethan Zane
Address: Creative Artists

Agency, 9830 Wilshire Blvd., Beverly Hills, CA 90212

PEABO BRYSON

Real Name: Robert Peabo Bryson
Birthplace: Greenville, SC
Birthdate: 4/13/51
Occupation: Singer
Debut: (Album) *Reaching for the Sky*, 1978
Signature: "Beauty and the Beast" (with Celine Dion)
Facts: In February 1992, became the first artist to have three separate records ("A Whole New World," "We Kiss in a Shadow," "By the Time This Night Is Over") at the top of four different charts (Hot 100, Hot Adult Contemporary, Classical Crossover, Contemporary Jazz).
Brought up on a farm, Peabo was the oldest of four children. "I was taught to work hard—man, I could slop hogs and pick cotton with the best of them."
Original Job: Backup singer for Al Freeman and the Upsetters
Relationship: Juanita Leonard
Child: Linda
Major Awards: Oscar, Best Song, "Beauty and the Beast," 1992; Grammy, Best Pop Performance—Duo or Group, "Beauty and the Beast," 1992; Grammy, Best Song Written Specifically for a Movie, "Beauty and the Beast," 1992; Oscar, Best Song, "A Whole New World" (with Regina Belle), 1993; Grammy, Best Pop Performance—Duo or Group, "A Whole New World" (with Regina Belle), 1993; Grammy, Song of the Year, "A Whole New World" (with Regina Belle), 1993
Address: Columbia Records, 51 West 52nd St., New York, NY 10019

JIMMY BUFFETT

Birthplace: Pascagoula, MS
Birthdate: 12/25/46
Occupation: Singer, songwriter
Education: University of Southern Mississippi
Debut: (Album) *Down to Earth*, 1970
Signature: "Margaritaville"
Facts: Has chaired Florida's Save the Manatee Club since its inception in 1981. In 1992, sued the parent Florida Audubon Society for independent control of the club, arguing that the society was "too cozy" with many of the businesses he felt were polluters.

Wrote a children's book, *The Jolly Man*, with his eight-year-old daughter in 1987. Also wrote two novels, including *Tales from Margaritaville* (1989). Has received a $3-million advance for a collection of tropical short stories.
In 1991, four Cuban exiles seeking political asylum swam to Buffett's Florida house. He handed them over to the authorities after offering them refreshments.
Also owns the Margaritaville Cafe franchise.
Original Job: Reviewer for *Billboard* magazine and freelance writer for *Inside Sports* and *Outside* magazines
Marriage: Jane Slagsvol
Children: Savannah, Sarah
Address: Frontline Management, 80 Universal City Plaza, 4th Fl., Universal City, CA 91608

SANDRA BULLOCK

Birthplace: Arlington, VA
Birthdate: 1967
Occupation: Actor
Education: East Carolina University, Neighborhood Playhouse with Sanford Meisner
Debut: (Film) *Fire on the Amazon*, 1990
Signature: *Speed*
Facts: Her mother was a European opera singer, so as a child Bullock shuttled between Austria, Germany, and the U.S.
Played lead actress in the short-lived TV series *Working Girl*.
Her role in *While You Were Sleeping* was originally offered to Demi Moore, whose salary demands were out of reach.
Original Job: Waitress
Famous Relative: Helga Bullock, mother, opera singer
Address: United Talent Agency,

9560 Wilshire Blvd., Beverly Hills, CA 90212

TIMOTHY BUSFIELD

Birthplace: Lansing, MI
Birthdate: 6/12/57
Occupation: Actor
Education: East Tennessee State University, Actor's Theatre of Louisville
Debut: (Stage) *Richard III* at Circle Rep.'s Young Playwrights Festival
Signature: *thirtysomething*
Facts: Busfield played Michael J. Fox's college buddy on *Family Ties* before joining the cast of *thirtysomething*.
Infamy: In March 1993, a 17-year-old actress filed a civil suit against Busfield, accusing him of sexually assaulting her on the Minnesota set of *Little Big League*. He denied the charges.
Marriages: Radha Delmarter (divorced), Jennifer Meriwen
Children: Willy, Daisy, Samuel Clark
Major Award: Emmy, Best Supporting Actor in a Drama Series, *thirtysomething*, 1991
Address: William Morris Agency, 151 El Camino Dr., Beverly Hills, CA 90212

BRETT BUTLER

Birthplace: Montgomery, AL
Birthdate: 1/30/58
Occupation: Actor, comedian
Debut: (TV) *Dolly*, 1988
Signature: *Grace Under Fire*
Facts: Writes short stories and poetry in her spare time.

Was named after Lady Brett Ashley in Ernest Hemingway's *The Sun Also Rises*.

Butler was discovered while working at the Lone Star Cafe Steak House in Georgia. A wealthy club owner asked her to figure a tip, and she responded, "I can't believe you've got 10 million dollars and your I.Q. matches your in-seam." She was hired on the spot.

Before achieving sitcom success, often occupied one of the nine boxes on *The Hollywood Squares*.
Original Job: Cocktail waitress
Marriages: Charles Wilson (divorced), Ken Ziegler
Address: International Creative Management, 8942 Wilshire Blvd., Beverly Hills, CA 90211

JOEY BUTTAFUOCO

Birthplace: Massapequa, NY
Birthdate: 1956
Occupation: Mechanic
Signature: Had an affair with Amy Fisher
Facts: On his first date with Mary Jo Buttafuoco in 1972, Joey took her to see *Deliverance*.

Owns a boat aptly named "Double Trouble," which he allegedly used for love trysts with Fisher.

In1988, entered a drug rehab program for cocaine abuse.
Infamy: In 1993, Joey was indicted for the statutory rape of Amy Fisher, sentenced to six months in prison, a $5,000 fine, and five years' probation.
Original Job: Mechanic at Complete Auto Body
Marriage: Mary Jo Buttafuoco
Children: Paul, Jessica
Address: Complete Auto Body & Fender, 1025 Merrick Rd., Baldwin, NY 11510

DAVID BYRNE

Birthplace: Dumbarton, Scotland
Birthdate: 5/14/52
Occupation: Singer, songwriter, director
Education: Attended Rhode Island School of Design
Debut: (Song) "Love Goes to Building on Fire," 1976
Signature: Talking Heads
Facts: Talking Heads' debut single was produced by Tony Bongiovi, uncle to Jon Bon Jovi.

In its first gig, the band opened for The Ramones.
Marriage: Adelle Lutz
Child: Malu
Major Awards: Grammy, Best Album Package, *Speaking in Tongues* (with Talking Heads), 1983; Oscar, Best Original Film Score, *The Last Emperor* (with Ryuichi Sakamoto and Gong Su), 1988; Grammy, Best Original Film Score, *The Last Emperor* (with Ryuichi Sakamoto and Gong Su), 1988
Address: Warner Brothers Recording, 3300 Warner Blvd., Burbank, CA 91505

NICOLAS CAGE

Real Name: Nicholas Coppola
Birthplace: Long Beach, CA
Birthdate: 1/7/64
Occupation: Actor
Education: High school dropout
Debut: (TV) *The Best of Times*, 1980; (Film) *Valley Girl*, 1983
Signature: *Raising Arizona*
Facts: Was expelled from elementary school.

Changed his last name to have an identity independent of his famous uncle. He assumed the name Cage in admiration of the avant-garde composer John Cage and comic-book character Luke Cage.

His method acting techniques have involved having wisdom teeth removed without Novocaine for his role as a wounded war veteran in *Birdy*, slashing his arm with a knife in *Racing with the Moon*, and eating a live cockroach for *Vampire's Kiss*.
Marriage: Patricia Arquette
Child: Weston (by ex-girlfriend Kristina Fulton)
Famous Relatives: Francis Ford Coppola, director, uncle; Talia Shire, actor, aunt
Address: International Creative Management, 8942 Wilshire Blvd., Beverly Hills, CA 90211

DEAN CAIN

Birthplace: Mt. Clemens, MI
Birthdate: 7/31/66
Occupation: Actor
Education: Princeton University
Debut: (Film) *The Stone Boy*, 1983; (TV) *The ABC Saturday Mystery*, 1990
Signature: *Lois & Clark: The New Adventures of Superman*
Facts: As a child, played baseball with Charlie Sheen and football with Chris Penn, and served on the student council with Rob Lowe.

Passed up 17 college football scholarships. He was a star defensive back (set an NCAA Division 1-AA record for interceptions in a season) and dated fellow student Brooke Shields for two years.

Was signed by the Buffalo Bills after his graduation in 1988, but injured his knee three days before his first preseason NFL game.

Had a recurring role in *Beverly Hills 90210* in, 1992, as Brenda Walsh's boyfriend, Rick.

Was turned down for the role of Jake on *Melrose Place*.
Original Job: Professional football player
Relationship: Gabrielle Reece
Famous Relatives: Sarah Thomas, actor, mother; Christopher Cain, director, stepfather
Address: Creative Artists Agency, 9830 Wilshire Blvd., Beverly Hills, CA 90212

MICHAEL CAINE

Real Name: Maurice Joseph Micklewhite
Birthplace: London, England
Birthdate: 3/14/33
Occupation: Actor
Debut: (Film) *A Hill in Korea*, 1956
Signature: *Alfie*
Facts: Fell in love with wife when he saw her on TV in a commercial for Maxwell House Coffee (1971).

Caine's brother David's existence in a mental hospital was kept secret from him for over 40 years, although his mother visited David regularly until she died in 1989.

Changed his last name to Caine after seeing the marquee for *The Caine Mutiny*, 1954.
Original Job: Cement mixer, dishwasher, driller, production office assistant
Marriages: Patricia Haines (divorced), Shakira Baksh
Children: Dominique, Natasha
Major Awards: Golden Globe, Best Actor in a Comedy, *Educating Rita*, 1984; Oscar, Best Supporting Actor, *Hannah and Her Sisters*, 1986; Golden Globe, Best Actor in a Miniseries, *Jack the Ripper*, 1989
Address: International Creative Management, 8942 Wilshire Blvd., Beverly Hills, CA 90211

NAOMI CAMPBELL

Birthplace: London, England
Birthdate: 5/22/70
Occupation: Supermodel
Education: Attended London School of Performing Arts
Debut: (Magazine) *British Elle*, 1985
Facts: In an effort to extend her talents beyond her modeling career, she wrote a novel, *Swan*, starred in the movie *Miami Rhapsody*, and recorded an album for Epic Records.

Has been romantically involved with Mike Tyson, Robert DeNiro, and U2's Adam Clayton.

Opened Fashion Cafe in 1995 in New York City with fellow supermodels Elle MacPherson and Claudia Schiffer.
Infamy: Staged an impromptu stripping episode during lesbian night at a Manhattan bar.
Address: Ford Models Inc., 334 East 59th St., New York, NY 10022

JENNIFER CAPRIATI

Birthplace: Long Island, NY
Birthdate: 3/29/76
Occupation: Tennis player
Education: High school
Facts: Capriati was the

youngest player (age 13) ever to turn pro, the youngest Grand Slam semi-finalist ever (age 14 in 1990 French Open), and the youngest to win at Wimbledon (1990).

Began swimming at one month and was competing with five-year-olds at local swim events by 15 months. At nine months, before she could walk, Capriati was climbing on the jungle gym and swinging from monkey bars.
Infamy: Police gave her a citation for allegedly shoplifting jewelry in December 1993.

Arrested in March 1994 for possession of marijuana in her hotel room. Went into a detox clinic for 30 days.
Major Titles: Semi-finalist, French Open, 1990; Wimbledon, 1990; Olympics, Gold Medal, 1992
Address: International Management Group, One Erieview Plaza, #1300, Cleveland, OH 44144

MARIAH CAREY

Birthplace: New York, NY
Birthdate: 3/27/70
Occupation: Singer
Education: High school
Debut: (Album) *Mariah Carey*, 1990
Signature: "Vision of Love"
Facts: Her vocal range spans five octaves.

Her wedding cost half a million dollars. She watched tapes of the 1981 wedding of Charles and Diana in preparation.
Infamy: Sued by her stepfather in 1992 for failing to share profits from her 1990 album.
Original Job: Waitress, hat checker, restaurant hostess
Marriage: Tommy Mottola
Major Awards: Grammy, Best Pop Vocal—Female, "Vision of Love," 1990; Grammy, Best New Artist, 1990
Address: Columbia/CBS Records, 51 West 52nd St., New York, NY 10019

MARY CHAPIN CARPENTER

Birthplace: Princeton, NJ
Birthdate: 2/21/58
Occupation: Singer, songwriter, guitarist
Education: Brown University
Debut: (Album) *Hometown Girl*, 1988
Signature: "He Thinks He'll Keep Her"
Facts: Father, Chapin Carpenter,

was a high-level *Life* magazine executive, so she spent her youth in Princeton, Tokyo, and Washington, DC.

Goes by the name Chapin, not Mary.

After college, considered music something to do for extra cash until she found her real career. Only after landing a nine-to-five job did she realize how much music meant to her, and began to focus on it.

Wrote Wynonna Judd's hit "Girls with Guitars" and co-wrote Cyndi Lauper's "Sally's Pigeon."
Infamy: Became an alcoholic after performing for years in bars.
Major Awards: Grammy, Best Country Vocal—Female, "Down at the Twist and Shout," 1991; Grammy, Best Country Vocal—Female, "I Feel Lucky," 1992; Grammy, Best Country Vocal—Female, "Passionate Kisses," 1993; Grammy, Best Country Vocal—Female, "Shut Up and Kiss Me," 1994; Grammy, Best Country Album, *Stones in the Road*, 1994
Address: Columbia Records, 51 West 52nd St., New York, NY 10019

JIM CARREY

Birthplace: Jacksons Point, Canada
Birthdate: 1/17/62
Occupation: Actor
Debut: (TV) *The Duck Factory*, 1984; (Film) *Finders Keepers*, 1984
Signature: *Ace Ventura: Pet Detective*
Fact: When his accountant father was laid off, he quit high school to make money doing janitorial work.

The $20 million he is receiving for *Cable Man*, due out next

summer, is the highest salary yet paid to a comedian.

A coalition of fire prevention groups demanded that his Fire Marshall Bill sketches on *In Living Color* be taken off the air because of the negative effect they were having on children.
Marriage: Melissa Womer (divorced), Lauren Holly (relationship)
Child: Jane
Address: United Talent Agency, 9560 Wilshire Blvd., Suite 500, Beverly Hills, CA 90212

JOHNNY CARSON

Birthplace: Corning, IA
Birthdate: 10/23/25
Occupation: Talk show host
Education: University of Nebraska
Debut: (TV) *Carson's Cellar*, 1951
Signature: *The Tonight Show*
Facts: Declined role to play lead in the series that became *The Dick Van Dyke Show*.

As a 12-year-old, performed at local parties as "The Great Carsoni."

His son Richard was killed when his car plunged off a road (1991).

Third wife Joanna Holland received $20 million in cash and property in divorce settlement, 1983.

Served with the U.S. Naval Reserve during World War II.
Original Job: Radio announcer, ventriloquist, magician
Marriages: Joan Wolcott (divorced), Joanne Copeland (divorced), Joanna Holland (divorced), Alexis Mass
Children: Christopher, Richard (deceased), Cory
Major Awards: Elected to the Emmy Hall of Fame in 1987; Kennedy Center honoree, 1993
Address: Carson Productions, P.O. Box 5474, Santa Monica, CA 90409

DAVID CARUSO

Birthplace: Queens, NY
Birthdate: 1/17/56
Occupation: Actor
Debut: (Film) *An Officer and a Gentleman*, 1982
Signature: *NYPD Blue*
Facts: Caruso used to stand in police lineups in New York's 112th Precinct, the same precinct in which *NYPD Blue* is set, for $25.

Producer Steven Bochco originally worked with Caruso in 1981,

when he played a tough Irish gang leader in the first three episodes of *Hill Street Blues*.

Made his acting debut as a stock boy who assists Margaret Hamilton in a Maxwell House ad.

After getting a taste of movie acting in *Kiss of Death*, Caruso decided his heart was really in films. His agent presented the producers of his TV series, *NYPD Blue*, with a list of extraordinary demands including a reported tripling of his salary to return to the show. The producers let him walk, to the outrage of many of the show's fans.
Infamy: Named in an $8-million palimony lawsuit in 1994 after leaving ex-girlfriend Paris Papiro.
Original Job: Loading dock worker, waiter
Marriages: Sherry Maugans (divorced), Rachel Ticotin (divorced), Margaret Buckley (relationship)
Children: Greta, Houston
Major Award: Golden Globe, Best Actor in a Drama Series, *NYPD Blue*, 1994
Address: United Talent Agency, 9560 Wilshire Blvd., Suite 500, Beverly Hills, CA 90212

DANA CARVEY

Birthplace: Missoula, MT
Birthdate: 4/2/55
Occupation: Actor
Edcation: San Francisco State University
Debut: (TV) *One of the Boys*, 1981(Film); *This Is Spinal Tap*, 1984
Signature: *Wayne's World*
Facts: Church Lady (character on *Saturday Night Live*) was a composite of several women at Carvey's Lutheran church who expressed indignation at his family's irregular attendance and less-than-complete commitment to the church.

His version of Garth is based on his real-life brother, Brad.
Original Job: Stand-up comedian
Marriage: Paula
Children: Dex, Thomas
Major Award: Emmy, Best Individual Performance in a Variety or Music Program, *The Saturday Night Live Presidential Bash*, 1993
Quote: "No dates . . . No proms. No football games. No driver's license. Basically, I was a fetus with shoes." (On his life in high school.)
Address: International Creative

Management, 8942 Wilshire Blvd., Beverly Hills, CA 90211

JOHNNY CASH

Real Name: J. R. Cash
Birthplace: Kingsland, AR
Birthdate: 2/26/32
Occupation: Singer, songwriter
Debut: (Song) "Hey Porter," 1955
Signature: "I Walk The Line"
Facts: Cash is one-fourth Cherokee Indian.

He cannot read music.

Created 75 cuts for his 1994 album, produced by Rick Rubin (of Beastie Boys fame), which included songs written for him by Red Hot Chili Pepper Flea and Glenn Danzig.

Known as "the Man in Black," which is the title of his 1975 autobiography. Cash adopted this persona while working in a trio that only wore matching black outfits.

Wrote a novel, *Man in White*, in 1986.

He chose John as a first name when the military wouldn't accept initials.
Infamy: Cash was addicted to Dexadrine in the '60s.
Original Job: Door-to-door appliance salesman, factory worker
Marriages: Vivian Liberto (divorced), June Carter
Children: Rosanne, Kathleen, Cindy, Tara, John Carter, stepdaughter Rebecca Carlene, stepdaughter Rozanna Lea
Major Awards: Grammy, Best Country Performance—Duo or Group, "Jackson" (with June Carter), 1967; Grammy, Best Country Vocal—Male, "Folsom Prison Blues," 1968; Grammy, Best Country Vocal—Male, "A Boy Named Sue," 1969; Grammy, Best Country Performance—Duo or Group, "If I Were a Carpenter" (with June Carter), 1970; Grammy, Best Spoken Word Recording, *Interviews from the Class of '55* (with others), 1986; Grammy, Legend Award, 1991; Grammy, Best Contemporary Folk Album, *American Recordings*, 1994; elected to Country Music Hall of Fame, 1980; elected to the Rock and Roll Hall of Fame, 1992
Address: Agency for the Performing Arts, 9000 Sunset Blvd., Suite 1200, Los Angeles, CA 90069

ROSANNE CASH

Birthplace: Memphis, TN
Birthdate: 5/24/55

Occupation: Singer, songwriter
Education: State Community College; attended Vanderbilt University and Lee Strasberg Theatre Institute
Debut: (Song) "Blue Moon with Heartache," 1979
Signature: "I Don't Know Why You Don't Want Me"
Fact: Never intended to become a musician. Her original ambition was to become a serious fiction writer.
Infamy: In 1982, entered a drug rehabilitation program for a cocaine dependency she had developed in 1979.
Original Job: Worked in wardrobe department during her father's tour. One day the tour managers asked her to come on stage and sing harmony.
Marriage: Rodney Crowell (divorced)
Children: Hannah, Caitlin, Chelsea
Famous Relatives: Johnny Cash, country singer, father; June Carter Cash, country singer, stepmother; Carlene Carter, country singer, step-sister
Major Award: Grammy, Best Country Vocal—Female, "I Don't Know Why You Don't Want Me," 1985
Address: Capitol Records, 1750 N. Vine Street, Hollywood, CA 90028

CHEVY CHASE

Real Name: Cornelius Crane Chase
Birthplace: New York, NY
Birthdate: 10/8/43
Occupation: Actor
Education: Bard College
Debut: (Film) *The Groove Tube*, 1974
Signature: *National Lampoon* movies
Facts: Worked as a writer for *Mad Magazine* (1969).

In 1968 signed as a recording artist with MGM Records.

While still at school, teamed up with friends to write an underground TV show that later became an off-off-Broadway show and movie, *The Groove Tube* (1974).
Infamy: Entered the Betty Ford rehabilitation center in 1986 due to an addiction to pain killers and alcohol.

Pleaded no contest in a 1995 arrest for drunk driving. His blood alcohol level tested at .18—more than twice California's legal limit.

In 1995, was the subject of a

$30-million lawsuit filed by his chauffeur for breach of contract and emotional distress over an incident that involved the illegal purchase of the drug Percoset.
Original Job: Magazine writer, tennis pro, bartender
Marriages: Jacqueline Carlin (divorced), Jayni
Children: Cydney Cathalene, Caley, Emily
Major Awards: Emmy, Best Supporting Actor in a Variety or Music Program, *Saturday Night Live*, 1976; Emmy, Best Writing in a Comedy, Variety, or Music Series, *Saturday Night Live*, 1976; Emmy, Best Writing in a Comedy, Variety, or Music Special, *The Paul Simon Special*, 1978
Address: Creative Artists Agency, 9830 Wilshire Blvd., Beverly Hills, CA 90212

DEEPAK CHOPRA

Birthplace: India
Birthdate: 1949
Occupation: Author
Education: All-India Institute of Medicine
Facts: Was a mainstream endocrinologist, and chief of staff at New England Memorial Hospital, before embracing alternative healing methods.

Dr. Chopra practices a form of ayurvedic medicine called Maharishi Ayur-Veda, named after the Indian spiritual leader who taught transcendental meditation to the Beatles. The system is based on a 5,000-year-old Indian holistic health system involving herbal remedies, massage, yoga, and transcendental meditation. (Ayur-Veda is derived from the Sanskrit roots for "life" and "knowledge.")
Marriage: Rita
Children: Gautam, Mallika
Address: Sharp Institute for Human Potential and Mind Body Medicine, 973B Lomas Santa Fe, Solana Beach, CA 92075

CONNIE CHUNG

Real Name: Constance Yu-Hwa Chung
Birthplace: Washington, DC
Birthdate: 8/20/46
Occupation: TV journalist
Education: University of Maryland
Facts: First joined CBS as a general assignment reporter in 1971, covering McGovern's presidential campaign and Watergate.

Tenth child; five of the Chungs'

first nine children died in their native China during World War II, when medical care was often unavailable for civilians. Her father was a diplomat in Chiang Kai-shek's government and moved to Washington, DC, in 1944.
Original Job: Copy clerk with a television station
Infamy: Created controversy when she broadcast Newt Gingrich's mother's comment that her son thought Hillary Clinton was a bitch, after promising Newt's mother the comment would stay just between them.

Fired from her job as co-anchor of the CBS Evening News in 1995 after a series of controversial on-air interviews, including the one with Newt Gingrich's mother.
Marriage: Maury Povich
Child: Adopted son Matthew
Major Awards: Emmy, "Shot in Hollywood," 1987; Emmy, "Interview with Marlon Brando," 1989
Address: Geller Media Management, 250 West 57th St., Suite 213, New York, NY 10019

TOM CLANCY

Birthplace: Baltimore, MD
Birthdate: 1947
Occupation: Author
Debut: (Book) *The Hunt for Red October*, 1984
Signature: Espionage thriller novels
Facts: First short story was rejected by *Analog* science fiction magazine. Had just one article (on the MX missile system) to his credit when *Hunt for Red October* was published.

In the U.S. Army Reserve Officers' Training Corps, his poor eyesight kept him from serving in the Vietnam War.

Part-owner of the Baltimore Orioles, he also led the effort to bring an NFL expansion team to Baltimore for the 1994 season.

Clear and Present Danger was the bestselling book of the '80s.
Original Job: Insurance agent
Marriage: Wanda Thomas (divorced)
Children: Michelle, Christine, Kathleen, Tom
Quote: "What do I care if someone reads my books a hundred years from now? I will be dead. And it's kind of hard to make money when you're dead."
Address: G. P. Putnam's Sons, 200 Madison Ave., New York, NY 10016

ERIC CLAPTON

Real Name: Eric Clapp
Birthplace: Ripley, England
Birthdate: 3/30/45
Occupation: Singer, guitarist, songwriter
Education: Attended Kingston Art School
Debut: (Album) *The Yardbirds,* 1963
Signature: "Layla"
Facts: At the Ealing Club in London, occasionally substituted for lead singer Mick Jagger in Blues, Incorporated.

Earned the nickname "Slowhand" because his powerful playing regularly broke his guitar strings, which he then changed onstage to the accompaniment of a slow handclap from listeners.

The song "Layla" was reportedly inspired by an affair that Clapton had at the time with George Harrison's wife Patti, and was dedicated "to the wife of my best friend."

Tragedy struck in 1991, when his four-and-a-half-year-old son died in a fall from Clapton's exgirlfriend's apartment. The song "Tears in Heaven" is a tribute to him.

Was among 1,080 Britons recognized on Queen Elizabeth's honors list at the end of 1994.
Infamy: After release of *Layla and Other Assorted Love Songs* (1970), dropped out of sight for two-and-a-half years because of a heroin addiction. He was brought out of seclusion by Pete Townshend of The Who. A bout with alcoholism followed. Now, he says he hasn't touched a drink since 1987.
Original Job: Construction worker
Marriage: Patricia Anne Boyd-Harrison (divorced)
Child: Conor (deceased)
Major Awards: Grammy, Album of the Year, *The Concert for Bangladesh* (with George Harrison and Friends), 1972; Grammy, Best Rock Vocal—Male, "Bad Love," 1990; Grammy, Album of the Year, *Unplugged,* 1992; Grammy, Best Rock Vocal—Male, "Layla," 1992; Grammy, Record of the Year, Song of the Year, and Best Pop Vocal—Male, "Tears in Heaven," 1992; Grammy, Best Traditional Blues Album, *From the Cradle,* 1994
Address: Creative Artists Agency, 9830 Wilshire Blvd., Beverly Hills, CA 90212

GEORGE CLOONEY

Birthplace: Lexington, KY
Birthdate: 5/6/61
Occupation: Actor
Education: Northern Kentucky University
Debut: (TV) *E/R,* 1984
Signature: *ER*
Facts: Got his Hollywood break playing a medical intern on the short-lived CBS comedy series *E/R,* set in a Chicago hospital emergency room. On NBC's *ER,* also set in a Chicago hospital emergency room, he graduated to full-fledged doctor.

Appeared as Roseanne's boss and Jackie's boyfriend during the first season of *Roseanne.*
Marriage: Talia Balsam (divorced)
Famous Relatives: Rosemary Clooney, singer, aunt; Nick Clooney, TV host, father; Miguel Ferrer, actor, cousin
Address: William Morris Agency, 151 El Camino Dr., Beverly Hills, CA 90212

GLENN CLOSE

Birthplace: Greenwich, CT
Birthdate: 3/19/47
Occupation: Actor
Education: William and Mary College
Debut: (Stage) *Love for Love,* 1974; (TV) *Too Far To Go,* 1979; (Film) *The World According to Garp,* 1982
Signature: *Fatal Attraction*
Facts: When she was 13, her father opened a clinic in the Belgian Congo (now Zaire) and ran it for 16 years. During most of that time, the Close children lived alternately in Africa and at boarding schools in Switzerland.

Owns a store in Bozeman,

Montana, and recently announced that it will no longer sell porn magazines.

Chosen by Andrew Lloyd Webber to replace Patti LuPone in *Sunset Boulevard,* 1994.
Infamy: When she went on a two-week vacation from *Sunset Boulevard* in 1995, the production company released erroneous box-office figures implying that Close's absence had no effect on ticket sales. Close sent a scathing letter of complaint to composer-producer Andrew Lloyd Webber, which was obtained and published in the media.
Original Job: Toured Europe and the U.S. as a member of Up With People
Marriages: Cabot Wade (divorced), James Marlas (divorced), Steve Beers (engaged)
Children: Annie Maude Starke (from relationship with John Starke)
Major Awards: Tony, Best Actress, *The Real Thing,* 1984; Tony, Best Actress, *Death and the Maiden,* 1992; Tony, Best Actress (Musical), *Sunset Boulevard,* 1995
Address: Creative Artists Agency, 9830 Wilshire Blvd., Beverly Hills, CA 90212

NATALIE COLE

Real Name: Stephanie Natalie Maria Cole
Birthplace: Los Angeles, CA
Birthdate: 2/6/49
Occupation: Singer
Education: University of Massachusetts at Amherst
Debut: (Album) *Inseparable,* 1975
Signature: "Unforgettable"
Facts: In the late '70s, was nicknamed Natalie "Queen" Cole by the media. Aretha "Queen of Soul" Franklin took offense at the comparison, and a feud developed between the two singers.

Often asked father to bring home latest Beatles records, which he did despite his dislike for the music. He would slip in records of Ella Fitzgerald.
Infamy: Was ruled incapable of handling her own affairs due to drug and alcohol dependency and, in 1983, her mother was named conservator of her estate. Cole entered drug treatment program at Hazelden Clinic in Minnesota and remained there for almost a year.
Original Job: Receptionist
Marriages: Marvin Yancy

(divorced), Andre Fischer (divorced)
Children: Robert, Elizabeth, Kyle
Famous Relatives: Nat "King" Cole, singer, father; Maria Hawkings Cole, singer, mother
Major Awards: Grammy, Best New Artist, 1975; Grammy, Best R&B Vocal—Female, "This Will Be," 1975; Grammy, Best R&B Vocal—Female, "Sophisticated Lady (She's a Different Lady)," 1976; Grammy, Record of the Year, "Unforgettable" (with Nat King Cole), 1991; Grammy, Album of the Year, *Unforgettable,* 1991; Grammy, Best Jazz Vocal, "Take a Look," 1993
Address: William Morris Agency, 151 El Camino Dr., Beverly Hills, CA 90212

SEAN CONNERY

Real Name: Thomas Connery
Birthplace: Edinburgh, Scotland
Birthdate: 8/25/30
Occupation: Actor
Debut: (Stage) *South Pacific,* 1951
Signature: James Bond
Facts: Connery grew up in a poor, industrial district of Scotland. At age seven, he took a job delivering milk before school, and by age 13 he quit school.

Served in the British Navy from 1947 to 1950. Was discharged due to ulcers.

In 1950, represented Scotland in London's Mr. Universe competition.
Original Job: Lifeguard, milkman, bricklayer, plasterer, coffin polisher, and usher
Marriages: Diane Cilento (divorced), Micheline Roquebrune
Child: Jason
Major Awards: Golden Globe, World Film Favorite, 1972 (with Charles Bronson); Oscar, Best Supporting Actor, *The Untouchables,* 1988; Golden Globe, Best Supporting Actor, *The Untouchables,* 1988
Address: Creative Artists Agency, 9830 Wilshire Blvd., Beverly Hills, CA 90212

HARRY CONNICK JR.

Birthplace: New Orleans, LA
Birthdate: 9/11/67
Occupation: Singer
Education: Attended Loyola University, Hunter College, Manhattan School of Music
Debut: (Album) *Harry Connick, Jr.,* 1987
Signature: "It Had To Be You"
Facts: Performed annually at the

New Orleans Jazz & Heritage Festival from the time he was eight.

He also recorded two albums of Dixieland music on little-known labels—the first when he was nine and the second when he was 10.

Learned jazz music from Ellis Marsalis, the patriarch of the Marsalis family at the New Orleans Center for the Creative Arts.

Infamy: Arrested for having a gun in his luggage at New York's JFK airport.

Marriage: Jill Goodacre

Major Awards: Grammy, Best Jazz Vocal—Male, *When Harry Met Sally,* 1989; Grammy, Best Jazz Vocal—Male, "We Are in Love," 1990

Address: Creative Artists Agency, 9830 Wilshire Blvd., Beverly Hills, CA 90212

DAVID COPPERFIELD

Real Name: David Kotkin
Birthplace: Metuchen, NJ
Birthdate: 9/16/56
Occupation: Magician
Education: Attended Fordham University
Debut: (TV) *The Magic of ABC,* 1977
Facts: In his act, has levitated a Ferrari, walked through the Great Wall of China, and made the Statue of Liberty disappear. He has also extricated himself from a safe in a building about to be demolished by explosives and a steel box on a raft heading for the Niagara Falls.

By age 12, had performed at local birthday parties for a fee of five dollars, under the name "Davino, the Boy Magician."

In 1982 developed Project Magic, a program designed to help people with physical and mental disabilities by teaching them magic.

Relationship: Claudia Schiffer (engaged)

Address: 9017 Wilshire Blvd., #500, Beverly Hills, CA 90210

FRANCIS FORD COPPOLA

Birthplace: Detroit, MI
Birthdate: 4/7/39
Occupation: Director and writer
Education: Hofstra University, UCLA Film School
Debut: (Film) *Dementia 13,* 1963
Signature: *The Godfather*
Facts: First dreamed of becoming a filmmaker at age 10, while

bedridden with polio. He put on shows for himself using puppets, a tape recorder, a film projector, and a television set.

Coppola's interest in producing a film about the automaker Preston Tucker: *The Man and His Dream,* (1988)—began when his father invested and lost $5,000 in the automaker's company.

Directed Michael Jackson in the 15-minute Epcot Center feature *Captain EO.*

First son, Gian Carlo, was killed in a boating accident in 1986.

Owns a vineyard in California's Napa Valley. Also owns a restaurant in San Francisco and property in Belize; he hopes to make that country the hub for a huge telecommunications center.

Original Job: Worked for famous B-movie director/producer Roger Corman as dialogue director, sound man, and associate producer

Marriage: Eleanor Neil
Children: Gian Carlo (deceased), Roman, Sofia
Famous Relatives: Talia Shire, actor, sister; Nicholas Cage, actor, nephew
Major Awards: Oscar, Best Original Screenplay, *Patton* (with Edmund H. North), 1970; Oscar, Best Adapted Screenplay, *The Godfather* (with Mario Puzo), 1972; Oscar, Best Director, *The Godfather Part II,* 1974; Oscar, Best Adapted Screenplay, *The Godfather Part II* (with Mario Puzo), 1974; Golden Globe, Best Director, *The Godfather,* 1972; Golden Globe, Best Screenplay, *The Godfather* (with Mario Puzo), 1972; Golden Globe, Best Director, *Apocalypse Now,* 1980; Golden Globe, Best Score, *Apocalypse Now* (with Carmine Coppola), 1980
Address: Creative Artists Agency, 9830 Wilshire Blvd., Beverly Hills, CA 90212

CHRIS CORNELL

Birthplace: Seattle, WA
Birthdate: 7/20/64
Occupation: Singer, songwriter, drummer
Debut: (Album) *Screaming Life,* 1987
Signature: Soundgarden
Facts: The group's name is borrowed from a sculpture in a waterfront park north of Seattle. When the wind blows, pipes in the sculpture make a

spooky, hooting noise that the bandmembers liked.
Major Awards: Grammy, Best Metal Performance, "Spoonman" (with Soundgarden), 1994; Grammy, Best Hard Rock Performance, "Black Hole Sun" (with Soundgarden), 1994
Quote: "A lot of people hated us, which I dug a lot. Sometimes it's fun to be hated. When you're always liked, you become self-conscious."
Address: A&M Records, 1416 N. La Brea Ave., Los Angeles, CA 90028

BILL COSBY

Birthplace: Philadelphia, PA
Birthdate: 7/12/37
Occupation: Actor, comedian, producer, author
Education: Attended Temple University; Doctor of Education, University of Massachusetts at Amherst
Debut: (TV) *I, Spy,* 1965; (Film) *Hickey and Boggs,* 1971
Signature: *The Cosby Show*
Facts: Grew up in a housing project in Philadelphia.

A gifted athlete, he was noticed by a scout for the Green Bay Packers.

Has played the drums since he was 11. A jazz aficionado, is president of the Rhythm and Blues Hall of Fame.

Original Job: Shined shoes, delivered groceries
Marriage: Camille Hanks
Children: Erika Ranee, Erinn Charlene, Ennis William, Ensa Camille, Evin Harrah
Major Awards: Emmy, Best Actor in a Drama Series, *I Spy,* 1966, 1967, 1968; Emmy, *Bill Cosby Special,* 1969; Emmy, *The New Fat Albert Show,* 1981; Emmy, Best Comedy Series, *The Cosby Show,* 1985; Golden Globe, Best Actor in a Comedy Series, *The Cosby Show,* 1985, 1986; elected to the Emmy Hall of Fame, 1991; NAACP Image Award, 1976; Grammy, Best Comedy Recording, *I Started Out as a Child,* 1964; *Why Is There Air,* 1965; *Wonderfulness,* 1966; *Revenge,* 1967; *To Russell, My Brother, Whom I Slept With,* 1968; *Bill Cosby,* 1969; *Those of You with or without Children, You'll Understand,* 1986; Grammy, Best Recording for Children, *Bill Cosby Talks to Kids About Drugs,* 1971; Grammy, Best Recording for Children, *The Electric Company*

(with Lee Chamberlin and Rita Moreno), 1972
Address: William Morris Agency, 151 El Camino Dr., Beverly Hills, CA 90212

ELVIS COSTELLO

Real Name: Declan McManus
Birthplace: London, England
Birthdate: 8/25/55
Occupation: Singer, songwriter
Education: High school dropout
Debut: (Album) *My Aim Is True,* 1977
Signature: Elvis Costello & The Attractions
Fact: Got his first contract with CBS Records by performing on the sidewalk in front of the hotel where the label's sales conference was in progress. Was arrested for disturbing the peace, but achieved his purpose.
Infamy: In a drunken argument in 1979, used racial epithets in referring to Ray Charles and James Brown. American disc jockeys took his records off their playlists, and he received numerous death threats.
Original Job: Computer operator at an Elizabeth Arden cosmetics factory
Marriages: Mary (divorced), Caitlin O'Riordan
Child: Matthew
Famous Relative: Ross McManus, singer, father
Address: Warner Brothers Recording, 3300 Warner Blvd., Burbank, CA 91505

KEVIN COSTNER

Birthplace: Lynwood, CA
Birthdate: 1/18/55
Occupation: Actor, director, producer
Education: California State University at Fullerton
Debut: (Film) *Sizzle Beach,* 1979
Signature: *Dances with Wolves*
Facts: At 18, built a canoe and paddled down the same rivers that Lewis and Clark had navigated on their way to the Pacific.

As a teenager, he sang in the church choir.

Turned down the leading role in *War Games* (played by Matthew Broderick) to play Alex, the character who commits suicide, in *The Big Chill.* Only two weeks before the film's release, Alex's part was cut. But director Lawrence Kasdan promised Costner that he would write a part for him in another film, and

tailored the role of Jake in *Silverado* (1985) for Costner.
Infamy: In 1995, Kevin Reynolds, the director of *Waterworld*, left the project abruptly during post-production. It was alleged that it was a "clash of Kevins" that led to his departure, though both Reynolds and Costner declined to comment.

In February 1995, Costner and his brother Dan began building an entertainment complex in the Black Hills of South Dakota, on land that the Lakota Indians consider sacred and have been trying to recover since 1887. Costner had been made an honorary Lakota in 1990 after working with them on *Dances with Wolves*.
Original Job: Worked in marketing, stage-managed Raleigh Studios in L.A.
Marriage: Cindy Silva (divorced)
Children: Annie, Lily, Joe
Major Awards: Oscar, Best Director, *Dances with Wolves*, 1991; Oscar, Best Picture, *Dances with Wolves* (produced with Jim Wilson), 1991; Golden Globe, Best Director, *Dances with Wolves*, 1991
Address: Creative Artists Agency, 9830 Wilshire Blvd., Beverly Hills, CA 90212

KATIE COURIC

Birthplace: Arlington, VA
Birthdate: 1/7/57
Occupation: Broadcast journalist
Education: University of Virginia
Signature: *Today*
Fact: After hearing Couric read a report on the air, the president of CNN banned the young assignment editor from further television appearances, complaining about her high-pitched, squeaky voice. Keeping her spirits, Couric began working with a voice coach.
Original Job: Desk assistant at ABC News in Washington, DC
Marriage: Jay Monahan
Child: Elinor Tully
Address: NBC, 30 Rockefeller Plaza, New York, NY 10122

COURTENEY COX

Birthplace: Birmingham, AL
Birthdate: 6/15/64
Occupation: Actor
Education: Attended Mt. Vernon College in Washington, DC
Debut: (TV) *Misfits of Science*, 1985; (Film) *Down Twisted*, 1987

Signature: *Friends*
Facts: Discovered in 1984 Brian De Palma video "Dancing in the Dark" with Bruce Springsteen.

Played Michael J. Fox's girlfriend on *Family Ties* and Jim Carrey's love interest in *Ace Ventura: Pet Detective*.
Original Job: Model
Relationship: Michael Keaton
Address: Creative Artists Agency, 9830 Wilshire Blvd., Beverly Hills, CA 90212

CINDY CRAWFORD

Birthplace: De Kalb, IL
Birthdate: 2/20/66
Occupation: Supermodel
Education: Attended Northwestern University
Debut: (Film) *Fair Game*, 1995
Signature: *House of Style*
Facts: Crawford was the valedictorian of her high school class, and received a full scholarship to study chemical engineering in college. There, a professor accused Crawford of cheating after she received a perfect score on a calculus midterm exam.

Supports P-FLAG (Parents and Friends of Lesbians and Gays) and leukemia research (her brother died of the disease at age three).
Infamy: Posed for the cover of *Vanity Fair* shaving lesbian singer k.d. lang, prompting a renewal of international rumors she and husband Richard Gere were each homosexual and maintained the marriage for appearances only. In May 1994, the couple took out a $30,000 ad in the *Times* of London denying the rumors.
Original Job: Spent summers during high school detasseling corn in fields
Marriage: Richard Gere (separated)
Address: William Morris Agency,

151 El Camino Dr., Beverly Hills, CA 90212

MICHAEL CRICHTON

Real Name: John Michael Crichton
Birthplace: Chicago, IL
Birthdate: 10/28/42
Occupation: Writer, director, producer
Education: Harvard, Harvard Medical School
Debut: (Book) *Odds On* (under the pseudonym John Lange), 1966; (Film) *Westworld*, 1973
Signature: *Jurassic Park*
Facts: Published a travel article in the *New York Times* when he was 14.

Developed FilmTrak, a computer program for film production and is creator of the computer game Amazon.
Infamy: In 1974 was fired as screenwriter of the film adaptation of *The Terminal Man* when his screenplay deviated too much from the book.
Original Job: Anthropology professor
Marriages: Joan Radam (divorced), Kathy St. Johns (divorced), Anne Marie Martin
Child: Taylor
Address: Creative Artists Agency, 9830 Wilshire Blvd., Beverly Hills, CA 90212

SHERYL CROW

Birthplace: Kennett, MO
Birthdate: 2/11/63
Occupation: Singer, songwriter
Education: University of Missouri
Debut: (Album) *Tuesday Night Music Club*, 1994
Signature: "All I Wanna Do"
Facts: Her mother and father played piano and trumpet, respectively, with a big band on weekends. Their four children

were encouraged to learn music and often practiced on the four pianos in the house simultaneously.

Sang backup for Michael Jackson's 18-month *Bad* tour and, later, for Don Henley.

Went through a severe depression in the late '80s and didn't get out of bed for six months.

Played at Woodstock '94.
Major Awards: Grammy, Record of the Year, "All I Wanna Do," 1994; Grammy, Best New Artist, 1994; Grammy, Best Pop Vocal—Female, "All I Wanna Do," 1994
Address: William Morris Agency, 151 El Camino Dr., Beverly Hills, CA 90212

TOM CRUISE

Real Name: Thomas Cruise Mapother IV
Birthplace: Syracuse, NY
Birthdate: 7/3/62
Occupation: Actor
Education: High school dropout
Debut: (Film) *Endless Love*, 1981
Signature: *Top Gun*
Facts: Dyslexia put him in remedial reading courses in school, but Cruise proved himself in sports.

At age 14, enrolled in a seminary to become a priest. Dropped out after one year.

Took up acting after losing his place on a high school wrestling team due to a knee injury.

Member of the Church of Scientology.
Infamy: Author Anne Rice publicly criticized David Geffen for casting Cruise in *Interview with a Vampire* in 1994. After Rice saw the film she admitted Geffen had been right.
Original Job: Busboy
Marriages: Mimi Rogers (divorced), Nicole Kidman
Children: Adopted daughter Isabella Jane, adopted son Connor Antony
Major Award: Golden Globe, Best Actor, *Born on the Fourth of July*, 1990
Quote: "I'm not the Stanislavski kind of actor. I just want to communicate with the people in the scene."
Address: Creative Artists Agency, 9830 Wilshire Blvd., Beverly Hills, CA 90212

BILLY CRYSTAL

Birthplace: New York, NY
Birthdate: 3/14/47

Occupation: Comedian, actor
Education: Attended Marshall University, Nassau Community College; New York University
Debut: (TV) *Soap*, 1977; (Film) *Rabbit Test*, 1978
Signature: *When Harry Met Sally . . .*
Facts: Went to college on a baseball scholarship and hosted a campus-radio talk show.

First theater job as a house manager for *You're a Good Man Charlie Brown*, 1968.

Studied directing under Martin Scorsese at New York University.
Infamy: Walked off the set of his first *Saturday Night Live* appearance after his seven-minute monologue was cut from the show.
Original Job: Substitute teacher, writer
Marriage: Janice Goldfinger
Children: Jennifer, Lindsay
Famous Relative: Milt Gabler, founded Commodore Records and later headed Decca Records, uncle
Major Awards: Emmy, Best Writing in a Variety or Music Program, *Midnight Train to Moscow*, 1990; Emmy, Best Individual Performance in a Variety or Music Program, *The 63rd Annual Oscars*, 1991; Emmy, Best Writing in a Variety or Music Program, *The 63rd Annual Oscars*, 1991; Emmy, Best Writing in a Variety or Music Program, *The 64th Annual Oscars*, 1992
Quote: "My father used to bring home jazz musicians at Passover. We had swinging seders."
Address: International Creative Management, 8942 Wilshire Blvd., Beverly Hills, CA 90211

MACAULAY CULKIN

Birthplace: New York, NY
Birthdate: 8/26/80
Occupation: Actor
Education: Attends the Professional Children's School
Debut: (Stage) *Bach Babies*, 1984
Signature: *Home Alone*
Facts: His allowance is $5 a day.

Didn't enjoy his first screen kiss (in *My Girl*) because it required 16 takes.

Studied one year of pre-ballet at the 92nd Street Y on a Harkness Scholarship in dance and the George Ballanchine School of American Ballet, and in 1987 appeared with the New York City Ballet at Lincoln Center in *The Nutcracker*.

Culkin's footage was edited out of the film *Born on the Fourth of July* (1989).
Famous Relatives: Christopher Culkin, stage actor, father; Bonnie Bedelia, actor, aunt; Shane Culkin, actor, brother; Kieran Culkin, actor, brother
Address: William Morris Agency, 151 El Camino Dr., Beverly Hills, CA 90212

JAMIE LEE CURTIS

Birthplace: Los Angeles, CA
Birthdate: 11/22/58
Occupation: Actor
Education: Choate; attended the University of the Pacific
Debut: (TV) *Operation Petticoat*, 1977; (Film) *Halloween*, 1978
Signature: *A Fish Called Wanda*
Facts: Very athletic, Curtis was trained as a dancer and appeared on *Circus of the Stars* as an acrobat.

Curtis became interested in her husband Christopher Guest when she saw his picture in *Rolling Stone*. She gave him her home number through an agent.
Infamy: Admitted to using cocaine, even with her father, although not abusing it. She quit completely in 1983.
Marriage: Christopher Guest
Child: Annie
Famous Relatives: Tony Curtis, actor, father; Janet Leigh, actor, mother
Major Awards: Golden Globe, Best Actress in a Comedy Series, *Anything but Love*, 1990; Golden Globe, Best Actress in a Comedy, *True Lies*, 1995
Address: Creative Artists Agency, 9830 Wilshire Blvd., Beverly Hills, CA 90210

BILLY RAY CYRUS

Birthplace: Flatwoods, KY
Birthdate: 8/25/61
Occupation: Singer
Education: Attended Kentucky's Georgetown College
Debut: (Album) *Some Gave All*, 1992
Signature: "Achy-Breaky Heart"
Facts: "Where Am I Gonna Live?" was written right after his wife threw him out of the house. He gave her half the royalties.

After a concert, one woman told Cyrus how her seven-year-old autistic boy spoke for the first time after hearing his song, and the first words out of his mouth were "achy-breaky heart."

Claims that a "psychic vibe" in his family convinced him to give up playing baseball and become a musician, which he did when he was 20.
Infamy: Songwriter Danny Mote filed a copyright infringement suit against Cyrus in 1993, claiming that Cyrus's song "She's Not Crying Anymore" was copied from Mote's song "Crying Eyes."
Original Job: Car salesman
Marriages: Cindy Smith (divorced), Leticia Finley
Children: Christopher Cody, Destiny Hope, Braison Chance
Famous Relative: Ronald Ray Cyrus, one of Kentucky's most popular politicians, father
Address: Mercury Nashville, 66 Music Square W., Nashville, TN 37203

ROSIE DALEY

Birthplace: South Seaville, NJ
Birthdate: 1961
Occupation: Chef, cookbook author
Debut: Head Chef at the Cal-a-Vie spa in San Diego
Signature: Oprah Winfrey's personal chef
Facts: Daley helped Winfrey lose 72 pounds in eight months. Before accepting the job as Oprah's personal chef, Daley refused similar offers from celebrities like Paula Abdul.

In the Kitchen with Rosie: Oprah's Favorite Recipes became the fastest-selling hardcover in history.
Original Job: Dishwasher in a roadside diner; worked in health food restaurants after high school while pursuing a career in art
Child: Marley
Address: Harpo Productions, 110 N. Carpenter St., Chicago, IL 60607

TYNE DALY

Real Name: Ellen Tyne Daly
Birthplace: Madison, WI
Birthdate: 2/21/46
Occupation: Actor
Education: Attended Brandeis University, studied at the American Music and Dramatic Academy
Debut: (TV) *The Virginian*, 1962; (Stage) *The Butter and Egg Man*, 1966; (Film) *John and Mary*, 1969
Signature: *Cagney & Lacey*
Fact: In 1983, 1984, and 1985

Tyne Daly and *Cagney & Lacey* costar Sharon Gless were up against each other for the Emmy for Best Actress in Dramatic Series. Daly won all three times.
Marriage: Georg Stanford Brown (divorced)
Children: Alisabeth, Kathryne, Alyxandra
Famous Relatives: James Daly, actor, father; Hope Newell, actor, mother; Timothy Daly, actor, brother
Major Awards: Emmy, Best Actress in a Drama Series, *Cagney & Lacey*, 1983, 1984, 1985, 1988; Tony, Best Actress (Musical), *Gypsy*, 1990
Address: 700 N. Westknoll Dr., #302, Los Angeles, CA 90069

CLAIRE DANES

Birthplace: New York, NY
Birthdate: 4/12/79
Occupation: Actor
Debut: (TV) *Law & Order*, 1992; (Film) *Little Women*, 1995
Signature: *My So-Called Life*
Facts: Winona Ryder was so taken with Danes's portrayal of Angela Chase on *My So-Called Life* that she called her *Little Women* director to suggest Danes for the part of Beth.

First auditioned for *My So-Called Life* when she was 13, but it took two more years for the show to get a firm commitment from ABC.
Major Awards: Golden Globe, Best Actress in a TV Drama, *My So-Called Life*, 1995
Address: ABC, 77 West 66th St., New York, NY 10023

JEFF DANIELS

Birthplace: Georgia
Birthdate: 2/19/55
Occupation: Actor
Education: Attended University of Central Michigan, apprentice at New York's Circle Rep
Debut: (Stage) *The Farm*, 1976; (Film) *Ragtime*, 1981
Signature: *The Purple Rose of Cairo*
Facts: In 1989, played guitar on Don Johnson's album, *Let It Roll*.

While Jim Carrey was paid $7 million for his role in *Dumb and Dumber*, Daniels was reportedly paid just $500,000.
Original Job: Lumberyard worker
Marriage: Kathleen Treado
Child: Ben
Address: International Creative Management, 8942 Wilshire Blvd., Beverly Hills, CA 90211

TED DANSON

Real Name: Edward Bridge Danson III
Birthplace: San Diego, CA
Birthdate: 12/29/47
Occupation: Actor
Education: Attended Stanford University, Carnegie-Mellon University
Debut: (TV) *Somerset*, 1975; (Film) *The Onion Field*, 1979
Signature: *Cheers*
Facts: Father was the director of a local Native American museum.

In 1981, was the Ramis man on TV ads for cologne and men's toiletry products.

While at Stanford, followed a good-looking waitress to an audition "just to be near her" and ended up winning a part. Tap dances.
Infamy: Appeared at companion Whoopi Goldberg's 1993 Friars Club roast in blackface.
Marriages: Randall Lee Gosch (divorced), Casey Coates (divorced), Mary Steenburgen (engaged)
Children: Kate, Alexis
Major Awards: Golden Globe, Best Actor in a Made-for-TV Movie, *Something About Amelia*, 1985; Emmy, Best Actor in a Comedy Series, *Cheers*, 1990, 1993; Golden Globe, Best Actor in a Comedy Series, *Cheers*, 1990, 1991
Address: Creative Artists Agency, 9830 Wilshire Blvd., Beverly Hills, CA 90212

JAYE DAVIDSON

Birthplace: Riverside, CA
Birthdate: 1967
Occupation: Actor, model
Education: High school
Debut: (Film) *The Crying Game*, 1992
Signature: *The Crying Game*
Facts: Studied ballet as a child but gave it up because it seemed too demanding.

Worked for the Walt Disney corporation in London.
Original Job: Hairdresser, sales clerk
Address: International Creative Management, 8942 Wilshire Blvd., Beverly Hills, CA 90211

GEENA DAVIS

Real Name: Virginia Davis
Birthplace: Wareham, MA
Birthdate: 1/21/57
Occupation: Actor
Education: Boston University

Debut: (Film) *Tootsie*, 1982; (TV) *Buffalo Bill*, 1983
Signature: *Thelma and Louise*
Facts: Six-foot Davis, two inches taller than the cutoff established by professional modeling agencies, worked as a waitress to pay her bills. Finally she lied about her height and was accepted by the Zoli agency.

While working as a saleswoman at Anne Taylor, Davis got a job as a human mannequin in the store window.
Marriages: Richard Emmolo (divorced), Jeff Goldblum (divorced), Renny Harlin
Major Award: Oscar, Best Supporting Actress, *The Accidental Tourist*, 1989
Address: Creative Artists Agency, 9830 Wilshire Blvd., Beverly Hills, CA 90212

DANIEL DAY-LEWIS

Birthplace: London, England
Birthdate: 4/29/57
Occupation: Actor
Education: Old Vic Theatre School
Debut: (Film) *Sunday, Bloody Sunday*, 1971
Signature: *My Left Foot*
Fact: At 16, accidentally overdosed on migraine medicine and suffered from two weeks of hallucinations. Because of this, he was mistakenly diagnosed as a heroin addict and placed in a mental hospital. To escape, he had to put on his "greatest performance of sanity."
Original Job: Loaded trucks
Relationship: Isabelle Adjani
Child: son (with Isabelle Adjani), name not released at press time
Famous Relatives: C. Day-Lewis, former poet laureate of Britain, father; Sir Michael Balcon, producer, grandfather; Jane Balcon, actress, mother
Major Award: Oscar, Best Actor, *My Left Foot*, 1989
Address: William Morris Agency, 151 El Camino Dr., Beverly Hills, CA 90212

ROBERT DE NIRO

Birthplace: New York, NY
Birthdate: 8/17/43
Occupation: Actor
Education: Attended the High School of Music and Art and dropped out, studied at the Dramatic Workshop, the Luther James Studio, the Stella Adler Studio, and the Actor's Studio
Debut: (Film) *Greetings*, 1969

Signature: *Taxi Driver*
Facts: Although commonly regarded as Italian-American, De Niro is more Irish in ancestry.

First acting experience was playing the Cowardly Lion in a Public School 41 production of *The Wizard of Oz*.

Co-owns Rubicon, a San Francisco restaurant, with Francis Ford Coppola.

The pop group Bananarama recorded a song (1984) called "Robert De Niro's Waiting." They originally wanted to use Al Pacino's name, but Pacino refused to let them.

De Niro grew up in New York City's Little Italy, just a few blocks away from his future friend, Martin Scorsese.
Marriage: Diahnne Abbott (divorced)
Child: Raphael
Major Awards: Oscar, Best Supporting Actor, *The Godfather Part II*, 1974; Oscar, Best Actor, *Raging Bull*, 1981; Golden Globe, Best Actor, *Raging Bull*, 1981
Address: Creative Artists Agency, 9830 Wilshire Blvd., Beverly Hills, CA 90212

ELLEN DEGENERES

Birthplace: New Orleans, LA
Birthdate: 1958
Occupation: Actor, comedian
Signature: *Ellen*
Facts: Considered becoming a professional golfer.

In the 1980s the Showtime cable network, looking to name someone Funniest Person in America, found DeGeneres at a comedy club in New Orleans. She was given the title, and toured the country in a Winnebago with a big nose above the front bumper. It earned her the scorn of other comics, who thought she received the title undeservedly.

Was the first female comic

ever to be invited to sit on Carson's couch in her first appearance on *The Tonight Show*.
Original Job: Vacuum cleaner saleswoman, waitress
Address: United Talent Agency, 9560 Wilshire Blvd., 5th Fl., Beverly Hills, CA 90212

DANA DELANY

Birthplace: New York, NY
Birthdate: 3/11/56
Occupation: Actor
Education: Phillips Andover Academy; attended Wesleyan University
Debut: (TV) *Love of Life*, 1979; (Film) *The Fan*, 1981; (Stage) *A Life*
Signature: *China Beach*
Facts: Delany's first real love affair was a three-year relationship with actor Treat Williams.

While struggling to become an actress, Delany spent her nights working at an after-hours club where Bruce Willis tended bar.
Original Job: Cocktail waitress
Major Award: Emmy, Best Actress in a Drama Series, *China Beach*, 1989, 1992
Address: International Creative Management, 8942 Wilshire Blvd., Beverly Hills, CA 90211

JOHNNY DEPP

Birthplace: Owensboro, KY
Birthdate: 6/9/63
Occupation: Actor
Education: High school dropout
Debut: (Film) *Nightmare on Elm Street*, 1984
Signature: *21 Jump Street*
Facts: Dropped out of school at age 16 and joined a series of garage bands, one of which (The Kids) opened for Iggy Pop. Moved to L.A., where his ex-wife introduced him to actor Nicolas Cage, who spawned Depp's career.

Once owned a painting of a clown by executed serial killer John Wayne Gacy; now Depp has a pathological fear of clowns.

Tattoos: "Betty Sue" and "Wino Forever" (formerly "Winona Forever").

Co-owns the Viper Room, the '30s-style nightclub in L.A., outside of which River Phoenix died (1994).

Member of the band P, with ex-Sex Pistol Steve Jones and Red Hot Chili Pepper Flea.
Infamy: Charged with trashing a $1,200/night hotel room in New York City in September 1994.

Original Job: Rock guitarist, sold pens over the phone
Marriages: Lori Anne Allison (divorced), Sherilyn Fenn (engaged, never married), Jennifer Grey (engaged, never married), Winona Ryder (engaged, never married), Kate Moss (relationship)
Address: International Creative Management, 8942 Wilshire Blvd., Beverly Hills, CA 90211

DANNY DEVITO

Birthplace: Neptune, NJ
Birthdate: 11/17/44
Occupation: Actor, director, producer
Education: American Academy of Dramatic Arts
Debut: (Stage) *The Man with a Flower in His Mouth,* 1969
Signature: *Taxi*
Facts: After high school he worked in his sister's hair salon and was known as "Mr. Danny."

Got his part in *One Flew Over the Cuckoo's Nest* (1975) through producer Michael Douglas, whom DeVito had met in summer stock a few years before. Kirk Douglas had directed DeVito in *Scalawag* in 1973.
Original Job: Hairdresser, theatrical makeup artist, valet
Marriage: Rhea Perlman
Children: Lucy Chet, Gracie Fan, Jake Daniel Sebastian
Major Awards: Golden Globe, Best Supporting Actor in a Comedy Series, *Taxi,* 1979; Emmy, Best Supporting Actor in a Comedy Series, *Taxi,* 1981
Address: Creative Artists Agency, 9830 Wilshire Blvd., Beverly Hills, CA 90212

LEONARDO DICAPRIO

Birthdate: 1975
Occupation: Actor

Debut: (TV) *Romper Room;* (Film) *Parenthood,* 1990
Signature: *This Boy's Life*
Facts: Rejected by a talent agent when he was 10 years old for having a bad haircut.

First memory is of wearing red-and-yellow tap shoes and being lifted onto a stage by his father to entertain people waiting for a concert.

First acting experience was in a Matchbox car commercial.
Address: Creative Artists Agency, 9830 Wilshire Blvd., Beverly Hills, CA 90212

CELINE DION

Birthplace: Charlemagne, Canada
Birthdate: 3/30/68
Occupation: Singer
Education: High school dropout
Fact: Celine had nine best-selling French albums behind her before she recorded *Unison* in 1990.
Infamy: In 1990, refused to accept a Quebec music award as anglophone artist of the year, declaring she was "proud to be Quebecoise." The anglophone press criticized her harshly for exploiting the incident for its publicity value.
Marriage: Rene Angelil
Major Awards: Grammy, Best Pop Performance—Duo or Group, "Beauty and the Beast" (with Peabo Bryson), 1992; Grammy, Best Song Written Specifically for a Movie, "Beauty and the Beast" (with Peabo Bryson), 1992
Address: 550 Music/Epic, 550 Madison Ave., New York, NY 10022

SHANNEN DOHERTY

Birthplace: Memphis, TN
Birthdate: 4/12/71
Occupation: Actor
Debut: (Film) *Night Shift,* 1982
Signature: *Beverly Hills 90210*
Facts: Before her role on *90210,* Doherty starred in *Little House on the Prairie* with Melissa Gilbert and *Our House* with Wilfred Brimley.

Led the Pledge of Allegiance at the Republican National Convention in 1992.

Subject of *I Hate Brenda* newsletter.
Infamy: Notorious for her antics off the set, including an alleged brawl with another woman at a nightclub.

Admits to abusing drugs and alcohol.
Marriage: Ashley Hamilton (divorced), Rob Weiss (relationship)
Address: William Morris Agency, 151 El Camino Dr., Beverly Hills, CA 90212

PHIL DONAHUE

Birthplace: Cleveland, OH
Birthdate: 12/21/35
Occupation: Talk show host
Education: Notre Dame University
Debut: (Radio) Radio KYW, Cleveland, 1957; (TV) KYW-TV, Cleveland, 1958
Signature: *Donahue*
Facts: With *The Phil Donahue Show* in 1967, he pioneered the concept of audience participation. He says, "Two or three shows in, I realized the audience was asking some very good questions during the commercials. Then, on some given day which I don't even remember, I jumped out of the chair and went into the audience. A woman stood up and asked the guest a question. And that, that was nirvana."

First met Marlo Thomas when she was a guest on his show.
Original Job: Salesman
Marriages: Marge Cooney (divorced), Marlo Thomas
Children: Michael, Kevin, Daniel, Jim, Mary Rose
Major Awards: Emmy, Best Host of a Talk Show, *Donahue,* 1977, 1979, 1980, 1982, 1983, 1985, 1986, 1988; elected to the Emmy Hall of Fame, 1992
Address: NBC, 30 Rockefeller Plaza, New York, NY 10112

MICHAEL DOUGLAS

Birthplace: New Brunswick, NJ
Birthdate: 9/25/44
Occupation: Actor, producer, director
Education: University of California, Santa Barbara
Debut: (TV) *The Experiment,* 1969; (Film) *Hail, Hero!,* 1969
Signature: *Fatal Attraction*
Facts: His film company, Big Stick Productions, produced *One Flew over the Cuckoo's Nest* (1975) and *The China Syndrome* (1979), in which he starred.

Directed two episodes of TV show *The Streets of San Francisco,* in which he costarred.

Flunked out of college during his freshman year.
Marriage: Diandra Luker (separated)
Child: Cameron

Famous Relatives: Kirk Douglas, actor, father; Diana Dill, actress, mother; Eric Douglas, comedian, half brother
Major Awards: Oscar, Best Actor, *Wall Street,* 1988; Golden Globe, Best Actor, *Wall Street,* 1988
Address: Creative Artists Agency, 9830 Wilshire Blvd., Beverly Hills, CA 90212

ROBERT DOWNEY JR.

Birthplace: New York, NY
Birthdate: 4/4/65
Occupation: Actor
Education: High school dropout
Debut: (Film) *Pound,* 1970
Signature: *Chaplin*
Facts: Was the live-in companion of actress Sarah Jessica Parker for seven years.

Is working on a musical career and has written over 30 original songs. His version of *Chaplin*'s theme song, "Smile," is on the soundtrack album.

In *Pound,* he was five years old and played a puppy.
Infamy: Claims he once resembled the fast-living cocaine addict he played in *Less Than Zero.* Drugs were condoned in his family, and he started abusing at an early age. "I was pulling 360s in the Universal parking lot and disappearing for three days for things one needs blood transfusions to recuperate from."
Original Job: Waiter
Marriage: Deborah Falconer
Child: Indio
Famous Relative: Robert Downey, underground filmmaker, father
Address: Creative Artists Agency, 9830 Wilshire Blvd., Beverly Hills, CA 90212

DR. DRE

Real Name: Andre Young
Birthplace: Compton, CA
Birthdate: 1965
Occupation: Rap artist, record producer
Debut: (Album) *Boyz N the Hood* (with N.W.A.), 1986; (Album) *The Chronic* (solo), 1993
Signature: *The Chronic*
Facts: Dre's signature "hopping" car is a black 1964 Chevrolet Impala.

Founding member of N.W.A., a group labeled "the Sex Pistols of rap," in his late 20s.
Efil4 Zaggin (with N.W.A.) was the first hardcore rap album to make it to No.1 on the *Billboard* pop charts.

Dre launched the rap career of his brother, Warren G, and his brother's friend, Snoop Doggy Dogg; his label, Death Row Records, released Snoop's debut album.

Took shock value to new levels with 1994 music video with Ice Cube for "Natural Born Killaz," which featured a graphic recreation of the Nicole Simpson/Ron Goldman slayings.

Infamy: TV show host Dee Barnes filed a multimillion-dollar law suit against Dre after he pushed her against the wall of a Hollywood nightclub in the early '90s.

Arrested in a New Orleans hotel lobby after a scuffle ended in the battery of an officer.

Former colleague Eazy-E, who died of AIDS, sued Dre under federal racketeering laws.

Convicted of a misdemeanor assault for breaking the jaw of an aspiring record producer.

Sentenced on August 30, 1994, to five months in a halfway house for violating the terms of his probation in a drunk driving incident. Dre was also ordered to pay a $1,053 fine and attend a 90-day alcoholism education program.

In 1995, became the object of a $10 million palimony suit filed by his ex-girlfriend, Vivian Morgan.

Children: Marcel, Summer
Major Award: Grammy, Best Rap Performance—Solo, "Let Me Ride," 1993
Address: Interscope Records, 10900 Wilshire Blvd., Suite 1230, Los Angeles, CA 90024

RICHARD DREYFUSS

Birthplace: Brooklyn, NY
Birthdate: 10/29/47
Occupation: Actor
Education: Attended San Fernando Valley State College
Debut: (Film) Valley of the Dolls, 1967; (Stage) In Mama's House, 1968
Signature: Close Encounters of the Third Kind
Facts: In 1978, at age 29, became the youngest man to win an Academy Award for Best Actor (for The Goodbye Girl).

Wife was diagnosed with Lupus (a disease that causes the body's immune system to attack its own tissue) and in 1986 newborn son Ben was diagnosed with Peter's Anomaly (a rare defect in which the cornea of the eye is fused to the iris). Dreyfuss and

his ex-wife donated $300,000 to a Lupus research lab at UCLA and have raised funds for an international eye-research facility at the University of California in San Diego.

As a conscientious objector during the Vietnam War, he worked two years in L.A. County General Hospital (1969–71).

Infamy: In 1982, got into an accident with his Mercedes and was arrested for illegal possession of cocaine and Percodan. The court ordered rehabilitation in lieu of a trial.

Marriage: Jeramie Rain (divorced)
Children: Emily, Benjamin, Harry
Major Awards: Oscar, Best Actor, The Goodbye Girl, 1977; Golden Globe, Best Actor in a Comedy, The Goodbye Girl, 1978
Address: International Creative Management, 8942 Wilshire Blvd., Beverly Hills, CA 90211

DAVID DUCHOVNY

Birthplace: New York, NY
Birthdate: 3/7/60
Occupation: Actor
Education: Princeton; master's degree from Yale
Debut: (Film) Julia Has Two Lovers, 1991
Signature: The X Files
Facts: Duchovny was working on his Ph.D. dissertation, "Magic and Technology in Contemporary Fiction," when he got his first acting job in a Lowenbrau beer commercial.

Played Denise the transvestite detective on Twin Peaks, 1990–91.

America Online has two separate folders devoted to messages about him; as one fan explained, "the drool is too heavy to be confined to one."

Original Jobs: Teaching assistant at Yale, bartender
Relationship: Perrey Reeves
Address: International Creative Management, 8942 Wilshire Blvd., Beverly Hills, CA 90211

BOB DYLAN

Real Name: Robert Zimmerman
Birthplace: Duluth, MN
Birthdate: 5/24/41
Occupation: Singer, songwriter
Education: Attended University of Minnesota
Debut: (Album) Bob Dylan, 1961
Signature: "Blowin' in the Wind"
Facts: Took stage name from Dylan Thomas.

His backup band, The Hawks, later evolved into The Band.

Motorcycle crash in July 1966 led to a brief retirement.

Became a born-again Christian in 1979.

Infamy: Sued by Ruth Tryangiel in 1994. She claims she was his lover on and off for 19 years, and that she cowrote much of his music and helped manage his career. The lawsuit asks for $5 million plus damages and palimony.

Original Job: Performed with a Texas carnival
Marriage: Sarah Lowndes (divorced)
Children: Jesse, Maria, Jakob, Samuel, Anna
Major Awards: Grammy, Best Album Cover—Photography, Bob Dylan's Greatest Hits, 1967; Grammy, Album of the Year, The Concert for Bangladesh (with George Harrison and Friends), 1972; Grammy, Best Rock Vocal—Male, "Gotta Serve Somebody," 1979; Grammy, Lifetime Achievement Award, 1991; Grammy, Best Traditional Folk Album, World Gone Wrong, 1994
Address: Columbia Records, 51 West 52nd St., New York, NY 10019

CLINT EASTWOOD

Birthplace: San Francisco, CA
Birthdate: 5/31/30
Occupation: Actor, director
Education: Los Angeles City College
Debut: (Film) Revenge of the Creature, 1955
Signature: Dirty Harry
Facts: He was drafted in 1951 but en route to Korea his plane crashed. He swam miles to shore and was made swimming instructor at a boot camp, where he met actors Martin Milner and David Janssen, who sparked his acting career.

Elected mayor of Carmel, CA, in 1986; reelected in 1988.

Jazz musician and self-taught piano player, he plays three songs in the movie In the Line of Fire. Also composed two Cajun-inspired instrumentals for A Perfect World.

Infamy: Slapped with palimony suit by former lover Sondra Locke

Original Job: Lumberjack, forest-fire fighter, steelworker
Marriages: Maggie Johnson (divorced)

Children: Kyle, Alison, Francesca
Major Awards: Golden Globe, Cecil B. DeMille Award, 1988; Oscar, Best Picture, Unforgiven, 1992; Golden Globe, Best Director, Unforgiven, 1993; Oscar, Irving G. Thalberg Memorial Award, 1995
Address: William Morris Agency, 151 El Camino Dr., Beverly Hills, CA 90212

ROGER EBERT

Birthplace: Urbana, IL
Birthdate: 6/18/42
Occupation: Film critic, writer
Education: University of Illinois; attended University of Cape Town, South Africa; University of Chicago
Debut: Film critic for the Chicago Sun-Times, 1967
Signature: Siskel & Ebert
Facts: While at the University of Illinois, Ebert was editor of the Daily Illini and president of the U.S. Student Press Association, 1963–64.

Ebert wrote the screenplay for the movie version of Beyond the Valley of the Dolls, 1970. He also wrote a novel, Behind the Phantom's Mask, which was released in 1993.

He is a member of the Studebaker Drivers' Club.

Major Award: Pulitzer Prize, 1975; Emmy, 1979
Marriage: Chaz Hammel-Smith
Address: c/o Donald Ephraim, 108 West Grand, Chicago, IL 60610

KENNETH "BABYFACE" EDMONDS

Birthplace: Indianapolis, IN
Birthdate: 1958
Occupation: Singer, songwriter, producer
Debut: (Album) Lovers, 1989
Facts: While in ninth grade, phoned concert promoters pretending to be his teacher, asking if musicians would grant his gifted young charge—actually himself—an interview. Through this ruse, chatted with Stevie Wonder, the Jackson 5, and Earth, Wind and Fire.

Given his moniker in the early '80s by funk guitarist Bootsy Collins because of his youthful looks.

Has written or produced hits for Mariah Carey, Whitney Houston, Bobby Brown, TLC, Boyz II Men, and Toni Braxton.

Marriages: Denise (divorced), Tracey McQuarn
Major Awards: Grammy, Best R&B Song, "It's No Crime," 1991; Grammy, Album of the Year (producer) *The Bodyguard*, 1993; Grammy, Producer of the Year, "Boomerang" (with L.A. Reid), 1993; Grammy, Best R&B Vocal—Male, "When Can I See You," 1994; Grammy, Best R&B Song, "I'll Make Love to You," 1994
Address: Epic Records, 2100 Colorado Ave., Santa Monica, CA 90404

ANTHONY EDWARDS

Birthplace: Santa Barbara, CA
Birthdate: 7/19/63
Occupation: Actor
Education: Attended University of Southern California
Debut: (TV) *The Killing of Randy Webster*, 1981; (Film) *Heart Like a Wheel*, 1982
Signature: *ER*
Facts: His classmates at USC included Forest Whitaker and Ally Sheedy.

Played a burnt-out surfer in 1982's *Fast Times at Ridgemont High*, and one of the two head nerds in 1984's *Revenge of the Nerds*.

Somewhat bored with acting, he was planning to direct a low-budget children's feature, *Charlie's Ghost Story*, when he was called for *ER*. Originally turned down the *ER* role when production dates for the two projects initially overlapped.
Original Job: Actor in commercials for McDonald's and Country Time Lemonade
Marriage: Jeanine Lobell
Child: Bailey
Address: NBC, 30 Rockefeller Plaza, New York, NY 10112

MELISSA ETHERIDGE

Birthplace: Leavenworth, KS
Birthdate: 5/29/61
Occupation: Singer, songwriter, guitarist
Education: Attended Berklee College of Music
Debut: *Melissa Etheridge*, 1988
Facts: Played in women's bars around L.A. for six years beginning in 1982.

Came out by leaping onstage at one of Bill Clinton's presidential inaugural bashes, kissing cult figure Elvira, and proclaiming herself a proud lifelong lesbian.
Relationship: Julie Cypher

Major Awards: Grammy, Best Rock Vocal—Female, "Ain't It Heavy," 1992; Grammy, Best Rock Vocal—Female, "Come to My Window," 1994
Quote: "I like to bring the sexual energy out by seducing the audience, and, when it's there, building on it. I would like to say that, maybe, going to a concert of mine is like foreplay."
Address: Island Records, 14 East 4th St., New York, NY 10012

NORA EPHRON

Birthplace: New York, NY
Birthdate: 5/19/41
Occupation: Screenwriter, director
Education: Wellesley College
Debut: (Book) *Wallflower at the Orgy*, 1970; (TV) *Perfect Gentleman*, 1978
Signature: *When Harry Met Sally . . .*
Facts: She was the subject of the play *Take Her, She's Mine*, written by her parents.

Her book *Heartburn* was adapted into a 1986 movie starring Jack Nicholson and Meryl Streep. Wrote screenplays for *Silkwood* and *When Harry Met Sally*.
Marriages: Dan Greenburg (divorced), Carl Bernstein (divorced), Nicholas Pileggi
Children: Jacob, Max
Famous Relatives: Henry Ephron, screenwriter, father; Phoebe Ephron, screenwriter, mother; Delia Ephron, writer, sister
Address: International Creative Management, 8942 Wilshire Blvd., Beverly Hills, CA 90211

FABIO

Real Name: Fabio Lanzoni
Birthplace: Milan, Italy
Birthdate: 3/15/61
Occupation: Model
Debut: (TV) *Acapulco H.E.A.T.*
Facts: Posed for more than 100 bodice-ripping romance novel covers in 1992 and earned up to $3,000 per book cover.

Broke his left leg at age 16, and rehabilitation started him on the road to bodybuilding. He shaves his 48-inch chest twice a week.

Has expanded his career to writing and developing exercise equipment and fitness techniques.

In 1993, wrote his own book, *Pirate*.

Often offers a date with himself as a prize for charity auctions.
Address: Roger Richman Agency, 9777 Wilshire Blvd., Suite 915, Beverly Hills, CA 90212

CHRIS FARLEY

Birthplace: Madison, WI
Birthdate: 2/15/64
Occupation: Actor
Education: Marquette University
Debut: (Film) *Wayne's World*, 1992
Signature: *Saturday Night Live*
Fact: His childhood heroes were John Belushi, Dan Aykroyd, and Bill Murray, and just like them he started out doing stand-up at Second City in Chicago.
Original Job: Worked at an oil company
Address: Brillstein-Grey Entertainment, 9150 Wilshire Blvd., Suite 350, Beverly Hills, CA 90212

MIA FARROW

Birthplace: Los Angeles, CA
Birthdate: 2/9/45
Occupation: Actor
Education: Attended Marymount in Los Angeles and Cygnet House in London
Debut: (Stage) *The Importance of Being Earnest*, 1963
Signature: *Rosemary's Baby*
Facts: Mother—biological or adoptive—of 13 kids.

Was on first cover of PEOPLE, March 4, 1974.
Infamy: Was awarded custody of the two children she and Woody Allen adopted, as well as their biological son, after a highly publicized case involving allegations of molestation by Allen.
Marriages: Frank Sinatra (divorced), Andre Previn (divorced)
Children: Soon-Yi, Keili-Shea, Tam, Lark, Daisy, Moses, Isaiah Justus, Fletcher, Matthew, Sascha, Seamus (formerly Satchel), Eliza (formerly Dylan), Gabriel Wilk
Famous Relatives: Maureen O'Sullivan, actress, mother; John Farrow, director, father
Address: William Morris Agency, 151 El Camino Dr., Beverly Hills, CA 90201

SALLY FIELD

Birthplace: Pasadena, CA
Birthdate: 11/6/46
Occupation: Actor

Education: Columbia Pictures Workshop, Actor's Studio
Debut: (TV) *Gidget*, 1965
Signature: *The Flying Nun*
Facts: Was a cheerleader in high school.

Won the lead role in *Gidget* from among 150 other finalists.

Though entertaining, *The Flying Nun* discouraged people from thinking of her as a serious actress; the producers of the movie *True Grit* refused even to give her an audition. She was paid $4,000 a week for the television show.
Marriages: Steve Craig (divorced), Alan Greisman (divorced)
Children: Peter, Eli, Samuel
Famous Relatives: Mary Field Mahoney, actress, mother; Jock Mahoney, actor, stepfather
Major Awards: Emmy, *Sybil*, 1977; Golden Globe, Best Actress, *Norma Rae*, 1979; Oscar, Best Actress, *Norma Rae*, 1979; Oscar, Best Actress, *Places in the Heart*, 1984
Address: Creative Artists Agency, 9830 Wilshire Blvd., Beverly Hills, CA 90212

RALPH FIENNES

Birthplace: Suffolk, England
Birthdate: 12/22/62
Education: London's Royal Academy of Dramatic Art
Debut: (Film) *Wuthering Heights*, 1992
Signature: *Schindler's List*
Facts: Fiennes gained 28 pounds to play Amon Goeth in *Schindler's List*, 1993. He was chosen for the role after director Steven Spielberg saw Fiennes's performance in the British TV movie *A Dangerous Man: Lawrence After Arabia*.
Marriage: Alex Kingston
Major Award: Tony, Best Actor (Drama), *Hamlet*, 1995
Address: Creative Artists Agency, 9830 Wilshire Blvd., Beverly Hills, CA 90212

LINDA FIORENTINO

Real Name: Clorinda Fiorentino
Birthplace: Philadelphia, PA
Birthdate: 3/9/60
Occupation: Actor
Education: Rosemont College
Debut: (Film) *Vision Quest*, 1985
Signature: *The Last Seduction*
Facts: Since *The Last Seduction* was shown on HBO before moving to theaters, she was ineligible to be nominated for an Academy Award.

In the late 1980s, passed up several jobs—including, reportedly, the Kelly McGillis role in *Top Gun*—to star as Andy Warhol waif Edie Sedgwick in *The War at Home*, a project that was pushed back numerous times until it was finally canceled two weeks before shooting.
Original Job: Bartender
Address: Creative Artists Agency, 9830 Wilshire Blvd., Beverly Hills, CA 90212

LAURENCE FISHBURNE

Birthplace: Augusta, GA
Birthdate: 7/30/61
Occupation: Actor
Education: Attended Lincoln Square Academy
Debut: (Stage) *Section D*, 1975; (Film) *Cornbread, Earl and Me*, 1975
Signature: *Boyz N the Hood*
Facts: Appeared regularly on soap opera *One Life to Live* for four years starting when he was nine.

At 14, went with his mother to the Philippines for what was supposed to be a three-month shoot for *Apocalypse Now*; the shoot lasted 18 months.

A theater buff, he wrote, directed, and starred in a play, *Riff Raff*, in 1994.
Marriage: Hanja Moss (divorced)
Children: Langston, Montana
Major Awards: Tony, Featured Actor, *Two Trains Running*, 1992; Emmy, Best Guest Actor in a Drama, *Tribeca*, 1993
Address: 10100 Santa Monica Blvd., 25th Fl., Los Angeles, CA 90067

CARRIE FISHER

Birthplace: Burbank, CA
Birthdate: 10/21/56
Occupation: Actor, novelist, screenwriter
Education: Dropped out of Beverly Hills High School, attended Sarah Lawrence College and Central School of Speech and Drama, London
Debut: (Stage) *Irene*, 1972
Signature: *Star Wars*
Facts: Sang in her mother's Las Vegas nightclub act.

Her first public appearance was in a *Life* magazine photograph with her mother shortly after her father had run off to marry Elizabeth Taylor.
Infamy: Was a user of LSD and Percodan; almost overdosed, 1985.

Marriage: Paul Simon (divorced)
Child: Billie
Famous Relatives: Debbie Reynolds, actress, mother; Eddie Fisher, singer, father
Quote: "You find me a kid that thinks he got enough affection and attention as a child and I'll show you Dan Quayle."
Address: Creative Artists Agency, 9830 Wilshire Blvd., Beverly Hills, CA 90212

BRIDGET FONDA

Birthplace: Los Angeles, CA
Birthdate: 1/27/64
Occupation: Actor
Education: Attended New York University, studied at the Lee Strasberg Institute and with Harold Guskin
Debut: (Film) *Aria*, 1987; (TV) *21 Jump Street*, 1989
Signature: *Point of No Return*
Facts: Named after Bridget Hayward, a woman her father loved who had committed suicide.

Her movie debut was in *Aria*, in which she stripped naked, had sex, then committed suicide during her eight minutes on screen with no dialogue.
Relationship: Eric Stoltz
Famous Relatives: Peter Fonda, actor, father; Susan Brewer, actor, mother; Henry Fonda, actor, grandfather; Jane Fonda, actor, aunt
Address: United Talent Agency, 9560 Wilshire Blvd., Suite 500, Beverly Hills, CA 90212

JANE FONDA

Birthplace: New York, NY
Birthdate: 12/21/37
Occupation: Actor, political activist, fitness instructor
Education: Attended Vassar College, studied method acting in Lee Strasberg's Actors Studio
Debut: (Film) *Tall Story*, 1960
Signature: *Barbarella*
Facts: Mother committed suicide in a sanitarium in 1953.

Jane Fonda's Workout is the bestselling nondramatic video in history.

Spent much of the '70s speaking for the Black Panthers and against the Vietnam War and was almost arrested for treason, earning her the nickname "Hanoi Jane."
Marriages: Roger Vadim (divorced), Tom Hayden (divorced), Ted Turner
Children: Vanessa, Troy, Garrity, Nathalie (stepdaughter)
Famous Relatives: Henry Fonda,

actor, father; Peter Fonda, actor, brother; Bridget Fonda, actor, niece
Major Awards: Oscar, Best Actress, *Klute*, 1971; Oscar, Best Actress, *Coming Home*, 1978. Golden Globe, World Film Favorite—Female, 1973, 1979, 1980; Emmy, Lead Actress in a Limited Series or Special, *The Dollmaker*, 1983
Address: Creative Artists Agency, 9830 Wilshire Blvd., Beverly Hills, CA 90201

HARRISON FORD

Birthplace: Chicago, IL
Birthdate: 7/13/42
Occupation: Actor, director
Education: Ripon College
Debut: (Film) *Dead Heat on a Merry-Go-Round*, 1966
Signature: Indiana Jones
Fact: Scar beneath his lower lip is the result of a motorcycle accident.
Original Job: Carpenter
Marriages: Mary Ford (divorced), Melissa Mathison
Children: Willard, Benjamin, Malcolm, Georgia
Quote: "I want to be bald, completely bald. Wouldn't it be great to be bald in the rain?"
Address: Pat McQueeney Management, 10279 Century Woods Dr., Los Angeles, CA 90067

JODIE FOSTER

Real Name: Alicia Christian Foster
Birthplace: Los Angeles, CA
Birthdate: 11/19/62
Occupation: Actor, director
Education: Yale University
Debut: (TV) *Mayberry RFD*, 1969; (Film) *Napoleon and Samantha*, 1972
Signature: *Silence of the Lambs*
Facts: Started at three years old as the bare-bottomed Coppertone child in the then ubiquitous advertisement. She got the job when, too young to wait in the car, she was noticed at her brother's casting call. By age eight, she had appeared in over 40 commercials.

At 13, played a hooker in *Taxi Driver*. Because she was so young, the film's producers hired her sister Constance to double for her in a nude scene. Before she got the role, she had to pass psychological tests. "I spent four hours with a shrink to prove I was normal enough to play a hooker. Does that make sense?"

As valedictorian in high

school, she gave her graduation speech in French.
Infamy: Object of would-be presidential assassin John Hinckley's obsession.
Famous Relative: Buddy Foster, actor, brother
Major Awards: Golden Globe, Best Actress, *The Accused*, 1988; Golden Globe, Best Actress, *The Silence of the Lambs*, 1991; Oscar, Best Actress, *The Accused*, 1988; Oscar, Best Actress, *The Silence of the Lambs*, 1991
Address: International Creative Management, 8942 Wilshire Blvd., Beverly Hills, CA 90211

MICHAEL J. FOX

Birthplace: Edmonton, Canada
Birthdate: 6/9/61
Occupation: Actor
Education: High school dropout
Debut: (TV) *Palmerstown, U.S.A.*, 1980; (Film) *Midnight Madness*, 1980
Signature: *Family Ties*
Facts: When he got the audition for *Family Ties*, he was $35,000 in debt, living on macaroni and cheese, and had been forced to sell off a sectional couch piece by piece to raise money.

Eric Stoltz was first cast in *Back to the Future*, but when he proved to be "too intense for the comedy," Fox got the role. For seven weeks he played Alex on *Family Ties* by day, then transformed himself into Marty McFly for the film.

Heavy smoker, but asks not to be photographed smoking to avoid becoming a negative role model for his younger fans.
Marriage: Tracy Pollan
Children: Sam Michael, Aquinnah Kathleen, Schuyler Frances
Major Awards: Emmy, Best Actor in a Comedy Series, *Family Ties*, 1985, 1986, 1987, 1988; Golden Globe, Best Actor in a Comedy Series, *Family Ties*, 1989
Address: Creative Artists Agency, 9830 Wilshire Blvd., Beverly Hills, CA 90212

ARETHA FRANKLIN

Birthplace: Memphis, TN
Birthdate: 3/25/42
Occupation: Singer
Education: High school dropout
Debut: (Song) "Rock-A-Bye Your Baby with a Dixie Melody," 1961
Signature: "Respect"
Facts: Started out as a gospel singer in her father's Baptist church in Detroit in the '50s. Her

father was minister of the New Bethel Baptist Church, one of the largest pastorates in the U.S., until 1979, when he went into a coma after being shot in his home by a burglar.

Infamy: Was sued for breach of contract in 1984 when she was unable to return in the Broadway musical *Sing, Mahalia, Sing,* mainly because of her fear of flying.

Marriages: Ted White (divorced), Glynn Thurman (divorced)

Children: Clarence, Edward, Teddy, Kecalf

Major Awards: Grammy, Best Rhythm and Blues Song, "Respect," 1967; Grammy, Best R&B Vocal—Female, "Respect," 1967; Grammy, Best R&B Vocal—Female, "Chain of Fools," 1968; Grammy, Best R&B Vocal—Female, "Share Your Love with Me," 1969; Grammy, Best R&B Vocal—Female, "Don't Play That Song," 1970; Grammy, Best R&B Vocal—Female, "Bridge over Troubled Water," 1971; Grammy, Best R&B Vocal—Female, *Young, Gifted, & Black,* 1972; Grammy, Best R&B Vocal—Female, "Master of Eyes," 1973; Grammy, Best R&B Vocal—Female, "Ain't Nothing Like the Real Thing," 1974; Grammy, Best R&B Vocal—Female, "Hold On I'm Comin'," 1981; Grammy, Best R&B Vocal—Female, "Freeway of Love," 1985; Grammy, Best R&B Vocal—Female, *Aretha,* 1987; Grammy, Best R&B Duo or Group, "I Knew You Were Waiting (For Me)" (with George Michael), 1987; Grammy Legend Award, 1991; inducted into the Rock and Roll Hall of Fame, 1987; NARAS Lifetime Achievement Award, 1994

Address: William Morris Agency, 151 El Camino Dr., Beverly Hills, CA 90212

DENNIS FRANZ

Birthplace: Chicago, IL
Birthdate: 10/28/44
Occupation: Actor
Debut: (TV) *The Chicago Story,* 1981
Signature: *NYPD Blue*
Facts: Claims he was the "worst postman in the history of the post office" before becoming an actor. "I used to start my route at daybreak, and I would finish long after dark. I'd stop for donuts, I'd play with animals, I'd go home with my bag of mail and just lay around the house a bit."

Served 11 months in Vietnam with an elite Airborne division.

Marriage: Joanie Zeck
Children: Stepdaughter Krista, stepdaughter Tricia
Major Awards: Emmy, Best Actor in a Drama Series, *NYPD Blue,* 1994; Golden Globe, Best Actor in a Drama Series, *NYPD Blue,* 1995
Address: Paradigm, 200 West 57th St., Suite 900, New York, NY 10019

ZSA ZSA GABOR

Real Name: Sari Gabor
Birthplace: Budapest, Hungary
Birthdate: 2/6/17
Occupation: Actor
Debut: (Film) *Lovely To Look At,* 1952
Signature: *Moulin Rouge*
Facts: Named Miss Hungary in 1936.

Her compendium of humorous advice on relationships, *Complete Guide to Men (How To Catch a Man, How To Marry a Man, How To Get Rid of a Man)* was published by Doubleday in 1970.

Actor George Sanders had been married to her older sister Magda before marrying Zsa Zsa in 1949.

While appearing in *Forty Carats* at a Philadelphia dinner theater in 1983, she walked off the stage, complaining that handicapped patrons were making too much noise.

Infamy: Involved in many highly publicized controversies, including disputes over unpaid hotel bills and unpaid parking tickets.

George Sanders once hired private detectives to obtain evidence for use in a divorce hearing. When the detectives broke in on her and caught her with South American playboy Porfirio Rubirosa, she served them champagne.

In 1989, found guilty of slapping a Beverly Hills cop who pulled her over her Rolls-Royce.

Marriages: Burhan Belge (divorced), Conrad Hilton (divorced), George Sanders (divorced), Herbert Hunter (divorced), Joshua Kosden, Jr. (divorced), Jack Ryan (divorced), Michael O'Hara (divorced), Felipe Alba (ceremony declared invalid), Prince Frederick von Anhalt, Duke of Saxony
Child: Francesca
Famous Relative: Eva Gabor, actor, sister
Major Award: Golden Globe, Most Glamorous Actress, 1958
Address: Kal Ross Management,

8721 Sunset Blvd., Los Angeles, CA 90069

ANDY GARCIA

Birthplace: Havana, Cuba
Birthdate: 4/12/56
Occupation: Actor
Education: Attended Florida International University in Miami
Debut: (TV) *Hill Street Blues* (pilot), 1981; (Film) *Blue Skies Again,* 1983
Signature: *The Godfather Part III*
Facts: Family fled from Castro's Cuba to Florida when he was a boy.

The 1990 movie *Internal Affairs* was written with Garcia in mind.

Married his high school sweetheart.

Original Job: Standup comedian, waiter
Marriage: Maria Victoria
Children: Dominique, Daniella
Address: Carlyle Agency, 639 N. Larchmont, Suite 207, Los Angeles, CA 90004

JAMES GARNER

Real Name: James Baumgarner
Birthplace: Norman, OK
Birthdate: 4/7/28
Occupation: Actor and producer
Education: Attended University of Oklahoma
Debut: (Film) *Toward the Unknown,* 1956
Signature: *The Rockford Files*
Facts: Part Cherokee Indian.

Received two Purple Hearts during the Korean War.

Original Job: Merchant marine, gas station attendant, traveling salesman, truck cleaner, carpet layer, hod carrier, maintenance man, swim-suit model
Marriage: Lois Clarke
Children: Kimberly, Gretta, Scott
Major Awards: Emmy, Best Actor in a Drama Series, *The Rockford Files,* 1977; elected to the Emmy Hall of Fame, 1990
Quote: "If you have any pride in your work, you don't go on TV."
Address: International Creative Management, 8942 Wilshire Blvd., Beverly Hills, CA 90211

JANEANE GAROFALO

Birthplace: New Jersey
Birthdate: 9/28/64
Occupation: Actor, comedian
Education: Providence College
Debut: (TV) *The Ben Stiller Show,* 1992; (Film) *Reality Bites,* 1994
Signature: *Larry Sanders Show*

Fact: Has "Think" tatooed on her arm.
Original Job: Bike messenger, receptionist
Marriage: Rob Cohn (divorced)
Quote: "If I've learned one thing in life, it's that I can always count on pinkeye at the most inappropriate moment."
Address: United Talent Agency, 9560 Wilshire Blvd., Suite 500, Beverly Hills, CA 90212

ANTHONY GEARY

Birthplace: Coalville, UT
Birthdate: 5/29/47
Occupation: Actor
Education: Attended University of Utah
Debut: (TV) *Bright Promise,* 1969; (Film) *Blood Sabbath,* 1969
Signature: *General Hospital*
Facts: Quit *General Hospital* in 1984 because he hated the heartthrob status. The character was originally designed to appear for only 13 weeks. He returned in 1990 as Luke Spencer's cousin Bill Eckert, a German-Italian machinist. Luke reemerged on October 29, 1993.

Has appeared on the stage at the Los Angeles Theater Center in productions of Ibsen and Tennessee Williams, and in a national stage tour of *Jesus Christ, Superstar.*

During time off from Luke, had a bawdy nightclub act with dancers called The Smut Queens.

Major Award: Emmy, Best Actor in a Daytime Drama, *General Hospital,* 1982
Address: c/o Raymond Katz, 345 North Maple Dr., Suite 235, Beverly Hills, CA 90210

DAVID GEFFEN

Birthplace: Brooklyn, NY
Birthdate: 2/21/43
Occupation: Producer, executive
Education: Dropped out of two colleges
Signature: Geffen Records
Facts: Graduated in the bottom 10 percent of his high-school class.

Diagnosed with terminal cancer in 1976 and retired soon after. Four years later, doctors told him his diagnosis had been a mistake.

Dated Cher and Marlo Thomas. Later claimed to be bisexual and, in 1992, pronounced himself gay.

Has produced such hits as

movies *Beetlejuice* and *Risky Business*, and Broadway musicals *Cats* and *Miss Saigon*.

Sold Geffen Records to MCA in 1990 for 10 million shares of stock (at the time worth $540 million). Eight months later MCA was sold to Matsushita and his shares soared to $710 million.

Was publicly criticized by *Interview with a Vampire* author Anne Rice for casting Tom Cruise in the movie's lead in 1994. After Rice saw the film she admitted Geffen had been right.

His DreamWorks SKG, formed with Jeffrey Katzenberg and Steven Spielberg, is the first completely new movie studio in 50 years.

Infamy: Admits to having been extremely promiscuous with men during his Studio 54 days in the 1970s.
Original Job: Television audience usher, mailroom worker at William Morris Talent Agency
Major Awards: Tony, Best Musical, *Cats*, 1983; Tony, Best Play, *M Butterfly*, 1988
Quote: "I wouldn't rather be smart than lucky. I'll take it however it comes. Because I'd rather win than be right."
Address: Geffen Records, 9130 Sunset Blvd., Los Angeles, CA 90069

RICHARD GERE

Birthplace: Philadelphia, PA
Birthdate: 8/31/48
Occupation: Actor
Education: Attended University of Massachusetts
Debut: (Film) *Report to the Commissioner*, 1975
Signature: *An Officer and a Gentleman*
Facts: Won a gymnastics scholarship to the University of Massachusetts.

In 1973, first studied the "middle way" of Siddhartha Gotama Buddha as preached by a Japanese sect. In 1982, switched faith to the Tibetan school of Buddhism. In 1986, became a student of the exiled Dalai Lama.

First three big film roles (*Days of Heaven*, 1978, *American Gigolo*, 1980, and *An Officer and a Gentleman*, 1982) were roles turned down by John Travolta.
Infamy: Took out a $30,000 ad with wife Cindy Crawford in the *Times* of London in May 1994 denying rumors of their homosexuality.
Original Job: Rock musician

Marriage: Cindy Crawford (separated)
Address: International Creative Management, 8942 Wilshire Blvd., Beverly Hills, CA 90211

MEL GIBSON

Birthplace: Peekskill, NY
Birthdate: 1/3/56
Occupation: Actor, director
Education: University of New South Wales
Debut: (Film) *Summer City*, 1977
Signature: *The Road Warrior*
Facts: Father moved the family from New York to Australia in the '60s so his sons wouldn't be drafted.

The night before his audition for *Mad Max*, he got into a barroom fight in which his face was badly beaten, an accident that won him the role.

Took up acting only because his sister submitted an application to the National Institute of Dramatic Art behind his back.
Marriage: Robyn Moore
Children: Hannah, Edward, Christian, Will, Lucian, Meggin
Famous Relative: Eva Mylott, opera singer, grandmother
Address: International Creative Management, 8942 Wilshire Blvd., Beverly Hills, CA 90211

KATHIE LEE GIFFORD

Real Name: Kathie Epstein
Birthplace: Paris, France
Birthdate: 8/16/53
Occupation: Talk show host, singer
Education: Attended Oral Roberts University
Debut: (TV) *$100,000 Name That Tune*, 1976
Signature: *Live! With Regis and Kathie Lee*
Facts: Despite having a Jewish father, became a born-again Christian at age 11.

Organized a folk singing group while at Oral Roberts University. Named her dog Regis.
Original Job: Gospel singer
Marriages: Paul Johnson (divorced), Frank Gifford
Children: Cody Newton, Cassidy Erin
Quote: "I am irreverent, I am opinionated, but I'm not perky."
Address: William Morris Agency, 151 El Camino Dr., Beverly Hills, CA 90212

MELISSA GILBERT

Birthplace: Los Angeles, CA
Birthdate: 5/8/64

Occupation: Actor
Education: Attended USC
Debut: (TV) *Little House on the Prairie*, 1974
Signature: *Little House on the Prairie*
Facts: Was involved with Rob Lowe for six years and broke up with him due to his infidelities.

There is a sign on the front lawn of Gilbert's house in California that says "Little House on the Valley."
Marriages: Bo Brinkman (divorced), Bruce Boxleitner
Child: Dakota
Famous Relatives: Sara Gilbert, actor, sister; Jonathan Gilbert, actor, brother; Robert Crane, creator of *The Honeymooners*, grandfather; Paul Gilbert, actor, father; Barbara Crane, dancer and actor, mother
Address: William Morris Agency, 151 El Camino Dr., Beverly Hills, CA 90212

VINCE GILL

Birthplace: Norman, OK
Birthdate: 4/12/57
Occupation: Singer, songwriter, guitarist
Education: High school
Debut: (Song) "Turn Me Loose," 1984
Signature: "When I Call Your Name"
Facts: After high school, contemplated a career as a pro golfer, but dropped that idea when offered a spot in a top progressive bluegrass group, Bluegrass Alliance.

Joined the band Sundance to play with its great fiddler, Bryon Berline; later joined The Cherry Bombs to be with singer-songwriter Rodney Crowell.

Lead singer for Pure Prairie League in the late 70s.

In the 1980s, worked in Nashville as a studio session vocalist and musician with such stars as Bonnie Raitt, Rosanne Cash, and Patty Loveless.

Dubbed "The Benefit King," he sponsors his own pro-celebrity golf tournament and annual celebrity basketball game and concert.
Marriage: Janis Oliver
Child: Jennifer
Major Awards: Grammy, Best Country Vocal—Male, "When I Call Your Name," 1990; Grammy, Best Country Vocal Collaboration (with Steve Wariner and Ricky Skaggs), "Restless," 1991; Grammy, Best Country Song, "I Still Believe in You" (with John Barlow Jarvis), 1992; Grammy,

Best Country Vocal—Male, "I Still Believe in You," 1992; Grammy, Best Country Instrumental "Red Wing" (with Asleep at the Wheel), 1993; Best Country Vocal—Male, "When Love Finds You," 1994
Address: William Morris Agency, 151 El Camino Dr., Beverly Hills, CA 90212

WHOOPI GOLDBERG

Real Name: Caryn Johnson
Birthplace: New York, NY
Birthdate: 11/13/49
Occupation: Actor, comedian
Education: School for the Performing Arts, New York
Debut: (Film) *The Color Purple*, 1985
Signature: *Ghost*
Facts: Kicked a heroin addiction in the '70s.

Began performing at age eight with the Helena Rubenstein Children's Theater and later enrolled in the Hudson Guild children's arts program.

Co-owns the West Hollywood restaurant Eclipse with Steven Seagal and Joe Pesci.
Infamy: Was roasted by black-faced companion Ted Danson at a Friars Club event, 1993.
Original Job: Bricklayer, hairdresser, bank teller, and makeup artist for a funeral parlor
Marriage: One prior marriage, David Claessen (divorced), Lyle Trachtenberg
Child: Alexandra Martin
Major Awards: Grammy, Best Comedy Recording, *Whoopi Goldberg*, 1985; Golden Globe, Best Actress, *The Color Purple*, 1986; Golden Globe, Best Supporting Actress, *Ghost*, 1991; Oscar, Best Supporting Actress, *Ghost*, 1990
Address: Creative Artists Agency, 9830 Wilshire Blvd., Beverly Hills, CA 90212

JEFF GOLDBLUM

Birthplace: Pittsburgh, PA
Birthdate: 10/22/52
Occupation: Actor
Education: Trained at Sanford Meisner's Neighborhood Playhouse
Debut: (Stage) *Two Gentlemen of Verona*, 1971; (Film) *Death Wish*, 1974
Signature: *The Big Chill*
Facts: Brother Rick died at 23 from a rare virus picked up on a North African trip.

Starred as a stockbroker-turned-P.I. with Ben Vereen in

the TV series *Tenspeed and Brownshoe*, 1980.
Marriages: Patricia Gaul (divorced), Geena Davis (divorced), Laura Dern (engaged)
Address: International Creative Management, 8942 Wilshire Blvd., Beverly Hills, CA 90211

JOHN GOODMAN

Birthplace: Afton, MO
Birthdate: 6/20/52
Occupation: Actor
Education: Southwest Missouri State University
Debut: (Film) *Eddie Macon's Run*, 1983
Signature: *Roseanne*
Facts: Made a living doing dinner and children's theater before Broadway debut in 1979 in *Loose Ends*.

Acted in college with Kathleen Turner and Tess Harper.

Appeared in commercials for Coors beer, Crest toothpaste, and 7UP.
Original Job: Bouncer
Marriage: Annabeth Hartzog
Child: Molly
Major Award: Golden Globe, Best Actor in a Comedy Series, *Roseanne*, 1993
Address: Creative Artists Agency, 9830 Wilshire Blvd., Beverly Hills, CA 90212

KELSEY GRAMMER

Birthplace: St. Thomas, Virgin Islands
Birthdate: 2/20/55
Occupation: Actor
Education: Attended Juilliard
Debut: (TV) *Another World*, 1983
Signature: *Frasier*
Facts: Father and sister were murdered; his two half brothers died in a scuba accident.

His unborn child died when his ex-wife attempted suicide.

Was nominated five times before finally winning an Emmy in 1994.
Infamy: Arrested for driving under the influence of drugs in 1987; failed to show up for two arraignments for a cocaine arrest in 1988; sentenced to community service and 30 days in prison in 1990.

In 1995, faced allegations of sexual assault by a 17-year-old, who claimed they had had sex when she was 15. The New Jersey grand jury declined to charge him.
Original Job: Theatrical painter
Marriages: Doreen Alderman (divorced), Barrie Buckner

(divorced), Cerlette Lamme (divorced), Leigh-Anne Csuhany (divorced), Tammi Baliszewski (engaged)
Children: Greer, Spencer
Major Award: Emmy, Best Actor in a Comedy, *Frasier*, 1994
Address: Paramount Television Productions, 5555 Melrose Ave., Los Angeles, CA 90038

AMY GRANT

Birthplace: Augusta, GA
Birthdate: 11/25/60
Occupation: Singer
Education: Attended Vanderbilt University
Debut: (Album) *Amy Grant*, 1976
Facts: "Baby, Baby" (Grant's first hit single) was written for her infant daughter, Millie.

Recorded her first album at age 16 and recorded eight more before her first truly big album, *Age to Age*, came out in 1980.
Infamy: When Grant moved from gospel to pop, some Christian radio stations refused to play her albums and condemned her for selling out her Christian values.
Marriage: Gary Chapman
Children: Matt, Millie, Sarah Cannon
Major Awards: Grammy, Best Gospel Performance—Contemporary, *Age to Age*, 1982; Grammy, Best Gospel Vocal—Female, "Ageless Medley Myrrh," 1983; Grammy, Best Gospel Vocal—Female, "Angels," 1984; Grammy, Best Gospel Vocal—Female, *Unguarded*, 1985; Grammy, Best Gospel Vocal, "Lead Me On," 1988
Address: P.O. Box 50701, Nashville, TN 37205

HUGH GRANT

Birthplace: London, England
Birthdate: 9/9/60
Occupation: Actor
Education: Attended New College, Oxford University
Debut: (Film) *Privileged*, 1982
Signature: *Four Weddings and a Funeral*
Facts: Grant opted not to do a nude scene with Andie MacDowell in *Four Weddings and a Funeral* when a makeup artist asked if he wanted definition painted on his body.

While at Oxford, formed a revue group, The Jockeys of Norfolk.

Grant is very popular in Japan, and there are two books on him published there, *Hugh Grant Vol. 1* and *Hugh Grant Vol. 2*.

Infamy: Arrested in June 1995 in Hollywood for picking up a prostitute.
Relationship: Elizabeth Hurley
Major Award: Golden Globe, Best Actor in a Comedy, *Four Weddings and a Funeral*, 1995
Quote: "So many dogs have their day. I'm having mine now—and though I'd love it to go on and on, I suspect I'll be back doing BBC radio drama next spring."
Address: Creative Artists Agency, 9830 Wilshire Blvd., Beverly Hills, CA 90212

LINDA GRAY

Birthplace: Santa Monica, CA
Birthdate: 9/12/40
Occupation: Actor
Education: Studied with Charles Conrad
Debut: (TV) *Marcus Welby, M.D.*, 1974
Signature: *Dallas*
Fact: Before landing any big acting roles, was a model and appeared in over 400 TV commercials.
Original Job: Model
Marriage: Ed Thrasher (divorced)
Children: Jeff, Kehly
Address: Agency for the Performing Arts, 9000 Sunset Blvd., Suite 1200, Los Angeles, CA 90069

WAYNE GRETZKY

Birthplace: Brantford, Canada
Birthdate: 1/26/61
Occupation: Hockey player
Education: High school dropout
Facts: Began skating at age two, entered the Branford Novice All-Star Team at age six, and was playing against 14-year-olds by age eight.

In the 1979–80 season Gretzky became the youngest player ever to score 50 or more goals and 100 or more points in a season, and the youngest player to be voted Most Valuable Player.

In 1994, surpassed hockey legend Gordie Howe's record for career goals, with 802.
Marriage: Janet Jones
Children: Paulina, Ty, Trevor
Major Awards: NHL MVP, 1980, 1981, 1982, 1983, 1984, 1985, 1986, 1987, 1989; NHL Sportsmanship Award, 1980, 1991, 1992; NHL leading scorer, 1980, 1981, 1982, 1983, 1984, 1985, 1986, 1987, 1990, 1991
Address: Los Angeles Kings, The

Forum, 3900 West Manchester Blvd., Inglewood, CA 90306

MELANIE GRIFFITH

Birthplace: New York, NY
Birthdate: 8/9/57
Occupation: Actor
Education: Attended Pierce College
Debut: (Film) *Night Moves*, 1975
Signature: *Working Girl*
Facts: Alfred Hitchcock, who was in love with Griffith's mother, gave Melanie a tiny wooden coffin containing a wax replica of her mother, outfitted in the same clothes she had worn in *The Birds*, on her sixth birthday

At 14, left home to move in with Don Johnson, who was then 22. She married him at 18 and was divorced a year later. In 1988, on her way to the Hazelden Clinic for rehab, she called Don from the plane and renewed their love.

Was clawed in the face by a lioness in the filming of *Roar* (1981).
Infamy: Was addicted to drugs and alcohol in the late '70s and early '80s, and studio executives refused to speak with her. In 1980, she was hit by a car while crossing Sunset Boulevard. She suffered a broken leg and arm, but her doctor said that if she hadn't been so drunk she probably would have been killed.
Original Job: Model
Marriages: Don Johnson (divorced), Steven Bauer (divorced), Don Johnson (separated), Antonio Banderas (relationship)
Children: Alexander, Dakota
Famous Relative: Tippi Hedren, actor, mother
Major Award: Golden Globe, Best Actress in a Comedy, *Working Girl*, 1989
Address: International Creative Management, 8942 Wilshire Blvd., Beverly Hills, CA 90211

NANCI GRIFFITH

Birthplace: Austin, TX
Birthdate: 7/6/53
Occupation: Singer, songwriter
Education: University of Texas
Debut: (Album) *There's a Light Beyond These Woods*, 1978
Signature: "From a Distance"
Facts: Began writing songs while in grade school.

Songs she wrote were recorded by Emmylou Harris,

Suzy Bogguss, and Kathy Mattea, among others.

Although her name has been connected to Ireland, she has no Irish blood (her mother's family came from Scotland).
Original Job: Elementary school teacher
Marriage: Eric Taylor (divorced)
Major Award: Grammy, Best Contemporary Folk Recording, *Other Voices/Other Rooms*, 1993
Address: MCA Music Entertainment Group, 70 Universal City Plaza, Universal City, CA 91608

JOHN GRISHAM

Birthplace: Arkansas
Birthdate: 1955
Occupation: Author
Education: Mississippi State, University of Mississippi Law School
Debut: (Book) *A Time To Kill*, 1989
Signature: *The Firm*
Facts: Little League baseball coach.

Wife edits his books as he writes them.

Was inspired to write *A Time To Kill* by testimony he heard at the De Soto County courthouse from a 10-year-old girl who was testifying against a man who had raped her and left her for dead.

Served as a Democrat in the Mississippi State Legislature for seven years (1983–90).

Shaves only once a week, before church on Sunday.

In 1989 formed Bongo Comics Group.
Original Job: Attorney
Marriage: Renee
Children: Ty, Shea
Address: Jay Garon-Brook Associates, 101 West 55th St., New York, NY 10019

CHARLES GRODIN

Real Name: Charles Grodinsky
Birthplace: Pittsburgh, PA

Birthdate: 4/21/35
Occupation: Actor, writer
Education: University of Miami, Pittsburgh Playhouse School, studied with Lee Strasberg and Uta Hagen
Debut: (Stage) *Tchin-Tchin*, 1962
Signature: *Midnight Run*
Facts: Grodin was almost cast in the lead role in *The Graduate* but lost it due to an argument with the producers over salary.

Only leases white or gray Cadillac DeVille sedans because he doesn't like to attract attention.

Took his "self-parodying loutishness," as one reviewer called it, to his own cable TV talk show in 1995, to entertaining results.
Marriages: Julia (divorced), Elissa
Children: Marion, Nicky
Quote: On a *Tonight Show* appearance, Grodin told Johnny Carson, "It's hard for me to answer a question from someone who really doesn't care about the answer." Carson banned Grodin from the show.
Address: United Talent Agency, 9560 Wilshire Blvd., Suite 500, Beverly Hills, CA 90212

MATT GROENING

Birthplace: Portland, OR
Birthdate: 2/15/54
Occupation: Cartoonist
Education: Evergreen College
Debut: (Comic Strip) *Life in Hell* (in the *Los Angeles Reader*), April 1980
Signature: *The Simpsons*
Facts: Elected student-body president in high school. Once elected, tried to rewrite the student government constitution to switch absolute power to himself.

In Los Angeles, ghostwrote the autobiography of an elderly film director who also employed him as a chauffeur, and worked as a landscaper for a sewage treatment plant.

The members of the Simpson family bear the same names as members of Groening's family (although Bart is an anagram for brat).

Groening's home in Venice, CA, is near a canal so he can canoe easily.
Original Job: Writer, rock critic
Marriage: Deborah Caplin
Children: Homer, Abraham
Major Award: Emmy, Outstanding Animated Program, *The Simpsons*, 1990, 1991

Address: Fox Broadcasting Co., 10201 West Pico Blvd., Los Angeles, CA 90035

GENE HACKMAN

Birthplace: San Bernardino, CA
Birthdate: 1/30/30
Occupation: Actor
Education: Pasadena Playhouse, attended University of Illinois, School of Radio Technique in NY
Debut: (Stage) *Any Wednesday*, 1964
Signature: *The French Connection*
Facts: Did his own driving in the car-chase scenes in *The French Connection*, 1971.

At the Pasadena Playhouse, he and classmate Dustin Hoffman were voted the two least likely to succeed.
Original Job: Doorman, truck driver, shoe salesman, soda jerk, furniture mover
Marriages: Faye Maltese (divorced), Betsy Arakawa
Children: Elizabeth, Leslie, Christopher
Major Awards: Oscar, Best Actor, *The French Connection*, 1971; Oscar, Best Supporting Actor, *Unforgiven*, 1992; Golden Globe, Best Actor, *The French Connection*, 1972; Golden Globe, Best Supporting Actor, *Unforgiven*, 1993
Address: Creative Artists Agency, 9830 Wilshire Blvd., Beverly Hills, CA 90212

ARSENIO HALL

Birthplace: Cleveland, OH
Birthdate: 2/12/59
Occupation: Talk show host
Education: Attended Ohio University, Kent State University
Debut: (TV) *The ABC 1/2 Hour Comedy Hour*, 1983
Signature: *The Arsenio Hall Show*
Facts: Appeared in the cult film *Amazon Women on the Moon*, 1987.

Became interested in magic at age seven, and later performed at birthday parties and bar mitzvahs, eventually leading to an appearance on a local TV special, *The Magic of Christmas*.

His interest in talk shows began early. While a young boy, he used to arrange the living room chairs for a make-believe show he pretended to host.

Has dated Emma Samms,

Paula Abdul, and Sinéad O'Connor.
Infamy: Reportedly angered at Paramount for "deserting" his talk show, in his final weeks on air in 1994 he booked Louis Farrakhan as a guest and told media executives to "kiss my black ass."
Original Job: Advertising
Address: Paramount Pictures, 5555 Melrose Ave., Los Angeles, CA 90038

BRIDGET HALL

Birthplace: Dallas, TX
Birthdate: 12/14/77
Occupation: Supermodel
Education: High school dropout
Facts: Her parents divorced when she was one year old.

Began modeling at age nine; three days after her mother took her to a Dallas modeling agency she was shooting for a J.C. Penney catalog. At 13, when the 5'8" Hall became too tall to model children's wear, her mother hired a makeup artist, hairstylist and photographer to take mature, bikini-clad portfolio pictures.

By age 16, had already graced the covers of 22 magazines.
Infamy: Moved to New York in 1993 into the New York City townhouse of modeling titans Eileen and Jerry Ford, but had to move out three months later for violating the nightly curfew.
Address: Ford Modeling Agency, 344 East 59th St., New York, NY 10022

HAMMER

Real Name: Stanley Kirk Burrell
Birthplace: Oakland, CA
Birthdate: 3/29/63
Occupation: Rap artist, dancer
Education: High school
Debut: (Song) "Ring 'Em," 1987; (TV) *Amen*, 1991
Facts: While doing impressions of James Brown on the Oakland Coliseum parking lot, was noticed by Charlie Finley, owner of the A's, who made him a bat-boy and later honorary executive vice president.

Joined Navy for three years and began intensive Bible studies.

Started Bust It Records with money from two Oakland ballplayers, selling singles from the trunk of his car.

Owns a racehorse, Dance Floor, that came in third in 1992 Kentucky Derby.

Infamy: Was sued by two Oakland ballplayers for reneging on their 1987 loan.
Marriage: Stephanie
Child: Akeiba Monique
Major Awards: Grammy, Best Rap Performance—Solo, and Best Rhythm and Blues Song, "U Can't Touch This" (as M.C. Hammer), 1990; Grammy, Best Music Video—Long Form, *Please Hammer Don't Hurt 'Em: The Movie* (as M.C. Hammer), 1990
Address: 1750 N. Vine St., Hollywood, CA 90212

TOM HANKS

Birthplace: Concord, CA
Birthdate: 7/9/56
Occupation: Actor
Education: Attended Chabot College, California State University–Sacramento
Debut: (Film) *He Knows You're Alone,* 1980
Signature: *Forrest Gump*
Facts: Attended at least five different elementary schools.

After a one-shot guest spot on *Happy Days,* producer Ron Howard asked him to read for a secondary part in *Splash,* but he got the lead instead.

Played Michael J. Fox's alcoholic uncle on the sitcom *Family Ties.*
Marriages: Samantha Lewes (divorced), Rita Wilson
Children: Colin, Elizabeth, Chester
Major Awards: Golden Globe, Best Actor in a Comedy, *Big,* 1989; Golden Globe, Best Actor, *Philadelphia,* 1994; Golden Globe, Best Actor, *Forrest Gump,* 1995; Oscar, Best Actor, *Philadelphia,* 1993; Oscar, Best Actor, *Forrest Gump,* 1994
Address: Creative Artists Agency, 9830 Wilshire Blvd., Beverly Hills, CA 90212

DARYL HANNAH

Birthplace: Chicago, IL
Birthdate: 12/3/60
Occupation: Actor
Education: Studied ballet with Maria Tallchief, studied at Chicago's Goodman Theater, attended UCLA
Debut: (Film) *The Fury,* 1976
Signature: *Splash*
Facts: When alone at home, sometimes wears Fred Astaire's shoes, which she bought at an auction.

Her childhood interest in movies grew out of a lifelong

battle with insomnia. Was diagnosed as "semiautistic" by psychiatrists.

In high school, was the only female member of the soccer team.

Played keyboard in some of ex-boyfriend Jackson Browne's videos. Sang backup vocals in his hit, "You're a Friend of Mine" (1975).

Seriously dated John Kennedy Jr., but broke up when he wouldn't marry her.
Famous Relatives: Page Hannah, actress, sister; Haskell Wexler, cinematographer, uncle
Address: International Creative Management, 8942 Wilshire Blvd., Beverly Hills, CA 90211

WOODY HARRELSON

Real Name: Woodrow Tracy Harrelson
Birthplace: Midland, TX
Birthdate: 7/23/61
Occupation: Actor
Education: Hanover College
Debut: (Film) *Wildcats,* 1986
Signature: *Cheers*
Facts: A hyperactive child, sometimes prone to violence, he was placed in a school for problem students. "Violence was almost an aphrodisiac for me." Took Ritalin.

His absent father was convicted of murdering a federal judge and sentenced to life in prison when Woody was a freshman in college.

Sang and composed for a 10-piece "blues-a-billy" band, Manly Moondog and the Three Kool Kats.

Dated Brooke Shields, Carol Kane, Glenn Close, and Moon Unit Zappa.
Infamy: Admits to having been a sex addict.
Original Job: Claims he had over 17 different jobs in one year, including waiting tables and short-order cooking, and was fired from almost all of them
Marriages: Nancy Simon (divorced), Laura Louie (relationship)
Child: Denni Montana
Major Award: Emmy, Best Supporting Actor in a Comedy Series, *Cheers,* 1989
Address: Creative Artists Agency, 9830 Wilshire Blvd., Beverly Hills, CA 90212

PHIL HARTMAN

Birthplace: Brantford, Canada
Birthdate: 9/24/48

Occupation: Actor, writer
Debut: (TV) *Our Time,* 1985
Signature: *Saturday Night Live*
Facts: When Hartman left *Saturday Night Live* in 1994, he had set a record for the longest run (eight seasons, 153 shows) by a regular cast member.

Hartman cowrote the film *Pee wee's Big Adventure* with Paul Reubens, and starred as Kap'n Karl on the TV show *Pee-wee's Playhouse.*
Original Job: Graphic designer (designed the Crosby, Stills, and Nash logo)
Marriages: Two prior marriages, Brynn Omdahl
Children: Sean, Birgen
Major Award: Emmy, Best Writing in a Variety or Music Program, *Murderers Among Us,* 1989
Address: William Morris Agency, 151 El Camino Dr., Beverly Hills, CA 90212

DAVID HASSELHOFF

Birthplace: Baltimore, MD
Birthdate: 7/17/52
Occupation: Actor
Education: Attended California Institute of the Arts
Debut: (TV) *The Young and the Restless,* 1975
Signature: *Knight Rider*
Facts: Hasselhoff is a successful recording star in Europe, and has toured Germany and Austria. He performed a concert in front of 500,000 people at the Berlin Wall.

Baywatch was the first American show to appear in mainland China. It is the most watched show on the planet, seen by almost a billion people every day.
Marriages: Catherine Hickland (divorced), Pamela Bach
Children: Taylor Ann, Hayley Amber
Address: JSO Management, 11342 Dona Lisa Dr., Studio City, CA 91604

TERI HATCHER

Birthplace: Sunnyvale, CA
Birthdate: 12/8/64
Occupation: Actor
Education: Attended De Anza Junior College
Debut: (TV) *The Love Boat,* 1985; (Film) *Tango & Cash,* 1989
Signature: *Lois & Clark: The New Adventures of Superman*
Facts: Played Penny Parker on *MacGyver* in 1985, a role that

later became a recurring character.
Infamy: Before *Lois and Clark,* she made an independent film, *Cool Surface,* with nudity and simulated sex scenes.
Original Job: Dancer
Marriage: Jon Tenney
Quote: "Despite the fact that I have a good-size pair of breasts . . . in *Lois & Clark* I have the opportunity to show the world they're not my only attribute."
Address: William Morris Agency, 151 El Camino Dr., Beverly Hills, CA 90212

ETHAN HAWKE

Birthplace: Austin, TX
Birthdate: 11/6/70
Occupation: Actor, director, writer
Education: Attended New York University, studied acting at the McCarter Theatre in Princeton, the British Theatre Association, and Carnegie-Mellon University
Debut: (Film) *Explorers,* 1985; (Stage) *The Seagull,* 1992
Signature: *Dead Poets Society*
Facts: Was seen out drinking and dancing with the married Julia Roberts in April 1994. He claims they were just discussing a possible movie project.

Starred in *Explorers* when he was 14 with River Phoenix.

His own singing was featured in the *Reality Bites* soundtrack.

Dropped out of Carnegie Mellon after two months to act in *Dead Poets Society.*

Co-founded the New York theater company Malaparte.
Relationship: Jane Pratt
Address: Creative Artists Agency, 9830 Wilshire Blvd., Beverly Hills, CA 90212

GOLDIE HAWN

Birthplace: Takoma Park, MD
Birthdate: 11/21/45
Occupation: Actor
Education: American University
Debut: (Film) *The One and Only Genuine Family Band,* 1968
Signature: *Private Benjamin*
Facts: Discovered while dancing in the chorus of an Andy Griffith TV special in 1967. Became a regular on *Laugh-In.*

Father performed as a musician at the White House.
Original Job: Go-go dancer
Marriages: Gus Trikonis (divorced), Bill Hudson (divorced), Kurt Russell (relationship)
Children: Katie, Oliver, Wyatt

Major Awards: Oscar, Best Supporting Actress, *Cactus Flower,* 1970; Golden Globe, Best Supporting Actress, *Cactus Flower,* 1970
Address: Creative Artists Agency, 9830 Wilshire Blvd., Beverly Hills, CA 90212

DON HENLEY

Birthplace: Linden, TX
Birthdate: 7/22/47
Occupation: Singer, songwriter, drummer, guitarist
Signature: The Eagles
Fact: Played in Linda Ronstadt's backup band, out of which the Eagles emerged.
Marriage: Sharon Summerall
Major Awards: Co-recipient (with other members of The Eagles) of Grammy Awards for best pop vocal performance by a group, 1975, for "Lyin' Eyes"; record of the year, 1977, *Hotel California;* best arrangement for voices, 1977, "New Kid in Town"; best rock vocal performance by a group, 1979, "Heartache Tonight"; solo Grammies for best rock vocal performance by a male, 1985 and 1989; Grammy, "The Boys of Summer," 1985; Grammy, "The End of the Innocence," 1990
Address: Geffen Records, 9130 Sunset Blvd., Los Angeles, CA 90069

KATHARINE HEPBURN

Birthplace: Hartford, CT
Birthdate: 11/8/07
Occupation: Actor
Education: Bryn Mawr College
Debut: (Stage) *The Czarina,* 1928; (Film) *A Bill of Divorcement,* 1932
Signature: *The African Queen*
Facts: In her strict New England home, where her father was a surgeon and her mother a militant suffragette, Hepburn and her siblings took cold showers every morning.

Since she was considered too much of a tomboy, she was educated by home tutors.

Decided to take up acting once she realized there was little opportunity for a woman to become a doctor.

According to a 1995 biography, she settled for Tracy after her true love, Catholic director John Ford, couldn't get a divorce from his wife.
Original Job: Sold balloons
Marriages: Ludlow Ogden Smith

(divorced), Spencer Tracy (relationship, deceased)
Major Awards: Oscar, Best Actress, *Morning Glory,* 1933; Oscar, Best Actress, *Guess Who's Coming to Dinner,* 1967; Oscar, Best Actress, *The Lion in Winter,* 1968; Emmy, Best Actress in a Drama Special, *Love Among the Ruins,* 1975; Oscar, Best Actress, *On Golden Pond,* 1981; Kennedy Center Honor for Lifetime Achievement, 1990
Quote: "I am revered rather like an old building."
Address: William Morris Agency, 151 El Camino Dr., Beverly Hills, CA 90212

DUSTIN HOFFMAN

Birthplace: Los Angeles, CA
Birthdate: 8/8/37
Occupation: Actor
Education: Attended Los Angeles Conservatory of Music, Santa Monica City College; studied at the Pasadena Playhouse and the Actor's Studio
Debut: (Stage) *Yes Is for a Very Young Man,* 1960; (Film) *Tiger Makes Out,* 1967
Signature: *The Graduate*
Facts: Played Tiny Tim in junior high school.

Slept on Gene Hackman's kitchen floor while looking for work.

Achieved Ratso's distinctive walk in *Midnight Cowboy* by putting pebbles in his shoe.

When taking the screen test for *The Graduate,* Hoffman said, "I don't think I'm right for the role. He's a kind of Anglo-Saxon, tall, slender, good-looking chap. I'm short and Jewish." During the screen test he forgot his lines and was nervous and clumsy.

Hoffman originally wanted to be a concert pianist. Also studied to be a doctor.
Original Job: Washing dishes, checking coats, waiting tables, cleaning a dance studio, selling toys at Macy's, attendant in a psychiatric institution
Marriages: Anne Byrne (divorced), Lisa Gottsegen
Children: Karina, Jenna, Jacob, Rebecca, Max, Alexandra
Major Awards: Oscar, Best Actor, *Kramer vs. Kramer,* 1980; Oscar, Best Actor, *Rain Man,* 1989; Emmy, Best Actor in a Made-for-TV Movie, *Death of a Salesman,* 1986
Address: Creative Artists Agency, 9830 Wilshire Blvd., Beverly Hills, CA 90212

LAUREN HOLLY

Birthplace: Geneva, NY
Occupation: Actor
Debut: (Film) *Band of the Hand,* 1986
Signature: *Picket Fences*
Facts: Personal tragedy struck in 1992 when her parents ended their 30-year marriage and, a short time later, her 14-year-old brother died in a house fire.

Her very public 1994 divorce from Anthony Quinn's struggling actor son, Danny, had him claiming that her careless spending squandered his fortune and her accusing him of having affairs and refusing to work.
Marriages: Danny Quinn (divorced), Jim Carrey (relationship)
Address: United Talent Agency, 9560 Wilshire Blvd., Suite 500, Beverly Hills, CA 90212

ANTHONY HOPKINS

Birthplace: Port Talbot, South Wales
Birthdate: 12/31/37
Occupation: Actor
Education: Welsh College of Music and Drama, Royal Academy of Dramatic Art, London
Debut: (Stage) *Julius Caesar,* 1964; (Film) *The Lion in Winter,* 1968
Signature: *The Silence of the Lambs*
Facts: Debuted as conductor with the New Symphony Orchestra at Royal Albert Hall, 1982.

Was knighted in 1993.

Understudied for Laurence Olivier in *Dance Of Death,* 1966.
Infamy: Had a long bout with alcohol addiction.
Original Job: Steelworker
Marriages: Petronella Barker (divorced), Jennifer Ann Lynton
Child: Abigail
Major Awards: Emmy, Best Actor in a Drama or Comedy Special, *The Lindbergh Kidnapping Case,* 1976; Emmy, Best Actor in a Miniseries, *The Bunker,* 1981; Oscar, Best Actor, *Silence of the Lambs,* 1991
Address: International Creative Management, 8942 Wilshire Blvd., Beverly Hills, CA 90211

WHITNEY HOUSTON

Birthplace: Newark, NJ
Birthdate: 8/9/63
Occupation: Singer
Education: High school

Debut: (Album) *Whitney Houston,* 1985
Facts: Got her start at age eight singing in the New Hope Baptist Junior Choir.

Sang backup for Chaka Khan, Lou Rawls, and Dionne Warwick.

As a model, appeared on the cover of *Seventeen.*

Was an actress in her early days, appearing on *Silver Spoons* and *Gimme a Break.*
Original Job: Model
Marriage: Bobby Brown
Child: Bobbi Kristina
Famous Relatives: Cissy Houston, singer, mother; Thelma Houston, singer, aunt; Dionne Warwick, singer, cousin
Major Awards: Emmy, Best Individual Performance in a Variety or Music Program, *The 28th Annual Grammy Awards,* 1986; Grammy, Best Pop Vocal—Female, "Saving All My Love for You," 1985; Grammy, Best Pop Vocal—Female, "I Wanna Dance with Somebody," 1987; Grammy, Best Pop Vocal—Female, "I Will Always Love You," 1993; Grammy, Record of the Year, "I Will Always Love You," 1993; Grammy, Album of the Year, *The Bodyguard Soundtrack,* 1993
Address: William Morris Agency, 151 El Camino Dr., Beverly Hills, CA 90212

HELEN HUNT

Birthplace: Los Angeles, CA
Birthdate: 6/15/63
Occupation: Actor
Education: Attended UCLA
Debut: (TV) *The Mary Tyler Moore Show,* 1970; (Film) *Rollercoaster,* 1977
Signature: *Mad About You*
Facts: Hunt studied acting, got an agent, and got a part in the TV movie *Pioneer Woman* by age nine.

Began a two-year romance with actor Matthew Broderick while working on *Project X* (1986).

Played Murray Slaughter's daughter on *The Mary Tyler Moore Show.*
Relationship: Hank Azaria
Famous Relatives: Gordon Hunt, director, father; Peter Hunt, director, uncle
Major Awards: Golden Globe, Best Actress in a Comedy Series, *Mad About You,* 1994, 1995
Address: Creative Artists Agency, 9830 Wilshire Blvd., Beverly Hills, CA 90212

HOLLY HUNTER

Birthplace: Conyers, GA
Birthdate: 3/20/58
Occupation: Actor
Education: Carnegie Mellon University
Debut: (Film) *The Burning*, 1981; (Stage) *Crimes of the Heart*, 1981
Signature: *The Piano*
Facts: Director Jane Campion was originally looking for a tall, statuesque Sigourney Weaver type for the lead in *The Piano*.

Youngest of seven children, grew up on a cattle and hay farm in Georgia, where she drove a tractor.

Appeared in pilot for television series *Fame* (1982).
Marriage: Janusz Kaminski
Major Awards: Emmy, Best Actress in a Miniseries, *Roe vs. Wade*, 1989; Emmy, Best Actress in a Miniseries, *The Positively True Adventures of the Alleged Texas Cheerleader-Murdering Mom*, 1993; Oscar, Best Actress, *The Piano*, 1993; Golden Globe, Best Actress, *The Piano*, 1993
Address: International Creative Management, 8942 Wilshire Blvd., Beverly Hills, CA 90211

ELIZABETH HURLEY

Birthplace: Hampshire, England
Birthdate: 6/10/65
Occupation: Actor, model
Education: Attended London Studio Centre
Debut: (Stage) *The Man Most Likely To . . .* , (Film) *Rowing in the Wind*, 1986
Signature: *Christabel*
Facts: Long recognized only as actor Hugh Grant's girlfriend. In 1995 when she accompanied Grant on a guest appearance on the *Joan Rivers* show, Rivers asked, "And who are you?" The two have dated since 1987.

She and Grant started the production company, Simian Films.

At the opening of Grant's movie *Four Weddings and a Funeral*, she wore a Versace dress held together by 24 safety pins.

Replaced Paulina Porizkova as the face of Estée Lauder cosmetics. Defied conventional stardom by beginning as an actress and becoming a supermodel at age 29.

Characterizes herself as an army brat; her father was an army major.

Notorious in her early 20s for her punk-rock phase. She pierced her nose, spiked and painted her hair pink and frequented punk rock bars.

Needlepoint is one of her favorite pastimes.

Was a candidate for the position of ambassador for the United Nations High Commissioner for Refugees.
Infamy: Was expelled from the London Studio Centre after leaving school and going to a Greek Island.
Relationship: Hugh Grant
Address: Creative Artists Agency, 9830 Wilshire Blvd., Beverly Hills, CA 90212-1825

ICE CUBE

Real Name: O'Shea Jackson
Birthplace: Los Angeles, CA
Birthdate: 6/15/69
Occupation: Rap artist, actor
Education: Phoenix Institute of Technology
Debut: (Album) *Boyz N the Hood* (with N.W.A.), 1986; (Album) *Amerikkka's Most Wanted* (solo), 1990
Signature: *Boyz N the Hood*
Facts: Former lyricist of the rap group N.W.A. His 1991 album, *Death Certificate*, stirred controversy because it contained racist attacks on Koreans and called for the murder of a Jewish man.

Began writing rap lyrics at age 14.
Child: O'Shea Jackson Jr.
Quote: "Rap is the network newscast black people never had."
Address: Priority Records, 6430 Sunset Blvd., Hollywood, CA 90028

ICE-T

Real Name: Tracy Morrow
Birthplace: Newark, NJ
Birthdate: 2/16/58
Occupation: Rap artist, actor
Debut: (Single) "The Coldest Rap," 1982; (Film) *Breakin'*, 1984;
Signature: *New Jack City*
Facts: Appeared in the films *Breakin'* and *Breakin' II*, among others.

Spent four years running with gangs in South Central Los Angeles.

Served four years as a ranger in the U.S. Army.

Was raised by an aunt in Los Angeles after both of his parents died by the time he was in seventh grade.
Relationship: Darlene

Children: Latisha, Ice Jr.
Major Award: Grammy, Best Rap Performance—Duo or Group, "Back on the Block" (with others), 1990
Address: William Morris Agency, 151 El Camino Dr., Beverly Hills, CA 90212

JEREMY IRONS

Birthplace: Isle of Wight, England
Birthdate: 9/19/48
Occupation: Actor
Education: Bristol Old Vic Theatre School
Debut: (Stage) *Godspell*, 1972
Signature: *The French Lieutenant's Woman*
Facts: At school, excelled at rugby, the fiddle, and clarinet and headed the cadet corps.

Made his mark with the BBC series *Brideshead Revisited*, 1981.

Played a dual role as twin brothers in *Dead Ringers*, a 1988 movie he considers his best work.
Original Job: Housecleaner, gardener, assistant stage manager, busker (singing and playing guitar outside movie theaters)
Marriage: Sinéad Moira Cusack
Children: Samuel James, Maximilian Paul
Major Awards: Tony, Best Actor, *The Real Thing*, 1984; Oscar, Best Actor, *Reversal of Fortune*, 1991; Golden Globe, Best Actor, *Reversal of Fortune*, 1991
Address: Creative Artists Agency, 9830 Wilshire Blvd., Beverly Hills, CA 90212

CHRIS ISAAK

Birthplace: Stockton, CA
Birthdate: 6/26/56
Occupation: Singer, songwriter, actor
Education: University of the Pacific
Debut: (Album) *Silvertone* (with Silvertone), 1985; (Film) *Married to the Mob*, 1988
Signature: "Wicked Game"
Facts: In 1987, performed "Blue Hotel" on TV show *The Last Resort*, which flopped in the U.S. but was a hit in France.

Appeared in movies *Silence of the Lambs* (1991) and *Little Buddha* (1993).
Original Job: Amateur boxer, tour guide for a film studio
Address: Warner Brothers, 3300 Warner Blvd., Burbank, CA 91510

ALAN JACKSON

Birthplace: Newnan, GA
Birthdate: 10/17/58
Occupation: Singer, songwriter
Education: Attended South Georgia College
Debut: (Album) *Here in the Real World*, 1989
Signature: "Neon Rainbow"
Facts: She got Jackson his big break. A flight attendant, she cornered Glen Campbell in the Atlanta airport and asked him to listen to her husband's tape.

Started wearing his trademark white Stetson to hide scars above his left eyebrow (a result of a childhood accident with a coffee table).
Original Job: Forklift operator, car salesman, home builder
Marriage: Denise
Child: Mattie
Address: Arista Records, 6 W. 57th St., New York, NY 10019

JANET JACKSON

Birthplace: Gary, IN
Birthdate: 5/16/66
Occupation: Singer, actor
Debut: (TV) *Good Times*, 1977
Facts: With 1986 song "When I Think of You," she and brother Michael became the first siblings in the rock era to have No. 1 songs as soloists.

Paula Abdul was Janet's choreographer before starting her own career.

Played Charlene DuPrey on the TV series *Diff'rent Strokes*.
Marriages: James DeBarge (annulled), Rene Elizondo (relationship)
Famous Relatives: Michael, singer, brother; La Toya, singer, sister; Tito, singer, brother; Randy, singer, brother; Marlon, singer, brother; Jermaine, singer, brother; Jackie, singer, brother
Major Awards: Grammy, Best Music Video—Long Form, *Rhythm Nation 1814*, 1989; Grammy, Best R&B Song, "That's the Way Love Goes," 1993
Address: Virgin Records, 1790 Broadway, New York, NY 10019

MICHAEL JACKSON

Birthplace: Gary, IN
Birthdate: 8/29/58
Occupation: Singer, songwriter, actor
Debut: (Stage) Mr. Lucky's, Gary, IN (with Jackson 5), 1966
Signature: *Thriller*

Facts: Built amusement park on property and maintains a menagerie of animals including Bubbles the Chimp.

Gave Elizabeth Taylor away at her marriage to Larry Fortensky in 1991.

Surgery includes four nose jobs, two nose adjustments, and cleft put in his chin. Randy Tarraborelli's unauthorized biography claims that Michael had the surgery to avoid resembling his abusive father as much as possible.

Infamy: Settled out of court a civil lawsuit alleging child molestation. The boy then refused to testify in a criminal proceeding, so prosecutors declined to press charges.

Famous Relatives: Janet, singer, sister; LaToya, singer, sister; Tito, singer, brother; Randy, singer, brother; Marlon, singer, brother; Jermaine, singer, brother; Jackie, singer, brother

Marriage: Lisa Marie Presley

Major Awards: Grammy, Best R&B Vocal—Male, "Don't Stop 'Till You Get Enough," 1979; Grammy, Album of the Year, *Thriller*, 1983; Grammy, Best Pop Vocal—Male, *Thriller*, 1983; Grammy, Best R&B Song, "Billie Jean," 1983; Grammy, Best R&B Vocal—Male, "Billie Jean," 1983; Grammy, Best Recording for Children, *E.T., the Extraterrestrial*, 1983; Grammy, Record of the Year, "Beat It," 1984; Grammy, Best Pop Vocal—Male, "Beat It," 1984; Grammy, Song of the Year, "We Are the World" (with Lionel Richie), 1985; Grammy, Best Music Video, Short Form, *Leave Me Alone*, 1989; Grammy, Legend Award, 1993

Address: Creative Artists Agency, 9830 Wilshire Blvd., Beverly Hills, CA 90212

SAMUEL L. JACKSON

Birthplace: Chattanooga, TN
Birthdate: 1949
Occupation: Actor
Education: Morehouse College
Debut: (Film) *Ragtime*, 1981
Signature: *Pulp Fiction*
Facts: Angry at Morehouse College's lack of African-American studies and its control by a white governing body, he participated in a protest involving locking up the school's board of trustees, and was expelled in 1969. He later returned to graduate.

In 1991's *Jungle Fever*, Jackson's performance as crackhead Gator won him the first-ever sup-

porting actor award given by the Cannes Film Festival.

Was Bill Cosby's stand-in for three years on *The Cosby Show*.
Infamy: Had a problem with drugs and alcohol for several years. Ironically, his first role after taking a vow of sobriety was as the crack addict Gator.
Original Job: Security guard
Marriage: LaTanya Richardson
Child: Zoe
Address: International Creative Management, 8942 Wilshire Blvd., Beverly Hills, CA 90211

MICK JAGGER

Birthplace: Dartford, England
Birthdate: 7/26/43
Occupation: Singer, songwriter
Education: Attended London School of Economics
Debut: (Song) "Come On" (cover of Chuck Berry original), 1963
Signature: The Rolling Stones
Facts: Went to elementary school with guitarist Keith Richards but lost touch with him until they met again on a London train in 1960.

Sang backup on Carly Simon's 1973 hit, "You're So Vain."

Co-owned the Philadelphia Furies, a soccer team, with Peter Frampton, Rick Wakeman, and Paul Simon.
Marriages: Bianca Peres Morena de Macias (divorced), Jerry Hall
Children: Karis, Jade, Elizabeth Scarlett, James Leroy Augustine, Georgia May
Major Awards: Grammy, Best Album Package, *Tattoo You* (with the Rolling Stones), 1981; Grammy, NARAS Lifetime Achievement Award, 1986; inducted into the Rock and Roll Hall of Fame (with the Rolling Stones), 1989; Grammy, Best Rock Album, *Voodoo Lounge* (with the Rolling Stones), 1994
Quote: "It's a good way of making a living. I think we'll just keep right on doing it."
Address: The Rolling Stones, 1776 Broadway, #507, New York, NY 10019

PETER JENNINGS

Birthplace: Toronto, Canada
Birthdate: 7/29/38
Occupation: Anchor, senior editor
Education: Attended Carleton University and Rider College
Debut: At age nine, hosted *Peter's People*, a CBC radio show for children, 1947
Signature: *ABC's World News Tonight*
Facts: At 26, was the youngest

network anchor ever. ABC removed him after three years. Took over as permanent anchor in 1983.
Original Job: Bank teller and late-night radio host
Marriage: One previous marriage (divorced), Valerie Godsoe (divorced), Kati Marton (divorced)
Children: Elizabeth, Christopher
Famous Relative: Charles Jennings, vice president of programming at CBC, father
Address: ABC, 77 West 66th St., New York, NY 10023

BILLY JOEL

Birthplace: Bronx, NY
Birthdate: 5/9/49
Occupation: Singer, songwriter, piano player
Education: High school
Debut: (Song) "You Got Me Hummin'" (cover of Sam and Dave original, with The Hassles), 1965
Signature: "Piano Man"
Facts: Had a suicidal period when he was in his early 20s; after taking pills and swallowing furniture polish, he spent three weeks in Meadowbrook Hospital.

As a Long Island teenager, was a local welterweight boxing champion.

Wrote "New York State of Mind" within 20 minutes of returning home from California in 1975.
Original Job: Rock critic for *Changes* magazine
Marriages: Elizabeth Weber (divorced), Christie Brinkley (divorced), Carolyn Beegan (relationship)
Child: Alexa Ray
Major Awards: Grammy, Record of the Year, "Just the Way You Are," 1978; Grammy, Song of the Year, "Just the Way You Are," 1978; Grammy, Album of the Year, *Billy Joel*, 1979; Grammy, Best Pop Vocal—Male, *52nd Street*, 1979; Grammy, Best Rock Vocal—Male, *Glass Houses*, 1980; Grammy, Best Recording for Children, *In Harmony 2* (with others), 1982; Grammy, Legend Award, 1991
Address: QBQ Entertainment, 341 Madison Ave., 14th Fl., New York, NY 10017

ELTON JOHN

Real Name: Reginald Kenneth Dwight
Birthplace: Pinner, England
Birthdate: 3/25/47

Occupation: Singer, songwriter, piano player
Education: Attended Royal Academy of Music, London
Debut: (Album) *Come Back Baby* (with Bluesology), 1965
Signature: "Rocket Man"
Facts: Took his name from first names of Bluesology members Elton Deal and John Baldry.

Wrote "Philadelphia Freedom" in 1975 for Billie Jean King.

Is godfather to Sean Lennon.

Along with Tim Rice of *Little Shop of Horrors* fame), scored the 1994 Disney movie *The Lion King*.

Attended London's Royal Academy of Music but quit three weeks before final exams.

Has donated more than $5.5 million—profits from his singles—to his nonprofit care and education foundation.
Infamy: In 1994, *Star* magazine alleged that he was in a romantic relationship with an Atlanta man. He denied being involved with the man and sued the magazine over the article.
Original Job: Worked at Mills Music Publishers
Marriage: Renate Blauer (divorced)
Major Awards: Grammy, Best Pop Performance—Duo or Group, "That's What Friends Are For" (with Dionne & Friends), 1986; Grammy, Best Pop Vocal Performance—Male, "Can You Feel the Love Tonight," 1994; inducted into the Rock and Roll Hall of Fame, 1994; Golden Globe, Best Original Song, "Can You Feel the Love Tonight," 1995
Address: c/o John Reid, 32 Galena Rd., London W6 OLT England

DON JOHNSON

Birthplace: Flat Creek, MO
Birthdate: 12/15/49
Occupation: Actor
Education: Attended University of Kansas, studied at the American Conservatory Theater in San Francisco
Debut: (Stage) *Fortunes and Men's Eyes*, 1969; (Film) *The Magic Garden of Stanley Sweetheart*, 1970
Signature: *Miami Vice*
Facts: At age 12, seduced his babysitter. At 16, moved out of his dad's place and moved in with a 26-year-old cocktail waitress. At the University of Kansas, became romantically involved with a drama professor.
Infamy: When he was 12, was

caught stealing a car and sent to a juvenile detention home.

Admits to having been addicted to alcohol and cocaine. Says he was sober for ten years, but was treated again for a drinking problem in 1994.
Original Job: Worked in a meat-packing plant
Marriages: Melanie Griffith (divorced, remarried, separated)
Children: Jesse (with Patti D'Arbanville), Dakota
Major Award: Golden Globe, Best Actor in a Drama Series, *Miami Vice*, 1986
Address: International Creative Management, 8942 Wilshire Blvd., Beverly Hills, CA 90211

MAGIC JOHNSON

Real Name: Earvin Johnson
Birthplace: Lansing, MI
Birthdate: 8/14/59
Occupation: Basketball player (retired)
Education: Attended Michigan State University
Facts: On November 7, 1991, announced that he was retiring from basketball after being diagnosed HIV positive. Was diagnosed only months after marrying longtime friend Earletha "Cookie" Kelly, who was in the early stages of pregnancy. Neither Cookie nor the child has tested positive for the disease.

After his diagnosis, became one of the world's major fundraisers and spokesmen for AIDS.

Given his nickname in high school by a local sportswriter after a game in which he scored 36 points and had 18 rebounds.
Infamy: In 1992, admitted he caught the AIDS virus from "messing around with too many women."
Marriage: Earletha "Cookie" Kelly
Children: Andre, Earvin III, adopted daughter Elisa
Major Awards/Titles: MVP, National Collegiate Athletic Association Final Four playoff tournament, 1979; MVP, NBA Championship Series, 1980, 1982, 1987; All-NBA First Team, 1983, 1984, 1985, 1986, 1987, 1988; MVP, NBA (regular season), 1987; Grammy, Best Spoken Word Album, *What You Can Do To Avoid AIDS* (with Robert O'Keefe), 1992
Address: Creative Artists Agency, 9830 Wilshire Blvd., Beverly Hills, CA 90212

QUINCY JONES

Birthplace: Chicago, IL
Birthdate: 3/14/33
Occupation: Composer, producer
Education: Attended Seattle University; Berklee College of Music, Boston Conservatory
Debut: Trumpeter, arranger, for Lionel Hampton Orchestra, 1950
Signature: Produced *Off the Wall*, *Thriller*, and *Bad*
Facts: Established his own label, Qwest, in 1981 and founded *Vibe* magazine.

Scored the TV series *Roots* in 1977.

Has worked with many prominent pop and jazz artists, including Ray Charles, Miles Davis, Ella Fitzgerald, Dizzy Gillespie, Ice-T, Chaka Khan, and Sarah Vaughan.

Middle name is Delight.
Marriages: Jeri Caldwell (divorced), Ulla Anderson (divorced), Peggy Lipton (divorced), Nastassja Kinski (relationship)
Children: Jolie, Martina-Lisa, Quincy III, Kidada, Rashida, Kenya
Major Award: Grammy, Album of the Year, *Back on the Block*, 1991; Oscar, Jean Hersholt Humanitarian Award, 1995
Address: William Morris Agency, 151 El Camino Dr., Beverly Hills, CA 90212

TOMMY LEE JONES

Birthplace: San Saba, TX
Birthdate: 9/15/46
Occupation: Actor
Education: Harvard University
Debut: (Stage) *A Patriot for Me*, 1969; (TV) *One Life To Live*, 1969; (Film) *Love Story*, 1970
Signature: *The Executioner's Song*
Facts: Roomed with Vice-President Al Gore while attending Harvard.

Is a champion polo player.

Raises Black Angus cattle on his ranch in San Antonio.
Original Job: Worked in oil fields
Marriages: Katherine Lardner (divorced), Kimberlea Gayle Cloughley (separated)
Children: Austin, Victoria
Major Awards: Emmy, Best Actor in a Miniseries, *The Executioner's Song*, 1983; Oscar, Best Supporting Actor, *The Fugitive*, 1994; Golden Globe, Best Supporting Actor, *The Fugitive*, 1994
Quote: "I like to cook. I'm really

interested in killing things and eating them."
Address: International Creative Management, 8942 Wilshire Blvd., Beverly Hills, CA 90211

MICHAEL JORDAN

Birthplace: Brooklyn, NY
Birthdate: 2/17/63
Occupation: Basketball player
Education: Attended the University of North Carolina
Facts: He was cut from the varsity basketball team in high school.

Though he said, "This is my dream," after hitting his first homer playing professional baseball in the minor leagues, he soon left baseball to return to basketball.

In his first game back against archrival Knicks in 1995, some fans paid scalpers more than $1,000 a ticket. They were not disappointed; he scored 55 points.
Marriage: Juanita Vanoy
Children: Jeffrey, Marcus, Jasmine
Major Awards/Titles: College Player of the Year, 1984; Olympic Gold Medal, 1984, 1992; NBA scoring leader, 1987, 1988, 1989, 1990, 1991, 1992, 1993; NBA All-Star team (7 seasons); NBA MVP, regular season, 1988, 1991, 1992; NBA MVP, finals, 1991, 1992, 1993
Address: Chicago Bulls, One Magnificent Mile, 980 N. Michigan Ave., Chicago, IL 60611

DONNA KARAN

Real Name: Donna Faske
Birthplace: Forest Hills, NY
Birthdate: 10/2/48
Occupation: Fashion designer
Education: Parsons School of Design
Signature: DKNY clothes
Facts: While in college, worked for designers Chuck Howard and Liz Claiborne.

After serving a long apprenticeship with the Anne Klein collection, at age 26 was given full creative control by the principal owner of the firm after Anne Klein died of cancer in 1974.

Close personal friend to many stars including Barbra Streisand.
Original Job: Sales clerk at a Long Island dress shop
Marriages: Mark Karan (divorced), Stephen Weiss
Child: Gabrielle
Major Awards: Coty Award, 1977, 1981; named to Coty Hall of Fame, 1984

Address: Donna Karan Co., 550 7th Ave., New York, NY 10018

JEFFREY KATZENBERG

Birthplace: New York, NY
Birthdate: 1950
Occupation: Studio executive
Education: Attended college
Facts: Left his multimillion-dollar job at Walt Disney several weeks after being refused the No. 2 spot vacated by the death of president Frank Wells. Had been with Disney for a decade, helping to take its film division from worst to first.

Credited with resuscitating the animated feature, a dormant art form when he got to Disney; created the 1994 blockbuster, *The Lion King*.

His DreamWorks SKG, formed with David Geffen and Steven Spielberg, is the first completely new movie studio in 50 years. Also co-owns the Century City eatery, Dive!, with Spielberg.
Infamy: In 1991, issued a 28-page memo criticizing many aspects of Disney operations. Intended for limited internal readership, it was widely circulated, to the embarrassment of many Disney staffers.
Original Job: Paramount mailroom worker
Marriage: Marilyn Siegel
Children: Laura, David
Address: DreamWorks SKG, 100 Universal City Plaza, Universal City, CA 91608

HARVEY KEITEL

Birthplace: Brooklyn, NY
Birthdate: 5/13/39
Occupation: Actor, producer
Education: Studied with Lee Strasberg at the Actor's Studio and Stella Adler
Debut: (Film) *Who's That Knocking at My Door?*, 1968
Signature: *Bad Lieutenant*
Facts: Joined the U.S. Marine Corps at age 16 and served in Lebanon.

Answered a newspaper ad placed by Martin Scorsese, then an NYU student director, seeking actors for his first film in 1965, which started their professional relationship.

Was cast as the lead in *Apocalypse Now*, but had a falling out with director Francis Ford Coppola and was fired on location in the Philippines. He was replaced by Martin Sheen.

As a child, Keitel had a severe stutter.

Unusual among Hollywood actors for his willingness to show frontal nudity in his films (The Piano, Bad Lieutenant).

Infamy: Was asked to leave the Alexander Hamilton Vocational School in Brooklyn because of truancy.

Original Job: Shoe salesman

Marriage: Lorraine Bracco (divorced)

Child: Stella

Address: William Morris Agency, 151 El Camino Dr., Beverly Hills, CA 90212

JOHN F. KENNEDY JR.

Birthplace: Washington, DC

Birthdate: 11/25/60

Occupation: Editor-in-chief of new political magazine, George

Education: Brown University, attended University of Delhi, India, New York University Law School

Facts: First baby in the White House since 1893.

Worked in the Peace Corps in Guatemala following a devastating earthquake.

Failed the bar exam twice.

Famous Relatives: John F. Kennedy, president, father; Jacqueline Onassis, first lady, mother; Ted Kennedy, senator, uncle

Relationship: Carolyn Bessette

Address: George, 1633 Broadway, 41st Floor, New York, NY 10019

NICOLE KIDMAN

Birthplace: Hawaii

Birthdate: 6/20/67

Occupation: Actor

Education: St. Martin's Youth Theatre, Melbourne, Australia

Debut: (Film) Bush Christmas, 1983

Signature: Dead Calm

Facts: Became an overnight star in Australia with her performance in the miniseries Vietnam, 1988.

Joined the Church of Scientology, of which husband Cruise is a devoted member.

Marriage: Tom Cruise

Children: Isabella Jane (adopted), Connor Antony (adopted)

Address: Creative Artists Agency, 9830 Wilshire Blvd., Beverly Hills, CA 90212

ANTHONY KIEDIS

Birthplace: Grand Rapids, MI

Birthdate: 11/1/62

Occupation: Singer

Education: Attended UCLA

Debut: (Album) Red Hot Chili Peppers, 1984

Signature: Red Hot Chili Peppers

Facts: He and fellow Chili Pepper Michael "Flea" Balzary were classmates at Hollywood's Fairfax High School.

Played Sylvester Stallone's son in the 1978 film F.I.S.T.

The group was originally called Tony Flow and the Miraculously Majestic Masters of Mayhem.

Quit taking drugs, drinking, and eating meat after guitarist Hillel Slovak died of a heroin overdose in 1988. The RHCP songs "Under the Bridge," "Knock Me Down," and "My Lovely Man" all relate to Slovak's death.

Infamy: Kiedis appeared in U.S. Health Department ads advocating the use of condoms to stop AIDS, but the ads never ran—government officials yanked them when they learned that Kiedis had once been charged with lewdness for exposing himself to a female University of Virginia student backstage after a concert.

Original Job: Actor

Famous Relative: Blackie Dammett, actor, father

Major Award: Grammy, Best Hard Rock Song, "Give It Away" (with Red Hot Chili Peppers), 1992

Address: Warner Brothers Recording, 3300 Warner Blvd., Burbank, CA 91505

VAL KILMER

Birthplace: Los Angeles, CA

Birthdate: 12/31/59

Occupation: Actor

Education: Hollywood Professional School, Juilliard

Debut: (Stage) Slab Boys, 1983; (TV) One Too Many, 1985; (Film) Top Secret!, 1984

Signature: The Doors

Facts: Grew up in Chatsworth, CA, across the road from the Roy Rogers ranch. Was the middle child of three boys.

His younger brother, Wesley, drowned right before he left for Juilliard.

At 17, was the youngest person ever accepted to Juilliard's drama school. Cowrote a play with Juilliard classmates, How It All Began; starred in an off-Broadway production at the New York Shakespeare Festival.

Met Joanne Whalley on the set of Willow in 1988. Pursued her persistently until she finally agreed to marry him.

Provided much of the vocals for the film The Doors.

Lives in a cabin in Santa Fe, NM. Is part Cherokee and spends his leisure time exploring the Southwest.

Marriage: Joanne Whalley (separated)

Child: Mercedes

Famous Relatives: Joyce Kilmer, poet, second cousin twice removed

Address: Creative Artists Agency, 9830 Wilshire Blvd., Beverly Hills, CA 90212

LARRY KING

Real Name: Lawrence Harvey Zeiger

Birthplace: Brooklyn, NY

Birthdate: 11/19/33

Occupation: Talk show host

Facts: In February of 1992, Ross Perot announced his bid for the presidency on Larry King Live.

Father died of a heart attack when he was 10, and he grew up on public assistance.

As a teenager, ran away to get married. Had the ceremony annulled shortly thereafter.

Graduated from high school just one point above passing.

Infamy: In December of 1971, he was arrested for stealing money a financier had given him for the New Orleans D.A.'s investigation into the death of John F. Kennedy. King had used the money to pay taxes after he had blown his own money on Cadillacs, expensive restaurants, and gambling debts. The charge was eventually dropped.

Original Job: Janitor at a local AM radio station in Florida

Marriages: Alene Akins (divorced, remarried, divorced), Mickey Sutphin (divorced), Sharon Leporte (divorced), Julie Alexander (divorced), Deanna Lund (engaged)

Child: Chaia

Address: CNN Larry King Live, 820 1st St., NE, Washington, DC 20002

STEPHEN KING

Birthplace: Portland, ME

Birthdate: 9/21/47

Occupation: Author

Education: University of Maine

Debut: (Book) Carrie, 1974

Signature: Horror novels

Facts: Family was deserted by father, who went out for a pack of cigarettes and never returned.

Wrote first short story at age seven.

Had his first story published in a comic book fan magazine, Comics Review, in 1965.

Was working as a high school English teacher at Hampden Academy, in Maine, when his first book was published.

Used the pseudonym Richard Bachman for five novels, including The Running Man (made into an Arnold Schwarzenegger film, 1987).

Original Job: Laborer in an industrial laundry

Marriage: Tabitha Spruce

Children: Joe, Owen, Naomi

Address: Creative Artists Agency, 9830 Wilshire Blvd., Beverly Hills, CA 90212

GREG KINNEAR

Birthplace: Logansport, IN

Birthdate: 1964

Occupation: Talk show host

Education: University of Arizona

Debut: (TV) Movietime, 1987

Signature: Talk Soup

Facts: Lived in Beirut, Lebanon, with family and then evacuated to Athens, Greece, when the Lebanese civil war broke out.

Worked on the advertising campaigns for such films as Space Sluts in the Slammer, The Imp, and the Ghoulies series.

Hosted syndicated action game show, College Mad House.

Address: William Morris Agency, 151 El Camino Dr., Beverly Hills, CA 90212

CALVIN KLEIN

Real Name: Richard Klein

Birthplace: New York, NY

Birthdate: 11/19/42

Occupation: Fashion designer

Education: Fashion Institute of Technology

Facts: Rescued his daughter from kidnappers in 1978.

As a boy in the Bronx, grew up around the corner from Ralph Lifshitz (now Ralph Lauren).

Former junk bond czar Michael Milken issued $80 million in high-interest Klein bonds in the '80s.

Infamy: Was addicted to valium and alcohol in the '80s, and attended a Minnesota rehabilitation center for 31 days in 1988.

Marriages: Jayne Centre (divorced), Kelly Rector

Child: Marci

Major Awards: Coty Award,

1973, 1974,1975; elected to American Fashion Critics Circle Hall of Fame, 1975; Council of Fashion Designers of America Award, 1994
Quote: "Anything I've ever wanted to do, I've done. Anyone I've wanted to be with, I've had."
Address: Calvin Klein, Ltd., 205 West 39th St., New York, NY 10018

TED KOPPEL

Birthplace: Lancashire, England
Birthdate: 2/8/40
Occupation: Broadcast journalist
Education: Syracuse University, Stanford University
Debut: (Radio) WMCA radio
Signature: *Nightline*
Facts: Author, *Adlai Stevenson: In the National Interest.*

When he joined ABC in 1963, he was the youngest news reporter ever to join a network.

Emigrated to the U.S. from England in 1953.
Marriage: Grace Anne Dorney
Children: Andrea, Deidre, Andrew, Tara
Major Award: Elected to the Emmy Hall of Fame, 1991
Address: ABC, 77 West 66th St., New York, NY 10023

KARL LAGERFELD

Birthplace: Hamburg, Germany
Birthdate: 9/10/38
Occupation: Fashion designer
Education: Lycée Montaigne
Debut: First prize, women's coat design, International Wool Secretariat contest, 1954
Facts: Drew illustrations for books as a child. Apprenticed to Pierre Balmain, designing clothes for Sophia Loren, Rita Hayworth, and Gina Lollobrigida.

Led the pret-à-porter wave of designers in the '60s in Paris, working at various times for Fendi furs and Charles Jourdan shoes.

Initiated art deco revival in early '70s.

Created the perfume Chloé for Elizabeth Arden (1975). Under the pen name Minouflet de Vermenou, he reviews books for French *Vogue.*
Infamy: Refused director Robert Altman access to his Paris show to film *Pret-a-Porter;* sued Altman after the film's release, claiming it referred to Lagerfeld as "a thief of ideas."
Address: 3 West 57th St., New York, NY 10019

RICKI LAKE

Birthplace: New York, NY
Birthdate: 9/21/68
Occupation: Actor, talk show host
Education: Attended Ithaca College
Debut: (Film) *Hairspray,* 1988
Signature: *The Ricki Lake Show*
Facts: This once-dumpy star of John Waters' cult films like *Cry Baby* lost 125 pounds over a three-year period.

Plays the flute, piccolo, clarinet, and piano.
Infamy: Arrested in 1994 for criminal mischief for her part in a People for the Ethical Treatment of Animals attack on the offices of designer Karl Lagerfeld.
Original Job: Cabaret singer, appeared off-Broadway in 1983
Marriage: Rob Sussman
Address: William Morris Agency, 151 El Camino Dr., Beverly Hills, CA 90212

K.D. LANG

Real Name: Katherine Dawn Lang
Birthplace: Consort, Canada
Birthdate: 9/2/61
Occupation: Singer, songwriter
Education: Attended college in Red Deer, Alberta, Canada
Debut: (Album) *A Truly Western Experience,* 1984
Facts: Acted in the movie *Salmonberries,* 1991.

Recorded a duet with Roy Orbison on a remake of his song "Crying" in 1988, shortly before he died.
Infamy: Her recordings have been boycotted in the conservative areas of the South and cattle ranching areas of central Canada because she is a lesbian and an animal rights activist.
Original Job: Performance artist
Major Awards: Grammy, Best Country Vocal—Collaboration,

"Crying" (with Roy Orbison), 1988; Grammy, Best Country Vocal—Female, "Absolute Torch and Twang," 1989; Grammy, Best Pop Vocal—Female, "Constant Craving," 1992
Quote: "I have a little bit of penis envy. They're ridiculous, but they're cool."
Address: Sire Records, 75 Rockefeller Plaza, New York, NY 10019

JESSICA LANGE

Birthplace: Cloquet, MN
Birthdate: 4/20/49
Occupation: Actor
Education: Attended University of Minnesota
Debut: (Film) *King Kong,* 1976
Signature: *The Postman Always Rings Twice*
Facts: Raised in a depression-prone family with an alcoholic father who moved the family repeatedly, Lange adopted a full-blown, travel-and-party lifestyle as a young adult.

Had a relationship (and a child) with Mikhail Baryshnikov.

The 1994 film *Blue Sky,* for which she won a best actress Academy Award (after four previous nominations), languished in a bank vault after it was made in 1991 because its studio, Orion Pictures, had declared bankruptcy.
Original Job: Dancer, model
Marriages: Paco Grande (divorced), Sam Shepard (relationship)
Children: Alexandra, Hannah, Walker
Major Awards: Oscar, Best Supporting Actress, *Tootsie,* 1982; Oscar, Best Actress, *Blue Sky,* 1994; Golden Globe, Best Actress, *Blue Sky,* 1995
Address: Creative Artists Agency, 9830 Wilshire Blvd., Beverly Hills, CA 90212

ANGELA LANSBURY

Birthplace: London, England
Birthdate: 10/16/25
Occupation: Actor
Education: Attended Webber-Douglas School of Singing and Dramatic Art, attended Feagin School of Drama and Radio
Debut: (Film) *Gaslight,* 1944
Signature: *Murder, She Wrote*
Facts: Immigrated with her family to the U.S. when the Germans began to bomb London in World War II.

In 1943, went to MGM to audition for *The Picture of*

Dorian Gray and was told the studio was looking for someone to play the role of the maid in *Gaslight.* She auditioned and got it.

In the seven years she was under contract to MGM, she appeared in 70 films.
Original Job: Ticket-taker in the theater in which her mother worked, clerk in department store
Marriages: Richard Cromwell (divorced), Peter Pullen Shaw
Children: Anthony Peter, Deidre Angela
Famous Relatives: Moyna McGill, actor, mother; David Lansbury, actor, nephew
Major Awards: Golden Globe, Best Supporting Actress, *The Picture of Dorian Gray,* 1946; Golden Globe, Best Supporting Actress, *The Manchurian Candidate,* 1963; Golden Globe, Best Actress in a TV Series—Drama, *Murder, She Wrote,* 1985, 1987, 1990, 1992; Tony, Best Actress (Musical), *Mame,* 1966; Tony, Best Actress (Musical), *Dear World,* 1969; Tony, Best Actress (Musical), *Gypsy,* 1975; Tony, Best Actress (Musical), *Sweeney Todd,* 1979
Address: William Morris Agency, 151 El Camino Dr., Beverly Hills, CA 90212

JOHN LARROQUETTE

Birthplace: New Orleans, LA
Birthdate: 11/25/47
Occupation: Actor
Debut: (TV) *Doctor's Hospital,* 1976
Signature: *Night Court*
Facts: Narrator of *The Texas Chainsaw Massacre.*

Played squadron member Robert Anderson in the TV series *Baa Baa Black Sheep,* 1976–78.

Larroquette is an alcoholic who sobered up without the help of Alcoholics Anonymous.
Original Job: Disc jockey
Marriage: Elizabeth
Children: Lisa, Jonathan, Benjamin
Major Award: Emmy, Best Supporting Actor in a Comedy Series, *Night Court,* 1985, 1986, 1987, 1988
Address: Creative Artists Agency, 9830 Wilshire Blvd., Beverly Hills, CA 90212

QUEEN LATIFAH

Real Name: Dana Owens
Birthplace: East Orange, NJ
Birthdate: 3/18/70
Occupation: Rap artist, actor

Education: High school
Debut: (Album) *All Hail the Queen*, 1989; (TV) *The Fresh Prince of Bel-Air*, 1991; (Film) *Jungle Fever*, 1991
Facts: Was a power forward on two state championship basketball teams in high school.

Trained in karate and use of firearms by her policeman father.

CEO of Flavor Unit, a management and production company whose clients have included Naughty by Nature and FU-Schnickens.

Brother Lance Owens Jr., died at age 24 in a motorcycle accident in 1992; "Winky's Theme" on the album *Black Reign* was dedicated to him.
Infamy: Charged in a municipal misdemeanor complaint in 1995 after 240 illegally copied tapes were found in a video store she had sold in 1994.
Original Job: Worked at Burger King, cashier at the Wiz
Major Award: Grammy, Best Rap Solo Performance, *U.N.I.T.Y.*, 1994
Address: Polygram Holding, Inc., 825 8th Ave., New York, NY 10019

MARTIN LAWRENCE

Birthplace: Frankfurt, Germany
Birthdate: 4/16/65
Occupation: Actor
Education: High school
Debut: (TV) *What's Happening Now*, 1985; (Film) *Do the Right Thing*, 1989
Signature: *Martin*
Facts: He was a *Star Search* winner, a street performer in Washington Square Park, and a stand-up comedian at the Improv's open-mike night.

Worked at Sears in Queens with Salt-N-Pepa and Kid 'N Play.
Infamy: After a 1994 appearance on *Saturday Night Live* in which he told women to "put a Tic-Tac in your ass" to remain clean, Lawrence was banned from all NBC productions.
Original Job: Gas station attendant, store clerk
Marriage: Patricia Southall
Address: United Talent Agency, 9560 Wilshire Blvd., Suite 500, Beverly Hills, CA 90212

PAMELA LEE

Birthplace: Comox, Canada
Birthdate: 7/1/67
Occupation: Actor
Education: High school
Debut: (TV) *Home Improvement*, 1991
Signature: *Baywatch*
Facts: Got her first commercial job after her image was projected on a giant scoreboard screen at a Canadian football game in 1989.

Says her mother encouraged her to pose for her several *Playboy* covers, telling her it was a compliment.

Writes fairy tales and poetry and regularly keeps a dream diary.

Married Motley Crüe drummer Tommy Lee in Cancun, Mexico, in 1995 wearing a tiny white bikini. (Lee wore white Bermuda shorts.)
Original Job: Beer company spokesmodel
Marriage: Tommy Lee
Address: 8730 Sunset Blvd., #220, Los Angeles, CA 90069

SPIKE LEE

Real Name: Shelton Lee
Birthplace: Atlanta, GA
Birthdate: 3/20/57
Occupation: Filmmaker, director
Education: Morehouse College, New York University
Debut: (Film) *She's Gotta Have It*, 1986
Signature: *Do the Right Thing*
Facts: Known as an unofficial New York Knick, sitting courtside and shouting out to players on both teams. During the 1994 Eastern Conference Championships, some fans felt that his harassment of an Indiana Pacer caused the player to score the most points in the game and defeat the Knicks.

Taught at Harvard as a visiting professor in 1992.

A film he made at NYU, *Joe's Barbershop: We Cut Heads*, was the first student work ever selected for Lincoln Center's "New Directors, New Films" showcase and won a student award from the Academy of Motion Pictures Arts and Sciences.
Infamy: Accused by the Anti-Defamation League of B'Nai Brith of fostering anti-Semitism through his films, most notably via his portrayal of two Jewish nightclub owners in *Mo' Better Blues*.
Original Job: Advertising copywriter
Marriage: Tonya Linette Lewis
Child: Satchel Lewis
Address: International Creative Management, 8942 Wilshire Blvd., Beverly Hills, CA 90211

JENNIFER JASON LEIGH

Real Name: Jennifer Morrow
Birthplace: Los Angeles, CA
Birthdate: 2/5/62
Occupation: Actor
Education: Lee Strasberg Institute
Debut: (Film) *Death of a Stranger*, 1971
Signature: *The Best Little Girl in the World*
Facts: In order to prepare for roles, she writes a complete imaginary diary for the character.

Dieted down to 86 pounds for her role as an anorexic in the TV movie *The Best Little Girl in the World*, 1981.

When her father, Vic Morrow, was killed in a helicopter accident while filming *Twilight Zone: The Movie*, Leigh and her family reportedly mourned by watching his old films through the night.
Famous Relatives: Vic Morrow, actor, father; Barbara Turner, screenwriter, mother; Mina Badie, actor, half sister
Major Award: Golden Globe, Special Achievement, *Short Cuts*, 1994
Address: International Creative Management, 8942 Wilshire Blvd., Beverly Hills, CA 90211

LAURA LEIGHTON

Real Name: Laura Miller
Birthplace: Iowa City, IA
Birthdate: 7/24/68
Education: High school
Signature: *Melrose Place*
Facts: In 1987, toured with the traveling singing troupe Young Americans.

Her role on *Melrose Place* was originally intended to last just two episodes.
Original Job: Pizza Hut commercial actress, waitress
Relationship: Grant Show (engaged)
Quote: "I didn't even have a television when I was growing up."
Address: 924 Westwood Blvd., 9th Fl., Los Angeles, CA 90024

JAY LENO

Real Name: James Leno
Birthplace: New Rochelle, NY
Birthdate: 4/28/50
Occupation: Talk show host, comedian
Education: Emerson College
Debut: (TV) *The Marilyn McCoo & Billy Davis Jr. Show*, 1977; (Film) *Silver Bears*, 1978
Signature: *The Tonight Show*

Facts: Collects antique cars and motorcycles.

Made his first appearance on *The Tonight Show* in 1977.

While in grade school, Leno executed such pranks as flushing tennis balls down the toilet and hiding a dog in his locker. His fifth grade teacher wrote on his report card, "If Jay spent as much time studying as he does trying to be a comedian, he'd be a big star."
Original Job: Rolls-Royce mechanic, deliveryman
Marriage: Mavis Nicholson
Address: International Creative Management, 8942 Wilshire Blvd., Beverly Hills, CA 90211

DAVID LETTERMAN

Birthplace: Indianapolis, IN
Birthdate: 4/12/47
Occupation: Talk show host
Education: Ball State University
Debut: (TV) *The Starland Vocal Band Show*, 1977
Signature: *Late Show with David Letterman*
Facts: While working as a weather announcer at a local TV station, he congratulated a tropical storm on being upgraded to a hurricane.

Was the announcer for the late-night movie program *Freeze Dried Movies*. On the program, he blew up a model of the television station at which he was working.
Infamy: Margaret Ray has continually stalked him at his New Canaan, CT, home. She was caught at or in his home eight times from 1988–1993.
Original Job: TV announcer, weatherman
Marriage: Michelle Cook (divorced), Regina Lasko (relationship)
Major Awards: Emmy, Best Host

of a Daytime Variety Series, *The David Letterman Show*, 1981; Emmy, Writing in a Variety or Music Show, *Late Night with David Letterman*, 1984, 1985, 1986, 1987
Address: Worldwide Pants Inc., 1697 Broadway, New York, NY 10019

JULIETTE LEWIS

Birthplace: San Fernando Valley, CA
Birthdate: 6/21/73
Occupation: Actor
Debut: (TV) *I Married Dora*, 1987; (Film) *My Stepmother Is an Alien*, 1988
Signature: *Cape Fear*
Facts: In 1987 went to court to become legally "emancipated" so that she would be exempt from laws that limit child actors to five hours of work on school days.

Lived with Brad Pitt for four years. She met him on the set of the TV movie *Too Young To Die* in 1989.
Famous Relative: Geoffrey Lewis, actor, father
Address: William Morris Agency, 151 El Camino Dr., Beverly Hills, CA 90212

RUSH LIMBAUGH

Birthplace: Cape Girardeau, MO
Birthdate: 12/12/51
Occupation: Talk show host
Education: Attended Southeastern Missouri State University
Debut: (Radio) *The Rush Limbaugh Show*
Facts: Claims he does not own a pair of blue jeans.

More than 300 "Rush rooms" have opened in restaurants nationwide for the purpose of broadcasting Rush Limbaugh's programs to patrons.

Met his current wife, Marta Fitzgerald, via electronic mail on CompuServe Information Service. They were married by Supreme Court Justice Clarence Thomas.
Infamy: In February 1994, the Florida Citrus Commission advertised orange juice on Limbaugh's show. The ads generated 7,500 calls to the Commission protesting their choice of such a controversial figure to promote their product. The National Organization for Women, as well as various gay and lesbian groups, urged people to boycott Florida orange juice. Meanwhile, about 30 Rush supporters bought out the entire supply of orange juice

at an Orlando, Florida store in a counterprotest.
Original Job: Disc jockey, PR man for the Kansas City Royals
Marriages: Roxy Maxine McNeely (divorced), Michelle Sixta (divorced), Marta Fitzgerald
Address: 924 Westwood Blvd., 9th Fl., Los Angeles, CA 90024

HEATHER LOCKLEAR

Birthplace: Los Angeles, CA
Birthdate: 9/25/61
Occupation: Actor
Education: Attended UCLA
Debut: (TV) *Dynasty*, 1981
Signature: *Dynasty*
Facts: Served over six years as the spokesperson for the Health and Tennis Corporation of America.

Played officer Stacy Sheridan on the crime drama series *T.J. Hooker* with William Shatner, 1982–87.

When she joined the cast of *Melrose Place*, the series's audience jumped 50 percent.
Marriage: Tommy Lee (divorced), Richie Sambora
Address: William Morris Agency, 151 El Camino Dr., Beverly Hills, CA 90212

JULIA LOUIS-DREYFUS

Birthplace: New York, NY
Birthdate: 1/13/61
Occupation: Actor
Education: Northwestern University
Debut: (TV) *Saturday Night Live*, 1982; (Film) *Hannah and Her Sisters*, 1986
Signature: *Seinfeld*
Facts: Parents were divorced when she was only one year old.

Met husband in college and worked with him on *Saturday Night Live*.

Her role in *Seinfeld* was not in the original mix created by Jerry Seinfeld and Larry David, but was imposed by the network, which felt a female perspective was needed.
Original Job: Member of the Second City comedy troupe
Marriage: Brad Hall
Child: Henry
Major Award: Golden Globe, Best Supporting Actress, *Seinfeld*, 1993
Address: United Talent Agency, 9560 Wilshire Blvd., Suite 500, Beverly Hills, CA 90212

COURTNEY LOVE

Real Name: Courtney Menely
Birthplace: San Francisco, CA

Birthdate: 7/9/64
Occupation: Singer, songwriter
Education: High school dropout
Debut: (Album) *Pretty on the Inside*, 1991
Signature: Hole
Facts: Ran away to Europe at 15; her grandfather's death left her a millionaire.

Mother was the psychologist who examined Katherine Anne Power ('60s radical and fugitive who recently confessed to being an accessory to bank robbery).

Appeared in the film *Straight to Hell*, 1987.

Before founding Hole, Love was lead vocalist for the San Diego rock band Faith No More in the early '80s "for about a week" (before they found Chuck Mosely). She also played with Kat Bjelland of the Minneapolis all-girl band Babes in Toyland and future L7 member Jennifer Finch in Sugar Baby Doll.

Named daughter after the '30s actress Frances Farmer, who is the subject of Nirvana song "Frances Farmer Will Have Her Revenge on Seattle."
Infamy: In her early teens, was sent to a juvenile detention center after stealing a Kiss T-shirt from a department store.

A *Vanity Fair* article described Love as shooting heroin while pregnant. Though she denied the charge, child-welfare authorities temporarily removed the baby after she was born.

Arrested in 1995 for verbally abusing a flight attendant aboard an Australian flight. She was not convicted, but ordered to remain on good behavior for one month.
Original Job: Danced in strip joints in L.A. and Alaska
Marriage: Kurt Cobain (deceased)
Child: Frances Bean
Famous Relatives: Linda Carroll, psychologist, mother; Hank Harrison, author, father
Address: William Morris Agency, 151 El Camino Dr., Beverly Hills, CA 90212

LYLE LOVETT

Birthplace: Klein, TX
Birthdate: 11/1/57
Occupation: Singer, songwriter
Education: Texas A&M
Debut: (Album) *Lyle Lovett*, 1986
Facts: Played guitar in coffee shops while in college.

Lives in a clapboard house built by his grandparents.

Is afraid of cows.

Marriage: Julia Roberts (separated)
Major Awards: Grammy, *Lyle Lovett and His Large Band*, 1989; Grammy, Best Pop Vocal Collaboration, "Funny How Time Slips Away" (with Al Green), 1994; Grammy, Best Country Group Performance with Vocal, "Blues for Dixie" (with Asleep at the Wheel), 1994
Address: International Creative Management, 8942 Wilshire Blvd., Beverly Hills, CA 90211

JON LOVITZ

Birthplace: Tarzana, CA
Birthdate: 7/21/57
Occupation: Actor
Education: Attended University of California–Irvine
Debut: (TV) *The Paper Chase*, 1984; (Film) *The Last Resort*, 1986
Signature: *Saturday Night Live*
Facts: Provided the voice for the animated sitcom *The Critic*. Has also provided voices for *The Simpsons* and the film *An American Tail 2: Fievel goes West*, 1991.

Had his own special, *The Please Watch the Jon Lovitz Special*, which aired in 1992.
Infamy: Grabbed Jamie Lee Curtis's breast during the American Comedy Awards in 1995. She looked shocked, then grabbed his crotch. Critics pounced on his lack of decorum, although Curtis later said it was a planned joke.
Original Job: Waiter, orderly, messenger
Quote: "Anybody who tells you he doesn't want to be famous is full of crap."
Address: Creative Artists Agency, 9830 Wilshire Blvd., Beverly Hills, CA 90212

ROB LOWE

Birthplace: Charlottesville, VA
Birthdate: 3/17/64
Occupation: Actor
Education: High school
Debut: (TV) *A New Kind of Family*, 1978
Signature: *St. Elmo's Fire*
Facts: As a child, he memorized all the lines to *The Wizard of Oz* and liked to dress up as Batman.

Played in the celebrity all-star game at Dodger Stadium while in high school, where his classmates included Emilio Estevez and Sean Penn.

Is deaf in his right ear.

Infamy: Lowe admitted to having sex with a teenage girl and recording the act, and was sued by her mother. He performed 20 hours of community service.
Marriage: Sheryl Berkoff
Child: Edward Matthew
Famous Relative: Chad Lowe, actor, brother
Address: William Morris Agency, 151 El Camino Dr., Beverly Hills, CA 90212

SUSAN LUCCI

Birthplace: Scarsdale, NY
Birthdate: 12/23/50
Occupation: Actor
Education: Marymount College
Debut: (TV) *All My Children,* 1969
Signature: *All My Children*
Facts: Was nominated 15 times for the best actress in a daytime series, and lost every time.

Made the semifinals in New York State Miss Universe pageant, 1968. Dropped out of the competition to finish her college exams.

As Erica Kane, Lucci has impersonated a nun, been kidnapped, rescued a lover from prison using a helicopter, and stared down a grizzly bear.
Original Job: "Color girl" for CBS, sitting for cameras as a new lighting system for color TV was being developed
Marriage: Helmut Huber
Children: Liza Victoria, Andreas Martin
Address: International Creative Management, 8942 Wilshire Blvd., Beverly Hills, CA 90211

JOAN LUNDEN

Real Name: Joan Blunden
Birthplace: Fair Oaks, CA
Birthdate: 9/19/50
Occupation: Television show host
Education: Attended Universidad de las Americas, American River Junior College
Signature: *Good Morning America*
Facts: Father died in a plane crash when she was 12; she claims that sparked her need to become "Miss Organization Freak," down to laying out her next day's clothes—in order—before she goes to sleep.

Co-author of parenting books *Joan Lunden's Mothers' Minutes* and *Your Newborn Baby;* author of the syndicated column "Parents Notes."

Original Job: Owner of charm school, TV reporter
Marriage: Michael Krauss (divorced)
Children: Jamie Beryl, Lindsay Leigh, Sarah Emily
Address: *Good Morning America,* ABC, 77 West 66th St., New York, NY 10023

LORETTA LYNN

Real Name: Loretta Webb
Birthplace: Butcher Hollow, KY
Birthdate: 4/14/35
Occupation: Singer, songwriter
Debut: (Single) "Honky Tonk Girl," 1960
Signature: "Coal Miner's Daughter"
Facts: First woman to earn a certified gold country album.

While her kids were still young, her husband gave her a guitar to accompany the singing she did around the house. She taught herself to play.

Her first No. 1 single, "Don't Come Home A-Drinkin' (With Lovin' on Your Mind)" was banned from several stations. Many of her songs have been banned, including "Rated X" and "The Pill."

Married when she was 13. "By the time I was 17, I had four kids, and I had never been anywhere." She was a grandmother at 31, one year after her twins (her last children) were born.
Marriage: Oliver Vanetta Lynn Jr.
Children: Betty Sue Lynn Markworth, Jack Benny (deceased), Clara Lynn Lyell, Ernest Ray, Peggy, Patsy
Famous Relative: Crystal Gayle, singer, sister
Major Awards: Grammy, Best Country Performance—Duo or Group, "After the Fire Is Gone" (with Conway Twitty), 1971; Grammy, Best Recording for Children, *Sesame Country* (with others), 1981; inducted into the Country Music Hall of Fame, 1988
Address: MCA Records, 70 Universal Plaza, Universal City, CA 91608

ANDIE MACDOWELL

Real Name: Rosalie Anderson MacDowell
Birthplace: Gaffney, SC
Birthdate: 4/21/58
Occupation: Actor
Education: Attended Winthrop College
Debut: (Film) *Greystoke: The*

Legend of Tarzan, Lord of the Apes, 1984
Signature: *Green Card*
Facts: After *Greystoke* was filmed, MacDowell's part was overdubbed with a British accent provided by Glenn Close.

Played Jimi Hendrix's "Angel" at her wedding.
Original Job: Elite model
Marriage: Paul Qualley
Children: Justin, Rainey, Sarah Margaret
Major Award: Golden Globe, Special Achievement, *Short Cuts,* 1994
Address: International Creative Management, 8942 Wilshire Blvd., Beverly Hills, CA 90211

KYLE MACLACHLAN

Birthplace: Yakima, WA
Birthdate: 2/22/59
Occupation: Actor
Education: University of Washington, Seattle
Debut: (Film) *Dune,* 1984
Signature: *Twin Peaks*
Fact: Read the Hardy Boys and imagined himself as one of the investigators.
Marriage: Linda Evangelista
Major Award: Golden Globe, Best Actor in a Drama Series, *Twin Peaks,* 1991
Address: United Talent Agency, 9560 Wilshire Blvd., Suite 500, Beverly Hills, CA 90212

SHIRLEY MACLAINE

Real Name: Shirley MacLean Beaty
Birthplace: Richmond, VA
Birthdate: 4/24/34
Occupation: Actor, author
Education: Washington School of Ballet
Debut: (Stage) *Oklahoma!,* 1950
Signature: *Terms of Endearment*
Facts: Starred in her own TV series, *Shirley's World* (1971–72).

Was performing with the Washington School of Ballet by the time she was 12, but soon grew too tall to be a ballerina.

Following a showbiz cliché, she got the lead in the 1954 Broadway show *The Pajama Game* when the lead hurt her ankle.

As a young girl, often had to come to the aid of her bookish and picked-on younger brother with fists blazing.
Infamy: Ridiculed for her oft-expressed beliefs in reincarnation, detailed in her best-selling books *Out on a Limb* and *Danc-*

ing in the Light. Satirized herself in the "Pavilion of Former Lives" in the film *Defending Your Life* (1991).

Had an open marriage with husband Parker, but was stunned to learn from a channeler (later confirmed by a private eye) that he had transferred millions of dollars to his girlfriend's account.

Wrote a tell-all book in 1995, detailing how Debra Winger mooned her and broke wind, and describing Frank Sinatra as "a perpetual kid" and "someone who muscled others." Sinatra's response to the book: "It's amazing what a broad will do for a buck."
Original Job: Dancer
Marriage: Steve Parker (divorced)
Child: Stephanie Sachiko
Famous Relative: Warren Beatty, actor, brother
Major Awards: Golden Globe, New Female Star of the Year, 1955; Golden Globe, Best Actress, *Some Came Running,* 1959; Golden Globe, Most Versatile Actress, 1959; Golden Globe, Best Actress in a Comedy, *The Apartment,* 1961; Golden Globe, Best Actress, *Irma la Douce,* 1964; Golden Globe, Best Actress, *Terms of Endearment,* 1984; Golden Globe, Best Actress, *Madame Sousatzka,* 1989; Emmy, Outstanding Comedy-Variety or Musical Special, *Shirley MacLaine: If They Could See Me Now,* 1974; Emmy, Outstanding Comedy-Variety or Musical Special, *Gypsy in My Soul,* 1976; Emmy, Outstanding Writing of Variety or Music Program, *Shirley MacLaine... Every Little Movement,* 1980; Oscar, Best Actress, *Terms of Endearment,* 1983
Address: International Creative Management, 8942 Wilshire Blvd., Beverly Hills, CA 90211

ELLE MACPHERSON

Real Name: Eleanor Gow
Birthplace: Sydney, Australia
Birthdate: 1965
Occupation: Supermodel, actor
Debut: *Sports Illustrated* swimsuit model, *Sirens,* 1994
Facts: Appeared in every issue of *Elle* magazine from 1982 to 1988.

Launched a designer lingerie line in Australia and New Zealand in 1991.

Opened Fashion Cafe in New York City in 1995 with super-

models Claudia Schiffer and Naomi Campbell.
Marriage: Gilles Bensimon (divorced), Tim Jeffries (relationship)
Address: International Creative Management, 8942 Wilshire Blvd., Beverly Hills, CA 90211

JOHN MADDEN

Birthplace: Austin, MN
Birthdate: 4/10/36
Occupation: Sportscaster
Education: California Polytechnic University
Debut: Assistant coach, Santa Maria, CA
Signature: CBS football analyst
Fact: Coached the Oakland Raiders for 10 years and had a record of 103-32-7.

Intensely afraid of flying, he always takes a train or a bus to cover games.
Marriage: Virginia Fields
Major Awards: American Football League Coach of the Year, 1960; American Sportscaster Association, Sports Personality of the Year, 1985; Emmy, Best Sports Personality—Analyst, 1982, 1983, 1985, 1986, 1987, 1988
Address: Fox Broadcasting Co., 10201 West Pico Blvd., Los Angeles, CA 90035

MADONNA

Real Name: Madonna Louise Veronica Ciccone
Birthplace: Bay City, MI
Birthdate: 8/16/58
Occupation: Singer
Education: Attended University of Michigan
Debut: Dancer, Alvin Ailey Dance Company, 1979
Signature: "Material Girl"
Facts: She starred in an exploitation film called *A Certain Sacrifice* in 1980.

Early in her career, posed nude for a New York photographer. Those photos later appeared in *Playboy*.

She appears in a nightclub scene from the 1983 movie *Vision Quest*, singing "Crazy for You" in the background.
Infamy: Swore 14 times while on *The Late Show with David Letterman*, to get revenge for his many jokes at her expense. She also handed Letterman a pair of her panties and told him to smell them.

Her video for "Justify My Love" (1990) was banned from MTV.

Her book *Sex* (1992) was originally banned in Japan, where it

is against the law to show pubic hair. Officials eventually relented since the book was being distributed anyway.
Original Job: Model, worked in a doughnut shop
Marriage: Sean Penn (divorced), Carlos Leon (relationship)
Major Awards: Grammy, Best Music Video—Long Form, *Madonna—Blonde Ambition World Tour Live*, 1991
Address: Creative Artists Agency, 9830 Wilshire Blvd., Beverly Hills, CA 90212

JOHN MALKOVICH

Birthplace: Christopher, IL
Birthdate: 12/9/53
Occupation: Actor
Education: Attended Eastern Illinois University, Illinois State University
Debut: (Stage) *True West*, 1982
Signature: *Dangerous Liaisons*
Facts: Played football and tuba in high school.

Took up acting in college when he fell for a female drama student.

Co-founded the Steppenwolf Theatre in Chicago, in 1976.
Original Job: Enrolled in Eastern Illinois University with plans of becoming an environmentalist
Marriages: Glenne Headly (divorced), Nicoletta Peyran
Children: Amandine, Lowey
Major Award: Emmy, Best Supporting Actor in a Made-for-TV Movie, *Death of a Salesman*, 1986
Address: International Creative Management, 8942 Wilshire Blvd., Beverly Hills, CA 90211

DAVID MAMET

Birthplace: Chicago, IL
Birthdate: 11/30/47
Occupation: Writer, director
Education: Goddard College, studied at the Neighborhood Playhouse in New York
Debut: (Stage) *The Duck Variations*, 1971
Signature: *Glengarry Glen Ross*
Facts: Wrote several children's plays and books, including, *Warm and Cold*, in 1985.

Has worked as a busboy, driven a cab, worked at *Oui* magazine, and waited tables. Was an assistant office manager for a real estate company and taught drama at Yale, New York University, and the University of Chicago.

Wrote the screenplays for *The Postman Always Rings Twice*

(1981), *The Verdict* (1982), and *The Untouchables* (1987).

Published his first novel, *The Village*, in 1994.

Still writes on a 25-year-old manual typewriter and uses a pencil.

Co-founded the Atlantic Theater Company as a summer workshop in Vermont for his NYU students.
Original Job: Worked backstage at the Hull House Theatre in Chicago
Marriages: Lindsay Crouse (divorced), Rebecca Pidgeon
Children: Willa, Clara, Zosia
Major Award: Pulitzer Prize, *Glengarry Glen Ross*, 1984
Address: P.O. Box 381589, Cambridge, MA 02238

BARRY MANILOW

Real Name: Barry Alan Pincus
Birthplace: Brooklyn, NY
Birthdate: 6/17/46
Occupation: Singer, songwriter
Education: Attended New York College of Music, Juilliard, City College of New York
Debut: (Album) *Barry Manilow I*, 1975
Signature: "I Write the Songs"
Facts: Arranged music for Bette Midler's band.

Wrote and sang jingles for Dr Pepper, Pepsi, and McDonald's ("You Deserve a Break Today").

Father deserted family when he was two years old, and he was left to be raised by his mother and grandparents.
Original Job: Worked in mail room at CBS
Marriage: Susan (divorced), Linda Allen (relationship)
Major Awards: Tony, *Concerts on Broadway*, 1976; Grammy, Best Pop Vocal—Male, "Copacabana (At the Copa)," 1978
Address: William Morris Agency, 151 El Camino Dr., Beverly Hills, CA 90212

WYNTON MARSALIS

Birthplace: New Orleans, LA
Birthdate: 10/18/61
Occupation: Trumpeter
Education: Attended Juilliard on a full scholarship
Debut: (Band) Art Blakey's Jazz Messengers, 1980
Facts: His first trumpet was a hand-me-down from bandleader Al Hirt.

Played with New Orleans Philharmonic at age 14.

Released his first classical album, *Trumpet Concertos*, in

1983. Was first artist ever to receive—or be nominated for—awards in both jazz and classical categories in a single year.
Children: Wynton, Simeon
Famous Relatives: Ellis Marsalis, musician, father; Branford Marsalis, musician, brother
Major Awards: Grammy, Best Jazz Performance—Soloist, "Think of One," 1983; Grammy, Best Jazz Performance—Soloist, "Hot House Flowers," 1984; Grammy, Best Jazz Performance—Soloist, "Black Codes from the Underground," 1985; Grammy, Best Jazz Performance—Group, "Black Codes from the Underground," 1985; Grammy, Best Jazz Performance—Group, "J Mood," 1986; Grammy, Best Jazz Performance—Group, *Marsalis Standard Time Volume I*, 1987
Address: 9000 Sunset Blvd., #1200, Los Angeles, CA 90069

PENNY MARSHALL

Real Name: Carole Penny Marshall
Birthplace: New York, NY
Birthdate: 10/15/42
Occupation: Actor, director
Education: Attended University of New Mexico
Debut: (TV) *The Danny Thomas Hour*, 1967
Signature: *Laverne and Shirley*
Facts: Even though the family was Congregationalist, Marshall's mother was convinced that Jewish men make the best husbands, so she sent Penny to a Jewish summer camp each year.

Lost the part of Gloria on TV's *All in the Family* to Sally Struthers.

Was first woman director to have a film take in more than $100 million at the box office (*Big*).
Original Job: Dance instructor, secretary
Marriages: Michael Henry (divorced), Rob Reiner (divorced)
Child: Tracy Lee
Famous Relatives: Garry Marshall, director, producer, brother; Tony Maschiarelli, producer, father
Address: Creative Artists Agency, 9830 Wilshire Blvd., Beverly Hills, CA 90212

STEVE MARTIN

Birthplace: Waco, TX
Birthdate: 8/14/45

Occupation: Actor, writer
Education: Attended Long Beach State College, UCLA
Debut: (TV) *The Smothers Brothers Comedy Hour*, 1967
Signature: *Comedy Is Not Pretty*
Facts: Lived behind Disneyland and got his start there performing magic tricks and playing the banjo.

Is a dedicated art collector.
Original Job: Sold guidebooks at Disneyland
Marriage: Victoria Tennant (divorced)
Major Awards: Emmy, Best Writing in a Comedy, Variety, or Music Program, *The Smothers Brothers Comedy Hour*, 1969; Grammy, Best Comedy Recording, *Let's Get Small*, 1977; Grammy, Best Comedy Recording, *A Wild and Crazy Guy*, 1978
Address: International Creative Management, 8942 Wilshire Blvd., Beverly Hills, CA 90211

MARLEE MATLIN

Birthplace: Morton Grove, IL
Birthdate: 8/24/65
Occupation: Actor
Education: William Rainey Harper College
Debut: (Film) *Children of a Lesser God*, 1986
Signature: *Children of a Lesser God*
Facts: Became deaf through a case of roseola infantum at the age of 18 months.

A devout baseball fan, she takes her own glove to games.

At age 21, youngest to win an Oscar for Best Actress (for *Children of a Lesser God*). Gave her acceptance speech in sign language.
Original Job: Policewoman (studied criminal justice in college)
Marriage: Kevin Grandalski
Major Awards: Oscar, Best Actress, *Children of a Lesser God*, 1987; Golden Globe, Best Actress, *Children of a Lesser God*, 1987
Address: International Creative Management, 8942 Wilshire Blvd., Beverly Hills, CA 90211

PAUL McCARTNEY

Real Name: James Paul McCartney
Birthplace: Liverpool, England
Birthdate: 6/18/42
Occupation: Singer, songwriter, bassist
Education: High school
Debut: Formed the Quarry Men, Moondogs, and the Silver Beatles with John Lennon and George Harrison, 1956–1962
Signature: The Beatles
Facts: When he wanted to use "Yesterday" in his 1984 film *Give My Regards to Broad Street*, he had to apply to the publishers for its use; he no longer owned the copyright of the most recorded song in history (over 2,500 cover versions exist).

Was the first Beatle to quit in 1970, releasing his solo album *McCartney* almost simultaneously with the band's release of *Let It Be*.

His version of "Mary Had a Little Lamb" hit No. 9 on the British charts in June 1972.

In the Paul McCartney Kindergarten in Krakow, Poland, children are taught English through McCartney's songs.
Infamy: Admitted to taking LSD and was arrested numerous times with Linda for possession of marijuana and for growing it at their Scotland farmhouse. Because of this, his application for a U.S. passport was refused many times.
Marriage: Linda Eastman
Children: James, Mary, Stella, stepdaughter Heather
Major Awards: Grammy, Best New Artist (with The Beatles), 1964; Grammy, Best Pop Vocal—Duo or Group, *A Hard Day's Night* (with The Beatles), 1964; Grammy, Song of the Year, "Michelle" (with John Lennon), 1966; Grammy, Best Rock Vocal, "Eleanor Rigby," 1966; Grammy, Album of the Year, *Sgt. Pepper's Lonely Hearts Club Band* (with The Beatles), 1967; Grammy, Best Score, *Let It Be* (with The Beatles), 1970; Grammy, Best Pop Performance—Duo or Group, *Band on the Run* (with Wings), 1974; Grammy, Hall of Fame Winner, *Sgt. Pepper's Lonely Hearts Club Band* (with The Beatles), 1992; Oscar, Best Score, *Let It Be* (with The Beatles), 1970; inducted into the Rock and Roll Hall of Fame (with The Beatles), 1988; NARAS Lifetime Achievement Award, 1990
Address: Capitol Records, 1750 N. Vine St., Hollywood, CA 90028

REBA McENTIRE

Birthplace: Chockie, OK
Birthdate: 3/28/55
Occupation: Singer, songwriter
Education: Southeastern State University
Debut: (Song) "I Don't Want To Be a One-Night Stand," 1976

Signature: "Is There Life out There?"
Facts: As a teenager, performed with her siblings in the Singing McEntires. Their first single was a tribute to her grandfather, rodeo rider John McEntire.

Appeared in the 1990 movie *Tremors*, as well as other film and TV roles.

Her longtime tour manager and seven of her band members died in a plane crash in 1991.
Original Job: Cattle rancher, rodeo barrel racer
Marriages: Charlie Battles (divorced), Narvel Blackstock
Child: Shelby Stephen
Major Awards: Grammy, Best Country Vocal—Female, "Whoever's in New England," 1986; Grammy, Best Country Female Vocalist, 1987; Grammy, Best Country Vocal—Collaboration, "Does He Love You" (with Linda Davis), 1993
Address: MCA Records, 70 Universal City Plaza, Universal City, CA 91608

MEAT LOAF

Real Name: Marvin Lee Aday
Birthplace: Dallas, TX
Birthdate: 9/27/51
Occupation: Singer
Education: High school
Debut: (Album) *Bat out of Hell*, 1977
Signature: *Bat out of Hell*
Facts: Weighed 240 pounds in seventh grade.

Nicknamed by his high school football coach.

Bat out of Hell, the third-best-selling album ever, still sells 15,000 copies a week, 16 years after its release.

Twenty-two lawsuits with his manager, publisher, and other associates led to $85 million in losses.

Acted in off-Broadway production of *The Rocky Horror Picture Show*, 1974.
Infamy: After his 1981 album, *Dead Ringer*, fell flat, went on a nine-month booze bender.
Original Job: Baseball coach
Marriage: Leslie
Children: Two children
Major Awards: Grammy, Best Solo Rock Vocal, "I'd Do Anything for Love (But I Won't Do That)," 1993
Address: MCA Records, 70 Universal City Plaza, Universal City, CA 91608

NATALIE MERCHANT

Birthplace: Jamestown, NY
Birthdate: 10/26/63
Occupation: Singer, songwriter
Education: Attended Jamestown Community College
Debut: (Album) *Human Conflict No. 5* (with 10,000 Maniacs), 1982
Signature: 10,000 Maniacs
Facts: The band mistakenly took its name from the B-movie *2000 Maniacs*.

Split from the group in the summer of 1993, citing the desire to work solo.

Between touring for *Blind Man's Zoo* and recording *Our Time in Eden*, volunteered at a Harlem daycare center for homeless kids.

Dated R.E.M.'s Michael Stipe on and off for three years.
Address: Elektra Entertainment, 75 Rockefeller Plaza, New York, NY 10019

LORNE MICHAELS

Real Name: Lorne Lipowitz
Birthplace: Toronto, Canada
Birthdate: 11/17/44
Occupation: Producer, writer
Education: University of Toronto
Debut: (TV) *Rowan and Martin's Laugh-In*, 1968 (writer)
Signature: *Saturday Night Live*
Facts: In addition to *Saturday Night Live*, Michaels produces *Late Night with Conan O'Brien*. He has also produced the films *Three Amigos* (1986), *Wayne's World* (1992), *Wayne's World 2* (1993), *The Coneheads* (1993), *Lassie* (1994), and *Stuart Saves His Family* (1995).
Marriages: Rosie Shuster (divorced), Susan Forristal (divorced), Alice Barry
Children: Henry Abraham, Edward
Major Awards: Writers Guild of America Awards (4); Emmy, Best Writing in a Comedy, Variety, or Music Special, *Lily*, 1974, 1976; Emmy, Best Writing in a Comedy, Variety, or Music Series, *Saturday Night Live*, 1976, 1977; Emmy, Best Writing in a Comedy, Variety, or Music Series, *The Paul Simon Special*, 1978; Emmy, Best Writing in a Variety or Music Program, *Murderers Among Us*, 1989
Address: Broadway Video, 1619 Broadway, 9th Fl., New York, NY 10019

DEMI MOORE

Real Name: Demetria Guynes
Birthplace: Roswell, NM
Birthdate: 11/11/62
Occupation: Actor
Education: Left high school to model in Europe, studied with Zina Provendie
Debut: (Film) *Choices*, 1981; (TV) *General Hospital*, 1981
Signature: *Ghost*
Facts: Was cross-eyed as a child and had an operation to correct it, wearing a patch over one eye.

Decided to become an actress in high school when she lived in the same building as Nastassja Kinski.

In order to play coke addict Jules in the 1985 movie *St. Elmo's Fire*, she had to sign a contract stipulating that she would stop her own alcohol and drug abuse, an agreement that caused her to turn her life around.

She and Bruce Willis were married on November 21, 1987, by singer Little Richard.
Infamy: Posed nude and pregnant on the cover of *Vanity Fair*.
Original Job: Model
Marriages: Freddy Moore (divorced), Bruce Willis
Children: Rumer Glenn, Scout Larue, Tallulah Belle
Address: Creative Artists Agency, 9830 Wilshire Blvd., Beverly Hills, CA 90212

TONI MORRISON

Real Name: Chloe Anthony Wofford
Birthplace: Lorain, OH
Birthdate: 2/18/31
Occupation: Author
Education: Howard University, Cornell University
Debut: (Book) *The Bluest Eye*, 1969
Signature: *Beloved*
Facts: Has served as an editor at Random House, helping to publish the works of other black Americans like Toni Cade Bambara, Angela Davis, and Muhammad Ali.

Has taught at Harvard, Yale, and Princeton.
Original Job: Textbook editor
Marriage: Harold Morrison (divorced)
Children: Harold Ford, Slade Kevin
Major Awards: National Book Critics Circle Award, *Song of Solomon*, 1977; Pulitzer Prize,

Beloved, 1988; Nobel Prize for Literature, 1993
Address: International Creative Management, 8942 Wilshire Blvd., Beverly Hills, CA 90211

VAN MORRISON

Real Name: George Ivan Morrison
Birthplace: Belfast, Northern Ireland.
Birthdate: 8/31/45
Occupation: Singer, songwriter
Education: High school dropout
Debut: (Song) "Don't Start Crying" (with Them), 1964
Signature: "Brown Eyed Girl"
Facts: Was lead singer of Them from 1964 to 1967 and has worked solo ever since.

In 1965, wrote "Gloria," which achieved moderate success but didn't hit the U.S. top ten until it was covered by The Shadows of Knight in 1966.
Marriage: Janet Planet (divorced)
Address: Polydor, 825 Eighth Avenue, 27th Floor, New York, NY 10019

ROB MORROW

Birthplace: New Rochelle, NY
Birthdate: 7/21/62
Occupation: Actor
Debut: (TV) *Tattingers*, 1988
Signature: *Northern Exposure*
Facts: In 1990, turned down a role in the proposed CBS series *The Antagonists* to appear in the play *The Substance of Fire*, in a part written for him. After he refused the TV role, his manager told him that he would never work again, and his agent wanted to dump him. Both forgave him very quickly after he landed the lead role in *Northern Exposure*, 1990.

In 1991, worked at Vassar College as director on a 20-minute film he wrote about a child reacting to his divorced mother's new relationship.
Original Job: Waiter, balloon messenger
Address: William Morris Agency, 151 El Camino Dr., Beverly Hills, CA 90212

EDDIE MURPHY

Birthplace: Hempstead, NY
Birthdate: 4/3/61
Occupation: Actor
Education: Attended Nassau Community College
Debut: (TV) *Saturday Night Live*, 1980
Signature: *Beverly Hills Cop*

Facts: Father was a policeman who died when Eddie was five.

Was voted most popular at Roosevelt Jr.-Sr. High School in New York, NY.

Created and produced the TV series *The Royal Family*, which was cut short upon the sudden death of the star Redd Foxx.

Co-owns the L.A. restaurant Georgia with Denzel Washington.
Original Job: Shoe store clerk
Marriage: Nicole Mitchell
Children: Bria, Myles Mitchell, Christian, Shayne Audra
Major Award: Grammy, Best Comedy Recording, *Eddie Murphy—Comedian*, 1983; Golden Globe, Best Actor, *Trading Places*, 1984
Address: International Creative Management, 8942 Wilshire Blvd., Beverly Hills, CA 90211

BILL MURRAY

Birthplace: Wilmette, IL
Birthdate: 9/21/50
Occupation: Actor, writer
Education: Loyola Academy, attended Regis College, attended Second City Workshop in Chicago
Debut: (TV) *Saturday Night Live*, 1977
Signature: *Ghostbusters*
Facts: Was a pre-med student at St. Regis College.

Provided the voice of Johnny Storm, the Human Torch, on Marvel Comics' radio show, *The Fantastic Four*. This is where he was heard by the producers of *Saturday Night Live*.

Bill's son, Homer Banks, is named after legendary Chicago Cub Ernie Banks.

In 1981, performed the song "The Best Thing (Love Song)" for John Waters' *Polyester*.
Original Job: Pizza maker
Marriage: Margaret Kelly
Children: Homer, Luke
Famous Relative: Brian Doyle-Murray, actor, brother
Major Award: Emmy, Best Writing in a Comedy Series, *Saturday Night Live*, 1977
Address: Creative Artists Agency, 9830 Wilshire Blvd., Beverly Hills, CA 90212

MIKE MYERS

Birthplace: Scarborough, Canada
Birthdate: 1964
Occupation: Actor, writer
Education: High school
Debut: (TV) *Mullarkey & Myers*, 1984

Signature: *Wayne's World*
Facts: He appeared in a TV commercial with Gilda Radner at age eight.

Met his wife at a hockey game.

Had been doing the Wayne character since high school. "I did him in kitchens at parties to make girls laugh."
Marriage: Robin Ruzan
Major Awards: Emmy, Outstanding Writing in a Comedy Series, *Saturday Night Live*, 1989; Emmy, Best Writing in a Variety or Music Program, *Murderers Among Us*, 1989
Address: United Talent Agency, 9560 Wilshire Blvd., Suite 500, Beverly Hills, CA 90212

LIAM NEESON

Birthplace: Ballymena, Northern Ireland
Birthdate: 6/7/52
Occupation: Actor
Debut: (Stage) *In the Risen*, 1976; (Film) *Excalibur*, 1981
Signature: *Schindler's List*
Facts: At age nine, joined a boxing team run by a priest. Nose was broken during an early match, and had it set on site by his manager. Quit boxing at age 17.

First starring role was the disfigured hero of the film *Darkman*, 1990.
Original Job: Forklift operator, architect's assistant, amateur boxer
Marriage: Natasha Richardson
Child: Micheál
Address: Creative Artists Agency, 9830 Wilshire Blvd., Beverly Hills, CA 90212

WILLIE NELSON

Birthplace: Abbott, TX
Birthdate: 4/30/33
Occupation: Singer, songwriter, guitarist, actor
Education: Attended Baylor University in Texas
Debut: (Album) *...And Then I Wrote*, 1962; (Film) *The Electric Horseman*, 1979
Signature: "Mamas, Don't Let Your Babies Grow Up To Be Cowboys"
Facts: Nelson taught at Baptist Sunday school until officials objected to him playing in seedy bars.

Sold his first song, "Family Bible," for $50 to feed his family; it became a huge hit, performed by more than 70 country artists.

Organized Farm Aid concerts

to help midwestern farmers stricken by drought and threatened with foreclosure.

Began writing songs at age seven.

Infamy: In 1991, after a seven-year dispute with the IRS over $16.7 million in back taxes, the government seized most of Nelson's possessions (country club, recording studio, 44-acre ranch, 20 other properties in four states, instruments, recordings, and memorabilia).

Arrested in 1994 for possession of marijuana. Charges were later dismissed.

Original Job: Janitor, door-to-door salesman (Bibles, encyclopedias, vacuum cleaners, sewing machines), hosted country music shows on Texas radio stations

Marriages: Martha Matthews (divorced), Shirley Collie (divorced), Connie Koepke (divorced), Annie D'Angelo

Children: Lana, Susie, Billy (deceased), Paula Carlene, Amy, Lukas Autry, Jacob Micah

Major Awards: Grammy, Best Country Vocal—Male, "Blue Eyes Cryin' in the Rain," 1975; Grammy, Best Country Vocal—Male, "Georgia on My Mind," 1978; Grammy, Best Country Performance—Duo or Group, "Mamas Don't Let Your Babies Grow Up To Be Cowboys" (with Waylon Jennings), 1978; Grammy, Best Country Song, "On the Road Again," 1980; Grammy, Best Country Vocal—Male, "Always on My Mind," 1982; Grammy, Best Country Song, "Always on My Mind," 1982; Grammy, Legend Award, 1990; inducted into the Country Music Hall of Fame in 1993

Address: Mark Rothbaum & Associates, P.O. Box 2689, Danbury, CT 06813

AARON NEVILLE

Birthplace: New Orleans, LA
Birthdate: 1/24/41
Occupation: Singer
Debut: (Single) "Over You," 1960
Signature: Singer with the Neville Brothers
Facts: Worked as a longshoreman on the docks in New Orleans to pay the record company for the studio time he used to record songs like "Over You" and "Tell It Like It Is."

A staunch Catholic, he credits his success to his faith in God. To this day he still offers novenas to

St. Jude. "There's always something impossible to pray for."

Infamy: Spent six months in jail for auto theft in 1959.

Marriage: Joel

Children: Ernestine, Ivan, Jason, Aaron Jr.

Famous Relatives: Art Neville, singer, brother; Charles Neville, singer, brother; Cyril Neville, singer, brother

Major Awards: Grammy, Best Pop Vocal—Duo or Group with Vocal, "Don't Know Much" (with Linda Ronstadt), 1989; Grammy, Best Pop Vocal—Duo or Group with Vocal, "All My Life" (with Linda Ronstadt), 1990; Down Beat Blues, Soul, R&B Award, 1990; Grammy, Best Country Vocal Collaboration, "I Fall to Pieces" (with Trisha Yearwood), 1994

Address: William Morris Agency, 151 El Camino Dr., Beverly Hills, CA 90212

PAUL NEWMAN

Birthplace: Cleveland, OH
Birthdate: 1/26/25
Occupation: Actor, director, producer
Education: Kenyon College, Attended Yale School of Drama, Actors Studio
Debut: (Film) *The Silver Chalice*, 1954
Signature: *The Hustler*
Facts: Briefly attended Ohio University and was allegedly asked to leave for crashing a beer keg into the president's car.

The Newman's Own food company he founded in 1987 with writer friend A.E. Hochner has donated more than $60 million to charity.

Has worked on more than nine movies with actor wife Joanne Woodward.

A die-hard, marching liberal, he founded in the leftist opinion-making magazine, *The Nation.*

Is a professional race car driver.

Marriages: Jacqueline Witte (divorced), Joanne Woodward
Children: Scott (deceased), Susan, Stephanie, Elinor "Nell" Teresa, Melissa Steward, Claire Olivia
Major Awards: Golden Globe, World Film Favorite—Male, *Hud*, 1963; Oscar, Lifetime Achievement, 1985; Oscar, Best Actor, *The Color of Money,* 1986; Oscar, Jean Hersholt Humanitarian Award, 1993
Address: Creative Artists

Agency, 9830 Wilshire Blvd., Beverly Hills, CA 90212

WAYNE NEWTON

Birthplace: Norfolk, VA
Birthdate: 4/3/42
Occupation: Entertainer
Education: High school dropout
Debut: (TV) *Jackie Gleason and His American Scene Magazine,* 1962; (Film) *80 Steps to Jonah,* 1969
Facts: Protégé of Jackie Gleason. Partly Native American.

Earns $250,000 a week for his Las Vegas performances.

Infamy: In 1992, declared bankruptcy, listing debts of more than $20 million.

In 1994 his creditors once again went to court, charging that, despite millions in current earnings, he continued spending lavishly on himself (including a reported $75,000 repairing his home pond for his pet penguins) and made little effort to pay what he owed them.

Marriages: Elaine Okamura (divorced), Kathleen McCrone
Child: Erin
Address: Atlantic Records, 75 Rockefeller Plaza, New York, NY 10019

JACK NICHOLSON

Birthplace: Neptune, NJ
Birthdate: 4/22/37
Occupation: Actor, director, producer, screenwriter
Education: Studied with the Players Ring acting group
Debut: (Stage) *Tea and Sympathy,* 1957; (Film) *Cry-Baby Killer,* 1958
Signature: *The Shining*
Facts: Recorded *The Elephant's Child,* a children's record, with Bobby McFerrin (1987).

Abandoned by his father in childhood, he was raised believing his grandmother was his mother and his real mother was his older sister. The truth was revealed to him years later when a *Time* magazine researcher uncovered the truth while preparing a story on the star.

Has been nominated ten times for the Academy Award.

Infamy: Known for being a ladies' man, Nicholson had a 17-year relationship with actress Anjelica Huston that ended in 1990 when Nicholson revealed that actress Rebecca Broussard, his daughter's best friend, was carrying his child.

During a later two-year falling out period with Broussard, he dated a 20-year-old and reportedly fathered her baby girl.

Reportedly used a golf club to strike the windshield of a '69 Mercedes that had cut him off in traffic in 1994. The driver's civil suit was settled out of court.

Original Job: Office boy in MGM's cartoon department
Marriages: Sandra Knight (divorced), Rebecca Broussard (relationship)
Children: Jennifer, Lorraine, Raymond
Major Awards: Golden Globe, Best Actor, *Chinatown,* 1975; Golden Globe, Best Actor, *One Flew over the Cuckoo's Nest,* 1976; Golden Globe, Best Supporting Actor, *Terms of Endearment,* 1984; Golden Globe, Best Actor in a Comedy, *Prizzi's Honor,* 1986; Oscar, Best Actor, *One Flew over the Cuckoo's Nest,* 1975; Oscar, Best Supporting Actor, *Terms of Endearment,* 1984; Grammy, Best Recording for Children, *The Elephant's Child,* 1987
Address: 15760 Ventura Blvd., Suite 1730, Encino, CA 91426

LESLIE NIELSEN

Birthplace: Regina, Canada
Birthdate: 2/11/26
Occupation: Actor, writer
Education: Attended Lorne Greene's Academy of Radio Arts, Toronto
Debut: (TV) *Actor's Studio,* 1950; (Film) *Forbidden Planet,* 1956
Signature: *Naked Gun*
Facts: Grew up in a log cabin 200 miles south of the Arctic Circle.

Suffered a childhood case of rickets. Legally deaf.

Served in the Royal Canadian Air Force during World War II.

Original Job: Radio announcer, disc jockey
Marriages: Monica Boyer (divorced), Sandy Ullman (divorced), Barbaree Earl
Children: Thea, Maura
Famous Relative: Eric Nielsen, member of Canadian Parliament, brother
Address: 15760 Ventura Blvd., #1730, Encino, CA 91436

CONAN O'BRIEN

Birthplace: Brookline, MA
Birthdate: 4/18/63
Occupation: Talk show host
Education: Harvard University

Debut: (TV) *Not Necessarily the News,* 1985
Signature: *NBC's Late Night with Conan O'Brien*
Facts: Has written for *Saturday Night Live* and *The Simpsons.*

While at Harvard, served as president of *The Harvard Lampoon* for two years, the first person to do so since Robert Benchley in 1912.

First TV producing credit was *Lookwell* (1991), a sitcom pilot starring Adam West as a former TV detective who becomes a real cop.
Major Award: Emmy, Best Writing in a Variety or Music Program, *Murderers Among Us,* 1989
Quote: "The nightmare is that you spend the rest of your life being funny at parties and people say, 'Why didn't you do *that* when you were on television?'"
Address: United Talent Agency, 9560 Wilshire Blvd., Suite 500, Beverly Hills, CA 90212

CHRIS O'DONNELL

Birthplace: Chicago, IL
Birthdate: 1970
Occupation: Actor, model
Education: Boston College, UCLA
Debut: (TV) *Jack and Mike,* 1986; (Film) *Men Don't Leave,* 1990
Signature: *Scent of a Woman*
Facts: Youngest of seven children (four sisters and two brothers), grew up in Winnetka, IL.

Began modeling and appearing in commercials in 1983, at age 13. Appeared in a McDonald's commercial opposite Michael Jordan.

Was 17 when he auditioned for *Men Don't Leave.* His mother had to promise him a new car to get him to try out. He is still waiting for that car.

Originally cast as Barbra Streisand's son in *Prince of Tides,* but she decided to have her real-life son play the role instead.

Took time off from pursuing a degree in marketing from Boston College in order to work with Al Pacino on *Scent of a Woman.*
Address: Creative Artists Agency, 9830 Wilshire Blvd., Beverly Hills, CA 90212

ROSIE O'DONNELL

Birthplace: Commack, NY
Birthdate: 1962
Occupation: Actor, comedian

Education: Attended Dickinson College and Boston University
Debut: (TV) *Gimme a Break,* 1986; (Stage) *Grease,* 1994
Facts: Won the *Star Search* comedy competition five times.

Fascinated with the blue-collar mundane, she began extensively collecting McDonald's Happy Meal figurines.

Against her agent's advice, she auditioned for—and won—the role of Betty Rizzo in the Broadway revival of *Grease* in 1994. She had no theater experience and says she'd never sung in public before.
Child: Parker Jaren (adopted)
Address: International Creative Management, 8942 Wilshire Blvd., Beverly Hills, CA 90211

ASHLEY OLSEN

Birthdate: 6/13/86
Occupation: Actor
Debut: (TV) *Full House,* 1987
Facts: Two minutes older than fraternal twin sister Mary-Kate and has a freckle under her nose.

Their mother says, "When they need someone to be more active or emotional, they let Ashley do it."

How is she different from her twin? "My voice is deeper."
Famous Relative: Jamie Olsen, former dancer with the Los Angeles Ballet, mother
Address: *Full House,* 4000 Warner Blvd., Burbank, CA 91522

MARY-KATE OLSEN

Birthdate: 6/13/86
Occupation: Actor
Debut: (TV) *Full House,* 1987
Facts: Wants to be a candymaker or a cowgirl when she grows up.

Both twins earn income not only from the show but also through sale of the talking Michelle doll.

"Mary-Kate is more serious, so she gets the serious lines to do," says her mother.
Famous Relative: Jamie Olsen, former dancer with the Los Angeles Ballet, mother
Address: *Full House,* 4000 Warner Blvd., Burbank, CA 91522

SHAQUILLE O'NEAL

Birthplace: Newark, NJ
Birthdate: 3/6/72
Occupation: Basketball player
Education: Attended Louisiana State University
Facts: His rap album, *Shaq*

Diesel, sold more than one million copies. Got his rap start by singing on "What's Up Doc," a song put out in 1993 by his favorite rap group, FU-Schnickens.

He stands seven feet one inch, weighs 303 pounds, and wears size 21 triple-E shoes.

His first name translates, ironically, to "little one."

Spent most of his adolescence in Germany, where his stepfather was an army sergeant.
Major Awards: NBA Rookie of the Year, 1993; Member, NBA All-Star Team, 1993, 1994; Gold Medal, World Basketball Championships, 1994
Address: Orlando Magic, One Magic Pl., Orlando, FL 32801

JULIA ORMOND

Birthplace: Epsom, England
Birthdate: 1965
Occupation: Actor
Education: Webber Douglas Academy, London
Debut: (TV) *Traffik,* 1990; (Film) *The Baby of Macon,* 1993
Signature: *Legends of the Fall*
Facts: Her stockbroker father became a millionaire by 30, but when the marriage collapsed, Julia, her mother, and sister had to move out of their 20-room mansion.

Her first casting call was for a television ad for cottage cheese; she got the job.

Starred in many London stage productions before venturing into movies.
Original Job: Waitress
Marriage: Rory Edwards (divorced)
Address: Creative Artists Agency, 9830 Wilshire Blvd., Beverly Hills, CA 90212

OZZY OSBOURNE

Real Name: John Michael Osbourne
Birthplace: Aston, England
Birthdate: 12/3/48
Occupation: Singer
Debut: (Album) *Black Sabbath,* 1970
Signature: Black Sabbath
Facts: In 1984, splintered glass from a broken mirror in the video for "So Tired" lodged in Osbourne's throat, but no permanent injury occurred.

Was sued, unsuccessfully, in 1987 by the parents of California teenager John McCollum. McCollum's parents claimed that Osbourne's song "Suicide

Solution" influenced the youth to kill himself. Osbourne said, "If I wrote music for people who shot themselves after listening to my music, I wouldn't have much of a following."
Infamy: Was a burglar until he spent two months in Winston Green Prison.

Osbourne bit the head off a dove during a meeting of Los Angeles record executives. Later he tried it at a concert with a bat and the bat bit him.

Admits to being heavily into LSD and other drugs during his Black Sabbath years. Has been treated for alcohol abuse several times.
Original Job: Slaughterhouse worker
Marriages: Thelma Osbourne (divorced), Sharon Arden
Address: William Morris Agency, 151 El Camino Dr., Beverly Hills, CA 90212

MICHAEL OVITZ

Birthplace: Encino, CA
Birthdate: 12/14/46
Occupation: President of Walt Disney Company
Education: UCLA
Facts: Began as a mailroom clerk in the William Morris Agency. Set up CAA, where he was superagent and chairman, after he was fired from William Morris.

Was pre-med student at UCLA.

Practices aikido, a Japanese form of martial arts. He discovered Steven Seagal, who was training him in martial arts.
Original Job: Tour guide at Universal Studios
Marriage: Judy Reich
Address: Walt Disney Studios, 500 S. Buena Vista St., Burbank, CA 91521

AL PACINO

Real Name: Alfredo James Pacino
Birthplace: New York, NY
Birthdate: 4/25/40
Occupation: Actor
Education: High School of the Performing Arts, Actor's Studio
Debut: (Stage) *The Peace Creeps,* 1966; (Film) *Me, Natalie,* 1969
Signature: *The Godfather*
Fact: Has been involved with actresses Jill Clayburgh, Marthe Keller, and Diane Keaton.
Original Job: Mail deliverer at *Commentary* magazine, mes-

senger, movie theater usher, building superintendent
Relationship: Lyndall Hobbs
Child: Julie Marie
Major Awards: Tony, Best Supporting Actor (Dramatic), *Does a Tiger Wear a Necktie?*, 1969; Tony, Best Actor, *The Basic Training of Pavlo Hummel*, 1977; Golden Globe, Best Actor, *Serpico*, 1974; Golden Globe, Best Actor, *Scent of a Woman*, 1993; Oscar, Best Actor, *Scent of a Woman*, 1992
Address: Creative Artists Agency, 9830 Wilshire Blvd., Beverly Hills, CA 90212

CHAZZ PALMINTERI

Real Name: Calogero Lorenzo Palminteri
Birthplace: Bronx, NY
Birthdate: 5/15/51
Occupation: Actor, playwright, screenwriter
Education: Theodore Roosevelt High School
Debut: (TV) *Hill Street Blues*, 1986
Signature: *A Bronx Tale*
Facts: Before Robert DeNiro purchased the manuscript for *A Bronx Tale*, Palminteri had rejected other million dollar studio bids for it. At that time, he only had $178 in the bank and was $14,000 in debt. He had written the screenplay as a vehicle for his acting career and was insistent on playing the title role, Sonny.

For the first 12 years of his acting career, he was the financial failure of the family.

Credits his father, Lorenzo, for teaching him reverence for women. Extremely devoted to his parents; he purchased them a Florida estate.

Wrote *Faithful*, a Paul Mazursky film, while engaged and musing about the sanctity of marriage.

When he was young, he insisted on only dating Italian girls.
Original Job: Nightclub doorman at The Limelight
Marriage: Gianna Ranado
Address: Creative Artists Agency, 9830 Wilshire Blvd., Beverly Hills, CA 90212

SARAH JESSICA PARKER

Birthplace: Nelsonville, OH
Birthdate: 3/25/65
Occupation: Actor

Education: American Ballet Theater, Professional Children's School in New York
Debut: (TV) *The Little Match Girl*, 1973; (Stage) *The Innocents*, 1976
Facts: Sang in Metropolitan Opera productions of *Hansel and Gretel, Cavalleria Rusticana, Pagliacci*, and *Parade*.

Starred as nerdy Patty Green on the CBS TV sitcom *Square Pegs*, 1982–83.

Played Annie in the Broadway musical, 1979–80.

Lived with Robert Downey Jr. for seven years.

Wears a size two.
Original Job: Dancer with Cincinnati Ballet and the American Ballet Theatre
Relationship: Matthew Broderick
Address: Creative Artists Agency, 9830 Wilshire Blvd., Beverly Hills, CA 90212

DOLLY PARTON

Birthplace: Sevierville, TN
Birthdate: 1/19/46
Occupation: Singer, songwriter
Education: High school
Debut: (Song) "Puppy Love," 1956
Signature: "9 to 5"
Facts: Met her husband in the Wishy Washy laundromat.

Has her own theme park, Dollywood, located in Gatlinburg at the edge of the Smoky Mountains. In her hometown of Sevierville, Tennessee, there is a statue of her on the Sevier County Courthouse lawn.
Marriage: Carl Dean
Major Awards: Grammy, Best Country Vocal—Female, *Here You Come Again*, 1978; Grammy, Best Country Vocal—Female, "9 to 5," 1981; Grammy, Best Country Performance—Duo or Group, *Trio* (with Linda Rondstadt and Emmylou Harris), 1987
Quote: "Left to my own, I'd rather look like trash. I love tacky clothes. My look came from a very serious honest place, and that was a country girl's idea of what glamour was."
Address: International Creative Management, 8942 Wilshire Blvd., Beverly Hills, CA 90211

JANE PAULEY

Real Name: Margaret Jane Pauley
Birthplace: Indianapolis, IN
Birthdate: 10/31/50

Occupation: Broadcast journalist
Education: Attended Indiana University
Debut: (TV) WISH-TV, Indiana, 1972
Signature: *Dateline NBC*
Facts: Succeeded Barbara Walters on the *Today* show two weeks shy of her 26th birthday in 1976; left 13 years later in a controversy over Deborah Norvile's role that generated enormous sympathy for Pauley.

Limits her children's TV viewing to one hour a day.
Marriage: Garry Trudeau
Children: Ross, Rachel, Thomas
Address: International Creative Management, 8942 Wilshire Blvd., Beverly Hills, CA 90211

LUCIANO PAVAROTTI

Birthplace: Modena, Italy
Birthdate: 10/12/35
Occupation: Singer
Education: Istituto Magistrale Carlo Sigonio
Debut: (Stage) *La Bohème*, 1961
Facts: Established Opera Company of Philadelphia/ Luciano Pavarotti Vocal Company, 1980.

Makes at least $100,000 per concert. His fortune is estimated to be between $25 and $50 million.

Dreads the anticipation of singing more than singing itself. "The 10 minutes before the performance you wouldn't wish on your worst enemies."

Half a billion people saw the televised "Three Tenors" concert (with Placido Domingo and José Carreras) in 1990.

In 1990, the only musicians who sold more recordings than Pavarotti were Madonna and Elton John.
Infamy: He was sued by the BBC when it found out that a 1992 Pavarotti concert it had bought for broadcast had really been lip-synched.
Original Job: Elementary school teacher, salesman
Marriage: Adua Veroni
Children: Lorenza, Cristina, Giuliana
Major Awards: Grammy, Best Classical Vocal Performance, *Luciano Pavarotti—Hits from London Center*, 1978; Grammy, Best Classical Vocal Performance, *O Sole Mio (Favorite Neapolitan Songs)*, 1979; Grammy, Best Classical Vocal Performance, *Live from Lincoln Center—Sutherland—Horne—Pavarotti* (with Joan Sutherland and Marilyn Horne), 1981;

Grammy, Best Classical Vocal Performance, *Luciano Pavarotti in Concert*, 1988; Grammy, Best Classical Vocal Performance, *Carreras, Domingo, Pavarotti in Concert* (with José Carreras and Placido Domingo), 1990
Address: 941 Via Giardini, 41040 Saliceta S. Giuliano, Modena, Italy

PEPA

Real Name: Sandra Denton
Birthplace: Queens, NY
Birthdate: 9/9/69
Occupation: Rap artist
Education: Queensborough Community College
Debut: (Album) *Hot, Cool & Vicious*, 1986
Signature: Salt-N-Pepa
Facts: Pepa and Salt both worked at Sears with Martin Lawrence and Kid 'N Play.

Received Grammy Award nomination in 1989 in the newly created rap category, but boycotted the show when the awards program did not televise the presentation of the award.
Original Job: Telephone customer service representative
Relationship: Anthony "Treach" Criss
Child: Tyran
Major Award: Grammy, Best Rap Performance by a Group or Duo, "None of Your Business," (with Salt-N-Pepa), 1994
Address: Next Plateau Records, 1650 Broadway, Room 1103, New York, NY 10019

ROSIE PEREZ

Birthplace: Brooklyn, NY
Birthdate: 1964
Occupation: Actress, choreographer
Education: Los Angeles City College
Debut: (TV) *Soul Train*; (Film) *Do the Right Thing*, 1989
Signature: *Do the Right Thing*
Facts: Was discovered as a dancer at the L.A. club Funky Reggae by Spike Lee, who offered her a role in *Do the Right Thing*.

Choreographer for the TV comedy/variety show *In Living Color*. Has choreographed numbers for Bobby Brown and Diana Ross.
Infamy: At age 12, cut a woman's neck and was placed in a group home.
Original Job: Dancer
Address: Creative Artists Agency, 9830 Wilshire Blvd., Beverly Hills, CA 90212

JOE PESCI

Birthplace: Newark, NJ
Birthdate: 2/9/43
Occupation: Actor
Education: High school dropout
Debut: (Radio) *Star Kids*, 1947; (Film) *Hey, Let's Twist!*, 1961
Signature: *My Cousin Vinny*
Facts: Played guitar for Joey Dee and The Starliters.

At age five appeared in Broadway musicals and Eddie Dowling plays. At age ten became a regular on TV's *Star Time Kids* doing impersonations and singing.

Was managing a restaurant in the Bronx when called by Robert De Niro and Martin Scorsese to play Jake LaMotta's brother in *Raging Bull*, 1978.

He appears in some of his films under the psuedonym Joe Ritchie.
Original Job: Has worked as a nightclub singer, stand-up comedian, barber, postal worker, delivery boy, produce manager, answering service worker, and restaurant manager
Marriages: Two prior marriages, Martha Haro
Child: Tiffany
Major Award: Oscar, Best Supporting Actor, *Goodfellas*, 1991
Address: Creative Artists Agency, 9830 Wilshire Blvd., Beverly Hills, CA 90212

TOM PETTY

Birthplace: Gainesville, FL
Birthdate: 10/20/52
Occupation: Singer, songwriter, guitarist
Education: High school dropout
Debut: *Tom Petty and the Heartbreakers*, 1977
Signature: "Free Fallin'"
Facts: Toured for two years as Bob Dylan's backing band.

Recorded two albums with The Traveling Wilburys, comprised of George Harrison, Bob Dylan, Roy Orbison, Jeff Lynne, and Petty.
Marriage: Jane
Children: Adria, Kim
Address: 8730 Sunset Blvd., 6th Fl., Los Angeles, CA 90069

MICHELLE PFEIFFER

Birthplace: Santa Ana, CA
Birthdate: 4/29/57
Occupation: Actor
Education: Attended Golden West College and Whitley College for Court Reporting
Debut: (TV) *Delta House*, 1979;

(Film) *The Hollywood Knights*, 1980
Signature: *The Fabulous Baker Boys*
Facts: Had one line on TV show *Fantasy Island*.

Got her first break by winning the Miss Orange County Beauty Pageant.

In 1993, she decided to be a single mother and adopted a baby girl, who was given the last name Kelley after Pfeiffer's marriage.

Had the leading role in *Grease 2*, 1982.
Original Job: Supermarket cashier, court reporter, model
Marriages: Peter Horton (divorced), David E. Kelley
Children: Claudia Rose (adopted), John Henry
Major Award: Golden Globe, Best Actress, *The Fabulous Baker Boys*, 1990
Address: International Creative Management, 8942 Wilshire Blvd., Beverly Hills, CA 90211

LIZ PHAIR

Birthplace: New Haven, CT
Birthdate: 4/17/67
Occupation: Singer, songwriter
Education: Oberlin College
Debut: *Exile in Guyville*, 1993
Facts: Was adopted at birth by a physician father and art instructor mother.

Guyville was named album of the year in a *Village Voice* poll of the nation's pop critics and Phair was tagged Best New Female Artist of 1993 by *Rolling Stone*.

Her lyrics are among the most frank and obscene in rock.
Original Job: Artist assistant
Marriage: Jim Staskauskas
Quote: "My lyrics are totally how I talk. I have a potty mouth. But I think it's termed explicit because I'm a girl."
Address: International Creative Management, 8942 Wilshire Blvd., Beverly Hills, CA 90211

DAVID HYDE PIERCE

Birthplace: Saratoga Springs, NY
Birthdate: 4/3/59
Occupation: Actor
Education: Yale
Debut: (Stage) *Beyond Therapy*, 1982; (Film) *The Terminator*, 1984; (TV) *Powers That Be*, 1991
Signature: *Frasier*
Facts: Realized he had a strong resemblance to his TV brother Frasier (Kelsey Grammer) after being mistaken for Grammer many times before he even

accepted the role. In the orginal storyline for *Frasier*, Pierce's character (Niles) didn't exist but was added after producers, who saw Pierce in *The Powers That Be*, noticed the resemblance.
Original Job: Clothing salesman, church organist
Address: J. Michael Bloom, 9255 Sunset Blvd., Suite 710, Los Angeles, CA 90069

DAVE PIRNER

Birthplace: Green Bay, WI
Birthdate: 4/16/64
Occupation: Singer, songwriter, guitarist
Debut: (Album) *Say What You Will*, 1984
Signature: Soul Asylum
Facts: Played drums at age 17 with group The Shitz. Joined Dan Murphy and Karl Mueller to form Loud Fast Rules and, later, Soul Asylum.

Likes trains, doesn't own a television or CD player.

The Minneapolis group had been together ten years and was on the verge of breaking up when their sixth album, 1992's *Grave Dancers Union*, hit the *Billboard* top ten.
Relationship: Winona Ryder
Address: Columbia Records, 51 West 52nd St., New York, NY 10019

BRAD PITT

Real Name: William Bradley Pitt
Birthplace: Shawnee, OK
Birthdate: 12/18/64
Occupation: Actor
Education: Attended University of Missouri at Columbia, studied acting with Roy London
Debut: (TV) *Dallas*; (Film) *Cutting Class*, 1989
Signature: *Legends of the Fall*
Facts: Got his big break when

he was seen in a sexy Levi's TV ad in 1989.

Was cast as the hitchhiker in the 1991 movie *Thelma and Louise* only after William Baldwin turned down the role, choosing to star in *Backdraft* instead.

Dated Robin Givens for six months when they both acted in the TV series *Head of the Class*. Also lived with Juliette Lewis for several years.

While at college, posed shirtless for a campus fundraising calendar.
Original Job: Chauffeur for Strip-O-Gram women, dressed up as the El Pollo Loco restaurant chicken
Relationship: Gwyneth Paltrow
Address: Creative Artists Agency, 9830 Wilshire Blvd., Beverly Hills, CA 90212

SUSAN POWTER

Birthplace: Sydney, Australia
Birthdate: 1957
Occupation: Weight-loss expert
Education: High school dropout
Debut: (Book) *Stop the Insanity!*, 1993
Facts: Attended a Dominican convent in Australia until she was ten, when her family moved to Pelham Manor, NY.

Dropped out of school in the ninth grade.

Her idol is Jean Harris, the murderer of the Scarsdale diet doctor.

Her program-length infomercial, *Stop the Insanity!*, sold $50 million of her weight-loss products in 1993—a record at the time.
Infamy: Her brother disputes her claim that she once weighed 260 pounds, saying that the "fat" photo she shows on her infomercial was during her pregnancy.

Filed for bankruptcy in early 1995, due, she says, to legal wrangles with business partners Gerald and Richard Frankel.
Original Job: Nurse's aide, secretary, topless dancer
Marriages: Nic Villareal (divorced), Lincoln Apeland
Children: Damien, Kiel
Address: RPR & Associates, 5952 Royal Ln., Suite 264, Dallas, TX 75230

LISA MARIE PRESLEY-JACKSON

Birthplace: Memphis,TN
Birthdate: 2/1/68
Signature: Daughter of Elvis and Priscilla Presley

426

Facts: Will likely inherit $150 million on her 30th birthday.

When Lisa Marie once said she had never seen snow, Elvis flew her to Utah.

Is a devoted follower of the Church of Scientology.

Marriages: Danny Keough (divorced), Michael Jackson

Children: Danielle, Benjamin

Address: Sony Music Entertainment, 2100 Colorado Ave., Santa Monica, CA 90404

PRISCILLA PRESLEY

Birthplace: Brooklyn, NY

Birthdate: 5/24/45

Occupation: Actor

Education: Studied with Milton Katselas, attended Steven Peck Theatre Art School, Chuck Norris Karate School

Debut: (TV) *Those Amazing Animals,* 1980

Signature: *Dallas*

Fact: Began dating Elvis in Germany when he was in the army and she was the 14-year-old daughter of an air force officer.

Formed Bis and Beau boutique with dress designer Olivia, and marketed their exclusive designs to Barbra Streisand, Cher, Julie Christie, and others.

Original Job: Wella Balsam model

Marriages: Elvis Presley (divorced), Marco Garibaldi (relationship)

Children: Lisa Marie, Navarone Anthony

Address: William Morris Agency, 151 El Camino Dr., Beverly Hills, CA 90212

DENNIS QUAID

Birthplace: Houston, TX

Birthdate: 4/9/54

Occupation: Actor

Education: Attended the University of Houston

Debut: (Film) *September 30, 1955,* 1978

Fact: Wrote songs for three of his films: *The Night the Lights Went Out in Georgia* in 1981, *Tough Enough* in 1983, and *The Big Easy* in 1987.

Shed 47 pounds over a three-month period before playing the scrawny Doc Holliday in 1994's *Wyatt Earp.*

Infamy: Admitted to having a cocaine addiction, a problem he overcame with help from then girlfriend Meg Ryan.

Marriages: Pamela Jayne Soles (divorced), Meg Ryan

Child: Jack Henry

Famous Relative: Randy Quaid, actor, brother

Address: 8942 Wilshire Blvd., Beverly Hills, CA 90211

BONNIE RAITT

Birthplace: Burbank, CA

Birthdate: 9/8/49

Occupation: Singer, songwriter

Education: Attended Radcliffe College

Debut: (Album) *Bonnie Raitt,* 1971

Facts: Grew up in a Quaker family in L.A.

Got her first guitar for Christmas when she was eight.

Founded the annual Rhythm & Blues Awards, to provide money to deserving R&B stars who may have been cheated in the early days by managers and/or record labels.

Infamy: Was an avid drinker until giving up all alcohol and drugs a decade ago.

Marriage: Michael O'Keefe

Child: One son, unnamed at press time

Famous Relative: John Raitt, actor, father

Major Awards: Grammies, Album of the Year, Best Rock Vocal—Female, and Best Pop Vocal—Female, "Nick of Time," 1989; Grammy, Best Pop Vocal—Female, "Something To Talk About," 1991; Grammy, Best Rock Vocal—Female, "Luck of the Draw," 1991; Grammy, Best Rock Duo with Vocal, "Good Man, Good Woman" (with Delbert McClinton), 1991; Grammy, Best Pop Album, *Longing in Their Hearts,* 1994

Address: P.O. Box 626, Los Angeles, CA 90078

DAN RATHER

Birthplace: Wharton, TX

Birthdate: 10/31/31

Occupation: Anchor, correspondent, editor

Education: Sam Houston State College

Debut: (TV) KHOU-TV, Houston, 1960

Signature: *CBS Evening News with Dan Rather*

Facts: Succeeded Walter Cronkite in anchoring the evening news upon Cronkite's retirement in 1981.

In his 1994 book, *The Camera Never Blinks Twice,* he devotes less than a page to his former co-anchor Connie Chung.

Infamy: Angry over a delay in the start of the news, he walked

off the set, leaving TV screens blank for six minutes. He also had a stormy pre-election interview with then vice-president George Bush in 1988.

Marriage: Jean

Children: Robin, Danjack

Major Awards: Emmy, Correspondent, Coverage of the Watergate Affair, 1973; Emmy, Correspondent, Shooting of Governor Wallace, 1973; Emmy, Correspondent, Agnew Resignation, 1974; Emmy, Correspondent, Watergate, the White House Transcripts, 1974; Emmy, Documentary Correspondent, The Senate and the Watergate Affair, 1974; Emmy, Correspondent, "The Computers Are Coming," 1983; Emmy, Correspondent, Afghanistan, 1984; Emmy, Correspondent, Geneva Summit: Mexican Earthquake, 1985; Emmy, "The Battle for Afghanistan," 1987; Emmy, Correspondent, "Inside Afghanistan," 1987

Address: CBS, 51 West 52nd St., New York, NY 10019

ROBERT REDFORD

Real Name: Charles Robert Redford Jr.

Birthplace: Santa Monica, CA

Birthdate: 8/18/37

Occupation: Actor, director, producer

Education: Attended University of Colorado, Pratt Institute of Design, the American Academy of Dramatic Arts

Debut: (Stage) *Tall Story,* 1959; (Film) *War Hunt,* 1962.

Signature: *Butch Cassidy and the Sundance Kid*

Facts: Went to college on a baseball scholarship but lost it due to alcohol abuse. Left school in 1957 to go to Europe; lived in Paris and Florence as a painter.

Founded the nonprofit Sundance Institute in Park City, UT, which sponsors an annual film festival and provides support for independent film production.

Infamy: As a teenager, Redford stole and resold hubcaps.

Original Job: Carpenter, shop assistant, oil field worker

Marriage: Lola Van Wagenen (divorced), Kathy O'Rear (relationship)

Children: Shauna, Amy Hart, David James

Major Awards: Oscar, Best Director, *Ordinary People,* 1981; Golden Globe, New Male Film Star, *Daisy Clover,* 1966; Golden Globe, Male World Film Favorite,

1975, 1977, 1978; Golden Globe, Best Director, *Ordinary People,* 1982; Golden Globe, Cecil B. DeMille Lifetime Achievement Award, 1994

Address: Creative Artists Agency, 9830 Wilshire Blvd., Beverly Hills, CA 90212

KEANU REEVES

Birthplace: Beirut, Lebanon

Birthdate: 9/4/64

Occupation: Actor

Education: High school dropout; studied with Jasper Deeter

Debut: (Film) *Youngblood,* 1986

Signature: *Bill and Ted's Excellent Adventure*

Facts: His father is Chinese-Hawaiian and his mother is English.

Hasn't seen his father, who is currently serving a ten-year prison term in Hawaii for cocaine possession, since he was 13.

His first name means "cool breeze over the mountains" in Hawaiian.

Had traveled around the world by the time he was two years old.

Was the MVP on his high school hockey team in Toronto. A skilled goalie, Reeves earned the name "The Wall."

Turned down the Al Pacino/Robert De Niro film *Heat* to play Hamlet on stage in Winnipeg, Canada. The February 1995 sold-out run was critically acclaimed.

He plays bass in the band Dogstar.

His mother was a costume designer for rock stars.

Address: Creative Artists Agency, 9830 Wilshire Blvd., Beverly Hills, CA 90212

PAUL REISER

Birthplace: New York, NY

Birthdate: 3/30/57

Occupation: Actor, comedian

Education: SUNY-Binghamton

Debut: (Film) *Diner,* 1982

Signature: *Mad About You*

Facts: Has appeared in several hit films, including *Beverly Hills Cop* (1984), *Aliens* (1986), and *Beverly Hills Cop II* (1987).

Dubbed by reporters as part of the Four Funniest Men in the World Club, which includes Jerry Seinfeld, Larry Miller, and Mark Schiff. The members meet every New Year's Day for lunch (once they even met in London when Reiser was there filming *Aliens*).

Original Job: Health food distributor
Marriage: Paula
Child: Ezra Samuel
Address: United Talent Agency, 9560 Wilshire Blvd., Suite 500, Beverly Hills, CA 90212

BURT REYNOLDS

Birthplace: Waycross, GA
Birthdate: 2/11/36
Occupation: Actor
Education: Attended Florida State University; Palm Beach Junior College; Hyde Park Playhouse
Debut: (Stage) *Mister Roberts*, 1956; (Film) *Angel Baby*, 1961
Signature: *Smokey and the Bandit*
Facts: Reynolds was signed to play football with the Baltimore Colts but a car accident pushed him into acting.

He is part Cherokee and part Italian.

His father was the chief of police in Palm Beach, FL.
Infamy: Appeared nude in centerfold of the April 1972 issue of *Cosmopolitan*.

In the late '80s, unfounded AIDS rumors circulated when Reynolds was suffering from temporomandibular joint disorder.
Original Job: Bouncer, dishwasher, stuntman
Marriages: Judy Carne (divorced), Loni Anderson (divorced), Pam Seals (relationship)
Child: Quinton (adopted)
Major Awards: Emmy, Best Actor in a Comedy Series, *Evening Shade*, 1991; Golden Globe, Best Actor in a Comedy Series, *Evening Shade*, 1992
Address: William Morris Agency, 151 El Camino Dr., Beverly Hills, CA 90212

TRENT REZNOR

Birthplace: Mercer, PA
Birthdate: 5/17/65
Occupation: Singer, keyboardist
Education: Attended Allegheny College
Debut: (Album) *Pretty Hate Machine*, 1989
Signature: Nine Inch Nails
Facts: Reznor makes all Nine Inch Nails albums himself, using a band only for live shows.

In 1990, misplaced video footage of a half-naked Reznor being thrown from a building landed in the hands of the FBI, who thought it was an actual

murder. They led an investigation and found Reznor, alive and well and on tour. The publicity helped put Nine Inch Nails in the spotlight.

Mixed the soundtrack LP for Oliver Stone's film *Natural Born Killers* in 1994.

Lived for a year in the Benedict Canyon, CA, house where Sharon Tate and others were murdered by Charles Manson followers.

In what he says was possibly an unconscious attempt to identify with Woodstock '94 fans, he tripped his guitar player on the way to the stage, who fell flat in the mud and started the whole band in a mud match. They performed covered in the stuff.
Original Job: Odd jobs—including cleaning toilets—at a recording studio
Major Awards: Grammy, Best Metal Performance, "Wish," 1992
Address: Nothing Records, 2337 West 11th St., Suite 7, Cleveland, OH 44113

ANNE RICE

Real Name: Howard Allen O'Brien
Birthdate: 10/4/41
Occupation: Writer
Education: North Texas State University, San Francisco State College
Debut: (Book) *Interview with a Vampire*, 1976
Facts: Is the author of a series of pornographic novels under the name A. N. Roquelaure (which means "cloak").

Is afraid of the dark.

Was originally named after her father and mother's maiden name; changed name to Anne by the time she was in first grade.

In 1972, her six-year-old daughter died of leukemia.
Original Job: Waitress, cook, insurance claims adjuster
Marriage: Stan Rice
Children: Michele (deceased), Christopher
Address: Alfred A. Knopf, 201 East 50th St., New York, NY 10022

MICHAEL RICHARDS

Birthplace: Culver City, CA
Birthdate: 7/21/48
Occupation: Actor
Education: Los Angeles Valley College, California Insitute of the Arts
Debut: (TV) *Fridays*, 1980
Signature: *Seinfeld*

Facts: Has appeared in guest spots on *Hill Street Blues* and *Miami Vice*.

Starred with Weird Al Yankovic in the film *UHF*, 1989.

He was drafted at the height of the Vietnam War in 1970: "When the drill sergeant yelled at me on the first day, I tried to explain the duffel bag was too heavy."
Original Job: Postal worker, schoolbus driver
Marriages: Cathleen (divorced), Ann Talman (relationship)
Child: Sophia
Major Award: Emmy, Best Supporting Actor in a Comedy Series, *Seinfeld*, 1992, 1993
Address: International Creative Management, 8942 Wilshire Blvd., Beverly Hills, CA 90211

NATASHA RICHARDSON

Birthplace: London, England
Birthdate: 5/11/63
Occupation: Actor
Education: Central School for Speech and Drama
Debut: (Stage) *On the Razzle*, 1983
Signature: *The Handmaid's Tale*
Facts: At age four, appeared as a bridesmaid of Vanessa Redgrave in *The Charge of the Light Brigade*

Was named after the heroine in Tolstoy's *War and Peace*.
Marriages: Robert Fox (divorced), Liam Neeson
Child: Micheál
Famous Relatives: Vanessa Redgrave, actor, mother; Tony Richardson, director, father; Joely Richardson, actor, sister; Lynn Redgrave, actor, aunt
Quote: "I've spent half my life trying to get away from being Vanessa Redgrave's daughter, and now I've got to get away from being Liam Neeson's wife."
Address: International Creative Management, 8942 Wilshire Blvd., Beverly Hills, CA 90211

JOAN RIVERS

Real Name: Joan Alexandra Molinsky
Birthplace: Brooklyn, NY
Birthdate: 6/8/37
Occupation: Talk show host
Education: Connecticut College for Women, Barnard College
Debut: (TV) *The Tonight Show*, 1965
Facts: Wrote for *Candid Camera* and *The Ed Sullivan Show*.
Original Job: Publicist at Lord & Taylor, fashion coordinator for

Bond Clothing Stores, temporary office secretary, syndicated columnist
Marriage: Edgar Rosenberg (deceased), Orin Lehman (relationship)
Child: Melissa
Major Awards: Clio Award, 1976, 1982; Emmy, Best Host of a Talk Show, *The Joan Rivers Show*, 1990
Address: William Morris Agency, 151 El Camino Dr., Beverly Hills, CA 90212

TIM ROBBINS

Birthplace: West Covina, CA
Birthdate: 10/16/58
Occupation: Writer, director, actor
Education: Attended New York University, SUNY-Plattsburgh, and UCLA
Debut: (Film) *No Small Affair*, 1984
Signature: *The Player*
Facts: Was kicked off the hockey team in high school for fighting.

Founded Los Angeles theater group Actors' Gang.

Has been an outspoken political activist and peace advocate.
Original Job: Factory worker
Relationship: Susan Sarandon
Children: Jack Henry, Miles
Major Awards: Golden Globe, Best Actor in a Comedy, *The Player*, 1993; Golden Globe, Special Achievement, *Short Cuts*, 1994
Address: International Creative Management, 8942 Wilshire Blvd., Beverly Hills, CA 90211

JULIA ROBERTS

Real Name: Julie Fiona Roberts
Birthplace: Smyrna, GA
Birthdate: 10/28/67
Occupation: Actor
Education: High school
Debut: (TV) *Crime Story*, 1986
Signature: *Pretty Woman*
Facts: Originally wanted to be a veterinarian.

In 1986, she played opposite her brother (actor Eric Roberts) in the film *Blood Red*.

Was set to marry Kiefer Sutherland in 1991, but canceled the wedding at the last minute with virtually no explanation.
Original Job: Worked in a shoe store and an ice cream shop
Marriage: Lyle Lovett (separated)
Famous Relatives: Eric Roberts, actor, brother; Lisa Roberts, actor, sister
Major Awards: Golden Globe, Best Supporting Actress, *Steel Magnolias*, 1990; Golden Globe, Best Actress in a Comedy, *Pretty Woman*, 1991
Address: International Creative Management, 8942 Wilshire Blvd., Beverly Hills, CA 90211

AXL ROSE

Real Name: William Bailey
Birthplace: Lafayette, IN
Birthdate: 1962
Occupation: Singer
Education: High school dropout
Debut: (EP) *Live ?!*@ Like a Suicide*, 1986 (with Guns N' Roses)
Signature: Guns N' Roses
Facts: Guns N' Roses' first full-length album, *Appetite for Destruction* (1987), has sold more than 18 million copies.

In the middle of a 1991 St. Louis concert, Rose jumped into the crowd to remove a camera from a fan. The band left the stage, and the crowd rioted. Sixty fans ended up in the hospital, the brand-new concert hall suffered $500,000 in damages, and all of the band's equipment was destroyed.

Discovered when he was 17 that his real surname was Rose (his biological father had left when Axl was a baby, and his mother remarried). He took his stage name from a band he used to play with in Indiana. Had his name officially changed to W. Axl Rose in 1986.
Infamy: By the time he was 20, he had been jailed on numerous occasions for battery, contributing to the delinquency of a minor, public intoxication, criminal trespass, and mischief.

In 1990, he was arrested for allegedly hitting a neighbor over the head with a bottle after she complained about loud music.

Ex-wife Erin Everly and ex-fiancée Stephanie Seymour have filed separate suits against Rose charging that he subjected them to physical abuse.

Marriages: Erin Invicta Everly (annulled)
Address: Geffen Records, 9130 Sunset Blvd., Los Angeles, CA 90069

ROSEANNE

Birthplace: Salt Lake City, UT
Birthdate: 11/3/53
Occupation: Actor
Education: High school dropout
Debut: (TV) *Funny*, 1983; (Film) *She-Devil*, 1989
Signature: *Roseanne*
Facts: Dropped out of high school to hitchhike across country, landing in a Colorado artists' colony at age 18.

Had cosmetic surgery and weight reduction in 1993. Breasts were reduced from 40DD to 38C.

Had a tattoo on her upper right thigh that read: "Property of Tom Arnold." When the pair split, she tattooed over it with a flying fairy and flowers.

Claims she was physically and sexually abused as a child. Suppressed memory of the abuse until an adult.

Gave up baby girl for adoption at age 18.

Born to Jewish parents but raised as a Mormon in Salt Lake City. Her dad sold crucifixes door to door.
Infamy: Grabbed her crotch, spat, and screeched while singing the national anthem at a San Diego baseball game in 1990.
Original Job: Window dresser, cocktail waitress
Marriages: Bill Petland (divorced), Tom Arnold (divorced), Ben Thomas
Children: Brandi, Jessica, Jennifer, Jake, Buck
Major Awards: Golden Globe, Best Actress in a Comedy Series, *Roseanne*, 1993; Emmy, Best Actress in a Comedy Series, *Roseanne*, 1993
Address: William Morris Agency, 151 El Camino Dr., Beverly Hills, CA 90212

MEG RYAN

Real Name: Margaret Hyra
Birthplace: Fairfield, CT
Birthdate: 11/19/61
Occupation: Actor
Education: Attended New York University
Debut: (Film) *Rich and Famous*, 1981; (TV) *As the World Turns*, 1983

Signature: *When Harry Met Sally . . .*
Fact: Became high school homecoming queen when the original queen was suspended.

Her strained relationship with her mother became tabloid-show fodder when her stepfather wrote an article about the pair's discord in a magazine in 1992. Ryan subsequently ended all contact with them.

Met husband Quaid on the set of the comedy film, *Innerspace*, in 1987. A year later, they professionally reunited for the unsuccessful film *D.O.A.*
Marriage: Dennis Quaid
Child: Jack Henry
Address: International Creative Management, 8942 Wilshire Blvd., Beverly Hills, CA 90211

WINONA RYDER

Real Name: Winona Laura Horowitz
Birthplace: Winona, MN
Birthdate: 10/29/71
Occupation: Actor
Education: High school
Debut: (Film) *Lucas*, 1986
Signature: *Beetlejuice*
Facts: Her childhood home in Elk, CA, had no electricity.

In junior high school, was attacked and beaten by fellow students during her first week at a new school, apparently because they mistook her for a boy.

Has read *The Catcher in the Rye* countless times, and travels with a copy.

Dated Christian Slater, was engaged to Johnny Depp.

Timothy Leary, the famous psychologist and countercultural philosopher, was her godfather.
Relationship: David Pirner
Major Award: Golden Globe, Best Supporting Actress, *The Age of Innocence*, 1994
Address: Creative Artists Agency, 9830 Wilshire Blvd., Beverly Hills, CA 90212

SALT

Real Name: Cheryl James
Birthplace: Brooklyn, NY
Birthdate: 3/8/64
Occupation: Rap artist
Education: Queensborough Community College
Debut: (Album) *Hot, Cool & Vicious*, 1986
Facts: Teamed with Pepa to create first female rap group to cross over to the *Billboard* Pop Chart with the gold single "Push It."

Both Salt and Pepa worked at Sears with Martin Lawrence and Kid 'N Play.
Original Job: Telephone customer service representative
Relationship: Gavin Wray (engaged)
Child: Corin
Major Award: Grammy, Best Rap Performance by a Group or Duo, "None of Your Business," (with Salt-N-Pepa), 1994
Address: Next Plateau Records, 1650 Broadway, Room 1103, New York, NY 10019

ADAM SANDLER

Birthplace: Brooklyn, NY
Birthdate: 9/9/66
Occupation: Comedian, actor
Education: New York University
Debut: (TV) *The Cosby Show*, 1987; (Film) *Shakes the Clown*, 1992
Signature: *Saturday Night Live*
Facts: Became a writer for *Saturday Night Live* in 1990, but his sketches were often too eccentric for others to make their own. He soon became a "featured player" doing those skits and, after the success of his Opera Man, became a regular cast member.

As a developing comic, was so taken by Rodney Dangerfield he memorized many of Dangerfield's routines.
Original Job: Stand-up comedian
Relationship: Margaret Ruden (engaged)
Address: Creative Artists Agency, 9830 Wilshire Blvd., Beverly Hills, CA 90212

SUSAN SARANDON

Real Name: Susan Abigail Tomalin
Birthplace: New York, NY
Birthdate: 10/4/46
Occupation: Actor
Education: Catholic University of America
Debut: (Film) *Joe*, 1970
Signature: *Thelma & Louise*
Facts: Her background is Welsh-Italian. Was one of nine children, and attended Catholic school.

Is 12 years older than beau Tim Robbins.

An activist for numerous political, cultural, and health causes, she digressed during her 1991 Academy Awards presentation to speak for a half-minute on behalf of Haitian refugees with AIDS.
Original Job: While in college,

worked in the drama department, modeled, and cleaned apartments

Marriages: Chris Sarandon (divorced), Tim Robbins (relationship)
Children: Eva Maria Livia, Jack Henry, Miles
Address: International Creative Management, 8942 Wilshire Blvd., Beverly Hills, CA 90211

DIANE SAWYER

Birthplace: Glasgow, KY
Birthdate: 12/22/45
Occupation: Broadcast journalist
Education: Wellesley College
Debut: (TV) WLKY-TV, Louisville, 1967
Signature: *Primetime Live*
Facts: Was national Junior Miss, largely on the strength of her interview and essays.

As a weathercaster in Louisville, KY, she spruced up forecasts with quotes from her favorite poems.

Served as staff assistant to former President Nixon and helped him research his memoirs.
Marriage: Mike Nichols
Major Awards: Emmy, "PanAm Flight 103," 1990; Emmy, "Murder in Beverly Hills," 1991
Address: ABC, 77 West 66th St., New York, NY 10023

CLAUDIA SCHIFFER

Birthplace: Dusseldorf, Germany
Birthdate: 8/24/71
Occupation: Supermodel
Education: High school
Facts: Tripped during her runway modeling debut in 1990.

Earns as much as $50,000 a day.

Opened Fashion Cafe in New York City in 1995 with fellow supermodels Elle MacPherson and Naomi Campbell.
Relationship: David Copperfield (engaged)
Address: 5 Union Sq., #500, New York, NY 10003

ARNOLD SCHWARZENEGGER

Birthplace: Graz, Austria
Birthdate: 7/30/47
Occupation: Actor, director, bodybuilder
Education: University of Wisconsin
Debut: (Film) *Hercules in New York,* 1969
Signature: *The Terminator*
Facts: After coming to the U.S. in the '60s, founded a bricklaying

business, Pumping Bricks, to finance his bodybuilding career.

Won the Austrian Junior Olympic weightlifting championship as well as Junior Mr. Europe and several curling titles.

In 1974, acted in *Happy Anniversary and Goodbye,* an unsold CBS sitcom pilot starring Lucille Ball and Art Carney.

Has killed over 275 people on screen.
Infamy: Named in a 1995 paternity suit by a Texas woman who claims he fathered her daughter 12 years earlier.
Original Job: Managed a Munich health club
Marriage: Maria Owings Shriver
Children: Katherine Eunice, Christina Maria Aurelia, Patrick
Major Award: Golden Globe, Best Newcomer in Films, *Stay Hungry,* 1977
Quote: "Everything I have ever done in my life has always stayed. I've just added to it...But I will not change. Because when you are successful and you change, you are an idiot."
Address: International Creative Management, 8942 Wilshire Blvd., Beverly Hills, CA 90211

MARTIN SCORSESE

Birthplace: New York, NY
Birthdate: 11/17/42
Occupation: Director
Education: New York University
Debut: (Film) *Boxcar Bertha,* 1972
Signature: *Taxi Driver*
Facts: Collaborated on the production of Michael Jackson's *Bad* video in 1987.

Was originally enrolled as an English major before switching to film.
Original Job: Faculty assistant and instructor in film department at NYU
Marriages: Larraine Marie Brennan (divorced), Julia Cameron (divorced), Isabella Rosellini (divorced), Barbara DeFina (separated)
Children: Catherine Terese, Domenica Elizabeth
Major Award: Cannes Film Festival, Palme d'Or, *Taxi Driver,* 1976
Address: Creative Artists Agency, 9830 Wilshire Blvd., Beverly Hills, CA 90212

STEVEN SEAGAL

Birthplace: Lansing, MI
Birthdate: 4/10/51
Occupation: Actor, producer

Education: Attended Orange Coast College
Debut: (Film) *Above the Law,* 1988
Signature: *Hard To Kill*
Facts: Founder, Aikido Ten Shin Dojo, Los Angeles.

First non-Asian to successfully open a martial arts academy in Japan.

In 1968, moved to Japan, where he taught English and wrote articles for Japanese magazines and newspapers.

Organized security for the departure of the Shah's family from Iran.

Commands the title of Shihan (Master of Masters).
Infamy: Was sued by a film assistant for sexual harassment. Paid money to settle out of court in 1990.

In 1994, was married to both his first and second wives simultaneously.

Scriptwriter Lars Hansson claimed in 1994 that Seagal threatened him with death after he refused to sell him film rights to a CIA hit-man story.

In 1995, was accused by ex-girlfriend Cheryl Shuman of harassing her. A judge threw out her lawsuit, calling it unintelligible.
Original Job: Martial arts instructor, bodyguard
Marriages: Miyako Fujitani (divorced), Adrienne LaRussa (annulled), Kelly LeBrock (separated)
Children: Kentaro, Ayako, Annalisa, Arissa, Dominick San Rocco
Address: Creative Artists Agency, 9830 Wilshire Blvd., Beverly Hills, CA 90212

JERRY SEINFELD

Birthplace: Brooklyn, NY
Birthdate: 4/29/55

Occupation: Actor, comedian
Education: Queens College
Debut: (Stand-up) Catch a Rising Star, Manhattan, 1976
Signature: *Seinfeld*
Facts: At his first stage appearance, he was so nervous he forgot his routine and only mumbled the words "The beach. Driving. Shopping. Parents," and walked off.

Owns several dozen pairs of sneakers, including a custom pair of "Air Seinfelds."

Has practiced yoga for 20 years and is a strict vegetarian.
Infamy: Created a stir when he began dating 18-year-old Shoshanna Lonstein in 1993.
Original Job: Sought the worst jobs possible, including selling light bulbs over the phone and costume jewelry on the streets of New York, to force himself to succeed at comedy
Major Awards: American Comedy Award, Funniest Male Stand-up, 1988; Emmy, Best Comedy Series, *Seinfeld,* 1993; Golden Globe, Best Actor in a Comedy Series, *Seinfeld,* 1994
Address: Creative Artists Agency, 9830 Wilshire Blvd. Beverly Hills, CA 90212

JANE SEYMOUR

Real Name: Joyce Frankenberg
Birthplace: Hillingdon, England
Birthdate: 2/15/51
Occupation: Actor
Education: Attended Arts Educational School, London
Debut: (Film) *Oh, What a Lovely War,* 1968
Signature: *Dr. Quinn, Medicine Woman*
Facts: Danced with the London Festival Ballet at 13.

Named Honorary Citizen of Illinois by Governor Thompson in 1977.
Original Job: Ballet dancer
Marriages: Michael Attenborough (divorced), Geoffrey Planer (divorced), David Flynn (divorced), James Keach
Children: Stepdaughter Katie, stepson Sean, Jennifer, Kalen
Major Awards: Golden Globe, Best Actress in a Miniseries, *East of Eden,* 1982; Emmy, Best Supporting Actress in a Miniseries, *Onassis,* 1988
Address: Creative Artists Agency, 9830 Wilshire Blvd., Beverly Hills, CA 90212

PAUL SHAFFER

Birthplace: Toronto, Canada
Birthdate: 11/28/49

Occupation: Musician, bandleader
Education: University of Toronto
Debut: (TV) *Saturday Night Live*, 1975
Signature: *Late Show with David Letterman*
Facts: Appeared in the movie *This Is Spinal Tap*, 1984.

Starred in sitcom *A Year at the Top*, which was canceled after only six episodes.
Marriage: Cathy Vasapoli
Daughter: Victoria Lily
Address: Worldwide Pants Inc., 1697 Broadway, New York, NY 10019

TUPAC SHAKUR

Birthplace: New York, NY
Birthdate: 1971
Occupation: Rap artist
Education: Attended Baltimore School for the Arts
Debut: (Film) *Juice*, 1992; (Album) *2Pacalypse Now* (solo), 1992
Facts: Made his acting debut at age 13 in a production of *A Raisin in the Sun*.

Nickname: "Rebel of the Underground."

Was a member of the rap group Digital Underground.

Grandfather Elmer Pratt, a member of the Black Panthers, is currently serving a life sentence for murder in California. His mother, an activist herself, testified at the trial of the Chicago Seven, and Tupac was almost born in jail.
Infamy: Convicted of attacking a former employee on a music video set. Served fifteen days in jail, forty-five days of community service, fined $2,000.

In 1993, arrested in Atlanta for allegedly shooting two off-duty police officers.

Convicted in 1994 on charges of sexually assaulting a female fan. In the midst of the trial, he was shot in the head and groin during an unrelated robbery attempt. Shakur was sentenced to a maximum term of four and one-half years in prison.

In 1995, married longtime girlfriend in New York's Clinton Correctional Facility.
Marriage: Keisha Morris
Famous Relative: Elmer Pratt, political activist, grandfather
Address: Interscope Records, 10900 Wilshire Blvd., Suite 1230, Los Angeles, CA 90024

GARRY SHANDLING

Birthplace: Chicago, IL
Birthdate: 11/29/49
Occupation: Actor, writer, comedian
Education: University of Arizona
Debut: (TV) *Sanford & Son*, 1976
Signature: *Larry Sanders Show*
Fact: Wrote for *Sanford & Son*, *Welcome Back, Kotter*, and *Three's Company*.

Named *The Tonight Show*'s permanent guest host in 1986 and was widely expected to be Johnny Carson's successor, but decided he didn't enjoy it enough so he left.
Address: Creative Artists Agency, 9830 Wilshire Blvd., Beverly Hills, CA 90212

WILLIAM SHATNER

Birthplace: Montreal, Canada
Birthdate: 3/22/31
Occupation: Actor, author, producer, director
Education: McGill University
Debut: (TV) *Goodyear TV Playhouse*, 1956
Signature: *Star Trek*
Facts: Has written a series of books, beginning with *TekWar*, which were turned into movies in which he stars.

Most celebrated pre-*Trek* experience was as a guest on one of the most famous *Twilight Zone* episodes, "Nightmare at 20,000 Feet," in 1963.

One of his leisure activities is breeding horses.

Became CEO of a special effects company, CORE Digital Pictures, in 1995.
Original Job: Novelist
Marriages: Gloria Rand (divorced), Marcy Lafferty (divorced)
Children: Leslie, Lisabeth, Melanie
Address: 100 Wilshire Blvd., Suite 1800, Santa Monica, CA 90401

CHARLIE SHEEN

Real Name: Carlos Irwin Estevez
Birthplace: Los Angeles, CA
Birthdate: 9/3/65
Occupation: Actor
Education: High school dropout
Debut: (TV) *The Execution of Private Slovik*, 1975; (Film) *Grizzly II: The Predator*, 1984
Signature: *Platoon*
Facts: Pitched on the Santa Monica High School baseball team. Was kicked off the team for skipping school.

A Peace of My Mind, a collection of his poetry, was published in 1991.

As a teenager, produced and directed over 200 Super-8 and video short films, some starring future stars such as Sean and Chris Penn, Rob and Chad Lowe, and his brother Emilio Estevez.
Infamy: Admits to having been addicted to drugs and alcohol.

Admits to having paid prostitutes employed by Heidi Fleiss at least $2,000 per encounter between 1991 and 1993.
Relationship: Donna Peel (engaged)
Child: Cassandra (with Ginger Lynn Allen)
Famous Relatives: Martin Sheen, actor, father; Emilio Estevez, actor, brother; Renee Estevez, actor, sister; Ramon Estevez, actor, brother
Major Awards: Emmy, Best Guest Actor in a Comedy, *Murphy Brown*, 1993
Address: International Creative Management, 8942 Wilshire Blvd., Beverly Hills, CA 90211

BROOKE SHIELDS

Birthplace: New York, NY
Birthdate: 5/31/65
Occupation: Actor
Education: Princeton University
Debut: (Film) *Alice, Sweet Alice*, 1978
Signature: *Pretty Baby*
Facts: Began her career as an Ivory Snow baby when she was 11 months old. Appeared on more than 30 magazine covers at age 16.

Says now that her overbearing ex-manager stage-mother, Teri, was an alcoholic. Shields was conceived out of wedlock and her father was around only for the first few months of her life.

Has been linked romantically to Liam Neeson, Prince Albert of Monaco, George Michael, Michael Bolton, and Michael Jackson.
Infamy: As the 12-year-old star of *Pretty Baby*, played a prostitute in various states of undress.
Original Job: Model
Relationship: André Agassi
Address: William Morris Agency, 151 El Camino Dr., Beverly Hills, CA 90212

GRANT SHOW

Birthplace: Detroit, MI
Birthdate: 2/27/62
Occupation: Actor

Education: UCLA, London Academy of Music and Dramatic Arts
Debut: (TV) *Ryan's Hope*
Signature: *Melrose Place*
Facts: Started out as friend of Luke Perry on *Beverly Hills 90210* before moving to the spin-off series *Melrose Place*.

Played police officer Rick Hyde on *Ryan's Hope*, but left the role to study acting in London.
Relationship: Laura Leighton (engaged)
Address: Creative Artists Agency, 9830 Wilshire Blvd., Beverly Hills, CA 90212

ANDREW SHUE

Birthplace: South Orange, NJ
Birthdate: 2/20/67
Occupation: Actor
Education: Dartmouth
Signature: *Melrose Place*
Facts: Played professional soccer for the Bulawayo Highlanders in Zimbabwe after graduating from Dartmouth.

Taught math in Zimbabwe.
Original Job: Professional soccer player, math instructor
Relationship: Jennifer Hageney (engaged)
Famous Relative: Elisabeth Shue, actor, sister
Address: Spelling Television, 5700 Wilshire Blvd., Los Angeles, CA 90036

ALICIA SILVERSTONE

Birthplace: San Francisco, CA
Birthdate: 1976
Occupation: Actor
Education: High school equivalency
Debut: (Film) *The Crush*, 1993
Signature: Aerosmith music video "Cryin'"
Facts: Filed for emancipation from her parents at 15 so she could work in films as an adult.

Won MTV's Villain of the Year

award in 1993 for her performance as the lovestruck psychopath in *The Crush*.
Quote: "People who say I'm sexy don't really understand what sexy means. I'm always dirty and always in sweats. That's the real me."
Address: Premiere Artists Agency, 8899 Beverly Blvd., Suite 102, Los Angeles, CA 90048

NEIL SIMON

Real Name: Marvin Neil Simon
Birthplace: Bronx, NY
Birthdate: 7/4/27
Occupation: Playwright, screenwriter, producer
Education: New York University
Debut: (Stage) *Adventures of Marco Polo, A Musical Fantasy,* 1959; (Film) *After the Fox,* 1966
Signature: *The Odd Couple*
Facts: Flew in the U.S. Air Force, 1945–46.

Met his third wife in 1985 when she was handing out perfume samples at the Beverly Hills Neiman Marcus store.

Owns Eugene O'Neill Theatre in New York.

Has written more than 27 Broadway shows.
Original Job: Mail room clerk
Marriages: Joan Baim (deceased), Marsha Mason (divorced), Diane Lander (divorced, remarried, divorced)
Children: Two daughters
Major Awards: Tony, Best Author (Dramatic), *The Odd Couple,* 1965; Tony, Special Award, 1975; Golden Globe, Best Screenplay, *The Goodbye Girl,* 1978; Tony, Best Play, *Biloxi Blues,* 1985; Tony, Best Play, *Lost in Yonkers,* 1991; Pulitzer Prize, Best Play, *Lost in Yonkers,* 1991
Address: c/o Gary DeSilva, 616 Highland, Manhattan Beach, CA 90266

PAUL SIMON

Birthplace: Newark, NJ
Birthdate: 10/13/41
Occupation: Singer, songwriter
Education: Queens College, attended Brooklyn Law School
Debut: (Song) "Hey Schoolgirl" (with Art Garfunkel, under the name Tom and Jerry), 1957
Signature: *Graceland*
Facts: In sixth grade, he played the White Rabbit to Garfunkel's Cheshire Cat in *Alice in Wonderland*.

Co-owned the Philadelphia Furies, a soccer team, with Mick

Jagger, Peter Frampton, and Rick Wakeman.
Marriages: Peggy Harper (divorced), Carrie Fisher (divorced), Edie Brickell
Children: Harper, Adrian Edward, Lulu
Famous Relative: Louis Simon, bassist, father
Major Awards: Grammy, Record of the Year, "Mrs. Robinson" (with Simon & Garfunkel), 1968; Grammy, Best Pop Performance—Duo or Group, "Mrs. Robinson" (with Simon & Garfunkel), 1968; Grammy, Best Soundtrack Album, *The Graduate* (with Dave Grusin), 1968; Grammy, Record of the Year, "Bridge over Troubled Water" (with Simon & Garfunkel), 1970; Grammy, Album of the Year, *Bridge over Troubled Water* (with Simon & Garfunkel), 1970; Grammy, Song of the Year, "Bridge over Troubled Water," 1970; Grammy, Best Rock/Contemporary Song, "Bridge over Troubled Water," 1970; Grammy, Album of the Year, *Still Crazy After All These Years,* 1975; Grammy, Best Pop Vocal—Male, "Still Crazy After All These Years," 1975; Grammy, Album of the Year, *Graceland,* 1986; Emmy, Best Writing in a Comedy, Variety, or Music Special, *The Paul Simon Special,* 1978; inducted into the Rock and Roll Hall of Fame (with Art Garfunkel), 1990
Address: 1619 Broadway, Suite 500, New York, NY 10019

O.J. SIMPSON

Real Name: Orenthal James Simpson
Birthplace: San Francisco, CA
Birthdate: 7/9/47
Occupation: Football player (retired), actor
Education: Attended City College of San Francisco, University of Southern California
Debut: Halfback, Buffalo Bills, 1969, (Film) *The Klansman,* 1974
Facts: Had rickets as a child, wore braces on his legs.

In 1979, his daughter Aaren drowned in the family swimming pool.

Films include *The Towering Inferno* and *The Naked Gun*.
Infamy: In 1994, was indicted for the murder of ex-wife Nicole and her friend Ronald Goldman. Reports that he had beaten Nicole during their marriage surfaced during the trial.

Major Awards: Heisman Trophy, 1968; set many NFL rushing records including first to gain 2,000 yards in season, 1973; Pro Football Hall of Fame, 1985
Marriages: Marquerite L. Whitley (divorced), Nicole Brown (divorced), Paula Barbieri (relationship)
Children: Arnelle, Jason, Aaren (deceased) (with Marguerite Whitley), Sydney, Justin
Address: International Creative Management, 8942 Wilshire Blvd., Beverly Hills, CA 90211

FRANK SINATRA

Real Name: Francis Albert Sinatra
Birthplace: Hoboken, NJ
Birthdate: 12/12/15
Occupation: Singer, actor
Education: Attended Drake Institute
Debut: (Radio) *Lucky Strike Hit Parade*
Signature: "My Way"
Facts: Provided a voice for the 1988 film *Who Framed Roger Rabbit*.

Weighed over 13 pounds at birth and was mistaken for stillborn until his grandmother held him under a cold water faucet.

Begged executives at Columbia to let him play the key role of Maggio in *From Here to Eternity,* and agreed to play the part for only $8,000.

Has recorded over fifteen hundred songs.
Infamy: Has been reportedly linked to the Mafia.
Original Job: Worked on the news truck of the *Jersey Observer,* later was a copy boy and covered college sports
Marriages: Nancy Barbato (divorced), Ava Gardner (divorced), Mia Farrow (divorced), Barbara Marx
Children: Nancy, Christine, Frank Jr.
Famous Relatives: Nancy Sinatra, singer, actor, daughter; Frank Sinatra Jr., actor, son; Christine Sinatra, producer, daughter
Major Awards: Special Academy Award, 1945; Oscar, Supporting Actor, *From Here to Eternity,* 1953; Grammy, Best Album, *Come Dance with Me,* 1959; Grammy, Best Album, *September of My Years,* 1965; Grammy, Best Album, *Moonlight,* 1966; Grammy, Record of the Year, "Moonlight," 1966; Grammy, Best Male Vocalist, 1959, 1965, 1966; Emmy,

Outstanding Musical Special, *Frank Sinatra: A Man and His Music,* 1965; Oscar, Jean Hersholt Humanitarian Award, 1970; Presidential Medal of Freedom, 1985
Address: Warner Brothers Recording, 3300 Warner Blvd., Burbank, CA 91505

SINBAD

Real Name: David Adkins
Birthplace: Benton Harbor, MI
Birthdate: 11/10/56
Occupation: Actor, comedian
Education: Attended University of Denver
Debut: (TV) *Comedy Tonight,* 1985; (Film) *That's Adequate,* 1989
Signature: *Sinbad*
Facts: Finalist in the comedy competition on *Star Search* in 1984.

Intended to play pro basketball.
Infamy: While in the Air Force, impersonated officers and went AWOL.
Marriage: Meredith (divorced)
Children: Paige, Royce
Address: William Morris Agency, 151 El Camino Dr., Beverly Hills, CA 90212

SLASH

Real Name: Saul Hudson
Birthplace: Stoke-on-Trent, England
Birthdate: 1965
Occupation: Guitarist
Debut: (EP) *Live ?!*@ & Like a Suicide,* 1986 (with Guns N' Roses)
Signature: Guns N' Roses
Facts: His mother, Ola, was a costume designer for The Pointer Sisters and David Bowie. His father Anthony designed album covers.

Grew up in California's Laurel Canyon. His next-door-neighbor was Joni Mitchell.

At Guns N' Roses' first official Los Angeles show, two people showed up.

When on tour with Aerosmith in 1987, their contract stipulated that consumption of chemical substances would be confined to their dressing room so as not to tempt Aerosmith members.
Infamy: The song "Coma" was based on his numerous heroin overdoses.
Marriage: Renee
Address: Geffen Records, 9130 Sunset Blvd., Los Angeles, CA 90069

CHRISTIAN SLATER

Real Name: Christian Hawkins
Birthplace: New York, NY
Birthdate: 8/18/69
Occupation: Actor
Education: Attended Dalton School, Professional Children's School
Debut: (TV) One Life To Live, 1976; (Film) The Legend of Billie Jean, 1985
Signature: Heathers
Facts: Began his career in the stage revival of The Music Man, at the age of nine.

Dated Winona Ryder, Christy Turlington, and Samantha Mathis.

Was born on the final day of Woodstock.
Infamy: Arrested twice for drunk driving, served ten days in jail in 1990.

Arrested in 1994 for attempting to carry a 9mm pistol through an airport metal detector. He was ordered to spend three days working with homeless children on a plea-bargained misdemeanor charge in 1995.

Was sued in 1995 for palimony seeking $100,000 plus property worth $2 million by ex-fiancée Nina Peterson Huang, who claims she had an agreement with Slater to put her career on hold during their five years of living together. Four months after they got engaged, Huang left the volatile actor and broke off the relationship.
Famous Relatives: Mary Jo Slater, casting director, mother; Michael Hawkins, stage actor, father
Address: Creative Artists Agency, 9830 Wilshire Blvd., Beverly Hills, CA 90212

WILL SMITH

Birthplace: Philadelphia, PA
Birthdate: 9/25/68
Occupation: Actor, rap artist
Education: High school
Debut: Rapper as part of DJ Jazzy Jeff & The Fresh Prince
Signature: The Fresh Prince of Bel Air
Facts: Turned down a scholarship to MIT to pursue music.

By 1989 had made and lost his first million dollars, the latter due to excessive spending.

Earned his nickname, the Prince, from a teacher in Overbrook High School because of his regal attitude and ability to talk his way out of difficult situations.
Original Job: Rap artist

Marriage: Sheree Zampino (separated)
Child: Willard C. "Trey" III
Major Awards: Grammy, Best Rap Performance—Solo, "Parents Just Don't Understand" (with D.J. Jazzy Jeff & The Fresh Prince), 1988; Grammy, Best Rap Performance—Duo or Group, "Summertime" (with D.J. Jazzy Jeff & The Fresh Prince), 1991
Address: Creative Artists Agency, 9830 Wilshire Blvd., Beverly Hills, CA 90212

WESLEY SNIPES

Birthplace: Orlando, FL
Birthdate: 7/31/62
Occupation: Actor
Education: Attended New York City's High School of the Performing Arts, SUNY-Purchase
Debut: (Film) Wildcats, 1985
Signature: New Jack City
Facts: Has studied martial arts, including the African/Brazilian version Capoeira, since his youth.

Appeared in commercials for Levi's 501 Jeans and Coca-Cola Classic.

Snipes came to director Spike Lee's attention when he played a young punk who threatens Michael Jackson in the Martin Scorsese–directed video Bad, 1987.
Infamy: Arrested in 1994 for reckless driving for speeding at up to 120 mph on his motorcycle in Florida, leading state troopers on a 30-mile chase. Sentenced to eighty hours of community service, six months' probation, and $7,000 in fines and court costs.
Original Job: Street and puppet theater in his troupe, Struttin' Street Stuff, installed telephones
Marriages: One marriage (divorced), Roshumba (relationship)
Child: Jelani
Major Award: ACE Award, Vietnam War Story, 1989
Address: Creative Artists Agency, 9830 Wilshire Blvd., Beverly Hills, CA 90212

SNOOP DOGGY DOGG

Real Name: Calvin Broadus
Birthplace: Long Beach, CA
Birthdate: 1971
Occupation: Rap artist
Education: High school
Debut: (Album) Doggystyle, 1993
Facts: Nickname "Snoop" was given to him by his mother;

"Doggy Dogg" came from a cousin who used to call himself Tate Doggy Dog.

Says his musical heroes are Al Green, Curtis Mayfield, and L. J. Reynolds of the Dramatics.
Infamy: One month after graduating from Long Beach Polytechnic High School, was arrested and incarcerated on a drug charge.

In 1993 went on trial for murder of Phil Woldermariam, having been arrested while driving the Jeep from which two fatal gunshots were fired by his bodyguard. It was reported that the victim was seen arguing with the rapper and his friend and brandishing a weapon prior to the shooting. Snoop's attorney claimed that Woldermariam (on probation after serving a one-year jail term for firing a firearm on public property) had previously assaulted the rapper with a gun, holding it to his head and threatening his life during the filming of a video.

In 1994, was arrested in Lake Charles, LA, when deputies attempting to deliver civil court papers smelled marijuana outside his hotel room. Charged with possession of marijuana and drug paraphernalia.
Original Job: Sold candy, delivered newspapers, bagged groceries
Address: International Creative Management, 8942 Wilshire Blvd., Beverly Hills, CA 90211

TOM SNYDER

Birthplace: Milwaukee, WI
Birthdate: 5/12/36
Occupation: Talk show host
Education: Attended Marquette University
Debut: (Radio) WRIT-AM, Milwaukee; (TV) KNBC-TV News, Los Angeles; 1970
Signature: Tomorrow
Facts: David Letterman, whose company is producing Snyder's new late-night talk show, Late Late Show with Tom Snyder, is the one who took over Snyder's time slot when NBC dropped Tomorrow in 1982.
Marriage: One marriage (divorced)
Child: One daughter
Major Award: Emmy, Best Host, Tomorrow, 1974
Address: CBS, 51 West 52nd St., New York, NY 10019

STEPHEN SONDHEIM

Birthplace: New York, NY
Birthdate: 3/22/30
Occupation: Composer, lyricist
Education: Williams College
Debut: (Stage) Girls of Summer, 1956
Signature: West Side Story
Facts: In May 1992, turned down the NEA's Medal of Arts Award, claiming the agency is "a symbol of censorship and repression rather than encouragement and support."

When Sondheim left home at age 15, he was taken in by Oscar Hammerstein II (lyricist of Oklahoma!), who taught him how to structure songs.
Original Job: Wrote for Topper TV series, 1953, crossword puzzle writer
Major Awards: Pulitzer Prize, Best Play, Sunday in the Park with George, 1985; Grammy, Best Cast Show Album, Company, 1970; Grammy, Best Cast Show Album, A Little Night Music, 1973; Grammy, Song of the Year, "Send in the Clowns," 1975; Grammy, Best Cast Show Album, Sweeney Todd, 1979; Grammy, Best Cast Show Album, Sunday in the Park with George, 1984; Grammy, Best Cast Show Album, West Side Story, 1985; Grammy, Best Cast Show Album Follies in Concert, 1986; Grammy, Best Cast Show Album, Into the Woods, 1988; Oscar, Best Song, "Sooner or Later (I Always Get My Man)," 1990; Tony, Best Score, Company, 1971; Tony, Best Score, Follies, 1972; Tony, Best Score, A Little Night Music, 1973; Tony, Best Score, Sweeney Todd, 1979; Tony, Best Score, Into the Woods, 1988; Tony, Best Score, Passion, 1994
Quote: "I like neurotic people. I like troubled people. Not that I don't like squared away people, but I prefer neurotic people.... Songs can't develop uncomplicated characters or unconflicted people. You can't just tell the sunny side and have a story with any richness to it."
Address: c/o F. Roberts, 65 East 55th St., #702, New York, NY 10022

AARON SPELLING

Birthplace: Dallas, TX
Birthdate: 4/22/23
Occupation: Producer, writer
Education: Attended the Sorbonne, Southern Methodist University

Signature: *Beverly Hills 90210*
Facts: Served in U.S. Army Air Force, 1942–45; awarded the Bronze Star and Purple Heart with Oak Leaf Cluster.

In 1969, founded Thomas-Spelling Productions with actor Danny Thomas.

Has produced network hit series such as *The Mod Squad*, *Starsky and Hutch*, *S.W.A.T.*, *Charlie's Angels*, *Family*, *Dynasty*, *Beverly Hills 90210*, and *Melrose Place*.
Original Job: Actor
Marriage: Carole Gene Marer
Children: Victoria "Tori" Davey, Randall Gene
Famous Relative: Tori Spelling, actor, daughter
Major Awards: Emmy, Outstanding Drama/Comedy Special, *Day One*, 1989; Emmy, Outstanding Made-for-TV Movie, *And the Band Played On*, 1993
Quote: "I just got tired of the critics saying that I was the master of schlock. It didn't bother me until my kids began growing up and reading it. Well, I'm proud of those entertainment shows they call schlock."
Address: Creative Artists Agency, 9830 Wilshire Blvd., Beverly Hills, CA 90212

STEVEN SPIELBERG

Birthplace: Cincinnati, OH
Birthdate: 12/18/47
Occupation: Director, producer
Education: California State College at Long Beach
Debut: (TV) *Night Gallery*, 1969
Signature: *E.T., the Extra-Terrestrial*
Facts: Made the film *Firelight* at age 16, about the reflecting telescope he made himself, and his father hired a Phoenix, AZ, movie house to show it.

Became a TV director at Universal Pictures at age 20 after finding an empty office and pretending he belonged there.

Was not accepted by the University of Southern California's film department.

Co-owns the L.A. restaurant Dive! with Jeffrey Katzenberg.

A 22-minute film he made in college, *Amblin'*, brought him the attention of Sidney Sheinberg, at the time head of Universal Television. It also provided the name for his production company.

Directed the first episode of

Columbo, as well as installments of *Marcus Welby, M.D.*

His DreamWorks SKG studio, formed in 1994 with David Geffen and Jeffrey Katzenberg, is the first new studio in 50 years.
Marriages: Amy Irving (divorced), Kate Capshaw
Children: Max, Sasha, Sawyer, stepdaughter Jessica, Theo (adopted)
Famous Relative: Anne Spielberg, screenwriter, sister
Major Awards: Oscar, Irving G. Thalberg Memorial Award, 1986; Oscar, Best Director, *Schindler's List*, 1993; Golden Globe, Best Director, *Schindler's List*; 1994, American Film Institute Lifetime Achievement Award, 1995
Address: Creative Artists Agency, 9830 Wilshire Blvd., Beverly Hills, CA 90212

BRUCE SPRINGSTEEN

Birthplace: Freehold, NJ
Birthdate: 9/23/49
Occupation: Singer, songwriter
Education: Attended Ocean City Community College
Debut: (Album) *Greetings from Asbury Park*, 1973
Signature: *Born in the USA*
Facts: E Street Band, formed in 1973, was named after the road in Belmar, NJ, where keyboardist David Sancious's mother lives.

After a 1976 Memphis concert, was caught climbing over the wall to Graceland.

Gave the song "Because the Night" to Patti Smith's producer, who was working in the adjacent recording studio.

In 1986, he rejected a $12-million offer from Lee Iococca to use "Born in the U.S.A." for Chrysler commercials.
Marriages: Julianne Phillips (divorced), Patti Scialfa
Children: Evan, Jessica, Sam
Major Awards: Grammy, Best Recording for Children, *In Harmony 2* (with others), 1982; Grammy, Best Rock Vocal, "Dancing in the Dark," 1984; Grammy, Best Rock Vocal, "Tunnel of Love," 1987; Grammy, Song of the Year, "Streets of Philadelphia," 1994; Grammy, Best Rock Vocal—Male, "Streets of Philadelphia," 1994; Grammy, Best Rock Song, "Streets of Philadelphia," 1994; Grammy, Best Song Written for a Motion Picture, "Streets of Philadelphia," 1994; Oscar, Best Song, "Streets of Philadel-

phia," 1994; Golden Globe, Best Song, "Streets of Philadelphia," 1994
Address: Columbia Records, 1801 Century Park W., Los Angeles, CA 90067

SYLVESTER STALLONE

Birthplace: Hell's Kitchen, New York
Birthdate: 7/4/46
Occupation: Actor, writer, director
Education: American School of Switzerland, attended University of Miami
Debut: (Film) *Bananas*, 1971
Signature: *Rocky*
Facts: When he was born, the forceps severed a nerve in his face and partially paralyzed his lip, chin, and half of his tongue.

Had rickets as a child.

In high school he played football, fenced, and threw discus.

His paintings have been featured in galleries.

In *Bananas* (1971), played a goon who was thrown off a subway by Woody Allen.

As a boy was kicked out of fourteen schools in eleven years.

In 1971 appeared in a softcore porn film, *A Party at Kitty & Stud's*.
Infamy: In March 1994, dumped longtime girlfriend Jennifer Flavin via letter sent FedEx. They have since reconciled.

Romanced Janice Dickinson, until DNA tests revealed that her newborn daughter wasn't his. She claimed to be pregnant by him again, then miscarried.
Original Job: Usher, fish salesman, zoo attendant, bookstore detective, teacher at American School of Switzerland
Marriages: Sasha Czack (divorced), Brigitte Nielsen (divorced), Jennifer Flavin (relationship)
Children: Sage, Seth (with Sasha Czack)
Famous Relative: Frank Stallone, musician, brother; Jacqueline Stallone, astrologer, mother
Address: Creative Artists Agency, 9830 Wilshire Blvd., Beverly Hills, CA 90212

DANIELLE STEEL

Real Name: Danielle Schuelein-Steel
Birthplace: New York, NY
Birthdate: 8/14/47
Occupation: Writer
Education: Lycée Français,

attended Parsons School of Design, New York University
Debut: (Book) *Going Home*, 1973
Facts: Wrote over 30 best-selling novels in 20 years, including *The Ring* (1980), *Secrets* (1985), and *Daddy* (1989).
Infamy: Two of her ex-husbands were convicts; she married one while he was still in prison, the other when she was eight months pregnant with his child.
Original Job: Vice president of public relations and new business for Supergirls, Ltd., a PR and ad agency
Marriages: Claude Eric Lazard (divorced), Danny Zugelder (divorced), Bill Toth (divorced), John Traina (separated)
Children: Beatrix, Nicholas, Samantha, Victoria, Vanessa, Max, Zara
Address: Bantam Doubleday Dell Publishing Group, 1540 Broadway, New York, NY 10036

HOWARD STERN

Birthplace: New York, NY
Birthdate: 1/12/54
Occupation: Radio DJ
Education: Boston University
Signature: *The Howard Stern Show*
Facts: 1994 Libertarian gubernatorial candidate in New York but dropped out of race before the elections.

Once fired for referring to station management as "scumbags" on the air during a salary dispute.

Practices transcendental meditation each morning in the limo ride to work.
Infamy: After angry listeners provided the FCC with transcripts of Stern's show about masturbating to Aunt Jemima and having rough sex with actress Michelle Pfeiffer, the commission fined Infinity Broadcasting, which owns WNBC-New York, $600,000.

Stern made fun of singer Selena Quintanilla Perez after her murder in April 1995, playing her music with sounds of gunfire in the background and parodying her mourners. The League of United Latin American Citizens said it intended to drive Stern's program off the air. Stern later apologized for his conduct.
Marriage: Alison Berns
Children: Emily, Debra
Address: K-ROCK-FM (WXRK),

600 Madison Ave., New York, NY 10022

JON STEWART

Real Name: Jon Stuart Liebowitz
Birthplace: Lawrence, NJ
Birthdate: 1963
Occupation: Talk show host, comedian, actor
Education: College of William and Mary
Debut: (TV) *Short Attention Span Theater*, 1991
Signature: *The Jon Stewart Show*
Facts: Got the idea to do stand-up at age twenty-four, when using puppets to teach schoolkids about disabled people—a gig that honed his prop-wielding skills. Went on the road doing stand-up for the next six years.

His parents divorced when he was nine, and his relationship with his dad became increasingly strained over the years as Stewart gleefully aired the family's dirty laundry in his club acts.
Original Job: Bartender, bike mechanic, porter in a bakery, research lab assistant
Quote: "As long as I can remember, I wanted to sleep late, stay up late and do nothing in between."
Address: William Morris Agency, 151 El Camino Dr., Beverly Hills, CA 90212

MARTHA STEWART

Birthplace: Nutley, NJ
Birthdate: 1942
Occupation: Entertainment and lifestyle consultant
Education: Barnard College
Debut: (Book) *Entertaining*, 1981
Signature: *Martha Stewart Living*
Facts: Has published more than a dozen books on entertaining.

Discovered her love for decorating, gardening, and cooking when she and her husband bought a Connecticut farmhouse and fixed it up themselves in 1971. Over the years, she added a barn-turned-party-room, a greenhouse, pool, vegetable gardens, orchards, an English border garden, and beehives, turkeys, chickens, and cats.

Sleeps four hours a night with the lights on so when she wakes up she can get right to work.
Original Job: Model, stockbroker, take-out gourmet food store owner

Marriage: Andy Stewart (divorced)
Child: Alexis
Address: *Martha Stewart Living*, 20 West 43rd St., New York, NY 10036

PATRICK STEWART

Birthplace: Mirfield, England
Birthdate: 7/13/40
Occupation: Actor, writer
Education: Attended Bristol Old Vic Theatre School
Debut: (Stage) *Treasure Island*, 1959
Signature: *Star Trek: The Next Generation*
Facts: Was so sure that he was going to be fired from the initial season of *Star Trek: The Next Generation* that he didn't unpack his bags for six weeks.
Original Job: Journalist
Marriage: Sheila (divorced)
Children: Sophie, Daniel
Quote: "I was brought up in a very poor and very violent household. I spent much of my childhood being afraid."
Address: International Creative Management, 8942 Wilshire Blvd., Beverly Hills, CA 90211

BEN STILLER

Birthplace: New York, NY
Birthdate: 1966
Occupation: Actor, director
Education: Attended UCLA
Debut: (Film) *Empire of the Sun*, 1987
Signature: *Reality Bites*
Facts: At age 10, began making Super-8 movies about getting revenge on bullies in his neighborhood.

His short film parody of *The Color of Money* landed him a job at *Saturday Night Live* and his own show on MTV.
Relationship: Jeanne Tripplehorn (engaged)
Famous Relatives: Jerry Stiller, comedian, father; Anne Meara, comedian, mother; Amy Stiller, actor, sister
Major Award: Emmy, Best Writing in Variety or Music Program, *The Ben Stiller Show* (with others), 1992
Address: Creative Artists Agency, 9830 Wilshire Blvd., Beverly Hills, CA 92012

STING

Real Name: Gordon Matthew Sumner
Birthplace: Newcastle upon Tyne, England

Birthdate: 10/2/51
Occupation: Singer, songwriter, actor
Education: Warwick University
Debut: (Song) "Fall Out" (with The Police), 1977
Signature: The Police
Facts: In 1978, rejected the part of the villain in James Bond film *For Your Eyes Only*.

He gained his nickname by wearing a black-and-yellow striped shirt, like a bee.

Received a seaman's card and worked as a bass player with The Ronnie Pierson Trio on Princess Cruise Lines at age 17.

Claimed in a 1993 *Rolling Stone* interview that by practicing meditation, he can make love for more than five hours at a time.
Original Job: Teacher, construction worker, clerk for Inland Revenue
Marriages: Frances Eleanor Tomelty (divorced), Trudie Styler
Children: Joseph, Katherine, Mickey, Jake, Coco
Major Awards: Grammy, Best Rock Performance—Duo or Group, "Don't Stand So Close to Me" (with The Police), 1981; Grammy, Song of the Year, "Every Breath You Take," 1983; Grammy, Best Pop Performance—Duo or Group, "Every Breath You Take" (with The Police), 1983; Grammy, Best Pop Vocal—Male, "Bring On the Night," 1987; Grammy, Best Rock Song/Vocal Performance, "Soul Cages," 1991; Grammy, Best Pop Vocal—Male, "If I Ever Lose My Faith in You," 1993; Grammy, Best Music Video—Long Form, *Ten Summoner's Tales*, 1993
Address: The Bugle House, 21A Noel St., London W1, England

MICHAEL STIPE

Birthplace: Decatur, GA
Birthdate: 1/4/60
Occupation: Singer, songwriter
Education: Attended Southern Illinois University and University of Georgia
Debut: *Chronic Town* (with R.E.M.), 1982
Signature: R.E.M.
Facts: In the early years of R.E.M., traveled to 49 states by the time he was 24.

Planned to record with friend Kurt Cobain. Cobain had tickets to come to Stipe's in Atlanta but called to cancel, and committed suicide soon after.

Infamy: Was rumored to have AIDS because, he says, he is thin, has bad skin, and is sexually ambiguous. He denies being HIV-positive.
Major Awards: Grammy, Best Alternative Performance, *Out of Time*, 1991; Grammy, Best Pop Vocal—Group, "Losing My Religion," 1991
Address: Warner Brothers Recording, 3300 Warner Blvd., Burbank, CA 91505

OLIVER STONE

Birthplace: New York, NY
Birthdate: 9/15/46
Occupation: Director, writer, producer
Education: Attended Yale University, New York University film school
Debut: (Film) *Seizure*, 1974
Signature: *Platoon*
Facts: Served in the U.S. Merchant Marine, 1966; in the Army in Vietnam, 1967–68. Awarded Bronze Star and Purple Heart with Oak Leaf Cluster.

Made acting debut as a bum in *The Hand* (1981), which he wrote and directed.
Original Job: Taxi driver in New York City, teacher at Free Pacific Institute in South Vietnam
Infamy: At least 10 real killings were linked to his ode to violence, *Natural Born Killers*, with one 14-year-old decapitator even telling friends he wanted to be famous like the killers in the movie.
Marriages: Majwa Sarkis (divorced), Elizabeth Burkit Cox (divorced)
Children: Sean, Michael
Major Awards: Oscar, Best Adapted Screenplay, *Midnight Express*, 1978; Oscar, Best Director, *Platoon*, 1986; Golden Globe, Best Director, *Platoon*, 1987; Oscar, Best Director, *Born*

on the Fourth of July, 1991; Golden Globe, Best Director, *Born on the Fourth of July*, 1990; Golden Globe, Best Screenplay, *Born on the Fourth of July* (with Ron Kovic), 1990; Golden Globe, Best Director, *JFK*, 1992
Address: Creative Artists Agency, 9830 Wilshire Blvd., Beverly Hills, CA 90212

SHARON STONE

Birthplace: Meadville, PA
Birthdate: 3/10/58
Occupation: Actor
Education: Attended Edinboro State University
Debut: (Film) *Stardust Memories*, 1981
Signature: *Basic Instinct*
Facts: She has an I.Q. of 154.
  Between 1977 and 1980, became one of the top 10 models at the Ford Agency.
Infamy: Posed nude for *Playboy* just days after finishing *Total Recall*, 1990.
Original Job: Model
Marriages: George Englund (divorced), Michael Greenburg (divorced), Bob Wagner (relationship)
Famous Relative: Michael Stone, actor, brother
Quote: "If I was just intelligent, I'd be OK. But I am fiercely intelligent, which most people find threatening.... I have a strong point of view based on my experience. It may or may not be the correct one, but it is an informed one, and I'm willing to fight for it. If I were a petite, brunette, ethnic lawyer then my behavior would be totally acceptable. But we Barbie Dolls are not supposed to behave the way I do."
Address: P.O. Box 7304, North Hollywood, CA 91603

MADELEINE STOWE

Birthplace: Los Angeles, CA
Birthdate: 8/18/58
Occupation: Actor
Education: Attended USC
Debut: (TV) *Baretta*, 1977; (Film) *Stakeout*, 1987
Signature: *The Last of the Mohicans*
Facts: Starred in first film, *Tropical Snow*, in 1986, but the film was not released until 1989. *Stakeout* was her first released film in 1987.
Marriage: Brian Benben
Major Award: Golden Globe, Special Achievement, *Short Cuts*, 1994
Address: United Talent Agency,

9560 Wilshire Blvd., Suite 500, Beverly Hills, CA 90212

MERYL STREEP

Real Name: Mary Louise Streep
Birthplace: Summit, NJ
Birthdate: 4/22/49
Occupation: Actor
Education: Vassar College; MFA, Yale University
Debut: (Stage) *Trelawny of the Wells*, NY Shakespeare Festival, 1975; (Film) *Julia*, 1977
Signature: *Sophie's Choice*
Facts: When she was 12, began studying with vocal coach Estelle Liebling, who had also taught diva Beverly Sills.
  In high school, was a cheerleader and homecoming queen.
  Formed a child support group with Annette Bening, Carrie Fisher, and Tracey Ullman, in which they watch each other's children.
  When New York theater giant Joseph Papp, who ran Shakespeare in the Park among others, knew he was dying, he asked Streep to succeed him; she turned him down so she could devote more time to her family.
Original Job: Waitress
Marriage: Don Gummer
Children: Henry, Mary Willa, Grace Jane, Louisa Jacobson
Major Awards: Emmy, Best Actress in a Miniseries, *Holocaust*, 1978; Golden Globe, Best Supporting Actress, *Kramer vs. Kramer*, 1980; Golden Globe, Best Actress, *The French Lieutenant's Woman*, 1982; Golden Globe, Best Actress, *Sophie's Choice*, 1983; Oscar, Best Supporting Actress, *Kramer vs. Kramer*, 1980; Oscar, Best Actress, *Sophie's Choice*, 1982
Address: Creative Artists Agency, 9830 Wilshire Blvd., Beverly Hills, CA 90212

BARBRA STREISAND

Real Name: Barbara Streisand
Birthplace: Brooklyn, NY
Birthdate: 4/24/42
Occupation: Singer, actor, director
Education: Attended Yeshiva University
Debut: (Stage) *Another Evening with Harry Stoones*, 1961; (Film) *Funny Girl*, 1968
Signature: "The Way We Were"
Facts: Her father died when she was 15 months old.
  She graduated from high school two years early.
  Although she had never sung

before an audience before, she won a talent contest in a Greenwich Village bar and won a singing job at another bar.
  Her Oscar for *Funny Girl* (1968) tied with Katharine Hepburn for *A Lion in Winter*, the only tie for a Best Actress Academy Award.
Original Job: Theater usher, switchboard operator, waitress
Marriage: Elliot Gould (divorced)
Child: Jason Emanuel
Famous Relative: Roslyn Kind, singer, sister
Major Awards: Emmy, Outstanding Program Achievements in Entertainment, *My Name is Barbra*, 1965; Oscar, Best Actress, *Funny Girl*, 1968; co-recipient Oscar, Best Song, "Evergreen," 1976; Golden Globe, Best Actress, *Funny Girl*, 1968; Golden Globe, Best Director, *Yentl*, 1984; Georgie Award, AGVA, 1977; Grammy, Best Female Pop Vocalist 1963–65, 1977, 1986; Grammy, Best Songwriter (with Paul Williams), 1977; Grammy, Legend Award, 1992; Tony, Special Award, 1970
Address: Creative Artists Agency, 9830 Wilshire Blvd., Beverly Hills, CA 90212

QUENTIN TARANTINO

Birthplace: Knoxville, TN
Birthdate: 3/27/63
Occupation: Director, writer, actor
Education: High school dropout
Debut: (Film) *Reservoir Dogs*, 1992 (writer, director, and actor)
Signature: *Pulp Fiction*
Facts: Studied movies while working at an L.A. video store for four years. Got the idea for *Reservoir Dogs* when he saw that no one had made a heist movie in a long time.
  Once played an Elvis impersonator on *The Golden Girls*.
  Is said to have an I.Q. of 160.

Had already tried his hand at screenwriting as a teenager, penning *Captain Peachfuzz and the Anchovy Bandit.*
Infamy: Once went to jail for failing to pay his parking tickets.
Original Job: Video sales clerk
Relationship: Grace Lovelace
Major Awards: Cannes Film Festival, Palme d'Or, *Pulp Fiction*, 1994; Oscar, Best Original Screenplay, *Pulp Fiction*, 1994; Golden Globe, Best Screenplay, *Pulp Fiction*, 1995
Quotes: "People ask me if I went to film school. And I tell them, 'No, I went to films.'"
Address: William Morris Agency, 151 El Camino Dr., Beverly Hills, CA 90212

ELIZABETH TAYLOR

Birthplace: London, England
Birthdate: 2/27/32
Occupation: Actor
Education: Byron House, Hawthorne School, Metro-Goldwyn-Mayer School
Debut: (Film) *There's One Born Every Minute*, 1942
Signature: *Cleopatra*
Facts: Almost died from pneumonia and had an emergency tracheotomy in 1961.
  When she was three years old she danced before Queen Elizabeth and Princess Margaret.
  After friend Rock Hudson died from AIDS, became the founding chair of the American Foundation for AIDS Research (AMFAR) in 1985.
  She met construction worker Larry Fortensky, whom she married in 1992, at the Betty Ford Clinic.
Infamy: Checked herself into the Betty Ford Clinic to overcome alcohol dependency, 1983. Returned in 1988 to overcome painkiller dependency.
Marriages: Nicholas Conrad Hilton Jr. (divorced), Michael Wilding (divorced), Mike Todd (deceased), Eddie Fisher (divorced), Richard Burton (divorced, remarried, divorced), John Warner (divorced), Larry Fortensky (separated)
Children: Michael, Christopher, Elizabeth, Maria Carson (adopted German orphan)
Major Awards: Oscar, Best Actress, *Butterfield 8*, 1960; Oscar, Best Actress, *Who's Afraid of Virginia Woolf*, 1966; Oscar, Jean Hersholt Humanitarian Award, 1992; French Legion of Honor, 1987; American Film

Institute Lifetime Achievement Award, 1993
Address: William Morris Agency, 151 El Camino Dr., Beverly Hills, CA 90212

JOHN TESH

Birthplace: Garden City, NY
Birthdate: 7/1/53
Occupation: Television host, composer, pianist
Education: Attended Juilliard during high school, North Carolina State University
Signature: *Entertainment Tonight*
Facts: Anchored local TV news in Durham, NC, Orlando, Nashville, and New York before signing with CBS Sports and, in 1986, *Entertainment Tonight*.

An incurable romantic, he proposed to Selleca by reserving an entire Monterey restaurant, hiring a string quartet to serenade her with a song he had written, "Concetta," and arranging for a fireworks display outside the window.

He and Selleca, who pledged to avoid premarital sex during their year-long courtship, starred in a late-night infomercial for a series of videos about relationships.

Composed songs for sporting events he was covering for CBS, including the Tour de France and the Pan-American Games, both of which won Emmys.

His own recording label, GTS Records, has sold more than two million of his CDs. His *Romantic Christmas*, with Selleca, went gold, selling more than 500,000 copies.
Original Job: TV reporter
Marriages: Julie Wright (divorced), Connie Selleca
Child: Prima
Major Awards: Emmy, best musical composition for a sports program, Pan-American Games, 1983; Emmy, musical score, Tour de France, 1987
Address: 5555 Melrose Ave., Los Angeles, CA 90038

EMMA THOMPSON

Birthplace: London, England
Birthdate: 4/15/59
Occupation: Actor
Education: Cambridge University
Debut: (Film) *Henry V*, 1989
Signature: *Howards End*
Facts: Wrote screenplay adaptation of *Sense and Sensibility* by Jane Austen, whose novels she began reading at age nine.

When first met her husband,

Kenneth Branagh, she "thought he had strange hair."

Lives on the street on which she was raised, opposite her mother and down the street from her younger sister, Sophie.
Marriage: Kenneth Branagh
Famous Relatives: Eric Thompson, producer, father; Phyllida Law, actor, mother; Sophie Thompson, actor, sister
Major Award: Oscar, Best Actress, *Howards End*, 1992; Golden Globe, Best Actress, *Howards End*, 1993
Address: Lorraine Hamilton Management, 19 Denmark St., London WC2H 8NA, England

UMA THURMAN

Birthplace: Boston, MA
Birthdate: 4/29/70
Occupation: Actor
Education: Attended Professional Children's School
Debut: (Film) *Kiss Daddy Good Night*, 1987
Signature: *Dangerous Liaisons*
Facts: Her father, a professor of Asian religion, named her Uma after a Hindu goddess.

Her Swedish mother, a psychotherapist, was once married to Timothy Leary.

The nearly six-foot actress quit school and headed for New York at age 16. Modeling jobs and movies quickly followed.
Original Job: Model, dishwasher
Marriage: Gary Oldman (divorced), Timothy Hutton (relationship)
Address: Creative Artists Agency, 9830 Wilshire Blvd., Beverly Hills, CA 90212

MARISA TOMEI

Birthplace: Brooklyn, NY
Birthdate: 12/4/64
Occupation: Actor
Education: Attended Boston University
Debut: (Film) *The Flamingo Kid*, 1984
Signature: *My Cousin Vinny*
Facts: Attended Boston University for one year, until she got a role on *As the World Turns*.

Played Lisa Bonet's roommate during the first season of *A Different World* (1987–88).
Major Award: Oscar, Best Supporting Actress, *My Cousin Vinny*, 1993
Address: William Morris Agency, 151 El Camino Dr., Beverly Hills, CA 90212

JOHN TRAVOLTA

Birthplace: Englewood, NJ
Birthdate: 2/18/54
Occupation: Actor
Education: High school dropout
Debut: (Film) *The Devil's Rain*, 1975; (TV) *Welcome Back, Kotter*, 1975
Signature: *Saturday Night Fever*
Facts: Holds the record for the most *Rolling Stone* covers for an actor: four.

An avid flyer since the age of 16, he turned down the lead in *An Officer and a Gentleman*, a part reportedly written for him, because the shooting conflicted with his attendance of American Airlines' month-long jet pilot training course. In 1995, a plane he owns and was piloting lost electrical power over Washington, DC, and had a mid-air near-miss with a commercial jetliner.

His first love, actor Diana Hyland, was 18 years older than the then 22-year-old Travolta. Nine months into the romance she died of cancer—in Travolta's arms.

Languished for nearly a decade in forgettable and/or unpopular films until *Pulp Fiction* restored him to Hollywood's A-list. He earned just $140,000 for his part in the film, far less than the millions-per-picture he once commanded.

Has been a member of the Church of Scientology for more than 20 years.
Marriage: Kelly Preston
Child: Jett
Famous Relatives: Ellen Travolta, actor, sister; Joey Travolta, actor, brother
Address: William Morris Agency,

151 El Camino Dr., Beverly Hills, CA 90212

JEANNE TRIPPLEHORN

Birthplace: Tulsa, OK
Birthdate: 1963
Occupation: Actor
Education: Attended Tulsa University, Juilliard
Debut: (TV) *The Perfect Tribute*, 1991
Signature: *Basic Instinct*
Quote: On a rough sex scene with Michael Douglas in *Basic Instinct:* "My head kept hitting the wall. That's what I call a hard day's work."
Original Job: Radio and television personality in Tulsa, OK
Relationship: Ben Stiller (engaged)
Address: Creative Artists Agency, 9830 Wilshire Blvd., Beverly Hills, CA 90212

CHRISTY TURLINGTON

Birthplace: Walnut Creek, CA
Birthdate: 1/2/69
Occupation: Supermodel
Education: Attended UCLA
Facts: Her face was used on mannequins at the Metropolitan Museum of Art's costume galleries.

Dated screenwriter Roger Wilson for seven years and they had a Buddhist service together, though they were never officially married.
Relationship: Jason Patric
Address: Ford Models Inc., 334 East 59th St., New York, NY 10022

KATHLEEN TURNER

Real Name: Mary Kathleen Turner
Birthplace: Springfield, MO
Birthdate: 6/19/54
Occupation: Actor
Education: Studied at London's Central School of Speech and Drama, attended Southwest Missouri State University, University of Maryland
Debut: (TV) *The Doctors*, 1977; (Stage) *Gemini*, 1978; (Film) *Body Heat*, 1981
Signature: *Peggy Sue Got Married*
Facts: Places pencil erasers at the back of her mouth to practice her sultry voice.

Daughter of a U.S. foreign service officer, she grew up in Canada, Cuba, Washington, DC, and Venezuela before settling in London.
Infamy: Husband was the lease-

holder of a building in New York City where 87 people were killed by a fire caused by arson. He pled guilty in 1992 to building code violations, paying $60,000 to be used by a Bronx community service center and performing fifty hours of community service.
Original Job: Waitress
Marriage: Jay Weiss
Child: Rachel Ann
Major Awards: Golden Globe, Best Actress in a Comedy, *Romancing the Stone*, 1985; Golden Globe, Best Actress in a Comedy, *Prizzi's Honor*, 1986
Address: International Creative Management, 8942 Wilshire Blvd., Beverly Hills, CA 90211

TED TURNER

Real Name: Robert Edward Turner III
Birthplace: Cincinnati, OH
Birthdate: 11/19/38
Occupation: Media executive, owner of Atlanta Braves and Hawks
Education: Attended Brown University
Debut: In 1970, bought failing Atlanta TV station, which he turned into WTBS
Signature: CNN
Facts: Won the America's Cup in his yacht, *Courageous*, in 1977.
Interested in owning a major TV network, he made a failed bid for CBS in 1985, and launched negotiations with NBC in 1994 that ultimately broke down.
Owns four bison ranches out west, making him America's largest private bison rancher.
Infamy: Was "asked to leave" Brown University in 1967 for having a girl in his room after hours; was later awarded an honorary degree.
Original Job: Selling space on billboards in family business
Marriages: Judy Nye (divorced), Jane Shirley Smith (divorced), Jane Fonda
Children: Laura Lee, Robert Edward IV, Rhett, Beau, Jennie
Major Award: Elected to the Emmy Hall of Fame, 1991
Address: Turner Broadcasting System, One CNN Center, Atlanta, GA 30348

TINA TURNER

Real Name: Anna Mae Bullock
Birthplace: Nutbush, TN
Birthdate: 11/26/39
Occupation: Singer, actor

Debut: (Song) "Fool in Love," 1960
Signature: "What's Love Go To Do with It?"
Facts: "River Deep, Mountain High" (1966) was No. 1 in Britain and earned The Ike and Tina Turner Revue the chance to open for The Rolling Stones in 1969.
Became a Buddhist in the early '80s.
Endured years of physical abuse and extramarital affairs by then husband Ike.
Marriage: Ike Turner (divorced), Erwin Bach (relationship)
Children: Stepson Craig, stepson Ronnie, Ike Jr., Michael
Major Awards: Grammy, Best R&B Duo or Group, "Proud Mary" (with Ike Turner), 1972; Grammy, Record of the Year and Best Pop Vocal—Female, "What's Love Got To Do With It?," 1984; Grammy, Best Rock Vocal of the Year, "Better Be Good to Me," 1985; Grammy, Best Rock Vocal of the Year, "One of the Living," 1986; Grammy, Best Rock Vocal of the Year, "Back Where You Started," 1986; Grammy, Best Rock Vocal of the Year, *Tina Live in Europe*, 1988; inducted into Rock and Roll Hall of Fame, 1991
Address: Creative Artists Agency, 9830 Wilshire Blvd., Beverly Hills, CA 90212

STEVEN TYLER

Real Name: Steven Tallarico
Birthplace: Boston, MA
Birthdate: 3/26/48
Education: High school dropout
Debut: (Album) *Aerosmith*, 1973
Signature: Aerosmith
Facts: Met future Aerosmith members Joe Perry and Tom Hamilton at Lake Sunapee, NH, where their families had vacation houses.
Seriously injured in a motorcycle accident in 1981, capping a long period of discord and debauchery among band members. "I lay there in the hospital crying and flipping out, knowing some other group was going to step into our space. Through the stupor of my medication, I pictured a spotlight. We walked out of it."
When the band reformed in 1984, they got a contract with Geffen but had to audition first.
Aerosmith co-owns the West Hollywood restaurant House of Blues with Dan Aykroyd and Jim Belushi.

Infamy: Alcohol and drug use including heroin addiction.
Children: Mia (with Cyrinda Tallarico), Liv (with Bebe Buell)
Major Awards: Grammy, Best Rock Performance by a Duo or Group with Vocal, "Janie's Got a Gun," 1990; Grammy, Best Rock Performance by a Duo or Group with Vocal, "Crazy," 1994
Quote: On what is left for his band to accomplish: "I'm looking to be the lounge act on the space shuttle so I can sing 'Walk This Way' on the ceiling."
Address: Geffen Records, 9130 Sunset Blvd., Los Angeles, CA 90069

MIKE TYSON

Birthplace: New York, NY
Birthdate: 7/1/66
Occupation: Boxer
Education: High school dropout
Signature: Youngest heavyweight champion ever, 1986
Facts: Has a 30,000 square-foot mansion near Cleveland with an indoor swimming pool shaped like a boxing glove.
Entered prison in 1992 a doughy 275 pounds, some 50 over his last fighting weight, but emerged a sculpted 216 pounds after patronizing the prison commissary (mostly for milk, cereal, and canned tuna) more than the prison mess.
Born a Catholic and baptized as a Baptist in 1988, he converted to Islam while in prison.
He lined his eight-by-eleven foot prison cell with more than 300 books, and was so impressed by the writings of Arthur Ashe and Mao Tse-tung that he had his biceps inscribed with their portraits by an inmate tattoo artist.
Infamy: Convicted in 1992 of raping 18-year-old beauty contestant Desiree Washington. Spent three years in prison; released on probation in the spring of 1995, with requirements to perform 100 hours of community service each year and undergo counseling for "sex problems." Washington has also sued for civil damages for injuries suffered during the assault.
Marriage: Robin Givens (divorced), Monica Turner (relationship)
Child: Michael
Major Awards/Titles: Heavyweight Boxing Champion, 1986–1990
Address: Don King Productions,

32 East 69th St., New York, NY 10021

BLAIR UNDERWOOD

Birthplace: Tacoma, WA
Birthdate: 8/25/64
Occupation: Actor
Education: Carnegie-Mellon University
Debut: (TV) *The Cosby Show*, 1985
Signature: *L.A. Law*
Facts: Underwood says he was stopped for speeding and a gun was put to his head when he reached for his driver's license. He said he is conscious of subtle racism: "You think twice about offering to help an elderly lady cross the street because she's going to scream 'rape' or think you're stealing."
Marriage: Desirée DaCosta
Address: 5200 Lankershim Blvd., #260, North Hollywood, CA 91601

JOHN UPDIKE

Birthplace: Shillington, PA
Birthdate: 3/18/32
Occupation: Writer
Education: Harvard College, Oxford University
Debut: (Book) *The Carpentered Hen and Other Tame Creatures*, 1958
Signature: *Rabbit, Run*
Facts: Collected Walt Disney comic books.
Marriages: Mary Entwhistle Pennington (divorced), Martha R. Bernhard
Children: Elizabeth, David, Miranda, Michael, three stepchildren
Major Awards: Pulitzer Prize, *Rabbit Is Rich*, 1982; American Book Award, *Rabbit Is Rich*, 1982
Address: Alfred A. Knopf, 201 East 50th St., New York, NY 10022

JEAN-CLAUDE VAN DAMME

Real Name: Jean-Claude Van Varenberg
Birthplace: Brussels, Belgium
Birthdate: 10/18/60
Occupation: Actor, martial arts expert
Debut: (Film) *Rue Barbare (Barbarous Street)*, 1983
Signature: *Kickboxer*
Facts: A middleweight champion in the Professional European Karate Association, he began studying karate at age 11.
Van Damme's fight scenes

are so intense that he won't film them in the United States for fear of being sued.

Changed his name to Frank Cujo in 1983; however, changed it again after the release of the Stephen King film *Cujo*.

Infamy: In 1989, sued for "willfully" gouging the eye of an extra in a swordfight while filming *Cyborg*.

Original Job: Ran the California Gym in Brussels before coming to the U.S. in 1981, worked as a limo and taxi driver, bouncer, carpet installer, and pizza deliveryman

Marriage: Two prior marriages, Gladys Portugues (divorced), Darcy LaPier

Children: Kristopher, Bianca

Address: International Creative Management, 8942 Wilshire Blvd., Beverly Hills, CA 90211

EDDIE VAN HALEN

Birthplace: Nijmegen, Holland
Birthdate: 1/26/55
Occupation: Singer, guitarist
Education: Attended Pasadena City College
Debut: (Album) *Van Halen*, 1978
Facts: When Van Halen wanted to propose to Valerie Bertinelli, he first asked her father for her hand.

Did guitar work on Michael Jackson's "Beat It," free of charge, as a favor.

Formed the group Broken Combs with brother Alex, later changed the name to Mammoth. Formed Van Halen in 1974.

Album, and recording studio that Eddie owns, 5150, is named after the New York police code for the criminally insane.

Infamy: A now reformed alcoholic, he and his band were notorious for backstage partying and obnoxious behavior; they even insisted that all brown M&Ms be removed from candy bowls backstage at their concerts.

Charged with trying to bring a loaded semiautomatic pistol on an airplane in 1995. Fined $1,000 and sentenced to a year of probation.

Marriage: Valerie Bertinelli
Child: Wolfgang
Famous Relative: Alex Van Halen, drummer, brother
Major Award: Grammy, Best Hard Rock Performance, *For Unlawful Carnal Knowledge* (with Van Halen), 1991
Address: Premier Agency, 3 East 54th St., New York, NY 10022

LUTHER VANDROSS

Birthplace: New York, NY
Birthdate: 4/20/51
Occupation: Singer, songwriter
Education: Attended Western Michigan University
Debut: (Song) "Everybody Rejoice (A Brand New Day)" from *The Wiz*, 1978
Signature: "Here and Now"
Facts: Started playing the piano at age three.

Sister was a member of the '50s group The Crests.

His first group, Listen My Brother, formed while he was a high school student, played at the Apollo and appeared on the first episode of *Sesame Street*.

Original Job: S&H Green Stamp defective-merchandise clerk
Major Awards: Grammy, Best R&B Vocal—Male, "Here and Now," 1990; Grammy, Best R&B Song, "Power of Love/Love Power," 1991; Grammy, Best R&B Vocal—Male, *Power of Love*, 1991
Address: International Creative Management, 8942 Wilshire Blvd., Beverly Hills, CA 90211

EDDIE VEDDER

Real Name: Eddie Mueller
Birthplace: Chicago, IL
Birthdate: 12/23/64
Occupation: Singer, songwriter
Education: High school
Debut: (Album) *Ten*, 1991
Signature: Pearl Jam
Facts: Vedder, a Red Hot Chili Peppers roadie, was introduced to future Pearl Jam members by Jack Irons.

"Vedder" is his mother's maiden name.

Parents divorced before he was two, and he grew up thinking his stepfather was his real father. His mother revealed the identity of his biological father only after the man had died. The song "Alive" chronicles his feelings on this discovery.

Voted "most talented" by his high school graduating class. Dropped out of high school his senior year (later passed equivalency exam).

Original Job: Worked at service station, waited tables
Marriage: Beth Liebling
Quote: "I think celebrities suck."
Address: Epic Records, 550 Madison Ave., New York, NY 10022

GIANNI VERSACE

Birthplace: Reggio di Calabria, Italy
Birthdate: 12/2/46
Occupation: Fashion designer
Facts: Has designed costumes for operas and ballets in Milan, Leningrad, Brussels, and other cities. Versace's collaboration with the French choreographer Maurice Bejart was the subject of a 1989 film by Sergio Salerni entitled *La Fortuna dell'Amicizia* (*The Good Fortune of Friendship*).

Versace's mother was a boutique owner and dressmaker.

Studied architectural design in Italy and earned a degree allowing him to work as an architect or building contractor's assistant.

Infamy: An article in London's *Independent* Sunday newspaper in 1994 claimed he was linked to the Mafia and questioned whether his revenues were high enough to support his extravagant lifestyle. Versace denied the accusations and sued the paper for libel. Was issued an apology by the paper and settled out of court for $158,000 in damages and legal costs.

Original Job: Part-time fashion buyer for his mother
Major Awards: The Cutty Sark American Award for Excellence in Men's Fashion, 1983, 1988; Italy's Occhio d'Oro (Golden Eye) Award, 1982, 1984, 1990, 1991; Council of Fashion Designers of America, International Award, 1993
Address: Gianni Versace Boutique, 816 Madison Ave., New York, NY, 10021

ROBERT JAMES WALLER

Birthplace: Rockford, Iowa
Birthdate: 8/1/39
Occupation: Author, professor of business management
Education: University of Northern Iowa, Indiana University
Debut: (Book) *The Bridges of Madison County*, 1991
Signature: *The Bridges of Madison County*
Facts: The books on his desk reportedly range from *A History of Mathematics* to issues of *Guns & Ammo*.

Won college basketball scholarship.

Wrote his second book, *Slow Waltz in Cedar Bend*, in 10 days.

Used an old door lain across a wooden sawhorse for a table

until he replaced it with a new $700 table he named "Steve."
Original Job: Taught management and economics, dean of business school
Marriage: Georgia Ann Wiedemeier
Child: Rachael
Address: Creative Artists Agency, 9830 Wilshire Blvd., Beverly Hills, CA 90212

BARBARA WALTERS

Birthplace: Boston, MA
Birthdate: 9/25/31
Occupation: Broadcast journalist
Education: Sarah Lawrence College
Debut: (TV) *The Today Show*, 1974
Signature: *20/20*
Facts: In 1957, Don Hewitt, now executive producer of *60 Minutes*, told Walters: "You're marvelous, but stay out of television."

Walters was the only woman reporter in the press group that accompanied President Nixon on his historic trip to China in 1972.

Original Job: Intent on becoming a teacher, went for her master's in education while working as a secretary
Marriages: Robert Henry Katz (annulled), Lee Guber (divorced), Merv Adelman (divorced), Sen. John Warner (relationship)
Child: Jacqueline Dena
Major Awards: Emmy, Best Host on a Talk Show, *Today*, 1975; Emmy, Best Interviewer, *The Barbara Walters Show*, 1982; elected to the Television Hall of Fame, 1990
Address: *20/20*, ABC, 77 West 66th St., New York, NY 10023

DENZEL WASHINGTON

Birthplace: Mt. Vernon, NY
Birthdate: 12/28/54
Occupation: Actor
Education: Fordham University, studied acting at the American Conservatory Theatre, San Francisco
Debut: (Film) *Carbon Copy*, 1981
Signature: *Malcolm X*
Facts: Played Malcolm X in *When The Chickens Come Home To Roost* on Broadway, as well as in the 1992 Spike Lee movie.

In college, played football and basketball and wrote poetry before deciding to try acting.

Original Job: Drama instructor
Marriage: Paulette Pearson

Children: John David, Katia, Malcolm, Olivia
Major Awards: Oscar, Best Supporting Actor, *Glory*, 1989; Golden Globe, Best Supporting Actor, *Glory*, 1989
Address: International Creative Management, 8942 Wilshire Blvd., Beverly Hills, CA 90211

WENDY WASSERSTEIN

Birthplace: Brooklyn, NY
Birthdate: 10/18/50
Occupation: Playwright
Education: Mount Holyoke College, City College of New York, Yale University School of Drama
Debut: (Stage) *Any Woman Can't,* 1973
Signature: *The Heidi Chronicles*
Facts: Almost enrolled in business school rather than pursuing drama.

Brother sent her a note prior to a premiere: "Can't come to play tonight. Am buying Nabisco."
Famous Relative: Bruce Wasserstein, investment banking star, brother
Major Awards: Pulitzer Prize, *The Heidi Chronicles*, 1988; Tony, *The Heidi Chronicles*, 1988
Address: Vintage Books, 201 East 50th St., New York, NY 10022

SIGOURNEY WEAVER

Real Name: Susan Weaver
Birthplace: New York, NY
Birthdate: 10/8/49
Occupation: Actor
Education: Stanford University; Yale University (MFA)
Debut: (Stage) *The Constant Wife* (with Ingrid Bergman), 1974
Signature: *Alien*
Facts: Took her name from a character in *The Great Gatsby.*

As a senior at Stanford, she dressed as an elf and lived in a treehouse with her boyfriend.

Accepted at Yale Drama School as "Mr." Sigourney Weaver.
Marriage: Jim Simpson
Child: Charlotte
Famous Relatives: Sylvester "Pat" Weaver, president of NBC, father; Elizabeth Inglis, actor, mother
Major Awards: Golden Globe, Best Actress, *Gorillas in the Mist*, 1989; Golden Globe, Best Supporting Actress, *Working Girl*, 1989
Address: International Creative

Management, 8942 Wilshire Blvd., Beverly Hills, CA 90211

ANDREW LLOYD WEBBER

Birthplace: London, England
Birthdate: 3/22/48
Occupation: Composer, producer
Education: Attended Magdelen College of Oxford University, Royal Academy of Music, Oxford, Guildhall School of Music, Royal College of Music
Debut: (Stage) *Joseph and the Amazing Technicolor Dreamcoat,* 1968
Signature: *The Phantom of the Opera*
Fact: In 1969, was commissioned by RCA to write an opera based on a single, "Jesus Christ Superstar."
Infamy: After firing Faye Dunaway from the play *Sunset Boulevard* in 1994 because, he said, she couldn't sing, Webber wrote a confidential letter of apology that he then allowed the *London Standard* to print in its entirety. Dunaway, claiming she could indeed sing, sued, and settled for a reported $1.5 million.
Marriages: Sarah Jane Tudor Hugill (divorced), Sarah Brightman (divorced), Madeleine Astrid Gurdon
Children: Nicholas, Imogen, Alastair
Famous Relative: William Webber, London College of Music director, father
Major Awards: Grammy, Best Cast Show Album, *Evita* (with Tim Rice), 1980; Grammy, Best Cast Show Album, *Cats*, 1983; Grammy, Legend Award, 1990; New York Drama Critics Award, *Evita*, 1980; Tony, Best Score, *Evita* (music; Tim Rice, lyrics), 1980; Tony, Best Score, *Cats* (music; T. S. Eliot, lyrics), 1983; Tony, Best Musical, *The Phantom of the Opera*, 1988
Address: Peter Brown, 909 Third Ave., 8th Fl., New York, NY 10022

ROBIN WILLIAMS

Birthplace: Chicago, IL
Birthdate: 7/21/52
Occupation: Actor
Education: Claremont Men's College, College of Marin, Juilliard
Debut: (TV) *Laugh-In,* 1977
Signature: *Mork and Mindy*
Facts: Grew up on a 30-room estate in Bloomfield Hills, MI.

Spent most of childhood playing with his 2,000 toy soldiers.

Second wife was a former nanny of Robin's children and his personal assistant. She served as a producer for *Mrs. Doubtfire*, 1994.
Infamy: Sued for $6.2 million in 1986 by former companion Michelle Tish Carter, who claimed that he gave her herpes during their two-year relationship. Williams countersued for extortion. The suits were settled out of court for an undisclosed amount.

Shared cocaine with John Belushi only a few hours before Belushi's death.
Original Job: Street mime
Marriages: Valeri Velardi (divorced), Marsha Garces
Children: Zachary, Zelda, Cody Alan
Major Awards: Golden Globe, Best Actor in a Comedy Series, *Mork and Mindy*, 1979; Emmy, Best Individual Performance in a Variety or Music Program, *A Carol Burnett Special*, 1987; Emmy, Best Individual Performance in a Variety or Music Program, *ABC Presents a Royal Gala*, 1988; Golden Globe, Best Actor in a Comedy, *Good Morning, Vietnam*, 1988; Golden Globe, Best Actor in a Comedy, *The Fisher King*, 1992; Golden Globe, Special Achievement, *Aladdin*, 1993; Golden Globe, Best Actor in a Comedy, *Mrs. Doubtfire*, 1994; Grammy, Best Comedy Recording, *Reality . . . What a Concept*, 1979; Grammy, Best Comedy Recording, *A Night at the Met*, 1987; Grammy, Best Comedy Recording, *Good Morning, Vietnam*, 1988; Grammy, Best Recording for Children, *Pecos Bill*, 1988
Address: Creative Artists Agency, 9830 Wilshire Blvd., Beverly Hills, CA 90212

BRUCE WILLIS

Real Name: Walter Bruce Willis
Birthplace: Idar-Oberstein, Germany
Birthdate: 3/19/55
Occupation: Actor
Education: Attended Montclair State College
Debut: (Stage) *Heaven and Earth*, 1977
Signature: *Die Hard*
Facts: Was student council president in high school.

The stammer he'd had since childhood disappeared whenever he performed.

Willis and Demi Moore were married on November 21, 1987, by singer Little Richard.

Has his own band, Bruno.

He and his family live in once sleepy Hailey, Idaho, in the Rockies. Attempting to revitalize the town, Willis bought nearly every building on Main Street.
Infamy: During his senior year in high school, was expelled after a racial disturbance and was only permitted to graduate because his father hired an attorney to get him reinstated.
Original Job: Du Pont plant worker, bartender, commercial actor for Levi's 501 jeans
Marriage: Demi Moore
Children: Rumer Glenn, Scout Larue, Tallulah Belle
Major Awards: Emmy, Best Actor in a Drama Series, *Moonlighting*, 1987; Golden Globe, Best Actor in a Comedy Series, *Moonlighting*, 1987
Address: William Morris Agency, 151 El Camino Dr., Beverly Hills, CA 90212

AUGUST WILSON

Real Name: Frederick August Kittel
Birthplace: Pittsburgh, PA
Birthdate: 4/27/45
Education: High school dropout
Occupation: Playwright
Debut: (Play) *Ma Rainey's Black Bottom*, 1981
Signature: *The Piano Lesson*
Fact: Founded the black activist theater company Black Horizon on the Hill in the 1960s.
Marriages: One prior marriage, Judy Oliver (divorced), Constanza Romero
Child: Sakina Ansari
Major Awards: Pulitzer Prize, Best Play, *Fences*, 1987; Pulitzer Prize, Best Play, *The Piano Lesson*, 1990; Tony, Best Play, *Fences*, 1987
Address: c/o Paul Weiss, 1285 Ave. of the Americas, New York, NY 10019

OPRAH WINFREY

Birthplace: Kosciusko, MS
Birthdate: 1/29/54
Occupation: Talk show host
Education: Tennessee State University
Debut: (Radio Reporter) WVOL, Nashville, 1971–72
Signature: *The Oprah Winfrey Show*
Facts: Delivered Easter sermon to congregation when she was two years old.

Once approached Aretha Franklin as she was stepping out of a limo and convinced Franklin that she had been abandoned. Aretha gave her $100, which Oprah used to stay in a hotel.

As a college sophomore, was the first African-American news co-anchor on a local TV station.

In college, won the title of Miss Tennessee and competed in the Miss Black America contest.

After being sexually abused at age nine by an older cousin and later by a family friend, she ran away from home at age 13.
Original Job: News reporter, WVOL radio, WTVF television, Nashville, TN
Relationship: Stedman Graham (engaged)
Major Awards: Emmy, Best Host of a Talk Show, *The Oprah Winfrey Show*, 1986, 1990, 1991, 1992, 1993, 1994
Address: Harpo Productions, 110 N. Carpenter St., Chicago IL 60607

DEBRA WINGER

Real Name: Mary Debra Winger
Birthplace: Cleveland, OH
Birthdate: 5/17/55
Occupation: Actor
Education: Attended California State University at Northridge
Debut: (TV) *Wonder Woman*, 1976
Signature: *An Officer and a Gentleman*
Facts: In 1972, moved to Israel and served in the army for three months.

At 18 was in a coma after an accident at an amusement park where she was working in a troll costume.

Played Wonder Woman's younger sister, Drusilla the Wonder Girl, in the 1976–77 TV show.

Provided the voice (mixed with that of an elderly woman) for the title character of *E.T., the Extra-Terrestrial*, 1982.
Original Job: Amusement park troll
Marriage: Timothy Hutton (divorced)

Child: Emmanuel Noah
Address: Creative Artists Agency, 9830 Wilshire Blvd., Beverly Hills, CA 90212

ELIJAH WOOD

Birthplace: Cedar Rapids, IA
Birthdate: 1/28/81
Occupation: Actor
Debut: (Film) *Back to the Future II*, 1989
Signature: *North*
Facts: His first acting role was when he was seven, playing the pint-sized executive in Paula Abdul's "Forever Your Girl" video.

Has appeared in more than 15 national commercials.

Gets more than 700 fan letters every week from adoring teenage girls.
Original Job: Model, commercial actor
Address: William Morris Agency, 151 El Camino Dr., Beverly Hills, CA 90212

ALFRE WOODARD

Birthplace: Tulsa, OK
Birthdate: 11/8/53
Occupation: Actor
Education: Boston University
Debut: (Stage) *Horatio*, 1974
Signature: *Cross Creek*
Facts: Played Dr. Roxanne Turner on the series *St. Elsewhere*, 1985–87.

Nominated for an Oscar for *Cross Creek*.
Marriage: Roderick Spencer
Children: Mavis (adopted), Duncan (adopted)
Major Awards: Emmy, Best Supporting Actress in a Drama Series, *Hill Street Blues*, 1984; Emmy, Best Guest Performer, *L.A. Law*, 1987
Address: International Creative Management, 8942 Wilshire Blvd., Beverly Hills, CA 90211

WYNONNA

Real Name: Christina Claire Ciminella
Birthplace: Ashland, KY
Birthdate: 5/3/64

Occupation: Singer
Education: High school
Debut: (Song) "Had a Dream" (with The Judds), 1984
Signature: *Wynonna*
Facts: Drives a 1957 Chevy and a turquoise Harley-Davidson.

Had asthma as a child.

Adopted her name after the town of Wynona, OK, mentioned in the song "Route 66."

The Judds got their first recording contract when mother Naomi, a nurse, gave a tape to patient Diana Maher, daughter of record producer Brent Maher.
Relationship: Arch Kelley III
Child: Elijah
Famous Relatives: Naomi Judd, country singer, mother; Ashley Judd, actor, sister
Major Awards: Best Country Performance by a Group or Duo, "Mama He's Crazy," 1984; "Why Not Me," 1985; "Grandpa (Tell Me 'Bout the Good Old Days)," 1986; "Give a Little Love," 1988; "Love Can Build a Bridge," 1991; Grammy, Best Country Song, "Love Can Build a Bridge," 1991
Address: 3907 Alameda Ave., 2nd Fl., Burbank, CA 91505

YANNI

Real Name: Yanni Chrysomallis
Birthplace: Kalamata, Greece
Birthdate: 11/4/54
Occupation: Musician, pianist
Education: University of Minnesota
Debut: (Album) *Optimystique*, 1986
Facts: Former member of the Greek National Swimming Team. Toured with the cult rock band Chameleon.

His music has been used on broadcasts of numerous sporting events, including the Tour de France, the Olympic Games, and the World Series.
Relationship: Linda Evans
Address: 6714 Villa Madera Dr., SW, Tacoma, WA 98499

ROBERT ZEMECKIS

Birthplace: Chicago, IL
Birthdate: 5/14/51
Occupation: Director, producer, screenwriter
Education: University of Southern California
Debut: (Film) *I Wanna Hold Your Hand*, 1978 (directing and cowriting)
Signature: *Forrest Gump*
Facts: Films he directed include *Romancing the Stone*, *Death Becomes Her*, *Who Framed Roger Rabbit*, and the trilogy of *Back to the Future*. Co-executive-produced HBO's *Tales from the Crypt*.

Is considered one of Hollywood's most accomplished techno-wonk filmmakers who use elaborate special effects in most of his films.

Met his frequent script collaborator Bob Gale at USC film school; in 1979 they wrote the ill-fated *1941* for Steven Spielberg.
Marriage: Mary Ellen Trainor
Child: Alex
Major Awards: Oscar, Best Director, *Forrest Gump*, 1994; Golden Globe, Best Director, *Forrest Gump*, 1995
Address: Creative Artists Agency, 9830 Wilshire Blvd., Beverly Hills, CA 90212

DAPHNE ZUNIGA

Birthplace: Berkeley, CA
Birthdate: 1962
Occupation: Actor
Education: Attended UCLA
Debut: (Film) *The Dorm That Dripped Blood*, 1981
Signature: *Melrose Place*
Facts: Played John Cusack's reluctant traveling companion in Rob Reiner's college romance film, *The Sure Thing*, 1985.

Said that therapy helped her to find a steady boyfriend.
Relationship: Billy Marti
Famous Relative: Jennifer Zuniga, actor, sister
Address: c/o Murphy, 2401 Main St., Santa Monica, CA 90405

THE REGISTER OF THOUSANDS

Here's a celebrity data base covering the multitudes of shakers and shapers, the near-great and notorious, those who grace the screen and the tube, the page and the stage—a resource to discover the real names, birthdates, birthplaces, occupations, and claims to fame of a large slice of pop culture. Those who are coy about their birthdates or are too new on the scene to be sufficiently well documented have been passed over for this year's list—but stay tuned.

AAMES, WILLIE (Willie Upton). Los Angeles, CA, 7/15/60. Actor. *Eight Is Enough.*

ABBOTT, JIM. Flint, MI, 9/19/67. One-handed baseball pitcher.

ABDUL, PAULA. Los Angeles, CA, 6/19/62. Singer, dancer, choreographer, divorced from Emilio Estevez. "Straight Up."

ABRAHAM, F. MURRAY. Pittsburgh, PA, 10/24/39. Actor. *Amadeus.*

ABRAHAMS, JIM. Milwaukee, WI, 5/10/44. Producer, writer, director. *Airplane!; The Naked Gun.*

ABRAHAMS, MICK. Luton, England, 4/7/43. Guitarist. Jethro Tull.

AD-ROCK, KING (Adam Horovitz). New York, NY, 10/31/66. Rap artist. The Beastie Boys.

ADAMS, BROOKE. New York, NY, 2/8/49. Actor. *Invasion of the Body Snatchers.*

ADAMS, BRYAN. Kingston, Canada, 11/5/59. Singer, songwriter. "(Everything I Do) I Do it for You."

ADAMS, DON. New York, NY, 4/19/26. Actor. Maxwell Smart on *Get Smart.*

ADAMS, DOUGLAS. Cambridge, England, 3/11/52. Novelist. *The Hitchhiker's Guide to the Galaxy.*

ADAMS, EDIE (Elizabeth Edith Enke). Kingston, PA, 4/16/29. Actor. *The Ernie Kovacs Show.*

ADAMS, MAUD (Maud Wikstrom). Lulea, Sweden, 2/12/45. Actor. *Octopussy.*

ADAMSON, STUART (William Adamson). Manchester, England, 4/11/58. Guitarist, singer. Big Country.

ADJANI, ISABELLE. Paris, France, 6/27/55. Actor. *Camille Claudel.*

AGAR, JOHN. Chicago, IL, 1/31/21. Actor, formerly married to Shirley Temple. *The Sands of Iwo Jima.*

AGNEW, PETE. Scotland, 9/14/46. Bassist, singer. Nazareth.

AGNEW, SPIRO. Baltimore, MD, 11/9/18. Politician. Resigned as vice president.

AGUTTER, JENNY. Taunton, England, 12/20/52. Actor. *Logan's Run.*

AIELLO, DANNY. New York, NY, 6/20/33. Actor, writer. *Moonstruck.*

AIKMAN, TROY KENNETH. Cerritos, CA, 11/21/66. Football player. Quarterback for the Dallas Cowboys.

AIMEE, ANOUK (Françoise Soyra Dreyfus). Paris, France, 4/27/32. Actor. *A Man and a Woman.*

AKERS, KAREN. New York, NY, 10/13/45. Cabaret singer.

ALBERT, EDDIE (Eddie Albert Heimberger). Rock Island, IL, 4/22/08. Actor, father of Edward. Oliver Wendell Douglas on *Green Acres.*

ALBERT, EDWARD. Los Angeles, CA, 2/20/51. Actor, son of Eddie. *Midway.*

ALBRECHT, BERNIE (Bernard Dicken). Salford, England, 1/4/56. Guitarist. Joy Division; New Order.

ALDA, ALAN (Alphonso D'Abruzzo). New York, NY, 1/28/36. Actor, writer, director, son of Robert Alda. Benjamin Franklin "Hawkeye" Pierce on *M*A*S*H.*

ALDRIN, BUZZ (Edwin Eugene Aldrin Jr.). Montclair, NJ, 1/20/30. Astronaut, businessman.

ALEXANDER, GARY. Chattanooga, TN, 9/25/43. Singer, guitarist. The Association.

ALEXANDER, JANE (Jane Quigley). Boston, MA, 10/28/39. Actor. *All the President's Men.* Head of the National Endowment for the Arts.

ALI, MUHAMMAD (Cassius Clay). Louisville, KY, 1/17/42. Boxing great.

ALLEN, DEBBIE. Houston, TX, 1/16/50. Choreographer, actor, sister of Phylicia Rashad. *Fame.*

ALLEN, DUANE. Taylortown, TX, 4/29/43. Singer. The Oak Ridge Boys.

ALLEN, JOAN. Rochelle, IL, 8/20/56. Actor. *Compromising Positions.*

ALLEN, KAREN. Carrollton, IL, 10/5/51. Actor. *Raiders of the Lost Ark.*

ALLEN, NANCY. New York, NY, 6/24/50. Actor. *Robocop.*

ALLEN, PAPA DEE (Thomas Allen). Wilmington, DE, 7/18/31. Keyboardist, singer. War.

ALLEN, RICK. Sheffield, England, 11/1/63. One-armed drummer. Def Leppard.

ALLEN, ROD (Rod Bainbridge). Leicester, England, 3/31/44. Bassist, singer. The Fortunes.

ALLEN, STEVE. New York, NY, 12/26/21. Writer, performer, variety show host, husband of Jayne Meadows. *The Steve Allen Show.*

ALLEN, VERDEN. Hereford, England, 5/26/44. Keyboardist. Mott The Hoople.

ALLEY, KIRSTIE. Wichita, KS, 1/12/55. Actor, married to Parker Stevenson. Rebecca Howe on *Cheers.*

ALLISON, JERRY. Hillsboro, TX, 8/31/39. Drummer. Buddy Holly & The Crickets.

ALLMAN, GREGG. Nashville, TN, 12/8/47. Keyboardist, guitarist, singer, formerly married to Cher. The Allman Brothers Band.

ALLSUP, MIKE. Modesto, CA, 3/8/47. Guitarist. Three Dog Night.

ALLYSON, JUNE (Ella Geisman). Westchester, NY, 10/7/17. Actor. *The Dupont Show Starring June Allyson; Lassie.*

ALMOND, MARC (Peter Almond). Southport, England, 7/9/59. Singer. Soft Cell.

ALONSO, MARIA CONCHITA. Cuba, 6/29/57. Actor. *The Running Man.*

ALPERT, HERB. Los Angeles, CA, 3/31/35. Trumpeter, band leader, cofounder of A&M Records. The Tijuana Brass.

ALSTON, BARBARA. Brooklyn, NY, 1945. Singer. The Crystals.

ALSTON, SHIRLEY (Shirley Owens). Passaic, NJ, 6/10/41. Singer. The Shirelles.

ALT, CAROL. Queens, NY, 12/1/60. Supermodel.

ALTMAN, ROBERT. Kansas City, MO, 2/20/25. Director, writer, producer. *The Player.*

ALVARADO, TRINI. New York, NY, 1/10/69. Actor. *Rich Kids.*

AMIN, IDI. Koboko, Uganda, 1/1/25. Political leader, former president of Uganda.

AMIS, SUZY. Oklahoma City, OK, 1/5/61. Actor. *Blown Away.*

AMOS, JOHN. Newark, NJ, 12/27/41. Actor. James Evans on *Good Times.*

AMOS, WALLY JR. Tallahassee, FL, 7/1/36. Business executive. Famous Amos chocolate chip cookies.

ANDERSON, ALFA. 9/7/46. Singer. Chic.

ANDERSON, HARRY. Newport, RI, 10/14/52. Actor. Judge Harry Stone on *Night Court.*

ANDERSON, IAN. Edinburgh, Scotland, 8/10/47. Singer, flautist. Jethro Tull.

ANDERSON, JON. Lancashire, England, 10/25/44. Singer, drummer. Yes.

ANDERSON, KEVIN. Illinois, 1/13/60. Actor. *Sleeping with the Enemy.*

ANDERSON, LAURIE. Chicago, IL, 6/5/50. Singer, performance artist.

ANDERSON, LONI. St. Paul, MN, 8/5/46. Actor. Receptionist Jennifer Marlowe on *WKRP in Cincinnati.*

ANDERSON, MELISSA SUE. Berkeley, CA, 9/26/62. Actor. Mary Ingalls Kendall on *Little House on the Prairie.*

ANDERSON, MELODY. Edmonton, Canada, 1/3/55. Actor. Dale Arden in *Flash Gordon.*

ANDERSON, RICHARD. Long Branch, NJ, 8/8/26. Actor. Oscar Goldman on *The Six Million Dollar Man* and *The Bionic Woman.*

ANDERSON, RICHARD DEAN. Minneapolis, MN, 1/23/50. Actor. *MacGyver.*

ANDERSON, RICK. St. Paul, MN, 8/1/47. Bassist. The Tubes.

ANDERSON, TERRY. 10/27/47. Journalist, former hostage.

ANDERSSON, BENNY (Goran Andersson). Stockholm, Sweden, 12/16/46. Keyboards, singer. Abba.

ANDERSSON, BIBI. Stockholm, Sweden, 11/11/35. Actor. *The Seventh Seal.*

ANDES, MARK. Philadelphia, PA, 2/19/48. Bassist. Spirit.

ANDRESS, URSULA. Berne, Switzerland, 3/19/36. Actor. *Dr. No.*

ANDRETTI, MARIO. Montona Trieste, Italy, 2/28/40. Auto racer.

ANDREW, PRINCE. London, England, 2/19/60. British royalty, son of Queen Elizabeth II.

ANDREWS, ANTHONY. London, England, 1/12/48. Actor. *Brideshead Revisited.*

ANDREWS, BARRY. London, England, 9/12/56. Keyboardist. XTC.

ANDREWS, JULIE (Julia Wells). Walton-on-Thames, England, 10/1/35. Actor, singer. *The Sound of Music.*

ANKA, PAUL. Ottawa, Canada, 7/30/41. Singer, songwriter. "Diana."

ANN-MARGRET (Ann-Margret Olsson). Valsjobyn, Sweden, 4/28/41. Actor, singer. *Viva Las Vegas.*

ANNAUD, JEAN-JACQUES. Draveil, France, 10/1/43. Writer, director. *Quest for Fire; The Lover.*

ANNE, PRINCESS. London, England, 8/15/50. British royalty, daughter of Queen Elizabeth II.

ANSPACH, SUSAN. New York, NY, 11/23/45. Actor. *Five Easy Pieces.*

ANT, ADAM (Stewart Goddard). London, England, 11/3/54. Singer. Adam & The Ants.

442

ANTHONY, MICHAEL. Chicago, IL, 6/20/55. Bassist. Van Halen.

ANTON, SUSAN. Oak Glen, CA, 10/12/50. Actor, singer. *Goldengirl.*

ANWAR, GABRIELLE. Laleham, England, 2/4/70. Actor. Tangoed with Al Pacino in *Scent of a Woman.*

APPICE, CARMINE. New York, NY, 12/15/46. Drummer. Vanilla Fudge.

APPLEGATE, CHRISTINA. Hollywood, CA, 11/25/72. Actor. Kelly Bundy on *Married . . . with Children.*

AQUINO, CORAZON. Tarlac, Philippines, 1/25/33. Political leader. Former president of the Philippines.

ARAFAT, YASIR. Cairo, Egypt, 8/24/29. Political leader. Head of the PLO.

ARCHER, ANNE. Los Angeles, CA, 8/25/47. Actor. Wife of Michael Douglas in *Fatal Attraction.*

ARENHOLZ, STEPHEN. The Bronx, NY, 4/29/69. Actor.

ARGENT, ROD. St. Albans, England, 6/14/45. Keyboardist. The Zombies.

ARKIN, ALAN. New York, NY, 3/26/34. Actor, director, writer, folk singer, member of Second City, father of Adam Arkin (*Chicago Hope*). *The In-Laws.*

ARMATRADING, JOAN. Basseterre, West Indies, 12/9/50. Singer, songwriter. "Me, Myself, I."

ARMSTRONG, BESS. Baltimore, MD, 12/11/53. Actor. Julia Peters on *On Our Own.*

ARMSTRONG, NEIL. Wapakoneta, OH, 8/5/30. Astronaut.

ARNAZ, DESI JR. Los Angeles, CA, 1/19/53. Actor, singer, son of Lucille Ball and Desi Arnaz. *Here's Lucy.*

ARNAZ, LUCIE. Los Angeles, CA, 7/17/51. Actor, daughter of Lucille Ball and Desi Arnaz, married to Laurence Luckinbill. *Here's Lucy.*

ARNESS, JAMES (James Aurness). Minneapolis, MN, 5/26/23. Actor, brother of Peter Graves. *Gunsmoke.*

ARQUETTE, PATRICIA. New York, NY, 4/8/68. Actor, granddaughter of Cliff Arquette, sister of Rosanna. *True Romance.*

ARQUETTE, ROSANNA. New York, NY, 8/10/59. Actor, granddaughter of Cliff Arquette, sister of Patricia, and inspiration for Toto song "Rosanna." *Desperately Seeking Susan.*

ARTHUR, BEATRICE (Bernice Frankel). New York, NY, 5/13/26. Actor. *Maude.*

ASH, DANIEL. 7/31/57. Guitarist, singer. Bauhaus; Love and Rockets.

ASHER, PETER. London, England, 6/22/44. Singer. Peter and Gordon.

ASHFORD, NICKOLAS. Fairfield, SC, 5/4/42. Singer. Ashford and Simpson.

ASHFORD, ROSALIND. Detroit, MI, 9/2/43. Singer. Martha & The Vandellas.

ASHLEY, ELIZABETH (Elizabeth Ann Cole). Ocala, FL, 8/30/39. Actor. *Evening Shade.*

ASNER, EDWARD. Kansas City, KS, 11/15/29. Actor. *Lou Grant.*

ASSANTE, ARMAND. New York, NY, 10/4/49. Actor. *The Doctors.*

ASTBURY, IAN. Heswall, England, 5/14/62. Singer. The Cult.

ASTIN, JOHN. Baltimore, MD, 3/30/30. Actor, formerly married to Patty Duke, father of Sean Astin. Gomez Addams on *The Addams Family.*

ASTIN, SEAN. Santa Monica, CA, 2/25/71. Actor, son of John Astin and Patty Duke. *Encino Man.*

ASTLEY, RICK. Warrington, England, 2/6/66. Singer, songwriter. "Never Gonna Give You Up."

ASTON, JAY. London, England, 5/4/61. Singer. Bucks Fizz.

ASTON, JOHN. England, 11/30/57. Guitarist. Psychedelic Furs.

ATKINS, CHET. Luttrell, TN, 6/20/24. Virtuoso guitarist.

ATKINS, CHRISTOPHER. Rye, NY, 2/21/61. Actor. *The Blue Lagoon.*

ATKINSON, PAUL. Cuffley, England, 3/19/46. Guitarist. The Zombies.

ATTENBOROUGH, RICHARD. Cambridge, England, 8/29/23. Actor, producer, director. *Gandhi.*

ATWOOD, MARGARET. Ottawa, Canada, 11/18/39. Author, poet. *The Handmaid's Tale.*

AUBERJONOIS, RENE. New York, NY, 6/1/40. Actor. Security Chief Odo on *Deep Space Nine.*

AUTRY, ALAN. Shreveport, LA, 7/31/52. Actor. Bubba Skinner on *In the Heat of the Night.*

AUTRY, GENE. Tioga, TX, 9/29/07. Screen's first singing cowboy. *The Gene Autry Show.*

AVALON, FRANKIE (Francis Thomas Avallone). Philadelphia, PA, 9/18/40. Singer, actor. *Beach Blanket Bingo.*

AVORY, MICK. London, England, 2/15/44. Drummer. The Kinks.

AXTON, HOYT. Duncan, OK, 3/25/38. Singer, songwriter, actor. *Gremlins.*

AZNAVOUR, CHARLES (Shahnour Varenagh Aznourian). Paris, France, 5/22/24. Singer, songwriter, actor. *The Tin Drum.*

BACALL, LAUREN (Betty Perske). New York, NY, 9/16/24. Actor, widow of Humphrey Bogart, formerly married to Jason Robards. *Key Largo.*

BACH, BARBARA. Queens, NY, 8/27/47. Actor, married to Ringo Starr. *The Spy Who Loved Me.*

BACHMAN, RANDY. Winnipeg, Canada, 9/27/43. Guitarist, singer. Bachman-Turner Overdrive; The Guess Who.

BACHMAN, ROBBIE. Winnipeg, Canada, 2/18/53. Drummer. Bachman-Turner Overdrive.

BACON, KEVIN. Philadelphia, PA, 7/8/58. Actor, married to Kyra Sedgwick. *Footloose.*

BADANJEK, JOHN. 1948. Drummer. Mitch Ryder & The Detroit Wheels.

BAEZ, JOAN. Staten Island, NY, 1/9/41. Folk singer and songwriter, peace and civil rights activist.

BAILEY, PHILIP. Denver, CO, 5/8/51. Singer, conga player, percussionist. Earth, Wind & Fire.

BAILEY, TOM. Halifax, England, 6/18/57. Singer, keyboardist. Thompson Twins.

BAIN, BARBARA. Chicago, IL, 9/13/34. Actor. *Mission: Impossible.*

BAIO, SCOTT. Brooklyn, NY, 9/22/61. Actor. Charles "Chachi" Arcola on *Happy Days.*

BAKER, ANITA. Detroit, MI, 12/20/57. R&B singer.

BAKER, CARROLL. Johnstown, PA, 5/28/31. Actor. *Kindergarten Cop.*

BAKER, CHERYL (Rita Crudgington). London, England, 3/8/54. Singer. Bucks Fizz.

BAKER, GINGER (Peter Baker). Lewisham, England, 8/19/40. Drummer. Cream; Blind Faith.

BAKER, JOE DON. Groesbeck, TX, 2/12/36. Actor. *Walking Tall.*

BAKER, KATHY. Midland, TX, 6/8/50. Actor. *Picket Fences.*

BAKER, MICKEY (McHouston Baker). Louisville, KY, 10/15/25. Singer. Mickey & Sylvia.

BAKKER, JIM. Muskegon, MI, 1/2/40. TV evangelist, participant in the PTL scandal.

BAKKER, TAMMY FAYE. International Falls, MN, 3/7/42. TV evangelist. Former wife of PTL founder Jim Bakker.

BAKSHI, RALPH. Haifa, Palestine, 10/29/38. Animator, writer, director. *Fritz the Cat.*

BAKULA, SCOTT. St. Louis, MO, 10/9/55. Actor. *Quantum Leap.*

BALABAN, BOB. Chicago, IL, 8/16/45. Actor. Roles in *Midnight Cowboy, Little Man Tate.*

BALDWIN, ADAM. Chicago, IL, 2/27/62. Actor. *My Bodyguard.*

BALIN, MARTY (Martyn Jerel Buchwald). Cincinnati, OH, 1/30/43. Singer. Jefferson Airplane/Starship.

BALL, DAVID. Blackpool, England, 5/3/59. Keyboardist. Soft Cell.

BALL, ROGER. Dundee, Scotland, 6/4/44. Alto and baritone saxophonist. Average White Band.

BALLARD, HANK. Detroit, MI, 11/18/36. Singer/songwriter. "Work with Me Annie."

BALLARD, KAYE (Catherine Gloria Balotta). Cleveland, OH, 11/20/26. Actor, singer.

BALSAM, MARTIN. New York, NY, 11/4/19. Actor. *On the Waterfront.*

BALSLEY, PHILIP. 8/8/39. Singer. Kingsmen; Statler Brothers.

BAMBAATAA, AFRIKA. The Bronx, NY, 1958. Rap/hip-hop DJ.

BANALI, FRANKIE. 11/14/55. Musician. Quiet Riot.

BANANA (Lowell Levinger). Cambridge, MA, 1946. Keyboardist, guitarist. The Youngbloods.

BANCROFT, ANNE (Anna Maria Italiano). The Bronx, NY, 9/17/31. Actor. Mrs. Robinson in *The Graduate.*

BANKS, TONY. East Heathly, England, 3/27/51. Keyboardist. Genesis.

BARBATA, JOHN. 4/1/45. Drummer. The Turtles; Jefferson Starship.

BARBEAU, ADRIENNE. Sacramento, CA, 6/11/45. Actor. Carol on *Maude.*

BARBIERI, RICHARD. 11/30/57. Keyboardist. Japan.

BARDOT, BRIGITTE (Camille Javal). Paris, France, 9/28/34. Sex goddess. *And God Created Woman.*

BARGERON, DAVE. Massachusetts, 9/6/42. Trombonist. Blood, Sweat and Tears.

BARKER, BOB. Darrington, WA, 12/12/23. Game show host. *The Price Is Right.*

BARKER, CLIVE. Liverpool, England, 10/5/52. Author. *The Inhuman Condition.*

BARNES, LEO. 10/5/55. Musician. Hothouse Flowers.

BARRE, MARTIN. 11/17/46. Guitarist. Jethro Tull.

BARRERE, PAUL. Burbank, CA, 7/3/48. Lead guitarist. Little Feat.

BARRETT, ASTON. Kingston, Jamaica, 11/22/46. Bassist. Bob Marley & The Wailers.,

BARRETT, MARCIA. St. Catherine's, Jamaica, 10/14/48. Singer. Boney M.

BARRETT, RONA. New York, NY, 10/8/36. News correspondent, columnist.

BARRETT, SYD (Roger Barrett). Cambridge, England, 1/6/46. Singer, guitarist. Pink Floyd.

BARRY, MARION. Itta Bena, MS, 3/6/36. Mayor of Washington, served six-month prison term for cocaine possession.

BARRYMORE, JOHN DREW. Beverly Hills, CA, 6/4/32. Actor, father of Drew Barrymore.

BARSON, MIKE. England, 5/21/58. Keyboardist. Madness.

BARTEL, PAUL. New York, NY, 8/6/38. Director, writer, actor. *Eating Raoul.*

BARTHOL, BRUCE. Berkeley, CA, 1947. Bassist. Country Joe & The Fish.

BARYSHNIKOV, MIKHAIL. Riga, Latvia, 1/27/48. Dancer, actor. *White Nights.*

BATEMAN, JASON. Rye, NY, 1/14/69. Actor, brother of Justine. David on *The Hogan Family.*

BATEMAN, JUSTINE. Rye, NY, 2/19/66. Actor, sister of Jason. Mallory Keaton on *Family Ties.*

BATES, ALAN. Allestree, England, 2/17/34. Actor. *An Unmarried Woman.*

BATTLE, KATHLEEN. Portsmouth, OH, 8/13/48. Opera singer.

BAUER, JOE. Memphis, TN, 9/26/41. Drummer. The Youngbloods.

BAUER, STEVEN (Steven Echevarria). Havana, Cuba, 12/2/56. Actor, formerly married to Melanie Griffith. *Wiseguy.*

BAUMGARTNER, STEVE. Philadelphia, PA, 10/28/67. Writer, actor. *My Best Friend's Girl.*

BAXTER, JEFF "SKUNK." Washington, DC, 12/13/48. Lead Guitarist. Steely Dan; The Doobie Brothers.

BAXTER, KEITH. Monmouthshire, Wales, 4/29/33. Actor.

BAXTER, MEREDITH. Los Angeles, CA, 6/21/47. Actor, formerly married to David Birney. Elyse Keaton on *Family Ties.*

BEACHAM, STEPHANIE. Hertfordshire, England, 2/28/47. Actor. Sable Scott Colby on *The Colbys.*

BEAKY (John Dymond). Salisbury, England, 7/10/44. Guitarist. Dave Dee, Dozy, Beaky, Mick and Tich.

BEALS, JENNIFER. Chicago, IL, 12/19/63. Actor. *Flashdance.*

BEARD, FRANK. Dallas, TX, 12/10/49. Drummer. ZZ Top.

BEASLEY, ALLYCE. Brooklyn, NY, 7/6/54. Actor. Agnes Dipesto on *Moonlighting.*

BEATRICE, PRINCESS. London, England, 8/8/88. British royalty, daughter of Prince Andrew and the Duchess of York.

BEATTY, NED. Lexington, KY, 7/6/37. Actor. *Deliverance.*

BECK (Beck Hansen). Los Angeles, CA, 1971. Singer, songwriter. "Loser."

BECK, JEFF. Wallington, England, 6/24/44. Guitarist. The Yardbirds; The Jeff Beck Group; The Jan Hammer Group.

BECK, JOHN. Chicago, IL, 1/28/43. Actor. Mark Graison on *Dallas.*

BECK, MICHAEL. Memphis, TN, 2/4/49. Actor. *Xanadu.*

BECKER, BORIS. Liemen, Germany, 11/22/67. Tennis player.

BECKER, WALTER. New York, NY, 2/20/50. Bassist. Steely Dan.

BECKLEY, GERRY. Texas, 9/12/52. Singer, guitarist. America.

BEDELIA, BONNIE. New York, NY, 3/25/46. Actor. *Presumed Innocent.*

BEDFORD, MARK. London, England, 8/24/61. Bassist. Madness.

BEEFHEART, CAPTAIN (Don Van Vliet). Glendale, CA, 1/15/41. Singer, high school friend of Frank Zappa. Captain Beefheart & The Magic Band.

BEERS, GARY. 6/22/57. Bassist, singer. INXS

BEGLEY, ED JR. Los Angeles, CA, 9/16/49. Actor. Dr. Victor Ehrlich on *St. Elsewhere.*

BEL GEDDES, BARBARA New York, NY, 10/31/22. Actor. *Dallas.*

BELAFONTE, HARRY. New York, NY, 3/1/27. Actor, singer, father of Shari. "The Banana Boat Song."

BELAFONTE, SHARI. New York, NY, 9/22/54. Actor, daughter of Harry. *Hotel.*

BELL, ANDY. Peterborough, England, 4/25/64. Singer. Erasure.

BELL, RICKY. Boston, MA, 9/18/67. Singer. New Edition.

BELL, ROBERT. Youngstown, OH, 10/8/50. Bassist. Kool & The Gang.

BELL, RONALD. Youngstown, OH, 11/1/51. Saxophonist. Kool & The Gang.

BELLADONNA, JOEY. Oswego, NY. Singer. Anthrax.

BELLAMY, GEORGE. Sunderland, England, 10/8/41. Guitarist. The Tornados.

BELLAMY, TONY. Los Angeles, CA, 9/12/40. Singer, guitarist. Redbone.

BELLO, FRANK. 7/9/65. Bassist. Anthrax.

BELMONDO, JEAN-PAUL. Paris, France, 4/9/33. Actor. *Breathless.*

BELUSHI, JIM. Chicago, IL, 6/15/54. Actor, brother of late John Belushi. *K-9.*

BENATAR, PAT (Pat Andrzejewski). Brooklyn, NY, 1/10/53. Singer. "Heartbreaker."

BENBEN, BRIAN. Newburgh, NY. Actor. Dream On. Married to Madeline Stowe.

BENEDICT, DIRK (Dirk Niewoehner). Helena, MT, 3/1/45. Actor. Lt. Templeton Peck on *The A-Team.*

BENJAMIN, RICHARD. New York, NY, 5/22/38. Actor, director. *Love at First Bite; Goodbye, Columbus.*

BENNETT, BRIAN. London, England, 2/9/40. Drummer. The Shadows.

BENNETT, ESTELLE. New York, NY, 7/22/44. Singer. The Ronettes.

BENNETT, PATRICIA. New York, NY, 4/7/47. Singer. The Chiffons.

BENSON, GEORGE. Pittsburgh, PA, 3/22/43. Singer, guitarist. "Give Me the Night."

BENSON, RENALDO. Detroit, MI, 1947. Singer. The Four Tops.

BENSON, ROBBY (Robby Segal). Dallas, TX, 1/21/56. Actor, writer, director. *Ice Castles.*

BERADINO, JOHN. Los Angeles, CA, 5/1/17. Actor, baseball player. Dr. Hardy on *General Hospital.*

BERENGER, TOM. Chicago, IL, 5/31/50. Actor. *Platoon.*

BERENSON, MARISA. New York, NY, 2/15/47. Actor. *Barry Lyndon.*

BERGEN, POLLY (Nellie Paulina Burgin). Knoxville, TN, 7/14/30. Singer, actor. *The Winds of War.*

BERGER, ALAN. 11/8/49. Bassist. Southside Johnny & The Asbury Jukes.

BERGMAN, INGMAR. Uppsala, Sweden, 7/14/18. Writer, director. *The Silence.*

BERKOWITZ, DAVID. New York, NY, 6/1/53. Serial killer. Son of Sam.

BERLE, MILTON (Milton Berlinger). New York, NY, 7/12/08. Actor. *The Milton Berle Show.*

BERNHARD, SANDRA. Flint, MI, 6/6/55. Actor, singer. *Roseanne.*

BERNSEN, CORBIN. Los Angeles, CA, 9/7/54. Actor, married to Amanda Pays. Arnie Becker on *L.A. Law.*

BERRI, CLAUDE (Claude Langmann). Paris, France, 7/1/34. Actor, director, producer of films.

BERRY, BILL. Hibbing, MN, 7/31/58. Drummer. R.E.M.

BERRY, CHUCK. San Jose, CA, 10/18/26. Rock and Roll legend, singer and guitarist. "Johnny B. Goode."

BERRY, JAN. Los Angeles, CA, 4/3/41. Singer. Jan & Dean.

BERTINELLI, VALERIE. Wilmington, DE, 4/23/60. Actor, married to Eddie Van Halen. Barbara Cooper Royer on *One Day at a Time.*

BETTS, DICKEY. West Palm Beach, FL, 12/12/43. Guitarist, singer. The Allman Brothers Band.

BIALIK, MAYIM. San Diego, CA, 12/12/75. Actor. *Blossom.*

BIEHN, MICHAEL. Anniston, AL, 7/29/56. Actor. *The Terminator.*

BIG FIGURE, THE (John Martin). 1947. Drummer. Dr. Feelgood.

BILLINGSLEY, BARBARA. Los Angeles, CA, 12/22/22. Actor. June Cleaver on *Leave It to Beaver.*

BILLINGSLEY, PETER. New York, NY, 1972. Child actor. *A Christmas Story.*

BILLINGSLEY, RAY. Wake Forest, NC, 7/25/57. Cartoonist. *Curtis.*

BIRD, LARRY. West Baden, IN, 12/7/56. Basketball great. Boston Celtics.

BIRNEY, DAVID. Washington, DC, 4/23/39. Actor, formerly married to Meredith Baxter. *St. Elsewhere.*

BIRRELL, PETE. Manchester, England, 5/9/41. Bassist. Freddie & The Dreamers.

BIRTLES, BEEB (Gerard Birtlekamp). Amsterdam, the Netherlands, 11/28/48. Guitarist. The Little River Band.

BISHOP, JOEY (Joseph Gottlieb). The Bronx, NY, 2/3/18. Actor. *The Joey Bishop Show.*

BISSET, JACQUELINE. Waybridge, England, 9/13/44. Actor. *The Deep.*

BIVINS, MICHAEL. 8/10/68. Singer. New Edition, Bell Biv DeVoe.

BLACK, CILLA (Cilla White). Liverpool, England, 5/27/43. Singer, TV personality.

BLACK, JET (Brian Duffy). England, 8/26/58. Drummer. The Stranglers.

BLACK, KAREN (Karen Ziegler). Park Ridge, IL, 7/1/42. Actor. *Easy Rider.*

BLACKMON, LARRY. New York, 5/29/56. Singer, drummer. Cameo.

BLACKMORE, RITCHIE. Weston-Super-Mare, England, 4/14/45. Guitarist. Deep Purple; Rainbow.

BLADD, STEPHEN JO. Boston, MA, 7/13/42. Drummer, singer. The J. Geils Band.

BLADES, RUBEN. Panama City, Panama, 7/16/48. Actor, singer. *The Milagro Beanfield War.*

BLAIR, BONNIE. Cornwall, NY, 3/18/64. Speed skater.

BLAIR, LINDA. Westport, CT, 1/22/59. Actor. *The Exorcist.*

BLAKE, ROBERT (Michael Gubitosi). Nutley, NJ, 9/18/33. Actor. *Baretta.*

BLAKELY, SUSAN. Frankfurt, Germany, 9/7/50. Actor. *Rich Man, Poor Man.*

BLAKLEY, ALAN. Bromley, England, 4/1/42. Guitarist. Brian Poole & The Tremeloes.

BLAND, BOBBY. Rosemark, TN, 1/27/30. Singer.

BLASS, BILL. Ft. Wayne, IN, 6/22/22. Fashion designer.

BLEDSOE, TEMPESTT. Chicago, IL, 8/1/73. Actor. Vanessa Huxtable on *The Cosby Show.*

BLOOM, CLAIRE. London, England, 2/15/31. Actor. *Richard III.*

BLOOM, ERIC. Long Island, NY, 12/1/44. Lead guitarist, keyboardist. Blue Öyster Cult.

BLOW, KURTIS (Kurtis Walker). New York, NY, 8/9/59. DJ, rapper.

BLUECHEL, TED JR. San Pedro, CA, 12/2/42. Singer, drummer. The Association.

BLUME, JUDY. Elizabeth, NJ, 2/12/38. Novelist. *Are You There God? It's Me Margaret.*

BLUNSTONE, COLIN. Hatfield, England, 6/24/45. Singer. The Zombies.

BOBBY G. (Bobby Gubby). London, England, 8/23/53. Singer. Bucks Fizz.

BOGARDE, DIRK (Derek Niven van den Bogaerde). Hampstead, England, 3/28/21. Actor. *Death in Venice.*

BOGERT, TIM. Richfield, NJ, 8/27/44. Bassist. Vanilla Fudge.

BOGLE, BOB. Portland, OR, 1/16/37. Guitarist, bassist. The Ventures.

BOGOSIAN, ERIC. Woburn, MA, 4/24/53. Actor, writer. *Talk Radio.*

BOLAN, MARC (Mark Feld). Hackney, England, 9/30/47. Singer, guitarist. T. Rex.

BOLDER, TREVOR. 6/9/50. Bassist. Spiders from Mars; Uriah Heep.

BOLOGNA, JOSEPH. Brooklyn, NY, 12/30/38. Actor. *Chapter Two.*

BONADUCE, DANNY. 8/13/59. Actor, radio personality. Danny on *The Partridge Family.*

BOND, RONNIE (Ronnie Bullis). Andover, England, 5/4/43. Drummer. The Troggs.

BONDS, GARY (Gary Anderson). Jacksonville, FL, 6/6/39. Singer.

BONET, LISA. San Francisco, CA, 11/16/67. Actor, formerly married to Lenny Kravitz. Denise Huxtable on *The Cosby Show.*

BONHAM-CARTER, HELENA. London, England, 5/26/66. Actor. *A Room with a View.*

BONNER, FRANK. Little Rock, AR, 2/28/42. Actor. Herb Tarlek on *WKRP in Cincinnati.*

BONO, CHASTITY. Los Angeles, CA, 3/4/69. Daughter of Sonny and Cher.

BONO, SONNY (Salvatore Bono). Detroit, MI, 2/16/35. Singer, actor, director, congressman, formerly married to Cher, father of Chastity. *The Sonny and Cher Comedy Hour.*

BONSALL, BRIAN. 12/3/82. Child actor. *Family Ties.*

BONSALL, JOE. Philadelphia, PA, 5/18/48. Singer. The Oak Ridge Boys.

BOONE, PAT. Jacksonville, FL, 6/1/34. Singer, actor. *The Pat Boone Show.*

BOONE, STEVE. North Carolina, 9/23/43. Bassist, singer. The Lovin' Spoonful.

BOOTHE, POWERS. Snyder, TX, 6/1/49. Actor. *Guyana Tragedy: The Story of Jim Jones.*

BORGNINE, ERNEST (Ernest Borgnino). Hamden, CT, 1/24/17. Actor. *McHale's Navy.*

BOSSON, BARBARA. Charleroi, PA, 11/1/39. Actor, married to producer Steven Bochco. Fay Furillo on *Hill Street Blues.*

BOSTWICK, BARRY. San Mateo, CA, 2/24/45. Actor. *The Rocky Horror Picture Show.*

BOTTOMS, JOSEPH. Santa Barbara, CA, 4/22/54. Actor. *The Black Hole.*

BOTTOMS, SAM. Santa Barbara, CA, 10/17/55. Actor. *Apocalypse Now.*

BOTTOMS, TIMOTHY. Santa Barbara, CA, 8/30/51. Actor. *Johnny Got His Gun.*

BOTTUM, RODDY. Los Angeles, CA, 7/1/63. Keyboardist. Faith No More.

BOUCHARD, JOE. Long Island, NY, 11/9/48. Bassist, singer. Blue Öyster Cult.

BOWE, RIDDICK. New York, NY, 8/10/67. Boxer, former heavyweight champion of the world.

BOWERS, TONY. 10/31/56. Bassist. Simply Red.

BOWIE, DAVID (David Jones). Brixton, England, 1/8/47. Singer, actor, married to Iman. *Ziggy Stardust and the Spiders from Mars.*

BOX, MICK. London, England, 6/8/47. Guitarist, songwriter. Uriah Heep.

BOXLEITNER, BRUCE. Elgin, IL, 5/12/50. Actor, married to Melissa Gilbert. *Scarecrow and Mrs. King.*

BOY GEORGE (George O'Dowd). Eltham, England, 6/14/61. Singer. Culture Club.

BOYLE, LARA FLYNN. Davenport, IA, 3/24/70. Actor. *Twin Peaks.*

BOYLE, PETER. Philadelphia, PA, 10/18/33. Actor. *Young Frankenstein.*

BRACCO, LORRAINE. Brooklyn, NY, 1955. Actor. *GoodFellas.*

BRADBURY, RAY. Waukegan, IL, 8/22/20. Novelist. *The Martian Chronicles.*

BRAGG, BILLY (Steven Bragg). Barking, England, 12/20/57. Punk/R&B singer, songwriter.

BRAID, LES (William Braid). Liverpool, England, 9/15/41. Bassist. The Swinging Blue Jeans.

BRAMLETT, BONNIE. Acton, IL, 11/8/44. Singer. Delaney & Bonnie.

BRAMLETT, DELANEY. Pontotoc County, MS, 7/1/39. Guitarist, singer. Delaney & Bonnie.

BRANDAUER, KLAUS MARIA. Altaussee, Austria, 6/22/44. Actor. *Out of Africa.*

BRATTON, CREED. Sacramento, CA, 2/8/43. Guitarist. The Grass Roots.

BRAUNN, ERIK. Boston, MA, 8/11/50. Guitarist, singer. Iron Butterfly.

BREATHED, BERKE. Encino, CA, 6/21/57. Cartoonist. *Bloom County.*

BRENNAN, EILEEN. Los Angeles, CA, 9/3/35. Actor. *Private Benjamin.*

BRENNEMAN, AMY. New London, CT, 6/22/64. Actor. *NYPD Blue.*

BRENNER, DAVID. Philadelphia, PA, 2/4/45. Stand-up comedian. *Nightlife.*

BREWER, DONALD. Flint, MI, 9/3/48. Drummer. Grand Funk Railroad.

BRICKELL, EDIE. Oak Cliff, TX, 1966. Singer, songwriter, married to Paul Simon. Edie Brickell and New Bohemians.

BRIDGES, BEAU (Lloyd Vernet Bridges III). Los Angeles, CA, 12/9/41. Actor, director, son of Lloyd, brother of Jeff. *The Fabulous Baker Boys.*

BRIDGES, LLOYD. San Leandro, CA, 1/15/13. Actor, father of Beau and Jeff. *Sea Hunt.*

BRIDGES, TODD. San Francisco, CA, 5/27/66. Actor. Willis Jackson on *Diff'rent Strokes.*

BRIGATI, EDDIE. Garfield, NJ, 10/22/46. Singer, percussionist. The (Young) Rascals.

BRIGGS, DAVID. Melbourne, Australia, 1/26/51. Guitarist. The Little River Band.

BRILEY, ALEX. 4/12/56. Singer. The Village People.

BRIMLEY, WILFORD. Salt Lake City, UT, 9/27/34. Actor. *Cocoon.*

BRINKLEY, DAVID. Wilmington, NC, 7/10/20. Pioneer news journalist and anchor. *This Week with David Brinkley.*

BRIQUETTE, PETE (Patrick Cusack). Ireland, 7/2/54. Bassist, singer. The Boomtown Rats.

BRITTANY, MORGAN (Suzanne Cupito). Los Angeles, CA, 12/5/51. Actor. Katherine Wentworth on *Dallas.*

BRITTON, CHRIS. Watford, England, 6/21/45. Guitarist. The Troggs.

BROLIN, JAMES (James Bruderlin). Los Angeles, CA, 7/18/40. Actor, father of Josh. Dr. Steven Kiley on *Marcus Welby, M.D.*

BRONSON, CHARLES (Charles Buchinsky). Ehrenfield, PA, 11/3/21. Actor, widower of Jill Ireland. *Death Wish.*

BROOKER, GARY. Southend, England, 5/29/45. Singer, keyboardist. Procol Harum.

BROOKS, ALBERT (Albert Einstein). Los Angeles, CA, 7/22/47. Actor, writer, director. *Defending Your Life.*

BROOKS, LALA. Brooklyn, NY, 1946. Singer. The Crystals.

BROTHERS, JOYCE (Joyce Bauer). New York, NY, 10/20/28. Psychologist.

BROWN, BLAIR. Washington, DC, 1948. Actor. *The Days and Nights of Molly Dodd.*

BROWN, BRYAN. Panania, Australia, 6/23/47. Actor, married to Rachel Ward. *FX.*

BROWN, DAVID. Houston, TX, 2/15/47. Bassist. Santana.

BROWN, ERROL. Kingston, Jamaica, 11/12/48. Singer. Hot Chocolate.

BROWN, GEORG STANFORD. Havana, Cuba, 6/24/43. Actor. *Colossus: The Forbin Project.*

BROWN, GEORGE. Jersey City, NJ, 1/5/49. Drummer. Kool and The Gang.

BROWN, HAROLD. Long Beach, CA, 3/17/46. Drummer. War.

BROWN, IAN. Sale, England, 2/20/63. Singer. Stone Roses.

BROWN, JAMES. Augusta, GA, 5/3/28. The Godfather of Soul.

BROWN, JIM. St. Simons Island, GA, 2/17/36. Football player, actor. *The Dirty Dozen.*

BROWN, JIMMY. Birmingham, England, 11/20/57. Drummer. UB40.

BROWN, MICHAEL (Michael Lookofsky). New York, NY, 4/25/49. Keyboardist. The Left Banke.

BRUCE, JACK. Glasgow, Scotland, 5/14/43. Singer, bassist. Cream.

BRUCE, MICHAEL. 3/16/48. Guitarist, keyboardist. Alice Cooper.

BRUFORD, BILL. London, England, 5/17/48. Drummer. Yes.

BRYAN, DAVID (David Rashbaum). New Jersey, 2/7/62. Keyboardist. Bon Jovi.

BRYON, DENNIS. Cardiff, Wales, 4/14/49. Drummer. Amen Corner.

BRZEZICKI, MARK. Slough, England, 6/21/57. Drummer. Big Country.

BUCHANAN, PAUL. Scotland. Singer, synthesizer player. Blue Nile.

BUCHHOLZ, FRANCIS. 2/19/50. Guitarist. Scorpions.

BUCK, PETER. Athens, GA, 12/6/56. Guitarist. R.E.M.

BUCK, ROBERT. Guitarist. 10,000 Maniacs.

BUCKINGHAM, LINDSEY. Palo Alto, CA, 10/3/47. Guitarist, singer. Fleetwood Mac.

BUCKLER, RICK (Paul Buckler). 12/6/56. Drummer, singer. The Jam.

BUCKLEY, BETTY. Big Spring, TX, 7/3/47. Actor. *Eight Is Enough.*

BUJOLD, GENEVIEVE. Montreal, Canada, 7/1/42. Actor. *Dead Ringers.*

BUNKER, CLIVE. Blackpool, England, 12/12/46. Drummer. Jethro Tull.

BUNNELL, DEWEY. Yorkshire, England, 1/19/51. Singer, guitarist. America.

BURCHILL, CHARLIE. Glasgow, Scotland, 11/27/59. Guitarist. Simple Minds.

BURDEN, IAN. 12/24/57. Synthesizer player. Human League.

BURDON, ERIC. Walker-on-Tyne, England, 5/11/41. Singer, songwriter. The Animals; War.

BURGHOFF, GARY. Bristol, CT, 5/24/43. Actor. Radar O'Reilly on *M*A*S*H.*

BURKE, DELTA. Orlando, FL, 7/30/56. Actor, married to Gerald McRaney. *Designing Women.*

BURKE, SOLOMON. Philadelphia, PA, 1936. Country-gospel-R&B singer, songwriter.

BURNEL, JEAN-JACQUES. London, England, 2/21/52. Bassist. The Stranglers.

BURNETT, CAROL. San Antonio, TX, 4/26/33. Actor. *The Carol Burnett Show.*

BURNS, BOB. Drummer. Lynyrd Skynyrd.

BURNS, GEORGE (Nathan Birnbaum). New York, NY, 1/20/1896. Actor and comedian. *The George Burns and Gracie Allen Show.*

BURR, CLIVE. 3/8/57. Drummer. Iron Maiden.

BURRELL, BOZ (Raymond Burrell). Lincoln, England, 1946. Bassist. Bad Company.

BURROWS, DARREN E. Winfield, KS, 9/12/66. Actor. Ed Chigliak on *Northern Exposure.*

BURSTYN, ELLEN (Edna Rae Gillooly). Detroit, MI, 12/7/32. Actor. *Alice Doesn't Live Here Anymore.*

BURT, HEINZ. Hargin, Germany, 7/24/42. Bassist. The Tornados.

BURTON, LEVAR. Landstuhl, Germany, 2/16/57. Actor. Geordi LaForge on *Star Trek: The Next Generation.*

BURTON, TREVOR. Aston, England, 3/9/44. Lead guitarist. The Move.

BUSEY, GARY. Goose Creek, TX, 6/29/44. Actor. *The Buddy Holly Story.*

BUSH, BARBARA. Rye, NY, 6/8/25. Former First Lady, married to George Bush.

BUSH, GEORGE. Milton, MA, 6/12/24. Political leader, husband of Barbara. Forty-first president of the U.S.

BUSH, KATE. Bexleyheath, England, 7/30/58. Singer, songwriter.

BUSHY, RONALD. Washington, DC, 9/23/45. Drummer. Iron Butterfly.

BUTKUS, DICK. Chicago, IL, 12/9/42. Football player, actor. *My Two Dads.*

BUTLER, GEEZER (Terry Butler). Birmingham, England, 7/17/49. Bassist. Black Sabbath.

BUTLER, JERRY. Sunflower, MS, 12/8/39. Singer. The Impressions.

BUTLER, JOE. Glen Cove, NY, 9/16/43. Drummer, singer. The Lovin' Spoonful.

BUTLER, RICHARD. Surrey, England, 6/5/56. Singer, lyricist. Psychedelic Furs.

BUTLER, TONY. Ealing, England, 2/13/57. Bassist. Big Country.

BUTTAFUOCO, JOEY. Massapequa, NY. 3/11/56. Mechanic. Had affair with Amy Fisher.

BUTTONS, RED (Aaron Chwatt). New York, NY, 2/5/19. Performer. *The Red Buttons Show.*

BUXTON, GLEN. Akron, OH, 11/10/47. Guitarist. Alice Cooper.

BUZZI, RUTH. Westerly, RI, 7/24/36. Actor. *Laugh-In.*

BYRNE, GABRIEL. Dublin, Ireland, 1950. Actor, formerly married to Ellen Barkin. *Miller's Crossing.*

BYRON, DAVID. Essex, England, 1/29/47. Singer. Uriah Heep.

CAAN, JAMES. The Bronx, NY, 3/26/39. Actor. *The Godfather.*

CADDY, ALAN. London, England, 2/2/40. Guitarist. The Tornados; Johnny Kidd & The Pirates.

CAESAR, SID. Yonkers, NY, 9/8/22. Performer. *Your Show of Shows.*

CAFFEY, CHARLOTTE. Santa Monica, CA, 10/21/53. Singer. The Go-Gos.

CAGE, JOHN. New York, NY, 9/5/12. Composer, author. Composed scores for choreography by Merce Cunningham.

CAIN, JONATHAN. Chicago, IL, 2/26/50. Keyboardist. Journey.

CALABRO, THOMAS. 2/3/59. Actor. Michael Mancini on *Melrose Place.*

CALE, JOHN. Garnant, Wales, 12/4/40. Bassist, keyboardist, violist, singer. The Velvet Underground.

CALIFORNIA, RANDY (Randy Wolfe). Los Angeles, CA, 2/20/51. Guitarist, singer. Spirit.

CALLOW, SIMON. London, England, 6/15/49. Actor. *A Room with a View.*

CALVERT, BERNIE. Burnley, England, 9/16/43. Bassist. The Hollies.

CAMERON, KIRK. Panorama City, CA, 10/12/70. Actor, brother of Candace. Mike Seaver on *Growing Pains.*

CAMP, COLLEEN. San Francisco, CA, 1953. Actor. Kristin Shepard on *Dallas.*

CAMPBELL, ALI (Alastair Campbell). Birmingham, England, 2/15/59. Lead singer, guitarist. UB40.

CAMPBELL, BILL. Chicago, IL, 1960. Actor. *The Rocketeer.*

CAMPBELL, BRUCE. Royal Oak, MI, 6/22/58. Actor, producer, screenwriter. *The Adventures of Briscoe County Jr.*

CAMPBELL, GLEN. Delight, AR, 4/22/36. Actor, singer. *The Glen Campbell Goodtime Hour.*

CAMPBELL, MIKE. Panama City, FL, 2/1/54. Guitarist. Tom Petty & The Heartbreakers.

CAMPBELL, ROBIN. Birmingham, England, 12/25/54. Lead guitarist, singer. UB40.

CAMPBELL, TISHA. Oklahoma City, OK, 10/13/70. Actor. *Martin.*

CAMPION, JANE. Wellington, New Zealand, 4/30/54. Director, screenwriter, daughter of Richard and Edith. *The Piano.*

CANN, WARREN. Victoria, Canada, 5/20/52. Drummer. Ultravox.

CANNON, DYAN (Samille Diane Friesen). Tacoma, WA, 1/4/37. Actor. *Bob & Carol & Ted & Alice.*

CAPALDI, JIM. Evesham, England, 8/24/44. Drummer, singer. Traffic.

CAPSHAW, KATE (Kathleen Sue Nail). Ft. Worth, TX, 1953. Actor, married to Steven Spielberg. *Indiana Jones and the Temple of Doom.*

CARA, IRENE. New York, NY, 3/18/59. Actor, singer. *Fame.*

CARAY, HARRY. Saugus, CA, 5/16/21. Announcer for the Chicago Cubs.

CARDIN, PIERRE. Venice, Italy, 7/7/22. Fashion designer.

CARDINALE, CLAUDIA. Tunis, Tunisia, 4/15/39. Actor. *The Pink Panther.*

CAREY, TONY. 10/16/53. Keyboardist. Rainbow.

CARLIN, GEORGE. New York, NY, 5/12/37. Actor. "Seven Dirty Words."

CARLISLE, BELINDA. Hollywood, CA, 8/16/58. Singer, songwriter. The Go-Gos.

CARLOS, BUN (Brad Carlson). Rockford, IL, 6/12/51. Drummer. Cheap Trick.

CARMEN, ERIC. Cleveland, OH, 8/11/49. Singer. The Raspberries.

CARNE, JUDY (Joyce Botterill). Northampton, England, 3/27/39. Actor. *Laugh-In.*

CARNEY, ART. Mt. Vernon, NY, 11/4/18. Actor and comedian. Ed Norton on *The Honeymooners.*

CAROLINE, PRINCESS. Monte Carlo, Monaco, 1/23/57. Daughter of Princess Grace of Monaco.

CARON, LESLIE. Paris, France, 7/1/31. Actor. *Lili.*

CARPENTER, JOHN. Carthage, NY, 1/16/48. Director, writer. *Halloween.*

CARPENTER, RICHARD. New Haven, CT, 10/15/46. Keyboardist, singer. The Carpenters.

CARR, DAVID. Leyton, England, 8/4/43. Keyboardist. The Fortunes.

CARRACK, PAUL. Sheffield, England, 4/21/51. Singer, songwriter. Squeeze; Ace; Mike and the Mechanics.

CARRADINE, DAVID. Hollywood, CA, 12/8/36. Actor, son of John Carradine, brother of Keith and Robert. *Kung Fu.*

CARRADINE, KEITH. San Mateo, CA, 8/8/49. Actor, son of John, brother of David and Robert, father of Martha Plimpton. *The Will Rogers Follies.*

CARRADINE, ROBERT. Hollywood, CA, 3/24/54. Actor, son of John, brother of David and Keith. *Revenge of the Nerds.*

CARRERA, BARBARA. Managua, Nicaragua, 12/31/51. Model, actor. *Dallas.*

CARROLL, DIAHANN (Carol Diahann Johnson). New York, NY, 7/17/35. Actor, singer, married to Vic Damone. *I Know Why the Caged Bird Sings.*

CARRY, JULIUS. Actor. Mitchell Baldwin on *Murphy Brown.*

CARTER, DIXIE. McLemoresville, TN, 5/25/39. Actor. Julia Sugarbaker on *Designing Women.*

CARTER, JIMMY. Plains, GA, 10/1/24. Political leader. Thirty-ninth president of the U.S.

CARTER, LYNDA. Phoenix, AZ, 7/24/51. Actor. *Wonder Woman.*

CARTER, NELL. Birmingham, AL, 9/13/48. Actor, singer. *Gimme a Break.*

CARTERIS, GABRIELLE. 1/2/61. Actor. Andrea Zuckerman on *Beverly Hills 90210.*

CARTWRIGHT, VERONICA. Bristol, England, 1950. Actor. *Alien.*

CASADY, JACK. Washington, DC, 4/13/44. Bass guitarist. Jefferson Airplane/Starship.

CASEY, HARRY WAYNE (Harold Casey). Hialeah, FL, 1/31/51. Singer, keyboardist. KC & The Sunshine Band.

CASS, PEGGY (Mary Margaret Cass). Boston, MA, 5/21/24. Actor. Panelist on *To Tell The Truth.*

CASSIDY, DAVID. New York, NY, 4/12/50. Actor, half brother of Shaun, son of Jack, step-son of Shirley Jones. Keith in *The Partridge Family.*

CASSIDY, ED. Chicago, IL, 5/4/31. Drummer. Spirit.

CASSIDY, JOANNA. Camden, NJ, 8/2/44. Actor. Jo Jo White on *Buffalo Bill.*

CASTRO, FIDEL (Fidel Ruz). Mayari, Cuba, 8/13/26. Political leader. President of Cuba.

CATES, PHOEBE. New York, NY, 7/16/63. Actor, married to Kevin Kline. *Fast Times at Ridgemont High.*

CATHERALL, JOANNE. Sheffield, England, 9/18/62. Singer. Human League.

CATTINI, CLEM. 8/28/39. Drummer. Johnny Kidd & The Pirates; Tornados.

CATTRALL, KIM. Liverpool, England, 8/21/56. Actor. *The Bonfire of the Vanities.*

CAVALIERE, FELIX. Pelham, NY, 11/29/44. Singer, keyboardist. The (Young) Rascals.

CAVETT, DICK. Gibbon, NE, 11/19/36. Actor, talk show host. *The Dick Cavett Show.*

CEASE, JEFF. Nashville, TN, 6/24/67. Guitarist. The Black Crowes.

CETERA, PETER. Chicago, IL, 9/13/44. Singer, songwriter. Chicago.

CHADWICK, LES (John Chadwick). Liverpool, England, 5/11/43. Bassist. Gerry & The Pacemakers.

CHAMBERLAIN, RICHARD (George Chamberlain). Los Angeles, CA, 3/31/35. Actor. *Dr. Kildare.*

CHAMBERLAIN, WILT. West Philadelphia, PA, 8/21/36. Basketball great.

CHAMBERS, GEORGE. Flora, MS, 9/26/31. Bassist, singer. The Chambers Brothers.

CHAMBERS, JOE. Scott County, MS, 8/24/42. Guitarist, singer. The Chambers Brothers.

CHAMBERS, LESTER. Flora, MS, 4/13/40. Harmonicist, singer. The Chambers Brothers.

CHAMBERS, MARTIN. Hereford, England, 9/4/51. Drummer. The Pretenders.

CHAMBERS, TERRY. England, 7/18/55. Drummer. XTC.

CHAMBERS, WILLIE. Flora, MS, 3/3/38. Guitarist, singer. The Chambers Brothers.

CHANDLER, CHAS (Bryan Chandler). Heaton, England, 12/18/38. Bassist. The Animals.

CHANDLER, GENE (Gene Dixon). Chicago, IL, 7/6/37. Singer, songwriter.

CHANNING, CAROL. Seattle, WA, 1/31/21. Actor. *Hello, Dolly!*

CHANNING, STOCKARD (Susan Williams Antonia Stockard). New York, NY, 2/13/44. Actor. *Grease.*

CHAO, ROSALIND. Los Angeles, CA. Actor. Soon-Lee on *M*A*S*H.*

CHAPLIN, GERALDINE. Santa Monica, CA, 7/31/44. Actor. *Dr. Zhivago.*

CHAPMAN, ROGER. Leicester, England, 4/8/44. Singer. Family.

CHAPMAN, TRACY. Cleveland, OH, 3/30/64. Folk singer, songwriter.

CHAQUICO, CRAIG. 9/26/54. Singer, guitarist. Jefferson Starship.

CHARISSE, CYD (Tula Ellice Finklea). Amarillo, TX, 3/8/22. Actor. *Brigadoon.*

CHARLES, RAY (Ray Robinson). Albany, GA, 9/23/30. Singer, songwriter. "Georgia on My Mind."

CHARLTON, MANUEL. 7/25/41. Guitarist, singer, songwriter. Nazareth.

CHARO. Murcia, Spain, 1/15/51. Actor, singer. *The Love Boat.*

CHECKER, CHUBBY (Ernest Evans). Spring Gulley, SC, 10/3/41. Singer, songwriter. Popularized the Twist and Limbo.

CHER (Cherilyn Sarkisian La Piere). El Centro, CA, 5/20/46. Singer, actor, formerly married to Sonny Bono and Gregg Allman. *Moonstruck.*

CHERRY, NENEH. Stockholm, Sweden, 3/10/64. Rap/pop singer, songwriter.

CHILD, JULIA. Pasadena, CA, 8/15/12. TV chef, author. *Mastering the Art of French Cooking.*

CHILES, LOIS. Alice, TX, 1950. Model, actor. *The Way We Were.*

CHILTON, ALEX. Memphis, TN, 12/28/50. Guitarist, singer. The Box Tops; Big Star.

CHONG, RAE DAWN. Vancouver, Canada, 1962. Actor, daughter of Thomas Chong. *The Color Purple.*

CHONG, THOMAS. Edmonton, Canada, 5/24/38. Singer, actor, writer, director, former partner of Cheech Marin, father of Rae Dawn Chong. *Up in Smoke.*

CHRISTIAN, GARRY. Merseyside, England, 2/27/55. Singer. The Christians.

CHRISTIAN, ROGER. 2/13/50. Singer. The Christians.

CHRISTIAN, RUSSELL. 6/8/56. Singer. The Christians.

CHRISTIE, JULIA. Chukua, India, 4/14/41. Actor. *Dr. Zhivago.*

CHRISTIE, LOU (Lugee Sacco). Glenwillard, PA, 2/19/43. Singer, songwriter. "Lightnin' Strikes."

CHRISTO (Christo Javacheff). Gabrovo, Bulgaria, 6/13/35. Artist. The Umbrellas.

CHRISTOPHER, WILLIAM. Evanston, IL, 10/20/32. Actor. Father Francis Mulcahy on *M*A*S*H.*

CHUCK D. (Charles Ridenhour). 1960. Rap artist. Public Enemy.

CHURCHILL, CHICK. Mold, Wales, 1/2/49. Keyboardist. Ten Years After.

CIPOLLINA, JOHN. Berkeley, CA, 8/24/43. Guitarist. Quicksilver Messenger Service.

CLAIBORNE, LIZ (Elisabeth Claiborne). Brussels, Belgium, 3/31/29. Fashion designer.

CLARK, ALAN. Durham, NC, 3/5/52. Keyboardist. Dire Straits.

CLARK, DAVE. Tottenham, England, 12/15/42. Drummer. The Dave Clark Five.

CLARK, DICK. Mt. Vernon, NY, 11/30/29. Producer, music/game show host. *American Bandstand.*

CLARK, GRAEME. Glasgow, Scotland, 4/15/66. Bassist. Wet Wet Wet.

CLARK, NEIL. 7/3/55. Guitarist. Lloyd Cole & The Commotions.

CLARK, PETULA. Surrey, England, 11/15/32. Actor, singer. *Downtown.*

CLARK, ROY. Meherrin, VA, 4/15/33. Country singer, songwriter. *Hee Haw.*

CLARK, STEVE. Hillsborough, England, 4/23/60. Guitarist. Def Leppard.

CLARKE, ALLAN (Harold Clarke). Salford, England, 4/5/42. Singer. The Hollies.

CLARKE, EDDIE. 10/5/50. Guitarist. Motörhead.

CLARKE, MICHAEL (Michael Dick). New York, NY, 6/3/44. Drummer. The Byrds.

CLARKE, VINCE. Basildon, England, 7/3/61. Keyboardist. Erasure.

CLAY, ANDREW DICE. Brooklyn, NY, 1958. Actor. *The Adventures of Ford Fairlaine.*

CLAYBURGH, JILL. New York, NY, 4/30/44. Actor. *An Unmarried Woman.*

CLAYTON, ADAM. Ireland, 3/13/60. Bassist. U2.

CLAYTON-THOMAS, DAVID (David Thomsett). Surrey, England, 9/13/41. Lead singer. Blood, Sweat & Tears.

CLEESE, JOHN. Weston-Super-Mare, England, 10/27/39. Actor. *Monty Python's Flying Circus.*

CLIFF, JIMMY (Jimmy Chambers). Somerton, Jamaica, 1949. Reggae singer, songwriter.

CLIFFORD, DOUG. Palo Alto, CA, 4/24/45. Drummer. Creedence Clearwater Revival.

CLINTON, BILL. Hope, AK, 8/9/46. Husband of Hillary Rodham, father of Chelsea. 42nd President of the United States.

CLINTON, CHELSEA. Arkansas, 2/27/80. Daughter of Bill and Hillary.

CLINTON, GEORGE. Kannapolis, NC, 7/22/40. Funk pioneer, singer. Parliament; Funkadelic.

CLINTON, HILLARY RODHAM. Park Ridge, IL, 10/26/47. Wife of Bill, mother of Chelsea. First Lady.

CLOONEY, ROSEMARY. Maysville, KY, 5/23/28. Actor, singer.

CLYDE, JEREMY. England, 3/22/44. Singer, guitarist. Chad & Jeremy.

COBURN, JAMES. Laurel, NE, 8/31/28. Actor. *The Magnificent Seven.*

COCA, IMOGENE. Philadelphia, PA, 11/18/08. Actor. *Your Show of Shows.*

COCHRANE, TOM. 5/14/53. Singer, guitarist. Red Rider.

COCKER, JOE (John Cocker). Sheffield, England, 5/20/44. Singer.

COEN, ETHAN. St. Louis Park, MN, 1958. Director, writer. Brother of Joel. *Raising Arizona.*

COEN, JOEL. St. Louis Park, MN, 1955. Director, writer. Brother of Ethan. *Raising Arizona.*

COGHLAN, JOHN. Dulwich, England, 9/19/46. Drummer. Status Quo.

COHEN, DAVID. Brooklyn, NY, 1942. Keyboardist. Country Joe & The Fish.

COHEN, LEONARD. Montreal, Canada, 9/21/34. Singer, songwriter, poet.

COLBERT, CLAUDETTE (Lily Chauchoin). Paris, France, 9/13/05. Actor. *It Happened One Night.*

COLE, BRIAN. Tacoma, WA, 9/8/42. Singer, bassist. The Association.

COLE, LLOYD. Derbyshire, England, 1/31/61. Singer, guitarist. Lloyd Cole & The Commotions.

COLEMAN, DABNEY. Austin, TX, 1/3/32. Actor. *Buffalo Bill.*

COLEMAN, GARY. Zion, IL, 2/8/68. Actor. Arnold Jackson on *Diff'rent Strokes.*

COLEY, DORIS. Passaic, NJ, 8/2/41. Singer. The Shirelles.

COLLA, JOHNNY. California, 7/2/52. Saxophonist, guitarist. Huey Lewis & The News.

COLLEN, PHIL. London, England, 12/8/57. Guitarist. Def Leppard.

COLLINS, ALLEN. Jacksonville, FL, 7/19/52. Guitarist. Lynyrd Skynyrd.

COLLINS, GARY. Boston, MA, 4/30/38. Actor, talk show host. *Home.*

COLLINS, JOAN. London, England, 5/23/33. Actor. Alexis Carrington Colby on *Dynasty.*

COLLINS, JUDY. Seattle, WA, 5/1/39. Folk/rock guitarist, singer, songwriter. "Send in the Clowns."

COLLINS, PHIL. Chiswick, England, 1/30/51. Singer, drummer. Genesis.

COLLINS, STEPHEN. Des Moines, IA, 10/1/47. Actor. *Tales of the Gold Monkey.*

COLOMBY, BOBBY. New York, NY, 12/20/44. Drummer, singer. Blood, Sweat & Tears.

COLT, JOHNNY. Cherry Point, NC, 5/1/66. Bassist. The Black Crowes.

COLUMBUS, CHRIS. Spangler, PA, 9/10/58. Director. *Home Alone.*

CONAWAY, JEFF. New York, NY, 10/5/50. Actor. Bobby Wheeler on *Taxi.*

CONNELLY, JENNIFER. New York, NY, 12/12/70. Actor. *The Rocketeer.*

CONNOLLY, BRIAN. Hamilton, Scotland, 10/5/49. Singer. Sweet.

CONNORS, JIMMY. Belleville, IL, 9/2/52. Tennis player.

CONNORS, MIKE (Krekor Ohanian). Fresno, CA, 8/15/25. Actor. *Mannix.*

CONROY, KEVIN. Westport, CT, 11/30/55. Actor. Voice of Batman in *Batman: The Animated Series.*

CONSTANTINE, MICHAEL (Constantine Joanides). Reading, PA, 5/22/27. Actor. *Room 222.*

CONTI, TOM. Paisley, Scotland, 11/22/41. Actor. *Reuben Reuben.*

CONWAY, KEVIN. New York, NY, 5/29/42. Actor. *Slaughterhouse Five.*

CONWAY, TIM (Thomas Daniel Conway). Willoughby, OH, 12/15/33. Actor. *The Carol Burnett Show.*

COODER, RY (Ryland Cooder). Los Angeles, CA, 3/15/47. Folk blues guitarist, composer.

COOK, JEFF. Fort Payne, AL, 8/27/49. Singer, fiddler, guitarist, keyboardist. Alabama.

COOK, NORMAN (Quentin Cook). Sussex, England, 7/31/63. Singer. The Housemartins.

COOK, PAUL. London, England, 7/20/56. Drummer. The Sex Pistols.

COOK, STU. Oakland, CA, 4/25/45. Bassist. Creedence Clearwater Revival.

COONCE, RICKY. Los Angeles, CA, 8/1/47. Drummer. The Grass Roots.

COOPER, ALICE (Vincent Furnier). Detroit, MI, 2/4/48. Singer, songwriter. Alice Cooper.

COOPER, JACKIE (John Cooper Jr.). Los Angeles, CA, 9/15/22. Actor, director. *Superman.*

COPE, JULIAN. Bargoed, Wales, 10/21/57. Singer, bassist. The Teardrop Explodes.

COPELAND, STEWART. Alexandria, Egypt, 7/16/52. Drummer, singer. The Police.

CORBIN, BARRY. Dawson County, TX, 10/16/40. Actor. Maurice Minnifield on *Northern Exposure.*

CORGAN, BILLY. Chicago, IL, 3/17/67. Singer, songwriter, guitarist. Smashing Pumpkins.

CORLEY, PAT. Dallas, TX, 6/1/30. Actor. Phil the bartender on *Murphy Brown.*

CORNICK, GLENN. Barrow-in-Furness, England, 4/24/47. Bassist. Jethro Tull.

CORNISH, GENE. Ottawa, Canada, 5/14/45. Guitarist. The (Young) Rascals.

CORNWELL, HUGH. London, England, 8/28/49. Singer, guitarist. The Stranglers.

CORT, BUD (Walter Edward Cox). New Rochelle, NY, 3/29/50. Actor. *Harold and Maude.*

COSTELL, DAVID. Pittsburgh, PA, 3/15/44. Bassist. Gary Lewis and the Playboys.

COULIER, DAVID. Detroit, MI. Actor. Joey Gladstone on *Full House*.

COVERDALE, DAVID. Saltburn-by-the-Sea, England, 9/22/49. Singer. Whitesnake.

COWSILL, BARRY. Newport, RI, 9/14/54. Bassist, singer. The Cowsills.

COWSILL, BILL. Newport, RI, 1/9/48. Guitarist, singer. The Cowsills.

COWSILL, BOB. Newport, RI, 8/26/49. Guitarist, singer. The Cowsills.

COWSILL, JOHN. Newport, RI, 3/2/56. Drummer. The Cowsills.

COWSILL, PAUL. Newport, RI, 11/11/52. Keyboardist, singer. The Cowsills.

COWSILL, SUE. Newport, RI, 5/20/60. Singer. The Cowsills.

COX, ANDY. Birmingham, England, 1/25/60. Guitarist. Fine Young Cannibals.

COX, COURTENEY. Birmingham, AL, 6/15/64. Actor. *Friends*.

COX, RONNY. Cloudcroft, NM, 8/23/38. Actor. *Beverly Hills Cop*.

COYOTE, PETER (Peter Cohon). New York, NY, 1942. Actor. *Jagged Edge*.

CRAIG, MIKEY. Hammersmith, England, 2/15/60. Bassist. Culture Club.

CRAVEN, WES. Cleveland, OH, 8/2/39. Director, novelist. *A Nightmare on Elm Street*.

CRAWFORD, JOHN. 1/17/60. Bassist, singer. Berlin.

CRAWFORD, MICHAEL (Michael Dumble-Smith). Salisbury, England, 1/19/42. Actor, singer. *The Phantom of the Opera*.

CRAWFORD, RANDY (Veronica Crawford). Macon, GA, 2/18/52. Rock-R&B singer, songwriter.

CRAY, ROBERT. Columbus, GA, 8/1/53. Contemporary blues singer, songwriter. "Smoking Gun."

CREGAN, JIM. 3/9/46. Guitarist. Steve Harley & Cockney Rebel.

CREME, LOL. Manchester, England, 9/19/47. Singer, guitarist. 10cc; Godley & Creme.

CRENNA, RICHARD. Los Angeles, CA, 11/30/27. Actor. *Rambo: First Blood Part II*.

CREWSDON, ROY. Manchester, England, 5/29/41. Guitarist. Freddie & The Dreamers.

CRISS, PETER (Peter Crisscoula). Brooklyn, NY, 12/27/47. Drummer, singer. Kiss.

CROFTS, DASH. Cisco, TX, 8/14/40. Singer, guitarist, mandolinist. Seals & Crofts.

CRONIN, KEVIN. Evanston, IL, 10/6/51. Singer. REO Speedwagon.

CRONKITE, WALTER. St. Joseph, MO, 11/4/16. News journalist and anchor. *CBS Evening News*.

CRONYN, HUME. London, Canada, 7/18/11. Actor, writer, director, widower of Jessica Tandy. *The Postman Always Rings Twice*.

CROPPER, STEVE. Willow Springs, MO, 10/21/41. Guitarist. Booker T. & The MG's.

CROSBY, CATHY LEE. Los Angeles, CA, 12/2/49. Actor. *That's Incredible!*

CROSBY, DAVID (David Van Cortland). Los Angeles, CA, 8/14/41. Singer, guitarist. The Byrds; Crosby, Stills, Nash & Young.

CROSBY, DENISE. Hollywood, CA, 1958. Actor, granddaughter of Bing Crosby. *Star Trek: The Next Generation*.

CROSBY, HARRY. Los Angeles, CA, 8/8/58. Actor, singer.

CROSS, BEN. London, England, 12/16/48. Actor. *Chariots of Fire*.

CROSS, CHRIS (Chris St. John). London, England, 7/14/52. Bassist, synthesizer player. Ultravox.

CROSS, CHRISTOPHER (Christopher Geppert). San Antonio, TX, 5/3/51. Guitarist, singer, songwriter. "Ride Like the Wind."

CROUSE, LINDSAY. New York, NY, 5/12/48. Actor. *The Verdict*.

CRYER, JON. New York, NY, 4/16/65. Actor. *The Famous Teddy Z*.

CULLIMORE, STAN. Hull, England, 4/6/62. Bassist. The Housemartins.

CULLUM, JOHN. Knoxville, TN, 3/2/30. Actor. Holling Vincoeur on *Northern Exposure*.

CULP, ROBERT. Oakland, CA, 8/16/30. Actor. *I Spy*.

CUMMINGS, BURTON. Winnipeg, Canada, 12/31/47. Singer, keyboardist. The Guess Who.

CUMMINGS, GEORGE. Meridian, MS, 7/28/38. Lead guitarist. Dr. Hook.

CUNNINGHAM, BILL. Memphis, TN, 1/23/50. Bassist, pianist. The Box Tops; Big Star.

CUNNINGHAM, TOM. Glasgow, Scotland, 6/22/65. Drummer. Wet Wet Wet.

CUOMO, MARIO. Queens, NY, 6/15/32. Political leader. Former Governor of New York.

CURRIE, ALANNAH. Auckland, New Zealand, 9/20/59. Singer, saxophonist, percussionist. Thompson Twins.

CURRIE, BILLY. Huddersfield, England, 4/1/52. Synthesizer player, keyboardist. Ultravox.

CURRIE, CHERRIE. Los Angeles, CA, 1960. Singer, married to Robert Hays. The Runaways.

CURRY, TIM. Cheshire, England, 4/19/46. Actor. *The Rocky Horror Picture Show*.

CURTIN, JANE. Cambridge, MA, 9/6/47. Actor. *Kate & Allie*.

CURTIS, CHRIS (Chris Crummy). Oldham, England, 8/26/41. Singer, drummer. The Searchers.

CURTIS, SONNY. Meadow, TX, 5/9/37. Guitarist. Buddy Holly & The Crickets.

CURTIS, TONY (Bernard Schwartz). New York, NY, 6/3/24. Actor, father of Jamie Lee Curtis, formerly married to Janet Leigh. *Some Like It Hot*.

CUSACK, CYRIL. Durban, South Africa, 11/26/10. Actor. *Fahrenheit 451*.

CUSACK, JOAN. Evanston, IL, 10/11/62. Actor. *Working Girl*.

CUSACK, JOHN. Chicago, IL, 6/28/66. Actor. *The Grifters*.

CUSACK, SINEAD. Ireland, 2/18/48. Actor, married to Jeremy Irons, daughter of Cyril Cusack.

D'ALEO, ANGELO. The Bronx, NY, 2/3/41. Singer. Dion & The Belmonts.

D'ANGELO, BEVERLY. Columbus, OH, 11/15/54. Actor. *Hair*.

D'ARBY, TERENCE TRENT. New York, NY, 3/15/62. R&B singer, songwriter. "Wishing Well."

DAFOE, WILLEM. Appleton, WI, 7/22/55. Actor. *Mississippi Burning*.

DALE, GLEN (Richard Garforth). Deal, England, 4/2/43. Guitarist, singer. The Fortunes.

DALLIN, SARAH. Bristol, England, 12/17/61. Singer. Bananarama.

DALTON, TIMOTHY. Colwyn Bay, Wales, 3/21/44. Actor. James Bond in *The Living Daylights*.

DALTREY, ROGER. London, England, 3/1/44. Lead singer. The Who.

DALY, GARY. Merseyside, England, 5/5/62. Singer. China Crisis.

DALY, TIMOTHY. New York, NY, 3/1/56. Actor. *Wings*.

DAMMERS, JERRY (Jerry Dankin). 5/22/54. Keyboardist. The Specials.

DAMONE, VIC (Vito Farinola). Brooklyn, NY, 6/12/28. Singer, married to Diahann Caroll. *The Vic Damone Show*.

DANCE, CHARLES. Worcestershire, England, 10/10/46. Actor. *The Jewel in the Crown*.

DANELLI, DINO. New York, NY, 7/23/45. Drummer. The (Young) Rascals.

DANGERFIELD, RODNEY (Jacob Cohen). Babylon, NY, 11/22/21. Actor. *Back to School*.

DANIEL, JEFFREY. Los Angeles, CA, 8/24/55. Singer. Shalamar.

DANIELS, WILLIAM. Brooklyn, NY, 3/31/27. Actor. *St. Elsewhere*.

DANKO, RICK. Simcoe, Canada, 12/9/43. Bassist, singer. The Band.

DANNER, BLYTHE. Philadelphia, PA, 2/3/43. Actor. *The Prince of Tides*.

DANTE, MICHAEL (Ralph Vitti). Stamford, CT, 1935. Actor. Crazy Horse in *Custer*.

DANZA, TONY. Brooklyn, NY, 4/21/51. Actor. Tony Micelli on *Who's the Boss?*

DAVIDOVICH, LOLITA. Ontario, Canada, 7/15/61. Actor. *Blaze*.

DAVIDSON, JOHN. Pittsburgh, PA, 12/13/41. Game show host. *Hollywood Squares*.

DAVIDSON, LENNY. Enfield, England, 5/30/44. Guitarist. The Dave Clark Five.

DAVIES, DAVE. Muswell Hill, England, 2/3/47. Singer, guitarist. The Kinks.

DAVIES, IVA. Australia, 5/22/55. Guitarist, singer. Icehouse.

DAVIES, RAY. Muswell Hill, England, 6/21/44. Singer, guitarist. The Kinks.

DAVIES, RICHARD. England, 7/22/44. Singer, keyboardist. Supertramp.

DAVIS, BILLY JR. St. Louis, MO, 6/26/40. Singer. The 5th Dimension.

DAVIS, CLIFTON. Chicago, IL, 10/4/45. Actor, singer, composer. *Never Can Say Goodbye*.

DAVIS, JIM. Marion, IN, 7/28/45. Cartoonist. *Garfield*.

DAVIS, MAC (Morris Mac Davis). Lubbock, TX, 1/21/42. Singer, songwriter, actor. *The Mac Davis Show*.

DAVIS, MARTHA. Berkeley, CA, 1/15/51. Singer. The Motels.

DAVIS, OSSIE. Cogdell, GA, 12/18/17. Actor, writer. *Evening Shade*.

DAVIS, PAUL. Manchester, England, 3/7/66. Keyboardist. Happy Mondays.

DAVIS, ROB. Carshalton, England, 10/1/47. Lead guitarist, singer. Mud.

DAVIS, SPENCER. Swansea, Wales, 7/17/42. Guitarist. The Spencer Davis Group.

DAVIS, WILLIE. 1940. Drummer. Joey Dee and the Starliters.

DAY, DORIS (Doris von Kappelhoff). Cincinnati, OH, 4/3/24. Actor, performer. *The Doris Day Show*.

DAY, MARK. Manchester, England, 12/29/61. Guitarist. Happy Mondays.

DE BURGH, CHRIS (Chris Davidson). Argentina, 10/15/48. Singer, songwriter. "Lady in Red."

DE HAVILLAND, OLIVIA. Tokyo, Japan, 7/1/16. Actor. *Gone with the Wind*.

DE LAURENTIIS, DINO. Torre Annunziata, Italy, 8/8/19. Producer. *King Kong; Conan the Barbarian*.

DEACON, JOHN. Leicester, England, 8/19/51. Bassist. Queen.

DEAN, JIMMY. Plainview, TX, 8/10/28. Performer. *The Jimmy Dean Show*.

DEBARGE, EL (Eldra DeBarge). Grand Rapids, MI, 6/4/61. Singer, keyboardist, record producer.

DEE, DAVE (Dave Harman). Salisbury, England, 12/17/43. Lead singer, tambourinist. Dave Dee, Dozy, Beaky, Mick and Tich.

DEE, JOEY (Joey DiNicola). Passaic, NJ, 6/11/40. Singer. Joey Dee and the Starliters.

DEE, KIKI. Bradford, England, 3/6/47. Pop singer.

DEE, RUBY. Cleveland, OH, 10/27/24. Actor. *Do the Right Thing.*

DEE, SANDRA (Alexandra Zuck). Bayonne, NJ, 4/23/42. Actor. *Gidget.*

DEFOREST, CALVERT. Brooklyn, NY, 1923. Actor, Larry "Bud" Melman.

DEKKER, DESMOND (Desmond Dacris). Kingston, Jamaica, 7/16/42. Reggae singer, songwriter.

DELON, ALAIN. Sceaux, France, 11/8/35. Actor. *Is Paris Burning?*

DELP, BRAD. Boston, MA, 6/12/51. Guitarist, singer. Boston.

DELUISE, DOM. Brooklyn, NY, 8/1/33. Actor. *The Dom DeLuise Show.*

DELUISE, PETER. Hollywood, CA, 1967. Actor. Doug Penhall on *21 Jump Street.*

DEMME, JONATHAN. Rockville Centre, MD, 2/22/44. Director, producer, writer. *The Silence of the Lambs; Swimming to Cambodia.*

DEMORNAY, REBECCA. Santa Rosa, CA, 8/29/62. Actor. *The Hand That Rocks the Cradle.*

DEMPSEY, PATRICK. Lewiston, ME, 1/13/66. Actor. *Loverboy.*

DENEUVE, CATHERINE (Catherine Dorleac). Paris, France, 10/22/43. Actor. *The Last Metro.*

DENNEHY, BRIAN. Bridgeport, CT, 7/9/39. Actor. *Cocoon.*

DENSMORE, JOHN. Los Angeles, CA, 12/1/45. Drummer. The Doors.

DENVER, BOB. New Rochelle, NY, 1/9/35. Actor. Gilligan on *Gilligan's Island.*

DENVER, JOHN (Henry Deutschendorf). Roswell, NM, 12/31/43. Country singer, songwriter, actor. "Country Roads."

DEPARDIEU, GERARD. Chateauroux, France, 12/27/48. Actor. *Green Card.*

DEREK, BO (Mary Cathleen Collins). Long Beach, CA, 11/20/56. Actor, married to John Derek. *10.*

DEREK, JOHN (Derek Harris). Hollywood, CA, 8/12/26. Actor, director, married to Bo Derek. *The Ten Commandments.*

DERN, BRUCE. Chicago, IL, 6/4/36. Actor, father of Laura. *Coming Home.*

DERN, LAURA. Los Angeles, CA, 2/10/67. Actor, daughter of Bruce Dern and Diane Ladd, engaged to Jeff Goldblum. *Jurassic Park.*

DERRINGER, RICK (Richard Zehringer). Fort Recovery, OH, 8/5/47. Singer, songwriter, producer. The McCoys.

DESTRI, JIMMY. 4/13/54. Keyboardist. Blondie.

DEVANE, WILLIAM. Albany, NY, 9/5/37. Actor. Greg Sumner in *Knots Landing.*

DEVITO, TOMMY. Montclair, NJ, 6/19/36. Singer, guitarist. The Four Seasons.

DEVOE, RONALD. 11/17/67. Singer. New Edition; Bell Biv DeVoe.

DEY, SUSAN. Pekin, IL, 12/10/52. Actor. *L.A. Law.*

DEYOUNG, CLIFF. Inglewood, CA, 2/12/45. Actor. *The Hunger.*

DEYOUNG, DENNIS. Chicago, IL, 2/18/47. Singer, keyboardist. Styx.

DIAMOND, NEIL (Noah Kaminsky). New York, NY, 1/24/41. Singer, songwriter. *The Jazz Singer.*

DIAMONDE, DICK (Dingeman Van Der Sluys). Hilversum, Holland, 12/28/47. Bassist. The Easybeats.

DIANA, PRINCESS (Diana Frances Spencer). Sandringham, England, 7/1/61. Princess of Wales. British royalty, married to (and separated from) Prince Charles.

DICKEN (Jeff Pain). 4/4/50. Singer. Mr. Big.

DICKERSON, B. B. (Morris Dickerson). Torrance, CA, 8/3/49. Bassist, singer. War.

DICKINSON, ANGIE (Angie Brown). Kulm, ND, 9/30/32. Actor. *Police Woman.*

DICKINSON, BRUCE (Paul Dickinson). Worksop, England, 8/7/58. Singer. Iron Maiden.

DIDDLEY, BO (Otha Bates). McComb, MS, 12/30/28. Legendary blues guitarist, singer, songwriter.

DIFFORD, CHRIS. London, England, 11/4/54. Singer, guitarist. Squeeze.

DILLER, PHYLLIS (Phyllis Driver). Lima, OH, 7/17/17. Actor. *The Phyllis Diller Show.*

DILLON, KEVIN. Mamaroneck, NY, 8/19/65. Actor. *The Doors.*

DILLON, MATT. New Rochelle, NY, 2/18/64. Actor. *The Outsiders.*

DIMAGGIO, JOE. Martinez, CA, 11/25/14. Baseball great. New York Yankees. Once married to Marilyn Monroe.

DIMUCCI, DION. The Bronx, NY, 7/18/39. Lead singer. Dion & The Belmonts.

DIO, RONNIE JAMES. Cortland, NY, 7/10/48. Singer. Rainbow; Black Sabbath.

DITKA, MIKE. Carnegie, PA, 10/18/39. NFL football player, coach.

DIXON, DONNA. Alexandria, VA, 7/20/57. Actor, married to Dan Aykroyd. *Bosom Buddies.*

DIXON, JEANE. Medford, WI, 1/4/18. Astrologer, author.

DOBSON, KEVIN. New York, NY, 3/18/43. Actor. *Knots Landing.*

DOHERTY, DENNY. Halifax, Canada, 11/29/41. Singer. The Mamas and the Papas.

DOLENZ, MICKEY (George Dolenz). Los Angeles, CA, 3/8/45. Singer, drummer. The Monkees.

DOMINO, FATS (Antoine Domino). New Orleans, LA, 2/26/28. Legendary singer, songwriter.

DONAHUE, TROY (Merle Johnson). New York, NY, 1/27/36. Actor. *Hawaiian Eye.*

DONALDSON, SAM. El Paso, TX, 3/11/34. News reporter and anchor. *Prime Time Live.*

DONEGAN, LAWRENCE. 7/13/61. Bassist. Lloyd Cole & The Commotions.

DONEGAN, LONNIE (Anthony Donegan). Glasgow, Scotland, 4/29/31. Folk/blues guitarist, banjoist, and singer.

DONOVAN (Donovan Leitch). Glasgow, Scotland, 2/10/46. Folk/psychedelic singer, songwriter, father of Ione Skye and Donovan Leitch. "Mellow Yellow."

DONOVAN, JASON. Malvern, Australia, 6/1/68. Singer, actor.

DORMAN, LEE. St. Louis, MO, 9/19/45. Bassist. Iron Butterfly.

DOUGHTY, NEAL. Evanston, IL, 7/29/46. Keyboardist. REO Speedwagon.

DOUGLAS, BUSTER (James Douglas). Columbus, OH, 4/7/60. Boxer. Defeated Mike Tyson.

DOUGLAS, DONNA (Dorothy Bourgeois). Baywood, LA, 9/26/35. Actor. Elly May Clampett on *The Beverly Hillbillies.*

DOUGLAS, KIRK (Issur Danielovitch). Amsterdam, NY, 12/9/16. Actor, producer, father of Michael. *Spartacus.*

DOW, TONY. Hollywood, CA, 4/13/45. Actor. Wally Cleaver on *Leave It to Beaver.*

DOWN, LESLEY-ANN. London, England, 3/17/54. Actor. *Dallas.*

DOWNEY, BRIAN. Dublin, Ireland, 1/27/51. Drummer. Thin Lizzy.

DOWNEY, MORTON JR., 12/9/33. Controversial talk show host, actor.

DOWNS, HUGH. Akron, OH, 2/14/21. Host, actor, commentator. *20/20.*

DOYLE, DAVID. Omaha, NE, 12/1/25. Actor. John Bosley on *Charlie's Angels.*

DOZY (Trevor Davies). Enford, England, 11/27/44. Bassist. Dave Dee, Dozy, Beaky, Mick and Tich.

DRAGON, DARYL. Los Angeles, CA, 8/27/42. Keyboardist. The Captain & Tennille.

DREJA, CHRIS. Surbiton, England, 11/11/44. Guitarist. The Yardbirds.

DRYDEN, SPENCER. New York, NY, 4/7/38. Drummer. Jefferson Airplane/Starship.

DUBROW, KEVIN. 10/29/55. Lead singer. Quiet Riot.

DUDIKOFF, MICHAEL. Redondo Beach, CA, 10/8/54. Actor. *American Ninja.*

DUFFY, BILLY. 5/12/61. Lead guitarist. The Cult.

DUFFY, JULIA. Minneapolis, MN, 6/27/50. Actor. *Newhart.*

DUFFY, PATRICK. Townsend, MT, 3/17/49. Actor. Bobby Ewing on *Dallas.*

DUKAKIS, OLYMPIA. Lowell, MA, 6/20/31. Actor. *Moonstruck.*

DUKE, DAVID. Tulsa, OK, 1951. White supremacist, politician.

DUKE, PATTY (Anna Marie Duke). New York, NY, 12/14/46. Actor, formerly married to John Astin, mother of Sean Astin. *The Patty Duke Show.*

DUKES, DAVID. San Francisco, CA, 6/6/45. Actor. *Sisters.*

DULLEA, KEIR. Cleveland, OH, 5/30/36. Actor. *2001: A Space Odyssey.*

DUNAWAY, DENNIS. Cottage Grove, OR, 12/9/48. Bassist. Alice Cooper.

DUNAWAY, FAYE. Bascom, FL, 1/14/41. Actor. *Mommie Dearest.*

DUNCAN, GARY (Gary Grubb). San Diego, CA, 9/4/46. Guitarist. Quicksilver Messenger Service.

DUNCAN, SANDY. Henderson, TX, 2/20/46. Actor. *Funny Face.*

DUNN, DONALD. Memphis, TN, 11/24/41. Bassist. Booker T. & The MG's.

DUNN, LARRY. Colorado, 6/19/53. Keyboardist. Earth, Wind & Fire.

DUNNE, GRIFFIN. New York, NY, 6/8/55. Actor. *After Hours.*

DURBIN, DEANNA (Edna Durbin). Winnipeg, Canada, 12/4/21. Actor. *One Hundred Men and a Girl.*

DURNING, CHARLES. Highland Falls, NY, 2/28/33. Actor. *Evening Shade.*

DURY, IAN. Upminster, England, 5/12/42. Singer. Ian Dury & The Blockheads.

DUTTON, CHARLES. Baltimore, MD, 1/30/51. Actor. *Roc.*

DUVALL, ROBERT. San Diego, CA, 1/5/31. Actor. *Tender Mercies.*

DUVALL, SHELLEY. Houston, TX, 7/7/49. Actor, producer. *The Shining.*

DYSART, RICHARD. Brighton, MA, 3/30/29. Actor. Leland McKenzie on *L.A. Law.*

EARLE, STEVE. Fort Monroe, VA, 1/17/55. Country/rock singer, songwriter. Guitar Town.

EASTON, ELLIOT (Elliot Shapiro). Brooklyn, NY, 12/18/53. Guitarist. The Cars.

EASTON, SHEENA (Sheena Orr). Bellshill, Scotland, 4/27/59. Rock/R&B singer.

EBSEN, BUDDY (Christian Ebsen Jr.). Belleville, IL, 4/2/08. Actor. Jed Clampett on *The Beverly Hillbillies.*

ECHOLS, JOHN. Memphis, TN, 1945. Lead guitarist. Love.

EDDY, DUANE. Corning, NY, 4/26/38. Legendary rock guitarist.

EDEN, BARBARA (Barbara Huffman). Tucson, AZ, 8/23/34. Actor. Jeannie in *I Dream of Jeannie.*

EDGE, GRAEME. Rochester, England, 3/30/42. Drummer. The Moody Blues.

EDGE, THE (David Evans). Wales, 8/8/61. Guitarist. U2.

EDMONTON, JERRY. Canada, 10/24/46. Drummer. Steppenwolf.

EDWARD, PRINCE. London, England, 2/19/60. British royalty, son of Queen Elizabeth II.

EDWARDS, BERNARD. Greenville, NC, 10/31/52. Bassist. Chic.

EDWARDS, BLAKE (William Blake McEdwards). Tulsa, OK, 7/26/22. Writer, director. The Pink Panther series.

EDWARDS, NOKIE. Washington, DC, 5/9/39. Lead guitarist. The Ventures.

EGGAR, SAMANTHA. London, England, 3/5/39. Actor. The Collector.

EIKENBERRY, JILL. New Haven, CT, 1/21/47. Actor. Ann Kelsey on L.A. Law.

EKBERG, ANITA. Malmo, Sweden, 9/29/31. Actor. La Dolce Vita.

EKLAND, BRITT. Stockholm, Sweden, 10/6/42. Actor. After the Fox.

ELIZONDO, HECTOR. New York, NY, 12/22/36. Actor. Freebie and the Bean.

ELLERBEE, LINDA. Bryan, TX, 8/15/44. News commentator. Our World.

ELLIOTT, BOBBY. Burnley, England, 12/8/42. Drummer. The Hollies.

ELLIOTT, CHRIS. New York, NY, 1960. Comedy writer, actor. Get a Life.

ELLIOTT, DENNIS. London, England, 8/18/50. Drummer. Foreigner.

ELLIOTT, JOE. Sheffield, England, 8/1/59. Singer. Def Leppard.

ELLIOTT, SAM. Sacramento, CA, 8/9/44. Actor. Tombstone.

ELLIS, RALPH. Liverpool, England, 3/8/42. Guitarist, singer. The Swinging Blue Jeans.

ELMORE, GREG. San Diego, CA, 9/4/46. Drummer. Quicksilver Messenger Service.

ELSWIT, RIK. New York, NY, 7/6/45. Guitarist, singer. Dr. Hook.

ELVIRA (Cassandra Peterson). Manhattan, KS, 9/17/51. Horror film hostess.

ELWES, CARY. London, England, 10/26/62. Actor. The Princess Bride.

EMERSON, KEITH. Todmorden, England, 11/1/44. Keyboardist. Emerson, Lake & Palmer.

ENGEL, SCOTT (Noel Engel). Hamilton, OH, 1/9/44. Singer. The Walker Brothers.

ENGLUND, ROBERT. Hollywood, CA, 6/6/49. Actor. Freddie Krueger in Nightmare on Elm Street series.

ENNIS, RAY. Liverpool, England, 5/26/42. Lead guitarist, singer. The Swinging Blue Jeans.

ENO, BRIAN. Woodbridge, England, 5/15/48. Synthesizer player, producer. Cofounder of Roxy Music.

ENTNER, WARREN. Boston, MA, 7/7/44. Singer, guitarist. The Grass Roots.

ENTWISTLE, JOHN. Chiswick, England, 10/9/44. Bassist. The Who.

ENYA (Eithne Ni Bhraona). Gweedore, Ireland, 1962. Singer, composer.

ERRICO, GREG. San Francisco, CA, 9/1/46. Drummer. Sly & The Family Stone.

ERVING, JULIUS. Roosevelt, NY, 2/22/50. Basketball great. Philadelphia 76ers.

ESIASON, BOOMER (Norman Julius Esiason Jr.). West Islip, NY, 4/17/61. NFL football player.

ESPOSITO, GIANCARLO. Copenhagen, Denmark, 4/26/58. Actor. Do the Right Thing.

ESSEX, DAVID (David Cook). Plaistow, England, 7/23/47. Drummer, singer, songwriter, actor. Stardust.

ESTEFAN, GLORIA (Gloria Fajardo). Havana, Cuba, 9/1/57. Latin pop singer. The Miami Sound Machine.

ESTEVEZ, EMILIO. New York, NY, 5/12/62. Actor, writer, divorced from Paula Abdul, son of Martin Sheen. Repo Man.

ESTRADA, ERIK. New York, NY, 3/16/49. Actor. Frank "Ponch" Poncherello on CHiPS.

EUGENIE, PRINCESS. London, England, 3/23/90. British royalty, daughter of Prince Andrew and the Duchess of York.

EVANGELISTA, LINDA. Canada, 6/10/65. Supermodel, married to Kyle MacLachlan.

EVANS, DALE (Francis Smith). Uvalde, TX, 10/31/12. Actor. The Yellow Rose of Texas.

EVANS, LINDA (Linda Evanstad). Hartford, CT, 11/18/42. Actor. Dynasty.

EVANS, MARK. Melbourne, Australia, 3/2/56. Bassist. AC/DC.

EVANS, MIKE (Michael Jonas Evans). Salisbury, NC, 11/3/49. Actor. Lionel on The Jeffersons.

EVERETT, CHAD (Raymond Lee Cramton). South Bend, IN, 6/11/36. Actor. Medical Center.

EVERLY, DON (Isaac Everly). Brownie, KY, 2/1/37. Singer, guitarist. The Everly Brothers.

EVERLY, PHIL. Chicago, IL, 1/19/39. Singer, guitarist. The Everly Brothers.

EVERT, CHRIS. Ft. Lauderdale, FL, 12/21/54. Tennis player.

EVIGAN, GREG. South Amboy, NJ, 10/14/53. Actor. B.J. and the Bear.

FABARES, SHELLEY (Michelle Marie Fabares). Santa Monica, CA, 1/19/44. Actor, married to Mike Farrell, niece of Nanette Fabray. Christine Armstrong on Coach.

FABIAN (Fabian Forte). Philadelphia, PA, 2/6/43. Singer, actor. American Bandstand.

FABRAY, NANETTE (Ruby Nanette Fabares). San Diego, CA, 10/27/20. Actor, aunt of Shelley Fabares. One Day at a Time.

FAGEN, DONALD. Passaic, NJ, 1/10/48. Singer, keyboardist. Steely Dan.

FAHEY, SIOBHAN. 9/10/60. Singer. Bananarama.

FAIRBANKS, DOUGLAS JR. New York, NY, 12/9/09. Actor. Gunga Din.

FAIRCHILD, MORGAN (Patsy McClenny). Dallas, TX, 2/3/50. Actor. Falcon Crest.

FAIRWEATHER-LOW, ANDY. Ystrad Mynach, Wales, 8/8/50. Singer, guitarist. Amen Corner.

FAITH, ADAM (Terence Nelhams). Acton, England, 6/23/40. Singer, actor, financial adviser.

FAITHFULL, MARIANNE. Hampstead, England, 12/29/46. Folk/rock singer.

FAKIR, ABDUL. Detroit, MI, 12/26/35. Singer. The Four Tops.

FALANA, LOLA (Loletha Elaine Falana). Philadelphia, PA, 9/11/43. Singer.

FALCO (Johann Hoelcel). Austria, 2/19/57. Singer, songwriter. "Rock Me Amadeus."

FALCONER, EARL. Birmingham, England, 1/23/59. Bassist. UB40.

FALK, PETER. New York, NY, 9/16/27. Actor. Columbo.

FALTSKOG, AGNETHA. Jonkoping, Sweden, 4/5/50. Singer. Abba.

FAMBROUGH, HENRY. 5/10/38. Singer. The (Detroit) Spinners.

FAME, GEORGIE (Clive Powell). Leigh, England, 9/26/43. Singer, keyboardist. Georgie Fame & The Blue Flames.

FARENTINO, JAMES. Brooklyn, NY, 2/24/38. Actor. Dynasty.

FARINA, DENNIS. Chicago, IL, 2/29/44. Actor. Crime Story.

FARNER, MARK. Flint, MI, 9/29/48. Singer, guitarist. Grand Funk Railroad.

FARR, JAMIE (Jameel Joseph Farah). Toledo, OH, 7/1/34. Actor. Maxwell Klinger on M*A*S*H.

FARRAKHAN, LOUIS (Louis Eugene Walcott). New York, NY, 5/11/33. Controversial Muslim minister.

FARRELL, BOBBY. Aruba, West Indies, 10/6/49. Singer. Boney M.

FARRELL, MIKE. St. Paul, MN, 2/6/39. Actor, writer, director, married to Shelley Fabares. B. J. Hunnicutt on M*A*S*H.

FARRIS, STEVE. 5/1/57. Guitarist. Mr. Mister.

FARRISS, ANDREW. Perth, Australia, 3/27/59. Keyboardist. INXS.

FARRISS, JON. Perth, Australia, 8/10/61. Drummer, singer. INXS.

FAULKNER, ERIC. Edinburgh, Scotland, 10/21/55. Guitarist. The Bay City Rollers.

FAWCETT, FARRAH. Corpus Christi, TX, 2/2/47. Actor. Jill Munroe on Charlie's Angels.

FELDMAN, COREY. Reseda, CA, 7/16/71. Actor. Stand By Me.

FELDON, BARBARA (Barbara Hall). Pittsburgh, PA, 3/12/41. Actor. Agent 99 on Get Smart.

FELDSHUH, TOVAH. New York, NY, 12/27/53. Actor. The Idolmaker.

FELICIANO, JOSE. Lares, Puerto Rico, 9/10/45. Singer, guitarist. Chico and the Man.

FELL, NORMAN. Philadelphia, PA, 3/24/24. Actor. Stanley Roper on Three's Company.

FENN, SHERILYN. Detroit, MI, 2/1/65. Actor. Twin Peaks.

FERGUSON, JAY (John Ferguson). Burbank, CA, 5/10/47. Singer. Spirit.

FERGUSON, LARRY. Nassau, Bahamas, 4/14/48. Keyboardist. Hot Chocolate.

FERGUSON, SARAH. London, England, 10/15/59. Duchess of York. Married to (and separated from) Prince Andrew.

FERRARO, GERALDINE. Newburgh, NY, 8/26/35. Politician, first woman vice-presidential candidate.

FERRER, MEL (Melchor Gaston Ferrer). Elberon, NJ, 8/25/12. Producer, director, actor, formerly married to Audrey Hepburn. Falcon Crest.

FERRER, MIGUEL. Santa Monica, CA, 2/7/54. Actor, son of Jose Ferrer and Rosemary Clooney. Twin Peaks.

FERRIGNO, LOU. Brooklyn, NY, 11/9/52. Actor, bodybuilder. The Incredible Hulk.

FERRIS, BARBARA. London, England, 10/3/40. Actor. The Strauss Family.

FERRY, BRYAN. Durham, England, 9/26/45. Singer, songwriter. Roxy Music.

FIEGER, DOUG. Detroit, MI, 8/20/52. Singer, guitarist. The Knack.

FIELDER, JIM. Denton, TX, 10/4/47. Bassist. Blood, Sweat & Tears.

FIELDS, KIM. Los Angeles, CA, 5/12/69. Actor. Dorothy "Tootie" Ramsey on The Facts of Life.

FIERSTEIN, HARVEY. Brooklyn, NY, 6/6/54. Actor, writer. Mrs. Doubtfire.

FILIPOVIC, ZLATA. Sarajevo, Bosnia-Herzegovina, 12/3/81. Author. Zlata's Diary.

FINCH, RICHARD. Indianapolis, IN, 1/25/54. Bassist. KC & The Sunshine Band.

FINER, JEM. Ireland. Banjoist. The Pogues.

FINGERS, JOHNNIE (Johnnie Moylett). Ireland, 9/10/56. Keyboardist, singer. The Boomtown Rats.

FINN, TIM (Te Awamutu). New Zealand, 6/25/52. Singer, keyboardist. Split Enz.

FINNEY, ALBERT. Salford, England, 5/9/36. Actor. Shoot the Moon.

FIRTH, COLIN. Grayshott, England, 9/10/60. Actor. Another Country.

FISH (Derek Dick). Dalkeith, Scotland, 4/25/58. Singer. Marillion.

FISHER, AMY. New York, NY, 1974. The "Long Island Lolita."

FISHER, EDDIE. Philadelphia, PA, 8/10/28. Singer, formerly married to Debbie Reynolds, Elizabeth Taylor, and Connie Stevens, father of Carrie Fisher. *The Eddie Fisher Show.*

FISHER, MATTHEW. Croydon, England, 3/7/46. Keyboardist. Procol Harum.

FISHER, ROGER. Seattle, WA, 2/14/50. Guitarist. Heart.

FITZGERALD, GERALDINE. Dublin, Ireland, 11/24/14. Actor. *Wuthering Heights.*

FLACK, ROBERTA. Black Mountain, NC, 2/10/39. Pop singer. "The First Time Ever I Saw Your Face."

FLEA (Michael Balzary). Melbourne, Australia. Singer, bassist. The Red Hot Chili Peppers.

FLEETWOOD, MICK. London, England, 6/24/42. Drummer. Fleetwood Mac.

FLEMING, PEGGY. San Jose, CA, 7/27/48. Ice skater. Olympic gold medalist.

FLETCHER, ANDY. Basildon, England, 7/8/60. Keyboardist. Depeche Mode.

FLETCHER, LOUISE. Birmingham, AL, 7/22/34. Actor. *One Flew over the Cuckoo's Nest.*

FLOYD, EDDIE. Montgomery, AL, 6/25/35. R&B singer, songwriter.

FOGELBERG, DAN. Peoria, IL, 8/13/51. Guitarist, singer, songwriter.

FOGERTY, JOHN. Berkeley, CA, 5/28/45. Singer, guitarist. Creedence Clearwater Revival.

FOLLOWS, MEGAN. Toronto, Canada, 3/14/68. Actor. *Anne of Green Gables.*

FONDA, PETER. New York, NY, 2/23/39. Actor, son of Henry Fonda, brother of Jane, father of Bridget. *Easy Rider.*

FONTAINE, JOAN (Joan de Havilland). Tokyo, Japan, 10/22/17. Actor, sister of Olivia de Havilland. *Suspicion.*

FONTANA, WAYNE (Glyn Ellis). Manchester, England, 10/28/40. Singer. Wayne Fontana & The Mindbenders.

FORD, FAITH. Alexandria, LA, 9/14/64. Actor. Corky Sherwood Forrest on *Murphy Brown.*

FORD, FRANKIE (Frankie Guzzo). Gretna, LA, 8/4/40. Singer.

FORD, LITA. London, England, 9/23/59. Lead guitarist. The Runaways.

FOREMAN, CHRIS. England, 8/8/58. Guitarist. Madness.

FOREMAN, GEORGE. Marshall, TX, 1/10/49. Boxer, actor. *George.*

FORSSI, KEN. Cleveland, OH, 1943. Bassist. Love.

FORSTER, ROBERT. Rochester, NY, 7/13/41. Actor. *Banyon.*

FORSYTHE, JOHN (John Freund). Penns Grove, NJ, 1/29/18. Actor. Blake Carrington on *Dynasty.*

FORTUNE, JIMMY. Newport News, VA, 3/1/55. Musician. Statler Brothers.

FORTUNE, NICK (Nick Fortuna). Chicago, IL, 5/1/46. Bassist. The Buckinghams.

FOSTER, MEG. Reading, PA, 5/14/48. Actor. *Cagney and Lacey.*

FOX, JACKIE. California, 1960. Bassist. The Runaways.

FOX, JAMES. London, England, 5/19/39. Actor. *The Loneliness of the Long Distance Runner.*

FOX, SAMANTHA. England, 4/15/66. Singer. "Naughty Girls (Need Love Too)."

FOX, TERRY (Terrance Stanley Fox). Winnipeg, Canada, 7/28/58. Track athlete, fund-raiser.

FOXTON, BRUCE. Woking, Surrey England, 9/1/55. Guitarist. The Jam.

FOXWORTH, ROBERT. Houston, TX, 11/1/41. Actor. Chase Gioberti on *Falcon Crest.*

FRAKES, JONATHAN. Bethlehem, PA, 1952. Actor. Commander William Riker on *Star Trek: The Next Generation.*

FRAME, RODDY. East Kilbride, Scotland, 1/29/64. Singer, guitarist. Aztec Camera.

FRAMPTON, PETER KENNETH. Beckenham, England, 4/22/50. Guitarist, singer, songwriter.

FRANCIOSA, ANTHONY (Anthony Papaleo). New York, NY, 10/25/28. Actor. *The Long Hot Summer.*

FRANCIS, ANNE. Ossining, NY, 9/16/30. Actor, former child model.

FRANCIS, BILL. Mobile, AL, 1/16/42. Keyboardist, singer. Dr. Hook.

FRANCIS, CONNIE (Concetta Franconero). Newark, NJ, 12/12/38. Singer. "Where the Boys Are."

FRANTZ, CHRIS (Charlton Frantz). Fort Campbell, KY, 5/8/51. Drummer. Talking Heads.

FRASER, ANDY. London, England, 8/7/52. Bassist. Free.

FRASER, BRENDAN. Indianapolis, IN, 1967. Actor. *Encino Man.*

FRAZIER, JOE. Beaufort, SC, 1/17/44. Boxer, former heavyweight champ.

FREDRIKSSON, MARIE. Sweden, 5/30/58. Singer. Roxette.

FREEMAN, BOBBY. San Francisco, CA, 6/13/40. Singer, songwriter.

FREEMAN, MORGAN. Memphis, TN, 6/1/37. Actor, director. *Driving Miss Daisy.*

FREHLEY, ACE (Paul Frehley). The Bronx, NY, 4/22/51. Guitarist, singer. Kiss.

FREIBERG, DAVID. Boston, MA, 8/24/38. Bassist. Quicksilver Messenger Service.

FREWER, MATT. Washington, DC, 1/4/58. Actor. *Max Headroom.*

FREY, GLENN. Detroit, MI, 11/6/48. Singer, songwriter. The Eagles.

FRICKER, BRENDA. Dublin, Ireland, 2/17/45. Actor. *My Left Foot.*

FRIPP, ROBERT. Wimborne Minster, England, 1946. Guitarist. King Crimson.

FROST, CRAIG. Flint, MI, 4/20/48. Keyboardist. Grand Funk Railroad.

FRY, MARTIN. Manchester, England, 3/9/58. Singer. ABC.

FUNICELLO, ANNETTE. Utica, NY, 10/22/42. Actor, Mouseketeer. *Beach Blanket Bingo.*

FUNT, ALLEN. New York, NY, 9/16/14. Producer. *Candid Camera.*

FURAY, RICHIE. Yellow Springs, OH, 5/9/44. Singer, guitarist. Buffalo Springfield; Poco.

FURUHOLMEN, MAGS. Oslo, Norway, 11/1/62. Keyboardist, singer. a-ha.

GABLE, JOHN CLARK. Los Angeles, CA, 3/20/61. Actor. Son of Clark Gable.

GABRIEL, PETER. Cobham, England, 5/13/50. Singer, songwriter. Genesis.

GAHAN, DAVE. Epping, England, 5/9/62. Singer. Depeche Mode.

GAIL, MAXWELL. Derfoil, MI, 4/5/43. Actor. Sergeant Stanley Wojohowicz on *Barney Miller.*

GALLAGHER, PETER. Armonk, NY, 8/19/55. Actor. *sex, lies and videotape.*

GARDNER, CARL. Tyler, TX, 4/29/27. Lead singer. The Coasters.

GARFAT, JANCE. California, 3/3/44. Bassist, singer. Dr. Hook.

GARFUNKEL, ART. New York, NY, 11/5/42. Singer, actor, former partner of Paul Simon. *Carnal Knowledge.*

GARLAND, BEVERLY. Santa Cruz, CA, 10/17/30. Actor. *My Three Sons.*

GARR, TERI. Lakewood, OH, 12/11/49. Actor. *Tootsie.*

GARRETT, BETTY. St. Joseph, MO, 5/23/19. Actor. *All in the Family.*

GARRITY, FREDDIE. Manchester, England, 11/14/40. Singer. Freddie & The Dreamers.

GARSON, GREER. County Down, Northern Ireland, 9/29/08. Actor. *Mrs. Miniver.*

GARTH, JENNIE. Champaign, IL, 4/3/72. Actor. Kelly Taylor on *Beverly Hills 90210.*

GARTSIDE, GREEN (Green Strohmeyer-Gartside). Cardiff, Wales, 6/22/56. Singer. Scritti Politti.

GARY, BRUCE. Burbank, CA, 4/7/52. Drummer. The Knack.

GATES, DAVID. Tulsa, OK, 12/11/40. Keyboardist, singer. Bread.

GATLIN, RUDY. 8/20/52. Singer. The Gatlin Brothers.

GATLIN, STEVE. 4/4/51. Singer. The Gatlin Brothers.

GAUDIO, BOB. The Bronx, NY, 11/17/42. Singer, organist. The Four Seasons.

GAYLE, CRYSTAL (Brenda Webb). Paintsville, KY, 1/9/51. Country singer.

GAYLORD, MITCH. Van Nuys, CA, 1961. Gymnast.

GAYNOR, MITZI (Francesca Marlene Von Gerber). Chicago, IL, 9/4/31. Actor. *Anything Goes.*

GAZZARA, BEN (Biago Gazzara). New York, NY, 8/28/30. Actor. *Inchon.*

GEARY, CYNTHIA. Jackson, MS, 3/21/66. Actor. *Northern Exposure.*

GEILS, J. (Jerome Geils). New York, NY, 2/20/46. Guitarist. The J. Geils Band.

GELDOF, BOB. Dublin, Ireland, 10/5/54. Singer. The Boomtown Rats.

GERARD, GIL. Little Rock, AR, 1/23/43. Actor. *Buck Rogers in the 25th Century.*

GERARDO. Ecuador, 1965. Rap artist. "Rico Suave."

GERTZ, JAMI. Chicago, IL, 10/28/65. Actor. *Less Than Zero.*

GESSLE, PER. 1/12/59. Guitarist, singer. Roxette.

GETTY, BALTHAZAR. 1/22/75. Actor, grandson of J. Paul Getty. *Where the Day Takes You.*

GETTY, ESTELLE. New York, NY, 7/25/23. Actor. Sophia Petrillo on *The Golden Girls.*

GHOSTLEY, ALICE. Eve, MO, 8/14/26. Actor. *Bewitched.*

GIAMMARESE, CARL. Chicago, IL, 8/21/47. Guitarist. The Buckinghams.

GIANNINI, GIANCARLO. Spezia, Italy, 8/1/42. Actor. *Seven Beauties.*

GIBB, BARRY. Isle of Man, England, 9/1/47. Singer, guitarist. The Bee Gees.

GIBB, CYNTHIA. Bennington, VT, 12/14/63. Actor. *Madman of the People.*

GIBB, MAURICE. Manchester, England, 12/22/49. Singer, bassist. The Bee Gees.

GIBB, ROBIN. Manchester, England, 12/22/49. Singer. The Bee Gees.

GIBBINS, MIKE. Swansea, Wales, 3/12/49. Drummer. Badfinger.

GIBBONS, BILLY. Houston, TX, 12/16/49. Guitarist, singer. ZZ Top.

GIBBONS, LEEZA. 3/26/57. TV personality. *Entertainment Tonight.*

GIBBS, MARLA (Margaret Bradley). Chicago, IL, 6/14/33. Actor. Florence Johnston on *The Jeffersons.*

GIBSON, DEBBIE. Long Island, NY, 8/31/70. Singer, songwriter.

GIBSON, HENRY. Germantown, PA, 9/21/35. Actor. Poet from *Laugh-In.*

GIFFORD, FRANK. Santa Monica, CA, 8/16/30. Football player turned sports commentator, married to Kathie Lee Gifford. *Monday Night Football.*

GIFT, ROLAND. Birmingham, England, 5/28/62. Singer. Fine Young Cannibals.

GIGUERE, RUSS. Portsmouth, NH, 10/18/43. Singer, guitarist. The Association.

GILBERT, GILLIAN. Manchester, England, 1/27/61. Keyboardist. New Order.

GILBERT, SARA (Rebecca Sara MacMahon). Santa Monica, CA, 1/29/75. Actor, sister of Melissa and Jonathan Gilbert. Darlene Conner on *Roseanne.*

GILES, MIKE. Bournemouth, England, 1942. Drummer. King Crimson.

GILL, PETER. Liverpool, England, 3/8/64. Drummer. Frankie Goes to Hollywood.

GILLAN, IAN. Hounslow, England, 8/19/45. Singer. Deep Purple.

GILLIAM, TERRY. Minneapolis, MN, 11/22/40. Writer, director, actor. *Monty Python and the Holy Grail.*

GILMORE, JIMMIE DALE. Tulia, TX, 1945. Country singer. "Dallas."

GILMOUR, DAVID. Cambridge, England, 3/6/44. Singer, guitarist. Pink Floyd.

GINTY, ROBERT. New York, NY, 11/14/48. Actor. *Baa Baa Black Sheep.*

GIVENS, ROBIN. New York, NY, 11/27/64. Actor, formerly married to Mike Tyson. *Head of the Class.*

GLASER, PAUL MICHAEL. Cambridge, MA, 3/25/43. Actor, director. Det. Dave Starsky on *Starsky and Hutch.*

GLASS, RON. Evansville, IN, 7/10/45. Actor. *Barney Miller.*

GLEASON, JOANNA. Winnipeg, Canada, 6/2/50. Actor, daughter of Monty Hall. *Into the Woods.*

GLENN, SCOTT. Pittsburgh, PA, 1/26/42. Actor. *The Right Stuff.*

GLESS, SHARON. Los Angeles, CA, 5/31/43. Actor. Chris Cagney on *Cagney and Lacey.*

GLITTER, GARY (Paul Gadd). Banbury, England, 5/8/40. Singer, songwriter.

GLOVER, CRISPIN. New York, NY, 9/20/64. Actor. George McFly in *Back to the Future.*

GLOVER, DANNY. San Francisco, CA, 7/22/47. Actor. *Lethal Weapon.*

GLOVER, JOHN. Kingston, NY, 8/7/44. Actor. *Shamus.*

GLOVER, ROGER. Brecon, Wales, 11/30/45. Bassist. Deep Purple.

GOBLE, GRAHAM. Adelaide, Australia, 5/15/47. Guitarist. Little River Band.

GODLEY, KEVIN. Manchester, England, 10/7/45. Singer, drummer. 10cc; Godley & Creme.

GOLD, TRACEY. New York, NY, 5/16/69. Actor. *Growing Pains.*

GOLDEN, WILLIAM LEE. Brewton, AL, 1/12/39. Singer. The Oak Ridge Boys.

GOLDING, LYNVAL. Coventry, England, 7/24/51. Guitarist. The Specials.

GOLDTHWAIT, BOBCAT. Syracuse, NY, 5/1/62. Actor. *Police Academy* series.

GOLDWYN, TONY. Los Angeles, CA, 5/20/60. Actor. *Ghost.*

GOLINO, VALERIA. Naples, Italy, 10/22/66. Actor. *Rain Man.*

GOODALL, JANE. London, England, 4/3/34. Anthropologist, author. *In the Shadow of Man.*

GOODEN, SAM. Chattanooga, TN, 9/2/39. Singer. The Impressions.

GOODING, CUBA JR. The Bronx, NY, 1968. Actor. *Boyz N the Hood.*

GORBACHEV, MIKHAIL. Privolnoye, Russia, 4/2/31. Former leader of the USSR.

GORE, ALBERT JR. Washington, DC, 3/31/48. Vice president of the United States.

GORE, LESLEY. New York, NY, 5/2/46. Singer.

GORE, MARTIN. Basildon, England, 7/23/61. Keyboardist. Depeche Mode.

GORHAM, SCOTT. Santa Monica, CA, 3/17/51. Guitarist. Thin Lizzy.

GORMAN, STEVE. Hopkinsville, KY, 8/17/65. Drummer. The Black Crowes.

GORME, EYDIE. New York, NY, 8/16/32. Singer. Steve and Eydie.

GORRIE, ALAN. Perth, Scotland, 7/19/46. Singer, bassist. Average White Band.

GORSHIN, FRANK. Pittsburgh, PA, 4/5/33. Actor. The Riddler on *Batman.*

GOSSETT, LOUIS JR. Brooklyn, NY, 5/27/36. Actor. *An Officer and a Gentleman.*

GOTTI, JOHN. New York, NY, 10/27/40. Reputed mob leader.

GOUDREAU, BARRY. Boston, MA, 11/29/51. Guitarist. Boston.

GOULD, BILLY. Los Angeles, CA, 4/24/63. Bassist. Faith No More.

GOULD, BOON. 3/14/55. Guitarist. Level 42.

GOULD, ELLIOTT (Elliott Goldstein). Brooklyn, NY, 8/29/38. Actor. Formerly married to Barbra Streisand. *Bob & Carol & Ted & Alice.*

GOULD, PHIL. 2/28/57. Drummer. Level 42.

GOULDMAN, GRAHAM. Manchester, England, 5/10/45. Singer, guitarist. 10cc.

GOULET, ROBERT (Stanley Applebaum). Lawrence, MA, 11/26/33. Singer, actor. *Blue Light.*

GRAF, STEFFI. Bruhl, Germany, 6/14/69. Tennis player, youngest woman to win French Open.

GRAHAM, BILLY. Charlotte, NC, 11/7/18. Evangelist. *Billy Graham Crusades.*

GRAHAM, LARRY. Beaumont, TX, 8/14/46. Bass guitarist. Sly & The Family Stone.

GRAMM, LOU. Rochester, NY, 5/2/50. Singer. Foreigner.

GRANDMASTER FLASH (Joseph Saddler). New York, NY, 1958. Rap artist. Grandmaster Flash; Melle Mel & The Furious Five.

GRANDY, FRED. Sioux City, IA, 6/29/48. Actor, politician. Burl "Gopher" Smith on *The Love Boat.*

GRANGER, FARLEY. San Jose, CA, 7/1/25. Actor. *Strangers on a Train.*

GRANT, EDDY (Edmond Grant). Plaisance, Guyana, 3/5/48. Reggae singer, songwriter.

GRANT, LEE (Lyova Rosenthal). New York, NY, 10/31/27. Actor, mother of Dinah Manoff. *Peyton Place.*

GRANTHAM, GEORGE. Cordell, OK, 11/20/47. Drummer, singer. Poco.

GRATZER, ALAN. Syracuse, NY, 11/9/48. Drummer. REO Speedwagon.

GRAVES, PETER (Peter Aurness). Minneapolis, MN, 3/18/26. Actor, brother of James Arness. Jim Phelps on *Mission: Impossible.*

GRAY, EDDIE. 2/27/48. Guitarist. Tommy James & The Shondells.

GRAY, LES. Carshalton, England, 4/9/46. Singer. Mud.

GRAY, SPALDING. Barrington, RI, 6/5/41. Actor, writer, performance artist. *The Killing Fields.*

GREBB, MARTY. Chicago, IL, 9/2/46. Keyboardist. The Buckinghams.

GREEN, AL (Al Greene). Forrest City, AR, 4/13/46. R&B singer, songwriter.

GREEN, KARL. Salford, England, 7/31/47. Bassist. Herman's Hermits.

GREENAWAY, PETER. Newport, Wales, 4/5/42. Director, writer. *The Cook, the Thief, His Wife and Her Lover.*

GREENFIELD, DAVE. Keyboardist. The Stranglers.

GREENSPOON, JIMMY. Los Angeles, CA, 2/7/48. Organist. Three Dog Night.

GREENWOOD, ALAN. New York, NY, 10/20/51. Keyboardist. Foreigner.

GREGG, BRIAN. Bassist. Johnny Kidd & The Pirates.

GREGORY, GLENN. Sheffield, England, 5/16/58. Singer. Heaven 17.

GREY, JENNIFER. New York, NY, 3/26/60. Actor, daughter of Joel. *Dirty Dancing.*

GREY, JOEL (Joel Katz). Cleveland, OH, 4/11/32. Musical comedy performer, father of Jennifer. *Cabaret.*

GRIER, DAVID ALAN. Detroit, MI, 6/30/55. Actor. *In Living Color.*

GRIER, ROSEY (Roosevelt Grier). Cuthbert, GA, 7/14/32. Football player, actor.

GRIFFITH, ANDY. Mt. Airy, NC, 6/1/26. Actor, writer, producer. *The Andy Griffith Show.*

GRILL, ROB. Los Angeles, CA, 11/30/44. Bassist, singer. The Grass Roots.

GROSS, MARY. Chicago, IL, 3/25/53. Actor, sister of Michael. *Saturday Night Live.*

GROSS, MICHAEL. Chicago, IL, 6/21/47. Actor, brother of Mary. Steven Keaton on *Family Ties.*

GRUNDY, HUGH. Winchester, England, 3/6/45. Drummer. The Zombies.

GUCCIONE, BOB. New York, NY, 12/17/30. Publisher, founder of *Penthouse.*

GUEST, CHRISTOPHER. New York, NY, 2/5/48. Actor, writer, married to Jamie Lee Curtis. *This Is Spinal Tap.*

GUEST, LANCE. Saratoga, CA, 7/21/60. Actor. *Knots Landing.*

GUEST, WILLIAM. Atlanta, GA, 6/2/41. Singer. Gladys Knight & The Pips.

GUILLAUME, ROBERT (Robert Williams). St. Louis, MO, 11/30/37. Actor. Benson DuBois on *Soap.*

GUINNESS, ALEC. London, England, 4/2/14. Actor. *The Bridge on the River Kwai.*

GULAGER, CLU. Holdenville, OK, 11/16/28. Actor. *The Last Picture Show.*

GUMBEL, BRYANT. New Orleans, LA, 9/29/48. News show host and sportscaster. *Today.*

GUSTAFSON, KARIN. Miami, FL, 6/23/59. Actor. *Taps.*

GUSTAFSON, STEVEN. Bassist. 10,000 Maniacs.

GUTHRIE, ARLO. New York, NY, 7/10/47. Folk singer, songwriter. "Alice's Restaurant."

GUTTENBERG, STEVE. Brooklyn, NY, 8/24/58. Actor. *Three Men and a Baby.*

GUY, BILLY. Attasca, TX, 6/20/36. Baritone. The Coasters.

GUY, BUDDY (George Guy). Lettsworth, LA, 7/30/36. Blues guitarist.

GUY, JASMINE. Boston, MA, 3/10/64. Actor. Whitley Gilbert on *A Different World.*

HAAS, LUKAS. West Hollywood, CA, 4/16/76. Actor. *Witness.*

HACK, SHELLEY. Greenwich, CT, 7/6/52. Actor. *Charlie's Angels.*

HACKETT, BUDDY (Leonard Hacker). Brooklyn, NY, 8/31/24. Actor. *It's a Mad Mad Mad Mad World; The Love Bug.*

HADLEY, TONY. Islington, England, 6/2/59. Singer. Spandau Ballet.

HAGAR, SAMMY. Monterey, CA, 10/13/47. Singer, guitarist. Van Halen.

HAGERTY, JULIE. Cincinnati, OH, 6/15/55. Actor. *Airplane!*

HAGMAN, LARRY (Larry Hageman). Fort Worth, TX, 9/21/31. Actor, son of Mary Martin. J. R. Ewing on *Dallas.*

HAHN, JESSICA. Massapequa, NY, 7/7/59. *Playboy* model, involved in PTL Jim Bakker scandal.

HAID, CHARLES. San Francisco, CA, 6/2/43. Actor, director, producer. Andrew Renko on *Hill Street Blues.*

HAIM, COREY. Toronto, Canada, 12/23/72. Actor. *The Lost Boys.*

HALE, BARBARA. DeKalb, IL, 4/18/22. Actor, mother of William Katt. Della Street on *Perry Mason*.

HALFORD, ROB. Birmingham, England, 8/25/51. Singer. Judas Priest.

HALL, ANTHONY MICHAEL. Boston, MA, 4/14/68. Actor. *Sixteen Candles*.

HALL, BRUCE. Champaign, IL, 5/3/53. Bassist. REO Speedwagon.

HALL, DARYL (Daryl Hohl). Pottstown, PA, 10/11/49. Singer, guitarist. Hall & Oates.

HALL, DEIDRE. 10/31/47. Actor. Marlena Evans on *Days of Our Lives*.

HALL, FAWN. Annandale, VA, 1959. Secretary for Oliver North. Iran-Contra scandal.

HALL, MONTY. Winnipeg, Canada, 8/25/24. TV personality. *Let's Make a Deal*.

HALL, TERRY. Coventry, England, 3/19/59. Singer. The Specials.

HAM, GREG. Australia, 9/27/53. Saxophonist, keyboardist, flautist. Men at Work.

HAM, PETE. Swansea, Wales, 4/27/47. Guitarist, pianist, singer. Badfinger.

HAMEL, VERONICA. Philadelphia, PA, 11/20/43. Actor. Joyce Davenport on *Hill Street Blues*.

HAMILL, DOROTHY. Chicago, IL, 7/26/56. Ice skater. Olympic gold medalist.

HAMILL, MARK. Oakland, CA, 9/25/52. Actor. Luke Skywalker in *Star Wars* trilogy.

HAMILTON, GEORGE. Memphis, TN, 8/12/39. Actor. *Love at First Bite*.

HAMILTON, LINDA. Salisbury, MD, 9/26/56. Actor. Sarah Connor in *The Terminator*.

HAMILTON, SCOTT. Haverford, PA, 8/28/58. Ice skater.

HAMILTON, TOM. Colorado Springs, CO, 12/31/51. Bassist. Aerosmith.

HAMLIN, HARRY. Pasadena, CA, 10/30/51. Actor. *L.A. Law*.

HAMLISCH, MARVIN. New York, NY, 6/2/44. Composer. *The Way We Were*; *The Sting*.

HAMMETT, KIRK. 11/18/62. Guitarist. Metallica.

HAMPSHIRE, SUSAN. London, England, 5/12/41. Actor. *The Forsythe Saga*.

HANCOCK, HERBIE. Chicago, IL, 4/12/40. Jazz pianist, composer. "Rockit."

HARDING, TONYA. Portland, OR, 11/12/70. Figure skater. Pled guilty to hindering prosecution in Nancy Kerrigan attack.

HARDISON, KADEEM. Brooklyn, NY, 7/24/66. Actor. Dwayne Wayne on *A Different World*.

HAREWOOD, DORIAN. Dayton, OH, 8/6/50. Actor. *Roots—The Next Generation*.

HARKET, MORTEN. Konigsberg, Norway, 9/14/59. Lead singer. a-ha.

HARLEY, STEVE (Steve Nice). London, England, 2/27/51. Singer. Steve Harley & Cockney Rebel.

HARMON, MARK. Los Angeles, CA, 9/2/51. Actor. *St. Elsewhere*.

HARPER, JESSICA. Chicago, IL, 10/10/49. Actor.

HARPER, TESS (Tessie Jean Washam). Mammoth Spring, AR, 8/15/50. Actor. *Crimes of the Heart*.

HARPER, VALERIE. Suffern, NY, 8/22/40. Actor. Rhoda Morgenstern on *The Mary Tyler Moore Show*.

HARRINGTON, PAT. New York, NY, 8/13/29. Actor. Dwayne Schneider on *One Day at a Time*.

HARRIS, BARBARA (Sandra Markowitz). Evanston, IL, 7/25/35. Actor. *Family Plot*.

HARRIS, ED. Tenafly, NJ, 11/28/50. Actor. *The Right Stuff*.

HARRIS, JULIE. Grosse Point, MI, 12/2/25. Actor. *Knots Landing*.

HARRIS, MEL (Mary Ellen Harris). Bethlehem, PA, 7/12/57. Actor. Hope Murdoch Steadman on *thirtysomething*.

HARRIS, RICHARD. Limerick, Ireland, 10/1/30. Actor. *A Man Called Horse*.

HARRISON, BILLY. Belfast, Ireland, 10/14/42. Lead guitarist. Them.

HARRISON, GEORGE. Liverpool, England, 2/25/43. Singer, lead guitarist. The Beatles.

HARRISON, GREGORY. Catalina Island, CA, 5/31/50. Actor. *Trapper John, MD*.

HARRISON, JENILEE. Northridge, CA, 6/12/59. Actor. Jamie Ewing Barnes on *Dallas*.

HARRISON, JERRY. Milwaukee, WI, 2/21/49. Keyboardist. Talking Heads.

HARRISON, NOEL. London, England, 1/29/35. Singer, actor. *The Girl from U.N.C.L.E.*

HARRY, DEBORAH. Miami, FL, 7/1/45. Singer. Blondie.

HART, MARY. Sioux Falls, SD, 11/8/50. TV hostess. *Entertainment Tonight*.

HART, MICKY (Michael Hart). New York, NY, 9/11/44. Drummer, songwriter. Grateful Dead.

HARTLEY, MARIETTE. New York, NY, 6/21/40. Actor. *Peyton Place*.

HARTMAN, DAVID. Pawtucket, RI, 5/19/35. Actor, talk show host. *Good Morning America*.

HARTMAN, JOHN. Falls Church, VA, 3/18/50. Drummer. The Doobie Brothers.

HASSAN, NORMAN. Birmingham, England, 11/26/57. Percussionist. UB40.

HATFIELD, BOBBY. Beaver Dam, WI, 8/10/40. Singer. The Righteous Brothers.

HATTON, BILLY. Liverpool, England, 6/9/41. Bassist. The Fourmost.

HAUER, RUTGER. Breukelen, Netherlands, 1/23/44. Actor. *Blade Runner*.

HAVENS, RICHIE. Brooklyn, NY, 1/21/41. Folk/blues guitarist, singer, songwriter.

HAWKING, STEPHEN. Oxford, England, 1/8/42. Theoretical physicist, author of *A Brief History of Time*.

HAY, COLIN. Scotland, 6/29/53. Singer. Men at Work.

HAY, ROY. Southend, England, 8/12/61. Guitarist, keyboardist. Culture Club.

HAYDOCK, ERIC. Stockport, England, 2/3/42. Bassist. The Hollies.

HAYES, CHRIS. California, 11/24/57. Lead guitarist. Huey Lewis & The News.

HAYES, ISAAC. Covington, TN, 8/20/42. R&B/rock saxophonist, keyboardist, singer, songwriter.

HAYS, ROBERT. Bethesda, MD, 7/24/47. Actor, married to Cherie Currie. *Airplane!*

HAYWARD, JUSTIN. Wiltshire, England, 10/14/46. Singer, songwriter. The Moody Blues.

HEADLY, GLENNE. New London, CT, 3/13/55. Actor, formerly married to John Malkovich. *Dirty Rotten Scoundrels*.

HEADON, NICKY. Bromley, England, 5/30/55. Drummer. The Clash.

HEALEY, JEFF. Toronto, Canada, 1966. Singer, songwriter, guitarist.

HEARD, JOHN. Washington, DC, 3/7/46. Actor. Father in *Home Alone*.

HEATON, PAUL. Birkenhead, England, 5/9/62. Singer, guitarist. The Housemartins.

HEDREN, TIPPI (Natalie Kay Hedren). New Ulm, MN, 1/19/35. Actor. Mother of Melanie Griffith. *The Birds*.

HEFNER, HUGH. Chicago, IL, 4/9/26. Publisher, founder of *Playboy*.

HELL, RICHARD (Richard Myers). Lexington, KY, 10/2/49. Bassist. Television.

HELLER, JOSEPH. New York, NY, 5/1/23. Author, dramatist. *Catch-22*.

HELLIWELL, JOHN. England, 2/15/45. Saxophonist. Supertramp.

HELM, LEVON. Marvell, AR, 5/26/42. Drummer, singer. The Band.

HELMSLEY, HARRY. New York, NY, 3/4/09. Businessman, married to Leona Helmsley.

HELMSLEY, LEONA. New York, NY, 7/4/20. Hotel executive, married to Harry Helmsley. Convicted of tax evasion.

HEMINGWAY, MARGAUX. Portland, OR, 2/1/55. Actor, model, granddaughter of Ernest Hemingway, sister of Mariel. *Lipstick*.

HEMINGWAY, MARIEL. Ketchum, ID, 11/22/61. Actor, granddaughter of Ernest Hemingway, sister of Margaux. *Manhattan*.

HEMSLEY, SHERMAN. Philadelphia, PA, 2/1/38. Actor. George on *The Jeffersons*.

HENDERSON, ALAN. Belfast, Ireland, 11/26/44. Bassist. Them.

HENDERSON, BILLY. Detroit, MI, 8/9/39. Singer. The (Detroit) Spinners.

HENDERSON, FLORENCE. Dale, IN, 2/14/34. Actor. Carol Brady on *The Brady Bunch*.

HENNER, MARILU. Chicago, IL, 4/6/52. Actor. Elaine Nardo on *Taxi*.

HENNING, DOUG. Fort Gary, Canada, 5/3/47. Magician. *The Magic Show*.

HENRIKSEN, LANCE. New York, NY, 5/5/40. Actor. *Aliens*.

HENRY, BUCK (Buck Zuckerman). New York, NY, 12/9/30. Actor, writer. *Get Smart*; *That Was the Week That Was*.

HENRY, CLARENCE. Algiers, LA, 3/19/37. Singer. "Ain't Got No Home."

HENRY, JUSTIN. Rye, NY, 5/25/71. Actor. *Kramer vs. Kramer*.

HENRY, PRINCE. London, England, 8/15/84. British royalty, son of Prince Charles and Princess Diana.

HENSLEY, KEN. England, 8/24/45. Keyboardist, guitarist, singer, percussionist. Uriah Heep.

HENSLEY, PAMELA. Los Angeles, CA, 10/3/50. Actor. C. J. Parsons on *Matt Houston*.

HERMAN, PEE-WEE (Paul Reubenfeld). Peekskill, NY, 8/27/52. Children's performer. *Pee-Wee's Playhouse*.

HERRMANN, EDWARD. Washington, DC, 7/21/43. Actor. *The Paper Chase*.

HERSHEY, BARBARA (Barbara Herzstein). Hollywood, CA, 2/5/48. Actor. *Hannah and Her Sisters*.

HERVEY, JASON. Los Angeles, CA, 4/6/72. Actor. Wayne Arnold on *The Wonder Years*.

HESSEMAN, HOWARD. Salem, OR, 2/27/40. Actor. Dr. Johnny Fever on *WKRP in Cincinnati*.

HESTON, CHARLTON (Charles Carter). Evanston, IL, 10/4/24. Actor. *The Ten Commandments*.

HETFIELD, JAMES. 8/3/63. Singer, guitarist. Metallica.

HEWETT, HOWARD. Akron, OH, 10/1/55. Singer. Shalamar.

HEYWARD, NICK. Kent, England, 5/20/61. Guitarist, singer. Haircut 100.

HICKS, CATHERINE. New York, NY, 8/6/51. Actor. *Peggy Sue Got Married*.

HICKS, TONY. Nelson, England, 12/16/43. Guitarist. The Hollies.

HILL, ANITA. Tulsa, OK, 7/30/56. Lawyer, law professor. Accused Supreme Court nominee Clarence Thomas of sexual harrassment.

HILL, ARTHUR. Saskatchewan, Canada, 8/1/22. Actor. *Owen Marshall, Counsellor at Law*.

HILL, DAVE. Fleet Castle, England, 4/4/52. Guitarist. Slade.

HILL, DUSTY. Dallas, TX, 5/19/49. Bassist, singer. ZZ Top.

HILL, FAITH. Star, MS, 1968. Singer. "Wild One."

HILL, STEVEN. Seattle, WA, 2/24/22. Actor. *Law and Order.*

HILLERMAN, JOHN. Denison, TX, 12/20/32. Actor. Jonathan Quayle Higgins III on *Magnum P.I.*

HILLERMAN, TONY. Sacred Heart, OK, 5/27/25. Novelist.

HILLMAN, CHRIS. Los Angeles, CA, 12/4/42. Singer, bassist. The Byrds.

HINES, GREGORY. New York, NY, 2/14/46. Actor, dancer. *The Cotton Club.*

HINGLE, PAT (Martin Patterson Hingle). Denver, CO, 7/19/23. Actor. *Gunsmoke.*

HINSLEY, HARVEY. Northampton, England, 1/19/48. Guitarist. Hot Chocolate.

HIRSCH, GARY "CHICKEN." England, 1940. Drummer. Country Joe & The Fish.

HIRSCH, JUDD. New York, NY, 3/15/35. Actor. Alex Rieger on *Taxi.*

HITCHCOCK, RUSSELL. Melbourne, Australia, 6/15/49. Singer. Air Supply.

HO, DON. Kakaako, HI, 8/13/30. Singer. "Tiny Bubbles."

HOBBS, RANDY. 3/22/48. Bassist. The McCoys.

HODGE, PATRICIA. Lincolnshire, England, 9/29/46. Actor. *The Elephant Man.*

HODGSON, ROGER. Portsmouth, England, 3/21/50. Guitarist. Supertramp.

HODO, DAVID. 7/7/50. Singer. The Village People.

HOFFS, SUSANNA. Newport Beach, CA, 1/17/57. Guitarist, singer. The Bangles.

HOGAN, HULK (Terry Gene Bollea). Augusta, GA, 8/11/53. Wrestler, former World Federation heavyweight champion.

HOGAN, PAUL. Lightning Ridge, Australia, 10/8/39. Actor. *Crocodile Dundee.*

HOLBROOK, HAL. Cleveland, OH, 2/17/25. Actor. *All the President's Men.*

HOLDER, NODDY (Neville Holder). Walsall, England, 6/15/50. Guitarist, singer. Slade.

HOLLAND, JOOLS (Julian Holland). 1/24/58. Keyboardist. Squeeze.

HOLLIMAN, EARL. Delhi, LA, 9/11/28. Actor. *Police Woman.*

HOLLIS, MARK. Tottenham, England, 1955. Singer, guitarist, keyboardist. Talk Talk.

HOLM, CELESTE. New York, NY, 4/29/19. Actor. *All About Eve.*

HOLMES, LARRY. Cuthbert, GA, 11/3/49. Boxer. Former heavyweight champ.

HOOK, PETER. Salford, England, 2/13/56. Bassist. Joy Division; New Order.

HOOKER, JOHN LEE. Clarksdale, MS, 8/22/17. Legendary blues guitarist, singer, songwriter.

HOOKS, JAN. Decatur, GA, 4/23/57. Actor. Carlene Frazier Dobber on *Designing Women.*

HOPE, BOB (Leslie Hope). Eltham, England, 5/29/03. Actor, performer for overseas troops. *The Road* movies with Bing Crosby.

HOPE, DAVE. Kansas, 10/7/49. Bassist. Kansas.

HOPKIN, MARY. Pontardawe, Wales, 5/3/50. Singer, discovered by the Beatles. "Those Were the Days."

HOPKINS, TELMA. Louisville, KY, 10/28/48. Singer, actor, former member of Tony Orlando & Dawn. *Family Matters.*

HOPPER, DENNIS. Dodge City, KS, 5/17/36. Actor, director. *Easy Rider.*

HOPPER, SEAN. California, 3/31/53. Keyboardist. Huey Lewis & The News.

HOPWOOD, KEITH. Manchester, England, 10/26/46. Guitarist. Herman's Hermits.

HORNE, LENA. Brooklyn, NY, 6/30/17. Singer, actor.

HORNSBY, BRUCE. Williamsburg, VA, 11/23/54. Singer, keyboardist, accordionist. Bruce Hornsby & The Range.

HOSKINS, BOB. Bury St. Edmunds, England, 10/26/42. Actor. *Who Framed Roger Rabbit.*

HOWARD, ALAN. Dagenham, England, 10/17/41. Bassist. Brian Poole & The Tremeloes.

HOWARD, ARLISS. Independence, MO, 1955. Actor. *Full Metal Jacket.*

HOWARD, KEN. El Centro, CA, 3/28/44. Actor. *The White Shadow.*

HOWARD, RON. Duncan, OK, 3/1/54. Actor, director. Richie Cunningham on *Happy Days.*

HOWE, STEVE. London, England, 4/8/47. Guitarist, singer. Yes; Asia.

HUCKNALL, MICK "RED." Manchester, England, 6/8/60. Singer. Simply Red.

HUDLIN, REGINALD. Centerville, IL, 12/15/61. Director, writer, producer, brother of Warrington. *House Party.*

HUDLIN, WARRINGTON. East St. Louis, IL, 1952. Producer, director, brother of Reginald. *House Party.*

HUDSON, GARTH. London, Canada, 8/2/37. Organist. The Band.

HUGG, MIKE. Andover, England, 8/11/42. Drummer. Manfred Mann.

HUGHES, GLENN. 7/18/50. Singer. The Village People.

HULCE, TOM. White Water, WI, 12/6/53. Actor. *Amadeus.*

HUMAN BEATBOX (Darren Robinson). 6/10/67. Rap artist. Fat Boys.

HUMPERDINCK, ENGELBERT (Arnold Dorsey). Madras, India,

5/2/36. Pop singer. *The Engelbert Humperdinck Show.*

HUMPHREYS, PAUL. London, England, 2/27/60. Keyboardist. Orchestral Manoeuvres in the Dark (OMD).

HUNT, BILL. 5/23/47. Keyboardist. Electric Light Orchestra (ELO).

HUNT, LINDA. Morristown, NJ, 4/2/45. Actor. *The Year of Living Dangerously.*

HUNTER, IAN. Shrewsbury, England, 6/3/46. Singer, guitarist. Mott The Hoople.

HUNTER, TAB (Arthur Gelien). New York, NY, 7/11/31. Actor. *Damn Yankees.*

HUPPERT, ISABELLE. Paris, France, 3/16/55. Actor. *Entre Nous.*

HURT, JOHN. Shirebrook, England, 1/22/40. Actor. *The Elephant Man.*

HURT, MARY BETH (Mary Beth Supinger). Marshalltown, IA, 9/26/48. Actor, formerly married to William Hurt. *The World According to Garp.*

HURT, WILLIAM. Washington, DC, 3/20/50. Actor, formerly married to Mary Beth Hurt. *Children of a Lesser God.*

HUSSEIN, SADDAM. Tikrit, Iraq, 4/28/37. Leader of Iraq.

HUSSEY, WAYNE. Bristol, England, 5/26/59. Guitarist, singer. The Mission.

HUSTON, ANJELICA. Santa Monica, CA, 7/8/51. Actor, daughter of John Huston. *Prizzi's Honor.*

HUTCHENCE, MICHAEL. Sydney, Australia, 1/22/60. Singer. INXS.

HUTTER, RALF. Krefeld, Germany, 1946. Keyboardist, drummer, singer. Kraftwerk.

HUTTON, DANNY. Buncrana, Ireland, 9/10/42. Singer. Three Dog Night.

HUTTON, LAUREN (Mary Hutton). Charleston, SC, 11/17/43. Actor, model. *American Gigolo.*

HUTTON, TIMOTHY. Malibu, CA, 8/16/60. Actor, director. *Ordinary People.*

HUXLEY, RICK. Dartford, England, 8/5/42. Guitarist. The Dave Clark Five.

HYNDE, CHRISSIE. Akron, OH, 9/7/51. Singer, divorced from Jim Kerr. The Pretenders.

IACOCCA, LEE (Lido Anthony Iacocca). Allentown, PA, 10/15/24. Auto executive, author. *Iacocca.*

IAN, JANIS (Janis Fink). New York, NY, 4/7/51. Folk/rock singer, songwriter.

IDLE, ERIC. Durham, England, 3/29/43. Actor. *Monty Python's Flying Circus.*

IDOL, BILLY (Billy Broad). Stanmore, England, 11/30/55. Singer, songwriter.

IGLESIAS, JULIO. Madrid, Spain, 9/23/43. Pop singer, songwriter.

ILLSLEY, JOHN. Leicester, England, 6/24/49. Bassist. Dire Straits.

IMAN. Mogadishu, Somalia, 7/25/55. Model, married to David Bowie.

INGELS, MARTY. Brooklyn, NY, 3/9/36. Actor, agent, married to Shirley Jones. *The Pruitts of Southampton.*

INGLE, DOUG. Omaha, NE, 9/9/46. Singer, keyboardist. Iron Butterfly.

INGRAM, JAMES. Akron, OH, 2/16/56. R&B singer, songwriter.

INNES, NEIL. Essex, England, 12/9/44. Singer, keyboardist. The Bonzo Dog Doo-Dah Band.

INNIS, ROY. Saint Croix, Virgin Islands, 6/6/34. Civil rights leader.

IOMMI, TONY. Birmingham, England, 2/19/48. Guitarist. Black Sabbath.

IRELAND, KATHY. Santa Barbara, CA, 3/8/63. Model, sister of Mary and Cynthia. *Sports Illustrated* swimsuit cover girl.

IRELAND, PATRICIA. Oak Park, IL, 10/19/45. Political activist. President of NOW.

IRVING, AMY. Palo Alto, CA, 9/10/53. Actor. *Yentl.*

IRVING, JOHN. Exeter, NH, 3/2/42. Author. *The World According to Garp.*

IRWIN, BILL. Santa Monica, CA, 4/11/50. Actor. *Eight Men Out.*

ISLEY, O'KELLY. Cincinnati, OH, 12/25/37. Singer. The Isley Brothers.

ISLEY, RONALD. Cincinnati, OH, 5/21/41. Lead singer. The Isley Brothers.

ISLEY, RUDOLPH. Cincinnati, OH, 4/1/39. Singer. The Isley Brothers.

IVEY, JUDITH. El Paso, TX, 9/4/51. Actor. *Designing Women.*

IVORY, JAMES. Berkeley, CA, 6/7/28. Director, producer. *Howard's End.*

JABS, MATTHIAS. 10/25/56. Guitarist. Scorpions.

JACKEE (Jackee Harry). Winston-Salem, NC, 8/14/56. Actor. *227.*

JACKSON, BO. Bessemer, AL, 11/30/62. Pro football, baseball player.

JACKSON, EDDIE. 1/29/61. Bassist, singer. Queensryche.

JACKSON, FREDDIE. New York, NY, 10/2/56. R&B singer, songwriter.

JACKSON, GLENDA. Birkenhead, England, 5/9/36. Actor. *Women in Love.*

JACKSON, JACKIE (Sigmund Jackson). Gary, IN, 5/4/51. Singer, brother of Michael and Janet Jackson. The Jacksons.

JACKSON, JERMAINE. Gary, IN, 12/11/54. Singer, brother of Michael and Janet. The Jacksons.

JACKSON, JESSE. Greenville, SC, 10/8/41. Civil rights leader, politician. Founded the Rainbow Coalition.

JACKSON, JOE. Burton-on-Trent, England, 8/11/55. Singer, songwriter.

JACKSON, KATE. Birmingham, AL, 10/29/48. Actor. Sabrina Duncan on *Charlie's Angels*.

JACKSON, MARLON. Gary, IN, 3/12/57. Singer, brother of Michael and Janet. The Jacksons.

JACKSON, PERVIS. 5/17/38. Singer. The (Detroit) Spinners.

JACKSON, TITO (Toriano Jackson). Gary, IN, 10/15/53. Singer, brother of Michael and Janet. The Jacksons.

JACKSON, TONY. Liverpool, England, 7/16/40. Singer, bassist. The Searchers.

JACKSON, VICTORIA. Miami, FL, 8/2/58. Actor. *Saturday Night Live*.

JACOBI, DEREK. London, England, 10/22/38. Actor. *The Day of the Jackal*.

JACOBI, LOU. Toronto, Canada, 12/28/13. Actor. *Irma La Douce*.

JAGGER, BIANCA. Managua, Nicaragua, 5/2/45. Socialite, actor. Divorced from Mick Jagger.

JAM MASTER JAY (Jason Mizell). New York, NY, 1965. DJ Run-D.M.C.

JAMES, CLIFTON. Portland, OR, 5/29/25. Actor. *Cool Hand Luke*.

JAMES, ETTA. Los Angeles, CA, 1/25/38. Singer. Bridged R&B and rock.

JAMES, RICK (James Johnson). Buffalo, NY, 2/1/52. Funk singer, songwriter. "Super Freak."

JAMES, TOMMY (Tommy Jackson). Dayton, OH, 4/29/47. Singer. Tommy James & The Shondells.

JANIS, CONRAD. New York, NY, 2/11/28. Actor, musician. Frederick McConnell on *Mork and Mindy*.

JARDINE, AL. Lima, OH, 9/3/42. Guitarist, singer. The Beach Boys.

JARREAU, AL. Milwaukee, WI, 3/12/40. Jazz singer, sang theme song to *Moonlighting*.

JAZZIE B. (Beresford Romeo). London, England, 1/26/63. Rap artist. Soul II Soul.

JEFFRIES, LIONEL. London, England, 6/10/26. Actor, director. *The Water Babies*.

JENNER, BRUCE. Mount Kisco, NY, 10/28/49. Track athlete, sportscaster. Olympic gold medalist.

JENNINGS, WAYLON. Littlefield, TX, 6/15/37. Country singer, songwriter. *The Dukes of Hazzard* theme song.

JETER, MICHAEL. Lawrenceburg, TN, 8/26/52. Actor. *Evening Shade*.

JETT, JOAN. Philadelphia, PA, 9/22/60. Singer, guitarist. "I Love Rock 'n' Roll."

JILLIAN, ANNE (Anne Nauseda). Cambridge, MA, 1/29/51. Actor. *It's a Living*.

JOHANSEN, DAVID. Staten Island, NY, 1/9/50. Actor, singer, a.k.a. Buster Poindexter. *Scrooged*.

JOHN, DR. (Malcolm Rebennack). New Orleans, LA, 11/21/40. Rock/cajun/ blues singer,

songwriter. "Right Place Wrong Time."

JOHN PAUL II, POPE. Wadowice, Poland, 5/18/20. First non-Italian pope since the Renaissance.

JOHNS, GLYNIS. Durban, South Africa, 10/5/23. Actor. *Glynis*.

JOHNSON, ARTE. Benton Harbor, MI, 1/20/29. Actor. *Laugh-In*.

JOHNSON, BEN. Pawhuska, OK, 6/13/18. Actor. *The Last Picture Show*.

JOHNSON, BEVERLY. Buffalo, NY, 10/13/52. Model, actor.

JOHNSON, HOLLY (William Johnson). Khartoum, Sudan, 2/19/60. Singer. Frankie Goes to Hollywood.

JOHNSON, HOWIE. Washington, DC, 1938. Drummer. The Ventures.

JOHNSON, LADY BIRD. Karnack, TX, 12/22/12. Former First Lady, wife of Lyndon.

JOHNSON, MATT. 8/15/61. Singer, guitarist. The The.

JOHNSON, VAN. Newport, RI, 8/25/16. Actor. *The Caine Mutiny*.

JOHNSON, WILKO (John Wilkinson). 1947. Guitarist. Dr. Feelgood.

JON, JOHN. 2/26/61. Musician. Bronski Beat.

JONES, ALAN. Swansea, Wales, 2/6/47. Baritone saxophonist. Amen Corner.

JONES, BOOKER T. Memphis, TN, 12/11/44. Keyboardist. Booker T. & The MG's.

JONES, DAVY. Manchester, England, 12/30/45. Singer, actor. The Monkees.

JONES, DEAN. Decatur, AL, 1/25/31. Actor. *The Shaggy D.A.*

JONES, GRACE. Spanishtown, Jamaica, 5/19/52. Singer, actor. *A View to a Kill*.

JONES, GRAHAM. North Yorkshire, England, 7/8/61. Guitarist. Haircut 100.

JONES, HOWARD. Southampton, England, 2/23/55. Singer, songwriter.

JONES, JAMES EARL. Arkabutla, MS, 1/17/31. Actor, voice of Darth Vader. *The Great White Hope*.

JONES, JEFFREY. Buffalo, NY, 9/28/47. Actor. Principal Ed Rooney in *Ferris Bueller's Day Off*.

JONES, JENNIFER (Phyllis Isley). Tulsa, OK, 3/2/19. Actor. *The Song of Bernadette*.

JONES, JOHN PAUL (John Paul Baldwin). Sidcup, England, 1/31/46. Bassist. Led Zeppelin.

JONES, KENNY. London, England, 9/16/48. Drummer. The Small Faces.

JONES, MICK. Brixton, England, 6/26/55. Guitarist, singer. The Clash; Big Audio Dynamite.

JONES, MICK. London, England, 12/27/44. Guitarist. Foreigner.

JONES, NEIL. Llanbradach, Wales, 3/25/49. Guitarist. Amen Corner.

JONES, PAUL (Paul Pond). Portsmouth, England, 2/24/42.

Singer, harmonicist. Manfred Mann.

JONES, RANDY. 9/13/52. Singer. The Village People.

JONES, RAY. Oldham, England, 10/22/39. Bassist. Billy J. Kramer & The Dakotas.

JONES, RICKIE LEE. Chicago, IL, 11/8/54. Rock/jazz singer, songwriter.

JONES, SAM J. Chicago, IL, 8/12/54. Actor. *Flash Gordon*.

JONES, SHIRLEY. Smithton, PA, 3/31/34. Actor, married to Marty Ingels. *The Partridge Family*.

JONES, STEVE. London, England, 9/3/55. Guitarist. The Sex Pistols.

JONES, TERRY. Colwyn Bay, Wales, 2/1/42. Actor, director, writer. *Monty Python's Life of Brian*.

JONES, TOM (Tom Woodward). Pontypridd, Wales, 6/7/40. Pop singer.

JORDAN, LONNIE (Leroy Jordan). San Diego, CA, 11/21/48. Keyboardist, singer. War.

JOURARD, JEFF. 1955. Guitarist. The Motels.

JOURDAN, LOUIS (Louis Gendre). Marseilles, France, 6/19/19. Actor. *Gigi*.

JOYCE, MIKE. Manchester, England, 6/1/63. Drummer. The Smiths.

JOYNER-KERSEE, JACKIE. St. Louis, IL, 3/3/62. Track athlete. Olympic gold medalist.

JUDD, NAOMI (Diana Judd). Ashland, KY, 1/11/46. Country singer, mother of Wynonna and Ashley. The Judds.

JUMP, GORDON. Dayton, OH, 4/1/32. Actor. Arthur Carlson on *WKRP in Cincinnati*.

JUSTMAN, SETH. Washington, DC, 1/27/51. Keyboardist, singer. The J. Geils Band.

KAHN, MADELINE. Boston, MA, 9/29/42. Actor. *Blazing Saddles*.

KALE, JIM. 8/11/43. Bassist. The Guess Who.

KANE, BIG DADDY. New York, NY, 9/10/68. Rap artist, songwriter. "Long Live the Kane."

KANE, CAROL. Cleveland, OH, 6/18/52. Actor. Simka Graves on *Taxi*.

KANTNER, PAUL. San Francisco, CA, 3/12/42. Guitarist. Jefferson Airplane; Starship.

KAPRISKY, VALERIE. Paris, France, 1963. Actor. *Breathless*.

KARPOV, ANATOLY. Zlatoust, Russia, 5/23/51. Chess player. International grandmaster, world champion.

KARRAS, ALEX. Gary, IN, 7/15/35. Former football player, actor. *Webster*.

KASPAROV, GARRY. Baku, Russia, 4/13/63. Chess player. International grandmaster, world champion.

KATH, TERRY. Chicago, IL, 1/31/46. Guitarist. Chicago.

KATT, WILLIAM. Los Angeles, CA, 2/16/55. Actor, son of Barbara Hale. *The Greatest American Hero*.

KATZ, STEVE. New York, NY, 5/9/45. Guitarist, harmonicist, singer. Blood, Sweat & Tears.

KAUKONEN, JORMA. Washington, DC, 12/23/40. Guitarist. Jefferson Airplane; Hot Tuna.

KAVNER, JULIE. Los Angeles, CA, 9/7/51. Actor. Voice of Marge Simpson on *The Simpsons*; *Rhoda*.

KAY, JOHN (Joachim Krauledat). Tilsit, Germany, 4/12/44. Guitarist, singer. Steppenwolf.

KAYE, STUBBY. New York, NY, 11/11/18. Actor. *Guys and Dolls*.

KAYLAN, HOWARD (Howard Kaplan). New York, NY, 6/22/47. Singer, saxophonist. The Turtles.

KAZURINSKY, TIM. Johnstown, PA, 3/3/50. Actor. *Saturday Night Live*.

KEACH, STACY (William Keach Jr.). Savannah, GA, 6/2/41. Actor. *Mickey Spillane's Mike Hammer*.

KEANE, BIL. Philadelphia, PA, 10/5/22. Cartoonist. *The Family Circus*.

KEATON, DIANE (Diane Hall). Los Angeles, CA, 1/5/46. Actor. *Annie Hall*.

KEATON, MICHAEL (Michael Douglas). Coraopolis, PA, 9/9/51. Actor. *Batman*.

KEEBLE, JON. London, England, 7/6/59. Drummer. Spandau Ballet.

KEEL, HOWARD (Harold Leek). Gillespie, IL, 4/13/17. Actor. Clayton Farlow on *Dallas*.

KEENAN, BRIAN. New York, NY, 1/28/44. Drummer. The Chambers Brothers; Manfred Mann.

KEESHAN, BOB (Robert James Keeshan). Lynbrook, NY, 6/27/27. TV personality, author. *Captain Kangaroo*.

KEFFORD, ACE (Christopher Kefford). Mosely, England, 12/10/46. Bassist. The Move.

KEITH, BRIAN. Bayonne, NJ, 11/14/21. Actor. Bill Davis on *Family Affair*.

KEITH, DAVID LEMUEL. Knoxville, TN, 5/8/54. Actor. *An Officer and a Gentleman*.

KELLER, MARTHE. Basel, Switzerland, 1/28/45. Actor. *Marathon Man*.

KELLERMAN, SALLY. Long Beach, CA, 6/2/37. Actor. Hot Lips in the movie *M*A*S*H*.

KELLEY, DEFOREST. Atlanta, GA, 1/20/20. Actor. Dr. Leonard "Bones" McCoy on *Star Trek*.

KELLEY, KITTY. Spokane, WA, 4/4/42. Unauthorized biographer.

KELLING, GRAEME. Paisley, Scotland, 4/4/57. Guitarist. Deacon Blue.

KELLY, GENE. Pittsburgh, PA, 8/23/12. Actor, dancer, director. *Singin' in the Rain*.

KELLY, MARK. Dublin, Ireland, 4/9/61. Keyboardist. Marillion.

KELLY, MOIRA. 1968. Actor. *The Cutting Edge.*

KEMP, GARY. Islington, England, 10/16/60. Guitarist, brother of Martin. Spandau Ballet.

KEMP, MARTIN. London, England, 10/10/61. Bassist, brother of Gary. Spandau Ballet.

KENDRICKS, EDDIE. Birmingham, AL, 12/17/39. Singer. The Temptations.

KENNEDY, GEORGE. New York, NY, 2/18/25. Actor. *Cool Hand Luke.*

KENNEDY, TED. Brookline, MA, 2/22/32. Politician, brother of John and Robert.

KENNIBREW, DEE DEE (Dolores Henry). Brooklyn, NY, 1945. Singer. The Crystals.

KENNY G (Kenneth Gorelick). Seattle, WA, 6/5/56. Jazz saxophone player.

KENSIT, PATSY. London, England, 3/4/68. Actor, married to Jim Kerr. *Lethal Weapon 2.*

KERNS, JOANNA (Joanna De Varona). San Francisco, CA, 2/12/53. Actor. Maggie Seaver on *Growing Pains.*

KERR, DEBORAH. Helensburg, Scotland, 9/30/21. Actor. *The King and I.*

KERR, JIM. Glasgow, Scotland, 7/9/59. Singer, married to Patsy Kensit. Simple Minds.

KERRIGAN, NANCY. Stoneham, MA, 10/13/69. Figure skater. Olympic silver medalist, victim of knee attack.

KHAN, CHAKA (Yvette Marie Stevens). Great Lakes, IL, 3/23/53. Singer. Rufus.

KIDD, JOHNNY (Frederick Heath). London, England, 12/23/39. Singer. Johnny Kidd & The Pirates.

KIDDER, MARGOT. Yellow Knife, Canada, 10/17/48. Actor. Lois Lane in *Superman.*

KIEL, RICHARD. Detroit, MI, 9/13/39. Actor. Jaws in *The Spy Who Loved Me.*

KILPATRICK, JAMES JR. Oklahoma City, OK, 11/1/20. Journalist. *60 Minutes.*

KIMBALL, BOBBY (Bobby Toteaux). Vinton, LA, 3/29/47. Lead singer. Toto.

KING, ALAN (Irwin Kniberg). Brooklyn, NY, 12/26/27. Producer, comedian. *The Andersen Tapes.*

KING, B. B. (Riley King). Itta Bena, MS, 9/16/25. Legendary blues guitarist, singer, songwriter.

KING, BEN E. (Ben E. Nelson). Henderson, NC, 9/23/38. Singer. The Drifters.

KING, BILLIE JEAN. Long Beach, CA, 11/22/43. Tennis player.

KING, CAROLE (Carole Klein). Brooklyn, NY, 2/9/42. Singer, songwriter.

KING, CORETTA SCOTT. Marion, AL, 4/27/27. Author, lecturer, widow of Martin Luther King Jr.

KING, DON. Cleveland, OH, 8/20/31. Boxing promoter.

KING, MARK. Isle of Wight, England, 10/20/58. Singer, bassist. Level 42.

KING, PERRY. Alliance, OH, 4/30/48. Actor. Cody Allen on *Riptide.*

KING, WILLIAM. Alabama, 1/30/49. Trumpeter, keyboardist. The Commodores.

KINGSLEY, BEN (Krishna Bhanji). Snaiton, England, 12/31/43. Actor. *Gandhi.*

KINSKI, NASTASSJA (Nastassja Nakszynski). Berlin, Germany, 1/24/60. Actor, daughter of Klaus Kinski. *Cat People.*

KIRBY, BRUNO (Bruce Kirby Jr.). New York, NY, 4/28/49. Actor. *City Slickers.*

KIRKE, SIMON. Wales, 7/28/49. Drummer. Bad Company; Free.

KIRKLAND, SALLY. New York, NY, 10/31/44. Actor. *Anna.*

KIRKMAN, TERRY. Salina, KS, 12/12/41. Singer, keyboardist. The Association.

KIRKPATRICK, JEANE. Duncan, OK, 11/19/26. Diplomat. Former U.S. representative to the U.N.

KISSINGER, HENRY. Fuerth, Germany, 5/27/23. Richard Nixon's secretary of state.

KITT, EARTHA. North, SC, 1/26/28. Actor, singer. *The Mark of the Hawk.*

KLEIN, DANNY. New York, NY, 5/13/46. Bassist. The J. Geils Band.

KLEIN, ROBERT. New York, NY, 2/8/42. Actor. *Comedy Tonight.*

KLEMPERER, WERNER. Cologne, Germany, 3/22/20. Actor. Colonel Wilhelm Klink on *Hogan's Heroes.*

KLINE, KEVIN. St. Louis, MO, 10/24/47. Actor, married to Phoebe Cates. *The Big Chill.*

KLUGMAN, JACK. Philadelphia, PA, 4/27/22. Actor. Oscar Madison on *The Odd Couple.*

KNIGHT, GLADYS. Atlanta, GA, 5/28/44. Singer. Gladys Knight & The Pips.

KNIGHT, JONATHAN. Boston, MA, 11/29/69. Singer. New Kids on the Block.

KNIGHT, JORDAN. Boston, MA, 5/17/71. Singer. New Kids on the Block.

KNIGHT, MERALD. Atlanta, GA, 9/4/42. Singer. Gladys Knight & The Pips.

KNIGHT, MICHAEL E. Princeton, NJ, 5/7/59. Actor. Tad Martin on *All My Children.*

KNIGHT, SHIRLEY. Goessell, KS, 7/5/36. Actor. *The Dark at the Top of the Stairs.*

KNIGHTS, DAVE. Islington, England, 6/28/45. Bassist. Procol Harum.

KNOPFLER, DAVID. Glasgow, Scotland, 12/27/52. Guitarist. Dire Straits.

KNOPFLER, MARK. Glasgow, Scotland, 8/12/49. Singer, guitarist. Dire Straits.

KNOTTS, DON. Morgantown, WV, 7/21/24. Actor. Barney Fife on *The Andy Griffith Show.*

KNOWLES, PATRIC (Reginald Lawrence Knowles). Horsforth, England, 11/11/11. Actor. *How Green Was My Valley.*

KNOX, BUDDY (Wayne Knox). Happy, TX, 4/14/33. Rock/country singer, songwriter.

KNUDSEN, KEITH. Ames, IA, 10/18/52. Drummer, singer. The Doobie Brothers.

KOCH, ED. New York, NY, 12/12/24. Former mayor of New York.

KOENIG, WALTER. Chicago, IL, 9/14/36. Actor, writer, director, producer. Pavel Chekov on *Star Trek.*

KOOL ROCK. (Damon Wimbley). 11/4/66. Rap artist. Fat Boys.

KOPELL, BERNIE. New York, NY, 6/21/33. Actor. Dr. Adam Bricker on *The Love Boat.*

KORMAN, HARVEY. Chicago, IL, 2/15/27. Actor. *The Carol Burnett Show.*

KOSSOFF, PAUL. London, England, 9/14/50. Guitarist. Free.

KOTTO, YAPHET. New York, NY, 11/15/37. Actor. *Live and Let Die.*

KRABBE, JEROEN. Amsterdam, The Netherlands, 12/5/44. Actor. *The Fugitive.*

KRAMER, BILLY J. (Billy J. Ashton). Bootle, England, 8/19/43. Singer. Billy J. Kramer & The Dakotas.

KRAMER, JOEY. New York, NY, 6/21/50. Drummer. Aerosmith.

KRANTZ, JUDITH. New York, NY, 1/9/28. Novelist. *Scruples.*

KRAVITZ, LENNY. New York, NY, 5/26/64. Singer, songwriter, formerly married to Lisa Bonet. "Are You Gonna Go My Way?"

KREUTZMANN, BILL JR. Palo Alto, CA, 5/7/46. Drummer. Grateful Dead.

KRIEGER, ROBBIE. Los Angeles, CA, 1/8/46. Guitarist. The Doors.

KRIGE, ALICE. Upington, South Africa, 6/28/55. Actor. *Chariots of Fire.*

KRISTOFFERSON, KRIS. Brownsville, TX, 6/22/36. Singer, songwriter, actor. *Amerika.*

KUBRICK, STANLEY. The Bronx, NY, 7/26/28. Director, producer, writer. *2001: A Space Odyssey.*

KUHLKE, NORMAN. Liverpool, England, 6/17/42. Drummer. The Swinging Blue Jeans.

KURALT, CHARLES. Wilmington, NC, 9/10/34. News reporter, commentator. *On the Road with Charles Kuralt.*

KURTZ, SWOOSIE. Omaha, NE, 9/6/44. Actor. *Sisters.*

KWAN, NANCY. Hong Kong, 5/19/39. Actor. *The World of Suzie Wong.*

LABELLE, PATTI (Patricia Holt). Philadelphia, PA, 5/24/44. Pop/soul singer.

LADD, CHERYL (Cheryl Stoppelmoor). Huron, SD, 7/12/51. Actor. Kris Munroe on *Charlie's Angels.*

LADD, DIANE (Diane Ladner). Meridian, MS, 11/29/32. Actor, mother of Laura Dern. *Alice Doesn't Live Here Anymore.*

LAHTI, CHRISTINE. Birmingham, MI, 4/4/50. Actor. *Swing Shift.*

LAINE, DENNY (Brian Hines). Jersey, England, 10/29/44. Singer, guitarist. The Moody Blues.

LAKE, GREG. Bournemouth, England, 11/10/48. Bassist, singer. Emerson, Lake & Palmer; King Crimson.

LAMARR, HEDY (Hedwig Kiesler). Vienna, Austria, 11/9/13. Actor. *Ecstasy.*

LAMAS, LORENZO. Los Angeles, CA, 1/20/58. Actor. Lance Cumson on *Falcon Crest.*

LAMBERT, CHRISTOPHER. New York, NY, 3/29/57. Actor. *Greystoke: The Legend of Tarzan, Lord of the Apes.*

LAMM, ROBERT. New York, NY, 10/13/44. Singer, keyboardist. Chicago.

LAMOUR, DOROTHY (Mary Dorothy Slaton). New Orleans, LA, 12/10/14. Actor. *Road to Singapore.*

LANCASTER, ALAN. London, England, 2/7/49. Bassist. Status Quo.

LANDAU, MARTIN. Brooklyn, NY, 6/20/31. Actor. *Mission: Impossible.*

LANDERS, AUDREY. Philadelphia, PA, 7/18/59. Actor. Afton Cooper on *Dallas.*

LANDESBERG, STEVE. The Bronx, NY, 11/3/45. Actor. Detective Arthur Dietrich on *Barney Miller.*

LANDIS, JOHN. Chicago, IL, 8/3/50. Director. *Twilight Zone—The Movie.*

LANE, ABBE. Brooklyn, NY, 12/14/35. Actor, formerly married to Xavier Cugat. *Xavier Cugat Show.*

LANE, CHARLES. New York, NY, 12/5/53. Director. *Sidewalk Stories.*

LANE, DIANE. New York, NY, 1/22/65. Actor. *Rumble Fish.*

LANE, RONNIE. Plaistow, England, 4/1/46. Bassist. The Small Faces.

LANG, BOB. Manchester, England, 1/10/46. Bassist. Wayne Fontana & The Mindbenders.

LANGE, HOPE. Redding Ridge, CT, 11/28/31. Actor. *The Ghost and Mrs. Muir.*

LANGE, TED. Oakland, CA, 1/5/47. Actor. Isaac Washington on *The Love Boat.*

LANGELLA, FRANK. Bayonne, NJ, 1/1/40. Actor. *Dracula.*

LANIER, ALLEN. 6/25/46. Guitarist, keyboardist. Blue Öyster Cult.

LANSING, ROBERT (Robert Brown). San Diego, CA, 6/5/29. Actor. *The Man Who Never Was.*

LAPREAD, RONALD. Alabama, 9/4/50. Bassist, trumpeter. The Commodores.

LARDIE, MICHAEL. 9/8/58. Musician. Great White.

LARUE, FLORENCE. Pennsylvania, 2/4/44. Singer. The 5th Dimension.

LASSER, LOUISE. New York, NY, 4/11/39. Actor, formerly married to Woody Allen. *Bananas.*

LAUDER, ESTEE. New York, NY, 7/1/08. Fashion designer.

LAUPER, CYNDI. New York, NY, 6/20/53. Singer, actor, professional wrestling promoter. *She's So Unusual.*

LAUREN, RALPH (Ralph Lifshitz). Bronx, NY, 10/14/39. Fashion designer.

LAURENT, YVES SAINT. Oran, Algeria, 8/1/36. Fashion designer.

LAURIE, PIPER (Rosetta Jacobs). Detroit, MI, 1/22/32. Actor. Mother in *Carrie.*

LAVERN, ROGER (Roger Jackson). Kidderminster, England, 11/11/38. Keyboardist. The Tornados.

LAVIN, LINDA. Portland, ME, 10/15/37. Actor, singer. *Alice.*

LAWRENCE, CAROL (Carol Laraia). Melrose Park, IL, 9/5/35. Actor, singer. *West Side Story.*

LAWRENCE, JOEY. Montgomery, PA, 4/20/76. Actor, singer. *Blossom.*

LAWRENCE, VICKI. Inglewood, CA, 3/26/49. Actor. *Mama's Family.*

LAWSON, LEIGH. Atherston, England, 7/21/45. Actor. *Tess.*

LAWTON, JOHN. 6/11/46. Singer. Uriah Heep.

LEA, JIMMY. Melbourne Arms, England, 6/14/52. Bassist, keyboardist, violinist. Slade.

LEACH, ROBIN. London, England, 8/29/41. TV host. *Lifestyles of the Rich and Famous.*

LEACHMAN, CLORIS. Des Moines, IA, 4/30/26. Actor. Phyllis Lyndstrom on *The Mary Tyler Moore Show.*

LEADON, BERNIE. Minneapolis, MN, 7/19/47. Guitarist, singer. The Eagles.

LEAR, FRANCES. Hudson, NY, 7/14/23. Magazine editor, formerly married to Norman. Founder of *Lear's.*

LEAR, NORMAN. New Haven, CT, 7/27/22. Producer, director, formerly married to Frances. *All in the Family.*

LEARNED, MICHAEL. Washington, DC, 4/9/39. Actor. Olivia on *The Waltons.*

LEBON, SIMON. Bushey, England, 10/27/58. Lead singer. Duran Duran.

LEE, ALVIN. Nottingham, England, 12/19/44. Guitarist, singer. Ten Years After.

LEE, ARTHUR. Memphis, TN, 1945. Guitarist, singer. Love.

LEE, BARBARA. New York, NY, 5/16/47. Singer. The Chiffons.

LEE, BEVERLY. Passaic, NJ, 8/3/41. Singer. The Shirelles.

LEE, BRENDA (Brenda Tarpley). Lithonia, GA, 12/11/44. Singer.

LEE, GEDDY. Willowdale, Canada, 7/29/53. Singer, bassist. Rush.

LEE, JASON SCOTT. Los Angeles, CA, 1966. Actor. *Dragon: The Bruce Lee Story.*

LEE, JOHNNY. Texas City, TX, 7/3/46. Singer. "Lookin' for Love."

LEE, MICHELE (Michele Dusiak). Los Angeles, CA, 6/24/42. Actor. Karen Fairgate MacKenzie on *Knots Landing.*

LEE, PEGGY (Norma Delores Egstrom). Jamestown, ND, 5/26/20. Actor, singer. *The Jazz Singer.*

LEE, RIC. Cannock, England, 10/20/45. Drummer. Ten Years After.

LEE, STAN. New York, NY, 12/28/22. Artist, writer, Marvel Comics legend.

LEE, TOMMY (Tommy Bass). Athens, Greece, 10/3/62. Drummer, married to Pamela Anderson, formerly married to Heather Locklear. Mötley Crüe.

LEEDS, GARY. Glendale, CA, 9/3/44. Drummer. The Walker Brothers.

LEESE, HOWARD. Los Angeles, CA, 6/13/51. Keyboardist, guitarist. Heart.

LEEVES, JANE. East Grinstead, England, 4/13/63. Actor. Daphne Moon on *Frasier.*

LEEWAY, JOE. London, England, 1957. Percussionist. Thompson Twins.

LEGUIZAMO, JOHN. Bogota, Columbia, 7/22/65. Actor. *Carlito's Way.*

LEIBMAN, RON. New York, NY, 10/11/37. Actor. *Kaz.*

LEIGH, JANET (Jeannette Helen Morrison). Merced, CA, 7/6/27. Actor, mother of Jamie Lee Curtis. *Psycho.*

LEITCH, DONOVAN. 8/16/68. Actor, son of folk singer Donovan, brother of Ione Skye.

LEMAT, PAUL. Rahway, NJ, 9/22/52. Actor. *American Graffiti.*

LEMIEUX, MARIO. Montreal, Canada, 10/5/65. NHL hockey player. Pittsburgh Penguins.

LEMMON, CHRIS. Los Angeles, CA, 1/22/54. Actor, son of Jack Lemmon. *Swing Shift.*

LEMMON, JACK. Boston, MA, 2/8/25. Actor, father of Chris Lemmon. *Some Like It Hot.*

LEMMY (Ian Kilmister). Stoke-on-Trent, England, 12/24/45. Bassist, singer. Motorhead.

LEMON, MEADOWLARK. Wilmington, NC, 4/25/32. Basketball player. Harlem Globetrotters.

LENNON, JULIAN (John Charles Julian Lennon). Liverpool, England,

4/8/63. Singer, songwriter, son of John Lennon.

LENNOX, ANNIE. Aberdeen, Scotland, 12/25/54. Singer, songwriter. Eurythmics.

LEONARD, ROBERT SEAN. Westwood, NJ, 2/28/69. Actor. *Dead Poets Society.*

LEONARD, SHELDON (Sheldon Bershad). New York, NY, 2/22/07. Producer, actor. *It's a Wonderful Life.*

LEONARD, SUGAR RAY. Wilmington, NC, 5/17/56. Boxer.

LERNER, MICHAEL. Brooklyn, NY, 6/22/41. Actor. *Barton Fink.*

LESH, PHIL (Phil Chapman). Berkeley, CA, 3/15/40. Bassist. Grateful Dead.

LESTER, ROBERT "SQUIRREL." 1/13/30. Singer. The Chi-Lites.

LEVERT, EDDIE. Canton, OH, 6/16/42. Singer. The O'Jays.

LEVIN, DRAKE. Guitarist. Paul Revere & The Raiders.

LEVY, EUGENE. Hamilton, Canada, 12/17/46. Actor, writer. *SCTV.*

LEWIS, AL (Alexander Meister). New York, NY, 4/30/10. Actor. *The Munsters.*

LEWIS, CARL (Carl Frederick Carlton). Birmingham, AL, 7/1/61. Track athlete. Olympic gold medalist.

LEWIS, EMMANUEL. New York, NY, 3/9/71. Actor. Webster Long on *Webster.*

LEWIS, GARY (Gary Levitch). New York, NY, 7/31/46. Singer, drummer, son of Jerry Lewis. Gary Lewis & The Playboys.

LEWIS, HUEY (Hugh Cregg III). New York, NY, 7/5/50. Singer. Huey Lewis & The News.

LEWIS, JERRY (Joseph Levitch). Newark, NJ, 3/16/26. Actor, father of Gary Lewis. *The Nutty Professor.*

LEWIS, JERRY LEE. Ferriday, LA, 9/29/35. Legendary rock keyboardist, singer, songwriter.

LEWIS, PETER. Los Angeles, CA, 7/15/45. Guitarist, singer. Moby Grape.

LIDDY, G. GORDON. New York, NY, 11/30/30. Watergate participant, talk show host. *The G. Gordon Liddy Show.*

LIFESON, ALEX. Fernie, Canada, 8/27/53. Guitarist. Rush.

LIGHT, JUDITH. Trenton, NJ, 2/9/49. Actor. Angela on *Who's the Boss?*

LIGHTFOOT, GORDON. Orillia, Canada, 11/17/38. Folk guitarist, singer, songwriter.

LINCOLN, ABBEY (Anna Marie Woolridge). Chicago, IL, 8/6/30. Singer, actor. *For Love of Ivy.*

LINDEN, HAL (Hal Lipschitz). The Bronx, NY, 3/20/31. Actor. *Barney Miller.*

LINDES, HAL. Monterey, CA, 6/30/53. Guitarist. Dire Straits.

LINDSAY, MARK. Eugene, OR, 3/9/42. Singer, saxophonist. Paul Revere & The Raiders.

LINDUP, MIKE. 3/17/59. Keyboardist, singer. Level 42.

LINKLETTER, ART. Moose Jaw, Canada, 7/17/12. TV personality. *People Are Funny.*

LINN-BAKER, MARK. St. Louis, MO, 6/17/54. Actor. Cousin Larry Appleton on *Perfect Strangers.*

LINVILLE, LARRY. Ojai, CA, 9/29/39. Actor. Frank Burns on *M*A*S*H.*

LIOTTA, RAY. Newark, NJ, 12/18/55. Actor. *GoodFellas.*

LITHGOW, JOHN. Rochester, NY, 10/19/45. Actor. *The World According to Garp.*

LITTLE EVA (Eva Narcissus Boyd). Bellhaven, NC, 6/29/45. Singer. "The Loco-Motion."

LITTLE RICHARD (Richard Penniman). Macon, GA, 12/5/35. Legendary singer, songwriter.

LIVGREN, KERRY. Kansas, 9/18/49. Guitarist. Kansas.

L.L. COOL J (James Todd Smith). New York, NY, 1/14/68. Rap artist.

LLOYD, CHRISTOPHER. Stamford, CT, 10/22/38. Actor. "Reverend Jim" Ignatowski on *Taxi.*

LLOYD, EMILY. London, England, 9/29/70. Actor. *Wish You Were Here.*

LOCKE, JOHN. Los Angeles, CA, 9/25/43. Keyboardist. Spirit.

LOCKE, SONDRA. Shelbyville, TN, 5/28/47. Actor. *The Gauntlet.*

LOCKHART, JUNE. New York, NY, 6/25/25. Actor. *Lost in Space.*

LOCKWOOD, GARY. Van Nuys, CA, 2/21/37. Actor. *2001: A Space Odyssey.*

LOCORRIERE, DENNIS. Union City, NJ, 6/13/49. Lead singer. Dr. Hook.

LODGE, JOHN. Birmingham, England, 7/20/45. Bassist. The Moody Blues.

LOFGREN, NILS. Chicago, IL, 6/21/51. Guitarist, keyboardist, singer, songwriter.

LOGGIA, ROBERT. Staten Island, NY, 1/3/30. Actor. *Mancuso, FBI.*

LOGGINS, KENNY. Everett, WA, 1/7/48. Singer, songwriter.

LOLLOBRIGIDA, GINA. Subiaco, Italy, 7/4/27. Actor. *Circus.*

LOM, HERBERT. Prague, Czechoslovakia, 1/9/17. Actor. *Spartacus.*

LONG, SHELLEY. Ft. Wayne, IN, 8/23/49. Actor. Diane Chambers on *Cheers.*

LONGMUIR, ALAN. Edinburgh, Scotland, 6/20/53. Bassist. The Bay City Rollers.

LONGMUIR, DEREK. Edinburgh, Scotland, 3/19/55. Drummer. The Bay City Rollers.

LORD, JACK (Jack Ryan). New York, NY, 12/30/30. Actor. *Hawaii Five-O.*

LORD, JON. Leicester, England, 6/9/41. Keyboardist. Deep Purple.

LORDS, TRACY (Norma Kuzma). Steubenville, OH, 5/7/68. Actor, former porn star. *Melrose Place.*

LOREN, SOPHIA (Sophia Scicolone). Rome, Italy, 9/20/34. Actor. *Two Women.*

LOUGANIS, GREG. El Cajon, CA, 1/29/60. Diver. Olympic gold medalist.

LOUGHNANE, LEE. Chicago, IL, 10/21/46. Trumpeter. Chicago.

LOUISE, TINA (Tina Blacker). New York, NY, 2/11/34. Actor. Ginger Grant on *Gilligan's Island.*

LOVE, MIKE. Baldwin Hills, CA, 3/15/41. Singer. The Beach Boys.

LOVELADY, DAVE. Liverpool, England, 10/16/42. Drummer. The Fourmost.

LOVELESS, PATTY. Belcher Holler, KY, 1/4/57 Singer.

LOWE, CHAD. Dayton, OH, 1/15/68. Actor, brother of Rob Lowe. *Life Goes On.*

LOWE, CHRIS. Blackpool, England, 10/4/59. Keyboardist. Pet Shop Boys.

LUCIA, PETER. 2/2/47. Drummer. Tommy James & The Shondells.

LUCKINBILL, LAURENCE. Fort Smith, AR, 11/21/34. Actor, married to Lucie Arnaz. *The Boys in the Band.*

LUDLUM, ROBERT. New York, NY, 5/25/27. Novelist, actor, producer. *The Gemini Contenders.*

LUFT, LORNA. Los Angeles, CA, 11/21/52. Actor, half-sister of Liza Minnelli, daughter of Judy Garland. *Where the Boys Are.*

LUKATHER, STEVE. Los Angeles, CA, 10/21/57. Lead guitarist. Toto.

LULU (Marie Lawrie). Glasgow, Scotland, 11/3/48. Singer, actor. *To Sir with Love.*

LUNDGREN, DOLPH. Stockholm, Sweden, 11/3/59. Actor. *Rocky IV.*

LUPONE, PATTI. Northport, NY, 4/21/49. Actor. *Life Goes On.*

LUPUS, PETER. Indianapolis, IN, 6/17/37. Actor. Willie Armitage on *Mission: Impossible.*

LWIN, ANNABELLA (Myant Aye). Rangoon, Burma, 10/31/65. Singer. Bow Wow Wow.

LYDON, JOHN. London, England, 1/31/56. Singer, a.k.a. Johnny Rotten. The Sex Pistols; Public Image Ltd.

LYNCH, STAN. Gainesville, FL, 5/21/55. Drummer. Tom Petty & The Heartbreakers.

LYNGSTAD, FRIDA (Anni-Frid Lyngstad). Narvik, Sweden, 11/15/45. Singer. Abba.

LYNNE, JEFF. Birmingham, England, 12/30/47. Singer, guitarist. Electric Light Orchestra (ELO).

LYNOTT, PHIL. Dublin, Ireland, 8/20/51. Singer, bassist. Thin Lizzy.

LYONS, LEO. Standbridge, England, 11/30/43. Bassist. Ten Years After.

LYTE, MC. New York, NY, 1971. Rap artist.

MA, YO-YO. Paris, France, 10/7/55. Cello virtuoso.

MACARTHUR, JAMES. Los Angeles, CA, 12/8/37. Actor, son of Helen Hayes. Danny Williams on *Hawaii Five-O.*

MACCHIO, RALPH. Long Island, NY, 11/4/62. Actor. *The Karate Kid.*

MACCORKINDALE, SIMON. Cambridge, England, 2/12/52. Actor. *Falcon Crest.*

MACDONALD, EDDIE. St. Asaph, Wales, 11/1/59. Bassist. The Alarm.

MACDONALD, ROBIN. Nairn, Scotland, 7/18/43. Guitarist. Billy J. Kramer & The Dakotas.

MACGOWAN, SHANE. Kent, England, 12/25/57. Guitarist, singer. The Pogues.

MACGRAW, ALI. Pound Ridge, NY, 4/1/38. Actor. *Love Story.*

MACKAY, ANDY. London, England, 7/23/46. Saxophonist, woodwindist. Roxy Music.

MACKAY, DUNCAN. 7/26/50. Keyboardist. Steve Harley & Cockney Rebel.

MACLEAN, BRYAN. Los Angeles, CA, 1947. Guitarist, singer. Love.

MACLEOD, GAVIN. Mt. Kisco, NY, 2/28/31. Actor. Captain Stubing of *The Love Boat.*

MACNAUGHTON, ROBERT. New York, NY, 12/19/66. Actor. *E.T., the Extra-Terrestrial.*

MACNEE, PATRICK. London, England, 2/6/22. Actor. *The Avengers.*

MACNEIL, ROBERT. Montreal, Canada, 1/19/31. Broadcast journalist. *MacNeil/Lehrer Report.*

MACNELLY, JEFF. New York, NY, 9/17/47. Cartoonist. *Shoe.*

MACNICOL, PETER. Dallas, TX, 4/10/54. Actor. *Sophie's Choice.*

MADIGAN, AMY. Chicago, IL, 9/11/51. Actor. *Places in the Heart.*

MADSEN, MICHAEL. Chicago, IL, 1959. Actor, brother of Virginia. *Reservoir Dogs.*

MADSEN, VIRGINIA. Winnetka, IL, 9/11/63. Actor, sister of Michael. *Electric Dreams.*

MAGNUSON, ANN. Charleston, WV, 1/4/56. Actor. Catherine Hughes on *Anything but Love.*

MAGUIRE, LES. Wallasey, England, 12/27/41. Keyboardist, saxophonist. Gerry & The Pacemakers.

MAHONEY, JOHN. Manchester, England, 6/20/40. Actor. Father of Dr. Crane on *Cheers* and *Frasier.*

MAJORS, LEE (Harvey Lee Yeary II). Wyandotte, MI, 4/23/40. Actor, formerly married to Farrah Fawcett. *The Six Million Dollar Man.*

MAKEPEACE, CHRIS. Montreal, Canada, 4/22/64. Actor. *My Bodyguard.*

MAKO (Makoto Iwamatsu). Kobe, Japan, 12/10/33. Actor. *The Sand Pebbles.*

MALDEN, KARL (Mladen Sekulovich). Gary, IN, 3/22/14. Actor, American Express

spokesperson. *The Streets of San Francisco.*

MALONE, DOROTHY. Chicago, IL, 1/30/25. Actor. *Written on the Wind.*

MALTIN, LEONARD. New York, NY, 12/18/50. Film critic. *Entertainment Tonight.*

MANDEL, HOWIE. Toronto, Canada, 11/29/55. Actor. Dr. Wayne Fiscus on *St. Elsewhere.*

MANDELA, NELSON. Umtata, South Africa, 7/18/18. President of South Africa.

MANDELA, WINNIE. Transkei, South Africa, 9/26/34. Political activist, formerly married to Nelson Mandela.

MANDRELL, BARBARA. Houston, TX, 12/25/48. Country singer. Barbara Mandrell & The Mandrell Sisters.

MANETTI, LARRY. Chicago, IL, 7/23/47. Actor. Rick on *Magnum, P. I.*

MANN, MANFRED (Michael Lubowitz). Johannesburg, South Africa, 10/21/40. Keyboardist. Manfred Mann.

MANN, TERRENCE. Kentucky, 1945. Actor. *Les Misérables.*

MANOFF, DINAH. New York, NY, 1/25/58. Actor, daughter of Lee Grant. Carol Weston on *Empty Nest.*

MANSON, CHARLES. Cincinnati, OH, 11/11/34. Murderer, cult leader.

MANTEGNA, JOE. Chicago, IL, 11/13/47. Actor. *The Godfather, Part III.*

MANZANERA, PHIL. London, England, 1/31/51. Guitarist. Roxy Music.

MANZAREK, RAY. Chicago, IL, 2/12/35. Keyboardist. The Doors.

MARCEAU, MARCEL. Strasbourg, France, 3/22/23. Actor, pantomimist. *Bip.*

MARCHAND, NANCY. Buffalo, NY, 6/19/28. Actor. *Lou Grant.*

MARCOS, IMELDA. Talcoban, the Philippines, 7/2/31. Wife of late Ferdinand Marcos.

MARCOVICCI, ANDREA. New York, NY, 11/18/48. Actor, singer. *Trapper John, MD.*

MARGO, MITCH. Brooklyn, NY, 5/25/47. Tenor singer. The Tokens.

MARGO, PHIL. Brooklyn, NY, 4/1/42. Bass singer. The Tokens.

MARIN, CHEECH (Richard Marin). Los Angeles, CA, 7/13/46. Actor, writer, former partner of Tommy Chong. *Up in Smoke.*

MARINARO, ED. New York, NY, 3/31/50. Actor, football player. *Hill Street Blues.*

MARK, MARKY (Mark Wahlberg). Dorchester, MA, 6/5/71. Rap artist, Calvin Klein underwear model, brother of Donny Wahlberg.

MARLEY, ZIGGY (David Marley). Jamaica, 1968. Singer, songwriter, son of Bob Marley. Ziggy Marley & The Melody Makers.

MARR, JOHNNY. Manchester, England, 10/31/63. Guitarist. The Smiths.

MARRIOTT, STEVE. Bow, England, 1/30/47. Singer, guitarist. The Small Faces.

MARS, MICK (Bob Deal). Terre Haute, IN, 4/4/55. Guitarist. Mötley Crüe.

MARSALIS, BRANFORD. Breaux Bridge, LA, 8/26/60. Jazz musician, bandleader, saxophonist. Brother of Wynton Marsalis. Former musical director of *The Tonight Show.*

MARSDEN, FREDDIE. Liverpool, England, 10/23/40. Drummer. Gerry & The Pacemakers.

MARSDEN, GERRY. Liverpool, England, 9/24/42. Singer, lead guitarist. Gerry & The Pacemakers.

MARSH, IAN. Sheffield, England, 11/11/56. Keyboardist. The Human League; Heaven 17.

MARSHALL, E. G. (Everett Marshall). Owatonna, MN, 6/18/10. Actor. *Twelve Angry Men.*

MARSHALL, PETER (Pierre La Cock). Huntington, WV, 3/30/30. TV personality. Host of *The Hollywood Squares.*

MARTELL, VINCE. New York, NY, 11/11/45. Guitarist. Vanilla Fudge.

MARTIN, ANDREA. Portland, ME, 1/15/47. Writer, actor. *SCTV.*

MARTIN, DEAN (Dino Crocetti). Steubenville, OH, 6/17/17. Actor, singer. Ex-partner of Jerry Lewis.

MARTIN, DEWEY. Chesterville, Canada, 9/30/42. Singer, drummer. Buffalo Springfield.

MARTIN, DICK. Battle Creek, MI, 1/30/23. Actor. Cohost of *Laugh-In.*

MARTIN, JIM. Oakland, CA, 7/21/61. Guitarist. Faith No More.

MARTIN, PAMELA SUE. Westport, CT, 1/15/53. Actor. *Dynasty.*

MARTINDALE, WINK (Winston Conrad Martindale). Bells, TN, 12/4/34. TV personality. Host of *Tic Tac Dough.*

MARTINI, JERRY. Colorado, 10/1/43. Saxophonist. Sly & The Family Stone.

MARVIN, HANK (Brian Rankin). Newcastle, England, 10/28/41. Lead guitarist. The Shadows.

MARX, RICHARD. Chicago, IL, 9/16/63. Singer, songwriter.

MASON, DAVE. Worcester, England, 5/10/47. Singer, guitarist. Traffic.

MASON, JACKIE. Sheboygan, WI, 6/9/34. Actor. *Chicken Soup.*

MASON, MARSHA. St. Louis, MO, 4/3/42. Actor. *The Goodbye Girl.*

MASON, NICK. Birmingham, England, 1/27/45. Drummer. Pink Floyd.

MASSI, NICK (Nick Macioci). Newark, NJ, 9/19/35. Singer, bassist. The Four Seasons.

MASTELOTTO, PAT. 9/10/55. Drummer. Mr. Mister.

MASTERSON, MARY STUART. Los Angeles, CA, 6/28/66. Actor, daughter of Peter. *Fried Green Tomatoes.*

MASTERSON, PETER. Houston, TX, 6/1/34. Actor, writer, director, father of Mary Stuar. *The Exorcist.*

MASTRANGELO, CARLO. The Bronx, NY, 10/5/39. Bass singer. Dion & The Belmonts.

MASTRANTONIO, MARY ELIZABETH. Oak Park, IL, 11/17/58. Actor. *The Color of Money.*

MASTROIANNI, MARCELLO. Fontana Liri, Italy, 9/28/24. Actor. *La Dolce Vita.*

MASUR, RICHARD. New York, NY, 11/20/48. Actor. *One Day at a Time.*

MATHERS, JERRY. Sioux City, IA, 6/2/48. Actor. Theodore "Beaver" Cleaver on *Leave It to Beaver.*

MATHESON, TIM. Glendale, CA, 12/31/47. Actor. *National Lampoon's Animal House.*

MATHEWS, DENISE (formerly Vanity). Niagara, Canada, 1/3/63. Former singer and actor (a.k.a. D.D. Winters), now Christian Evangelist, bible student, married to L.A. Raiders defensive end Anthony Smith. *The Last Dragon.*

MATHIS, JOHNNY. San Francisco, CA, 9/30/35. Pop singer.

MATLOCK, GLENN. 8/27/56. Bassist. The Sex Pistols.

MATTHAU, WALTER (Walter Matuschanskayasky). New York, NY, 10/1/20. Actor. *The Odd Couple.*

MATTHEWS, IAN (Ian McDonald). Lincolnshire, England, 6/16/45. Singer, guitarist. Matthew's Southern Comfort.

MATURE, VICTOR. Louisville, KY, 1/29/15. Actor. *Samson and Delilah.*

MAUS, JOHN. New York, NY, 11/12/43. Singer. The Walker Brothers.

MAXFIELD, MIKE. Manchester, England, 2/23/44. Lead guitarist. Billy J. Kramer & The Dakotas.

MAY, BRIAN. Twickenham, England, 7/19/47. Guitarist. Queen.

MAY, ELAINE (Elaine Berlin). Philadelphia, PA, 4/21/32. Actor, director, writer. *Ishtar.*

MAY, PHIL. Dartford, England, 11/9/44. Singer. The Pretty Things.

MAYALL, JOHN. Macclesfield, England, 11/29/33. Singer, keyboardist, harmonicist. The Bluesbreakers.

MAYFIELD, CURTIS. Chicago, IL, 6/3/42. Singer, songwriter, record producer, paralyzed in an accident during a concert. "Superfly."

MAYS, WILLIE. Fairfield, AL, 5/6/31. Baseball player. San Francisco Giants.

MAZAR, DEBI. Queens, NY, 1964. Actor. *Civil Wars; L.A. Law.*

MAZURSKY, PAUL. Brooklyn, NY, 4/25/30. Producer, director, writer, actor. *Down and Out in Beverly Hills.*

M.C. ERIC. 8/19/70. Rap artist. Technotronic.

MCA (Adam Yauch). Brooklyn, NY, 8/15/67. Rap artist. The Beastie Boys.

MCBRIDE, MARTINA. Sharon, KS, 7/29/66. Singer.

MCCALLUM, DAVID. Glasgow, Scotland, 9/19/33. Actor. *The Great Escape.*

MCCARTHY, ANDREW. Westfield, NJ, 11/29/62. Actor. *Less Than Zero.*

MCCARTHY, KEVIN. Seattle, WA, 2/15/14. Actor. *Invasion of the Body Snatchers.*

MCCARTNEY, LINDA (Linda Eastman). New York, NY, 9/24/42. Pianist, singer, percussionist, photographer, married to Paul McCartney.

MCCARTY, JIM. Liverpool, England, 7/25/44. Drummer. The Yardbirds; Mitch Ryder & The Detroit Wheels.

MCCAULEY, JACKIE. Coleraine, Ireland, 12/14/46. Keyboardist. Them.

MCCAULEY, PATRICK. Northern Ireland, 3/17/44. Drummer. Them.

MCCLANAHAN, RUE. Healdton, OK, 2/21/34. Actor. Blanche Devereaux on *The Golden Girls.*

MCCLARY, THOMAS. 10/6/50. Lead guitarist. The Commodores.

MCCLINTON, DELBERT. Lubbock, TX, 11/4/40. Singer, songwriter.

MCCLURG, EDIE. Kansas City, MO, 7/23/50. Actor. *The Hogan Family.*

MCCLUSKEY, ANDY. Wirral, England, 6/24/59. Singer. Orchestral Manoeuvres in the Dark (OMD).

MCCOO, MARILYN. Jersey City, NJ, 9/30/43. Singer, cohost of *Solid Gold.* The 5th Dimension.

MCCREADY, MIKE. 4/5/66. Guitarist. Pearl Jam.

MCCULLOCH, IAN. Liverpool, England, 5/5/59. Singer. Echo & The Bunnymen.

MCDANIELS, DARRYL D. New York, NY, 1964. Rap artist. Run-D.M.C.

MCDONALD, COUNTRY JOE. El Monte, CA, 1/1/42. Guitarist, singer. Country Joe & The Fish.

MCDONALD, IAN. London, England, 6/25/46. Saxophonist. King Crimson.

MCDONALD, MICHAEL. St. Louis, MO, 12/2/52. Singer, songwriter, keyboardist. The Doobie Brothers.

MCDONALD, PAT. 8/6/52. Musician. Timbuk 3.

MCDONNELL, MARY. Ithaca, NY, 1952. Actor. *Dances with Wolves.*

MCDORMAND, FRANCES. Illinois, 1958. Actor. *Mississippi Burning.*

MCDOWALL, RODDY. London, England, 9/17/28. Actor. *Planet of the Apes.*

MCDOWELL, MALCOLM. Leeds, England, 6/19/43. Actor. *A Clockwork Orange.*

MCENROE, JOHN JR. Wiesbaden, Germany, 2/16/59. Tennis player.

Formerly married to Tatum O'Neal, relationship with Patty Smyth.

MCFERRIN, BOBBY. New York, NY, 3/11/50. Singer. "Don't Worry, Be Happy."

MCGAVIN, DARREN. Spokane, WA, 5/7/22. Actor. *The Night Stalker.*

MCGEOCH, JOHN. Guitarist. Siouxsie & The Banshees.

MCGILLIS, KELLY. Newport Beach, CA, 7/9/57. Actor. *Witness.*

MCGOVERN, ELIZABETH. Evanston, IL, 7/18/61. Actor. *Ragtime.*

MCGOVERN, MAUREEN. Youngstown, OH, 7/27/49. Singer, actor. "The Morning After."

MCGRAW, TIM. Start, LA, 5/1/67. Singer.

MCGUINN, ROGER "JIM" (James Joseph McGuinn). Chicago, IL, 7/13/42. Singer, guitarist. The Byrds.

MCGUINNESS, TOM. Wimbledon, England, 12/2/41. Bassist. Manfred Mann.

MCINTOSH, LORRAINE. Glasgow, Scotland, 5/13/64. Singer. Deacon Blue.

MCINTYRE, FRITZ. 9/2/58. Keyboardist. Simply Red.

MCINTYRE, JOE. Needham, MA, 12/31/73. Singer. New Kids on the Block.

MCINTYRE, ONNIE. Lennox Town, Scotland, 9/25/45. Guitarist. Average White Band.

MCJOHN, GOLDY. 5/2/45. Organist. Steppenwolf.

MCKAGAN, DUFF ROSE (Michael McKagan). Seattle, WA. Bassist. Guns N' Roses.

MCKEAN, MICHAEL. New York, NY, 10/17/47. Actor, writer. Lenny Kosnowski on *Laverne & Shirley.*

MCKELLAR, DANICA. La Jolla, CA. Actor. Winnie Cooper on *The Wonder Years.*

MCKELLEN, IAN. Burnley, England, 5/25/39. Shakespearian actor.

MCKEON, NANCY. Westbury, NY, 4/4/66. Actor. Jo Polniaczek on *The Facts of Life.*

MCKEOWN, LESLIE. Edinburgh, Scotland, 11/12/55. Singer. The Bay City Rollers.

MCKUEN, ROD. Oakland, CA, 4/29/33. Poet. *Laugh-In.*

MCLAGAN, IAN. England, 5/12/46. Keyboardist. The Faces.

MCLEAN, DON. New Rochelle, NY, 10/2/45. Singer, songwriter.

MCLEMORE, LAMONTE. St. Louis, MO, 9/17/39. Singer. The 5th Dimension.

MCMAHON, ED. Detroit, MI, 3/6/23. Announcer and host. *The Tonight Show; Star Search.*

MCNALLY, JOHN. Liverpool, England, 8/30/41. Singer, guitarist. The Searchers.

MCNEIL, MICK. Scotland, 7/20/58. Keyboardist. Simple Minds.

MCNICHOL, KRISTY. Los Angeles, CA, 9/11/62. Actor. Barbara Weston on *Empty Nest.*

MCPHERSON, GRAHAM. Hastings, England, 1/13/61. Singer. Madness.

MCQUEEN, BUTTERFLY. Tampa, FL, 1/8/11. Actor. Prissy in *Gone with the Wind.*

MCRANEY, GERALD. Collins, MS, 8/19/48. Actor, married to Delta Burke. John D. "Mac" MacGillis on *Major Dad.*

MCVIE, CHRISTINE (Christine Perfect). Birmingham, England, 7/12/44. Keyboardist, singer. Fleetwood Mac.

MCVIE, JOHN. London, England, 11/26/45. Bassist. Fleetwood Mac.

MEADOWS, AUDREY. Wu Chang, China, 2/8/26. Actor. Alice Kramden on *The Honeymooners.*

MEADOWS, JAYNE (Jayne Cotter). Wu Chang, China, 9/27/20. Actor, quiz show regular, married to Steve Allen, sister of Audrey.

MEANEY, COLM. Dublin, Ireland, 1953. Actor. Miles O'Brien on *Star Trek: The Next Generation.*

MEARA, ANNE. Brooklyn, NY, 9/20/29. Actor, partner/married to Jerry Stiller, mother of Ben Stiller. *The Out-of-Towners.*

MEDLEY, BILL. Santa Ana, CA, 9/19/40. Singer. The Righteous Brothers.

MEDRESS, HANK. Brooklyn, NY, 11/19/38. Tenor singer. The Tokens.

MEHTA, ZUBIN. Bombay, India, 4/29/36. Conductor.

MEINE, KLAUS. 5/25/48. Singer. Scorpions.

MEISNER, RANDY. Scottsbluff, NE, 3/8/47. Bassist, singer. The Eagles; Poco.

MELLENCAMP, JOHN. Seymour, IN, 10/7/51. Guitarist, singer, songwriter.

MENDOZA, MARK. Long Island, NY, 6/13/54. Bassist. Twisted Sister.

MENKEN, ALAN. New Rochelle, NY, 1949. Composer. *Beauty and the Beast.*

MERCHANT, JIMMY. New York, NY, 2/10/40. Singer. Frankie Lymon & The Teenagers.

MEREDITH, BURGESS. Cleveland, OH, 11/16/07. Actor. The Penguin on *Batman.*

MESSINA, JIM. Maywood, CA, 12/5/47. Guitarist, singer. Poco.

METCALF, LAURIE. Edwardsville, IL, 6/16/55. Actor. Jackie Conner Harris on *Roseanne.*

METHENY, PAT. Lee's Summit, MO, 8/12/54. Jazz guitarist. "Offramp."

MEYERS, ANN. San Juan, Puerto Rico, 4/6/70. Actor. Emma McArdle on *Kate & Allie.*

MEYERS, AUGIE. San Antonio, TX, 5/31/40. Keyboardist. Texas Tornados.

MIALL, TERRY LEE. England, 11/8/58. Drummer. Adam & The Ants.

MICHAEL, GEORGE (Georgios Kyriacou Panayiotou). London,

England, 6/25/63. Singer, songwriter. Wham!

MICK (Michael Wilson). Amesbury, England, 3/4/44. Drummer. Dave Dee, Dozy, Beaky, Mick and Tich.

MIDLER, BETTE. Paterson, NJ, 12/1/45. Actor, singer. "The Rose."

MIDORI. Osaka, Japan, 10/25/71. Violinist.

MIFUNE, TOSHIRO. Tsingtao, China, 4/1/20. Actor. Throne of Blood.

MIKE D. (Mike Diamond). New York, NY, 11/20/65. Rap artist. The Beastie Boys.

MILANO, ALYSSA. New York, NY, 12/19/72. Actor. Samantha Micelli on Who's the Boss?

MILANO, FRED. The Bronx, NY, 8/26/40. Tenor singer. Dion & The Belmonts.

MILES, SARAH. Ingatestone, England, 12/31/41. Actor. Ryan's Daughter.

MILES, SYLVIA. New York, NY, 9/9/34. Actor. Midnight Cowboy.

MILES, VERA (Vera Ralston). Boise City, OK, 8/23/29. Actor. Psycho.

MILKEN, MICHAEL. Van Nuys, CA, 1946. Financier. Convicted of securities violations.

MILLER, ANN (Lucille Ann Collier). Chireno, TX, 4/12/23. Actor. On the Town.

MILLER, CHARLES. Olathe, KS, 6/2/39. Saxophonist, clarinetist. War.

MILLER, DENNIS. Pittsburgh, PA, 11/3/53. TV personality. Saturday Night Live.

MILLER, JERRY. Tacoma, WA, 7/10/43. Guitarist. Moby Grape.

MILLER, PENELOPE ANN. Santa Monica, CA, 1/13/64. Actor. Carlito's Way.

MILLER, STEVE. Milwaukee, WI, 10/5/43. Singer, guitarist. The Steve Miller Band.

MILLS, HAYLEY. London, England, 4/18/46. Actor, daughter of John Mills, sister of Juliet Mills. The Parent Trap.

MILLS, JOHN. Suffolk, England, 2/22/08. Actor, father of Hayley and Juliet Mills. Ryan's Daughter.

MILLS, JULIET. London, England, 11/21/41. Actor, daughter of John Mills, sister of Hayley Mills. Nanny and the Professor.

MILLS, MIKE. 12/17/58. Bassist. R.E.M.

MILLS, STEPHANIE. New York, NY, 3/22/57. Actor, singer. The Wiz.

MILLWARD, MIKE. Bromborough, England, 5/9/42. Guitarist, singer. The Fourmost.

MIMIEUX, YVETTE. Los Angeles, CA, 1/8/39. Actor. The Black Hole.

MINNELLI, LIZA. Los Angeles, CA, 3/12/46. Singer, actor, daughter of Vincente Minnelli and Judy Garland, half-sister of Lorna Luft. Cabaret; The Sterile Cuckoo.

MINNESOTA FATS. New York, NY, 1913. Billiards player. Portrayed by Jackie Gleason in The Hustler.

MINOGUE, KYLIE. Melbourne, Australia, 5/28/68. Actor, singer.

MIOU-MIOU (Sylvette Hery). Paris, France, 2/22/50. Actor. Going Places.

MIRABELLA, GRACE. Maplewood, NJ, 6/10/30. Fashion editor, publishing executive. Mirabella.

MITCHELL, JONI (Roberta Anderson). Fort McLeod, Canada, 11/7/43. Folk singer, songwriter.

MITCHELL, LIZ. Clarendon, Jamaica, 7/12/52. Singer. Boney M.

MITCHELL, MITCH (John Mitchell). Middlesex, England, 7/9/46. Drummer. The Jimi Hendrix Experience.

MITCHELL, NEIL. Helensborough, Scotland, 6/8/67. Keyboardist. Wet Wet Wet.

MITCHUM, JAMES. Los Angeles, CA, 5/8/41. Actor, son of Robert. Thunder Road.

MITCHUM, ROBERT. Bridgeport, CT, 8/6/17. Actor, father of James. Cape Fear; The Night of the Hunter.

MODINE, MATTHEW. Loma Linda, CA, 3/22/59. Actor. Vision Quest.

MOFFAT, DONALD. Plymouth, England, 12/26/30. Actor. Clear and Present Danger; Tales of the City.

MOLL, RICHARD. Pasadena, CA, 1/13/42. Actor, stands 6' 8". Bailiff Nostradamus "Bull" Shannon on Night Court.

MOLLAND, JOEY. Liverpool, England, 6/21/48. Guitarist, keyboardist, singer. Badfinger.

MONARCH, MICHAEL. Los Angeles, CA, 7/5/50. Guitarist. Steppenwolf.

MONDALE, WALTER "FRITZ." Ceylon, MN, 1/5/28. Politician, former Vice President of the United States, former presidential candidate.

MONEY, EDDIE (Eddie Mahoney). Brooklyn, NY, 3/2/49. Singer.

MONTALBAN, RICARDO. Mexico City, Mexico, 11/25/20. Actor. Fantasy Island.

MONTANA, JOE. New Eagle, PA, 6/11/56. Football great.

MONTGOMERY, GEORGE (George Letz). Brady, MT, 8/29/16. Actor. The Texas Rangers.

MONTGOMERY, JOHN MICHAEL. Lexington, KY, 1/20/65. Country singer.

MOODY, MICKY. 8/30/50. Guitarist. Whitesnake.

MOONEY, KEVIN. England, 5/5/62. Bassist. Adam & The Ants.

MOORE, DUDLEY. Dagenham, England, 4/19/35. Actor. Arthur.

MOORE, MARY TYLER. Brooklyn, NY, 12/29/36. Actor. The Mary Tyler Moore Show.

MOORE, MELBA (Beatrice Hill). New York, NY, 10/29/45. R&B singer, actor. Purlie.

MOORE, ROGER. London, England, 10/14/27. Actor, replaced Sean Connery as James Bond. Live and Let Die.

MOORE, SAM. Miami, FL, 10/12/35. Singer. Sam & Dave.

MORAN, ERIN. Burbank, CA, 10/18/61. Actor. Joanie Cunningham on Happy Days.

MORANIS, RICK. Toronto, Canada, 4/18/54. Actor, writer. Honey, I Shrunk the Kids.

MOREAU, JEANNE. Paris, France, 1/23/28. Actor. Jules et Jim.

MORENO, RITA (Rosita Dolores Alverio). Humacao, PR, 12/11/31. Actor. West Side Story.

MORGAN, LORRIE (Loretta Lynn Morgan). Nashville, TN, 6/27/59. Singer.

MORIARTY, CATHY. The Bronx, NY, 11/29/60. Actor. Raging Bull.

MORIARTY, MICHAEL. Detroit, MI, 4/5/41. Actor. Law and Order.

MORITA, NORIYUKI "PAT." Isleton, CA, 6/28/32. Actor. The Karate Kid.

MORRIS, GREG. Cleveland, OH, 9/27/34. Actor. Mission: Impossible.

MORRIS, STEPHEN. Macclesfield, England, 10/28/57. Drummer. New Order.

MORRISON, STERLING. East Meadow, NY, 8/29/42. Singer, bassist, guitarist. The Velvet Underground.

MORRISON, VAN (George Ivan Morrison). Belfast, Northern Ireland, 8/31/45. Singer, songwriter. "Brown Eyed Girl."

MORRISSEY (Stephen Morrissey). Manchester, England, 5/22/59. Singer. The Smiths.

MORSE, DAVID. Hamilton, MA, 10/11/53. Actor. St. Elsewhere.

MORTON, JOE. New York, NY, 10/18/47. Actor. Terminator 2: Judgment Day.

MORVAN, FABRICE. Guadeloupe, 5/14/66. "Singer." Milli Vanilli.

MOSLEY, BOB. Paradise Valley, CA, 12/4/42. Bassist. Moby Grape.

MOSS, JON. Wandsworth, England, 9/11/57. Drummer. Culture Club.

MOSS, KATE. London, England, 1/16/74. Supermodel.

MOST, DONNY. New York, NY, 8/8/53. Actor. Ralph Malph on Happy Days.

MOSTEL, JOSH. New York, NY, 12/21/46. Actor. City Slickers.

MOULDING, COLIN. Swindon, England, 8/17/55. Bassist, singer. XTC.

MOUNT, DAVE. Carshalton, England, 3/3/47. Drummer, singer. Mud.

MOYERS, BILL. Hugo, OK, 6/5/34. Journalist, commentator. Bill Moyers' Journal.

MOYET, ALISON (Genevieve Moyet). Basildon, England, 6/18/61. Singer. Yazoo.

MUDD, ROGER. Washington, DC, 2/9/28. Broadcast journalist, newscaster.

MULDAUR, DIANA. New York, NY, 8/19/38. Actor. Capt. Kathryn Janeway on Star Trek: Voyager.

MULGREW, KATE. Dubuque, IA, 4/29/55. Actor. Ryan's Hope.

MULHARE, EDWARD. County Cork, Ireland, 4/8/23. Actor. Knight Rider.

MULHERN, MATT. Philadelphia, PA, 7/21/60. Actor. 2nd Lt. Gene Holowachuk on Major Dad.

MULL, MARTIN. Chicago, IL, 8/18/43. Actor. Mary Hartman, Mary Hartman.

MULLEN, LARRY JR. Dublin, Ireland, 10/31/61. Drummer. U2.

MULLIGAN, RICHARD. New York, NY, 11/13/32. Actor. Dr. Harry Weston on Empty Nest.

MUMY, BILLY. El Centro, CA, 2/1/54. Actor. Lost in Space.

MURPHY, MICHAEL. Los Angeles, CA, 5/5/38. Actor. Manhattan.

MURPHY, PETER. 7/11/57. Singer. Bauhaus.

MURRAY, DAVE. London, England, 12/23/58. Lead guitarist. Iron Maiden.

MUSIC, LORENZO. Brooklyn, NY, 5/2/37. Actor, writer. Carlton the Doorman on Rhoda.

NABORS, JIM. Sylacauga, GA, 6/12/32. Actor. Gomer Pyle on The Andy Griffith Show.

NADER, RALPH. Winsted, CT, 2/27/34. Political activist, author. Unsafe at Any Speed.

NAMATH, JOE. Beaver Falls, PA, 5/31/43. Football great, endorser.

NASH, BRIAN. Liverpool, England, 5/20/63. Guitarist. Frankie Goes to Hollywood.

NASH, GRAHAM. Blackpool, England, 2/2/42. Guitarist. The Hollies; Crosby, Stills, Nash & Young.

NAUGHTON, DAVID. West Hartford, CT, 2/13/51. Actor. An American Werewolf in London.

NAUGHTON, JAMES. Middletown, CT, 7/6/45. Actor. The Good Mother.

NAVRATILOVA, MARTINA. Prague, Czechoslovakia, 10/10/56. Tennis player.

NEAL, PATRICIA. Packard, KY, 1/20/26. Actor. Hud.

NEGRON, CHUCK. The Bronx, NY, 6/8/42. Singer. Three Dog Night.

NEIL, VINCE (Vince Wharton). Hollywood, CA, 2/8/61. Singer. Mötley Crüe.

NEILL, SAM. Ireland, 9/14/47. Actor. Jurassic Park.

NELLIGAN, KATE. London, Canada, 3/16/51. Actor. The Prince of Tides.

NELSON, CRAIG T. Spokane, WA, 4/4/46. Actor, writer. Hayden Fox on Coach.

NELSON, DAVID. New York, NY, 10/24/36. Actor, son of Ozzie and Harriet, brother of Ricky. David Nelson on The Adventures of Ozzie and Harriet.

NELSON, JUDD. Portland, ME, 11/28/59. Actor. *The Breakfast Club.*

NELSON, SANDY. Santa Monica, CA, 12/1/38. Rock/jazz drummer.

NELSON, TRACY. Santa Monica, CA, 10/25/63. Actor, daughter of Rick Nelson. *Father Dowling Mysteries.*

NEMES, LES. Surrey, England, 12/5/60. Bassist. Haircut 100.

NESMITH, MIKE (Robert Nesmith). Houston, TX, 12/30/42. Singer, guitarist, actor. The Monkees.

NEVILLE, ART. New Orleans, LA, 12/17/37. Singer, keyboardist. The Neville Brothers.

NEVILLE, CHARLES. New Orleans, LA, 12/28/38. Saxophonist. The Neville Brothers.

NEVILLE, CYRIL. 1/10/48. Singer, percussionist. The Neville Brothers.

NEWHART, BOB (George Newhart). Chicago, IL, 9/5/29. Actor, comedian. *The Bob Newhart Show.*

NEWLEY, ANTHONY. Hackney, England, 9/24/31. Actor, composer. "The Candy Man."

NEWMAN, RANDY. Los Angeles, CA, 11/28/43. Singer, songwriter.

NEWTON, JUICE. Lakehurst, NJ, 2/18/52. Country singer. "Angel of the Morning."

NEWTON-JOHN, OLIVIA. Cambridge, England, 9/26/48. Singer, actor. *Grease.*

NGUYEN, DUSTIN. Saigon, Vietnam, 1962. Actor. *21 Jump Street.*

NICHOL, AL. Winston-Salem, NC, 3/31/46. Guitarist, keyboardist, singer. The Turtles.

NICKS, STEVIE. Phoenix, AZ, 5/26/48. Singer. Fleetwood Mac.

NIELSEN, RICK. Rockford, IL, 12/22/46. Singer, guitarist. Cheap Trick.

NIELSON, BRIGITTE. Denmark, 7/15/63. Actor, formerly married to Sylvester Stallone. *Red Sonja.*

NIMOY, LEONARD. Boston, MA, 3/26/31. Actor, director. Mr. Spock on *Star Trek.*

NOIRET, PHILIPPE. Lille, France, 10/1/31. Actor. *Cinema Paradiso.*

NOLAN, MIKE. Dublin, Ireland, 12/7/54. Singer. Bucks Fizz.

NOLTE, NICK. Omaha, NE, 2/8/40. Actor. *48 Hrs.*

NOONAN, PEGGY. New York, NY, 9/7/50. Author, presidential speechwriter. Responsible for phrase "a kinder, gentler nation."

NOONE, PETER. Manchester, England, 11/5/47. Singer. Herman's Hermits.

NORRIS, CHUCK (Carlos Ray). Ryan, OK, 3/10/40. Karate champion, actor. *Good Guys Wear Black.*

NORTH, OLIVER. San Antonio, TX, 10/7/43. Presidential aide, senatorial candidate. Iran-Contra.

NORTON, KEN. Jacksonville, IL, 8/9/45. Boxer, actor. *The Gong Show.*

NOURI, MICHAEL. Washington, DC, 12/9/45. Actor. *Flashdance.*

NOVAK, KIM (Marilyn Novak). Chicago, IL, 2/13/33. Actor. *Vertigo.*

NOVELLO, DON. Ashtabula, OH, 1/1/43. Actor. Father Guido Sarducci.

NUGENT, TED. Detroit, MI, 12/13/48. Hard rock guitarist, actor.

NUMAN, GARY (Gary Webb). Hammersmith, England, 3/8/58. Singer. "Cars."

O'CONNOR, CARROLL. New York, NY, 8/2/24. Actor. Archie Bunker in *All in the Family.*

O'CONNOR, DONALD. Chicago, IL, 8/28/25. Actor. *Singin' in the Rain.*

O'CONNOR, SANDRA DAY. El Paso, TX, 3/26/30. Supreme Court Justice.

O'CONNOR, SINEAD. Dublin, Ireland, 12/8/66. Singer.

O'HARA, BRIAN. Liverpool, England, 3/12/42. Guitarist, singer. The Fourmost.

O'HARA, CATHERINE. Toronto, Canada, 3/4/54. Actor. Mother in *Home Alone.*

O'HARA, MAUREEN (Maureen FitzSimons). Dublin, Ireland, 8/17/21. Actor. *How Green Was My Valley.*

O'NEAL, ALEXANDER. 11/14/53. Songwriter.

O'NEAL, RYAN (Patrick Ryan O'Neal). Los Angeles, CA, 4/20/41. Actor, father of Tatum O'Neal. *Love Story.*

O'NEAL, TATUM. Los Angeles, CA, 11/5/63. Actor, daughter of Ryan, formerly married to John McEnroe. *Paper Moon.*

O'NEILL, ED. Youngstown, OH, 4/12/46. Actor. Al Bundy on *Married . . . with Children.*

O'NEILL, JENNIFER. Rio de Janeiro, Brazil, 2/20/49. Actor, former model. *Summer of '42.*

O'NEILL, JOHN. 8/26/57. Guitarist. The Undertones.

O'SHEA, MILO. Dublin, Ireland, 6/2/26. Actor. *The Verdict.*

O'SULLIVAN, GILBERT (Raymond O'Sullivan). Waterford, Ireland, 12/1/46. Singer, songwriter.

O'SULLIVAN, MAUREEN. Byle, Ireland, 5/17/11. Actor, mother of Mia Farrow. *Hannah and Her Sisters.*

O'TOOLE, ANNETTE (Annette Toole). Houston, TX, 4/1/53. Actor. *Superman III.*

O'TOOLE, MARK. Liverpool, England, 1/6/64. Bassist. Frankie Goes to Hollywood.

O'TOOLE, PETER. Connemara, Ireland, 8/2/32. Actor. *Lawrence of Arabia.*

OAKEY, PHILIP. Sheffield, England, 10/2/55. Singer. The Human League.

OAKLEY, BERRY. Chicago, IL, 4/4/48. Bassist. The Allman Brothers Band.

OATES, JOHN. New York, NY, 4/7/49. Singer, guitarist. Hall & Oates.

OCASEK, RIC (Ric Otcasek). Baltimore, MD, 3/23/49. Singer, guitarist. The Cars.

OCEAN, BILLY (Leslie Charles). Fyzabad, Trinidad, 1/21/50. Rock/R&B singer, songwriter.

OLDFIELD, MIKE. Reading, England, 5/15/53. Bassist, composer. "Tubular Bells."

OLDMAN, GARY. New Cross, England, 3/21/58. Actor, formerly married to Uma Thurman, engaged to Isabella Rossellini. *Bram Stoker's Dracula.*

OLIN, KEN. Chicago, IL, 7/30/54. Actor, director. Michael Steadman on *thirtysomething.*

OLIN, LENA. Stockholm, Sweden, 3/22/55. Actor. *Havana.*

OLMOS, EDWARD JAMES. East Los Angeles, CA, 2/24/47. Actor. Martin Castillo on *Miami Vice.*

ONTKEAN, MICHAEL. Vancouver, Canada, 1/24/46. Actor. *Twin Peaks.*

OPPENHEIMER, ALAN. New York, NY, 4/23/30. Actor. Gene Kinsella on *Murphy Brown.*

ORANGE, WALTER. Florida, 12/10/47. Singer, drummer. The Commodores.

ORBACH, JERRY. The Bronx, NY, 10/20/35. Actor. *Law and Order.*

ORLANDO, TONY (Michael Cassivitis). New York, NY, 4/3/44. Singer. Tony Orlando & Dawn.

ORR, BENJAMIN (Benjamin Orzechowski). Cleveland, OH, 8/9/55. Singer, bass guitarist. The Cars.

ORZABAL, ROLAND (Roland Orzabal de la Quintana). Portsmouth, England, 8/22/61. Guitarist, keyboardist. Tears for Fears.

OSBORNE, JEFFREY. Providence, RI, 3/9/48. Singer, songwriter, drummer. L.T.D.

OSGOOD, CHARLES. New York, NY, 1/8/33. Broadcast journalist, author.

OSKAR, LEE (Oskar Hansen). Copenhagen, Denmark, 3/24/46. Harmonicist. War.

OSMOND, ALAN. Ogden, UT, 6/22/49. Singer, member of the Osmond family. The Osmonds.

OSMOND, DONNY. Ogden, UT, 12/9/57. Singer, member of the Osmond family. *The Donny & Marie Show.*

OSMOND, JAY. Ogden, UT, 3/2/55. Singer, member of the Osmond family. The Osmonds.

OSMOND, MARIE (Olive Marie Osmond). Ogden, UT, 10/13/59. Singer, member of the Osmond family. *The Donny & Marie Show.*

OSMOND, MERRILL. Ogden, UT, 4/30/53. Singer, member of the Osmond family. The Osmonds.

OSMOND, WAYNE. Ogden, UT, 8/28/51. Singer, member of the Osmond family. The Osmonds.

OTIS, CARRE. Model, actor, married to Mickey Rourke.

OTIS, JOHNNY (John Veliotes). Vallejo, CA, 12/28/21. R&B drummer, pianist, and songwriter.

OWEN, RANDY. Fort Payne, AL, 12/13/49. Singer, guitarist. Alabama.

OWENS, SHIRLEY. Passaic, NJ, 6/10/41. Lead singer. The Shirelles.

OXENBERG, CATHERINE. New York, NY, 9/21/61. Actor. Amanda Carrington on *Dynasty.*

OZ, FRANK. Hereford, England, 5/25/44. Puppeteer, film director. *The Muppet Show.*

PACULA, JOANNA. Tamaszow Lubelski, Poland, 1/2/57. Actor. *Gorky Park.*

PAGE, JIMMY. Heston, England, 1/9/44. Guitarist. Led Zeppelin.

PAICE, IAN. Nottingham, England, 6/29/48. Drummer. Deep Purple.

PAICH, DAVID. Los Angeles, CA, 6/25/54. Keyboardist, singer. Toto.

PALANCE, JACK (Walter Palanuik). Lattimer, PA, 2/18/20. Actor. *City Slickers.*

PALIN, MICHAEL. Sheffield, England, 5/5/43. Actor, writer. *Monty Python's Flying Circus.*

PALMER, BETSY. East Chicago, IN, 11/1/26. Actor, panelist on *I've Got a Secret.*

PALMER, CARL. Birmingham, England, 3/20/51. Drummer. Emerson, Lake & Palmer; Asia.

PALMER, JOHN. 5/25/43. Keyboardist. Family.

PALMER, ROBERT (Alan Palmer). Batley, England, 1/19/49. Singer, songwriter. "Addicted to Love."

PANKOW, JAMES. Chicago, IL, 8/20/47. Trombonist. Chicago.

PANOZZO, CHUCK. Chicago, IL, 9/20/47. Bassist. Styx.

PANOZZO, JOHN. Chicago, IL, 9/20/47. Drummer. Styx.

PAQUIN, ANNA. Wellington, New Zealand, 1982. Actor. *The Piano.*

PARAZAIDER, WALTER. Chicago, IL, 3/14/45. Saxophonist. Chicago.

PARE, MICHAEL. Brooklyn, NY, 10/9/59. Actor. *Eddie and the Cruisers.*

PARFITT, RICK (Richard Harrison). Redhill, England, 10/25/43. Guitarist, singer. Status Quo.

PARILLAUD, ANNE. France, 1961. Actor. *La Femme Nikita.*

PARKER, FESS. Fort Worth, TX, 8/16/25. Actor. *Daniel Boone.*

PARKER, GRAHAM. Deepcut, England, 11/18/50. Singer. Graham Parker & The Rumour.

PARKER, JAMESON. Baltimore, MD, 11/18/47. Actor. *Simon and Simon.*

PARKER, MARY-LOUISE. Ft. Jackson, SC, 8/2/64. Actor. *Fried Green Tomatoes.*

PARKER, RAY JR. Detroit, MI, 5/1/54. Singer, songwriter. "Ghostbusters."

PARSONS, ESTELLE. Lynn, MA, 11/20/27. Actor. *Roseanne.*

PARTRIDGE, ANDY. Malta, 11/11/53. Guitarist, singer. XTC.

PATERSON, GERRY. Winnepeg, Canada, 5/26/45. Drummer. The Guess Who.

PATINKIN, MANDY (Mandel Patinkin). Chicago, IL, 11/30/52. Actor. Yentl.

PATRIC, JASON (Jason Patrick Miller). Queens, NY, 1966. Actor. Rush.

PATRICK, ROBERT. Marietta, GA, 1959. Actor. Evil T-1000 in Terminator 2: Judgment Day.

PATTEN, EDWARD. Atlanta, GA, 8/2/39. Singer. Gladys Knight & The Pips.

PATTERSON, LORNA. Whittier, CA, 6/1/57. Actor. Private Benjamin.

PATTERSON, MELODY. Los Angeles, CA, 1947. Actor. Wrangler Jane on F Troop.

PATTINSON, LES. Ormskirk, England, 4/18/58. Bassist. Echo & The Bunnymen.

PATTON, MIKE. Eureka, CA, 1/27/68. Lead singer. Faith No More.

PATTON, WILL. Charleston, SC, 6/14/54. Actor. No Way Out.

PAYCHECK, JOHNNY (Donald Eugene Lytle). Greenfield, OH, 5/31/41. Singer. "Take This Job and Shove It."

PAYNE, BILL. Waco, TX, 3/12/49. Keyboardist. Little Feat.

PAYS, AMANDA. Berkshire, England, 6/6/59. Actor, married to Corbin Bernsen. The Flash.

PAYTON, DENIS. Walthamstow, England, 8/11/43. Saxophonist. The Dave Clark Five.

PAYTON, LAWRENCE. Detroit, MI. Singer. The Four Tops.

PAYTON, WALTER. Columbia, MS, 6/25/54. Football player.

PEARL, MINNIE (Sarah Colley). Centreville, TN, 10/25/12. Actor. Hee Haw.

PEARSON, DELROY. Romford, England, 4/11/70. Singer. Five Star.

PEARSON, DENIECE. Romford, England, 6/13/68. Lead singer. Five Star.

PEARSON, DORIS. Romford, England, 6/8/66. Singer. Five Star.

PEARSON, LORRAINE. Romford, England, 8/10/67. Singer. Five Star.

PEARSON, STEDMAN. Romford, England, 6/29/64. Singer. Five Star.

PEART, NEIL. Hamilton, Canada, 9/12/52. Drummer. Rush.

PECK, GREGORY (Eldred Peck). La Jolla, CA, 4/5/16. Actor, producer. To Kill a Mockingbird.

PEEK, DAN. Panama City, FL, 11/1/50. Singer, guitarist. America.

PELE, PEROLA NEGRA (Edson Arantes do Nascimento). Tres Coracoes, Brazil, 10/23/40. Soccer legend.

PELLOW, MARTI (Mark McLoughlin). Clydebank, Scotland, 3/23/66. Singer. Wet Wet Wet.

PENA, ELIZABETH. Elizabeth, NJ, 9/23/61. Actor. La Bamba.

PENDER, MIKE (Michael Prendergast). Liverpool, England, 3/3/42. Singer, lead guitarist. The Searchers.

PENDERGRASS, TEDDY. Philadelphia, PA, 3/26/50. R&B singer, songwriter, drummer.

PENDLETON, AUSTIN. Warren, OH, 3/27/40. Actor. What's Up Doc?

PENDLETON, BRIAN. Wolverhampton, England, 4/13/44. Guitarist. The Pretty Things.

PENGILLY, KIRK. 7/4/58. Guitarist, saxophonist, singer. INXS.

PENN, SEAN. Burbank, CA, 8/17/60. Actor, director, formerly married to Madonna. Fast Times at Ridgemont High.

PENNY, JOE. London, England, 9/14/56. Actor. Jake Styles on Jake and the Fatman.

PERKINS, CARL (Carl Lee Perkings). Ridgely, TN, 4/9/32. Legendary singer, songwriter. "Blue Suede Shoes."

PERKINS, ELIZABETH. Queens, NY, 11/18/61. Actor. Big.

PERLMAN, RHEA. Brooklyn, NY, 3/31/48. Actor, married to Danny DeVito. Carla Tortelli LeBec on Cheers.

PERLMAN, RON. New York, NY, 4/13/50. Actor. The Beast in Beauty and the Beast.

PEROT, HENRY ROSS. Texarkana, TX, 6/27/30. Self-made billionaire businessman, former presidential candidate.

PERRINE, VALERIE. Galveston, TX, 9/3/43. Actor. Lenny.

PERRY, JOE. Boston, MA, 9/10/50. Guitarist. Aerosmith.

PERRY, LUKE (Perry Coy III). Fredericktown, OH, 10/11/66. Actor. Beverly Hills 90210.

PERRY, STEVE. Hanford, CA, 1/22/53. Singer. Journey.

PERRY, WILLIAM "THE REFRIGERATOR." Aiken, SC, 12/16/62. Very large football player. Chicago Bears.

PESCOW, DONNA. Brooklyn, NY, 3/24/54. Actor. Saturday Night Fever.

PETERS, BERNADETTE (Bernadette Lazzara). New York, NY, 2/28/48. Actor, performer. Pennies from Heaven.

PETERS, BROCK. New York, NY, 7/2/27. Actor, singer. To Kill a Mockingbird.

PETERS, MIKE. Prestatyn, Wales, 2/25/59. Guitarist, singer. The Alarm.

PETERSEN, WILLIAM. Chicago, IL, 1953. Actor. To Live and Die in L.A.

PETERSON, DEBBI. Los Angeles, CA, 8/22/61. Drummer, singer. The Bangles.

PETERSON, SYLVIA. New York, NY, 9/30/46. Singer. The Chiffons.

PETERSON, VICKI. Los Angeles, CA, 1/11/58. Guitarist, singer. The Bangles.

PETERSON, TOM. Rockford, IL, 5/9/50. Singer, bassist. Cheap Trick.

PETTY, LORI. Chattanooga, TN. Actor. A League of Their Own.

PFISTERER, ALBAN. Switzerland, 1947. Drummer, keyboardist. Love.

PHANTOM, SLIM JIM (Jim McDonnell). 3/20/61. Drummer. The Stray Cats.

PHILBIN, REGIS. New York, NY, 8/25/34. Talk show host. Live with Regis and Kathie Lee.

PHILIP, PRINCE (Philip Mountbatten). Corfu, Greece, 6/10/21. Husband of Queen Elizabeth II, Duke of Edinburgh.

PHILLIPS, CHYNNA. Los Angeles, CA, 4/29/68. Singer, half-sister of Mackenzie, daughter of John and Michelle, married to Billy Baldwin. Wilson Phillips.

PHILLIPS, JOHN. Parris Island, SC, 8/30/35. Singer, formerly married to Michelle, father of Mackenzie and Chynna. The Mamas & the Papas.

PHILLIPS, LOU DIAMOND (Lou Upchurch). Philippines, 2/17/62. Actor. La Bamba.

PHILLIPS, MACKENZIE (Laura Mackenzie Phillips). Alexandria, VA, 11/10/59. Actor, daughter of John Phillips, half-sister of Chynna. Julie Cooper Horvath on One Day at a Time.

PHILLIPS, MICHELLE (Holly Gilliam). Santa Ana, CA, 6/4/44. Actor, formerly married to John, mother of Chynna. Anne Matheson on Knots Landing.

PHILTHY ANIMAL (Philip Taylor). Chesterfield, England, 9/21/54. Drummer. Motorhead.

PICKETT, WILSON. Prattville, AL, 3/18/41. Singer, songwriter. "In the Midnight Hour."

PIERSON, KATE. Weehawken, NJ, 4/27/48. Organist, singer. The B-52's.

PILATUS, ROBERT. New York, NY, 6/8/65. "Singer." Milli Vanilli.

PINCHOT, BRONSON. New York, NY, 5/20/59. Actor. Balki Bartokomous on Perfect Strangers.

PINDER, MIKE. Birmingham, England, 12/12/42. Keyboardist. The Moody Blues.

PINKNEY, BILL. Sumter, NC, 8/15/25. Bassist. The Drifters.

PIRRONI, MARCO. England, 4/27/59. Guitarist. Adam & The Ants.

PISCOPO, JOE. Passaic, NJ, 6/17/51. Actor. Saturday Night Live.

PITNEY, GENE. Hartford, CT, 2/17/41. Singer, songwriter.

PLACE, MARY KAY. Tulsa, OK, 9/23/47. Actor. The Big Chill.

PLANT, ROBERT. Bromwich, England, 8/20/48. Singer. Led Zeppelin.

PLESHETTE, JOHN. New York, NY, 7/27/42. Actor. Richard Avery on Knots Landing.

PLESHETTE, SUZANNE. New York, NY, 1/31/37. Actor. Emily Hartley on The Bob Newhart Show.

PLOWRIGHT, JOAN. Brigg, England, 10/28/29. Actor, widow of Laurence Olivier. Enchanted April.

PLUMB, EVE. Burbank, CA, 4/29/58. Actor. Jan Brady on The Brady Bunch.

PLUMMER, AMANDA. New York, NY, 3/23/57. Actor, daughter of Christopher Plummer. The Fisher King.

PLUMMER, CHRISTOPHER. Toronto, Canada, 12/13/27. Actor, father of Amanda Plummer. Baron von Trapp in The Sound of Music.

POINTER, ANITA. East Oakland, CA, 1/23/48. Singer. Pointer Sisters.

POINTER, BONNIE. East Oakland, CA, 6/11/51. Singer. Pointer Sisters.

POINTER, JUNE. East Oakland, CA, 11/30/54. Singer. Pointer Sisters.

POINTER, RUTH. East Oakland, CA, 3/19/46. Singer. Pointer Sisters.

POITIER, SIDNEY. Miami, FL, 2/20/27. Actor. Guess Who's Coming to Dinner.

POLANSKI, ROMAN. Paris, France, 8/18/33. Director, writer. Rosemary's Baby.

POLLACK, SYDNEY. South Bend, Indiana, 7/1/34. Director, producer, actor. The Way We Were.

POLLAN, TRACY. New York, NY, 6/22/60. Actor, married to Michael J. Fox. Family Ties.

POOLE, BRIAN. Barking, England, 11/2/41. Singer. Brian Poole & The Tremeloes.

POP, IGGY (James Osterburg). Ann Arbor, MI, 4/21/47. Singer, songwriter.

POPCORN, FAITH. New York, NY, 5/11/43. Trend analyst, consultant.

PORCARO, STEVE. Los Angeles, CA, 9/2/57. Keyboardist, singer. Toto.

PORTZ, CHUCK. Santa Monica, CA, 3/28/45. Bassist. The Turtles.

POST, MARKIE. Palo Alto, CA, 11/4/50. Actor. Christine Sullivan on Night Court.

POTTER, CAROL. Tenafly, NJ, 5/21/48. Actor. Beverly Hills 90210.

POTTS, ANNIE. Nashville, TN, 10/28/52. Actor. Mary Jo Shively on Designing Women.

POUNDSTONE, PAULA. Alabama, 12/29/60. Comedian, actor.

POVICH, MAURY. Washington, DC, 1/7/39. Talk show host, married to Connie Chung. A Current Affair.

POWELL, BILLY. Florida, 6/3/52. Keyboardist. Lynyrd Skynyrd.

POWELL, COLIN. New York, NY, 4/5/37. Military leader.

POWELL, DON. 9/10/50. Drummer. Slade.

POWERS, STEPHANIE (Stefania Federkiewicz). Hollywood, CA, 11/12/42. Actor. Jennifer on *Hart to Hart.*

PRENTISS, PAULA (Paula Ragusa). San Antonio, TX, 3/4/39. Actor. *What's New Pussycat?*

PRESLEY, REG (Reginald Ball). Andover, England, 6/12/43. Singer. The Troggs.

PRESTON, KELLY. Honolulu, HI, 10/13/62. Actor, married to John Travolta. *52 Pick-Up.*

PRICE, ALAN. Fairfield, Durham, 4/19/41. Keyboardist. The Animals.

PRICE, LLOYD. Kenner, LA, 5/9/33. Singer, songwriter.

PRICE, RICK. 6/10/44. Bassist. Wizzard.

PRIDE, CHARLEY. Sledge, MS, 3/18/38. Country singer, songwriter.

PRIEST, STEVE. London, England, 2/23/50. Bassist. Sweet.

PRIESTLEY, JASON. Vancouver, Canada, 8/28/69. Actor. Brandon Walsh on *Beverly Hills 90210.*

PRIESTMAN, HENRY. 7/21/58. Singer. The Christians.

PRIME, JAMES. Kilmarnock, Scotland, 11/3/60. Keyboardist. Deacon Blue.

PRINCE MARK D. 2/19/60. Rap artist. Fat Boys.

PRINCIPAL, VICTORIA. Fukuoka, Japan, 1/3/50. Actor. Pam Ewing on *Dallas.*

PRITCHARD, BARRY. Birmingham, England, 4/3/44. Guitarist, singer. The Fortunes.

PROBY, P. J. (James Smith). Houston, TX, 11/6/38. Singer, actor.

PROWSE, JULIET. Bombay, India, 9/25/36. Actor, dancer.

PRYCE, JONATHAN. North Wales, 6/1/47. Actor. *Miss Saigon.*

PRYOR, NICHOLAS. Baltimore, MD, 1/28/35. Actor. *Risky Business.*

PRYOR, RICHARD. Peoria, IL, 12/1/40. Actor. *Stir Crazy.*

PUERTA, JOE. 7/2/51. Bassist, singer. Bruce Hornsby & The Range.

PULLMAN, BILL. Hornell, NY, 1954. Actor. *Ruthless People; Malice.*

PURCELL, SARAH. Richmond, IN, 10/8/48. TV personality. Cohost on *Real People.*

QADDAFI, MUAMMAR. Sirta, Libya, 1942. Political leader. Libyan head of state.

QUAID, RANDY. Houston, TX, 10/1/50. Actor, brother of Dennis. *The Last Picture Show.*

QUAIFE, PETE. Tavistock, England, 12/31/43. Bassist. The Kinks.

QUATRO, SUZI (Suzi Quatrocchio). Detroit, MI, 6/3/50. Singer, songwriter, actor.

QUAYLE, DAN. Indianapolis, IN, 2/4/47. Vice president under George Bush.

QUAYLE, MARILYN. Indianapolis, IN, 7/29/49. Lawyer, author,

married to Dan. *Embrace the Serpent.*

QUINLAN, KATHLEEN. Mill Valley, CA, 11/19/54. Actor. *Clara's Heart.*

QUINN, AIDAN. Chicago, IL, 3/8/59. Actor. *The Playboys.*

QUINN, ANTHONY. Chihuahua, Mexico, 4/21/15. Actor. *Zorba the Greek.*

QUINN, DEREK. Manchester, England, 5/24/42. Lead guitarist. Freddie & The Dreamers.

QUIVERS, ROBIN. 1953. Radio personality, author. *The Howard Stern Show.*

RABBITT, EDDIE. New York, NY, 11/27/44. Singer, songwriter. "I Love a Rainy Night."

RAFFERTY, GERRY. Paisley, Scotland, 4/16/47. Singer, songwriter. "Baker Street."

RAFFI. Cairo, Egypt, 7/8/48. Singer, songwriter, children's performer. *Everything Grows.*

RAFFIN, DEBORAH. Los Angeles, CA, 3/13/53. Actor. *Once Is Not Enough.*

RALPH, SHERYL LEE. Waterbury, CT, 12/30/56. Actor. *The Distinguished Gentleman.*

RALPHS, MICK. Hereford, England, 3/31/44. Guitarist. Mott The Hoople; Bad Company.

RAMIS, HAROLD. Chicago, IL, 11/21/44. Writer, director, actor. Egon Spengler in *Ghostbusters.*

RAMONE, DEE DEE (Douglas Colvin). Fort Lee, VA, 9/18/52. Bassist. The Ramones.

RAMONE, JOEY (Jeffrey Hyman). Forest Hills, NY, 5/19/52. Singer. The Ramones.

RAMONE, JOHNNY (John Cummings). Long Island, NY, 10/8/48. Guitarist. The Ramones.

RAMONE, TOMMY (Thomas Erdelyi). Budapest, Hungary, 1/29/49. Drummer. The Ramones.

RAMOS, LARRY JR. (Hilario Ramos Jr.). Kauai, HI, 4/19/42. Singer, guitarist. The Association.

RAMPLING, CHARLOTTE. Surmer, England, 2/5/46. Actor. *The Verdict.*

RAMSEY, AL. New Jersey, 7/27/43. Guitarist. Gary Lewis & The Playboys.

RANDALL, TONY (Leonard Rosenberg). Tulsa, OK, 2/26/20. Actor. Felix Unger on *The Odd Couple.*

RAPHAEL, SALLY JESSY. Easton, PA, 2/25/43. talk show hostess. *Sally Jessy Raphael.*

RAPP, DANNY. Philadelphia, PA, 5/10/41. Lead singer. Danny & The Juniors.

RAREBELL, HERMAN. 11/18/49. Drummer. Scorpions.

RASCHE, DAVID. St. Louis, MO, 8/7/44. Actor. *Sledge Hammer.*

RASHAD, AHMAD. Portland, OR, 11/19/49. Football player, sportscaster, husband of Phylicia.

RASHAD, PHYLICIA. Houston, TX, 6/19/48. Actor, sister of Debbie

Allen, wife of Ahmad. Clair Huxtable on *The Cosby Show.*

RATZENBERGER, JOHN. Bridgeport, CT, 4/6/47. Actor. Cliff Claven on *Cheers.*

RAWLS, LOU. Chicago, IL, 12/1/36. R&B singer. "Lady Love."

RAY, JAMES EARL. Alton, IL, 3/10/28. Assassin. Killed Martin Luther King Jr.

REA, CHRIS. Middlesbrough, England, 3/4/51. Singer, songwriter, guitarist.

REAGAN, NANCY. New York, NY, 7/6/21. Former First Lady, married to president Ronald Reagan.

REAGAN, RONALD. Tampico, IL, 2/6/11. Politician, actor, father of Ron Jr., husband of Nancy. Fortieth U.S. president. *Bedtime for Bonzo.*

REAGAN, RONALD JR. Los Angeles, CA, 5/20/58. Performer, son of former president Ronald Reagan.

REASON, REX. Berlin, Germany, 11/30/28. Actor. *This Island Earth.*

RECORD, EUGENE. 12/23/40. Lead singer. The Chi-Lites.

REDDING, NOEL. Folkestone, England, 12/25/45. Bassist, The Jimi Hendrix Experience.

REDDY, HELEN. Melbourne, Australia, 10/25/42. Pop singer. *The Helen Reddy Show.*

REDGRAVE, CORIN. London, England, 6/16/39. Actor, brother of Lynn and Vanessa. *A Man for All Seasons.*

REDGRAVE, LYNN. London, England, 3/8/43. Actor, sister of Corin and Vanessa. *House Calls.*

REDGRAVE, VANESSA. London, England, 1/30/37. Actor, sister of Corin and Lynn. *Playing for Time.*

REED, LOU (Louis Firbank). Long Island, NY, 3/2/43. Singer, songwriter. The Velvet Underground.

REED, OLIVER. Wimbledon, England, 2/13/38. Actor. *The Three Musketeers.*

REED, PAMELA. Tacoma, WA, 4/2/53. Actor. *The Right Stuff.*

REEMS, HARRY (Herbert Streicher). The Bronx, NY, 8/27/47. Actor. *Deep Throat.*

REEVE, CHRISTOPHER. New York, NY, 9/25/52. Actor. *Superman.*

REEVES, MARTHA. Alabama, 7/18/41. Lead singer. Martha & The Vandellas.

REEVES, STEVE. Glasgow, MT, 1/21/26. Actor. *Hercules.*

REGALBUTO, JOE. Brooklyn, NY. Actor. Frank Fontana on *Murphy Brown.*

REID, DON. Staunton, VA, 6/5/45. Musician, brother of Harold. Statler Brothers.

REID, HAROLD. Staunton, VA, 8/21/39. Musician, brother of Don. Statler Brothers.

REID, JIM. East Kilbride, Scotland, 1961. Guitarist, singer. The Jesus & Mary Chain.

REID, TIM. Norfolk, VA, 12/19/44. Actor, producer. Gordon "Venus Flytrap" Sims on *WKRP in Cincinnati.*

REID, WILLIAM. East Kilbride, Scotland, 1958. Guitarist, singer. The Jesus & Mary Chain.

REINER, CARL. New York, NY, 3/20/22. Actor, writer, and director. *The Dick Van Dyke Show.*

REINER, ROB. New York, NY, 3/6/45. Actor, writer, producer, director, son of Carl, formerly married to Penny Marshall. Mike Stivic on *All in the Family.*

REINHOLD, JUDGE (Edward Ernest Reinhold Jr.). Wilmington, DE, 5/21/57. Actor. Rosewood in *Beverly Hills Cop.*

REINKING, ANN. Seattle, WA, 11/10/49. Actor, dancer. *Annie.*

REITMAN, IVAN. Komarno, Czechoslovakia, 10/26/46. Director, producer. *Ghostbusters.*

RETTIG, TOMMY. Jackson Heights, NY, 12/10/41. Actor. *Lassie.*

REVERE, PAUL. Harvard, NE, 1/7/38. Keyboardist. Paul Revere & The Raiders.

REYNOLDS, DEBBIE (Mary Frances Reynolds). El Paso, TX, 4/1/32. Actor, formerly married to Eddie Fisher, mother of Carrie Fisher. *Singin' in the Rain.*

REYNOLDS, MARJORIE. Buhl, ID, 8/12/21. Actor. *The Life of Riley.*

RHODES, NICK (Nicholas Bates). Mosely, England, 6/8/62. Keyboardist. Duran Duran.

RIBEIRO, ALFONSO. New York, NY, 9/21/71. Actor, dancer. *Fresh Prince of Bel Air.*

RICH, ADAM. New York, NY, 10/12/68. Actor. Nicholas Bradford on *Eight Is Enough.*

RICHARD, CLIFF (Harry Webb). Lucknow, India, 10/14/40. Singer, drummer. The Shadows.

RICHARDS, KEITH. Dartford, England, 12/18/43. Guitarist. The Rolling Stones.

RICHARDSON, MIRANDA. Lancashire, England, 3/3/58. Actor. *The Crying Game.*

RICHARDSON, SUSAN. Coatesville, PA, 3/11/52. Actor. Susan Bradford on *Eight Is Enough.*

RICHIE, LIONEL. Tuskegee, AL, 6/20/49. Singer, songwriter. The Commodores.

RICHRATH, GARY. Peoria, IL, 10/18/49. Guitarist. REO Speedwagon.

RICKLES, DON. New York, NY, 5/8/26. Actor. *The Don Rickles Show.*

RICKMAN, ALAN. Hammersmith, England, 1946. Actor. *Die Hard.*

RIDGELEY, ANDREW. Windlesham, England, 1/26/63. Guitarist. Wham!

RIEGERT, PETER. New York, NY, 4/11/47. Actor. *Crossing Delancey.*

RIGBY, CATHY. Long Beach, CA, 12/12/52. Gymnast, actor.

RIGG, DIANA. Doncaster, England, 7/20/38. Actor. Emma Peel on *The Avengers*.

RIGGS, BOBBY. Los Angeles, CA, 2/25/18. Tennis player, defeated by Billie Jean King.

RILEY, PAT. Rome, NY, 3/20/45. Basketball coach. Former New York Knicks coach.

RINGWALD, MOLLY. Sacramento, CA, 2/18/68. Actor. *Sixteen Candles*.

RITTER, JOHN. Burbank, CA, 9/17/48. Actor, producer. Jack Tripper on *Three's Company*.

RIVERA, CHITA. Washington, DC, 1/23/33. Singer.

RIVERA, GERALDO. New York, NY, 7/4/43. Talk show host and reporter. *Geraldo*.

RIVERS, JOHNNY (John Ramistella). New York, NY, 11/7/42. Soul/rock singer, songwriter.

RIZZUTO, PHIL. New York, NY, 9/25/18. Baseball great, sports announcer.

ROBARDS, JASON. Chicago, IL, 7/26/22. Actor, formerly married to Lauren Bacall. *Inherit the Wind*.

ROBERTS, ERIC. Biloxi, MS, 4/18/56. Actor, brother of Julia. *The Pope of Greenwich Village*.

ROBERTS, ORAL. Ada, OK, 1/24/18. Evangelist. Oral Roberts University.

ROBERTS, TANYA (Tanya Leigh). The Bronx, NY, 10/15/55. Actor. *Charlie's Angels*.

ROBERTS, TONY. New York, NY, 10/22/39. Actor. *Play It Again, Sam*.

ROBERTS, XAVIER. Cleveland, GA, 10/31/55. Businessman. Creator of Cabbage Patch Kids.

ROBERTSON, BRIAN. Glasgow, Scotland, 9/12/56. Guitarist. Thin Lizzy.

ROBERTSON, CLIFF. La Jolla, CA, 9/9/25. Actor. *Charly*.

ROBERTSON, PAT (Marion Gordon Robertson). Lexington, VA, 3/22/30. Evangelist, TV personality. Founder of Christian Broadcasting Network.

ROBERTSON, ROBBIE (Jaime Robertson). Toronto, Canada, 7/5/44. Guitarist, singer. The Band.

ROBINSON, CHRIS. Atlanta, GA, 12/20/66. Singer. The Black Crowes.

ROBINSON, CYNTHIA. Sacramento, CA, 1/12/46. Trumpeter. Sly & The Family Stone.

ROBINSON, JAY. New York, NY, 4/14/30. Actor. *The Robe*.

ROBINSON, RICH. Atlanta, GA, 5/24/69. Guitarist. The Black Crowes.

ROBINSON, SMOKEY (William Robinson). Detroit, MI, 2/19/40. Motown singer, songwriter. Smokey Robinson & The Miracles.

ROCK, CHRIS. New York, NY, 1967. Actor. *Saturday Night Live*.

ROCKER, LEE (Leon Drucher). 1961. Double bassist. The Stray Cats.

ROCKWELL (Kenneth Gordy). Detroit, MI, 3/15/64. Singer, son of Berry Gordy. "Somebody's Watching Me."

RODGERS, NILE. New York, NY, 9/19/52. Guitarist. Chic.

RODGERS, PAUL. Middlesbrough, England, 12/17/49. Singer. Free; Bad Company.

ROE, TOMMY. Atlanta, GA, 5/9/42. Singer, songwriter.

ROGERS, KENNY. Houston, TX, 8/21/38. Country singer, actor. "The Gambler."

ROGERS, MIMI. Coral Gables, FL, 1/27/56. Actor. Formerly married to Tom Cruise. *Someone To Watch Over Me*.

ROGERS, MISTER (Fred Rogers). Latrobe, PA, 3/20/28. Children's host, producer. *Mr. Rogers' Neighborhood*.

ROGERS, ROY (Leonard Slye). Cincinnati, OH, 11/5/12. TV cowboy, singer. *Happy Trails with Roy and Dale*.

ROGERS, WAYNE. Birmingham, AL, 4/7/33. Actor. Trapper John on *M*A*S*H*.

ROGERS, WILL JR. New York, NY, 10/20/12. Actor, lecturer. *The Story of Will Rogers*.

ROKER, ROXIE. Miami, FL, 8/28/29. Actor, mother of Lenny Kravitz. Helen Willis on *The Jeffersons*.

ROLLE, ESTHER. Pompano Beach, FL, 11/8/22. Actor. *Driving Miss Daisy*.

ROLLINS, HOWARD JR. Baltimore, MD, 10/17/50. Actor. *In the Heat of the Night*.

ROMAN, RUTH. Boston, MA, 12/23/24. Actor. *The Long Hot Summer*.

RONSTADT, LINDA. Tucson, AZ, 7/15/46. Singer, actor. *The Pirates of Penzance*.

ROONEY, ANDY. Albany, NY, 1/14/20. News commentator. *60 Minutes*.

ROONEY, MICKEY (Joe Yule Jr.). Brooklyn, NY, 9/23/20. Actor. *National Velvet*.

ROSE, PETE. Cincinnati, OH, 4/14/41. Baseball player and manager. Cincinnati Reds.

ROSS, DIANA. Detroit, MI, 3/26/44. Singer, actor, former member of the Supremes. *Lady Sings the Blues*.

ROSS, KATHARINE. Hollywood, CA, 1/29/43. Actor. *The Graduate*.

ROSS, MARION. Albert Lea, MN, 10/25/28. Actor. Marion Cunningham on *Happy Days*.

ROSS, RICKY. Dundee, Scotland, 12/22/57. Singer. Deacon Blue.

ROSSELLINI, ISABELLA. Rome, Italy, 6/18/52. Actor, formerly married to Martin Scorsese, engaged to Gary Oldman. *Blue Velvet*.

ROSSI, FRANCIS. Forest Hill, England, 4/29/49. Guitarist, singer. Status Quo.

ROSSINGTON, GARY. Jacksonville, FL, 12/4/51. Guitarist. Lynyrd Skynyrd.

ROTH, DAVID LEE. Bloomington, IN, 10/10/55. Singer. Van Halen.

ROTH, TIM. London, England, 1961. Actor. *Reservoir Dogs*.

ROTHERY, STEVE. Brampton, England, 11/25/59. Guitarist. Marillion.

ROTHWELL, RIC. Stockport, England, 3/11/44. Drummer. Wayne Fontana & The Mindbenders.

ROUNDTREE, RICHARD. New Rochelle, NY, 9/7/42. Actor. *Shaft*.

ROURKE, MICKEY. Schenectady, NY, 7/16/53. Actor, married to Carre Otis. *9 1/2 Weeks*.

ROWLAND, KEVIN. Wolverhampton, England, 8/17/53. Singer, guitarist. Dexy's Midnight Runners.

ROWLANDS, GENA. Cambria, WI, 6/19/34. Actor. *Gloria*.

RUDD, PHILIP. Australia, 5/19/46. Drummer. AC/DC.

RUDNER, RITA. Miami, FL, 9/11/55. Actor, comedian.

RUEHL, MERCEDES. Queens, NY, 2/28/48. Actor. *Lost in Yonkers*.

RUFFIN, DAVID. Meridian, MS, 1/18/41. Singer. The Temptations.

RUNDGREN, TODD. Philadelphia, PA, 6/22/48. Singer, songwriter.

RUSHDIE, SALMAN. Bombay, India, 6/19/47. Author. *The Satanic Verses*.

RUSSELL, GRAHAM. Nottingham, England, 6/1/50. Singer. Air Supply.

RUSSELL, JACK. 12/5/60. Singer. Great White.

RUSSELL, JANE. Bemidji, MN, 6/21/21. Actor, pinup girl. *The Outlaw*.

RUSSELL, KURT. Springfield, MA, 3/17/51. Actor, cohabitant of Goldie Hawn. *Tombstone*.

RUSSELL, LEON (Hank Wilson). Lawton, OK, 4/2/41. Country/blues singer, songwriter.

RUSSELL, NIPSEY. Atlanta, GA, 10/13/24. Actor. Car 54, Where Are You?

RUSSELL, THERESA (Theresa Paup). San Diego, CA, 3/20/57. Actor. *Black Widow*.

RUTHERFORD, MIKE. Guildford, England, 10/2/50. Guitarist. Genesis; Mike & The Mechanics.

RUTHERFORD, PAUL. Liverpool, England, 12/8/59. Singer. Frankie Goes to Hollywood.

RUTTAN, SUSAN. Oregon City, OR, 9/16/48. Actor. Roxanne on *L.A. Law*.

RYAN, TOM. Anderson, IN, 6/6/26. Cartoonist. *Tumbleweeds*.

RYDER, MITCH (William Levise Jr.). Detroit, MI, 2/26/45. Singer. Mitch Ryder & The Detroit Wheels.

RYDER, PAUL. Manchester, England, 4/24/64. Bassist. Happy Mondays.

RYDER, SHAUN. Little Hulton, England, 8/23/62. Singer. Happy Mondays.

SABATINI, GABRIELA. Buenos Aires, Argentina, 5/16/70. Tennis player.

SADE (Helen Folasade Adu). Ibadan, Nigeria, 1/16/59. Singer.

SAGAL, KATEY. Los Angeles, CA, 1956. Actor. Peg on *Married . . . with Children*.

SAGAN, CARL. New York, NY, 11/9/34. Astronomer. *Cosmos*.

SAGET, BOB. Philadelphia, PA, 5/17/56. Actor. *Full House*.

SAHM, DOUG. San Antonio, TX, 11/6/41. Singer, guitarist. Sir Douglas Quintet.

SAINT, EVA MARIE. Newark, NJ, 7/4/24. Actor. *On the Waterfront*.

SAINT JAMES, SUSAN (Susan Miller). Los Angeles, CA, 8/14/46. Actor. Kate on *Kate & Allie*.

SAJAK, PAT. Chicago, IL, 10/26/46. Game show host. *Wheel of Fortune*.

SALAZAR, ALBERTO. Havana, Cuba, 8/7/58. Track athlete, won New York City Marathon.

SALES, SOUPY (Milton Supman). Franklinton, NC, 1/8/30. TV personality. *The Soupy Sales Show*.

SALINGER, J. D. (Jerome David Salinger). New York, NY, 1/1/19. Author. *The Catcher in the Rye*.

SALT, JENNIFER. Los Angeles, CA, 9/4/44. Actor. *Midnight Cowboy*.

SAMBORA, RICHIE. 7/11/59. Guitarist, married to Heather Locklear. Bon Jovi.

SAMMS, EMMA. London, England, 8/28/60. Actor. Fallon Carrington Colby on *Dynasty* and *The Colbys*.

SAMPRAS, PETE. Washington, DC, 8/12/71. Tennis player.

SAMWELL-SMITH, PAUL. Richmond, England, 5/8/43. Bassist. The Yardbirds.

SAN GIACOMO, LAURA. Denville, NJ, 11/14/61. Actor. *sex, lies and videotape*.

SANDERS, RICHARD. Harrisburg, PA, 8/23/40. Actor. Les Nessman on *WKRP in Cincinnati*.

SANDS, JULIAN. Yorkshire, England, 1/15/58. Actor. *A Room with a View*.

SANDY, GARY. Dayton, OH, 11/3/46. Actor. Andy Travis on *WKRP in Cincinnati*.

SANFORD, ISABEL. New York, NY, 8/29/17. Actor. Louise on *The Jeffersons*.

SANTANA, CARLOS. Autlan de Navarro, Mexico, 7/20/47. Guitarist, singer. Santana.

SANTIAGO, HERMAN. New York, NY, 2/18/41. Singer. Frankie Lymon & The Teenagers.

SARANDON, CHRIS. Beckley, WV, 7/24/42. Actor, former husband of Susan. Leon in *Dog Day Afternoon*.

SASSOON, VIDAL. London, England, 1/17/28. Hairstylist.

SAVAGE, FRED. Highland Park, IL, 7/9/76. Actor, brother of Ben. Kevin Arnold on *The Wonder Years*.

SAVAGE, JOHN (John Youngs). Long Island, NY, 8/25/49. Actor. *The Deer Hunter.*

SAVAGE, RICK. Sheffield, England, 12/2/60. Bassist. Def Leppard.

SAVANT, DOUG. 6/21/64. Actor. *Melrose Place.*

SAWYER, RAY. Chickasaw, AL, 2/1/37. Lead singer. Dr. Hook.

SAYER, LEO (Gerard Sayer). Shoreham-by-Sea, England, 5/21/48. Singer, songwriter. "You Make Me Feel Like Dancing."

SCABIES, RAT (Chris Miller). Kingston-upon-Thames, England, 7/30/57. Drummer. The Damned.

SCACCHI, GRETA. Milan, Italy, 2/18/60. Actor. *Presumed Innocent.*

SCAGGS, BOZ (William Scaggs). Ohio, 6/8/44. Guitarist, singer, songwriter. "Lowdown."

SCALIA, JACK. Brooklyn, NY, 11/10/51. Actor. *Wolf.*

SCARPELLI, GLENN. Staten Island, NY, 7/6/68. Actor. Alex Handris on *One Day at a Time.*

SCHACHER, MEL. Flint, MI, 4/3/51. Bassist. Grand Funk Railroad.

SCHEIDER, ROY. Orange, NJ, 11/10/35. Actor. Chief Brody in *Jaws.*

SCHELL, MAXIMILIAN. Vienna, Austria, 12/8/30. Actor. *Judgment at Nuremberg.*

SCHENKER, RUDOLPH. 8/31/48. Guitarist. Scorpions.

SCHERMIE, JOE. Madison, WI, 2/12/45. Bassist. Three Dog Night.

SCHNEIDER, FRED. Newark, GA, 7/1/51. Keyboardist, singer. The B-52's.

SCHNEIDER, MARIA. Paris, France, 3/27/52. Actor. *Last Tango in Paris.*

SCHNEIDER-ESLEBEN, FLORIAN. Dusseldorf, Germany, 1947. Keyboardist, drummer, singer, woodwindist. Kraftwerk.

SCHOLZ, TOM. Toledo, OH, 3/10/47. Guitarist, keyboardist. Boston.

SCHON, NEAL. San Mateo, CA, 2/27/54. Guitarist. Journey.

SCHORR, DANIEL. New York, NY, 8/31/16. Broadcast journalist. NPR.

SCHRODER, RICK. Staten Island, NY, 4/13/70. Actor. *Lonesome Dove.*

SCHULTZ, DWIGHT. Baltimore, MD, 11/24/47. Actor. H. M. "Howling Mad" Murdock on *The A-Team.*

SCHULZ, CHARLES. Minneapolis, MN, 11/26/22. Cartoonist. *Peanuts.*

SCHWARZKOPF, NORMAN. Trenton, NJ, 8/22/34. Retired army general, Gulf War hero.

SCHYGULLA, HANNA. Katlowitz, Germany, 12/25/43. Actor. *Dead Again.*

SCIORRA, ANNABELLA. New York, NY, 1964. Actor. *The Hand That Rocks the Cradle.*

SCOLARI, PETER. New Rochelle, NY, 9/12/54. Actor. *Bosom Buddies.*

SCOTT, ANDY. Wrexham, Wales, 6/30/51. Guitarist. Sweet.

SCOTT, BON (Ronald Scott). Kirriemuir, Scotland, 7/9/46. Singer. AC/DC.

SCOTT, GEORGE C. Wise, VA, 10/18/27. Actor, married to Trish Van Devere. *Patton.*

SCOTT, GORDON (Gordon Werschkul). Portland, OR, 8/3/27. Actor. *Tarzan's Hidden Jungle.*

SCOTT, HOWARD. San Pedro, CA, 3/15/46. Guitarist, singer. War.

SCOTT, MIKE. Edinburgh, Scotland, 12/14/58. Singer, guitarist. The Waterboys.

SCOTT, RIDLEY. South Shields, England, 11/30/37. Director, brother of director Tony. *Thelma and Louise.*

SCOTT, WILLARD. Alexandria, VA, 3/7/34. Weatherman. *Today.*

SEAL, ELIZABETH. Genoa, Italy, 8/28/33. Actor. *Irma La Douce.*

SEALE, BOBBY. Dallas, TX, 10/20/36. Political activist, author. Cofounder of the Black Panthers.

SEALS, JIM. Sidney, TX, 10/17/41. Singer, guitarist, saxophonist, violinist. Seals & Crofts.

SEAVER, TOM. Fresno, CA, 11/17/44. Baseball pitcher.

SEBASTIAN, JOHN. New York, NY, 3/17/44. Singer, guitarist, harmonicist, autoharpist. "The Lovin' Spoonful."

SEDAKA, NEIL. Brooklyn, NY, 3/13/39. Pop singer, songwriter. "Laughter in the Rain."

SEDGWICK, KYRA. New York, NY, 8/19/65. Actor, married to Kevin Bacon.

SEEGER, PETE. New York, NY, 5/3/19. Folk singer, songwriter, guitarist, social activist. Founded The Weavers.

SEGAL, GEORGE. New York, NY, 2/13/34. Actor. *Look Who's Talking.*

SEGER, BOB. Dearborn, MI, 5/6/45. Singer, songwriter. The Silver Bullet Band.

SELLECCA, CONNIE (Concetta Sellecchia). The Bronx, NY, 5/25/55. Actor, married to John Tesh. *Hotel.*

SELLECK, TOM. Detroit, MI, 1/29/45. Actor. *Magnum, P.I.*

SENDAK, MAURICE. New York, NY, 1/10/28. Author, illustrator. *Where the Wild Things Are.*

SENSIBLE, CAPTAIN (Ray Burns). England, 4/23/55. Bassist. The Damned.

SERAPHINE, DANNY. Chicago, IL, 8/28/48. Drummer. Chicago.

SERGEANT, WILL. Liverpool, England, 4/12/58. Guitarist. Echo & The Bunnymen.

SETZER, BRIAN. 4/10/60. Guitarist, singer. The Stray Cats.

SEVERIN, STEVE. 9/25/55. Bassist. Siouxsie & The Banshees.

SEYMOUR, STEPHANIE. San Diego, CA, 7/23/68. Supermodel.

SHALIT, GENE. New York, NY, 1932. Critic. *Today.*

SHAPIRO, HELEN. Bethnal Green, England, 9/28/46. Singer, actor, cabaret performer.

SHARIF, OMAR (Michel Shalhoub). Alexandria, Egypt, 4/10/32. Actor. *Dr. Zhivago.*

SHARKEY, FEARGAL. Londonderry, Northern Ireland, 8/13/58. Singer. The Undertones.

SHARP, DAVE. Salford, England, 1/28/59. Guitarist. The Alarm.

SHARPTON, AL. Brooklyn, NY, 1954. Politician, activist, clergyman.

SHAVER, HELEN. St. Thomas, Canada, 2/24/51. Actor. *The Amityville Horror.*

SHAW, SANDIE (Sandra Goodrich). Dagenham, England, 2/26/47. Pop singer.

SHAW, TOMMY. Montgomery, AL, 9/11/52. Lead guitarist. Styx.

SHAWN, WALLACE. New York, NY, 11/12/43. Playwright, actor. *My Dinner with Andre.*

SHEA, JOHN. North Conway, NH, 4/14/49. Actor. *Lois & Clark.*

SHEARER, HARRY. Los Angeles, CA, 12/23/43. Actor. *This Is Spinal Tap.*

SHEEDY, ALLY. New York, NY, 6/13/62. Actor. *WarGames.*

SHEEHAN, FRAN. Boston, MA, 3/26/49. Bassist. Boston.

SHEEN, MARTIN (Ramon Estevez). Dayton, OH, 8/3/40. Actor, father of Charlie Sheen and Emilio Estevez. *Apocalypse Now.*

SHEILA E. (Sheila Escovedo). Oakland, CA, 12/12/59. Drummer, singer.

SHELDON, SIDNEY. Chicago, IL, 2/11/17. Novelist, producer. *The Other Side of Midnight.*

SHELLEY, CAROLE. London, England, 8/16/39. Actor. *The Elephant Man.*

SHELLEY, PETE (Peter McNeish). Lancashire, England, 4/17/55. Guitarist, singer. The Buzzcocks.

SHEPARD, SAM (Sam Rogers). Ft. Sheridan, IL, 11/5/43. Playwright, actor. *True West; The Right Stuff.*

SHEPHERD, CYBILL. Memphis, TN, 2/18/50. Actor. Maddie Hayes on *Moonlighting.*

SHERIDAN, JIM. Dublin, Ireland, 1949. Director, writer. *My Left Foot.*

SHERIDAN, NICOLLETTE. Worthington, England, 11/21/63. Actor, model. *The Sure Thing.*

SHIRE, TALIA (Talia Rose Coppola). Lake Success, NY, 4/25/46. Actor, sister of Francis Ford Coppola. *Rocky I–V.*

SHORROCK, GLENN. Rochester, England, 6/30/44. Singer. The Little River Band.

SHORT, MARTIN. Toronto, Canada, 3/26/50. Actor. Ed Grimley on *Saturday Night Live.*

SHOWALTER, MAX (Casey Adams). Caldwell, KS, 6/2/17. Actor. First Ward Cleaver in the *Leave It to Beaver* pilot, "It's a Small World."

SHRIVER, MARIA. Chicago, IL, 11/6/55. Broadcast journalist,

married to Arnold Schwarzenegger. *First Person with Maria Shriver.*

SIEGEL, JAY. Brooklyn, NY, 10/20/39. Baritone singer. The Tokens.

SIEGEL, JERRY. Cleveland, OH, 10/17/14. Cartoonist. *Superman.*

SIKKING, JAMES B. Los Angeles, CA, 3/5/34. Actor. Lt. Howard Hunter on *Hill Street Blues.*

SILLS, BEVERLY. New York, NY, 5/25/29. Opera singer.

SILVER, RON. New York, NY, 7/2/46. Actor, director. *Reversal of Fortune.*

SILVERMAN, JONATHAN. Los Angeles, CA, 8/5/66. Actor. *Brighton Beach Memoirs.*

SIMMONS, GENE (Chaim Witz). Haifa, Israel, 8/25/50. Long-tongued bassist, singer. Kiss.

SIMMONS, JEAN. London, England, 1/31/29. Actor. *The Thorn Birds.*

SIMMONS, JOSEPH. Queens, NY, 1964. Rap artist. Run-D.M.C.

SIMMONS, PATRICK. Aberdeen, WA, 1/23/50. Guitarist, singer. The Doobie Brothers.

SIMMONS, RICHARD. New Orleans, LA, 7/12/48. Health guru. *Sweatin' to the Oldies.*

SIMON, CARLY. New York, NY, 6/25/45. Singer, songwriter, childrens' book author.

SIMONE, NINA. Tryon, NC, 2/21/33. Singer. Soundtrack for *The Crying Game.*

SIMONON, PAUL. Brixton, England, 12/15/55. Bassist. The Clash.

SINCLAIR, MADGE. Kingston, Jamaica, 4/28/38. Actor. *Trapper John, MD.*

SINGER, LORI. Corpus Christi, TX, 5/6/62. Actor. *Fame.*

SINGLETON, JOHN. Los Angeles, CA, 1/6/68. Director, writer. *Boyz N the Hood.*

SINGLETON, STEPHEN. Sheffield, England, 4/17/59. Saxophonist. ABC.

SIOUX, SIOUXSIE (Susan Dallon). Chiselhurst, England, 5/27/57. Singer. Siouxsie & The Banshees.

SISKEL, GENE. Chicago, IL, 1/26/46. Critic. *Siskel & Ebert & The Movies.*

SIXX, NIKKI (Frank Ferrano). Seattle, WA, 12/11/58. Bassist. Mötley Crüe.

SKELTON, RED (Richard Skelton). Vincennes, IN, 7/18/13. Actor. *The Red Skelton Show.*

SKERRITT, TOM. Detroit, MI, 8/25/33. Actor. *Picket Fences.*

SKYE, IONE (Ione Leitch). London, England, 9/4/71. Actor, daughter of folk singer Donovan, sister of Donovan Leitch. *Say Anything.*

SLATER, HELEN. New York, NY, 12/15/65. Actor. *Supergirl.*

SLATER, RODNEY. Lincolnshire, England, 11/8/44. Saxophonist, trumpeter. The Bonzo Dog Doo-Dah Band.

SLEDGE, DEBBIE. Philadelphia, PA, 7/9/54. Singer. Sister Sledge.

SLEDGE, JONI. Philadelphia, PA, 9/13/56. Singer. Sister Sledge.

SLEDGE, KATHY. Philadelphia, PA, 1/6/59. Singer. Sister Sledge.

SLEDGE, KIM. Philadelphia, PA, 8/21/57. Singer. Sister Sledge.

SLEDGE, PERCY. Leighton, AL, 11/25/41. Singer. "When a Man Loves a Woman."

SLICK, GRACE (Grace Wing). Chicago, IL, 10/30/39. Singer. Jefferson Airplane/Starship.

SLIWA, CURTIS. New York, NY, 3/26/54. Founder of the Guardian Angels.

SMIRNOFF, YAKOV (Yakov Pokhis). Odessa, Russia, 1/24/51. Actor. *What a Country!*

SMITH, ADRIAN. Huckney, England, 2/27/57. Guitarist. Iron Maiden.

SMITH, BOB. Buffalo, NY, 11/27/17. Entertainer. *Howdy Doody.*

SMITH, BOBBIE. 4/10/36. Singer. The (Detroit) Spinners.

SMITH, CHARLES MARTIN. Los Angeles, CA, 10/30/53. Actor. *American Graffiti.*

SMITH, CLAYDES (Charles Smith). Jersey City, NJ, 9/6/48. Guitarist. Kool & The Gang.

SMITH, CURT. Bath, England, 6/24/61. Singer, bassist. Tears for Fears.

SMITH, JACLYN. Houston, TX, 10/26/47. Actor. Kelly Garrett on *Charlie's Angels.*

SMITH, JEFF. Seattle, WA, 1/22/39. TV personality, chef, author. *The Frugal Gourmet.*

SMITH, JEROME. Miami, FL, 6/18/53. Guitarist. KC & The Sunshine Band.

SMITH, LARRY. Oxford, England, 1/18/44. Drummer. The Bonzo Dog Doo-Dah Band.

SMITH, LIZ. Fort Worth, TX, 2/2/23. Gossip columnist.

SMITH, MAGGIE. Ilford, England, 12/28/34. Actor. *Sister Act.*

SMITH, MIKE. Neath, Wales, 11/4/47. Tenor saxophonist. Amen Corner.

SMITH, MIKE. Edmonton, England, 12/12/43. Singer, keyboardist. The Dave Clark Five.

SMITH, PATTI. Chicago, IL, 12/31/46. Singer, songwriter.

SMITH, PHIL. 5/1/59. Saxophonist. Haircut 100.

SMITH, ROBERT. Crawley, England, 4/21/59. Guitarist, singer. The Cure.

SMITS, JIMMY. New York, NY, 7/9/55. Actor. Victor Sifuentes on *L.A. Law.*

SMOTHERS, DICK. New York, NY, 11/20/39. Actor, singer, brother of Tom. *The Smothers Brothers Comedy Hour.*

SMOTHERS, TOM. New York, NY, 2/2/37. Actor, singer, brother of Dick. *The Smothers Brothers Comedy Hour.*

SMYTH, PATTY. New York, NY, 6/26/57. Singer, relationship with John McEnroe. "The Warrior."

SNEED, FLOYD. Calgary, Canada, 11/22/43. Drummer. Three Dog Night.

SNODGRESS, CARRIE. Chicago, IL, 10/27/46. Actor. *Diary of a Mad Housewife.*

SOMERS, SUZANNE (Suzanne Mahoney). San Bruno, CA, 10/16/46. Actor. *Three's Company.*

SOMERVILLE, JIMMY. Glasgow, Scotland, 6/22/61. Dance/rock singer, keyboardist.

SOMMER, ELKE (Elke Schletz). Berlin, Germany, 11/5/40. Actor. *A Shot in the Dark.*

SORVINO, PAUL. New York, NY, 4/13/39. Actor. *GoodFellas.*

SOTHERN, ANN (Harriet Lake). Valley City, ND, 1/22/09. Actor. *The Ann Sothern Show.*

SOUL, DAVID (David Solberg). Chicago, IL, 8/28/43. Actor. Kevin "Hutch" Hutchinson on *Starsky and Hutch.*

SOUTH, JOE. Atlanta, GA, 2/28/40. Rock/country guitarist, singer, songwriter.

SOUTHSIDE JOHNNY (Johnny Lyon). Neptune Park, NJ, 12/4/48. Singer. Southside Johnny & The Asbury Jukes.

SPACEK, SISSY (Mary Elizabeth Spacek). Quitman, TX, 12/25/49. Actor. *Coal Miner's Daughter.*

SPADER, JAMES. Boston, MA, 2/7/60. Actor. *sex, lies, and videotape.*

SPANO, JOE. San Francisco, CA, 7/7/46. Actor. Henry Goldblume on *Hill Street Blues.*

SPANO, VINCENT. New York, NY, 10/18/62. Actor. *Rumble Fish.*

SPEAR, ROGER. London, England, 6/29/43. Saxophonist, kazooist. The Bonzo Dog Doo-Dah Band.

SPECTOR, PHIL. New York, NY, 12/26/40. Music producer. Wall of sound.

SPECTOR, RONNIE (Veronica Bennett). New York, NY, 8/10/43. Lead singer. The Ronettes.

SPELLING, TORI. Los Angeles, CA, 5/16/73. Actor, daughter of Aaron Spelling. Donna on *Beverly Hills, 90210.*

SPENCE, ALEXANDER. Windsor, Canada, 4/18/46. Guitarist, lead singer. Moby Grape.

SPENCER, JEREMY. West Hartlepoole, England, 7/4/48. Guitarist. Fleetwood Mac.

SPILLANE, MICKEY (Frank Morrison). New York, NY, 3/9/18. Author. Mike Hammer detective stories.

SPINKS, LEON. St. Louis, MO, 7/11/53. Boxer, former heavyweight champion, brother of Michael.

SPINKS, MICHAEL. St. Louis, MO, 7/29/56. Boxer. Olympic gold medalist, brother of Leon.

SPOCK, BENJAMIN. New Haven, CT, 5/2/03. Physician, author. *Common Sense Book of Baby Care.*

SPOONER, BILL. Phoenix, AZ, 4/16/49. Guitarist. The Tubes.

SPRINGFIELD, DUSTY (Mary O'Brien). Hampstead, England, 4/16/39. Folk/pop singer.

SPRINGFIELD, RICK (Richard Spring Thorpe). Sydney, Australia, 8/23/49. Singer, actor. *General Hospital.*

SQUIER, BILLY. Wellesley, MA, 5/12/50. Singer. "Everybody Wants You."

SQUIRE, CHRIS. London, England, 3/4/48. Bassist. Yes.

SQUIRE, JOHN. Sale, England, 11/24/62. Lead guitarist. The Stone Roses.

ST. JOHN, JILL (Jill Oppenheim). Los Angeles, CA, 8/19/40. Actor, married to Robert Wagner. *Diamonds Are Forever.*

STACK, ROBERT. Los Angeles, CA, 1/13/19. Actor. Eliot Ness on *The Untouchables.*

STAFFORD, JIM. Eloise, FL, 1/16/44. Singer, songwriter. "Spiders and Snakes."

STAMOS, JOHN. Cypress, CA, 8/19/63. Actor. *Full House.*

STAMP, TERENCE. London, England, 7/23/39. Actor. *Superman II.*

STANLEY, PAUL (Paul Eisen). Queens, NY, 1/20/50. Guitarist, singer. Kiss.

STANSFIELD, LISA. Rochdale, England, 4/11/66. Singer, songwriter. "All Around the World."

STANTON, HARRY DEAN. West Irvine, KY, 7/14/26. Actor. *Paris, Texas.*

STAPLES, NEVILLE. 4/11/56. Singer, percussionist. The Specials.

STAPLES, PETE. Andover, England, 5/3/44. Bassist. The Troggs.

STAPLETON, JEAN (Jeanne Murray). New York, NY, 1/19/23. Actor. Edith Bunker on *All in the Family.*

STAPLETON, MAUREEN. Troy, NY, 6/21/25. Actor. *Airport.*

STARR, RINGO (Richard Starkey). Liverpool, England, 7/7/40. Drummer, singer, actor, married to Barbara Bach. The Beatles.

STAUBACH, ROGER. Cincinnati, OH, 2/5/42. NFL football player. Dallas Cowboys.

STAX, JOHN (John Fullegar). London, England, 4/6/44. Bassist. The Pretty Things.

STEEL, JOHN. Gateshead, England, 2/4/41. Drummer. The Animals.

STEELE, DAVID. Birmingham, England, 9/8/60. Keyboardist, bassist. Fine Young Cannibals.

STEELE, MICHAEL. 6/2/54. Bassist, singer. The Bangles; The Runaways.

STEELE, TOMMY (Thomas Hicks). Bermondsey, England, 12/17/36. Guitarist, singer, actor.

STEENBURGEN, MARY. Newport, AR, 2/8/53. Actor, engaged to Ted Danson. *Parenthood.*

STEIGER, ROD. Westhampton, NY, 4/14/25. Actor. *In the Heat of the Night.*

STEIN, CHRIS. Brooklyn, NY, 1/5/50. Guitarist. Blondie.

STEIN, MARK. Bayonne, NJ, 3/11/47. Singer, organist. Vanilla Fudge.

STEINBERG, DAVID. Winnipeg, Canada, 8/9/42. Actor, director. *Paternity.*

STEINEM, GLORIA. Toledo, OH, 3/25/34. Women's rights activist.

STERBAN, RICHARD. Camden, NJ, 4/24/43. Singer, bassist. The Oak Ridge Boys.

STERN, DANIEL. Bethesda, MD, 8/28/57. Actor, narrator of *The Wonder Years. City Slickers.*

STERN, ISAAC. Kreminiecz, Russia, 7/21/20. Violinist.

STERNHAGEN, FRANCES. Washington, DC, 1/13/30. Actor. *Driving Miss Daisy.*

STEVENS, ANDREW. Memphis, TN, 6/10/55. Actor, son of Stella. *Dallas.*

STEVENS, CAT (Steven Georgiou). Soho, England, 7/21/47. Folk singer, songwriter—left recording upon conversion to Islam.

STEVENS, CONNIE (Concetta Ann Ingolia). Brooklyn, NY, 8/8/38. Actor. *Hawaiian Eye.*

STEVENS, FISHER. Chicago, IL, 11/27/63. Actor. *Short Circuit.*

STEVENS, RAY (Ray Ragsdale). Clarksdale, GA, 1/24/39. Singer. *Andy Williams Presents Ray Stevens.*

STEVENS, SHAKIN' (Michael Barratt). Ely, Wales, 3/4/48. Singer, actor.

STEVENS, STELLA (Estelle Eggleston). Hot Coffee, MS, 10/1/36. Actor, mother of Andrew. *Santa Barbara.*

STEVENSON, DON. Seattle, WA, 10/15/42. Drummer. Moby Grape.

STEVENSON, MCLEAN. Bloomington, IL, 11/14/29. Actor. Lt. Colonel Henry Blake on *M*A*S*H.*

STEVENSON, PARKER. Philadelphia, PA, 6/4/52. Actor, married to Kirstie Alley. *Falcon Crest.*

STEWART, AL. Glasgow, Scotland, 9/5/45. Guitarist, singer, songwriter.

STEWART, DAVE. Sunderland, England, 9/9/52. Keyboardist, guitarist. Eurythmics.

STEWART, ERIC. Manchester, England, 1/20/45. Singer, guitarist. 10cc.

STEWART, JIMMY. Indiana, PA, 5/20/08. Actor. *It's a Wonderful Life.*

STEWART, MARTHA (Martha Haworth). Bardwell, KY, 10/7/22. Actor. *Holocaust.*

STEWART, ROD. Highgate, England, 1/10/45. Singer, songwriter.

STIERS, DAVID OGDEN. Peoria, IL, 10/31/42. Actor. Dr. Charles Emerson Winchester on *M*A*S*H*.

STILES, RAY. Carshalton, England, 11/20/46. Bassist, singer. Mud.

STILLER, JERRY. New York, NY, 6/8/31. Actor, partner/married to Anne Meara, father of Ben Stiller.

STILLS, STEPHEN. Dallas, TX, 1/3/45. Singer, guitarist. Buffalo Springfield; Crosby, Stills, Nash & Young.

STOCKDALE, JAMES. Abington, IL, 12/23/23. Vietnam POW, running mate of presidential candidate Ross Perot.

STOCKWELL, DEAN. Hollywood, CA, 3/5/35. Actor. Al Calavicci on *Quantum Leap*.

STOCKWELL, JOHN (John Samuels). Galveston, TX, 3/25/61. Actor. *My Science Project*.

STOLTZ, ERIC. American Samoa, 9/30/61. Actor. *Mask*.

STONE, DEE WALLACE (Deanna Bowers). Kansas City, MO, 12/14/48. Actor. Mother in *E.T., the Extra-Terrestrial*.

STONE, FREDDIE. Dallas, TX, 6/5/46. Guitarist. Sly & The Family Stone.

STONE, ROSIE. Vallejo, CA, 3/21/45. Singer, keyboardist. Sly & The Family Stone.

STONE, SLY (Sylvester Stewart). Dallas, TX, 3/15/44. Singer, keyboardist, guitarist. Sly & The Family Stone.

STORCH, LARRY. New York, NY, 1/8/23. Actor. *F Troop*.

STORM, GALE (Josephine Cottle). Bloomington, TX, 4/5/22. Actor. *My Little Margie*.

STRASSMAN, MARCIA. New York, NY, 4/28/48. Actor. Julie Kotter on *Welcome Back Kotter*.

STRATHAIRN, DAVID. San Francisco, CA, 1949. Actor. *Matewan*.

STRATTON, DENNIS. London, England, 11/9/54. Guitarist. Iron Maiden.

STRAUSS, PETER. Croton-on-Hudson, NY, 2/20/47. Actor. *The Jericho Mile*.

STRICKLAND, KEITH. Athens, GA, 10/26/53. Drummer. The B-52's.

STRITCH, ELAINE. Detroit, MI, 2/2/25. Actor. *September*.

STRUMMER, JOE (John Mellors). Ankara, Turkey, 8/21/52. Singer, guitarist. The Clash.

STRUTHERS, SALLY. Portland, OR, 7/28/48. Actor. Gloria Bunker Stivic on *All in the Family*.

STRYKERT, RON. Australia, 8/18/57. Guitarist. Men at Work.

STUART, CHAD. England, 12/10/43. Singer, guitarist. Chad & Jeremy.

STUART, HAMISH. Glasgow, Scotland, 10/8/49. Singer, guitarist. Average White Band.

STUBBS, LEVI (Levi Stubbles). Detroit, MI, 6/6/36. Lead singer. The Four Tops.

SUCH, ALEC. 11/14/56. Bassist. Bon Jovi.

SULLIVAN, SUSAN. New York, NY, 11/18/44. Actor. Maggie Gioberti Channing on *Falcon Crest*.

SULLIVAN, TOM. Boston, MA, 3/27/47. Singer, actor, composer. "If You Could See What I Hear."

SUMMER, DONNA (LaDonna Gaines). Boston, MA, 12/31/48. Disco/pop singer. "Love To Love You Baby.".

SUMMERS, ANDY (Andrew Somers). Poulton le Fylde, France, 12/31/42. Guitarist, singer. The Police.

SUMNER, BARNEY (Bernard Dicken). Salford, England, 1/4/56. Guitarist, singer. New Order.

SUTHERLAND, DONALD. St. John, Canada, 7/17/34. Actor, father of Kiefer. *Ordinary People*.

SUTHERLAND, KIEFER. Los Angeles, CA, 12/18/66. Actor, son of Donald. *Flatliners*.

SUZMAN, JANET. Johannesburg, South Africa, 2/9/39. Actor. *Nicholas and Alexandra*.

SVENSON, BO. Goreborg, Sweden, 2/13/41. Actor. *Walking Tall*.

SWAGGART, JIMMY. Ferriday, LA, 3/15/35. Evangelist.

SWANN, LYNN. Alcoa, TN, 3/7/52. NFL football player.

SWAYZE, PATRICK. Houston, TX, 8/18/52. Actor, dancer. *Dirty Dancing*.

SWEENEY, D. B. (Daniel Bernard Sweeney). Shoreham, NY, 1961. Actor. *The Cutting Edge*.

SWEET, DERRELL. 5/16/47. Drummer, percussionist, singer. Nazareth.

SWEET, MATTHEW. Lincoln, NE, 10/6/64. Singer, songwriter, guitarist. "Girlfriend."

SWENSON, INGA. Omaha, NE, 12/29/32. Actor. Gretchen Kraus on *Benson*.

SWIT, LORETTA. Passaic, NJ, 11/4/37. Actor. Margaret "Hot Lips" Houlihan on *M*A*S*H*.

SYLVIAN, DAVID (David Batt). Lewisham, England, 2/23/58. Singer, guitarist. Japan.

T, MR. (Lawrence Tero). Chicago, IL, 5/21/52. Actor and wrestler. Bosco "B.A." Baracus on *The A-Team*.

TAJ MAHAL. New York, NY, 5/17/42. Singer, songwriter, composer. "Sounder."

TAKEI, GEORGE. Los Angeles, CA, 4/20/39. Mr. Sulu on *Star Trek*.

TALBOT, MICK. London, England, 9/11/58. Keyboardist. The Style Council.

TALLEY, GARY. Memphis, TN, 8/17/47. Guitarist. The Box Tops/Big Star.

TALLEY, NEDRA. New York, NY, 1/27/46. Singer. The Ronettes.

TAMBLYN, RUSS. Los Angeles, CA, 12/30/34. Actor. *West Side Story*.

TAMBOR, JEFFREY. San Francisco, CA, 7/8/44. Actor. *Hill Street Blues*.

TANDY, RICHARD. Birmingham, England, 3/26/48. Bassist. Electric Light Orchestra (ELO).

TARKENTON, FRAN. Richmond, VA, 2/3/40. Football player, sportscaster. *Monday Night Football*.

TAUPIN, BERNIE. Sleaford, England, 5/22/50. Lyricist. Wrote for Elton John.

TAYLOR, ANDY. Tynemouth, England, 2/16/61. Guitarist. Duran Duran.

TAYLOR, CLIVE. Cardiff, Wales, 4/27/49. Bassist. Amen Corner.

TAYLOR, DICK. Dartford, England, 1/28/43. Lead guitarist. The Pretty Things.

TAYLOR, JAMES. South Carolina, 8/16/53. Lead singer. Kool & The Gang.

TAYLOR, JAMES. Boston, MA, 3/12/48. Folk-oriented singer, songwriter.

TAYLOR, JOHN. Birmingham, England, 6/20/60. Bassist. Duran Duran.

TAYLOR, LARRY. Brooklyn, NY, 6/26/42. Bassist. Canned Heat.

TAYLOR, LILI. Chicago, IL, 1967. Actor. *Mystic Pizza*.

TAYLOR, ROD. Sydney, Australia, 1/11/29. Actor. *The Time Machine*.

TAYLOR, ROGER. King's Lynn, England, 7/26/49. Drummer. Queen.

TENCH, BENMONT. Gainesville, FL, 9/7/54. Keyboardist. Tom Petty & The Heartbreakers.

TENNANT, NEIL. Gosforth, England, 7/10/54. Singer. Pet Shop Boys.

TENNANT, VICTORIA. London, England, 9/30/50. Actor, formerly married to Steve Martin. *L.A. Story*.

TENNILLE, TONI. Montgomery, AL, 5/8/43. Singer. The Captain & Tennille.

TERRANOVA, JOE. 1/30/41. Baritone. Danny & The Juniors.

THICKE, ALAN. Ontario, Canada, 3/1/47. Actor. *Growing Pains*.

THISTLETHWAITE, ANTHONY. Leicester, England, 8/31/55. Saxophonist. The Waterboys.

THOMAS, B. J. (Billy Joe Thomas). Hugo, OK, 8/7/42. Pop singer. "Raindrops Keep Fallin' on My Head."

THOMAS, BETTY. Saint Louis, MO, 7/27/48. Actor. Lucy Bates on *Hill Street Blues*.

THOMAS, DAVE. Saint Catharines, Canada, 6/20/49. Actor. Doug MacKenzie on *SCTV*.

THOMAS, HENRY. San Antonio, TX, 9/8/72. Actor. Elliot in *E.T., the Extra-Terrestrial*.

THOMAS, JAY. New Orleans, LA, 7/12/48. Actor, radio personality. *Murphy Brown*.

THOMAS, MARLO (Margaret Thomas). Detroit, MI, 11/21/38. Actor, married to Phil Donahue,

daughter of Danny Thomas. *That Girl*.

THOMAS, MARY. Brooklyn, NY, 1946. Singer. The Crystals.

THOMAS, PHILIP MICHAEL. Columbus, OH, 5/26/49. Actor. Ricardo Tubbs on *Miami Vice*.

THOMAS, RAY. Stourport-on-Severn, England, 12/29/42. Flautist, harmonicist, singer. The Moody Blues.

THOMAS, RICHARD. New York, NY, 6/13/51. Actor. John Boy on *The Waltons*.

THOMPKINS, RUSSELL JR. Philadelphia, PA, 3/21/51. Lead singer. The Stylistics.

THOMPSON, LEA. Rochester, MN, 5/31/61. Actor. *Back to the Future*.

THOMPSON, PAUL. Jarrow, England, 5/13/51. Drummer. Roxy Music.

THOMPSON, SADA. Des Moines, IA, 9/27/29. Actor. *Family*.

THOMPSON, TONY. 11/15/54. Drummer. Chic.

THOMSON, DOUGIE. Glasgow, Scotland, 3/24/51. Bassist. Supertramp.

THORN, TRACEY. Hartfordshire, England, 9/26/62. Singer. Everything but the Girl.

THORNE-SMITH, COURTNEY. 11/8/68. Actor. *Melrose Place*.

THORNTON, BLAIR. Vancouver, Canada, 7/23/50. Guitarist. Bachman-Turner Overdrive.

THOROGOOD, GEORGE. Wilmington, DE, 1951. Singer, guitarist. George Thorogood and the Delaware Destroyers.

TICH (Ian Amey). Salisbury, England, 5/15/44. Lead guitarist. Dave Dee, Dozy, Beaky, Mick and Tich.

TIEGS, CHERYL. Alhambra, CA, 9/25/47. Model, author. *The Way to Natural Beauty*.

TIFFANY (Tiffany Renee Darwish). Norwalk, CA, 10/2/71. Singer.

TILBROOK, GLENN. London, England, 8/31/57. Singer, lead guitarist. Squeeze.

TILLIS, MEL. Pahokee, FL, 8/8/32. Singer, songwriter, father of Pam Tillis.

TILLIS, PAM. Plant City, FL, 7/24/57. Singer, daughter of Mel Tillis.

TILLY, MEG. Texada, Canada, 2/14/60. Actor, sister of Jennifer. *The Big Chill*.

TILTON, CHARLENE. San Diego, CA, 12/1/58. Actor. Lucy Ewing Cooper on *Dallas*.

TIM, TINY (Herbert Khaury). New York, NY, 4/12/22. Entertainer. "Tiptoe Through the Tulips."

TIPTON, GLENN. Birmingham, England, 10/25/48. Guitarist. Judas Priest.

TOLHURST, LOL (Laurence Tolhurst). 2/3/59. Keyboardist. The Cure.

TOLKAN, JAMES. Calumet, MI, 6/20/31. Actor. Principal in *Back to the Future*.

TOMLIN, LILY (Mary Jean Tomlin). Detroit, MI, 9/1/39. Actor. *Rowan & Martin's Laugh-In*.

TONE-LOC. Los Angeles, CA, 3/3/66. Rap artist. "Wild Thing."

TOPHAM, ANTHONY "TOP." England, 1947. Guitarist. The Yardbirds.

TORK, PETER (Peter Halsten Thorkelson). Washington, DC, 2/13/44. Keyboardist, bassist, actor. The Monkees.

TORME, MEL. Chicago, IL, 9/13/25. Singer.

TORN, RIP. (Elmore Rual Torn Jr.). Temple, TX, 2/6/31. Actor. *Blind Ambition*.

TORRENCE, DEAN. Los Angeles, CA, 3/10/40. Singer. Jan & Dean.

TOWNSEND, ROBERT. Chicago, IL, 2/6/57. Actor. *Hollywood Shuffle*.

TOWNSHEND, PETE. Chiswick, England, 5/19/45. Guitarist. The Who.

TOWNSON, RON. St. Louis, MO, 1/20/33. Singer. The 5th Dimension.

TRAVANTI, DANIEL J. Kenosha, WI, 3/7/40. Actor. Captain Frank Furillo on *Hill Street Blues*.

TRAVERS, BILL. Newcastle-upon-Tyne, England, 1/3/22. Actor, producer, director. *Born Free*.

TRAVERS, BRIAN. Birmingham, England, 2/7/59. Saxophonist. UB40.

TRAVIS, RANDY (Randy Traywick). Marshville, NC, 5/4/59. Country singer, songwriter.

TREBEK, ALEX. Sudbury, Canada, 7/22/40. Game show host. *Jeopardy!*

TRESVANT, RALPH. Boston, MA, 5/16/68. Singer. New Edition.

TREVOR, CLAIRE (Claire Wemlinger). New York, NY, 3/8/09. Actor. *Key Largo*.

TREWAVAS, PETER. Middlesborough, England, 1/15/59. Keyboardist. Marillion.

TRITT, TRAVIS. Marietta, GA, 2/9/63. Country singer, songwriter.

TROWER, ROBIN. Southend, England, 3/9/45. Guitarist. Procol Harum.

TRUDEAU, GARRY (Garretson Beckman Trudeau). New York, NY, 1948. Cartoonist, married to Jane Pauley. *Doonesbury*.

TRUGOY THE DOVE (David Jolicoeur). 9/21/68. Musician. De La Soul.

TRUMP, DONALD. New York, NY, 6/14/46. Real estate developer, author. Married to Marla Maples, formerly married to Ivana Winkelmayr Trump.

TRUMP, MARLA MAPLES. 10/27/63. Actor. Married to Donald Trump. *The Will Rogers Follies*.

TUCKER, JIM. Los Angeles, CA, 10/17/46. Guitarist. The Turtles.

TUCKER, MICHAEL. Baltimore, MD, 2/6/44. Actor, married to Jill Eikenberry. *L.A. Law*.

TUCKER, MICK. Harlesden, England, 7/17/49. Drummer. Sweet.

TUCKER, TANYA. Seminole, TX, 10/10/58. Pop singer. "Delta Dawn."

TUFANO, DENNIS. Chicago, IL, 9/11/46. Guitarist, lead singer. The Buckinghams.

TUNE, TOMMY. Wichita Falls, TX, 2/28/39. Actor, director, choreographer, dancer.

TURBO B. (Durron Maurice Butler). Pittsburgh, PA, 4/30/67. Rap artist. Snap.

TURNER, C. F. Winnipeg, Canada, 10/16/43. Bassist, singer. Bachman-Turner Overdrive.

TURNER, IKE. Clarksdale, MS, 11/5/31. Singer, songwriter, formerly married to Tina Turner. Ike & Tina Turner.

TURNER, JANINE (Janine Gauntt). Lincoln, NE, 12/6/63. Actor. *Northern Exposure*.

TURNER, LONNIE. Berkeley, CA, 2/24/47. Bassist, singer. The Steve Miller Band.

TUROW, SCOTT. Chicago, IL, 4/12/49. Author. *The Burden of Proof*.

TURTURRO, JOHN. Brooklyn, NY, 2/28/57. Actor. *Barton Fink*.

TWIGGY (Lesley Hornby). London, England, 9/19/49. Model, actor. *The Boy Friend*.

TWIST, NIGEL. Manchester, England, 7/18/58. Drummer. The Alarm.

TYLER, BONNIE (Gaynor Hopkins). Swansea, Wales, 6/8/53. Singer. "Total Eclipse of the Heart."

TYLER, RICHARD. Sunshine, Australia, 1948. Designer.

TYSON, CICELY. New York, NY, 12/19/33. Actor. *The Autobiography of Miss Jane Pittman*.

UECKER, BOB. Milwaukee, WI, 1/26/35. Actor. *Mr. Belvedere*.

UGGAMS, LESLIE. New York, NY, 5/25/43. Singer, actor. Kizzy in *Roots*.

ULLMAN, TRACEY. Hackbridge, England, 12/30/59. Actor. *The Tracey Ullman Show*.

ULLMANN, LIV. Tokyo, Japan, 12/16/39. Actor. *Persona*.

ULVAEUS, BJORN. Gothenburg, Sweden, 4/25/45. Guitarist, singer. Abba.

URICH, ROBERT. Toronto, Canada, 12/19/46. Actor. *Spenser: For Hire*.

VACCARO, BRENDA. Brooklyn, NY, 11/18/39. Actor. *Midnight Cowboy*.

VADIM, ROGER (Roger Vadim Plemiannikov). Paris, France, 1/26/28. Movie director, formerly married to Jane Fonda.

VALE, JERRY. New York, NY, 7/8/32. Pop singer. "Innamorata."

VALE, MIKE. 7/17/49. Bassist. Tommy James & The Shondells.

VALENTINE, HILTON. North Shields, England, 5/21/43. Guitarist. The Animals.

VALENTINE, SCOTT. Saratoga Springs, NY, 6/3/58. Actor. Nick Moore on *Family Ties*.

VALLI, FRANKIE (Frank Castelluccio). Newark, NJ, 5/3/37. Lead singer. The Four Seasons.

VALLONE, RAF (Raffaele Vallone). Tropea, Italy, 2/17/18. Actor. *Obsession*.

VALORY, ROSS. San Francisco, CA, 2/2/49. Bassist. Journey.

VAN ARK, JOAN. New York, NY, 6/16/43. Actor. Val Ewing *Knots Landing*.

VAN DEVERE, TRISH (Patricia Dressel). Englewood Cliffs, NJ, 3/9/45. Actor, married to George C. Scott. *The Day of the Dolphin*.

VAN DOREN, MAMIE (Joan Lucile Olander). Rowena, SD, 2/6/31. Actor. *Ain't Misbehavin'*.

VAN DYKE, DICK. West Plains, MO, 12/13/25. Actor and performer, brother of Jerry. *The Dick Van Dyke Show*.

VAN DYKE, JERRY. Danville, IL, 7/27/31. Actor, brother of Dick. *Coach*.

VAN HALEN, ALEX. Nijmegen, Holland, 5/8/55. Drummer. Van Halen.

VAN PATTEN, DICK. New York, NY, 12/9/28. Actor. *Eight Is Enough*.

VAN PEEBLES, MARIO. New York, NY, 1/15/57. Actor, director, writer, son of Melvin. *Posse*.

VAN PEEBLES, MELVIN. Chicago, IL, 8/21/32. Actor, writer, composer, father of Mario. *Sweet Sweetback's Badasssssss Song*.

VAN ZANDT, DONNIE. Florida, 6/11/52. Singer, guitarist. .38 Special.

VAN ZANDT, STEVIE. Boston, MA, 11/22/50. Bassist. E Street Band.

VANDA, HARRY (Harry Vandenberg). The Hague, The Netherlands, 3/22/47. Guitarist. The Easybeats.

VANDERBILT, GLORIA. New York, NY, 2/20/24. Fashion designer. Gloria Vanderbilt Jeans.

VANIAN, DAVE (David Letts). 10/12/56. Singer. The Damned.

VANNELLI, GINO. Montreal, Canada, 6/16/52. Singer, songwriter. "Living Inside Myself."

VARNEY, JIM. Lexington, KY, 6/15/49. Actor. *Ernest Goes to Camp*.

VAUGHN, ROBERT. New York, NY, 11/22/32. Actor. *The Man from U.N.C.L.E.*

VEE, BOBBY (Robert Velline). Fargo, ND, 4/30/43. Singer, songwriter.

VEGA, SUZANNE. New York, NY, 8/12/59. Folk-oriented guitarist, singer, songwriter. "Luka."

VELEZ, EDDIE (Edwin Velez). New York, NY, 6/4/58. Actor. *Extremities*.

VELJOHNSON, REGINALD. Queens, NY, 8/16/52. Actor. *Family Matters*.

VENDELA (Vendela Kirsebom). Sweden, 1/12/67. Supermodel.

VERDON, GWEN. Culver City, CA, 1/13/25. Actor, dancer, choreographer. *The Cotton Club*.

VEREEN, BEN. Miami, FL, 10/10/46. Actor, performer. Chicken George Moore on *Roots*.

VERLAINE, TOM (Thomas Miller). Mt. Morris, NJ, 12/13/49. Singer, lead guitarist. Television.

VERUSCHKA. 1943. Model, actor. *Blow Up*.

VESTINE, HENRY. Washington, DC, 12/25/44. Guitarist. Canned Heat.

VICKERS, MIKE. Southampton, England, 4/18/41. Guitarist. Manfred Mann.

VIDAL, GORE (Eugene Luther Vidal). West Point, NY, 10/3/25. Author, dramatist. *Lincoln: A Novel*.

VINCENT, JAN-MICHAEL. Denver, CO, 7/15/44. Actor. *The Mechanic*.

VINTON, BOBBY. Canonsburg, PA, 4/16/35. Singer, songwriter.

VIRTUE, MICKEY. Birmingham, England, 1/19/57. Keyboardist. UB40.

VOIGHT, JON. Yonkers, NY, 12/29/38. Actor. *Midnight Cowboy*.

VOLMAN, MARK. Los Angeles, CA, 4/19/47. Singer, saxophonist. The Turtles.

VON BULOW, CLAUS. Copenhagen, Denmark, 8/11/26. Businessman. Subject of the motion picture *Reversal of Fortune*.

VON SYDOW, MAX. Lund, Sweden, 7/10/29. Actor. *The Greatest Story Ever Told*.

VONNEGUT, KURT JR. Indianapolis, IN, 11/11/22. Author. *Slaughterhouse Five*.

WAAKTAAR, PAUL. Oslo, Norway, 9/6/61. Guitarist, singer. a-ha.

WAGGONER, LYLE. Kansas City, KS, 4/13/35. Actor. *Wonder Woman*.

WAGNER, JACK. Washington, MO, 10/3/59. Actor, singer. Frisco Jones on *General Hospital*.

WAGNER, LINDSAY. Los Angeles, CA, 6/22/49. Actor. *The Bionic Woman*.

WAGNER, ROBERT. Detroit, MI, 2/10/30. Actor, widower of Natalie Wood, married to Jill St. John. Jonathan Hart on *Hart to Hart*.

WAHL, KEN. Chicago, IL, 2/14/56. Actor. Vinnie Terranova on *Wiseguy*.

WAHLBERG, DONNIE. Dorchester, MA, 8/17/70. Singer, brother of Marky Mark. New Kids on the Block.

WAILER, BUNNY (Neville O'Riley Livingston). Kingston, Jamaica, 4/10/47. Singer, percussionist. Bob Marley & The Wailers.

WAITE, JOHN. Lancaster, England, 7/4/54. Singer, songwriter.

WAITS, TOM. Pomona, CA, 12/7/49. Singer, actor, composer. *Short Cuts*.

WALKEN, CHRISTOPHER. Astoria, NY, 3/31/43. Actor. *The Deer Hunter*.

WALKER, ALICE. Eatonton, GA, 2/9/44. Author. *The Color Purple*.

WALKER, CLINT. Hartford, IL, 5/30/27. Actor. *Cheyenne*.

WALKER, DAVID. Montgomeryville, AL, 5/12/43. Keyboardist. Gary Lewis & The Playboys.

WALKER, JIMMIE. New York, NY, 6/25/48. Actor. J. J. Evans on *Good Times*.

WALKER, JUNIOR (Autry DeWalt II). Blytheville, AR, 1942. Saxophonist, singer. Junior Walker & The All-Stars.

WALKER, MORT. El Dorado, KS, 9/3/23. Cartoonist. *Beetle Bailey*.

WALLACE, MIKE (Myron Leon Wallace). Brookline, MA, 5/9/18. News reporter and interviewer, anchor. *60 Minutes*.

WALLACH, ELI. Brooklyn, NY, 12/7/15. Actor. *The Good, the Bad and the Ugly*.

WALLER, GORDON. Braemar, Scotland, 6/4/45. Singer. Peter and Gordon.

WALLINGER, KARL. Prestatyn, Wales, 10/19/57. Keyboardist, guitarist. World Party.

WALSH, JOE. Cleveland, OH, 11/20/47. Guitarist, singer. The Eagles; The James Gang.

WALSH, M. EMMET. Ogdensburg, NY, 3/22/35. Actor. *Blood Simple*.

WALSTON, RAY. New Orleans, LA, 11/22/17. Actor. Uncle Martin on *My Favorite Martian*.

WALTER, JESSICA. Brooklyn, NY, 1/31/40. Actor. *Play Misty for Me*.

WALTER, TRACEY. Jersey City, NJ. Actor. Bob the Goon in *Batman*.

WANG, VERA. New York, NY, 1949. Designer.

WARD, BILL. Birmingham, England, 5/5/48. Drummer. Black Sabbath.

WARD, BURT. Los Angeles, CA, 7/6/46. Actor. *Batman*.

WARD, FRED. San Diego, CA, 12/30/42. Actor. *Henry and June*.

WARD, RACHEL. London, England, 1957. Actor. *Against All Odds*.

WARD, SELA. Meridian, MS, 7/11/56. Actor. *Sisters*.

WARDEN, JACK (Jack Warden Lebzelter). Newark, NJ, 9/18/20. Actor. Harry Fox on *Crazy Like a Fox*.

WARE, MARTYN. Sheffield, England, 5/19/56. Synthesizer player. The Human League; Heaven 17.

WARFIELD, MARSHA. Chicago, IL, 3/5/55. Actor. Roz Russell on *Night Court*.

WARNER, DAVID. Manchester, England, 7/29/41. Actor. *The Omen*.

WARNER, JULIE. New York, NY, 1965. Actor. *Doc Hollywood*.

WARNER, MALCOLM-JAMAL. Jersey City, NJ, 8/18/70. Actor. Theo Huxtable on *The Cosby Show*.

WARNES, JENNIFER. Orange County, CA, 1947. Pop singer.

WARREN, LESLEY ANN. New York, NY, 8/16/46. Actor. *Mission: Impossible*.

WARRICK, RUTH. St. Joseph, MO, 6/29/15. Actor. Phoebe Wallingford on *All My Children*.

WARWICK, CLINT (Clinton Eccles). Birmingham, England, 6/25/40. Bassist. The Moody Blues.

WARWICK, DIONNE (Marie Warrick). East Orange, NJ, 12/12/40. Gospel/pop singer.

WATERS, JOHN. Baltimore, MD, 4/22/46. Director, writer, actor. *Hairspray; Pink Flamingos; Serial Mom*.

WATERS, ROGER. Great Bookham, England, 9/9/44. Singer, bassist. Pink Floyd.

WATERSTON, SAM. Cambridge, MA, 11/15/40. Actor. *The Killing Fields*.

WATLEY, JODY. Chicago, IL, 1/30/59. Singer. Shalamar.

WATSON, BRUCE. Ontario, Canada, 3/11/61. Guitarist. Big Country.

WATT, BEN. 12/6/62. Guitarist, keyboardist, singer. Everything but the Girl.

WATTS, CHARLIE. Islington, England, 6/2/41. Drummer. The Rolling Stones.

WATTS, OVEREND (Peter Watts). Birmingham, England, 5/13/49. Bassist. Mott The Hoople.

WAXMAN, AL. Toronto, Canada, 3/2/34. Actor. Bert Samuels on *Cagney and Lacey*.

WAYANS, KEENEN IVORY. New York, NY, 6/8/58. Actor, director, writer. *In Living Color*.

WAYBILL, FEE (John Waldo). Omaha, NE, 9/17/50. Singer. The Tubes.

WAYNE, CARL. Mosely, England, 8/18/44. Singer. The Move.

WAYNE, PATRICK. Los Angeles, CA, 7/15/39. Actor, son of John. *McClintock!*

WEATHERS, CARL. New Orleans, LA, 1/14/48. Actor. Apollo Creed in *Rocky*.

WEAVER, BLUE (Derek Weaver). Cardiff, Wales, 3/3/49. Organist. Amen Corner.

WEAVER, DENNIS. Joplin, MO, 6/4/25. Actor. *McCloud*.

WEAVER, FRITZ. Pittsburgh, PA, 1/19/26. Actor. *Marathon Man*.

WEBB, PAUL. 1/16/62. Bassist. Talk Talk.

WEIDER, JOHN. England, 4/21/47. Bassist. Family.

WEIR, BOB. San Francisco, CA, 10/6/47. Guitarist. Grateful Dead.

WEITZ, BRUCE. Norwalk, CT, 5/27/43. Actor. Mick Belker on *Hill Street Blues*.

WELCH, BRUCE (Bruce Cripps). Bognor Regis, England, 11/2/41. Guitarist. The Shadows.

WELCH, RAQUEL (Raquel Tejada). Chicago, IL, 9/5/40. Actor. *One Million Years B.C.*

WELD, TUESDAY (Susan Weld). New York, NY, 8/27/43. Actor. *Looking for Mr. Goodbar*.

WELLER, PAUL. 5/25/58. Singer, bassist. The Jam.

WELLER, PAUL. Woking, England, 5/25/58. Singer, guitarist. The Style Council.

WELLER, PETER. Stevens Point, WI, 6/24/47. Actor. *Robocop*.

WELLS, CORY. Buffalo, NY, 2/5/42. Singer. Three Dog Night.

WELLS, KITTY (Muriel Deason). Nashville, TN, 8/30/19. Country singer.

WELNICK, VINCE. Phoenix, AZ, 2/21/51. Keyboardist. The Tubes.

WENDT, GEORGE. Chicago, IL, 10/17/48. Actor. Norm Peterson on *Cheers*.

WEST, ADAM (William Anderson). Walla Walla, WA, 9/19/29. Actor. *Batman*.

WEST, JOHN. Uhrichsville, OH, 7/31/39. Guitarist. Gary Lewis & The Playboys.

WEST, RICK. Dagenham, England, 5/7/43. Lead guitarist. Brian Poole & The Tremeloes.

WESTHEIMER, RUTH (Karola Ruth Siegel). Frankfurt, Germany, 6/4/28. Sex therapist. *Ask Dr. Ruth*.

WETTON, JOHN. Derbyshire, England, 7/12/49. Lead singer, bassist. Asia.

WEYMOUTH, TINA. Coronado, CA, 11/22/50. Bassist. Talking Heads.

WHALEY, FRANK. Syracuse, NY, 1963. Actor. *The Doors*.

WHALLEY-KILMER, JOANNE. Manchester, England, 8/25/64. Actor, formerly married to Val Kilmer. *Willow*.

WHELCHEL, LISA. Fort Worth, TX, 5/29/63. Actor. Blair Warner on *The Facts of Life*.

WHITAKER, FOREST. Longview, TX, 7/15/61. Actor. *The Crying Game*.

WHITAKER, JOHNNY. Van Nuys, CA, 12/13/59. Actor. Jody on *Family Affair*.

WHITE, BARRY. Galveston, TX, 9/12/44. R&B singer, songwriter.

WHITE, BETTY. Oak Park, IL, 1/17/22. Actor. Rose Nylund on *The Golden Girls*.

WHITE, CHRIS. Barnet, England, 3/7/43. Bassist. The Zombies.

WHITE, DAVE (David Tricker). Philadelphia, PA, 9/1/40. Singer. Danny & The Juniors.

WHITE, JALEEL. Los Angeles, CA, 11/27/76. Actor. Steve Urkel on *Family Matters*.

WHITE, MARK. Sheffield, England, 4/1/61. Guitarist. ABC.

WHITE, MAURICE. Memphis, TN, 12/19/41. Singer, drummer, kalimba player. Earth, Wind & Fire.

WHITE, VANNA (Vanna Rosich). North Myrtle Beach, SC, 2/18/57. Letter turner extraordinaire. *Wheel of Fortune*.

WHITE, VERDINE. Illinois, 7/25/51. Singer, bassist. Earth, Wind & Fire.

WHITELAW, BILLIE. Coventry, England, 6/6/32. Actor. *Charlie Bubbles*.

WHITFORD, BRAD. Winchester, MA, 2/23/52. Guitarist. Aerosmith.

WHITMORE, JAMES. White Plains, NY, 10/1/21. Actor. *Will Rogers, USA*.

WHITNEY, CHARLIE. Leicester, England, 6/4/44. Guitarist. Family.

WIEST, DIANNE. Kansas City, MO, 3/28/48. Actor. *Hannah and Her Sisters*.

WILCOX, LARRY. San Diego, CA, 8/8/47. Actor. Officer Jon Baker on *CHiPs*.

WILDE, KIM (Kim Smith). London, England, 11/18/60. Singer, songwriter.

WILDER, ALAN. 6/1/59. Singer, synthesizer player. Depeche Mode.

WILDER, GENE (Jerome Silberman). Milwaukee, WI, 6/11/35. Actor, director, writer, widower of Gilda Radner. *Young Frankenstein*.

WILLIAM, PRINCE. London, England, 6/21/82. British royalty, son of Prince Charles and Princess Diana.

WILLIAMS, ANDY. Wall Lake, IA, 12/3/30. Pop singer. "Where Do I Begin?"

WILLIAMS, BARRY. Santa Monica, CA, 9/30/54. Actor. Greg on *The Brady Bunch*.

WILLIAMS, BILLY DEE. New York, NY, 4/6/37. Actor. *Lady Sings the Blues*.

WILLIAMS, CINDY. Van Nuys, CA, 8/22/47. Actor. Shirley Feeney on *Laverne & Shirley*.

WILLIAMS, CLARENCE III. New York, NY, 8/21/39. Actor. Lincoln Hayes on *The Mod Squad*.

WILLIAMS, CLIFF. Rumford, England, 12/14/29. Bass guitarist. AC/DC.

WILLIAMS, DENIECE (Deniece Chandler). Gary, IN, 6/3/51. Gospel/pop singer.

WILLIAMS, ESTHER. Los Angeles, CA, 8/8/23. Actor, swimmer, widow of Fernando Lamas. *Bathing Beauty*.

WILLIAMS, HANK JR (Randall Hank). Shreveport, LA, 5/26/49. Country singer, songwriter. "Texas Women."

WILLIAMS, JOBETH. Houston, TX, 1953. Actor. *The Big Chill*.

WILLIAMS, JOHN TOWNER. Queens, NY, 2/8/32. Composer, conductor. *Jaws; Star Wars*.

WILLIAMS, MAISIE. Montserrat, West Indies, 3/25/51. Singer. Boney M.

WILLIAMS, MILAN. Mississippi, 3/28/48. Keyboardist, trombonist, guitarist, drummer. The Commodores.

WILLIAMS, MONTEL. Baltimore, MD, 7/3/56. Talk show host. *The Montel Williams Show*.

WILLIAMS, OTIS (Otis Miles). Texarkana, TX, 10/30/49. Singer. The Temptations.

WILLIAMS, PAUL. Birmingham, AL, 7/2/39. Singer. The Temptations.

WILLIAMS, TREAT (Richard Williams). Rowayton, CT, 12/1/51. Actor. *Prince of the City.*

WILLIAMS, VANESSA. New York, NY, 3/18/63. Model, pop singer, actor, first black Miss America (lost crown for violating moral codes).

WILLIAMS, WALTER. 8/25/42. Singer. The O'Jays.

WILLIAMS, WENDY O. (Wendy Orlean Williams). Rochester, NY, 1946. Entertainer, singer.

WILLIAMSON, NICOL. Hamilton, Scotland, 9/14/38. Actor. *Excalibur.*

WILLIG, GEORGE. New York, NY, 6/11/49. Actor, stuntman. Climbed World Trade Center.

WILSON, AL "BLIND OWL." Boston, MA, 7/4/43. Guitarist, singer, harmonicist. Canned Heat.

WILSON, ANN. San Diego, CA, 6/19/51. Lead singer. Heart.

WILSON, BARRY J. London, England, 3/18/47. Drummer. Procol Harum.

WILSON, BRIAN. Inglewood, CA, 6/20/42. Bassist, keyboardist, singer, father of Wendy and Carnie. The Beach Boys.

WILSON, CARL. Hawthorne, CA, 12/21/46. Guitarist, singer. The Beach Boys.

WILSON, CARNIE. Los Angeles, CA, 4/29/68. Singer, daughter of Brian, sister of Wendy. Wilson Phillips.

WILSON, CASSANDRA. Jackson, MS, 1955. Jazz singer.

WILSON, CINDY. Athens, GA, 2/28/57. Guitarist, singer. The B-52's.

WILSON, DEMOND. Valdosta, GA, 10/13/46. Actor. *Sanford and Son.*

WILSON, DON. Tacoma, WA, 2/10/37. Guitarist. The Ventures.

WILSON, FLIP (Clerow Wilson). Jersey City, NJ, 12/8/33. Actor. *The Flip Wilson Show.*

WILSON, JOYCE. Detroit, MI, 12/14/46. Singer. Tony Orlando & Dawn.

WILSON, MARY. Greenville, MS, 3/6/44. Singer. The Supremes.

WILSON, NANCY. Chillicothe, OH, 2/20/37. R&B singer.

WILSON, NANCY. San Francisco, CA, 3/16/54. Guitarist, singer. Heart.

WILSON, TOM. Grant Town, WV, 8/1/31. Cartoonist. *Ziggy.*

WILSON, TONY. Trinidad, 10/8/47. Bassist, singer. Hot Chocolate.

WILSON, WENDY. Los Angeles, CA, 10/16/69. Singer, sister of Carnie, daughter of Brian. Wilson Phillips.

WINCHELL, PAUL. New York, NY, 12/21/22. Ventriloquist, actor. *The Paul Winchell-Jerry Mahoney Show.*

WINDOM, WILLIAM. New York, NY, 9/28/23. Actor. *Murder She Wrote.*

WINFIELD, DAVE. Saint Paul, MN, 10/3/51. Baseball player.

WINFIELD, PAUL. Los Angeles, CA, 5/22/40. Actor. *Sounder.*

WINKLER, HENRY. New York, NY, 10/30/45. Actor, producer, director. Arthur "The Fonz" Fonzarelli on *Happy Days.*

WINNINGHAM, MARE. Phoenix, AZ, 5/6/59. Actor. *St. Elmo's Fire.*

WINSTON, JIMMY (James Langwith). London, England, 4/20/45. Organist. The Small Faces.

WINTER, EDGAR. Beaumont, TX, 12/28/46. Blues/rock keyboardist, brother of Johnny.

WINTER, JOHNNY. Beaumont, TX, 2/23/44. Blues/rock guitarist, brother of Edgar.

WINTERS, JONATHAN. Dayton, OH, 11/11/25. Actor. *The Jonathan Winters Show.*

WINTERS, SHELLEY (Shirley Schrift). St. Louis, MO, 8/18/22. Actor. *The Poseidon Adventure.*

WINWOOD, MUFF (Mervyn Winwood). Birmingham, England, 6/14/43. Singer, songwriter, bassist. The Spencer Davis Group.

WINWOOD, STEVE. Birmingham, England, 5/12/48. Singer, songwriter. The Spencer Davis Group; Traffic; Blind Faith.

WITHERS, BILL. Slab Fork, WV, 7/4/38. Pop singer, songwriter, guitarist.

WITHERS, JANE. Atlanta, GA, 4/12/26. Actor. Josephine the Plumber on TV commercials.

WOLF, PETER (Peter Blankfield). New York, NY, 3/7/46. Singer. The J. Geils Band.

WOLTERS, JOHN. 4/28/45. Drummer, singer. Dr. Hook.

WOMACK, BOBBY. Cleveland, OH, 3/4/44. Gospel/R&B singer, songwriter, guitarist.

WONDER, STEVIE (Steveland Morris). Saginaw, MI, 5/13/50. Singer, songwriter, formerly married to Syreeta Wright.

WONG, B. D. San Francisco, CA, 10/24/62. Actor. *M. Butterfly.*

WOOD, DANNY. Boston, MA, 5/14/71. Singer. New Kids on the Block.

WOOD, RON. London, England, 6/1/47. Guitarist. The Rolling Stones.

WOOD, ROY (Ulysses Adrian Wood). Birmingham, England, 11/8/46. Singer, guitarist, cellist. Electric Light Orchestra (ELO); Wizzard; The Move.

WOOD, STUART. Edinburgh, Scotland, 2/25/57. Guitarist. The Bay City Rollers.

WOODS, JAMES. Vernal, UT, 4/18/47. Actor. *Salvador.*

WOODWARD, EDWARD. Croydon, England, 6/1/30. Actor. *The Equalizer.*

WOODWARD, JOANNE. Thomasville, GA, 2/27/30. Actor, married to Paul Newman. *The Three Faces of Eve.*

WOODWARD, KEREN. Bristol, England, 4/2/61. Singer. Bananarama.

WORLEY, JO ANNE. Lowell, IN, 9/6/37. Actor, singer. *Laugh-In.*

WRAY, FAY. Alberta, Canada, 9/10/07. Actor. *King Kong.*

WRIGHT, ADRIAN. Sheffield, England, 6/30/56. Projector operator for on-stage slides and films. The Human League.

WRIGHT, LITTLE STEVIE. Leeds, England, 12/20/48. Singer. The Easybeats.

WRIGHT, MAX. Detroit, MI, 8/2/43. Actor. Willie Tanner on *ALF.*

WRIGHT, PAT. Brooklyn, NY, 1945. Singer. The Crystals.

WRIGHT, RICK. London, England, 7/28/45. Keyboardist. Pink Floyd.

WRIGHT, STEVEN. Burlington, MA, 12/6/55. Comedian.

WRIGHT, SYREETA. Pittsburgh, PA, 1946. Singer, songwriter, formerly married to Stevie Wonder.

WUHL, ROBERT. Union City, NJ, 10/9/51. Actor, writer. *Bull Durham.*

WYATT, JANE. Campgaw, NJ, 8/13/12. Actor. *Father Knows Best.*

WYMAN, BILL (William Perks). London, England, 10/24/36. Bassist. The Rolling Stones.

WYMAN, JANE (Sarah Jane Fulks). St. Joseph, MO, 1/4/14. Actor, formerly married to Ronald Reagan. Angela Channing on *Falcon Crest.*

WYNETTE, TAMMY (Virginia Wynette Pugh). Itawamba County, MS, 5/5/42. Country singer. "Stand by Your Man."

YAMAGUCHI, KRISTI. Hayward, CA, 7/12/71. Skater, Olympic gold medalist.

YANKOVIC, WEIRD AL (Alfred Matthew Yankovic). Los Angeles, CA, 10/23/59. Singer, spoof artist. "Like a Surgeon."

YANOVSKY, ZAL. Toronto, Canada, 12/19/44. Guitarist, singer. The Lovin' Spoonful.

YARROW, PETER. New York, NY, 5/31/38. Composer, author, singer. Peter, Paul and Mary.

YEARWOOD, TRISHA. Monticello, GA, 9/19/64. Singer.

YELTSIN, BORIS. Burka, Russia, 2/1/31. Russian political leader.

YESTER, JIM. Birmingham, AL, 11/24/39. Singer, guitarist. The Association.

YOAKAM, DWIGHT. Pikesville, KY, 10/23/56. Country singer. "Honky Tonk Man."

YORK, MICHAEL. Fulmer, England, 3/27/42. Actor. *Logan's Run.*

YORK, PETE. Redcar, England, 8/15/42. Drummer. The Spencer Davis Group.

YOUNG, ANGUS. Glasgow, Scotland, 3/31/59. Guitarist. AC/DC.

YOUNG, GEORGE. Glasgow, Scotland, 11/6/47. Guitarist. The Easybeats.

YOUNG, JAMES. Chicago, IL, 11/14/48. Guitarist. Styx.

YOUNG, JESSE COLIN (Perry Miller). New York, NY, 11/11/41. Guitarist, bassist, singer. The Youngbloods.

YOUNG, LORETTA (Gretchen Young). Salt Lake City, UT, 1/6/13. Actor. *The Farmer's Daughter.*

YOUNG, MALCOLM. Glasgow, Scotland, 1/6/53. Guitarist. AC/DC.

YOUNG, NEIL. Toronto, Canada, 11/12/45. Singer, songwriter, guitarist. Buffalo Springfield; Crosby, Stills, Nash & Young.

YOUNG, PAUL. Luton, England, 1/17/56. Singer, songwriter.

YOUNG, ROBERT. Chicago, IL, 2/22/07. Actor. *Marcus Welby, M.D.*

YOUNG, RUSTY. Long Beach, CA, 2/23/46. Pedal steel guitarist. Poco.

YOUNG, SEAN. Louisville, KY, 11/20/59. Actor. *No Way Out.*

YOUNG MC (Marvin Young). London, England, 1968. Rap artist.

YOUNGMAN, HENNY (Henry Youngman). Liverpool, England, 1/12/06. Actor. "Take my wife... please!"

ZADORA, PIA. New York, NY, 5/4/56. Actor. *Naked Gun 33 1/3.*

ZAHN, PAULA. Naperville, IL, 2/24/56. Broadcast journalist. *CBS This Morning.*

ZAL, ROXANA. Los Angeles, CA, 11/8/69. Actor. *Something About Amelia.*

ZANDER, ROBIN. Rockford, IL, 1/23/53. Singer, guitarist. Cheap Trick.

ZAPPA, DWEEZIL. Los Angeles, CA, 9/5/69. Guitarist, son of Frank, brother of Moon Unit. MTV.

ZAPPA, MOON UNIT. Hollywood, CA, 9/28/68. Singer, daughter of Frank, sister of Dweezil. "Valley Girl."

ZEVON, WARREN. Chicago, IL, 1/24/47. Singer, songwriter. "Werewolves of London."

ZIERING, IAN. 4/30/64. Actor. *Beverly Hills 90210.*

ZIMBALIST, STEPHANIE. Encino, CA, 10/8/56. Actor, daughter of Efrem. Laura Holt on *Remington Steele.*

ZMED, ADRIAN. Chicago, IL, 3/4/54. Actor. Vince Romano on *T. J. Hooker.*

HAPPY BIRTHDAY! THE GREATS' NATAL DATES

JANUARY 1
Idi Amin
Frank Langella
Don Novello
J.D. Salinger

JANUARY 2
Jim Bakker
Gabrielle Carteris
Chick Churchill
Joanna Pacula

JANUARY 3
Melody Anderson
Dabney Coleman
Mel Gibson
Robert Loggia
Victoria Principal
Stephen Stills
Bill Travers

JANUARY 4
Bernie Albrecht
Dyan Cannon
Matt Frewer
Ann Magnuson
Michael Stipe
Barney Sumner
Jane Wyman

JANUARY 5
Suzy Amis
George Brown
Jeane Dixon
Robert Duvall
Diane Keaton
Ted Lange
Walter Mondale
Chris Stein

JANUARY 6
Syd Barrett
Mark O'Toole
John Singleton
Kathy Sledge
Loretta Young
Malcolm Young

JANUARY 7
Nicolas Cage
Katie Couric
Kenny Loggins
Maury Povich
Paul Revere

JANUARY 8
David Bowie
Stephen Hawking
Robbie Krieger
Butterfly McQueen
Yvette Mimieux
Charles Osgood
Soupy Sales
Larry Storch

JANUARY 9
Joan Baez
Bill Cowsill
Bob Denver

Scott Engel
Crystal Gayle
David Johansen
Judith Krantz
Herbert Lom
Jimmy Page

JANUARY 10
Trini Alvarado
Pat Benatar
Donald Fagen
George Foreman
Bob Lang
Cyril Neville
Maurice Sendak
Rod Stewart

JANUARY 11
Naomi Judd
Vicki Peterson
Rod Taylor

JANUARY 12
Kirstie Alley
Anthony Andrews
Per Gessle
William Lee Golden
Cynthia Robinson
Vendela
Henny Youngman

JANUARY 13
Kevin Anderson
Patrick Dempsey
Robert "Squirrel"
    Lester
Julia Louis-Dreyfus
Graham McPherson
Penelope Ann Miller
Richard Moll
Robert Stack
Frances
    Sternhagen
Gwen Verdon

JANUARY 14
Jason Bateman
Faye Dunaway
L.L. Cool J
Andy Rooney
Carl Weathers

JANUARY 15
Captain Beefheart
Lloyd Bridges
Charo
Martha Davis
Chad Lowe
Andrea Martin
Pamela Sue Martin
Julian Sands
Peter Trewavas
Mario Van Peebles

JANUARY 16
Debbie Allen
Bob Bogle
John Carpenter

Bill Francis
Kate Moss
Sade
Jim Stafford
Paul Webb

JANUARY 17
Muhammad Ali
Jim Carrey
David Caruso
John Crawford
Steve Earle
Joe Frazier
Susanna Hoffs
James Earl Jones
Vidal Sassoon
Betty White
Paul Young

JANUARY 18
Kevin Costner
David Ruffin
Larry Smith

JANUARY 19
Desi Arnaz Jr.
Dewey Bunnell
Michael Crawford
Phil Everly
Shelley Fabares
Tippi Hedren
Harvey Hinsley
Robert MacNeil
Robert Palmer
Dolly Parton
Jean Stapleton
Mickey Virtue
Fritz Weaver

JANUARY 20
Buzz Aldrin
George Burns
Arte Johnson
DeForest Kelley
Lorenzo Lamas
David Lynch
John Michael
    Montgomery
Patricia Neal
Paul Stanley
Eric Stewart
Ron Townson

JANUARY 21
Robby Benson
Geena Davis
Mac Davis
Jill Eikenberry
Richie Havens
Billy Ocean
Steve Reeves

JANUARY 22
Linda Blair
Balthazar Getty
John Hurt
Michael Hutchence
Diane Lane

Piper Laurie
Chris Lemmon
Steve Perry
Jeff Smith
Ann Sothern

JANUARY 23
Richard Dean
    Anderson
Princess Caroline
Bill Cunningham
Earl Falconer
Gil Gerard
Rutger Hauer
Jeanne Moreau
Anita Pointer
Chita Rivera
Patrick Simmons
Robin Zander

JANUARY 24
Ernest Borgnine
Neil Diamond
Jools Holland
Nastassja Kinski
Michael Ontkean
Oral Roberts
Yakov Smirnoff
Ray Stevens
Warren Zevon

JANUARY 25
Corazon Aquino
Andy Cox
Richard Finch
Etta James
Dean Jones
Dinah Manoff

JANUARY 26
Jazzie B
David Briggs
Scott Glenn
Wayne Gretsky
Eartha Kitt
Paul Newman
Andrew Ridgeley
Gene Siskel
Bob Uecker
Roger Vadim
Eddie Van Halen

JANUARY 27
Mikhail
    Baryshnikov
Bobby Bland
Troy Donahue
Brian Downey
Bridget Fonda
Gillian Gilbert
Seth Justman
Nick Mason
Mike Patton
Mimi Rogers
Nedra Talley

JANUARY 28
Alan Alda
John Beck
Brian Keenan
Marthe Keller
Nicholas Pryor
Dave Sharp
Dick Taylor
Elijah Wood

JANUARY 29
David Byron
John Forsythe
Roddy Frame
Sara Gilbert
Noel Harrison
Eddie Jackson
Anne Jillian
Greg Louganis
Victor Mature
Tommy Ramone
Katharine Ross
Tom Selleck
Oprah Winfrey

JANUARY 30
Marty Balin
Phil Collins
Charles Dutton
Gene Hackman
William King
Dorothy Malone
Steve Marriott
Dick Martin
Vanessa Redgrave
Joe Terranova
Jody Watley

JANUARY 31
John Agar
Harry Wayne Casey
Carol Channing
Lloyd Cole
John Paul Jones
Terry Kath
John Lydon
Phil Manzanera
Suzanne Pleshette
Jean Simmons
Jessica Walter

FEBRUARY 1
Mike Campbell
Don Everly
Dennis Farina
Sherilynn Fenn
Margaux
    Hemingway
Sherman Hemsley
Rick James
Terry Jones
Billy Mumy
Lisa Marie Presley-
    Jackson
Ray Sawyer
Boris Yeltsin

FEBRUARY 2
Christie Brinkley
Garth Brooks
Alan Caddy
Farrah Fawcett
Gale Gordon
Peter Lucia
Graham Nash
Liz Smith
Tom Smothers
Elaine Stritch
Ross Valory

FEBRUARY 3
Joey Bishop
Thomas Calabro
Angelo D'Aleo
Blythe Danner
Dave Davies
Morgan Fairchild
Eric Haydock
Fran Tarkenton
Lol Tolhurst

FEBRUARY 4
Gabrielle Anwar
Michael Beck
Clint Black
David Brenner
Alice Cooper
Florence LaRue
Dan Quayle
John Steel

FEBRUARY 5
Bobby Brown
Red Buttons
Christopher Guest
Barbara Hershey
Jennifer Jason Leigh
Charlotte Rampling
Roger Staubach
Cory Wells

FEBRUARY 6
Rick Astley
Tom Brokaw
Natalie Cole
Fabian
Mike Farrell
Zsa Zsa Gabor
Alan Jones
Patrick Macnee
Ronald Reagan
Rip Torn
Robert Townsend
Michael Tucker
Mamie Van Doren

FEBRUARY 7
David Bryan
Miguel Ferrer
Jimmy Greenspoon
Alan Lancaster
James Spader
Brian Travers

FEBRUARY 8
Brooke Adams
Brian Bennett
Creed Bratton
Gary Coleman
John Grisham
Robert Klein
Ted Koppel
Jack Lemmon
Audrey Meadows
Vince Neil
Nick Nolte
Mary Steenburgen
John Williams

FEBRUARY 9
Mia Farrow
Carole King
Judith Light
Roger Mudd
Joe Pesci
Janet Suzman
Travis Tritt
Alice Walker

FEBRUARY 10
Laura Dern
Donovan
Roberta Flack
Jimmy Merchant
Mark Spitz
Robert Wagner
Don Wilson

FEBRUARY 11
Sheryl Crow
Conrad Janis
Tina Louise
Leslie Nielsen
Burt Reynolds
Sidney Sheldon

FEBRUARY 12
Maud Adams
Joe Don Baker
Judy Blume
Cliff DeYoung
Arsenio Hall
Joanna Kerns
Simon
　MacCorkindale
Ray Manzarek
Joe Schermie

FEBRUARY 13
Tony Butler
Stockard Channing
Roger Christian
Peter Hook
David Naughton
Kim Novak
Oliver Reed
George Segal
Bo Svenson
Peter Tork

FEBRUARY 14
Hugh Downs
Roger Fisher
Florence Henderson
Gregory Hines
Meg Tilly

Paul Tsongas
Ken Wahl

FEBRUARY 15
Mick Avory
Marisa Berenson
Claire Bloom
David Brown
Ali Campbell
Mikey Craig
Matt Groening
John Helliwell
Harvey Korman
Kevin McCarthy
Jane Seymour

FEBRUARY 16
Sonny Bono
LeVar Burton
James Ingram
William Katt
John McEnroe Jr.
Andy Taylor

FEBRUARY 17
Billie Joe Armstrong
Alan Bates
Jim Brown
Brenda Fricker
Hal Holbrook
Michael Jordan
Lou Diamond
　Phillips
Gene Pitney
Raf Vallone

FEBRUARY 18
Robbie Bachman
Randy Crawford
Sinead Cusack
Dennis DeYoung
Matt Dillon
George Kennedy
Toni Morrison
Juice Newton
Jack Palance
Molly Ringwald
Herman Santiago
Greta Scacchi
Cybill Shepherd
John Travolta
Vanna White

FEBRUARY 19
Mark Andes
Justine Bateman
Francis Buchholz
Lou Christie
Jeff Daniels
Falco
Tony Iommi
Holly Johnson
Smokey Robinson

FEBRUARY 20
Edward Albert
Robert Altman
Charles Barkley
Walter Becker
Ian Brown
Randy California
Cindy Crawford
Sandy Duncan

J. Geils
Kelsey Grammer
Jennifer O'Neill
Sidney Poitier
Andrew Shue
Peter Strauss
Gloria Vanderbilt
Nancy Wilson

FEBRUARY 21
Christopher Atkins
Jean-Jacques
　Burnel
Mary Chapin
　Carpenter
Tyne Daly
David Geffen
Jerry Harrison
Gary Lockwood
Rue McClanahan
Nina Simone
Vince Welnick

FEBRUARY 22
Drew Barrymore
Jonathan Demme
Julius Erving
Ted Kennedy
Sheldon Leonard
Kyle MacLachlan
John Mills
Miou-Miou
Robert Young

FEBRUARY 23
Peter Fonda
Howard Jones
Mike Maxfield
Steve Priest
David Sylvian
Brad Whitford
Johnny Winter
Rusty Young

FEBRUARY 24
Barry Bostwick
James Farentino
Steven Hill
Paul Jones
Edward James
　Olmos
Helen Shaver
Lonnie Turner
Paula Zahn

FEBRUARY 25
Sean Astin
George Harrison
Mike Peters
Sally Jessy Raphael
Bobby Riggs
Stuart Wood

FEBRUARY 26
Michael Bolton
Jonathan Cain
Johnny Cash
Fats Domino
John Jon
Tony Randall
Mitch Ryder
Sandie Shaw

FEBRUARY 27
Adam Baldwin
Garry Christian
Chelsea Clinton
Eddie Gray
Steve Harley
Howard Hesseman
Paul Humphreys
Ralph Nader
Neal Schon
Grant Show
Adrian Smith
Elizabeth Taylor
Joanne Woodward

FEBRUARY 28
Mario Andretti
Stephanie Beacham
Frank Bonner
Charles Durning
Phil Gould
Robert Sean
　Leonard
Gavin MacLeod
Bernadette Peters
Mercedes Ruehl
Bubba Smith
Joe South
Tommy Tune
John Turturro
Cindy Wilson

MARCH 1
Harry Belafonte
Dirk Benedict
Roger Daltrey
Timothy Daly
Jimmy Fortune
Ron Howard
Alan Thicke

MARCH 2
John Cowsill
John Cullum
Mark Evans
John Irving
Jennifer Jones
Eddie Money
Jay Osmond
Lou Reed
Al Waxman

MARCH 3
Willie Chambers
Jance Garfat
Jackie Joyner-
　Kersee
Tim Kazurinsky
Dave Mount
Mike Pender
Miranda
　Richardson
Tone-Loc
Blue Weaver

MARCH 4
Chastity Bono
Harry Helmsley
Patsy Kensit
Catherine O'Hara
Paula Prentiss
Chris Rea

Chris Squire
Shakin' Stevens
Bobby Womack
Adrian Zmed

MARCH 5
Alan Clark
Samantha Eggar
Eddy Grant
James B. Sikking
Dean Stockwell
Marsha Warfield

MARCH 6
Tom Arnold
Marion Barry
Kiki Dee
David Gilmour
Hugh Grundy
Ed McMahon
Shaquille O'Neal
Rob Reiner
Mary Wilson

MARCH 7
Tammy Faye Bakker
Paul Davis
Matthew Fisher
John Heard
Willard Scott
Lynn Swann
Daniel J. Travanti
Chris White
Peter Wolf

MARCH 8
Mike Allsup
Cheryl Baker
Clive Burr
Cyd Charisse
Mickey Dolenz
Ralph Ellis
Peter Gill
Randy Meisner
Gary Numan
Aidan Quinn
Lynn Redgrave
Claire Trevor

MARCH 9
Trevor Burton
Jim Cregan
Linda Fiorentino
Martin Fry
Marty Ingels
Emmanuel Lewis
Mark Lindsey
Jeffrey Osborne
Mickey Spillane
Robin Trower
Trish Van Devere

MARCH 10
Neneh Cherry
Prince Edward
Jasmine Guy
Chuck Norris
James Earl Ray
Tom Scholz
Sharon Stone
Dean Torrence

MARCH 11
Douglas Adams
Sam Donaldson
Bobby McFerrin
Susan Richardson
Ric Rothwell
Mark Stein
Bruce Watson

MARCH 12
Barbara Feldon
Mike Gibbins
Marlon Jackson
Al Jarreau
Paul Kantner
Liza Minnelli
Brian O'Hara
Bill Payne
James Taylor

MARCH 13
Adam Clayton
Dana Delany
Glenne Headly
Deborah Raffin
Neil Sedaka

MARCH 14
Michael Caine
Billy Crystal
Megan Follows
Boon Gould
Quincy Jones
Walter Parazaider

MARCH 15
Ry Cooder
David Costell
Terence Trent D'Arby
Fabio
Judd Hirsch
Phil Lesh
Mike Love
Bret Michaels
Rockwell
Howard Scott
Sly Stone
Jimmy Lee Swaggart

MARCH 16
Michael Bruce
Erik Estrada
Isabelle Huppert
Jerry Lewis
Kate Nelligan
Nancy Wilson

MARCH 17
Harold Brown
Lesley-Anne Down
Patrick Duffy
Scott Gorham
Mike Lindup
Rob Lowe
Patrick McCauley
Kurt Russell
John Sebastian

MARCH 18
Bonnie Blair
Irene Cara
Kevin Dobson
Peter Graves

472

John Hartman
Wilson Pickett
Charley Pride
John Updike
Vanessa Williams
Barry J. Wilson

MARCH 19
Ursula Andress
Paul Atkinson
Glenn Close
Terry Hall
Clarence Henry
Derek Longmuir
Ruth Pointer
Bruce Willis

MARCH 20
John Clark Gable
Holly Hunter
William Hurt
Spike Lee
Hal Linden
Carl Palmer
Slim Jim Phantom
Carl Reiner
Mr. Rogers
Theresa Russell

MARCH 21
Matthew Broderick
Timothy Dalton
Cynthia Geary
Roger Hodgson
Gary Oldman
Rosie Stone
Russell
   Thompkins Jr.

MARCH 22
George Benson
Jeremy Clyde
Randy Hobbs
Werner Klemperer
Andrew
   Lloyd Webber
Karl Malden
Marcel Marceau
Stephanie Mills
Matthew Modine
Lena Olin
Pat Robertson
William Shatner
Harry Vanda
M. Emmet Walsh

MARCH 23
Princess Eugenie
Chaka Khan
Ric Ocasek
Marti Pellow
Amanda Plummer

MARCH 24
Lara Flynn Boyle
Robert Carradine
Norman Fell
Lee Oskar
Donna Pescow
Dougie Thomson

MARCH 25
Hoyt Axton
Bonnie Bedelia
Aretha Franklin
Paul Michael Glaser
Mary Gross
Jeff Healey
Elton John
Neil Jones
Sarah Jessica
   Parker
Gloria Steinem
John Stockwell
Maisie Williams

MARCH 26
Alan Arkin
James Caan
Leeza Gibbons
Jennifer Grey
Vicki Lawrence
Leonard Nimoy
Teddy Pendergrass
Diana Ross
Fran Sheehan
Martin Short
Curtis Sliwa
Richard Tandy
Steven Tyler

MARCH 27
Tony Banks
Mariah Carey
Judy Carne
Andrew Farriss
Austin Pendleton
Maria Schneider
Tom Sullivan
Quentin Tarantino
Michael York

MARCH 28
Dirk Bogarde
Ken Howard
Reba McEntire
Chuck Portz
Salt
Dianne Wiest
Milan Williams

MARCH 29
Jennifer Capriati
Bud Cort
Hammer
Eric Idle
Bobby Kimball
Christopher
   Lambert

MARCH 30
John Astin
Warren Beatty
Tracy Chapman
Eric Clapton
Richard Dysart
Graeme Edge
Peter Marshall
Paul Reiser

MARCH 31
Rod Allen
Herb Alpert

Richard
   Chamberlain
Liz Claiborne
William Daniels
Albert Gore
Sean Hopper
Shirley Jones
Ed Marinaro
Al Nichol
Rhea Perlman
Mick Ralphs
Christopher Walken
Angus Young

APRIL 1
John Barbata
Alan Blakley
Billy Currie
Rudolph Isley
Gordon Jump
Ronnie Lane
Ali MacGraw
Phil Margo
Toshiro Mifune
Annette O'Toole
Debbie Reynolds
Mark White

APRIL 2
Dana Carvey
Glen Dale
Buddy Ebsen
Mikhail Gorbachev
Alec Guinness
Linda Hunt
Pamela Reed
Leon Russell
Keren Woodward

APRIL 3
Alec Baldwin
Jan Berry
Marlon Brando
Doris Day
Jennie Garth
Jane Goodall
Marsha Mason
Eddie Murphy
Wayne Newton
Tony Orlando
Barry Pritchard
Mel Schacher

APRIL 4
Maya Angelou
Robert Downey Jr.
Steve Gatlin
Dave Hill
Kitty Kelley
Graeme Kelling
Christine Lahti
Mick Mars
Nancy McKeon
Craig T. Nelson
Berry Oakley

APRIL 5
Allan Clarke
Agnetha Faltskog
Maxwell Gail
Frank Gorshin
Peter Greenaway

Mike McCready
Michael Moriarty
Gregory Peck
Colin Powell
Gale Storm

APRIL 6
Stan Cullimore
Marilu Henner
Jason Hervey
Ari Meyers
John Ratzenberger
John Stax
Billy Dee Williams

APRIL 7
Mick Abrahams
Patricia Bennett
Francis Ford
   Coppola
Buster Douglas
Spencer Dryden
James Garner
Bruce Gary
Janis Ian
Elaine Miles
John Oates
Wayne Rogers

APRIL 8
Patricia Arquette
Roger Chapman
Steve Howe
Julian Lennon
Edward Mulhare

APRIL 9
Jean-Paul
   Belmondo
Les Gray
Hugh Hefner
Mark Kelly
Michael Learned
Carl Perkins
Dennis Quaid

APRIL 10
Peter MacNicol
John Madden
Steven Seagal
Brian Setzer
Omar Sharif
Bobbie Smith
Bunny Wailer

APRIL 11
Stuart Adamson
Joel Grey
Bill Irwin
Louise Lasser
Delroy Pearson
Peter Riegert
Richie Sambora
Lisa Stansfield
Neville Staples

APRIL 12
Alex Briley
David Cassidy
Claire Danes
Shannen Doherty
Andy Garcia
Vince Gill

Herbie Hancock
John Kay
David Letterman
Ann Miller
Ed O'Neill
Will Sergeant
Tiny Tim
Scott Turow
Jane Withers

APRIL 13
Peabo Bryson
Jack Casady
Lester Chambers
Jimmy Destri
Tony Dow
Al Green
Garry Kasparov
Howard Keel
Jane Leeves
Brian Pendleton
Ron Perlman
Rick Schroder
Paul Sorvino
Lyle Waggoner

APRIL 14
Ritchie Blackmore
Dennis Bryon
Julie Christie
Larry Ferguson
Anthony Michael
   Hall
Buddy Knox
Jay Robinson
Pete Rose
John Shea
Rod Steiger

APRIL 15
Claudia Cardinale
Graeme Clark
Roy Clark
Samantha Fox
Emma Thompson

APRIL 16
Edie Adams
Ellen Barkin
Jon Cryer
Lukas Haas
Gerry Rafferty
Bill Spooner
Dusty Springfield
Bobby Vinton

APRIL 17
Boomer Esiason
Liz Phair
Pete Shelley
Stephen Singleton

APRIL 18
Barbara Hale
Hayley Mills
Rick Moranis
Conan O'Brien
Les Pattinson
Eric Roberts
Alexander Spence
Mike Vickers
James Woods

APRIL 19
Don Adams
Tim Curry
Dudley Moore
Alan Price
Larry Ramos Jr.
Mark Volman

APRIL 20
Craig Frost
Jessica Lange
Joey Lawrence
Ryan O'Neal
George Takei
Luther Vandross
Jimmy Winston

APRIL 21
Paul Carrack
Tony Danza
Queen Elizabeth II
Charles Grodin
Patti LuPone
Andie MacDowell
Elaine May
Iggy Pop
Anthony Quinn
Robert Smith
John Weider

APRIL 22
Eddie Albert
Joseph Bottoms
Glen Campbell
Peter Kenneth
   Frampton
Ace Frehley
Chris Makepeace
Jack Nicholson
Aaron Spelling
John Waters

APRIL 23
Valerie Bertinelli
David Birney
Steve Clark
Sandra Dee
Jan Hooks
Lee Majors
Alan Oppenheimer
Captain Sensible

APRIL 24
Eric Bogosian
Doug Clifford
Glenn Cornick
Billy Gould
Shirley MacLaine
Paul Ryder
Richard Sterban
Barbra Streisand

APRIL 25
Andy Bell
Michael Brown
Stu Cook
Meadowlark Lemon
Paul Mazursky
Al Pacino
Talia Shire
Bjorn Ulvaeus

APRIL 26
Carol Burnett
Duane Eddy
Giancarlo Esposito

APRIL 27
Anouk Aimee
Sheena Easton
Pete Ham
Coretta Scott King
Jack Klugman
Kate Pierson
Marco Pirroni
Clive Taylor

APRIL 28
Ann-Margret
Saddam Hussein
Bruno Kirby
Jay Leno
Madge Sinclair
Marcia Strassman
John Wolters

APRIL 29
Andre Agassi
Duane Allen
Stephen Arenholz
Keith Baxter
Daniel Day-Lewis
Lonnie Donegan
Carl Gardner
Celeste Holm
Tommy James
Rod McKuen
Zubin Mehta
Kate Mulgrew
Michelle Pfeiffer
Chynna Phillips
Eve Plumb
Francis Rossi
Jerry Seinfeld
Uma Thurman
Carnie Wilson

APRIL 30
Turbo B
Jill Clayburgh
Gary Collins
Perry King
Cloris Leachman
Al Lewis
Willie Nelson
Merrill Osmond
Bobby Vee
Ian Ziering

MAY 1
John Beradino
Judy Collins
Johnny Colt
Steve Farris
Nick Fortune
Bobcat Goldthwait
Joseph Heller
Ray Parker Jr.
Phil Smith

MAY 2
Jon Bon Jovi
Lesley Gore
Lou Gramm

Engelbert
  Humperdinck
Bianca Jagger
Goldy McJohn
Lorenzo Music
Benjamin Spock

MAY 3
David Ball
James Brown
Christopher Cross
Bruce Hall
Doug Henning
Mary Hopkin
Pete Seeger
Pete Staples
Frankie Valli
Wynonna

MAY 4
Nickolas Ashford
Jay Aston
Ronnie Bond
Ed Cassidy
Jackie Jackson
Randy Travis
Pia Zadora

MAY 5
Gary Daly
Lance Henriksen
Ian McCulloch
Kevin Mooney
Cathy Moriarty
Michael Murphy
Michael Palin
Bill Ward
Tammy Wynette

MAY 6
George Clooney
Willie Mays
Bob Seger
Lori Singer
Mare Winningham

MAY 7
Michael Knight
Bill Kreutzmann Jr.
Darren McGavin
Rick West

MAY 8
Philip Bailey
Rick Derringer
Chris Frantz
Melissa Gilbert
Gary Glitter
David Lemuel Keith
James Mitchum
Don Rickles
Paul Samwell-
  Smith
Toni Tennille
Alex Van Halen

MAY 9
Candice Bergen
Pete Birrell
James L. Brooks
Sonny Curtis
Nokie Edwards
Albert Finney

Richie Furay
Dave Gahan
Paul Heaton
Glenda Jackson
Billy Joel
Steve Katz
Mike Millward
Tom Petersson
Dave Prater
Lloyd Price
Tommy Roe
Mike Wallace

MAY 10
Jim Abrahams
Bono
Henry Fambrough
Jay Ferguson
Graham Gouldman
Dave Mason
Danny Rapp

MAY 11
Eric Burdon
Les Chadwick
Louis Farrakhan
Faith Popcorn
Natasha
  Richardson

MAY 12
Stephen Baldwin
Bruce Boxleitner
George Carlin
Lindsay Crouse
Billy Duffy
Ian Dury
Emilio Estevez
Kim Fields
Susan Hampshire
Katharine Hepburn
Ian McLagan
Tom Snyder
Billy Squier
David Walker
Steve Winwood

MAY 13
Beatrice Arthur
Peter Gabriel
Harvey Keitel
Danny Klein
Lorraine McIntosh
Paul Thompson
Overend Watts
Stevie Wonder

MAY 14
Ian Astbury
Jack Bruce
David Byrne
Tom Cochrane
Gene Cornish
Meg Foster
Fabrice Morvan
Danny Wood
Robert Zemeckis

MAY 15
Brian Eno
Graham Goble
Mike Oldfield

MAY 16
Pierce Brosnan
Harry Carey Jr.
Tracey Gold
Glenn Gregory
Janet Jackson
Barbara Lee
Gabriela Sabatini
Derrell Sweet
Ralph Tresvant

MAY 17
Bill Bruford
Dennis Hopper
Pervis Jackson
Jordan Knight
Sugar Ray Leonard
Maureen O'Sullivan
Trent Reznor
Bob Saget
Taj Mahal
Debra Winger

MAY 18
Joe Bonsall
Pope John Paul II

MAY 19
Nora Ephron
James Fox
David Hartman
Dusty Hill
Grace Jones
Nancy Kwan
Joey Ramone
Philip Rudd
Pete Townshend
Martyn Ware

MAY 20
Warren Cann
Cher
Joe Cocker
Sue Cowsill
Tony Goldwyn
Nick Heyward
Brian Nash
Bronson Pinchot
Ronald Reagan Jr.
Jimmy Stewart

MAY 21
Mike Barson
Peggy Cass
Ronald Isley
Stan Lynch
Carol Potter
Judge Reinhold
Leo Sayer
Mr. T
Hilton Valentine

MAY 22
Charles Aznavour
Richard Benjamin
Naomi Campbell
Michael Constantine
Jerry Dammers
Iva Davies
Morrissey
Bernie Taupin
Paul Winfield

MAY 23
Rosemary Clooney
Joan Collins
Betty Garrett
Bill Hunt
Anatoly Karpov

MAY 24
Gary Burghoff
Roseanne Cash
Thomas Chong
Bob Dylan
Patti LaBelle
Priscilla Presley
Derek Quinn
Rich Robinson

MAY 25
Dixie Carter
Justin Henry
Robert Ludlum
Mitch Margo
Ian McKellen
Klaus Meine
Frank Oz
John Palmer
Connie Sellecca
Beverly Sills
Leslie Uggams
Paul Weller

MAY 26
Verden Allen
James Arness
Helena Bonham-
  Carter
Ray Ennis
Levon Helm
Wayne Hussey
Lenny Kravitz
Peggy Lee
Stevie Nicks
Gerry Paterson
Philip Michael
  Thomas
Hank Williams Jr.

MAY 27
Cilla Black
Todd Bridges
Louis Gossett Jr.
Tony Hillerman
Henry Kissinger
Siouxsie Sioux
Bruce Weitz

MAY 28
Carroll Baker
John Fogerty
Roland Gift
Gladys Knight
Sondra Locke
Kylie Minogue

MAY 29
Annette Bening
Larry Blackmon
Gary Brooker
Kevin Conway
Roy Crewsdon
Melissa Etheridge
Anthony Geary

Bob Hope
Clifton James
Lisa Whelchel

MAY 30
Lenny Davidson
Keir Dullea
Marie Fredriksson
Nicky Headon
Ted McGinley
Clint Walker

MAY 31
Tom Berenger
Clint Eastwood
Sharon Gless
Gregory Harrison
Augie Meyers
Joe Namath
Johnny Paycheck
Brooke Shields
Lea Thompson
Peter Yarrow

JUNE 1
Rene Auberjonois
David Berkowitz
Pat Boone
Powers Boothe
Pat Corley
Jason Donovan
Morgan Freeman
Andy Griffith
Mike Joyce
Peter Masterson
Lorna Patterson
Jonathan Pryce
Graham Russell
Alan Wilder
Ron Wood
Edward Woodward

JUNE 2
Joanna Gleason
William Guest
Tony Hadley
Charles Haid
Marvin Hamlisch
Stacy Keach
Sally Kellerman
Jerry Mathers
Charles Miller
Milo O'Shea
Max Showalter
Michael Steele
Charlie Watts

JUNE 3
Michael Clarke
Tony Curtis
Ian Hunter
Curtis Mayfield
Billy Powell
Suzi Quatro
Scott Valentine
Deniece Williams

JUNE 4
Roger Ball
John Drew
  Barrymore
El DeBarge
Bruce Dern

Michelle Phillips
Parker Stevenson
Eddie Velez
Gordon Waller
Dennis Weaver
Ruth Westheimer
Charlie Whitney

JUNE 5
Laurie Anderson
Richard Butler
Spalding Gray
Kenny G.
Robert Lansing
Marky Mark
Bill Moyers
Don Reid
Freddie Stone

JUNE 6
Sandra Bernhard
Gary Bonds
David Dukes
Robert Englund
Harvey Fierstein
Roy Innis
Amanda Pays
Tom Ryan
Levi Stubbs
Billie Whitelaw

JUNE 7
James Ivory
Tom Jones
Liam Neeson
Prince

JUNE 8
Kathy Baker
Mick Box
Barbara Bush
Russell Christian
Griffin Dunne
Mick "Red" Hucknall
Neil Mitchell
Chuck Negron
Doris Pearson
Robert Pilatus
Nick Rhodes
Joan Rivers
Boz Scaggs
Jerry Stiller
Bonnie Tyler
Keenen Ivory Wayans

JUNE 9
Trevor Bolder
Johnny Depp
Michael J. Fox
Billy Hatton
Jon Lord
Jackie Mason

JUNE 10
Shirley Alston
Human Beatbox
Linda Evangelista
Lionel Jeffries
Grace Mirabella
Shirley Owens
Prince Philip

Rick Price
Andrew Stevens

JUNE 11
Adrienne Barbeau
Joey Dee
Chad Everett
John Lawton
Joe Montana
Bonnie Pointer
Donnie Van Zandt
Gene Wilder
George Willig

JUNE 12
Timothy Busfield
George Bush
Bun Carlos
Vic Damone
Brad Delp
Jenilee Harrison
Jim Nabors
Reg Presley

JUNE 13
Tim Allen
Christo
Bobby Freeman
Ben Johnson
Howard Leese
Dennis Locorriere
Mark Mendoza
Deniece Pearson
Ally Sheedy
Richard Thomas

JUNE 14
Rod Argent
Boy George
Marla Gibbs
Steffi Graf
Jimmy Lea
Will Patton
Donald Trump
Muff Winwood

JUNE 15
Jim Belushi
Simon Callow
Courteney Cox
Mario Cuomo
Julie Hagerty
Russell Hitchcock
Noddy Holder
Helen Hunt
Waylon Jennings
Jim Varney

JUNE 16
Eddie Levert
Ian Matthews
Laurie Metcalf
Corin Redgrave
Joan Van Ark
Gino Vannelli

JUNE 17
Norman Kuhlke
Mark Linn-Baker
Peter Lupus
Barry Manilow
Dean Martin
Jason Patric

Joe Piscopo

JUNE 18
Tom Bailey
Roger Ebert
Carol Kane
E.G. Marshall
Paul McCartney
Alison Moyet
Isabella Rossellini
Jerome Smith

JUNE 19
Paula Abdul
Tommy DeVito
Larry Dunn
Louis Jourdan
Nancy Marchand
Malcolm McDowell
Phylicia Rashad
Gena Rowlands
Salman Rushdie
Kathleen Turner
Ann Wilson

JUNE 20
Danny Aiello
Michael Anthony
Chet Atkins
Olympia Dukakis
John Goodman
Billy Guy
Martin Landau
Cyndi Lauper
Alan Longmuir
John Mahoney
Lionel Richie
John Taylor
Dave Thomas
James Tolkan
Brian Wilson

JUNE 21
Meredith Baxter
Berke Breathed
Chris Britton
Mark Brzezicki
Ray Davies
Michael Gross
Mariette Hartley
Bernie Kopell
Joey Kramer
Juliette Lewis
Nils Lofgren
Joey Molland
Jane Russell
Doug Savant
Maureen Stapleton
Prince William

JUNE 22
Peter Asher
Gary Beers
Bill Blass
Klaus Maria Brandauer
Amy Brenneman
Bruce Campbell
Tom Cunningham
Green Gartside
Howard Kaylan
Kris Kristofferson

Michael Lerner
Alan Osmond
Tracy Pollan
Todd Rundgren
Jimmy Somerville
Meryl Streep
Lindsay Wagner

JUNE 23
Bryan Brown
Adam Faith
Karin Gustafson

JUNE 24
Nancy Allen
Jeff Beck
Colin Blunstone
Georg Stanford Brown
Jeff Cease
Mick Fleetwood
John Illsley
Michele Lee
Andy McCluskey
Curt Smith
Peter Weller

JUNE 25
Tim Finn
Eddie Floyd
Allen Lanier
June Lockhart
Ian McDonald
George Michael
David Paich
Walter Payton
Carly Simon
Jimmie Walker
Clint Warwick

JUNE 26
Billy Davis Jr.
Chris Isaak
Mick Jones
Larry Taylor

JUNE 27
Isabelle Adjani
Julia Duffy
Bob Keeshan
Lorrie Morgan
Henry Ross Perot

JUNE 28
Kathy Bates
Mel Brooks
John Cusack
Dave Knights
Alice Krige
Mary Stuart Masterson
Noriyuki "Pat" Morita

JUNE 29
Maria Conchita Alonso
Gary Busey
Fred Grandy
Colin Hay
Little Eva
Ian Paice
Stedman Pearson

Roger Spear
Ruth Warrick

JUNE 30
David Alan Grier
Lena Horne
Hal Lindes
Andy Scott
Glenn Shorrock
Adrian Wright

JULY 1
Wally Amos Jr.
Pamela Anderson
Dan Aykroyd
Claude Berri
Karen Black
Roddy Bottum
Delaney Bramlett
Genevieve Bujold
Leslie Caron
Olivia De Havilland
Princess Diana
Jamie Farr
Farley Granger
Deborah Harry
Estee Lauder
Carl Lewis
Sydney Pollack
Fred Schneider
John Tesh
Mike Tyson

JULY 2
Pete Briquette
Johnny Colla
Imelda Marcos
Brock Peters
Joe Puerta
Ron Silver
Paul Williams

JULY 3
Paul Barrere
Betty Buckley
Neil Clark
Vince Clarke
Tom Cruise
Johnny Lee
Montel Williams

JULY 4
Leona Helmsley
Gina Lollobrigida
Kirk Pengilly
Geraldo Rivera
Eva Marie Saint
Neil Simon
Jeremy Spencer
John Waite
Al "Blind Owl" Wilson
Bill Withers

JULY 5
Shirley Knight
Huey Lewis
Michael Monarch
Robbie Robertson

JULY 6
Allyce Beasley
Ned Beatty

Gene Chandler
Rik Elswit
Nanci Griffith
Shelley Hack
Bill Haley
Jon Keeble
Janet Leigh
James Naughton
Nancy Reagan
Glenn Scarpelli
Sylvester Stallone
Burt Ward

JULY 7
Pierre Cardin
Shelley Duvall
Warren Entner
Jessica Hahn
David Hodo
Joe Spano
Ringo Starr

JULY 8
Kevin Bacon
Andy Fletcher
Anjelica Huston
Graham Jones
Raffi
Jeffrey Tambor
Jerry Valy

JULY 9
Marc Almond
Frank Bello
Brian Dennehy
Tom Hanks
Jim Kerr
Kelly McGillis
Mitch Mitchell
Fred Savage
Bon Scott
O.J. Simpson
Debbie Sledge
Jimmy Smits
John Tesh

JULY 10
David Brinkley
Ronnie James Dio
Ron Glass
Arlo Guthrie
Jerry Miller
Neil Tennant
Max Von Sydow

JULY 11
Giorgio Armani
Tab Hunter
Peter Murphy
Leon Spinks
Sela Ward

JULY 12
Milton Berle
Bill Cosby
Mel Harris
Cheryl Ladd
Christine McVie
Liz Mitchell
Richard Simmons
Jay Thomas
John Wetton
Kristi Yamaguchi

JULY 13
Stephen Jo Bladd
Lawrence Donegan
Harrison Ford
Robert Forster
Cheech Marin
Roger "Jim"
  McGuinn
Patrick Stewart
Spud Webb

JULY 14
Polly Bergen
Ingmar Bergman
Chris Cross
Rosey Grier
Frances Lear
Harry Dean Stanton

JULY 15
Willie Aames
Alex Karras
Peter Lewis
Brigitte Nielsen
Linda Ronstadt
Jan-Michael
  Vincent
Patrick Wayne
Forest Whitaker

JULY 16
Ruben Blades
Phoebe Cates
Stewart Copeland
Desmond Dekker
Corey Feldman
Tony Jackson
Mickey Rourke

JULY 17
Lucie Arnaz
Geezer Butler
Diahann Carroll
Spencer Davis
Phyllis Diller
David Hasselhoff
Art Linkletter
Donald Sutherland
Mick Tucker
Mike Vale

JULY 18
Papa Dee Allen
James Brolin
Terry Chambers
Hume Cronyn
Dion DiMucci
Glenn Hughes
Audrey Landers
Robin MacDonald
Nelson Mandela
Elizabeth
  McGovern
Martha Reeves
Red Skelton
Nigel Twist

JULY 19
Allen Collins
Alan Gorrie
Anthony Edwards
Pat Hingle

Bernie Leadon
Brian May

JULY 20
Paul Cook
Chris Cornell
Donna Dixon
John Lodge
Mike McNeil
Diana Rigg
Carlos Santana

JULY 21
Lance Guest
Edward Herrmann
Don Knotts
Leigh Lawson
Jon Lovitz
Jim Martin
Matt Mulhern
Henry Priestman
Isaac Stern
Cat Stevens
Robin Williams

JULY 22
Estelle Bennett
Albert Brooks
George Clinton
Willem Dafoe
Richard Davies
Louise Fletcher
Danny Glover
Don Henley
John Leguizamo
Alex Trebek

JULY 23
Dino Danelli
David Essex
Martin Gore
Woody Harrelson
Andy Mackay
Larry Manetti
Edie McClurg
Stephanie Seymour
Terence Stamp
Blair Thornton

JULY 24
Heinz Burt
Ruth Buzzi
Lynda Carter
Lynval Golding
Kadeem Hardison
Robert Hays
Laura Leighton
Michael Richards
Chris Sarandon

JULY 25
Ray Billingsley
Manuel Charlton
Estelle Getty
Barbara Harris
Iman
Jim McCarty
Verdine White

JULY 26
Blake Edwards
Dorothy Hamill
Mick Jagger

Stanley Kubrick
Duncan Mackay
Jason Robards
Roger Taylor

JULY 27
Peggy Fleming
Norman Lear
Maureen McGovern
John Pleshette
Al Ramsey
Betty Thomas
Jerry Van Dyke

JULY 28
George Cummings
Jim Davis
Terry Fox
Simon Kirke
Sally Struthers
Rick Wright

JULY 29
Michael Biehn
Neal Doughty
Peter Jennings
Geddy Lee
Martina McBride
Marilyn Quayle
Michael Spinks
David Warner

JULY 30
Paul Anka
Delta Burke
Kate Bush
Larry Fishburne
Buddy Guy
Anita Hill
Ken Olin
Rat Scabies
Arnold Schwarz-
  enegger

JULY 31
Daniel Ash
Alan Autry
Bill Berry
Dean Cain
Geraldine Chaplin
Norman Cook
Karl Green
Gary Lewis
Wesley Snipes
John West

AUGUST 1
Rick Anderson
Tempestt Bledsoe
Ricky Coonce
Robert Cray
Dom DeLuise
Joe Elliott
Jerry Garcia
Giancarlo Giannini
Arthur Hill
Yves Saint Laurent
Robert James
  Waller
Tom Wilson

AUGUST 2
Joanna Cassidy
Doris Coley
Wes Craven
Garth Hudson
Victoria Jackson
Carroll O'Connor
Peter O'Toole
Mary-Louise Parker
Edward Patten
Max Wright

AUGUST 3
Tony Bennett
B.B. Dickerson
James Hetfield
John Landis
Beverly Lee
Gordon Scott
Martin Sheen

AUGUST 4
David Carr
Frankie Ford

AUGUST 5
Loni Anderson
Neil Armstrong
Rick Derringer
Rick Huxley
Jonathan Silverman

AUGUST 6
Paul Bartel
Dorian Harewood
Catherine Hicks
Abbey Lincoln
Pat McDonald

AUGUST 7
Bruce Dickinson
Andy Fraser
John Glover
David Rasche
Alberto Salazar
B. J. Thomas

AUGUST 8
Richard Anderson
Philip Balsley
Princess Beatrice
Keith Carradine
Harry Crosby
Dino De Laurentiis
The Edge
Andy Fairweather-
  Low
Chris Foreman
Dustin Hoffman
Donny Most
Connie Stevens
Mel Tillis
Larry Dee Wilcox
Esther Williams

AUGUST 9
Kurtis Blow
Sam Elliott
Melanie Griffith
Billy Henderson
Whitney Houston
Ken Norton
Benjamin Orr

David Steinberg

AUGUST 10
Ian Anderson
Rosanna Arquette
Antonio Banderas
Veronica Bennett
Michael Bivins
Riddick Bowe
Jimmy Dean
Jon Farriss
Eddie Fisher
Bobby Hatfield
Lorraine Pearson

AUGUST 11
Erik Braunn
Eric Carmen
Hulk Hogan
Mike Hugg
Joe Jackson
Jim Kale
Denis Payton
Claus Von Bulow

AUGUST 12
John Derek
George Hamilton
Roy Hay
Sam J. Jones
Mark Knopfler
Pat Metheny
Marjorie Reynolds
Pete Sampras
Suzanne Vega
Jane Wyatt

AUGUST 13
Kathleen Battle
Danny Bonaduce
Fidel Castro
Dan Fogelberg
Pat Harrington
Don Ho
Feargal Sharkey

AUGUST 14
Halle Berry
Dash Crofts
David Crosby
Alice Ghostley
Larry Graham
Jackee
Magic Johnson
Steve Martin
Susan Saint James
Danielle Steel

AUGUST 15
Princess Anne
Julia Child
Mike Connors
Linda Ellerbee
Tess Harper
Matt Johnson
MCA
Bill Pinkney
Rose-Marie
Pete York

AUGUST 16
Bob Balaban
Angela Bassett

Belinda Carlisle
Robert Culp
Frank Gifford
Kathie Lee Gifford
Eydie Gorme
Timothy Hutton
Madonna
Fess Parker
Carole Shelley
James Taylor
Reginald
  Veljohnson
Lesley Ann Warren

AUGUST 17
Robert De Niro
Steve Gorman
Colin Moulding
Maureen O'Hara
Sean Penn
Kevin Rowland
Gary Talley
Donnie Wahlberg

AUGUST 18
Dennis Elliott
Martin Mull
Roman Polanski
Robert Redford
Christian Slater
Madeleine Stowe
Ron Strykert
Patrick Swayze
Malcolm-Jamal
  Warner
Carl Wayne
Shelley Winters

AUGUST 19
Ginger Baker
Bill Clinton
John Deacon
Kevin Dillon
Peter Gallagher
Ian Gillan
Billy J. Kramer
M.C. Eric
Gerald McRaney
Diana Muldaur
Jill St. John
John Stamos

AUGUST 20
Joan Allen
Connie Chung
Doug Fieger
Rudy Gatlin
Isaac Hayes
Don King
Phil Lynott
James Pankow
Robert Plant

AUGUST 21
Kim Cattrall
Wilt Chamberlain
Carl Giammarese
Kenny Rogers
Kim Sledge
Joe Strummer
Melvin Van Peebles
Clarence

Williams III

AUGUST 22
Ray Bradbury
Valerie Harper
John Lee Hooker
Roland Orzabal
Debbi Peterson
Norman
    Schwarzkopf
Cindy Williams

AUGUST 23
Ronny Cox
Barbara Eden
Bobby G.
Gene Kelly
Shelley Long
Vera Miles
Shaun Ryder
Richard Sanders
Rick Springfield

AUGUST 24
Yasir Arafat
Mark Bedford
Jim Capaldi
Joe Chambers
John Cipollina
Jeffrey Daniel
David Freiberg
Steve Guttenberg
Ken Hensley
Marlee Matlin
Claudia Schiffer

AUGUST 25
Anne Archer
Sean Connery
Elvis Costello
Billy Ray Cyrus
Mel Ferrer
Rob Halford
Monty Hall
Van Johnson
Regis Philbin
John Savage
Gene Simmons
Tom Skerritt
Blair Underwood
Joanne Whalley-
    Kilmer
Walter Williams

AUGUST 26
Jet Black
Bob Cowsill
Macaulay Culkin
Chris Curtis
Geraldine Ferraro
Michael Jeter
Branford Marsalis
Fred Milano
John O'Neill

AUGUST 27
Barbara Bach
Tim Bogert
Jeff Cook
Daryl Dragon
Pee-Wee Herman
Alex Lifeson
Glenn Matlock

Harry Reems
Tuesday Weld

AUGUST 28
Clem Cattini
Hugh Cornwell
Ben Gazzara
Scott Hamilton
Donald O'Connor
Wayne Osmond
Jason Priestley
Roxie Roker
Emma Samms
Elizabeth Seal
Danny Seraphine
David Soul
Daniel Stern

AUGUST 29
Richard
    Attenborough
Rebecca DeMornay
Richard Gere
Elliott Gould
Michael Jackson
Robin Leach
George Montgomery
Sterling Morrison
Isabel Sanford

AUGUST 30
Elizabeth Ashley
Timothy Bottoms
John McNally
Micky Moody
John Phillips
Kitty Wells

AUGUST 31
Jerry Allison
James Coburn
Debbie Gibson
Buddy Hackett
Van Morrison
Harold Reid
Rudolph Schenker
Daniel Schorr
Anthony
    Thistlethwaite
Glenn Tilbrook

SEPTEMBER 1
Greg Errico
Gloria Estefan
Bruce Foxton
Barry Gibb
Lily Tomlin
Dave White

SEPTEMBER 2
Rosalind Ashford
Jimmy Connors
Sam Gooden
Marty Grebb
Mark Harmon
Fritz McIntyre
Steve Porcaro
Keanu Reeves

SEPTEMBER 3
Eileen Brennan
Donald Brewer
Al Jardine

Steve Jones
Gary Leeds
Valerie Perrine
Charlie Sheen
Mort Walker

SEPTEMBER 4
Martin Chambers
Gary Duncan
Greg Elmore
Mitzi Gaynor
Judith Ivey
Merald Knight
Ronald LaPread
Jennifer Salt
Ione Skye

SEPTEMBER 5
John Cage
William Devane
Carol Lawrence
Bob Newhart
Al Stewart
Raquel Welch
Dweezil Zappa

SEPTEMBER 6
Dave Bargeron
Jane Curtin
Swoosie Kurtz
Claydes Smith
Paul Waaktaar
Jo Anne Worley

SEPTEMBER 7
Alfa Anderson
Corbin Bernsen
Susan Blakely
Chrissie Hynde
Julie Kavner
Peggy Noonan
Richard Roundtree
Benmont Tench

SEPTEMBER 8
Sid Caesar
Brian Cole
Michael Lardie
David Steele
Henry Thomas

SEPTEMBER 9
Doug Ingle
Michael Keaton
Sylvia Miles
Cliff Robertson
Adam Sandler
Dave Stewart
Roger Waters

SEPTEMBER 10
Chris Columbus
Siobhan Fahey
Jose Feliciano
Johnnie Fingers
Colin Firth
Danny Hutton
Amy Irving
Big Daddy Kane
Charles Kuralt
Pat Mastelotto
Joe Perry
Don Powell

Fay Wray

SEPTEMBER 11
Anne Bancroft
Harry Connick Jr.
Lola Falana
Mickey Hart
Earl Holliman
Amy Madigan
Virginia Madsen
Kristy McNichol
Jon Moss
Tommy Shaw
Mick Talbot
Dennis Tufano

SEPTEMBER 12
Barry Andrews
Gerry Beckley
Tony Bellamy
Darren E. Burrows
Linda Gray
Neil Peart
Brian Robertson
Peter Scolari
Barry White

SEPTEMBER 13
Barbara Bain
Jacqueline Bisset
Nell Carter
Peter Cetera
David Clayton-
    Thomas
Claudette Colbert
Randy Jones
Richard Kiel
Joni Sledge
Mel Torme

SEPTEMBER 14
Pete Agnew
Barry Cowsill
Faith Ford
Morten Harket
Walter Koenig
Paul Kossoff
Sam Neill
Joe Penny
Nicol Williamson

SEPTEMBER 15
Les Braid
Jackie Cooper
Prince Henry
Tommy Lee Jones
Oliver Stone

SEPTEMBER 16
Lauren Bacall
Ed Begley Jr.
Joe Butler
Bernie Calvert
David Copperfield
Peter Falk
Anne Francis
Allen Funt
Kenny Jones
B.B. King
Richard Marx
Susan Ruttan

SEPTEMBER 17
Anne Bancroft
Elvira
Jeff MacNelly
Roddy McDowall
Lamonte McLemore
John Ritter
Fee Waybill

SEPTEMBER 18
Frankie Avalon
Ricky Bell
Robert Blake
Joanne Catherall
Kerry Livgren
Dee Dee Ramone
Jack Warden

SEPTEMBER 19
Jim Abbott
John Coghlan
Lol Creme
Lee Dorman
Jeremy Irons
Joan Lunden
Nick Massi
David McCallum
Bill Medley
Nile Rodgers
Twiggy
Adam West

SEPTEMBER 20
Alannah Currie
Crispin Glover
Sophia Loren
Anne Meara
Chuck Panozzo
John Panozzo

SEPTEMBER 21
Leonard Cohen
Henry Gibson
Larry Hagman
Stephen King
Ricki Lake
Rob Morrow
Bill Murray
Catherine Oxenberg
Philthy Animal
Alfonso Ribeiro
Trugoy the Dove

SEPTEMBER 22
Scott Baio
Shari Belafonte
David Coverdale
Joan Jett
Paul LeMat

SEPTEMBER 23
Jason Alexander
Steve Boone
Ronald Bushy
Ray Charles
Lita Ford
Julio Iglesias
Ben E. King
Elizabeth Pena
Mary Kay Place
Mickey Rooney
Bruce Springsteen

SEPTEMBER 24
Phil Hartman
Gerry Marsden
Linda McCartney
Anthony Newley

SEPTEMBER 25
Gary Alexander
Michael Douglas
Mark Hamill
John Locke
Heather Locklear
Onnie McIntyre
Juliet Prowse
Christopher Reeve
Phil Rizzuto
Steve Severin
Will Smith
Cheryl Tiegs
Barbara Walters

SEPTEMBER 26
Melissa Sue
    Anderson
Joe Bauer
George Chambers
Craig Chaquico
Donna Douglas
Georgie Fame
Bryan Ferry
Linda Hamilton
Mary Beth Hurt
Winnie Mandela
Olivia Newton-John
Tracey Thorn

SEPTEMBER 27
Randy Bachman
Wilford Brimley
Greg Ham
Jayne Meadows
Meat Loaf
Greg Morris
Sada Thompson

SEPTEMBER 28
Brigitte Bardot
Jeffrey Jones
Marcello
    Mastroianni
Helen Shapiro
William Windom
Moon Unit Zappa

SEPTEMBER 29
Gene Autry
Anita Ekberg
Mark Farner
Bryant Gumbel
Patricia Hodge
Madeline Kahn
Jerry Lee Lewis
Larry Linville
Emily Lloyd

SEPTEMBER 30
Marc Bolan
Angie Dickinson
Deborah Kerr
Dewey Martin
Johnny Mathis
Marilyn McCoo

Sylvia Peterson
Victoria Tennant
Barry Williams

OCTOBER 1
Julie Andrews
Jean-Jacques
  Annaud
Jimmy Carter
Stephen Collins
Rob Davis
Richard Harris
Howard Hewett
Jerry Martini
Walter Matthau
Philippe Noiret
Randy Quaid
Stella Stevens
James Whitmore

OCTOBER 2
Richard Hell
Freddie Jackson
Donna Karan
Don McLean
Philip Oakey
Mike Rutherford
Sting
Tiffany

OCTOBER 3
Lindsey
  Buckingham
Chubby Checker
Barbara Ferris
Pamela Hensley
Tommy Lee
Gore Vidal
Jack Wagner
Dave Winfield

OCTOBER 4
Armand Assante
Clifton Davis
Jim Fielder
Charlton Heston
Chris Lowe
Anne Rice
Susan Sarandon

OCTOBER 5
Karen Allen
Clive Barker
Leo Barnes
Josie Bissett
Eddie Clarke
Jeff Conaway
Brian Connolly
Bob Geldof
Glynis Johns
Bil Keane
Mario Lemieux
Carlo Mastrangelo
Steve Miller

OCTOBER 6
Kevin Cronin
Britt Ekland
Bobby Farrell
Thomas McClary
Matthew Sweet
Bob Weir

OCTOBER 7
June Allyson
Toni Braxton
Kevin Godley
Dave Hope
Yo-Yo Ma
John Mellencamp
Oliver North
Martha Stewart

OCTOBER 8
Rona Barrett
Robert Bell
George Bellamy
Chevy Chase
Michael Dudikoff
Paul Hogan
Jesse Jackson
Sarah Purcell
Johnny Ramone
Hamish Stuart
Sigourney Weaver
Tony Wilson
Stephanie
  Zimbalist

OCTOBER 9
Scott Bakula
Jackson Browne
John Entwistle
Michael Pare
Robert Wuhl

OCTOBER 10
Charles Dance
Jessica Harper
Martin Kemp
Martina Navratilova
Alan Rachins
David Lee Roth
Tanya Tucker
Ben Vereen

OCTOBER 11
Joan Cusack
Daryl Hall
Ron Leibman
David Morse
Luke Perry
Grant Shaud

OCTOBER 12
Susan Anton
Kirk Cameron
Sam Moore
Luciano Pavarotti
Adam Rich
Dave Vanian

OCTOBER 13
Karen Akers
Tisha Campbell
Sammy Hagar
Beverly Johnson
Nancy Kerrigan
Robert Lamm
Marie Osmond
Kelly Preston
Nipsey Russell
Demond Wilson

OCTOBER 14
Harry Anderson
Marcia Barrett
Greg Evigan
Billy Harrison
Justin Hayward
Ralph Lauren
Roger Moore
Cliff Richard

OCTOBER 15
Mickey Baker
Richard Carpenter
Chris De Burgh
Sarah Ferguson
Lee Iacocca
Tito Jackson
Linda Lavin
Penny Marshall
Tanya Roberts
Don Stevenson

OCTOBER 16
Tony Carey
Barry Corbin
Gary Kemp
Angela Lansbury
Dave Lovelady
Tim Robbins
Suzanne Somers
C.F. Turner
Wendy Wilson

OCTOBER 17
Sam Bottoms
Beverly Garland
Alan Howard
Margot Kidder
Michael McKean
Howard Rollins Jr.
Jim Seals
Jerry Siegel
Jim Tucker
George Wendt

OCTOBER 18
Chuck Berry
Peter Boyle
Mike Ditka
Russ Giguere
Keith Knudsen
Melina Mercouri
Erin Moran
Joe Morton
Gary Richrath
George C. Scott
Vincent Spano

OCTOBER 19
Richard Dreyfuss
Patricia Ireland
John Lithgow
Karl Wallinger

OCTOBER 20
Joyce Brothers
William Christopher
Alan Greenwood
Mark King
Ric Lee
Jerry Orbach
Tom Petty

Will Rogers Jr.
Bobby Seale
Jay Siegel

OCTOBER 21
Charlotte Caffey
Julian Cops
Steve Cropper
Eric Faulkner
Lee Loughnane
Steve Lukather
Manfred Mann

OCTOBER 22
Eddie Brigati
Catherine Deneuve
Joan Fontaine
Annette Funicello
Jeff Goldblum
Valeria Golino
Derek Jacobi
Ray Jones
Christopher Lloyd
Tony Roberts

OCTOBER 23
Johnny Carson
Freddie Marsden
Perola Negra Pele
Weird Al Yankovic
Dwight Yoakam

OCTOBER 24
F. Murray Abraham
Jerry Edmonton
Kevin Kline
David Nelson
B.D. Wong
Bill Wyman

OCTOBER 25
Jon Anderson
Anthony Franciosa
Matthias Jabs
Midori
Tracy Nelson
Rick Parfitt
Minnie Pearl
Helen Reddy
Marion Ross
Glenn Tipton

OCTOBER 26
Hillary Rodham
  Clinton
Cary Elwes
Keith Hopwood
Bob Hoskins
Ivan Reitman
Pat Sajak
Jaclyn Smith
Keith Strickland

OCTOBER 27
Terry Anderson
John Cleese
Ruby Dee
Nanette Fabray
John Gotti
Simon LeBon
Marla Maples
Carrie Snodgress

OCTOBER 28
Jane Alexander
Steve Baumgartner
Michael Crichton
Wayne Fontana
Dennis Franz
Jami Gertz
Telma Hopkins
Bruce Jenner
Hank Marvin
Stephen Morris
Joan Plowright
Annie Potts
Julia Roberts

OCTOBER 29
Ralph Bakshi
Kevin Dubrow
Kate Jackson
Denny Laine
Melba Moore
Winona Ryder

OCTOBER 30
Harry Hamlin
Grace Slick
Charles Martin
  Smith
Otis Williams
Henry Winkler

OCTOBER 31
King Ad-Rock
Barbara
  Bel Geddes
Tony Bowers
Bernard Edwards
Dale Evans
Lee Grant
Deidre Hall
Sally Kirkland
Annabella Lwin
Johnny Marr
Larry Mullen Jr.
Jane Pauley
Dan Rather
Xavier Roberts
David Ogden Stiers

NOVEMBER 1
Rick Allen
Ronald Bell
Barbara Bosson
Keith Emerson
Robert Foxworth
Mags Furuholmen
James Kilpatrick Jr.
Lyle Lovett
Eddie MacDonald
Betsy Palmer
Dan Peek

NOVEMBER 2
k.d. lang
Brian Poole
Bruce Welch
Alfre Woodard

NOVEMBER 3
Adam Ant
Roseanne Arnold
Charles Bronson

Mike Evans
Larry Holmes
Steve Landesberg
Lulu
Dolph Lundgren
Dennis Miller
James Prime
Gary Sandy

NOVEMBER 4
Martin Balsam
Art Carney
Walter Cronkite
Chris Difford
Ralph Macchio
Delbert McClinton
Markie Post
Kool Rock
Mike Smith
Loretta Swit

NOVEMBER 5
Bryan Adams
Art Garfunkel
Peter Noone
Tatum O'Neal
Roy Rogers
Sam Shepard
Paul Simon
Elke Sommer
Ike Turner

NOVEMBER 6
Sally Field
Glenn Frey
Ethan Hawke
P.J. Proby
Doug Sahm
Maria Shriver
George Young

NOVEMBER 7
Billy Graham
Joni Mitchell
Johnny Rivers

NOVEMBER 8
Alan Berger
Bonnie Bramlett
Alain Delon
Mary Hart
Rickie Lee Jones
Terry Lee Miall
Bonnie Raitt
Esther Rolle
Rodney Slater
Courtney Thorne-
  Smith
Roy Wood
Roxana Zal

NOVEMBER 9
Spiro Agnew
Joe Bouchard
Lou Ferrigno
Alan Gratzer
Hedy Lamarr
Phil May
Pepa
Carl Sagan
Dennis Stratton

NOVEMBER 10
Glen Buxton
Greg Lake
MacKenzie Phillips
Ann Reinking
Jack Scalia
Roy Scheider

NOVEMBER 11
Bibi Andersson
Paul Cowsill
Chris Dreja
Stubby Kaye
Patric Knowles
Roger Lavern
Charles Manson
Ian Marsh
Vince Martell
Demi Moore
Andy Partridge
Kurt Vonnegut Jr.
Jonathan Winters
Jesse Colin Young

NOVEMBER 12
Errol Brown
Tonya Harding
John Maus
Leslie McKeown
Stephanie Powers
Wallace Shawn
Neil Young

NOVEMBER 13
Whoopi Goldberg
Joe Mantegna
Richard Mulligan

NOVEMBER 14
Frankie Banali
Prince Charles
Freddie Garrity
Robert Ginty
Brian Keith
Alexander O'Neal
Laura San
    Giacomo
McLean Stevenson
Alec Such
Yanni
James Young

NOVEMBER 15
Edward Asner
Petula Clark
Beverly D'Angelo
Yaphet Kotto
Frida Lyngstad
Tony Thompson
Sam Waterston

NOVEMBER 16
Lisa Bonet
Dwight Gooden
Clu Gulager
Burgess Meredith

NOVEMBER 17
Martin Barre
Danny DeVito
Ronald DeVoe
Bob Gaudio
Lauren Hutton

Gordon Lightfoot
Mary Elizabeth
    Mastrantonio
Lorne Michaels
Martin Scorsese
Tom Seaver

NOVEMBER 18
Margaret Atwood
Hank Ballard
Imogene Coca
Linda Evans
Kirk Hammett
Andrea Marcovicci
Graham Parker
Jameson Parker
Elizabeth Perkins
Herman Rarebell
Susan Sullivan
Brenda Vaccaro
Kim Wilde

NOVEMBER 19
Dick Cavett
Jodie Foster
Larry King
Jeane Kirkpatrick
Calvin Klein
Hank Medress
Kathleen Quinlan
Ahmad Rashad
Meg Ryan
Ted Turner

NOVEMBER 20
Kaye Ballard
Jimmy Brown
Mike D
Bo Derek
George Grantham
Veronica Hamel
Richard Masur
Estelle Parsons
Dick Smothers
Ray Stiles
Joe Walsh
Sean Young

NOVEMBER 21
Goldie Hawn
Dr. John
Lonnie Jordan
Laurence Luckinbill
Lorna Luft
Juliet Mills
Harold Ramis
Nicollette Sheridan
Marlo Thomas

NOVEMBER 22
Aston Barrett
Boris Becker
Tom Conti
Jamie Lee Curtis
Rodney Dangerfield
Terry Gilliam
Mariel Hemingway
Billie Jean King
Floyd Sneed
Stevie "Little
    Steven" Van
    Zandt

Robert Vaughn
Ray Walston
Tina Weymouth

NOVEMBER 23
Susan Anspach
Bruce Hornsby

NOVEMBER 24
Donald Dunn
Geraldine
    Fitzgerald
Chris Hayes
Dwight Schultz
John Squire
Jim Yester

NOVEMBER 25
Christina
    Applegate
Joe DiMaggio
Amy Grant
John F. Kennedy Jr.
John Larroquette
Ricardo Montalban
Steve Rothery
Percy Sledge

NOVEMBER 26
Cyril Cusack
Robert Goulet
Norman Hassan
Alan Henderson
John McVie
Charles Schulz
Tina Turner

NOVEMBER 27
Charlie Burchill
Dozy
Robin Givens
Eddie Rabbitt
Bob Smith
Fisher Stevens
Jaleel White

NOVEMBER 28
Beeb Birtles
Ed Harris
Hope Lange
Judd Nelson
Randy Newman

NOVEMBER 29
Felix Cavaliere
Denny Doherty
Barry Goudreau
Jonathan Knight
Diane Ladd
Howie Mandel
John Mayall
Andrew McCarthy
Garry Shandling

NOVEMBER 30
John Aston
Richard Barbieri
Dick Clark
Kevin Conroy
Richard Crenna
Roger Glover
Rob Grill
Robert Guillaume

Billy Idol
Bo Jackson
G. Gordon Liddy
Leo Lyons
Mandy Patinkin
June Pointer
Rex Reason
Ridley Scott

DECEMBER 1
Woody Allen
Carol Alt
Eric Bloom
John Densmore
David Doyle
Bette Midler
Sandy Nelson
Gilbert O'Sullivan
Richard Pryor
Lou Rawls
Charlene Tilton
Treat Williams

DECEMBER 2
Steven Bauer
Ted Bluechel Jr.
Cathy Lee Crosby
Julie Harris
Michael McDonald
Tom McGuinness
Rick Savage
Howard Stern

DECEMBER 3
Brian Bonsall
Ozzy Osbourne
Andy Williams

DECEMBER 4
Tyra Banks
Jeff Bridges
John Cale
Deanna Durbin
Chris Hillman
Wink Martindale
Bob Mosley
Gary Rossington
Southside Johnny
Marisa Tomei

DECEMBER 5
Morgan Brittany
Jeroen Krabbe
Charles Lane
Little Richard
Jim Messina
Les Nemes
Jack Russell

DECEMBER 6
Peter Buck
Rick Buckler
Tom Hulce
Janine Turner
Ben Watt
Steven Wright

DECEMBER 7
Larry Bird
Ellen Burstyn
Mike Nolan
Tom Waits
Eli Wallach

DECEMBER 8
Gregg Allman
Kim Basinger
Jerry Butler
David Carradine
Phil Collen
Bobby Elliott
Teri Hatcher
James MacArthur
Sinead O'Connor
Paul Rutherford
Maximilian Schell
Flip Wilson

DECEMBER 9
Joan Armatrading
Beau Bridges
Dick Butkus
Rick Danko
Kirk Douglas
Morton Downey Jr.
Dennis Dunaway
Douglas
    Fairbanks Jr.
Buck Henry
Neil Innes
John Malkovich
Michael Nouri
Donny Osmond
Dick Van Patten

DECEMBER 10
Frank Beard
Kenneth Branagh
Susan Dey
Ace Kefford
Dorothy Lamour
Mako
Walter Orange
Tommy Rettig
Chad Stuart

DECEMBER 11
Bess Armstrong
Teri Garr
David Gates
Jermaine Jackson
Booker T. Jones
Brenda Lee
Rita Moreno
Nikki Sixx

DECEMBER 12
Bob Barker
Dickey Betts
Mayim Bialik
Clive Bunker
Jennifer Connelly
Sheila E.
Connie Francis
Terry Kirkman
Ed Koch
Rush Limbaugh
Mike Pinder
Cathy Rigby
Frank Sinatra
Mike Smith
Dionne Warwick

DECEMBER 13
Jeff "Skunk" Baxter
John Davidson

Ted Nugent
Randy Owen
Christopher
    Plummer
Dick Van Dyke
Tom Verlaine
Johnny Whitaker

DECEMBER 14
Patty Duke
Cynthia Gibb
Bridget Hall
Abbe Lane
Jackie McCauley
Mike Scott
Dee Wallace Stone
Cliff Williams
Joyce Wilson

DECEMBER 15
Carmine Appice
Dave Clark
Tim Conway
Reginald Hudlin
Don Johnson
Paul Simonon
Helen Slater

DECEMBER 16
Benny Andersson
Steven Bochco
Ben Cross
Billy Gibbons
Tony Hicks
William Perry
Liv Ullmann

DECEMBER 17
Sarah Dallin
Dave Dee
Bob Guccione
Eddie Kendricks
Eugene Levy
Mike Mills
Art Neville
Paul Rodgers
Tommy Steele

DECEMBER 18
Chas Chandler
Ossie Davis
Elliot Easton
Ray Liotta
Leonard Maltin
Brad Pitt
Keith Richards
Steven Spielberg
Kiefer Sutherland

DECEMBER 19
Jennifer Beals
Alvin Lee
Robert
    MacNaughton
Alyssa Milano
Tim Reid
Cicely Tyson
Robert Urich
Maurice White
Zal Yanovsky

479

DECEMBER 20
Jenny Agutter
Anita Baker
Billy Bragg
Bobby Colomby
John Hillerman
Chris Robinson
Little Stevie Wright

DECEMBER 21
Phil Donahue
Chris Evert
Jane Fonda
Josh Mostel
Kurt Waldheim
Carl Wilson
Paul Winchell

DECEMBER 22
Barbara Billingsley
Hector Elizondo
Maurice Gibb
Robin Gibb
Lady Bird Johnson
Rick Nielsen
Ricky Ross
Diane Sawyer

DECEMBER 23
Corey Haim
Jorma Kaukonen
Johnny Kidd
Susan Lucci
Dave Murray
Eugene Record
Ruth Roman
Harry Shearer
James Stockdale

Eddie Vedder

DECEMBER 24
Ian Burden
Lemmy

DECEMBER 25
Jimmy Buffett
Robin Campbell
O'Kelly Isley
Annie Lennox
Shane MacGowan
Barbara Mandrell
Noel Redding
Hanna Schygulla
Sissy Spacek
Henry Vestine

DECEMBER 26
Steve Allen
Abdul Fakir

Alan King
Donald Moffat
Phil Spector

DECEMBER 27
John Amos
Peter Criss
Gerard Depardieu
Tovah Feldshuh
Mick Jones
David Knopfler
Les Maguire

DECEMBER 28
Alex Chilton
Dick Diamonde
Lou Jacobi
Stan Lee
Charles Neville
Johnny Otis
Maggie Smith

Denzel Washington
Edgar Winter

DECEMBER 29
Ted Danson
Mark Day
Marianne Faithfull
Mary Tyler Moore
Paula Poundstone
Inga Swenson
Ray Thomas
Jon Voight

DECEMBER 30
Joseph Bologna
Bo Diddley
Davy Jones
Jack Lord
Jeff Lynne
Mike Nesmith
Sheryl Lee Ralph

Russ Tamblyn
Tracey Ullman
Fred Ward

DECEMBER 31
Barbara Carrera
Rosalind Cash
Burton Cummings
John Denver
Tom Hamilton
Anthony Hopkins
Val Kilmer
Ben Kingsley
Tim Matheson
Joe McIntyre
Sarah Miles
Pete Quaife
Patti Smith
Donna Summer
Andy Summers

1996'S WATERSHED BIRTHDAYS

The following folks will have reason to celebrate (or toast themselves) a little harder this year as they reach birthday milestones.

TURNING 100

George Burns

TURNING 80

Walter Cronkite
Olivia DeHavilland
Kirk Douglas
Van Johnson
George Montgomery
Gregory Peck
Daniel Schorr
James Whitmore

TURNING 75

John Agar
Steve Allen
Dirk Bogarde
Charles Bronson
Harry Carey Jr.
Carol Channing
Rodney Dangerfield
Hugh Downs
Deanna Durbin
Brian Keith
Deborah Kerr
Johnny Otis
Prince Philip
Nancy Reagan
Marjorie Reynolds
Jane Russell

TURNING 70

Don Adams
Richard Anderson
Beatrice Arthur
Kaye Ballard
Tony Bennett
Chuck Berry
Mel Brooks
Fidel Castro
John Derek
Alice Ghostley
Peter Graves
Andy Griffith
Hugh Hefner
Lionel Jeffries
Jeane Kirkpatrick
Jerry Lewis
Audrey Meadows
Patricia Neal
Leslie Nielsen
Milo O'Shea
Betsy Palmer
Steve Reeves
Don Rickles
Tom Ryan
Harry Dean Stanton
Claus Von Bulow
Fritz Weaver
Jane Withers

TURNING 65

Papa Dee Allen
Carroll Baker

Anne Bancroft
Claire Bloom
Leslie Caron
Ed Cassidy
George Chambers
Lonnie Donegan
Olympia Dukakis
Robert Duvall
Anita Ekberg
Mitzi Gaynor
Mikhail Gorbachev
Larry Hagman
Tab Hunter
Dean Jones
James Earl Jones
Don King
Martin Landau
Hope Lange
Hal Linden
Gavin Macleod
Robert MacNeil
Imelda Marcos
Willie Mays
Rita Moreno
Toni Morrison
Anthony Newley
Leonard Nimoy
Philippe Noiret
Dan Rather
William Shatner
Jerry Stiller
James Tolkan
Rip Torn
Ike Turner
Mamie Van Doren
Jerry VanDyke
Barbara Walters
Tom Wilson
Boris Yeltsin

TURNING 60

Alan Alda
Wally Amos Jr.
Ursula Andress
Joe Don Baker
Hank Ballard
Rona Barrett
Marion Barry
Jim Brown
Solomon Burke
Ruth Buzzi
David Carradine
Dick Cavett
Wilt Chamberlain
Glenn Campbell
Bruce Dern
Tommy Devito
Troy Donahue
Keir Dullea
Hector Elizondo
Chad Everett
Albert Finney
Louis Gossett Jr..

Billy Guy
Buddy Guy
Dennis Hopper
Englebert
    Humperdinck
Marty Ingels
Glenda Jackson
Walter Koenig
Kris Kristofferson
Yves Saint Laurent
John Madden
Zubin Mehta
Mary Tyler Moore
David Nelson
Juliet Prowse
Lou Rawls
Burt Reynolds
Bobby Seale
Bobbie Smith
Tom Snyder
Tommy Steele
Stella Stevens
Levi Stubbs
Bill Wyman

TURNING 50

Peter Agnew
Alfa Anderson
Loni Anderson
Benny Andersson
Carmine Appice
Paul Atkinson
Banana
Martin Barre
Aston Barrett
Syd Barrett
Bonnie Bedelia
Candice Bergen
Eddie Brigati
Lala Brooks
Harold Brown
Jimmy Buffett
Clive Bunker
Boz Burrell
Richard Carpenter
Cher
Connie Chung
Bill Clinton
John Coghlan
Jim Cregan
Tim Curry
Tyne Daly
Charles Dance
Donovan
Neal Doughty
Patty Duke
Gary Duncan
Sandy Duncan
Jerry Edmonton
Greg Elmore
Greg Errico
Marianne Faithful
Sally Field

Matthew Fisher
Nick Fortune
Robert Fripp
J. Geils
Marla Gibbs
Lesley Gore
Alan Gorrie
Larry Graham
Les Gray
Marty Grebb
Al Green
Justin Hayward
John Heard
Gregory Hines
Patarcia Hodge
Keith Hopwood
Ian Hunter
Ralf Hutter
Doug Ingle
John Paul Jones
Tommy Lee Jones
Naomi Judd
Terry Kath
Diane Keaton
Ace Kefford
Danny Klein
Bill Kreutzman Jr.
Robbie Kreiger
Ronnis Lane
Bob Lane
Allen Lanier
John Lawton
Johnny Lee
Eugene Levy
Gary Lewis
Lee Loughnane
Andy Mackey
Barry Manilow
Cheech Marin
Jackie McCauley
Ian McDonald
Ian McLagan
Michael Milken
Hayley Mills
Liza Minnelli
Mitch Mitchell
Josh Mostel
Craig T. Nelson
Al Nichol
Rick Nielsen
El O'Neill
Gilbert O'Sullivan
Michael Ontkean
Lee Oskar
Michael Ovitz
Dolly Parton
Sylvia Peterson
Ruth Pointer
Charlotte Rampling
Ivan Reitman
Alan Rickman
Cynthia Robinson
Linda Ronstadt

Philip Rudd
Susan Saint James
Pat Sajak
Gary Sandy
Susan Sarandon
Bon Scott
Howard Scott
Helen Shapiro
Talia Shire
Ron Silver
Gene Siskel
Patti Smith
Carrie Snodgrass
Suzanne Somers
Joe Spano
Alexander Spence
Sylvester Stallone
Ray Stiles
Freddie Stone
Oliver Stone
Nedra Talley
Mary Thomas
Donald Trump
Jim Tucker
Dennis Tufano
Robert Urich
Ben Ver*een
Gianni Versace
Burt Ward
Lesley Ann Warren
John Waters
Wendy O. Williams
Carl Wilson
Demond Wilson
Joyce Wilson
Edgar Winter
Peter Wolf
Roy Wood
Syreeta Wright
Rusty Young

TURNING 40

Bernie Albrecht
Joan Allen
Barry Andrews
Steven Bauer
Robby Benson
Michael Biehn
Larry Bird
Larry Blackmon
Tony Bowers
Alex Briley
Peter Buck
Rick Buckler
Delta Burke
Richard Butler
Joey Buttafuoco
David Caruso
Kim Cattrall
Russell Christian
Paul Cook
David Copperfield
John Cowsill

Timothy Dalton
Dana Delany
Bo Derek
Mark Evans
Johnnie Fingers
Carrie Fisher
Andy Garcia
Green Gartside
Mel Gibson
Dorothy Hamill
Linda Hamilton
Tom Hanks
Anita Hill
Peter Hook
James Ingram
Chris Isaak
Matthias Jabs
Jackee
Freddie Jackson
Kenny G.
Sugar Ray Leonard
John Lydon
Ann Magnuson
Ian Marsh
Glenn Matlock
Joe Montana
Martina Navratilova
Joe Penny
Sheryl Lee Ralph
Eric Roberts
Brian Robertson
Mimi Rogers
Mickey Rourke
Katey Sagal
Bob Saget
Sinbad
Joni Sledge
Michael Spinks
Neville Staples
Alec Such
Barney Sumner
Dave Vanian
Sela Ward
Martyn Ware
Montel Williams
Adrian Wright
Dwight Yoakam
Paul Young
Pia Zadora
Paula Zahn
Stephanie
    Zimbalist

TURNING 30

King Ad-Roc
Troy Aikman
Rick Astley
Stephen Baldwin
Justine Bateman
Helena Bonham-
    Carter
Edie Brickell
Todd Bridges

Darren E. Burrows
Dean Cain
Graeme Clark
Johnny Colt
Cindy Crawford
John Cusack
Paul Davis
Patrick Dempsey
Samantha Fox

Cynthia Geary
Valeria Golino
Kadeem Hardison
Jeff Healey
Janet Jackson
Nicole Kidman
Kool Rock
Jason Lee Scott

Robert
    Macnaughton
Mary Stuart
    Masterson
Martina McBride
Mike McCready
Nancy McKeon
Fabrice Morvan
Sinead O'Connor

Jason Patric
Doris Pearson
Marti Pellow
Luke Perry
Chris Robinson
Adam Sandler
Jonathan Silverman
Lisa Stansfield
Ben Stiller

Kiefer Sutherland
Tone-Loc
Mike Tyson

TURNING 21

Drew Barrymore
Mayim Bialik
Leonardo DiCaprio
Balthazar Getty
Sara Gilbert

TURNING 20

Jennifer Capriati
Lukas Haas
Joey Lawrence
Fred Savage
Alicia Silverstone
Jaleel White